P9-CQC-560

PSYCHOLOGY

SECOND EDITION

PSYCHOLOGY

John M. Darley
Sam Glucksberg
Leon J. Kamin
Ronald A. Kinchla

Princeton University

PRENTICE-HALL, INC.
Englewood Cliffs, New Jersey 07632

Library of Congress Cataloging in Publication Data

Main entry under title:

Psychology.

Includes bibliographies and indexes.
1. Psychology.   I. Darley, John M.
BF121.P78 1984   150   83-19085
ISBN   0-13-733147-9

© 1984, 1981 by Prentice-Hall, Inc., Englewood Cliffs, N.J. 07632

Printed in the United States of America

10   9   8   7   6   5   4   3   2   1

Development Editor: Marjorie Weiser
Production Editor: Linda Benson
Photo Research: Anita Duncan, Teri Leigh Stratford
Book Design and Page Layout: Levavi & Levavi
Assistant Art Director: Linda Conway
Cover Design: Chris Wolf
Cover Photo: Trudy Glucksberg
Manufacturing Buyer: Ray Keating
Line Art: J & R Technical Services; Fine Line, Inc.

ISBN 0-13-733147-9

Prentice-Hall International, Inc., *London*
Prentice-Hall of Australia Pty. Limited, *Sydney*
Editora Prentice-Hall do Brasil, Ltda., *Rio de Janeiro*
Prentice-Hall Canada Inc., *Toronto*
Prentice-Hall of India Private Limited, *New Delhi*
Prentice-Hall of Japan, Inc., *Tokyo*
Prentice-Hall of Southeast Asia Pte. Ltd., *Singapore*
Whitehall Books Limited, *Wellington, New Zealand*

(Acknowledgments appear on p. 653, which constitutes a continuation of the copyright page.)

Overview

Contents

Part Three   LEARNING AND COGNITIVE PROCESSES

Preface

The unique task of psychology is to provide scientific explanations for human thought, emotion, and action. This generates the need for theories covering vast domains ranging from the biological functioning of humans to their social functioning in society. To tell students what we understand about human behavior, something about how we come to these understandings, and finally to make clear what we do not yet understand were the tasks we took on when we wrote the first edition of the textbook. The first edition was often well-received by teachers and students, and so it was with considerable enthusiasm that we began work on this edition. We now had an opportunity not only to update the text with recent developments in the many fields of psychology, but also to improve it on the basis of users' suggestions.

Again the basic form of our text is not unusual; indeed we wanted our table of contents to look comfortably familiar to teachers of introductory psychology. It was not at this level that we intended to compete with other successful texts. Rather, we wanted our book to present the commonly accepted content of introductory psychology in a clear, accurate, and interesting manner. Thus much of our creative efforts went into presenting concepts clearly and choosing interesting and effective examples to illustrate them.

We feel that one reason for the success of our text is the number of years each of us has taught introductory psychology. Furthermore, while the diversity of our individual areas of research allows us to bring some expertise to each of the areas we cover, we have often team taught the course so that we share a common sense of psychology which helped us to integrate the various sections of the text.

The book is divided into several parts, with an appendix on statistical measurement. This division is relatively standard and accurately reflects a broad consensus about how the field is generally organized. As a historical introduction, Part One provides the basic facts about humans as biological organisms. Part Two deals with how we experience the world—our sensory systems of sight, hearing, touch, taste, smell, and so on; our perceptual system, which makes sense of our sensations; and our consciousness and states of awareness. Part Three deals with issues of the mind—how we learn, remember, and think. Part Four turns to the wellsprings of behavior—motivation and emotion. How we grow, develop, and change with age and experience are treated in Part Five. Part Six deals with some of the most intriguing and complex problems in psychology, concerning the organization of the human personality, how that organization can go astray, and how therapy may be able to restore it to normal functioning. Finally, Part Seven provides an in-depth description and analysis of human interaction, the area of social psychology.

In doing this revision we have gone over every paragraph in the book looking for ways to say things better. We have also reduced coverage of some material and added new information. In both cases we are greatly indebted to the comments from faculty and students who had used the book.

In Chapter 1, we expanded the section on basic and applied research and included coverage of Gestalt psychology. One of the more visible features of the revision is the use of full color artwork in Chapters 2, 3, and 4 to show information more clearly than could be done with black and white figures. The rapid pace of developments in brain chemistry is reflected in a more extensive treatment of nerve conduction and of neurotransmitters in Chapter 2, of psychoactive drugs and substance abuse in Chapter 5, and of the biochemistry of behavior in Chapters 10 and 17. Also in Chapter 5, we have expanded our treatment of meditation, with particular emphasis on how it has been demystified and employed to relieve hypertension and anxiety.

Chapter 6 contains a new boxed Highlight that presents recent developments in the theoretical understanding of animal conditioning. New material has been added on the application of behavior modification principles in an industrial setting. And finally, there is a new boxed Highlight on the dramatically successful use of biofeedback to control visceral responses. In the chapter on memory (Chap. 7), new material has been added on the possible types of knowledge (semantic, episodic, and procedural) and how they may be represented in human memory. Chapter 8 presents new work on decision making, including research studies by Kahneman and Tversky on the power of framing effects and on peoples' insensitivity to sample size. Chapter 9 presents a new boxed Application containing a case study illustrating an abuse of IQ testing in the school system, new material on the concept of test bias and on the testing of minority groups, and an updated summary of research on the heritability of IQ based on the results of recent adoption studies.

Chapter 10 includes updated research on obesity and weight-loss programs. Chapter 11 includes several new sections on human sexual expression, intrinsic and extrinsic motivational orientations, and motivation in the workplace.

In the chapter on childhood (Chap. 12), new material has been added on children's ability to think and on the development of self-control. In Chapter 13, a new boxed Highlight describes the use of (and the problems in the use of) tests and interest inventories to help young adults make career decisions. Recent research updates the sections on old age and marriage and widowhood.

Chapter 14 has individual sections on nomothetic and ideographic personality theories. The next chapter, on stress and coping, updates information on the relationship between stress and illness and includes recent research on the psychological effects of chronic job stress. In the abnormal psychology chapter (Chap. 16), the section on clinical classification and diagnosis has been revised in terms of the DSM-III, including the five axes used in assessing an individual's problem. A new table is included that shows the classification of psychological disorders in the DSM-III. A section discusses the strengths and difficulties of the medical model. There is increased coverage of the topic of depression, as well as a new boxed Highlight on diet and abnormal behavior. Chapter 17 includes material on cognitive behavioral therapy and expands the sections on biofeedback and family therapy.

Chapter 18 includes new sections on self-fulfilling prophecies, the formation of attitudes, and social exchange in long-term relationships, as well as a new boxed Highlight on liking and loving and a new boxed Application on the relationship between violence on television and violent behavior. The chapter on social influence and group processes (Chap. 19) has a new section on organizational settings and a new boxed Application called "A Matrix Analysis of the Armaments Race."

ACKNOWLEDGMENTS

This revision was greatly facilitated by the advice we received from a number of knowledgeable reviewers, many of whom used the first edition in their teaching.

James R. Averill, University of Massachusetts

Ellen Banks, Daemen College

Ilene L. Bernstein, University of Washington

J. Kathryn Bock, Cornell University

John P. Brockway, Davidson College

Aaron J. Brownstein, The University of North Carolina at Greensboro

Andrew Caggiula, University of Pittsburgh

Thomas H. Carr, Michigan State University

Patricia Carrington, Princeton University

Jerome M. Chertkoff, Indiana University

Frances Cohen, University of California, San Francisco

William Cooper, University of Iowa

James Coyne, University of California, Berkeley

Helen J. Crawford, The University of Wyoming

Jennifer Crocker, Northwestern University

Robert G. Crowder, Yale University

Stephen F. Davis, Emporia State University

William S. Edell, University of Massachusetts

Ronald Finke, University of California, Davis

Irene Hanson Frieze, University of Pittsburgh

Alan Gilchrist, Rutgers—The State University

William C. Gordon, The University of New Mexico

Bernard S. Gorman, Nassau Community College

Joseph H. Grosslight, Florida State University

Carl R. Gustavson, North Dakota State University

Larry W. Hall, North Seattle Community College

Albert A. Harrison, University of California, Davis

Robert Hendersen, University of Illinois at Champaign

E. Tory Higgins, New York University

Daniel R. Ilgen, Michigan State University

Barry L. Jacobs, Princeton University

William A. Johnston, The University of Utah

Alan E. Kazdin, University of Pittsburgh

John F. Kihlstrom, University of Wisconsin

Daniel Kortenkamp, University of Wisconsin—Stevens Point

Gloria M. Lewis, Tennessee State University

Herschel Liebowitz, The Pennsylvania State University

Jacqueline Liederman, Boston University

James Mazur, Harvard University

Stuart J. McKelvie, Bishop's University

George J. Meyer, Suffolk County Community College

Richard Miller, Western Kentucky University

William R. Miller, The University of New Mexico

Susan Mineka, University of Wisconsin

Sarah O'Dowd, Community College of Rhode Island

Thomas Oltmanns, Indiana University

Ronald Peters, Iowa State University

Robert Plomin, University of Colorado, Boulder

Alan D. Poling, Western Michigan University

Jay B. Pozner, Jackson Community College

Robert W. Proctor, Auburn University

Alan Randich, University of Iowa

Jeffrey G. Reed, State University College at Genesco

Robert W. Rice, State University of New York at Buffalo

Damaris J. Rohsenow, University of Wisconsin

Milton E. Rosenbaum, The University of Iowa

Richard Schiffman, Rutgers—The State University

Miriam W. Schustack, Harvard University

Linda Smolak, Kenyon College

Sigfrid D. Soli, University of Maryland

Bonnie Spring, Harvard University

Robert M. Stern, The Pennsylvania State University

Charles E. Sternheim, University of Maryland

Colleen F. Surber, University of Wisconsin

James Terborg, University of Oregon

Edward Thrasher, San Bernardino Valley College

Katherine Van Giffen, University of California, Irvine

Marcia L. Weinstein, Salem State College

Jeremy M. Wolfe, Massachusetts Institute of Technology

Diane S. Woodruff, Temple University

Mark P. Zanna, University of Waterloo

Antonette Zeiss, Veteran's Administration Medical Center, Palo Alto, California

We mentioned several people in the first edition who made contributions to the text. They have our continued gratitude. Some people who made contributions to this first revision are Pat Carrington (Chapter 5), Thane Pittman (Chapter 11), Jeanne Smith (Chapter 14), and Peggy Thoits (Chapter 15).

Several of our colleagues continue to volunteer suggestions and informal guidance—Joel Cooper, Ron Comer, Ned Jones, Barry Jacobs, and Carl Olson.

Finally we want to thank some of the people at Prentice-Hall, particularly Linda Benson, Colette Conboy, Marge Weiser, and Susanna Lesan, for their encouragement and editorial help (and patience), and John Isley for keeping up our morale.

We cannot end without two more acknowledgments. The first is to the readers—teachers and students—of the first edition who made so many genuinely worthwhile suggestions for the second edition.

Writers of textbooks discover that they have committed themselves to keeping track of new developments in research psychology. After reviewing developments of the past few years, we have a sense of how far and how fast psychology has moved in that time. What we present in this text is the product of the labor and the insights of hundreds, perhaps thousands, of research psychologists. Our largest debt is to them, and we gratefully acknowledge it. The reader must think of our index of authors as a set of heartfelt acknowledgments, as we do.

While we are grateful to all of these people for their positive contributions to this book, we take full responsibility for any errors in fact.

J. M. D.
S. G.
L. J. K.
R. A. K.

1. Introduction to Psychology

There are very many people who are called psychologists, and what they have in common may not be immediately obvious. Psychologist A, for example, is a clinical psychologist. He works with people who have "psychological problems." A student comes to the college's counseling center, complaining that she feels depressed and lethargic. Perhaps also she has had some difficulty sleeping and some loss of appetite. Another student is suffering from a far more pervasive psychological disturbance. Perhaps he has recently begun to act strangely. He is often silent and withdrawn but occasionally bursts into almost incoherent speech. He believes that there is a widespread plot against him: His professors are spying on him and reporting slanderous information to the college authorities and the police. Recently he has noticed that the food served to him in the college cafeteria tastes peculiar, and he believes that "they" are trying to poison him. He has been referred to the psychologist after creating a disturbance in the cafeteria. The clinical psychologist is an expert—as expert as the present state of knowledge will allow—in the understanding and treatment of all the problems we have described. He works with patients in such places as mental health clinics, state hospitals, prisons, and school systems.

Psychologist B seems to be a very different kind of psychologist. She is a physiological psychologist, and she has never counseled a patient in her life. She spends most of her working hours in a laboratory, surrounded by complex (and expensive) pieces of apparatus. She wants to understand more about how the brain controls and influences human behavior and feelings. To acquire such understanding, she has had to learn neuroanatomy (the physical structure of the nervous system and brain) and biochemistry. She is studying rats—she can perform many experiments on them that, for obvious reasons, cannot be performed on human subjects. Psychologist B probably holds a university professorship and is thus teaching as well as performing research. Or she may be working full-time at research, perhaps in a government laboratory devoted to health problems or in the laboratories of a private drug manufacturer.

Psychologist C is also a college teacher, but at the moment he is in a courtroom, where he is about to appear as an expert witness for the defense. He has conducted research on human cognitive processes, particularly on human memory. He knows a great deal about the way in which the "memories" reported by eye witnesses can be influenced by changes in the wording of questions. The defense hopes that his testimony may help to discredit earlier testimony elicited from an eyewitness by the prosecution.

Psychologist D is employed full-time as a researcher in a government laboratory. She is designing visual displays that mimic or simulate what an astronaut would see when landing a craft on a planet with an atmosphere very different from that of earth. By such practice under simulated conditions here on earth, the safety of future space flights is increased considerably.

The four specimen psychologists we have described give some indication of the scope of modern psychology. There are some psychologists whose interests seem very close to those of biologists or biochemists. There are others whose interests seem close to those of sociologists, anthropologists, and social philosophers. The reason for this wide scope should be obvious. Psychology is concerned with human behavior, and humans are both biological and social creatures. To ignore either our biological or social nature is to guarantee defeat in any effort truly to understand ourselves. To understand, on the other hand, how our biological and social natures interact and unite would be the crowning achievement of human thought. The task set out for modern psychology—to become nothing less than the integrator of the biological and social sciences—is neither an easy nor a boring one. Psychologists specialize in interests and knowledge at some point in their careers, but they must remain sensitive to, and informed about, the many different areas of psychology. Despite their inevitable specialization, psychologists do talk to one another, and they tend to share a common point of view. This chapter is concerned with that common point of view—how it developed, what it includes, and what it excludes.

SOME HISTORICAL PERSPECTIVES

There is, today, little if any disagreement among psychologists about what it is that they ought to be studying. This was not always true. The first group of people who regarded themselves as scientific psychologists flourished in Germany in the second half of the nineteenth century, around the pioneer figure of Wilhelm Wundt (1832–1920). Their interests and activities seem, from today's perspective, surprisingly narrow. They were chiefly concerned with the problem of how the mind constructs sensations and perceptions out of the raw nerve messages delivered to the brain by the sense organs. They had been trained in the physiology of the sense organs and the nervous system. Their unique contribution was to be an analysis of the contents of the mind itself, in an effort to understand the relations between physiological events and conscious mental experience.

To undertake such studies, the appropriate experimental method was that of **introspection.** The first experimental psychologists sat in a quiet laboratory and examined their own mental experiences. They would expose themselves to controlled sensory stimulation of various sorts—perhaps a complex sound or a film of color on a textured surface. The introspecting subjects would analyze carefully the conscious experience produced by such stimuli and report what "elementary sensations" were combined to produce the complex experience, or perception, evoked by the stimulus. This method assumed the existence of a kind of "mental chemistry." The basic notion was that, through the sense organs, the mind contained a fixed number of basic sensations. These sensations were analogous to the elements in chemistry. Complex conscious mental experience might ultimately be understood as the result of various recombinations of these basic mental elements. These recombinations were analogous to compounds. It was quite in keeping with such a viewpoint to ask a conscientious and patient introspecting subject to describe in detail the sensations created by the complex experience of being tickled—perhaps some pressure, a little pain, and just a touch of warmth.

Clearly these early psychologists regarded their subject matter as the mind itself and felt that the life of the mind could be revealed by the technique of careful introspection. In emphasizing "direct access" to the mind, however, they paid a price. First, many minds—such as those of animals, young children, and mentally disturbed people—were simply inaccesssible. Second, even in the well-trained, normal, adult human subject some mental operations might simply not be reflected in consciousness. It is noteworthy that these early workers seem not to have been much concerned with the actual behavior of their subjects. What do people *do* with the sensations and perceptions that are forever cluttering up their minds? How do perceptions and experience influence behavior? How are they used to help the individual adjust to the vicissitudes of living on this earth?

In the United States a kind of revolution took place in experimental psychology in the early twentieth century. The major figure, at least in terms of popular impact, was John B. Watson (1878–1958). To Watson it seemed that early psychologists had attempted to study something that was too vague and subjective—perhaps even too "unreal"—to be a proper subject for scientific study. What is this thing called "mind"? How can we rely on the reports of introspectors about what is going on in their (to us) unobservable mind? What do we do when different introspectors give contradictory reports about the same stimulus? For psychology to become a genuine science, Watson argued, it had better concentrate on a definite subject matter that could be directly observed by all interested investigators. The proper study of psychology is, then, **behavior.** We can all observe the behavior of a subject and agree that it occurred in a particular way at a definite time and place. We ought to discover what the determiners of behavior are. What stimuli produce what observable responses? How do the relations between stimuli and responses change with experience? This kind of program, as Watson noted, could profoundly extend the scope of experimental psychology. The *behavior* of animals, infants, and the "insane"—unlike their "minds"—could be directly studied.

For a period, at least, Watson's arguments appeared to have enormous force, not so much because of their logic, perhaps, as because of the vast expansion of psychological research the behaviorist perspective encouraged. Then, too, there was disillusionment with the meager results of early introspectionism. Whatever the reason, it seems correct to say that at least until 1950 the vast majority of American psychologists agreed that psychology is the science of behavior. The mind, consciousness, and mental processes tended to be—so far as possible—ignored in psychological research. The behaviorists made no attempt to argue that the mind did not exist or that it was of no interest. They simply stressed the methodological simplicity of studying observable behavior.

Though Watson's behaviorism tended to dominate the American scene, a vigorous dissenting point of view was that of **Gestalt** psychology, a school founded by Max Wertheimer (1880–1943). The Gestalt psychologists, whose leaders immigrated to the United States from Germany before World War II, objected both to the "atomism" of behavioristic psychology and to the short shrift which it gave to perceptual processes. The Gestalt principles of perceptual organization (discussed in Chapter 4) led these workers to argue that complex psychological wholes could not be reduced to a mere sum of separate parts and that many forms of psychological organization—contrary to Watson's emphasis—were unlearned and innate.

But some experimental psychologists always felt that the facts of behavior had to be interpreted in terms of mental processes. Behaviorism stressed simple, straightforward connections between stimuli and responses (it was often called S-R psychology). Some stimuli and responses were simply and reliably related in this reflexlike way. With many stimuli, and with some kinds of subjects, however, it seemed obvious that the stimulus input was operated upon, transformed, processed, or mulled over before it was reponded to. That kind of internal processing—events taking place within the organism between the stimulus input and the response output—is what we mean when we talk about thinking or about mental processes. The existence of those internal events made it necessary to replace a simple S-R psychology with a more complex S-O-R psychology, where O stands for the organism that interposes its internal processes between observable stimuli and responses. Those internal events, of course, are not directly observable. They must be *inferred*—and they are inferred from the relations that we observe between stimuli and responses. Psychology in this respect is like any other science. To understand the phenomena that we directly observe, we have to construct "models" of *un*observable structures and processes that make sense out of our observations. Models and inferences constructed to explain one set of observations may have to be revised (or even abandoned) in the face of later and different observations. The goal is to collect those kinds of observations that seem to demand interpretation in terms of a particular model of mental processes. Psychologists, as later chapters will indicate, have been reasonably successful in devising experimental procedures that seem to reveal some of the properties of internal mental processes. The structure of the mind, and mental processes, are thus very much a part of the subject matter of scientific psychology, along with the analysis of behavior.

We should note that mental processes inferred in this way do not necessarily correspond to the results of introspection, for these mental processes may be entirely unobservable even to the organism in which they are occurring. This was, in fact, a central belief of the extremely influential (and nonexperimental) branch of psychology founded by Sigmund Freud (1856–1939). **Psychoanalytic theory** was developed by Freud to account for the often bizarre behaviors exhibited by neurotic patients who came to him seeking relief from their problems and symptoms. The behaviors and symptoms could be understood, Freud believed, in terms of the operation of powerful mental forces of which patients themselves were entirely unaware. According to the Freudian model, **unconscious** impulses, wishes, and sym-

Sigmund Freud, the founder of psychoanalytic theory, working in his study on the last book he wrote.

bolisms profoundly affect the behavior of all of us. The techniques Freud used to infer and argue for such unconscious mental processes were, if not entirely convincing, at least stunningly original and ingenious. We shall examine Freud's model in some detail in Chapter 14. For the present it is enough to say that modern experimental psychologists often proceed in basically the same way. For example, we might wish to know what mental processes are engaged when we instruct a subject to search through a printed page trying to locate each example of the letter "e." There is little sense in asking the subject to tell us; even after considerable experience with the task, the subject cannot do so. But there are experimental procedures that make possible highly plausible inferences about the mental processes involved in such a task.

Psychology thus seems to have come to a comfortable and sensible resolution of a problem that disturbed the first century of its development. What do we study? We study the observable behavior of people and of animals. From that observable behavior we construct logical inferences about the kinds of internal mental processes that underlie the observed behavior.

THE METHODS OF PSYCHOLOGY

Perhaps the least you might expect from psychologists is that they should agree among themselves about what the subject matter of their science is. They tend to agree, happily, on much more than just that. They have a strong predilection for the **experimental method** in acquiring reliable knowledge, and there are good and sufficient reasons to prefer the experimental method to all others. It is not always possible to use this method, however, so students of psychology should be aware not only of the virtues of the experimental method but also of the virtues—and the pitfalls—of nonexperimental methods.

The starting point for all knowledge about the world is the observation of some regularity in the flow of events. Thus people long ago observed the movements of the planets and calculated their orbits. They were regular, and this made possible the development of the science of astronomy. We came to understand the movements of the planets long before it was possible to perform experiments on the orbits of bodies in space. In psychology, too, we can and do make systematic observations about events with which we cannot interfere experimentally. Suppose, for example, you were interested in discovering what factors produce successful and happy marriages. Perhaps people who are alike should marry one another—or perhaps not. You cannot force people to marry one another for your experimental convenience, but you can measure the personality characteristics of people who are already married. Then, if you can devise an accurate measure of the "success" and "happiness" of a marriage, you can observe whether couples with very similar personalities tend to have more or less happy marriages than average. This kind of **survey method** is often used in psychological research.

The major drawback of psychological surveys is that the facts and regularities observed are often open to many different interpretations. Suppose you discovered that couples with very similar personalities did enjoy happier and more successful marriages. Would you then feel confident in advising young people to select mates with similar personalities? That would be rash

A student responds to questions asked in connection with a survey study.

counsel. Perhaps people who are happily married tend *as a result of that fact* to become like each other in personality. The mere observation that two things (similar personalities and happy marriages) occur together does not tell us which causes which, or even if one causes the other at all.

The facts revealed by a survey are basically **correlational:** We merely observe that some things tend to occur together in the real world. In the above example, successful marriages correlated with similar personalities of both spouses. The existence of a correlation may suggest many different interpretations. The actual cause cannot, of course, violate any of the facts observed, but it may not be suggested by those facts alone. We can, of course, conduct more and more elaborate surveys, collecting more and more different facts. Perhaps a convincing interpretation will finally emerge from the data, but it is also possible that we will miss the answer in a sea of true but uninterpretable facts.

Many surveys have demonstrated that college graduates earn considerably larger incomes than other people. This has often been interpreted to mean that college equips you with the skills and habits of mind that are necessary to earn a good income. Perhaps, consciously or not, knowledge of this fact had something to do with your deciding to attend college. But the truth is that nobody knows how, if at all, what you learn in college affects your ultimate income level. The people who attend college tend to come from certain backgrounds and to possess certain abilities and personality characteristics. Thus it is entirely possible that those same people, if turned loose in the real world at age 18, might earn the same relatively high incomes without ever attending college. Further it is also possible that a college degree is an irrelevant "credential" that serves as a passport to better job opportunities. That is, what one *learns* in college might be irrelevant to the economic benefits that flow from merely possessing a college degree.

Within some areas of psychology, the case-study method has been an invaluable technique for gaining important information and drawing hypotheses. The **case study** may be regarded as a special form of the survey method: The number of subjects surveyed (one) is, of course, very much smaller than in the usual survey, but the number of possibly relevant facts collected about that individual is very large. The case study involves very detailed knowledge about a single individual. Thus if you observed some striking behavior in a person, you can sift through your knowledge of that person's history and make guesses about the causes of that behavior. Your guesses may be wrong, but they can be tested by studying new and additional cases. For example, if you knew the detailed life history of a certain person with a severe stuttering problem, you might be struck by the fact that he had an unusually domineering father who often punished him severely. Perhaps your intuition would suggest that people with domineering fathers have trouble expressing themselves and may thus become severe stutterers. This is just the sort of hunch or tentative hypothesis that psychologists derive from a case study. In this case, though, the hunch is wrong; there is no indication that stutterers have more domineering parents than do nonstutterers. The danger of the case-study method is that it may confuse a striking coincidence with a true relationship.

Controlled Experimental Intervention

To illustrate the advantages of the experimental method, we shall first describe an experiment that, although it cannot ever be performed, could answer an important question. Then we shall describe some actual examples of how a straightforward experimental approach has helped to clarify interesting psychological problems. Finally we shall introduce a few useful technical terms that help you understand the basic structure of psychological experiments.

In the case study method only one subject may be involved or studied, but the amount of information gathered about that subject is much more than can be gathered through the survey method.

The available survey data establish beyond all doubt that cigarette smokers tend to die young—from lung cancer, heart disease, and many other illnesses. The data are so clear and overwhelming that no one can seriously question the fact that cigarette smoking is hazardous to health. There is not, however, any *experimental* evidence that smoking causes cancer, heart disease, or anything else in humans. What other interpretation of the survey data is possible?

There is an apparent psychological component in many diseases, as is discussed in Chapter 15. There is good reason to suppose that smokers and nonsmokers differ in their psychological makeup. The heavy smoker is often a tense and "nervous" individual. Possibly, then, tense and nervous individuals tend to die young from various diseases that are the result of their psychological traits. The correlation between cigarette smoking and early death might be nothing more than that—a correlation, and not a cause-and-effect relationship.

This line of reasoning seems more clever than wise, but it is hard to find fault with the logic. What about the fact, established by surveys, that heavy smokers who give up the habit improve their chances of living a long life? That can easily be explained away. We can ask, who *are* the heavy smokers who give up the habit? Possibly, they are tense and nervous people who at last have learned to live more comfortable and relaxed lives, and thus have improved their health.

The point by now may seem repetitious, but it is an important one: Without an *experimental* analysis, survey and correlational data are open to many different interpretations. Theoretically we could provide an unambiguous interpretation of the connection between cigarette smoking and early death by performing a simple experiment. Take 1,000 children 10 years old. Force half of them, selected at random, to smoke three packs a day for as long as they live. Forbid the other half to ever smoke. Then observe how long each subject in this experiment lives and also observe the cause of death of each subject. Presuming that the smokers die younger (it seems a safe bet), we would *know* that it is smoking—and not psychological traits correlated with smoking—that causes early death. We could also safely conclude that those causes of death that occur excessively in the smokers are the result of their smoking. Theoretically it is possible that *some* of the causes of death now associated with heavy smoking might not occur excessively among the subjects who had been experimentally forced to smoke.

The ethical sense of anyone seriously proposing such an experiment would be grossly defective, but the experimental analysis outlined does have the simplicity and definiteness to which science aspires. We want clear and certain answers to our questions. We are much more likely to obtain such answers if, rather than passively observing what occurs in nature, we actively arrange an experiment.

Experimenters intervene, arrange, prepare, manipulate, and plan. Thus in a sense they are in control of what is about to occur, and they are especially prepared to record accurately both what has happened and the circumstances that were in effect when it happened. They can—within ethical and practical limits—vary those circumstances at will and observe how, if at all, the phenomenon in which they are interested is affected. That, in essence, is what the celebrated experimental method is all about. Wherever it can be applied, it provides a certainty of knowledge that cannot be duplicated by any other technique. Experimenters can repeat their experiment and obtain the same

Psychometricians develop testing instruments that evaluate intellectual, personality, educational, or social characteristics. These tests may then be administered by any one of several different types of psychologists: school and educational, clinical and counseling, developmental, or personality.

result. Thus they come to feel that they can produce the phenomenon in which they are interested at will; they can turn it on or off by arranging the conditions of their experiment appropriately.

The purpose of conducting experiments, however, is not merely to control and to predict phenomena but also to understand them. To achieve an understanding of behavior, psychologists, like other scientists, use the results of experiments to construct **theories.** Theories—which are stated in general terms—explain many different and individual phenomena as the result of the operation of a small set of general principles. They enable us to see regularity and order in what would otherwise be an unending flow of unique events. They thus make our world more understandable.

Examples of Experimental Analysis

We turn now to some actual examples of experimental analysis applied to psychological problems. The experiments described here are not especially complex, but they illustrate the kinds of questions that can be meaningfully answered by an experimental approach to psychology.

DO FISH GET JEALOUS?   We will first use the experimental method to investigate the emotional life of a fish. The fish is the three-spined stickleback, a fish richly endowed with numerous "instinctive" or "species-specific" behaviors, as we will discuss in Chapter 10. The work of Tinbergen (1951) with this fish serves as a brilliant example of how a patient and straightforward experimental analysis can help to clarify what might otherwise appear to be a mysterious problem.

The male stickleback tends to stake out a patch of water as his own territory. Within that territory, during the mating season, he courts the female. The courtship behavior is quite complicated, and it follows a stereotyped and highly predictable pattern. When another male stickleback intrudes during

The Practice of Psychology

While all psychologists have been trained at the graduate level, the particular material learned as well as the techniques and methods employed differ considerably from area to area. The major subfields of psychology include

1. *Experimental psychology*. The term *experimental psychologist* may properly be applied to any psychologist who uses the experimental method to conduct research. But historically the term has been applied primarily to those who study sensation and perception; human performance; learning; motivation and emotion; language, thinking, and problem solving; and the physiology of behavior. Some two-thirds of experimental psychologists so defined work at colleges and universities, where they teach and conduct research. Many others work for government agencies, research foundations, or private research centers and industries.

2. *Clinical and counseling psychology*. The clinician diagnoses and treats individuals who suffer from emotional or adjustment problems. The clinician may conduct psychotherapy in private practice; in a state or private institution, such as a Veterans Administration Hospital; or in a number of varied settings such as juvenile courts, probation offices, prisons, or institutions for the mentally retarded. The clinician may also be a member of the psychology faculty of a university, teaching courses, training clinical graduate students, and perhaps also conducting therapy.

The counseling psychologist is similar to the clinician in both academic background and function. The counseling psychologist is employed in an educational setting, offering both vocational and emotional guidance to high school and college students.

3. *Industrial and organizational psychology*. Industrial psychology is an applied field. Psychologists in this area are primarily practitioners who apply psychological principles to the work setting, though some also conduct research to solve on-the-job prob-lems. Industrial psychologists are concerned with the "human factor" in the technological setting—how satisfied workers are with their jobs, how to increase morale and productivity, how to increase the quality of the industry's services, and how to develop better training and placement procedures. Industrial psychologists must be able to translate psychological knowledge and skills to practical settings, and also to communicate psychological principles to an audience with little or no background in the field.

4. *Engineering psychology*. The majority of engineering psychologists are employed in industry, where they aid in the design of equipment and training devices that are appropriate to human capacities. They also design and implement training programs to ensure the efficient functioning of human-machine systems. Other engineering psychologists work in governmental agencies or in private consulting firms.

5. *School and educational psychology*. School psychologists are concerned with problems of adjustment, mental health, and academic achievement

the mating season, the owner of the territory will attack and fight with the intruder. The attack and fighting behavior, like the courtship behavior, is stereotyped and predictable. The question is: What makes the male stickleback attack other males at this time? Those of us who have felt savage passions stir in our own breasts might be tempted to believe that the fish is in a jealous rage. To saddle a stickleback with an Othello complex, however, seems a bit extreme. Tinbergen's careful analysis of the problem followed more prosaic lines.

To answer the question, Tinbergen isolated the male stickleback in a special laboratory tank. The experimenter had provided himself with a number of wooden models of sticklebacks, and he proceeded to drop these into the tank one at a time. The models differed in various ways, as shown in Figure 1–1. Some were lifelike representations of male sticklebacks, while others were chunks of wood with little resemblance to a fish. The point was to discover what properties a model must have in order to elicit attack from the live fish. The result was clear: Any model with red paint on its bottom side tended to be attacked, but even very lifelike models without red paint on the underside were not attacked. The stickleback is so constructed that during the mating season it attacks things with a red underside that drift into its territory. That is, red-on-the-underside is a "releasing stimulus" for stereotyped and instinctive attack behavior. This may seem strange, but perhaps not so strange

in school children. They may also administer intelligence and proficiency tests to the students, assess problem behaviors and refer affected children to counseling agencies, and design and evaluate special education projects.

Educational psychologists are primarily concerned with the application of psychological principles and techniques to problems in education. They analyze educational needs, develop curriculum and teaching materials, and evaluate instructional programs.

6. *Psychometric psychology*. Psychometric psychologists develop testing instruments that evaluate intellectual, personality, educational, or social characteristics and adapt or develop statistical techniques for the analysis of such test data. They also evaluate testing instruments to determine if they are consistent and valid indicators of what is measured. The field of psychometrics overlaps with many of the other areas of psychology; for example, a psychometrician may construct measuring instruments in clinical, personality, or developmental psychology.

7. *Developmental psychology*. The developmental psychologist focuses on the human life span: infancy, childhood, adolescence, adulthood, and old age. Specific issues that the developmental psychologist may study include the acquisition of language and reasoning skills; the development of altruistic behavior and moral reasoning; the development of social skills and perceptions of self and others; and issues of adjustment in adulthood, and old age.

8. *Social psychology*. Social psychologists study the interactions between people, their perceptions of one another, and the effects that groups have on the behavior of the individual. Some of the topics studied by social psychologists are: social perception and impression formation, aggression and violence, the formation and change of attitudes, sex roles, and conformity and social influence.

Most social psychologists hold positions in colleges and universities; some hold research positions at private foundations and governmental agencies; still others are employed in more applied settings such as public opinion and market research consulting firms.

9. *Personality psychology*. The field of personality psychology overlaps with both social and developmental psychology and is also the field in which many psychometricians work. Personality psychology is both a research area and an area of concentration in educational and clinical psychology. Personality psychology is the study of individual differences —how people differ in terms of characteristics such as authoritarianism or emotional stability.

More than half of the positions held by personality psychologists are in universities, where both teaching and research is conducted. In addition, personality psychologists are employed by the government and private foundations.

Psychologists trained in any and all of the above fields often find employment and build careers using their psychological training in a wide variety of nontraditional settings. Some examples of such careers are given in another Application in this chapter.

when you learn another fact about sticklebacks: Glandular changes that take place in the male at the beginning of the mating season turn his belly red. To design the fish so that it attacks red-on-the-underside means that in its natural environment it will be attacking other males during the mating season.

The experiment, of course, does not answer all questions about this striking behavioral adjustment. We have no idea how the visual system of the fish is hooked up to its brain and its motor system in such a way as to produce this result. Physiologists, biochemists, psychologists, and others will be working for a very long time before we can begin to provide answers to such questions. This kind of experiment has in the meantime provided real clarification and has helped to "demystify" instinctive behavior. We may wonder how widely the implications of such studies can be generalized. In many other species the releasing stimuli for various instinctive behaviors have been discovered in a similar manner. We might wonder—and investigate—whether humans too are so constructed that certain stimuli tend automatically to trigger certain emotional reactions.

Of course, the experimental method can be used to analyze the behavior and mental processes of more complex organisms than fish. Since so many experimental psychologists work in a university setting, college students—who are easily accessible and often cooperative—have served as subjects in many significant psychological studies. We shall briefly describe one more experiment, which deals with a distinctively human problem and some very complicated social behavior. We include it to illustrate that the experimental method is fruitfully employed in all the various branches of psychology, including social psychology.

ARE CITY DWELLERS HEARTLESS? The interest of social psychologists in "bystander intervention" was spurred by a brutal incident that occurred in New York City in 1964 and was very widely reported in the press. A young woman was stabbed to death on the street of a residential neighborhood during the early morning hours. She screamed for help, and the loud and protracted disturbance awakened many people in the neighborhood. Police investigation later established that at least 38 people had observed part or all of the murderous attack, many watching from their windows. However, not one person went to the aid of the victim. Perhaps even more remarkable, not one even telephoned the police!

This apparently heartless and inhumane behavior provoked much editorializing and philosophizing. The incident was said to reveal the dehumanizing effect of modern urban living and our callous lack of concern for our fellow beings. Some observers thought that episodes of this sort signaled the breakdown of modern civilization. Two social psychologists, however, decided to subject "bystander intervention" (or lack of it) to experimental test. To do so, it was necessary to simulate an apparently lifelike emergency that would call for intervention by a bystander. The simulation devised by Darley and Latané (1968) seems to pass muster.

The college students who served as subjects in their study were temporarily misled, and it might be well to comment now on the ethical considerations involved in studies that use human subjects. The experiment must cause no harm to the subject. Further, when the study is completed, a careful "debriefing" session should be held in which the purpose of the experiment is explained in full to the subject, as well as the reason for any necessary deception by the experimenter. In institutions that regularly conduct research with human subjects, special review panels assess the procedures and purposes of a study before it is begun to ensure that appropriate ethical standards are maintained.

The subjects in the Darley and Latané study were at first led to believe that the experiment concerned how groups of human subjects went about solving certain problems under conditions of controlled communication. Thus, each member of the group was assigned to his or her own "isolation booth." The booths were interconnected so that verbal messages could be passed from one booth to another, but each subject was otherwise isolated from all the others.

Each subject was told this "cover story" after arriving at the laboratory. The detailed rules of the "problem-solving" experiment were also explained. Some subjects were led to believe that they were part of a 2-person group, while other were told that they were in 3-, 4-, or all the way up to 10-person groups. Each subject was escorted to an isolation booth and at no point saw the other members of the "group." The only communication allowed was through the push-button and signal-light network that linked all the booths.

The subject was never in fact a member of any group. The other students supposed to be in other booths did not exist. The "messages" the subject believed came from other booths as he or she worked on a collective task were sham messages generated by the experimenters. The critical point of the experiment came when, as the subject sat alone in the booth, a dramatic

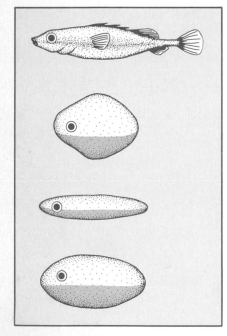

FIGURE 1–1
The three models shown with red on the underside elicited an attack from the male stickleback even though they bore little resemblance to a stickleback. On the other hand, the lifelike model at the top was not attacked, because it did not have red on the underside. (After Tinbergen, 1951)

message from a "fellow student" suddenly passed through an audio channel into the booth. The fellow student explained that he was not feeling well, that he really felt quite badly, that he was an epileptic, that he sometimes had severe seizures, that one seemed to be coming on, wouldn't someone please go get help? Then, through sound effects, it became clear that the student who had transmitted this appeal for help was having a convulsion. The dramatic message, however, was not genuine; it was an acted tape recording. The question of interest in this experiment is whether the real subject would do anything about the counterfeit appeal for help. The most obvious thing to do, evidently, would be to leave the booth and search for the victim's booth. The measurement recorded by the experimenter was a simple one: How many subjects emerged from the booth and how long did it take them to act after hearing the simulated emergency?

The results of this part of the study are indicated in Table 1–1. The variable manipulated by the experimenter was the number of people whom the subject believed to be in the group. The table shows that the subject was most likely to act and act quickly if told that he or she was the only other member of the group. In general, the larger the number of "bystanders" when an emergency takes place, the less likely is a given subject to intervene. The theoretical analysis of bystander intervention has been advanced well beyond this first study, as we will discuss in Chapter 19. For the moment the point is how an ingenious application of the experimental method to even very complex human social behaviors can produce orderly and theoretically significant results.

Size of Group	Number of Subjects	% Response	Mean Time (sec)
2 (Subject and victim)	13	85	52
3 (Subject, victim, and 1 other)	26	12	93
6 (Subject, victim, and 4 others)	13	31	166
Adapted from Darley and Latané (1968).			

Table 1–1: Effect of Group Size on Likelihood and Speed of Response.

The Nature of Psychological Experiments

INDEPENDENT AND DEPENDENT VARIABLES. We stated earlier that psychologists prefer the experimental method. It should be obvious by now that they agree that this method can be usefully applied to the whole range of phenomena with which they are concerned. The basic features of the experimental method are identical, regardless of the subject matter to which it is applied. Two terms that are very useful in understanding the structure of any experiment are independent variable and dependent variable.

The **independent variable** is something that there is reason to suppose might affect the dependent variable and that can be manipulated by the experimenter. Thus the makeup of the models dropped into the fish tank and the number of "bystanders" in the **experimental group** are both independent variables. In each of these experiments two or more values of each independent variable were subjected to deliberate study by the experimenter. The goal in each case was to observe whether different values of the independent variable produced different effects on the behavior of subjects.

The **dependent variable** is always some measurable aspect of the behavior of a subject, be it fish or human. Thus, whether the stickleback attacks a model and whether the subject emerges from the booth to get help are dependent variables. The dependent variable cannot be manipulated by the experimenter in the same direct fashion as the independent variable can. The value of the dependent variable, however, may be determined by the value of the independent variable that the experimenter has arbitrarily chosen for a given subject. The purpose of the experiment is in fact to discover whether such relations between the independent and dependent variables exist. In the two experiments we discussed, the dependent variable was clearly related to the independent variable.

There is often—thank goodness—a clear functional relationship between the values of the independent and dependent variables studied in a psychological experiment. For example, in the study of bystander intervention the time subjects took to emerge from their booths was smoothly related to the number of other subjects whom they believed to be present. The data showing this relationship are clear and orderly. The probability of an individual bystander's intervening *is a function of* the number of other bystanders who are present. We would like, obviously, to discover many such functional relationships. Whenever such functional relationships are established, we accumulate information to guide us in the construction of models and theories about the underlying processes that account for the relationships. If the theories are good ones they will not only account for the data already obtained, they will also suggest the existence of functional relationships that have not yet been established. Thus theory and experiment depend very much on each other. Without experimental facts we have precious little to theorize about. Without theories we would have no clear idea of how or where to find important experimental facts, what they mean when we find them, or how to relate them to other facts.

CONTROL GROUPS. The bare-bones description of the structure of an experiment suggests that the carrying out of a meaningful experimental study is as simple as child's play. Unfortunately that is not the case. Psychologists must often cudgel their brains in order to include in their studies appropriate **control groups.** We can best illustrate the logic of, and the necessity for,

The photos on this and the facing page show some examples of experimental psychologists, and of their subjects, at work: above, a graduate student cares for laboratory pigeons; below, a rat learns a maze; p. 15 top, a subject prepares to participate in a study of reaction times; p. 15 bottom, the developing perceptual abilities of an infant are tested.

control groups by describing a hypothetical example—which is, by the way, not at all farfetched.

Psychologist X wondered whether a particular drug really made people feel cheerful. To test this possibility, he recruited a large number of volunteer subjects. The subjects were asked to rate how cheerful they felt on a scale ranging from 1 ("abysmally depressed") to 7 ("ecstatically delighted"). The average self-rating of the subjects was 4.3—just a trifle more toward the cheerful end of the scale than the neutral scale value of 4. Then the subjects were each given a standard dose of the drug being tested. Psychologist X waited a long enough time to be certain that the drug had been absorbed into the subjects' bloodstream, then asked them to rate their cheerfulness once again. The subjects now reported an average rating of 6.1—a little short of ecstasy, but evidently much more cheerful than they had been. With appropriate statistical formulas, Psychologist X demonstrated that so large a change in average self-rating could not reasonably be attributed to mere chance. Thus he concluded that, just as the drug manufacturer had asserted, the drug really does make people feel cheerful. Psychologist X is either in the pay of the drug manufacturer or he knows very little about how to design a psychological experiment.

The same experiment was performed in a different way by Psychologist Y. The subjects studied were randomly divided into two different groups. One group was treated exactly the same as Psychologist X had treated all his subjects. First they rated their moods, then they took the same drug dosage, then they rated their moods once again. The results were virtually identical to those obtained by Psychologist X. The cheerfulness ratings increased from about 4.3 to about 6.1. The subjects in the second group were also treated in the same way, with one very important difference. They were given the same instructions and made the same mood ratings before and after receiving a pill. However, the pill did not contain the drug being tested—it contained only inactive ingredients. The cheerfulness ratings of this group *also* increased from about 4.3 to about 6.1. Thus Psychologist Y properly concluded that the drug does *not* affect cheerfulness. The second group served as a check or control over the interpretation of the results. This control group demonstrated a truism known to psychologists and physicians: People often respond to drugs and treatments in the way they think they "should." The bitter taste of a worthless patent medicine may convince some people that it is good for them, and they may then report that their symptoms are much improved.

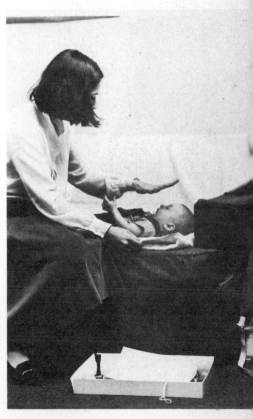

The necessity for appropriate control groups, as the following chapters will repeatedly demonstrate, applies to all areas of psychology. The point of a control group should be clear. We are often unaware of the effects that we, or unsuspected features of the experimental treatment, may exert upon our subjects. We are conscious of manipulating one thing deliberately, but we may well be manipulating other things at the same time. Thus, in our example, the important aspect of the experimental treatment was not the contents of the pill but the suggestion to subjects that the thing they swallowed might make them feel better. To guard against such possibilities, it is essential that a control group and an experimental group be treated identically in *every respect but one*. Then, if the behavior of the two groups differs significantly, we can logically attribute the difference to the one respect (the independent variable) in which they differed.

We might note that the purposes of a control group are sometimes accomplished in an experiment without designating any particular group of subjects as the control group. Suppose the drug experiment had been carried out with subjects randomly divided into four experimental groups, all of which received the same-sized pill and the same instructions. The pills contained, for different groups, either 1, 2, 3, or 4 grams of the drug substance. If there were significant differences in the mood ratings of the four groups, we could conclude that the drug did affect cheerfulness. However, the inclusion of a **placebo** control—a group that receives a zero dosage of the real drug—would obviously provide a clearer picture of the drug's effect.

Experimental psychologists must also be extraordinarily rigorous in the use of a variety of procedural controls. With a drug study of the sort described, it would not be gilding the lily to insist that the experimenter, no less than the subject, not know which subjects receive the real drug and which the placebo. There are several nasty possibilities here. The experimenter, without realizing it, might use a different tone of voice when instructing those subjects who are to receive the drug. This could easily influence those subjects' behavior. The experimenter might also mishear, misread, or miscalculate the responses of the subjects in such a way as to bias the results systematically. To guard against this kind of thing, many studies are now conducted with a **double-blind** procedure. That is, the experimenter who actually deals with the subject (like the subject himself) is unaware of the experimental group to which the subject has been assigned. The pitfalls into which "experimenter expectancy" may lead an unwary researcher have been documented in detail by Rosenthal (1967).

Basic and Applied Research

Within all sciences, there are two research traditions: One emphasizes basic or "pure" research, while the other emphasizes applied or "practical" research. Basic research assumes that discovering knowledge for its own sake is an appropriate and justifiable enterprise, while applied research is concerned with the immediate usefulness of experimental results. Although various subfields of psychology may emphasize either basic or applied research, in general the distinction between the two is not at all neat. In fact, much research bridges both orientations. Despite this, the basic-versus-applied-research distinction has created some tensions in the field of psychology. Basic research has been criticized as producing a body of literature that is of interest only to other psychologists. Particularly when public funds have been used, basic research has been criticized for wasting time and money to answer far-out questions that do not seem to be linked to pressing human problems. Within academic circles, applied research has often been criticized for a lack of theory, and thus a lack of general interest.

Kurt Lewin (1951), a distinguished social psychologist, struggled to amalgamate both theoretical and applied interests in psychology. He argued that psychology should not only increase the scientific understanding of human behavior, but also improve the quality of human life. By the late 1960s, in the subfield of social psychology, many were ready to follow Lewin by conducting theory-oriented research in real-world settings. There was a general call to take psychology "out of the laboratory" and into the social world. Some recent examples of "social-action" research in the Lewinian tradition include McClelland and Cook (1980), who studied energy conservation in an apartment building by using financial incentives; Kassin and Wrightsman (1980), who constructed "mock" juries to test the Supreme Court's assumption that jurors

The American Psychological Association (Woods, 1976) has conducted a survey aimed at locating trained psychologists engaged in unusual or nontraditional careers. The range of such occupations was very wide, indicating that psychological skills are found to be useful in a great variety of employment settings. The complete range is only suggested by the samples mentioned here.

In occupations concerned with social issues, psychologists were employed as: consultant to a Public Defender's office; legislative assistant to a United States Senator, focusing on health-care legislation; developmental psychologist working as consultant for children's television programming; president of a nonprofit environmental research foundation; psychologist in accident research; psychologist in social-urban planning; editor for a feminist publishing house, concerned with sex-role stereotypes; and warden at a center for young offenders.

In the clinical-counseling areas, psychologists were working as: administrator and consultant in the criminal justice system; assistant commissioner of public welfare; child psychologist consultant for day-care centers; vocational counselor in a rehabilitation agency; and rehabilitation psychologist. Trained educational and school psychologists were employed as evaluators of children's television programs; private consultants to schools, colleges, and state Departments of Education; and guidance specialists with foreign students. In the industrial field, psychologists worked as: consultants to management-development programs; researchers in the insurance industry; researchers on human-computer interactions; and engineering psychologist for the military.

Still other psychologists built careers as: researcher for a drug company in the treatment of psychiatric disorder; development of curriculum materials and specialized learning devices for insurance underwriters; researcher in human fertility issues; psychologist-editor for a medical publishing company; government researcher in highway safety; researcher and consultant for museums on visitor behavior; private practitioner concerned with animal-behavior problems; social psychologist organizer of volunteer work; and nursing-home consultant.

The comments offered by the individuals who responded to this survey made it clear that the broad training in basic psychological principles that they had received had both made it possible for them to enter these careers and had been useful in guiding their day-to-day work. There seem to be few, if any, areas of human concern to which psychological training is irrelevant.

do not allow a forced confession to influence their decisions; and Maniscalco, Doherty, and Ullman (1980), who conducted a study to discover whether applicants to graduate school were discriminated against because of a physical handicap. These kinds of studies, as Lewin noted in 1951, occur when and "if the theorist does not look toward applied problems with highbrow aversion or with a fear of social problems, and if the applied psychologist realizes that there is nothing so practical as a good theory" (p. 169).

The Assumption of Orderliness

The use of experimental methods in psychology must obviously be based on the belief that behavior subjected to such an analysis will turn out to be orderly, regular, and lawful. There are, as the following chapters will indicate, good grounds for such a belief. Psychological experiments have made sense out of a very large number of puzzling behavioral phenomena. Time and again psychologists have been able to show that many different behaviors are regular and lawful functions of many different independent variables. There will be at least some instances, as you read this book, when the addition of a new control group to an experimental procedure will suddenly cast a flood of light on a previously insoluble problem. However, in a sense the very successes of experimental psychology make it difficult to achieve what we would all like—a simple and complete understanding of human behavior. Probably the most difficult challenge for psychologists is the fact that behavior is simultaneously determined by *many* variables.

To predict, to control, and to understand the behavior of a gas in a cylinder,

Will *the* Real Psychological Truth Please Stand Up?

To acquire knowledge about the real world it is first of all necessary to observe it. The performing of an experiment is really nothing more than a very special and sophisticated form of observation. We can derive information about the world from any form of honest and careful observation of it. There are sometimes occasions, however, when our observations are impeded by precon-

ceptions and prejudices. This seems to be a special problem for students of psychology, since all of us carry around as part of our intellectual and cultural baggage a large number of psychological "facts" that are simply untrue. People have clearly been interested in other people, and in themselves, since people first appeared on the earth. From the myriad observations that people make of themselves and others it seems obvious and inevitable that a reasonable set of psychological facts should gradually be acquired by ev-

ery socialized human being and that these facts should be passed on as part of the cultural tradition. There are indeed all sorts of folk sayings, maxims, and proverbs that express the accumulated psychological knowledge of the human race. For example, all of us learn early in life that you can't teach an old dog new tricks. This homely saying seems to capture a number of profoundly important psychological truths. Plasticity is required for learning, plasticity lessens with age, old habits interfere with the learning of new

we need concern ourselves with only a very few variables. The color of the cylinder is not one of them. The behavior of human subjects, on the other hand, may well be influenced by the color of a room's wall—not to mention a quarrel earlier that day, a missed lunch, and the fact that their father died when they were three. To bring order to human behavior, and to predict it, is a far more complicated task than any faced by the other sciences. We can make many statements of the form: If all else is equal, then B will follow A. The problem is, of course, that in the real world all else never is equal. But that does not prevent us from coming to understand some things well and from learning that some variables are much more important than others in determining behavior.

RESISTANCE TO PSYCHOLOGICAL UNDERSTANDING

The attempt to develop a science of psychology sometimes meets with considerable skepticism, if not downright resistance. One type of objection seems largely theological. That is the argument that some aspects of human behavior and of the human spirit are outside the grasp of science. That may or may not be true, but the argument is not relevant to what psychologists are trying to do. Psychologists want to understand as much as they can as definitely as they can. To do this, they use the techniques and principles that have helped expand human understanding of the natural world. The use of those techniques and principles has helped us to make progress in understanding human behavior. We do not know how far we can progress—after all, in historical perspective, we have not been practicing the science of psychology very long. Perhaps the most we can ever achieve is very partial understanding. Even so, to replace ignorance with partial understanding seems to us worthwhile. Psychologists do, however, acknowledge that there are ways of coming to understand humanity outside of science: There is no danger that the advance of psychological science will cancel the value of Shakespeare in understanding the human condition.

habits. The difficulty with this analysis is that we also learn another folksaying: You're never too old to learn. Will the Real Psychological Truth please stand up?

There are many other examples of contradictory bits of psychological "knowledge" in our common heritage. Thus, "Absence makes the heart grow fonder"; but, "Out of sight, out of mind." Or, "You can't make a silk purse out of a sow's ear"; but, "Clothes make the man." We can make a reasonable guess about the history that lies behind such "popular psychology." We want to understand the behavior of ourselves and of other people. When a piece of behavior has already occurred, we can always "explain" it by dipping into the large grab bag of popular psychology and selecting out whatever psychological "law" best fits the occasion. Thus, if Grandfather first takes flying lessons at the age of 70, we have available two contradictory "laws" that between them will "explain" any outcome. Pretty obviously, true psychological laws should not contradict one another; and just as obviously, a knowledge of psychological principles should enable us to *predict* people's behavior, rather than "explaining" it *after* it has occurred. The point should be clear. We cannot rely on the practical, everyday psychology that has been passed on to all of us in the process of growing up. To the degree that it is possible to do so, it seems wise for students of psychology to discard preconceptions, or at least to be suspicious about the psychology which they think they already know.

Another common objection to psychology can be answered more simply. This argument is that human behavior is too "spontaneous" or unpredictable to be captured by scientific laws. This is just plain wrong. In many areas of human behavior highly accurate predictions are made by all of us every day. When the traffic light in front of you turns green, you can be reasonably certain that if you drive ahead, drivers from your left and right will not ram into you. There is little doubt that if you were now to read that on p. 118 of this book there is a vivid account of the sexual problems of college students many of you would stop reading this dreary argument and turn at once to p. 118. The odds are very high that nobody you know has engaged in incestuous sexual relations but that most of the people you know have had incestuous dreams. There are innumerable examples of human behavior that is both predictable and controllable—the task is to understand why and how.

Still another common objection to experimental psychology is that despite its high-flown promises, much experimental psychology turns out to be trivial. The facts and the data may be true enough, but they are neither interesting nor important. The experiments often involve animal subjects rather than humans. The problems analyzed often seem small-scale and unrelated to the real problems of human life. Why perform experiments that you know cannot provide answers to the truly significant questions?

There is a very good reason for performing "simple" experiments that seem artificial and contrived. To discover the laws that govern falling bodies we do not stand passively at the foot of the Empire State Building waiting for whatever happens to drop down. We instead set up a quiet corner of a laboratory and deliberately roll balls down inclined planes. The advantages are obvious. We are prepared to make particular observations at a particular time, with as many disturbing influences as possible eliminated. We deliberately isolate, and then manipulate, a *simple system*. There is too much going on in the real world all at once for us to grasp the relations between events. We are thus better off observing a simple system, with only a few variables at work, so that we can systematically make one thing happen after another. The history of science indicates that the general principles unearthed by the observation of artificially simple systems also operate in the wider world. The same principles that account for the motions of billiard balls in the laboratory also explain the grander movements of the planets in heaven. The "simple" experiments described throughout this text are attempts to isolate principles that can be applied to the understanding of many phenomena. We shall point to as many such applications as we can. We should repeat, however, that even the "simple" systems studied by psychologists are extraordinarily complex. To understand the movements of a white rat through a maze is doubtless easier than to understand the movements of a person through life, but it is still not easy. And the complexity in a slab of nervous tissue removed from a human brain makes balls and planes look like a child's playthings.

Despite resistance to the psychological perspective and the difficulty of the tasks, it is certain that the work of psychologists will continue for at least two obvious reasons. First, the subject matter of psychology is enormously interesting. There is little likelihood that people will ever lose interest in trying to understand "what makes them tick," and that is what psychology is about. Second, the results of psychological inquiry and speculation are relevant both to public policy and to the more private concerns of our personal lives. If we are to live better, we *need* to know more about psychology than we do now.

Psychologists do not yet know everything about human behavior; but what we already know is of interest, and it is also useful. There are a number of widespread beliefs about psychology that have little or no basis in fact but that have considerable impact and influence on many people. We hope that reading this book will help you to distinguish between valid and invalid claims about psychology. To use psychology effectively, it is necessary not only to know true facts, but also to have enough understanding to reject unfounded assertions. We hope and believe that the knowledge you acquire from the study of psychology will help you to understand better both yourself and others.

SUMMARY

1. Early psychologists were concerned with elementary sensations and consciousness; their chief method was introspection. Wilhelm Wundt was a pioneer in this field.

2. In the United States, John B. Watson revolutionized experimental psychology and claimed that psychology is the study of behavior.

3. The Gestalt psychologists and others, however, stressed the role of perceptual and other mental processes, both innate and learned.

4. At approximately the same time as Wundt, Freud developed his theories of psychoanalysis, in which the unconscious mind was a prominent idea.

5. Methods used by psychologists to acquire data vary, just as the various disciplines within psychol-

ogy vary. Among the various methods are *experimental method, survey method,* and *case studies.*

6. The experimental method involves beginning with a hypothesis and then testing it. Experiments must be carefully planned and repeated so that coincidence and accidental occurrences will not be misinterpreted as proof of the hypothesis.

7. In an experiment, the *independent variable* is the factor being tested; it is under the direct control of the experimenter. The *dependent variable* is some measurable aspect of a subject's behavior that may be affected by the independent variable. The purpose of an experiment is to discover whether such relations between the independent and dependent variables exist.

8. In an experiment, the control group—which should be as similar as possible to the experi-

mental group—experiences all of the same conditions as experimental subjects *except* for the independent variable. Control groups are necessary for the correct interpretation of the experimental results: Because the control group and the experimental group are treated identically in every way except for the independent variable, then it is logical to conclude that any differences in behavior are a result of the independent variable being tested.

9. Types of experimental controls are *placebo control, procedural control,* and the *double-blind procedure.*

10. Basic research is conducted for the sake of knowledge, whereas applied research is concerned with putting the results to immediate and practical use. In recent years social psychologists, in particular, have attempted to bridge the gap by conducting theory-oriented research in real-world settings.

Suggested Readings

BORING, E. E. *A history of experimental psychology* (2nd ed.). Englewood Cliffs, N.J.: Prentice-Hall, 1950. This is considered the classic overview of experimental psychology. The book begins with the rise of scientific psychology in the early nineteenth century and continues through to the modern period with a discussion of such areas as behavioral and Gestalt psychology.

CRAIG, J. R., & METZE, L. P. *Methods of psychological research.* Philadelphia: Saunders, 1979. This book is also an introduction to research methods. It discusses the scientific approach to problem solving, how to use research literature, and how to define variables and design research. Several research designs are discussed. In addition, the authors discuss ethical issues in research. The final section of the book instructs the reader in how to write a research report.

EVANS, R. I. *The making of psychology: Discussions with creative contributors.* New York: Knopf, 1976. This book consists of dialogues with prominent psychologists representing the major areas of psychology. The interviews introduce the reader to the contributor's major ideas and the historical antecedents of his or her field. The psychologists interviewed include B. F. Skinner, Jean Piaget, Gordon Allport, Konrad Lorenz, Carl Rogers, Leon Festinger, C. G. Jung, and Erik Erikson.

GUTHRIE, R. V. *Even the rat was white: A historical view of psychology.* New York: Harper & Row, 1976. The first half of this book explores the social antecedents of psychology by outlining the relationship between psychology and anthropology. The author reviews early research approaches to black/white differences. The second half of the book discusses the impact of psychology on the education of black people and the contributions of black American psychologists.

SHERMAN, R. *A career in psychology.* Washington, D.C.: American Psychological Association, 1965; WOODS, P. J. (Ed.). *Career opportunities for psychologists.* Washington, D.C.: American Psychological Association, 1976; WOODS, P. J. *The psychology major: Training and employment strategies.* Washington, D.C.: American Psychological Association, 1979. These three books discuss career opportunities and educational requirements in all areas of psychology. In addition, the American Psychological Association has several pamphlets on careers in psychology, which can be obtained by writing the APA, 1200 17th St. N.W., Washington, D.C. 20036.

WATSON, R. I. *The great psychologists.* Philadelphia: Lippincott, 1978. An examination of the historical unfolding of psychology through the works of its chief proponents. Drawing heavily on original sources, the book discusses the writings of Plato and Aristotle, Descartes, Kant, Wundt, Binet, James, Cattell, Watson, French, and contemporary American and European psychologists.

WERTHEIMER, M. *A brief history of psychology.* New York: Holt, Rinehart & Winston, 1979. A very readable little book that traces the emergence of psychology from the writings of the ancient Greeks and other philosophical traditions to the development of psychology as a separate field through the nineteenth and twentieth centuries. This is a good source to launch the reader on a historical exploration of psychology.

2. The Biological Framework

Psychology is primarily concerned with what organisms (people and animals) *do*—that is, how they behave. But, as we saw in Chapter 1, there are many different types of psychologists, and they take different approaches to this concern. One major difference is in their attitude toward studying what is *inside* an organism—in particular, the anatomy (structure) and physiology (functioning) of its nervous system. The two most extreme points of view are held by the behaviorists on the one hand and the physiological psychologists on the other.

The behaviorists, led by B. F. Skinner, maintain that what goes on inside an organism is none of their concern. They believe that a psychologist should try to predict an organism's response in a given situation on the basis of its past experiences, and never mind what goes on underneath its skin. This is sometimes called the "black box" approach because the organism is regarded as being enclosed and concealed—you can expose it to stimuli and record its response, but you can't open it and look inside. Physiological psychologists adopt the opposite strategy: They are primarily interested in what's inside the black box. The assumption is that an organism's behavior will become predictable when enough is known about its anatomy and physiology.

The two extreme positions can be likened to two ways of learning about a machine such as a car. The first method is to see what happens when you press the various buttons and pedals, and when you put (or fail to put) gasoline into the gas tank. The second method is to look under the hood and see which wire is connected to what, and which gear turns what other gear. Obviously, both methods are valid and would lead, in time, to a fairly good understanding of the behavior of the car. But neither method alone can give us the complete picture—for that, we need *both* methods. Thus in this book we shall combine the two approaches. In this chapter we will introduce you to the body mechanisms that are of chief concern to psychologists. In subsequent chapters we will examine the organism's behavior and then try to make connections with what is found "under the hood."

HEREDITY

All the instructions for building a car—including the "recipes" for the steel of the axles, the plastic of the dashboard, and the glass of the headlights—fill several thick volumes. Yet the instructions for making the infinitely more complex human body—including the "recipes" for the hard surface of the teeth, the flexible fibers of the muscles, and the transparent surface of the eye—can be fit into the microscopic area of a single cell. These instructions are contained in the **genes.**

Not only do genes determine whether you have blue eyes or brown, curly hair or straight; they also provide the directions for the construction of the nervous system, the endocrine system, the sense organs, the muscles. We sometimes think of genes as being primarily involved in producing *differences* among people; it is important to remember that they are also responsible for the many things that all humans have in common.

Genes and Chromosomes

Located within the nucleus of every cell in the body of an organism, genes are composed of DNA (deoxyribonucleic acid). This complex molecule, shaped

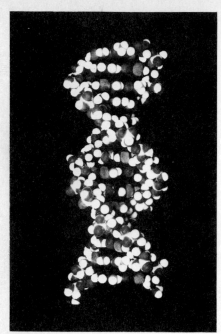

like a spiral staircase, has the remarkable ability to break in half lengthwise and form two new molecules identical to the first. The information in each gene is coded within the structure of the long helical DNA molecule by the precise ordering of its four organic bases (adenine, guanine, cytosine, and thymine). This code determines which of the 20 amino acids will be used, and in what order, in forming the protein that is synthesized by the cell. The kinds of protein that are consequently produced determine, in turn, the course of development. In other words, the information coded within the gene determines whether development results in a grasshopper, a sea anemone, a cow, or a human.

A large number (a thousand or more) genes grouped together in a specific order form a **chromosome.** Chromosomes occur in pairs in the nuclei of the cells of the body. The number of chromosomes varies from species to species—fruit flies have 8, frogs 26, rats 42, chimpanzees 48, and chickens, oddly enough, have 78. Humans have a relatively modest number: 46 (23 pairs). In each of these pairs one chromosome is inherited from the father and one from the mother.

When a human egg cell (ovum) or sperm cell is formed, it receives just one chromosome selected at random from each pair. Thus an ovum and a sperm cell each contain only 23 chromosomes instead of 46. When a sperm cell unites with an ovum at the moment of conception, the chromosomes from the mother join with those from the father, giving the fertilized ovum the full complement of 46. Since the chances are equal of getting either member of the mother's 23 pairs of chromosomes and either member of the father's 23 pairs, a given couple could theoretically produce 2^{23} times 2^{23} different combinations of chromosomes. Thus, genetically speaking, each of us had only one chance in about 70 trillion of being conceived! Despite this genetic diversity, a child still tends to resemble its parents, for the simple reason that half of its genes are shared with its mother and half with its father.

Figure 2–1 shows the 46 chromosomes of the normal male (left) and female (right). Genetic sex is determined by the so-called sex chromosomes.

A model of a DNA molecule showing its "interwoven spiral staircases" form (a double helix).

FIGURE 2–1
On the left are the 23 pairs of chromosomes of a normal male, and on the right the 23 pairs of chromosomes of a normal female. This figure shows the result of a process known as karyotyping, in which a dividing cell is flattened and stained, and a magnified photograph is taken of the chromosomes. The picture of each individual chromosome is then cut out, and they are arranged and numbered according to a standardized system.

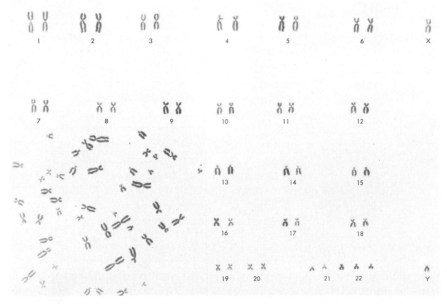

There are two sorts of sex chromosomes, X chromosomes and Y chromosomes. Every fertilized egg contains one **X chromosome** that is contributed by the mother. The second member of the pair, contributed by the father, may be either another X chromosome—in which case a female is formed—or a **Y chromosome**—which produces a male. Since only males have the Y chromosome, the genetic sex of a child is entirely determined by which one of the father's two sex chromosomes the child inherits. Occasionally something goes wrong with this process and a child is produced with only one X chromosome, or two Xs and a Y, or two Ys and an X. At other times hormonal abnormalities may cause a child whose genetic sex is male to appear female and be reared as a girl, or vice versa. (Such cases are discussed in Chapter 10, Biological Bases of Motivation.)

The 44 other chromosomes normally occur in matched pairs, although here again there are occasional genetic errors. In the most common of these there are 3 chromosomes instead of 2 in the 21st set; the result is a child born with **Down's syndrome** (formerly called "mongolism"), which consists of mental deficiency combined with various physical abnormalities.

Although the transmission of information from one generation to the next via the genes usually works very well, on occasion something goes awry. In a process called **mutation** one or more genes in an ovum or sperm cell is altered. Mutations can affect the structure and development of an organism in ways that may be beneficial or harmful; or they may have no significant effect on the organism. The causes of mutations are varied and include exposure to X-rays and certain chemicals.

Although chromosomes are large enough to be visible through a good microscope, this is not the case with genes. No one knows exactly how many genes there are in a human cell (the total number has been estimated to be somewhere between 20,000 and 125,000) or in exactly what order they are arranged on the chromosomes. Most of what is known about genetic action is derived by inference from breeding experiments, such as those that Gregor Mendel performed on pea plants more than a century ago. Geneticists often use fruit flies for their experiments, partly because it is possible to produce three or four generations of fruit flies in the time it takes for one pea plant to mature.

SINGLE-GENE TRAITS.   The genes for any particular trait are believed to be located at the same place on each of the two chromosomes that make up a normal pair. At a given location, a gene might occur in any one of several different forms, called **alleles.** Consider, for example, a trait that is controlled by a single gene, such as eye color in the fruit fly. We'll assume that two alleles are possible: one for red eyes (which we'll call E) and one for white eyes (e). If a fly has two of the same kind of allele, either EE or ee, it is *homozygous* for the trait. If allele E appears at the eye-color locus on one chromosome and e on the other, then the fly is *heterozygous* for the trait. In the latter case, the fly will have red eyes, because the red gene is **dominant** and the white **recessive.** The recessive version of a trait (white eyes, in this example) only appears when an individual is homozygous (ee) for the recessive gene.

If we mate a pair of red-eyed fruit flies that are each heterozygous for eye color (Ee), half of the offspring (on the average) will be heterozygous for the eye-color gene and will have red eyes. Half will be homozygous. A quarter will have the EE combination and will have red eyes; the remaining quarter will have the ee combination and will have white eyes (see Figure 2–2). Of course,

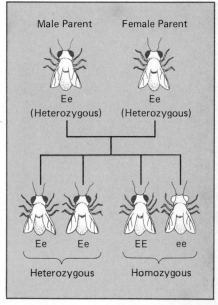

FIGURE 2–2
Eye color in the fruit fly is a single-gene trait. The gene for red eyes (E) is dominant over the gene for white eyes (e). Each offspring fly represents one-quarter of the offspring. Of course, since genes pair randomly, the offspring of any given pair of flies may deviate considerably from the expected proportions.

two white-eyed flies (both *ee*) can only produce white-eyed offspring, just as two homozygous red-eyed flies (both *EE*) can only produce red-eyed offspring.

A number of human traits are believed to be controlled in this way by single pairs of genes. For example, albinism appears to be a single-gene recessive trait: Two normally pigmented parents who are each carrying the albinism gene have one chance in four of producing an albino (unpigmented) child. An albino who marries a person without the albinism gene will produce only normally pigmented children; half of them, however, will be heterozygous carriers of the trait. On the other hand, the mutant gene that produces achondroplasia, the most common form of dwarfism, is dominant. If an achondroplastic dwarf marries a normal-sized individual, half of their children will be dwarfs. A union between a homozygous dwarf and a heterozygous dwarf would have only one chance in four of having a normal-sized child.

SEX-LINKED TRAITS.   The situation becomes more complicated when the gene for a trait is located on the sex chromosomes. In that case, it is known as a **sex-linked trait,** and the chances of having it generally depend on whether you're male or female. The two best-known examples of sex-linked traits are colorblindness and hemophilia (the condition in which the blood does not clot normally). The genes for these abnormalities are located on the X chromosome. A female has *two* X chromosomes, and if either one contains a normal gene for these traits, the abnormalities will not be expressed because they are recessive. A female can only be colorblind or hemophiliac in the unlikely event that she inherits one gene for the defect from each parent. But a male lacks a second X chromosome, so if the single X chromosome contains a gene for hemophilia, there is no allele to dominate it, and the child is born with the condition. Both colorblindness and hemophilia can be inherited by a son only from the *mother,* since a male always receives his X chromosome from his female parent. The female is a *carrier* of the sex-linked recessive gene.

POLYGENIC TRAITS.   Very few human traits are fully controlled by a single pair of genes; most of a person's characteristics, such as height and skin color, are **polygenic traits**—determined by the action of more than one gene pair. Even human eye color, although following fairly well the pattern of a single-gene trait (brown dominant, blue recessive) is probably a polygenic trait. Two blue-eyed parents *can,* on rare occasion, produce a brown-eyed child.

The Study of Heredity

Breeding experiments have been used to study polygenic traits in animals. Tryon (1942) performed a classic **selective breeding** experiment starting with an unselected sample of laboratory rats. The original rats differed considerably in the number of errors they made while learning to negotiate a complex maze for a food reward. The rats were separated into a "bright" group and a "dull" group based on their maze-running performance. Then bright females were mated with bright males, dull females with dull males. In the second generation this procedure was repeated, and so on for several generations. Tryon found that by the eighth generation he had two distinct strains of rats, "brights" and "dulls," with hardly any overlap between the two. Just about every member of the group that was bred for "brightness" was better at maze-running than an average rat of the first generation; just about every member of the group bred for "dullness" was worse.

The Tryon study demonstrated clearly that differences in the number of errors made while running the maze were somehow determined by inheritance. But it is not the case that Tryon's two strains of rats differed in *general* "brightness" or "dullness." In fact, later studies showed that even small changes in the particular makeup of Tryon's maze were enough to eliminate all differences in maze-running between his two strains. It is possible, for example, that Tryon's groups differed in their willingness to leave safe corners for open spaces—and that different mazes differed in the arrangement of corners and open spaces. We do know that selective breeding experiments have been performed—with results similar to Tryon's—using active versus inactive rats, emotional versus phlegmatic rats, and even alcoholic versus sober rats! These results come as no surprise to animal breeders, whose efforts have produced such diverse specimens as the Chihuahua, the bulldog, and the Great Dane.

HEREDITY AND ENVIRONMENT.   Tryon's rats were presumably treated alike—they all lived in the same kinds of cages, ate the same type of food, and had the same amount of maze-running experience. Thus any systematic differences in the scores made by the two groups of rats can be confidently attributed to differences in **heredity.** More commonly, experimenters use rats or mice that have been inbred (by breeding sisters to brothers for a number of generations) until genetic variations among them are minimized and the individual members of the strain are practically carbon copies of one another. Then differences in environment are introduced—for example, one subgroup is raised in bare cages, the other in an "enriched" environment. Any nonrandom differences that are found between the two subgroups can therefore be safely attributed to differences in environment.

In fact, differences in maze performance as large as those between Tryon's "bright" and "dull" strains of rat can be produced in either strain, simply by varying the complexity of their early environment (Cooper & Zubek, 1958). Thus it is important to distinguish between the specific genetic makeup of an organism, its **genotype,** and the manner in which these genes are expressed in a particular organism's development, its **phenotype.** The same genotype may yield quite different phenotypes depending on the organism's environment.

Such techniques cannot, of course, be used with human beings. A perennial question asked of psychologists is: How much of human behavior is inherited and how much is due to the effects of environment? Often it is impossible to answer this question because there is generally no way to hold environment constant and vary only heredity (as Tryon did), or to hold heredity constant and vary only environment (as experimenters with inbred rats do).

TWIN STUDIES.   Nature, however, occasionally provides us with the perfect opportunity to view heredity held constant. In the United States 1 out of every 86 births results in twins. Of these, the major proportion—about three-quarters—are **fraternal twins** (see Figure 2–3). Fraternal twins are conceived when a woman's ovaries release two ova instead of one, and each

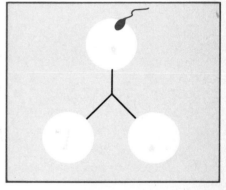
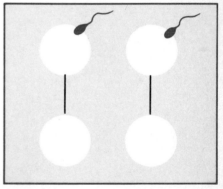

FIGURE 2–3
Identical twins (top) are produced when a fertilized ovum (zygote) subdivides to form two embryos. The resulting **monozygous twins** *will be genetically identical, since they each inherit the same parental genes. Fraternal twins (bottom), on the other hand, result when two ova released at the same time are each fertilized. Such* **dizygous twins** *are genetically no more alike than siblings conceived and born at different times.*

ovum is fertilized separately by a different sperm. Thus fraternal twins are no more closely related than ordinary siblings—on the average, they share 50 percent of their genes with each other (the same proportion that they share with each of their parents). Fraternal twins do not even have to have the same father: There are several authenticated cases of twins fathered by two different men.

The other quarter of twins are **identical.** Sometimes a fertilized egg, for unknown reasons, splits in two and forms two embryos instead of one. The genetic material in these two twins is identical—they have 100 percent of their genes in common—so any differences between them must be due to environment. Bear in mind, though, that "environment" includes what happens *before* birth as well as after. One member of a pair of twins is often more favorably situated in the uterus than the other; birth weights of twins often differ considerably. There is also an advantage to the baby born first—the second-born is more likely to suffer the ill effects of having been deprived of oxygen for a longer period of time.

The Study of Nature and Nurture

Many human characteristics have been studied with the goal of determining the relative contributions of heredity and environment. The methods employed are, of course, necessarily less direct than the technique of selective breeding—and the results, accordingly, are sometimes ambiguous. **Family studies** often indicate that a particular trait occurs more frequently among the parents, siblings, and other relatives of some family lines than in the population at large. However, such data do not make clear whether the cause of such "running in families" is the genetic similarity of close relatives, or the fact that their environments are similar, or both. **Twin studies** try to provide an answer by comparing, for the trait in question, the similarity of identical twins with the similarity of fraternal twins. Since identical twins have 100 percent of their genes in common, while fraternal twins have only about 50 percent, identical twins should be more alike than fraternals if the trait is genetically determined. However, since it is known that identical twins experience more similar environments than do fraternals, environment is not in fact held constant when the two types of twins are compared. Finally, **adoption studies** focus upon children given up for adoption at a very early age and thus reared without contact with their biological relatives. The aim of an adoption study is to *separate* genetic from environmental variables; such studies depend upon the assumption that the placement of children into adoptive homes has been essentially random. Complications arise if, for example, the biological children of "superior" parents tend to be placed into equally "superior" adoptive homes.

Twin and adoption studies have focused on a number of physical, mental, and behavioral traits. The results of such studies will be reported and critically evaluated where they are relevant throughout this book.

These and other studies have made it clear that genes do not *directly* produce mental illness or any other psychological trait: Genes simply provide the directions for building a body. When a psychological trait is shown to be hereditary it means that it's the product of some inherited characteristic of the body—probably some anatomical, physiological, or chemical variation in the nervous system or the endocrine system. These two important body systems will be the focus of the remainder of this chapter.

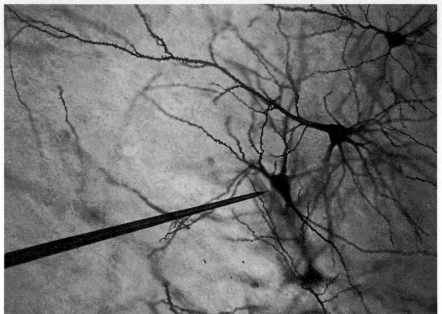

FIGURE 2–4
Golgi stained neurons from the cortex of a
monkey. The approximate 1 out of 100 cells
which take up the stain stand out in dark
against the unstained ones. This is a
microscopic view in which the cells are
magnified 500 diameters.

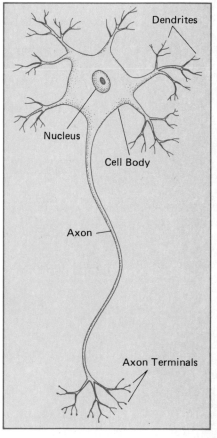

FIGURE 2–5
An idealized diagram of a typical neuron. Actual neurons vary tremendously in shape and size. Neurons receive stimulation through their dendrites or the cell body; the message is transmitted along the axon, which may be as much as a meter in length.

THE NERVOUS SYSTEM

In everyday language, "nervous" means "anxious" or "excitable," and "nerves" are what you're a bundle of when you're particularly anxious (not to be confused with "nerve," which is what you have a lot of when you're not anxious *enough*). Physiologically speaking, however, "nervous" simply means "having to do with nerves," the parts of the body that specialize in transmitting information. You may have disected a frog or a cat in a biology lab and isolated long stringy gray strands of tissue that were called nerves. These are really bundles of individual cells too small to be seen by the naked eye. Even under a microscope it is difficult to make out individual cells because their boundaries are so indistinct. In fact it wasn't until 1875 that an Italian anatomist named Carrillo Golgi found a way to see the individual nerve cells. Golgi discovered that certain chemicals completely stained a small number of cells while leaving the rest completely unstained. The structure of the stained cells could then be clearly seen under a microscope (Figure 2–4). What Golgi saw were **neurons,** the basic message-carrying cells of the nervous system. The unstained cells were both nonneural cells and other neurons (only about 1 out of 100 neurons absorb the Golgi stain, for reasons that are still not completely understood).

An idealized diagram of a common type of neuron is shown in Figure 2–5. Its major components are: the **cell body** (which contains the nucleus of the cell), short limblike structures called **dendrites** extending from the cell body, and a longer thinner extension called an **axon.** (Actual neurons differ considerably in size, number of dendrites, and length of axon.) Through a process we will consider later, neurons receive messages at the dendrite or cell body and relay them out along the axon to other neurons.

A Spanish contemporary of Golgi named Ramon Cajal used Golgi's methods to study the nervous system. (His drawing of neural structure, made in 1888, is shown in Figure 2–6.) Cajal demonstrated that neurons were discrete, well-defined cells whose interconnections seemed highly organized and specific. While many other staining methods have since been developed (see Figure 2–7 and 2–8), Cajal's use of Golgi's methods revealed much of the basic structure of our nervous system. (In 1906 the two researchers were awarded a Nobel prize for their work.)

The nervous system can be divided into two basic parts: the **central nervous system,** consisting of all the neurons that are entirely within the brain and the spinal cord; and the **peripheral nervous system,** consisting of all the neurons that are partly or completely outside the brain and the spinal cord. The peripheral nervous system can be further divided into **sensory neurons,** which carry information toward the central nervous system; and **motor neurons,** which carry signals from the central nervous system toward the muscles. Everything you know about the world outside yourself, everything you know about what goes on inside your body, has traveled to your central nervous system by sensory neurons. And every effect you have had on the world was carried out, in one way or another, through the action of motor neurons.

Neurons arose quite early in the course of evolution; animals as primitive as jellyfish have sensory and motor neurons. Neurons haven't even changed very much: A squid or a leech has basically the same kind of neurons a human has. In fact, much of our knowledge of neural functioning has come from studies of the nervous system of the squid.

In simple animals like the jellyfish, sensory neurons transmit their signals

FIGURE 2–6
In 1888 Cajal sketched this view of the Golgi stained neurons in a rat's visual cortex. It clearly revealed a complex network of interconnections between neurons.

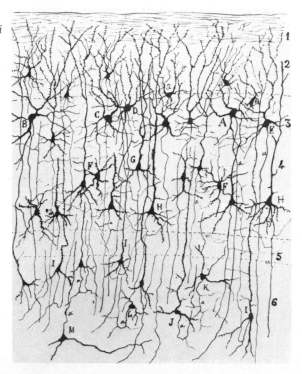

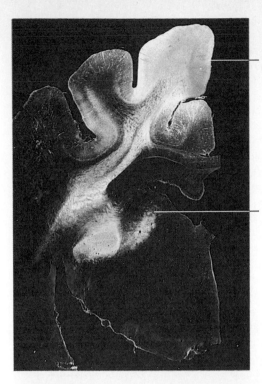

Visual cortex where horseradish peroxidase was injected

Horseradish peroxidase traveled through axons to lateral gerriculate

FIGURE 2–7
One way of studying neural pathways is to inject a substance called horseradish peroxidase into living nervous tissue. It enters neurons and is carried throughout their axons by a process called axonal transport. This photograph shows a slice of cat brain in which horseradish peroxidase appears white. It was originally injected into the cat's visual cortex, then spread along axons revealing the pathways connecting that area of cortex to the lateral geniculate.

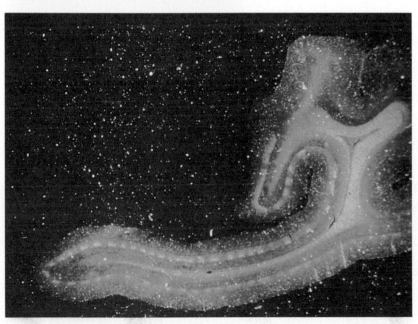

FIGURE 2–8 Organization of Neurons in the Visual Cortex.
Radioactive amino acid injected into a monkey's right eye traveled through neurons to his visual cortex. A slice of this cortex was placed on photographic film for several months producing this autoradiograph. The lighter bands indicate neurons containing the radioactive amino acids from the right eye which affected the film. The alternate dark bands indicate neurons associated with the left eye.

directly to motor neurons. But only a little higher on the evolutionary ladder —for example, in *Ascaris,* a parasitic roundworm—a third class of neurons intervenes between the sensory and the motor neurons. These intermediate neurons, called **interneurons,** process the signals sent to them by sensory neurons and by other interneurons. Then, on the basis of all the information they receive, they may or may not send a signal to the motor neurons for transmission to the muscles. Clearly, this three-stage system is capable of producing more complex forms of behavior than a two-stage system.

In *Ascaris* and other invertebrates, bunches of interneurons form clumps called **ganglia.** In general, both the proportion of neurons in the interneuron class and the total number of cells in the nervous system are greater in the more highly developed species.

By the time we get to the vertebrates (fish, amphibians, reptiles, birds, and mammals), the ganglion has become a full-fledged brain. We like to believe that the brain has reached its highest state of development in the human species—and perhaps it has, judging by some of our achievements. But it is well to remember that humans have neither the largest brains in the animal kingdom (elephants and porpoises have larger brains) nor even the highest brain-weight-to-total-weight ratio (it is about 1:50 in humans, but 1:20 in certain monkeys). There is no need, though, to feel overly humble. The human brain has somewhere between 10^{10} and 10^{11} neurons, or between 10 billion and 100 billion—as many as there are stars in our galaxy!

Development of the Nervous System

Even more remarkable, just about all these neurons are present in the human brain at birth—and all grow from the single cell that is the fertilized ovum. That means that brain-cell formation during the 9 months of fetal life must proceed at an average rate of 250,000 per minute! Of course, the rate of cell formation is not the same throughout development, because cells increase in number geometrically rather than arithmetically—one cell becomes two, two become four, and so on. Looking at it this way, it only takes about 36 generations of neurons to complete the human brain, or one division every 7 or 8 days during gestation.

In recent years it has been discovered that in many regions of the brain far more neurons are originally generated than eventually survive. Many seem to die during critical periods of development. Furthermore, there is evidence that sensory input to the developing brain determines in part which particular neurons survive. For example, certain cells in a rat's brain have been shown to receive sensory input from certain whiskers on its nose. These brain cells develop differently depending on the stimulation received by the whiskers (Figure 2–9). The more a particular whisker is stimulated, the more brain cells associated with that whisker will survive. The survival of cells in the developing visual system has also been shown to depend partially on visual stimulation. This sort of evidence has led to a growing belief that exposure to normal patterns of environmental stimulation may be critical during certain stages of human development. For example, children whose hearing mechanism doesn't work properly early in life may suffer irreversible damage to those areas of their brain that process sounds, even if the hearing mechanism itself is repaired later in life. This is why surgeons have begun to perform certain types of corrective ear (and eye) surgery on infants, when previously they preferred to wait until the infants were older and more sturdy.

GROWTH OF THE BRAIN AFTER BIRTH.   Approximately 9 months after conception, neurons in the human nervous system lose their ability to divide. Unlike most other cells in the body, neurons that die are not replaced. (Outside the central nervous system, however, an axon that is severed may be regenerated if the cell body remains intact.) Despite the fact that no new neurons are formed

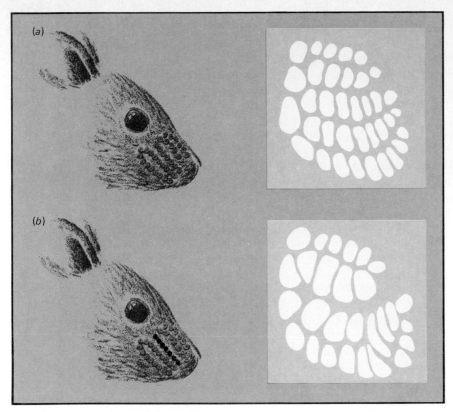

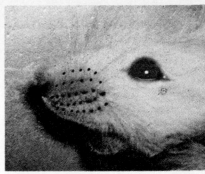

FIGURE 2–9
The photo of a mouse's snout shows how the animal's whiskers are arranged in rows. The blue-green stained tissue from a mouse's cortex reveals corresponding rows of sensory cells. The same thing (rows of whiskers and clusters of cortical cells) is shown in the upper drawing (a). The lower drawing (b) shows how removal of one row of whiskers from a newborn mouse's snout results in a subsequent loss of a row of cortical cells as the rat develops.

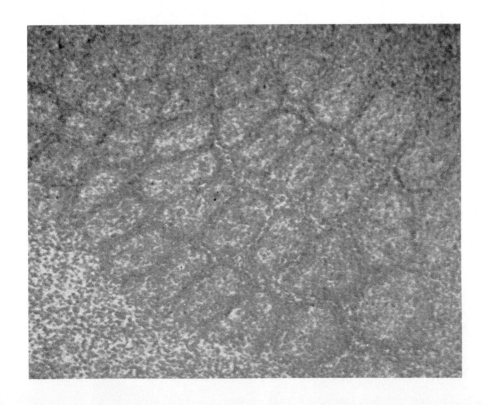

after birth, the brain continues to grow, from about 350 grams in a newborn infant to about 1,400 grams at puberty. This quadrupling in weight is partly due to an increase in the size of individual cells. In addition, the axons of many cells gradually grow a multilayered jacket of insulation made up of fatty cells called **myelin.** Since the transmission of neural impulses is as much as 20 times faster in myelinated fibers, the process of myelination is essential to the maturation of the nervous system. About half the cells in the nervous system eventually acquire a myelin sheath.

Probably the most important factor in the brain's growth in size during childhood is the proliferation of a second kind of brain cell, the **glial cell.** Unlike neurons, glial cells continue to divide; by adulthood they are 10 times as numerous as neurons. When a neuron dies, a glial cell grows to fill the gap.

Glial cells were once thought to serve primarily to hold the neurons together ("glial" comes from a Greek word meaning "sticky oil"). Now it is known that they have several other functions. They are responsible for the myelination of axons in the brain, they direct the growth of neuronal pathways or interconnections, and they play a general role in nervous system metabolism.

We have said that no new neurons are formed after fetal development. Neurons are able to live as long as people do and for the same reason: Parts of them are continuously being replaced as they wear out or are used up. In a neuron, all replacement parts are manufactured in the cell body and must be transported from there to wherever they are needed. A slow-moving system known as **axonal transport** carries the new cellular components down the axon to their destination. Cells in the brain are no more than a few centimeters in length, but in the peripheral nervous system—where an axon may extend more than a meter from its cell body—it may take weeks for the replacement parts to reach their intended site.

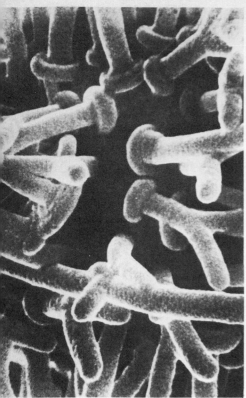

A *photograph of axons and axon terminals taken with a scanning electron microscope and magnified 5,000 times.*

How Neurons Work

The most important property of neurons is their ability to carry information from one place to another. This information is in the form of **nerve impulses** which travel along the neuron, normally from the dendrite or cell body out to the ends of the axon. The passage of nerve impulses can be recorded by inserting a tiny, needlelike electrical contact (microelectrode) into the liquid-filled interior of the neuron. Since only the tip of the needle is not insulated, we can measure the difference in electrical potential between the inside and outside of the cell. The electrical potential is measured in millivolts (mV). Figure 2–10 shows how the normally negative (about -70 mV) interior of the neuron periodically goes positive (about 55 mV). The normal negative state is called the neuron's **resting potential,** while each brief reversal of electric charge or *polarity* is a nerve impulse or **action potential.** One of the action potentials in Figure 2–10 is shown spread out in time to reveal more of its detail. Notice that after each positive phase or "spike" the interior of the neuron falls, becoming even more negative (about -80 mV) before returning to the resting potential.

What causes the sequence of electrical changes during an action potential? Basically, the successive opening and closing of microscopic channels in the "skin" or membrane of the neuron allow electrically charged ions to flow in and out. Ions are molecules that have lost (negative ions) or gained (positive ions) electrons. Large negative ions called organic anions (A^-) are produced

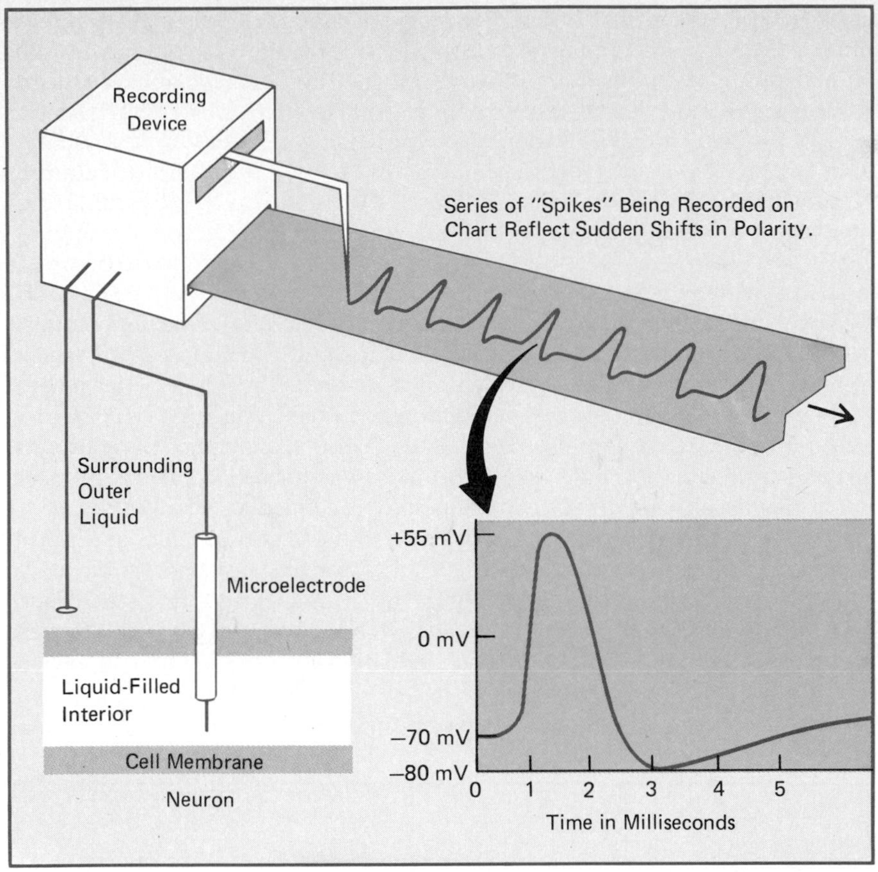

FIGURE 2–10
Recording nerve impulses. Detail shows the specific sequence of voltage changes of one nerve impulse over time. Each nerve impulse appears as a "spike" on the graph produced by the recording device.

within the neuron and remain there because they are too big to pass out through the membrane. Other smaller ions, such as the negative chloride (Cl^-), the positive sodium (Na^+), and the positive potassium (K^+), can sometimes pass through the membrane. Normally, a process called the ionic pump keeps the outside of the neuron about 10 times richer in potassium (K^+) ions than sodium (Na^+) ions, with this ratio just about reversed on the inside. A neuron's resting potential reflects the distribution of ions produced by the ionic pump, as well as the negative anions (A^-) trapped inside. (The inside is about −70 mV with respect to the outside.)

An action potential is triggered at a particular point on the membrane if the resting potential is sufficiently reduced at that point (e.g., by direct electrical stimulation). The action potential begins when microscopic sodium channels in the membrane suddenly open for about 1 millisecond. This allows *positive sodium (Na^+) ions to flow in,* quickly reversing the polarity of the neuron (the inside becomes about +45 mV with respect to the outside). This immediately causes other potassium channels to open for 1 or 2 milliseconds, allowing *positive potassium (K^+) ions to flow out,* leaving the interior even more negative (−80 mV) than it was at first. Finally, with both types of channels closed, the ionic pump restores the normal resting potential (−70 mV). The whole sequence takes only 4 or 5 milliseconds.

An important feature of the action potential is its **all-or-none property:** Once the sodium channels open, the entire electrochemical sequence occurs.

Furthermore, when the sodium channels close and the potassium channels open, it is impossible to initiate a second action potential (at that point on the neuron) until the potassium channels close. This is called the **absolute refractory period.** It is possible, but more difficult, to trigger a second action potential during the period when both types of channels have closed and the ionic pump is restoring the resting potential. This is called the **relative refractory period** (see Figure 2–11). These refractory periods limit the number of nerve impulses a neuron can transmit in a fixed period of time (e.g., pulses per second), since some minimum time must elapse between successive pulses.

Why do nerve impulses seem to travel along a neuron? If an action potential occurs at one point, it triggers off another action potential next to itself, which in turn triggers another one next to itself, and so on. The whole series moves like a wave along the neuron. A new action potential is triggered only in front of the traveling nerve impulse because the region just behind it is still in its absolute refractory period. This, then, is how information, in the form of nerve impulses (waves of action potentials), is carried along a neuron.

While nerve impulses travel faster along thicker axons, really rapid travel occurs only along axons that are partially enclosed and insulated by fatty cells called myelin. Action potentials only occur at unenclosed junctions called **nodes,** between these fatty cells. Nodes are found every 1 or 2 millimeters along the axon. When an action potential occurs at one junction (node), it

FIGURE 2–11
Relationship between the chemical and electrical changes that occur during an action potential.

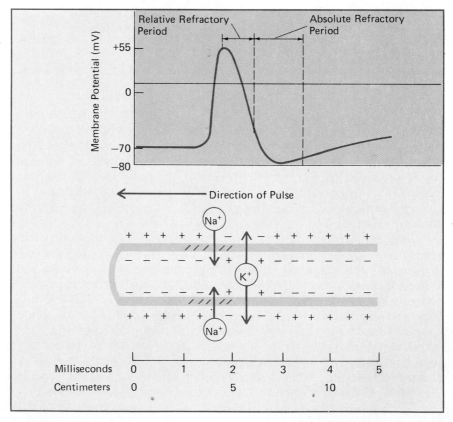

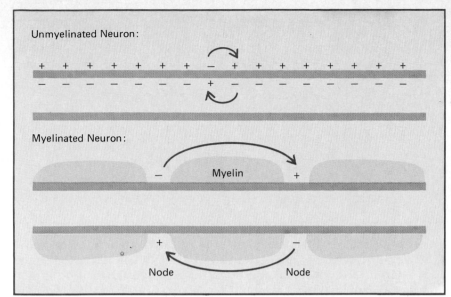

FIGURE 2–12
Propagation of nerve impulses along unmyelinated and myelinated neurons. Note that action potentials saltate or leap from node to node in the myelinated neuron, which allows them to travel faster than they do in unmyelinated neurons.

quickly triggers one at the next junction, instead of moving continuously along the axon, as it does in the absence of the myelin (see Figure 2–12). This rapid jumping from node to node along a myelinated neuron is called **saltatory conduction** (*saltation* means "leaping"). Thus, depending on the thickness and myelination of a neuron, its speed of information transmission varies from about $\frac{1}{5}$ to 120 meters per second.

Until now we have considered only how a nerve impulse, once triggered, moves along a neuron. We shall now consider how this triggering normally occurs and how the information traveling along one neuron is carried over to another.

Synapses and Neurotransmitters

Nerve impulses traveling along one neuron affect the activity of other neurons at points of interaction called **synapses.** These normally occur where the axon of one neuron terminates on the dendrite or cell body of another. Here, a nerve impulse (action potential) reaching the end of its axon can trigger an impulse in another neuron. In this way, information can be relayed from neuron to neuron. However, this is really too simple a picture of the interactions between neurons. Although they can relay information in this simple fashion, they often do far more. They combine, modify, transform, and process information in ways that we are only just beginning to understand and that are far more complex than the internal mechanism of the most advanced electronic computer. While much of this complexity need not be considered in a course on introductory psychology, some appreciation of it seems appropriate. In particular we should be aware of the variety of ways in which one neuron can affect another and the chemical nature of this interaction.

Figure 2–13 shows how the axons of many neurons (sometimes hundreds) can form synapses with a single neuron. Each point where the knobby ending of an axon (*synaptic knob*) contacts the neuron is an individual synapse. Between each synaptic knob and the other neuron is a very narrow (about

FIGURE 2–13

Synapses between many axons and the cell
body and dendrites of a single neuron. On
the neuron cell body and its branching dendrites are numerous synaptic knobs. These
are the terminals of the axons of other neurons. Note that the axon of this neuron
(shown at right) will in turn synapse with
another neuron.

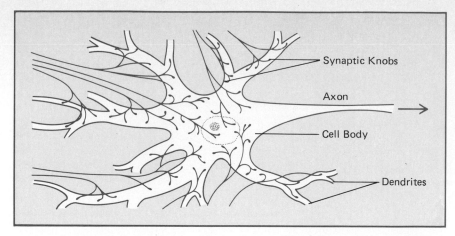

2 billionth of a meter), fluid-filled gap called the **synaptic cleft.** The arrival
of an action potential causes the synaptic knob to release chemicals into the
synaptic cleft. Those chemicals that are taken up by the other neuron so as to
directly increase (*excitatory synapse*) or decrease (*inhibitory synapse*) the
occurrence of an action potential are called **neurotransmitters.** (Other
chemicals act indirectly and are called **neuromodulators;** e.g., see Figure A
in the Highlight on endorphin and enkephalin.)

At first it was believed that there was only one kind of neurotransmitter,
acetycholine. It is now clear, however, that there are many neurotransmitters, only some of which have been clearly identified—norepinephrine,
dopamine, serotonin, and histamine, to name a few. Most neurons manufacture a particular type of neurotransmitter that is stored within each synaptic
knob in microscopic containers called *vesicles.* Figure 2–14 shows how an
action potential causes some vesicles to release neurotransmitters into the
synaptic cleft. These can be taken up at specific *receptor sites* on the other
neuron and affect that neuron's activity. Each neurotransmitter fits like a "key"
into a specific receptor site "lock." This whole process, called *synaptic transmission,* takes place in less than $\frac{1}{2}$ millisecond at some synapses. Any excess
neurotransmitter is quickly broken down or reabsorbed into the synaptic
knob (a process known as *reuptake*), so that the entire sequence can reoccur
within a few milliseconds.

FIGURE 2–14

A single synaptic knob of an axon is shown
on the dendrite of another neuron. Inside the
synaptic knob are vesicles or sacs containing
neurotransmitter (shown in purple). During
an action potential, some vesicles release neurotransmitter into the synaptic cleft. The detail shows how a filled vesicle successively (1)
makes contact with the presynaptic membrane, (2) empties its neurotransmitter into
the cleft, and (3) moves back into the synaptic knob where it can again become filled
with neurotransmitter.

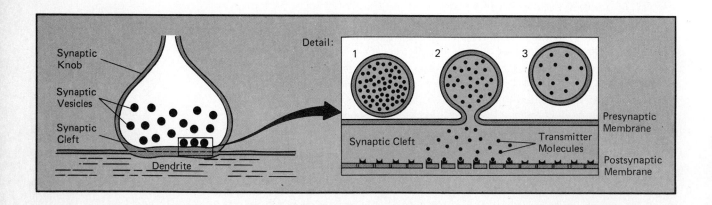

The Peripheral Nervous System

As we have seen, the nervous system is organized in a hierarchy of divisions. The first division is between the *central nervous system* (the brain and the spinal cord) and the *peripheral nervous system* (the neurons that are located, entirely or in part, outside of the central nervous system). The peripheral nervous system, in turn, can be divided into two classes of neurons: sensory and motor. Sensory neurons are connected to receptor cells located in the skin, in muscles and joints, in internal organs, and in the sense organs. They carry information from these receptors toward the spinal cord or the brain. Motor neurons carry information away from the spinal cord or brain; they form synapses with muscle cells at places called *neuromuscular junctions.*

The terms **afferent** and **efferent** are often used instead of *sensory* and *motor.* Afferent (from Latin *ad,* "toward," and *ferre,* "to carry") fibers carry impulses *toward* the central nervous system; efferent (from Latin *ex,* "away from," and *ferre*) fibers carry impulses *away* from it.

Motor neurons can be divided into two classes: **somatic** and **autonomic.** The somatic motor system is in charge of the skeletal or striated muscles. The autonomic motor system controls the *smooth* muscles (located in the digestive system, other internal organs and glands, and the walls of the blood vessels) and the *cardiac* muscles in the heart. Sometimes striated muscles are described as "voluntary" and smooth muscles as "involuntary," but this distinction is at best a rough approximation. The smooth muscles of the bladder are readily brought under voluntary control, whereas many involuntary movements—called **reflexes**—are performed by skeletal muscles.

Every synapse between an axon and the cell membrane of a skeletal muscle employs the neurotransmitter acetylcholine (ACh). Thus, a substance that interferes with the action of ACh can prevent nerve impulses from crossing these synapses and thus can produce paralysis. If the paralysis involves the muscles used in breathing, the results can be fatal. The deadly effects of *Botulinus* toxin come about in precisely this way, by blocking the release of ACh. (Botulinus toxin is sometimes present in improperly canned foods; it can be destroyed if the food is boiled for 5 minutes before eating.)

Other poisons block the uptake of ACh by the postsynaptic membrane; these include curare and cobra venom. Still others, such as the venom of the black widow spider and certain nerve gases developed for chemical warfare, cause too much ACh to build up in the synaptic space, so that eventually the neuron can no longer respond to it.

Neurons in the body are generally collected into nerves, which are bundles of parallel fibers covered by membrane. Nerves from the head and neck enter the central nervous system directly into the brain; these are the 12 pairs of *cranial nerves.* Those from below the neck enter the spinal cord as *spinal nerves.* Perhaps the best known nerve is the one that rudely announces its presence when you hit your so-called funny bone: It is the ulnar nerve, which passes close to the surface at the outside of the elbow.

Most nerves contain a mix of sensory and motor fibers. However, the fibers of the spinal nerves are sorted out before they enter the spinal cord. Sensory fibers enter from the back or dorsal side, forming the *dorsal root;* motor fibers enter from the front or ventral side, forming the *ventral root.*

Peripheral nerves are composed primarily of axons. A somatic motor neuron, for example, has its cell body within the spinal cord and sends out one

Endorphin and Enkephalin: The Body's Own Painkillers

Recently it has been discovered that two chemicals produced within the body, **endorphin** and **enkephalin**, are intimately involved with our sensitivity to pain. The manner in which successive findings have lead to this conclusion is a kind of scientific detective story that illustrates the very rapid, exciting interplay of experimentation and conjecture in modern neuroscience.

In 1973 several researchers (e.g., Pert & Snyder, 1973) published studies showing that certain regions of the brain and spinal cord are particularly sensitive to morphine, the analgesic (pain-killing) drug derived from the opium poppy. Fragments of neural tissue taken from these regions were shown to bind with (take up) radioactively labeled opiate compounds. Furthermore, this binding could be inhibited by a chemical called *naloxone*, which blocks the analgesic action of opiates such as morphine (naloxone is an *opiate antagonist*). Thus these regions of the nervous system appeared to be *opiate receptor sites*—that is, regions where opiates were taken up or received by the system. It was also noted that many of these regions were known to be involved in the perception of pain by humans and other mammals; indeed, electrical stimulation of some of these sites had previously been found to reduce pain.

Why should the nervous system have receptor sites for exotic foreign (**exogenous**) substances such as the opiate morphine? Suspicion grew that these sites normally function as receptors for internally produced (**endogenous**) chemicals similar to the exogenous opiates. Supporting this conjecture was evidence that electrical stimulation of the brain reduced the perception of pain in ways quite similar to that of opiates. For example:

1. Sites where electrical stimulation reduced pain were also found to be opiate receptor sites (Pert, Kuhar, & Snyder, 1976).
2. Both electrical stimulation and opiates caused neural signals to be sent along the same pathways from the brain to the spinal cord, where they blocked the transmission of pain signals.
3. The analgesic effect of both electrical stimulation and opiates diminishes with repetition, a phenomenon called **tolerance.** Furthermore, the tolerance developed through repeated use of one produces tolerance for the other, a phenomenon called **cross-tolerance** (Mayer & Hayes, 1975).
4. The analgesic effect of electrical stimulation is at least partially blocked by the opiate antagonist naloxone.

All this is what would be expected to happen *if the electrical stimulation caused the release of endogenous opiates that were then picked up by the same receptors that picked up morphine.* Sure enough, in 1975 scientists in Scotland isolated endogenous brain chemicals that would bind tightly to opiate receptors and could be blocked by naloxone (Hughes, Smith, Kosterlitz, Fothergill, Morgan, & Morris, 1975). They named these chemicals *enkephalins* (based on Greek words meaning "in the head"). Within a year other scientists had identified another group of endogenous, opiatelike substances they named *endorphins* (a contraction of *endogenous* and *morphine*).

Once the existence of these endogenous opiatelike substances was established, the next question was whether they had analgesic effects similar to those of morphine. The first answers to this question came from experiments on rats. For example, the tail-flick test is a commonly used measure of pain sensitivity in rats. It measures the speed with which a rat will move or flick its tail when a hot beam of light is focused on the tail. Even low dosages of morphine cause measurable decreases in the speed of tail flicking. This seems to reflect the analgesic effect of the morphine. Soon after the discovery of endorphin and enkephalin, it was established that injections of endorphin—either directly into the brain (Jacquet & Marks, 1976) or into the bloodstream (Tseng, Loh, & Li, 1976)—produced such analgesic effects on rats and that this analgesia could be blocked by the opiate antagonist naloxone. Furthermore, the analgesic effect of the endorphin was reduced in rats that had earlier developed tolerance to morphine (endorphin was shown to have a cross-tolerance with morphine). Similar research employing enkephalins was less clear, demonstrating a much weaker and shorter-lived effect than that of the endorphins. One reason for this may be that enkephalin seems to be broken down much more rapidly in our bodies than endorphin. (A rapid breakdown of this sort is common in neurotransmitters, since their persistence at the synaptic junction for too long would make a neuron unable to refire rapidly.)

Enkephalin does seem to play a role in regulating the transmission of pain information from peripheral pain receptors to the brain. This regulation or "gating" of pain information occurs in the spinal cord, as

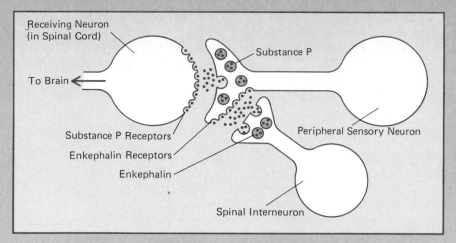

Receiving Neuron
(in Spinal Cord)

Substance P

To Brain ←

Substance P Receptors

Enkephalin Receptors

Enkephalin

Peripheral Sensory Neuron

Spinal Interneuron

Regulation or "gating" of pain information takes place at synapses in the spinal cord. The neurotransmitter substance P is carried in the axon of pain neurons. At the synapse these axons encounter enkephalin, the neurotransmitter released by interneurons. Enkephalin appears to control or modulate the release of substance P, so that the receiving neuron which sends pain impulses to the brain actually is receiving less substance P and therefore less pain information. Thus enkephalin acts as a neuromodulator.

illustrated in the figure. Peripheral pain neurons send signals into the spinal cord, where they form synapses with neurons leading upward toward the brain. The excitatory neurotransmitter at these synapses is believed to be a chemical known as *substance* P. It has been shown that enkephalin can block the release of substance P from sensory neurons. It has also been shown that enkephalin is present in interneurons (those neurons intervening between sensory and motor neurons), which also form synapses with the axon terminals of the peripheral pain neurons. We saw above that both morphine and electrical brain stimulation cause neural signals to be sent from the brain to the spinal cord, where they block transmission of pain signals to the brain. It appears that they do this through the release of enkephalin, which blocks the release of substance P from the peripheral pain axon—that is, enkephalin acts as a *neuromodulator*.

While there is much current speculation concerning the exact role of the endogenous opiates in normal body function, the picture is far from complete. They sometimes function quite locally at specific synaptic

junctions as neurotransmitters or neuromodulators and other times more globally, affecting whole systems of neurons. One of the most interesting conjectures is that they reduce our sensitivity to pain so that we can continue to function in highly stressful circumstances. For example there have been many stories of seriously wounded soldiers or accident victims who continued to function with little awareness of pain for some time after they were wounded. Under stress, did their bodies produce their own painkilling drug, an endogenous opiate? One research strategy employed to test this idea has been to see whether experimentally induced "stress" produces temporary analgesia. For example, Madden (1977) reported that after 30 minutes of discontinuous electric shock, rats showed increased levels of endogenous opiates and slower responses on the tail-flick test of analgesia. Similarly, Miller (1981) showed that humans exposed to repeated foot shocks had temporarily higher pain thresholds and that this temporary analgesia could be blocked by naloxone. Yet the results of other studies have been mixed. This may be because something as

complex as "stress" is difficult to define and also because some "painful" stimuli may involve non-opiate pain-control systems (Watkins & Mayer, 1982).

In any case, research on this fascinating topic continues, along with conjecture. For example, it has been shown that a runner's endorphin level rises during a long-distance race (Colt, Wardlaw, & Frantz, 1981). Also, it appears that strenuous exercise increases endorphin levels and that this increase is even greater with regular physical training. Does this mean that the exhilaration and freedom from pain reported by long-distance runners, the "runner's high," is caused by the release of endogenous opiates? Do runners become "addicted" to this "high," needing more and more endogenous opiates as their tolerance to them increases? Do they experience something akin to "withdrawal symptoms" when they are unable to run? Given what we know now, these are reasonable and intriguing questions.

It seems likely that some other endogenous chemicals also act much like familiar drugs. In the Highlight on endogenous benzodiazepines in Chapter 5 for example, we will examine endogenous chemicals that seem to act like the tranquilizers Librium and Valium.

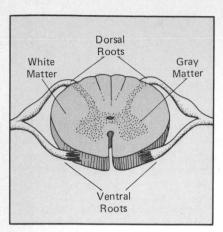

FIGURE 2–15
The diagram shows a cross section of the spinal cord, with the dorsal and ventral roots and gray and white matter.

extremely long axon that may reach all the way to the toe. In the autonomic motor system, on the other hand, the (generally shorter) journey is made in two or three stages: One axon leaves the spinal cord and forms a synapse with another cell, which either goes the rest of the way or synapses with a third cell. The many neurons that make up an autonomic nerve all have their synapses and cell bodies in the same place—within a ganglion, visible as a bulge on the nerve. Peripheral sensory nerves also have their cell bodies clustered in ganglia; these are located just outside the spinal cord, on the **dorsal** root.

The Spinal Cord

This column of neural tissue, only about 2 centimeters in diameter, runs downward from the brain through the hollow bones of the spine like a thread through a string of beads. A cross section of the spinal cord (see Figure 2–15) shows two areas that differ somewhat in appearance: a butterfly-shaped area of "gray matter" in the middle, surrounded by "white matter." The grayish area consists mostly of cell bodies; the whitish area, of myelinated axons that carry neural impulses upward, downward, or across the cord.

The spinal cord has two major jobs: to carry information back and forth between the body and the brain and to provide the necessary connections between the sensory and motor neurons involved in reflexes.

REFLEXES.   During a physical examination your legs may be struck with a rubber hammer just below the kneecap. Unless you inhibit it by tensing your muscles, your leg swings up in the familiar "knee-jerk" reflex. This is a good example of the simplest kind of reflex: the monosynaptic reflex arc. The doctor's hammer strikes a tendon that pulls a muscle and causes it to stretch. The movement fires sensory neurons that go from the muscle all the way to the spinal cord. In the spinal cord the sensory neurons synapse directly onto motor neurons, which lead back to the knee. Thus, the impulses received in the spinal cord are "reflected" right back to the muscle, causing it to contract. Figure 2–16 shows the neural pathway of the knee-jerk reflex.

Because the knee-jerk reflex is so easily tested, it serves as a ready, if rough, measure of nervous-system health. It is one of a large number of reflexes that make it possible to stand and walk erect. Such reflexes enable you to keep your balance when, for example, someone pushes down unexpectedly on your shoulders or knocks you sideward.

Few reflexes, however, are as simple as the knee jerk. Most involve at least one additional neuron, an interneuron. For instance, when you touch something that is hot and your hand withdraws automatically, the sensory neurons from the finger carry the message to the spinal cord. The message to the arm to withdraw the hand comes out of a *different* level of the spinal cord. To transmit the signal from the sensory neuron at one level to the motor neuron on another, at least one more neuron—and two more synapses—are required. Interneurons are also needed whenever the reflex crosses the spinal cord to the opposite side of the body. If you're barefoot and you step on something sharp, not only does the hurt foot withdraw, but the *other* leg stiffens so that you won't fall down.

The signals from the burnt hand or the hurt foot do not stop at the spinal cord. They continue upward to the brain. Only when the message gets to the brain do you become aware of the sensation of pain—by which time your

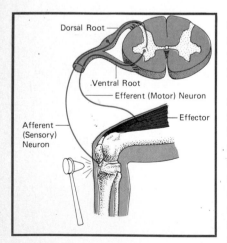

FIGURE 2–16
The neural pathway of the knee-jerk reflex, a monosynaptic reflex arc.

hand or foot has already jerked back. A person whose spinal cord is severed in an accident cannot feel any stimulation from the areas of the body inner-vated (supplied with nerves) by the part of the spinal cord below the break. Yet many reflexes remain intact.

THE BRAIN

Although the brain makes up only 2 or 2.5 percent of the weight of an adult human body, its rich supply of blood vessels furnishes it with about a fifth of the body's circulating blood. It uses a fifth of the body's supply of glucose (blood sugar), and a fifth of the oxygen. If the supply of oxygen is cut off for only 7 or 8 seconds, unconsciousness results; after 1 minute neurons start to degenerate. The same results follow if the supply of glucose is cut off—for example, by an overdose of insulin.

The interior portions of the brain have an additional circulatory system. This is the series of interconnected hollows (ventricles) that are filled with *cerebrospinal fluid,* a plasmalike liquid that aids in the nourishment of brain tissue and the disposal of wastes.

Removed from its protective bony case and deprived of its blood supply, the surface of the brain is grayish in color. This is the **gray matter** or **cerebral cortex** which forms a coating 2 or 3 millimeters thick over most of the outside of the human brain. It is composed chiefly of cell bodies. Under-neath is the **white matter,** composed primarily of myelinated axon fibers.

Almost everything that is visible in the intact brain is **cerebrum** (see Figure 2–17). The two hemispheres of the cerebrum, with their wrinkled wrapping of cerebral cortex, resemble the two connected halves of a walnut meat. Poking out from beneath the rear of the cerebrum is the **cerebellum,** with an even more heavily convoluted surface.

Extending downward from between the **cerebral hemispheres** is the lower portion of the **brain stem,** which continues through a hole in the base of the skull and becomes the spinal cord. There is not a clear-cut separation between the top of the spinal cord and the bottom of the brain; as in many other brain areas, the transition is gradual. But something very important is happening during that transition. Most of the fibers coming from the left side of the spinal cord are crossing over to the right, and vice versa. The left side of the spinal cord serves the left side of the body, but in the brain there is a reversal of this pattern. For reasons that may always remain a mystery, *the left side of the brain controls the right side of the body,* and *the right side controls the left side of the body.* Thus when a person suffers a stroke and develops paralysis in the left hand or the left side of the face, physicians know that the damage (usually caused by a blocked blood vessel) occurred in the right side of the brain. Fortunately, some recovery of function is usually possible, since unaffected brain areas may take over certain functions of the dead neurons.

Neurotransmitters in the Brain

When it comes to synaptic transmission in the brain, the neurotransmitter situation is incredibly complicated. Dozens of substances are involved, with different transmitters used in different brain areas and for different functions.

In order for the brain to work correctly, the proper neurotransmitter must

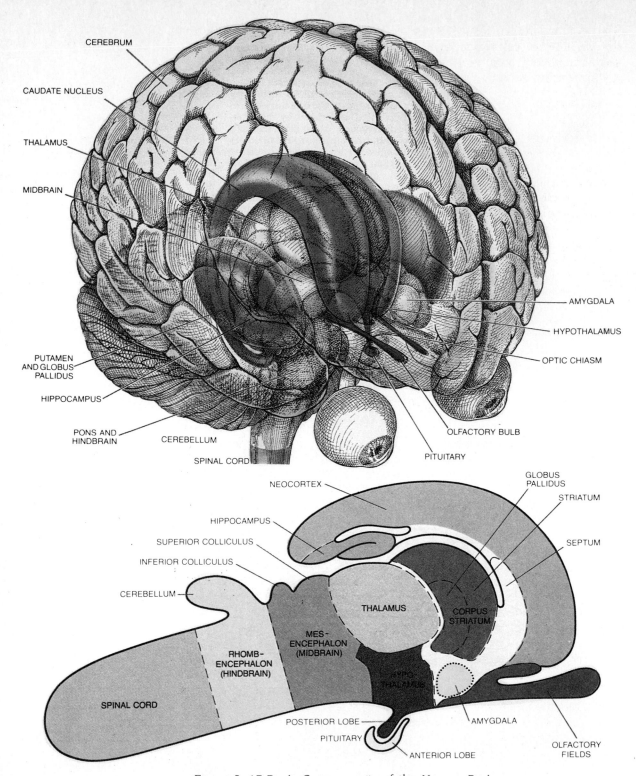

FIGURE 2–17 Basic Components of the Human Brain.
The corpus callosum, which connects the two cortical hemispheres, is located just above the thalamus at the base of the fold or crevice between the two hemispheres.

be produced in the proper synapse at just the right time; this substance must be received by the postsynaptic cell and then be inactivated soon enough so that it will not interfere with the next transmission, but not *too* soon. Given the complexity of the process, it is not surprising that things sometimes go wrong.

NEUROTRANSMISSION DISORDERS.   Two neurological disorders that have been traced to malfunctions of neurotransmission are Parkinson's disease and Huntington's chorea. *Parkinson's disease* is characterized by tremors and muscular rigidity (especially of the face) and by difficulty in making voluntary movements. This disorder has been traced to a deficiency of dopamine in certain parts of the brain. *Huntington's chorea* is a hereditary disease that first appears in middle age. It is characterized by jerky, uncoordinated motions of the face and body and by progressive mental deterioration. A deficiency of the neurotransmitter GABA is believed to be responsible. Huntington's chorea is carried by a dominant gene so that each child of an affected individual has a 50 percent chance of developing the disease.

You might think that such disorders can be treated simply by supplying the missing substances. This is not always possible, however, because of the **blood-brain barrier.** Nature has evolved a system for protecting the brain from toxic substances that might reach it through its rich supply of blood vessels. Blood vessels in the brain are less permeable than in other parts of the body; in addition, they are closely surrounded by glial cells. Only certain substances, such as oxygen, carbon dioxide, and glucose (blood sugar), can pass through this mesh. Large molecules are generally not able to get through, unless they are soluble in the fatty membranes of the glial cells. Thus, neither dopamine nor GABA can enter the brain from the bloodstream. For dopamine, an alternative has been found: A chemical called L-DOPA, which is metabolized into dopamine in the brain, does pass through the blood-brain barrier. L-DOPA has been used successfully in the treatment of Parkinson's disease. (Unfortunately, no metabolic precursor of GABA has yet been found that will penetrate the brain; thus, there is still no effective treatment for Huntington's chorea.)

An even more exciting way of increasing dopamine production may now be possible using a technique based on earlier work with lower organisms (Wuerthele, Freed, Olson, Morihisa, Spoor, Wyatt, & Hoffer, 1981). Recently, a potentially revolutionary operation was performed in which dopamine-producing brain cells were actually transplanted into the dopamine-deficient brain area of a Parkinsonian patient. Because the body's immune system works through the bloodstream, the blood-brain barrier prevented the transplanted brain tissue from being rejected by the body. It was hoped that the transplanted tissue would produce enough dopamine in its new site to relieve the patient's symptoms. While the results of this experiment are not yet clear, it opens up a whole realm of new possibilities. Since so much of the brain's activity is chemical in nature, it may be possible to transplant specific chemical-producing cells without concern for the precise synaptic connections. This would be, in effect, a kind of **brain transplant.**

PSYCHOACTIVE SUBSTANCES AND NEUROTRANSMISSION.   The psychological effects of many **psychoactive drugs** result from their action on neurotransmission.

Hallucinogenic drugs such as mescaline and psilocybin are structually similar to dopamine and norepinephrine and may mimic the effects of these neurotransmitters at certain sites in the brain. The lysergic acid diethylamide (LSD) molecule resembles the neurotransmitter serotonin, which is believed to be involved in sensory perception. The stimulant caffeine affects neurotransmission in a more complex way: It increases the amount of a substance (cylic adenosine monophosphate, or cyclic AMP) that initiates the action of neurotransmitters such as norepinephrine and dopamine. Another stimulant, **cocaine,** interferes with the mechanism that normally inactivates the neurotransmitters. This slows the recycling of these substances so that more transmitter remains in the synapse. Several antidepressant drugs, such as imipramine (Tofranil), work in a similar way, by slowing the reuptake of norepinephrine and serotonin.

Finally, neurotransmitters are now believed to be involved in several types of mental disorder. The most common of these, schizophrenia, has been tentatively linked with an abnormally high level of dopamine in the brain. Antipsychotic drugs such as chlorpromazine (Thorazine) seem to work by interfering with the uptake of dopamine by the postsynaptic membrane. The causes and treatments of mental disorders will be covered more fully in Chapters 16 and 17.

The Organization of the Brain

Neuroanatomists generally divide the brain into three parts: hindbrain, midbrain, and forebrain. In the adult human being, however, this division makes little sense because almost everything is forebrain, and most of the rest is hindbrain. These three divisions arose from structures that serve separate functions in simpler vertebrates: the hindbrain for balance and coordination of movement, the midbrain for vision, and the forebrain for smell. Although the organization of the human brain is considerably different and markedly more complicated, the three divisions can still be seen in the human embryo, arising as three separate lumps at the head end of the developing nervous system.

The Hindbrain

The hindbrain consists of the **medulla,** the **pons,** and the *cerebellum.* The medulla and the pons are two adjacent swellings of the brain stem, just above the spinal cord. The medulla controls some very important involuntary functions such as breathing, heartbeat, and digestion. In addition, several of the cranial nerves enter the brain at this point. Other cranial nerves enter at the pons, which serves mainly as a way station for neural pathways going to other brain areas.

The cerebellum (the name means "little cerebrum") is in charge of body equilibrium, muscle tone, and particularly the regulation of smoothly coordinated movements. Disorders of this brain area, sometimes seen in elderly people, lead to a characteristic kind of tremor that is most noticeable when the hand is making (or attempting to make) a purposeful movement.

The Midbrain

In the submammalian vertebrates, the **midbrain** is the primary area for processing sensory information from the eyes and ears. In mammals, this function is largely taken over by the cerebral cortex, and the midbrain shrinks in relative size and importance. Some visual and auditory fibers still travel to the midbrain, however. In primates, including humans, the midbrain's role in vision involves the control of eye movements; it sends out three pairs of cranial nerves to the eye muscles.

The midbrain possesses one other characteristic worthy of note. Many of the neurons that use the neurotransmitter dopamine originate in this area and send their projections upward to the forebrain. These pathways have been implicated in the regulation of complex movements and of emotional responses.

The hindbrain and the midbrain together make up the *brain stem.*

The Reticular Formation

Scattered through the brain stem is an intricate network of cells known collectively as the **reticular formation.** These cells receive inputs from several sensory systems; they send outputs upward to the forebrain. The reticular formation plays an important role in sleep and arousal. When the reticular formation of a sleepy animal is given a small electric shock through an electrode implanted in its brain, the animal immediately becomes alert and attentive.

The Forebrain

The forebrain is composed of two parts: the *diencephalon* and the *cerebrum* (*telencephalon*). The diencephalon contains the **thalamus,** a fairly large bilobed area at the midline of the brain. In mammals, whose cerebral cortex is the main locus for sensory processing, the thalamus is an important way station for receiving information from the various sense organs and relaying it—in an orderly fashion—to the cortex. For example, 80 percent of the axons of the optic nerve go directly to the *lateral geniculate nucleus* in the thalamus. (A nucleus is a ganglion located in the brain.) There these optic fibers form synapses with other neurons that project to the visual area of the cortex. Other nuclei in the thalamus receive information from the ears and from the sensory fibers that come up the spinal cord. This area also receives inputs from the reticular formation and from feedback fibers coming down from the cortex. Clearly, this is a major center for collecting and integrating sensory information.

The other part of the diencephalon is the **hypothalamus,** located (as its name implies) below the thalamus. This is an extremely important part of the brain because of its role in maintaining balance in many of the body's systems. For example, damage to the hypothalamus can disrupt temperature regulation, resulting in death from fever. Another important function of the hypothalamus is the regulation of motivated behavior (such as eating, drinking, and sexual activity) and of emotional responses. The hypothalamus has been somewhat irreverently described as being in charge of the four Fs: fleeing, fighting, feeding, and mating.

Hanging from the hypothalamus like an apple from a tree is the **pituitary gland.** Although this organ is an endocrine gland and not really part of the nervous system, it receives neural inputs from the hypothalamus. Thus, there is a connection between neural and hormonal mechanisms in the brain.

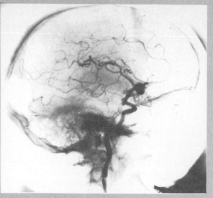
The Cerebrum

As Figure 2–18 shows, it is the cerebrum that has undergone the most dramatic increase in size going up the evolutionary ladder from fish to humans. The human cerebrum is composed of two heavily wrinkled hemispheres, which are (in appearance) almost perfect mirror images of each other. The gray carpet of **cortex**—a layer of cells roughly 2 millimeters thick—extends into the fissures and down the two flat facing sides of the hemispheres, until it is stopped by the **corpus callosum,** a wide band of white matter that connects the two halves (see the Highlight on split brains).

Under the cortex are several brain areas, known collectively as the *basal ganglia,* that are primarily concerned with the regulation of movement. One of these areas, the **corpus striatum,** receives dopamine-containing fibers from the midbrain. It is the corpus striatum that is affected by a deficiency of dopamine, thus causing Parkinson's disease, as we saw in the earlier section on neurotransmission disorders.

The remainder of the cerebrum can be subdivided into the **limbic system** and the **neocortex.** The limbic system is an oddly assorted set of structures

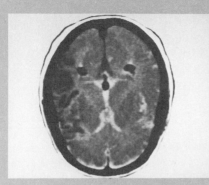

C. CAT *scan*

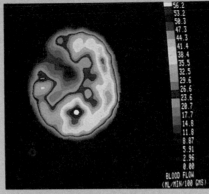

D. PET *scan*

called **computerized axial tomography**, or **CAT**, for short (*tomo* is from Greek word meaning "cut" or "slice"). Pictures of additional brain "slices" can be made in the same fashion, by simply sliding the patient along the axis of rotation.

While the CAT scan has already become an important medical and research tool, it has one important limitation. It reveals only the structure of the brain—not its neural activity. Another computerized method for generating pictures of narrow brain slices has recently been developed that does reveal aspects of neural activity. This method is called

positron emission tomography, or **PET**, because it is based on the release (emission) of positively charged particles (positrons) during neural activity. The emission occurs because some chemical involved in the neural activity has been radioactively tagged and introduced into the patient (e.g., by injection or inhalation). Each positron emitted as the chemical is used in neural action immediately collides with an electron, emitting *two gamma-ray photons that travel off in exactly opposite directions*. Photon detectors arrayed in a ring around a patient's head feed into a

computer, which calculates sites of high neural activity based on the simultaneous detection of photons by particular pairs of detectors. Using such information, the computer constructs images like the one shown in Figure D.

The major difference between CAT scans and PET scans is illustrated by Figures C and D. Both are images of a stroke patient's brain. The patient had recently suffered a stroke that blocked the blood flow to the left hemisphere of the brain. The CAT scan reveals considerable structural detail but only a slight structural alteration. The blood blockage was too recent to produce such changes. However, it had already caused major changes in neural activity as revealed in the PET scan shown in Figure D.

By using a variety of radioactively tagged chemicals, which enter into neural activity in different ways, PET scans may reveal how each chemical is being used in the living brain. Increasingly sophisticated versions of both the CAT and PET appear to be leading to major insights into the structure and function of the brain.

(including the hippocampus, the amygdala, and the septum) that are grouped together on the basis of function rather than anatomy. These structures are responsible for the production and control of emotional responses.

The limbic system receives dopamine-containing fibers from the midbrain; abnormally high levels of dopamine have been found in this area in the brains of deceased schizophrenics (Iverson, 1979). There are also close neural ties between the limbic system and the hypothalamus. In fact, on a strictly functional basis, parts of the hypothalamus can be considered part of the limbic system.

The role of the limbic system in emotionality has been shown by recent experiments performed with animals. Such experiments have shown that electrical stimulation of the amygdala or of certain parts of the hypothalamus (by electrodes permanently implanted in an animal's brain) produces all the signs of rage in laboratory animals. A cat, for example, hisses and bares its teeth and claws. Destruction of the amygdala has a taming effect in most species, resulting in an animal that is totally lacking in aggressiveness. Lesions in the septal area, on the other hand, tend to produce an increase in fear and anger reactions. Sexual disturbances, either hypersexuality or reduced sexuality, are also associated with damage to various parts of the limbic system. Perhaps the most interesting result is the finding of so-called pleasure centers in the limbic system and the related areas of the hypothalamus (see the Highlight).

THE NEOCORTEX

At last we come to the part of the brain that is responsible for all the things that distinguish humans from animals. The neocortex (often called simply the "cortex") is the outer layer of the cerebrum. This part of the brain began as a thin layer of cells in rodents, developed a few wrinkles in carnivores such as cats, expanded dramatically in the primates, and then suddenly swelled to tremendous proportions—pushing out the walls of the skull in the process—in human beings. The human neocortex has been estimated to contain "no fewer than 70 percent of all the neurons in the central nervous system" (Nauta & Feirtag, 1979). Neuroanatomists divide the neocortex of each hemisphere into four regions or *lobes* (see Figure 2–19); these lobes are separated from one another by landmarks such as the *central fissure* (which goes over the top of the head, cutting across both hemispheres) and the *lateral fissure* (on the side of each hemisphere).

Our knowledge of the functions of the neocortex has been greatly expanded by modern techniques of brain surgery. The Canadian neurosurgeon Wilder Penfield perfected a technique in which the patient remains conscious during the operation. The surgeon can then "map" areas of the cortex by

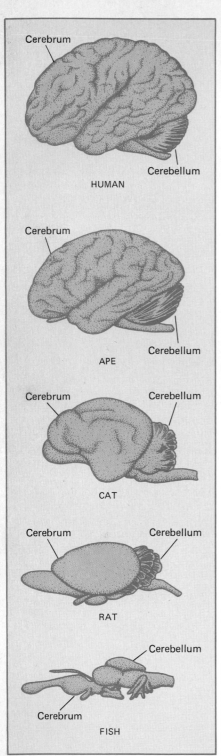

FIGURE 2–18
The brains of some representative vertebrates.

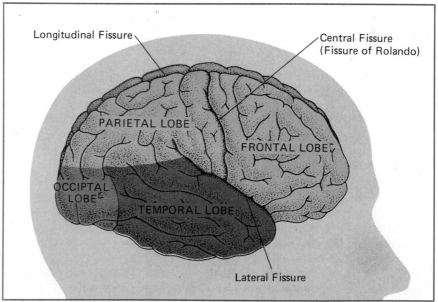

FIGURE 2–19
The four lobes of the neocortex and several important cortical areas are shown.

"Pleasure Centers" in the Brain

The discovery was made in 1953, at McGill University in Canada. James Olds, who was then a postdoctoral student, and Peter Milner, a graduate student, were testing the effects of electrical stimulation of the reticular formation, using electrodes permanently implanted in the brains of rats. One day an electrode aimed for the reticular formation went astray and ended up—as it was later discovered—in a nerve pathway near the hypothalamus. The rat recovered from the surgery and became a subject in Olds and Milner's experiment: A series of tiny electric shocks, each three or four volts in magnitude, were administered to its brain through the implanted electrode.

The results were surprising. The rat was free to run around in a large cage, and if it happened to be in a certain corner of the cage when the shock went on, it would tend to return to that corner. Olds and Milner soon discovered that they could induce the rat to remain in any part of the cage they chose, simply by administering the shocks only when the rat was in that location. It was clear that the rat was actively seeking electrical stimulation of the brain (ESB) and that it must have found the stimulation in some way pleasurable or rewarding (Olds & Milner, 1954).

Later, a lever was put in the rat's cage. Each time the rat pushed the lever it received an ESB lasting about a second. The animal quickly learned to press the lever and was soon administering ESBs to itself at a rate of 1 every 5 seconds. Olds and his associates went on to test many other brain sites and found that some electrode placements produced even higher rates of responding, up to 5,000 an hour. Rats with electrodes in these sites preferred to stimulate their brains rather than eat or sleep. One rat pressed the lever continuously for 26 hours straight before collapsing in exhaustion.

The brain locations involved include the limbic system and parts of the hypothalamus and the midbrain, all closely linked by extensive neural interconnections. In a rat's brain, that covers a lot of territory: Olds has estimated that almost a third of a rat's brain produces positive ESB results. A much smaller number of brain areas produce negative reactions—the rat will press the lever once by chance but will thereafter avoid it. These aversive brain sites are often located quite close to the positive sites.

Olds coined the term "pleasure centers" to describe the parts of the brain that produce a positive response to ESB. Rats are not the only species with pleasure centers: The original findings have since been extended to many other animal species, including goldfish, chickens, guinea pigs, rabbits, cats, dogs, dolphins, and monkeys.

There has been considerable speculation about the rewarding effects of ESB. It was quickly noticed that some male rats had ejaculations with ESB, and it was thought that the stimulation produced its effects through sexual gratification—that these rats were treating themselves to as many as thousands of orgasms an hour! Clearly, though, sex is not the only motivation. Some positive brain areas are associated with the hunger drive, others with thirst. A leading theory (Deutsch, 1960) of positive ESB effects is that the brain stimulation creates or increases the drive and at the same time relieves it. However, some brain areas that yield positive ESB results do not seem to be tied to a single drive.

Naturally, one is interested in knowing what effects this kind of ESB would have on a human being. Could one turn a person into a lever-pressing zombie by implanting electrodes in a human brain? Probably not, judging from the small amount of data that is presently available. There are some indications of pleasurable sensations (Sem-Jacobsen & Torkildsen, 1960), but these appear to be fairly mild compared with what animal experiments have led us to expect.

---

applying a small electric current and noting what the patient reports or what movements occur.

Sensory and Motor Areas of the Neocortex

The human neocortex, like that of other mammals, is partly taken up by sensory and motor functions. Two areas that have been extensively mapped are the **somatosensory area** and the **motor area.** These lie in a band that goes over the top of the brain, just behind and just in front of the central fissure.

THE MOTOR CORTEX. Mild electrical stimulation of a specific point on the motor cortex causes a movement of a specific part of the body. If a point on the right hemisphere is stimulated, a body part on the left side will respond, and vice versa. Moving the electrode to a different spot produces movement of another part of the body. Penfield found that some regions of the body—for instance, the fingers and the face—are represented by relatively large areas of the motor cortex, whereas other parts—the trunk and the legs—are allotted relatively small areas. The right side of Figure 2–20 is a graphic depiction of the resulting map of the motor cortex. In this picture, called a **motor homunculus,** each part of the body is shown larger or smaller, according to how much motor cortex is devoted to it. This is an approximate index of how many neurons serve that body part, which reflects the precision with which it can be controlled.

THE SOMATOSENSORY CORTEX. A similar mapping procedure on the posterior side of the central fissure produces a **somatosensory homunculus,** shown on the left side of Figure 2–20. In this case, the result of the electrical stimulation is a sensation somewhere in the body (again, on the opposite

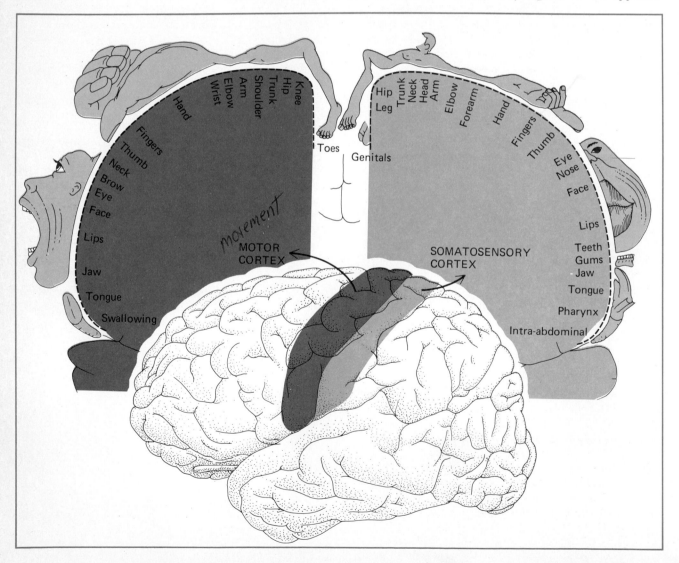

FIGURE 2–20
(Blue) A cross-section of the somatosensory cortex, and a somatosensory homunculus. (Red) A cross-section of the motor cortex of the human cerebrum and a motor homunculus. The sizes of the body parts are drawn in proportion to the amount of cortex devoted to them. (After Penfield & Rasmussen, 1950)

side). The two homunculi are quite similar—the parts of the body, such as the face and hands, that take up a lot of motor cortex also take up a lot of somatosensory cortex. Note that *all* somatosensory information is represented in this brain area: warmth, cold, pressure, pain, and awareness of location and motion of body parts. This information comes from the somatosensory neurons of the spinal cord and of the cranial nerves and assembles in the thalamus before reaching the cortex. The neural pathways that serve the sense of taste also end up on the somatosensory cortex.

THE AUDITORY CORTEX.   Auditory information from the ears is projected to the auditory cortex, which is just below the lateral fissure. The auditory cortex on each hemisphere receives inputs from *both* ears; however, each hemisphere gets more of its information from the ear on the opposite side of the head. Most neurons in the auditory cortex are "tuned" to sounds of a particular frequency or pitch. That is, a given neuron fires rapidly when sounds of a certain frequency are heard; it fires at slower rates to higher or lower frequencies. Different neurons are tuned to different frequencies.

THE VISUAL CORTEX.   Information from the eyes is carried to the brain by the two optic nerves and ultimately reaches the occipital lobe, in the very back of the head. Information from both eyes reaches both hemispheres, but it is divided up in a rather peculiar way: Neural signals from the right side of each eye reach the right side of the brain, those from the left go to the left side of the brain. This means that the visual field is divided in two. If you stare at the crease between the left- and right-hand pages of this book, the left-hand page is represented on your *right* occipital lobe, the right-hand page on your *left!* In order to accomplish this partition, each optic nerve has to split in half, with the two halves nearest the nose crossing over to go to the opposite side of the brain. The point where they cross is known as the **optic chiasm.**

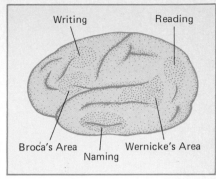

FIGURE 2–21
The usual locations of the brain areas that serve language functions are shown on the left cerebral hemisphere. The locations of these language centers vary somewhat from person to person; in some individuals they are on the right hemisphere.

Association Areas of the Neocortex

If we subtract all sensory and motor areas from the neocortex, the parts that remain are called **association areas.** It is to these areas that we owe our ability to speak, to read, to think, and to laugh. The association areas receive no direct inputs from the outside world; nor do they produce any outputs that result directly in motor responses. As the British brain biochemist Steven Rose (1975) has put it, "Neurons of the association areas talk only to one another and to other cortical neurons."

SPEECH AREAS.   The first part of the neocortex to be correctly assigned a specific function was a region known as **Broca's area,** located near the part of the motor cortex that controls movements of the mouth and jaws (see Figure 2–21). The discovery that this area plays an important role in the production of speech was made in 1861 by the French neurologist Paul Broca. One of Broca's patients was a man called "Tan," who totally lacked meaningful speech, although he was able to communicate with gestures. After Tan's death Broca examined his brain and found a lesion just above the lateral fissure, on the left hemisphere.

The disorder from which Tan had suffered is called **aphasia.** People with Broca's aphasia are able to understand speech and to use their vocal apparatus in other ways (they can sing, for instance); but they speak—if at all—only with great difficulty. Words are wrested out one by one, and they do not form complete sentences.

A second kind of aphasia was described by Carl Wernicke in 1874. It is associated with a brain area called **Wernicke's area,** located on the lower side of the lateral fissure near the auditory cortex. Damage to Wernicke's area produces a type of language difficulty in which both comprehension and speech are affected. People with Wernicke's aphasia speak fluently and in recognizable sentences, but the content of their speech is often bizarre or nonsensical.

The kind of brain damage that produces Broca's or Wernicke's aphasia usually involves only one hemisphere—the left, in most cases. Injuries to the same areas on the right side generally do not affect language ability. This fact, noted by Broca himself, was the first indication that the two hemispheres are not identical in function. We will now take a closer look at the differences between the two sides of the brain.

Right and Left Brain

The connection between speech and handedness has been known for over a century; it was too obvious to miss. When a person suffers a massive injury to the **left hemisphere** of the brain (most often because of a stroke), there are usually two results: paralysis of all or part of the right side of the body and a loss of the use of language. Perhaps a double-edged tragedy of this kind served as the inspiration for the Psalmist who wrote: "If I forget thee, O Jerusalem, let my right hand forget her cunning. If I do not remember thee, let my tongue cleave to the roof of my mouth" (Psalm 137). Most people use the left side of the brain to process language, and the right hand—which is controlled by the left side of the brain—to perform tasks that require skill. A little more than 90 percent of humans are right-handed, and this preponderance has prevailed for at least 5,000 years (Coren & Porac, 1977) and probably goes back to the earliest hominids (Dart, 1949). Apes, however, like subprimate vertebrates, do not tend to right-dominance. In most animal species individual members may favor one paw over the other, but the favored side is as likely to be the left as the right (Corballis & Beale, 1976).

The fact that the left side of the brain generally controls both the dominant hand and the ability to speak led some to dub it the "dominant hemisphere" and to wonder whether the right side might be just another one of those useless parts that we have inherited from our animal ancestors. For two reasons this view has been discarded: First, there is the problem of left-handers. Second, there is the fact, recognized only in recent years, that the right side of the brain has its uses, too.

LEFT-HANDED PEOPLE.   If right-hand, left-brain dominance is characteristically human, how do we account for left-handers? One possibility is that they were simply formed backward, like "mirror-image" twins. There *are* sets of twins whose hair and fingerprints whorl in opposite directions, but the overwhelming majority of twins—and of left-handed people—have their insides formed just like everybody else's: The asymmetrical locations of the heart, the stomach, and the intestines are normal. There are very, very few truly "mirror-image" people, and they are not necessarily left-handed.

Another puzzle is that although the speech centers of right-handers are almost invariably in the left hemisphere, in left-handers these centers are not always in the **right hemisphere.** As Table 2–1 shows, most left-handers process language with the hemisphere associated with their *non*dominant hand. Still more perplexing, a considerable proportion have speech centers on *both* sides of the brain.

	Right-Handed People	Left-Handed and Ambidextrous People
Speech on left hemisphere	92%	69%
Speech on right hemisphere	7%	18%
Speech on both hemispheres	1%	13%

Table 2–1: The Location of the Brain Area Devoted to Speech, and Its Relationship to Handedness.[a]

[a]Based on the effects of accidental lesions to the left or right hemisphere. From Milner, Branch, and Rasmussen (1966).

Some psychologists have proposed that these atypical cases are the results of early brain injuries: If the left side of the brain is injured (at birth, say), the right takes over some of its duties. That this can happen is unquestionable. As we have seen, stroke victims often regain many of their abilities, as cells surrounding the damaged tissue, or in the same location on the opposite hemisphere, take over some of the functions of the dead neurons. If an injury to the left hemisphere occurs early enough—in the first year or two of life—there is often no language deficit. However, there is no evidence that brain damage is responsible for left-handedness. Quite the contrary: Left-handers are known to recover their language abilities after a stroke more rapidly than right-handers, and this would not be likely if part of the brain had already been damaged. People who are right-handed but have close relatives who are left-handers also have a more favorable prognosis for recovery of speech after a stroke.

Clearly, there is a hereditary component to handedness. If both your parents are right-handed, the probability of your being left-handed is only 8 percent; if one parent is left-handed, it is 20 percent; if both are left-handed, it is 55 percent (Rife, 1940). Note that if left-handedness were a simple one-gene recessive trait, the children of two left-handers should all be left-handed.

A theory to account for all of these findings was first proposed by Annett (1972) and later elaborated by Corballis and Beale (1976). According to this theory, two factors are involved in the lateralization (sidedness) of the hand and brain: an inherited component and a random component. You inherit either a tendency toward lateralization or a tendency toward symmetry. In the former case, you are right-handed and have your speech centers on the left hemisphere. In the latter case, you have no innate tendency toward lateralization, and the random component takes over: Both handedness and lateralization of the brain are determined by chance.

WHAT THE OTHER HEMISPHERE DOES.   An ordinary right-handed person with speech centers in the normal place on the left hemisphere *does* suffer deficits if damage occurs to the right side of the brain. For example, there is an impairment of the ability to perceive the emotional responses of other people (Geshwind, 1979). An ordinary person with a lesion on the language side of the brain may not understand the meaning of what someone else is saying but will understand that the speaker is angry, or is joking. In contrast, a person with a lesion on the right hemisphere will understand the words but may be unable to recognize the emotional tone. This person may show further signs of emotional impairment, such as unconcern about any other disabilities that resulted from the brain injury.

Many other specialized functions are believed to be represented primarily on the right hemisphere: for example, perception of melody, of nonverbal patterns, and of spatial relationships. However, the two sides of the brain

HIGHLIGHT□
Split Brains:
Two Brains in One Body?

In addition to providing for routine communication between two sides of the brain, the corpus callosum allows the abnormal electrical discharges that cause epileptic seizures to spread from one hemisphere to another. In an attempt to control this disability and confine the seizures to one hemisphere, a daring surgical procedure was carried out in 1961 by P. J. Vogel and J. E. Bogen.* They severed the corpus callosum and one or two other smaller commissures (nerve bundles) that link the two sides of the cerebrum together.

The "split-brain" operation served the purpose it was designed for; in fact, it eliminated almost all epileptic attacks, even those confined to one hemisphere. More remarkably, the small group of people who underwent this surgery appeared to the casual observer to be completely normal. These **split-brain subjects** showed no noticeable changes either in intelligence or in personality. One patient awoke after the operation and, still drowsy from the anesthetic, joked that he had a "splitting headache" (Gazzaniga, 1967).

*Vogel and Bogen, then at the California College of Medicine, were encouraged in this work by experiments on split-brain cats in the early 1950s by Ronald Meyers and Roger Sperry at the California Institute of Technology and by the even earlier, but inconclusive, use of the split-brain procedure on epileptics by a New York neurosurgeon named William Van Wagenen in 1940.

It took some fairly subtle psychological testing to reveal the strange kinds of deficits that the surgery produced. A series of experiments reported by Gazzaniga demonstrated these deficits. When an object such as a pencil was placed in the right (dominant) hand of the split-brain subjects, they easily identified it by touch and said "pencil." But if the pencil was placed in their left hands and the subjects couldn't see it, they could not say what the object was. Yet there was nothing wrong with the hand itself: The subjects could identify the object by pointing (with their left hands) to a card on which the word *pencil* was printed, or they could use their left hands to pick out a pencil from among a group of objects hidden from view behind a screen. Information from the left hand was being delivered to the right hemisphere, but the right hemisphere could not speak. Because the corpus callosum had been severed, the information in the right hemisphere could not cross over to the speech centers in the left hemisphere. The left hemisphere didn't have the slightest idea what the left hand was holding!

Similar results were found when words or pictures were shown to only one hemisphere. This experiment made use of the fact that the visual field is split down the middle, with half going to the left hemisphere and half to the right. If a normal person looks at a point on a screen and a picture is flashed on the screen too briefly to allow eye movements, the part of the picture to the right of the point goes to the left hemisphere; the part to the left goes to the right hemisphere. This

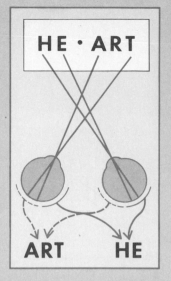

FIGURE A

technique was used with the split-brain subjects. In one experiment the word *heart* was flashed on the screen with *he* on one side of the point and *art* on the other (Figure A). If the subjects were asked what they saw, they said "art"—the part of the word transmitted to the left (speaking) side of the brain. But if they were asked instead to point with their left hand to the word they had seen, they pointed to a card that said "he." Notice that neither hemisphere knew that the word had been "heart." Notice also that although the right hemisphere was unable to speak, it was able to read and to understand spoken commands.

In another experiment (Levy, Trevarthen, & Sperry, 1972), split-brain patients were shown composite photographs combining the left half of one face with the right half of another (Figure B). These photographs are often called **chim-**

56   *Chapter 2: The Biological Framework*

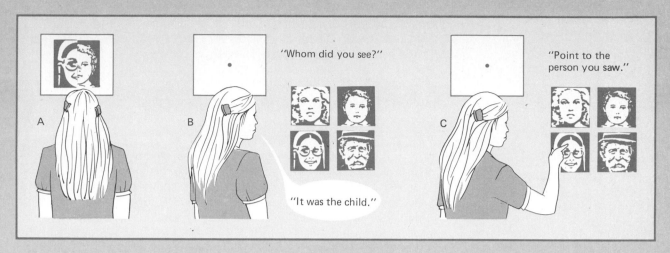

Figure B

eric stimuli after the mythical chimera, whose appearance kept changing. They were flashed briefly on a screen positioned in the subjects' view so that their left hemispheres received the right half of the image and their right hemispheres the left half. The subjects were then shown four normal faces, among which were the two contributing to the composite, and were asked which one they had seen. While they seemed totally unaware of the chimeric or conflicting nature of the briefly flashed image, their answer typically depended on how they were told to report. If they were told to *vocalize* their answer, they choose the face containing the half "seen" by the left hemisphere (the right half of the composite image). If told to *point* (using either hand), they choose the face whose half had gone to the right hemisphere (the left half of the composite). It was *as if* the verbal response was controlled by the left hemisphere and the pointing by the right (although

fine control of each hand is governed by the opposite hemisphere, gross movements can be controlled by either hemisphere).

The split-brain patient seems in the curious position of having two separate minds in a single body. The left mind has language and can readily communicate its experiences. The right mind, though not as verbal, can perform many acts independently. It can actually do some things better than the left mind. For instance, it seems to be better at arranging blocks to match a given pattern and at drawing pictures of figures such as cubes. The drawings made with the left hand are clumsy but fairly accurate; the drawings made with the right hand are neater but wrong.

The two minds of a split-brain patient are each capable of learning and remembering, but the memories of each are not accessible to the other side. Experiments with split-brain animals have made this apparent. When the corpus callosum of an

animal is severed, the result is two approximately equal hemispheres. If the right hemisphere of such an animal is taught to discriminate (with its left paw) between two different shapes, it turns out that the left hemisphere has learned nothing. It takes the left hemisphere just as long to learn the discrimination as it took the right hemisphere (Sperry, 1964).

The fact that split-brain animals and people have two independent minds should not be taken to mean that everybody else also has. In the intact brain there is complete, immediate, and constant communication between the two hemispheres. Learning and memories are shared. Each side has full access to the special talents and abilities of the other half. That is why consciousness in a person with a complete corpus callosum is unitary. The Russian poet Osip Mandelstam has written, "A leap—and my mind is whole."

normally work together, and there are usually no signs of their differing roles. Information is carried freely back and forth between the two hemispheres by the wide band of tissue known as the corpus callosum.

THE AUTONOMIC NERVOUS SYSTEM AND THE ENDOCRINE GLANDS

Earlier we said that the motor division of the peripheral nervous system has two parts: somatic and autonomic. So far we have concentrated primarily on the somatic motor system, which innervates striated (skeletal) muscles. Now we return to the autonomic motor system, which innervates two kinds of muscles: the smooth muscles of the glands and internal organs and the specialized cardiac muscles of the heart. It is because these muscles generally function without voluntary control (although voluntary control can be imposed upon some of them) that we call this system *autonomic* ("self-governed").

The autonomic system itself has two divisions: **sympathetic** and **parasympathetic.** Most organs and glands are innervated by both the sympathetic and the parasympathetic systems, which have opposing effects on them. The sympathetic system is concerned, to a large extent, with emergency situations and stress, whereas the parasympathetic system maintains the routine "vegetative" functions such as digestion. Another way of putting it is that the sympathetic system is associated with activation and expenditure of energy, while the parasympathetic system tends to conserve energy.

Inputs to the autonomic nervous system come from a number of areas of the central nervous system. In general, such inputs do not come directly but make many connections along the way. One important pathway starts in the sensory areas of the neocortex and filters downward through the association areas, the limbic system, the hypothalamus, the reticular formation, and the spinal cord. This pathway would be used when, for example, you see or hear something frightening. The physiological responses that accompany the feeling of fear—accelerated heart rate and breathing, increase in blood pressure, inhibition of digestion, and so on—are produced by the action of the sympathetic nervous system. These physiological responses are counteracted by the opposing effects of the parasympathetic nervous system, which tends to return the activity of the organs to their normal levels.

Anatomy of the Autonomic Nervous System

SYMPATHETIC.   Neurons of the sympathetic system exit from the central portion of the spinal cord, below the neck and above the small of the back. Each of these neurons synapses immediately within one of the ganglia of the *sympathetic chains.* There are two of these long chains of ganglia, one lying along each side of the spinal cord.

Some of the axons that leave the sympathetic chain go directly to the organs they innervate. Others travel to secondary ganglia and synapse with another set of neurons that go the rest of the way. A secondary sympathetic ganglion is known as a *plexus;* the best known of these is the solar plexus, located behind the stomach.

Because all the neurons of the sympathetic system come together in the

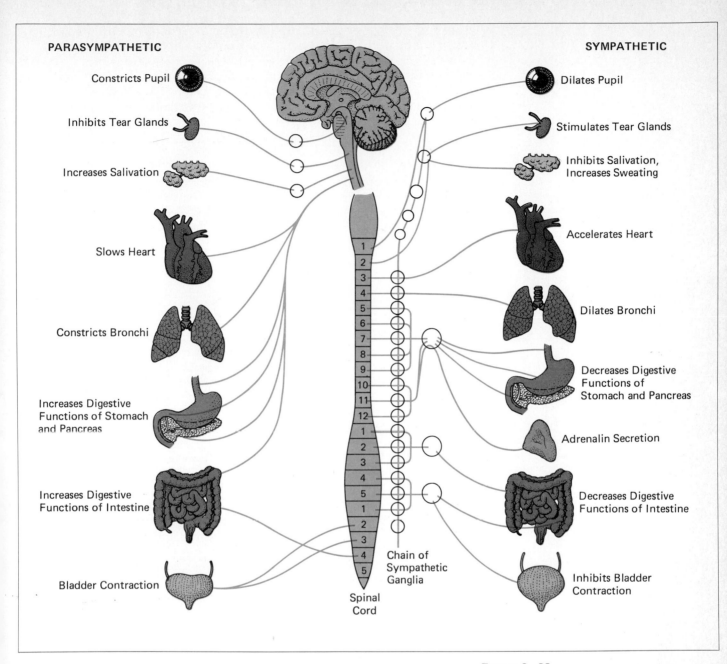

PARASYMPATHETIC

Constricts Pupil

Inhibits Tear Glands

Increases Salivation

Slows Heart

Constricts Bronchi

Increases Digestive Functions of Stomach and Pancreas

Increases Digestive Functions of Intestine

Bladder Contraction

SYMPATHETIC

Dilates Pupil

Stimulates Tear Glands

Inhibits Salivation, Increases Sweating

Accelerates Heart

Dilates Bronchi

Decreases Digestive Functions of Stomach and Pancreas

Adrenalin Secretion

Decreases Digestive Functions of Intestine

Inhibits Bladder Contraction

Chain of Sympathetic Ganglia

Spinal Cord

FIGURE 2—22
The parasympathetic (left) and sympathetic (right) nervous systems. Parasympathetic nerves arise from the brain and from the base of the spinal cord, sympathetic nerves from the remainder of the spinal cord. Nevertheless, the two sets of nerves serve the same organs.

sympathetic chain, they tend to work in unison. The effects produced by this system and by the parasympathetic system are shown in Figure 2–22.

PARASYMPATHETIC. Parasympathetic motor fibers leave the central nervous system from one of two locations: from the very bottom of the spinal cord, or directly from the brain in a cranial nerve. One of the cranial nerves, the *vagus* nerve, is the only exception to the rule that cranial nerves serve the head and neck. Some of the axons·in this nerve provide the parasympathetic innervation of the heart, the lungs, and the digestive system.

Parasympathetic neurons also form ganglia, but these are generally located near the organs they help control. Because the parasympathetic system has no unifying structure like the sympathetic chain, the parasympathetic ganglia are more independent of one another than the sympathetic ganglia, and do not necessarily act in concert. Moreover, some parts of the body receive sympathetic innervation but not parasympathetic—the sweat glands, the hair follicles, and the smaller blood vessels.

The Endocrine System

The glands of the endocrine system interact closely with one another and with the autonomic nervous system to regulate a number of vital metabolic and physiological functions. **Endocrine glands** are *ductless*—that is, they secrete their **hormones** or "chemical messengers" directly into the bloodstream, which carries the hormones all over the body. A list of the major endocrine glands and their principal hormones is given in Table 2–2.

Each hormone exerts its effects on a target organ somewhere in the body. In some cases, the target organs themselves are other endocrine glands. Hormones that control the secretion of other hormones are described as *tropic*.

The primary secretor of tropic hormones is the *pituitary gland,* located at the base of the brain and attached by a stalk to the hypothalamus. Because of its influence on many of the other endocrine glands, this tiny organ is often called the "master gland."

The pituitary consists of two parts, the *anterior* and the *posterior.* The anterior pituitary puts out several tropic hormones that regulate the functions of other glands. It, in turn, is regulated by the hypothalamus. For example, if the blood level of the hormone *thyroxin* becomes too low, the hypothalamus reacts by stimulating the anterior pituitary to secrete the hormone *thyrotropin.* Thyrotropin, released into the bloodstream, reaches the thyroid gland (located in the neck) and causes it to secrete more thyroxin. Thyroxin is important in the maintenance of the body's rate of metabolism. Too little thyroxin produces a condition known as **hypothyroidism,** which is associated with depression and fatigue. Hypothyroidism is particularly dangerous in childhood, when it causes a serious retardation of growth and mental development. Too much thyroxin also has ill effects: It produces **hyperthyroidism,** which leads to irritability, restlessness, and weight loss.

The anterior pituitary puts out several other important hormones. One of these is the *growth hormone,* too much of which results in a giant, too little in a dwarf. The *gonadotropic hormones* stimulate the ovaries to secrete the female sex hormones, the testes to secrete the male sex hormones.

Table 2–2: Major Glands and Hormones of the Endocrine System.

Gland	Hormone	Main Effect
Pituitary		
Anterior lobe	Adrenocorticotropic hormone (ACTH)	Stimulates adrenal cortex to produce steroids
	Growth hormone	Stimulates growth
	Thyrotropin	Stimulates thyroid to produce thyroxin
	Follicle-stimulating hormone (FSH)	Development of ova and sperm
	Luteinizing hormone (LH)	Maturation of ova and sperm; ovulation
	Prolactin	Production of milk in nursing female
Posterior lobe	Antidiuretic hormone (Vasopressin)	Prevents excess loss of fluids through urination
	Oxytocin	Uterine contractions, release of milk during nursing
Adrenal		
Cortex	Steroids (e.g., Cortisol)	Increase of blood glucose. Maintenance of metabolism and level of minerals in body
Medulla	Epinephrine (Adrenalin)	Increases blood pressure, heart rate, blood glucose, and perspiration. Stimulates production of ACTH
	Norepinephrine	Increases blood pressure, slows heart rate. Stimulates production of ACTH
Thyroid	Thyroxin	Increases metabolism
Pancreas		
Alpha cells	Glucagon	Increases blood glucose
Beta cells	Insulin	Enables body cells to use glucose (thereby decreasing blood glucose)
Parathyroid	Parathormone	Maintains level of calcium in blood
Ovaries (in female)	Estrogens	Development of female reproductive organs, secondary sex characteristics, and sexual behavior
	Progesterone	Thickening of lining of uterus and maintenance of pregnancy
Testes (in male)	Androgens (e.g., Testosterone)	Development of male reproductive organs, secondary sex characteristics, and sexual behavior

STRESS HORMONES.   Two endocrine glands act with the autonomic nervous system to generate the body's reaction to fear and other forms of stress. The hormonal response to stress begins when the hypothalamus triggers the anterior pituitary to release **adrenocorticotropic hormone (ACTH).** The target of this hormone is the outer surface (cortex) of the **adrenal glands,** located on top of the kidneys. In response to stimulation by ACTH, the adrenal cortex secretes hormones called *steroids,* which regulate the blood levels of glucose and of certain minerals (sodium, potassium, and chloride). In addition, the hypothalamus acts through the sympathetic nervous system to stimulate the inner part of the adrenal gland—the adrenal medulla—to secrete **epinephrine** (also called **adrenalin**) and **norepinephrine.** These hormones complement the action of the sympathetic nervous system. For example, they increase glucose levels and raise blood pressure. Their effects will be examined in more detail in Chapter 11, Human Motivation and Emotion, in the section on emotion.

We have already discussed norepinephrine in its role as a neurotransmitter in the brain. The same substance, secreted by the adrenal medulla instead of by the presynaptic membrane, acts as a hormone. The two functions of norepinephrine are kept separate by the blood-brain barrier, which prevents most of the circulating norepinephrine from entering the brain.

We are only beginning to understand the complex relationships between hormones and neurotransmitters, between chemistry and behavior. Research in this field is currently very active and likely to produce exciting results.

SUMMARY

1. A person's heredity is determined by the *genes,* located on the *chromosomes* in the nuclei of body cells.

2. The nervous system has two divisions: the *central nervous system,* consisting of the brain and spinal cord, and the *peripheral nervous system,* consisting of all the neurons outside the brain and spinal cord. Peripheral neurons are either *sensory* or *motor.*

3. A neuron is a cell that transmits information in the form of *nerve impulses;* these normally travel from a *dendrite* or the *cell body* out to the tips of the axon (*axon terminals*), where they can affect other neurons.

4. The inside of a neuron is normally electrically negative with respect to its outside. This is called its *resting potential.* When a nerve impulse reaches a particular point on the neuron, the interior becomes momentarily positive at that point. This reversal of polarity, called an *action potential,* is caused by the opening and closing of microscopic channels in the membrane, thereby allowing electrically charged ions to move in and out of the neuron.

5. The transfer of information between two neurons takes place at a junction called the *synapse;* for a message to cross the synaptic space, a substance called a *neurotransmitter* is released, sending a chemical signal from one neuron to another.

6. The spinal cord carries information between the brain and the body and also provides the connections between the sensory and motor neurons involved in spinal reflexes.

7. The hindbrain consists of the *medulla,* the *pons,* and the *cerebellum;* the cerebellum is in charge of equilibrium, muscle tone, and coordination. The hindbrain and the midbrain comprise the *brain stem.*

8. Scattered throughout the brain stem is an intricate network of cells known as the *reticular formation;* this system has a role in sleep and arousal.

9. The forebrain consists of the *thalamus,* the *hypothalamus,* and the *cerebrum.* The thalamus is an important collection and integration center for sensory information; the hypothalamus regulates motivated behavior and maintains a balance in many body systems.

10. The cerebrum includes the *limbic system,* which plays a major role in emotional behavior, and the *neocortex,* which contains about 70 percent of all neurons in the central nervous system.

11. Some areas of the neocortex have specialized functions; these areas include the *motor cortex,* the *visual cortex,* the *auditory cortex,* and the *somatosensory cortex* (which receives sensory information from the skin, joints and muscles, and internal organs). Such abilities as thinking, speaking, and reading are localized in the *association areas* of the cortex.

12. The cerebrum consists of a right hemisphere and a left hemisphere; the left hemisphere controls the right side of the body. Language abilities are generally localized in the left hemisphere; the right hemisphere may function in abilities such as spatial relationships and perception of nonverbal patterns.

13. The peripheral motor system has two divisions: *somatic* and *autonomic.* The somatic motor system innervates skeletal muscles. The autonomic system is composed of two subdivisions, the *sympathetic* and the *parasympathetic.* The sympathetic

system is associated with activation and expenditure of energy (especially in stress situations), and the parasympathetic system is associated with the maintenance of routine functions such as digestion.

14. The *endocrine system* consists of glands which secrete hormones that regulate a number of vital metabolic and physiologic functions; the endocrine system interacts closely with the autonomic nervous system.

Suggested Readings

BLAKEMORE, C. *Mechanics of the mind.* Cambridge, Eng.: Cambridge University Press, 1978. A richly illustrated, eclectic review of the current state of knowledge about the human brain.

The Brain (A Scientific American Book). San Francisco: W. H. Freeman & Company, Publishers, 1979. This is a paperback edition of the September 1979 issue of *Scientific American* containing 11 articles by eminent brain researchers. Superbly illustrated.

CORBALLIS, M. C., & BEALE, I. L. *The psychology of left and right.* Hillsdale, N.J.: Erlbaum, 1976. Left-right confusions, mirror images, and the psychology and biology of handedness and brain lateralization.

GAZZANIGA, M. S. *The bisected brain.* New York: Appleton, 1970. A leading investigator describes in detail the effects of split-brain surgery.

KAPLAN, A. R. (Ed.). *Human behavior genetics.* Springfield, Ill.: Thomas, 1976. Discusses genetic aspects of behavior, twin studies, schizophrenia, personality, and intelligence.

LEVINTHAL, C. F. *Introduction to physiological psychology* (2nd ed.). Englewood Cliffs, N.J.: Prentice-Hall, 1983. Lucid coverage of a wide range of topics in physiological psychology. Particularly informative on hormones, neurotransmitters, and nervous-system chemistry.

McFARLAND, R. A. *Physiological psychology: The biology of human behavior.* Palo Alto, Calif.: Mayfield, 1981. An excellent introduction to the biological bases of behavior.

ROSE, S. *The conscious brain.* New York: Knopf, 1975. A personal account of brain research by a British scientist. Written in a clear and interesting manner, but with a strong anti-American bias.

SPRINGER, S. P., & DEUTSCH, G. *Left brain, right brain.* San Francisco: W. H. Freeman & Company, Publishers, 1981. A comprehensive review of research indicating different functions for the right and left hemispheres.

3. Sensation

All our lives our brains remain in total darkness, insulated from the outside world by layers of flesh and bone. Knowledge of that world is carried into the brain through the sensory systems. These systems respond to certain aspects of the environment to produce subjective sensations such as light, sound, and taste. This chapter considers exactly how this is done by each sensory system.

Sensations are private or subjective events. You may describe your sensations to others, but no one else can directly experience them. Nevertheless, if a particular change in the physical environment evokes similar reports from many different people, it seems reasonable to assume that they experienced similar sensations. For example, turning up the volume control on a phonograph causes most listeners to describe the sound as growing louder. This shows a consistent relationship between a physical stimulus (the amount of energy coming from the loudspeaker) and the listeners' sensations (or at least their descriptions of what they hear). Relations of this sort are often referred to as **psychophysical relations,** since they seem to relate physical and psychological variables (stimuli and sensations).

We must be very careful in making inferences about sensations on the basis of verbal reports. Such reports are not only limited by a subject's verbal skills but are also easily influenced by what subjects expect to experience. Magicians often make use of spectators' expectations to trick them into believing they saw or heard or felt things that didn't actually occur. If you hold an open paper bag at arm's length and covertly snap a finger against the bag while passing the other hand above the bag, observers will usually report seeing you drop something into the bag. The sound of something striking the bag influences their visual perception, because the sequence of sound and arm movement is so highly correlated with the event they thought they had seen.

Such judgmental biases and expectancies play a role not only in magicians' illusions but also in almost all of your everyday experience, most often in ways that aid perception. The underlying reason for this is that activity in your various sensory systems is highly correlated, or **redundant.** For example, when people speak to you, the movement of their lips is highly correlated with the sound of their voice. We use this correlation or redundancy between the visual and auditory sensations so automatically that ventriloquists can trick us into attributing the source of their voice to their dummy, simply because it is the dummy's mouth that moves. In many circumstances this automatic connection of sight and sound is very useful; it allows us, for example, to visually keep track of a person's conversation at a crowded party when voice sounds are sometimes partially obscured. In fact, many deaf people learn to understand speech through lip reading alone.

The redundancy that operates in all normal perceptual processes makes it difficult to judge just what was involved in any one sensory event. Only by carefully controlling stimulus redundancy and by asking subjects very simple questions about their sensations is it possible to reveal consistent psychophysical relationships that shed light on the nature of our sensory systems. Thus, before describing the individual sensory systems, we shall consider some generally useful techniques for establishing psychophysical relationships.

MEASURING SENSORY CAPACITIES

Sensory Limits

Each sensory system is sensitive to some form of physical energy. Our auditory system responds to certain rapid variations in air pressure (sound), while our visual system responds to specific forms of electromagnetic energy (light). But we aren't sensitive to every aspect of our environment; there are limits to our sensitivity. First, we can only sense forms of energy for which we have "receivers" or **receptor organs** (eyes, ears, etc.). For example, we are surrounded by electromagnetic energy coming from many radio and television stations, yet unless we have the radio or television turned on we see and hear none of it. Second, energy must be intense enough to produce a noticeable sensation: A source of light must be strong enough for us to see it; a source of sound must be intense enough for us to hear it.

Some of the earliest work in experimental psychology (by Fechner in 1860) was aimed at assessing our sensory limits. Psychologists found that by varying the strength or intensity of a stimulus, they could determine the minimum level capable of evoking a sensation. This level, called the **absolute threshold** for the stimulus, marks the boundary between energy levels strong enough to evoke a noticeable sensation and those too weak to do so. Another kind of sensory limit was defined by our ability to notice a *change* in sensation. For example, a source of light has to be changed (increased or decreased) a minimum amount for someone to notice that change. Again, early experimental psychologists tried to measure exactly how small a difference in a physical stimulus would be noticed. They referred to this as the **difference threshold.**

The methods developed to measure absolute and difference **thresholds** were the earliest attempts at precise measurement in psychology. They are still of interest, not only on historical grounds, but also because they are simple and adequate for most purposes.

MEASURING ABSOLUTE AND DIFFERENCE THRESHOLDS

You can obtain a rough measure of an absolute threshold simply by asking a subject to adjust a stimulus in intensity until it just begins to evoke a sensation; for example, "Slowly increase the energy level of this light source by turning this knob until you just begin to see the light." For many purposes, the **method of adjustment** is a perfectly good procedure and leads to a reasonably consistent measure of the absolute threshold. Yet certain problems emerge when you attempt to be more precise. First of all, subjects won't be entirely consistent if asked to repeat this procedure; they will set the threshold intensity at a slightly different value each time. Nor will they indicate exactly the same threshold intensity if asked to reverse the procedure—that is, to begin with a high intensity and slowly reduce it until the sensation disappears.

In an attempt to obtain more consistent threshold measures, the **method of constant stimuli** was developed. A fixed set of stimulus intensities was repeatedly presented in a randomly determined sequence over a series of test

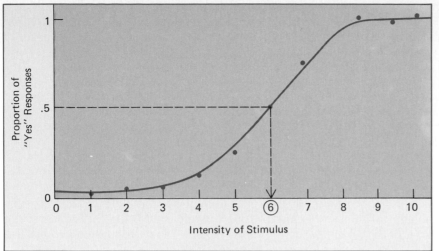

FIGURE 3–1
The absolute threshold of a stimulus is the intensity that has a 50 percent chance of evoking a sensation. A smooth curve has been fitted to the data points, and it appears that a stimulus intensity of about 6 will evoke a yes response about 50 percent of the time. Thus, the absolute threshold is about 6.

trials. On each trial one intensity was presented and subjects reported whether or not they experienced any sensation; for example, "Yes, I saw the light that time," or "No, I didn't see anything that time." Ideally this method would reveal an intensity level above which subjects always reported a sensation, and below which they never did. Unfortunately, things are not quite that simple. The nature of the problem is illustrated in Figure 3–1. Between the high intensities, which almost always evoked a yes report, and the very low intensities, which almost never did, there was a middle range where the proportion of reported sensations gradually increased with the intensity. Stimuli in this range sometimes evoked a sensation and at other times did not. What, then, should be called the absolute threshold? It was decided that the most reasonable answer was to call the absolute threshold the intensity that had a 50 percent chance of evoking a sensation. Figure 3–1 shows how this threshold was calculated.

In measuring difference thresholds, instead of varying the absolute level of the stimulus, a series of stimulus *differences* was presented to a subject, who reported whether or not they evoked different sensations. ("Did the light seem to change its appearance?" "Is this sound louder than that sound?") The same general pattern of results emerged: There was a range of stimulus differences so small they almost never evoked a reported change in sensation, a range of large differences that almost always did, and a middle range in which the proportion of noticeable differences increased slowly with the size of the stimulus difference. Thus the graph in Figure 3–1 is also characteristic of difference threshold data, only here the units would refer to the size of the stimulus difference. Again, the best measure of the difference threshold seems to be the physical difference that is noticed 50 percent of the time. This difference threshold has often been referred to as the **just noticeable difference (JND).**

A very general feature of difference thresholds was apparent long before formal measurement techniques were developed: People are usually more sensitive to changes in weak stimuli than they are to similar changes in stronger or more intense stimuli. For example, if you were listening to a voice in an otherwise quiet room, you would readily notice the addition of a second voice. Yet the addition of one voice to the chatter of many voices at a large

Table 3–1: Some Typical Values of Weber's Constant for Various Types of Stimuli.

Type of Stimulus	Weber's Constant
Electric Shock	.01
Heaviness	.02
Length	.03
Vibration	.04
Loudness	.05
Brightness	.08

After Teghtsoonian (1971).

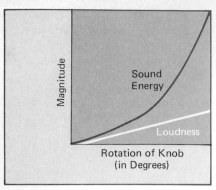

FIGURE 3–2
In order for loudness to increase equally for each degree of rotation, energy must increase progressively more and more.

cocktail party would probably go unnoticed. Similarly, you would probably notice a difference in weight between an empty paper cup and one containing a penny, yet you wouldn't notice a difference between a cup containing 100 pennies and one holding 101, even though the difference in weight (one penny) is exactly the same in both cases.

In 1834 a German psychophysicist named Ernst Weber suggested that the difference threshold (JND) for each type of stimulus is a constant fraction or proportion (k) of the stimulus intensity (I) being changed; that is,

$$JND = kI.$$

This is often referred to as **Weber's law,** and the constant of proportionality (k) is called **Weber's constant.** For example, Weber's constant for lifted weights, or heaviness, is about .02. This means that the JND for a 50-gram weight is .02 times 50 grams, or 1 gram, while the JND for a 500-gram weight is .02 times 500 grams, or 10 grams. Table 3–1 indicates some typical values of Weber's constant for other types of stimuli.

More recent research indicates that Weber's law should be viewed as only a rough characterization of our sensitivity to changes in stimulation. It fails in the case of very weak or very intense stimuli and is only approximately true for the middle range of stimuli. Nevertheless, it is a useful, general approximation of human sensitivity to stimulus differences.

Psychophysical Scaling

Sensory limits are only one aspect of our sensory capacities. Another aspect is how the strength or quality of a sensation changes as the physical stimulus is changed. For example, how rapidly does loudness grow with increases in the physical intensity of a sound? How does brightness grow as the energy level of a light source is increased? Attempts to answer such questions have produced measurement techniques called *psychophysical scaling*. The function of such techniques can be shown by the following practical problem.

Suppose you were asked to design a volume control for a phonograph that produced a subjectively constant increase in loudness as the control knob is turned clockwise for one full revolution (360 degrees); that is, each degree of rotation should seem to increase the loudness by the same amount. You might consider building the control so that the physical sound energy coming from the loudspeakers increased at a constant rate as the knob turned (each degree of rotation produced exactly the same increase in energy). If you did this, you would be disappointed, for the same amount of rotation (the same increase in energy) would produce much larger changes in loudness at the lower volume settings than at the higher ones. A more satisfactory system—and the one actually used in most volume controls—is indicated in Figure 3–2. Only if a given rotation produces progressively larger increases in sound energy as the knob is turned will listeners hear a constant growth in loudness (broken line).

You might argue, as did Gustav Fechner in 1860, that the relation between sound energy and loudness could be predicted from Weber's study of difference thresholds. The argument goes something like this. If the JND is the smallest noticeable difference in sensation, then larger differences could be considered the sum of many JNDs. Since Weber's law states that the size of a JND increases as stimulus intensity increases, progressively larger increases in

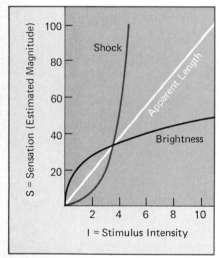

FIGURE 3–3
The graph shows the average estimated magnitude of sensation (S) for various intensities (I) of light, line length, and electrical shock. These curves can be described by Stevens's power law, $S = kI^b$, with the exponent b equal to .33 for brightness, 1 for apparent length, and 3.5 for shock. (Stevens, 1961)

intensity should be required to produce the same difference in sensation. Fechner showed that this argument implies that the relation between physical stimulus intensity (I) and the strength of sensation (S) is logarithmic; specifically,

$$S = c \log I$$

where c is simply a constant that depends on your unit of intensity. This logarithmic relation, often referred to as **Fechner's law,** implies that an increase in weight from 50 to 100 grams, for example, should produce the same increase in the sensation of heaviness as an increase from 25 to 50 grams, or from 100 to 200. The same *ratio* of stimulus intensities produces the same difference in sensation.

Fechner's law has proven to be less generally applicable than he had hoped. This is partly because Weber's law itself is only a rough approximation (it tends to fail at extreme intensity levels), and partly because there are more direct ways of measuring the relations between physical stimulus variables and sensation.

In 1956 S. S. Stevens showed that you could ask subjects to specify the strength of a sensation simply by assigning it a number. He called this method **magnitude estimation.** For example, you could present a stimulus of a certain light intensity and tell subjects that it has a brightness of 10, then present another light intensity and ask them to assign it a number indicating its relative brightness. If subjects believe the second light is twice as bright as the first, they should assign it the number 20; if they think it is only half as bright, they should give it the number 5, and so on. You could repeat this procedure with many different light intensities until you had a clear picture of the average number assigned to each. The black line in Figure 3–3 shows the type of relation defined in this way. Increases in light intensity produce progressively smaller changes in perceived brightness—the same general conclusion Fechner drew from Weber's law. However, Stevens argued that this is only true for certain types of stimulation. For example, magnitude estimation of the sensation evoked by electrical shock grows slowly at first, and then more rapidly as the shock is increased (the color line in Figure 3–3)—the opposite of the result predicted by Fechner's law.

Stevens proposed a more general way of characterizing such relations. This is referred to as **Stevens's power law,** since it asserts that sensation (S) is proportional to stimulus intensity (I) raised to some power (b):

$$S = kI^b$$

where k is a constant that depends on the unit of measurement being used. The three curves in Figure 3–3 follow this rule, with b equal to .33 for brightness, 1 for apparent length, and 3.5 for electrical shock. When b is less than 1, as it is for brightness, sensation grows progressively more slowly as intensity increases, but when b is greater than 1, as it is for shock, sensation grows progressively more rapidly as intensity increases. When b equals 1, as it does for apparent length, sensation is directly proportional to intensity.

Signal Detection Theory

While the traditional techniques for measuring sensory thresholds and sensitivity to changes in sensation are adequate for most purposes, there are some

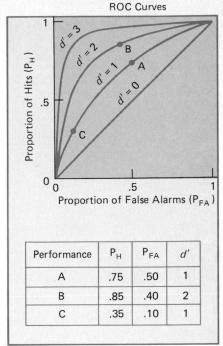

ROC Curves

Performance	P_H	P_{FA}	d'
A	.75	.50	1
B	.85	.40	2
C	.35	.10	1

Figure 3–4 Plotting ROC Curves
Performance of a detection task can be summarized by the proportion of times the subject reports signals when they are presented, "hits" (P_H), and the proportion of times a signal is erroneously reported when none was presented, "false alarms" (P_{FA}). Any performance can be represented as a point on the type of graph shown here. For example, point A indicates a performance in which P_H equals .75 and P_{FA} equals .5. It has been found that instructing a subject to be more or less conservative in reporting signals shifts the performance point along a curve called a receiver operating characteristic (ROC). Thus, giving subjects "conservative instructions" might shift their performance from point A to point C along the same ROC curve, labeled $d' = 1$. In contrast, increasing signal intensity slightly might shift performance from point A to point B, which lies on another ROC curve, labeled $d' = 2$. Notice that the higher the value of d', the closer the subject can come to perfect discrimination (the upper left corner of the graph where P_H equals 1 and P_{FA} equals 0). Thus d' is a measure of sensitivity or discriminability. It is independent of the subject's tendency to be "liberal" or "conservative," since this only shifts performance along a particular ROC curve, indicating the same value of d'.

problems. Underlying the concept of a "threshold" or a "JND" is the idea that people either do, or do not, detect a test stimulus each time it is presented. Yet subjects often say they are uncertain whether they detect anything; for example, "I thought I might have heard something that time, but I'm really not sure." If subjects are instructed to report a detection even when they are uncertain ("liberal instructions"), they tend to report more detections, and this liberal reporting *lowers* the measured threshold. On the other hand, if subjects are discouraged from reporting a detection when they are uncertain ("conservative instructions"), they tend to report fewer detections, and this *raises* the measured threshold. Thus these two different types of instruction produce results that reflect shifts in subjects' judgmental standards rather than any real change in their sensitivity to the test stimuli. It would be useful to have a measure of sensitivity that isn't influenced by instructional effects. Such a measure, termed d' is provided by the **signal detection theory** (Green & Swets, 1966). The way in which this measure is obtained is illustrated in Figure 3–4. The central idea is that the sensations evoked by very weak test stimuli may also occur in their absence, due to random firing of nerves or random motions of air molecules. Thus subjects' interpretation of such sensations is a sort of statistical decision or inference. They must decide whether the sensations were really evoked by a test stimulus, or were simply a product of irrelevant background "noise" in their own sensory system.

To understand the sorts of things that can influence a statistical decision, suppose you are spending the night in an old house. Such houses spontaneously generate a variety of sounds as they expand or contract with the temperature, old pipes rattle in their fittings, or loose shingles and shutters are tossed by the wind. Lying in bed, you hear a sound. Is it a prowler or simply part of the normal background noise? Your decision will be influenced by at least two factors: how unusual the sound is compared to the usual noises of the house, and how worried you are about prowlers. Certainly a rash of recent burglaries or a warning from the sheriff would increase your tendency to suspect a prowler. In other words, you would be influenced by your estimate of how likely it is that a prowler would be there. This is often referred to as your **expectancy.** And if you know there has been a recent series of homicides in the neighborhood, you would be far more likely to investigate the noise than if you knew there had been incidents of simple prowling. Thus the cost or *consequence* of an erroneous decision is also an important consideration. While such judgmental factors also influence your interpretation of weak stimuli, they do *not* affect the d' measure of sensitivity shown in Figure 3–4.

HEARING

Auditory Stimuli

The type of environmental stimulus that normally produces the sensation of sound is a rapid variation in air pressure next to your ears. This is usually caused by a similar variation introduced into the air some distance away and slightly earlier in time. If you were high in the stands watching the half-time

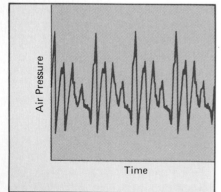

FIGURE 3–5
This is a typical waveform of the speech sound "ah." Even as simple a speech sound as this one involves a complex variation in air pressure over time. (Denes & Pinson, 1963)

show at a football game, you would see the bass drum being struck a few moments before you heard the sound. The rapid variations in air pressure produced by the vibrating surface of the drum spread through the air at about 1,100 feet per second, so that a similar, but weaker, pattern of variation is eventually produced next to your ears. If the drummer were 1,100 feet away, the sound would take 1 second to reach your ear. You would see the drum being hit before this, since light travels much faster than sound (186,000 miles per second). Other sources of sound (horns, cheering fans, a plane overhead) produce additional patterns of pressure variation that could reach your ears at the same time as those from the drum, mixing with and adding to them to produce an even more complex pattern of variation. Even a single human voice is a very complex pattern of pressure variations. Figure 3–5 shows the variations produced by a speaker making the sound "ah."

PURE TONES.   It is possible to consider complex patterns of the sort shown in Figure 3–5 as being made up of much simpler patterns called *pure tones*. Figure 3–6 illustrates particular pure tones. They consist of a rapid increase and decrease of air pressure over time in a regular pattern called a *sine wave*. All pure tones have this general form, although they differ in frequency and in amplitude. The **frequency** of a pure tone is defined as the number of complete cycles of pressure variation occurring in 1 second. (A complete cycle is the sequence of change from the highest pressure down to the lowest pressure and back to the highest pressure again.) Frequency is usually expressed in cycles per second or **hertz (Hz).** The **amplitude** of a pure tone is the greatest change from normal air pressure level produced during the cyclic variation in pressure. Figure 3–6 shows pure tones that differ in frequency and amplitude. Roughly speaking, the sensation of **pitch** is determined by the frequency of a tone, and its loudness by the amplitude. For example, the higher-pitched notes on a piano are produced by shorter strings that vibrate more rapidly, while the lower-pitched tones are produced by longer strings that vibrate more slowly. The harder a particular key is struck, the more the string vibrates back and forth, producing a higher-amplitude tone, which sounds louder.

Most people can only hear tones whose frequencies are between 20 and 20,000 Hz, and people vary in their sensitivity to tones within this range. Figure 3–7 illustrates the range of pure tones we normally hear. The lower curve is known as an **audiometric function.** It shows the lowest audible (threshold) energy for each frequency. The upper curve shows the highest tolerable energy (anything higher causes pain and damage to the ear). Notice that sound energy is expressed in bels. The **bel,** or **decibel, scale** (1 bel equals 10 decibels) is named in honor of Alexander Graham Bell. One bel represents a tenfold (10^1) increase in energy, two bels a hundredfold (10^2) increase, and three bels a thousandfold increase (10^3). Zero on the bel scale corresponds to the normal threshold energy for a 1,000 Hz tone. The threshold energy of a 20 Hz tone is over 80 dB or (8 bels); thus the threshold energy for a 20 Hz tone is more than 10^8 times as great as that for a 1,000 Hz tone.

The average energy level of the sound frequencies we hear in normal conversation is about 60 dB or 6 bels. This means it is 10^6 or 1,000,000 times the threshold level of a 1,000 Hz tone. Prolonged exposure to sounds above 80 or 90 dB can produce permanent hearing loss. For example, a normal conversation is about 60 dB, while the sounds at a rock music concert may be as high as 150 dB for those standing near the speakers.

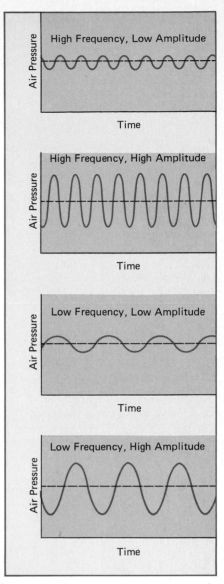

FIGURE 3–6
The graph shows four pure tones that differ in how rapidly the cycles of air pressure variation occur (frequency) and in the magnitude of that variation (amplitude).

Hearing Loss and Treatment

There are a number of ways in which the hearing mechanism can break down, starting with the eardrum and working inward. Damage to the eardrum itself can occur in many ways, the most common being the effect of external pressure (a blow to the ears, a nearby explosion, or extreme water pressure during a scuba dive). Ordinarily the pressure within the middle ear is matched to the external air pressure by means of the air entering the *Eustacian tube*, a small channel that runs from the rear of your mouth to the middle ear. However, a difference in external air pressure may puncture the eardrum when changes in pressure occur too rapidly, or if the Eustachian tube is blocked because of a heavy cold or a failure to swallow frequently enough (which opens the tubes) during changes in pressure (during a

scuba dive or when an airplane takes off or lands). If the puncture isn't too severe, this damage may be repaired through ear surgery, but the scar tissue in the repaired eardrum may produce permanent changes in the ear's response to various frequencies.

In another common form of deafness, the tiny bones in the middle ear fuse because of calcium deposits, and this fusion effectively blocks the mechanical transmission of sound to the cochlea. Delicate surgical techniques can break the calcium deposits and restore the flexibility of the bones. This surgery produces a dramatic and almost complete return of normal hearing.

The basilar membrane is susceptible to damage in a number of ways. First of all, there is the progressive deterioration due to age, which seems to affect the high-frequency regions of the membrane first. This produces heightened thresholds for the higher frequencies. A *hearing aid*, which selectively amplifies the higher frequencies, can restore normal hearing

to many elderly people.

A very similar pattern of hearing loss occurs if a patient is given extensive doses of mycine, which seems to cause progressive damage to the hair cells in the basilar membrane similar to the degeneration caused by age. Again, a hearing aid may restore normal hearing if the damage is not too extensive.

Exposure to very intense sounds can also cause damage to the basilar membrane. If the sound is primarily of one frequency, there may be damage to only one region, producing a *tonal gap*; that is, a loss of sensitivity to a narrow range of tones.

A device for automatically measuring audiometric functions was developed by auditory scientist George von Békésy, a winner of the Nobel prize. The device is called a *Békésy audiometer*. The person being tested simply listens for the sound of a tone, pressing a button when it is heard and releasing the button when it fades away. The button controls a tone generator constructed so that the intensity of the tone slowly decreases when the button is

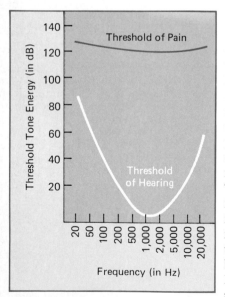

FIGURE 3–7
The graph above shows the range of pure tones we normally hear. The white curve is the normal audiometric function.

COMBINATIONS OF PURE TONES.   We rarely hear a single pure tone under normal circumstances, although the sound of a single note played on a flute comes close to it. Pure tones can be produced electronically for such purposes as tests of hearing or the composition of "electronic music." (If you have ever heard electronic music, you probably noticed the unnatural purity of the individual notes.) A single note played on most other musical instruments is really a mixture of pure tones. This can be seen in Figure 3–8, which shows the same note (C) produced by an *oscillator* (an electronic device capable of producing a pure tone) and a piano. The piano produces several tones at once—the fundamental tone (128 Hz for C) and several overtones. The **fundamental tone** is the basic frequency of the note and sounds the loudest. The **overtones** are multiples of the fundamental and sound softer than the fundamental. On the piano you can hear as many as 15 overtones besides the fundamental tone. These overtones (also called **harmonics**) blend with the fundamental tone to give the note its characteristic quality or **timbre.** The timbre, or pattern of overtones, varies with each instrument. It is determined by the material the instrument is made of, its design, and the way it is played. It is the timbre that makes the same note sound different when it comes from a tuba, a piano, or a human voice.

Most of the sounds we hear contain a wide range of frequencies. In fact, the sound of a shower running in an empty bathtub includes approximately equal amounts of all the audible frequencies. Such a sound is often called *white noise.* Other sounds, such as speech, may contain constantly shifting mixtures

pressed and slowly increases when it is released. Thus the tone intensity tends to vary around the subject's threshold, increasing until it becomes audible and the button is pressed, then decreasing until it becomes inaudible and the button is released. If, in addition, the frequency of the tone is slowly increased from 20 to 20,000 Hz, the subject's threshold is revealed for each frequency. The top graph shown here is a normal audiometric function obtained with the Békésy audiometer. The ragged curve reflects the alternate growth and decline in tone intensity around the threshold value as the button was alternately pressed and released. As the frequency of the tone slowly increased the threshold changed in the normal manner shown in Figure 3–7. The lower graph was obtained in a similar fashion from a person with a tonal gap around 5,000 Hz. As the frequency approached 5,000 Hz, the subject released the button longer until the intensity rose high enough to hear the tone again.

Again, if damage is not too great, a special hearing aid that amplifies only those frequencies to which sensitivity is reduced may restore normal hearing. Fortunately, there is tremendous redundancy in most sounds, which means that the ability to hear only a small part of the total frequency range may be all that is necessary for comprehension. People with tonal gaps are often unaware of any problem, since their brain automatically compensates for the loss.

Finally, there are various forms of nerve damage in the acoustic pathways or in the auditory projection areas in the cortex. These may be caused by a variety of factors, including birth defects, disease, blows to the head, and tumors. It is hard to make up for the loss of hearing caused by nerve damage. One way is to use another sensory system that provides the same information in a different form. For example, deaf people become quite adept at interpreting speech from lip movements (lip reading). While normal people also rely on lip movements to some extent, it is only when hear-

ing is lost that most people fully use the redundant visual information to interpret speech

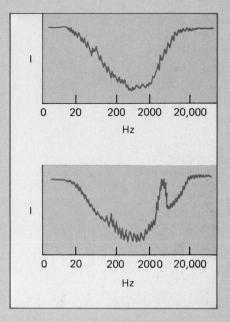

Audiometric functions showing threshold intensity for various frequencies from (top) a normal subject and (bottom) a subject with a tonal gap around 5,000 Hz.

of energy at various frequencies. Since we are not equally sensitive to all frequencies, the loudness of a sound made up of many frequencies depends on the specific amount of energy at each frequency.

The Ear

The ear is made up of three major structural components: the outer ear, the middle ear, and the cochlea. The outer ear, or *pinna,* is essentially a funnel that channels the air pressure variations into the head, where they are concentrated against the surface of a flexible membrane called the **eardrum,** causing it to vibrate (see Figure 3–9). These movements of the eardrum are then transmitted through the **middle ear** by a series of three small bones called the *hammer,* the *anvil,* and the *stirrup.* The hammer connects the eardrum to the anvil, which, in turn, is connected by the stirrup to another flexible membrane covering a small opening in the **cochlea,** or inner ear. This membrane, called the **oval window,** is much smaller than the eardrum. The bones connecting the two cause movements of the eardrum to produce smaller but more powerful movements of the oval window.

It is in the cochlea that the movements begun by pressure variations against the eardrum are changed into patterns of neural activity that produce the sensation of hearing. The amplified pressure variations on the oval window are transmitted through liquid-filled channels within the cochlea. When the liquid or fluid in the channel moves, it twists the **basilar membrane,** which

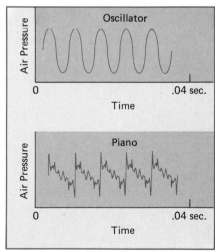

FIGURE 3–8

(Top) A pure tone of 128 Hz produced by an oscillator contains only that frequency. (Bottom) The note C_3 on a piano has the same fundamental frequency (128 Hz) but also contains other overtones.

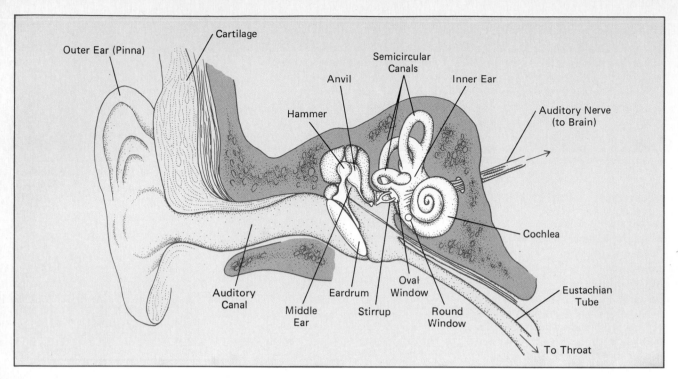

FIGURE 3–9

A *diagram of the ear, showing the outer ear, the middle ear, and the cochlea.*

is the wall of one channel. Hair cells in the basilar membrane are attached to neurons that fire (transmit a neural impulse) when the hair cell is twisted by the movement of the membrane. Figure 3–10A shows the snail-shaped cochlea; a better view of the liquid filled channels within the cochlea is shown in Figure 3–10B, which is an "uncoiled" drawing of the normally coiled structure. Notice how the pressure vibrations enter by the oval window, pass through a liquid-filled channel to the end of the cochlea, and pass back through another channel to the **round window,** where they are absorbed.

Theories of Hearing

Neural impulses are transmitted from neurons in the hair cells of the basilar membrane. The main question about hearing is how these neural impulses are coded to give different kinds of information—for instance, how do we know that a tone is a certain pitch (how do we tell middle C from a note an octave below that)?

One theory of pitch perception, called the **place theory,** is based on the idea that different sound frequencies (different pitches) actually trigger different neurons. It has been found that the frequency of vibrations determines which portion of the basilar membrane is moved or twisted most (Békésy, 1955). Thus the pitch information could be conveyed according to which neurons on which part of the membrane are stimulated. Electrophysiological studies have, in fact, shown that individual neurons in the cat's auditory nerve are "tuned" (most sensitive) to specific frequencies (see Figure 3–11).

One problem with this theory is that not all frequencies seem to cause the basilar membrane to twist more in one place than another. In fact, only high and (to some extent) middle frequencies seem to do this; pitch information about low frequencies must be transmitted in another way.

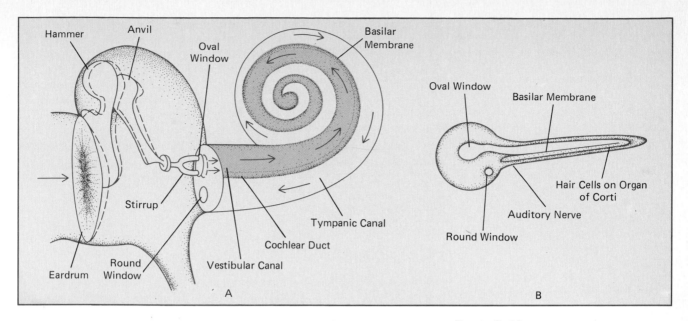

FIGURE 3–10

A. *The cochlea, or inner ear, is a coiled, snail-shaped canal; it is the part of the ear that contains the organ of hearing, called the organ of Corti.*

B. *An "uncoiled" drawing of the normally coiled structure of the cochlea. It is easier to see here how the pressure vibrations enter through the oval window, pass through a liquid-filled channel to the end of the cochlea, and pass back through another channel to the round window.*

An alternative way in which pitch information could be coded into neural activity is in terms of the rate (rather than the place) at which neurons are triggered. This is called the **frequency theory** of pitch perception (Wever & Bray, 1937). In fact, it can be shown that the rate or frequency of pulses traveling up the auditory nerve to the brain matches that of a tone over a wide range of frequencies. This is not too surprising for low frequencies, since individual nerves can respond over and over at these low rates. Yet it is impossible for a single fiber to fire, recover, and fire again as fast as would be necessary to follow a high-frequency tone. However, such high firing rates could be the product of several different sets of fibers, each firing in turn at a lower rate, but combining to produce the higher overall rate (just as when you listen to ten carpenters hammering, you hear many more hammer blows per minute than any one carpenter could make). This is often referred to as the **volley principle,** named for the way in which rows of soldiers in the Revolutionary War could load, fire, and reload one after another to produce more frequent volleys than could one row alone.

FIGURE 3–11

Tuning curves for three neurons in a cat's auditory nerve are consistent with the place theory of audition. Each curve indicates the sensitivity of a single neuron to various frequencies of tone as registered by a microelectrode inserted into the neuron. Measures are taken of the minimal (threshold) intensity of tone that, at each frequency, increases neuronal activity (increases the frequency of action potentials). The lower the threshold intensity, the greater is that neuron's sensitivity to that frequency. Notice that neurons I, II, and III are "tuned" (most sensitive) to progressively higher frequencies, as if they were carrying information from a particular place on the basilar membrane. (For the use of similar electrophysical methods to measure visual sensitivity, see the Highlight on receptive fields.) (Adapted from Kiang, Watanabe, Thomas, & Clark, 1962)

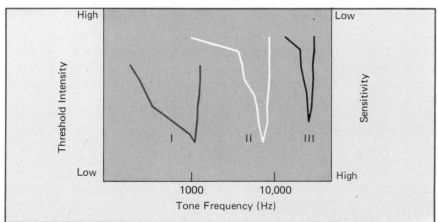

While pure-tone stimuli are adequate to measure basic properties of human hearing, most of the sounds we hear are complex combinations of tones. Of special interest are the shifting combinations of tones that make up human speech. In fact, certain regions of our sensory cortex may only respond to such stimuli (Lieberman & Studdart-Kennedy, 1978). These same regions may also be involved in speech production. For example, electrical stimulation of certain points in a person's brain can simultaneously alter perception of speech *and* cause speechlike movements in facial muscles (Ojemann & Mateer, 1979). We are really just beginning to explore these complex aspects of hearing. (Speech perception will be considered further in Chapter 8.)

SEEING

Visual Stimuli

Our eyes are sensitive to a narrow range of electromagnetic energy, wavelengths between 400 and 760 nanometers. This range is referred to as the **visual spectrum,** or, more simply, *light.* Particular sources of light vary in their brightness and color, depending on (among other things) the amount of energy present from each part of the spectrum—the light's spectral composition. Furthermore, most of our visual experience involves complex patterns of light—spatial patterns defined by variations in light across our field of view, and temporal patterns defined by variations in light over time. There are limits to our ability to discern both sorts of patterns. You've probably taken an eye test (called a *Snellen test*) that determined your ability to read progressively smaller rows of letters. Such tests measure **visual acuity,** the ability to discern fine details in spatial patterns of light. Your acuity is best in the very center of your field of view, and much poorer everywhere else. You

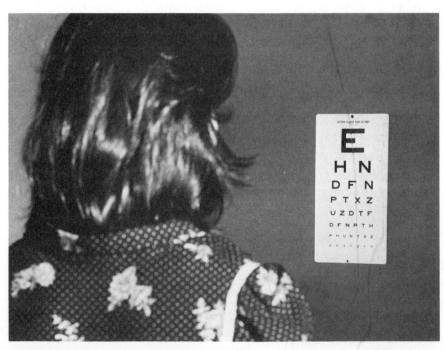

A Snellen chart is a standard set of letters of various sizes. It is used to measure visual acuity. If the smallest row of letters a subject can read at 20 feet corresponds to the smallest row of letters a normal (average) person can read at 20 feet, the person is said to have normal acuity, or "20/20 vision." However, if the smallest row of letters the subject can read at 20 feet corresponds to the smallest row a person with normal vision could read at an even greater distance, say 50 feet, the subject would be said to have below-normal acuity, or "20/50 vision."

An example of better than normal acuity would be someone with "20/10 vision," since this would mean they could see the letters as clearly at 20 feet as a normal person at only 10 feet.

normally don't notice this, since you can easily shift your eyes to gaze directly at any detail of interest (as you do when you read). Your ability to discern rapid variations in light in temporal patterns is also limited. For example, an ordinary fluorescent bulb isn't really on all the time; it is actually flickering off and on 60 times a second. The light projected onto a motion picture screen is actually flickering off and on about 64 times a second, yet the picture seems to be illuminated continuously. This phenomenon is called *flicker fusion.*

What light in your visual environment reaches your eyes? If you stood in the center of a large circle, the combined field of view from both eyes—your **visual field**—would include over 200 degrees of the circle's 360-degree circumference. The size of an object as it appears in this visual field depends both on its physical size and its distance from you . This is why it is often useful to describe the size of an object by how much of your visual field it occupies; that is, by how many degrees of the imaginary surrounding circle's circumference it would cover. This is referred to as an object's size in degrees or **visual angle.** A convenient reference is that your fingernail seen at arm's length has a width of about 1 degree visual angle (whereas the moon is only ½ a degree).

The Eye

In 1637 the philosopher-scientist René Descartes removed the eye from a dead bull, carefully scraped away the covering from the rear of the eyeball, and replaced it with a thin paper film. He then held a lighted candle in front of the eye. Clearly visible on the paper at the rear of the eye was an upside-down image of the candle. Since then, scientists have learned considerably more about the eye, but its basic property was clear to Descartes: It projects an image of the scene in front of the eye onto the rear wall of the eye. On this rear wall is a complicated tapestry of tissue called the **retina.** It is in the retina that light-sensitive cells convert the projected pattern of light into patterns of neural activity.

Figure 3–12 is a schematic cross section of the eye, showing some of its major parts. The optical system at the front of the eye that projects the image **cornea** and an inner component called the **lens.** Fine adjustment in the shape of the lens is required to focus either near or far objects onto the retina.

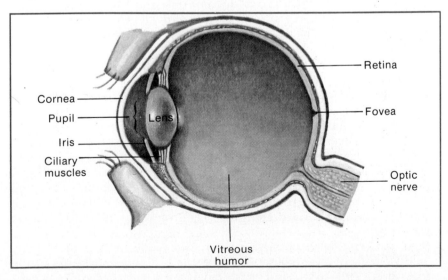

FIGURE 3–12
A *cross section of the eye.*

HIGHLIGHT☐
Sinusoidal Gratings: The Pure Tones of Vision

In recent years interest has developed in a type of visual stimulus that may be as useful in the study of vision as pure tones have been in the study of audition. In fact, the two types of stimuli have much in common. Where a pure tone is a regular cyclical variation in air pressure over time, the visual stimulus is a regular cyclical variation in brightness across space. Because the formal mathematical name for such cyclical variation is a **sine wave**, the patterns are often referred to as **sinusoidal gratings.** An example of one is shown in Figure A.

Just as a pure tone can be described or specified in terms of its frequency and amplitude, a grating has two corresponding properties called spatial frequency and contrast. **Spatial frequency** refers to how rapidly the brightness variations occur across space, and **contrast** refers to the difference in brightness between the lightest and darkest parts of the grating.

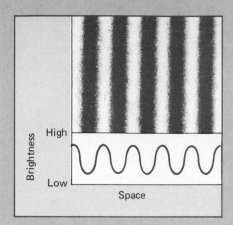

FIGURE A

A sinusoidal grating is shown above with a curve below showing how brightness varies in a regular, cyclical (sinusoidal) fashion across space. Other gratings can differ in how rapidly the cycles occur (frequency) and the difference in brightness between the lightest and darkest parts of the pattern (contrast).

We can see certain spatial frequencies better than others, just as we can hear certain frequencies of tones better than others. We require less amplitude in order to hear some tones, and we require less contrast in order to see some spatial frequencies. This aspect of vision is immediately apparent when you look at the pattern of brightness variations shown in Figure B. This pattern consists of sinusoidal gratings whose frequency increases as you go from left to right and whose contrast increases as you go from bottom to top. Thus, the higher up on the graph you must go to see each frequency of grating, the more contrast you need in order to see it; i.e., the less sensitive you are to that spatial frequency.

For most people, the boundary between those gratings they can see and those they can't is shaped like the curve shown in Figure B (if you view the page at normal reading distance). Notice that this is a sort of threshold curve much like the audiometric function shown in Figure 3–7, only here it indicates your sensitivity to various spatial frequencies. Traditional measures of acuity, such as the Snellen chart, only indicate our limited ability to see fine detail (high spatial frequencies). The curve shown in Figure B also indicates our limited abil-

---

shape of the lens is required to focus either near or far objects onto the retina. These fine adjustments are termed **accommodation** and are produced by changes in the tension of small muscles, the *ciliary muscles,* connected to the lens. Between the cornea and the lens is a richly pigmented structure called the **iris** (from the Greek word for rainbow). The pigments in the iris determine whether the eye is blue, black, brown, or hazel. A small, ringlike opening in the iris forms the round, black **pupil.** The size of this circular opening controls the amount of light entering the eye and varies as a function of the level of illumination. The diameter of the pupil is greatest in a dimly illuminated environment and smallest in a brightly lighted environment. Inside the pupil the light passes through the lens, which focuses it onto the retina, the inner lining of the back of the eyeball.

There are two major landmarks on the retina: the fovea and the blind spot (see Figure 3–13). The **fovea** is a tiny spot on the retina positioned behind the lens. It corresponds to the center of your field of view, where your visual acuity is highest. The **blind spot,** the center of a radiating web of blood vessels, is the point where blood vessels and neurons pass out through the wall of the eye. The blind spot is totally insensitive to light. (You aren't normally aware of this because the blind spot is at a different point in the visual field of each eye, so that what one eye misses, the other eye sees.)

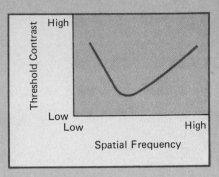

FIGURE B
The stimulus pattern (left) contains sinusoidal gratings that increase in frequency from left to right and in contrast from bottom to top. For most people, the boundary between the gratings they can see and those they can't is shaped like the curve shown on the graph (above). This indicates sensitivity to each spatial frequency: the less contrast required to make it visible, the greater the sensitivity. Compare this to Figure 3–7.

ity to see brightness variations that occur too slowly (low spatial frequencies).

Just as complex sounds can be interpreted as combinations of many pure tones, complex spatial patterns of brightness variation can be interpreted as combinations of many sinusoidal gratings. Thus, further specification of our ability to see various gratings may prove as useful in the study of vision as pure tones have in the study of audition.

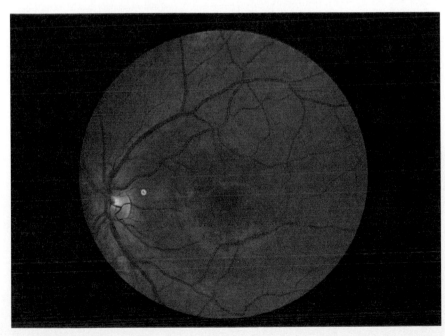

FIGURE 3–13
A view of the retina as seen through an opthalmoscope, a device invented by Helmholtz and now used in most medical examinations to inspect the blood vessels in patients' eyes. Two major landmarks are the fovea (the dark area in the center) and the blind spot where the optic nerve leaves the eyes (the large yellow circle from which blood vessels radiate). The circular area of the retina in this view has a diameter of about 10 mm or 36 degrees visual angle.

Adaptation to a Righted or Displaced Retinal Image

In 1637 René Descartes saw the inverted image of the world projected onto the rear of a dead bull's eye (see text) and wondered how the brain turned it right-side up. His solution (shown in Figure A) depended on a network of "pores" to carry "nervous spirits" away from the retina. The "pores" were simply interwoven to reinvert the image before it reached the pineal gland, "the home of our soul." While Descartes' "explanation" seems childishly simple in light of our present knowledge of neurology, the question still puzzles many students of sensation: Why don't we see the world upside down if the image on our retina is inverted?

The answer lies in an understanding of **sensory codes,** the form in which information about the outside world is carried from our sensory receptors to our brains. Each receptor converts certain aspects of our environment into complex patterns of nerve impulses. Basically all the brain requires is a consistent relationship between these sensory codes and the *information* they carry about the environment. There is no "little man in the head" (*homunculus*) looking at a "picture" sent from our retina. Rather, the activity of specific neurons in our brain is controlled by specific patterns of stimulation on the retina. (See the Highlight on receptive fields later in this chapter.) Although the manner in which these patterns of neural activity produce our experience of seeing is still not completely understood, certain experiments suggest that this process is remarkably flexible or adaptable.

In 1896 a psychologist named Stratton constructed a lens system which inverted the image entering his eye, thereby turning the image on the retina right side up. At first Stratton felt terribly disoriented; things looked not only upside down but also somehow "strange." He had difficulty walking and reaching things. As time passed, however, he began to adjust to the lenses. This was particularly true when he viewed parts of his own body. Finally on the eighth and last day of the experiment he wrote:

> As long as the . . . localization of my body was clear, the general experience was harmonious and everything was right-side up. But, when . . . the pre-experimental localization of my body was prominently in mind, . . . I seemed to be viewing the scene from an inverted body.

Stratton concluded that, in time, he would have completely adapted to the inverting lenses. Years later, another experimenter named Kohler (1947) wore inverting spectacles for almost a week and reported that he finally began to see the world right-side up. Both Stratton and Kohler found that it took some time to readjust when the spectacles were first taken off. Stratton didn't see the world upside down but had difficulty moving about. Kohler actually reported seeing the world inverted at first.

This sequence of gradual adaptation to distorted visual input, followed by a period of readaptation when the distortion was removed, has also been encountered in another type of study. The famous German sensory physiologist Hermann Von Helmholtz (1925) described a demonstration using *prism spectacles,* which shift the apparent position of objects to the right of their true position (Figure B):

> At first, without bringing the hand into the field, look closely at some definite object within reach.

Then close the eyes, and try to touch the object with the forefinger. The usual result will be to miss it by thrusting the hand too far to the right. But after trying for some little while, or, more quickly still, by inserting the hand in the field and under the guidance of the eye, touching the objects with it . . . then on trying the above experiment again, we shall discover that now we do not miss the objects, but feel for them correctly. Having learned how to do this, suppose now we take off the prisms and remove the hand from the field of view, and then after gazing steadily at some object, close our eyes and try to take hold of it. We find then that the hand will miss the object by being thrust too far to the left; until after several failures, our judgment of the direction of the eyes is rectified again.

A similar demonstration is often employed in lectures for introductory psychology courses. A student volunteer, preferably a quarterback on the football team, is asked to put on the prism spectacles and throw a few passes to another student. As shown in Figure C, his initial passes are off the mark to the *right* (where he sees the receiver because of the prisms). With practice however he soon learns to adjust his throws. Then, after removing the spectacles, he is asked to throw one last pass. This is usually off the mark to the *left,* showing the lingering effect of his adaptation to the prisms.

Our ability to adapt to distorted sensory input indicates a flexibility or "plasticity" in the way our brain utilizes sensory information. One can even adapt to as profound a change in the sensory code as Stratton's inversion of the normal retina image.

Subsequent research involving distorted visual input has revealed more about the adaptation process. For example, subjects who can actively reach out and touch objects

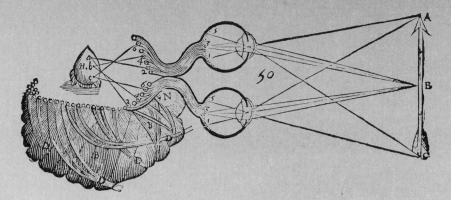

FIGURE A
Descartes used this drawing to show how the "upside-down" image on the retina was "righted" on its way to the pineal gland. (Blakemore, 1977)

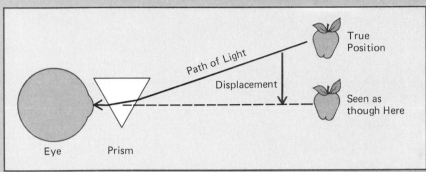

FIGURE B
A prism bends (refracts) light so that objects appear displaced to one side of their real position.

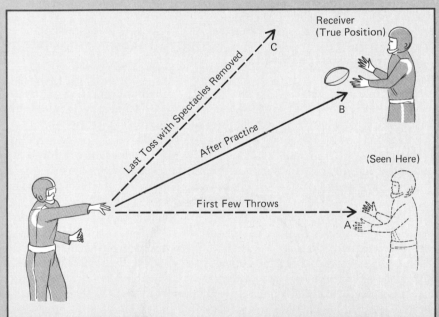

FIGURE C
When a football player wears prism spectacles, the first few tosses go where the receiver is seen to be (A). After practice (adaptation) the tosses go where the receiver really is (B). Then, when the prism spectacles are removed and one more toss is taken, the aftereffect of adaptation causes the toss to go to the left (C) of the receiver.

adapt more rapidly to inverting and prism spectacles than those who remain passive and are moved by the experimenter (Held, 1965; Kohler, 1962). It is *as if* the brain learns to adjust its motor (efferent) commands to the distorted sensory input, and this is what alters its interpretation of the sensory code.

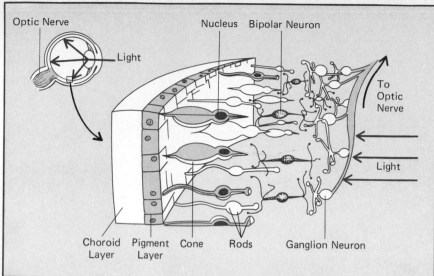

FIGURE 3–14

A cross section of the retina. Note that light has to pass through blood vessels and nerve cells before reaching the rods and cones, which are named for their shapes. Indeed, it has been said that the rods and cones have their backs to the light. (Adapted from Rubin, 1977, p. 73)

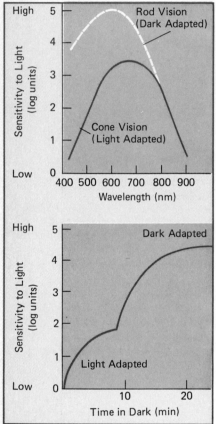

FIGURE 3–15

Two things happen as your eyes adapt to the dark. They gradually become more sensitive to light (the threshold becomes lower) and their sensitivity to various wavelengths of light (spectral sensitivity) shifts from the pattern typical of cones to that typical of rods. The process shown above takes approximately 40 minutes, with the break in the curve occurring after approximately 13 minutes. It represents the point at which the early cone-adaptation levels off while the rods continue to adapt.

Rods and Cones

There are approximately 120 million rods and 6 to 8 million cones on the retina (see Figure 3–14). Most of the cones are on the fovea, which is the center of the field of vision, where acuity is highest. **Cones** are primarily responsible for the ability to see fine detail; they function best in daylight or bright light and are also responsible for the ability to see color.

Rods are distributed on the retina outside of the fovea. We depend on the rods for our ability to see at night or in dim light. Rods do not distinguish colors—this is why at night you do not see colors, only black and white and gray. You may have also noticed that at night you see things better out of the corners or sides of your eye—this is because you are depending on your rods for night vision, and they are located off the center of the retina.

It is in the rods and cones that light energy triggers a complex photo-chemical process that results in neural activity that we experience as sight. The critical step in this process seems to be the breaking down or bleaching of photosensitive pigment in these cells by light. This chemical activity stimulates the neurons attached to the rods or cones, and this firing of the neurons is signalled to the brain. Then the chemicals recombine to form new pigment.

VISUAL ADAPTATION.   Rods and cones differ in their sensitivity to light and in the rate at which the bleaching and recombination of pigment takes place. This difference is important in *visual adaptation,* the adjustment in visual sensitivity in response to changes in the level of illumination. On a clear dark night we can see a single candle flame over 50 kilometers away. We can also see quite well on a sunny, snow-covered ski slope where the levels of light energy affecting our eyes may be over one trillion times greater than that of the candle flame. However, to function effectively in both situations, our visual system needs time to adjust its sensitivity to the level of illumination. This process of adjustment is called adaptation. **Dark adaptation** begins when you leave a brightly lighted environment and enter a darkened one; for example, when you leave a sunny street to enter a darkened movie theater. **Light adaptation** begins when this sequence is reversed; for example, when

FIGURE 3–16
First stare continuously for about 10 seconds at the black dot in the center of the upper rectangle. Then shift your gaze to the black dot in the lower rectangle and hold it steady. Within a moment or so, you should see an illusionary vertical gray area against a whiter background. This negative afterimage occurs because the region of your retina previously exposed to the white region in the upper rectangle has slightly light adapted (become less sensitive), while the parts of your retina previously exposed to the black regions in the upper rectangle slightly dark adapted (became more sensitive). When you shifted your gaze to the lower rectangle, the central part of your retina which was less sensitive produced a ''grayer'' region than the more sensitive areas on either side.

you leave the theater and step back into the sunlight. Your sensitivity to light is often so low on entering a darkened theater that you find it difficult to locate a seat. Yet gradually, over a period of minutes, your sensitivity increases until even the faces of the audience are clearly visible. When you eventually emerge from the theater, your eyes are so sensitive to the previously comfortable sunlight that you may squint for a few moments until you adapt to the light.

How does this take place? As we have seen, the basic process of vision is a photochemical one—the breaking down or bleaching of chemical pigments in rods and cones. It seems possible to account for much (but not all) of light and dark adaptation in terms of the balance between the bleaching and reconstitution of pigments in the rods and cones.

Pigment in the rods is much more sensitive to light than pigment in the cones. This means that it takes a less intense light stimulus to start the breaking down of the pigment in rods than it does in cones (see Figure 3–15). In fact, when you are light adapted you are relying primarily on the less-sensitive cones for vision, because most of the highly sensitive pigment in the rods is depleted. Only when you remain in a dimly illuminated environment long enough to dark adapt completely does the highly sensitive pigment in the rods reach its highest concentration. This allows you to see very dim stimuli that are too weak to affect the less-sensitive cones.

Adaptation makes a big difference in the visual threshold: To be detected in a light-adapted state, a stimulus must be 100,000 times as intense as in a dark-adapted state.

Exposing parts of your retina to different amounts of light for even a few seconds produces differences in their level of light adaptation. If you then look at an evenly illuminated screen, that part of your retina made less sensitive to light causes you to see an illusionary darker region on the screen, called a **negative afterimage.** You can experience this for yourself by looking at Figure 3–16. The part of your retina exposed to the vertical white bar becomes locally light adapted, that is, less sensitive to light. When you then look at the all-white rectangle, you ''see'' an illusionary vertical gray bar. This is because the less sensitive (more light-adapted) part of your retina sends weaker sensations to the brain, as if there were actually less light reflected from that part of the image.

NEURAL ACTIVITY IN THE RETINA.   The firing of a single rod or cone is not communicated to the brain in a simple one-retinal-cell-to-one-brain-cell fashion.

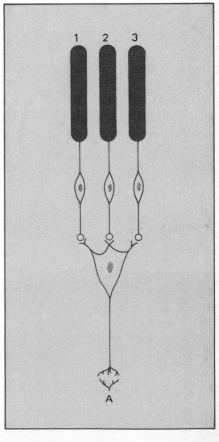

FIGURE 3–17
Cells 1, 2, and 3 converge on a single cell (cell A). Because of this convergence, there is no way of knowing whether activity at cell A was initiated by cell 1, 2, or 3—or any combination of the three.

Receptive Fields

One method of studying the relation between visual stimuli and neural activity at various points in the visual system, then present various of **receptive fields**. The basic strategy is to insert a tiny microelectrode into a neuron somewhere in the visual system, then present various types of visual stimulation to determine which ones influence the activity (pattern of action potentials) of that neuron. The type of stimulus and its location on the retina define the receptive field for that neuron. For example, one neuron might exhibit a change in its normal activity only when a vertical bar of light is presented 4 degrees to the left of the fovea. Another neuron might al-

ter its activity only when a small spot of light is projected within a small area on the far right of the fovea. In each case the type and location of stimulation that influence the activity of that neuron define its receptive field.

The accompanying figure (Figure A) illustrates the experimental setup devised by David H. Hubel and Torsten N. Wiesel (1959) to study the receptive fields of neurons in a cat's visual cortex. First, the cat was anesthetized and made completely motionless. A microelectrode was then slowly inserted into the cat's visual cortex through a hole in its skull. The position of the electrode was fixed when the pattern of electrical activity indicated it was positioned within a single neuron. The cat's eye was held open and focused on a screen, so that light stimuli,

rear-projected onto the screen, would in turn be projected onto the cat's retina. Various stimuli were then projected onto the screen to determine which would influence the electrical activity in the neuron.

To define a particular receptive field, a single dot of light was successively presented at various points on the screen (and therefore projected onto different parts of the cat's retina). At most locations the light might have no effect on the tagged neuron, but then the experimenter might notice a sudden inhibition (decrease) of neural firing. This effect can be recorded by lightly marking the screen at that location with a minus (−) sign to indicate that a dot of light presented at that spot reduced neural activity. The dot of light would then be presented at neighboring points on the screen, and these points would be marked with a minus (−) if the dot reduced the neural activity or with a plus (+) if it increased activity.

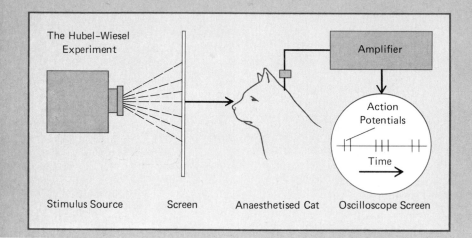

The Hubel–Wiesel Experiment

Amplifier

Action Potentials

Time

Stimulus Source   Screen   Anaesthetised Cat   Oscilloscope Screen

FIGURE A
The Hubel-Wiesel Experiment

Considerable interaction in neural activity occurs in the network of cells lying just above the rods and cones in the retina. Rods and cones connect to *bipolar cells*, which in turn connect to *ganglion cells* whose axons exit the eye through the optic nerve. There are also horizontal interconnections between each of these cells, as shown in Figure 3–14. This network of cells is really a sort of peripheral brain that carries out the first steps in the analysis of the visual image. Two important types of neural interaction that take place in the retina are convergence and lateral inhibition. **Convergence** is the flowing together of neural activity into common paths, much as automobiles leave their driveways to go into a common street. An example of this would be several rods or cones all influencing the same ganglion cell (see Figure 3–17). The firing of any one or more of these receptor elements could trigger activity in the same ganglion cell, so that the ganglion cell would respond to stimu-

The cluster of pluses and minuses labeled Neuron A in Figure B indicates one type of receptive field that Hubel and Weisel were able to "map" in this manner. Notice that light in the center of the cluster tended to increase neural firing, whereas light on the periphery tended to reduce firing (dots of light presented further away had no effect). This common type of simple receptive field is often called a "center-on" field. The type of stimulus that would evoke the most activity in the neuron was a small dot of light falling in the facilitating (+) center of the receptive field, surrounded by darkness so that no light fell on the inhibiting (−) peripheral regions. Thus this neuron could be thought of as a sort of small-white-dot detector. A dot of light that is too large would fall onto *both* + and − regions of the field, with inhibiting effects cancelling out some or all of the facilitating effects.

The receptive fields of two other neurons, labeled B and C, are also shown. See whether you can deduce the type of stimulus pattern that would evoke the most activity in each neuron. Neuron B should respond most actively to the vertical boundary, or "edge," between a lighted area on the left and a dark area on the right, positioned so that the light fell only on the + regions of the field, and dark only on the − regions. This would produce the maximum facilitation with no inhibition. Thus Neuron B could be thought of as a vertical-edge detector. In contast, Neuron C could be considered a horizontal-white-bar detector, since a horizontal white bar (of an appropriate thickness) could be positioned to fall on all the + regions of the field but not on the − regions. Many other types of fields have been mapped in this fashion, including some that seem designed to detect certain patterns of light *moving* in specific directions (e.g., a vertical white bar moving from left to right). In general, neurons in the visual cortex have the largest and most complex receptive fields, with neurons closer to the retina (such as Neuron A) having simpler and smaller fields.

By carefully mapping the receptive fields of neurons at various points in the visual cortex, Hubel and Wiesel have revealed much about its organization. For example, Figure C shows how an electrode can be inserted at right angles to the cortex (I) or diagonally (II). The small dashes next to the path of each electrode show the type of stimulus that neurons penetrated at that point seem designed to detect. It seems as if the neurons are organized in columns. Within a column, the neurons seem to detect stimuli having one orientation (I), with the particular orientation changing gradually from one column to the next (II). In 1981 Hubel and Wiesel were awarded a Nobel prize for their research on receptive fields.

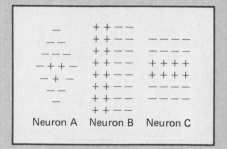

FIGURE B
Three types of receptive field

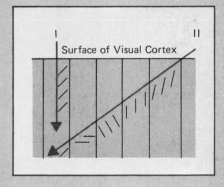

FIGURE C
Electrodes inserted along the path indicated by arrow I encounter neurons that detect stimuli of the same orientation. Those inserted along the path of arrow II encounter neurons that detect progressively rotated stimuli, revealing an organization in columns.

lation over a wider region of the retina than could a single rod or cone, and in that sense be more sensitive. However, this increase in area of sensitivity would be accompanied by a loss in spatial information, since firing of the ganglion cell wouldn't identify which of the converging rods or cones had been stimulated. Thus, neural convergence involves a loss of the type of spatial information most important for acuity. It is clear that there is considerable convergence of retinal elements; although there are about 120 million rods and 6 to 8 million cones, only 1 million neurons leave the eye in the optic nerve. Convergence occurs primarily in the periphery of the retina and mostly in the rods; there is hardly any convergence of the cones on the fovea. This is consistent with the high degree of acuity in the center of our visual field, and the lower acuity on the periphery.

Another basic form of neural interaction on the retina is **lateral in-**

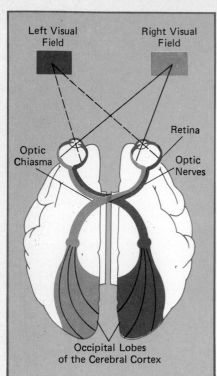

FIGURE 3–18

This diagram shows how information from the eyes is transmitted to the brain. The left side of the visual field falls on the right side of the retina of each eye. The nerves from the right side of each retina project to the right hemisphere of the brain. Similarly, the right side of the visual field falls on the left side of the retina, whose neurons project to the left hemisphere.

hibition. Here the firing of one neuron causes an inhibition (reduction) of activity in nearby cells. In a sense, the image represented in the firing of rods and cones is similar to a line drawing, since lateral inhibition makes the contours of the image sharper. This actually aids acuity, so it is not surprising that lateral inhibition is most characteristic of the interactions of the cones in the fovea, where acuity is highest.

Optic Pathways to the Brain

Figure 3–18 shows the pathways between the retina and the brain. A major feature of this system is that signals from the left half of each retina are transmitted to the left hemisphere of the brain, while signals from the right half of each retina project to the right hemisphere of the brian. Half of the neurons in each optic nerve cross over at a point called the *optic chiasm* and come together with neurons carrying information from the corresponding half of the retina in the other eye. There they join with new nerve bundles to carry the information to the visual cortex. However, this does not mean that each cortical hemisphere receives information from only one half of the visual field. The two hemispheres have many interconnections through which information can be transferred from one side of the brain to the other, as we discussed in Chapter 2.

Color Vision

There are three dimensions used to describe our sensation of color: brightness, hue, and saturation. *Brightness* refers to the amount of energy present in the light rays. As the amount of energy or intensity increases, a stimulus appears brighter. Brightness also depends on the context in which we see the stimulus, the general level of illumination, and other elements, which we will discuss in Chapter 4, "Perception."

Hue corresponds to our names for colors. When we differentiate between red and blue, for example, we are talking about two different hues. As the wavelength varies on the visual spectrum we see different hues (see Figure 3–19). But hue and wavelength are not interchangeable—any hue can be produced either by a single wavelength or by a mixture of quite different wavelenths (see color circle in Figure 3–20). "Light rays of different wavelength can be mixed together in infinite variations without affecting each other—when 'red light' and 'green light' add together to form 'yellow,' the yellow is in us, not in the light, which remains unchanged by the mixing" (Hochberg, 1978, p. 30).

The third dimension is **saturation** or purity of color. This quality is based on how much one wavelength predominates in the stimulus. If all energy is concentrated at a single wavelength, the hue seems very pure; as other wavelengths are added, the hue becomes grayer, more diluted. These three dimensions are illustrated in the color solid shown in Figure 3–21.

MIXTURES OF WAVELENGTHS.   Most of what we see is a mixture of many wavelengths. The particular mixture, or **energy spectrum,** is determined first of all by the original source of light, since each source emits a particular amount of energy at each wavelength. The particular mixture of light can be further modified by **filtering** or **reflection** of some light source (see Figure 3–22). Only the wavelengths we see as green are transmitted through the green part

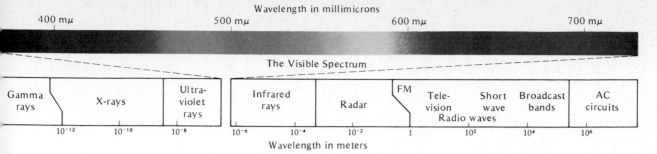

Wavelength in millimicrons

| 400 mμ | 500 mμ | 600 mμ | 700 mμ |

The Visible Spectrum

| Gamma rays | X-rays | Ultra-violet rays | Infrared rays | Radar | FM Tele-vision | Short wave | Broadcast bands | AC circuits |

Radio waves

10^{-12} 10^{-10} 10^{-8} 10^{-6} 10^{-4} 10^{-2} 1 10^2 10^4 10^6

Wavelength in meters

FIGURE 3–19 THE COLOR SPECTRUM
The color spectrum can be produced by passing white light through a prism. The fact that different wavelengths bend at different angles as they pass through glass causes the white light to be broken up into its component colors as shown above. The rainbow appears in the sky when sunlight passes through droplets of water falling from rain clouds, producing the same prismatic effect.

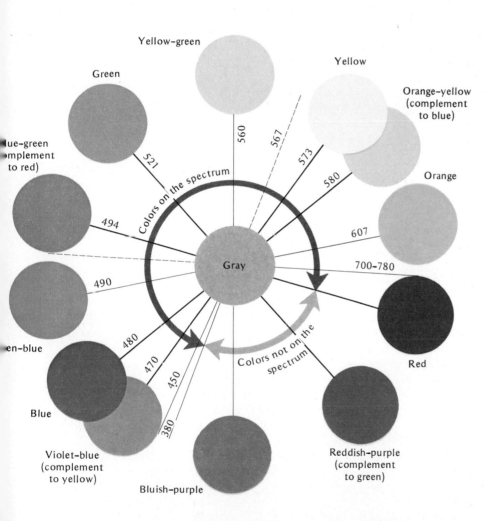

FIGURE 3–20 THE COLOR CIRCLE
The colors on this circle are laid out in identical order in which they appear in the spectrum, and a few nonspectral colors are added. The distance (along the circumference) between each of the colors is such that colors opposite one another are complementaries. A mixture of two complements will produce a neutral gray. Mixing noncomplementary hues will produce a hue midway between the two along the circumference of the circle.

of a stained glass window; the rest are filtered out. Green grass reflects only those wavelengths we see as green; the rest are absorbed (converted to heat energy).

There are basically two different ways to produce a particular mixture of wavelengths. You can *add* different sources of light to produce an **additive mixture** or you can reflect light off various pigments that *subtract* or absorb specific wavelengths to produce a **subtractive mixture.** For example, an

APPLICATION □
Visual Impairment and Treatment

One way of reviewing how the eye normally works is to consider how things can go wrong and the ways such problems can be treated. For example, the cornea, which accomplishes about 70 percent of the focusing in the eye, is normally very clear. However, various injuries and diseases (such as cataracts) can leave it so scarred or clouded that vision is lost or seriously impaired. Fortunately, surgeons are able to replace a damaged cornea with a clear one taken from the eye of a donor. While antibodies in our blood normally attack foreign tissue, the cornea is protected from such rejection because it contains no blood vessels, getting its nourishment instead from the watery aqueous humor behind it and the tears with which it is constantly bathed. A more common defect of the cornea is an irregular shape that makes it impossible to bring all parts of an image into focus at the same time. This condition, called *astigmatism*, can be corrected by eyeglasses ground to make up for the irregular shape of the cornea.

The colorfully pigmented tissue of the iris normally limits the light entering the eye through its small round opening, the pupil. However, albinos suffer from a lack of pigmentation and their pale, unpigmented iris is incapable of effectively blocking light. In bright environments they must wear darkened contact lenses or heavily tinted glasses to reduce the glare.

The lenses of the eyes often stiffen with age, until the ciliary muscles can no longer adjust their shape to focus on near or far objects. Benjamin Franklin invented a solution to this problem: the bifocal lens, the upper half of which provides a sharp image of distant objects, and the lower half of near objects. Even if the lens in your eye is naturally flexible, it can't alter its shape enough to make up for an eyeball that is too long or too short. The figure here illustrates the problem of focusing on distant objects when the retina is too long (a condition called *myopia* or *nearsightedness*) and the problem of focusing on near objects when the retina is too short (a condition called *hyperopia* or *farsightedness*). Each of these conditions can be corrected by contact lenses or eyeglasses that give the eye more focusing power.

A disease called *glaucoma* causes a

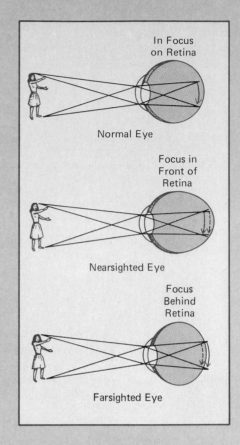

The figure shows the problem of focusing on distant objects when the retina is too long (nearsightedness), and the problem of focusing on near objects when the retina is too short (farsightedness).

FIGURE 3–21 THE COLOR SOLID
The color solid contains all of the distinguishable sensations of color. Hue varies as one travels around the circumference of the solid. The horizontal dimension depicts brightness and the vertical dimension depicts saturation. A complete solid would contain about 350,000 patches of discriminable colors.

Of course, not all visual problems are correctable, and many people have to adjust to a life without vision. Blind people often show amazing skill in their ability to use information from other sensory systems. They can identify people by the sound of their step or the odor of their perfume and can sense obstacles or the shape of a room by the way sounds echo.

The accompanying photo shows the alphabet of raised dots developed by Louis Braille. The Braille alphabet allows blind people to read more than 50 words a minute with the tips of their fingers. Recent advances in computer technology have made it possible for blind people to use hand-held optical scanning devices that automatically translate print into patterns of pressure stimulation, or even computer-generated speech sounds.

progressive increase in the internal pressure of the eye that eventually destroys the retina. An early symptom of this disease is a loss of flexibility in the eyeball caused by the building internal pressure. (Surprisingly, one of the most successful drugs for controlling this pressure increase is marijuana. In 1976 someone suffering from glaucoma became the first person in the United States to use marijuana legally on a prescription basis.)

There can be problems with the retina itself. Sometimes a blow to the head tears or detaches a small part of the retina from the rear surface of the eyeball (the *sclera*). This can often be repaired using a recently developed surgical technique. A tiny, high-intensity laser beam is briefly focused on the retina, causing a tiny burn. The resulting spot of scar tissue reconnects the retina to the rear surface of the eye, much like a tiny thumbtack.

additive mixture occurs if you project two colored light sources onto the same area of a white screen; a subtractive mixture occurs when you mix paints together. The general laws of color mixing are shown in Figure 3–23.

THEORIES OF COLOR VISION. How is the sensation of color produced in the brain? One clue to this puzzle is that we see colors quite well in very bright light when only the cones are responding, whereas we don't distinguish colors under very weak illumination, when only the rods are sensitive enough to respond. For example, a dark-adapted person could recognize forms in a color photograph by the light of the moon, but they would appear in shades of gray. This suggests that the cones are primarily responsible for translating spectral (wavelength) information into the neural patterns (codes) that signal colors to the brain.

It has been known since at least the time of Isaac Newton that it is possible to create virtually all colors by mixing blue, green, and red light. The British

Normally, a mixture of paints is subtractive (each pigment absorbs or "subtracts" wavelengths). However, in the technique used in pointillist paintings, such as the one shown here, the colors reflected by each daub of paint (see detail) mix in an additive fashion when the viewer is too far away to see the individual dots of color (the light reflected from adjacent daubs of color blurs together).

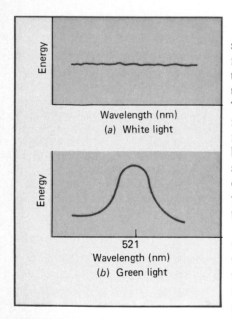

FIGURE 3–22
The spectral composition of white (a) and green (b) light. All wave lengths are present in white light, while mostly green wave lengths are present in green light. White light can be made green by passing it through a green filter or reflecting it off a green surface to remove certain wave lengths.

scientist Sir Thomas Young speculated in 1802 that only three types of color receptors are required to see all colors: one primarily sensitive to blue, one to green, and one to red. According to this theory, the stronger each of the three colors is in the visual stimulus, the stronger each type of receptor reacts. Thus, if the visual stimulus contains a lot of blue light the blue receptors will respond strongly; if it contains mostly red or green light the red or green receptors will react. The resulting *pattern* of neural responses is interpreted by the brain as color. If the stimulus contains energy from all parts of the spectrum, all three types of receptors respond and the sensation of white is evoked. If only the green and red receptors are stimulated, the sensation is yellow. Any visual stimulus that produces the same *pattern* of activity in the three types of receptors is seen as the same color.

This provides an explanation of negative-color afterimages of the sort illustrated in Figure 3–24. As you stare at the black dot in rectangle *a*, the red bar will primarily light-adapt (make less sensitive) your red receptors, whereas your green and blue receptors are less affected. When you then shift your gaze to stare at the dot in the center of the white rectangle *b*, you will soon "see" an illusionary green bar. This negative- (opposite-) color afterimage occurs because the red receptors don't respond as strongly as the yellow and green receptors, because the red receptors have just been partially light-adapted (made less sensitive). This produces a *pattern* of activity in the three types of receptors that mimics the pattern produced by a real green bar. Just the opposite explanation can be made for the illusionary aftereffect that you can "see" after staring at the green bar in rectangle *c*.

Young's three-receptor theory was elaborated some 50 years ago by Helmholtz and became known as the **Young-Helmholtz theory.** To this day, it

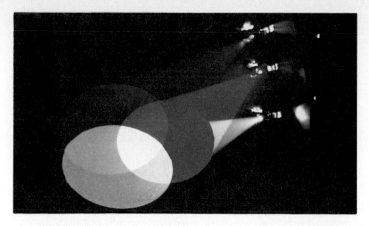

FIGURE 3–23 COLOR MIXING

The area of overlap of the red, green, and blue lights shows what happens when the three primaries are additively mixed: All three lights together yield white. But, since paint pigments absorb most wavelengths and reflect only a few, a mixture of the three primaries of paint is subtractive and all wavelengths are absorbed, producing black.

is one of the two most influential theories of color vision. In fact, modern measuring techniques have shown that there actually are three types of cones, each primarily sensitive to a different part of the spectrum (see Figure 3–25). However, while the Young-Helmholtz theory provides a reasonable interpretation of many aspects of color vision, it is not as successful in explaining others, for example, **color blindness.** By far the most common form of color blindness is an inability to discriminate red from green (about 7 percent of all males and 1 percent of all females have this problem). A less common type is the inability to distinguish blue from yellow. And there are even some people who see the world only in shades of gray, like a black and white photograph (see Figure 3–26).

Ewald Hering, a German physiologist and contemporary of Helmholtz, was the author of the second leading theory of color vision, the **opponent-process theory.** Hering argued that there were three separate color systems: red-green, blue-yellow, and black-white. According to this theory, the effect of the two components in each system is opposite (antagonistic), so that each system's signal to the brain indicates how much of each component is in the visual stimulus. Hering argued that **dichromats,** people who can't distinguish red from green or who can't distinguish blue from yellow, are simply missing one of the antagonistic color systems. **Monochromats,** people who can see the world only in shades of gray, are missing both color systems (only their black-white system is functional).

Elaboration of Hering's opponent-process theory over the years (Hurvich, 1978) has provided an interpretation for most of the phenomena of color vision (see Figure 3–27). Furthermore, it has become clear that it is not incompatible with the Young-Helmholtz theory. It seems likely that color vision really involves some combination of a three-cone system in the retina of the sort envisioned by Young, and the three opponent-process systems in the retina or further along the optic pathways envisioned by Hering.

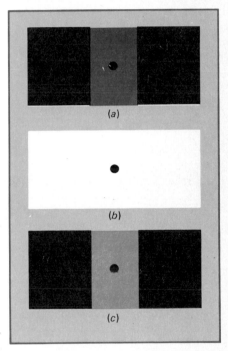

FIGURE 3–24

Negative-color afterimages can be seen by first staring continuously at the black dot in the center of the red or green bar for about 10 seconds, then shifting your gaze to the black dot in the center of the all-white rectangle. In a second or so you should see an illusionary bar in the color of the opposite side of the color circle (Figure 3–20). In terms of the Young-Helmholtz theory (Figure 3–25), prior stimulation of one (or primarily one) of the three types of cones reduces its sensitivity. The remaining types of cones are then more stimulated when you look at the white rectangle.

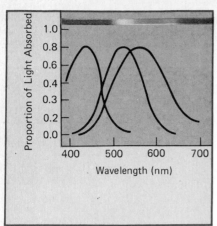

FIGURE 3–25
The Young-Helmholtz theory of color vision is based on the existence of three types of cones, each type primarily sensitive to wavelengths on a different part of the spectrum, as shown here.

FIGURE 3–26
A *photograph of balloons and 2 chips used to test for color blindness are shown as they would appear to four types of people.* (A) A normal person *sees all the colors in the photograph and can make out the snake-like path in the chip on the right and the number 48 in the chip on the left.* (B) A red-green blind person *cannot distinguish red from green in the photograph and cannot see the number 48 in the left chip.* (C) A yellow-blue blind person *cannot distinguish yellow from blue in the photograph and cannot see the snake-like path in the right chip.* (D) A totally color blind person *cannot see any colors in the photograph or the forms in the chips. Notice how each type of color blindness could be interpreted as a failure of either the red-green or blue-yellow opponent process system (see Figure 3–27) or, in the case of total color blindness, of both.*

(a) Photo and chips as seen by normal person

(b) Photo and chips as seen by red-green blind person

(c) Photo and chips as seen by yellow-blue blind person

(d) Photo and chips as seen by totally colorblind person

OTHER SENSES

Clearly, vision and audition are the most highly developed of our senses. However, each of our other senses also provides important information about our environment.

Taste

The physical stimuli for taste are chemical substances (sugar, wine, pizza) that touch the surface of the tongue or, to some extent, the soft palate, the pharynx, and the larynx. Yet the sensation of taste produced by these substances is heavily influenced by other factors, such as color, texture, temperature, and smell. This is why margarine is colored yellow and fruits are dyed before being put on sale. What is popularly meant by "taste" is really a complex perception involving other senses as well. Nevertheless, it is possible to study taste alone. There appear to be four primary taste qualities: sweet, sour, salt, and bitter. Békésy applied various substances to very tiny areas of the tongue and found that each small area responded primarily to one of the four sensations. Normally the substances we taste are spread over the whole surface of the tongue and we experience combinations or patterns of these basic tastes, which may seem quite different from any one of them. Furthermore, some tastes arise more slowly than others. For example, a wine taster might describe a sip of wine as "first fruity, followed by a huskier mellow flavor, and finally a golden aftertaste."

Taste buds are the main receptors for taste. There are about 9,000 of these tiny structures, located mostly on the tip, sides, and rear of the tongue. An example of one type of taste bud is shown in Figure 3–28. Each bud consists of about a dozen individual taste cells clustered together. Liquids, or substances dissolved in saliva, affect the individual taste cells and trigger impulses in neurons attached to each bud. By recording the electrical activity in individual cells, it is possible to show that each cell responds mainly (but not exclusively) to sweet, sour, salty, or bitter substances. Although two cells on the same taste bud may be "tuned" to respond primarily to different tastes, the cells on the tip of the tongue are mainly sensitive to sweet and salty tastes, those on the sides to sour, and those at the back to bitter. These cells are constantly dying and being replaced, so that a whole new set of cells is produced over any 7-day period. If you temporarily lose part of your taste sense by burning some of your taste buds with hot coffee, you can count on recovery within 7 days as new buds replace the injured ones. However, as we age, some of our taste buds die and aren't replaced, and a permanent change occurs in our sense of taste.

Smell

The basic stimuli for the sense of smell (**olfaction**) are airborne molecules that enter our nasal cavities. In order to produce a sensation of odor, these molecules must be soluble in the water or fat found in our nasal passages. Little more can be said regarding the relation between the physical character of the molecules and the odor they evoke. Although many people have tried to set up catgories of odor, there is no generally accepted classification scheme. One such attempt was a seven-category system—camphoraceous,

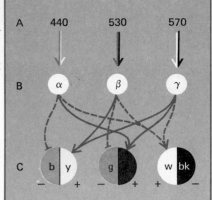

FIGURE 3–27
Hering's opponent-process theory of color vision is based on the existence of three separate color systems: green-red, blue-yellow, and white-black. Since the effect of the two components in each system is opposite, each system's signal to the brain shows the relevant amount of each component in the visual stimulus. (Based on Hurvich & Jameson, 1957)

FIGURE 3—28
The diagram shows the structure of a taste bud, the main receptor for taste. In the photo on the right, the taste buds responding to sour substances have triggered impulses in the neurons attached to the cells, causing a strong reaction to the sour taste of the lemon.

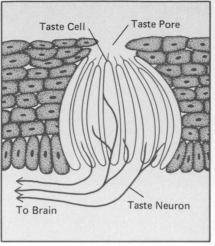

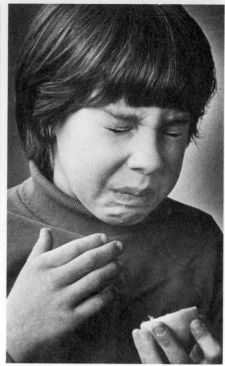

pungent, ethereal, floral, pepperminty, putrid, and musty (Amoore, 1964). However, even these odors may be broken down into more categories. At present the variety of classification schemes serves mainly to illustrate the complexity of odors.

The olfactory receptors are located on the *olfactory epithelium*. It consists of two surfaces located deep inside our two nasal cavities. The basic receptor units are cells buried in and under the epithelium that project their tips (bulbs), along with small hairlike cilia, into the layer of mucus covering the epithelium. It is the reaction of the bulbs and cilia to the soluble molecules trapped in the mucus that triggers the nervous impulse. The actual coding of the smell information is not well understood.

One reason so little is known about the olfactory system is that it is difficult to reach or electrically record from the receptor cells in the epithelium. Furthermore, it is difficult to control the presentation of stimuli (airborne, soluble molecules), although there have been elaborate attempts to do so. The movement of air in our nasal passages is very complicated. It is known that the act of sniffing alters the shape of the cavities so that more air passes over the olfactory epithelium, thereby exposing it to molecules of matter in the air that stimulate the odor sense. The congestion of the nasal passages when you have a cold makes it harder for the soluble molecules to reach the sense bulbs, which is why your sensitivity to odors is reduced when you have a cold.

Skin Sensations

Many different types of physical stimuli cause sensations in the skin. For scientific purposes, the sensation of pressure may be evoked by pressing the

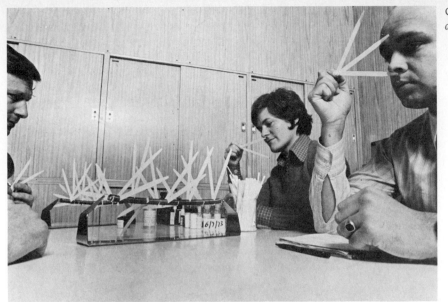

Comparing odors in an experiment in olfaction.

tip of a tiny hair against the skin. Warmth or cold may be evoked by touching the skin with a tiny metal point of a certain temperature. Pain may be evoked by intense application of either pressure or temperature stimuli. It is possible to "map" **skin sensitivity** by drawing a small grid on the skin and then systematically applying each type of stimulus to each square of the grid. Figure 3–29 shows a typical distribution of sensitivity for each sensation. If enough pressure, heat, or cold is applied at one point, its effect will be distributed over a wider area, so these maps are based on low levels of stimulation. Very hot water will stimulate both cold *and* warmth receptors, producing a sensation of "hot." A curious property of these spots of sensitivity is that stimulation of a cold spot with a warm metal tip evokes the sensation of cold, while stimulation of a warm spot with a cold tip evokes the sensation of warmth (this is known as *paradoxical cold* or *warmth,* respectively). Of course, under most circumstances our skin is stimulated over large areas, so that whole populations of these spots are stimulated in unison or rapid succession.

The distribution of sensitivity spots varies considerably from one part of the body to another. For example, there are many more pressure-sensitive spots on your lips and fingertips than on your back. This can be demonstrated by measuring how far apart two stimulated points must be for you to notice that two, rather than only one, points are being applied to the skin. It turns out that the smallest discernible separation on your back is over 35 times as great as on your fingertips.

Neurons in the skin have a variety of endings: Some are attached to the base of hair follicles, some have a type of enclosed or encapsulated ending, and some have free endings. At one time it was believed that specific sensitivity (warm, cold, or pain) was determined by the type of nerve ending. But close examination of the skin tissue identified as a cold, warm, or pain spot failed to reveal any consistent association between the type of nerve ending and sensitivity. It is clear that the neurons attached to hair follicles generally respond to light pressure. However, we are also sensitive to light pressure on skin areas that have no hair, such as the lips or fingertips.

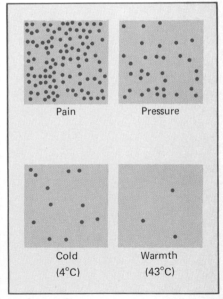

FIGURE 3–29
The diagrams above show a map of the typical distribution of skin sensitivity to pain, pressure, cold, and warmth.

Most of the skin sensations we experience should be thought of as complex patterns of stimulation involving multiple receptor systems. For example, the successive stimulation of adjacent pressure spots produces the sensation of being tickled.

Sensations of Bodily Position

As you move about in the world your body is influenced by gravity and inertia. Your muscles constantly flex and relax in relation to these forces. For example, you hold your body erect against the pull of gravity, or you put an arm in motion and then brake it as your fork approaches a plate. Considering the number of cooperative muscles involved, it is truly amazing that you can bring a fork to rest precisely under several peas, let alone perform a gymnast's back somersault on a narrow balance beam. While vision is an important part of these processes, two other sensory systems cooperate in feeding your brain the information required to perform these complex acts: the **kinesthetic sense** and the **equilibratory sense.**

KINESTHESIS.   Sense organs in the joints and muscles send signals to the brain that indicate the position of the joints and the degree of tension in the muscles. These sensors are responsible for our kinesthetic sense. Ballet dancers unconsciously use these sensors to monitor the position of their limbs, just as you do when you perform the more mundane acts of walking, sitting, or lifting. A rare form of disease called *tabes dorsalis* robs its victims of the kinesthetic sense in their legs. They compensate for this by visually monitoring their position in order to walk. Their slow, oddly shuffling gait is a vivid illustration of the importance of kinesthesis. Most people become aware of the importance of kinesthesis only when temporarily robbed of it: for example, when the dentist puts your tongue to sleep by a shot of novocaine and your speech becomes slurred, or when your leg "goes to sleep" because you have sat on it too long.

EQUILIBRATORY SENSE.   Two sensory organs located next to the cochlea in the inner ear are responsible for our general sense of equilibrium or balance. They are the semicircular canals and the vestibular sacs.

The **semicircular canals** are three ringlike structures, each oriented in a different plane at right angles to the other, just like the three surfaces forming the corner of a box. They are filled with fluid that moves in the canals when they are rotated, just as the water in a glass will rotate with respect to the glass when the glass is turned. The movement of the liquid twists small hair cells, triggering neurons attached to these cells. Any bodily movement influences the three separate semicircular canals in a specific way, and the pattern of neural activity signals the direction of motion to the brain.

The **vestibular sacs** are located between the cochlea and the semicircular canals. These sacs are filled with a jellylike substance containing small bones called **otoliths.** Hair cells embedded in the jellylike substance are twisted by the gravitational pull on the otoliths, producing nerve impulses. While the semicircular canals only respond to movement or shifts in position, gravitational pull on the otoliths in the vestibular sacs continuously signals the head's position even when the head is motionless. Disease or infection of the middle ear can produce an almost constant sense of *vertigo* (dizziness) because this signaling function is interrupted.

The emphasis in this chapter has been on the sensory systems that constantly send information about the outside world and other parts of our bodies back to the brain. It is in the brain that this information is integrated and interpreted. It is here that warmth, pressure, odor, and visual sensations become your experience of being held by your mother, and that a pattern of light and dark contours on the retina becomes the words of a novel. This is the process of perception to which we turn in the next chapter.

SUMMARY

1. All knowledge of the world is carried into the brain through the various sensory systems; activity in these systems is highly correlated, or *redundant* (e.g., the sound of a person's voice and the sight of their lips moving is highly correlated or redundant).

2. Before we can sense any form of energy, the stimulus must be at or above the *absolute threshold.* Before we can sense a stimulus change, the stimulus must be greater than the *difference threshold.*

3. Three basic *psychophysical relations* that characterize the association between changes in sensation and changes in stimulus intensity are *Weber's law,* JND = kI; *Fechner's law,* S = clogI; and *Stevens's power law,* S = kI^b.

4. Auditory stimuli are complex patterns of variations of air pressure; in the auditory system, stimuli are converted into patterns of neural activity that we experience as sound. An *audiometric function* indicates the absolute threshold for each frequency of tone.

5. The sensation of *pitch* is determined primarily by the *frequency* of a tone; *loudness* is determined by the *amplitude* of the tone.

6. The *place theory* of pitch perception is based on the idea that different sound frequencies (different pitches) actually trigger different neurons. An alternative way in which pitch information could be coded into neural activity is in terms of the rate at which neurons are triggered; this is the *frequency theory* of pitch perception.

7. The *visible spectrum,* or *light,* is the range of wavelengths of electromagnetic radiation between 400 and 760 nanometers (for normal vision).

8. The optical system at the front of the eye—consisting of the *cornea* and the *lens*—projects an image onto the *retina.* The eye's receptors are the rods and the cones of the retina.

9. When the *rods* and *cones* receive light energy, this triggers a complex photochemical process, resulting in neural activity that we experience as sight.

10. The *Young-Helmholtz theory of color vision* assumes that there are three types of cones, each primarily sensitive to a different part of the spectrum. Hering's *opponent-process theory* identifies three antagonistic pairs of color systems in the retina or along the optic pathways. It seems likely that color vision involves a combination of these theories.

11. The physical stimuli for taste are chemical substances (generally food) that touch the *taste buds* on the tongue.

12. Other factors influencing the sense of taste are color, texture, temperature, and smell.

13. The basic stimuli for smell (*olfaction*) are airborne molecules that enter the nasal cavities; the olfactory receptors are buried in and under the *olfactory epithelium,* located deep inside the nasal cavities.

14. Many different types of physical stimuli evoke skin sensations; these sensations include pressure, warm, cold, and pain.

15. Two sensory systems that provide the brain with information needed for the body to move properly are the *kinesthetic sense* and the *equilibratory sense.*

16. Sense organs in the joints and muscles define the kinesthetic sense; *semicircular canals* and *vestibular sacs* in the inner ear are responsible for equilibrium (balance).

Suggested Readings

Cornsweet, T. M. *Visual perception.* New York: Academic Press, 1971. An advanced review of the experimental methodology employed in the study of vision.

Egan, J. P. *Signal detection theory and ROC analysis.* New York: Academic Press, 1975. A quantitative development of signal detection theory for advanced students.

Geldard, F. *The human senses* (2nd ed.). New York: Wiley, 1972. A comprehensive development of the human sensory systems, suitable for advanced students.

Levine, M. W., & Shefner, J. M. *Fundamentals of sensation and perception.* Reading, Mass.: Addison-Wesley, 1981. A fairly advanced but very clearly written book that emphasizes sensory processes but also deals with perception.

Lindsay, P. H., & Norman, D. A. *Human information processing* (2nd ed.). New York: Academic Press, 1977. The senses are discussed as components of an information-processing system, with analogies drawn from computer pattern recognition.

Ludel, J. *Introduction to sensory processes.* San Francisco: W. H. Freeman & Company, Publishers, 1978. A detailed treatment of basic sensory processes, including physics and biochemistry relevant to these processes.

McBurney, D., & Collings, V. *Introduction to sensation and perception.* Englewood Cliffs, N.J.: Prentice-Hall, 1977. A clearly written and concise general introduction to sensation and perception.

Sciffman, H. R. *Sensation and perception* (2nd ed.). New York: John Wiley, 1982. A well-written introduction to a broad range of topics in sensation and perception.

4. Perception

Your senses are constantly affected by such aspects of the environment as electromagnetic radiation entering your eyes, rapid variations in air pressure next to your ears, and mechanical deformation of your touch receptors. Yet you aren't normally aware of isolated sensations. Instead you experience "things": see a person, a car, a printed word; hear a voice, a car's horn; feel the touch of a hand, or cool rain on your face. This interpretation of the information provided by your sensory systems is often referred to as **perception.** Ordinarily this process of interpretation is so automatic, rapid, and successful that you aren't even aware of it. Only when you are in error and perceive an **illusion,** or when stimuli are highly ambiguous, do you think much about the interpretations that you ordinarily make so easily.

A major goal of this chapter is to make you aware that almost all your perceptions are to some degree educated guesses about the world based on prior experience. To do this, we will deal primarily with visual perception, both because it is the richest source of sensory information and because it illustrates general perceptual principles that apply to other sensory modes as well. (Speech perception will be discussed in Chapter 8, "Language and Thought.") We will first consider some general principles of perception and then show how they apply to a variety of important perceptual processes.

SOME GENERAL PRINCIPLES

Redundancy and Perception

If one part of a message can be inferred from another, the parts are said to be redundant (just as material repeated by a lecturer is redundant). There is a considerable repetition of information, **redundancy,** in the sensory messages sent to our brain, and this plays a major role in perception.

A newborn infant does not understand the relationship between the sound of its mother's voice, the sight of her face, and the feel of her bodily warmth, but it rapidly learns that these are all closely related aspects of a single thing, "mother." Soon one sensation becomes a reliable *signal* or *cue* for the experience of the others: For instance, the sound of her voice often comes just before the sight of her face above the crib, or the sensation of being held. Almost every aspect of our experience involves relationships of this sort. As these relationships are learned, they begin to color every sensory experience we have. Individual sensations are interpreted as signals or cues for things in the world that can be reliably inferred from them.

Figure 4–1 shows how your knowledge of the *structural redundancy* in a face (the predictable relationships among its parts) allows you to infer or fill in the missing parts in a photograph.

Another example of redundancy is that between the sight of a person's lip movements and the sounds you hear. While you normally make little use of this, it allows you to be fooled by a ventriloquist. You attribute the speech sounds coming from the ventriloquist to the dummy because you see the dummy's lips move. Deaf people learn to lip-read—that is, to infer speech from lip movements.

The dominant view of perception over the last 100 years or so has been that sensory redundancy, which you know through experience, allows you to draw broad inferences about the world from very limited sensory informa-

FIGURE 4–1

This photograph has been cut into 10 equal columns, which have been arranged with alternate columns on two levels. Note that you can infer quite a lot about the five odd-numbered columns above from the five even-numbered columns below (and vice versa). This is because you know a great deal about the structure of faces and about how one part is related to another. You know, that is, about structural redundancy.

tion. These inferences are usually so accurate, highly practiced, and practically automatic that you are almost totally unaware of making them. This is why one of the early proponents of the view, Hermann von Helmholtz (1925/1962), referred to them as *unconscious inferences.*

For example, our language is highly redundant—you can often finish a sentence in your mind after hearing or seeing only part of it. When most people read the phrases in the triangles in Figure 4–2, they simply ignore the extra word in each phrase. Clearly, they make rapid inferences about each phrase, based on prior experience, without actually reading each word. While such automatic or unconscious inferential processes may have misled you in this instance, they are normally an efficient and useful aid to reading, allowing you to read rapidly without stopping to examine each word.

This view of perception has been challenged by the work of James J. Gibson (1966) and others. Gibson argued that traditional perceptual research failed to consider the active, information-seeking interaction between organisms and their environments. He believed that human sensory systems have evolved to extract far more complex forms of information from our environments than the stimuli used in traditional perception research. Rather than simply supplying cues from which our brain subsequently draws inferences, our sensory systems have evolved to be perceptual systems in their own right, systems sensitive to complex aspects of our environment sufficient to evoke immediate perceptual experience without any intervening inferential process. Proponents of Gibson's view (Neisser, 1967, 1976; Shaw & Bransford, 1977; Turvey & Shaw, 1978) have called for more ecologically valid experiments in perception, experiments that involve the complex patterns of stimulation encountered as we move about in normal environments, rather than those that have traditionally been used in sensory research. (See Highlight on Gibsonian invariants.)

Attention: Selectivity in Perception

Another basic principle of perception is that we are unable to deal with all potentially perceptible aspects of our environment at the same time. The study of how we selectively perceive one aspect or another is the study of **attention.** For example, you are probably sitting as you read this. Without moving, shift your attention to the sensations produced by the pressure of your body against the surfaces supporting it. Exactly where is the chair pressing against your back? Which parts of your left foot are pressing against something? As you attempt to answer questions of this sort, you selectively attend to sensory activity that was present earlier but unnoticed.

Have you ever been at a party gazing with apparent interest into the eyes of someone speaking to you, only to realize that you're really listening to a conversation going on behind you? Both voices, your partner's and the one you're really attending to, are entering your ears and evoking patterns of sensory activity. Yet you selectively perceive only one of them, finding it difficult to listen closely to both conversations at the same time. Thus you may occasionally switch your full attention back to your partner in order to keep the conversation going.

This "cocktail-party phenomenon" has been studied experimentally. Subjects heard two voices speaking at the same time (usually one voice in the right ear and a different voice in the left). They were sometimes instructed to listen primarily to one voice, sometimes to the other, and sometimes to try to listen to both simultaneously. Figure 4–3 shows the sort of "tradeoff" that was generally found between a subject's comprehension of each voice: Increased comprehension of one voice is generally associated with reduced comprehension of the other. To explain this negative relationship, an English psychologist named Donald Broadbent (1958) proposed that subjects have the capacity to listen to only one voice at a time; the negative relationship between the comprehension of each voice reflects the proportion of time subjects spent listening to each voice.

This sort of tradeoff between attending to one voice or another, however, can also be explained as a simultaneous sharing of attention rather than switching. That is, you may attend primarily to one voice, but at the same time allocate some small portion of your attention to the other voice. This view, sometimes referred to as the *filter theory,* was advanced by Anne Triesman (1964) to account for subjects' apparent sensitivity to certain kinds of information presented to the nonattending ear. For example, they were likely to notice it if the nonattended voice said a stimulus such as their own name.

Another view of attention (Norman, 1979) is that selection occurs not by selectively blocking or filtering sensory information, but by selective *processing* of information already evoked or activated in memory by incoming sensory information. Highly practiced and familiar stimuli (such as your own name) often seem to be perceived so automatically that it is almost impossible to ignore them (Schneider & Shiffrin, 1977). A good example of such *automaticity* in perception is the so-called *Stroop effect* (Stroop, 1935). Subjects are shown words that are printed in different colors of ink. They are told to ignore the words and just name the ink colors. They have little difficulty doing this, except when the words are names of different colors. For example, if the word "red" is printed in green ink, subjects often hesitate or stumble in saying "green," as if they have difficulty ignoring the word's meaning (the Stroop effect). Normally the highly practiced and almost automatic perception of word meaning facilitates reading. However, this same automaticity makes it difficult to ignore meaning and pay attention only to certain other aspects of the stimulus. Thus, the Stroop effect is a failure of selective perception (see Figure 4–4).

At present there is no general agreement concerning the mental processes that control attention. It seems likely that many different processes are responsible for selectivity in perception (Kinchla, 1980).

ORGANIZATION

As we have seen, we are seldom aware of isolated sensations. Our minds constantly organize sensory activity to perceive *things*. Complex sequences of auditory stimulation are perceived as words, a car motor, water running. Complex patterns of visual stimulation are seen as people, cars, printed words. Much of our ability to organize or structure complex patterns of sensory activity into meaningful forms depends on experience (see Figure 4–5). However, certain kinds of perceptual organization seem so universal and natural that it has been proposed they are innate rather than the product of earlier experience.

GESTALT PRINCIPLES OF ORGANIZATION. The **Gestalt** psychologists (Koffka, 1935; Köhler, 1940) believed that a number of innate organizational tendencies influence the way we see. While many contemporary psychologists feel that

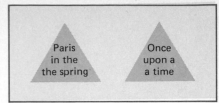

FIGURE 4–2
Read the phrases in the two triangles. Did you notice something wrong? Most people do not notice that there is an extra word in each phrase. This is because we really don't examine every word when we read. Rather, we make rapid, almost automatic assumptions about entire phrases from the few words on which we do fixate directly.

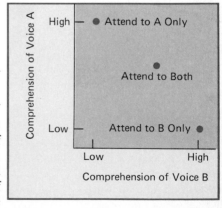

FIGURE 4–3
The graph shows the negative relation between a subject's comprehension of each voice when listening to two voices at the same time—increased comprehension of one is generally associated with reduced comprehension of the other. (Broadbent, 1958)

Gibsonian Invariants

The late psychologist James J. Gibson (1966; Gibson & Gibson, 1972) argued that traditional perceptual research ignored many aspects of our natural visual environment that serve as important perceptual cues. Look at Figure A shown on the right. While the scenes differ in many respects, they share one feature—a gradual shift in the average pattern of detail as you go from top to bottom. This shift is called a **texture gradient**; it is an almost invariant feature of nature when one is looking out across a surface. The retinal size of all objects diminishes with distance; thus this gradient is a strong cue for the perception of depth. While it is tempting to think of this cue as something the mind constructs out of the constituent details, Gibson argued that the sensation of a gradient may be as primitive and fundamental a sensory experience as hue or pitch.

Another example of a Gibsonian invariant is the pattern of retinal stimulation produced when you look at something as you move toward it. As you pass objects, their contours tend to stream off to the periphery of your retina in an accelerated fashion. In fact, some may be moving so fast that they are essentially blurred lines radiating toward the periphery of your field of view. This is illustrated in Figure B. Although the details of other images might differ, the **peripheral streaming** would still be a cue for movement. Again, this may provide a primitive cue for movement that is as immedi-

FIGURE A
These photos show how texture gradients can be a strong cue for depth.

FIGURE B
This photo shows how peripheral streaming is a strong cue for motion.

ate and direct as any other aspect of your visual experience.

Gibson's work has encouraged perceptual psychologists to take a fresh look at the patterns of visual stimulation encountered in natural environments. Earlier laboratory work may have been limited by a preoccupation with simple, easily manipulated, physical dimensions of light such as wavelength and intensity. Texture gradients and peripheral streaming are only two of the more complex invariants of our natural visual experience that play a major role in perception.

these tendencies are the result of experience and learning, all agree that they are strong and virtually universal tendencies.

Examples of such apparently universal organizational tendencies are the Gestalt *principles of grouping.* These refer to the human tendency to organize sets of isolated stimuli into groups on the basis of *proximity* (closeness), *similarity, closure, continuity,* and *symmetry.* These principles are illustrated and explained in Figure 4–6.

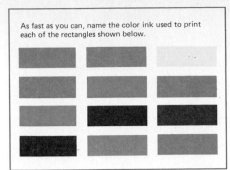

As fast as you can, name the color ink used to print each of the rectangles shown below.

FIGURE 4–4
Notice how difficult it is to ignore what the words say. You seem to automatically read the color names, and this interferes with naming the color of the ink. This is called the Stroop effect after the experimenter who devised this demonstration of automatic perception.

Now, as fast as you can, name the color ink used to print each word shown below, *ignoring what each word says.*

BLUE	GREEN	BROWN
RED	ORANGE	RED
YELLOW	GREEN	BLUE
RED	BLACK	ORANGE

FIGURE-GROUND ORGANIZATION. Another basic organizational tendency that the Gestalt psychologists argued is innate is referred to as **figure-ground organization**—the tendency to perceive things (figures) standing out against a background (ground). For example, as you read this page, the words are black figures standing out against the white background of the paper. Normally this type of organization is so efficient and automatic that it occurs unnoticed. However, consider the pattern shown in Figure 4–7. Here the normal figure-ground organization suggested by the generally white back-

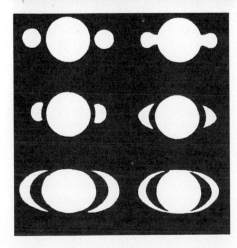

FIGURE 4–5
Organization is highly dependent on experience. Today's television generation of children would quickly recognize the planet Saturn as a sphere surrounded by a ring, as shown in the two photographs above, but an early astronomer who didn't know anything about Saturn couldn't "see" it correctly, as his drawings indicate (bottom, left). Without a clue (e.g., man on a horse) you may have the same problem "seeing" (organizing) a comprehensible form in the figure on the right.

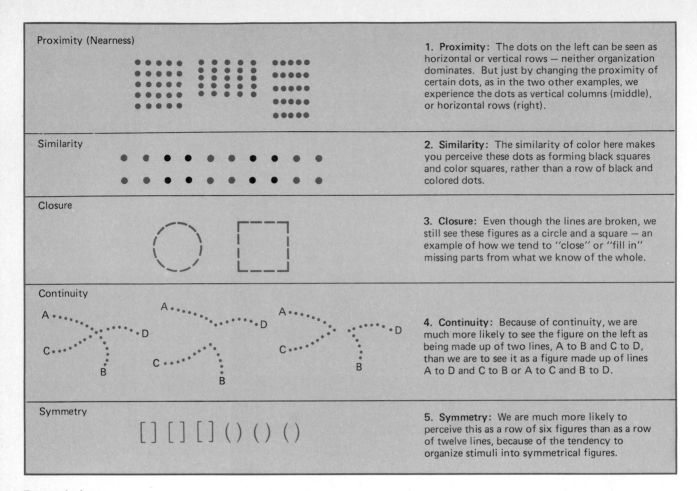

Proximity (Nearness)

1. **Proximity:** The dots on the left can be seen as horizontal or vertical rows — neither organization dominates. But just by changing the proximity of certain dots, as in the two other examples, we experience the dots as vertical columns (middle), or horizontal rows (right).

Similarity

2. **Similarity:** The similarity of color here makes you perceive these dots as forming black squares and color squares, rather than a row of black and colored dots.

Closure

3. **Closure:** Even though the lines are broken, we still see these figures as a circle and a square — an example of how we tend to "close" or "fill in" missing parts from what we know of the whole.

Continuity

4. **Continuity:** Because of continuity, we are much more likely to see the figure on the left as being made up of two lines, A to B and C to D, than we are to see it as a figure made up of lines A to D and C to B or A to C and B to D.

Symmetry

5. **Symmetry:** We are much more likely to perceive this as a row of six figures than as a row of twelve lines, because of the tendency to organize stimuli into symmetrical figures.

FIGURE 4–6

FIGURE 4–7
Because most words printed on white pages are black "figure" and white "ground" you tend to "see" (organize) the accompanying pattern as a jumble of odd-shaped black "figures" on the white "ground." If you try to reverse this figure-ground organization you will eventually see the word "house" as white letters ("figures") against a black "ground."

ground of the page encourages you to see the black regions as "figure" and the white regions as "ground." Only after some time and effort can you reverse this original organization and see the word "house" as a white figure against a black background.

While figure-ground organization has traditionally referred to visual perception, there seem to be similar organizational processes in hearing. For example, the "cocktail-party phenomenon" can be interpreted as a choice of which voice to hear as "figure" standing out against a background of another voice (or voices). Similarly, the particular stream of notes one chooses to hear as a single melodic line in a Bach fugue also seem to be a "figure" heard against a background of the other notes.

BISTABLE OR REVERSIBLE STIMULUS PATTERNS. One of the most convincing ways to illustrate the importance of organizational processes in perception is to consider stimulus patterns that are perceived in very different ways depending on your choice of organization. If there are only two alternative organizations, the stimulus patterns are often referred to as *bistable* or *reversible* patterns. Each organization produces a stable perception, although it is impossible to experience both simultaneously. One organization must be changed or reversed in order to experience the other perception.

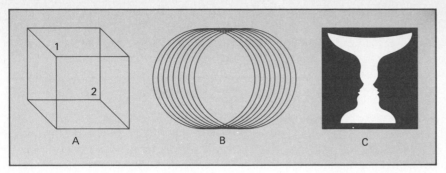

FIGURE 4–8
These are examples of reversible patterns. They can also be described as ambiguous figures, since it is not clear which pattern should predominate, unlike Figure 4–6, in which the pattern that revealed the word "house" is clearly the more appropriate organization. In Pattern A you can see a cube with either corner 1 or corner 2 closer to you. Pattern B can be seen as a cylinder lying on its side with its closer end on the left or on the right. Pattern C looks like a goblet if the white area is seen as "figure," or like two faces in profile if the white area is organized as "ground" (background).

Figure 4–8 presents several examples of stimuli susceptible to multiple organizations. Some of the patterns could also be described as *ambiguous,* since it is unclear which organization is appropriate. Fortunately, most of the things we see occur in contexts that provide ample cues for resolving such ambiguity.

Constancies: *Invariance amidst Change*

Although sensory activity may vary enormously from moment to moment, you perceive many aspects of the world as stable and invariant. For example, a person seen from different angles or distances produces different patterns of stimulation on your retina, yet you still "see" the same person. You draw similar inferences about the world from different patterns of sensory activity. Such inferences give a stability or constancy to your perceptions of the world despite great changes in sensory activity. We will discuss this phenomenon, **perceptual constancy,** in regard to size, shape, and color.

SIZE CONSTANCY. If a person walking away from you casts a smaller and smaller image onto your retina, why do you see that person's size as remaining constant? One explanation is that your interpretation of an object's size depends on both the size of its image on your retina (see Figure 4–9) and how far away you perceive it to be. Two objects casting the same-size image onto your retina would be perceived as different in size if they appear to be at different distances. The object that looks farther away from you would seem to be larger. Thus **size constancy** is the almost automatic tendency to compensate for changes in the size of the retinal image caused by changes in viewing distance.

Some psychologists argue that this process of compensation is unnecessary to explain size constancy. They say that size constancy occurs because both the object and its surroundings change together as the distance of the object

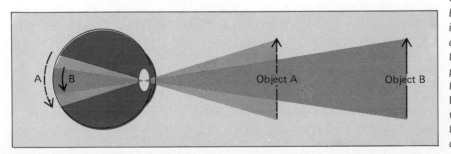

FIGURE 4–9
Object A and Object B are the same size, but because A is closer it casts a much larger image on the retina than B. However, because we are able to take into account distance cues and our experience of objects and people, we do not always experience things as the size of the image they cast on the retina. If A and B were people, for instance, we would not think that person A was twice as tall as person B. This is the principle of size constancy.

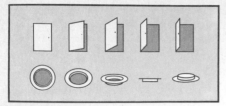

FIGURE 4-10

Two examples of shape constancy are shown here. The opening door is actually many different shapes, yet we still see it as basically a rectangular door. The different retinal images evoke an unchanging (constant) perception of shape. Only your perspective seems to change. The same is true of the hat seen from different perspectives.

changes. In other words, your friend at a distance looks smaller, but so do the buildings around her, and the trees and the cars. When close up, all of these—your friend and her surroundings—look larger, but they are in the same *relationship* to one another. In other words, size remains constant because the relationship between the object and its surroundings stays the same.

SHAPE CONSTANCY.   **Shape constancy** is the tendency to perceive objects as having the same shape in spite of variations in the shape they cast onto your retina (see Figure 4-10). As you watch a door opening, your view of it may change from a rectangle to a trapezoid. However, your past experience with doors causes you to infer or understand automatically that the door itself is not changing shape, but only your particular view of it.

Shape constancy depends on both familiarity with the shapes of objects and knowledge of their position in space relative to you. You may have had the experience of sitting far to one side in a movie theater and, at least at first, being keenly aware of the distortion produced by your perspective of the screen. However, you are capable of rapidly accommodating to the situation, and before long you were probably able to follow the movie without even noticing the distortion.

The Ames room uses a visual illusion to pit size constancy against shape constancy. In Figure 4-11 you seem to be looking at a normal room with one very tall, one average-sized, and one very short man in it. But this is really a very distorted room in which the rear wall is tilted away from you at an extreme angle, and you are really looking at it from the side (as if you were sitting on one side of a movie theater, as in the earlier example). The man who seems to be very short is really much farther away from you and produces a much smaller image on your retina than the other two men. Instead of seeing the three men as similar in height but at different distances from you, you perceive both ends of the rear wall to be equally far away and automatically infer that the men are of different heights. The strange shape of the room produces this misinterpretation.

The Ames room illusion is possible because you have a very strong expectancy concerning the shapes of normal rooms. And although you know there is something wrong about the difference in height among the three men, shape constancy wins out over size constancy. Because you don't perceive the true shape of the room the size distortion occurs. In order to see the room as normal, you must ignore distance cues.

When people have a chance to explore the Ames room, particularly if they are allowed to touch the walls and experience for themselves the way they slant, the illusion is gradually reduced. But just explaining it to someone, even showing a diagram, does not seem to destroy the illusion. Look at the photograph again. Can you see the room differently now that you know the trick? Intellectual knowledge seems to have little effect on perception—that's how magicians stay in business. The effects of perceptual cues are so *automatic* that we often cannot turn them off.

COLOR CONSTANCY.   The light reflected into your eyes from a person's skin varies a lot with the type of illumination in the room (firelight, sunlight, moonlight, fluorescent light), yet the color of the skin does not seem to change. This is called **color constancy,** another perceptual process that gives stability to our perceptions.

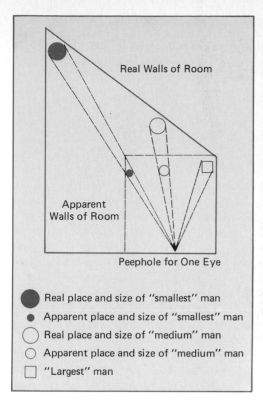

Real Walls of Room

Apparent
Walls of Room

Peephole for One Eye

● Real place and size of "smallest" man

● Apparent place and size of "smallest" man

○ Real place and size of "medium" man

○ Apparent place and size of "medium" man

□ "Largest" man

FIGURE 4–11
The Ames room is really a very distorted room, as shown in the diagram on the left. The distortion causes a visual illusion that pits size constancy against shape constancy. Your expectancy of the shape of normal rooms causes you to see these three men as varying in size.

Learning and expectation have a lot to do with color constancy. If you are shown an orange or a banana under hidden colored lights that distort its natural color, you still tend to perceive the orange as orange or the banana as yellow. If you are shown colored pieces of paper under the same conditions, even if you are told what colors they are "supposed" to be, your perceptions will probably be more highly influenced by the colored lights.

DEPTH PERCEPTION

How do we make inferences about a three-dimensional world on the basis of the two-dimensional patterns of light projected onto each retina? We use **depth (distance) cues: monocular cues** that are available from the retina of a single eye and the **binocular cues** that depend on combining information from both eyes.

Monocular Cues for Depth

Cover one of your eyes with your hand and look about you with the other eye. You still have a clear sense of seeing things at different distances, although not quite so vivid, perhaps. Now hold one finger out in front of the uncovered eye. Notice that when you focus on the finger, the background is out of focus and blurred, and when you focus on the background, the reverse is true. Thus focusing, or **accommodation,** produces a strong monocular depth cue: differences in the sharpness of objects at different distances. Although an artist could paint what you saw given a particular accommodation, the blurred and

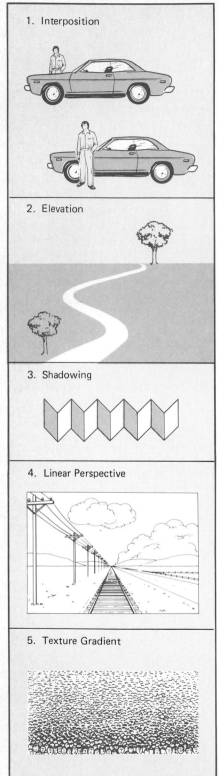

1. Interposition

2. Elevation

3. Shadowing

4. Linear Perspective

5. Texture Gradient

unblurred parts of the painting wouldn't change as you refocused your eye. This is probably why artists seldom use this as a major cue for depth. Monocular cues that *are* often used to represent depth in paintings are *interposition,* **elevation,** *shadowing,* **linear perspective,** and *texture gradient* (see Figure 4–12).

Binocular Cues for Depth

Since your eyes are separated by a few centimeters, the view from one is almost never exactly the same as the view from the other. The left eye sees more of the left side of an object, and the right eye sees more of the right side (see Figure 4–13). These two monocular views are automatically combined into a single subjective view, sometimes called the *cyclopean view* after the mythical one-eyed Cyclops. The difference between these two views is called **binocular disparity,** and it plays a major role in the perception of depth or distance.

If a contour is projected onto the same part of the retina in each eye, there is no difference in the representation of that contour in each monocular view, and the contour is perceived as flat. Such a contour will be seen clearly and vividly in the combined cyclopean view, a process termed **binocular fusion.** However, if a given contour is projected onto *different* parts of the two retinas, there will be a difference or disparity in its representation in each monocular view. If the disparity is small, the contour may still be fused. But if the disparity is large, the contour will not appear clear and vivid in the cyclopean view. It may appear as a double image or fade and fluctuate at times.

If there is a well-defined contour in one monocular view and a homogeneous region (no details or contours) in the corresponding part of the other monocular view, the contour will tend to dominate and be seen in the cyclopean view. However, suppose there are inconsistent contours in corresponding regions of the two monocular views (different contours are projected onto a particular part of the retina in each eye). You will alternately see one or the other, but usually not both, in the cyclopean view. This fluctuation usually occurs every second or so and is referred to as **binocular rivalry,** since the inconsistent contours in the two monocular views seem to compete for inclusion in the cyclopean view.

Why aren't we more aware of binocular disparity and rivalry? The principal reason is that when you attend to some detail, you rotate your eyes to minimize binocular disparity for that detail, thereby producing fusion. You do this by aiming your eyes so that the detail of current interest is projected onto each fovea. If this detail is some distance away, the two eyes may be pointing virtually straight ahead. However, when you attend to something closer, it's

FIGURE 4–12
1. *Interposition: If one object seems to be covering another, it will be perceived as being closer.*
2. *Elevation: The higher the object in the horizontal plane, the farther away it seems to be.*
3. *Shadowing: Shadows or shading tend to give an impression of depth.* 4. *Linear perspective: Parallel lines seem to converge at a point in the distance, which is what gives the illusion of depth to this drawing.* 5. *Texture gradient: As distance increases, the texture of objects becomes finer. This variance in texture is a strong clue to depth. (See the Highlight on Gibsonian invariants and the Dutch engraver M. C. Escher's Three Worlds, reproduced later in this chapter.)*

necessary to turn each eye slightly inward to point directly at the same detail. This inward rotation is called **convergence.** The nearer the detail is to you, the greater the convergence required to produce fusion. You can illustrate this for yourself by looking at your finger at arm's length and then slowly bringing it close to your nose. You can feel the inward rotation (convergence) of your eyes that is required to see it as it moves closer. Since different amounts of convergence are required to fuse details at different distances, fusion of details at one distance usually produces binocular disparity for details at other distances. (Look at your finger up close and notice the double images behind it.) As you successively attend to details at different distances, you shift convergence, successively producing fusion and disparity for things at each distance. The brain automatically interprets the shifts in convergence, fusion, and disparity as cues indicating relative distance. This whole process, termed binocular perception or **stereopsis,** is a major part of our sense of a third dimension (depth) in vision.

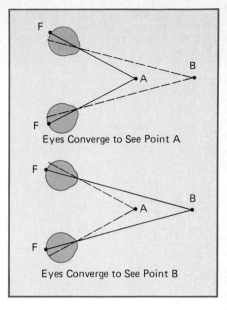

FIGURE 4–13

TOP. *If you rotate your eyes inward toward your nose (converge them) so as to see point A, the image of point A will fall on the fovea (F) of each retina, while the image of point B will fall on quite different parts of each retina.* BOTTOM: *If you converge your eyes to see the more distant point B, the opposite is true. Thus, the differences in convergence required to see objects at different distances is a convergence cue for depth.*

PERCEPTION OF PICTURES

Most of the characteristics of perception that we have discussed can be demonstrated in terms of how we look at pictures (paintings, drawings, or photographs). As with all perception, we draw as much from our earlier experiences (what we expect to see) as we do from the actual signals our eyes send to our brain. This process of interpretation is so automatic that we are usually unaware of what is happening. In this section we shall slow down the process to show exactly what happens when you look at a picture.

Eye Movements

When you look at a photograph or a painting you may think that you take in the whole image at once, but actually you build up a perception of the whole picture based on a series of separate looks. These are produced by successively moving your eye (such movement is called a **saccade**) and briefly (for about 150 msec) holding it still (this is called a **fixation**). Almost the whole image of the picture is cast onto some part of the retina during each fixation. As we discussed in Chapter 3, the ability to see detail lies in the fovea—acuity falls off very rapidly on the periphery of the eye. Thus, you move your eyes over the picture so that the fovea can pick up the details. This process of making a number of fixations is like making a picture from a series of snapshots, each of which shows most of the image but with only a small part in sharp focus.

The fixations are not random. They seem to concentrate on parts of the picture that are particularly informative and only rarely on highly redundant parts that can easily be inferred from the rest of the image. For example, in Figure 4–14 most of a subject's fixations were on details of the face; parts of the head and the neck, which could easily be guessed from the rest of the image, were sampled infrequently. This is an example of the sort of dynamic information-seeking interaction between the person and the environment that was emphasized by Gibson (1966), as we discussed earlier.

The fact that it takes time to see a picture, even though you feel you took it all in a single look, is clearly shown in the way you "see" impossible

HIGHLIGHT□
Experience and Perception: Size Constancy

The photograph below shows the kind of densely foliated tropical rain forest inhabited by the pygmies of the Congo. Anthropologist Colin Turnbull has described these people and their way of life. Many pygmies never leave this world. Turnbull describes what happened when a man named Kenge took his very first trip out of the dense mountain forest into the valley.

Then he saw the buffalo, still grazing lazily several miles away,

far down below. He turned to me and said, "What insects are those?" At first I hardly understood; then I realized that in the forest the range of vision is so limited that there is no great need to make an automatic allowance for distance when judging size. Out here in the plains, however, Kenge was looking for the first time over apparently unending miles of unfamiliar grasslands, with not a tree worth the name to give him any basis for comparison.

When I told Kenge that the insects were buffalo, he roared with laughter and told me not to tell such stupid lies. Kenge still did not believe, but he strained his eyes to see more clearly and asked what kind of buffalo were so small. I told him they were sometimes nearly twice the size of a forest buffalo, and he shrugged his shoulders and said we would not be standing out there in the open if they were. I tried telling him they were possibly as far away as from Epulu to the village of Kopu, beyond Eboyo. He began scraping the mud off his arms and legs, no longer interested in such fantasies. . . .

The road led on down to within about half a mile of where the herd was grazing, and as we got closer the "insects" must have seemed to get bigger and bigger. Kenge, who was now sitting on the outside, kept his face glued to the window, which nothing would make him lower. I even had to raise mine to keep him happy. I was never able to discover just what he thought was happening—whether he thought that the insects were changing into buffalo, or that they were miniature buffalo growing rapidly as we approached. His only comment was that they were not real buffalo, and he was not going to get out of the car again until we left the park. (Turnbull, 1962, pp. 252–253)

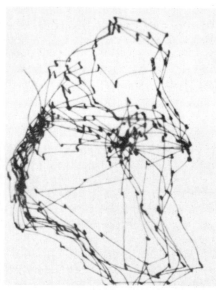

FIGURE 4–14
The network of lines on the right is a pattern of eye movements made by someone looking at a photograph of a piece of sculpture (Egyptian Queen Nefertiti) on the left. The pattern was recorded by bouncing a beam of light off a tiny mirror attached to the eye as the person looked at the photograph for 2 minutes. (Yarbus, 1967)

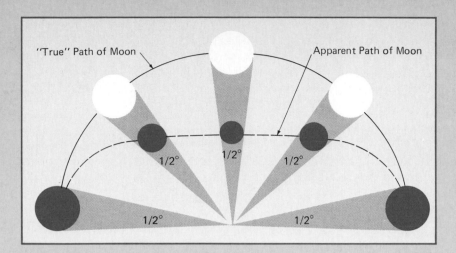

"True" Path of Moon

Apparent Path of Moon

1/2° 1/2° 1/2°

1/2° 1/2°

The moon always subtends (has) the same visual angle ($\frac{1}{2}$ degree) in your field of view. But if you "see" it as being further away at the horizon (broken line) the principle of size constancy implies that it is larger near the horizon.

How limited Kenge's perceptions seem to us! He was apparently so used to viewing objects at very close range in the dense underbrush of the tropical rain forest that he couldn't maintain size constancy when viewing objects at the un-familiar distances he encountered in the valley. But are our perceptions any less limited?

Almost everyone has seen a full moon close to the horizon and marveled at how much larger it seemed than when viewed directly overhead. In fact, there isn't real difference in the size of the moon—it always subtends a visual angle of about one-half degree. Rather, this *moon illusion* seems to be a failure of size constancy. We seem to judge its size as if it were closer to us when seen overhead than when near the hori-

zon (as shown in the photograph and in the figure). One explanation for this (Gregory, 1973) is that the outlines of objects near the horizon are powerful depth cues indicating that the moon is even farther away than the horizon. These depth cues are missing when the moon is overhead, so it seems closer (and therefore smaller, since its visual angle is the same). This interpretation is consistent with the fact that viewing the moon through a rolled-up magazine or other tube eliminates these depth cues, and the moon illusion.

The size illusions experienced in the Ames room shown earlier in Figure 4–10 also show how experience affects our perception. Even after you are told the true shape of the room, the illusion tends to persist. However, if you are allowed to move about in the room, to explore its shape actively, to reach into one corner after another with a long stick, the illusion gradually disappears. No doubt Kenge's lack of size constancy would also slowly disappear as he gained more experience outside the rain forest. Who knows, perhaps even the moon illusion will gradually disappear as humans become more experienced with extra-terrestrial space.

figures, such as the one in Figure 4–15. The various parts of such figures seem to make sense until you try to put them together. Note how reasonable each part of the picture appears at first. Each separate fixation by your eyes takes in a seemingly logical detail of the figure; it is only when you put them all together, or try to, that you realize there are impossible contradictions in the separate parts.

Three Dimensions from Two

When you think about it, it is amazing that a pattern of light and dark pigments on a flat two-dimensional surface can evoke the perception of a three-dimensional world. Indeed, this was a challenge that had puzzled painters for centuries. It is only fairly recently that artists have been completely successful in creating this illusion. To create the illusion, painters use a number of the depth cues mentioned earlier in the chapter.

M. C. Escher, a Dutch engraver, wanted to portray different levels of psychological space that could be evoked by two-dimensional images. In Figure 4–16 you first perceive the representation of a three-dimensional world containing

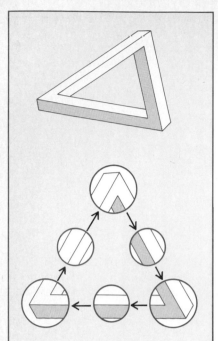

FIGURE 4–15
If you made the series of fixations on the triangle that is indicated here, each of your
high-acuity foveal views (as shown in the circles below) would be entirely acceptable alone,
but it would be impossible to put them together to form an acceptable perception of the
whole object. (After Lindsay & Norman,
1972, p. 25.)

some objects on a table top: a bottle, a drawing pad, and a book on which some lizards appear to be crawling. Follow the lizards as they climb a geo-metrically shaped object and down over a cup onto the drawing tablet. They appear to merge into the drawing page, becoming flat figures drawn onto it. As you scan the drawing, one of the flat lizards suddenly becomes three-dimensional, and another climbs up onto the book. The lizards exist in three distinct levels of psychological space. First, you're obviously aware that Figure 4–16 is a flat figure in your own book. In it you see another three-dimensional world containing the table top on which are located the drawing pad, the book, and the lizards. Finally, there is still another world represented by the drawings in the pad. By having the lizards move in and out of the normally isolated worlds, Escher provokes the viewer into an appreciation of their separate psychological existence.

Illusions Induced
by Two-Dimensional Depth Cues

The mind's ability to use these two-dimensional cues for three-dimensional space is so automatic and deeply ingrained that it can produce strong illu-sionary effects. For example, suppose you were asked to judge the length of each man in Figure 4–17 as a ruler would measure them. Naturally, you should ignore the converging lines, since they are irrelevant to your judg-ment. However, such lines normally serve as strong linear-perspective cues for depth. Even though you try to ignore them, it is almost impossible not to "see" the man on the right as longer than the other two. In fact, all three men measure exactly 26 mm. Thus they all project exactly the same size image onto

FIGURE 4–16
M. C. Escher, Reptiles.

M. C. Escher, *Rippled Surface*. Of this print, the artist wrote: "Two raindrops fall into a pond and, with the concentric, expanding ripples that they cause, disturb the still reflexion of a tree with the moon behind it. The rings shown in perspective afford the only means whereby the receding surface of the water is indicated."

your retina (subtend the same visual angle). However, when you perceive the representation as a three-dimensional space (a perception strongly suggested by the linear perspective), the figure on the right will be seen as farthest away. Thus, according to the "automatic" rules of size constancy, the figure on the right must be much larger than those on the left, since it projects the same-size retinal image.

Two other illusions that have been explained in a similar fashion (Gregory, 1973) are shown here. The *Ponzo illusion* (Figure 4–18) seems to involve linear perspective cues much like those in Figure 4–17. The *Müller-Lyer illusion* (Figure 4–19) may also be interpreted as involving linear perspective cues—in one case those seen in the corner of a room, and in the other those seen on the outside corner of a building. In each case, these two-dimensional cues may automatically evoke an unconscious perception of a three-dimensional space. The illusionary appearance of differing lengths would then be consistent with the rules of size constancy.

MOVEMENT PERCEPTION

The images cast onto your retina constantly shift and change as you shift the direction of your gaze or move about, and yet your brain is remarkably good at maintaining **location constancy:** A room doesn't seem to move just because you move or look about. There is an invariance or constancy in your perception of where things are, even though their representation on your retina changes considerably. Your mind constantly takes into account changes in the direction of your gaze and the position of your body. Only when these two factors seem insufficient to account for changes in the location of objects in your visual field do you perceive them as moving.

M. C. Escher, *Three Worlds*. Notice the texture gradient of the leaves. The "three worlds" of the title are, according to Escher, "the autumn leaves which show the receding surface of the water, the reflexion of three trees in the background and, in the foreground, the fish seen through the clear water."

FIGURE 4–17
The converging straight lines in this figure give a strong sensation of depth, an example of the use of linear perspective. This in turn produces the illusion that the figure on the right is longer than the one on the left.

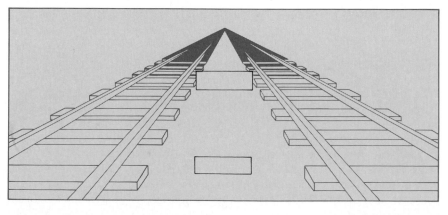

FIGURE 4–18
The kind of linear perspective shown here in real life in a photograph is what creates the Ponzo illusion in the drawing beneath it. Thus the cues given by this linear perspective make it seem that one band is longer than the other, whereas both are exactly the same size.

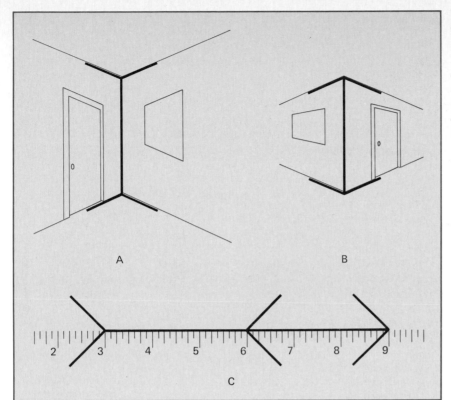

FIGURE 4–19
The Müller-Lyer illusion is shown in two different ways here. In both cases the line between the arrows is exactly the same length, although in each case one seems visibly longer than the other. Notice that in c, even though the figures appear against a ruler, quite clearly showing that the two lines are the same length, the illusion persists.

Absolute and Relative Retinal Movement

It is useful to distinguish between the absolute and relative position of objects within your visual field (on your retina). For example, as you read this line of text, a word's absolute position within your visual field changes each time you move your eyes. However, the relative position of (separation between) words doesn't change, since the words all shift across the field (retina) together. You don't perceive the words as moving simply because their absolute position within your visual field changes. You automatically interpret these changes as due to eye movements. Since your brain initiates the efferent commands that move your eyes, it can compare that movement with the absolute movement of objects across your retina. Only if the two differ do you perceive movement. You can demonstrate this for yourself: Close one eye and slightly move the other one by pressing it from the side with your finger. Since your brain didn't send out any efferent command to move your eye, the absolute movement of the image across your retina is perceived as movement of the scene "out there," almost as if you were seeing movements of a huge photograph that filled your whole visual field.

Another situation in which a misperception of absolute movement occurs is when you watch a small, *stationary* point of light in an otherwise totally dark room. After a while you tend to see the light as slowly moving about even though it really remains stationary. This is the so-called **autokinetic effect.** It can be shown that the primary cause of this illusion is your inability to keep

Many modern ideas about human perception have come from efforts to program computers to recognize patterns. One of the most important of these ideas is the concept of image structure (how the parts of an image are related). The accompanying figure shows how an image can be "parsed" or analyzed into a hierarchy of forms. This procedure, called **syntactic scene analysis**, reveals the structure of an image (a scene) in the same way that parsing a sentence reveals its grammatical structure (**syntax**). It is possible to program a computer to use knowledge of image structure, taking advantage of the structural redundancy in most images (the predictable relationships among an image's parts).

For example, computers have been taught to sort mail by searching a television image for the recipient's zip code. The computer program may first attempt to identify higher-order forms such as "stamp," "return address," and "recipient's address." It could then analyze the "recipient's address" to identify lower-order forms such as the recipient's "name," "street address," "city and state," and "zip code." Each phase of this "top-down" process could be guided by predictable relations among the various forms—that is, by structural redundancy. For example, "recipient's address" is usually found in the center of the envelope and contains the desired "zip code" below or next to "city and state."

It has been proposed that human perceptual processes use knowledge of such structural redundancy in much the same way. Early theories (Selfridge, 1959) emphasized a "bottom-up" perceptual sequence: Lower-order (smaller) features such as lines, points, and intersections are perceived first and then synthesized into higher-order (larger) forms. For example, recognition of an eye would be a strong cue for perception of a head. This view was encouraged by the work on receptive fields, as we discussed in Chapter 3: Simple **feature detectors** in the retina seem to feed into progressively more complex receptive fields as one progresses to higher visual centers.

Other theories have emphasized a "top-down" sequence of perception in which higher-order (larger) forms are recognized first, then analyzed into lower-order (smaller) forms (Navon, 1977; Broadbent, 1977). Thus recognition of a head is a strong cue for perception of two small circular components as eyes. This top-down sequence seems to occur when you look at the impossible figure shown in Figure 4–15. Only after a while do you realize that the lower-order components (each separate angle) are inconsistent with the higher-order form (a triangle) you first see.

There are also theories that propose the occurrence of both sequences of processing. In one such theory, **analysis-by-synthesis** (Neisser, 1967), analysis of some lower-order form is aided by a tentative synthesis of a higher-order form.

track of exactly where your eyes are pointing. You believe your eyes are stationary, but they really have shifted position slightly. This produces absolute movement of the light across your retina, which is erroneously interpreted as movement of the light rather than of your eyes. Why isn't your lack of perfect control over the position of your eyes a problem in other situations—for instance, in a well-lighted room? Probably because interpreting absolute movement of the image on your retina as movements of the room is so implausible (in the absence of sounds and other sensations suggesting something like an earthquake) that you automatically attribute the image motion to small eye movements (Kinchla & Allan, 1969).

There is still another situation in which you may misperceive (misinterpret) absolute retinal movement. Sitting next to the window on a train, you may perceive another adjacent train slowly begin to move. Then suddenly your realize that it is really your own train beginning to move. You erroneously attributed the absolute movement of the adjacent train's image across your retina to that train's movement rather than your own. Ordinarily you don't make mistakes like this, since other cues clearly indicate your own body motion (kinesthetic, tactile, auditory). However, when a train begins to move very slowly and smoothly, these cues may not be available.

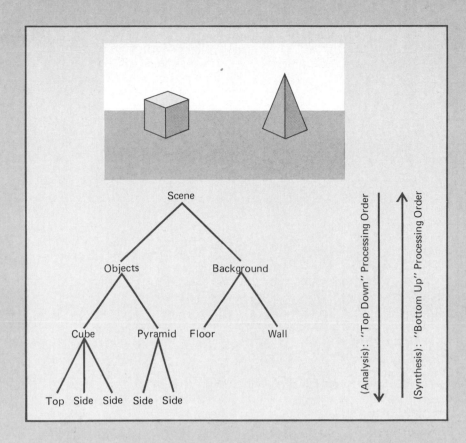

(Analysis): "Top Down" Processing Order

(Synthesis): "Bottom Up" Processing Order

but are capable of learning it as well (Raphael, 1976). Winston (1975) developed a program that can make the computer learn such abstract structural concepts as the class of forms called "arches" or "tables." It learns by being shown numerous examples of these classes, much as a child learns the alphabet in school. It then abstracts a general structural description to use in classifying new forms.

It seems clear that this sort of work should influence theories of human perceptual development and learning, as well as more general theories of human cognition.

Recently, even more sophisticated programs for computer pattern recognition have been developed that not only utilize structural knowledge

Fortunately, you rarely if ever have to rely solely on absolute retinal motion. Objects are ordinarily seen to move in well-illuminated visual fields against complex backgrounds. Thus the relative motion of object and background within your visual field is a strong cue for motion. The advantage of such cues is evident if you have ever tried to discern the movement of a small cloud high overhead in an otherwise clear blue sky. If the cloud is moving slowly, its movement may be hard to see. However, if you can view the cloud in reference to some stationary point, such as the edge of a roof, its motion may be easily discerned. In addition to changes in the separation between cloud and roof (relative movement), the cloud may actually slowly pass behind the edge of the roof. This progressive covering up of one object by another is another strong cue for motion that arises whenever objects move against clearly visible backgrounds. Relative motion or **motion parallax** is a cue for both depth and motion perception (see Figure 4–20).

People often misperceive relative retinal movement when a small spot of light is projected onto a large screen. If the screen is suddenly moved slightly, people often perceive the spot as moving. This is called *induced motion.* In most environments we have little difficulty discerning stationary reference points when interpreting relative retinal movement.

FIGURE 4–20
Notice how your successive views of the man, house, and tree would change as you drove past them in a car. The tree would seem to move from left to right behind the house, while the person would move from right to left in front of the house. This sort of relative movement or motion parallax is a strong cue for both motion and depth perception.

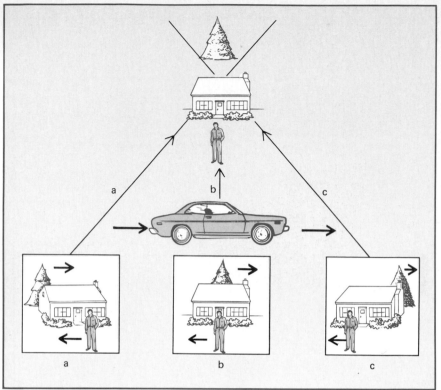

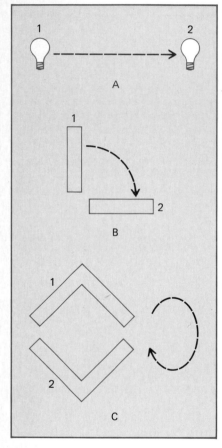

FIGURE 4–21
If after just the right delay (50 to 100 msec) form 1 is replaced by form 2 in A, B, or C, stroboscopic motion will be perceived, as indicated by the dotted line. In A this will be a smooth horizontal motion of the point from left to right. In B it will be a smooth "tipping" of the bar from vertical to horizontal. In C the angular form will appear to flip over. These effects suggest that there is a cognitive or interpretive aspect to stroboscopic motion: You perceive the most "reasonable" pattern of movement.

Stroboscopic Motion

An important aspect of visual motion perception is that a succession of still (static) images can produce the perception of smooth continuous motion. Called the **phi illusion** or **stroboscopic motion** (Figure 4–21), this is what makes a string of successively illuminated lights on a theater marquee appear to move. It also causes us to perceive smooth motion when watching a movie, though we are looking at a series of still photographs flashed in rapid succession on a screen.

The succession of images must be sufficiently fast to produce the phi illusion. You probably have seen early films in which the movement is jerky. This is because only 16 pictures a second were taken in these early movies. Modern films show up to 24 separate pictures a second to produce the illusion of smooth motion. Television presents up to 30 separate images a second.

READING

Reading is clearly one of our most important, efficient, and highly practiced information-processing skills. Just as with most forms of perception, you are unconscious of the many components of this skill because the process has become so automatic. In this section we will examine these complex components. We begin with an earlier view of the reading process, which grew out of early research on eye movements during reading and is still advanced by many companies selling speed-reading courses. We shall then raise some

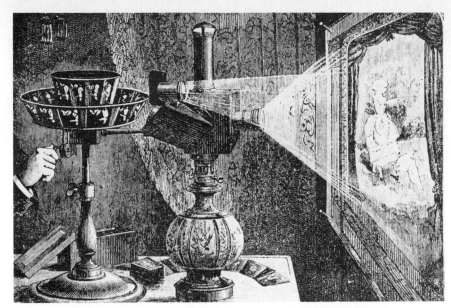

An early device for producing motion pictures (stroboscopic motion). A succession of static but slightly altered images are cast on the screen and seen as continuous movement.

questions about it and finally present an alternative view and the modern research that supports it.

Early Ideas about Reading

One of the first people to study eye movements was G. T. Buswell (1922). He recorded these movements by bouncing a light from a tiny mirror on the edge of a subject's contact lens onto a photographic film. He found that the eye successively makes a quick (1 or 2 msec) move (a saccade), then briefly (150 to 200 msec) holds still (a fixation). Figure 4–22 shows the patterns of eye movements during silent reading of both slow and fast readers. Slow readers make many fixations per line of text and often go back over parts of the line they have already passed. Such right-to-left shifts in fixation are called *recursions*.

In contrast, fast readers usually make only three or four fixations per line in an orderly left-to-right sequence without going back over the line. This suggested to early investigators that fast readers have learned to move their eyes in a more efficient manner, taking in more information during each fixation than poor or slow readers. They also discovered that when fast silent readers read out loud, their pattern of eye movements becomes more similar to those of slow silent readers; that is, there are many more fixations per line and more recursions. Maybe, investigators thought, slow readers simply haven't learned to read silently and are still trying to voice each word as they read. In fact, many slow silent readers could be seen to move their lips as they read, just as beginning readers often do. If this were the problem, then slow readers might be helped by teaching them not to vocalize during silent reading and to move their eyes in the more efficient pattern adopted by fast readers, taking in more information during each fixation.

But how much information does a good reader take in during a single fixation? To answer this question, early investigators used a device called a **tachistoscope,** which flashes printing onto a screen for precise periods of

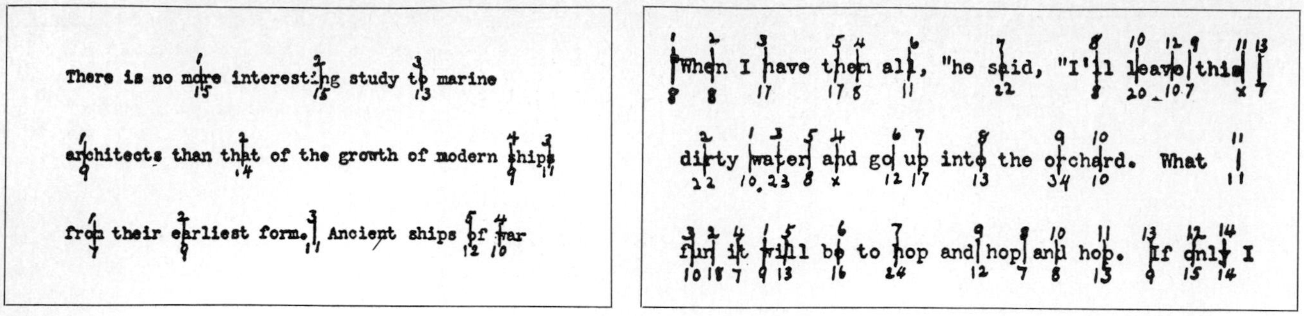

There is no more interesting study to marine
architects than that of the growth of modern ships
from their earliest form. Ancient ships of far

When I have them all, "he said, "I'll leave this
dirty water and go up into the orchard. What
fun it will be to hop and hop and hop. If only I

FIGURE 4–22

Eye movements by a fast reader (left) and a slow or beginning reader (right) during silent reading. The center of each fixation is shown by a vertical slash, the number above which shows the order in which the fixations occurred (the number below it shows the duration of fixations in quarters of a second). The slow reader takes many more fixations per line and often moves back over the line. The fast reader makes only four or five fixations per line and few recursions.
(Buswell, 1922)

time. For example, a test subject could be asked to fixate on a particular part of the screen and then a sentence could be projected onto the screen for perhaps 100 msec. This was sufficiently fast to ensure that the subject held only a single fixation while the sentence was on the screen. The experimenters were amazed to find that with practice subjects seemed able to read almost a whole sentence during a single presentation. Perhaps, then, subjects could be trained to read whole lines of text with a single 100-msec fixation. Since the rapid eye movement between fixations only takes 2 or 3 msec, subjects might be trained to read up to 10 lines a second. This is the basic strategy behind many speed-reading courses. Students are encouraged to break old reading habits and absorb a whole line of text in a single fixation. This is done first by tachistoscopic presentation and then by training students to fix their gaze briefly on the center of each line of text during regular reading. To make this easier, students are often told to slowly run the tip of their finger down the center of each page, fixating briefly on each line as the tip of the finger passes that line. In addition, they are encouraged to pick out key words and main ideas. To assess the effectiveness of such training, students are given comprehension tests to determine how well they understood the material they read. In fact, prospective customers of speed-reading courses are often asked to read something at their normal reading speed and then given a comprehension test. For example, they might read eight pages in 10 minutes and correctly answer 80 percent of the questions on the comprehension test. They are then given an initial speed-reading lesson. After it they are asked to "speed-read" the same number of pages in a comparable text. They may read eight pages in 5 minutes and then correctly answer 75 percent of the questions on a subsequent comprehension test. This usually convinces prospective students they have "doubled their reading speed" (8 pages in 5 minutes instead of 10 minutes) with "virtually no loss of comprehension" (75 percent correct instead of 80 percent).

Some Questions

This approach to speed reading seems based on rather convincing evidence. However, let's examine this evidence in light of modern reading research (Carver, 1972; Carpenter & Just, 1977; Smith, 1970). Can we really read a whole line of text during a single 100-msec fixation? There are really two parts to this question: *When* do we actually read the material? *How much* of it do we really read?

It would seem that we read it during the 100 msec it appears on the screen. However, it can easily be demonstrated that this is not so (e.g., Sperling, 1960). If a second line of text is presented immediately after the first and in the same

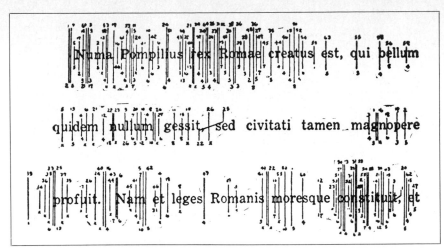

FIGURE 4–23
This figure shows a fast English reader learning to read Latin. As you can see, a normally fast reader reverts to a beginner's pattern of eye movements when learning to read another language. This indicates that eye movements reflect familiarity with the material being read rather than simply good (or bad) reading habits. (Buswell, 1922)

position on the screen, this second line will normally prevent us from reading the first line by obscuring or *masking* it. Therefore we don't fully read the first line during the 100 msec it is on the screen; we complete our reading after it disappears. If the second line of text is presented up to 1 second after the first, it may interfere with our reading of the first line. It's almost as if a picture of the first line persists briefly in our visual system after the 100-msec presentation, and it is this picture that we actually read. The idea that we can read a new line of text every 100 msec seems untenable in light of these poststimulus masking effects.

The second question about speed reading is how much we actually read in a single look. What do we mean by this? Suppose you were reading a story about farmers. Consider the following sentence, in which some letters have been replaced by a capital letter X:

XXX XARMER PLOWED THE FIXXX.

Could you guess the missing parts of the sentence from the parts you can see? Most people would quickly guess that the complete sentence is: The farmer plowed the field. How about the following sentence?

XXX XRACTOR WAS IN THE BXXX.

Again, given the context, you would quickly read it as: The tractor was in the barn. Because language is *redundant,* you can infer a great deal about the missing parts of the sentence from the parts you can see. Your ability to make inferences of this sort depends on your knowledge of the structure of language. The more you know, the less you need of a sentence to guess the rest. This suggests that the number of fixations a reader makes along a line depends on how easy it is to infer one part of the sentence from another part; that is, the degree of redundancy in the sentence. The more redundancy, the fewer fixations. In fact, even fast readers make many more fixations per line when the material is less redundant (see Figure 4–23).

The high degree of redundancy in most written material also makes it difficult to design accurate measures of comprehension. For example, a comprehension test to assess your understanding of the story about farmers might contain the following question:

The farmer wore _____ when he worked.
(a) a suit   (c) a dress
(b) overalls   (d) shorts

While the correct answer might have been stated explicitly in the story, you could make an educated guess based on other knowledge you had gained from the story (or from just the word "farmer" in the question). It is very difficult to devise comprehension questions whose answers could *not* be deduced from only partial knowledge of the material. Simply by guessing on all of the questions of a multiple-choice test with four alternatives for each question, you should get about 25 percent correct. If you had any knowledge at all of the material, you could do appreciably better. Notice that the poorer the speed-reading comprehension test, the easier it would be to impress prospective customers. Since such courses are a lucrative business, we would expect the salespeople to encourage prospective students.

To read 8 pages in 5 minutes instead of 10 minutes with a drop in comprehension of only 5 percent (from 80 percent to 75 percent) seems impressive. However, suppose someone who hadn't even read the material took the comprehension test and got 70 percent of the answers correct. That would change the interpretation of the earlier evidence completely. In fact, many of the comprehension tests used in speed-reading courses are not well designed, and people who haven't even read the material could do as well as 70 percent correct answers.

An Alternate View

Thus it would seem that good readers are fast because they need only sample parts of each line to draw accurate inferences about the whole line. This is what allows them to read with only a few fixations per line. *They aren't good readers because of the way they move their eyes; they can move their eyes the way they do because they are good readers.*

Does this mean that speed-reading courses are a sham and don't really teach you anything? No—simply that these courses might better be described as *speed-skimming courses* (Carver, 1972). They train you to skim rapidly and remember the major features of the text, key ideas, terms, and concepts. This is a very useful skill. Many people don't realize how much they can get out of many books and articles merely by skimming them. This level of reading is adequate and even desirable for much material, and slower, more careful reading would be a waste of time. Many people do not vary their speed of reading to fit material and the goals they have in mind, and for them a course that shows how to skim material rapidly could be very helpful.

SUMMARY

1. One sensation can be a cue for the experience of other sensations; because sensory data are *redundant,* we can make inferences from limited sensory input.

2. *Selectivity* or *attention* is the name given to the process that allows us to attend to certain sensory stimuli at a particular time while screening out other stimuli.

3. According to Gestalt principles of organization, we tend to organize visual stimuli into groups on the basis of *proximity, similarity, symmetry, closure,* and *continuity.*

4. Another Gestalt organization principle is figure-ground organization, the tendency to perceive things (figures) standing out against a background (ground).

5. *Bistable* or *reversible figures* are stimulus patterns that have two alternative organizations. *Ambiguous figures* are those open to multiple organizations.

6. Although sensory activity may vary enormously from moment to moment, we perceive many aspects of the world as stable and invariant, because of *perceptual constancy,* which includes *size constancy, shape constancy,* and *color constancy.*

7. Monocular cues for depth perception include *accommodation, interposition, elevation, shadowing, relative size,* and *texture gradients.*

8. The left eye and the right eye see slightly different versions of the same object, because each sees it from a slightly different angle. These differences are called *binocular disparity. Convergence* of the eyes may reduce this disparity enough to cause *fusion,* a single *cyclopian* view.

9. *Binocular perception* or *stereopsis* is the process by which the brain automatically interprets the shifts in convergence, fusion, and disparity as cues indicating relative distance.

10. *Syntactic scene analysis* yields a hierarchical representation of *image structure,* which, like parsing a sentence, reveals the relationships among its parts.

11. Perception of pictures involves eye movements (*saccades*) and *fixations;* the eyes move over the picture so that the fovea can pick up the details. These eye movements are concentrated on the most informative parts of the picture.

12. The *autokinetic effect* and *induced motion* are two examples of misperception of retinal movement. In the *phi illusion,* a succession of static images produces the perception of continuous motion.

13. Fast readers need few fixations because they can use the redundancy in language; they are not fast readers because they make fewer eye movements than slow readers.

Suggested Readings

CROWDER, R. G. *The psychology of reading.* New York: Oxford University Press, 1982. An introduction to a wide range of reading research.

GIBSON, J. J. *The senses considered as perceptual systems.* Boston: Houghton Mifflin, 1966. Gibson's influential and controversial refutation of traditional perception research.

GREGORY, R. L. *The intelligent eye.* New York: McGraw-Hill, 1970. A lively introduction to some fascinating aspects of visual perception, including a number of stereographic illustrations.

GREGORY, R. L. *Eye and brain: The psychology of seeing.* New York: McGraw-Hill, 1973. A beautifully illustrated and highly readable introduction to visual perception.

HABER, R. N., & HERSHENSON, M. *The psychology of visual perception* (2nd ed). New York: Holt, Rinehart and Winston, 1980. An advanced text covering a wide range of experimental work on visual perception.

HOCHBERG, J. *Perception* (2nd ed.). Englewood Cliffs, N.J.: Prentice-Hall, 1978. A detailed discussion of past and current theories of perception; includes a chapter on social perception and communication.

LACHMAN, R., MISTLER-LACHMAN, J., & BUTTERFIELD, E. C. *Cognitive psychology and information processing: An introduction.* Hillsdale, N.J.: Erlbaum, 1979. An advanced and comprehensive review of the modern information-processing approach to human perception.

LINDSAY, P. H., & NORMAN, D. A. *Human information processing* (2nd ed.). New York: Academic Press, 1977. Discusses perception from the point of view of computer science and biology.

SCHIFF, W. *Perception: An applied approach.* Boston: Houghton Mifflin, 1980. A Gibsonian approach to perception, emphasizing the function (utility) of natural human perception.

5. Altered States of Awareness

A t the beginning of the twentieth century, the distinguished American psychologist William James had this to say about the variety of conscious states:

Our normal waking consciousness . . . is but one special type of consciousness, whilst all about it, parted from it by the filmiest of screens, there lie potential forms of consciousness entirely different. We may go through life without suspecting their existence; but apply the requisite stimulus, and at a touch they are all there in all their completeness, definite types of mentality which probably somewhere have their field of application and adaptation. No account of the universe in its totality can be final which leaves these other forms of consciousness quite disregarded. How to regard them is the question—for they are so discontinuous with ordinary consciousness. Yet they may determine attitudes though they cannot furnish formulas, and open a region though they fail to give a map. At any rate, they forbid a premature closing of our accounts with reality. (James, 1890)

What is a "normal" state of consciousness? What is an "altered state"? How many are there? Even today, there is considerable debate concerning the answers to these questions. In this chapter we shall consider four of the more generally accepted types of altered states: sleep (and dreaming), hypnotic states, meditation, and drug-induced states.

SLEEP AND DREAMING

People spend one-third of their lives asleep. For most of us that means about 25 years will be spent in an unconscious state. Why do we sleep? One theory (Cohen, 1979) is that our sleep-wake cycle had survival value during our evolution as a species: Primitive humans were simply more likely to survive if they stayed quiet at night, hidden from predators, conserving their energy to be used in the daily hunt. Although emotional problems, drugs (e.g., caffeine, alcohol), or simply erratic sleeping habits may disrupt normal sleep patterns, most people suffer only occasional **insomnia,** the inability to sleep. Normally, the longer one is deprived of sleep, the harder it is to stay awake. Surprisingly, however, researchers have found that if sleep-deprived individuals are properly motivated, they perform both physical and cognitive tasks as well as ever (e.g., Webb, 1975).

Though people probably have been fascinated by the topic of sleep since they first thought about it, only in the last 30 years has scientific investigation begun its rapid development. Most of this work is conducted in "sleep laboratories," where volunteers agree to spend the night (or nights) hooked up to various electronic recording devices: the **EEG (electroencephalogram),** which records the patterns of brain waves; the EOG (electrooculogram), which measures eye movements; and EMG (electromyogram), which measures muscle tension or electrical activity in the muscles.

The actual moment of sleep onset is not best measured by any of these methods, but by optical reaction to light. In a typical study, subjects participating in the experiment have their eyelids taped open, and a bright light is repeatedly flashed into their eyes. They are instructed to press a button whenever they see the light, and at some point the pressing stops; that is the point at which sleep begins. (What is really amazing in this demonstration is that sleep has the power to overcome what seem to be overwhelming odds. Could you fall asleep with someone flashing a light in your taped-open eyes?)

Stages of Sleep

There are four stages of sleep that we go through in fairly repetitive cycles throughout the night. These four stages can be identified by different EEG patterns. These brain waves become increasingly irregular as sleep becomes deeper and as the person moves from Stage 1 to Stage 4 (see Figure 5–1). The brain waves of relaxed wakefulness (**alpha waves**) are quite regular. When

FIGURE 5–1
(Top) This person is participating in an experiment in a sleep laboratory. The wires attached to her head produce an EEG pattern similar to the one shown below. (Bottom) The EEG here shows brain wave patterns of the four stages of NREM sleep and Stage 1 REM sleep. Note the appearance of spikes in Stages 2–4 as sleep becomes deeper and the brain wave pattern becomes more irregular. (Luce & Segal, 1966)

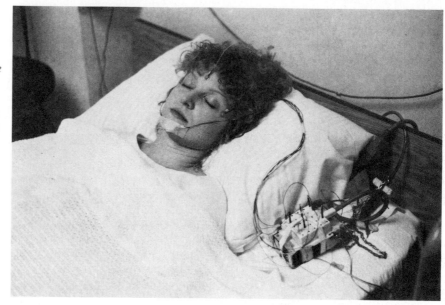

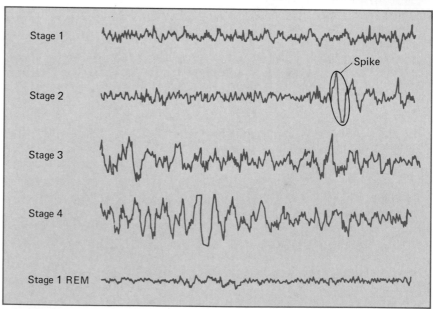

sleep begins and the person enters Stage 1, the brain-wave pattern remains regular, but the amplitude or height of the waves decreases. A few minutes later, sleep becomes deeper, and the sleeper enters Stage 2, in which the EEG pattern starts to become irregular, and the other brain wave types, called *spikes,* appear. Several minutes later, the sleeper experiences Stage 3, with still greater EEG irregularity. After about 10 minutes the deepest period of sleep is reached, Stage 4, which is characterized by many spikes. Sleepers in Stage 4 are difficult to waken; in children, this is the stage in which sleep walking, night terrors, and bed-wetting may occur (Dement, 1974).

This progression from Stage 1 to Stage 4 and back again to Stage 1 can take anywhere from 40 to 80 minutes. At this point, as a second sleep cycle begins and as the EEG pattern returns to Stage 1, something new is added: the presence of **rapid eye movements,** or **REMs.** The existence of this different type of sleep was discovered in 1953 by Aserinsky and Kleitman. It is called **REM sleep** because of the rapid eye movements that distinguish it from the four stages of non-REM or **NREM sleep.**

REM *Sleep*

Almost 25 percent of our sleep each night ($1\frac{1}{2}$ to 2 hours) is REM sleep. The REM periods occur with considerable regularity, about every 90 minutes, with different stages of NREM sleep occurring in the intervals between (see Figure 5–2). As the night goes on, Stages 3 and 4 of NREM tend to occur less frequently; the sleeper alternates mainly between longer REM periods and Stage 2. Near the end of the sleep cycle there are also short periods of wakefulness.

During REM sleep, the muscles become relaxed to the point of paralysis, as measured by an electromyogram (EMG). REM sleep is sometimes referred to as "paradoxical sleep," because the brain-wave pattern is similar to that of a waking person, but the person is deep in sleep with no tension in the muscles and no response to outside stimuli.

The amount of normal sleep and the percent of it that is REM sleep change throughout our lives. Figure 5–3 shows this. A 1-week-old baby sleeps about 16 hours a day, with 50 percent of that being REM sleep. By age 5, the amount of REM sleep is about the same as in adulthood, 20 percent, but the total sleep time continues to decline throughout life.

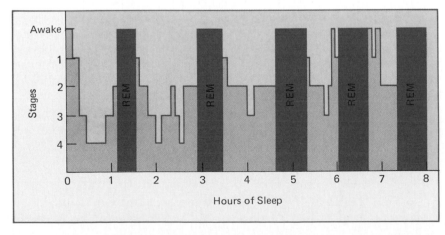

Hours of Sleep

FIGURE 5–2
The chart shows the typical progression through the night of NREM Stages 1–4 and Stage 1 REM sleep. Stages 1–4 are indicated on the x axis, and REM stages are represented by darker bars on the graph. As noted in the text, the REM periods occur about every 90 minutes throughout the night. (Dement, 1974)

FIGURE 5–3

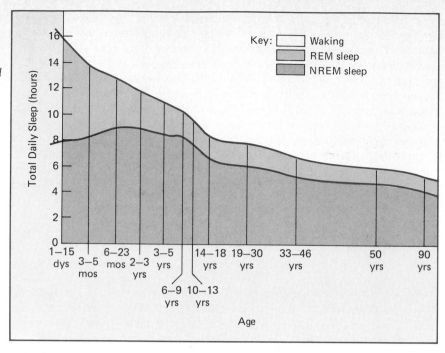

The average amount of sleep and the percent of it that is REM sleep changes throughout our lives. For example, in the first few weeks of life babies sleep about 16 hours a day, and half of that is REM sleep. By middle age, adults sleep a bit less than 7 hours a night, with about 25 percent of it being REM sleep. (Roffwarg et al., 1966)

Soon after the discovery of two different types of sleep, it was proposed by Dement and Kleitman (1957) that rapid eye movements indicate that the sleeper is dreaming, whereas dreaming does not take place during NREM sleep. To prove this they tried waking subjects each time the EOG indicated a pattern of rapid eye movements; about 85 percent of the subjects were able to recall a dream when they were awakened during a REM period. However, not all REM sleep is associated with dreams—and some dreams occur during NREM periods.

There have been several explanations of what rapid eye movements mean. One theory was that rapid eye movements are actually attempts by the sleeper to visually follow the course of the dream, much like watching a movie; now, however, it seems more likely that rapid eye movements are simply indications of the intense brain activity occurring during these periods of sleep. What is not known is what function REM sleep serves in humans. It is clear, however, that it is very important. If people are deprived of REM sleep, by being awakened as soon as they enter the REM period, they become irritated and uncomfortable. Sleepers will tend to compensate for REM deprivation in one night by increasing the number of REM periods on the next night or nights (a phenomenon called "REM rebound"). A similar effect does not occur with NREM sleep. In one experiment, a volunteer was awakened four successive nights each time he entered a REM period. On the fifth night, his sleep pattern showed 30 REM periods, over four times what the normal amount would be (Dement, 1974).

Why We Dream

To Sigmund Freud (1900/1953), dreams were the "royal road to the unconscious." During sleep, the conscious mind is, for the most part, not active. As a result, many of those disturbing ideas, feelings, and recollections that we try to avoid thinking about when we are awake spill over when we are asleep, because the conscious mind is not an effective monitor during sleep. Nevertheless, even during sleep we defend against threatening thoughts by disguising them, often in fantastic images. These images make up our **dreams,** and an interpretation of dreams can provide insight into the hidden, repressed corners of the mind. (Freud's theories are discussed in greater detail in Chapter 14.)

Some sleep and dream researchers are not receptive to Freud's view. McCarley, for example, suggests that dreams do not indicate "a process of disguise or concealment, but a process of activation" (1978, p. 72). He feels that this might explain why so many dream reports mention strenuous activity such as running, climbing, and so on.

There is also a theory proposing that the dream is a way of processing hidden memories of daytime experiences (Palumbo, 1978). So many events, big and small, impinge on us daily that if we were to stop and consider each one we would become confused and overwhelmed. Nevertheless, much of this information is important to our adequate functioning and should be examined. As these waking events come crowding in on us, they are held, many unevaluated, in a limited memory system. These experiences remain in the system until we fall asleep, when they are released. Our dreams process, evaluate, and organize our experiences for whatever use we may later find for them. According to this theory, we need to dream in order to sort out the events and solve some of the problems that might have arisen during the day.

Consistent with this idea is the finding that dreams show a pattern of alternating buildups of emotional tension followed by a release of tension; the number of buildup-release cycles appears to depend on the amount of tension present during the waking period (Cartwright, 1978).

Dream Content

Whatever the function of the dream, its content can be dazzling. Yet as vivid and strange as the content may be, it still contains glimpses of the commonplace. The setting might be your home or somewhere near it, and the characters might be friends, relatives, and your pet dog, even though in the dream the dog might be dancing to the latest disco tune. The point is that we draw on familiar material to stock the content of our dreams. But what about other events? Suppose there is a quite audible sound, though not loud enough to awaken the sleeper; will that sound be fed into the dream? Certainly, this sometimes happens. For example, most people have had the experience of integrating the sound of the alarm clock into an ongoing dream. Some sleep-laboratory research has addressed this issue.

In one experiment, various stimuli were presented to 4-year-old children during REM sleep. The stimuli might be a few drops of water, a puff of air, or the like. The children were then awakened and asked to describe their dreams. One girl reported, after the air puff was administered, that she dreamed of sailing in a boat with the wind blowing in her face. The drops of water resulted in a dream about being sprayed with a hose; and when a ball of cotton was rubbed lightly on her skin, she dreamed of her sister playing with a cuddly toy lion (Foulkes, Larson, Swanson, & Rardin, 1969). In a similar demonstration, 5 to 10 minutes after the onset of REM sleep adults were presented with the first name of a person. Though the names were not always integrated into a dream, there was a substantial number of cases where it had influence. "Robert" resulted in a dream about a rabbit, for example.

In a more recent experiment, which attempted to assess the role of visual factors in dream content, individuals wore red goggles on several days during their entire waking activity. The goggles, obviously, gave their whole visual environment a reddish hue. On the nights following the days in which the red goggles were worn, these subjects experienced four times as many dreams with a tint near the red end of the color spectrum (red, orange, or yellow) as they did when they did not wear the goggles (Hoffman, 1978). While many people claim that they dream in color, and others that they dream in black and white, it is almost impossible to confirm their statements. For example, when someone describes the grass in a dream as green, it may simply be an instance of reconstructed memory, in which people add details that they feel should be there.

Remembering Dreams

One of the most striking observations about dreams is that they are usually quite difficult to remember after only a short period of wakefulness. Results from the sleep laboratory indicate that about 80 to 85 percent of dreams from REM sleep, and fewer from NREM sleep, are recalled. But this high proportion occurs only if the individual reports the dream immediately upon awakening and only if he or she is awakened while in the midst of the dream or directly after it has ended. With delays, the memory for dreams deteriorates rapidly (Goodenough, 1978). This also helps explain why, when dreams are recalled, it is usually the last dream of the night that is remembered best. Of course, as Cartwright (1978) points out, the last dream of the night is also the longest, strangest, and most exciting—other factors that probably have strong effects on memory.

HYPNOSIS

Hypnosis is another condition in which people seem to lose consciousness. Contrary to popular belief, though, there are only superficial similarities between hypnosis and sleep. In fact, sleep and hypnosis differ in several basic ways—for instance, a hypnotized person does not show the same brain-wave pattern as a sleeping person—the pattern in hypnosis is similar to that of a waking person. There are some similarities, however; in the hypnotic-trance state, people are thinking, perceiving, and often acting out their perceptions—but, as in sleep, they appear to be unaware of the world around them.

What Is Hypnosis?

The term **hypnosis** comes from the Greek word *hypnos,* which means sleep. It can be defined as "that state or condition in which subjects are able to respond to appropriate suggestions with distortions of perception and memory" (Orne, 1977, p. 19). The psychological characteristics of someone under hypnosis include an increase in suggestibility, the limiting of attention

This is a painting of an early class in hypnosis given by Charcot, a French doctor who was a teacher of Sigmund Freud and a clinician in his own right. It was due to Charcot that the French Academy of Sciences accepted hypnotism as a legitimate form of treatment.

to a very small stimulus field, and the acceptance of illusionary perceptions and irrational arguments.

Early researchers believed that subjects in a hypnotic trance would be able to perform tasks that they would normally find impossible, and that the deeper the trance, the more profound the differences in performance would be. Actually, the hypnotic trance itself is not so dramatic as many people believe. Swinging pendants and whirling disks are not necessary to induce a trance; all that is required is a responsive person and some simple suggestions from the hypnotist—your arm is getting heavy, your eyes are closing, you are finding it difficult to move your hands, and so on. One performing hypnotist has commented on the simplicity of including the trance state: "Hypnotism is easy once you get the knack of it. The knack comes to most people easily; I hypnotized my first subject on the first trial" (Wolff, no date, p. 3).

A common but false belief about hypnosis is that hypnotized people will do things that they wouldn't ordinarily do—jumping out of windows, shooting themselves in the foot, or whatever. (Orne, 1977). A hypnotized person is neither unperceptive nor out of control, even though the nature of the control might change somewhat. Some voluntary acts, such as brushing one's hair when a certain word is heard, might become less voluntary, but the person is still in contact with reality and is still able to make judgments. If people under hypnosis are told to look at a blank wall and it is suggested that there is a picture of a ship there, they will be able to see and describe the picture. But they will know that the picture they are "seeing" is not real, that it is a hallucination. It might float around or it might be possible to see through it as if it were an apparition. Similarly, people are unlikely to dive out of a 20-story window under the mistaken impression that they are taking a dip in the back-yard swimming pool. They know that the window is not a ground-level diving board.

FIGURE 5-4

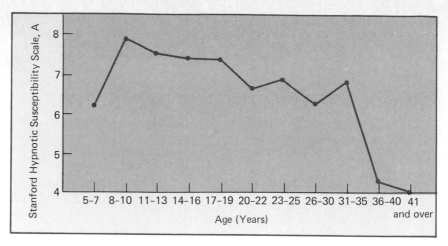

Hypnotic Responsiveness

About 15 percent of the population can be greatly affected by hypnotic suggestion, while 5 to 10 percent show no effect at all (they seem unable to be hypnotized); the rest of the population falls somewhere between these extremes. These individual differences in responsiveness are the subject of much research.

The great variation in the degree to which people respond to hypnosis is one of the most important discoveries in this field. In general, hypnotic susceptibility rises in childhood to a maximum in the preteenage years, then declines slowly thereafter (see Figure 5–4). But the variation in scores in this cycle is quite low; susceptibility to hypnosis is essentially stable over time. An individual who is highly responsive to hypnosis today will be highly responsive 10 years from now, and a person who has low hypnotic responsivity is not likely to develop high responsivity in the future. This suggests a genetic component; for example, identical twins are more likely to have the same level of hypnotic responsiveness than fraternal twins (Hilgard, 1975).

High responsivity to hypnosis is not a general personality trait, however—the person who is responsive to hypnosis is not likely to be more suggestible than other people in nonhypnotic situations, and easily hypnotized people are not more compliant than others in a nonhypnotic condition (Orne, 1977).

In recent research, Evans (1977) has found that people who are highly susceptible to hypnosis are more likely to be able to voluntarily control sleep. That is, they can fall asleep easily and in different locations, take daytime naps, and so on. These individuals may have a general ability to control their level of consciousness. People who are highly susceptible to hypnosis also learn meditation techniques rapidly.

Individual differences in hypnotic responsiveness have received more research attention than the trance state itself. In reviewing the research findings, Hilgard (1975) has concluded that the responsiveness is due more to the subject's characteristics than to the hypnotically induced state. In fact, some investigators feel that equal, or even stronger, effects can be produced by having subjects simulate the hypnotic condition rather than by actually inducing a trance.

What does it mean to simulate or make believe one is hypnotized? Barber and Wilson (1977) asked subjects "to feel as if you're looking at a TV program." They asked them to let their thinking and imagination move with the suggestion by recalling a TV program they liked and letting themselves "see" it again in their mind's eye. "I'd like you to respond in the way in which you'll benefit most . . . and that is to focus your thinking and to imagine to the best of your ability. Just let your thinking and your creative imagination go along with the instructions so you can fully experience the many interesting things your mind can do" (pp. 36–37). No attempt is made to induce a hypnotic trance; in fact, the instructions emphasize just the opposite.

During the use of this procedure, the subjects were asked to feel as if their finger was anesthetized, time was slowing down, or they were attending elementary school as a child. A comparison of people who were simulating hypnosis with other people in a trance state showed that the simulators were more responsive to suggestion; their fingers felt more anesthetized or they were more able to recreate the age-regressed state of a child. In other words, the trance state might not be necessary. The subjects might simply be trying to do what they think is expected of them—that is, playing a role (Sarbin & Coe, 1972). But just because simulation can mimic real hypnosis doesn't mean that there is no such thing as hypnosis (Orne, 1977). We don't prove that some effect is a fake or a nonphenomenon simply by showing that it can be produced in another way.

In one case, subjects were given a posthypnotic suggestion to run their hand through their hair whenever they heard the word *experiment*. Both simulators and hypnotized subjects complied with the suggestion when they were in the psychological laboratory. But outside the laboratory, in their normal everyday world, the simulators no longer responded. Subjects who had actually been hypnotized, however, continued to run their hands through their hair when they heard the word. It was as if the simulators dropped the role they were playing when they thought it was no longer relevant. The hypnotized subjects, on the other hand, went on responding to the special effect of posthypnotic suggestion. Orne, who with his colleagues conducted this demonstration (Orne, Sheenan, & Evans, 1968), later added: "regardless of how we describe hypnosis, it is real in the sense that the subject believes in his experience and is not merely acting as if he did" (Orne, 1977). This is not to say that simulators don't play their role quite well, some even reporting visual or auditory hallucinations. But when later questioned about their experiences and cautioned to answer honestly, many denied that the hallucinations were ever experienced, while others described events that were hardly as moving as those they had earlier reported (Bowers, 1967).

Pain Reduction through Hypnosis

The best example of a practical application of hypnosis is its use in reducing chronic pain. It has proven to be a remarkably effective **anesthetic;** indeed, the widespread use of hypnosis as a medical anesthetic in surgery in the nineteenth century was halted only by the introduction of ether and chloroform as more acceptable anesthetics.

In the typical laboratory investigations of pain reduction, two types of pain have been studied most extensively. In research into *ischemic pain,* a blood pressure cuff or tourniquet is attached to the person's arm and tightened; this is followed by exercising the hand and fingers. There is almost no pain at first, then very severe pain starts, becoming almost intolerable by 10 to 20 minutes

Hypnosis: Its Checkered Past

The history of hypnosis is a check-ered past filled with intrigue, dra-matic personalities, and a murky stew of garbled thinking occasionally clarified by a legitimate scientific in-sight. It was this kind of past that threw hyponosis into disrepute and delayed the development of our current knowledge.

The story starts with Friedrich An-ton Mesmer (1734–1815) of Vienna, who believed that magnets could influence the functioning of the hu-man body. He applied this notion in his medical practice to relieve pa-tients of long-term paralyses and other symptoms. Through a mixture of medical prowess, sheer egotism, and a flair for drama, Mesmer acci-dentally stumbled onto a process for inducing hypnosis. Mesmer be-lieved quite sincerely that he pos-sessed an above-normal amount of "magnetic fluid" and that this influence could be channelled to-

Mesmer (left) and his patients seated around a tub filled with iron fragments.

from the time the tourniquet is applied. Ischemic pain caused in this way resembles the pain that follows surgery (Hilgard, 1971). In research into *cold-pressor –pain,* the person's hand and arm are placed in ice water. The pain is severe and increases very rapidly; 30–45 seconds are as much as most people can tolerate.

Under hypnosis it is suggested to subjects that they will feel no pain from either of these two procedures. With the cold-pressor test, 67 percent of subjects who are highly responsive to hypnosis show substantial pain reduc-tion through hypnosis. Only 17 and 13 percent of subjects who have medium or low responsiveness, respectively, experience significant pain reduction through hypnosis (Hilgard, 1975). There is some positive effect through hyp-nosis for all subjects, however, regardless of the individual level of re-sponsiveness. Tests with ischemic pain have yielded comparable results. In the cases of ischemic pain, moreover, when the pain disappears the corre-sponding blood-pressure rise is also eliminated (Hilgard, 1975).

Of course, other agents can be administered for the relief of pain, such as aspirin or morphine. How does hypnosis compare to these drugs? Stern and his colleagues compared the effects of hypnosis, acupuncture, morphine, diazepam (the main ingredient in the tranquilizer Valium), aspirin, and a placebo (Stern, Brown, Ulett, & Sletten, 1977). In both the cold-pressor and ischemic tests, the greatest reduction of pain occurred in the hypnotic condi-

ward his patients. Seating his patients—up to 30 of them at a time—around a tub filled with iron fragments, "Mesmer, wearing a coat of lilac silk, walked up and down carrying a long iron wand, with which he touched the bodies of the patients, and especially those parts that were diseased. Often laying aside the wand, he magnetized them with his eyes, fixing his gaze on theirs" (Binet & Frere, 1901, in Sarbin, 1962, pp. 753–754).

According to our present knowledge of mental disorders, Mesmer's patients were probably suffering from hysterical conversion reactions—that is, their disorders had a predominantly psychological cause. Thus, the power of suggestion was very strong; indeed, the patients' belief that he could cure them was an important element in his success. The trappings of the chamber that housed the tub, and the flamboyant manner and dress of a man who probably looked like a medieval wizard, all helped to enhance the strong effects of suggestion.

Mesmer's results were undeniably impressive, and it took only a short time before word of them reached the established scientific community. In 1784, a royal commission was convened in Paris, the city where Mesmer conducted most of his healing sessions. The American ambassador, Benjamin Franklin, presided. The investigators found no evidence of actual magnetic powers and therefore supposed the cause to be a secret of Mesmer's, for how could he possibly produce these effects without knowing how he did it?

The French government is said to have offered him 20,000 francs to disclose the secret and Mesmer to have refused—refused, of course, to tell what he never knew, for he had no secret to disclose. As a result he gradually fell into disrepute, and finally, denounced as an imposter, he withdrew to Switzerland, where he died in 1815.

The confusion and reputation that surrounded hypnosis were the result then, of the way it was first de-scribed and the questionable behavior of Mesmer and other early practitioners. When later investigators dealt with hypnosis more soberly, the real advances in the field began. Braid, in the mid-nineteenth century, proposed two basic ideas about hypnosis that proved to be correct. One was that concentration on a particular idea could be so intense that memories would not carry over from the hypnotic to the normal state. The other was that suggestion was basic to hypnosis (Sarbin, 1962).

Later Charcot, a teacher of Sigmund Freud and an expert clinician in his own right, saw the relationship between hypnosis and instances of paralysis and amnesia (conversion reactions) brought on by psychological stresses. Thus, the study of hypnosis was well along on its march to respectability and, largely because of Charcot's work, the French Academy of Sciences finally accepted the phenomenon as legitimate.

tion; morphine was second, and acupuncture was a close third. Diazepam, aspirin, and the placebo were ineffective in reducing the type of pain produced in these experiments. Once again, the superiority of hypnosis in pain reduction was more prominent among those individuals who were highly responsive to hypnosis.

Hypnosis is also helpful in treating the *fear* of pain, with its resulting hypersensitivity. If we think something is going to hurt, it often hurts all the more; anxiety is often our worst enemy. Some situations such as major surgery are actually less painful than most people suppose, because there are not many pain receptors below the level of the skin. Anesthesia is often administered not so much to prevent pain (except in the first incision of the knife) as to reduce anxiety and tenseness and prevent shock (Barber, Spanos, & Chaves, 1974). Psychological factors are an important element in the perception of pain, and we have all witnessed at one time or another how powerful and unpleasant they can be.

In one case, a man with an intense neurotic fear of dental pain consulted a psychotherapist for help. Hypnotic suggestions that his mouth would be anesthetized and that he would feel no pain seemed to do no good, so the therapist tried a different approach. Placing the patient in a hypnotic trance, the therapist suggested that it would be the patient's left hand that would be "excruciatingly hypersensitive." In fact, no mention was made of mouth pain at all. The patient was assured that the dentist would be extremely careful not to touch his left hand. It worked: The overwhelming fear of dental pain was shifted to the hand, and the dentist was able to complete "extensive dental work . . . *without* any direct suggestions of anesthesis or use of chemical agents" (Beahrs, 1971, pp. 83–84).

Why is it that hypnosis works so well in reducing pain? A theory to account for the effects has been proposed by Ernest Hilgard, one of the most active researchers in the field. The theory has two components. The first simply involves waking suggestion—we just try to tell ourselves that the pain will be reduced, or we try not to think about it, depending on a "diversion of attention, relaxation, and reduced anxiety" (Hilgard, 1977). This path is open to anyone, whether of high, medium, or low responsiveness to hypnosis, and it can be used by people who are not hypnotically responsive at all. At most, however, this waking suggestion will reduce the perception of pain by about 20 percent. The second component accounts for the remaining 80 percent reduction, and it seems to be available only to those individuals who have high hypnotic responsivity. Hilgard describes it as an "amnesic-like" process in which hypnosis prevents the perception of pain from entering the person's awareness (Hilgard, 1977).

Posthypnotic Effects

In **posthypnotic suggestion,** a person is given a suggestion during hypnosis that is to be acted on only when the person is no longer hypnotized. For example, one might be told that an ear will itch whenever the hypnotist says "dog." The idea is that the effects of the suggestion will carry over from the hypnotic to the normal state. Since this is often an undesired outcome, most hypnotists make it a point to prevent it by telling the subjects that they will not remember suggestions made in the trance state when they come out of it. After all, the stage hypnotist does not want the subject to leave the theater still hallucinating that there is a hippopotamus standing next to him, nor would the psychotherapist in the case mentioned earlier want the patient to leave the dentist's office continuing to believe that his left hand is hypersensitive. It is believed that the signal to cancel the prior suggestion does prevent this from happening, and, when it doesn't, there is usually some simple explanation, as in the following example:

> Evans likewise suggested amnesia to the number 6 to a group of subjects. He intended this amnesia to last for the duration of the session, but one subject misunderstood the instruction to mean that the amnesia for the number 6 was to last until a later scheduled session. The subject was a high school mathematics teacher, who proceeded to experience great teaching difficulty in the classroom during the interim. (Perry, 1977, p. 264)

Suppose the hypnotist forgets to cancel the suggestion or the subject misinterprets the instruction—will the subject continue to respond to it for days, years, a lifetime? Actually, there seems to be little or no risk that these dire outcomes will occur. In most cases, unless a specific posthypnotic suggestion is given, the trance effects simply disappear by themselves. It is as if subjects give themselves a signal to cancel the suggestion. In some cases, subjects actually instruct themselves to remove the suggestion.

MEDITATION

Meditation seems to be a way in which people can limit reception of multiple stimuli by directing their attention to a single unchanging or repetitive stimulus. Meditation resembles some forms of self-hypnosis, but differs from it both in having no "goal" and in that self-suggestions are not given during the meditative state. Also, many people who are "unhypnotizable" by standard measurements are able to learn meditation easily (Morse, 1977).

Meditation is usually practiced seated, in a quiet environment. The object of the meditator's attention may be a mentally repeated sound (*mantra*), the breath, or any other appropriate focal point. When attention wanders, the meditator is directed to bring it back to the attentional object in an easy, unforced manner.

This basically simple procedure has been used in numerous societies throughout recorded history to alter consciousness in a way that has generally been perceived as deeply beneficial. Traditionally, the benefits of meditation have been defined as spiritual in nature, and it is used as an integral part of many religious practices. Recently, however, modern forms of meditation, simplified and divested of mystery and religious overtones, have been used for stress management, and this use has had promising results. Such adaptations of meditation are increasingly being used along with other forms of therapy to effect desired personality changes (Carrington, 1977).

Among the new "westernized" forms of meditation, the most extensively studied to date is Transcendental Meditation (TM). Perhaps more transitional than transcendental, TM retains certain ancient features such as the *puja* (a Hindu religious ceremony) and is taught by an organization that does not permit mental-health practitioners to assume an active role in its clinical management (unless they are TM teachers). Despite its popularity with the general public, therefore, the TM method has not been widely used in clinical settings.

Of the clinically oriented techniques, Clinically Standardized Meditation (CSM) (Carrington, 1978) and the Respiratory One Method (ROM) (Benson, 1975) are the best known. Both these techniques were originated with clinical objectives in mind and are noncultic. The two methods differ from each other in several respects, CSM being more permissive in its instructions and not linking the internally repeated sound to breathing as does ROM. Each method seems to appeal to a somewhat different sort of person, and often the client is given a choice between them.

Much research suggests that meditation can reduce the amount of stress that people experience. In a recent experiment performed in England, investigators attempted to find out whether individuals who practiced meditation would react less to stressful stimulation than a group of matched control subjects. In the laboratory, subjects were exposed to loud, grating sounds, the kind that "set your teeth on edge." While the nonmeditators tended to become tense during the experiment, the meditators showed very few arousal or "alarm" reactions, most of the time remaining quietly relaxed (Daniels, 1977).

In another study, meditators and nonmeditators were shown a film depicting grizzly carpentry-shop accidents. This film has been used as a stimulus in much research on stress and never fails to generate heightened alarm reactions in those who view it. Physiological measures and the reports of the

Meditation and Stress

Can some form of meditation, practiced daily, improve health and reverse stress-related illness? Research has shown that this simple practice may indeed have an effect on certain components of stress-related illnesses (Carrington et al., 1980). Meditation has been correlated, for example, with improvement in the breathing patterns of patients with bronchial asthma (Honsberger & Wilson, 1973); decreased blood pressure in hypertensive patients (Benson, 1977; Patel, 1973, 1975); reduced premature ventricular contractions in patients with ischemic heart disease (Benson et al., 1975); reduction of abnormally elevated serum cholesterol levels (Cooper & Aygen, 1979); reduced sleep-onset insomnia (Woolfolk et al., 1976; Miskiman, 1978); amelioration of stuttering (McIntyre et al., 1974); and reduction of symptoms of psychiatric illness (Glueck & Stroebel, 1975). Those for whom meditation brings improvement of a medical condition must keep on meditating regularly to maintain their gains, however. In such cases, meditation is like a change of diet that eliminates symptoms only as long as the diet is faithfully followed.

In terms of the actual, measurable, physiological effects of meditation, evidence indicates that during meditative states the individual consumes less oxygen (10 to 20 percent lower than during wakefulness), breathes more slowly, and has a slower heart rate. The galvanic skin response (GSR) also rises and shows less spontaneous fluctuation, indicative of a calm bodily state. Moreover, brain-wave patterns of meditators indicate a preponderance of alpha waves (typical of presleep or relaxed, drowsy states).

If incessant stimulation of the sympathetic nervous system is largely responsible for the incidence of stress-related illness, then the quiescence of the nervous system during meditation may well be a step toward improved health. We will discuss stress-related illness in depth in Chapter 15.

A question as yet unanswered, however, is whether other relaxation methods, for example progressive relaxation, may not accomplish the same objectives as meditation. If so, the effects of meditation would not be unique. Some physiological response patterns seen in the meditative state do differ from those seen in the quiet state brought about by progressive relaxation (Lehrer et al., 1980). But perhaps the most salient feature of meditation is that it is the most readily learned of all relaxation techniques and, according to many people, the easiest and pleasantest to practice. Thus meditation possesses some important practical advantages for clinical application. For many people, meditation may possess a special appeal that tends to keep them practicing it more faithfully than other self-help methods (Carrington, 1977).

subjects themselves indicated that the meditators tolerated the film with less stress than the nonmeditators (Goleman & Schwartz, 1976). These and other findings suggest that meditators may actually develop some immunity to stress.

People who meditate have also been shown to handle tasks in a more efficient manner. Groups of meditators have exhibited faster reaction times on visual tasks than nonmeditators (Appelle & Oswald, 1974), have discriminated more accurately among different sounds (Pirot, 1978), and have achieved better scores on tests of manual dexterity (Rimol, 1978).

Another benefit of meditation may be its antiaddictive properties (Shafii et al., 1974, 1975). Subjects who continue meditating over an extended period of time (usually a year or more) may spontaneously cut down on their intake of drugs, cigarettes, or alcohol. Regular practice of meditation has also been associated with increased productivity (Frew, 1977), lessened irritability (Carrington et al., 1980), improvement in low-grade chronic depression (meditation does not seem useful for severe depression) (Carrington et al., 1980), and greater self-assertion (Carrington, 1977). In addition to its usefulness for handling certain problems, meditation is also frequently used for purposes of self-development, such as improving physical coordination and speed in athletics or simply increasing the general enjoyment of life.

Just why limiting attention to a repetitive stimulus in this manner should have such far-flung results is a matter for speculation. One reason may be that regularly repeated sounds or rhythmic movements are inherently soothing.

Parents the world over, for example, pick up an agitated infant and rock it with an intuitive awareness of the soothing effects that these rhythmic actions have on the child. The tranquilizing properties of rhythm may be a key to some of meditation's effects, for rhythm is a basic component of meditation. The rhythm of the mantra is obvious but, in addition, the more subtle rhythms of breathing and heartbeat may come sharply into awareness during the inner stillness of any type of meditation. Some people have likened the experience of meditating to being rocked dreamily, "as though one were in a small boat bobbing at anchor in a gentle sea." The feeling of well-being that typically results from meditation may thus be related to its rhythmical nature.

Meditating can also be viewed as an erasing or "desensitizing" procedure. When thoughts or images of the stresses of ordinary life pass through our minds in this deeply relaxed and peaceful state, they may be partially neutralized. Such a "global desensitization" process, regularly repeated, may attune our nervous systems to being less easily aroused by stress.

In addition to such technical explanations, there are the obvious practical benefits of interrupting one's life periodically to become inwardly still. At the very least, meditation can give the mind a rest—a brief vacation from stress and worry. When focusing all of our attention on a mantra or meditative object, we cannot simultaneously be paying attention to stressful events or thoughts. Perhaps meditation allows the meditator to temporarily shut down those information-processing mechanisms of the brain that are ultimately responsible for producing stress. This short vacation from stress could then revive coping abilities, giving the meditator a more balanced outlook and increased energy for dealing with whatever difficulties may be presenting themselves.

While helpful to many people, meditation is clearly not a panacea. Patricia Carrington (1977), an authority on the clinical use of meditation, has written about the difficulties that can occur if meditation is used incorrectly:

1. *An occasional person may be hypersensitive to meditation, so that he or she needs much shorter sessions than the average.* Such people cannot tolerate the usual 15-to-20 minute sessions prescribed in many modern forms of meditation and may require drastic reductions in meditation time before they can benefit from the technique. Most problems of this sort, however, can be successfully overcome by careful adjustment of meditation time to suit the individual's needs.
2. *Overmeditation can be dangerous.* On the theory that "if one pill makes me feel better, taking the whole bottle should make me feel exceptionally well!" some people may decide to meditate 3 or 4 hours (or more) per day instead of the prescribed 15 to 20 minutes once or twice a day. Just as with a tonic or medicine, meditation may cease to have beneficial effects if taken in too heavy doses, and it may be detrimental instead. The technique should always be practiced in moderation, with the meditator following instructions given in a reliable meditation-training program.
3. *Even normal amounts of meditation can produce temporary discomforts.* Mild discomforts such as muscles cramping or stiffness from holding a single position are occasionally reported by some meditators. Others may feel somewhat disoriented in the first moments after they stop meditating. Carrington calls these "tension-release side effects" and describes them as a useful part of the meditative process, serving to release tension. However, meditators experiencing such side effects without having been informed

about them may be unnecessarily discouraged. Such people need to be taught how to handle these temporary annoyances—another reason why thorough training in the management of meditation is important.

Anyone deciding to learn meditation for the first time is advised to select a well-researched meditation technique. Some forms of meditation, even though they may have been in existence for thousands of years, are not suitable for the average person. For example, one venerable form of Indian meditation requires the meditator to gaze unblinkingly into a candle flame until tears run down the cheeks. While it is claimed that this practice is beneficial for Yogi practitioners, it can produce eyestrain when practiced incorrectly. Unless one studies under the guidance of an expert instructor who is trained to impart a traditional form of meditation with great care, it is safest to use those methods which have been scientifically studied and found to be appropriate for the average person.

"DRUGS" AND SUBSTANCE USE

Technically, any substance other than food that alters our bodily or mental functioning is a **drug.** Of particular interest in this chapter are the so-called **psychoactive drugs,** drugs that seem to affect one's state of consciousness. Many people mistakenly believe the term *drug* refers only to some sort of medicine or an illegal chemical taken by drug addicts. They don't realize that familiar substances such as alcohol and tobacco are also drugs. This is why the more neutral term *substance* is now used by many physicians and psychologists. For example, the phrase "substance abuse" is often used instead of "drug abuse" to make clear that the misuse of substances such as alcohol and tobacco can be just as destructive as heroin and cocaine.

We live in a society in which the medicinal and social use of substances (drugs) is pervasive: an aspirin to quiet a headache, some wine to be sociable, coffee to get going in the morning, a cigarette for the nerves, perhaps even a tranquilizer to deal with periods of extreme stress. When do these socially acceptable and apparently constructive uses of a substance become misuse? First of all, most substances must be taken in moderation or they produce negative effects such as intoxication or intense perceptual distortions. Repeated use of a substance can also lead to physical addiction or **substance dependence.** This is marked by, first, an increased tolerance, with more and more of the substance required to produce the desired effect, and second the appearance of unpleasant withdrawal symptoms when the substance is discontinued.

Psychoactive substances are commonly grouped according to whether they are stimulants, depressants, or hallucinogens. Stimulants initially speed up or activate the central nervous system, whereas depressants slow it down ("uppers" and "downers," in street parlance). Subsequent effects of substances in these categories may be more complex, however. For example, a stimulant may activate some part of the central nervous system (CNS) that then inhibits or depresses activity in another part. Hallucinogens have their primary effect on perception, distorting and altering it in a variety of ways. These are the substances Humphrey Osmond called *psychedelic* (from the Greek word meaning "mind-manifesting") because they seemed to alter radically one's state of consciousness.

Some substances don't fit into the preceeding three categories, seeming to require a special category of their own. Two that we shall consider are marijuana (and other forms of cannabis) and PCP or "angel dust." Table 5–1 presents a summary of the substances we consider in each category. You may be surprised at the way some drugs are categorized. For example, many people think of alcohol as a stimulant, whereas it is actually a depressant, or they think of nicotine (the active ingredient in cigarettes) as a depressant, whereas it is actually a stimulant. The drugs we shall consider in most detail are those which are often abused. We do this partly because it's important to understand the dangers of such drugs (many of which are illegal), and partly because many of these drugs have been studied more extensively than those which seem less dangerous.

Stimulants

Stimulants act to energize the central nervous system. Some, like the nicotine in cigarettes or the caffeine in coffee, are so common and relatively mild in action that we hardly think of them as stimulants at all. Others, such as amphetamines and cocaine, produce a high psychological dependence and are more likely to be seriously abused.

In moderate amounts, stimulants increase alertness and reduce fatigue. In higher doses they can produce anxiety and irritability. People who take stimulants often experience a feeling of inexhaustible energy and become excited and euphoric; in physiological terms, the pupils dilate, the pulse rate and blood pressure increase, and appetite is suppressed because the blood sugar level is raised. When the initial effect of the stimulant wears off, however, the user often experiences a letdown or "crash," with depression, anxiety, and fatigue.

COCAINE.   Since prehistoric times, the natives of such South American countries as Peru and Bolivia have chewed the bark of the coca plant as a source of energy and refreshment. In 1865 **cocaine,** the active ingredient in the plant, was first extracted. This odorless, white, fluffy powder, although illegal, is now widely used by millions of people and is the most powerful known natural stimulant.

Cocaine is usually taken by sniffing it up the nose ("snorting"), after which it passes into the bloodstream through the mucous membrane. Others prefer the more powerful effects obtained either by injecting it intravenously or by smoking a concentrated form ("base") in a pipe or cigarette.

The initial effect of cocaine is a euphoric rush of pleasure and well-being as it begins to stimulate the central nervous system. Its specific action is to block the natural breakdown of the neurotransmitter norepinephrine, so that synapses involving this neurotransmitter become more active. The user feels excited, talkative, and energetic. As more cocaine is taken, lower areas of the central nervous system are affected (the thalamus, hypothalamus, and reticular formation). The heart beats faster, blood pressure goes up, breathing becomes faster and deeper, and the person feels even more aroused and alert. More cocaine can lead to a state of *cocaine intoxication,* with confusion, anxiety, distorted speech, paranoia, and even hallucinations. If no more cocaine is taken, these effects subside, to be followed by a letdown that may include headache, dizziness or even fainting, and extreme fatigue leading to heavy and prolonged sleep. Usually the person awakes within 24 hours with

Table 5–1: Classification of Substances (Drugs) Discussed in This Chapter.

I. Stimulants
    Nicotine
    Caffeine
    Cocaine
    Amphetamines
        Amphetamine (Benzedrine)
        Dextroamphetamine
          (Dexedrine)
        Methamphetamine
          (Methadrine)

II. Depressants
    Alcohol
    Opioids (Narcotics)
        Opium
        Morphine
        Heroin
        Codeine
        Methadone
    Sedative-Hypnotics
        Barbiturates
        Benzodiazepines (minor
          tranquilizers)
          Diazepam (Valium)
          Chlordiazepoxide (Librium)

III. Hallucinogens
    Lysergic acid diethylamide
      (LSD)
    Mescaline (peyote)
    DOM (STP)
    Dimethyltryptine (DMT)

IV. Marijuana and Other Forms of
    Cannabis

V. Phencylidine (PCP or "Angel
    Dust")

A *cocaine user inhaling (snorting) the white powdery substance.*

few or no residual effects, unless the dose of cocaine was excessive (or unless it was mixed with some other drug, such as alcohol or heroin; then the sleep may lead to coma and even death). Cocaine also affects temperature-regulating mechanisms in the brain and the ability to perspire. This is why overdosage sometimes leads to death from high temperature.

Extended use of cocaine produces increased tolerance and, according to some, physical dependence with unpleasant withdrawal symptoms. Although there is some disagreement as to whether physical addiction actually occurs, there is little doubt that heavy users of cocaine find withdrawal a very unpleasant process.

The extreme expensiveness of cocaine is probably a major factor in limiting its abuse. Most people simply can't afford to use enough of it. On the other hand the very expense adds to its glamour and snob appeal, so that it is often referred to as the drug for rich people.

AMPHETAMINES.   These stimulants are manufactured in the laboratory. Some common **amphetamines** are *amphetamine,* trade-named Benzedrine; *dextroamphetamine,* trade-named Dexedrine; and *methamphetamine,* trade-named Methedrine. Most amphetamines are taken as pills or capsules, although some heavy users inject the drug directly for a faster and more powerful effect. Although amphetamines have much the same effect as cocaine, they cause it by increasing the release of the neurotransmitter norepinephrine (rather than slowing its breakdown, as cocaine does). In low dosages, this causes an increase in alertness and energy and a reduction in appetite. For this reason, amphetamines until quite recently were widely used for weight reduction. As the dangers of amphetamine use have become better understood, however, this practice has been largely abandoned. People who take amphetamines soon develop a tolerance, requiring more and more to produce the same effect. Furthermore, when they stop taking amphetamines, they suffer depression and fatigue similar to that experienced by people who stop using cocaine. Also, just as with cocaine, excessive use of amphetamine produces intoxication with paranoia, confusion, and hallucination. Chronic abusers ("speed freaks") may come to need 200 times or more the initial dosage because of increased tolerance. They also "crash" into deep depression and fatigue when they try to stop. Overdosage can lead to death through respiratory failure or uncontrolled variation in body temperature.

Depressants

Depressants reduce or "depress" the activity of the central nervous system (although their initial effects sometimes seem stimulating, because they reduce some inhibitory processes). While there are numerous depressants, here we shall consider only three of the most important types: alcohol; opiates and similar substances; and sedative-hypnotics.

ALCOHOL.   Archaeological evidence suggests that humans began drinking one form of **alcohol** or another before 6000 B.C. In moderation, drinking seems to make most people feel relaxed, sociable, and easy-going. When used to excess, however, it leads to dullness of sensation, degraded sensory-motor performance, impaired thought processes, sleep, and eventually even coma and death. Indeed, alcoholism is the 3rd-leading cause of death in the United States.

All alcoholic beverages contain the ingredient *ethyl alcohol;* but they don't all pack the same "punch." Hard liquors, for example, have much higher concentrations of alcohol than beer and wine. When an alcoholic drink is consumed, it enters the stomach, where about 20 percent of the alcohol passes through the stomach lining and is absorbed directly into the blood-stream (food in the stomach tends to slow this process). Later, the remaining alcohol is absorbed into the bloodstream as it passes through the small intestine.

The bloodstream carries the alcohol to the central nervous system, where it has its psychoactive effect. Although many people think that alcohol is a stimulant, it really acts to slow down the central nervous system; it is a *CNS depressant.* The first CNS centers to be affected seem to be those controlling judgment and inhibition. Thus, the drinker often becomes less inhibited, more talkative, and more outgoing. Reduced social inhibitions may lead to relaxation and a sense of well-being (although some people react by becoming morose or even aggressive). Notice that while a person may appear more stimulated and active, this is really the result of a reduction in inhibition (i.e., a disinhibition) produced by *depressing* certain regions of the central nervous system.

The extent of alcohol's effect on the body and behavior is primarily dependent on the proportion, or percentage, of it in the bloodstream. For example, 2 ounces of alcohol in the bloodstream of a large person will have less effect than 2 ounces in a small person. The percentage of blood alcohol depends not only on body size and how much is drunk, but also on how rapidly the person drinks. Alcohol is not chemically broken down by digestion. About 90 percent of it is converted into carbon dioxide and water by your liver, while the remaining 10 percent is eliminated directly through breathing, perspiring, or urinating. The liver can only deal with about $\frac{1}{3}$ to $\frac{1}{2}$ ounce of alcohol per hour (the equivalent of about 2 ounces of hard liquor, 6 ounces of wine, or 12 ounces of beer). If alcohol is consumed more rapidly than this, the concentration in the bloodstream builds up (and the liver is overburdened and abused). As the percentage of alcohol increases, its negative effects as a CNS depressant become more apparent: Coordination is lost; the perception of sensations such as temperature and pain is dulled; speech is slurred; thought processes are impaired; and vision becomes hazy. Larger doses lead to general sedation, sleep, coma, and eventually death (see Table 5–2). The exact relation between blood alcohol level and these behavioral changes depends on many factors, including age, familiarity with drinking, physical health, and length of time since previous drinking. The legal definition of "drunk" varies from state to state. In Utah, you are legally drunk if more than 0.08 percent of your blood volume is alcohol, while some states allow up to 0.15 percent before classifying you as drunk.

Alcohol's effect on emotional behavior is inconsistent, varying from one person to another. Some become friendly or silly; others become sad or uncommunicative. Apparently, these large individual differences involve a complex interaction of such factors as the basic personality of the drinker, the social setting, the reason for drinking, and so on. For example, it has been noted that alcohol tends to remove inhibitions. But one individual might be more inhibited than another before drinking, and therefore the behavioral effect of drinking will vary. Also, one person may normally inhibit aggression, exposing it only when drinking, while another who normally inhibits positive social activities becomes more gregarious and friendly when drinking.

Table 5–2: "Tale of D's"—The Relationship between Percentage of Blood Alcohol and Behavior.

At	One Is
.3%	dull and dignified
.5%	dashing and debonair
1%	perhaps dangerous and devilish
20%	likely dizzy and disturbing
25%	disgusting and disheveled
30%	delirious, disoriented, and surely drunk
35%	dead drunk
60%	probably dead

Adapted from Ray (1972, p. 45)

Most people who use alcohol keep their drinking within reasonable limits, usually having only one or two drinks in social settings, with very occasional overindulgence leading to intoxication. Others, however, fall into a pattern of alcohol abuse; they regularly drink to excess and feel they "need" alcohol in order to handle certain situations. Their drinking may begin to interfere with their social and occupational activities. They have frequent arguments because of their drinking, and they begin to be absent from work and may even lose their jobs. Extended alcohol abuse usually leads to actual alcohol dependence, in which unpleasant withdrawal symptoms occur when no alcohol is taken: Within hours, people dependent on alcohol may begin to shake, experience extreme fatigue, and become nauseous and vomit. Their hearts beat faster, and their blood pressure increases. They feel anxious and depressed and are easily irritated. In extreme cases, they may experience what is formally called *alcohol withdrawal delirium,* also known as *delirium tremors* or the *DTs.* They become mentally confused and suffer frightening visual hallucinations, such as being attacked by small animals or insects. All these withdrawal symptoms disappear within a week if the person does not drink during that time. Chronic alcohol abuse can cause enlargement and scarring of the liver (cirrhosis of the liver), which is often fatal. Since alcohol has no food value, alcoholics are often undernourished and fall easy prey to other diseases. Ray (1972) found that 70 percent of the males killed in car accidents were legally intoxicated, and Chafetz (1975) estimates that almost half of the murders, assaults, and rapes committed in this country involve excessive use of alcohol. More than 18 million people in the United States are heavy drinkers, consuming alcohol almost every day; the average adult alone consumes 9 quarts of alcohol annually. Although alcohol is legal, highly accessible, and alluringly advertised (sales amount to 20 or 30 billion dollars per year), in many ways it is the most dangerous drug in our society.

What leads some people to alcohol abuse and **alcoholism,** while others remain modest social drinkers? Many factors may be involved, among them anxiety, work pressures, and numerous opportunities to drink. Some people, citing twin studies and other evidence, believe that there is a genetic predisposition toward alcoholism. At present, however, this evidence is too sketchy, and it is accompanied by too many obvious social factors, to rule out a purely environmental explanation of alcoholism. It has also been suggested that there is a particular personality type, the "addictive personality," that is prone to abuse many substances, including food and cigarettes as well as alcohol.

OPIOIDS.   Natural products of the opium poppy, together with similar but synthetic substances such as methadone, are classified as **opioids.** The best-known natural opioids include opium, the least-processed form, and its derivatives heroin, morphine, and codeine. **Opium** has been used for thousands of years. It is produced from the dried milklike fluid that comes from the seedpods of the poppy. Smoking opium produces a warm, disembodied-feeling euphoria. While early physicians used it to reduce stomach cramps and ease the physical and emotional pain of patients, many people took it simply to escape into euphoria. In either case, users rapidly developed a physical dependence on the drug: If they stopped taking it, they experienced extreme discomfort.

In 1804, a new substance called **morphine** was derived from opium. (We owe its name to Morpheus, the Greek god of sleep.) It appeared to have all of opium's painkilling properties, quickly calming patients and helping them to sleep. Best of all, it was believed, morphine was not addictive. This is why morphine was used extensively during the Civil War to relieve pain. Unfortunately, it soon became apparent that morphine was just as addictive as opium.

Further efforts to produce a nonaddictive form of opium led in the late 1800s to a derivative named **heroin.** Again, however, just as with morphine, early enthusiasm and wide usage gave way to frustration: Heroin was also highly addictive. Finally, in 1917 it was concluded that there were *no non-addictive forms of opium,* and all were made illegal in the United States for other than medical uses. Since then, other derivatives of opium have been discovered (e.g., c*odeine*), and synthetic opioids have been developed. The latter are artificially synthesized drugs (e.g., *methadone*) that seem to act on the nervous system in much the same fashion that natural opium and its derivatives do. Both the natural and the synthetic opioids are now referred to as **narcotics.**

Although illegal and extremely dangerous, heroin is used illicitly by many people for the euphoria it produces. They introduce it into their bodies in a variety of ways: smoking it with tobacco, inhaling it ("snorting"), or injecting it just under the skin ("skin popping") or directly into the bloodstream ("mainlining"). Unfortunately, the initial highly pleasurable "rush" (particularly intense with injection) and subsequent few hours of euphoric high lead almost inevitably to heroin addiction, with increased tolerance and physical dependence, including exceedingly painful withdrawal symptoms. It is estimated that today there are about one-half million heroin addicts in the United States alone.

During the few hours of euphoric "high," when centers of emotion in the central nervous system are depressed, the heroin user is almost lethargic. The pupils constrict to tiny points; there are no pains or anxieties. Neither food nor sex holds much interest. Then, as this stage passes, the person once again returns to reality. Not only do addicts require extremely large doses of heroin because of their increased tolerance, but they also experience unpleasant withdrawal symptoms almost as soon as they come down from their "high." They feel anxious, perspire heavily, breath rapidly, and show many of the symptoms of a bad head cold. Most of all, they start to worry about obtaining their next dose of heroin ("fix"). Life for many addicts is a constant cycle of brief highs interspersed with desperate efforts to obtain more heroin. Not only do they run the risk of arrest for purchasing an illegal drug, but their increased tolerance may force them to spend up to several hundred dollars a day to support their habit. Often, this money can only be obtained through burglary, prostitution, or other criminal activities.

Heroin can kill if taken in excess. An overdose depresses the respiratory centers in the central nervous system to a point where breathing stops. A user who is awake can fight this to some extent by making a conscious effort to breathe. But a user who is asleep simply dies. Because the drug is obtained illegally, it is often difficult to determine how much the heroin has been "cut" (mixed with other substances). Many overdoses occur because the user obtains an unusually pure form of heroin. The user is also vulnerable to toxic impurities in the drug and to unsterile injections that may transmit disease. It is estimated that 2 percent of all heroin addicts die from their addiction, usually from an overdose (Dupont, 1971). In Chapter 17 we will consider some of the ways in which heroin addicts have been treated.

SEDATIVE-HYPNOTICS.   In general, sedative-hypnotic substances induce a state of relaxed drowsiness. At low dosages they simply calm the user and are called **sedatives.** At higher dosages they induce sleep and are called **hypnotics.**

The most widely employed sedative-hypnotic substances are called **barbiturates.** Since their development in the late nineteenth century they have been widely used, both to calm and to induce sleep. In recent years, however, with the development of tranquilizers, the barbiturates are now used primarily as a hypnotic (sleep-inducer). Taken in pill or capsule form, they depress CNS centers in much the same way that alcohol does. Low dosages calm and relax the user. Higher dosages inhibit the activity of neurons entering arousal centers in the reticular formation and thus induce sleep. At still higher dosages, barbiturates can cause respiratory failure.

Not until the 1950s did doctors begin to appreciate the dangers of barbiturates. Not only is there the risk of death through accidental or suicidal overdose, but barbiturates are also physically addictive. Chronic use leads to increased tolerance and to unpleasant withdrawal symptoms much like those of alcohol (e.g., nausea, vomiting, fatigue, anxiety, and depression). A particularly dangerous aspect of the increased tolerance is that while more and more of the substance is required to induce sleep, there is no change in the dosage that can be lethal. Thus, to achieve sleep, the chronic user eventually needs a dose that is almost lethal. Given the often groggy and confused state of the user, this leads to thousands of accidental deaths each year. Such accidents and suicidal overdoses cause approximately 5000 deaths in the United States each year (Seymour, 1979). Illegal (nonprescription) use of barbiturates and other sedative-hypnotics (e.g., *methaqualone,* trade-named Qualude) has become a major substance-abuse problem. Often such abuse begins with the legal (prescription) use of a barbiturate or other sedative-hypnotic as a sleeping pill. The user, finding that the pill also produces a pleasant and very relaxed state if taken during the day, turns to illegal sources of supply to maintain a growing dependence on such use of the drug.

In the 1950s a group of sedatives called *benzodiazepines* were developed to treat anxiety. These include *diazepam,* trade-named Valium, and *chlordiazepoxide,* trade-named Librium. They are often referred to as *antianxiety drugs* or minor **tranquilizers** (the "major tranquilizers" were the phenothiazenes, such as *thorazine,* now referred to as *antipsychotic drugs* rather than as tranquilizers). As antianxiety drugs, the minor tranquilizers (benzodiazipines) seem superior to barbiturates in several respects: First, they reduce anxiety without making the person drowsy; second, they act at very low dosages and are less likely to produce addiction; and third, they have less of an effect on respiratory centers, reducing the risk of a fatal overdose. In part, they have these unique properties because they act on CNS sites that are unaffected by barbiturates, although they also do affect some of the same sites that both barbiturates and alcohol affect (indeed, excessive use can lead to markedly similar patterns of intoxication). Identification of receptor sites for benzodiazepines has led to speculation that our bodies may produce substances that are chemically similar to the minor tranquilizers, providing a natural way of controlling anxiety (see the Highlight on endogenous benzodiazepines). The wide and enthusiastic use of Librium and Valium that began in the 1950s, however, has now been sharply curtailed as their addictive properties and potential for abuse have become more apparent. Nevertheless, they remain the most widely used antianxiety drugs.

Hallucinogens

Hallucinogens are drugs that alter our sensations and perceptions to the extent that we experience both our inner and outer worlds in radically different ways. Perhaps the best-known and most powerful hallucinogen is **LSD (lysergic acid diethylamide),** which was discovered in 1938 by a chemist named Albert Hoffman. Here is his own description of what happened after he unknowingly consumed a tiny amount of the new substance:

> In the afternoon of 16 April, 1943, when I was working on this problem I was seized by a peculiar sensation of vertigo and restlessness. Objects, as well as the shape of my associates in the laboratory appeared to undergo optical changes. I was unable to concentrate on my work. In a dream-like state I left for home where an irresistible urge to lie down overcame me. I drew the curtains and immediately fell into a peculiar state similar to drunkenness characterized by an exaggerated imagination. With my eyes closed, fantastic pictures of extraordinary plasticity and intensive color seemed to surge toward me. After two hours this state gradually wore off. (Hofmann, in Goodman & Gilman, 1975)

Later experiments revealed that Hoffman had probably consumed no more than 0.1 milligram of LSD, an amount that would barely cover the head of a pin. We now know that such minute doses can produce bizarre alterations of consciousness. Within an hour of ingesting the drug, perceptions, especially visual ones, become highly intensified. Colors seem more intense. Previously insignificant details of a scene leap out in incredibly fine detail. Inanimate objects move and alter their form. Hallucinations may occur, such as rapidly moving geometric forms that appear and disappear. In addition to these visual distortions, other senses are affected as well: There are strange sensations of hot and cold, and amplified sounds, both real and totally imagined. *Synesthesia,* a crossover in one's sensations, may occur: Sounds are "seen" and colors "heard." Time may crawl, with minutes seeming to pass like hours.

While the emotional effects of LSD can be euphoric, many people feel depersonalized and detached, and they may even suffer extreme anxiety or panic. Such "bad trips" can lead to serious accidents as the frightened user flees or fights off imagined danger.

LSD appears to affect the central nervous system through its interactions with the neurotransmitter serotonin. Systems of serotonin-releasing neurons begin in the brain stem and project all the way into various regions of the forebrain. When these neurons are activated by sensory input, they actually inhibit the firing of neurons in the visual and emotional centers of the forebrain. It is as if they acted to filter or regulate the flow of visual and emotional input. LSD has been shown to reduce activity in the serotonin system, which may eliminate the normal regulation of visual and emotional input and thus cause distortions of normal consciousness.

The psychoactive properties of LSD are still not well understood. Early interest centered on its apparent ability to induce a schizophrenic distortion of reality. In the 1950s and 1960s Timothy Leary and others argued that it produced profound new insights into one's self. Others have argued that the risk of "bad trips," lingering aftereffects, and even genetic damage make it a highly dangerous drug. In any case, it remains a potent hallucinogen, capable of profoundly distorting one's sense of reality in a highly unpredictable fashion, even at tiny dosages.

Endogenous Benzodiazepines —Does the Body Produce Its Own Tranquilizers?

In Chapter 2 we considered evidence that our own bodies produce a substance that acts like opiates to kill pain (see the Highlight on endorphin and enkephalin in that chapter). More recently, researchers have begun to suspect that another internally produced (endogenous) substance may control anxiety in much the same fashion that the benzodiazepine tranquilizers (e.g., Valium and Librium) do. The way in which research has led to this speculation resembles the story of the endogenous opiates.

In 1977, research groups in Denmark (Mohler & Okada, 1977) and Switzerland (Squires & Braestrup, 1977) discovered binding sites in the brain for benzodiazepines— that is, specific brain tissue that takes up benzodiazepines in a lock-and-key fashion (other sedatives, such as barbiturates, did not bind to these sites). Furthermore, the degree to which specific benzodiazepines were taken up reflected their relative effectiveness as tranquilizers (Mohler & Okada, 1977).

It was also noticed that the location of the benzodiazepine binding sites was generally consistent with the effects of tranquilizers (Young & Kuhar, 1980). For example, many of these sites were found in parts of the brain known to be involved in regulating emotions (see the accompanying figure).

Just as the discovery of opiate receptors in the central nervous system led to a search for endogenous opiates, the discovery of benzodiazepine receptors (binding sites) seemed to imply the existence of some internally produced tranquilizer (i.e., an endogenous benzodiazepine). This search is still going on, but enough has been learned to produce reasoned speculation (Snyder, 1981). Benzodiazepines seem to interact in some complicated way with GABA (gamma aminobietyric acid), the inhibitory neurotransmitter released by about 30 percent of the neurons in the brain. Anxiety is believed to be associated with excessive firing (hyperexcitability) of certain neural

There are many other hallucinogenic drugs, both naturally occurring and synthetic. *Mescaline* is the active ingredient of the *peyote* cactus. For centuries, Indians in Mexico and the southwestern United States have chewed peyote to induce hallucinations ("visions") during certain religious ceremonies. *DOM* is a long-lasting (12 hours) hallucinogen originally developed by the DOW Chemical Company and now illegally traded on the street as STP. A much more short-term hallucinogen is *DMT* (dimethyltryptine), the effects of which last only about an hour.

Marijuana and Other Forms of Cannabis

Marijuana is a mixture of the crushed leaves and flowering tops of the hemp plant (*Cannabis sativa*). The plant contains a substance called *THC* (tetrahydrocannabinal) that has a combination of psychoactive properties which defy simple categorization. It produces euphoria and release from inhibition much like the depressant alcohol; the relaxation or even fatigue of a sedative; and hypnotic, sensory, and perceptual distortions like a mild hallucinogen (which ordinarily increases wakefulness). This is why marijuana and other cannabis drugs are treated as a unique category of psychoactive substance in the *DSM III: Diagnostic and Statistical Manual of Mental Disorders* (1980). The various forms of cannabis differ chiefly in their concentration of THC. Of the natural forms of cannabis, marijuana is the least potent, and **hashish** (pure plant resin) the most potent. Recently an almost pure form of THC has been artificially synthesized in the laboratory.

Cannabis is most frequently taken by smoking it in a cigarette or pipe. It can also be eaten (Alice B. Toklas, a friend of the poet Gertrude Stein, is said to have baked delicious marijuana brownies). At low dosages, most users quickly develop a feeling of relaxed euphoria. Some become more talkative, while others become quiet and contemplative. Many describe their perceptions and

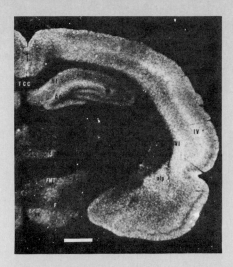

A *radioactively tagged benzodiazepine tranquilizer was administered to a rat. He was then sacrificed and a slice of his brain was placed on film for several weeks. The lightest areas in the developed film show where the benzodiazepine was taken up in the rat's brain (benzodiazepine receptor sites).*

pathways. This may trigger an increase in the release of GABA to produce a compensatory inhibition.

The binding of benzodiazepines seems to facilitate the uptake of GABA at its closely associated receptor sites. Thus both GABA and some as yet undiscovered endogenous benzodiazepine may act as tranquilizers. Chronic use of tranquilizers may produce tolerance because GABA production diminishes as its effects are magnified. Withdrawal symptoms may occur because the sudden reduction in benzodiazepines takes place when GABA production is low, leaving little inhibition of the anxiety-evoking neural activity.

The major point to be made here is *not* that we know exactly how tranquilizers affect the brain. It is, rather, that psychoactive drugs affect our minds in a complicated fashion. Recent research on brain chemistry and neurotransmitters seems to be opening the door to an understanding of these processes.

sensory experiences as intensified and unusual. Previously unnoticed colors and sounds become vivid and important. Space and forms may appear distorted, and time slows. However, while many people feel only pleasant or interesting effects, others become anxious and irritable. The particular pattern of one's reactions depends much on the particular situation and the behavior of those who are nearby.

There are physical symptoms as well. The eyes redden as blood vessels dilate, the mouth dries as saliva flow is inhibited, and the heart beats faster. Appetite often increases, a condition described by users as an "attack of the munchies."

As more THC enters the bloodstream, the user feels more and more drowsy. Speech may become slurred and thinking distorted. Things may seem hysterically funny and inspire long spells of giggling. Finally, the user falls into a deep sleep.

For many centuries, cannabis was used in Asia as an anesthetic and medication for maladies ranging from insomnia to rheumatism. In the mid-nineteenth century, Western European doctors began to prescribe it for neuralgia, menstrual pain, and migraine headaches. In the early twentieth century, its medical use was widely promoted in the United States by the drug company Parke-Davis. By the 1930s, however, doctors were prescribing such other drugs as morphine, aspirin, and barbiturates instead. Marijuana began to be used simply for pleasure and was distributed illegally. This period was marked by progressively harsher antidrug laws, and by 1937, marijuana, incongruously lumped with opium and heroin, was completely outlawed. During the 1960s marijuana use underwent a resurgence, with growing recognition that the harsh legal penalties seemed inconsistent with its apparent low level of danger. The *National Survey of Drug Abuse* (1979) reported that during 1979 more than 26 million Americans used cannabis at least once, including 31 percent of adolescents under 18 (10 percent of all high-school seniors), 68 percent of individuals between 18 and 25, and 20 percent of those over 26.

It is clear that earlier efforts to characterize cannabis as a "killer weed" were counterproductive exaggerations. Concerning its safety, however, real doubts still remain. Some evidence suggests that it is addictive. Chronic users may develop tolerance (Nowlan & Cohen, 1977) and experience withdrawal symptoms such as loss of appetite, running nose, diarrhea, and sweating (Jones, 1977). Also, the potency of illegally obtained cannabis has increased, and there are more instances of accidents related to cannabis intoxication (Marijuana Research Findings, 1980). Longer-term dangers may include susceptability to lung disease (Tashkin, Calvarese, & Simmons, 1978) and reduced fertility (Hembree, Nabias, & Huang, 1979).

PCP *or* "Angel Dust"

In 1959 a substance named **phencyclidine** (**PCP**) was developed for use as a powerful painkiller and an alternative to the highly addictive opiates. It seemed to control pain, not so much by eliminating it, but by producing a state of detachment from bodily sensations so that the pain could be ignored. PCP is chemically distinct from all the other drugs we have discussed, and it produces a sufficiently unique pattern of effects to warrant its own special category in *DSM III*.

In 1967, only 4 years after it first appeared on the market as a prescription drug, certain negative aspects of PCP had become so apparent that its use by humans was made illegal. Nevertheless, it soon began to be sold illegally on the street, where it is often referred to as "angel dust." It comes in a variety of forms, including pills, powder, rock crystals, and liquid. It can be swallowed, inhaled ("snorted"), injected, or even sprayed on tobacco and smoked. In fact, since it is cheaply and easily produced, it is often secretly added to other illicit drugs such as marijuana or cocaine to increase their apparent potency.

Shortly after taking PCP, many users feel mildly euphoric, while others become nervous and agitated. Moods swing rapidly: The user may feel elated and powerful one moment and fearful the next. Judgment is impaired, and the person may grow aggressive and start fights. Perception, including the sense of time, may be distorted. Physical changes include uncontrolled movement of the eyes, loss of pain sensitivity, increased blood pressure and heart rate, and loss of muscular control.

Larger doses of PCP produce even more negative effects. The user often feels detached from reality. Hallucinations occur and thought processes are seriously disturbed to the point of delirium. Paranoia and outbursts of violence are common. Strangly, these negative symptoms may occur either shortly after the PCP is taken or days later, after the user seems to have totally recovered.

Not surprisingly, the irrational thought processes, insensitivity to pain, paranoia, and outbursts of violence produced by high doses of PCP have led to numerous instances of severe injury, suicide, and accidental death (Siegal, 1978; Burns & Lerner, 1976). Sufficiently high doses of PCP have even led directly to coma and death through a depression of respiratory centers.

In spite of its dangers, PCP has become an increasingly popular illicit drug. It does produce some pleasant sensations. Its very unpredictability may appeal to some. It is inexpensive and easy to manufacture and, as yet, does not appear to produce tolerance or withdrawal symptoms.

SUMMARY

1. *NREM sleep* has four stages, which differ in terms of brain wave patterns and muscular changes. *REM sleep,* characterized by rapid eye movements and *dreaming,* occurs at 90-minute intervals throughout the sleep cycle.

2. There are a number of theories about why people dream. Freud believed that a dream is the expression of unconscious impulses and thoughts when a person's conscious defenses are lowered during sleep. Other theorists believe that dreams are a way of processing daytime memories, or of "recharging" the higher brain centers.

3. *Hypnosis* can be defined as a condition in which subjects are able to respond to appropriate suggestions with distortions of perception and memory.

4. Individual differences exist in responsiveness to hypnosis; about 15 percent of the population can be greatly affected by hypnotic suggestion, while about 5 to 10 percent show no effect at all; the rest fall somewhere between these two extremes.

5. Pain reduction through hypnosis has been tested with both *ischemic* and *cold-pressor pain;* those who are highly responsive to hypnosis show substantial pain reduction, while the results are less dramatic with those who are of medium or low responsiveness to hypnosis.

6. *Meditation* is concentration on one thought or word (in Transcendental Meditation, the word is called a *mantra*) in order to block out all other sensations and thoughts.

7. Drugs affecting behavior or consciousness are called *psychoactive drugs;* they include stimulants, depressants, and hallucinogens, as well as other substances such as cannabis and PCP.

Suggested Readings

BOWERS, K. *Hypnosis for the seriously curious.* Monterey, Calif.: Brooks/Cole, 1976. An extensive review of experimental studies of hypnosis.

CARRINGTON, P. *Freedom in meditation.* New York: Doubleday, 1977. A demystified, practical approach to meditation as a means of reducing tension.

CARTWRIGHT, R. A. *A primer of sleep and dreaming.* Reading, Mass.: Addison-Wesley, 1978. A simple, readable introduction to research on sleep and dreaming.

DEMENT, W. *Some must watch while some must sleep.* New York: Norton, 1978. A more advanced treatment of modern experimental methods of studying sleep.

GOLEMAN, D., & DAVIDSON, R. J. (Eds.). *Consciousness: Brain, states of awareness, and mysticism.* New York: Harper & Row, 1979. A collection of articles about consciousness, ranging from neuroscience to mysticism in approach.

GRINSPOON, L., & HEDBLOM, P. *The speed culture: Amphetamine use and abuse in America.* Cambridge, Mass.: Harvard University Press, 1975. An extensive and technical review of the use of stimulants.

HILGARD, E. R. *Divided consciousness.* New York: Wiley, 1977. An excellent introduction to hypnosis and altered states of consciousness by one of the foremost investigators in the field.

JAYNES, J. *The origin of consciousness in the breakdown of the bicameral mind.* Boston: Houghton Mifflin, 1977. A fascinating, if controversial, view of consciousness as a relatively recent evolutionary development in human history.

JOUVET, M. The states of sleep. *Scientific American,* 1967, *216,* 62–72. A brief, highly readable, and well-illustrated introduction to sleep research.

NARANJO, C., & ORNSTEIN, R. E. *On the psychology of meditation.* New York: Penguin, 1977. An introduction to meditation, its history and current practice.

ORNSTEIN, R. E. *The psycholgy of consciousness* (2nd ed.). New York: Harcourt Brace Jovanovich, 1977. An introductory level review of a wide range of work on human consciousness from a humanistic point of view.

WOLMAN, B. *Handbook of dreams: Research, theories, and applications.* New York: Van Nostrand, 1979. A broad collection of articles on dreaming.

6. Conditioning and Learning

The behavior of people, and of animals, is continually changed by the experiences that they have in the world. To be once bitten is to be twice shy; and the burnt child avoids the flame. Practice, we are told, makes perfect—and experience is the great teacher. We can define **learning** as the relatively permanent changes in behavior that are a result of past experience. Those changes, for the most part, serve to adjust us to the world in which we live. We can and do learn some maladjustive behaviors, but most of us profit from experience most of the time. The obvious function of learning is to make us able to go about the business of living in an effective way. The newborn mammal knows nothing about the world and depends for its survival on parental care. Through learning—as well as through growth—it is transformed into a knowledgeable and effective adult creature.

The experimental analysis of learning has occupied the attention of very many psychologists. The search for basic principles of learning, with wide applicability, has often involved the use of animals as experimental subjects. The emphasis in this chapter will be on those relatively simple forms of learning that can be most effectively manipulated and studied in animal subjects. Though such learning may be relatively simple, it is of fundamental importance, and, as we shall see, it occurs in humans in much the same way as in humbler creatures. The effects of humans' more complex learning processes, made possible by their enormous cerebral cortex and by their unique capacity for language, will be evident in later chapters. This "higher" learning does not take the place of the more primitive processes that we share with other animals. To understand some areas of human behavior—and especially behavior involving strong emotions—a thorough knowledge of **conditioning** is needed.

PAVLOV'S BASIC DISCOVERIES

The name of Ivan Pavlov (1849–1936) is known to almost everybody, and with good reason. The phenomena of conditioning were first discovered and analyzed in great detail in his laboratory. Pavlov's research, carried out over a period of many years, represented a genuine intellectual revolution. This work was a brilliant application of the methods of natural science to problems of learning and behavior that had previously been untouched. The long-lasting significance of Pavlov's contribution can be seen in the fact that, even today, the technical vocabulary used by psychologists when they discuss learning is largely Pavlovian. This is all the more remarkable when you consider that Pavlov was not a psychologist—and, indeed, had little respect for, or sympathy with, those psychologists who were his contemporaries.

Before his work on conditioned reflexes, Pavlov had won a Nobel prize (1904) for his research on the physiology of the digestive system. Pavlov's interest in conditioning—and his whole approach to it—was a logical outgrowth of his interest as a physiologist in the digestive glands. In his work on the digestive system Pavlov used dogs as experimental subjects. The salivary glands play an important role in the digestive process, and Pavlov developed a special operation to study their functioning in intact dogs. This made it possible for him to collect, and to measure precisely, the salivary secretions of his subjects. In this way he could examine the amount of salivary secretion that occurred when chemicals of various sorts were placed on the dog's tongue or when the dog ate. The saliva that flowed when food was placed in the dog's mouth was the sort of thing with which an experimental physiologist could deal routinely.

Pavlov noted, however, that at times a dog would salivate a great deal, even though no food was placed in its mouth. There was no good "physiological" reason for such salivation, but, on the other hand, it did not seem to occur at random. The "nonphysiological" salivary flow was very likely to occur if the dog smelled food, or heard the food bowls clattering in the laboratory kitchen, or caught sight of the attendant who usually fed it. This sort of salivary flow had been called "psychic secretion," to distinguish it from the more "respectable" and orderly physiological salivary flow that Pavlov had been studying. This kind of distinction made no sense to Pavlov. The salivary glands secreted only one kind of saliva, and "psychic secretion" meant that some of the activity of the salivary glands was influenced by the brain. Thus, if one wished really to understand the functioning of the digestive system, the physiology of still another organ—the brain—had also to be studied.

Pavlov decided to begin an experimental analysis of the elusive phenomena of "psychic secretion." This was *not* conceived as a study of learning and behavior. To Pavlov, his studies of conditioned reflexes were a way of investigating the physiological functioning of the brain. Throughout his life Pavlov was less interested in the behavioral phenomena he so brilliantly analyzed than in the hypothetical brain processes which, he inferred, must be causing the behaviors. The final irony is that Pavlov's "brain physiology" has been superseded by modern knowledge of neuroanatomy and neurophysiology. The permanent contribution made by Pavlov's work on conditioned reflexes belongs not to physiology, but to behavioral psychology.

The Basic Experiment

To show the various phenomena of conditioning, Pavlov thought up a simple and effective experimental procedure, illustrated in Figure 6–1. The subject was a dog, surgically prepared so that careful measurements of salivary flow could be obtained. The dog was held in a stock and isolated in a sound-proofed chamber. Through various mechanical devices, meat powder could either be placed directly on the dog's tongue or put in a food dish set before

FIGURE 6–1
Pavlovian dog, surgically prepared for measurement of salivary flow, restrained in a conditioning chamber.

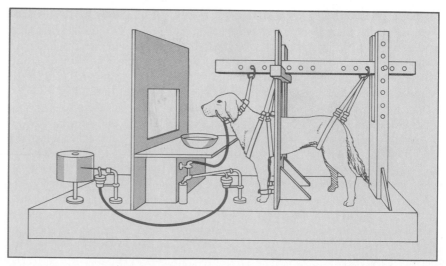

the dog. The experimenter could present, as desired, any of several controlled stimuli, such as the sound of a metronome or the flashing of a light.

The starting point for Pavlov's demonstration was the unconditioned reflex or **unconditioned response** (UR) of salivation. The unconditioned reflex is an innate, built-in reaction or response to a stimulus. Whenever meat powder is placed on the tongue of a normal dog, the response of salivation will occur. The nerve pathways that underlie this reflexive response are, so to speak, prewired. The sound of a metronome, on the other hand, will not cause a normal dog to salivate. The sound will probably elicit some response from the dog—its ears may prick up, or it may turn to look at the source of the sound. We can be quite certain, however, that it will not salivate. Pavlov now proceeded to make the dog salivate in response to the sound of the metronome. The trick is very simple: We merely sound the metronome, and shortly after we present the dog with meat powder. This sequence—metronome sound followed by meat powder—is repeated for a number of trials. The dog, on the first couple of trials, salivates only when the meat powder (the **unconditioned stimulus,** or US) is presented. After a few trials, however, it begins to salivate when the metronome sound (the **conditioned stimulus,** or CS) is presented. Salivation now occurs before the meat powder is presented. The sound of the metronome, which before had no relation to salivation, now reliably elicits a salivary response. When salivation occurs to a previously neutral CS, such as the sound of the metronome, we refer to it as a conditioned reflex, or a **conditioned response** (CR). The basic procedure for establishing a conditioned response is outlined in Figure 6–2.

Pavlov's basic experiment is a clear example of what has come to be known as the law of **"classical" conditioning:** Whenever a previously neutral stimulus (CS) is presented *in close temporal contiguity* (close in time) with an unconditioned stimulus (US), a response like that made to the US will come to be made to the CS. This is, of course, a law about learning. The experience of the regular sequence, metronome sound followed by food, has adaptively modified the dog's behavior. The CR is not always identical to the unconditioned response (UR); but it does seem that the response anticipates, and thus helps the animal to prepare for, delivery of the US. There are other occasions when the CR, although obviously related to the UR, may be opposite in form (see the Application on examples of classical conditioning).

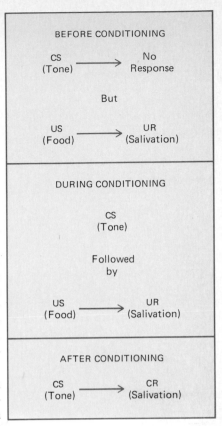

FIGURE 6–2
The relations between stimuli and responses during three phases of the establishment of a conditioned response.

Acquisition, Extinction, and Reinforcement

The course of a typical conditioning experiment in Pavlov's laboratory is shown in Figure 6–3. Note that on the very early trials there is no salivation to the CS. The conditioned response is gradually acquired over a number of trials. The bank of trials during which the animal is learning the conditioned response is called, logically enough, **acquisition.** The basic rule followed by the experimenter during acquisition is: Whenever the CS is presented, follow it with the US. That procedure—the CS followed by the US—is called **reinforcement.** The reinforcement of the CS with the US is the necessary condition for establishing a conditioned response.

What happens if, after the subject has acquired a conditioned response, we stop reinforcing the CS? That procedure, called **extinction,** leads to the gradual disappearance of the conditioned response, as shown in the center of Figure 6–3. Thus it is clear that to maintain a conditioned response one must continue reinforcing the response. Presentation of the CS without the US leads to extinction of the conditioned response.

FIGURE 6–3

The acquisition, extinction, spontaneous recovery, and reacquisition of a conditioned salivary response. Typically, the measure of conditioning is the number of drops of saliva elicited by the CS on each trial. Note that on the day following extinction, the first presentation of the CS elicits quite a large response.

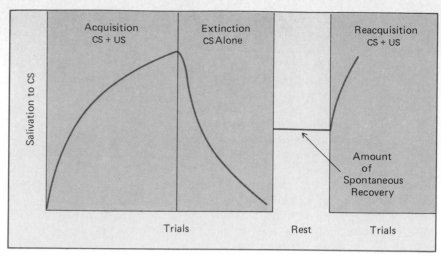

The extinction of a response, however, does not mean that the response has been "forgotten." That was shown clearly by further experiments demonstrating what Pavlov called **spontaneous recovery.** A dog that was subjected to acquisition and then extinction of a conditioned response was returned to its home cage. The next day it was placed into the conditioning chamber once again, and the metronome was sounded. The dog now salivated to the sound of the metronome for a couple of trials, without being reinforced, even though the response had seemed to be completely extinguished the day before. This spontaneous recovery of the response shows that extinction did not "erase" the conditioned response; as one might expect, after a cycle of acquisition and extinction, *reacquisition* of the response will occur much more rapidly than did the original acquisition. The extinction procedure evidently teaches the dog that—at least for the time being—the CS is no longer followed by the US. The fact that the US once followed it, however, is not forgotten. Without deliberate extinction training, in fact, animals retain conditioned responses intact over a period of several years.

Generalization

When a conditioned response has been established to a particular CS, stimuli similar to that CS will also tend to elicit the response, a process that is called **generalization.** The more similar the new stimulus is to the original CS, the greater will be the strength of the response. The nature of generalization was illustrated clearly in a simple example by Pavlov. The CS was a mechanical scratching of the dog's skin, which had been paired with meat powder (the US). When the conditioned response (salivation) had been firmly established, the dog was tested with scratches on different parts of its body. The closer the scratch was to the point at which the original CS had been applied, the more the dog salivated.

Generalization in human beings can easily be shown. The **galvanic skin response (GSR),** a change in the electrical resistance of the skin related to sweating, is an unconditioned emotional reaction (see Chapter 11). When college students receive an electric shock (US), *one* of their emotional reactions (UR) is a marked GSR. The GSR is easily conditioned: If a pure tone is sounded shortly before the students receive a shock, after only 1 or 2 trials they show a pronounced GSR to the tone alone. When students were conditioned to a particular tone, higher and lower tones also elicited a GSR. The GSR was greater when the test tone was close to the tone used as a CS during conditioning (Hovland, 1937). The typical form of a generalization gradient is shown in Figure 6–4.

With people, the similarity of one stimulus to another may depend critically on language and symbolization. Thus Diven (1936) conditioned college students to make a GSR in response to the word "barn" embedded in a list of recited words. This was easily accomplished by following the word "barn" with an electric shock. When conditioning had been established, the subjects also displayed GSRs to such rural words as "cow" or "hay"—but not to such neutral words as "table" or "chair." The generalization in this case has nothing to do with the physical similarity of one word to another but obviously depends on the meanings of the words.

The fact that conditioned responses generalize to stimuli similar to the CS has obvious adaptive value. The precise measurement and control over CSs that is possible in the laboratory is not much like what happens in real life, where stimuli are always changing from one occasion to the next. If a tiger has clawed you once, you are very likely to display a GSR and other conditioned emotional reactions the next time you see a tiger. The conditioning would not be very useful, however, if as a result of your first experience you responded only to the sight of a tiger approaching from your right with a distinctive wart on its nose.

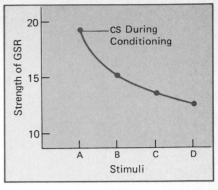

FIGURE 6–4

An example of generalization. The subjects had been conditioned originally to a CS (A) of a given frequency. When tested with the original tone, and with tones B, C, and D of differing frequencies, a clear generalization gradient appeared. The closer the frequency of the test tone to the frequency of tone A, the greater was the magnitude of the response to the tone. (Hovland, 1937)

Discrimination

Though conditioning generalizes to stimuli similar to the CS, it is possible to learn *not* to respond to similar stimuli, while continuing to respond to the CS itself. This is known as **discrimination.** Also studied by Pavlov, discrimination is a logical supplement to generalization. The procedure used by Pavlov to demonstrate discrimination is, in retrospect, perfectly obvious. We can condition a dog to respond to a tone of, let us say, 1,000 hertz (Hz). When conditioning is established, we find that the dog also salivates—though not as much—to tones of 900 or 1,100 Hz. To establish discrimination, we now present in a scrambled order tones of 900, 1,000, and 1,100 Hz. Whenever the 1,000 Hz tone is presented it is reinforced. When the 900 and 1,100 Hz tones are presented they are *not* reinforced. The result is that, after a fair number of trials, the dog will salivate to the 1,000 Hz tone while no longer salivating to the other tones. With a procedure of this sort, Pavlov was able to show that his dogs could discriminate between tones of 1,000 and 1,012 Hz.

This procedure, as Pavlov noted, seems ideally suited to the study of the sensory capacities of animals. Whenever the animal learns to discriminate between two similar stimuli, we know that it can tell the two stimuli apart. The usefulness of discrimination should be obvious. Without some check on the generalization process, you might find yourself making terrified emotional responses to the sight of a caged tiger, or even to an alley cat.

Higher-Order Conditioning

The fact that conditioning always involves, at the outset, an unconditioned reflex might seem to set limits on its implications for human behavior. While we do learn conditioned responses having to do with food, pain, and other biologically important events, much of human learning at least is far removed from such primitive considerations. That did not stop Pavlov from speculating that *all* learning might involve nothing more than long chains of conditioned responses. To support this idea, Pavlov pointed to the phenomenon of higher-order conditioning.

To establish a higher-order conditioned response, Pavlov began as usual by pairing a neutral CS with meat powder (the US). This CS might be the sound of a metronome, and we shall refer to it as CS_1. When CS_1 had been firmly conditioned, Pavlov moved on to a new neutral CS, such as a flashing light, which we shall call CS_2. CS_2, however, was never paired with meat powder. Instead, CS_2 was presented just before CS_1, and the pairing of CS_2 with CS_1 was *not* followed by meat powder. The earlier conditioning of CS_1, however, guaranteed that the animal would salivate when CS_1 was presented. In most cases, after a number of CS_2/CS_1 pairings the animal was conditioned to salivate to CS_2. The important point to note is that CS_2 has never been paired with meat powder; rather, it has been paired with CS_1, which earlier had been paired with meat powder. This process is called higher-order conditioning because a well-conditioned CS, such as CS_1, can itself serve as a US. The role played by CS_1 in establishing conditioning to CS_2 is very much like the role normally played by the US, the meat powder.

To drive the point home, Pavlov went on to still another new CS, called CS_3. The CS_3 (perhaps the smell of camphor) was paired with CS_2, which, as a result of higher-order conditioning, now caused salivation. With some dogs, at least, Pavlov was able to establish a "third-order" conditioned response. This kind of outcome encouraged his belief that much human learning depended on higher-order conditioning, with nonbiological stimuli (especially words) serving in effect as USs. Thus, in humans, a verbal threat may be as effective a reinforcer in making one afraid of the threatener as a physical attack would have been. Presumably, during childhood, threatening gestures and words had in fact been paired with actual physical attack and pain.

There is no doubt that higher-order conditioning does occur, and that fact clearly extends the boundaries of conditioning well beyond meat powder and other biological reinforcers. To speculate that all learning is nothing but a chain of conditioned responses, however, goes wildly beyond any observable facts. Pavlov's excessive enthusiasm was that of a pioneer, dazzled by sights never before observed.

Conditioned Inhibition

Many other conditioning phenomena were first discovered by Pavlov, and they are still of major concern to students and theorists of the learning process. We shall conclude this brief discussion with one more example. In another series of experiments, Pavlov used several neutral stimuli while working with the same dog. The dog was first conditioned to salivate to each of two stimuli, CS_1 and CS_2. This was of course done in the usual way, by pairing each of these CSs with meat powder. Then, on some trials, Pavlov presented a new stimulus, CS_3, at the same time as CS_1. Whenever the combination CS_3 plus CS_1 was presented, there was no reinforcement. There were trials when CS_1 was presented by itself, without CS_3. Whenever that occurred, CS_1 was reinforced. This is a kind of discrimination training. When CS_1 occurs alone, food always follows; but when CS_1 occurs together with CS_3, food never follows. There is nothing surprising in the fact that, after a number of trials, the dog comes to respond reliably to CS_1, while not responding to the combination of CS_1 and CS_3.

While this discrimination was being learned, Pavlov continued on some trials to present CS_2, which was always reinforced. Then, after the discrimination had been learned, Pavlov presented the dog with a new combination of stimuli, CS_2 and CS_3. The dog did *not* salivate to that combination—in spite of the fact that a conditioned response would surely have occurred if CS_2 had been presented alone. That meant, Pavlov reasoned, that CS_3 had been made into a *conditioned inhibitor* of responding. Though CS_3 had signalled non-reinforcement only when presented with CS_1, the conditioning had obviously given CS_3 a more general property. The dog now behaved as if CS_3 were a generalized signal for nonreinforcement of all conditioned responses. When CS_3 is presented together with any normally effective CS, it inhibits the conditioned response that would otherwise occur.

Variables That Affect Classical Conditioning

Many variables affect the strength of conditioned responses and the rate at which they are acquired. The more intense the US (for example, intensity of shock or amount of meat powder), the more rapid the conditioning and the stronger the response. The same thing occurs when the intensity of the CS is varied (that is, when a metronome CS is made louder, or a light CS is made brighter, the conditioned response is more rapidly acquired, more strongly performed, etc.).

Perhaps the most critical variable of all is the time relation between the CS and the US. The CS can be presented a little before the US, it can be presented at the same time as the US, or it can be presented a little after the US. The outcomes of these three basic arrangements differ very widely, as can be seen in Figure 6–5. The figure shows the results of a study with human subjects, using a conditioned finger–withdrawal response. The procedure involves the pairing of a tone (CS) with a shock (US) given to the subject's finger. The unconditioned response to shock on the finger is to jerk the finger away. When conditioning occurs, the finger is withdrawn in response to the tone (Spooner & Kellogg, 1947).

The backward conditioning procedure—in which the CS is presented *after* the US—results in virtually no conditioning. With simultaneous conditioning procedures—when CS and US occur at the same time—there is also very little, if any, conditioning. The forward conditioning procedure (CS presented before US) is effective, but how effective it is depends on the time interval between the CS and US. The strongest conditioning takes place when the CS is presented about 500 milliseconds before the US. When the time between the two stimuli is either more or less than that, the amount of conditioning drops off quite quickly. With conditioned finger-withdrawal in humans, an interval of only a couple of seconds between CS and US is long enough to eliminate almost all traces of conditioning. This pattern of results is characteristic of many human conditioning studies and of some animal studies as well. There are many animal studies, however, in which effective conditioning has been observed with much longer time intervals—on the order of minutes— between CS and US (Kamin, 1965). In such studies, however, it is still the case that backward and simultaneous conditioning procedures are relatively ineffective. Further, as might be expected, conditioning weakens as the time interval between CS and US is increased.

Perhaps you have been wondering how conditioning can be assessed when the CS and US are presented either simultaneously or close together in time.

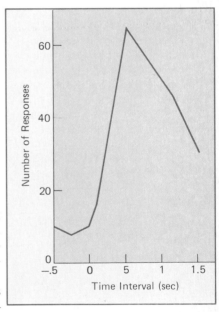

FIGURE 6–5
The strength of conditioned finger withdrawal in humans as a function of the time interval between CS and US. (Negative time intervals refer to a procedure in which the US is presented before the CS.)

APPLICATION□
Some Examples of Classical Conditioning

The technique for bringing reflex responses under the control of previously ineffective stimuli can have some unusual and interesting applications. The basic logic of the classical conditioning procedure led Mowrer and Mowrer (1938) to develop a simple treatment for enuresis (bed-wetting) in children. The reasoning was that in many cases of enuresis the child has simply failed to learn to wake up in response to the stimuli arising from a full bladder. This necessary bit of learning could be brought about by imaginative use of conditioning.

The ringing of a loud bell can be thought of as an unconditioned stimulus, which reliably awakens a sleeping child. What will happen if we follow the stimulation from a full bladder (CS) with the sound of a loud bell (US)? The principle of classical conditioning tells us that after a few such paired presentations, the response of waking up—at first a UR made only to the bell—should begin to occur in response to the stimulation from a full bladder. Then, of course, the child can go to the bathroom instead of wetting the bed while asleep.

There is no great trick in arranging for a bell to ring shortly after the child's bladder is full. The child sleeps on a special fine mesh sheet so constructed that the first drop of urine closes a circuit that sets off the alarm bell. The arrangement guarantees that shortly after the sleeping child is stimulated by a full bladder, he or she will be awakened by the bell. With a few nights of this treatment, most children begin to wake up in reponse to the stimulation from a full bladder—before wetting the bed.

The treatment of enuresis may seem a homely and unimportant matter, but Siegel's (1976) application of a classical conditioning model to some of the phenomena of drug tolerance appears to have profound and obvious medical significance. When people use a drug such as morphine or heroin, they rapidly develop a tolerance for the drug. That is, larger and larger drug doses are required to produce the same (or any) effect on behavior and feeling. The physiological basis for such tolerance effects is beginning to be understood (see Chapter 2), but Siegel's studies suggest that classical conditioning may play a large role.

When a neutral CS precedes injection of a drug, the response conditioned to the CS is often a *compensatory* response, the opposite of the immediate effect of the drug itself. The compensatory response makes it possible to understand some striking results reported by Siegel. Morphine, of course, lessens sensitivity to pain. Thus, when a rat is injected for the first time with morphine, it will not pull its paw away from the surface of an experimental hot-plate as quickly as it normally would. With repeated injections of the drug, however, the increased pain tolerance slowly diminishes. When the drug-tolerant rat is now given a placebo injection of saline, it shows supersensitivity to pain. That is, it withdraws its paw from the hot plate almost immediately. The salt solution, of course, has no effect on pain sensitivity. Presumably, then, the conditioned stimuli association with injections have elicited a conditioned response *opposite* to the pain-reducing effect of the drug itself.

This gradually conditioned compensatory effect, Siegel argues, is reponsible for the gradual development of drug tolerance. For the human drug addict, the gradually developing compensatory response must be counteracted by the continually increasing drug dosage.

The remarkable observation made by Siegel is that such conditioned effects are very sensitive to the precise environmental cues associated with the injection. Thus a rat that has been repeatedly injected with morphine in a particular room will show drug tolerance as long as the injections are given in the same room. When an injection is given in a distinctively different room, however, the full effect of the drug is restored. This indicates that drug tolerance effects are not an inevitable consequence of repeated drug usage. The tolerance effect, like all conditioned responses, is sensitive to changes in the conditioned stimuli.

When this is done, how can one know whether a response is an unconditioned reaction to the US or a conditioned reaction to the CS? The solution is to randomly insert "catch" or test trials along with the reinforced acquisition trials. The CS is presented alone, without the US, on such test trials, so that any response occurring on a test trial is obviously a conditioned response.

The effects of varying the time relations between CS and US are consistent with the idea that conditioning basically serves a signalling function. We are so built that we learn to respond in an appropriate preparatory way to signals that tell us something important is *about* to happen. From this point of view, the failure to obtain simultaneous or backward conditioning makes good sense. There is no reason to "prepare" for events that have already taken place. We should note, however, that the failure to observe a conditioned response does not necessarily mean that the subject has not learned that the CS and US regularly occur in sequence. There is no doubt that human subjects, who fail to show conditioned finger–withdrawal when two seconds or more elapse between CS and US, become quite aware of the fact that the CS means that shock will soon occur. Perhaps the failure to obtain conditioning with longer times between CS and US in humans reflects the fact that, with a couple of seconds to think matters over, there is time enough for complicated cognitive processes to override the basic conditioning process. We do know that, in humans, instructions to try to enhance or to inhibit conditioned responding have a considerable effect.

Classical Conditioning in Overview

Pavlov's analysis of salivary conditioning in dogs laid bare the structure of a fundamental learning process that has very wide applicability. There have been successful studies of conditioning performed on a wide variety of animal species. The unconditioned stimuli (and thus the conditioned responses) that have been used are many, and almost all forms of stimulation for which animals have senses have served as conditioned stimuli.

The core concept of conditioning is an ancient one, well appreciated by Aristotle and by the English empiricist philosophers. Pavlovian conditioning obviously involves a process of **association.** Put very loosely, one might say that the dog has learned to associate the sound of a metronome with the delivery of food because the two things repeatedly occur close together in time. Therefore, it salivates when it hears the metronome. To put matters so loosely, however, would be to ignore Pavlov's main message. To Pavlov, conditioning was an automatic, blind, "stamping-in" kind of process. There had to be definite, quantitative laws that determined the rate at which conditioning occurred and that could be discovered by experimental analysis. To talk glibly about the "association of ideas" or about the metronome's making the dog "think about" or "expect" food had nothing to do with science. There was no need, Pavlov stressed, to talk about the animal's "mind" at all. We could observe the CSs and the USs, the conditioned and unconditioned responses, and we could isolate variables that systematically affected conditioning. To Pavlov, of course, the aim of it all was to discover what physical processes in the brain were involved in conditioned associations. The unconditioned reflex obviously depended on the existence of a definite pathway within the nervous system, connecting stimulus and response. The conditioned reflex, in Pavlov's view, had to depend on no less definite a pathway—but new, conditioned pathways must be gradually stamped in during the course of conditioning. This remains an entirely logical inference. We are not, however, much closer to actual observation of such pathways—or to detailed knowledge of how they might be made—than Pavlov was.

OPERANT CONDITIONING

Pavlovian conditioning provides a mechanism through which previously ineffective or neutral stimuli come to elicit responses that were formerly elicited only by an unconditioned stimulus. That is, Pavlovian conditioning vastly extends the range of stimuli to which an organism can respond. Taken by itself, however, Pavlovian conditioning does not directly affect responses. The animal that came into the world with nothing but a Pavlovian learning mechanism might learn to salivate and to jerk its paw in response to a great many previously neutral stimuli, but it would not be capable of doing much else. There must, one might speculate, be a learning mechanism that works in a more direct way to change and to shape responses. There is; today this process is usually called **operant conditioning.**

Thorndike's Pioneer Studies

The first studies of what has come to be known as operant conditioning were done in the United States by Edward L. Thorndike, at about the same time that Pavlov began his experiments on conditioned reflexes. Though Thorndike and Pavlov shared a basically mechanistic approach toward their studies, Thorndike, as a psychologist, was much less interested in hypothetical brain processes than Pavlov. Influenced by the implications of Darwin's evolutionary theory, Thorndike set about to study the way in which "animal intelligence" served to adjust the animal to the world in which it must live. The cat was Thorndike's preferred subject; and to present it with the kind of problem it might have to learn to adjust to in the world outside the laboratory, he used what he called a puzzle box, shown in Figure 6–6. Before being put in the box, the cat had been given no food for some time. There was a bit of fish or liver on a dish outside the box, easily visible (and smellable) to the cat. The problem for the hungry cat is obvious enough: how to get out of the box and get the food. The box had been built so that if the cat brushed against a loop of string inside the box a latch would open, permitting the cat to step outside the box and get the food.

To measure learning in this situation, Thorndike recorded the time it took the cat, on consecutive trials, to escape from the box. This *latency* measure is simply the amount of time between the moment the cat is put inside the box and the moment it gets out. Presumably, if the cat learns to solve this problem, the time it takes to get out of the box will become less as trials progress. The

FIGURE 6–6
(Left) The original "puzzle box" used by Thorndike in his pioneering studies of animal learning.
(Right) This is one of the earliest "learning curves" in the history of the experimental study of conditioning. The time required by one of Thorndike's cats to escape from the puzzle box gradually decreased with trials, but with obvious reversals.

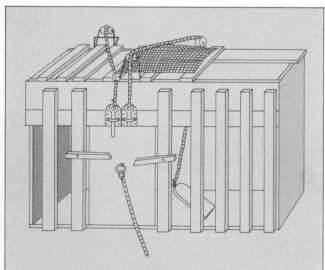

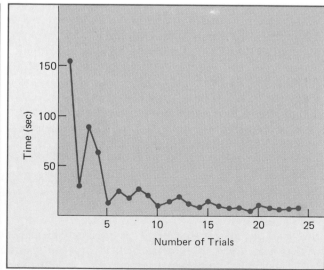

Contingency, Contiguity, and Conditioning

For many years it was believed that a CR was automatically "stamped in" whenever a US occurred close together in time with a CS. Thanks to more recent work by Rescorla (1967, 1969), it is now widely recognized that such a view is too simple.

The major point made by Rescorla was that animals were clearly sensitive to the *contingency* between CS and US. When the US is contingent upon the CS, the CS has predictive value. That is, the CS tells the animal something about how likely it is that a US is about to occur. To calculate contingency, it is necessary to *compare* the probability that the US will occur just after the CS with the probability that the US will occur at all *other* times. When the probability of US occurrence is higher immediately after CS presentation than at other times, we can speak of a positive contingency. When the probability of US occurrence is *lower* immediately after the CS than at other times we can speak of a negative contingency. Of course, it is possible for the probability of US occurrence to be equal at all times; in such a case there is no contingency between CS and US.

Traditionally, as in Pavlov's example, studies of conditioning presented the US *only* immediately after the CS. The US never occurred between trials. This meant that the US was *both* contiguous with *and* contingent upon the CS. To separate contingency from contiguity, and thus to study their separate roles, Rescorla's studies sprinkled neutral CSs and shock USs throughout lengthy experimental sessions, with contingency and contiguity experimentally varied for different groups of subjects. When CSs and USs were delivered on a random (non-contingent) basis, no conditioning to the CS occurred—even though, by chance, a number of CS–US pairings (contiguity) had occurred during the session. When positive contingency existed between CS and US, animals learned conditioned fear reactions to

the CS. For such conditioning to occur, it was not necessary that the CS always be followed by the US, nor was it necessary that no USs occur during the lengthy intervals between CSs. What *was* necessary was merely that the probability of a US be higher immediately following a CS than at other times. During the experimental session, when such was the case, the CS functioned as a predictor that the US was now somewhat more likely to occur. Similarly, if a negative contingency existed between CS and US, the CS became a *conditioned inhibitor* of fear reactions.

These results indicate that Pavlovian conditioning is a more complicated process than many had believed, but they do not answer the question of how the animal seems to "calculate contingencies." That problem has been addressed by Rescorla and Wagner (1972) and by Wagner and Rescorla (1972). Their ingenious but complicated theory shows how such "calculations" could arise as a consequence of the elementary, "stamping-in" kind of associative process already described.

---

results for a typical cat are given in Figure 6–6. The behavior of a subject, as shown in a graph, is known as a learning curve. The language in which Thorndike described this learning curve has had a profound influence on theories of conditioning and learning.

The cat took quite a lot of time to escape from the box during the early trials, but—with some reversals—it gradually required less. Finally, after a number of trials, the cat escaped from the box very promptly. The gradual nature of the learning curve caused Thorndike to talk about "trial-and-error" learning. The reason why so much time is needed during the early trials is because the cat is making or emitting, more or less at random, one response after another. The cat might run to the front of the box, then hurl itself against the side, then jump up and down, then yowl. These trial-and-error responses, however, don't work. They don't change anything much, and they certainly don't solve the problem. The *first* solution of the problem seems to occur quite by accident; eventually, in the course of prowling around the box, the cat brushes against the string, gets out of the box, and eats the food. When put in the box for the next trial, the cat does *not* promptly brush against the string. The same kinds of responses made on the first trial, and perhaps some new ones, will tend to occur. The cat will eventually hit the string, and perhaps this will happen sooner on the second trial than on the first. Probably still less time will be needed on the third trial, and less again on the fourth.

What is happening, said Thorndike, is that the response (brushing the string) that is followed by a good and satisfying effect is being gradually strengthened. The ineffective responses are not strengthened and, as a result, tend to drop out. The final outcome of this gradual process is the rapid and smooth performance of the "correct" response. The **law of effect,** as proposed by Thorndike, states that responses that are followed in time by a "good effect" tend to be repeated when the animal is next in the same situation. The gradual strengthening of an effective response was viewed by Thorndike as a blind and automatic "stamping-in" process. The animal did not "size up" the situation in a blinding flash of insight—this was shown by the slow and gradual way in which the learning curve progressed. The animal was so built that the *consequence* of a response would affect to some degree the likelihood that the response would be made again. This is obviously adaptive, and it is hard to imagine how animals that did not follow some such principle could survive in the world. However, it is important to note that the law of effect does not refer to the *logical* consequences of a response—it refers only to whatever actually does happen right after a response is made. The fact that, in Thorndike's experiment, there was a connection between brushing the string and opening the latch is an unnecessary coincidence as far as the cat's learning is concerned. The law of effect says that, if Thorndike had opened up the puzzle box every time the cat scratched its left ear, the cat would have learned to scratch its left ear in much the same way that it learned to brush against the string.

Skinner's Experiments

Thorndike's law of effect remains very much alive, although both his dated language and his primitive apparatus have been replaced. We no longer talk about "good" or "satisfying" effects. The Pavlovian term reinforcement is now applied to operant as well as classical conditioning. In operant conditioning, a **positive reinforcer** is some event (such as food) that, if presented just after a response, increases the likelihood that the response will be repeated. There are also **negative reinforcers.** They are events (such as electric shock) that, if stopped when a response is made, also increase the likelihood that the response will be repeated.

The most productive and influential analyst of operant conditioning and reinforcement—indeed, the man who gave it its name—has been B. F. Skinner. To study operant conditioning in fine detail, Skinner created the operant conditioning chamber, now universally known as the **Skinner box.** Though the size and the precise contents of a Skinner box vary for different species, the basic idea remains the same. The animal is put in a light- and sound-proofed chamber, within which not much can go on. There is always, however, within the box a device of some sort that the animal can use to make a response. For rats, for example, a small lever is usually placed on one wall of the box (see Figure 6–7). The rat can push the lever with its paws; for that matter, it can also push the lever with its nose, or in any other way it sees fit. A pigeon can peck at a small illuminated disk placed on one wall. In the box there must also be something to deliver reinforcers. In the box shown in Figure 6–7 an automatic feeder can put a small pellet of food in a cup near the lever. There are other boxes built so that a small dipper of water can be given to the rat when it responds correctly. The typical reinforcer for the pigeon is brief access to a hopper full of grain. Whatever species, response

FIGURE 6–7
The rat in a Skinner box. Normally, of course, the Skinner box is placed into a light- and soundproofed chamber. The visible equipment is used to program events (reinforcers, lights, tones, shocks) taking place inside the box.

device, or reinforcer may be used, the basic principle remains the same. When a response is made on the device, it is promptly followed by a reinforcer. The first response is often made as an accidental byproduct of exploring the box, although, as we shall see later, "shaping" procedures are often used to encourage that first response. In any event, when the first response is made it is followed right away by a reinforcer. The effect of the reinforcer is predictable: The animal tends to repeat the response, and thus to get more reinforcers. This increased likelihood of responding does not occur, of course, unless responses are reinforced.

The basic measure of learning used in operant conditioning of this kind is the *rate* of the occurrence of the response over time. The outcome of an operant conditioning study is shown on a *cumulative recorder* (Figure 6–8). The recorder is hooked up to the lever (or other device) in such a way that each time the animal responds a pen is moved one step upward on a roll of paper moving under it at a constant speed. As the animal makes more responses over time, the pen continues to move up one step with each response. Thus the animal's rate of response is reflected in the slope of the *cumulative record* drawn by the pen. When the animal is responding rapidly, the slope of the cumulative record is steep. When the animal is not responding at all, the cumulative record has no slope—the pen merely traces a horizontal line on the moving paper. Figure 6–9 is the cumulative record of a rat placed in a Skinner box and rewarded with a food pellet each time it responded.

Shaping

We have already referred to the procedure of **shaping.** This technique was known to, and widely practiced by, animal trainers long before Skinner studied it. To illustrate shaping, imagine how you would train a dog to roll over. The basic principle of operant conditioning tells you that, if you reward a hungry dog with food every time it rolls over, it should learn to roll over. The

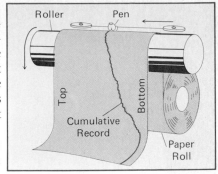

FIGURE 6–8
The working parts of a cumulative recorder, keeping track of the responses made by an animal in a Skinner box.

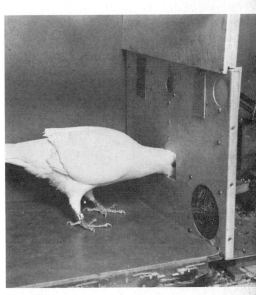

A pigeon in a Skinner box, consuming its reinforcer (grain).

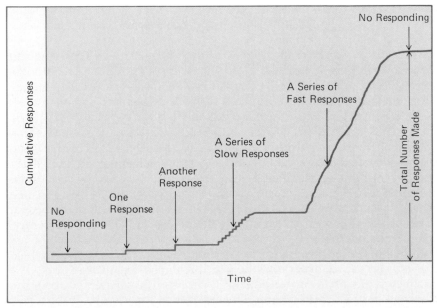

FIGURE 6–9
The cumulative record made by a rat reinforced with a small food pellet for each lever press made in a Skinner box.

The technique of shaping was used by animal trainers long before psychologists studied it. Whoever trained this tiger could not afford to wait until it spontaneously began balancing so adroitly. This balancing act was achieved instead through gradual reinforcement of successive approximations.

problem is that, even though you are armed and ready with food as a reinforcer, the dog is not very likely to roll over out of the blue. And if the desired behavior does not occur, there will be no opportunity to reinforce it. This, it should be noted, is a basic difference between Pavlovian and operant conditioning. There is a real sense in which you can force a dog to salivate and thus condition the dog to salivate to a chosen CS—you simply put food powder in its mouth to cause salivation. To get a dog to roll over—and to condition rolling over by reinforcing the response—is much more complicated.

The trick is to reinforce **successive approximations** of the desired behavior (sitting down, lying down, lying on its side, and, finally, rolling over). When the dog sits, perhaps helped along by a shove in that direction, the trainer, early in the game, reinforces sitting. This increases the likelihood that the dog will sit. The next approximation is lying down. Then, when the dog has made progress, the required response is made tougher. To get reinforcement the dog must now lie on its side. The art of shaping means gradually extending the required response, sometimes dropping back and reinforcing earlier, simpler responses, until at length the judicious dispensing of reinforcers has shaped the animal's behavior all the way along to the final goal. The amazing feats of circus animals have been built up by gradual reinforcement of successive approximations. This is a clear and powerful demonstration of operant conditioning acting to modify (shape) responses.

Partial Reinforcement and Reinforcement Schedules

So far our examples of operant conditioning have involved *continuous reinforcement.* That is, each time the response occurs, it is reinforced. That, however, is by no means necessary. The experimenter can choose to reinforce a given response only some of the time. There is a very predictable outcome to such a *partial reinforcement* procedure: When a response is acquired through partial reinforcement, and extinction is then undertaken (when the response is no longer reinforced), the response persists much more strongly than it would have if it had been reinforced every time it occurred. (This partial reinforcement effect has also been observed in classical conditioning, though it has more often been studied in operant conditioning.)

The effect of partial reinforcement in producing extreme **resistance to extinction** is not as strange as it might seem at first. When, during acquisition, the response is reinforced only part of the time, the animal is being trained to continue responding even though many responses are not reinforced. Persistence "pays off," and eventually the response will be reinforced (Amsel, 1967). Thus, when extinction training begins, the conditions are not dramatically changed from those prevailing during acquisition. Think of a vending machine that delivers candy bars for coins 50 percent of the time. When you are used to the sporadic payoffs of such a machine (many seem to be located in public places), you are not likely to notice right away if the machine breaks down entirely. There is a good likelihood that you will put in several coins—show resistance to extinction—before concluding that the response is no longer rewarded. That will not happen if, in the past, the machine has always delivered each time you put in a coin; in such a case, once the machine stops paying off, you will probably quickly stop putting in coins.

The partial-reinforcement effect is both powerful and widespread, but there are many practical training situations in which it seems to be totally

If in the past a vending machine has always delivered each time you put in a coin, once the machine stops paying off, one of your reactions will probably be to quickly stop putting in coins.

ignored. For example, suppose that you wish to train a child to perform a socially desirable behavior. While common sense suggests that this could best be done by rewarding the behavior each time it occurs, the partial reinforcement effect suggests otherwise. We usually want to "build-in" desirable behaviors in our children; the behavior should persist even when it is no longer followed by the direct rewards that seem right for children. To build in such persistence and resistance to extinction, partial reinforcement seems a better bet than continuous reinforcement.

The attempt to break an undesirable habit very often runs afoul of the partial reinforcement effect. Thus, imagine a little girl who cries each night when put to bed. The parents come to realize that they have unknowingly reinforced this behavior by picking up and comforting her. To break her now bothersome habit, her parents adopt a psychologically sound principle: The habit will no longer be reinforced. When she cries on future nights, they will no longer comfort her. This withholding of reinforcement should gradually eliminate the habit. The difficulty is that after a few nights of listening to the child cry herself to sleep, her parents relent and—just this once—pick her up and comfort her. The child has now experienced partial reinforcement of her bed-time crying. The habit will now be harder than ever to extinguish.

There are many different arrangements between responses and the occasional use of reinforcement, all of which are partial reinforcement procedures. The relation set up between a response and its reinforcer is called a **schedule of reinforcement.** The outcomes of many different reinforcement schedules have been described in detail by Ferster and Skinner (1957). The most interesting fact is that the same schedule has very much the same effect, no matter what response, what reinforcer, and what species are involved. The cumulative record produced by a pigeon pecking a key for grain under a certain kind of schedule cannot be distinguished from the cumulative record produced by a person pulling a plunger for cigarette rewards under the same schedule.

The wide variety of different reinforcement schedules can be conveniently broken down along two different dimensions. First, reinforcement can de-

FIGURE 6–10

The typical outcome of four partial reinforcement schedules, in the form of cumulative records. Slash mark indicates delivery of a reinforcement. The pause after each reinforcement is very characteristic of fixed-ratio schedules, while the "scalloped" shape of the record is typical of fixed-interval schedules.

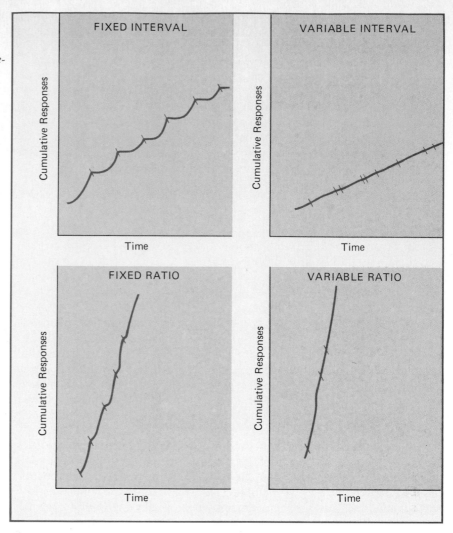

pend upon either the passage of a certain amount of *time* since the last reinforcement, or upon the animal's having performed a certain *number of responses* since the last reinforcement. Second, the amount of time (or number of responses) required since the last reinforcement can be either *fixed* or *variable.* This simplified classification gives rise to four basic reinforcement schedules. The outcomes of the four basic schedules are indicated in the cumulative records shown in Figure 6–10. The results are what you might expect.

With a **fixed-interval schedule,** the rule is that a certain amount of time (say, three minutes) must pass between two reinforcements. Thus, when a response has been rewarded, nothing the animal does during the next three minutes can produce another reward. The first response to be made *after* the passage of three minutes is the next one to be reinforced. The animal's behavior, after some experience with this schedule, seems quite sensible. There is no responding for some time after receipt of a reinforcer. Then, as the three minute mark begins to approach, the animal starts to respond at a growing rate until it receives its reinforcer. The cycle then begins again. The animal is obviously engaging in a form of timing behavior, though its timing is not entirely accurate. In somewhat the same way, students often stop studying right after a test and then gradually start up again as the date of the next test approaches.

The results produced by a **variable-interval schedule** are very different. With a three-minute variable-interval schedule, the *average* time between two reinforcers is three minutes, but the actual times between pairs of reinforcers differ widely and unpredictably. Thus, very occasionally, two reinforcers may be delivered only a few seconds apart; on other occasions, ten minutes may pass before the next reinforcer is made available. There is no way for the animal to know whether its *next* reinforcer will be made available in a matter of seconds, or only after many minutes. The result is a very steady rate of response over time: The cumulative record closely approximates a straight line with moderate slope. This means that the animal will receive almost all the reinforcers made available to it by the schedule, almost as soon as they are made available. (The reinforcers are "set up" by an automatic timing device and then released by the next response to occur.) Teachers could, for example, discourage the stop-start study pattern described earlier by giving unannounced spot quizzes. Since students would not know when they were to be tested, they wouldn't be as likely to stop studying for any great length of time.

In a **fixed-ratio schedule,** a reinforced response must be followed by a definite number of responses (say, 50) before the next reinforcement occurs. The faster the 50 responses are made, the sooner the animal receives its next reward. The animal can increase the frequency and thus the amount of reward by working at a rapid rate. The animal subjected to a fixed-ratio schedule works hard; it makes a great many responses very rapidly and thus earns many reinforcers. There is often a pause or "break" right after a reinforcer has been received, but the animal soon sets to work again with a vengeance.

Probably the most rapid rates of response, however, are produced by a **variable-ratio schedule.** With such a schedule, the number of responses required for the next reinforcement varies unpredictably. There may be one or two occasions when the next response is reinforced, while on other occasions several hundreds, or even thousands, of responses may be required. With this kind of schedule, the animal can again get the most rewards by working rapidly, and it does so. When the animal has had some experience with variable-ratio reinforcement, it can be induced to make literally thousands of responses between reinforcers. Chronic gamblers, who are exposed to a variable-ratio reinforcement schedule, literally cannot quit. The occasional and unpredictable reinforcement is—to the delight and profit of the casinos—enough to keep the gambler going through very long stretches without any reinforcement.

Factory work is normally reinforced on a fixed-interval schedule, with weekly paychecks depending on the time spent at work. Piecework tries to increase workers' output by relating reinforcement to the amount of work, rather than to time.

Variables That Affect Operant Conditioning

Many phenomena observed in operant conditioning seem very similar to those already noted in Pavlovian conditioning. Thus, at the simplest level, acquisition, extinction, and spontaneous recovery occur in the same way; acquisition depends on reinforcing a response, and extinction occurs when reinforcement is withheld. Further, generalization and discrimination are

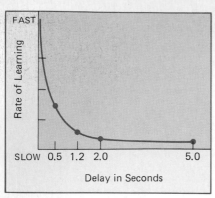

FIGURE 6–11

A *delay-of-reward gradient observed in operant conditioning in rats. Note that even a very small delay between responding and the subsequent reinforcement can drastically slow down the rate of learning.* (After Grice, 1948)

easily shown in operant conditioning studies. When, for example, a pigeon has been reinforced for pecking at a key illuminated by light of a given wavelength, it will also peck—but at lower rates—at lights of different wavelengths. There is no great trick to teaching the pigeon to discriminate between two different wavelengths—you simply reinforce its responses to one wavelength, while not reinforcing responses to the other wavelength.

The acquisition of operant conditioning is affected, in an obvious way, by the magnitude of reinforcement—just as Pavlovian conditioning is a function of the strength of the US. There is also a critical time interval that profoundly affects operant conditioning. To maximize operant conditioning, the reinforcer must be delivered just after the response occurs. The time (if any) between a response and the subsequent reinforcement is referred to as the *delay of reinforcement*. With animals, at least, even quite short delays of reinforcement—on the order of 5 or 10 seconds—are often enough to prevent operant conditioning from taking place at all; and any delay, no matter how short, slows down the rate of acquisition (see Figure 6–11). Though delay of reinforcement is also an important variable in human studies, it is less significant than with lower animals. Language and symbolic thought make it possible for humans to bridge very long time spans between responses and their reinforcement.

Reward and Punishment

The facts of operant conditioning indicate that whether or not a response will be repeated depends on events that follow it. Most studies of operant conditioning have examined the effects of positive reinforcers, or rewards. There are also studies in which a response has the effect of stopping or removing a negative reinforcer. Thus, if a rat is dropped onto an electrified grid floor and can stop the shock by pressing a lever, it will learn to do so. With successive trials the rat will press the lever more and more rapidly. The termination of shock is reinforcing in much the same way that the presentation of food or water is.

In everyday speech, however, the opposite of reward is **punishment.** We speak of punishment when we follow a response by presenting a negative reinforcer such as shock. Perhaps it seems obvious that the effect of punishment should be the exact opposite to that of reward. Where reward "stamps in" preceding responses, punishment might be expected to stamp them out. The effect of punishment, however, has been a matter of great dispute, in part because of the views of B. F. Skinner.

The effect of punishing a formerly rewarded response, Skinner argued, was to *suppress* performance of the response temporarily. The punishment would not permanently eliminate the animal's tendency to make the response. When punishment ended, the animal would once again perform the forbidden response. The effective way to eliminate an unwanted response is to make sure that it is no longer positively reinforced (to extinguish it)—or to reinforce positively those responses that are incompatible with it. Punishment is a notoriously ineffective way of changing our behavior, said Skinner—look at the results of our penal system! Perhaps the reason why we continue to use ineffective punishment procedures is because the delivery of punishment is positively reinforcing to those who dish it out!

Though Skinner's moral arguments against the use of punishment may be justified, there is no doubt that punishment, if strong enough, does "work."

That is, in experiments, previously reinforced responses that are immediately followed by punishment no longer occur; and, as is the case with reward, a delay between a response and its punishment weakens the effect considerably. The "suppression" of a punished response can, for all practical purposes, be made permanent. Thus, in practice, despite Skinner's talk about "temporary suppression," intense punishment can eliminate an unwanted response at least as effectively as ordinary extinction can. There are nevertheless some serious drawbacks to the use of punishment. Punishment affects much more than the particular response that it follows; that is, the punished animal seems *generally* suppressed and inhibited. The punished animal becomes generally fearful of the situation in which punishment occurs and will tend to avoid whomever (or whatever) is handing out punishment. Further, quite unlike reward, punishment does not tell the punished individual what to do; it merely says what *not* to do, without providing satisfactory alternatives. Therefore, when using punishment, one way to make it more effective is to give the person (or animal) rewarded alternatives to the undesired, to-be-punished response.

Secondary Reinforcement

The phenomenon of **secondary reinforcement** in operant conditioning is very similar to Pavlovian higher-order conditioning. The majority of reinforcers that have been used in experimental studies have (like Pavlovian USs) obvious biological bases. We can, however, transform a previously neutral stimulus into a reasonably effective reinforcer of operant responses. The sound of a buzzer is not normally reinforcing to a rat. When the only consequence of pressing a Skinner box lever is the sound of a buzzer, very little lever-pressing occurs. The results are quite different if, before being placed in the Skinner box, the animal is exposed to a number of paired presentations of the buzzer and food. The animal, during these buzzer-food pairings, does not need to perform any response to get the food. Then, if lever-pressing produces the buzzer, the animal will make a fair number of presses in the Skinner box—even though the presses are *not* followed by food or by any other primary reinforcer. The buzzer has become—as a result of its pairing with a primary reinforcer, food—a *secondary reinforcer*. The secondary reinforcer can be used in operant conditioning in the same way as a primary reinforcer, but its capacity to reinforce operant responses is a product of learning. The principle involved in establishing a secondary reinforcer is very similar to Pavlovian conditioning: Present the stimulus close together in time with a primary reinforcer.

Once established, the power of a secondary reinforcer seems to be quite general. Thus, a buzzer previously paired with food will reinforce lever presses made when the animal is no longer hungry, but merely thirsty (Estes, 1949). In most studies, however, the effectiveness of a secondary reinforcer is rather short-lived. The secondary reinforcer will indeed work for a while, but the animal will not continue to perform indefinitely for secondary reinforcement alone. To extend the "useful life" of a secondary reinforcer, one obvious technique is to use partial reinforcement procedures. Thus, when the buzzer-food association is being established, the buzzer is only sometimes followed by food. Then, in the Skinner box, lever-pressing is only sometimes followed by the buzzer. This partial-reinforcement procedure can result in a rat's making many thousands of lever presses with no reward other than

Eric Heiden's five gold medals, which he won at the 1980 Winter Olympics, are a good example of a secondary reinforcer.

secondary reinforcement (Zimmerman, 1957). There have been many learning theorists who, like Pavlov, have thought that much human behavior might be understood as the result of a long chain of secondary reinforcements. Thus you might think of money as a once neutral stimulus that, in your past, has been paired with a number of different primary reinforcers. The effectiveness of money as a reinforcer of human behavior is obvious, and it seems clear that people may continue to work for money in and of itself, and no longer only to satisfy needs. The smiling approval of fellow humans might also be thought of as a secondary reinforcer. When we are growing up, smiling human faces (often parental) are paired with the delivery of basic primary reinforcers.

Avoidance Learning

This rather special form of operant conditioning has been at the center of a number of interesting disagreements among theorists of animal learning. In a procedure for **avoidance learning,** the animal is presented with a warning signal (CS) that occurs a few seconds before delivery of a noxious US, often an electric shock. The animal, however, can avoid the shock by performing some specified response to the CS, *before* the shock is scheduled to occur. Thus, if it performs the required response quickly enough, the animal can avoid the shocks entirely. It can be shown that animals can learn such avoidance responses with great efficiency. Further, once they are learned, they can persist for thousands of trials during which the animal continues to avoid all shock (Solomon, Kamin, & Wynne, 1953).

What reinforces avoidance responding? For a *cognitive* theory of learning, such as those described in the final section of this chapter, avoidance learning poses no special problems. The pairing of the warning signal with shock has taught the animal to expect shock when the signal occurs. When shock is expected, the animal sensibly performs the response required in order to avoid shock. Within the more mechanistic framework of operant and Pavlovian conditioning theories, one cannot talk about animals "expecting" shocks or about animals acting "purposefully" to avoid some future event. What, therefore, is in the here-and-now that can possibly be "stamping in" the avoidance response?

The typical avoidance-learning experiment has been performed in such a way that, when the avoidance response is made, not only does the animal cause shock to be omitted on that trial; the response is also followed by the immediate termination of the warning signal itself. This, as reflection should suggest, might very well be a reinforcing event. The warning signal is at first a neutral stimulus; but, once it has been paired a few times with shock, it should become a secondary negative reinforcer. That is, any response that is followed by stopping the warning signal is in theory being reinforced. The "avoidance" respose might be learned not because it serves to avoid a threatened shock, but because it is followed by the prompt turning off of the warning signal! (Note that this view implies that avoidance learning involves a mixture of both Pavlovian and operant conditioning.)

These speculations, if correct, suggest that an animal should learn to perform a response that has no effect at all on whether the shock occurs but that does serve to terminate the warning signal preceding shock. This has been shown to be the case. When an animal's response is followed by termination of a warning buzzer—and is nevertheless followed on each trial by an unavoidable shock—the response is acquired (Kamin, 1956). When the response is followed by a slightly *delayed* termination of the buzzer, it is less

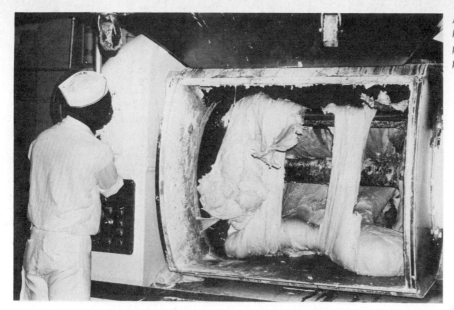

A bakery employee tending a dough-kneading machine. Dr. Judy Komaki used photos such as this to show bakery workers potentially hazardous work procedures.

effectively learned than when termination promptly follows the response. When termination of the buzzer is delayed as little as five seconds following the response, rats fail to learn an avoidance response at all. This failure to learn occurs even when, on trials when the response is made, shock is entirely avoided. Thus, delayed termination of the warning signal in an avoidance-learning experiment acts like any other delay-of-reward in operant conditioning (Kamin, 1957; see Figure 6–11). These and similar results suggest that much animal learning with all the earmarks of "foresight" may be understood more simply in terms of the "blind" and mechanical processes of conditioning. There are, however, other studies which show that even when no warning signal precedes the delivery of regularly scheduled shocks, rats can learn to make a response that postpones the occurrence of shock (Sidman, 1953).

Behavior Modification

Though the fine details of operant conditioning can be studied most effectively with animal subjects, there is every reason to suppose that the same processes also apply in human learning. To show the power of operant conditioning techniques in humans, you might try to repeat for yourself the verbal conditioning procedure described in the accompanying box. The box also describes a fascinating case study of the use of operant conditioning procedures in a mental hospital. This kind of practical application of operant conditioning ideas is the basis of a growing technology of **behavior modification.** (When such techniques are applied to changing abnormal behavior, the term **behavior therapy** is used; see Chapter 17.)

The systematic application of ideas derived from the study of operant conditioning is nicely illustrated by the work of Komaki, Barwick, and Scott (1978). They designed a program to reduce the number of accidents among workers in a large bakery. The first step was for the investigators to identify, by close observation of the work process, safe and unsafe work practices.

APPLICATION □
The Use of Operant Conditioning Techniques

With just a little planning, and without any apparatus at all, it should be possible for you to demonstrate some of the basic phenomena of operant conditioning—while apparently engaging in casual conversation with a friend. The following experiment was reported by Verplanck (1955), and can easily be repeated by anyone.

The basic rule of operant conditioning, of course, is to follow a particular response with the delivery of a reinforcer. The response selected for reinforcement was any statement of opinion made in the course of conversation. That is, whenever the subject uttered a sentence beginning with "It seems to me" or "I think" or "I believe," the experimenter reinforced the statement. The reinforcer was verbal agreement, perhaps given with a nod of smiling approval. Thus, whenever the subject expressed an opinion, the experimenter responded with some such remark as "That's true," or "I agree," or "How right you are!" The delivery of such verbal reinforcement had a marked effect on the subject's behavior. There was a clear increase in the frequency with which the subject made statements of opinion. To clinch matters, the experimenter went on to demonstrate that extinction could be brought about simply by withholding further reinforcement. When this happened, the statements of opinion decreased markedly.

Two notes of caution must be sounded for readers who wish to repeat this experiment. First, you may have to wait some time before your subject utters a first statement of opinion (recall that in operant conditioning a response must occur before it can be reinforced). Second, it is possible that your subject may "catch on" to what you are doing.

The following case study, taken from Ayllon (1963), illustrates an ingenious and systematic use of basic operant conditioning concepts in a mental hospital setting. The patient was a schizophrenic woman who, among other symptoms, wore enormous amounts of clothing—many sweaters, shawls, dresses, underclothes, and even sheets and towels wrapped around her body. The total weight of her clothing was 25 pounds.

To get the patient to give up this odd symptom, Ayllon made effective use of shaping technique, with food as a reinforcer. To get into the hospital dining room, the patient had to step on a scale, and to weigh less than a target weight selected by the experimenter. Thus, at first, the patient had to reduce the weight of her clothing to 23 (rather than 25) pounds. When this limit was met, a stricter limit was used, and so on. Though the patient missed a few meals during this shaping process, in a few months she was wearing only 3 pounds of clothing. The systematic use of food as a reinforcer had gradually eliminated a bizarre psychiatric symptom.

The conditioning treatment, of course, in no way "cured" the patient of her schizophrenia. However, as Ayllon pointed out, once the odd symptom was eliminated, other patients in the hospital were more likely to talk to and interact with the woman. Her family, in fact, took her home for a visit for the first time in 9 years, pointing out that the patient no longer looked like a "circus freak."

Then such identified practices were photographed and the resulting slides were shown to the workers. Next, for a period, workers were reinforced with positive feedback for performing the safe practices. The feedback included a posted "thermometer" graph, displaying the increasing number of safe practices by the group, as well as verbal approval given to individuals by supervisors for safe practices. With such positive feedback, the proportion of safely performed operations increased from 74 to 98 percent. Then, experimentally, the feedback reinforcement was withheld. The extinction procedure caused the proportion of safe operations to drop back down to 72 percent. The bakery's management decided to adopt the reinforcement procedure permanently. The result was a significant decline in the number of accidents and injuries. The bakery's safety rating changed from poor to excellent.

The ethical problems and some of the philosophical considerations involved in controlling people's behavior through the use of reinforcement have been discussed at length by Skinner, in such works as *Beyond Freedom and Dignity.* Perhaps the major point made by Skinner is that long before we could talk about it very intelligibly, we were already controlling one another's behavior by giving and withholding reinforcement. The rational use of reinforcement in designing human cultures and societies may result in increased efficiency, but it introduces nothing fundamentally new.

PAVLOVIAN AND OPERANT CONDITIONING COMPARED

We have now looked in some detail at two different forms of conditioning. There are some obvious differences between them, but there are also some important similarities. We shall now, in addition to comparing one form of conditioning with the other, try to understand how, in practice, the two conditioning processes relate to one another. We shall also try to see whether, armed with no other concepts than those provided by the study of conditioning, we can account adequately for *all* animal learning.

The *differences* between Pavlovian and operant conditioning seem fairly obvious. The Pavlovian kind of experiment is performed on a basically passive animal, generally kept under rather severe restraints. The sequence of CS followed by US is continually repeated, and the animal begins to make a reflexlike response to the CS. In operant conditioning, on the other hand, the animal quite literally operates actively on its environment. The animal must itself push the lever, or peck the key, before its response can be followed by reinforcement. Without activity on the animal's part—often motivated by a strong drive state such as hunger—there could be no operant conditioning. The basic principle of shaping, moreover, allows for progressive (and sometimes quite startling) changes in the response itself. The control over a fixed response is not merely "switched" from one stimulus to another; the response itself changes.

With all these apparent differences in mind, it is also the case that both kinds of conditioning clearly involve very basic processes of association. The (operant) association between a response and a subsequent reinforcing stimulus does not seem fundamentally different in kind from the (Pavlovian) association between a conditioned and an unconditioned stimulus. The kind of "stamping-in" process envisioned by both Pavlov and Thorndike could easily include both of these (as well as other) associations. In short, there may be a single basic associative learning process that underlies both types of conditioning. This seems even more likely when one recognizes that, in fact, it is extraordinarily difficult to design an experimental situation in which one or the other kind of conditioning takes place in "pure" form. The reinforcers used in studies of operant conditioning are typically Pavlovian USs as well, and vice-versa.

There have been some attempts to argue that the two types of conditioning may apply to two different types of **responses.** Thus, the suggestion has often been made that Pavlovian conditioning might only affect responses controlled by the autonomic nervous sytem, while operant conditioning might apply only to responses controlled by the skeletal nervous system. The same basic distinction has been made more loosely, by contrasting "involuntary" with "voluntary" responses.

Theories of learning aside, it is a matter of considerable practical importance to discover whether *operant* reinforcement can condition responses controlled by the autonomic nervous system. Consider the rate at which the heart beats. This is controlled by the autonomic nervous system. There are people with medical conditions that require them to develop a slower heart

Biofeedback and the Learned Control of Visceral Responses

Working with paralyzed hospital patients, Miller and Brucker (1979) have reported some fascinating results concerned with the voluntary control of human blood pressure. They worked first with a man whose spinal cord had been severed by a gunshot wound and who, although he had strong arms and shoulders, had been unable to walk with crutches and braces. The man's problem, a consequence of his injury, was severe postural hypotension. That is, whenever he was placed in an upright position, his blood pressure fell so low that he promptly fainted. To combat the hy-

potension, an apparatus was hooked up to the patient in such a way that whenever his systolic pressure increased slightly, an audible tone was produced. This enabled the patient to learn, with practice, to produce very large increases in his blood pressure. That in turn made it possible for him, when placed upright, to boost his blood pressure enough so that he did not faint. The remarkable results are illustrated in the figure, which shows the patient's blood pressure in the first few minutes after being placed in a standing position. When he did not try to control his blood pressure, it fell to a dangerously low level within two minutes; but by producing a voluntary increase just before standing, he was able to maintain normal pressure. This enabled him to learn to walk with crutches and braces, and at last report he had been doing so

for more than three years.

Biofeedback can be defined as a procedure that gives subjects information about their own internal processes, allowing them to monitor and modify a number of normally involuntary responses. To assure themselves that the spectacular result with their first paralyzed patient was not a fluke or an artifact, Miller and Brucker then worked with 10 additional patients. All were paralyzed by severe spinal injuries. During practice sessions *without* feedback, none of the patients could learn to raise their blood pressure. However, when feedback was provided, 9 of 10 patients learned to produce large increases within 25 practice sessions. Moreover, the changes in pressure observed over the course of the 25 sessions produced a typical, Thorndike-like learning curve.

These results suggest that bio-

rate. What, if anything, can we do to teach such people to slow down their heart rates?

The animal research of Miller and DiCara (1967) was directed toward problems of this sort. The experiments are of necessity quite complex. For example, one must rule out reflexive changes of heart rate brought about by skeletal responses rather than by operant reinforcement. Thus, a man told that he would receive a large reward for speeding up his heart rate could easily do so; all he needs to do is run up a few flights of stairs. This kind of reflexive change in heart rate is obviously not a direct effect of an operant reinforcer on heart action itself. To rule out this kind of response, the animals' muscles were paralyzed by a drug, which in turn made artificial respiration necessary. There are not many operant reinforcements that can be given to paralyzed and artificially respirated subjects, but stimulation of a "pleasure center" in the brain, through a depth electrode, is one (see Chapter 2). The procedure adopted for one group of animals was to provide a reinforcing brain stimulation whenever a spontaneous small increase in heart rate occurred. With another group of animals, small *decreases* in heart rate were promptly followed by the same brain stimulation. This kind of shaping procedure was effective; those animals rewarded for increased heart rates sped up their heart rates quite a lot during a session, while those animals reinforced for decreased heart rates did the opposite.

These and other impressive results were at one time routinely reported from Miller's laboratory (Miller, 1969). Theoretically, the data showed that autonomic nervous system responses, like all others, are influenced by operant reinforcers that follow them in time. Practically, the results held out considerable promise for the development of behavioral medicine in humans. There is in principle no reason why conditioning techniques cannot be

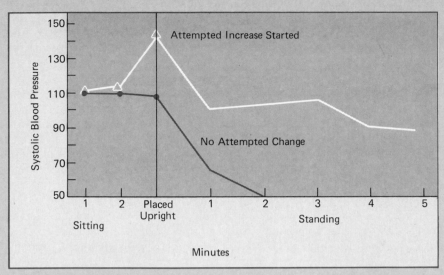

(Adapted from Miller & Brucker, 1979)

controlled by the autonomic nervous system can indeed be operantly conditioned. There seems little likelihood that the Miller and Brucker results are based on reflexive consequences of voluntary movements. First, the patients were almost totally paralyzed. Second, the patients learned a very *specific* response of increasing blood pressure. Though reflexive responses normally involve a simultaneous increase of both blood pressure and heart rate, the patients learned to increase blood pressure *without* increasing heart rate. Finally, a number of control studies have indicated that changes in breathing, and the few muscular contractions of which the patients were capable, did not produce the large blood-pressure changes that had been learned through biofeedback training.

feedback techniques based upon operant shaping and reinforcement principles have great promise as therapeutic procedures. They also suggest that, at least in humans, some visceral responses normally

used—together with drugs and surgery—to affect the functioning of the internal organs. The first flush of enthusiasm, however, may have been excessive. The impressive early successes first reported by Miller and DiCara have not been routinely repeated (Miller & Dworkin, 1974; Miller, 1978; Roberts, 1979). There is, on the other hand, an accumulating number of successful—and sometimes spectacular—therapeutic results reported by practitioners of behavioral medicine (see Highlight on biofeedback).

When the basic phenomena of Pavlovian and operant conditioning were being discovered, there was a tendency for many workers in the field to believe that—whether or not they were basically one process—the two forms of conditioning would between them provide an entirely adequate account of at least animal learning. Perhaps, it was even suggested, with the right modifications to account for the conditioning of language, even all of human learning could be understood in this way. That early enthusiasm has now faded. There is no question but that conditioning plays an important part in the learning of animals, and in humans. There are more *cognitive* learning processes, however, that not only play the major role in human learning but also seem quite evident in animal experimentation. We shall, in the next section of this chapter, describe some studies of "cognitive" learning in animals. For the moment, we can point out that a main way conditioning applies in humans may be precisely in that area where cognition and reason seem so ineffective—in the conditioning of emotional and of normally involuntary responses.

The pioneers who began the systematic study of animal learning often assumed that the general laws of learning would be very much the same in all animal species. Thus, it made no real difference if one studied rats, pigeons, goldfish, or flatworms. The effects of delay of reinforcement, or of

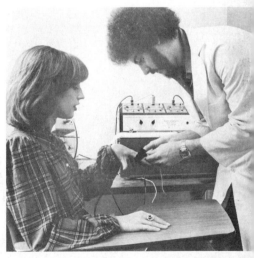

Experiments have shown that when subjects are given feedback of their present bodily states in the form of audible tones, moving graphs, or dials, they can in turn learn to control such bodily reactions as brain wave pattern, blood pressure, and muscle tension. The biofeedback technique has been successfully applied as an adjunct to treatment for chronic headaches.

partial reinforcement, might equally well be studied in any of these species. Further, the particular stimuli chosen for use in an experiment were not thought to matter; that is, any neutral CS might be paired with any US, and the course of conditioning would be much the same. In recent years these views have changed considerably, in large measure due to the remarkable work on **bait shyness** reportd by Garcia and his associates (Garcia & Koelling, 1966; Garcia, McGowan, & Green, 1972). The bait-shyness phenomenon is clearly demonstrated in the behavior of the rat. When a rat eats poisoned food, it will not—assuming it survives—eat the poisoned bait a second time. This learning to avoid a normally favored food takes place in only one trial. This happens even though the illness produced by poison may not occur until several hours after the rat has eaten the poisoned food. How does the rat know that the food—eaten long ago—caused its illness?

It must be, Garcia has argued, that evolution has given the rat a tendency to associate internal bodily states, such as illness, with the smell and taste of food—even when long time periods pass between eating and the subsequent illness. This kind of learning would obviously be adaptive in the rat's natural environment. The rat, needless to say, will not learn to associate the sound of a buzzer with an illness that occurs six hours later; but it *will* associate a particular food with an illness occurring hours later.

The tendency for some unconditioned stimuli to be preferentially associated with particular conditioned stimuli is not unique to bait shyness, or to the rat. For example Foree and LoLordo (1973) exposed pigeons to a compound stimulus consisting of both a light and a tone. When the compound stimulus was paired with a *food* US, the pigeons learned to associate the light, but not the tone, with the US. However, when the same compound stimulus was paired with *shock,* the pigeons learned to associate the tone much more than the light with shock. Note that neither the light nor the tone is the "stronger" CS; the association depends upon the particular US that is being presented.

Results of this kind indicate that individual species may be specially "prepared" to form associations between particular sets of stimuli (see Chapter 11). This in turn limits our ability to generalize to other species "laws" based on laboratory studies of individual species. These and similar results also suggest that, by studying animals in the laboratory rather than in their natural habitats, we are likely to overlook some special characteristics of individual species. That in no way denies, however, the fact that the basic findings discussed in this chapter have been observed repeatedly across a wide range of species. The bait-shyness phenomenon itself can be viewed as a remarkable modification of the normal effects of the time between CS and US, rather than as an utterly new phenomenon. In experimental studies of bait shyness, it is clearly the case that the longer the interval between eating the food and the following illness, the less the tendency to avoid the distinctive food. This seems quite in accord with basic Pavlovian principles.

COGNITIVE LEARNING IN ANIMALS

Though most studies of animal learning have been performed in a conditioning framework, critics have been quick to point out that—real though the phenomena of conditioning may be—such studies do not tap the more "mental" or "cognitive" forms of learning. The most vigorous criticism of early conditioning studies came from the Gestalt psychologists (see Chapter 4). They argued that the learning observed by Pavlov and by Thorndike seemed blind, robot-like, and automatic exactly because the experimental situations into which the animals had been placed did not allow for truly intelligent or insightful behavior. There is not much chance for a beast to display its cleverness when it is caged in a virtually empty Skinner box or locked into a conditioning stock. To study **insight**—a form of learning and problem solving that depends on complex cognitive activity—it is necessary to observe animals in a freer experimental situation. The experimenter must take pains to make available all the various elements that, when appropriately related to one another by the animal, yield an insightful solution.

Insight Learning

The classical studies of **insight learning** were reported in 1925 by Wolfgang Köhler. The subjects of his studies were chimpanzees. That is not surprising: The cognitive processes involved in insightful learning are characteristic of higher animals with a well-developed cortex. The chicken or the snail, though easily conditioned, would not be a good bet for experiments on insight.

The kind of procedure used by Köhler can best be seen in the two-stick problem. The chimp is in its cage, and easily visible on the floor outside the cage is a tempting banana. There is a short stick on the floor of the cage, and a longer stick on the floor just outside the cage. When presented with this problem the chimp is most likely, first of all, to reach between the cage bars in a futile effort to obtain the banana. When this fails, the chimp may fly into a temper tantrum. When calm returns, the eye of the chimp may suddenly fall on the stick inside its cage. Then, very quickly, the chimp picks up the short stick, runs to the front of the cage, and tries to rake the banana in with the stick. The stick, however, is not long enough. This failure may produce a *real* temper tantrum. To shorten the story, a bright chimp will eventually notice the long stick just outside the cage. Then, quick as a flash—we talk of the "flash of insight"—the chimp will rake in the long stick with the short stick, and immediately use the long stick to rake in the banana. (The same kind of insightful solutions occurred when the banana was suspended from the cage ceiling, out of reach, and three boxes were scattered about the cage floor. The chimps, after sizing up the situation, would stack the three boxes into a kind of tower, climb the tower, and obtain the banana.)

These problem solutions, in Köhler's view, depended on the chimp's ability to restructure cognitive elements into new and purposeful wholes. The chimp clearly seems to be thinking, much as you and I do. The insight, Köhler stressed, was not the result of blind, Thorndikeian trial-and-error, random responses. When the chimp got the point, the insight came very suddenly— and irreversibly. When an animal (or person) learns something insightfully, rather than by rote (repetitive drill), it is less likely to forget the solution, Köhler maintained. There is a basically arbitrary nature to the associations which, in conditioning studies, experimenters impress upon their subjects. With insight studies, the elements the animal is allowed to relate to one another form a meaningful whole and a sensible cognitive structure.

Learning Sets

The gap between gradual conditioning and sudden insight may not be quite as fundamental as Köhler maintained. Though Köhler did not stress the fact, the chimps with which he worked had lived free in the wild before serving as experimental subjects. They doubtless had had previous experience in

Conditioning, Attention, and Surprise

The kinds of data that have encouraged cognitive analyses of conditioning are well illustrated by the phenomena of **blocking** (Kamin, 1968). When the CS in a conditioning study is made up of two different stimuli (say, a light and a noise presented at the same time), rats normally condition to each of the two stimuli. When tested alone, the light and the noise will each elicit a conditioned response. That seems obvious enough—each of the stimuli has been paired close together in time with the US (say, a shock). The results are very different, however, if the animal is first conditioned to either the light alone paired with the US or the noise alone paired with the US. Then, despite continued reinforcement of the compound with the US, the animal fails to condition to the new, added CS element. The previous conditioning of Stimulus A in some way *blocks* conditioning to Stimulus B when the AB compound is later reinforced.

Possibly the blocking of conditioning occurs because the previously conditioned element (Stimulus A) engages so much of the animal's attention that it simply does not notice the newly added Stimulus B and thus fails to condition to it. There are many indications, however, that this is not the case. Thus, if, when Stimulus B is first added on to the previously conditioned Stimulus A, reinforcement is withheld, the animal rapidly learns that Stimulus B is a conditioned inhibitor, a signal of nonreinforcement. To have learned this, the animal must have been paying attention to Stimulus B. Possibly, then, the animal stops paying attention to Stimulus B only when, as in the usual blocking experiment, Stimulus B provides no new information. When Stimulus B is added to Stimulus A, and the compound is followed by the very same US that A alone has previously signalled, B is a *redundant* (noninformative) stimulus. Perhaps animals learn to ignore, or "tune out," CSs that prove to be redundant, and thus do not condition to them. This kind of theory of the blocking phenomenon has been advanced by Mackintosh (1975).

In a similar vein, Kamin (1968) has suggested that the kinds of associations normally formed during conditioning are made when, and only when, the US *surprises* the animal. With a normal conditioning procedure, using only one CS, the US is—at least on early trials—a surprising and important event. The surprise makes the animal "look back," or scan, its memory of very recent events. When the animal "locates" the CS, it forms an association between CS and US—but only as a consequence of having been surprised by the US. The dog, so to speak, having been surprised by the sudden appearance of meat powder, wonders what on earth could have produced the meat. Thinking back over what has recently happened, the dog remembers the metronome sound and thus associates metronome sound with meat.

This kind of cognitive account obviously fits the data of blocking experiments. When Stimulus A has earlier become conditioned, its occurrence informs the animal that the US is about to follow. The addition of Stimulus B to Stimulus A at this point will not be followed by any surprising event—only by the same old US. Thus, the animal will *not* form an association between B and the US, even though they have occurred close together in time. When the addition of B to A is followed by a changed US, or the withholding of the US, the animal is surprised—and learns what Stimulus B signals.

using sticks and climbing structures. The insightful solutions did not really come out of the blue. Presumably, the chimps' accumulation of past experiences had played some role in the appearance of an insightful problem solution.

The way in which previous problem solutions transfer to aid the prompt solution of a new problem has been studied in detail by Harlow (1949). The subjects of Harlow's experiments were monkeys, tested in the kind of apparatus shown in Figure 6–12. The problem put to the monkey is a two-choice discrimination. There is a small food reward that, on each trial, is consistently placed under one of two objects. For example, in the first problem the monkey may be presentd with a square box and a round box. The food is always under the square box, which is sometimes presented to the monkey's right and other times to the monkey's left. To get the food reward on any trial, the monkey must reach out and lift the square box; there is no reward on trials when the monkey lifts the round box. When first presented with such a

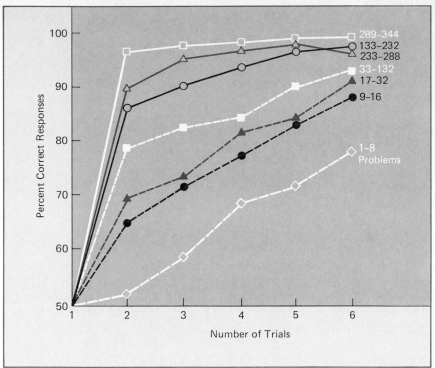

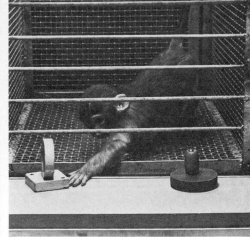

FIGURE 6–12
(Left) These curves summarize the results of Harlow's learning set studies. Note that during the first eight problems the monkey performs little better than chance (50 percent correct) for the first six trials. By the time 289 problems have been solved, the monkey is almost always correct on the second trial of any new problem. (Harlow, 1949)
(Right) The monkey in a Harlow learning set experiment reaching for the one of two objects under which the food reward has been placed.

problem, the animal will operate on a chance basis and will tend to select the correct box on about 50 percent of the trials. With later trials, however, the monkey's performance will improve until, finally, it is correct on 100 percent of the trials. Then the animal is presented with a *new* two-choice discrimination. This time, for example, a black triangular box and a white triangular box might be used, with food always under the black box. The monkey will gradually solve this problem, too—and it will probably need fewer trials to master the second discrimination than were taken to learn the first. The monkey is given a whole series of new two-choice discriminations to learn, with the results shown in Figure 6–12.

The monkey eventually arrives at a state in which any new two-choice discrimination is solved immediately. When first presented with two new objects, the monkey reaches at random for one or the other. When its first choice happens to be correct, the monkey stays with it on all following trials never bothering to pick up the other object. When its first choice happens to be incorrect, the monkey immediately switches to the other object and selects it on all following trials. This "insightful" behavior provides impressively rapid solutions to new problems; but note that the insight is itself the product of a gradual trial-and-error learning process. The improvement in the rate of solution of new problems, as a consequence of experience with past problems, is referred to as the acquisition of a **learning set.** The animal, while gradually solving a particular problem, is learning more than particular responses; it is also *learning how to learn.* That is, it may also learn general techniques and approaches that will be useful in the solution of new problems. The monkey, needless to say, is more likely to acquire learning sets than is the rat.

Latent Learning

The importance of cognitive factors in animal learning was clearly shown by the maze studies done by Edward C. Tolman and his followers. The kind of multiple-entry maze used in such studies can be seen in Figure 6–13. The hungry rat must work its way from the start box to the end box, in which there is a food reward. There are many possible blind alleys on the way. When the rat is first put in the maze it will enter many blind alleys (make many errors) as it goes from the start box to the goal box. With more trials, learning is shown by a steady decrease in the number of errors.

Though it is possible to theorize that reward in the goal box stamps in a particular sequence of right-turning and left-turning responses, Tolman argued that this was not the case. What the rat learns, according to Tolman, is a kind of "cognitive map," or mental picture, of the maze. That kind of learning—the storing of information about the world—takes place even when there is no reinforcement. To make these points, Tolman did experiments on **latent learning.** The outcome of a classic study by Tolman and Honzik (1930) is shown in Figure 6–14. Three different groups of rats were run through the same maze. The first group received a food reward in the goal box on each trial. These animals gradually reduced their number of errors to a near-zero level, and there is nothing surprising about that. The second group of rats received no reinforcement in the goal box. Though their errors declined slightly over time, they continued to make many more errors than did the reinforced group. There is again nothing surprising in this. The most interesting result is that for the third group. They received no reinforcement during the first 10 days. Then, on the 11th day, for the first time food was given in the goal box. When placed into the maze on the next (12th) day, these

FIGURE 6–13
Floor plan and photo of the type of maze used in the study of latent learning in rats. (Tolman & Honzik, 1930)

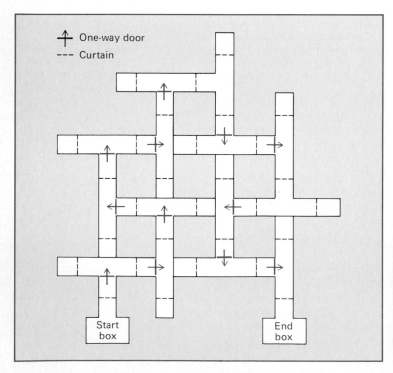

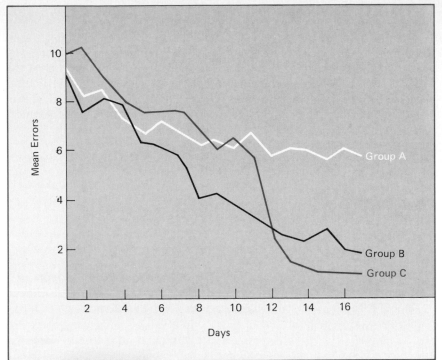

FIGURE 6–14
The results of the classic study of latent learning. Group A never received a food reward in the maze, while Group B was rewarded on each day. The reward was given to Group C for the first time on Day 11. Note the immediate change in their behavior on Day 12. (Tolman & Honzik, 1930)

animals made almost no errors. The single reinforcement brought about a dramatic improvement in their performance, so that they ran the maze about as well as the group that had been rewarded on all the earlier days. The rats had shown, in Tolman's term, *latent learning.* The early days of wandering through the maze without reinforcement had led to the building up of a mental picture of the maze. Then, when the animals were shown on the 11th day that the goal box now contained reinforcement, they used this latent cognitive learning to run through the maze without errors.

The latent learning studies, in addition to pointing toward the operation of cognitive factors in animal learning, force us to make a clear distinction between **learning** and **performance.** The performance of an animal may not change much from trial to trial, but that does not necessarily mean that the animal is not learning. The learning may involve cognitive restructuring that remains latent until some event—such as the sudden introduction of reinforcement—prompts the animal to use what it has learned. The distinction between learning and performance is often made by students who do poorly on an exam. Though the exam performance was very poor, students may argue, it did not really reflect what they insist they learned from the course. The grading systems of schools, however, are geared to performance, not to latent learning.

There are, as we have seen, many forms of animal learning that seem to demand interpretation in terms of cognitive factors. There is also the possibility that even such simple forms of learning as conditioning may involve cognition. As mentioned earlier, we can think of the CS as causing the animal to "expect" the US, and we can think of the animal as "expecting" that a particular reponse will be followed by reinforcement. Though most theorists have argued that such language only serves to complicate simple processes, in recent years "cognitive-type" language and concepts have been worked into theoretical accounts of elementary conditioning.

With the steady accumulation of knowledge over the years, many of the controversies that once dominated the study of animal learning have pretty well disappeared. We now know that *some* animal learning can be understood in terms of the "stamping-in" theory of Pavlov and Thorndike. We know also that other forms of animal learning demand more cognitive forms of theoretical explanation, such as those of Köhler and of Tolman. The widespread importance of conditioning as a basic building block of animal—and of human—learning has been clearly established.

SUMMARY

1. Pavlov's basic experiment is a clear example of what has come to be known as the law of classical conditioning: Whenever a previously neutral stimulus (CS) is presented in close temporal contiguity with an unconditioned stimulus (US), a response like the one made to the US will come to be made to the CS.

2. The basic rule followed by the experimenter during acquisition is: Whenever the CS is presented, follow it with the US. That procedure—CS followed by US—is called *reinforcement.* If the CS is no longer reinforced, the conditioned response disappears—this is known as *extinction. Spontaneous recovery* of a response occurs after extinction, indicating that extinction does not completely erase the conditioned response.

3. When a conditioned response has been established to a particular conditioned stimulus, stimuli similar to that CS will also tend to elicit the response, in a process called *generalization*. In *discrimination,* the subject learns not to respond to similar stimuli while continuing to respond to the CS itself.

4. Pavlov noted that a CS established in one series of trials could then, on its own, act as a US in a second series of trials. This is called *higher-order conditioning*. Much human learning depends on such conditioning.

5. In operant conditioning, the *presentation* of a positive reinforcer increases the likelihood that a response will be repeated. The *termination* of a negative reinforcer also increases the likelihood that the response will be repeated.

6. *Shaping* is the technique used to modify or change responses. In shaping, one reinforces the successive approximations of a particular response until the desired behavior is performed.

7. In general, reinforcing every correct response is less effective than some type of partial reinforcement, which leads to learning that is more resistant to extinction. Schedules of reinforcement can be based on either the number of responses (ratio) or the time elapsed between responses (interval), and can be either variable or fixed. The four basic schedules are thus *fixed-interval, variable-interval, fixed-ratio,* and *variable-ratio.*

8. *Punishment* is the opposite of reward or reinforcement. There are a number of serious drawbacks to punishment: It tends to generally suppress and inhibit responding; it causes the person or animal to become fearful of the situation in which it occurred and of the person who administered it; and it does not tell a person or animal what to do, it merely says what *not* to do, without presenting satisfactory alternatives.

9. A *primary reinforcer* is one that is rewarding by itself, without any association with other reinforcers. The value of a *secondary reinforcer* must be learned by associating it with primary reinforcers.

10. *Insight,* a form of learning and problem solving that depends on cognitive activity, was studied by Köhler, who described it as the ability to restructure cognitive elements into new and purposeful wholes.

11. Trial-and-error learning and insightful learning can be combined in learning how to learn—that is, in acquiring a *learning set,* which was studied by Harlow.

12. *Latent learning* shows a clear distinction between learning and performance. If some event such as the use of reinforcement prompts the animal to use what it has learned, its performance may change immediately, showing that such learning has in fact taken place.

Suggested Readings

FLAHERTY, C. F., HAMILTON, L. W., GANDELMAN, R. J., & SPEAR, N. E. *Learning and memory.* Chicago: Rand McNally, 1977. A wide-ranging, clearly spelled out text on animal learning, with much material on human learning and memory as well.

HILGARD, E. R., & BOWER, G. H. *Theories of learning,* 5th ed. Englewood Cliffs, N.J.: Prentice-Hall, 1981. As implied by the title, the emphasis is on theory, not data. Much material of historical interest.

HONIG, W. K., & STADDON, J. E. R. (Eds.). *The handbook of operant behavior.* Englewood Cliffs, N.J.: Prentice-Hall, 1977. Individual chapters by different authorities, covering a wide range of subject matters, each in considerable detail.

MACKINTOSH, N.J. *The psychology of animal learning.* New York: Academic Press, 1974. *The* comprehensive text on animal learning, but difficult going for the beginner.

RACHLIN, H. *Introduction to modern behaviorism,* 2nd ed. San Francisco: W. H. Freeman and Company Publishers, 1976. This brief volume reviews most of the facts and concepts of both classical and operant conditioning, placing them in an historical context.

SCHWARTZ, B. *Psychology of learning and behavior.* New York: Norton, 1978. An up-to-date and thorough text, especially strong on recent developments.

SCHWARTZ, B., & LACEY, H. *Behaviorism, science, and human nature.* New York: Norton, 1982. A brief summary of basic conditioning phenomena, with an emphasis on operant techniques and some of their applications. Includes a thoughtful critique of the philosophy underlying behavior theory, and of its limitations.

SKINNER, B. F. *Beyond freedom and dignity.* New York: Knopf, 1971. The inventor of the Skinner box as cultural guru and philosopher.

7. Memory

After you make an appointment with someone, you may simply hope you will remember it, or you may jot it down in your calendar. That is, you either rely on your own internal **memory** or use some sort of external memory. Fortunately, given the enormous amount of information we wish to retain and the limits of our internal memory, there are many forms of external memory systems, ranging from a string tied to a finger to huge computer memories. A **memory system** is simply an aid to the retention of information over time. Thus a book, a tape recording, and a photograph are all external memory systems. Each preserves information in a particular form, and each is best suited to preserving certain types of information.

DESCRIBING MEMORY SYSTEMS

Psychological ideas about internal memory are often expressed as analogies with external forms of memory. For this reason, although our central interest in this chapter is internal human memory, it is useful to begin by considering some external memory systems and some of the terminology used to describe them. Next we will consider how people perform a variety of memory tasks and some factors that lead to forgetting. Finally, we will consider theories of human memory and discuss some ways of improving memory that have been suggested by these theories.

External Memory Systems

The terms "encoding," "retention," and "retrieval" are often used to describe three basic aspects of memory systems. **Encoding** refers to the way information is first stored or represented in a system. **Retention** refers to the way the information is preserved in a system over time. And **retrieval** refers to the way the information is finally recovered from a system. The three aspects can be illustrated in terms of that most familiar external memory system, a book. Information is first *encoded* into patterns of ink in the form of words when the book is printed. It is *retained* over time by the persistence of this pattern, although information can be lost if the ink or paper is of a poor quality, or if the book is physically damaged (by water or fire, etc.). Finally, the information in the book is *retrieved* or recovered when it is read.

The same distinctions can also be made in terms of another external memory system, a tape recording. Here information—for example, a lecturer's voice—is encoded in the form of magnetic patterns laid down on the tape as it moves past the recording head. Retention of the information depends on the persistence of this pattern over time. Again, information can be lost if the tape is physically damaged or exposed to strong magnetic fields, or if another recording is made over the first. Finally, information is retrieved from the tape by playing it back.

We will use the phrase *information loss* in a very general way to refer to what happens when anything interferes with the accurate retrieval of information. Information loss can occur during encoding, retention, or retrieval. For example, a tape recorder could lose information because of improper recording (encoding), accidental erasure during retention, or a broken playback system that prevents retrieval. Note that if the defective playback system were repaired, it would then be possible to recover any information that was still

A tape recorder is one kind of memory system. Information is encoded as magnetic patterns, retained (unless accidentally erased), and retrieved when the tape is played.

Table 7–1: Examples of Codes.

English:	hat
French:	chapeau
Morse code:	. . . . , . _ . , _
Braille:	●○　●○　●○ ●●　○○　●● ○○,　○○,　●○

The same information can be represented in many different forms or codes. For example, the concept of "hat" can be represented by the 4 codes shown here: English, French, Samuel Morse's telegraphic code of dots and dashes, and the system of raised dots invented for blind readers by Louis Braille.

on the tape. The point is that although failure to recover information from a memory system is an instance of information loss, the information is not necessarily permanently beyond retrieval. This point can be illustrated in another way. Suppose you consulted a card catalogue in a library and then went to the place where the book should be shelved. If it wasn't there, and hadn't been checked out, you couldn't retrieve the information in that book. The book might have been permanently lost or simply misplaced. You might make an exhaustive search of the stacks for the missing book—another retrieval process. But even if this failed, the book might eventually turn up, or you might be able to locate another copy in another library or bookstore. So, you couldn't consider the loss permanent. Later we shall consider similar issues in human memory, when it is difficult to decide whether information is permanently lost or only temporarily irretrievable.

Notice that information is represented in different ways in each of the memory systems we have considered (printed letters, magnetic patterns, etc.). Each of these representations or **codes** has its special properties, such as the ease and speed with which you can encode various forms of information and the sorts of things that will interfere with retention. For example, the nature of a person's voice is normally easier to store on magnetic tape than on the printed page, although a good writer may describe a voice quite accurately. Also, the retention of printed words is uninfluenced by magnetic fields, but a tape recording can be completely erased by such fields.

A number of different codes may also be used in the same memory system. For example, a novel printed in different languages would be an encoding of the same information in the same form of memory system (a book) using a different code (French or English). Table 7–1 illustrates a variety of codes for representing the same concept.

Information held in a memory system may also be **recoded,** either by retrieving the information from that system and coding it into another system, or by recoding it into the same system. Suppose you had a friend make a tape recording of a lecture you had to miss. You might listen to the tape that evening and then either write a summary of the main ideas into another memory system, your notebook, or simply make another tape recording of your summary. In either case, there are two important aspects of this recoding process: the information loss or reduction involved, and the reorganization of the information. **Information reduction** occurs because there is less information about the lecture in the recoded summary than there was on the original tape. Even if the lecture were typed out verbatim, some reduction would be inevitable because the typed pages wouldn't contain the sounds of the lecturer's voice. In any case, many details of the lecture (jokes, illustrations, etc.) are purposely left out of a summary. Organization of information can also be changed during the recoding process. The information on the tape is in the exact sequence in which the lecturer presented it. You might choose to summarize the principal points in a very different sequence if such a **reorganization** seems simpler.

It should be emphasized that recoding doesn't always involve information reduction. In fact, some coding processes involve **elaborative** processes that may actually add to the retrieved information (see Figure 7–1). **Reconstructive** or **reintegrative** processes would allow you to fill in text in an old manuscript that had been partly destroyed, or to bridge gaps caused by static on a tape recording of a human voice. In each case you reconstruct the missing information through educated guessing based on the information that

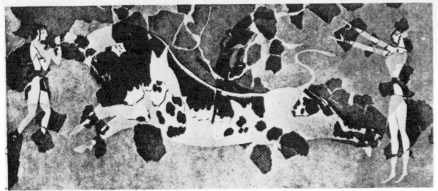

wasn't lost and your knowledge of linguistic redundancy. This is the same sort of inferential process that occurs so automatically in perception, as we discussed in Chapter 4. For example, you often infer parts of a scene or printed sentence that you don't gaze at directly from those you do. Elaboration may also occur when you code or recode information. For example, when you rewrite lecture notes you might expand on a point made by the lecturer with an example drawn from your own experience.

Memory systems can be also described in terms of their *capacity*. For example, a sales rep might use a small pocket notebook to record appointments during the day, then at the end of the day transfer these appointments to a larger notebook in her office. The pocket notebook has a lower capacity for storing information than the large office notebook. However, the pocket notebook has compensating advantages, such as its physical size and transportability, that make it easier and faster to use during the day. The office notebook has a greater capacity, but in order to retrieve information from it during the day, the sales rep must return to, or at least phone, her

Magnetic tape (left) was an early form of mass storage memory for computers.

The miniaturization of memory into tiny chips (right) has increased the capacity and reduced the cost of computer memory.

office. Thus the 2 memory systems differ in speed of encoding and retrieval as well as capacity.

Perhaps the richest source of ideas about external memory systems has been computer science. Computers are distinguished in terms of their memory (e.g., random access, disc, tape). Information is represented and organized in a variety of ways and elaborate strategies developed for information retrieval.

Human Memory Systems

As we have seen, it is possible to describe external memory systems in terms of such properties as their capacity, codes, speed of encoding and retrieval, susceptibility to interference, and so on. Even though the human memory system is an internal one, it can usefully be described in similar terms. We can often infer quite a bit about a memory system from the way it functions or behaves, even if we can't examine it directly. In the next section we will examine some of the ways in which human memory has been studied. Careful observation of how humans perform various memory tasks has suggested a variety of theoretical conjectures about the nature of human memory. Many of these theoretical approaches involve analogies between human memory and external memory systems, and in particular with electronic computers.

MEMORY TASKS: ASSESSING HUMAN MEMORY

The first systematic experiments on human memory were conducted around 1876 by a German named Hermann Ebbinghaus (Ebbinghaus, 1885). He developed a number of simple memory tasks and carefully observed how people performed them. Similar tasks have since been employed in hundreds of memory experiments. We will look briefly at three different types of tasks: recall, recognition, and relearning.

Recall

One of the simplest ways to test human memory is to allow subjects to study a list of words, and then to ask them to **recall** as many as possible, either by naming them or writing them down. Take a minute to study the list of words in the margin on p. 193. Now cover the list and write out as many of the items as you can remember. The color curve in Figure 7–2 shows the relationship between the length of time subjects study lists of this sort and the number of items they can successfully recall during a 1-minute period. Not surprisingly, the longer they study, the more study time is required for them to recall one additional word (a "diminishing return"). Another feature of recall tasks is indicated by the white curve in Figure 7–2. This shows how many items were recalled after various periods of study, given a 3-minute instead of a 1-minute recall period. Items that aren't recalled in 1 minute may still be recalled when subjects are given enough time.

Some common recall tasks are naming each state in the United States, or answering such questions as "What is her name?" or "What is your phone number?" The more you use or study an item of information, the more likely you are to recall it. However, recall may often take some time, even when you

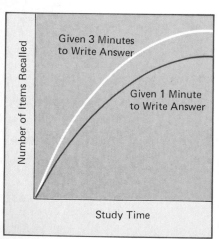

FIGURE 7–2
The colored line shows the relation between how long subjects studied a list of words and how many terms they could recall in the 1-minute recall period. The white line shows how many terms were recalled with a longer recall period of 3 minutes.

are quite confident that it will occur promptly. How often have you felt that the correct answer is on the tip of your tongue, and you have not been able to produce it? This **tip-of-the-tongue (TOT) phenomenon** suggests that recall is an active process that requires both time and concentration. Sometimes you may have the TOT experience and finally give up trying to recall some fact, only to find a few moments later that the fact pops into your mind without any further conscious effort on your part.

In order to control more precisely the amount of time each word in a recall list is available for study, experimenters often present the words serially (one after another), so that subjects see each word for the same length of time. With this kind of presentation, words at the beginning and end of the list are more likely to be recalled than those in the middle. This is called the **serial position effect** and is illustrated in graph form in Figure 7–3. The higher recall of the words at the beginning of the list is referred to as a **primacy effect;** the higher recall of words at the end of the list (the most recently presented words) is called a **recency effect.**

Distribution of practice also has a very strong effect on recall. For example, suppose you were trying to learn a list of Spanish vocabulary words. You would probably recall more words after four separate (spaced) half-hour study sessions (perhaps one session a day for four days) than after a single concentrated (massed) two-hour session, even though you had a total of two hours' practice in each case. This effect is often referred to as the *advantage of spaced* (spread-out) *over massed* (close-together or concentrated) *practice.* The same effect has also been demonstrated in subjects' ability to recall words presented twice within a single list: The more words that intervene between the first and second presentation of the word, the better will be the recall (see Figure 7–4).

The ability to recall something can be strongly influenced by other stimuli presented at the time of recall. Such stimuli are often referred to as **recall cues.** For example, your ability to recall someone's name might be aided by such recall cues as hearing his or her voice or seeing a picture of the person. In fact, simply asking someone to recall something can be considered a recall cue. There is no doubt that such stimuli as "What is your address?" or "What items were on the list you just read?" influence what you remember. Stimuli present at the time you learn something are likely to be good recall cues, a phenomenon Tulving (1978) called **encoding specificity.**

The fact that contiguous or repeatedly paired stimuli make each a good recall cue for the other explains a phenomenon called **state-dependent learning.** Things learned in a particular environment (indoors, outdoors, a noisy dormitory, a quiet library) or in a particular physiological state (fatigue, intoxication, cold, warm) are often recalled better in the same environment or state. For instance, if you studied for an exam in a cold, small room, you might not recall the information as well in a warm, large room as you would in a cold, small one. Similarly, the bodily sensations associated with mild intoxication could serve as recall cues for things learned in that state.

In some of the earliest recall experiments, Ebbinghaus used nonsense syllables such as DAK, MIF, BIP, and RUC. Since these had virtually no prior associations or meaning for his subjects, almost everything they learned about them could be introduced in the laboratory. In studies of cued recall, subjects were first shown two nonsense syllables at a time (e.g., DAK–VOP, BIP–TIF, ZOX–VAM). Later they were shown only the first member of each pair and asked to recall the second (e.g., if they were shown DAK, they should respond

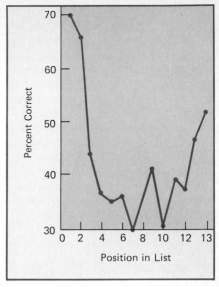

FIGURE 7–3
This graph shows the serial position effect: The position of the words in the list, which determines the order in which they are presented, affects recall. Higher recall of words at the beginning of the list is called the primacy effect, and higher recall of words at the end of the list (the most recently presented words) is called the recency effect.

house
tree
car
grass
coin
candle
barn
bus
gun
soup

FIGURE 7–4

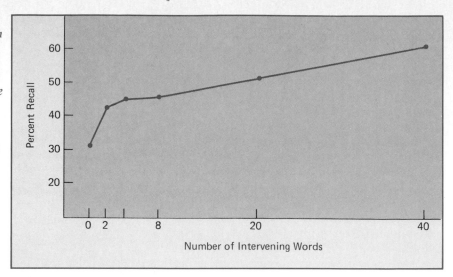

Distribution of practice affects recall. Madigan (1969) serially presented subjects with a list of 48 words. Each of 24 words occurred twice in this list, separated by varying numbers of intervening words. The further apart were the 2 presentations of the same word, the more likely it was to be recalled. For example, if a word appeared twice in immediate succession (0 words intervening), only about 30 percent of the subjects recalled it. However, as the 2 presentations (practices) of a word were spaced further apart, more subjects recalled it—with about 60 percent of subjects recalling a word for which 40 words intervened. This is an example of the advantage of spaced over massed practice.

VOP, or if they were shown BIP, they should respond TIF). Thus the first member of each pair served as a recall cue for the second member. By repeatedly pairing the two associates, then testing the ability of one to evoke recall of the other, Ebbinghaus was able to measure the gradual growth of associations.

Ebbinghaus developed his experimental approach to the study of memory at the end of the nineteenth century, and it became the dominant style of research on memory for verbal material well into the 1950s. However, there

FIGURE 7–5

"The War of Ghosts," a nineteenth century American Indian myth, and its recall by one of Bartlett's subjects. (Bartlett, 1932, p. 65)

(a) Original Indian Myth

The War of the Ghosts

One night two young men from Egulac went down to the river to hunt seals, and while they were there it became foggy and calm. Then they heard war-cries, and they thought: "Maybe this is a war-party." They escaped to the shore, and hid behind a log. Now canoes came up, and they heard the noise of paddles, and saw one canoe coming up to them. There were five men in the canoe, and they said:

"What do you think? We wish to take you along. We are going up the river to make war on the people."

One of the young men said, "I have no arrows."

"Arrows are in the canoe," they said.

"I will not go along. I might be killed. My relatives do not know where I have gone. But you," he said, turning to the other, "may go with them."

So one of the young men went, but the other returned home.

And the warriors went on up the river to a town on the other side of Kalama. The people came down to the water, and they began to fight, and many were killed. But presently the young man heard one of the warriors say: "Quick, let us go home; that Indian has been hit." Now he thought: "Oh, they are ghosts." He did not feel sick, but they said he had been shot.

So the canoes went back to Egulac, and the young man went ashore to his house, and made a fire. And he told everybody and said: "Behold I accompanied the ghosts, and we went to fight. Many of our fellows were killed, and many of those who attacked us were killed. They said I was hit, and I did not feel sick."

He told it all, and then he became quiet. When the sun rose he fell down. Something black came out of his mouth. His face became contorted. The people jumped up and cried.

He was dead.

(b) Typical recall by a student in Victorian England

The War of the Ghosts

Two men from Edulac went fishing. While thus occupied by the river they heard a noise in the distance.

"It sounds like a cry," said one, and presently there appeared some in canoes who invited them to join the party of their adventure. One of the young men refused to go, on the ground of family ties, but the other offered to go.

"But there are no arrows," he said.

"The arrows are in the boat," was the reply.

He thereupon took his place, while his friend returned home. The party paddled up the river to Kaloma, and began to land on the banks of the river. The enemy came rushing upon them, and some sharp fighting ensued. Presently someone was injured, and the cry was raised that the enemy were ghosts.

The party returned down the stream, and the young man arrived home feeling none the worse for his experience. The next morning at dawn he endeavoured to recount his adventures. While he was talking something black issued from his mouth. Suddenly he uttered a cry and fell down. His friends gathered round him.

But he was dead.

Victorian college students tended to systematically forget, distort, and revise details of a North American Indian myth in ways that made the recalled story less unusual to them.

were those who felt that Ebbinghaus lost something very important when he chose to use nonsense syllables. They argued that normal human memory dealt with material rich in associations, organization, and meaning and that these played a major role in human memory. For instance, the English psychologist Frederic Bartlett (1932/1964) felt that memory research should use meaningful material instead of nonsense syllables. One gets very different views of human memory from considering the work of Ebbinghaus and Bartlett, because Bartlett's work dealt with aspects of human memory that Ebbinghaus purposely tried to avoid through the use of nonsense syllables.

In one of his studies, Bartlett had subjects read a short but strange and complicated story, *The War of the Ghosts.* Then, after some time had elapsed, he had them recall as much of the story as they could (see Figure 7–5). *The War of the Ghosts* is a legend told by nineteenth-century Indians on the northwest coast of Canada. Barlett purposely chose a story that would not only be unfamiliar to his Victorian English subjects, but that also came from a culture quite different from their own. Bartlett wondered whether the cultural differences would affect his subjects' recall of the story. He found that subjects had a systematic tendency to forget, distort, and add details in a way which would make the recalled story less strange and unusual to them. For example, the subject whose recall is shown in Figure 7–5 changed "to hunt seals" to "went fishing," "war cries" to "a cry," and "arrows are in the canoe" to "arrows are in the boat." For other subjects "something black came out of his mouth" became "frothed at the mouth" or simply "vomited."

grass	heart	gun
bike	car	bus
phone	soup	bridge
coin	tree	cliff
house	door	barn
boat	bat	rifle

Recognition

Another way to test memory is to use a **recognition** task. Consider the list of words in the margin on this page. Some of these terms were in the list you saw earlier; others are new or *distractor* items. Check those items you remember seeing in the earlier list.

Notice that in this case a word is presented and you must decide whether or not you recognize it from a previous list. This is similar to asking someone "Is that Mary?" or "Is your phone number 621-7753?" rather than "Who is that?" or "What is your phone number?" as in the recall task. Here the answer to the recall question is actually there, and you must say whether or not you recognize it.

In general, people are more likely to recognize an item than to recall it. This may be simply because presentation of the item is itself a good recall cue. This idea was explored by Tulving and Watkins (1973), with the results shown in Figure 7–6. They varied how much of an item was present at the time of recall by varying the number of its letters shown to the subject. When no letters were shown, as in a simple recall task, recall was low. The more letters shown, the better the recall, indicating that presentation of even part of an item serves as a recall cue. Finally, when the whole item was presented, as in a conventional recognition task, subjects were most likely to recall seeing the item earlier. So recognition may be thought of as a special case of recall, in which the item itself serves as a recall cue.

Relearning

Even when people seem to have totally forgotten something they learned earlier, **relearning** it may take less time than the original learning. This reduction in time to learn, or **savings,** suggests that they actually had some

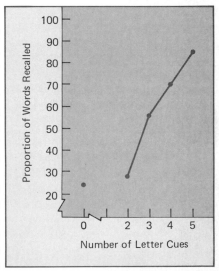

FIGURE 7–6
In this experiment Tulving and Watkins varied how much of an item (a 5-letter word) was presented to subjects to see how it would affect recall of the item. Their results are shown in the graph above: When no letters are shown, as in a simple recall task, recall is low; the more letters shown, the better the recall; and when the whole item is presented, as in a recognition task, recall is highest. (Tulving & Watkins, 1973)

memory of the material before they began to relearn it. Suppose subjects study a list of 20 items for successive 1-minute periods with a recall test following each study period. Proceeding in this way, it might take 15 study periods (minutes) before all 20 items can be recalled on the following test. Several weeks later the subjects might claim they can't recall any of the words.

Now suppose they relearn the words, using exactly the same procedure as before. A perfect performance on the recall test might occur after only 10 study periods, a savings score of 5 minutes (time for the original learning minus time for relearning). The savings score in this case is one-third of the total original study time, or $33\frac{1}{3}$ percent. This savings suggests that the subjects actually did remember something from the original learning, even though they couldn't recall any of the items before the relearning session.

FORGETTING: INFORMATION LOSS IN HUMAN MEMORY

We saw earlier that information is lost in external memory systems in ways that are characteristic of each system. Of course, information loss or forgetting also occurs in human memory. The ways in which this occurs, and the factors that influence it, have led to a variety of theories concerning the nature of human memory, which we will examine later in this chapter.

The Effect of Retention Time

The most obvious factor in forgetting is the passage of time. In general, the longer the interval between learning and recall (the retention interval), the less likely it is that we will remember something (see Figure 7–7). Yet there are many exceptions to this general rule. You often remember events that occurred during a time of crisis, such as the death of a friend or a moment of personal peril, even though they took place many years ago. It is remarkable, in fact, how clearly most people can remember things of this sort. On

FIGURE 7–7
The most obvious factor in forgetting is the passage of time, as shown in this graph. Note that retention decreases very rapidly at first, then much more slowly after the first 9 hours. (Ebbinghaus, 1885)

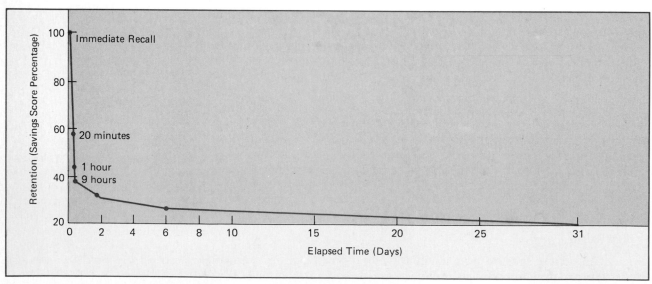

the other hand, you may forget the name of someone just introduced to you before you finish shaking hands. Thus the passage of time alone is not a reliable indicator of whether something will be remembered. More important, it seems, is how well the information was learned or encoded originally, what happens to the person during the retention period, and the situation in which retrieval is attempted.

Distraction and Attentional Problems

You are unlikely to remember people's names if you don't pay attention when they are introduced. Nor will you find it easy to remember the details of your last psychology lecture while driving at high speed through heavy traffic. There is a difference between these two examples. Distractions that occur while you are trying to retrieve information usually affect your memory only temporarily (you probably will remember the lecture once you are safely home). But if your attention is distracted when information is first presented, you may never be able to remember it, as if it was not even encoded. In Chapter 4 we considered a number of attentional problems, such as being able to attend closely to only one person's voice at a time. If someone else is speaking at the same time, you neither perceive nor remember much of what that person says. Thus an important determinant of what you remember is what you attend to.

Even if you do attend to information as it is presented, distraction immediately afterward may also produce information loss. You may, for instance, have noticed you're more likely to forget someone's name if you are distracted right after being introduced. An experiment by Peterson and Peterson (1959) illustrates this effect. Their subjects heard 3-consonant trigrams, such as P, T, K or L, C, J, which they were then asked to recall after retention intervals ranging from 3 to 18 seconds. If allowed to attend solely to this task, the subjects could perform it perfectly. However, if they had to perform a distracting task during the retention interval (counting backwards by 3's from a number seen right after hearing the trigram), recall was hindered until there was almost no recall after 18 seconds (see Figure 7–8). It is clear that attending to information as it is presented *and* not being distracted immediately afterward are both required to avoid forgetting.

Interference from Other Memories

Your ability to remember something may be impaired, or interfered with, by memories of other things, particularly things that are quite similar or conceptually related. Suppose you have been shown through several homes by a real estate agent. Thinking back, you might have difficulty recalling which homes had specific features, sometimes erroneously remembering a feature of one house as belonging to another, or sometimes being unsure whether you really saw a particular feature at all, since you saw so many. The more similar the houses and the more of them you saw, the more likely you would be to experience confusions of this sort.

Phenomena very much like this have been studied experimentally. Subjects are shown several word lists and then asked to recall items from a particular list. The more lists they are shown, and the more similar the words in the lists, the more poorly the subjects perform (see Figure 7–9). The simplest form of this experiment requires 3 groups of subjects and 2 lists of words. Two groups

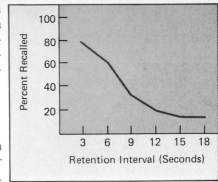

FIGURE 7–8
In this experiment, subjects who heard 3-consonant trigrams (such as P, T, K) were asked to recall them after retention intervals ranging from 3 to 18 seconds. Subjects performed a distracting task during the retention interval (counting backward). The letters were rapidly forgotten, with almost no recall after 18 seconds. (Peterson & Peterson, 1959)

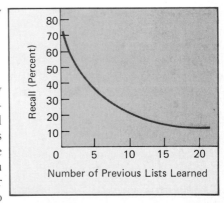

FIGURE 7–9
When subjects are shown a series of word lists and then asked to recall items from a particular list, the more lists they are shown, and the more similar the words in the lists, the more poorly they perform.

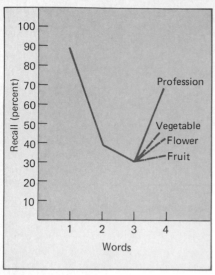

FIGURE 7-10
The graph shows evidence of a release from interference if there is a distinct category shift in the fourth word presented in the list. That is, there is less proactive interference if the item is unrelated to the words already retained in memory. (Wickens, 1972)

of subjects learn only 1 list, either List A or List B. The third group learns both lists, first A and then B. The 2-list group is typically poorer at recalling either list than the corresponding 1-list group. This indicates both that learning List A interferes with recall of B, and that learning List B interferes with recall of A. The interference of A with recall of B is termed **proactive interference,** since A was learned before B. The interference of B with recall of A is called **retroactive interference.** Both types of interference depend on the similarity of the words on each list. For example, there will be more interference if both lists are vegetable names than if one is vegetables and the other is fruit.

These effects can be demonstrated in even simpler form. Wickens (1972) presented subjects with a series of words and then tested their recall. While the list was much longer, only recall of the first 4 words is of interest here. The first 3 words on each subject's list were names of fruits; the fourth word varied for different groups of subjects—it was the name of either a fruit, a vegetable, a flower, or a profession. The rest of the list was identical for all subjects. Figure 7-10 shows how recall gradually falls off for the first 3-words as proactive interference increases the primacy effect shown earlier (in Figure 7-3). However, the amount of proactive interference indicated on the fourth item clearly depends on its similarity to the first three. It is as if there is a *release from interference* when there is a distinct *category shift*.

It seems, then, that the likelihood of forgetting something because of interference from other information in memory depends on the item's relation to that information.

Emotional Factors

We seem to remember most vividly an event to which we have had a strong emotional response. Moments of great elation or excitement, grief, or sorrow are often sharply etched in our memories. Every detail seems to stand out. Of course, such events are ones we may discuss often. Each time we describe the event or someone mentions it, we have another opportunity to encode information about it. This is surely one reason we remember such events better than others. Another reason is that things we feel strongly about usually command our attention and make us less likely to be distracted by other things. For example, a difference of opinion between family members can cause them to focus attention on the issue and on their interactions and not be distracted by other events. This may be why we remember quarrels so vividly.

Of course, while our attention is directed to our emotional involvement, we are likely to forget other kinds of information. For example, great anxiety can distract you from listening to a lecture. You may spend your time looking nervously about the classroom at your fellow students, or looking out the window thinking about your problems.

Freud (1933) argued that many of the seemingly innocent failures of memory that occur in everyday life are the product of unconscious motives and emotions. Forgetting your car keys may be caused by an unconscious desire to stay home from work. Forgetting someone's name or an appointment may be an expression of unconscious anger. Freud called such unconsciously purposeful forgetting **repression** and made the gradual uncovering of such repressed memories, particularly those associated with traumatic experiences, a central goal of psychoanalysis. He argued that when patients finally remember such events, they are freed from feelings of anxiety and maladaptive behavior caused by such repressed memories, a process he called **catharsis.**

Emotional problems can produce almost total failure of memory for even recent events that are too painful for a person to deal with. A mother may be unable to remember anything that happened on the day her child drowned. A man may leave his home for work one day, then find himself in a distant city months later with no memory of what has happened to him since he left home. Such **fugue states** seem to satisfy some psychological or emotional need and are discussed in more detail in Chapter 16.

Organic Causes of Forgetting

Some causes of forgetting have a clear organic basis. These **organic amnesias** are usually caused by some sort of damage to the brain resulting from disease, injury to the head, or brain surgery. For example, in **Alzheimer's disease,** which affects some older people, gradual reduction in the brain's oxygen supply and general atrophy of the brain produce an overall reduction in cognitive function, including memory.

More specific effects on memory may be produced by other types of brain damage. If the damage causes loss of memory only for events occurring *after* it, it is termed **anterograde amnesia.** If it affects events occurring *before* it, it is termed **retrograde amnesia.** Combinations of retrograde and anterograde amnesia also occur.

Korsakoff's syndrome is a disease associated with chronic alcoholism and the resulting malnutrition; it causes permanent brain damage. While victims of this disease have some retrograde amnesia, they can remember most of their earlier life. However, they don't remember new information for more than a few minutes. People with this chronic anterograde amnesia can meet someone, or read a magazine, and a few minutes later fail to recognize

Retrograde amnesia is often caused by a blow to the head. Depending on the severity of the blow, the amnesia may extend back a few moments or a few weeks. The rider in this accident may not later remember any of the events leading up to it.

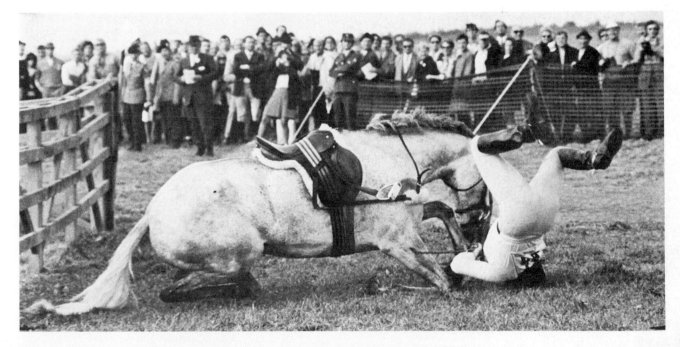

the person, or read the magazine as if it were new. Each day they start afresh with memories only of their early life. Similar chronic patterns of anterograde amnesia can be produced by damage to the hippocampus. Milner (1970) studied a patient, H. M., whose hippocampus was surgically lesioned to reduce epileptic seizures. The patient had a normal IQ but couldn't remember new information for more than a few minutes.

Retrograde amnesias are usually temporary and often caused by a blow to the head. (They can also be caused by electroconvulsive shock, which is sometimes used to treat severely depressed mental patients.) These amnesias may extend back a few moments, days, or even weeks, depending on the severity of the blow to the head. As time passes, the older events are usually recalled first, until finally there is no amnesia. Sometimes, however, memory of events that occurred during the last few minutes before the injury (or electroconvulsive shock) seems to be permanently lost. It is almost as if these events were never completely encoded.

THEORIES OF HUMAN MEMORY

Some Early Ideas

Early ideas about memory were closely related to ideas about learning. Plato likened human memory to soft wax on which experiences produce imprints or traces; forgetting occurs as successive traces gradually obliterate earlier ones. Plato's conception was elaborated by Aristotle to include associations of these traces: Retrieving one memory could lead to others through an organized network of associations.

The conception of learning as the formation of associations has been central to many theories of learning up to the present day. Formation of associations was often attributed to simple **temporal contiguity.** Things that happen at the same time tend to become associated. Memory of one will then evoke a memory of the other. This was the view of Ebbinghaus (1885), whose paired-association method for studying human memory we considered earlier in this chapter.

Some theorists thought of the associations between memory traces as "neural paths." Like footpaths across a field, neural paths were supposed to become more defined through repeated use; if not used they would gradually decay or fade away. Notice the difference between the idea of forgetting as simple decay through disuse and Plato's conception of new impressions overlying and obscuring old ones. Arguments as to whether forgetting occurs because of decay or simply the interfering effects of new memories have continued to this day.

The concept of associated neural traces was elaborated in **consolidation theory** (Müller & Pilzecker, 1900). According to this theory, the neural paths "reverberate" or remain active for some time after they are formed, and this continued activity is necessary for them to "consolidate" or become permanent. An explanation of retrograde amnesia is offered by consolidation theorists in support of their view: The traumatic events (a blow to the head or electroconvulsive shock) that cause the amnesia prevent consolidation of the traces laid down by immediately preceding events, causing a loss of memory for such events. Similar effects were shown in lower animals given electroconvulsive shock immediately after learning.

Multiprocess Theories of Human Memory

Early learning theorists hoped to account for all learning, by both humans and lower organisms, in terms of a few basic models—for example, by association based on contiguity, or by reinforcement as in Pavlovian or operant conditioning. It was hoped that memory could be accounted for in the same way. However, by the 1950s many psychologists had grown pessimistic about achieving a unified theory. Influenced by work on communication theory, decision making, and computer science, they began to develop models for specific aspects of human information processing. Some concentrated on how humans retain information for intervals as brief as a few minutes or even seconds. Others, less interested in short-term memory, studied how people retain and retrieve information over periods of days, weeks, and even years. Still other psychologists focused on how people remember visual images or sounds, how they remember particular experiences or episodes rather than facts, and so on.

Out of this varied work emerged a picture of human memory *not* as a single memory system, but as a number of interrelated memory systems, each with its own special properties. This multiprocess view of human memory is reflected in the highly influential theory proposed by Atkinson and Shiffrin (1971, 1977). They attempted to integrate earlier work on both short-term and long-term memory systems (see Figure 7–11). Sensory information is briefly retained in **sensory memory systems;** some of it is then recoded into **short-term memory,** where it may be maintained through a process called **rehearsal.** The longer the information resides in short-term memory, the more likely it is to be finally recoded or transferred into **long-term memory.** Retention in long-term memory was assumed to be virtually permanent, although effective strategies were required for successful retrieval. Let's consider this and other multiprocess theories of memory and some of the things they were designed to explain.

Sensory Memory

A simple example of visual persistence can be seen when a brightly glowing cigarette is moved rapidly back and forth in the dark. It seems to have a tail behind it, indicating that you continue to see light a short time after it has

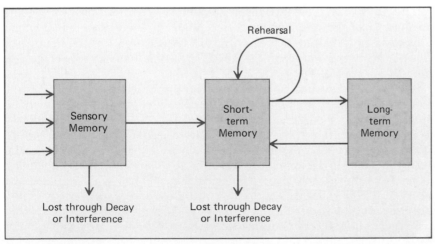

FIGURE 7–11
Atkinson and Shiffrin's multiprocess view of human memory is shown in this model. Sensory information is briefly retained in some type of sensory memory system; some of it is then recoded into short-term memory, where it may be retained through rehearsal. The longer it remains in short-term memory, the more likely it is to be transferred into long-term memory. While information can be lost from sensory and short-term memories through decay or interference, retention in long-term memory is assumed to be virtually permanent.

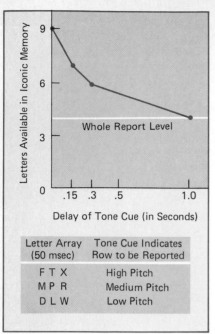

FIGURE 7–12 SPERLING'S CUED PARTIAL
RESPONSE PROCEDURE
*Sperling (1960) visually presented a 3-by-3
array of letters for 50 milliseconds followed by
an auditory tone cue indicating which row of
letters the subject was to report. Sperling estimated the total number of letters available in iconic memory by multiplying
the number of letters correctly reported from
the cued row by the number of rows (3). The
results suggest a large-capacity iconic
memory that "fades away" (decays) in about
1 second.*

ceased falling on a particular part of the retina. Is this persistence in visual sensation a form of memory? Certainly information about an image is being retained over time, even though that time is very brief, so it would seem to meet the basic definition of a memory system.

This and other evidence has led to the idea of an **iconic memory system** (an *icon* is an image or pictorial representation) that is able to retain at least some information about visual images for periods up to 1 or 2 seconds. Such information appears to be in a form or code quite similar to the original sensation. It also seems susceptible to disturbance by other visual stimulation. For example, as we pointed out in Chapter 4, while subjects can read short sentences presented on a screen for only 100 milliseconds, reading can be prevented (or at least reduced) by highly contoured patterns presented up to 1 second after the sentence. Since reading can be disrupted by a *subsequent* "masking" pattern, it must occur at least partly *after* the exposure. It is as if subjects continue to read from an iconic memory of the sentence. This effect has been interpreted as a form of retroactive interference that produces information loss in the iconic memory system.

A now-classic experiment on iconic memory was conducted by George Sperling (1960), who was interested in measuring how much people could "see" in a briefly presented visual image. In what he termed a *whole-report procedure* subjects were shown a 3-by-3 array of 9 letters for only 50 milliseconds and asked to name as many of the letters as they could. While they could usually name only about 4 or 5 of the letters, they reported "seeing" all 9 of them. Sperling surmised that their problem wasn't "seeing" the letters but simply remembering them long enough to report them (just as you would have difficulty repeating back a list of 9 letters someone read aloud to you). He devised a *cued partial-report procedure* (Figure 7–12) in which the subject was only required to report 1 of the 3 rows of letters. The particular row was indicated by a tone cue sounded *after* the letter array had been presented: A high, medium, or low tone indicated, respectively, that the top, middle, or bottom row of letters was to be reported.

Sperling's reasoning went like this: If an iconic memory persisted until the tone cue sounded, the subject need only "read out" and remember for report the 3 letters in the cued row, a relatively easy memory task. Even if only some of the 9 letters remained available in iconic memory when the cue sounded, the subject could at least report these. Thus, if you multiplied the average number of letters reported from the cued row, times the number of rows (3), you would have an estimate of the total number of letters available in iconic memory when the cue sounded. For example, if the average was 2 letters correctly reported from the cued row, this would imply that 2 times 3 (that is, 6) letters were, on average, available in iconic memory when the cue sounded.

Figure 7–12 shows how Sperling's estimate of the "letters available in iconic memory" depended on the timing of the tone cue. If the cue was sounded immediately after the letters were shown (0 delay) all 3 letters in the cued row were usually reported correctly (the "letters available" equaled 3 × 3 or 9). However, as the delay of the tone cue increased, the estimate of available letters diminished. For example, when the tone occurred 0.3 seconds after the letters were shown, only about 2 letters in the cued row were reported (the available letters equaled 2 × 3 or 6). At delays of 1 second or more, the subjects reported no more letters from the cued row than would be expected from their whole-report performance.

Sperling's results were seen as supporting the idea of a *high-capacity, rapidly decaying, iconic memory system.* In this system, information was coded in a form similar to the original stimulus (since other visual stimulation could produce interference or "masking").

Certain characteristics of hearing may be evidence of an **echoic memory system** (Neisser, 1967). As with iconic memory, the information retained seems to be in a form or code quite similar to the original sensation and susceptible to disturbance by other auditory stimulation. For example, the ability to discriminate the pitch of a briefly presented tone can be reduced by the subsequent presentation of an auditory masking tone (Massaro, 1970). This retroactive masking effect occurs at delays of up to a quarter of a second. (It should be pointed out that this does not prove that the echoic memory system retains information for only a quarter of a second; it may simply be that pitch recognition is completed in a quarter of a second, so that longer retention doesn't affect pitch judgments.)

Iconic and echoic memory systems represent what many theorists, including Atkinson and Shiffrin, have referred to as **sensory memory systems.** Such systems have been suggested for other senses as well as for vision and hearing. They seem to briefly retain a representation of sensory information in a code quite similar to the original sensation and are susceptible to disturbance by subsequent stimulation of the same sort. These systems may hold sensory information until it can be selectively processed and recoded into a short-term memory system. For example, Sperling interpreted the limit of 4 or 5 letters reported in his whole-report procedure as the capacity of a short-term verbal memory system rather than as the capacity of iconic memory.

Short-Term Memory

The idea that short-term memory has a capacity of only a few items goes back at least to Ebbinghaus, who reported that the longest list of nonsense syllables we can recall perfectly after only one presentation is about 6 or 7. Similarly, the number of digits (**digit span**) a normal adult can successfully recall immediately after hearing them spoken is about 7 or 8. A variety of evidence suggesting that the capacity of short-term memory is somewhere between 5 and 9 is discussed in a famous paper by George Miller (1956) entitled "The Magic Number Seven Plus or Minus Two." Miller pointed out that these 5 to 9 items should be thought of as "chunks" of information rather than individual units. For example, Figure 7–13 illustrates how subjects can be taught to "chunk" sets of 3 binary digits (1's or 0's) into a single octal digit (0 through 7). Their immediate memory for the binary digits was originally about 7; after training on the chunking or recoding procedure they could remember almost 7 octal digits, which correspond to about 21 binary units. Thus, recoding into more parsimonious "chunks" can effectively increase your short-term memory capacity.

REHEARSAL AND TRANSFER.   Atkinson and Shiffrin (see Figure 7–11) believed that information could be retained in short-term memory through a process of *rehearsal,* repeating it over and over. The longer the rehearsal period, the more likely that the information would be transferred to long-term memory. This theory provides an interpretation of the Peterson and Peterson experiment we described earlier. Distracting subjects immediately after they heard

HIGHLIGHT □
Short-Term Memory for Letters:
Two Kinds of Code?

A basic feature of any memory system is the way in which information is represented or coded in that system. An elegantly simple experiment by Thorsen, Hochhaus, and Stanners (1976) illustrates how questions of this sort can be addressed experimentally.

On each of a series of trials, subjects were shown 2 letters, with intervals between the letters of up to 2 seconds. On each trial, as rapidly as possible after seeing the second letter, subjects were to press 1 of 2 buttons to indicate whether the letters were the same (e.g., an F followed by an F) or different (an X followed by a Y). On a random half of the trials the letters were the same, and on the rest of the trials they were different.

The experimenters were primarily interested in a subject's reaction times on trials when the letters were *different*. They reasoned that if the first letter were represented (coded) in a visual form—a *structural code*—subjects would have the most

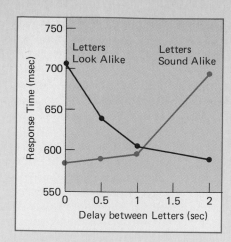

FIGURE A
Average time to respond "different" at various interletter intervals for visually similar letters (P/R, X/Y, K/X) and for acoustically similar letters (E/D, P/E, X/S).

difficulty (take longest) distinguishing letters that looked alike (had a similar structure), such as P and R or X and Y. On the other hand, if the first letter were represented in memory by its name or sound—an *acoustical code*—then subjects should have the most difficulty (take longest) distinguishing letters that sounded alike, such as E and P or X and S.

The most important aspects of their results are shown in Figure A.

The black line shows the average time to respond "different" to 2 letters that look alike (but don't sound alike) for intervals between the letters of either 0, 0.5, 1.0, or 2 seconds. The color line shows the corresponding times for responses to letters that sound alike but don't look alike.

Notice that when the letters are presented in immediate succession, subjects take longer to distinguish those that look alike than those that sound alike, as if the comparison were based on a visual or structural code. However, as the interval between letters increases, this pattern gradually changes until it is totally reversed for intervals of 2 seconds. Then subjects take longer to distinguish letters that sound alike, as if the comparison were based on an acoustical code.

Many psychologists interpret these and other results as indicating that visual information about a letter is initially represented in memory in a structural code, then rapidly recoded into an acoustical code during the first 1 or 2 seconds. Whether this is the *only* interpretation of these results is open to debate. Nevertheless, this experiment illustrates how psychologists have attempted to identify the nature of representation or coding in memory.

---

a trigram prevents rehearsal, so the trigram is rapidly lost and unlikely to enter long-term memory.

A similar explanation can be given for the shape of the serial position curve (see Figure 7–3) in recall. Rundus (1971) conducted an experiment in which subjects were slowly shown a list of words, one word at a time. They were instructed to "rehearse out loud" any words they wished as the list was presented. This allowed Rundus to count how often each word was rehearsed. The primacy effect can be explained by the more frequent rehearsal of early items, thereby (according to Atkinson and Shiffrin) allowing them more opportunity to transfer into long-term memory. The recency effect can be attributed to those items remaining in short-term memory after the list · is presented.

The rehearsal explanation provides an alternative to consolidation theory's interpretation of retrograde amnesia caused by trauma. It proposes that trauma causes loss of information from short-term memory before it can be rehearsed and transferred to long-term memory. This loss, rather than the failure to consolidate a memory trace, causes retrograde amnesias.

Three-Digit Binary Code		One-Digit Octal Code
000	=	0
001	=	1
010	=	2
011	=	3
100	=	4
101	=	5
110	=	6
111	=	7

Binary Number:	110	101	111	001	100	110	111
Recoded into Octal Number:	6	5	7	1	4	6	7

The pattern of memory in patients who have Korsakoff's syndrome also seems consistent with the idea of separate short- and long-term memory systems. Perhaps these patients have normal short-term memories but have lost the ability to transfer new information into long-term memory.

Notice how closely related the idea of short-term memory is to the concept of consciousness. Information in short-term memory seems readily accessible. It is information we are currently working with, transforming, rehearsing, recoding. In fact, it is the almost immediate accessibility of information in working memory that distinguishes it from the larger store of information in longer-term memory systems, which seem to involve lengthier retrieval processes.

Long-Term Memory

Consider how long it can take you to recall what you did three summers ago, or the way your bedroom looked when you were in high school. Are you retrieving information from a separate **long-term memory system,** with a much greater capacity than short-term but requiring lengthier and more complicated retrieval processes? Many psychologists believe so. Some also believe that there are different types of long-term memory, specialized for different types of knowledge. For example, one distinction is that between propositional (declarative) knowledge and procedural knowledge (Anderson, 1976; Ryle, 1949). **Propositional** or **declarative knowledge** is factual knowledge, such as "5 is larger than 4," "I walked to school," or "ice is cold." Each statement is a *proposition,* a relation between 2 or more concepts (for example, the relation "larger than" between the concepts "5" and "4"). Each proposition is a declaration of fact and is either true or false. Such knowledge can often be acquired through a single experience and represented in a purely symbolic form (as by the words on this page). In contrast, **procedural knowledge** is knowledge of how to do something, whether tying your shoes or programming a computer. Such knowledge is usually gained slowly, through repeated experience or practice, and is evidenced by how well (or poorly) you perform some task.

HIGHLIGHT☐

Retrieving Information from Short-Term Memory

Sternberg (1966) devised an experimental method for studying how fast people can retrieve information from short-term memory. This method, often referred to as Sternberg's *memory-scanning procedure*, is a simple form of recognition task. On each of a series of trials, subjects are shown a small set of items, called the *memory set*; then, a few moments later, another item, called a *probe*. The subjects' task is to decide as quickly as possible whether or not the probe was one of the memory set shown on that trial. For example, in Sternberg's original experiments, each memory set consisted of from 1 to 6 digits, shown one after another. The probe was also a digit shown 2 seconds after the last digit of the memory set. Subjects were to quickly press one button if the probe was also in the memory set, a "yes" response, or another button if it wasn't, a "no" response. Both types of trials occurred equally often in a random order.

Table A gives several examples of such trials. Notice that the number of digits in the memory set ranges from 1 in Example A to 6 in Example C. Sternberg wondered how the variation in the size of the memory set would influence the speed of a subject's response. He speculated that the more items a subject had to re-

Table A: Examples of Test Trials.

Example	Memory Set	Probe	Correct Response
A	2,5	5	yes
B	8	3	no
C	6,8,5,9 2,0	2	yes
D	9,3,6	0	no
E	2,1,9,4,7	2	yes

tain in short-term memory, the longer it would take to retrieve or "scan" those items, to decide if one matched the probe.

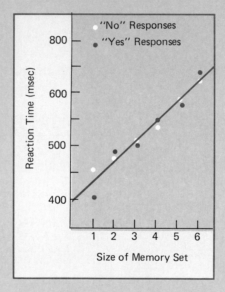

FIGURE A
The average time to answer "yes" (color circles) or "no" (white circles) for memory sets. (Sternberg, 1966)

Figure A shows the approximately linear relation Sternberg found between the number of items in the memory set and average response time. Each additional item in the memory set added about 38 milliseconds to that time. This suggested to Sternberg that subjects "scanned" or compared the items in a short-term memory one after another (serially), with each item taking about 38 milliseconds—a *high-speed, serial-scanning process*.

A surprising feature of Sternberg's results was the fact that both "yes" and "no" responses could be described by linear functions with the same slope. This is not what one would expect if the serial-scanning process ended as soon as an item in the memory set was found to match the probe.

A *self-terminating process* of this sort would require you to scan all the items to decide "no," but (on the average) only half the items to decide "yes." Thus the slope of the "yes" response function in Figure A should be only half that of the "no" response function. This led Sternberg to propose that *all* items are scanned before either a "yes" or "no" decision is made, an *exhaustive process*.

It is now clear that there are other ways of interpreting Sternberg's data, but his interpretation is elegantly simple and difficult to disprove. It remains a fine example of the interplay between theory and data in the study of human memory.

PROPOSITIONAL OR DECLARATIVE KNOWLEDGE,   Tulving (1972) argued that there are really two forms of propositional or declarative knowledge, episodic and semantic, each represented in its own memory system. **Episodic knowledge** consists of propositions regarding specific experiences or episodes in your past, such as "I walked to school this morning," "I spoke to John last night," or "we talked until midnight." In contrast, the propositions of **semantic knowledge** are declarations of facts independent of *when* you learned or experienced them, such as "5 is larger than 3," "a pelican is a bird," or "Hartford is in Connecticut."

An incident involving a neurologist and a brain-damaged patient (Claparede, 1911) is sometimes cited as evidence of separate propositional and episodic memory systems. The doctor once hid a sharp pin in his hand before shaking hands with the patient. He wanted to see how the pain of the pinprick would affect her memory for the event. Later when the doctor again offered his hand to her, she refused, saying only that "doctors sometimes hide pins in their hands." It was as if she had forgotten the specific painful episode (a failure of episodic memory) but remembered a general fact (semantic memory).

Tulving (1972) also pointed out that the verbal learning research of Ebbinghaus was really the study of episodic rather than semantic memory. Subjects recalled such things as "DAX was one of the nonsense syllables I just read" or "crystal was one of the words in the first list you read to me." The subject was *not* concerned with the (semantic) meaning of *DAX* or *crystal,* but simply with whether or not they had been presented at a particular time (episodic knowledge). Thus much of the research on verbal learning discussed earlier in this chapter could be considered research on episodic rather than semantic memory.

The study of semantic memory is more in the tradition of Bartlett. It is concerned with the *meanings* of words and with memory for progressively larger meaningful units such as sentences (Anderson & Paulson, 1977), paragraphs (Kintsch & Bates, 1977), and stories (Rumelhart, 1977; Bower, Black, & Turner, 1979).

Many theoretical ideas about semantic memory stem from the gradual (step-by-step) way we often retrieve information from long-term memory. The desired information isn't recalled immediately but is remembered only after we first recall related information. Aristotle referred to this gradual process of recall as "recollection" and argued that it reflected a sequence of associations between ideas. The recollection of one idea leads through association to the next, and so on, until you finally recall the desired information. Put another way, *each recalled idea in turn becomes a recall cue for another idea.*

The idea of knowledge as a *network of associations* has had a long history in psychology. A modern version of this view is that human memory should be thought of as a *network of interrelated propositions* (Anderson & Kintsch, 1974; Norman & Rumelhart, 1975). This stems in large part from computer scientists' use of such networks to represent knowledge in computer programs, especially those designed to process language or recognize forms (see the Highlight on computer pattern recognition in Chapter 4). A simple illustration of knowledge represented by a propositional network can be made in terms of the following sentence:

Jackson hit a high pop-up to Cerone, the catcher for the Yankees.

The information (knowledge) in this sentence could be broken down into 3 simpler propositions:

A. Jackson hit a pop-up to Cerone.
B. The pop-up was high.
C. Cerone was the catcher for the Yankees.

The network of interrelations among these 3 propositions is represented graphically in Figure 7–14. Again, each proposition specifies a relation between 2 or more concepts; for example, Proposition C specifies that the

FIGURE 7–14
A graphic representation of the network of interrelated propositions (A, B, C) in the statement "Jackson hit a high pop-up to Cerone,
the catcher for the Yankees."

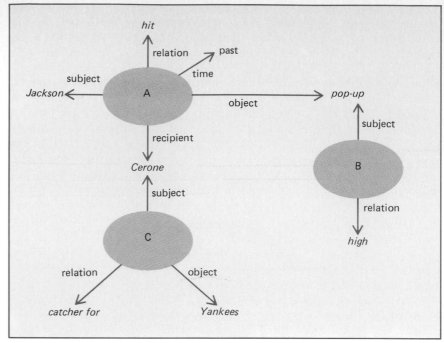

concept "Cerone" (the player) has the relation "catcher for" with the concept "Yankees" (the baseball team). Other aspects of each proposition, such as tense (time), subject, object, or recipient of an action, are indicated next to the arrows in Figure 7–14. The psychological reality of such representations is suggested by experiments in which people were asked to recall sentences (e.g., Anderson, 1976). They were much better at recalling the information represented in individual propositions than in recalling the actual sequence of words (*surface form*) of the sentences. For example, they might remember the full sentence represented in Figure 7–14, but in this form:

The high pop-up hit by Jackson went to the Yankee catcher Cerone.

The information in the individual propositions (A, B, and C) would have been recalled, but not the surface form.

Recall of information from a propositional network is often described in terms of *activating* particular propositions, thereby making them easier to recall. It is assumed that a proposition is activated either by some external event (cue) or the earlier activation of a related proposition. In other words, there is a **spread of activation** from an activated proposition to closely related propositions. A good *recall cue* either activates the desired informa-tion directly or activates it indirectly by first activating related information. This is one explanation for the tip-of-the-tongue (TOT) phenomenon dis-cussed earlier: Closely related information is activated first, with activation finally spreading to the desired word.

Spread of activation would also explain a phenomenon called **priming:** Information is often recalled more easily (rapidly) if closely related informa-tion has recently been recalled or activated (primed). For example, Meyer and Schvaneveldt (1971) asked subjects to decide as quickly as possible whether the items in pairs of letter strings were *both* words (e.g., first—truck) or not (e.g., roast—frist; flact—brive). Subjects recognized a pair of words faster if

Production:	One way to make a noun plural.
IF	the goal is to generate a plural noun and the noun ends in a hard consonant,
THEN	generate the noun with an "s" on the end.
Production:	Changing from first to second gear in one kind of car.
IF	the car is in first gear and the car is going faster than 10 mph and there is a clutch and there is a stick shift,
THEN	depress the clutch and move the stick to the upper right and release the clutch.

Adapted from Anderson (1980)

Table 7–2: Examples of Two Productions.
Each production consists of conditions (IF) and a procedure (THEN) to be followed when the conditions are met. Anderson's ACT theory represents human procedural knowledge as a combination of propositional networks and procedures of this sort.

the 2 items were closely related (e.g., bread—butter; farm—barn) than if they weren't (e.g., rope—crystal; nurse—steak). It was as if the first word the subjects processed activated or primed knowledge that was closely related, thus making a closely related word easier to recognize.

It has been argued that knowledge can be represented in long-term memory as images or pictures as well as by propositional or verbal codes. This dual-coding view (Paivio, 1971) was encouraged by experiments of the sort described in the Highlight on visual memory. An alternative view (e.g., Anderson, 1978) is that information in long-term memory is always represented in a propositional code. We may simply construct a "mental image" as we retrieve this information, just as we visualize a scene described verbally in a novel.

PROCEDURAL KNOWLEDGE. We learn how to do things, and we can remember (or forget) how to do them. Thus we have some sort of memory for procedural knowledge. Applied psychologists have long been interested in how we learn such perceptual-motor skills as aiming a rifle or hitting a golf ball (see Keele & Summers, 1976, for a review of such work). More recently, cognitive psychologists have become interested in cognitive skills such as adding two numbers, playing chess, or running a meeting. How is such procedural knowledge represented in memory?

A theory of procedural knowledge has recently been proposed (Anderson, 1980). Called ACT theory, it combines a propositional network of the sort we considered earlier with the step-by-step procedures, resulting in a *production* (Newell, 1973; Simon, 1978). Some examples of productions are shown in Table 7–2. Notice that each procedure is to be carried out when certain conditions (indicated by propositions) are met.

Procedural knowledge can also be represented as a *script* (Schank & Abelson, 1977), a generalized program that outlines how to do something and that we can modify to fit particular circumstances. For example, subjects were asked to describe the 20 most important steps in "eating in a restaurant" (Bower et al., 1979). While there were many individual differences, most agreed on several basic steps or "scenes" (see Table 7–3). Each scene also tended to have a typical internal structure; for example, in scene 5 the main course is eaten before dessert. This basic script could be modified to fit special circumstances such as "eating at a cafeteria." One can easily think of scripts for other activities, such as making an airplane reservation, getting dressed, or going to a party.

Table 7–3: The Restaurant Script.

Scene 1
Enter restaurant
Scene 2
Be seated.
Scene 3
Look over menu.
Scene 4
Order meal.
Scene 5
Eat meal.
Scene 6
Pay bill.
Scene 7
Leave restaurant.

Depth of Processing: An Alternative to the Multiprocess View

The multiprocess view of human memory sees knowledge as represented in a number of interacting memory systems. For example, according to the Atkinson and Shiffrin model (Figure 7–11), transfer of information from short-term to long-term memory depends only on the length of time it remains in short-term memory. Thus transfer is more likely to occur if the subject maintains the information in short-term memory through rehearsal.

It seems clear, however, that one does many things to information in short-term memory beyond the simple rehearsal process suggested by Atkinson and Shiffrin. First of all, information may be combined with other information to form more complex representations or codes, a process sometimes referred to as *elaboration.* For example, on hearing the word "boat," you might encode it into short-term memory. You might then retrieve information held in long-term memory and visualize a boat you had previously sailed on. Thus you would now have a representation of a word just spoken, plus information of an earlier experience. The more you thought about boats, the more complex representations you might develop. Any of these may be encoded and available for retrieval later. The question arises: Is it simply the amount of time an item spends in short-term memory that increases its long-term retention, or is retention increased by the multiplicity and complexity of representations that the item evokes as you continue to think about it?

Craik and Lockhart (1972) proposed the latter view as an alternative to Atkinson and Shiffrin's multiple memory system. They argued that we ignore most of the information available in our ongoing sensory experiences, so it is never elaborated into more complex representations. This is why it is unlikely to be remembered. For example, as you drive down a street many signs are projected onto your retina. Some you attend to and think about to varying degrees, others go totally unnoticed. A stop sign usually requires only a small amount of attention or thought, while a sign advertising a movie you recently saw could evoke a complex series of thoughts drawing on a large amount of associated information in memory. Thus it could be argued that the

What you will remember of this scene would probably depend on whether you were hungry, sleepy, or low on gas. You would "process" certain information more "deeply" in each case.

depth of processing we give any experience determines the number and complexity of its encodings and therefore how likely we are to recall it in the future.

Craik and Tulving (1975) conducted an experiment to evaluate depth of processing. They presented a series of words to subjects along with questions asking something about each word. Some questions—such as "Is the word in capital letters?"—only required a surface analysis of the word. Other questions required deeper processing—for example, "Would the word fit in the sentence 'The boy played the _____?'" Later, when subjects were given an unexpected recognition test, their ability to recognize a word was directly related to the depth of processing required by the earlier question about that word.

A closely related aspect of depth of processing is the organization and structuring that occur during elaboration. This can involve reordering material from the sequence in which it was experienced into a sequence more consistent with some logical structure. You often do this when abstracting or summarizing a lecture, particularly when the lecturer's organization of the material seems less satisfactory than your own. Note that such recoding or reorganization of information is one way in which our general world knowledge (general rules or principles, facts, etc.) may derive from our ongoing experience. Memory for particular sequences of our own experiences (episodic memory) and memory for general knowledge (semantic memory) may simply reflect different levels or forms of organization rather than different memory systems.

We mentioned earlier that stimuli that were present when something was originally learned (encoded) may later serve as effective recall cues, a phenomenon Tulving (1978) called *encoding specificity*. If as you originally learned something you organized it into catgories and thought about those category names, the names might later serve as useful recall cues. For example, suppose you were asked to remember the list of foods in the margin. After looking at the list for a few moments you would probably notice that it contains the names of 3 fruits, 3 vegetables, and 3 meats. Thus you could reorganize it to reflect this structure, as shown in Figure 7–15. In attempting to recall the list, you could first retrieve a category name, which then, according to encoding specificity, would serve as a cue for the recall of items in that category.

Your understanding of a story's structure (see Figure 7–16) might aid recall in a very similar fashion. In thinking about the story structure, you could develop more elaborate codes (**schemas,** *scripts*) to characterize the story—for example: "There were 4 main scenes in the story—the setting, crises, solution, and reward." This code, which would probably be easier to recall

peach
potato
beef
pork
pear
beet
plum
radish
chicken

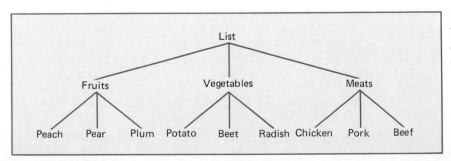

FIGURE 7–15
The 9-word list of foods shown in the margin above can be organized or structured in terms of the categories fruits, vegetables, and meats.

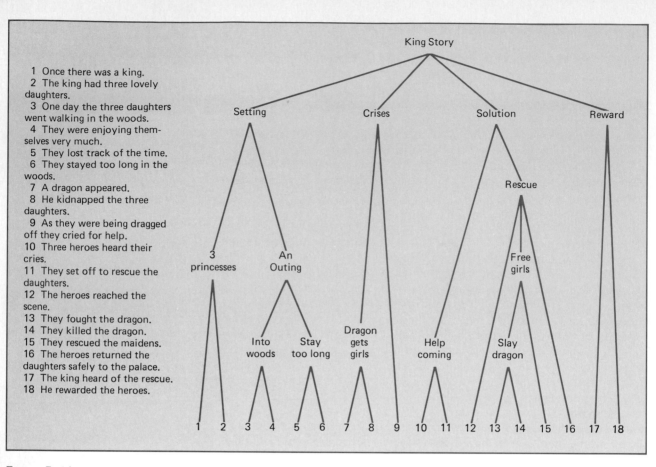

1 Once there was a king.
2 The king had three lovely daughters.
3 One day the three daughters went walking in the woods.
4 They were enjoying themselves very much.
5 They lost track of the time.
6 They stayed too long in the woods.
7 A dragon appeared.
8 He kidnapped the three daughters.
9 As they were being dragged off they cried for help.
10 Three heroes heard their cries.
11 They set off to rescue the daughters.
12 The heroes reached the scene.
13 They fought the dragon.
14 They killed the dragon.
15 They rescued the maidens.
16 The heroes returned the daughters safely to the palace.
17 The king heard of the rescue.
18 He rewarded the heroes.

FIGURE 7–16
Understanding a story's structure can aid recall. In thinking about the structure of the King Story shown here, you might develop more elaborate codes to characterize the story; these codes would serve as cues for recalling details of the story. (Pollard-Gott, McCluskey, & Todres, 1979)

than the details of the story, could serve as a cue for recalling these details, just as did the category names (fruits, vegetables, and meats) in the preceding examples.

Constructive Memory

In Chapter 4 we emphasized the role of stimulus redundancy in perception. Because different aspects of a stimulus are often correlated (redundant), we can infer things about one aspect from another. (Linear perspective is a strong cue for depth.) It appears that the same sort of thing happens when information is retrieved from human memory. Suppose, for example, you were asked to describe someone you met only briefly a year ago. You might first recall that the person was an automobile salesman. You might then recall that he had an outgoing personality, was quite verbal, and argued persuasively. But wait! Is this information based on your actual experience with this man or on your *stereotype* of car salesmen (that is, on what you believe to be the typical personality characteristics of car salesmen)? Certainly people's choice of occupation is often correlated with their personality. It would be possible, but very surprising, to find an introverted, inarticulate car salesman who couldn't argue very persuasively. Thus remembering a person's occupation often allows us to make useful inferences about his or her personality. In fact, we make such inferences so often and so automatically that we may not even be sure whether we are recalling our actual experiences with people or inferring what their behavior was like on the basis of what we remember about their occupation. Inferences of this sort can sometimes distort our recollection of people so that we treat them unfairly, just as our perceptions can sometimes be biased because of inappropriate inferences. (Our ways of interpreting events and people, and some inherent biases in the process, will be discussed at length in Chapter 18.) However, most such inferences aid retrieval, just as they do perception. Even if you can recall only a few major details of some past event, you can often fill in or construct details you can't recall on the basis of your knowledge of redundancy.

In her book *Eyewitness Testimony,* Elizabeth Loftus (1979) considers how witnesses recall a crime or accident. In one experiment, all subjects were shown a filmed auto accident. Half of the subjects were then asked, "How fast were the cars going when they *smashed into* each other?" The other subjects were asked," "How fast were the cars going when they *hit* each other?" The "smashed into" phrasing elicited much higher speed estimates than the "hit" phrasing. Furthermore, this effect on the subjects' memories was still evident a week later when they were asked (among other questions), "Did you see any broken glass?" Almost twice as many of the "smashed into" subjects remembered broken glass, even though no broken glass was shown in the film. It was as if the verbs in the original question colored their reconstruction of the event, with "smashed into" evoking a memory of a more violent accident than "hit."

One interesting aspect of constructive processes in memory is the difficulty it produces in interpreting the recall of dreams. Suppose you are trying to recall a dream you had the night before. You remember dreaming you were sitting in your kitchen and then, a short while later, driving your car. Now, in the real world it would be impossible to get from your kitchen to your car without leaving the house and walking to your car. In other words, the two events you do remember—sitting in your kitchen and driving a car—are almost perfectly correlated with the intermediate event of moving from the kitchen to the car (they are among the scripts that you have for traveling). If you were recalling these events from real life instead of from a dream, you would be quite safe in assuming you had moved from the kitchen to the car. In fact, you might find it hard to tell whether you really remember walking to the car or have simply inferred it from events you do recall. You probably make such automatic inferences during your attempts to recall dreams, but in the dream world, events aren't constrained by the rules of physical reality. Therefore we have no way of determining how much people really remember about their dreams and how much they automatically infer during reconstruction on the basis of inappropriate physical laws.

IMPROVING MEMORY

Methods for improving memory are called **mnemonic techniques** or simply **mnemonics.** They can be as trivial as tying a string around your finger, or highly elaborate strategies that themselves take considerable time to learn. Many of these techniques were developed hundreds of years ago by actors, politicians, scholars, magicians, and priests. While the originators of these techniques weren't familiar with modern theories of human memory, most

Visual Memory: When Remembering Seems like Seeing

Can you remember how many right turns you normally make when walking from one campus building to another? Or how many windows there are in the front of your house? Many people say they would answer such questions by taking an imaginary walk across the campus and noticing how often they turned right, or creating a mental image of their house and "looking at it" to count the windows. This suggests that remembering may sometimes be like seeing. Although this is a controversial issue, there are a number of studies that seem to support this view.

Both the work on iconic memory and the study by Thorsen and Hoch-haus (1976) described in an earlier box suggest very short-term visual memory systems (1 to 2 seconds). Other experiments imply that retrieval of information over much longer retention intervals may also have "visual" properties.

Paivio (1978) asked subjects to recall how clocks looked at various times and to compare the angles formed by the hour and minute hands. For example, he asked, "Is the angle larger at 4:25 or 9:10?" As can be seen in Figure A, the angle in this case is larger at 9:10. The graph in Figure A indicates how the average reaction time (time to decide) decreased as the *difference* between the 2 angles increased. Thus when the angles are similar in size (for example, 12:05 and 1:10), answers are given more slowly than when they are very different (for example, 4:25 and 9:10).

The important point is that this pattern of results is similar to that

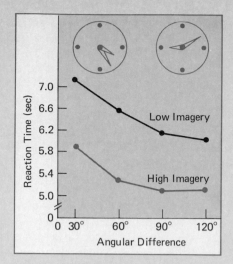

FIGURE A
When asked to mentally compare the angles formed by the two hands of a clock at different times, the reaction time to decide which was larger decreased as angular differences increased. (Paivio, 1978)

mnemonics can be understood in terms of these theories, and they seem to involve only a few basic principles.

Basic Principles

It seems clear that the more you think about something, the more likely you are to remember it. However, as we have seen, this usually means more than simple repetitive rehearsal of the information. It also involves elaboration and reorganization of the information, which produce multiple encodings and useful recall cues. The importance of such cues is obvious if you consider how information is usually retrieved from long-term memory. The process can take some time and often has discernible stages. Each retrieved piece of information aids the retrieval of more information—thus the retrieval process may require several steps to recover information gradually. In other words, if you can't immediately recall a particular fact, you may find it possible to recall something that will serve as an effective recall cue for the information you want to remember. Thus a common feature of most mnemonic techniques is the use of recall cues that are easier to retrieve than the information they subsequently help you to remember.

How does one select appropriate cues and how does something come to function as a cue? First of all, a cue will serve no useful purpose unless it can be recalled. Second, it is of no use to recall the cue if it isn't an effective one. For example, a string tied around your finger is an external memory cue that may help you remember something else. It has the advantage of being easily

Mnemonics may help you learn your lines in a play.

obtained when the subjects are actually shown 2 clock faces and asked to compare the angles. Thus, when asked to compare how 2 times would look from memory, subjects act *as if* they were seeing a mental image.

Kosslyn, Ball, and Reiser (1978) had subjects memorize a map similar to the one shown in Figure B. They then asked them to "visualize" the map from memory, focusing on a particular object such as the "hut" in the lower left corner of the island. The subjects were then told to "imagine a black dot moving from that object to another point on the map"; for example, to the "marsh" in the upper left of the island. As indicated on the graph in Figure B, the time it took to visualize the dot moving from one point to another was a linear function of the actual distance on the map. Again, it was as if subjects were actually seeing a dot move across a remembered image of

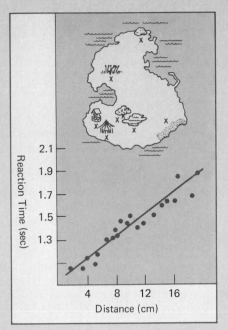

FIGURE B
If asked to visualize a dot moving from one point (X) to another in a previously memorized map, visualization time was a linear function of distance on the map. (Kosslyn et al., 1978)

the map, since the further it had to move, the longer it took.

If remembering how something looked is really like seeing it again, such visualization may interfere with normal vision. Segal and Fusella (1970) asked subjects to either form a visual image (for example, the image of a horse) or an auditory image (for example, the sound of a doorbell). They found that when subjects formed visual images they were poorer at detecting visual signals than when they imagined sounds. Similar *modality-specific interference* during visualization has been demonstrated by Brooks (1968) and Byrne (1974).

retrieved, but it may not be an effective recall cue. You may be aware that the knot on your finger was put there to remind you of something but be totally unable to remember what that something was.

The phenomenon of encoding specificity suggests one principle for making cues effective. The cue should be present at the time you originally encoded the information. For example, you were thinking about something when you tied the string around your finger; thus, according to the principle of encoding specificity, seeing the string may be a good cue for remembering those thoughts. This principle should apply not only to physical, contextual cues but also to cognitive cues. Visiting the house you grew up in may be an effective cue for many childhood memories, but simply visualizing the house may also serve to evoke similar memories.

Something may also serve as a cue if it is closely related to the information you want to remember. This relation may be as simple as "rhymes with" or "has the same first letter"; or more complex, such as a category name. For example, you might remember that your shopping list included "vegetables," which, in turn, would help you recall specific members of this category. Similarly, suppose you want to remember the information in a chapter or story. The title of a specific section or structural component of the material could serve as a recall cue for information in that component. For example, the structure of the king story was illustrated earlier in Figure 7–16. The terms "setting," "crises," "solution," and "reward" could serve as recall cues for various major parts of the story (e.g., "crises" for the information in sentences 7, 8, and 9). Outlining material helps you remember it because the phrases you use to characterize each section can function as recall cues.

Unusual Memories

It is popularly believed that some people are born with an extraordinary ability to remember things, a sort of super-memory. Actually, there is very little hard evidence to support this belief, even though psychologists have long been interested in studying such people.

Many of those who claim to have super-memories make their living on the stage, and are referred to as *mnemonists*. Like magicians, many mnemonists are quite secretive about their methods. However, there is little reason to believe they actually have super-memories. Like magicians, many simply employ outright deception, such as a confederate in the audience or a hidden radio system. Others use mnemonic techniques that, with sufficient practice, could be used just as effectively by anyone. Of course, such mnemonists would like their audiences to believe they are using extraordinary mental powers rather than elaborations of the basic mnemonic techniques described in this chapter.

One interesting case of someone who actually seemed to combine mnemonic techniques with unusual mental abilities is presented in the book *The Mind of a Mnemonist* by the Russian neurophysiologist Alexander Luria (1920/1968). His subject seemed to have an unusually well-developed capacity for visualization, which he used to recall information. He reported being able to associate information with visual experience quite easily. In fact, his subjective experiences could be described as synesthetic. *Synesthesia* refers to experiences in one sensory mode evoked by stimulation of another. Luria's subject had intense visual associations to nonvisual stimuli. Thus he often described auditory tones as having a vivid color. He wasn't very good at remembering certain things, particularly aspects of a stimulus that didn't lend themselves to visualization. Other interesting studies of mnemonists have been reported by Aitkin (1962), Hunt and Love (1972), and Coltheart and Glick (1974).

Another type of super-memory is **eidetic imagery** or, as it is more commonly called, **photographic memory.** This is an ability to remember how something looked in such vivid detail that it is like actually seeing it again. Strangely, considering how many people claim to know, or have heard of, or be related to someone who has this ability, there is very little evidence that such an ability exists. Early studies of eidetic imagery use such questionable methods that it is difficult to draw any clear conclusions from them. More recently Leask, Haber, and Haber (1969) tested 500 schoolchildren and classified only about 7 percent as eidetic, and even these children could have been described as simply having very good imagery rather than a photographic memory.

What appeared to be the first really convincing evidence of true eidetic imagery was reported by Stromeyer and Psotka in 1973. Their subject was shown one member of a pair of random-dot stereograms on one day, and then saw the second a day later. The two patterns were such that, when fused stereoptypically, a viewer would see a digit standing out against a background. Each pattern by itself consisted of thousands of tiny black-and-white squares arranged in a totally random pattern. It would seem impossible for subjects to identify the digit unless they had a virtually photographic memory of the first pattern, which they could then "fuse" with the pattern seen a day later. The apparent ability of one subject to do this has been cited as finally proving the existence of eidetic imagery. Unfortunately, that subject subsequently refused to demonstrate her skill, and the study has never been successfully repeated. Thus it is still questionable whether true eidetic imagery exists.

Mnemonics

One of the oldest mnemonics was used by ancient Greek orators to help them remember the sequence of points they wanted to discuss in a speech. The technique is called the **method of loci.** The basic idea is to use some well-learned sequence of locations as a series of cues for the information you want to remember. For example, suppose you wanted to remember the following shopping list: milk, cereal, eggs, and bread. You could use the familiar sequence of locations encountered on entering your own house as an easily recalled sequence of cues. These might be in sequence: your front porch, the hallway inside the front door, the living room, and the kitchen. One of the best ways to make each of these a cue is to associate each location with one of the items to be remembered. Clearly visualize each location cue and the associated grocery item. Thus you might imagine milk covering your front porch and dripping down the steps. Next you might visualize your front hall ankle deep in cereal, crunching underfoot as you waded through it. Your living room could be completely covered with eggs—splattered against the wall, breaking under your feet. Finally, you could visualize your kitchen full of loaves of bread, fluffy loaves piled one upon the other, pouring out of your oven and filling the whole kitchen. Then when you reached the store, you could take a mental walk through your house, using each location as a cue for a particular item.

A related mnemonic involves learning a series of **peg words** in order. You start with an easily recalled series, the numbers 1 to 10. These numbers will be the cues for words that rhyme with each number. These words, in turn, will be cues for things you wish to remember. For example, the numbers can be used to recall the list of rhyming words in the margin. After only a few moments of practice each number should become an effective cue for its rhyming word. In order to use these words as cues for the items you wish to remember, you must somehow associate them in your memory. This can be done in much the same fashion as in the method of loci: Each item to be remembered is visualized in conjunction with the cue word. For example, suppose you wanted to use this method to remember the same shopping list (milk, cereal, eggs, bread). You could first visualize a bun with milk; perhaps an overturned milk bottle with a soggy bun in a puddle of milk. Next a shoe filled with cereal. Then a green tree growing up through an enormous pile of pure white eggs, or a tree with eggs in place of fruit. And finally, a loaf of bread caught in a closing door. Then you would use the numbers as cues for the rhyming words, which would, in turn, cue a recall of the visualization and the grocery item.

one	bun
two	shoe
three	tree
four	door
five	hive
six	sticks
seven	heaven
eight	date
nine	vine
ten	hen

Many techniques for remembering take advantage of the fact that certain stimuli are presented to you when you need to recall something, and such stimuli are particularly useful as recall or retrieval cues. Consider the **keyword method** developed by Atkinson and Raugh (1975) for learning foreign languages. At first foreign words may not be good direct cues for their English equivalent. However, they can often be used as an indirect recall cue. Many foreign words are good cues for English words that rhyme with them. For example, the word "maison" in French corresponds to "house" in English. "Maison" approximately rhymes with the English word "mason," and it is easy to visualize a stonemason building a house. Thus "maison" would be a cue for mason, which would be a cue for house.

A generally useful sort of cue is an abbreviation or reductive coding of a more complex phrase. An **acronym** is a word made up from parts of the words in a more complex phrase—a type of "chunking" procedure. Comsat, for example, is an abbreviation of "communication satellite." Not only is it an abbreviation, but it is a good cue for the longer title.

How to Remember

The preceding mnemonic techniques may be useful in special instances. More importantly, however, they illustrate general strategies that may be applied whenever you want to remember something. Here are some things you can do to aid your memory:

1. Think about the information you want to remember as long, and as often, as possible. (Remember, spaced practice is often better than massed practice.)

2. Don't just repeat it over and over. Try to elaborate, rephrase, and reorganize it.

3. If possible, ask questions about the material you wish to remember. In addition to giving you more time to think about it, this also forces you to consider different aspects and details of the material.

4. Think of ways in which you might use recall cues. What do you associate with the material that may be easier to recall and could then act as a recall cue? Are there key words you could learn to recall through rhyming or visualization? They would serve as good recall cues.

5. Outline or think about the structure of the information. Is there a way of naming or describing major components of the structure so that these names might serve as recall cues?

6. Is the information redundant? Could you recode or reduce the information to a simpler form from which it would be easy to reconstruct the rest? In other words, what are the key ideas? Can you summarize or abbreviate?

7. Practice retrieval. Don't just study material, put it aside occasionally and practice remembering it. Can you remember things in sequence so that one thing serves as a recall cue for the next thing? Practice going through these sequences, and try to devise better ones.

SUMMARY

1. *Encoding* is the way information is first stored in a memory system; *retention* is the way information is preserved over time; and *retrieval* is the way information is recovered from memory.

2. Three basic types of memory tasks are *recall, recognition,* and *relearning.* Skilled performance is another way of demonstrating memory.

3. In general, people are better at recognition tasks than recall tasks; the items used in recognition tests seem to act as recall cues. People are often able to relearn a task faster than they originally learned it; the reduction in learning time is called *savings.*

4. Factors involved in forgetting include passage of time, distraction or attentional problems, interference from other memories, emotional factors, and organic causes.

5. Multiprocess theories of memory assume that knowledge is represented in a variety of interacting memory systems. For example, the Shiffrin and Atkinson model proposes three systems: *sensory memory, short-term memory,* and *long-term memory.*

6. Different kinds of knowledge may be retained in different memory systems. Two kinds of knowledge are *procedural* ("knowing how") and *propositional* or *declarative* ("knowing that"). Propositional knowledge in turn may be either *semantic* or *episodic.*

7. *Depth of processing* is essentially a "single-process" view of memory: Differences in the way we remember things arise because we process them differently, not because they are held in different memory systems. As we process things more "deeply" we may associate, organize, structure, visualize, and elaborate them, thereby making them easier to recall.

8. Memory appears to involve *reconstructive processes* that cause us to fill in gaps in our recall with what seems reasonable or likely.

9. Mnemonic techniques involve the effective use of recall clues. Some effective methods include the *method of loci, peg words,* the *key-word method,* and the use of reductive coding or *acronyms.*

Suggested Readings

ANDERSON, J. R. *Cognitive psychology and its implications*. San Francisco: W. H. Freeman & Company, Publishers, 1980. A good introduction to modern theories of how knowledge is represented in memory.

BOWER, G. H. (Ed.). *Human memory: Basic processes*. New York: Academic Press, 1977. A collection of articles for advanced students on theories and issues in human memory. Includes updates by the authors of the articles, commenting on their earlier research and conclusions.

KIHLSTROM, J., & EVANS, F. *Functional disorders of memory*. Hillsdale, N.J.: Erlbaum, 1979. The authors approach the study of human memory through an examination of failures of normal memory.

KLATZKY, R. *Human memory: Structures and processes* (2nd ed.). San Francisco: W. H. Freeman & Company, Publishers, 1980. An excellent and widely used undergraduate text in human memory.

LACHMAN, R., LACHMAN, J., & BUTTERFIELD, E. *Cognitive psychology and information processing: An introduction*. Hillsdale, N.J.: Erlbaum, 1979. An up-to-date review of research in memory from an information-processing point of view.

LOFTUS, E. F. *Eyewitness testimony*. Cambridge, Mass.: Harvard University Press, 1979. A survey of memory research bearing on eyewitness testimony.

LURIA, A. R. *The mind of a mnemonist*. New York: Basic Books, 1968. (Originally published in 1920.) A fascinating and detailed account of a mnemonist by a famous Russian scientist.

NORMAN, D. *Memory and attention: An introduction to human information processing* (2nd ed.). New York: John Wiley, 1976. A highly readable introduction to information-processing theories of memory and experimental methods used in studying human memory.

8. Language and Thought

High-speed digital computers with vast memories and incredibly fast computing capabilities have revolutionized many areas of science, technology, and commerce. Yet these machines, with all their computing power, cannot do what a child of two or three can already do; they cannot understand and produce simple, ordinary human conversation. In the late 1950s the availability of computers raised hopes for the eventual design and production of machines that could scan a printed text and convert the patterns of light and dark on a printed page into sounds, enabling the blind to "read." In the last decade, such machines became a reality. For example, a Kurzweil machine can scan the pages of a book or magazine and convert the optical information into reasonably comprehensible speech. The synthesized speech that it produces, however, sounds dull and somewhat mechanical. More importantly, this machine has no understanding of what it is reading, and so it cannot decide how to pronounce such words as *lead,* to guide, and *lead,* a heavy metal. A great deal of effort was also devoted to developing computer programs that could translate material automatically from one language into another and that could understand the meaning of either printed or spoken language. Neither of these more complicated efforts has yet fully succeeded.

When the first attempts to duplicate human speech capabilities on computers were made, we were relatively ignorant about the complexity of human language. Now we know much more about how people perceive speech sounds and interpret the meanings of those sounds and thus we now know some of the problems and difficulties that are involved in designing language-understanding machines. Because holding an ordinary conversation seems as easy and natural to us as breathing or walking, it has taken a long time for us to appreciate how complex human language use really is. But when we look carefully at the nature of human language and the mental activities that must take place when we speak, listen to speech, or think, we realize the complexity of the processes involved. As we describe the activities involved in language, keep in mind the sorts of things a machine or computer program must "know" if it is to deal efficiently and appropriately with ordinary human discourse.

THE NATURE OF HUMAN LANGUAGE

Language Universals

On the surface, languages such as Chinese or Turkish seem quite different from one another. They sound different, seem to have different grammatical rules, and, to a native English speaker, they may not even sound like languages at all. The stream of speech coming from someone speaking a totally foreign language may not even sound as though there are separate words; it sometimes sounds like a continuous rush of gibberish.

Roger Brown (1965) has summarized the minimal design features of all human languages. First, all languages use a limited number of speech sounds, called **phonemes** (see the Highlight on speech sounds and speech perception). Most languages use fewer than 100 phonemes. English, for example, has about 45 phonemes, while Hawaiian manages with even fewer, about 13. With so few phonemes, a language such as Hawaiian has to render the English "Merry Christmas" as "Melly Kalikamaka." Each of the speech sounds of a

Speech Sounds and Speech Perception

A New Yorker, a Texan, an Iowan, and a Vermonter can all say the word "ball" and can be understood perfectly well by one another. Yet the precise sound of the vowel represented by the letter *a* will be different in each case. Similarly, the sounds represented by the letter *p* in the words "pin" and "spin" are also different, yet we tend to hear those two *p* sounds as identical. In each of these two examples, a single phoneme—the vowel sound in "ball" in one case, the sound of the letter *p* in the other—is heard and recognized correctly, despite marked differences in the physical sound itself. This poses an intriguing question: When are two speech sounds functionally the same, and when are they different?

For any specific language, two speech sounds are different phonemes if substitution of one for another actually changes the meanings of words in which they appear. For example, changing the sound of *r* to the sound of *l* in the word "rip" changes the word itself. In contrast, changing the quality of the sound of *r* from the typical English pronunciation to the trilling Scots pronunciation does not change the word "rip" into another word. Therefore, *r* and *l* are considered two separate

and distinct phonemes in English, while the trilled and untrilled *r*'s are merely variants (**allophones**) of the same phoneme. Are the sounds of *r* and *l* inherently more "different" or more discriminable than the two variants of *r*? Not to speakers of Japanese, a language that does not treat *r* and *l* as two separate phonemes. This does not, of course, indicate defective hearing among Japanese. We who speak English also do not hear some of the differences between the phonemes of other languages. For example, the sounds represented by the letters *k* and *c* in the phrase "keep cool" sound exactly alike to us, yet they are actually different sounds and are treated as such in Arabic. (Note the placement of the tongue for the sound of *k* in "keep," where it touches the roof of the mouth toward the back, and the more forward placement for the sound of *c* in "cool.") When we learn a language, one of the first things we learn is to hear differences among those speech sounds that are specifically important in that language and to ignore others.

We also learn to categorize certain physically different speech sounds as the same. For example, the *d* sounds in the syllables "dee" and "doo" sound exactly alike to us, even though the physical stimuli for these two sounds are quite different (as shown in the illustration above). In doing these things, people use

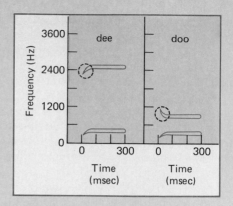

not only the stimulus information in the sounds themselves, but the context as well. People are better able to recognize speech sounds when they form words than when they form nonsense syllables (Stevens & House, 1972). Common words are heard more clearly than uncommon ones (Pollack, Rubenstein, & Decker, 1959), and grammatical and meaningful sentences are heard more clearly than nonsensical sentences (Miller & Isard, 1963). Most computerized pattern-recognition devices—like the kind that recognizes the computer-patterned letters and numerals on bank checks—can use only the physical stimuli that they are given and must rely completely on them. People, on the other hand, can tolerate a remarkable amount of variability and distortion by using their knowledge of the language and of the world to identify accurately the sounds that occur in ordinary conversation.

---

language is meaningless on its own. For example, the consonant that we represent by the letter *k* has no meaning. These meaningless units can be combined to form meaningful units such as words in virtually limitless ways—the 45 phonemes of English can be combined and recombined to form hundreds of thousands of words, just as can the 13 phonemes of Hawaiian.

This is a second way in which all languages are alike: They all have a small number of meaningless speech units that can be combined to form a virtually infinite number of *meaningful* speech units. This property—having both meaningless and meaningful language units—is technically known as *duality of structure*. Third, in all languages most meanings are assigned to words arbitrarily. That is, a word does not have to sound like the thing it refers to. Therefore, we are free to coin new words, change the meanings of old words, and in general build a vocabulary to suit our communicative and symbolic needs.

Finally, all languages combine words in systematic ways to form sentences. In principle the number of sentences that can be generated, starting with a finite and small set of phonemes, is infinite. Every language spoken on earth has these 4 characteristics and also has the capacity to create an unlimited set of sentences that can be used to express any conceivable set of ideas.

Morphemes, Words, and Meanings

The smallest unit of speech that has meaning is the **morpheme.** A morpheme may be a word or a part of a word. Common prefixes and suffixes, as in the words "*a*typical," "*non*sense," "jump*ed*," and "lesson*s*," are one type of morpheme. These morphemes must always be used with at least one other morpheme to form a word, and so they are called *bound* morphemes. *Free* morphemes correspond roughly to words: Words like "man" and "page" are simultaneously single morphemes and words. Finally, many words consist of several morphemes put together, both free and bound, such as "*de* + compos*ed*," "*counter* + attack*ed*," and so on.

Morphemes and words are made by combining phonemes according to the morphophonemic rules of the language. The phonological rules of English describe our implicit knowledge of the sound system of our language. For example, most native English speakers would agree that "spab," even though it is not a word in the language, is a possible sound sequence, whereas "sbab" is not. The particular rule, in this case, says that a voiced consonant may not follow the sound represented by the letter *s*.

A voiced consonant is sounded with vocal-chord vibration, called *voicing*. Voiceless consonants do not include such vibration. You can appreciate this difference by putting your fingers on your Adam's apple (the larynx) while you alternate pronouncing "zzzz" and "ssss." The former is voiced; the latter is not. For consonants such as /b/, the "buzz" of voicing starts about 35 milliseconds after the onset of the consonant when it is voiced, as in *boo,* but not until the following vowel when it is unvoiced, as in *poo.* Among the voiced consonants of English are /v/ as in *voo* and /d/ as in *do*. Their unvoiced counterparts are /f/ as in *foo* and /t/ as in *too.* Because of the phonological rule that an /s/ sound may not be followed by a voiced consonant, not only "sbab" but also "svab" and "sdad" are "illegal." We know this intuitively, although few of us can state the rule explicitly.

The grammar of a language contains rules for the allowable sequences of sounds and for morpheme combinations, but, as we mentioned earlier, there are essentially no rules for assigning meanings to words. With a very few exceptions, the meanings of words are assigned arbitrarily—the words bear no physical resemblance to the things they name. Because meanings are assigned arbitrarily, we can have as many words as we need. Indeed, if word sounds had to resemble the things or concepts that they symbolize, how could a language have words like "justice" or "poverty"?

ASPECTS OF MEANING: DENOTATIVE AND CONNOTATIVE.   Words such as "and," "or," "on," and "of" are function words. Their function is to specify relations among things, and they are the parts of speech such as prepositions and conjunctions.

Nouns, verbs, adjectives, and adverbs are content words. Content words symbolize at least two different kinds of meanings, denotative and connotative.

The **denotative** meaning of a word is usually defined as the thing or class of things that the word can label. This meaning is like a dictionary definition of a word. But dictionary definitions are, at best, only rough guides to what a word denotes. In order for a dictionary to be useful, one must already have a good command of the language and a reasonable knowledge of one's physical and social world. For example, a partial dictionary definition of the word "chaste" is "innocent of unlawful sexual intercourse." A third grader who had been assigned this word to look up in a dictionary did so, and when asked to use the word in a sentence, wrote "The amoeba is a chaste animal." Clearly, one aspect of the the word's denotative meaning had been understood, but not several other important aspects, such as that the word can only be sensibly applied to adult human beings. If we include this kind of knowledge of what words mean, then the meanings of words would look more like encyclopedia entries than dictionary entries. For example, a dictionary entry for the word "dog" is "a carnivorous domesticated mammal probably descended from the common wolf" (Merriam-Webster, 1973). An encyclopedia would provide the additional information that dogs are furry, that they make excellent pets, that some dogs are used for hunting and others for herding, that they come in a variety of sizes and shapes, and so on. The denotative meaning of the word "dog," then, is really the sum total of the ideas shared by people in our culture of what a "dog" is.

When the word "dog" is used in a conversation, one or more aspects of our conception of what a dog is may be appropriate to the intended meaning of the sentence. For example, if someone says that her dog only eats prime beef, then the word "dog" clearly refers to a pet. However, if someone says that the movie he went to last week was a real dog, then the word "dog" refers to a particular property or attribute of dogs, in this case a rather negative property. These examples illustrate one of the primary characteristics of word meanings in isolation. Virtually any word, when considered out of context, can be interpreted in many ways. Clearly, when we refer to a word's meaning, we can really refer to a range or class of meanings that the word may have when used in sentences or conversational contexts.

It would be difficult enough to program a computer to interpret the denotative meanings of words because, as we have seen, virtually all words can be interpreted in more than one way. This difficulty is compounded by the **connotative,** or emotional, meanings of words. This emotional (sometimes called **affective**) meaning of a word essentially reflects how we feel about the thing that the word represents. This meaning is measured by the **semantic differential,** a technique devised by Osgood, Suci, and Tannenbaum (1957). The semantic differential is a set of rating scales. Each scale has a pair of opposite adjectives, as shown in Figure 8–1. The word to be rated is put at the top of the scale, and people are asked to rate that word on each of the scales below it. "Home," for example, might be rated as more round than angular, more passive than active, good rather than bad, rather warm, and relaxed. The word "prison" might be rated as more angular than round, bad rather than good, and relatively cold. If a word is rated as good, then it will probably also be rated as smooth rather than rough, and relaxed rather than tense. Because the ratings on some scales tend to go together (that is, they *correlate* with one another), the ratings of the 10 scales can be summarized in terms of three general scales, or *dimensions,* of connotative meaning. These three general

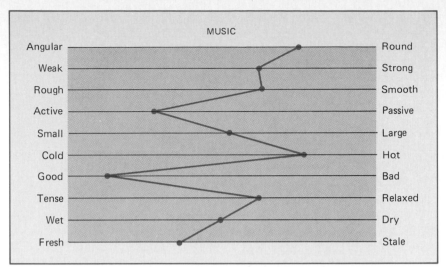

FIGURE 8–1

How one person rated the word "music" on the semantic differential. How would you rate "music" on these scales? (Glucksberg & Danks, 1975)

summary scales are the good-bad scale, the active-passive scale, and the strong-weak scale, representing the three major dimensions of connotative meaning, respectively: *evaluation, activity,* and *potency.*

Just as the denotative meanings of words will vary with context, so will connotative meanings. Sometimes even a small change in context will have a sizable effect. For example, the evaluative and activity connotations of the word "inventive" would be quite different in the phrases "an inventive assassin" and "an inventive poet."

Are the three dimensions of connotative meaning—evaluation, activity, and potency—unique to the English language, or do they also characterize the connotative meanings of words in other languages? Obviously, the connotative meaning of any particular word may vary considerably from one language and culture to another. For example, "peasant" may be rated as bad, passive, and weak by Americans, and good, active, and strong by mainland Chinese. This is to be expected when peoples differ in culture, ideology, and experience. However, extensive cross-cultural research by Osgood and his colleagues (1975) has revealed a striking universality in the structure of connotative meaning. Using the semantic differential in many different cultures and languages, including American, Dutch, French, Finnish, and Japanese (among others), the same three major dimensions of connotative meaning appear again and again. Of the world's peoples that have been tested so far, all seem to judge the connotative meanings of words in similar ways, using the same three dimensions of evaluation, activity, and potency.

Sentences and Messages

In every langauge, words are combined into sentences according to set rules. These word-combining rules form the **syntax** of a language, and they can be used to generate all the grammatical sentences of a language. To date, no such complete grammar has been written for any language, but theoretical linguists such as Noam Chomsky (1957) have argued convincingly that any such grammar would need at least two types of rules—phrase structure rules and transformational rules.

Phrase-structure rules govern the organization of the various parts of a sentence. To illustrate how phrase-structure rules can be used to generate the sentences of a language, let us assume that there is a language with just four types of words: nouns, verbs, articles, and adjectives. Using the symbol → to mean "can be rewritten as," we can represent the lexicon (vocabulary) of this language as follows:

Nouns: N → man, woman, horse, dog, etc. . . .
Verbs: V → saw, heard, hit, etc. . . .
Articles: Art → a, the. . . .
Adjectives: Adj → happy, sad, fat, timid, etc. . . .

Thus, wherever the symbols [N → man] appear, we can substitute the word "man" for the symbol *N*. Phrase-structure or rewrite rules such as this one can refer to parts of sentences, such as noun phrases and verb phrases, as well as to single words. The sentence "A fat man hit the dog" can, under the rewrite rules of this partial grammar, be described in terms of its parts: The first three words are a noun phrase (NP), the last three words are a verb phrase (VP).

These parts can be broken down even further. The noun phrase consists of an article, an adjective, and a noun. The verb phrase consists of a verb plus a noun phrase. These relationships can be summarized in two ways. One way is in terms of a tree structure diagram, as in Figure 8–2. The other way, which is equivalent to the diagram, is in the form of a set of phrase-structure (rewrite) rules:

Rule 1. S → NP + VP. This rule states that a sentence, S, consists of, or can be rewritten as, a noun phrase (NP) plus a verb phrase (VP).

Rule 2. NP → Art + [Adj] + N. This rule states that a noun phrase (NP) consists of an article (Art) plus, optionally, an adjective (Adj), plus a noun.

Rule 3. VP → V + NP. This rule states that a verb phrase (VP) consists of a verb (V) plus a noun phrase (NP).

FIGURE 8–2
Phrase-structure analysis of the sentence, "A fat man hit the dog."

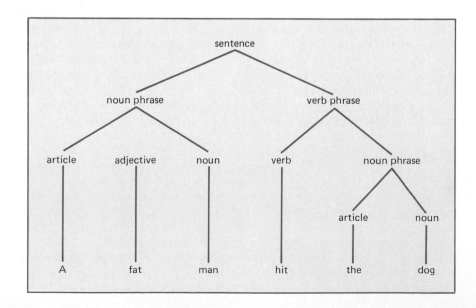

This grammar, which was devised for illustrative purposes by Victoria Fromkin (1976), can, with just the 13-word lexicon listed above, generate 4,800 sentences.

Notice, however, that these 4,800 sentences represent a tiny fraction of the kinds of sentences that could occur in English. For example, all the verbs are in the simple past tense. All the nouns are in singular form, and they refer only to animate beings. Only simple declarative sentences can be generated—this small grammar does not generate questions, commands, or any of the many other kinds of sentences we normally use. Yet, with very small additions to the rules, the number of sentences that can be generated can increase enormously. Merely by allowing each verb to appear in present as well as past tense, we double the number of verb phrases and so double the number of different sentences we can have. If we also double the number of available nouns by allowing each to appear in both singular and plural form, we could then generate 36,400 different sentences (80 different NPs multiplied by 480 different VPs). How many sentences could we generate if we now again double the number of available nouns by simply adding four new ones in both singular and plural form?[*]

Phrase structure rules not only tell us how sentences can be constructed, they also provide a description of those sentences. For example, the sentences

John saw Mary.
Peter heard Sally.

strike us as being quite similar to each other, even though the words are different. One way they are similar is that they have the same grammatical structure—they have both been generated by the same phrase-structure rules (in this case, S → NP + VP; NP → N; VP → V + NP). However, some sentences that appear similar to one another have quite different structures. Consider the following two sentences:

John saw Mary.
Mary was seen by John.

Here we have two sentences with different phrase structures, yet they are obviously related; indeed, they mean roughly the same thing. In each case, John is the person who saw someone and Mary is the person who was seen. The grammatical rules that describe the relationships *between* sentences are called **transformational rules.** These are rules that specify how various types of sentences are related to one another. They do this by showing how one string (sequence) of words can be rewritten or transformed into another. For example, one set of transformational rules allows us to rewrite

Mary hit the ball.

into

The ball was hit by Mary.

SURFACE STRUCTURE AND DEEP STRUCTURE. Essentially, these types of phrase structure and transformational rules make explicit some of the intuitions we

[*]This would give us 160 NPs and 960 VPs, which can yield 153,600 different sentences.

have about our language. For example, most of us feel, intuitively, that the two sentences

John is easy to please.
John is eager to please.

are similar to and yet different from one another. They share a surface similarity in that they differ by just one word—"eager" versus "easy." They have the same **surface structure.** However, they differ quite markedly in terms of their underlying organization and intent, that is, their **deep structure.** This intuition of ours, that these two sentences are really basically different, can be demonstrated by applying the same transformation to each sentence.

John is easy to please.   It is easy to please John.
John is eager to please.   It is eager to please John.

The difference between the original two sentence types is now obvious and explicit. The first can be transformed in this way and still make sense, but the second cannot. Therefore, the original two sentences have different deep structures; they are basically different sentence types.

FORM AND MEANING.   The surface structure of a sentence is known as its surface form. We have already seen how the same meaning can be expressed in different surface forms. What do people remember about a sentence—its form, its meaning, or both? Under most circumstances people tend to forget the verbatim form of sentences and remember only the meaning. Jaqueline Sachs (1967) asked people to listen to short stories and then tested to see if they could remember the exact wording of selected sentences in those stories. If the test came immediately after hearing the original sentence, then people could easily recognize any changes in wording, as in:

Original sentence: He sent a letter about it to Galileo.
Test sentence: A letter about it was sent to Galileo.

However, if the test sentence came a mere 27 seconds later in the story, then people could not tell whether it was the same as the original. In contrast, people could easily tell when the meaning had been changed, as in:

Galileo sent him a letter about it.

even after longer delays, when memory for exact wording becomes particularly poor (Anderson & Paulson, 1977).

Memory for exact wording can be quite good when that wording is important for one reason or another. Memorized prose, poetry, and song lyrics can be retained verbatim for years, often for a lifetime (Rubin, 1977). Similarly, the intent of jokes or insults often depends upon the exact words that are used, and we all too often remember such material verbatim. People also tend to remember the surface form for statements with personal significance such as sarcasm, personal criticism, and humorous remarks (Keenan et al., 1977). Such statements are just the kind that cannot survive paraphrasing, and so it is not surprising that the original wording is remembered.

LITERAL, INTENDED, AND CONVEYED MEANINGS.   The grammatical rules of a language could, in principle, be used to specify the literal meanings of all the sentences of that language. But would such a set of rules enable a computer to interpret the meanings of ordinary language? Unfortunately it would not, because people often go beyond the *literal* meanings of sentences in order to understand what a speaker intends to convey. This meaning is the *intended* or *conveyed* meaning of an utterance. For example, the literal meaning of the statement "Can you pass the salt" is, roughly, "Are you physically or otherwise capable of passing the salt?" In most ordinary contexts, such as when people are sitting around a table eating lunch, the literal meaning of that sentence makes no sense. The intended meaning—"please pass the salt"—does. Similarly, if you say to someone who is standing by a closed window "Gee, it's hot in here," it would probably be understood that you are not merely commenting on the weather but are asking that a window be opened.

These examples illustrate how people combine the information they have about the language, about the situation they are in, and about other people, to figure out the meaning of the speech they hear or read. The information that people have about their langauge is their *linguistic competence*. The information about the situation and about the people involved in the conversation is *contextual knowledge*.

Both linguistic competence and contextual knowledge are necessary for understanding, but they are not enough. People must also know about the principles of conversational exchanges. Grice (1975) was among the first philosophers of language to point out that people who participate in a conversation follow the "Cooperative Principle." Speakers are assumed to be informative, truthful, relevant, and concise. Listeners assume that speakers indeed do try to be informative, truthful, relevant, and concise. When a speaker seems to violate these maxims of conversation, the listener is led to seek some alternative interpretation. For example, if someone remarks "seems to be raining a bit" in the midst of a torrential downpour, this would be a violation of the maxim to be informative, and so the remark is interpreted as irony or sarcasm rather than as a mere description of the weather. The statement "can you pass the salt" is hardly relevant as a question about ability, and so it is interpreted as a request. Similarly, a statement such as "my aunt Sarah is a baby" is not likely to be literally true, and so, on the assumption that the speaker is trying to be truthful, it is interpreted metaphorically—Aunt Sarah behaves childishly.

Finally, people go beyond both the literal and conveyed meanings of utterances to draw inferences about matters that are related to an utterance. If someone were to say to you, "Peter forgot to close the door," you would get far more information than is contained in the literal interpretation of that sentence. For example, you would probably be left with the following beliefs, among others: that Peter was supposed to or intended to close the door; that Peter was able to do so; that the door was indeed open at some time; that something undesirable might have happened or did happen because the door was left open; that the undesirable consequences of Peter's forgetfulness might have been a robbery, or rain soaking the floor, or that a canary or dog had escaped, and so on. And, just as important, you would be learning something about Peter's reliability and, of course, about the speaker's attitudes and feelings about poor old Peter. Whenever we deal with speech in meaningful ways, we bring to bear our knowledge of the language, the world, and, perhaps most of all, our knowledge about ourselves and other people.

LEARNING A FIRST LANGUAGE

Most children utter their first words toward the end of their first year. By the time they are 2, most children have an active vocabulary of more than 200 words and can speak in short simple sentences. Within 3 to 4 years of their birth, children have acquired the basic grammar of their language. The apparent ease and speed of first-language learning has led some theorists to postulate an innate **language-acquisition device,** or **LAD** (Chomsky, 1975). The LAD can be defined as some characteristic property of the human mind that is uniquely and specially tuned for language acquisition. As we describe the various steps children go through on their way to full language competence, we shall see that there may be many LADs, each consisting of a specific characteristic of the human organism that helps in learning one or another aspect of language.

Is Language Learned or Innate?

Until Noam Chomsky revolutionized linguistics with his theory of transformational generative grammar, people believed that language was learned in the same ways that other skills and habits are learned. Speech sounds were learned by **imitation.** Word meanings were learned by associating the sound of a word with the thing that the word named. Finally, syntax—the set of rules for combining words to form sentences—was learned by making associations between words. Thus, the expression "the red ball" would be learned by associating "the" with "red," and "red" with "ball."

This simple form of learning undoubtedly does occur during language acquisition. Some aspects of word meanings can be acquired by classical (Pavlovian) conditioning. For example, if a word or nonsense syllable is repeatedly paired with an unpleasant event, then that word itself becomes unpleasant (Staats & Staats, 1957). Operant-conditioning techniques have been used to teach simple word meanings to such special types of people as autistic children and mentally retarded patients. If a child is positively reinforced for making an appropriate sound (for example, the word "truck" in the presence of a toy truck), then the child could gradually learn to associate the word and its referent—the thing it names.

Chomsky's contribution to the psychology of language acquisition was to point out convincingly that some aspects of language could not, in principle, be learned by conditioning or by imitation but require, instead, knowledge of complex rules.

Rules are involved at every level of language learning, from the sounds of language to the grammar. The sounds of a language are not composed of a set of independent, discrete sounds. Instead, the sounds of a language form a phonological system, obeying the kinds of rules we described earlier. Word meanings, while arbitrary, are not just labels for things but also represent complex concepts. For example, knowing the word *dog* implies that one knows what dogs are, how they differ from cats, and how they differ from everything else we know about in the world. Finally, learning the syntax of a language must involve rule-discovery procedures. The syntactic rules of a language are not transparent—they are not given explicitly in speech. Indeed, most of us cannot readily describe the rules we use to form grammatical

Speech Acts and How to Make a Promise

According to speech-act theorists such as John Searle (1979), language is used in five general ways: to tell people how things are; to get people to do things; to express feelings and attitudes; to commit ourselves to something; and to accomplish things directly (as when we make a declaration such as "I now pronounce you husband and wife"). Whenever we interpret an utterance, we must decide what the speaker is trying to do: tell us something, get us to do something, and so on. The surface form of the sentence is usually not enough to let us know just what speech act is being performed. For example, the simple declarative sentence "It is raining" can be a descriptive act, or it can be a request to shut a window, an expression of lack of confidence in the weather-forecasting system, or a commitment to do something that depends on rain, such as plant the garden.

Listeners must use their knowledge of the person who is talking and the context of the conversation to interpret correctly even the simplest of utterances. Both listeners and speakers must also follow the implicit rules of speech-act theory if they are to understand one another. The rules of speech-act theory specify the conditions for well-formed speech acts. Consider the conditions that must be satisfied when someone wants to make a promise.

a. The promise must be spoken in the presence of a listener, unless it is a promise to oneself.
b. The utterance describes a future action by the speaker.
c. The listener would prefer that the speaker take that action, and the speaker assumes that this is indeed so.
d. Neither the speaker nor the listener expect that the promised action would normally have been taken without this promise.
e. The speaker sincerely intends to perform the action.
f. By promising, the speaker takes on an obligation to carry out the promised action.
g. The speaker intends to inform the hearer that the speaker is taking on that obligation.

These "rules" for how to make a well-formed promise are, like the rules of syntax, implicitly known by all adult members of the speech community. Test your own intuitions by judging which of the following speech acts are well-formed promises and which violate one or more of the implicit how-to-promise rules described above.

1. Mother to 10-year-old child: "You misbehave and I promise to tell your father when he comes home."
2. Teacher to class: "I promise that the final examination will not be easy."
3. Husband to wife: "I promise to breathe tomorrow."
4. Weather forecaster to TV audience: "I promise that it will not rain all weekend."
5. Child to teacher: "I promise that I did do my homework last night."
6. Young lady to friend: "I promised Harry that I would marry him, but he doesn't know it yet."

See below for answers.*

sentences, but the fact that we can do so is an incontrovertible sign that the rules are there. If the rules are not explicitly laid out in the speech that a child hears, and if parents don't teach the rules explicitly, then how could imitation and reinforcement learning work?

Chomsky and his followers believe that children are born with an **innate** knowledge of the general form of linguistic rules. Others believe that children can discover such rules during the course of growing up in a speaking community. In either case, there is general agreement that language learning involves more complicated learning mechanisms than imitation and conditioning, even though these simpler mechanisms are involved.

The mistakes young children make illustrate that they are learning rules, and not just imitating the speech they hear. When children say "Daddy runned" or "This is my bestest color," they are not imitating the speech that they have heard; they are using a rule that they have somehow discovered.

*All of these violate one or more how-to-promise rules: 1 and 2 violate rule c; 3 violates d, f, and g; 4 violates b, e, f, and g; 5 violates b, e, f, and g; 6 violates a, f, and g.

From Prespeech to Speech

From the moment they are born, infants prepare for learning language by learning many of the prerequisites for language. They learn to distinguish between speech and nonspeech sounds—between words and the sneezes, coughs, grunts, and all those other noises that people make. They learn how to produce the speech sounds of their native language. They learn to differentiate between self and others, and they learn concepts of objects. And, of course, they learn that things have names. Infants also learn, even if only in the crudest of terms, about communicative *intentions*—that when their mother or father makes speech sounds, some meaning or communication is intended (Bruner, 1974/75). Once this idea has been grasped, children can begin to figure out *what* meanings are being expressed (MacNamara, 1972).

INFANT PERCEPTION AND VOCALIZATIONS. Until quite recently very little was known about newborns' perceptual abilities, or about the development of their vocal abilities. Beginning in the early 1970s, scientists began to investigate these two aspects of language development, with surprising results.

It had long been believed that the newborn's auditory sensitivity is quite poor, and that the ability to distinguish among minimally different speech sounds could develop only with learning and experience. This is undoubtedly true for many speech sounds, but human infants have a head start in being able to discriminate among *some* important speech sounds virtually at birth. Eimas and his colleagues (1971) discovered that infants between 1 and 4 months discriminated between the syllables [ba] and [pa] exactly as adults do. This early ability to hear at least some of the important speech sounds, especially those that are common to most human languages, surely must be helpful to children as they begin to pick up the sound patterns of speech. Furthermore, the infant brain seems to be especially prepared to acquire language. For most right-handed adults, speech is localized in the left hemisphere. Preterm infants as young as 35 weeks after conception already display this hemispheric asymmetry. Speechlike sounds evoked more cortical (brain) responses from the left than from the right hemispheres in these infants (Molfese & Molfese, 1980), suggesting that brain specialization for speech develops quite early indeed. Of course, such early specialization would not be particularly useful if infants did not hear much speech, but they do. Both male and female adults talk incessantly to infants, even newborns, providing them with early and extensive speech experience (Rheingold & Adams, 1980).

In contrast to the very early appearance of speech-perception abilities, the human infant's ability to produce speech sounds at birth is very poor indeed. The major reason for this is the shape and structure of the baby's vocal tract (see Figure 8–3). At birth, it is more like the vocal tract of a chimpanzee than the vocal tract of an adult human. The larynx is relatively high, and the tongue takes up virtually all of the space in the oral cavity. These two factors provide a very small resonance chamber that cannot be adjusted very much to produce differences in vowel sounds. This means that the infant simply does not have the vocal machinery to produce speech sounds at birth (Oller & Warren, 1976).

While this vocal tract structure is not suited for speech, it is perfectly suited for sucking and drinking without gagging or choking. This configuration of tongue, larynx, and epiglottis virtually guarantees that the infant can breathe only through the nose, and that the epiglottis will protect the breathing

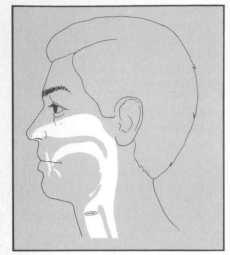

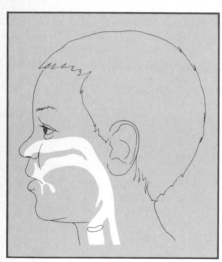

FIGURE 8–3

(Top) *The typical vocal tract of a human adult. The oral cavity is relatively large and its shape and size can be varied rather extensively by moving the tongue around.*
(Bottom) *The typical vocal tract of a human infant at birth. The infant's oral cavity is quite small because the tongue takes up so much space and because the larynx is high up in the throat. This vocal tract cannot be varied much at all, and so cannot produce a variety of speech sounds.*

passages from any liquids or solids taken by mouth. It is as if Mother Nature intended the infant to eat first, talk later.

From birth to 6 weeks, infant vocalizations are mostly reflexive. The baby cries, fusses, spits, sneezes, and coughs. From 6 weeks to about 4 months, the baby begins to combine these vocalizations with the speechlike sounds of cooing and gurgling. These sounds somewhat resemble consonant-vowel syllables, and are usually addressed to the caretaker. By about 4 months, the shape and structure of the baby's vocal tract have matured, and the baby begins to produce a variety of speechlike sounds.

Babies seem to practice one or two types of sounds at a time. For example, an infant might spend 4 weeks producing "raspberries," then two days of high-pitched squealing, usually making these sounds while looking at people or at interesting objects. This vocal play appears to serve 2 functions. First, it obviously attracts attention and plays a role in communication between the infant and other people. Second, it enables infants to learn what they can do with their vocal apparatus, preparing for the learning that will occur between 6 months and 1 year.

By the 6th month, infants can voluntarily control some consonant sounds, and they engage in a characteristic form of baby talk called **reduplicated babbling.** Typically, this consists of a consonant and a vowel, such as "da da da da da" or "ma ma ma ma ma." It may not be coincidental that the words for father and mother in many human languages sound like this babbling— virtually all infants, regardless of the language spoken in the home, say things like this. Almost as soon as infants have achieved control of simple consonant-vowel sounds, they stop making them, and instead use **expressive jargon.** This involves a variety of syllables, with far less repetition than reduplicated babbling, and with a surprising similarity to the intonation patterns of adult speech. Indeed, it sounds very much like normal adult speech, but not a bit of it is intelligible. It is almost as if infants have learned the broad characteristics of the sounds of the language, including many of the vowels, consonants, and the intonation patterns, and are now practicing their new-found vocal skills.

SOCIAL AND COGNITIVE DEVELOPMENT.   During this first year of life other prerequisites to language learning become established. Babies begin to *imitate* adult actions. Nonverbal communication occurs in a variety of settings—play, feeding, dressing, bathing, bedtime. Baby and parent begin to understand one another's intentions, motivations, and behaviors. This interpersonal understanding is a necessary step toward learning the meanings of words. It is much like visiting a foreign country and figuring out the names of things. The most common way is to notice that someone is talking about, say, bread or cheese, and then associating the words you hear with the appropriate things. This requires that you know what a person is talking about *before* you understand the language. Similarly, young children "learn their language by first determining, independent of language, the meaning which a speaker intends to convey to them, and by then working out the relationship between the meaning and the language. To put it another way, the infant uses meaning as a clue to language, rather than language as a clue to meaning" (MacNamara, 1972, p. 1).

The behaviors of parents and infants seem designed to maximize the chances of their understanding one another before they can rely on spoken language. A mother will try to capture an infant's attention when naming something. Infants, by their fourth month, will tend to look at what their

mother is looking at, thus ensuring that when infant and mother interact, they are paying attention to the same thing (Bruner, 1974/75). In these as well as in other more subtle ways, an infant can find out what the mother is saying and talking about and so can begin to learn the meanings of the words that the mother uses.

Acquiring a Vocabulary

When children utter their first words, they do so one at a time. For example, a child might say "doggie," or "milk," or "Mama." What could each of these utterances mean? During this stage of one-word utterances the child may often use a single word to express a whole message. For example, the word "milk" could mean "I want more milk" or "Where is the milk?" These one-word utterances can never be interpreted without considering the specific situation the child is in, and what the child and others are doing at the moment. They are called **holophrastic** utterances because just one word expresses a whole message.

Single words can also be used by young children to refer to several different things. The word "dog," for example, may often be used to refer to other furry, four-legged animals, such as cats, horses, or sheep. This kind of **over-extension** of a word's meaning is quite common. Sometimes such an over-extension is a sign that the child has not yet learned the precise meaning of a word. At other times, it could simply be a child's way of talking about something whose name isn't yet known. In this latter case, the word "dog" would be used holophrastically to express the meaning "an animal that is like a dog."

At first, new words are learned rather slowly. Gradually the rate of learning increases, and then accelerates quite rapidly, so that by 24 months an average working vocabulary of almost 300 words is not unusual, with many of the words having been learned toward the end of the second year (see Figure 8–4).

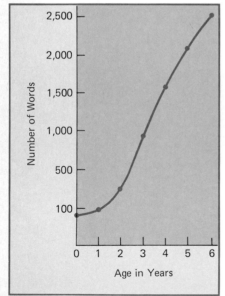

FIGURE 8–4
Starting with a few words at the age of 1 year, children learn, on the average, about 270 words by age 2, and by age 6 have a vocabulary of over 2,500 words. (Lenneberg, 1967; Smith, 1926)

By the time children are about 3 years old they display a characteristic and efficient pattern of word learning. Carey and Bartlett (1983) studied the ways that 3-year-olds learned the meaning of a single new word, *chromium*. They used *chromium* to refer to the color *olive* and introduced this new word by saying to children "You see those two trays over there. Bring me the chromium one. Not the red, the chromium one." The children could easily follow this direction by picking out the tray that wasn't red, and virtually all of them did so. More interestingly, virtually all gave clear indications that they had heard a new word by repeating the word *chromium*. Noticing that a new word has been spoken is the first important aspect of children's word-learning strategies. After this one single exposure about half the children realized that the new word was a name of a color but did not seem to know that the color was olive. This is the second efficient strategy for word-learning: knowing the general category of the word. Once children realized that *chromium* is a color word, then the next time it is used they can discover just what color it refers to. After a total of only 5 exposures to this new word over a period of 10 weeks, about 70 percent of the children seemed to understand that it referred to the color olive. Apparently, young children can learn the meanings of new words with only minimal exposure to them, provided that the new words are used meaningfully in natural, conversational settings.

What do children talk about during the early part of language acquisition? Katherine Nelson watched 18 children as they spoke their first 50 words. Her observations suggest that children do not learn words passively, or by merely imitating what their parents say. Instead, they tend to talk about what interests them (Nelson, 1973).

Among the first 10 words used by every child were the names for animals, food, and toys. Not once in the first 50 words did "diaper," "pants," "sweater," or "mittens" appear, even though parents must have used these words quite often. In general, young children seem to name the things that they handle or play with directly, and the things that do something, like move or make noises. They do not name things that just sit there, like furniture, or grass, or stores.

During this naming and learning period parents prepare the way for the next advance, two-word and three-word utterances. In addition to talking in short sentences themselves, parents will often expand a child's short utterances. If a child says "milk," a parent might say "Does Tommy want more milk?" This reply is based on the parent's best guess about the child's communicative intent. If the parent has guessed correctly, the reply can serve as a model for an expanded utterance. If the parent has guessed incorrectly, the reply tells the child that his or her one-word utterance is sometimes inadequate and ambiguous. In either case, children can get useful information about language and communication.

From Words to Sentences

Some time around the middle of the second year the one-word utterances of holophrastic speech begin to be replaced by the child's first sentences—two-word utterances. The particular words that children put together in these early and primitive sentences are carefully chosen. In many respects they resemble the kinds of word choices we make when we compose telegrams. We leave out relatively unimportant words, and include only those words we absolutely need to get our message across.

Young children who are unable to put together more than two or three words at a time tend to be **telegraphic** in this sense. They do not, of course, deliberately decide which words to omit. They do, however, use the few words and limited grammar that they have to good effect. Like the single-word utterances of holophrastic speech, two-word utterances are used to express a wide variety of meanings. Thus, the sentence "Mommy lunch" might be used to express any one of several different meanings: "That lunch belongs to Mommy," or "Mommy is eating lunch," and so on (Bloom, 1970, 1973).

Children throughout the world, in different cultures and in different language communities, behave in pretty much the same ways during this stage of language development. They all proceed from holophrastic speech to telegraphic two-word sentences, and they all talk about the same kinds of

Table 8–1: Two Word Sentences in Child Speech from Several Languages.

FUNCTION OF UTTERANCE	LANGUAGE				
	English	*German*	*Russian*	*Finnish*	*Samoan*
LOCATE, NAME	there book that car see doggie	buch da [book there] gukuk wauwau [see doggie]	Tosya tam [Tosya there]	tuossa Rina [there Rina] vettä siinä [water there]	Keith lea [Keith there]
DEMAND, DESIRE	more milk give candy want gum	mehr milch [more milk] bitte apfel [please apple]	yeshchë moloko [more milk] day chasy [give watch]	anna Rina [give Rina]	mai pepe [give doll] fia moo [want sleep]
NEGATE	no wet no wash not hungry allgone milk	nicht blasen [not blow] kaffee nein [coffee no]	vody net [water no] gus' tyu-tyu [goose gone]	ei susi [not wolf] enää pipi [anymore sore]	le 'ai [not eat] uma mea [allgone thing]
DESCRIBE EVENT OR SITUATION	Bambi go mail come hit ball block fall baby highchair	puppe kommt [doll comes] tiktak hängt [clock hangs] sofa sitzen [sofa sit] messer schneiden [cut knife]	mama prua [mama walk] papa bay-bay [papa sleep] korka upala [crust fell] nashla yaichko [found egg] baba kresio [grandma armchair]	Seppo putoo [Seppo fall] talli 'bm-bm' [garage 'car']	pa'u pepe [fall doll] tapale 'oe [hit you] tu'u lalo [put down]
SHOW POSSESSION	my shoe mama dress	mein ball [my ball] mamas hut [mama's hat]	mami chashka [mama's cup] pup moya [navel my]	täti auto [aunt car]	lole a'u [candy my] polo 'oe [ball your] paluni mama [balloon mama]
MODIFY, QUALIFY	pretty dress big boat	milch heiss [milk hot] armer wauwau [poor dog]	mama khoroshaya [mama good] papa bol'shoy [papa big]	rikki auto [broken car] torni iso [tower big]	fa'ali'i pepe [headstrong baby]
QUESTION	where ball	wo ball [where ball]	gde papa [where papa]	missä pallo [where ball]	fea Punafu [where Punafu]

From Slobin (1971).

things (Slobin, 1971). All children name things and people. All children have a way of announcing that they have noticed something (for instance, "Hi doggie!"). All children have simple ways of expressing important things such as the hoped-for reappearance of something, like "More milk," or the equally important facts of disappearance, like "Allgone cookie." The kinds of semantic relations and functions of language expressed by children the world over are the same (see Table 8–1).

Once children have mastered two-word utterances, they begin to learn the syntax of the language. One of the more sensitive measures of a child's level of language development is the number of words (or morphemes) used per utterance. This measure, devised by Roger Brown at Harvard, is called MLU— mean length of utterance (1973). With increasing cognitive and linguistic sophistication, children's utterances tend, on average, to get longer (see Figure 8–5). This reflects at least two kinds of developmental changes. First, it reflects the child's capacity to organize and produce longer sequences of words, irrespective of the grammatical complexity of those sequences. Second, it reflects the child's learning of more complex grammatical forms. In early speech, a child might say "Go home?" Later, the same meaning might be expressed in the adultlike "Can we go home now?"

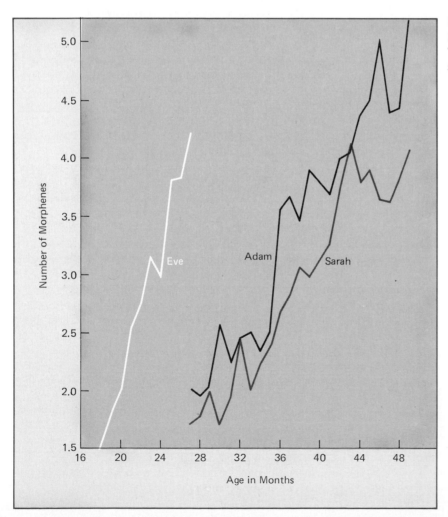

FIGURE 8–5
Mean length of utterance increases with age. This increase is shown for three children studied by Brown (1973).

FIGURE 8–6

This is the test used to assess children's knowledge of pluralization rules. (Berko, 1958)

Children's acquisition of the syntax of the language involves more than learning how to string more and more words together. It also involves learning the syntactic rules that make it possible for them to produce new sentences, as well as to make some revealing mistakes. Sometimes when children first learn to express the past tense in English, they will use the standard form, as in "walk-ed," and sporadically also use irregular forms, like "went." When they really learn the rule—adding the suffix *-ed* to a verb stem—they apply this rule to all verbs and say things like "goed" instead of "went," "breaked" instead of "broke," and so on. It then takes several years to learn the exceptions to the rule. This pattern of rule-learning, then overgeneralizing the rule, and finally learning the exceptions to the rule has been observed in every language that has these kinds of rules and exceptions.

The rules of grammar, even though they may lead to some mistakes, greatly simplify the task of language learning. Once we have a rule, we need not memorize every form of every word in the language. We can even generalize the grammar to words that don't exist. In an ingenious experiment, Jean Berko (1958) taught nonsense names to 5- and 6-year-old children. A child would be shown a drawing of an unfamiliar animal (see Figure 8–6), and told, "this is a wug." Then Berko would point to a second picture and say, "There are two of them. There are two _____." The children then completed the sentence and said "wugs," indicating that they indeed knew the rule for pluralization in English.

Of course, knowing a rule does not mean that we are conscious of that knowledge, or that we can describe the rule. Even literate adults can know rules without being aware of them. For example, what rules do we follow to produce *tag questions,* such as "John went home yesterday, didn't he?" or "John didn't go home yesterday, did he?" What are the rules that specify that the phrase "a large red Turkish truck" is correct, while the phrase "a Turkish red large truck" is incorrect? We must know these rules because we follow them when we speak, but, clearly, we don't know them consciously.

From Sentences to Conversation

A telephone rings, and a 3-year-old child answers. The caller asks, "Is your mommy home?" The child immediately puts the phone down and calls for Mother to answer the phone. This child has understood the *intent* of the caller—to speak to Mother. At this age, most children use the immediate situation to help them interpret what people say. They may very often ignore the details of the speech they hear. Somewhat older children may go to the other extreme. They will rely completely on the literal meaning of a sentence and ignore the social or conversational context. Thus, a 4-year-old who is asked "Is your mommy home?" may very well answer "Yes," and wait for the conversation to continue.

From about 3 to 6 years, children learn a great deal about conversational behavior. This includes learning how to tell whether to take a statement literally or not, as in our telephone example. It also includes the development of awareness and sensitivity to other people's feelings and their needs for information. Young children tend to ask for things or tell people to do things directly. They will say "Swing me," or "I want a cookie." Older children, starting at about 4 to 5 years of age, will use adultlike, indirect requests. They will say "Do you want to swing me?" or "Can I have a cookie?" They will also provide reasons for requests, like "Gimme the hammer—I *need* it."

This shift away from direct requests to indirect and rationalized statements

 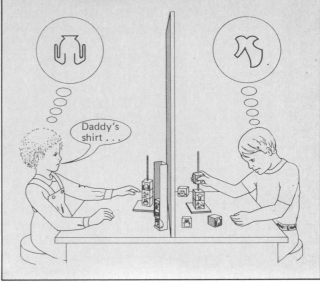

reflects an increasing understanding of social and interpersonal factors in communication. When adults talk to one another they routinely tailor their speech to suit their listeners. For example, when two strangers are given a communication problem that involves talking about unusual geometric forms (as in Figure 8–7), they begin by using long descriptive phrases, and then gradually shorten those phrases as they tacitly develop a two-person code (Krauss & Glucksberg, 1977). When nursery school children are given a version of this task (Figure 8–8), they behave as if a tacit code had already been developed. The descriptions they give to one another are short, idiosyncratic, and virtually uninformative to the listeners (Glucksberg, Krauss, & Weisberg, 1966).

With further development of their language and social skills, children learn when and how to adjust what they say and how they say it, depending upon who their listeners are. Four-year-olds appear to know how to adjust their speech in some obvious situations. For example, they will use longer sentences and more complex grammatical constructions when talking to adults than when talking to 2-year-olds (Shatz & Gelman, 1973). Further elaboration and development of these social-linguistic skills will enable them to make the same subtle and fine-tuned adjustments that adults make during ordinary conversation (Asher, 1979).

FIGURE 8–7 (LEFT)
In the adult communication task, the speaker had to describe six odd designs on a paper in front of him and give the number that went with each; a listener on the other side of an opaque barrier had to assign the correct number to copies of the same designs. Adult speakers communicated successfully by giving detailed descriptions the first time a design was used; when the same form appeared in later trials, speakers shortened their descriptions (for example, "The spaceman's helmet," and then just "helmet"), and continued to be well understood by listeners. (Krauss & Glucksberg, 1977)

FIGURE 8–8 (RIGHT)
In the children's version of the task, the speaker had to describe the design on blocks appearing at the base of a dispenser and then stack the blocks on a peg. The listener's task was to select the correct blocks from a randomly ordered collection and stack them in the same order. The youngest speakers gave noncommunicative descriptions that were usually misunderstood. (Krauss & Glucksberg, 1977)

LANGUAGE AND THOUGHT

Can animals other than humans learn a humanlike language? Can animals who have no such language reason or solve problems? Is there any connection between being able to talk and being able to think?

Nonhuman Language

All animals communicate with one another. A honey bee returning from a food source will perform a dance in the hive that informs the other bees

Examples of cats and non-cats. What properties do cats have that the non-cats don't have?

Cat

Non-cat

Cat

Non-cat

where the food is (von Frisch, 1967). Wolves, lions, and other pack-hunting animals communicate with one another when coordinating a hunt. Until recently, however, no animal has learned even the rudiments of a human language.

People have always wondered whether animals, and particularly chimpanzees, could be taught a humanlike language. Early attempts to teach chimpanzees to talk were complete failures (Kellogg & Kellogg, 1933; Hayes, 1951). Allen and Beatrice Gardner, of the University of Nevada, suspected that chimps could not talk because they lacked the necessary vocal apparatus, not because they weren't smart enough. Acting on this hunch, they decided to teach American Sign Language (ASL)—used by many American deaf people—to a young female chimp, Washoe. Washoe learned to sign, and after about two years she began to combine signs into short simple sequences—much like the early sentences of human children (Gardner & Gardner, 1969).

Washoe, like a human child, was able to produce word combinations that could be interpreted quite readily. Her combinations seemed to express the same semantic relations that are expressed universally in young children's utterances (see Table 8–1). Furthermore, Washoe used virtually all of her combinations spontaneously, without having them taught to her or having any opportunity to imitate them.

Since the Gardners' pioneering work with Washoe, several other chimpanzees—and at least one gorilla—have been taught fairly complex communication systems. Some of these were based on signs adapted from Ameslan, others on artificial signing systems. In each case, the animals were able to acquire and use label-referent terms (see the Application on whether an ape can learn language). There is, however, some question about two aspects of their langauge use. First, there is considerable doubt as to whether apes can proceed beyond two-sign utterances of any complexity. Second, the apes who have learned these skills have not yet shown any evidence of using their communication systems conversationally, either with people or with other apes. In general, their spontaneous communications consist primarily of requests and, occasionally, casual object-naming. The linguistic capabilities of chimpanzees and gorillas have yet to be unambiguously determined.

Concepts

A concept is our knowledge about a category of objects or events. When we have a concept of, say, *chairs,* we can recognize that something is a chair even if we have never seen it or one just like it before. We would also know that it belongs to a larger category of things called *furniture.* Having such concepts is enormously useful and efficient. Most of the things and events we encounter

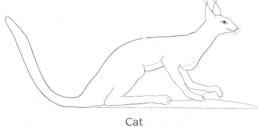
Cat

Cat

Non-cat

APPLICATION☐
Can an Ape Learn Language?

The Gardners taught the chimpanzee Washoe a crude version of American Sign Language, ASL. Other chimpanzees have been taught to communicate with people and to construct sentencelike strings of symbols in different ways. David Premack (1976) taught the chimpanzee Sarah to make symbol strings by placing magnetized plastic forms on a magnetic board (see below, left). Duane Rumbaugh (1977) taught a chimpanzee named Lana to use a computerlike keyboard with illuminated push buttons to communicate in a system he called *Yerkish* (see photo). In each of these cases it was claimed that the chimpanzee had mastered an essential component of natural language, the ability to create a sentence.

Herbert Terrace has reported the results of an intensive study of a chimpanzee named Nim Chimpsky (pun was intended). Over a period of several years Nim made more than 19,000 multiple-sign utterances in the version of ASL that Terrace taught him. These utterances were then carefully analyzed for evidence of syntactic regularities. According to Terrace, most of the multiple-sign utterances were either simple repetitions, like "tickle me tickle" or "hug me Nim," or they were inadvertently cued by a human teacher. Terrace analyzed the film records of other chimpanzees who had been taught ASL, including Washoe, and concluded that they did not clearly demonstrate that the chimpanzees had mastered even an elementary form of syntax. Terrace concluded that "apes can learn many isolated symbols (as can dogs, horses, and other nonhuman species), but they show no unequivocal evidence of having mastered the conversational . . . or syntactic organization of language" (Terrace, Petitto, Sanders, & Bever, 1979, p. 901).

The key word in this quotation is "unequivocal." The Gardners strongly disagree with Terrace's conclusion. They argue that Washoe did use languagelike rules, and that she did show "conversational give-and-take" between herself and human companions (Gardner & Gardner, 1980). The evidence is, then, equivocal, and we will have to wait for more complete studies of chimpanzees' learning to "talk" before the final answer is in. Can an ape learn to create a sentence? Maybe.

Leaving aside the question about creating sentences, can an ape learn arbitrary linguistic reference? Sue Savage-Rumbaugh and her colleagues (Savage-Rumbaugh et al, 1980) taught two young chimpanzees the meanings of two labels—one for edibles (foods), the other for nonedibles (tools). The chimpanzees were then tested to see if they could categorize novel objects and novel labels as foods or as tools on the basis of the previously learned "names." They clearly could, suggesting that chimps are capable of learning at least this aspect of humanlike language—arbitrary symbolic reference. Interestingly, Lana, who had received extensive languagelike training in Yerkish (see above), failed to learn these two new category-words.

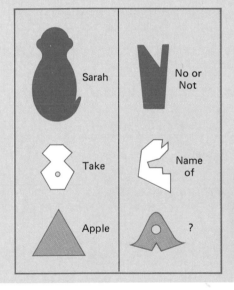

Sarah

No or Not

Take

Name of

Apple

?

every day are examples of well-known categories, even though they may be new to us in many ways. By having a concept of what a thing or event is we can classify something new as an instance of a familiar category, thus saving us an enormous amount of unnecessary learning.

For example, my concept of *cats* allows me to recognize any one of an infinite number of different animals as cats, and to classify accurately almost any animal I might see as being a cat or not. I also know where cats fit in the animal kingdom, and I can compare them with other animals such as dogs,

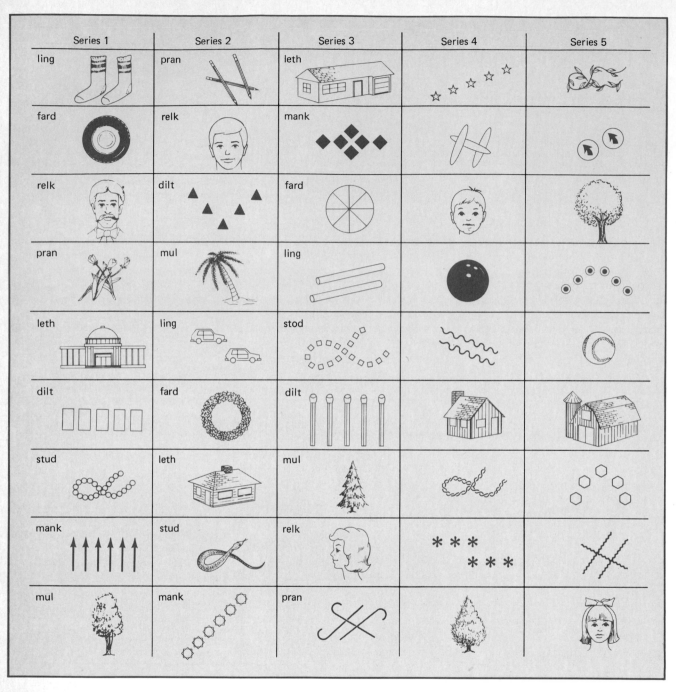

FIGURE 8–9

The nine pictures of Series 1 were shown one at a time together with their labels. This was followed by Series 2, then 3, 4, and 5, and people had to learn which labels went with which pictures. Concrete object concepts, such as faces, were learned most quickly. Spatial form and pattern concepts, such as circle, were more difficult. Most difficult were concepts based on number, such as two objects. Can you provide the correct labels for the pictures in Series 4 and 5? If you can, then you have learned the concepts that are labeled ling, fard, and so on. (After Heidbreder, 1947)

elephants, or fish. I know pretty much what to expect from any cat I might meet, and, therefore, I would know what to do if I should meet one.

How do we acquire such concepts? One way is to learn a set of rules that defines a category. In an influential study of concept formation, Heidbreder (1947) found that people learn classification rules based on concrete ideas more easily than rules based on abstract properties like numbers (see Figure 8–9). The relative difficulty of concrete and abstract concepts can also be seen in the developing child. Children's early concepts are primarily concrete, including such things as dogs, people, toys and candy. Later, concepts like *living things* come in, as well as such concepts as *fairness, honesty,* and *truth*. At first, these abstract concepts are quite simple: *truth* may be defined as "not lying." In adulthood, the concept of *truth* is far more complex, and few of us would even try to define it.

Concepts can also be easy or difficult to learn depending on the types of rules that define them. When a single rule defines a concept, it is a *simple* concept. In this sense, all of the concepts shown in Figure 8–9 are *simple* concepts, whether they are abstract or concrete. When the rules become more complicated, then the concepts become more difficult to learn. Bruner and Goodnow (1956) used arbitrary concepts to see what kinds of classification rules were hardest to learn. When classification decisions had to be based on two or more rules, it took longer to learn the concept than when only one rule was required. When something must have two or more features or characteristics in order to qualify as a member of the category it is called a **conjunctive concept.** The concept of *registered voter* is a conjunctive concept. In order to qualify as a registered voter, a person must be 18 years old, a citizen, and a resident of a particular district and also must have his or her name entered on a particular roster of names.

Even more difficult are **disjunctive concepts.** These involve "either–or" rules. For example, the category *U.S. citizen* is defined as someone (1) who was born in the United States; *or* (2) either of whose parents were United States citizens; *or* (3) who was naturalized in a U.S. District Court. If any one of these conditions is met, then the person is a citizen.

When the rules for classifying examples of a concept can be stated explicitly, then that concept is well defined. Many everyday concepts (for example, *citizen* and *voter*) are well defined, but many others are not. For such fuzzy concepts, we do not seem to use simple rules to define categories. Instead, we can classify things in terms of their similarity to the most typical examples of that category. Consider the category of things we call *birds*. All birds share certain characteristics: they all have wings, and they all have feathers. However, it would not bother us to learn that someone had discovered a wingless bird, or that someone had managed to breed a wingless and featherless bird for the domestic poultry market. This means that wings and feathers are not necessary or defining features of birds, although they are certainly characteristic of them. Other features that we associate with birds are their ability to fly, sing, build nests, and so on.

Our concept of *bird,* then, consists of what we expect birds to look and act like. On this basis, people agree that robins and sparrows are highly typical birds. Chickens and turkeys are not quite as typical, and penguins and ostriches are highly atypical (Rosch, 1977). Similarly, our concept of *fruit* enables us to classify things as fruits and also to know that apples, pears, and oranges are typical fruits, while watermelons, papayas, and blueberries are atypical. Atypical fruits differ from typical fruits in one or more ways. Watermelons are larger than most fruits, papayas have an unusual texture and taste, and blueberries are small and, of course, blue (how many other blue fruits are there?). Notice that we do not use the technical definition of fruit in our everyday life, and so tomatoes and cucumbers are not included in the fruit category despite the fact that they are technically fruits.

How do we learn everyday concepts like these if we do not learn a set of defining rules? Rosch (1977) has suggested that after extensive experience with members of a category, such as birds, we gradually learn what most birds are like. This includes things such as their average size, their most usual coloring, their common behavior patterns, and everything else about them that is *birdlike*. It would *not* include such things as having two eyes or warm blood, because lots of other kinds of animals have these features too. In other words, we learn what most birds have in common with one another, and what most birds have that other kinds of animals do not. This enables us to distinguish between birds and all the other animals that are not birds, and also gives us a notion of what a typical bird is like. Our concept of *bird,* then, is the sum total of what we have learned about birds and about other kinds of animals.

The Functions of Language in Thought

The chimpanzees who have learned languagelike communication systems also provide striking illustrations of some of the noncommunicative uses of language. Obviously, languages and languagelike signs or symbol systems are designed primarily for communicative functions. But the ability to express ideas, urges, or concepts in words or in signs can also have profound effects on other behaviors. For example, people can express aggression or anger either physically (by hitting someone), or verbally. Can chimpanzees who have learned languagelike communications systems use them to express similar emotions? When Nin Chimpsky was being trained he would sometimes threaten and bite people. After he had learned the sign for "bite," he seldom actually threatened or bit—he simply signed "bite" and that seemed enough to do two things. First, it told people that he was angry; second, it seemed to vent his anger. The chimp seldom bit people after symbolically expressing his anger (Terrace, 1979). This was particularly surprising because Terrace and his colleagues had used the results of their work with Nim to challenge the contention that chimps could learn sentences.

Nevertheless, Nim's languagelike abilities finally did serve him well. The research program at Columbia had been concluded, and so Nim was sent to a primate research laboratory in Oklahoma. He was then donated to a medical research laboratory in New York, where he was kept in a small cage and was scheduled to receive hepatitus virus and other potentially painful treatments. Terrace and others who knew of his plight protested vigorously. Nim, after all, had grown up in social contact with people. He even knew some "words" and apparently protested vigorously himself by signing "out! out!" to the medical laboratory personnel. After his case was publicized in the daily newspapers, he was released and sent back to Oklahoma, where he can live out his life with other chimpanzees in relative peace and freedom. Having a language, even a minimal one, can help when one is in trouble.

Having a language can also help in solving conceptual problems. One problem that is difficult for chimpanzees to solve is *cross-modal matching*— telling whether or not two objects are the same or different when one of the objects can be seen but not touched, and the other object can be touched but not seen. Lana, a chimp who was taught a computer-based sign system, could solve such problems easily when the objects involved were ones that she had names for. She had much more difficulty with objects that she had no names for (Rumbaugh et al., 1979).

Children, too, display changes in their abilities to solve certain kinds of problems when they learn how to use language. One such problem is the *far transposition* test. A child is first taught that to find a toy or a piece of candy he or she must choose the smaller of two boxes. After learning this, the child is given two new boxes, both of which are quite different in size from the original training pair. Children who could not express the original learning in words—"pick the smaller one"—generally could not succeed in transferring the knowledge they gained in the first test to the second test. Most of the children who could express the answer verbally did succeed (Kuenne, 1946).

Language, then, does more than serve communicative functions. It can help us to control and guide our behavior, and it can be useful in thinking and problem solving.

Linguistic Relativity

In the late nineteenth century and early part of this century, linguists and anthropologists worked primarily with exotic cultures and languages—for example, American Indian, Samoan, tribal African, and Eskimo. The languages that they studied were strikingly different from the familiar European languages, and the modes of thinking and action also seemed strikingly different. Did the culture influence the development of the language or could it be that modes of thought and conceptualization are prisoners of the language—that what and how people think depends upon the particular language they speak?

This idea—that the particular language a person speaks determines how the world is perceived and conceptualized—is known as the Whorfian hypothesis, after Benjamin Whorf (1940), who with Edward Sapir (1912/1958) was among the early proponents of **linguistic relativity.**

There is ample evidence that the way we describe things can affect how those things might be perceived, remembered, or thought about. The labels we give to ambiguous stimuli will influence how they are seen and how they are remembered. Look at Figure 8–10. It can be seen either as two strings with beads on them, or as a bear cub climbing the far side of a tree. In a classic experiment, people were shown drawings that could be named in either of two ways (see Figure 8–11). The names given to the drawings substantially influenced the drawings that subjects later reproduced from memory (Carmichael, Hogan, & Walter, 1932).

These kinds of experiments suggested a way to test the Whorfian hypothesis. If different languages provide different sets of names for, say, colors, then people who speak different languages should show differential color memory. For example, in ordinary English we have about six basic color terms—red, orange, yellow, green, blue, and violet (plus, of course, black and white). In the language of the Dani, a tribe in Western New Guinea, there are only two color words. One term refers to all the dark, cool colors, the other to all the light, warm colors. Do English speakers conceptualize colors differently from speakers of Dani?

Eleanor Rosch Heider and Daniel Olivier (1972) tested Dani natives and American college students for their ability to remember and discriminate

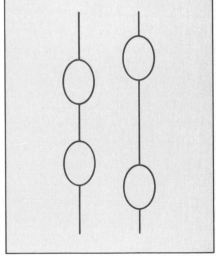

FIGURE 8–10

What is this a picture of? See the text for an explanation.

Are Some Languages Better than Others?

Is English better than French? Is Portuguese better than Hungarian? Except for reasons of snobbery or chauvinism, the answer to both these questions is no. All known languages, from the Dani of Western New Guinea to the English of the Court of St. James, are equally complex and equally grammatical. There are no criteria that would enable us to judge whether any one language is better or worse than any other.

What about the dialects of a single language? Are some versions of English better than others? Is a Vermont or Maine accent better than a Texas or Louisiana accent? Are all of these regional accents inferior to "standard" English? If so, what is "standard" English, and who speaks it?

In England, the standard was once defined by the type of people who spoke it. In 1931, a British linguist wrote this definition of the "best" English: "Every one knows that there is a kind of English which is neither provincial nor vulgar, a type which most people would willingly speak if they could, and desire to speak if they do not. . . . It is the type spoken by members of the great Public* Schools, and by those classes in society which normally frequent these. . . . This is the best kind of English

*The "public" schools of England are really the expensive and exclusive private schools.

. . . because it is spoken by those often very properly called 'the best people'" (Wyld, 1931, p. 605).

What is the American equivalent to this? Perhaps the kind of radio and television broadcast English that has no trace of a regional accent. The more obvious the regional accent, the less standard the speech. Obviously, this criterion is as arbitrary as the social class criterion used by Mr. Wyld in 1931. Ultimately, our feelings about regional and ethnic accents reflect our feelings about the people themselves. If a particular group has high status, then its members' accents are acceptable (for example, an upper class British or sophisticated French accent). If a group has low status, then its members' accents are judged as unacceptable.

among colors. The Americans and the Danis were equal in their ability to discriminate shades of difference among colors. The Americans were slightly better at remembering which one of 40 different color chips had been shown to them 30 seconds before. However, these two groups of very different people fundamentally perceive and conceptualize color in identical ways. Both Danis and Americans link together the same colors. Colors that are only somewhat similar to Americans are also only somewhat similar to the Danis. The colors that Americans confuse in memory are the same ones that the Dani confuse in memory. In other words, the perceived degrees of similarity and

FIGURE 8–11

The drawings in the center column were shown to people together with the labels of List 1 or the labels of List 2. When asked to draw the original pictures from memory, people tended to make the pictures more like their labels than the original was. (Carmichael, Hogan, & Walter, 1932)

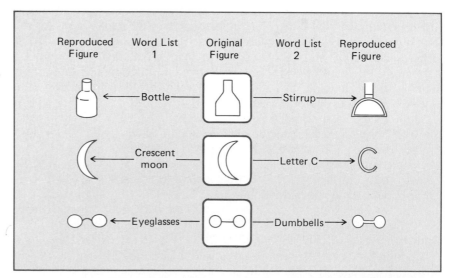

difference among colors are the same in these two language groups. The color names available to these two groups of people have not influenced basic aspects of perception and knowledge of colors.

These findings as well as many others offer no support for the Whorfian hypothesis, at least with respect to naming practices. The influence of language upon thought may be pervasive, but the differences among human languages do not seem to cause important differences in how people perceive and conceptualize the world (Glucksberg & Danks, 1975).

THINKING

Many different mental activities are called *thinking*. At one extreme there is the conscious but idle daydreaming that we all do occasionally. At the other is the unconscious creative thought of the scientist, writer, or artist that few of us ever engage in. In this section we examine the thinking that goes into everyday reasoning, problem solving, and decision making.

Reasoning

Do kangaroos have livers? Even if you have never learned this fact directly (and it's most unlikely that you have), you can still answer the question correctly. The answer is not recalled or remembered, but generated by **reasoning.** In **deductive reasoning,** the steps are explicit and the conclusions firm. In order to answer the kangaroo question deductively, we could transform the question into a syllogism (a three-term reasoning format):

All kangaroos are mammals.
All mammals have livers.
Conclusion: Kangaroos have livers.

We could also answer the question by using **inductive reasoning:**

> Many animals that I know have livers. The kangaroo resembles these animals in many ways. Therefore, it is more than likely that kangaroos have livers. But I wouldn't bet my life on it.

In both cases, information that we already have permits us to generate additional information. This is one of the more important functions of reasoning.

We also use reasoning to judge the validity of arguments. In general, college students are quite good at detecting logical flaws in syllogisms. For example, many students would agree that this argument is false:

All Xs are Y.
All Zs are Y.
Therefore, all Xs are Zs.

This same logic problem, however, can be made either easier or more difficult by changing the particular terms used. For example, it is most clearly recognized as false if we already know that the conclusion is, in the real world, false:

All Israelis are people.
All Egyptians are people.
Therefore, all Israelis are Egyptians.

In contrast, if we tend to agree with the conclusion, then it is more difficult to detect the logical flaw:

Welfare is giving to the poor.
Charity is giving to the poor.
Therefore, welfare is charity.

These examples illustrate how our knowledge and our biases can interfere with our ability to use deductive logic (Wason & Johnson-Laird, 1972).

HYPOTHESIS TESTING.   Reasoning also seems to be easier if the problem is relatively concrete rather than abstract. When people are asked to test a simple **hypothesis,** they usually look for evidence in favor of the hypothesis, disconfirm or falsify that hypothesis. This tendency is called the *confirmatory bias.* This bias is stronger with relatively abstract material, as illustrated by a study of hypothesis testing and reasoning by Johnson-Laird and Wason (1977). College students were given the problem of testing a simple hypothesis about letters and numbers that were printed on file cards. Four cards were placed on a table, as in Figure 8–12. The subjects were told that each of the four cards had a letter on one side and a number on the other. The hypothesis to be tested was

If a card has a vowel on one side, then it has an odd number on the other side.

In formal terms, this hypothesis can be stated as:

If p then q,

where p represents any vowel and q represents any odd number. This hypothesis can be tested by turning over those cards that would provide the relevant information. The problem is, What is the minimal number of cards that must be turned over, and which cards are they?

Most people either turn over more cards than are necessary, or the wrong

FIGURE 8–12

Problem Form	Test the Hypothesis: If p then q			
Formal	p	$not\text{-}p$	q	$not\text{-}q$
Abstract	A	B	5	2

ones. Everyone turns the *p* card, with the vowel A on one side, to see if that has an odd number (*q*) on the other side. Should the *q* card, with a 5 on it, also be turned over? Most people do, but this card provides no useful information at all. If the 5 card has a vowel on the other side, then it is consistent with the hypothesis. If the 5 card does *not* have a vowel on the other side, then it is still consistent with the hypothesis. Remember that the hypothesis, or rule, does not say that *only* cards with vowels have odd numbers on the other side, so it really makes no difference what letter is on cards with odd numbers on them. The only other informative card is the card with an even number on it (*not-q*—that is, the card with a 2 on it). If that card has a vowel on the other side, then the hypothesis (if vowel, then odd number) is false.

Very few people spontaneously choose just these two informative cards, the *p* (vowel) card and the *not-q* (even number) card. However, when this same problem is presented in a concrete and plausible form, then most people solve it immediately (see Figure 8–13). The hypothesis is given in the form of a rule:

If an envelope is sealed, then it must have first-class postage (20¢ stamp) on it.

In formal terms, this is the same as the vowel and number problem, if *p* then *q*. Now *p* is a sealed envelope and *q* is a 20¢ stamp. With our knowledge of the postal system and the goal of making sure that first class mail has enough postage on it, people do choose to inspect the sealed envelope (*p*) to make sure that the correct postage is on it, and the envelope with the 13¢ stamp (*not-q*) to make sure that it is not sealed. In formal logical terms, to test the hypothesis

If *p* then *q*,

the only relevant evidence involves *p* and *not q*; *p* to make sure that *q* is there, and *not-q* to be sure that *p* is not there.

Of course, people do not usually think in such formal and abstract terms. If we did, then doing this problem first in the easy, concrete form should make the other versions of the problem easier. It does not. People make the same mistakes on the abstract and formal versions of the problem whether or not they are first given the easy, concrete form (Johnson-Laird et al., 1972).

FIGURE 8–13

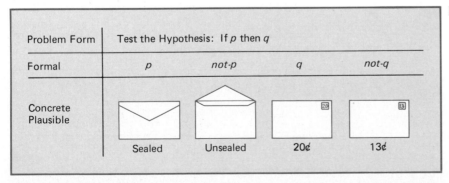

Problem Form	Test the Hypothesis: If *p* then *q*			
Formal	*p*	*not-p*	*q*	*not-q*
Concrete Plausible	Sealed	Unsealed	20¢	13¢

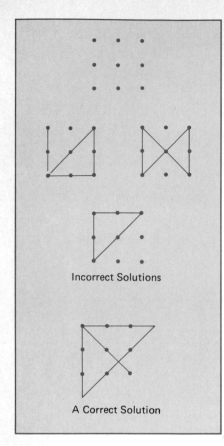

Incorrect Solutions

A Correct Solution

FIGURE 8–14
The nine-dot problem. Connect the dots by drawing only four straight lines. Do not retrace any lines, and do not lift your pencil from the paper.

There seems to be virtually no transfer of learning from one form of this reasoning problem to other forms. This suggests that formal training in such subjects as logic may not be very useful for thinking outside the logic classroom.

Problem Solving

Problems are novel situations that require novel behaviors, or situations for which no one has ever found satisfactory solutions or for which there *are* no satisfactory solutions. When we can't answer a question by using our memory, or when we can't deal with a situation by doing what we did the last time, then we are faced with a problem. Some problems are difficult to solve because, for one reason or another, they set us off on the wrong track. These kinds of problems involve **negative set.** Other kinds of problems are difficult because they require putting together information in new and original ways; they require creativity.

NEGATIVE SET.   Someone faced with a problem can go off on the wrong track for any one of several reasons. In the nine-dot problem (in Figure 8–14), the spatial characteristics of the arrangement implicitly influence people to stay within the imaginary square formed by the dots. In Luchins' water jar problems (Table 8–2), people have to figure out how to get a specified amount of water from three jars with different fluid capacities. An incorrect or negative set can easily be established. The first problem is simple enough. Problems 2 through 6 can be solved by the same method: Jar B minus Jar A, minus twice Jar C. Problems 7 and 8 can also be solved this way, but notice that they can be solved much more easily by using only two jars. Problem 9 cannot be solved at all in the usual three-jar way. People who have learned to solve problems 2 through 6 often continue to use the habitual three-jar solution for problems 7 and 8, and get stuck on problem 9. People who have not had this set-inducing experience have no difficulties at all with problem 9 (Luchins, 1942).

Max Wertheimer, in his book *Productive Thinking* (1945/1959), describes a classroom example of this kind of negative set. Children who had already learned how to find the area of a rectangle applied that formula (the product of two sides) to the problem of finding the area of a parallelogram. The teacher then taught the class the correct formula: area = base × altitude (see Figure 8–15A). Wertheimer decided to find out what the children had learned by giving the class an area problem with the parallelogram shown in Figure

Table 8–2: Luchins' Water Jar Problems.
How do you measure out the right amount of water using Jars A, B, and C?

| PROBLEM NUMBER | JARS AVAILABLE FOR USE | | | REQUIRED AMOUNT |
	A	B	C	
1	29	3		20
2	21	127	3	100
3	14	163	25	99
4	18	43	10	5
5	9	42	6	21
6	20	59	4	31
7	23	49	3	20
8	15	39	3	18
9	28	76	3	25

From Luchins (1942).

FIGURE 8–15
Children were first taught to find the area of parallelograms, using the diagram shown in A. They were then given the parallelogram shown in B and asked to find the area. One kind of solution attempt, C, indicated a complete lack of understanding. The solution method illustrated in D demonstrated that the child understood the nature of the problem and the solution. (Wertheimer, 1945/1959)

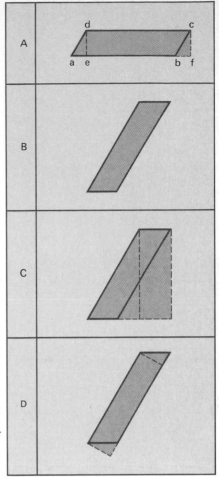

8–15B. Two kinds of solutions were attempted. The attempt shown in Figure 8–15C shows a complete lack of understanding and a rote and inappropriate application of the method. Figure 8–15D shows an appropriate application of the method, along with an understanding of that method.

Habitual ways of thinking about ordinary objects can also lead to a kind of negative set called **functional fixedness** (Duncker, 1945). One such problem is shown in Figure 8–16. When people are asked to mount a candle on the wall, with only tacks in a box and a book of matches, as many as 50 percent fail to notice that the tack box can be used as a candle holder. When, however, the box is explicitly labeled as a *box,* all the people tested solved the problem in less than a minute (Glucksberg & Weisberg, 1966). In effect, telling people that a box was available short-circuited the usual response of trying to use tacks or melted wax alone to make a candle holder.

This result suggests that information that would be helpful to solve a problem may well be in long-term memory but may still be unavailable when it is needed. Experiments on the effects of practice on such problem solving suggest the same thing. Weisberg and his colleagues (1978) trained people to associate the box and candle with one another and then gave them the candle problem to solve. The prior association of *box* with *candle* did not help at all, unless the subjects had been informed that what they had learned earlier might be useful in the problem situation. Using somewhat different types of problems, Gick and Holyoak (1980) found the same thing. Unless you are explicitly informed that one experience is relevant to another, chances are

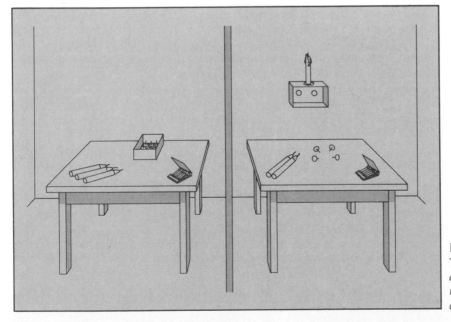

FIGURE 8–16
The candle problem: Using only the materials on the table, how can the candle be mounted on the wall? The solution is shown on the right. (Glucksberg & Weisberg, 1966)

you will *not* use something you learned in one situation in a different but related new situation. This failure of transfer in problem solving is analogous to the failure of transfer in reasoning that we described earlier.

Decision Making

The problems that we have been discussing up to now involve certainties. They contain full information for solution, and each has a single correct answer. In daily life, however, we encounter problems where we must make decisions under conditions of uncertainty. We do not have full information, and there may be no single, correct answer. Instead, the information that we have is probabilistic, and the decisions that we make are really our best bets about the future. How good are we at making such decisions?

In general, people seem to get along quite well amidst the uncertainties of daily life. At the same time, people are also susceptible to subtle biases. Too often, the way a situation is worded, or *framed,* can have significant biasing effects. Assume that you have just entered a theater lobby and discover that you've lost your ticket, for which you had paid $25.00. Would you buy another ticket for $25.00 to see the show? Many people decide that they would not do so, possibly on the grounds that the show is not worth $50.00. Now consider a slight variant of this situation. You have just entered a theater lobby to buy a $25.00 ticket. You discover that you have lost $25.00 sometime during the day. Would you still buy a ticket for $25.00? In this context, most people say that they would. Notice that the only difference in the two situations is the subjective impression that in one case it costs $50.00 to see the show, but only $25.00 in the other. But in both cases you are out of pocket by $50.00. The different decisions, then, are not rational in any economic sense, but they do seem to make intuitive psychological sense.

Kahneman and Tversky (1982) were among several psychologists to demonstrate the power of such **framing effects,** the effects of how a problem is worded. These effects can be particularly pronounced when decisions involve serious risks. Consider this problem:

> Imagine that the government is preparing for an outbreak of a rare disease that is expected to kill 600 people. Two programs are available. If program A is adopted, then 200 people will be saved. If program B is adopted, then there is a $\frac{1}{3}$ chance that 600 people will be saved, and a $\frac{2}{3}$ chance that nobody will be saved. Which program should be adopted?

When the issue is framed in this way, most people prefer program A over program B. This avoids the $\frac{2}{3}$ risk that nobody will be saved. Now consider a similar problem involving the same disease and the same expectation that if nothing is done, 600 people will die:

> Two programs are available. If program C is adopted, then 400 people will die. If program D is adopted, then there is a $\frac{1}{3}$ chance that nobody will die, and a $\frac{2}{3}$ chance that 600 people will die.

When the issue is framed in this way, most people prefer program D over program C, avoiding the certain consequence that 400 people will die. This might seem reasonable to you until you realize that programs A and C have precisely the same outcomes: Of the original 600 people at risk, 200 will live and 400 will die. Programs B and D are also precisely the same:—$\frac{1}{3}$ chance of 600 people being saved is the same as a $\frac{1}{3}$ chance of nobody dying. We may be too easily swayed by how such problems are worded!

Decisions are often based on our beliefs about the relative likelihood of things happening—the price of real estate next year, the availability of jobs for engineers in the year you expect to graduate, whether the romance of the moment will last through marriage, and so on. People estimate the likelihood of such things by relying on rather general and useful strategies called **heuristics.**

In one of these strategies, the *representative heuristic,* we use the similarity between objects or events to help us estimate probabilities. For example, we might be told that "George is quiet and shy. He likes to be helpful to others but is generally uninterested in people or in daily events. He is very concerned with tidiness, order, and neatness in every detail." What is the likelihood that George is a librarian rather than a farmer? Most people would guess that George is a librarian because he matches our stereotype of librarians. This would be a perfectly valid inference in this case, if the stereotype were in fact true. Nevertheless, this heuristic can lead us astray by diverting our attention from other important factors, such as the laws and principles of probability. Imagine that you were given the description of George and then were told: "George belongs to a club that has 5 librarians and 20 farmers. What is the likelihood that George is a librarian?" This additional information about the relative number of librarians and farmers should influence your answer, but unfortunately, it rarely does. This information about *prior probability* is simply ignored by most people, even though it is important and informative.

The representativeness heuristic is also responsible for another common type of error. Suppose you tossed a coin 6 times in a row. Which of the following sequences would be more likely to occur, A or B:

A: Head, Head, Head, Tail, Tail, Tail
B: Head, Tail, Tail, Head, Tail, Head

Most people choose B because it looks more like our stereotype of a random sequence than does A. A moment's reflection, however, should convince you that A and B are equally likely. With any given proportion of heads and tails, any one sequence is just as likely as any other.

People also tend to ignore sample size as an important source of information. Suppose that you polled 5 Californians and found that all 5 drank ginger ale for breakfast. Would you then believe that most Californians drink ginger ale in the morning? Probably not, but when the problem is somewhat more subtle, sample size tends to be ignored. Tversky and Kahneman (1974) demonstrated people's insensitivity to sample size with a problem like this one:

A town has two hospitals, a large one and a small one. About 50 babies are born every day in the large hospital, and 10 babies every day in the small hospital. As everyone knows, about 50 percent of all babies born are boys, but of course the exact percentage will fluctuate from day to day, sometimes being higher than 50 percent, sometimes lower. In one particular year both hospitals kept a record of the days on which more than 60 percent of the babies born were boys. Which hospital was more likely to record such days?

About half of the college students who were given this problem judged that the likelihood was the same for both hospitals, while the other half split evenly between choosing the larger and the smaller hospitals. The correct judgment is that the smaller hospital is more likely to have such deviant days. This becomes crystal clear in the extreme case of a really small hospital that records just one birth a day. If half the babies born in a year are boys, then on half of the days of the year this hospital would record 100 percent boys! If a hospital had two babies born a day, then on one-quarter of the days of a year it would record 100 percent boys (on half of the days of the year, on average, one boy and one girl would be born; on the other half, two boys or two girls). These examples illustrate the general principle: Small samples are deviant far more often than large samples. Yet people assume that they will be just as representative as large samples.

The *availability heuristic* is another method that people use to estimate the relative frequency of events or things. If you are asked which is more common in small towns, American or foreign cars, how would you decide? One way is to try to remember specific instances of American and foreign cars in small-town settings. If you can think of more American instances than foreign, you would infer that American cars are more frequent. In this way, we can make a frequency estimate without actually counting. Instead, we count a small sample of instances, with the more available instances in our memory having the most influence. Because more frequent or common events or things are more available in memory, this is generally a useful and informative strategy. However, this heuristic can also lead us astray if availability of instances does not accurately reflect true frequency.

Imagine that you are sampling words that are four or more letters long from a book written in English. After sampling several hundred at random, will you have more words that start with the letter *r* or more words with *r* as the third letter? Most people judge that there are more words with *r* as first letter than words with *r* as third letter (e.g., more words like *road* than like *cartoon*). This is because it is easier to think of words that begin with *r* than to think of words that have *r* in the third-letter position. The availability heuristic leads to the judgment that words with initial letter *r* are relatively frequent. But just the opposite is true. There are far more words with *r* in third position than in first. This last sentence, for example, had no words starting with r, but 4 with *r* in third position—*far, more, words,* and *first.*

These examples suggest that people in general do not think clearly, particularly under conditions of uncertainty. We tend to overuse such generally valid but intuitive strategies as the representativeness and availability heuristics, and to underuse formal, logical, and statistical strategies (Nisbett & Ross, 1980). While this is certainly true, the occasions and situations in which we are led astray may be relatively rare. Perhaps explicit training in scientific and statistical reasoning would make those occasions rarer still.

Creativity

The kinds of laboratory puzzles we have been dealing with bear little overt resemblance to the problems faced by scientists, engineers, or creative artists.

Creativity *consists of making new combinations of previous known ideas. Gutenberg wanted to produce an affordable Bible to replace costly hand-written versions. His invention of moveable and reusable type drew on familiar elements from wood-block printing and coin-casting; the printing press itself owed a debt to the wine press then widely in use. In this bas-relief from the pedestal of a statue of Gutenberg in the city of Mainz in Germany, we see the printer reading a proof sheet while an assistant turns the press to ink another proof. On a line strung across the print shop, proofs hang to let the ink dry.*

They do, however, share one important property with real-world problems: The person begins either by not knowing at all what to do, or by going off on the wrong track. Both the laboratory puzzles and the real-world problems require novel behavior—a change of habitual modes of acting and thinking.

Real-world problems often are far more complex and require much more work to be solved. Many creative problem solutions and discoveries seem to occur in four stages: preparation, incubation, illumination, and verification. Gutenberg's invention of the printing press illustrates these stages. The **preparation stage** consisted of several substages. The first was his explicit goal— to reproduce the Bible economically. The second consisted of learning about and considering several ways to print letters. He considered and thought about how wood block printing is done by rubbing paper or material on a carved and inked block. Because carving a page of letters in wood is laborious and slow, he searched for alternatives that would allow individual letters to be reused. He got the idea of type-casting from coin-stampings and seals. In his own words, "Do you not see that you can repeat as many times as necessary the seal covered with signs and characters?" (Gutenberg, in Koestler, 1964, p. 123).

Many, if not all, of the elements of the printing press were now available in Gutenberg's mind. However, he was still stuck with the notion of rubbing to make an imprint—he was on the wrong track. The idea of making an imprint by pressure did not occur to him until after a period of **incubation**—a period of time during which no progress seemed to be made, and during which little conscious thought seemed to be applied to the problem. The moment of **illumination** came to Gutenberg when, as he put it, "I took part in the wine harvest. I watched the wine flowing, and going back from the effect to the cause, I studied the power of this press. . . ." Suddenly, the idea

Table 8–3: A Test of Creativity: The Remote Associates Test (RAT).

Find a word that is associated with all three of these words:

rat	blue	cottage

Answer: cheese

Here are four other examples*:

1. railroad	girl	class
2. book	blood	gear
3. writer	cast	blood
4. sky	note	room

*Answers: working, worm, type, blue.

(After Mednick, 1962).

occurs—put together the seal and the wine-press, and the letter-press is created! The **verification** follows. Will the idea actually work?

Many first-hand accounts of important discoveries follow this pattern. A goal is clearly set, and then potentially relevant information is gathered. This preparation done, a period of apparent inactivity follows. This can often be a period of incubation involving a great deal of unconscious mental activity. Sometimes, this leads to a flash of illumination or insight. Finally, if the idea is promising, it is tested and verified.

The moment of illumination itself often involves the coming together of familiar elements in new ways. The gifted mathematician Henri Poincaré wrote, "to create consists of making new combinations of associative elements that are useful" (1929). A psychologist who devised a test of creativity (see Table 8–3) described creative thinking as "the forming of associative elements into new combinations which either meet new requirements or are in some way useful" (Mednick, 1962, p. 221).

This definition of creative behavior brings us full circle to the child learning language—putting together elements (like words) into new combinations that are useful (sentences).

SUMMARY

1. All languages share certain features: (a) a limited number of speech sounds, called *phonemes;* (b) combinations of phonemes to form countless words; (c) meanings assigned arbitrarily to words; (d) words combined in systematic ways to form a theoretically infinite number of sentences. Because all languages share these features, any idea or concept that can be expressed in one language can also be expressed in any other language.

2. The *morpheme* is the smallest unit of speech that has meaning. The *denotative meaning* of a word is the thing or class of things the word can label. The *connotative meaning* reflects how we feel about the thing the word stands for.

3. The *semantic differential* is a rating scale of the three major dimensions of connotative meaning: evaluation, activity, and potency.

4. Words are combined into sentences according to rules, which form the *syntax* of a language. *Phrase-structure rules* govern the organization of various parts of a sentence; *transformational rules* specify the relationships between sentences and spell out how one type of sentence can be transformed into another.

5. Chomsky believes that children are born with an innate *language acquisition device (LAD)*. Others believe that children discover basic linguistic rules as part of growing up in a speaking community.

6. By the sixth month infants engage in *reduplicated babbling*. In the next phase, they use *expressive jargon,* vocalizations that sound like adult speech but are unintelligible.

7. The one-word utterances of children are called *holophrastic* utterances because just one word can express a whole phrase or sentence. A child's first sentences, which are two-word utterances, are *telegraphic* in the use of words—only the most important words are included.

8. One of the noncommunicative uses of language is to help solve conceptual problems; being able to label things and to express what we have learned in words helps in thinking and problem solving.

9. Whorf's *linguistic-relativity hypothesis*—that differences in languages cause important differences in the way people perceive and conceptualize the world—does not seem to be borne out in recent experiments.

10. Some problems are difficult to solve because they set us off on the wrong track; such problems involve *negative set.* One kind of negative set is *functional fixedness,* in which habitual ways of thinking about ordinary objects block the solution of the problem.

11. Our knowledge and our biases can interfere with our ability to reason—if we agree with a conclusion it is harder to detect a flaw in the logic involved.

12. Creativity is often the result of a four-stage process involving *preparation, incubation, illumination,* and *verification.*

Suggested Readings

ANDERSON, J. R. *Cognitive psychology and its implications.* San Francisco: W. H. Freeman & Company Publishers, 1980. An introduction to the field of cognitive psychology, with excellent treatments of concept formation, problem solving, and reasoning.

CLARK, H. H., & CLARK, E. V. *Psychology and language: An introduction to psycholinguistics.* New York: Harcourt Brace Jovanovich, 1977. A comprehensive survey of linguistics and psychology, with particular attention to the mental processes people use to comprehend language.

GLUCKSBERG, S., & DANKS, J. H. *Experimental psycholinguistics.* Hillsdale, N.J.: Erlbaum, 1975. A clear introduction to the concepts of speech perception, semantics, and syntax in the context of the experimental psychology of language.

JOHNSON-LAIRD, P. N., & WASON, P. C. (Eds.). *Thinking: Readings in cognitive science.* Cambridge, Eng.: The University Press, 1977. Covers literature on thinking and includes work from computer science, linguistics, and philosophy.

KAHNEMAN, D., & TVERSKY, A. The psychology of preferences. *Scientific American,* 1982, *246* (1), 160–173. A readable summary of research on how people's choices may be biased away from objectivity.

MILLER, G. A. *Language and speech.* San Francisco: W. H. Freeman & Company Publishers, 1981. An elegant introduction to the science of language by an eminent scholar in the field.

NISBETT, R., & ROSS, L. *Human inference: Strategies and shortcomings of social judgment.* Englewood Cliffs, N.J.: Prentice-Hall, 1980. The controversial book that claims that people "lack the machinery for bringing the relevant facts into conscious view" and so are doomed to error and irrationality.

ROSCH, E., & LLOYD, B. B. (Eds.). *Cognition and categorization.* Hillsdale, N.J.: Erlbaum, 1978. Reviews the literature on categorization and concept formation, bringing together a representative set of essays from various disciplines and approaches.

SMITH, E. E., & MEDIN, D. L. *Categories and concepts.* Cambridge, Mass.: Harvard University Press, 1981. Surveys the psychological literature on concept formation during the last ten years.

WEISBERG, R. W. *Memory, thought and behavior.* New York: Oxford University Press, 1980. Argues convincingly that the role of memory in thinking and problem solving has been seriously overlooked and shows how selective retrieval of relevant information from memory can play critical roles in creative thinking and problem solving.

9. Intelligence

F ew, if any, applications of psychology have had as much impact on our lives as the intelligence test. That you are a college student reading this book makes it almost certain that your score on a standardized intelligence test is higher than average—and the fact that you were known to have a higher than average score may be responsible for your being in college at all. The kinds of courses you were encouraged to take in high school were very likely influenced by teachers' knowledge of your intelligence-test score. The college you are attending almost certainly examined your score on a "scholastic aptitude" test—a kind of intelligence test—before deciding to admit you. The results of intelligence tests have deeply affected the personal lives and careers of millions of people.

The data collected by intelligence testers have also played a prominent role in influencing our ideas about education and, for that matter, about social policy in general. We know, for example, that similar intelligence-test scores tend to run in families. That is, parents with high test scores tend to have children with high test scores—just as parents with low test scores tend to have children with low test scores. Furthermore, there are quite large average differences in measured intelligence among social classes and ethnic and racial groups. These differences are also somehow passed on from one generation to the next. Do these facts mean, as some have suggested, that differences in intelligence are largely a matter of heredity? Do they mean, as others have argued, that intelligence test scores are largely determined by environment, which in turn is shared by members of the same family, social class, or race? Are individual differences *within* a race largely determined by heredity, while differences in the average test scores *between* races are largely determined by environment? If differences in test scores are mostly determined by the genes, would that mean that education and other environmental influences cannot increase intelligence beyond some genetically fixed level? These are obviously important and controversial questions, which we shall try to answer in this chapter.

BINET AND THE IQ

The Background of Binet's Test

The first useful intelligence test was devised in France by Alfred Binet and his collaborator, Theophile Simon. The first version of their test, published in 1905, marked a radical departure from earlier efforts to measure intelligence or mental ability. The first impetus toward the development of "mental tests" had been given by Charles Darwin's cousin, Francis Galton. The differences among people were in Galton's view largely caused by heredity; and humanity could improve itself, Galton argued, if gifted individuals were encouraged to mate with other gifted people, and if the ungifted were discouraged (or prevented) from mating at all. These ideas were adopted by the eugenics movement, founded by Galton. To support his arguments about the importance of heredity, Galton demonstrated that "eminence" in British life tended to run in families. The sons and grandsons of eminent jurists were more likely than the average person to themselves become eminent jurists, for example. This and other such facts suggested to Galton the importance of the genes in allowing a given person to become eminent. There were also,

Galton noted, differences among races in the frequency of eminent people or people of genius—there were many such superior individuals to be found among the British, and, he believed, virtually none in Africa or India.

Throughout his life, Galton maintained an active interest in measuring and testing human "specimens," recording, cataloguing, and calculating the differences among them. The quantitative "mental tests" used by Galton and his early followers, however, were very simple. Perhaps because of his strong biological leanings, Galton concentrated on such "laboratory-like" tests as simple reaction time, and on measures of sensory thresholds and capacities. These could be measured with precision, and there were large differences among individuals on such tests. The difficulty was that performance on such tests did not seem to be related to what most people would recognize as signs of real intelligence or mental ability. For example, it was not the case that an excellent student reacted more quickly to the sound of a buzzer than did an inferior student.

The task that faced Binet was much more down-to-earth and practical than Galton's concern with eugenics. The school authorities in the city of Paris had asked Binet to develop a testing procedure that could help to pick out students with low academic aptitude—that is, those students who would not profit much from the regular school curriculum, and for whom special classes should be set up. That meant, of course, that the test Binet made had to be related to—had to be able to *predict*—a child's performance in school.

The Concept of Mental Age

The point of departure for Binet was a simple but powerful idea: Normally, as children grow older, their mental powers increase. We do not expect a normal 2-year-old to learn the multiplication tables, no matter how often they are recited in his or her presence. However, if the same child has failed to learn the multiplication tables by the age of 12, we might well be concerned that the child is not very intelligent. (That assumes, of course, that the child has been exposed repeatedly to the multiplication tables, at school or elsewhere.)

The normal growth of mental power with age suggested to Binet the concept of **mental age.** That is, it is reasonable to expect the average 9-year-old to possess certain pieces of knowledge and to be able to solve certain kinds of "intellectual" problems. Whatever intellectual skills the average 9-year-old possesses define the mental age of 9. Further, children who are only 7 or 8 years of age should have difficulty coping with test material that is appropriate for 9-year-olds. Older children, of course, should find the 9-year-old material very easy.

Binet next set about interviewing and examining numbers of Paris school children, trying to find out precisely what intellectual accomplishments were characteristic of children of different ages. From his point of view, a good item for inclusion in his test was one that most (but not all) children of a given age could answer correctly. Further, the proportion of children younger than that age who could answer the item should be small, while the proportion of older children answering successfully should be large. In practice, Binet selected items that about three-fourths of children of a given age could answer. If one found, as Binet did, a number of such items for 9-year-olds, the child who could answer those items was said to have a mental age of 9. That same child usually could answer the items that Binet had placed on his 8-year-old scale; but he or she would have difficulty with items on the 10-year-old scale.

Year 3

1. Point to eyes, nose, and mouth
2. Repeat two digits
3. Identify objects in a picture
4. Repeat a sentence of six syllables

Year 7

1. Show right hand and left ear
2. Describe a picture
3. Carry out three commands given simultaneously
4. Count the value of six coins

Year 15

1. Repeat seven digits
2. Find three rhymes for a given word in one minute
3. Repeat a sentence of 26 syllables
4. Interpret a set of given facts

The kinds of items that Binet included in his scales dealt directly with knowledge, thinking, reasoning, and judgment—the kinds of materials involved in successful school performance. Table 9–1 lists a number of representative tasks that Binet's test required children of different ages to perform.

The child who could answer the items on the scale for 10-year-olds was assigned a mental age of 10. To assess the child's brightness or dullness, however, the child's mental age had to be compared to his or her chronological age. For an 8-year-old to have a mental age of 10 means one thing; for a 12-year-old to have a mental age of 10 means something else. The first child seems to be obviously bright, while the second child may seem to be dull.

The Concept of IQ

For Binet it was enough simply to compare the child's mental and chronological ages. His original concern was to be able to pick out, for special-education classes, children who would not profit from the regular school curriculum. To Binet it seemed clear that a young child whose mental age lagged behind his or her chronological age by as much as 2 years was backward and needed special educational attention.

The concept of **intelligence quotient,** or IQ, was introduced by a German psychologist, William Stern. The IQ, as proposed by Stern, represented the *ratio* of a child's mental age to his or her **chronological age.** To be rid of fractions, the ratio was multiplied by 100. This meant that, for any chronological age, the average IQ was 100. Obviously, if a child's mental age was greater than the chronological age, the IQ would be above 100. If the mental age were lower than the chronological age, the IQ would be below 100. For a 10-year-old child with a mental age of 12, the formula for calculating IQ gives the following result:

$$\text{IQ} = \frac{\text{Mental Age}}{\text{Chronological Age}} \times 100 = \frac{12}{10} \times 100 = 120$$

If the same 10-year-old had a mental age of 8, the IQ would be calculated as 80.

The Stanford-Binet Test

The **Stanford-Binet test,** a translated and modified version of Binet's original scale, was introduced into the United States by Lewis Terman, a professor at Stanford University, in 1916. The standardization of test items—determining what items corresponded to what mental ages—had of course to be revised, using a standardization sample of American children. A **standardization sample,** at least in theory, is representative of the entire population, and thus provides the norms, or standards of performance, to which the performance of any individual can then be compared. The Stanford-Binet test has been modified and restandardized on new samples of children in 1937, in 1960, and in 1972. Note that, with the passage of time, any intelligence test must be restandardized. When given the same test items that had been used in 1937, American children of 1972 performed at a considerably higher level than their 1937 predecessors. This might reflect changed schooling conditions, or the impact of exposure to television. Whatever the cause, it is important to understand that the IQ is a relative, not an absolute, measure. It expresses an individual's standing relative to the performance of some specific standardization sample. The same performance that was typical of 5-year-olds in 1937 is inferior to the performance of today's 5-year-olds; but the average IQ of 5-year-olds has, of course, remained at 100.

Though the Stanford-Binet test contains scales for adults, it is mostly used with children between 2 and 14 years of age. The basic Binet procedure of separate items for each mental age level has been kept, and the items are of much the same sort as those used by Binet. For each age level, there is a scale consisting of 6 different items. To determine a child's IQ, the first step is to discover his or her *basal* mental age. That is the highest mental age level at which the child can pass all 6 items. When the basal age level has been discovered, the tester continues with items from the next-highest mental age level. This process continues until a mental age level is reached at which the child can pass no items at all. The child's mental age is the basal age plus some credit for each item passed in scales above the basal age level. Since each mental age scale contains 6 items, each passed item above the basal mental age level is worth 2 more months of mental age.

With earlier versions of the Stanford-Binet test, a literal intelligence quotient was calculated, and the child's mental age was divided by the chro-

FIGURE 9–1
The approximate distribution of IQs in the population.

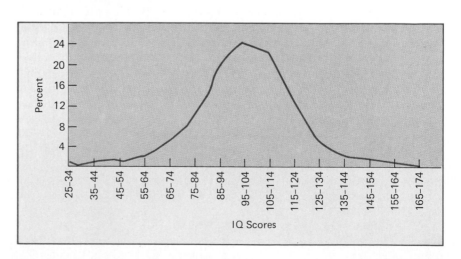

nological age. This is no longer done, however. The performance of the children in the standardization sample has now been scored in such a way that the average IQ at each age is 100, *and* the standard deviation at each age is 16. The standard deviation of 16 means that IQ scores are symmetrically distributed around an average of 100, with about 95 percent of all IQs falling between 68 and 132. The approximate distribution of IQs is shown in Figure 9–1.

Stability of IQ

Do children's IQs remain stable as they grow older? That is, will bright 5-year-olds (compared to other 5-year-olds) be equally bright when, 7 years later, they are compared to 12-year-olds? The answer is that they are quite likely to remain relatively bright, but that there are many individual exceptions.

We would not, of course, expect individuals' measured IQs to remain exactly the same each time they are tested; if nothing else, there is some error of measurement involved in mental testing, as there is in all forms of measurement. The **reliability** of the Stanford-Binet is such that we should not be surprised if a child's measured IQ changes by as much as 10 points from week to week. A perfectly reliable test would be one that, when it was given to the same individuals on 2 separate occasions, produced exactly the same scores each time. In such a test, the agreement between the 2 sets of scores would be expressed in a **correlation coefficient.** In a perfectly reliable test, the correlation coefficient would be 1.00; if there were no relation or only chance agreement between the scores, the correlation coefficient would be .00. There is a clear and obvious tendency for IQs taken early in childhood to be highly correlated with IQs taken in later childhood, or in adulthood. The correlations in IQ scores of the same individuals tested at different ages are illustrated in Table 9–2. The IQ at any age is obviously correlated with the IQ at any other age; but it is also the case (sensibly enough) that the correlations are smaller when many years separate the 2 tests.

The fact that, for the most part, IQ remains relatively stable throughout life should not obscure the equally obvious fact that many dramatic changes in IQ—clearly involving more than measurement error—do take place. Thus, for example, Honzik, Macfarlane, and Allen (1948) tested a group of children repeatedly between the ages of 2 and 18 and reported that 37 percent of the subjects showed IQ differences of at least 20 points between 2 different testings. Hindley and Owen (1978) report that about half of the children tested changed IQ by at least 10 points between the ages of 3 and 17. Figure 9–2 illustrates 2 examples of IQs changing progressively, and dramatically, over time. These examples should serve as a caution against premature labeling and tracking of a child with a low (or high) IQ. There are clearly individual cases in which IQ does change very markedly.

The Test Defines Intelligence

For practical purposes, what psychologists mean by the word "intelligence" has been pretty well defined by the content of the Stanford-Binet and other widely used intelligence tests. In other words, you are an intelligent person if you can do well on the sorts of questions asked by intelligence tests. This may seem to be an empty statement, but it is not entirely so. The validity of

Table 9–2: Correlations among IQ Scores at Different Ages.

Test Age (Years)	RETEST AGE (YEARS)				
	5	7	10	14	18
2	.32	.46	.37	.28	.31
5		.73	.71	.61	.56
7			.77	.75	.71
10				.86	.73
14					.76

From Honzik, Macfarlane, & Allen (1948).

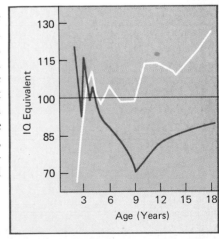

FIGURE 9–2
The changes in IQ over time of two different children, who were tested repeatedly from age 2 to age 18. (Honzik, Macfarlane, & Allen, 1948)

the test items was established by the fact that children who did well on the test also did well in their school subjects. **Validity** is the degree to which scores on a test correlate with some criterion independent of the test itself—in this case, school grades. To Binet, it was essential that teachers' judgments of the brightness or dullness of students should correspond to the same students' scores on the test. This was in fact found to be the case. Ever since Binet's time, revised or new tests of intelligence have been validated by their correlation with school grades—or by their correlation with Binet's test. Thus it is no accident that a child's IQ score can be used to predict his or her performance in school. The precise magnitude of the correlation varies with a number of conditions, but as a general rule, IQ correlates in the neighborhood of .40 to .60 with school grades. That is a substantial, but very far from perfect, correlation. That is, other things besides IQ also determine school grades.

The fact that IQ tests have been validated against performance in school has an interesting consequence. We are defining as "intelligence" precisely those skills that are involved in the learning of academic subjects in school. If the curriculum of the Paris school system had been vastly different from what it in fact was in 1904, today's intelligence tests might contain very different kinds of items. That form of nimble-wittedness involved in "street smarts"—a smartness highly adaptive for modern urban street life—seems scarcely represented in IQ tests.

The Test as Diagnostic Instrument

Though IQ scores can be used to predict school performance, Binet had much more than that in mind. He thought of the test as a diagnostic instrument. The test was to be used to help identify those children who would do very poorly in school. The problem with those children, Binet believed, was that their intelligence had not yet been developed enough. The task of the educator, once the test had located such backward children, was to *develop and increase* their intelligence by special educational procedures. Thus Binet definitely did not think of the test as measuring some fixed or unchangeable quantity. He argued that the right instruction—a form of "mental orthopedics" —could increase the intelligence of lagging children. This optimistic attitude about test scores and the possibility of training children to become more intelligent has not been very common among testers who followed Binet. To the degree that IQ tests serve a diagnostic purpose, they are usually used to help assign children to classes thought right for their measured level of intelligence. The basic assumption is made that the IQ will remain constant, and that classroom experience will neither increase nor decrease the IQ.

Achievement, Aptitude, and Capacity

We live in a society that uses many different kinds of tests for many different purposes. It is important to understand both the purpose of a particular test and the assumptions that underlie its use. There are, at one extreme, **achievement tests.** Their purpose is to measure, as accurately as possible, how much you have learned before taking the test. Thus, when you finish a college course, you usually take an exam. The purpose of the exam is to assess how much of the course content you have learned. Though it is possible that students with high IQs may receive higher exam grades, they receive no special credit for having a high IQ. The slower, plodding student who works hard may receive a higher grade than the brilliant student who did not study.

This is wholly appropriate, since the only purpose of the exam, as an achievement test, is to measure how much of the tested material has in fact been learned.

There are other occasions, however, when tests are used to *predict* some future performance. For example, the military wants to predict the likelihood that a given candidate for aircraft pilot training will successfully complete the complicated and expensive course of training. To fly a plane well requires, among other things, good physical coordination and a good sense of mechanical matters. Thus, all candidates for pilot training are normally given a battery of **aptitude tests,** including tests of mechanical aptitude and of eye-hand coordination, which will be used to predict how well they'll do in the training program. People with poor scores on such tests tend to fail pilot training.

The distinction between an achievement test and an aptitude test thus depends on the purpose to which the test is put. It is difficult, if not impossible, to distinguish between the 2 types of tests on other grounds. The very same item can be—and often is—included in both achievement and aptitude tests. Think back to the entrance examination you took before being accepted by your college. The college thought of that exam as an aptitude test, from which they predicted that you would do well in college. That is, your "scholastic aptitude" was found to be high. The questions you answered, however, were very similar to questions that you had earlier answered in high-school course examinations. The same questions were then regarded as part of an achievement test. When you did poorly on such an achievement test in high school, you might have argued that the test did not reflect your **aptitude**—only the fact that you had not studied enough for it. Those who do poorly on a test of scholastic aptitude can just as reasonably argue that the test reflects nothing more than their failure to study enough—but in this instance, the failure to study would have occurred over a long time span. The failure to have studied, it should be obvious, does not necessarily mean that person *could* not have mastered the material on the aptitude test.

People—including psychologists—often make the mistake of thinking that an aptitude test can somehow measure a person's *capacity* to learn. The assumption is made that everyone has some fixed limit to his or her learning ability, and that that limit is at least partly determined by heredity. That may be a plausible assumption, but it is clearly wrong to believe that any test can directly measure a person's hereditary potential or capacity. The results of *all* tests necessarily depend upon a person's past experiences, present motivation, and many other factors. There is not and cannot be any direct test of "innate intelligence." These points have been made clearly by a distinguished committee of mental-test specialists appointed by the American Psychological Association (Cleary, Humphreys, Kendrick, & Wesman, 1975). These authorities were clear in pointing out that the assumption that all members of our society had had an "equal opportunity" to learn the materials presented in IQ tests was not correct. Of course, it is possible to argue that *most* people have had *almost* equal opportunities, and that tests are therefore more or less *approximate* indicators of mental capacity. When language is this imprecise, however, the potential for disagreement and controversy is obvious.

Intelligence and Age

It is obvious that, throughout childhood, intellectual capability continues to increase with age. For that reason, different kinds of items must be introduced into the scales that are used to measure the IQs of older children. The items for older children are, of course, more complex and difficult. What, however, happens to intellectual capability beyond childhood, as people pass through adulthood and old age?

To answer this question, it is necessary to compare the performances of adults of differing ages when tested with the same material. The early studies of intelligence and age (for example, Jones & Conrad, 1933) suggested that a gradual decline in intelligence began in the early 20s, and that the average decline in intellectual powers by the age of 60 was very large. We now know, however, that at least a good part of this apparent decline was an effect produced by **cross-sectional studies** of the aging process. Within a study that is cross-sectional in design, different individuals are tested at different ages. Thus, for example, we might test some 20-year-olds, some 40-year-olds, and some 60-year-olds, all on the same day. When the performances of older and younger subjects are compared, we not only observe the effects of biological age, we are also comparing groups of subjects born at different times and exposed to differing educational practices and cultural conditions. The more satisfactory way of studying the effects of age is in **longitudinal studies.** These studies continually test the *same* subjects as they grow older. The difficulty with longitudinal studies is that, for obvious reasons, they take a very long time to carry out. There is also a problem posed by subjects dropping out of the study as time passes. These "dropouts" are not a random sampling of the original group of subjects. Figure 9–3 summarizes the results of a study that combined cross-sectional and longitudinal methods. The best data now available suggest that performance on IQ-test material may increase until about the age of 25, then hold relatively steady until about 40. From about 40 on there appears to be some decline, and a sharper decline sets in at about age 60 (Schaie, Labouvie, & Buech, 1973). The relevant data from both longitudinal and cross-sectional studies have been discussed in detail by Botwinick (1977).

These trends, however, are true only of average scores. There is evidence to indicate that highly educated people, who tend to keep up intellectual interests and activities throughout life, show very little decline. There is also

FIGURE 9–3
The graph shows the results of a study combining cross-sectional and longitudinal methods. The results show a decline in mental-test scores with age. (Schaie, Labouvie, & Buech, 1973)

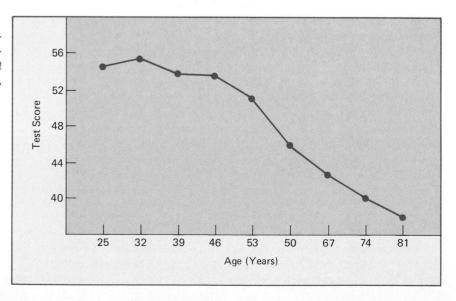

evidence that not all mental abilities are equally likely to decline with age. For example, vocabulary and verbal skills may even improve with age, while skills involving spatial visualization and deductive reasoning may decline. In general, tasks that require quick responding are especially vulnerable to aging.

Children with Low IQs

The original purpose of Binet's test was to identify backward students. The test, and others based on it, is still used in an effort to diagnose the "mentally retarded." To be so diagnosed, an IQ below 70 is usually regarded as a necessary—but not sufficient—condition. That is, it is only when a low IQ is coupled with inadequate social and occupational adjustment that the label of retardation is correctly applied. There are many low-IQ children who appear definitely retarded in the classroom, but not on the playground or in their home environments. These children usually, after leaving school, are able to find productive employment and to function successfully and independently. They merge imperceptibly into the rest of the normal population.

Typically, distinctions are made among various degrees of **mental retardation.** Mild retardation, with IQs ranging from about 55 to 69, occurs in about 2 percent of the population; among such people, prospects for successful adaptation to independent adult life are reasonably good. Moderate retardation, with IQs between 40 and 54, occurs in about .1 percent of the population. Severe retardation—with IQs below 40—is much rarer, occuring in some .003 percent of the population. The severely retarded usually need institutional care throughout their lives. With the right training they can be taught many self-help skills, and the quality of their lives can be improved.

For most mentally retarded people, no clear physical cause can be found. This type of relatively mild retardation is often called "familial-cultural." Those so diagnosed are generally born to parents with low IQs and have been reared in depressed and deprived conditions. There are other cases of retardation —often very severe—that are clearly related to catastrophic biological accidents of some kind, or to known genetic defects. For example, prenatal infection of the mother, or a lack of adequate oxygen during birth, may result in brain damage to the fetus, producing severe retardation. The sometimes severe retardation known as **Down's syndrome** (once called "mongolism") is known to be caused by the presence of an extra 47th chromosome in the cells of the affected child. The extra chromosome produces a number of characteristic physical abnormalities, as well as mental retardation. The risk of having a child with Down's syndrome is very much higher among mothers in their 40s than among younger mothers. Advances in education and health care have maximized the abilities and improved the physical condition of individuals who have Down's syndrome.

Phenylketonuria (PKU) is a rare form of retardation, thought to depend on the inheritance of a particular recessive gene. It was first noted in 1934 that a few retarded children, some of whom were siblings, excreted phenylpyruvic acid in their urine. We now know that the mental retardation of these children was in some way produced by the overaccumulation of that amino acid in their bodies. Thus, a defect in metabolism caused by inheritance of a particular gene must ultimately injure the central nervous system in such a way as to produce this form of mental retardation. Happily, a successful treatment for this genetic defect is available. The child must be fed a diet very low in phenylalanine. The dietary treatment, if begun early enough, prevents the

This child was born with Down's syndrome, which is caused by the presence of an extra, 47th chromosome in the cells. This extra chromosome produces a number of physical abnormalities, as well as mental retardation.

accumulation of the responsible amino acid, and the child develops with a normal IQ. PKU, it must be stressed, is a rare form of retardation. Unfortunately, there are no similarly successful treatments—nor such clearly understood causes—for most forms of retardation.

Children with High IQs

Terman, in 1925, began to study a large group of California schoolchildren with very high IQs, averaging about 150. The original children, numbering over 1,000, have been followed through life for more than 50 years. The project was often referred to by Terman as a study of "genius," but "children with high IQs" seems to be a more accurate description. These children, selected at a young age because of outstandingly high IQs, for the most part went on to live productive and "successful" lives. They earned many college and advanced degrees, and many became doctors, lawyers, professors, or novelists. They wrote many books and scientific papers. They earned good incomes. They weighed more at birth than the average infant, and they were taller and healthier than most children throughout childhood. They seemed as adults to be socially well-adjusted members of their communities, and to be content with the way they had lived their lives.

These findings clearly disprove the notion that high-IQ children are in some way unbalanced or "freakish." They also indicate that, if all we know about a school child is that he or she has a very high IQ, it is a good bet that he or she will go on to lead the kind of "successful" life described above—though, it should be said, not *all* of Terman's subjects succeeded. There is no indication, however, that these very high-IQ children produced works of genuinely creative genius. There is really no proof, either, that their successes had been *caused* by their very high IQs. Almost all of Terman's subjects had been born into professional and well-to-do families. This kind of family background might well be responsible for their good childhood health and for much of their adult success—quite apart from their high IQs. We do not know, for example, whether the lower-IQ sisters and brothers of Terman's selected subjects were any less successful than the subjects themselves. Though Terman would doubtless have expected such a difference, we do not in fact have the necessary data.

TYPES OF INTELLIGENCE TESTS

The benchmark against which more recently developed IQ tests have been measured is the Stanford-Binet test. When new tests are proposed, their validity as IQ tests is often demonstrated by showing that they are highly correlated with Stanford-Binet scores. The Stanford-Binet test does have scales that can be used with adults, but it was basically designed to test children. To measure adults, a number of awkward assumptions had to be made; for instance, by assuming that mental growth stopped at age 16, and by assigning that "chronological age" to all adults, approximate "IQs" could be calculated.

Testing Individuals: The Wechsler Scale

The measurement of adult IQ was greatly advanced by the development of the **Wechsler Adult Intelligence Scale** (**WAIS**). First presented in 1939, this test was revised in 1955 and most recently restandardized in 1981. The success

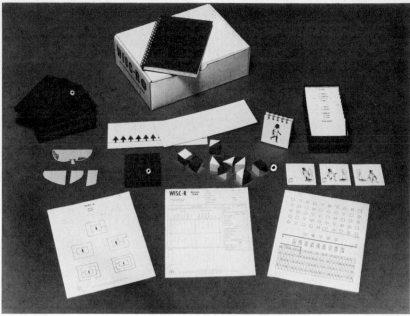

The testing kit for the Wechsler Intelligence Scale for Children is shown in the photo on the right. On the left, a child is working on the Object Assembly portion of the test. She has before her pieces with part of a picture on each and must put them together to form an object (in this case, a horse).

of his adult scale prompted Wechsler to develop the **Wechsler Intelligence Scale for Children** (**WISC-R**), revised in 1974 and designed for children aged 6–16. Most recently, for even younger children, the Wechsler Preschool and Primary Scale of Intelligence has been presented.

The various Wechsler scales, although designated for different age groups, are very much alike in their basic form and types of content. They are all substantially correlated with the Stanford-Binet, with which they have much in common, but from which they differ in some important ways. The outstanding similarity is that both the Stanford-Binet and Wechsler tests are designed to be administered by a trained examiner to one person at a time. The examiner must use training and judgment in deciding whether or not the answer to a given item is correct. The one-on-one testing session takes about an hour in each case, and a skilled examiner can note not only the child's answers but also his or her mannerisms, emotional state, cooperativeness, and so on.

DEVIATION IQ. The Wechsler scales were the first to use the concept of a **deviation IQ.** The decision was made that the average test score for people of any age should be 100, and that the standard deviation of these IQs should be 15 at every age. (This and other statistical concepts are explained in the Appendix.) This result is accomplished by statistical adjustment of the actual raw scores obtained in the standardization samples among people of different ages. That is, one's IQ is determined by comparing one's performance to that of people one's own age in the standardization sample for the test. To have a Wechsler IQ of 130 means that you have done better on the test than about 97.5 percent of people *your age* in the standardization sample. Thus, if you have recently taken the WAIS, you are being compared to a standardization sample studied shortly before 1981. The deviation-IQ procedure also means that if you are 18 years old, and your 65-year-old grandparent has done just a little worse than you in answering the test questions, your grandparent will have a considerably higher IQ than you. That is so because, in the standard-

Table 9–3: Sample Questions from the Wechsler Adult Intelligence Scale.

Verbal Scale	
Information	What is steam made of? What is pepper?
Comprehension	Why is copper often used in electrical wires? Why do some people save sales receipts?
Arithmetic	It takes 3 people 9 days to paint a house. How many would it take to do it in 3 days? An automobile goes 25 miles in 45 minutes. How far would it go in 20 minutes?
Digit Repetition	Repeat the following numbers in order: 1, 3, 7, 2, 5, 4 Repeat the following numbers in reverse order: 5, 8, 2, 4, 9, 6
Similarities	In what way are a circle and a triangle alike? In what way are an egg and a seed alike?
Vocabulary	What is a hippopotamus? What does "resemble" mean?
Performance Scale	
Picture Arrangement	A story is told in 3 or more cartoon panels placed in the incorrect order; put them together to tell the story.
Picture Completion	Point out what's missing from each picture.
Block Design	After looking at a pattern or design, try to arrange small colored cubes in the same pattern.
Object Assembly	Given pieces with part of a picture on each, put them together to form such objects as a hand or a profile.
Digit Symbol	Learn a different symbol for each number and then fill in the blank under the number with the correct symbol.

ization sample, the average 65-year-old could answer fewer questions than the average 18-year-old.

The Wechsler scales also differ from the Stanford-Binet by breaking down the total IQ into 2 separate components—a verbal IQ and a performance IQ. The Stanford-Binet contains many different kinds of testing material mixed together, and provides a single "global" IQ score. The WAIS, however, separates its material into 11 different subscales, which are shown in Table 9–3. The first 6 scales together are combined to give a verbal IQ, while the last 5 scales give a performance IQ. The total IQ is basically the average of the 2. The verbal and performance IQs are substantially correlated with each other, and each is correlated with the Stanford-Binet IQ—the verbal IQ somewhat more so. There are individual cases, however, in which the verbal and performance IQs are very different. This can often be informative, and might indicate language difficulty, or reading or perceptual disabilities.

Testing Groups

Group tests of intelligence sacrifice the detail and the kinds of intimate personal knowledge available from an individual testing session, but they are obviously necessary if very large groups of people are to be examined. The first impetus for group tests came at the time of World War I, when the United States Army decided to test draftees. Two group tests—the Alpha and the

FIGURE 9–4
Specimen items from the Army Alpha and Beta Tests of World War I.

Beta—were quickly developed; sample items from each are given in Figure 9–4. Typically, group tests are administered at the same time to large numbers of people, with paper, pencil, and multiple-choice answer blanks. Though some of the items included in the Alpha test seem amusing and unfair today, the basic form of the Alpha test is very similar to that of many verbal paper-and-pencil tests in use today. The Army General Classification Test of World War II and its more recent replacements are more sophisticated than the old Alpha, as are most of the group tests now used in school systems and in industry. The Beta test of World War I is rather unusual. The test was designed as a *performance* test. To measure accurately the IQs of illiterate or foreign-born draftees, the test had to be "nonverbal"—it couldn't depend on reading skill or familiarity with the English language. The kinds of material shown in Figure 9–4 were made up with that aim in mind. The test, however, had to be given to large groups of men. The instructions were thus given in "pantomime." Readers may decide for themselves whether this performance test fairly measured the IQs of the foreign-born and the illiterate.

Performance Tests and "Culture Fairness"

To say that one has measured "intelligence," rather than what a person happens to have learned, it is necessary that the test be fair in allowing the testees to *use* their intelligence. It is obvious that much verbal material is highly specialized knowledge, not available to all people. Thus, an item such as "Wundt is to Wertheimer as Watson is to _____?" might be a fair test of the intelligence of someone who has studied psychology, but clearly not for anybody else. The item "Sunday is to Monday as January is to _____?" would

APPLICATION□
An Abuse of Testing

The limits of intelligence tests as measures of learning ability are clearly understood in theory, but they are sometimes ignored in practice. This can sometimes lead to serious injustices, as the following true story makes clear.

Alicia P. was 4½ years old when she came, with her parents, from Puerto Rico to an industrial state in the northeast. Placed in a nursery school at the age of 5, Alicia, who spoke very little English, was given the Stanford-Binet IQ test with the help of a Spanish-speaking interpreter. The examining psychologist did not assign a specific IQ score to Alicia but wrote into her record that she was a "Potentially Severe Learning Disability Case." The next year, when she was to enroll in the first grade, another psychologist tested her, again with the Stanford-Binet, but this time in English. The IQ score assigned to Alicia was 47—though the examiner noted that she was "well-poised and socially responsive" and gave off "an impression of mental alertness not borne out by the testing." The psychologist wrote that an IQ of 47 "places Alicia in the category of moderately retarded mentally, usually accepted as trainable." The recommendation was made and accepted that she be placed into a special class for trainable mental retardates.

Within 2 weeks, the teacher of the special class for retardates had written to the school superintendent to point out that Alicia was incomparably in advance of all other students in her class and did not seem at all retarded. The decision was then made to place her into a slightly higher-level class for "educable mental retardates." Three years later, under state law, it was necessary to test Alicia once more. This time, in an attempt to get around language problems, she was tested with the performance scale only of the WISC-R. Her performance IQ was now 76. The psychologist wrote that since 3 years in a class for retardates had increased her IQ from 47 to 76, the class was obviously good for her!

By this time, Alicia's Spanish-speaking parents, who had noticed that she seemed to be learning very little at school, had become aware that she had been placed in a class for retardates. They demanded that their child be tested by a Spanish-speaking psychologist, who employed a specially translated version of the WISC-R and indicated that Alicia's IQ was an entirely normal 95. The school authorities, now in some doubt, had her tested yet again, by still another psychologist. That tester reported that Alicia stated that she preferred to be tested in English. Her IQ, again on the WISC-R, was now said to be 73—with a verbal IQ of 66 and a performance IQ of 86. The Child Study Team in charge of Alicia's case met to consider all these apparently contradictory findings. They concluded that, since the Spanish-speaking psychologist had not had access to Alicia's past records (did not know of her earlier IQ score of 47), they would be guided by the opinion of the tester who said that her present IQ was 73. That tester called her a borderline case and suggested that she remain in the class for retardates.

Some years later, prodded by a lawyer hired by Alicia's parents, the child was tested once again with the WISC-R, by the same school psychologist who had reported her IQ to be 73. This time, however, the psychologist's report stated that she "preferred to have this examination administered in the Spanish language." Her IQ was now 103—with a verbal IQ of 96 and a performance IQ of 110. The psychologist now wrote that "the classification of educable mentally retarded can no longer be sustained . . . I am at a loss to explain the wide discrepancy between the two IQ evaluations." It is hard to believe that this tester failed to recognize the role of language difficulties in Alicia's test scores—but the stigmatizing effect of a scientific-looking IQ number like 47 can blind even sophisticated people to the obvious.

Finally, after 10 long years, Alicia was placed for the first time into an ordinary classroom. She was far behind her classmates, however. When her parents asked for special tutoring for her, they were told that such help was available only for retarded pupils—which the test now showed she was not! Testing, clearly, has not been of much help to Alicia, nor has it been to some other children like her.

probably be regarded as fair by most test-makers, at least for people who speak English. They assume that everyone has been exposed over and over to the names and sequences of the days and the months. That is, if material is "equally" familiar to everyone, it is fair game for an IQ test. The other approach to fairness, in theory, is to use material with which everybody is equally *un*familiar; for example, the testee may be asked to see relationships among groups of unusual geometric forms.

Performance tests of IQ try to avoid some of the more obvious biases of verbal materials by concentrating on materials such as making designs from blocks, completing incomplete drawings, fitting the right peg into the right hole, seeing relations among geometric forms, and so on. Cattell (1949) called his version of such a test "culture free." Perhaps the most widely used such test is Raven's Progressive Matrices (1947), which depends entirely on seeing relations among geometric figures.

To call any test "culture free" is obviously an exaggeration. To begin with, the instructions must be communicated to the testee in some way. Further, members of some cultures find the very idea of being tested strange or offensive. The best that might be hoped for is that some tests might be relatively more "culture fair" than others. The differences among human cultures, however, are enormous, complex, and subtle. We cannot be sure that by reducing the verbal content of a test we are making it fair to all cultures and subcultures. The attempt to develop **culture-fair tests** seems on the whole to have been disappointing. Within the United States, at least, results obtained with them have not differed greatly from those obtained with more traditional tests. Perhaps, in view of the substantial correlation between the verbal and performance scales in Wechsler's tests, this is not at all surprising.

More recently, test-makers have been concerned with the question of whether tests are *biased* against members of minority groups. Bias, in this technical usage of the term, refers to whether or not the same test score, earned by members of 2 different groups, predicts the same academic (or other) performance. For college students at least, tests do not seem to be biased in this sense against minority groups (Jensen, 1980). For example, black and white students with the same scores on the Scholastic Aptitude Test tend to receive about the same grades in college courses. The lack of bias, however, does not necessarily mean that the test score is a fair assessment of the academic *potential* of minority students. The difference between groups in average score on an "unbiased" test may reflect an unfair distribution of educational and other resources in society at large. The test score is being used merely to predict college grades of high-school graduates in society as it now exists. Those students who have high SAT scores are somewhat more likely to receive better grades—whether they are black or white.

Factorially Designed Tests

Though Wechsler did split the total IQ into verbal and performance IQs, he agreed entirely with Binet in stressing the importance of "general intelligence." This was wholly in keeping with the views of a pioneering English psychologist, Charles Spearman. Test items, in Spearman's view, all measured a general mental capacity, labelled *g*. They did so, however, with different degrees of purity. That was because all items also measured some *specific* ability (*s*), and different items measured different specific abilities in different amounts. When all the items were combined into a single test of general intelligence, the various specific abilities contained in the many different items tended to cancel one another out. The result, assuming the right mixture of different kinds of specific items, was a fair measure of general intelligence.

This might be clearer if you think of it in terms of athletic ability instead of intelligence. Some people seem to be good at all athletic skills, and some seem to be poor at them all, even after serious effort. That is, all sports tap some abilities in common. However, there are also some who are good at one sport but not at others. It would be hard to imagine a petite gymnast playing center on a basketball team in the NBA, and it would be hard to imagine an NBA center on the balance beam. The same kind of specificity sometimes holds true for mental abilities.

Spearman's "2-factor" theory of test items was supported by his work with the mathematical procedure of **factor analysis.** This procedure, by examining the intercorrelations among large numbers of items and tests, attempts to "extract out" what all the items have in common. Factor analysis is discussed in more detail in Chapter 14.

Within the United States, Louis Thurstone (1938) challenged Spearman's views. Thurstone argued that a single IQ score was misleading, often covering over sharp differences—within the same individual—in several different mental abilities. For example, a person skilled in the use of words might be backward in the use of numbers, and it is better to know this than to state (accurately) that he or she has an average IQ on a test containing both kinds of items. Thurstone, by analyzing the intercorrelations among a large number of different tests given to the same people, felt that he had discovered at least 7 independent or "pure" factors of mental ability. Thus he developed, and marketed, 7 separate subtests. The 7 factors, each with its own test, were verbal comprehension, word fluency, number, space, memory, perceptual speed, and reasoning.

There is nothing sacred about Thurstone's 7 factors. Had he done his work in factor analysis using other kinds of items, or other subjects, he would no doubt have discovered somewhat different factors. Further, the 7 factors reported by Thurstone are *not* independent of one another. That is, people high on one factor tend to be high on all other factors as well, to a significant degree. This intercorrelation among the factors, of course, brings us back to Spearman, *g*, and the idea of general intelligence.

The other tack, however, has been taken by a distinguished American factor analyst, J. P. Guilford. The "structure of intellect" theory presented by Guilford (1967) states that there are no fewer than 120 factors of intelligence, each representing a different intellectual ability. The idea of sitting still while taking 120 tests will not appeal to many!

Though it seems clear that in many instances a "profile" or breakdown of different mental skills should be more informative than a single number representing IQ, the fact is that tests measuring general IQ (sometimes divided into verbal vs. performance or verbal vs. quantitative parts) are still much more commonly used. Probably that is because the general IQ tests, lumping together many different skills, do a reasonable job of predicting average school performance. There is no evidence that the factorially designed tests do any better, or even as well.

Tests of Divergent Thinking

The search by Guilford for 120 separate factors of mental ability encouraged him and his followers to develop radically different kinds of mental tests. Perhaps the most interesting of them are based on the distinction between **convergent** and **divergent thinking.** With many problems—as with most problems in IQ tests—the solution depends on logically "narrowing down" or converging on the one correct answer. With other problems, the solution depends on being able to let one's thoughts "roam" creatively along different or divergent pathways, resulting in original and surprising ideas—*not* arriving at one predetermined answer. To test divergent thinking ability—which has sometimes been identified with creativity—Guilford and Hoepfner (1971) have used such items as: "Name as many uses as you can think of for a toothpick," or "Imagine all of the things that might possibly happen if all national and local laws were suddenly abolished." To do well on such a test the subject must respond not with one correct answer but with many novel ideas.

Though a number of tests of divergent thinking have been developed, it has turned out that, at least to a considerable degree, scores on such tests are correlated with scores on "convergent" IQ tests. This seems to be mostly because people with low IQ scores tend also to have low divergent thinking or "creativity" scores. Within groups with high traditional IQs, however, there is a lot of variation in divergent thinking ability. Many high-IQ people, in fact, are quite poor at divergent thinking.

We do not know to what degree, if any, people with high scores on divergent-thinking tests are in fact creative in real life. There are no doubt many factors involved in real-life creativity that are not captured by simple divergent-thinking tests. We do know that divergent-thinking scores are not as correlated with school grades as IQ is. The relations among IQ, genuinely creative thinking, school grades, and accomplishment are obviously complex. Thus, for example, Albert Einstein had an indifferent school career, and James Watson, who solved the riddle of the DNA molecule, had an unspectacular IQ of 115. There are school counselors, however, who advise students not to attempt college unless they have an IQ of 120! The prediction from IQ or from school grades to actual accomplishment clearly cannot be made with anything like certainty.

NATURE, NURTURE, AND TEST SCORES

The Concept of Heritability

There are some people with high IQs, many people with average IQs, and some people with low IQs. That is to say, there is much variation among people in IQ-test scores. What causes these differences among people? To what extent are they produced by the different genes that people inherit? To what extent are they produced by the different environments that people experience as they grow up? These questions, having to do with the relative importance of nature and of nurture, have given rise to much controversy—and not a little passion—since the birth of IQ testing.

Everyone agrees, of course, that human genes are a necessary precondition for the development of human intelligence and of IQ. There is no environment that can raise the intellectual level of a fish, a bird, or a monkey to that of a normal human being. Everyone also agrees that exposure to human language and society is an absolute necessity for the development of those skills measured by IQ tests. Without this, having normal human genes alone cannot result in a normal IQ score. Thus it is obviously correct to state that *both* genes *and* environment are inextricably involved in the development of IQ—or, for that matter, the development of any other trait.

The controversy has to do with the differences in IQ among normal human beings, all of them possessing normal sets of human genes. There are, within normal limits, great differences in the sets of genes that all of us inherit from our parents. The question is, are these undoubted differences in our genes largely, moderately, or only slightly related to the differences among us in IQ test scores?

The concept of the **heritability ratio** is one effort to give a quantitative answer to this question. In theory, the heritability of IQ can be estimated by comparing the IQ correlations of various types of biological relatives. For example, we know that parents and children have 50 percent of their genes in common. Grandparents and grandchildren have only 25 percent of their genes in common. Put very simply, if the heritability of IQ were very high, we would expect the IQ correlation between parent and child to be about .50, and that between grandparent and grandchild to be about .25. The actual procedures used in calculating heritability are quite complex, but the basic idea is to see how closely the resemblance in IQ of relatives corresponds to their resemblance in genetic makeup (that is, the proportion of genes they have in common).

Arthur Jensen, in an influential 1969 article, summarized a number of studies of IQ correlations among relatives within the white population. The data, Jensen argued, indicated that the heritability of IQ among whites was about .80. That figure, if correct, would indicate that 80 percent of the variance in IQ among individuals is due to the fact that they have different genes. The **variance,** as a statistical measure, is simply the square of the standard deviation; the variance in IQ, thus, is 225—the square of the standard deviation of 15. Thus, as matters now stand, about 95 percent of whites have IQs between 70 and 130. To say that the heritability of IQ is .80 is to imply that if all whites were to be brought up in the *same* (average) environment, the variance in IQ would then be .80 times 225, or 180. That is, the standard deviation of IQ would be 13.4, so that 95 percent of IQ scores would fall between about 73 and 127. This large remaining variation in IQ scores would be *entirely* the product of genetic differences among people since, in our hypothetical example, all individuals had been reared in the same environment. The same kinds of calculations indicate that if the heritability of IQ were .20, rearing all individuals in the same average environment should compress the range of IQs so that 95 percent of all scores would fall between 87 and 113.

We must note, however, that very great difficulties are involved in calculating the heritability of a human trait. The basic problem is that close biological relatives not only have many genes in common, they also tend to have highly similar environments. The more closely related people are biologically, the more similar their environments are likely to have been. This **covariance** of genes and environment, together with other difficulties, has convinced at least some authorities (Feldman & Lewontin, 1975; Layzer, 1974) that accurate or meaningful heritability estimates cannot be made for human populations. (With animals or plants, no such problem exists. The breeding of individual plants or animals can be controlled, and offspring can be assigned at random to strictly controlled environments.)

The paragraphs that follow will examine the data from which Jensen and many others have tried to calculate the heritability of IQ. We shall not be concerned, however, with attempting to estimate a precise heritability ratio. We shall ask—more modestly, but more realistically—do the available data suggest that genetic differences are responsible for a large, moderate, or small proportion of the differences in IQ among people? These terms may seem very imprecise, but—as we shall see—so are the available data. Throughout our examination of the relevant research studies, we shall try to focus on a critical question: Does this study effectively separate the effects of heredity from those of environment? To the extent that genes and environment are allowed to covary in any study, a meaningful answer about the relative importance of each cannot be obtained.

Genetic Relatedness and IQ

The simplest way—in theory, at least—of studying the genetic basis of IQ is to study identical twins who have been brought up apart from each other. Pairs of identical twins are the only individuals in the world whose genes are entirely the same. Thus it is obvious that if IQ is largely determined by inheritance, pairs of identical twins ought to resemble each other greatly in IQ scores. This should be true even if the twins have been reared in entirely different environments. Most twin pairs, of course, grow up in the same household and share very similar environments. There are, however, a few rare cases of identical twins who have been separated very early in life and brought up in different families. Those rare cases—separated identical twins—make up a kind of natural experiment on heredity and environment. The basic logic is simple. Two separated identical twins have their heredity in common, but not their environments. Thus, if their IQs are very similar, that similarity must be due to the one factor they have in common—their heredity.

STUDIES OF SEPARATED IDENTICAL TWINS.   There have been, for obvious reasons, few studies of separated twins. Four investigators, however, have gathered large enough samples to make some statistical analysis possible. The largest and apparently most impressive study was made in England by the late Sir Cyril Burt (1966). The Burt study, said to be based on 53 pairs of separated twins, reported a very high IQ correlation between twins. Further, Burt indicated that there was no correlation at all in the socioeconomic status levels of the households in which the separated twins had beeen reared. Twins reared in households with vastly different socioeconomic levels resembled each other greatly in IQ—just as did twins reared in very similar households. Taken at face value, Burt's study appeared to provide very strong evidence for an overwhelming genetic effect on IQ. However, it has now become clear that Burt's study cannot be taken at face value. There is clear evidence that much of Burt's published work was fraudulent, and much of his data invented. Psychologists are now unanimous—regardless of their views about heredity and environment—in rejecting Burt's suspect data.

The second largest study was also done in England by Shields (1962), who managed to test 40 pairs of separated twins. The IQ correlation obtained by Shields was .77—not as high as Burt's, but still very substantial. The difficulty, however, is that in the Shields study most of the twins seem to have been reared in quite similar environments. Some were not separated at all until they were 7 or 8 years old, and 27 of the 40 pairs were actually brought up in related branches of the same family. The twins had usually been born into poor families, and the mother had felt unable to take on the burden of 2 more infants at the same time. The most common single pattern was for the mother to keep one child and to give the other to her sister (or to the father's sister) to rear. This, of course, tended to result in the "separated" twins having similar environments. Thus, Shields says of one pair: "The paternal aunts decided to take one twin each, and they have brought them up amicably, living next-door to one another in the same Midlands colliery village. . . .

Separated at birth, the Mallifert twins meet accidently.
(Drawing by Chas. Addams; © 1981 The New Yorker Magazine, Inc.)

They are constantly in and out of each other's houses" (p. 164). This kind of close contact and highly similar environment also occurred even when the twins were brought up by unrelated families. Thus, Shields writes of another pair: "Brought up within a few hundred yards of one another. . . . Told they were twins after girls discovered it for themselves, having gravitated to one another at school at the age of 5 . . . they were never apart, wanted to sit at the same desk . . ." (p. 189).

For the 27 Shields pairs reared in related branches of the same family, the IQ correlation was .83. For the 13 pairs reared in unrelated families, the correlation was a significantly lower .51. That is clear evidence that "separated" identical twins resemble each other more if the environments in which they have been reared are similar. We cannot deduce what the IQ correlation would be if—as Burt falsely claimed—there were *no* systematic similarities in the environments of separated pairs. The correlation, if such an ideal experiment could in fact be performed, might conceivably be .00, though few psychologists would expect this outcome. There is some reason to suppose that the correlation might be lower than the .51 observed among the Shields pairs reared by unrelated families. We have seen that even among these pairs there were substantial similarities in environment.

The two remaining studies reported results basically similar to those of Shields. The 19 pairs studied in the United States by Newman, Freeman, and Holzinger (1937) correlated .67, while the 12 pairs studied in Denmark by Juel-Nielsen (1965) correlated .62. These correlations seem substantial, but they cannot be attributed entirely to heredity. The twins in these studies, like those observed by Shields, tended to be reared in quite similar environments and often had considerable contact with each other. Further, there is reason to believe that the particular IQ tests used in these studies were not accurately standardized for age and for sex (Kamin, 1974). Since a pair of identical twins is always of the same age and same sex, any tendency for the test to favor a

APPLICATION☐
Cyril Burt: Science, Fraud, and Policy

The late Sir Cyril Burt (1883–1971) was doubtless England's most distinguished psychologist—knighted by his monarch, and given a medal by the American Psychological Association. Burt served for many years as a school psychologist of the London County Council. He was the first person in the English-speaking world to hold such a position. Throughout his long life, Burt conducted research on the inheritance of mental ability. He reported that he had managed to locate 53 pairs of separated identical twins. With the assistance of two collaborators, J. Conway and Margaret Howard, the twins had been IQ tested. Though the twins were said to have been reared in wholly unrelated environments, they resembled one another dramatically in IQ. Burt was also the only investigator who was able to test, in the same population, large numbers of pairs of biological relatives of every sort—grandparents and grandchildren, second cousins, uncles and nieces, etc. The IQ correlations that Burt reported for various kinds of relatives corresponded with remarkable precision to the values one would expect if IQ were almost entirely determined by the genes. Professor Arthur Jensen (1972) clearly spoke for many when he wrote that Burt's work was "the most satisfactory attempt" to estimate the heritability of IQ; and that Burt's "larger, more representative samples than any other investigator had ever assembled" would "secure Burt's place in the history of science."

Things began to unravel when it was first pointed out (Kamin, 1973) that in later published papers, as the size of Burt's twin samples grad-

ually increased, the IQ correlations remained identical to the third decimal place! That is so unlikely an outcome as to be unbelievable. There were many other mutual contradictions and inconsistencies revealed by cross-checking of Burt's many published papers. There was also a disturbing ambiguity in Burt's research reports—no details were given about what IQ tests had been used, or when or where the testing had been carried out. By 1974, Jensen was ready to agree that Burt's data were "useless for hypothesis testing." But Jensen maintained that Burt had been merely careless, not fraudulent—and that data other than Burt's ("the most satisfactory") also supported the idea of a high heritability of IQ.

In 1976 Oliver Gillie, a reporter for the *London Sunday Times*, charged in a front-page article that Burt had perpetrated the most sensational scientific fraud of the century. Burt's "collaborators" and "coauthors"—J. Conway, Margaret Howard, and others—appeared never to have existed. Testimony was available that Burt himself had written papers using their names and that at the least they were unknown to anybody, and clearly not in England, during the time when they were supposedly testing twins! This frank labeling of Burt as a fraud was attacked by some IQ-testing authorities as "unfounded defamation" (Jensen, 1976) and "McCarthyism . . . character assassination" (Eysenck, 1977).

The argument about whether Burt was careless or a fraud has now been put to rest. The authorized Burt biography by Leslie Hearnshaw was published in 1979. With Burt's private papers and documents available to him, Hearnshaw was reluctantly forced to conclude that at least much of Burt's data was the result of systematic fraud.

With the disappearance of Burt's "data," the *least* that can be said is that the case for substantial heritability of IQ has been weakened. The unhappy Burt story, moreover, provokes some troublesome thoughts. Why did Burt invent false data? Throughout his life, Burt was interested in—and had great influence upon—educational policy in England. He argued that the "11-plus exam"—a form of IQ test given at age 11—should be given to all school children, and that the result of that exam was a measure of the "innate intelligence" of the child. Thus, in Burt's view, it was proper to use this test result as the basis for "streaming" children, irreversibly, into one of 3 educational channels. There was only one track—requiring a very high test score—that led on to a university training. With Burt's great influence, this policy was in fact adopted. Further, Burt (1943) argued that limited educational resources in the school system should go primarily to the "gifted." The majority were genetically too inferior to profit much from academic training. The "data" provided by Burt were used by him to support his policy recommendations.

Perhaps more disturbing than the fact that a distinguished psychologist could lie—there have been a few celebrated frauds in almost all the sciences—is the fact that so many accepted Burt's data, uncritically, at face value. This must mean that preconceived ideas about what is true prevent scientists in at least some areas from exercising their normal critical judgments. With hindsight, the embarrassing flaws and discrepancies in Burt's published work are painfully obvious. That flawed and fraudulent work, however, was communicated to a whole generation of students of psychology, education, and genetics as serious science.

particular age group or sex will tend to make the twins appear more similar in IQ than they really are.

Within the past few years, considerable newspaper and television publicity has been given to an ongoing study of separated identical twins at the University of Minnesota. At this writing, this project has not yet yielded any published scientific report. There seems little reason to suppose, however, that new data from this study will change the basic picture. Presumably, the twins will resemble one another in IQ, but the degree both of effective separation and of environmental similarity will be questionable.

To sum up, the actual studies of separated identical twins have produced results much less conclusive than might have been obtained in an ideal—but in practice impossible to perform—experiment. The twins who have been studied do resemble each other in IQ, but —once Burt's data are rejected— they have also experienced quite similar environments. Thus there is no way to know how much of the observed IQ correlation might be due to identical genes, and how much to similar environments. There is obviously much room for disagreement in interpreting these data; if there were not, the argument about heredity, environment, and IQ would long since have ended.

STUDIES OF ADOPTED CHILDREN.　The practice of adoption makes possible other kinds of studies that, in principle, might be able to unravel the combined effects of heredity and environment on IQ. A number of interesting and relevant questions can be asked about the IQs of adopted children. We might ask, first, do adopted children tend to have normal IQs? The answer is very clear: The average IQ of adopted children is distinctly superior. This tends to be the case even when the biological parents of the adopted children have very low IQs. For example, 100 adoptees in Iowa had an average IQ of 117 (Skodak & Skeels, 1949). The biological mothers of the same children had an average IQ of only 87. We can safely conclude that the source of the superior IQs of the adopted children must have been the excellent environment that most adoptive parents give their children. Those families that choose to adopt children—and that are selected by adoption agencies as suitable parents—tend to be highly advantaged. They obviously provide environments that foster the development of high IQ in their children.

The beneficial effect of an adoptive environment has been dramatically illustrated, and precisely quantified, in a recent French adoption study (Schiff, Duyme, Dumaret, & Tomkiewicz, 1982). The authors located a number of children whose biological parents were unskilled workers and who had been adopted shortly after birth into upper-middle-class families. The adopted children, however, had biological siblings or half-siblings who were reared by their natural parents. There is no reason to expect any genetic difference between the adopted children and their siblings or half-sibs. Nevertheless, the adoptees, at school age, had an average IQ 14 points higher than that of their sibs. Perhaps of more social importance, the adopted children had had to repeat one or more school grades only one-fourth as often as did the sibs reared by their own parents. These facts tell us that environment can have a large effect on IQ and school performance. They tell us little, however, about the *relative* importance of heredity and environment. The results do tell us that we could reduce the school-failure rates and increase the IQs of the children of unskilled workers—by providing them with the kinds of environments typical of middle-class adopting families.

There have been a number of attempts to compare the IQ correlation between adopted parents and adopted children with that between ordinary, biological parents and children. Biological children living in normal families have received both their genes and their environment from their parents. Adopted children, however, have received only their environment from their adoptive parents. Thus, to the extent that genes are important determiners of IQ, one would expect the correlation between biological parent-child pairs to be larger than that between adoptive parent-child pairs.

The earliest studies of adopted children showed clearly that the IQ correlation between adoptive parent and child was relatively small—and clearly smaller than that observed between parent and child in ordinary biological families (Burks, 1928; Leahy, 1935). This kind of comparison, however, may be misleading. We have already noted that adoptive parents, having been rigorously selected by adoption agencies, are a very special kind of people. There is relatively little variation among them in IQ, and relatively little variation in the excellence of the environments they provide for their adopted children. When there is little variation in a measurement, correlations involving that measure tend to be low. The special and unique characteristics of adoptive families make it hazardous to compare them to ordinary families.

Many adoptive families, however, contain not only an adopted child, but also a *biological* child of the same parents. These families seem especially suited for investigating the nature–nurture problem. They are all "special" families, all having wished to adopt a child, and all having been selected as suitable by adoption agencies. Within each family, the adopted child has received only the environment from the parents, and the biological child has received both genes and environment from the very same parents. To the degree that IQ is passed on through the genes, it is obvious that within such families the correlation between parent and biological child should be larger than that between parent and adopted child.

In two recent adoption studies, the necessary data were collected from a reasonably large number of these special families. The correlations between the *mother* and her two kinds of children, in each of the studies, are given in Table 9–4 (top). There is obviously no significant difference between the 2 correlations, within either study. The child's IQ resembles the mother's IQ to the same degree, whether or not the child and mother are genetically related. This result clearly does not support the idea that IQ is a very heritable trait. The study by Scarr and Weinberg (1977), it might be noted, has one rather unusual feature. The adopted children are black, and the adoptive parents—as well as the biological children of the parents—are white.

The picture seems rather different, however, when the correlations between the *father* and his 2 kinds of children are considered. These data, given

	Texas Adoption Project (Horn et al., 1979)	Transracial Adoption (Scarr & Weinberg, 1977)
Correlation of mother and biological child	.20 (N = 162)	.34 (N = 100)
Correlation of mother and adopted child	.22 (N = 151)	.29 (N = 66)
Correlation of father and biological child	.28 (N = 163)	.34 (N = 102)
Correlation of father and adopted child	.12 (N = 152)	.07 (N = 67)

Table 9–4: Mother-Child and Father-Child IQ Correlations in Adoptive Families with Biological Children.

in Table 9–4 (bottom), show that the father more closely resembles his biological than his adopted child. That is especially the case in Scarr and Weinberg's transracial adoption study. There is no obvious reason why the data for fathers and for mothers should differ in this way, although it is possible to invent plausible reasons. They would not be very convincing, however, without further and more detailed studies.

We can also look at correlations between various types of siblings in these 2 studies. The families contain some pairs of biological siblings. That is, the parents have had 2 or more biological children of their own. Within each of these families there are also 1 or more adopted children. There are therefore 2 kinds of biologically unrelated sibling pairs. There are some pairs of genetically unrelated adopted children reared by the same parents; and there are some genetically unrelated pairs consisting of 1 biological child and 1 adopted child of the same parents. The correlations for all 3 types of sibling pairs, in each study, are given in Table 9–5. The samples are in some cases relatively small, and the correlations fluctuate somewhat. What is clear, however, is that there is no tendency for the biologically related pairs to be more highly correlated than the unrelated pairs. Within the Scarr and Weinberg study, the biological pairs are all white, the adopted pairs are all black, and the biological-adopted pairs consist of 1 white and 1 black child each.

The Texas Adoption Project was able to obtain the IQ scores of the biological mothers of the adopted children. Their average IQ was lower, by about 6 points, than that of the adoptive mothers. Despite this, the adopted children and the biological children of the adoptive parents each had the same average IQ of 112. Thus it is clear that the adoptive parents were able to transmit high IQs equally to *all* their children—whether or not they shared genes with them. These IQ averages, according to the authors of the Texas Project, suggest "a heritability of IQ that is close to zero" (Horn, Loehlin, & Willerman, 1979). From a consideration of all the correlational data in their study, the same authors suggested that "moderate heritabilities" are indicated. These conclusions have some special force, since the authors had begun their study expecting to find a very high heritability of IQ, presumably in the neighborhood of .80.

Perhaps the best summary we can make of modern, well-designed adoption studies is that their data are not consistent with a very high heritability of IQ. Depending on which aspects of the data one chooses to emphasize (not all the data have been reviewed here), heritability appears to be somewhere between moderate and very low.

COMPARISON OF IDENTICAL AND FRATERNAL TWINS.   Identical twins occur when a single sperm fertilizes a single ovum and, early in the process of development,

Table 9–5: Sibling IQ Correlations in Adoptive Families with Biological Children.

	Texas Adoption Project (Horn et al., 1979)	Transracial Adoption (Scarr & Weinberg, 1977)
Biological-biological (related) pairs	.35 (N = 46)	.37 (N = 75)
Adopted-adopted (unrelated) pairs	_____	.49 (N = 21)
Biological-adopted (unrelated) pairs	.29 (N = 197)	.30 (N = 134)

an extra split occurs. This results in the birth of 2 individuals who have identical genes. These 2 individuals are always of the same sex, and almost always they are strikingly similar in physical appearance. The more common type of twins, fraternal twins, occurs when 2 separate sperm fertilize 2 separate ova. Thus, fraternal twins are no more alike genetically than ordinary sibling pairs. They are in fact ordinary siblings who happen to be born at the same time. They can be of the same or opposite sex, and their physical resemblance is no greater than that of ordinary siblings. They share on average, like ordinary siblings, 50 percent of their genes.

These facts suggest that a comparison of identical and fraternal twins might help to illuminate the roles of heredity and environment. The two types of twins have in common that each has been born and reared in the same family environment. To the degree that being of the same age is likely to increase the similarity of environmental experience, the 2 types of twins are again equated. The obvious difference is that identical twins are much more alike genetically—to be precise, twice as much alike—than are fraternal twins. Thus, if IQ is heritable, the correlation between identical twins should be much larger than that between fraternal twins.

There have been literally dozens of studies comparing the IQ correlations of identical and of same-sexed fraternal twins. (The studies typically include only same-sex fraternal pairs, since all identical pairs are necessarily of the same sex.) The studies agree, almost without exception, in reporting a higher IQ correlation for identical twins. The typical correlation found for identical twins is about .85, while that found for fraternal twins is about .61 (Bouchard & McGue, 1981). This result is consistent with a substantial heritability of IQ—but it is also open to different interpretations.

There is a large body of evidence indicating that identical twins in fact experience much more similar environments than do fraternal twins. This is presumably a consequence of their striking physical similarity, which evidently encourages their parents, teachers, and peers to regard and treat them very much the same. Further, identical twins appear to be much more closely attached to each other than are same-sex fraternal twins. The result of all this is that identical twins are much more likely to play and spend time together, to have the same friends and teachers, to sleep in the same room, and to wear the same clothes than are fraternal twins (Loehlin & Nichols, 1976). When parents are asked whether or not they have tried to treat their twins "exactly the same," parents of identicals much more often say that they have tried to do just that. We are thus forced to note once more that, in the real world, genes and environment tend to covary—much to the annoyance of investigators of the nature–nurture problem. The difference in IQ correlations between identicals and fraternals must at least in part be caused by the differentially similar environments they have experienced. We have no way of knowing how large a part of the difference to assign to heredity, and how large a part to environment.

The Loehlin and Nichols study contains a further bit of information which indicates that the especially similar treatment given to identical twins does in fact increase the correlation of their IQs. There were 502 pairs of identical twins in the study, and in about half the cases the parents indicated that they had tried to treat the 2 twins "exactly the same." Those identical twins whose parents did treat them exactly the same resembled each other significantly more in IQ than did those whose parents did not treat them alike. This *must* be an environmental effect, since all identical twin pairs have identical genes.

The older twins are fraternal twins; the younger twins are identical. As noted by Loehlin and Nichols (1976), identical twins are much more likely to play and spend time together, to have the same friends and teachers, to sleep in the same room, and to wear the same clothes than are fraternal twins.

The fact that similar treatment affects the IQ correlation of even identical pairs, put together with the fact that identicals are much more likely than fraternals to receive similar treatment, makes clear that some part (perhaps most) of the correlation difference between the 2 types of twins is environmentally produced.

FAMILY STUDIES OF IQ CORRELATIONS.   There have been many studies designed to show that biological relatives have similar IQs, and there is no doubt about this correlation. Further, the closer the biological relation, the higher the IQ correlation (Bouchard & McGue, 1981). This is what one would expect if IQ were highly heritable; but it would also follow from the obvious fact that the more closely related two people are biologically, the more similar are their environments. We cannot deduce, from the fact that similar IQ-test scores tend to run in families, the degree to which genetic and environmental factors are involved.

The family studies have recently been summarized by two prominent behavior geneticists (Plomin & DeFries, 1980). They concluded that, although older data suggested a heritability of about .80, more recent studies suggest a heritability of about .50. Thus, where Jensen (1969) had implied that heredity was about four times as important as environment in determining IQ differences among whites, Plomin and DeFries now imply that heredity and environment are about equally effective. The Plomin and DeFries estimate of heritability seems high, however, compared to recent detailed statistical analyses of the family correlations by still other geneticists. Thus Rice, Cloninger, and Reich (1980) have suggested a heritability of .30, while Rao, Morton, Lalouel, and Lew (1982)—who had earlier suggested a much higher figure—now suggest .31.

When viewed as a whole, the data on IQ correlations among relatives within the white population suggest, at most, rather moderate heritability, and perhaps very little heritability. With the collection of new data, and with the improvement of techniques for analyzing the data, heritability estimates have clearly been declining. At the same time, there are too many inconsistencies to place much confidence in any particular numerical estimate. That, at least, is the conclusion of the present authors, after reviewing a large and somewhat ambiguous set of research studies.

Group Differences in IQ Scores

From the earliest days of intelligence testing, researchers have spent considerable effort in examining differences among groups of various sorts in average IQ scores. These studies have, if anything, created more controversy than have studies of individual differences in IQ—and, as we shall see, they have been even less revealing about the nature of IQ, or the ways in which nature and nurture interact in the development of IQ.

SEX DIFFERENCES.   Two large groups of considerable interest to most people are the male and female sexes. The answer to the question of whether the 2 sexes differ in measured IQ is straightforward: No, they do not. This might be due, however, to the fact that test-makers do not believe that males and females *should* differ in IQ. The tests of general intelligence in common use have all been standardized so as to do away with, or at least to minimize, possible sex differences. The choice of which items to include in an intelligence test is, after all, arbitrary. The test-makers have deliberately eliminated from their tests items that disproportionately favored one sex or the other. Where this has not been done, items favoring one sex have been deliberately balanced by items favoring the other. The equality of the sexes in IQ may thus be more a fact of test construction than a fact of nature. The point is that it would be easy to construct a test with all the surface characteristics of an IQ test to make *either* sex look more "intelligent." For example, Willerman (1979) has reported that among a Texas sample of husbands and wives, one item was successfully passed by 70 percent of males and only 30 percent of females. The item is actually included in the Wechsler test, and it asks what is the temperature at which water boils.

When specialized tests have not been deliberately standardized to remove sex differences, there is some suggestion that males may do a little better on quantitative items, and females a little better on verbal items. These are not large differences, however, and they are not consistently reported in all studies. The most consistently found sex difference—at least after early childhood—is on tasks involving spatial visualization, on which males tend to do better. We do not know to what extent the sex difference in spatial abilities is genetic, and to what extent it is cultural. The fact that wives are less knowledgeable than their husbands about the temperature at which water boils should not be taken to indicate a genetic intellectual inferiority of females! We might also note from this example that inability to answer an IQ test question does not necessarily imply a handicap in adjusting to the demands of the real world. The Texas wives were probably at least as adept as their husbands in the constructive use of boiling water in the kitchen.

SOCIAL-CLASS DIFFERENCES.   There are large and clear differences in the average IQs of members of different social classes and occupations, and they are not surprising in nature. Put most simply, people who work with their heads—and especially professional people—do very well on IQ tests. People who work with their hands do less well, with unskilled laborers having lower scores than skilled laborers. The World War II testing program of the United States Army, using the Army General Classification Test, found distinctively different average IQs across a wide range of civilian occupations. These are illustrated in Figure 9–5; note that there is considerable variation in IQ *within* any given occupation. There is no evidence, by the way, to indicate that within an occupation people with the higher IQs perform their jobs much better.

Perhaps of more interest, children born to parents of different social classes also differ in average IQ—but the differences are not so large as those among their parents. The 1937 restandardization of the Stanford-Binet test found substantial differences among children whose parents had been classified into 7 occupational classes. These data are given in Table 9–6. The same kind of social-class differences were again observed when the WISC-R test was restandardized in 1974 (Kaufman & Doppelt, 1976). The 6- to 16-year-old children of "professional and technical workers" had an average IQ of 109.4, compared to 92.1 for the children of "laborers, farm laborers, and farm foremen."

The existence of IQ differences among adults of different occupations and classes says nothing at all about the genetic and environmental bases of IQ. People with high IQs, no matter how they got them, tend to end up in the more prestigious and economically rewarding occupations. We do not even know whether high IQ is really a *cause* of entering a higher occupation.

FIGURE 9–5
The averages and ranges of IQs in a number of different occupations. There are distinctly different average IQs across the range of occupations, and there is also considerable variation within any given occupation. (Harrell & Harrell, 1945)

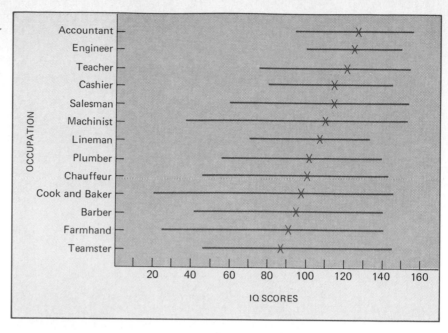

Table 9–6: Average IQ of Children (Ages 2–18) According to Father's Occupation.

Father's Occupation	Children's Average IQ
Professional	115.9
Semiprofessional and managerial	111.9
Clerical, skilled trades, and retail businesses	107.1
Rural owners	94.2
Semiskilled, minor clerical, minor business	104.4
Slightly skilled	99.1
Day laborers, urban and rural	96.3

From McNemar (1942).

Possibly, for example, family background, possession of a diploma, or non-intellectual social skills are much more important than IQ in determining occupational level (Jencks, 1972).

The fact that children born into different social classes have different IQs can be—and, as we might by now expect, has been—interpreted in different ways. There is no doubt that the environments of children differ widely across social classes, and it seems reasonable to believe that this produces the observed IQ differences. The data summarized in Table 9–6 make clear, however, that social-class differences in IQ appear even before 5 years of age. That means that environmental differences assumed to affect IQ must be operating before that age, and before the child has been exposed to formal schooling. The other interpretation is to assume that social classes differ genetically, and that genes making for high IQ occur more often in the upper social classes. This idea was argued vigorously by the early American translators of Binet's test (Terman, 1916; Goddard, 1920; Yerkes & Foster, 1923). The same notion has been proposed more recently by Herrnstein (1973), who argued that in a free society, people born with "good" genes tend to rise in social class and to transmit their good genes to their offspring. This must result, according to Herrnstein, in a "meritocracy"—a society in which the upper classes are genetically gifted, and in which the genetically superior children of upper-class parents necessarily (and justifiably) remain in the upper class. This idea and variants of it seem to be as old as civilized man. Plato, for example, argued that slaves were by nature born to be slaves, and that Athenians were born to be free men. The evidence to support the hereditary basis of social-class membership has not become much more convincing since Plato's time.

We can note that the 1937 restandardization of the Stanford-Binet test also indicated (Table 9–7) that children born in farm areas had much lower average IQs than children born in cities. This seems an obvious consequence of the greater educational and environmental opportunities available in cities (at least in 1937). The argument has also been made, however, that genetically bright people tended to migrate to the stimulating and rewarding cities, leaving a residue of duller folk, who have genetically dull children, in rural areas. This hypothetical argument is not likely to convince many farmers—no more so than similar arguments about a genetic basis for low black IQ scores have convinced black people, or people sensitive to the effects of racial prejudice and discrimination. Further, by the time the WISC-R was restandardized in 1974, the urban–rural difference in average IQ had sunk to a mere 2 IQ points. That, as Kaufman and Doppelt (1976) suggested, might well be attributed to the increasing impact of mass media on rural families and to improved educational facilities.

Table 9–7: Average IQ of Children (Ages 2–18) in Urban, Suburban, and Rural Areas.

Type of Area	Children's Average IQ
Urban	106.2
Suburban	104.9
Rural	96.6

From McNemar (1942).

BLACK–WHITE DIFFERENCES. The most inflamed arguments about the heritability of IQ have involved the fact that, in the United States, black people on average tend to score some 10 to 15 points lower in IQ than do white people. This fact has been known for a long time. The Army testing program of World War I indicated such a difference—and it also indicated that black people in some northern states had a higher average IQ than whites in some southern states. To some, the data proclaimed that black people were genetically inferior to white people. To others, the data indicated that IQ was determined by educational and environmental opportunities.

The influential article by Jensen (1969), already cited, not only argued that the heritability of IQ among white people was .80, but it also maintained that the difference in average IQ between black people and white people was probably of genetic origin. Further, in Jensen's view, attempts at compensatory education of underprivileged children—such programs as Head Start and other interventions aimed at increasing intellectual competence of the children—had failed, and were bound to fail. That was so, said Jensen, because of the high heritability of IQ.

There are few more obvious social facts than the overwhelming discrimination to which black people have been exposed throughout American history. The clear environmental differences between black people and white people seem, to most social scientists, obviously related to the difference in average IQ. The fact is, however, that black people and white people do inherit somewhat different genes, which affect, among other things, skin color, hair texture, etc. Thus, it is difficult to *disprove* the idea that genetic differences between the races *might* be responsible for the IQ difference. (*Why* one would want to prove or disprove such an idea is another question—perhaps better left untouched in this textbook.)

There seems little point in attempting to summarize in detail the multitude of research studies on black–white IQ differences. The topic seems almost to have obsessed some American researchers, which, in view of the importance of race in American society, seems scarcely surprising. There are studies to show that light-skinned black people have higher IQs than dark-skinned black people. This has been interpreted as indicating that degree of black ancestry is a predictor (genetically) of IQ. The same result, however, has also been interpreted as a consequence of the lesser discrimination against light-skinned black people. The fact that northern blacks have higher IQs than southern blacks (and than southern whites in some states) has been interpreted as a result of better educational opportunity—but it has also been interpreted as a consequence of selective migration of genetically bright black people from the South to the North, or as a result of greater black–white intermarriage in the North. The point should be obvious: Until and unless black people have the same environmental experiences as white people, those who wish to argue about the basis of the observed IQ difference will be free to do so. Their arguments may be ingenious, but they will be without convincing evidence. The pity is that in a society which supposedly treats people as individuals, and not as specimens belonging to particular groups, so much time and energy has been wasted on an irrelevant and, strictly speaking, unanswerable question. (See the accompanying box on race and IQ.)

Most present-day psychologists agree that there is *no* evidence that clearly supports a genetic interpretation of black–white IQ differences. Perhaps a smaller proportion, but still a majority, agree that what is known about environmental and cultural differences between the races seems adequate to explain the observed IQ difference.

Though Jensen (1969) asserted that the heritability of IQ among whites is .80, our own review has indicated that this number is unrealistically high. The fact is, though, that even if IQ heritability *were* very high, both within the white and black populations, this would *not* necessarily mean that a difference between the 2 races in *average* IQ had *any* genetic basis! To see this clearly, imagine 2 sacks, each containing the same mixture of seeds from many different genetic varieties of corn. The seeds from the white sack are all planted in a patch of very fertile soil, with very uniform environmental conditions. The seeds from the black sack are all planted in uniformly poor soil. Now, *within* each of the 2 plots of land, the differing heights to which the various corn plants grow will be determined entirely by heredity (the seed). The *average* height of corn plants, however, will be less in the poorer soil—even though exactly the same mixture of seeds has been planted in each plot. The different results *between* the 2 plots will be determined entirely by environment. This type of example should make clear to you the difficulty—or even absurdity—of asking whether heredity or environment is responsible for differences between human groups. The (highly disputable) existence of high IQ heritability *within* one or both races does not, despite Jensen's assertions, have any implications for understanding the different averages *between* the 2 groups. (The use of the term "poor soil" in this example is not meant to imply that the environment and culture of black people is generally deficient or defective. The environment of most American blacks, however, has not been such as to lead to high scores on standardized IQ tests.)

The final point to be made has to do with the concept of heritability itself. The concept is relevant only to *differences* among individuals in some measured trait—not to the average level of that trait. Thus, for example, any environmental treatment that immediately doubled everyone's IQ would have

Race and IQ

There are many kinds of studies that make it very implausible to suggest that the black–white difference in average IQ is genetically determined. Lee (1951) studied black children who had arrived in Philadelphia with their migrating parents from the South. When first tested the children had very low IQs, but after enrolling in the Philadelphia schools and living in the city for some time their IQs increased steadily, by an average of about 6 points. There was no such increase in IQ over time observed among a control group of black children who had been born in Philadelphia. This result indicates that superior educational and cultural opportunities in the city (at least at the time of Lee's study) served to elevate the environmentally depressed IQ scores of southern black children.

There is clearly no support for a genetic interpretation in a study by Eyferth (1961), conducted in Germany. The children in this study were all born out of wedlock to white German mothers. The fathers were American servicemen, some black and some white. The race of the father made no overall difference in the average IQs of the children. Other researchers (Willerman, Naylor, & Myrianthopoulos, 1974) studied 101 white women who had borne children by black fathers, and 28 black women who had borne children by white fathers. There is no genetic reason to suppose that the IQs of these two types of interracial children should be different, and there were no significant differences between the two sets of parents in socioeconomic status. The average IQ of interracial children born to white mothers was 102, compared to 93 for equally interracial children born to black mothers.

This outcome makes no genetic sense, but it is open to a number of environmental interpretations—for instance, the mother is the main "teacher" of the child, and white mothers had not experienced racial prejudice while growing up.

The effects of transracial adoption (at least on IQ) have been studied by Scarr and Weinberg (1976). The average IQ of 99 black and interracial children adopted before they were 1 year old by advantaged white families was a very high 110. That average score is considerably higher than would have been observed if the children had not been adopted. The families adopting these children were obviously able to endow them with high IQs by nongenetic means. That is not to say that the adoption of black children by white families is necessarily a good policy; and it is not to say that being reared in a *white* family increased the adopted children's IQs. If the same children had been adopted into advantaged *black* families, the same IQ result would presumably have occurred. We have no information about what would happen if white children were adopted into black families, since such adoptions are very rare in our society.

Those studies that have most directly examined whether there might be a genetic black–white IQ difference have consistently failed to find supporting evidence. We cannot prove the nonexistence of such a difference, but we cannot prove the nonexistence of unicorns, either. We should be aware that our persistent interest in this question may well have nonscientific roots. A word to the wise is sufficient.

no effect on the heritability of IQ. Those who had average IQs before the new environmental treatment would still have average IQs—but average IQs would now be 200. The fact that the heritability of a trait is high in no way implies that its *average* level cannot be profoundly affected by appropriate environmental intervention.

IQ TESTING AND SOCIETY

The controversy now surrounding the use and interpretation of IQ tests has a long and sometimes unpleasant history. Perhaps hindsight makes ethical judgments easier than they appeared at the time, but the social biases and racism of the early mental-testing movement in the United States seem shocking by today's standards. When Lewis Terman first published his Stanford-Binet test in 1916 he wrote confidently that black and Mexican children *would* be found to have lower average IQs than whites and that such differences could never be eradicated by educational or cultural changes. He argued that such children ". . . should be segregated in special classes. . . . They cannot master abstractions, but they can often be made efficient workers. . . . There is no possibility at present of convincing society that they should not be allowed to reproduce. . . . They constitute a grave problem because of their unusually prolific breeding" (p. 92). Writing later of children in the low IQ ranges, Terman (1917) urged society to "curtail the increasing spawn of degeneracy" (p. 165).

The major social involvement of the early IQ testers, however, was with the long national debate over immigration policy that took place before and after World War I. The United States Public Health Service in 1912 invited Henry Goddard to apply the new mental tests to samples of European immigrants arriving at Ellis Island, New York. The tests, Goddard reported, showed that 83 percent of Jews, 80 percent of Hungarians, 79 percent of Italians, and 87 percent of Russians were "feeble-minded." There was no problem, Goddard believed, posed by the fact that immigrants did not know English. The verbal tests could be translated, and they could be supplemented with "culture-fair" performance tests. The use of mental tests "for the detection of feeble-minded aliens," Goddard proudly reported (1917), had greatly increased the number of would-be immigrants deported from Ellis Island.

Those who opposed immigration from the countries of southeastern Europe were greatly encouraged by IQ data collected by the United States Army during World War I (Yerkes, 1921). The first mass mental testing in history took place during the war, when people drafted into the Army were given one of two specially developed group IQ tests. The Alpha test was a typical paper-and-pencil verbal test, while the Beta test was a performance test specially designed for those who were illiterate or who could not understand English-language instructions. The data from some 2 million tested draftees, as we have already seen, indicated that black people had a lower average score than white people. The most immediately relevant findings, however, concerned the IQs of immigrants who had been drafted into the Army. The data indicated clearly that the highest IQs were scored by immigrants from England, Scotland, Canada, and the countries of northern and western Europe. The lowest IQs were those of immigrants from southeastern Europe—Italians, Russians, Poles, and Jews. The psychologists who summarized these findings wrote simply: "The Latin and Slavic countries stand low" (Yerkes, 1921).

The Army immigrant data were analyzed in great detail by Carl Brigham in his book *A Study of American Intelligence* (1923). Those immigrants who had lived in America for 20 years or more before being tested in the Army, Brigham reported, had IQs every bit as high as native-born Americans. The immigrants who had lived in the country fewer than 5 years tended with alarming frequency to be feeble-minded. These facts might have suggested that IQ scores were heavily influenced by familiarity with American culture and language, even when "nonverbal" performance tests were used. That was not Brigham's interpretation. "We must assume," Brigham declared, "that we are measuring native inborn intelligence." The explanation, according to Brigham, was that immigrants who had arrived in the country 20 years ago were mostly from northern and western Europe, with much "Nordic blood." The more recent immigrants, from southeastern Europe, contained inferior "Alpine" and "Mediterranean" blood.

The conclusion of Brigham's book is a profound embarrassment today, but at the time—only some 60 years ago—it was taken as serious and responsible

science. The genetically inferior, Brigham wrote, were reproducing their poor stock at an alarming rate. Further, ". . . we are incorporating the negro into our racial stock, while all of Europe is comparatively free from this taint. . . . The steps that should be taken . . . must of course be dictated by science and not by political expediency. . . . The really important steps are those looking toward the prevention of the continued propagation of defective strains in the present population" (p. 210). The "prevention" of reproduction by defective stocks already in the country, Brigham urged, should be coupled with a law designed to reduce the number of inferior Alpine and Mediterranean immigrants.*

The Army data, and Brigham's book, were cited repeatedly as Congress debated the new immigration law of 1924. The new law did in fact dramatically reduce the proportion of immigrants coming from southeastern Europe. This was done by assigning each European country an annual quota of allowable immigrants—and by basing the quotas on the United States census of 1890, before the massive influx of southeastern Europeans had begun. The naïve genetic interpretation of the Army IQ data, widely accepted among psychologists of the time, helped in some measure to pass a racist immigration law that transformed American society. The overconfident and ethnocentric interpretation of IQ data can have profound consequences. The relevance of this early episode in the history of IQ testing to today's concern over black–white differences seems obvious. Psychologists know more about their own creation, IQ tests, than does anybody else, and their conflicting opinions will be listened to. There is no more reason to allow psychologists

---

*At a later date (1930), Brigham publicly retracted his earlier analysis of the Army data, confessing that he had been wrong and "pretentious." By that time the new immigration law had already been in effect for 6 years, and Brigham had become Secretary of the College Entrance Examination Board. There he developed a test with which many students are familiar, the Scholastic Aptitude Test.

to have the final say about the uses of IQ tests, however, than there is to allow physicists to have the final word about the use of atomic bombs, or of nuclear power plants.

SUMMARY

1. Alfred Binet set out to devise a test that would predict a child's performance in school. He used the concept of *mental age* (*MA*) to assess the child's mental ability as compared to his or her *chronological age* (*CA*). Stern developed the concept of the *intelligence quotient* (*IQ*), the ratio of MA to CA multiplied by 100; at any given chronological age the average IQ is 100.

2. The Stanford-Binet test was a revised version of Binet's test, which was introduced in the U.S. by Lewis Terman in 1916. Since then, the test items have been modified and restandardized in 1937, 1960, and 1972.

3. *Achievement tests* measure how much one has learned before taking the test; *aptitude tests* are used to predict some future performance. The difference between the 2 lies more in the purpose to which the test is put than in the types of questions asked.

4. People are considered mentally retarded if they have an IQ below 70 coupled with inadequate social and occupational adjustment. For the great majority of retarded persons, no physical cause can be specified; some cases of severe retardation are related to biological accidents or genetic disorders such as Down's syndrome.

5. A 50-year study begun by Terman in 1922 showed that people with very high IQs tend to live productive and successful lives, disproving the notion that such people are somehow "freakish."

6. Both the Stanford-Binet test and the Wechsler Intelligence Scales are individual tests, designed to be administered by a trained examiner to one person at a time. The Wechsler scales were the first to use the concept of a *deviation IQ,* comparing a person's score to the scores of others of the same age in the standardization sample.

7. The Army Alpha and Beta tests are examples of group tests; they were developed to test draftees in World War I. The Alpha test is a verbal paper-and-pencil test; the Beta test was designed as a performance test for illiterate or foreign-born draftees.

8. Thurstone argued that there were seven independent or "pure" factors of mental ability—verbal comprehension, word fluency, number, space, memory, perceptual speed, and reasoning.

9. Guilford proposed 120 factors of intelligence, each representing a different intellectual ability. Guilford and his followers developed radically different mental tests, some of the most interesting of which tested *divergent* rather than *convergent thinking.*

10. Whether intelligence is inherited or whether it is a function of environment is the subject of much controversy. The *heritability ratio* is one effort to answer the question quantitatively.

11. Various ways of trying to control for one factor or the other include studying identical twins raised apart; comparing adopted children's IQs to those of both their adoptive and biological parents; and studying adopted children in families that also have biological children. There are difficulties in all these approaches, and we can only say that heritability appears to be somewhere between moderate and low.

12. Researchers have also examined differences among groups in average IQ scores based on sex, race, and social class. There are such differences, but we cannot say whether they are genetically or environmentally based.

Suggested Readings

BLOCK, N. J., & DWORKIN, G. *The IQ controversy.* New York: Pantheon, 1976. A well-selected and broad set of relevant readings, some old and some new.

BRODY, E. B., & BRODY, N. *Intelligence: Nature, determinants, and consequences.* New York: Academic Press, 1976. An advanced and thorough review, with balanced coverage of the nature–nurture controversy.

EYSENCK, H. J. vs. KAMIN, L. *The intelligence controversy.* New York: John Wiley, 1981. A debate, complete with rebuttals, between two protagonists with very different views.

JENSEN, A. R. *Genetics and education.* New York: Harper & Row, 1972. Reprints several of the author's articles, including the 1969 *Harvard Educational Review* article that rekindled the nature–nurture debate.

KAMIN, L. J. *The science and politics of I.Q.* Hillsdale, N.J.: Erlbaum, 1974. Reviews much of the same material covered by Eysenck and Kamin's book, but with a clearly environmental emphasis.

LOEHLIN, J. C., LINDZEY, G., & SPUHLER, J. N. *Race differences in intelligence.* San Francisco: W. F. Freeman & Company, Publishers, 1975. Though focused on data relevant to race differences, this book is also broadly concerned with the heritability of IQ.

SAMUDA, R. J. *Psychological testing of American minorities: Issues and consequences.* New York: Dodd, Mead, 1975. Testing from a minority perspective.

10. Biological Bases of Motivation

THEORIES OF MOTIVATION
Historical theories
Homeostasis and drive theory

HUNGER
Physiological mechanisms and food intake regulation
APPLICATION: Specific Hungers
Human obesity

THIRST
What starts drinking?
What stops drinking?

SEXUALITY AND MATING
Sexual differentiation
Mating behavior
HIGHLIGHT: Mating and Parental Behavior in the Ring Dove

PARENTING
HIGHLIGHT: Sociobiology and Altruistic Behavior

AGGRESSION
Kinds of aggressive behavior
Physiological factors in aggression

SUMMARY

SUGGESTED READINGS

What makes the jogger jog, the canary sing, the dolphin come up for air? Why does the cat stalk the mouse, the stallion seek the mare? When we ask questions like this we are asking questions about **motivation.** In nonscientific terms, motivation is "the reason for a person's or an animal's actions."

The word "motivation" comes from the same Latin root as the words "motion" and "motor." When psychologists study motivation, the central problems sound a lot like those for the physics of motion: What starts a person or an animal moving, what keeps it moving, what determines the direction of its movement, and what stops it? Hunger is a motivator; so are thirst, pain, excessive heat or cold, and many other physical and psychological conditions.

In this chapter we will first discuss theories of motivation and then examine some specific motivators, such as hunger and thirst. The emphasis here will be on the basic motivations shared by animals and people. The kinds of motivation that are considered characteristically human will be covered in Chapter 11.

THEORIES OF MOTIVATION

The concept of motivation is extremely important in psychology. The goal of any science is the ability to make accurate predictions; thus, many psychologists feel that the primary goal of psychology is to predict behavior. But whereas the planets move around the sun or hydrogen combines with oxygen in a perfectly predictable fashion, behavior appears to be quite variable. A chief source of this variability is motivation. For example, we can't always tell how much an animal knows just by observing a small piece of its behavior: If it isn't motivated, it may not perform an act that it has previously learned. We can put a rat in a maze through which it has run accurately a hundred times before, and if it is not hungry or thirsty it might wander aimlessly or just go to sleep. This is referred to as the *difference between learning and performance*. In order to predict performance, we have to know about motivation.

Historical Theories

FREE WILL VERSUS DETERMINISM.   People have always been interested in the question of what makes us do what we do. Before Darwin presented his evidence that human beings are simply a more elaborate animal, most people believed that the rules for human behavior were quite different from the rules for animal behavior. The prevalent belief from the time of Plato and Aristotle through the Middle Ages and probably even today is that people's behavior is under the control of their minds and that they are free to choose what they will do. Although their decisions might be influenced by outside stimuli and by internal needs and desires, their actions are controlled by human reason. This view is referred to as the doctrine of **free will.** For someone who believes in free will, a scientific theory of human motivation is useless, because it is impossible to predict what a person will choose to do.

Even in the time of Plato there were people who argued with the idea of free will. The Greek philosopher Democritus believed that all events in nature are the results of inflexible chains of cause and effect. If we knew all the laws of cause and effect we would be able to predict perfectly the behavior of people, as well as the motions of inanimate objects. This doctrine is called **determinism.**

The deterministic viewpoint became increasingly popular after the publication of Charles Darwin's *On the Origin of Species* (1859) and the eventual acceptance of Darwin's ideas by the scientific community. If humans and animals have the same ancestral origins and are closely related biologically, it is reasonable to assume that human behavior—like animal behavior—is subject to the laws of cause and effect. B. F. Skinner, in his book *Beyond Freedom and Dignity* (1971), argued that our traditional belief in "free will" is a dangerous illusion. Only when we realize how much of our behavior is determined by reinforcement contingencies set up by advertisers, politicians, and other social manipulators will we organize society so as to maximize personal development.

INSTINCTS.   A very important concept that Darwin did not originate but that he did help to bring into prominence was the concept of **instinct.** To Darwin, an instinct was basically just a complicated reflex: an innate pattern of behavior that is emitted in response to some stimulus. Natural selection, he held, operated in the same way on instincts as on any other innate characteristic: Slight variations of a given instinct occur in a population, and the variation that is most successful is preserved (because its possessor is more likely to survive) and is passed on.

Some later theorists believed that instincts provided not only the behavior itself but the *motivation* behind the behavior. For example, William James (1890) assumed that a hen possesses not only the innate behavior pattern for sitting on eggs, but—more important—an innate tendency to *want* to sit on eggs. In James's own words:

> To the broody hen the notion would probably seem monstrous that there should be a creature in the world to whom a nestful of eggs was not the utterly fascinating and precious and never-to-be-too-much-sat-upon object which it is to her. (p. 210)

James felt that "man has a far greater variety of impulses than any lower animal," so, therefore, man must possesses more instincts.

The belief that the motivation behind human behavior is provided chiefly by instincts reached its height in the second decade of the twentieth century. Unconscious instincts, such as repressed sexual desire, played a central role in the theories of Sigmund Freud (see Chapter 14). In the United States, some psychologists drew up lists of "instincts" such as curiosity, pugnacity, and gregariousness. Almost every kind of human behavior could then be attributed to the motivating force of some instinct or other: A man who washed his hands was impelled by the Instinct of Cleanliness; a woman who bought a pencil was responding to the Instinct of Acquisitiveness. The problem was that saying that a behavior was motivated by an instinct didn't help at all in understanding the behavior—saying that people have an instinct of cleanliness doesn't tell us any more than saying that they generally keep themselves clean. To poke fun at the way the concept had outgrown its usefulness, Ayres (1921) published a paper subtitled "The Instinct of Belief-in-Instincts."

While there are some modern versions of instinctual theory (see the Highlight on sociobiology and altruistic behavior), the term itself is now rarely used in any technical sense. It is simply acknowledged that genes define the potential for species-specific behaviors, which may only be realized under particular environmental conditions.

Homeostasis and Drive Theory

The idea that replaced the concept of instinct was based on the notion of **homeostasis.** The physiologist Walter Cannon (1939) introduced this term to describe the way the body maintains a balance or equilibrium in its internal environment. For instance, if the temperature of the body drops just a little, the blood vessels in the skin constrict so that less heat escapes into the air (see Figure 10–1). If the temperature goes up, the blood vessels in the skin dilate and the sweat glands begin to function. Thus, the temperature of a healthy person normally remains within narrow limits, thanks to the body's internal "thermostat." In a similar way, if the amount of water in the tissues is too high, the excess is excreted in the urine; if it is too low, the person becomes thirsty and will drink the necessary amount of fluids. In general, whenever the body deviates too far in one direction or another from its ideal state, a response is triggered that restores it to equilibrium. The term *homeostasis* is used to mean both the ideal balanced state and the process by which the state is maintained; the bodily functions that accomplish this are called **homeostatic mechanisms.**

What does homeostasis have to do with motivation? The clearest statement of the theory came from Clark Hull (1943). To Hull, any deviation from homeostatic balance produces a **need.** A need, in turn, produces a **drive.** A drive is a motivational force, an inciter of action. For example, an animal deprived of nourishment for a day or two has a need for food. The need creates a drive; in this case the drive is called *hunger.* The drive motivates the animal to search for food and to eat it when it is found. Eating the food soon restores the animal to a state of homeostasis. The result is what Hull called **drive reduction.** Drive reduction, according to this theory, is what gives positive reinforcers (such as food) their power to increase the probability of a response in operant conditioning (see Chapter 6).

Needs do not only result from a *lack* of something. Pain or any strong stimulus is assumed to produce a deviation from homeostatis. The result is a drive to escape the stimulus. The cessation of pain is a highly effective primary reinforcer.

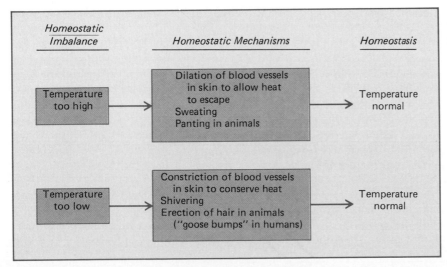

FIGURE 10–1
This chart shows how homeostasis works in the area of temperature regulation in humans and animals.

What "need" produces this man's "drive" to collect comic books?

PROBLEMS WITH DRIVE THEORY.   One problem with drive theory is that all needs do not produce drives. For example, a person exposed to carbon monoxide might be dying for lack of oxygen, but oxygen deprivation creates no drives. The recent popularity of hot tubs has provided some additional tragic evidence of homeostatic imbalance without a drive. People have died while immersed to the neck in hot water, because their bodies gave them no signal that they were becoming dangerously overheated. (The usual physiological mechanisms for controlling body temperature don't work under water.)

There can be needs without drives; there also can be drives without needs. Motivation sometimes seems to arise as a result of external stimuli, instead of from some internal physiological imbalance. An external stimulus of this sort, one that has the capacity to motivate behavior even if a drive was apparently not present initially, is called an **incentive.** A good example of an incentive is an attractive member of the opposite sex—to a male rat, for instance, a receptive female rat. The presence of this incentive is likely to arouse a sex drive that was previously quiescent. Another incentive, to most humans and to animals of many species, is anything that tastes sweet, whether it reduces the hunger drive or not. Rats will press a lever to receive a drop of saccharin solution, and will continue to do so over months of testing. Moreover, sweet foods retain their incentive value even in the absence of a need for nutrition. You might have just finished a big meal and not be the least bit hungry, but when offered a tempting dessert you may not be able to resist it.

Even when the drive-inducing qualities of external stimuli are added, there is a great variety of human and animal behavior that cannot be explained in terms of the kinds of drives we have been discussing. The concept of homeostasis originally pertained to physiological changes in body parts such as the blood vessels, heart, lungs, and kidneys. Drive theorists applied the notion to the organism as a whole. Some assumed that if the organism is not suffering from a physiological deprivation or motivated to escape from a strong stimulus, it will do nothing at all. But that is not the case. Animals act as though they *want* to be stimulated, want novelty, want to explore. Monkeys will learn to solve mechanical puzzles even if they are never rewarded for it (Harlow, Harlow, & Meyer, 1950), and they will perform work in order to see interesting things—a toy train, for example—through a window (Butler, 1953). Even rats will learn to press a lever just to make the illumination in their cages increase and decrease (Roberts, Marx, & Collier, 1958) or to gain access to a running wheel (Collier & Hirsch, 1971). And human beings do all sorts of bizarre things that drive theory can't account for: They scare themselves with ghost stories and roller coaster rides, eat food spicy enough to stimulate the pain receptors in the mouth, and go to movies designed to arouse the sexual drive but not to satisfy it. Many psychologists believe that organisms are born with an "exploratory drive" and that they have an innate need for a certain amount of stimulation. Lack of stimulation is what makes solitary confinement a universally dreaded punishment.

The instinct theorists of the 1920s spoke of an "instinct of curiosity." Are we any further along when we speak of an "exploratory drive"? The concept of drive has one theoretical advantage over the concept of instinct. Instincts are assumed to provide both the energy or motivation behind a given action and, in addition, to specify the action itself. Drives are assumed only to provide the energy for action. Thus, a given sample of behavior can be analyzed into 2 components: the action itself (say, pressing a lever) and the motivation behind the action (say, the hunger drive produced by a certain period of food deprivation).

The concept of drives has often been useful. It is most useful when we are talking about relatively clearcut states of physiological deprivation such as hunger and thirst. However, even in these cases there are difficulties with the traditional view of drive as a product of homeostatic imbalance. We will discuss some of these difficulties in the next section of this chapter, where specific drives are covered in greater detail.

HUNGER

Everyone has felt hunger. It is a universal source of motivation. Because it is easily produced in the laboratory and easily satisfied, and because an organism does not quickly die if its food needs are not met, hunger has been studied more thoroughly than any other motivation. Yet there is still much that we do not understand about this very complicated subject. One problem is that mechanisms that regulate food intake appear to differ in different species. Thus we cannot be sure that experimental results found with dogs will hold true for rats, or that results found with rats will hold true for people. Humans, of course, are the most difficult species to study. Their eating behavior is controlled by social and cognitive factors as well as by physical ones. And many of the experiments that have been most helpful to our understanding of hunger and feeding behavior in animals cannot, for obvious reasons, be performed on humans.

Physiological Mechanisms and Food Intake Regulation

Organisms must regulate their food intake both on a day-to-day basis, to meet their immediate physiological requirements, and on a long-term basis, to maintain a stable (adult) body weight. A large animal, such as a horse or a cow, that eats food low in caloric value (such as grass) must eat almost continuously to get enough nutrition. But humans and most animals that have been studied in the laboratory (mainly dogs, cats, rats, mice, and guinea pigs) eat *meals*. That is, they eat for a while, and then they stop eating. After a lapse of time they eat again. The number of meals taken a day (when allowed free access to food) varies: Humans generally take 2 to 4, cats 9 to 10, rats 12 to 15, guinea pigs 22 to 25. The basic questions here are: What makes an organism start eating? What makes it stop? What determines the size of a meal?

THE STOMACH AND THE MOUTH. An obvious place to look for the origin of hunger and satiety is the stomach. Surprisingly, though, the stomach does not seem to play an important role in regulating food intake. People whose stomachs have been removed for medical reasons still get hungry and eat normal amounts of food. And rats that have had all the nerves from the stomach to the brain cut also maintain their normal food intake (Morgan & Morgan, 1940).

Additional information about the stomach's role in food-intake regulation comes from experiments with rats in which a plastic tube is surgically inserted into the stomach or the esophagus (the passageway from the mouth to the stomach). It is then possible to place food or liquid directly into a rat's stomach, bypassing its mouth. In one experiment (Miller & Kessen, 1952) milk or a saline solution was injected directly into rats' stomachs. The rats learned to go to the place where they received the milk injections (in preference to the place where they received the saline), even though they were never able to taste or swallow it. Tasting or swallowing does have an effect, though: Rats that received a quantity of milk directly into their stomachs drank more additional milk than ones that had taken the same quantity in the normal way, by mouth (Berkun, Kessen, & Miller, 1952). And hospitalized people being maintained on intravenous feeding still report feeling hungry, although they do not actually eat much if offered food.

MONITORING OF BLOOD SUGAR.   One plausible way for the body to regulate food intake would be through the level of glucose (blood sugar) in the circulatory system. Jean Mayer (1953) proposed that the changing level of glucose is monitoried by "glucostats" in the brain. The mechanism has to be a fairly complex one though—not one that simply equates hunger with low glucose levels and satiety with high levels. Diabetics have elevated glucose levels, yet they tend to eat more, not less, than healthy people. The mechanism postulated by Mayer would keep track of the *rate* at which glucose is being used by the body's cells: A low rate would produce hunger, a high rate satiety. The rate can be measured (in the laboratory and, theoretically, in the body) by comparing the amount of glucose in the outgoing blood in the arteries with that in the incoming blood in the veins. Mayer found that the difference between these 2 measurements was largest a little while after a big meal, then gradually grew smaller. Subjects' reports of hunger coincided with the times when the difference was minimal. According to this theory, diabetics feel hungry because they have a lot of glucose in *both* arterial and venous blood, so the *difference* is small. Similarly, injections of insulin, which lower glucose levels in *both* arterial and venous blood, also produce hunger. Nondiabetic rats given daily injections of insulin overeat and become fat.

There apparently are other substances in the blood, besides glucose, that help to regulate intake of food. If blood from a satiated rat is transfused into a hungry one, the hungry rat eats much less than usual. Transfusions in the opposite direction, however, have no effect: The satiated rat does not begin to eat again after receiving blood from a hungry animal (Davis, Gallagher, & Ladlove, 1967). One candidate for this mysterious "satiety factor" is a hormone called cholecystokinin, which is produced by the small intestine soon after a meal. When this hormone is injected into hungry animals it temporarily inhibits eating (Gibbs, Young, & Smith, 1973).

THE ROLE OF THE HYPOTHALAMUS.   The search for mechanisms that control hunger and satiety has led most often to the part of the brain known as the **hypothalamus** (see Chapter 2). The hypothalamus itself is composed of a number of sub-areas that can be distinguished anatomically and on the basis of their functions. One of these sub-areas is the *lateral hypothalamus,* or lateral nucleus. This part of the brain has been identified as an excitatory area for eating and drinking. When a rat's lateral hypothalamus is destroyed, it will at first neither eat nor drink, and it will die unless it is forcefed (Teitelbaum & Epstein, 1962). If kept alive, it will eventually resume eating and drinking, but it will only eat foods that taste good. Electrical stimulation of the lateral hypothalamus causes a previously satiated rat to become hungry and thirsty. If food is not immediately available, the rat will press a lever to obtain it (Hoebel, 1971).

This rat's ventromedial nucleus has been damaged, with the result that it has gained so much weight that it weighs 3 times what a normal rat would weigh.

Part of Hypothalamus	Destroyed (by lesioning)	Activated (by electrical stimulation)
Ventromedial nucleus	Animals overeat (hyperphagia)	Hungry animals won't eat; if eating when activated, they stop immediately
Lateral nucleus	Animals stop eating entirely (aphagia)	Animals start eating immediately, even if they have just eaten

Table 10–1: Roles of the 2 Parts of the Hypothalamus in Regulation of Eating as Evidenced by the Results of the Destruction or Activation of Each Part.

If the electrode is located in a different part of the hypothalamus, the ventromedial nucleus, stimulation will cause a hungry rat to *stop* eating. The *ventromedial hypothalamus* (VMH for short) has been called the satiety center—that is, the center where "glucostats" (the blood-sugar monitors) are believed to be located.

If a rat's VMH is damaged or destroyed, the animal will eat more food at each meal and will soon weigh 2 or 3 times as much as a normal rat (see Table 10–1). What's interesting is that the rat won't continue to gain weight indefinitely. At some point its weight will level off and it will eat just enough to maintain itself at that new weight (Teitelbaum, 1961). Moreover, although this rat eats more than a normal rat, in some ways it seems *less* hungry: It is more finicky about what it eats and it won't work as hard to get food (Miller, Bailey, & Stevenson, 1950; Teitelbaum, 1957).

A rat with brain lesions in the VMH will maintain itself at a higher weight than before its surgery; similarly, a rat with lesions in the lateral hypothalamus will eventually maintain itself at a new, lower weight (Keesey & Powley, 1975). In both cases it looks like the homeostatic "thermostat" is still working but that the setting has simply been changed. This is the **set-point theory** of food regulation (Nisbett, 1972). According to this theory, the feeding-regulation mechanisms of the obese rat and the obese human are not out of order—they are just set at a higher set point. As long as the weight is below the set point, the person or animal is hungry. Like rats with VMH lesions, many obese people tend to eat more, eat faster, be less active, and be more finicky about what they eat. We will return to the problem of human obesity shortly.

CRITICISM OF HOMEOSTATIC THEORIES OF EATING.   From the homeostatic viewpoint, an animal is assumed to begin a meal whenever some physiological mechanism signals a certain level of depletion or need. Some psychologists have presented strong arguments against this view (Collier, Hirsch, & Hamlin, 1972; Collier, Hirsch, & Kanarek, 1977). For example, when food is readily available, the amount taken in a meal is not related to the length of time since the last meal, and perhaps not even to the amount taken in the last meal (Panksepp, 1973). Mealtimes seem to depend not on the level of depletion but on the time of day (cats and rats do most of their eating at night) and on the availability of alternative activities such as running in wheels. Collier believes that healthy animals in natural environments have developed behavior that assures an adequate intake of food—they *anticipate* their needs rather than respond to them. An example is the behavior of large ruminants such as cows. These animals have a tremendous storage capacity and it takes them a long time to digest their food. They must continually take in food to provide the

Specific Hungers

Experiments have shown that some kinds of animals are able to regulate their intake of specific nutritional substances, such as fats, carbohydrates, proteins, and various vitamins and minerals. Is this also true of humans?

In a famous experiment with 3 toddlers performed in a hospital setting, the children proved able to regulate their diets satisfactorily when free to select from a variety of nutritious foods (Davis, 1928). Whether the results would have been the same if cake and candy had been among the alternatives is difficult to say. There have certainly been many reported cases of people who have sickened or died from malnutrition because they have chosen (for one reason or another) to adhere to a diet that did not meet their nutritional needs. And thousands of people died of scurvy before it became commonly ac-

cepted in the early 1800s that citrus fruits would prevent this dreaded disease—a fact that had been reported half a century earlier by the Scottish physician James Lind.

Most of the work on specific hungers has been done with rats. Rats are able to balance their intake of fats, carbohydrates, and proteins and will press levers for hours to supply themselves with one of these nutrients if it is missing from their diet—even if the other substances are freely available (Collier, Hirsch, & Kanarek, 1977). They will consume large quantities of calcium after removal of the parathyroid glands (which regulate calcium balance), and large quantities of salt after removal of the adrenal glands (which regulate the body's salt content). In the case of salt, the preference for salty foods follows immediately after salt depletion—no learning seems to be necessary.

Choosing other necessary substances, however, seems to require experience. Rats fed on a diet deficient in a vitamin such as

thiamine will gradually eat less and less of that diet, and their weight will drop. When offered a different type of food they will accept it eagerly, although rats are generally very cautious about eating anything new. The old diet will always be avoided unless there is nothing else to eat. Evidently they have learned to associate it with feeling ill. The same thing happens when a rat is fed some kind of poison: Even if hours elapse between when the rat eats a particular kind of food and when it becomes ill, it is unlikely to try that food again (Garcia & Koelling, 1966; Rozin & Kalat, 1971).

Whether this sort of ability—obviously very important for rat survival—exists in other species remains to be shown. Rats seem to be particularly good at maintaining their diet an an optimal level. For example, when given a diet high in bulk and low in calories, rats eat enough to maintain a constant caloric intake. Cats, on the other hand, will eat a constant amount of bulk and will therefore lose weight.

raw material for the fermentation process. If they waited until their previous meal was digested and assimilated before they began to eat again, they would be in trouble. And animals such as wolves and lions, which must expend large amounts of energy to procure food, could scarcely afford to wait until their supply of energy was depleted before they began to look for more food. Thus, according to Collier, through the course of evolution each species of animal has evolved feeding patterns that are suited to its ecological niche but are flexible enough to be modified if the environment changes. A good example of this kind of flexibility is the hyena's hunting pack. If the available game is small and a successful hunt results in only the dominant animals eating well and the rest going hungry, the pack splits up into smaller packs. When large game again becomes available, so that a kill will feed many animals, the packs reassemble into larger units (Kruuk, 1972).

Human Obesity

One rarely sees an overweight animal in a natural environment (unless it is getting ready to hibernate). Only humans and a few of the species that humans have domesticated seem to have the capacity to become obese under normal conditions. What causes the normal motivation to eat to go wrong?

DEFINING OBESITY.   In humans **obesity** is often defined as being more than about 15 percent over the "ideal" weight, given a person's height and overall body build. However, Mayer (1955) has pointed out that a 6-foot-tall football player weighing 200 pounds is "overweight" according to the charts, yet may have very little body fat. On the other hand, a very inactive person whose weight is at or even below the "ideal" weight may be so lacking in muscle tissue that an abnormally high percentage of that weight consists of fat. Mayer has defined obesity as the condition that is present "when the fat content reaches 30 percent of the body weight." The size of fat deposits can be roughly determined by measuring the thickness of a skin fold, or by measurements of body density. It should be noted that the proportion of body fat increases in normal animals as they age, and at a given age it is higher in females than in males.

CHARACTERISTICS OF OBESE PEOPLE.   As we mentioned earlier, there are some interesting parallels between the behavior of obese humans and that of rats that overeat because of lesions in their ventromedial hypothalamus. Schachter (1971) has spelled out these similarities in detail. First, both obese humans and VMH rats are more sensitive than their normal counterparts to the taste of food. When food or drink is adulterated with quinine, a harmless substance with a bitter taste, obese humans and rats take less of it than normal subjects. When the food tastes good, the obese eat more.

Obese subjects are also less willing to work for food than the nonobese. When rats are rewarded with a pellet of food for each lever press, VMH rats press more than normals. But when they have to press a number of times for each pellet, they press *less* than normal rats (Teitelbaum, 1957). Schachter found a similar result with humans. In a cleverly designed experiment, subjects were invited to help themselves from a bagful of almonds. The almonds were either shelled or unshelled. Nonobese people accepted the offer and ate some nuts about half the time, whether they were shelled or not shelled. Obese subjects almost always accepted the offer of nuts without shells but almost never accepted when the nuts had to be shelled.

Other reported similarities include general activity level (the obese are less active), emotional responsiveness (the obese react more emotionally), num-

Table 10–2: Some Shared Characteristics of Obese Humans and Rats with VMH Lesions.

1. Eat more when good-tasting food is available.
2. Eat less when the food tastes bad.
3. Are less willing to work for food.
4. Eat faster.
5. Eat fewer meals per day (but more per meal).
6. Tend to be more emotionally reactive.
7. Are generally less active.

From Schachter (1971).

ber of meals eaten per day (the obese eat fewer), and speed of eating (the obese eat faster). Some of Schachter's comparisons are summarized in Table 10–2.

A THEORY OF OBESITY.   Schachter's theory about these VMH rats and obese humans is that they differ from normal-weight organisms not so much in their mechanisms for food-intake regulation as in their general level of responsiveness to all external stimuli: "When a food-relevant cue is present the obese are more likely to eat and to eat a great deal than are normals. When such a cue is absent, the obese are less likely to try to eat or complain about hunger." The reason they are less willing to work for their food, says Schachter, is simply because food that has to be worked for is more remote and therefore provokes less of a food-acquiring response.

There is evidence for this hypothesis from human subjects. Overweight and normal-weight people had to lift weights with their fingers to get food. There were 4 conditions: They worked for sandwiches wrapped either in clear plastic or in opaque white paper, and they either did or did not get a sample piece of sandwich. Figure 10–2 shows that when there were 2 food cues (transparent wrapper plus sample sandwich), obese subjects worked almost twice as hard as the nonobese. With no food cues, the nonobese subjects worked harder (Johnson, 1970). While Schachter's theory has been quite influential, it has also been criticized. For example, Rodin (1981) claimed that his review of research on human obesity failed to support Schachter's view.

THE SET-POINT THEORY.   Earlier we mentioned Nisbett's theory that overweight people and VMH rats have a higher set-point weight. The assumption is that when they are below this set point, they are in a state of deprivation or homeostatic imbalance, even if their weight is above normal levels. Nisbett believes that this state of deprivation is responsible for the distinctive characteristics of obese people, and not the obesity itself or the mechanisms that caused the obesity.

This theory has been tested in a series of experiments reported by Herman and his colleagues (Herman & Mack, 1975; Herman & Polivy, 1975; Hibscher & Herman, 1977). The experimenters divided their subjects into 2 categories on the basis of their answers to a series of questions: either "restrained eaters" (dieters) or "nonrestrained eaters" (nondieters). They assumed that restrained eaters, whether they are obese or of normal weight, weigh less than their set-point weight and are therefore in a state of chronic deprivation. Nonrestrained eaters, obese or nonobese, are assumed to be at or near their set-point weights.

The experimental results supported the set-point theory. College men or women who were concerned about their weight and restrained their eating (dieters) showed many of the same traits that Schachter had found in his obese subjects, even if they were at a normal weight at the time of the experiment. Conversely, obese subjects who didn't care about their weight and ate as much as they wanted (nondieters) behaved more like Schachter's nonobese subjects. For example, both obese and nonobese dieters ignored internal cues and ate a lot of ice cream after they had been given 2 milkshakes to drink as part of a "rating experiment." The milkshakes evidently broke down the dieters' normal restraint, because dieters who hadn't had the milkshakes ate less of the ice cream (as shown in Figure 10–3). This was exactly the opposite of what was found with nondieters (both obese and normal weight).

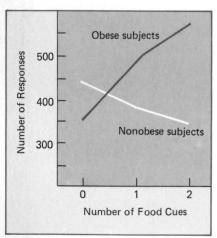

FIGURE 10–2
When there are a number of food cues, obese subjects will work almost twice as hard as the nonobese subjects to get food. With no food cues, the nonobese subjects worked harder. (Johnson, 1970)

Another experiment showed that normal-weight subjects who are dieters show the same kind of emotional responsiveness that had previously been linked with obesity. Hibscher and Herman (1977) even showed that both obese dieters and nonobese dieters have elevated blood levels (compared with nondieters) of certain substances known as "free fatty acids." The free-fatty-acid content of the blood has been shown to go up in response to food deprivation (Gordon, 1960).

FAT CELLS. According to Nisbett's theory, the set-point weight determines whether or not a person can maintain a socially acceptable weight without being hungry all the time. But what determines the set-point weight? Nisbett claims that it is the number of fat cells in the body. In one study, fat cells were found to be 3 times as numerous in obese people as in nonobese (Knittle & Hirsch, 1968). Knittle (1975) believes that the number of fat cells in the body is pretty well fixed by the age of 2; it is determined partly by heredity and partly by eating habits in infancy. According to this theory, overeating simply causes the fat cells to increase in size and dieting causes them to shrink, but the number of these cells stays approximately the same. Thus, when an obese person loses weight, the fat cells are supposedly "starved," which accounts for the state of chronic deprivation found in habitual dieters.

Not all psychologists believe in the fat-cell theory. Some who *do* believe in it think that it only accounts for a certain kind of obesity—the kind that produces a moderately overweight child who becomes a moderately over-weight adult. There are many other types of obesity. Undoubtedly we will eventually find that there are a number of different causes for obesity, some primarily emotional, some primarily physiological, and some primarily due to social or environmental causes. In a society where almost everyone has a car and no one walks, lack of exercise may be an important factor. This idea has led Mayer (1955) to wonder "whether there is not a direct relationship between recent improvements in transportation and increased prevalence of overweight."

The situation for the obese individual is not as hopeless as it would seem from some of the theories we have discussed. Many of these people *do* lose weight, by themselves, under a physician's supervision, or through an organized program. Among the most promising programs of weight control are those, such as Weight Watchers International, that employ behavior-modification techniques to alter basic eating habits. Their focus is on learning to eat properly, eating more slowly, and encouraging patience with the weight-loss process. Coupled with appropriate social supports, such programs may produce permanent weight change rather than the typically transient loss produced by a "diet" (Brownell & Venditti, 1983; Stunkard, 1983). People who have successfully lost weight through these or other programs do not show the symptoms of depression or irritability that might be expected from the set-point theory. On the contrary, weight loss has been associated with favorable changes in emotional and social adjustment (Wilson, 1978).

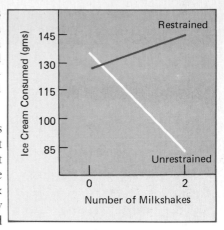

FIGURE 10–3

In one of a series of experiments done by Herman and his colleagues, the set-point theory was upheld—both obese and nonobese subjects who were dieters (restrained eaters) ate more ice cream after consuming two milk shakes than similar subjects who weren't dieters (unrestrained eaters). (Hibscher & Herman, 1977)

THIRST

People who have suffered from severe water deprivation describe extreme thirst as a much more excruciating sensation than extreme hunger. It is also much more life threatening: We can survive for weeks without food, but only for a few days without water.

We lose water all the time. An average of 2½ liters passes from our bodies each day in urine, feces, and exhaled air. This water must all be replaced by drinking liquid or eating foods with a high moisture content. Under normal conditions, organisms do not experience extreme thirst because their patterns of water intake (like their patterns of food intake) *prevent* severe depletion from occurring.

What Starts Drinking?

Most of us would immediately claim that thirst is equivalent to the sensation of a dry mouth and throat. During dehydration, there is usually a reduced salivary flow, and that makes the mouth feel dry. But dryness of the mouth does not play an essential role in the regulation of water intake. This has been shown in several ways. People given drugs that cause dryness of the mouth and those who were born without salivary glands drink more frequently, but their total intake is about normal. The same is true of dogs that have had their salivary glands tied off (Montgomery, 1931).

THE HYPOTHALAMUS.   We saw in the previous section that the mechanisms that produce hunger are located primarily in the hypothalamus and not in the stomach. The situation is similar for thirst: The mechanisms are again located primarily in the hypothalamus, rather than in the mouth or throat. Several hypothalamic areas have been implicated; one of these is the lateral hypothalamus, which was previously mentioned in connection with hunger. Lesions in this region interfere with drinking as well as eating—in fact, the effect on drinking seems to be more severe and more persistent. The *preoptic area,* at the very front of the hypothalamus, has also been shown to be involved in thirst. Electrical stimulation of the preoptic area, or the injection of minute quantities of salty water, causes goats to drink excessively (Andersson, 1952; Andersson & McCann, 1955).

In order for the hypothalamus to regulate water intake, it must have some way of obtaining information about the body's need for fluids. This is accomplished by two independent mechanisms, one based on **osmoreceptors,** the other on **volumetric receptors.** These are sometimes called, respectively, the *intracellular mechanism* and the *extracellular mechanism.* The first kind responds to the amount of fluid inside the body's cells, the second to the fluid outside the cells, especially that contained in the circulatory system.

OSMORECEPTORS.   The fluids in the body, both within the cells and outside of them, normally contain about 0.9 percent salt (sodium chloride). When an organism has been deprived of water for a while, the extracellular fluid becomes more concentrated (in other words, saltier). Now there are different concentrations of salt on the two sides of the cell wall, and the result is **osmosis**—the movement of fluids through a semipermeable membrane. In this case, water moves through the cell wall from inside the cell to outside, decreasing the saltiness of the extracellular fluid but at the same time depleting the cell of water. It is believed that certain cells in the hypothalamus, the osmoreceptors, are sensitive to this depletion. When water moves out of these cells, a response is triggered, and signals are sent to other cells in the brain. One result is that the organism becomes thirsty. Another is that the hypothalamus stimulates the pituitary gland to release a hormone (the *antidiuretic* hormone) that causes the kidneys to produce more highly concentrated urine. This means that less water is lost through excretion.

The functioning of the osmoreceptors has been demonstrated experimentally by injecting salty water (more than 0.9 percent salt) into the stomachs or blood vessels of animals. This has the same effect as water deprivation: Because the extracellular fluid becomes saltier than that within the cells, the cells lose water. Such injections cause animals to become thirsty, even if they were previously satiated with water. The same thing happens to people who drink sea water or eat salty foods.

VOLUMETRIC RECEPTORS. People who do not get *enough* salt also become thirsty. In this case the fluid outside of the cells is less salty than that within, and osmosis causes extracellular water to enter the cells. Now the quantity of extracellular fluid (mainly blood) is depleted. The mechanism that responds to this depletion, called a *volumetric receptor,* is the same one that produces intense thirst in wounded people who have lost a lot of blood. Although, in the case of blood loss, there has been no change in the body's concentration of salts, the total *volume* of extracellular fluid has decreased. The result is a drop in blood pressure.

Where are the receptors that detect a drop in blood volume and pressure? Apparently, they are in several places. For example, if the blood supply to the kidneys or the heart is reduced, there is an increase in drinking (Fitzsimmons, 1972). It seems that there are pressure receptors in the left ventricle of the heart and in the blood vessels leading to the kidneys (Carlson, 1980).

When a drop in blood volume or pressure is detected, it triggers the release of an enzyme called *renin* from the kidneys. Renin is responsible for the production of a substance called *angiotensin.* Angiotensin reaches the brain through the bloodstream and stimulates thirst receptors. While there is some debate about the exact location of these receptors (Carlson, 1980), injections of angiotensin into the brain of an experimental animal is the surest way to produce drinking behavior (Epstein, Fitzsimmons, & Rolls, 1970).

What Stops Drinking?

The mechanisms we have described initiate drinking when intracellular or extracellular fluids get low. What stops it? A stomach-load of water is only 25 percent absorbed in 15 minutes; yet dogs (for example) are able to replace their water deficits quite accurately, on 1 or 2 short bouts of drinking (Adolph, 1939). What tells them when they have had enough?

A number of experiments have been performed in attempts to answer this question. Many of these experiments have made use of the technique in which a plastic tube is surgically inserted into an animal's esophagus. Water can be put directly into the animal's stomach through the tube, or water that the animal drinks can be prevented from reaching its stomach. The results of such experiments have led to the conclusion that no one factor can account for the cessation of drinking. Three factors seem to be involved: (1) the actual number of licks or swallows of water the animal takes; (2) the volume of water in the animal's stomach; and (3) absorption of water from the stomach and intestines, and the consequent replenishment of intracellular and extracellular fluids.

SEXUALITY AND MATING

The motivations we have studied so far in this chapter have an important element in common: If the needs that underlie them are not met, the organism dies. The sex drive is different. As far as we know, no one has ever died for lack of sex. In fact, it might be described as a drive without a need, because it involves no deviation from homeostasis and is to a certain extent independent of deprivation and satiation. Deprivation and satiation play *some* role, but not nearly so great as with hunger and thirst.

Although it is not necessary to the survival of the individual, the sex or mating drive is essential to the survival of the species. The drive is maintained by the process of natural selection: Organisms endowed with little or no desire to mate are unlikely to bear young. In the human species the expression of the drive is somewhat fettered by social laws and customs, but it remains a powerful source of motivation. Some evidence of this is provided by TV and magazine advertisements, which use sex to sell everything from cars to toothpaste.

Sexual Differentiation

GENETIC SEX.   Nature has happily provided almost every species with two sexes, male and female. Usually an organism's sex is determined at the time of conception. In humans and other mammals, as we saw in Chapter 2, an egg carrying an X chromosome unites with a sperm carrying an X chromosome to produce a genetic female, or with a sperm carrying a Y chromosome to produce a genetic male. Thus a cell from a normal female contains two X chromosomes, and a cell from a normal male contains one X chromosome and one Y.

Not all humans, however, fall into the simple XX or XY classification. For example, there are men with an XXY pattern. These people have underdeveloped but clearly male genitals. As adults they prove to be sterile and have a somewhat feminine body build. There are also men with an XYY pattern. They are taller than average, and sometimes have genital abnormalities. It was at first thought that this chromosomal pattern is associated with a higher degree of impulsiveness or aggressiveness, because prison populations have a higher incidence of XYY individuals. However, XYY men in the nonprison population do not seem to be any more aggressive than normal XY men (Owen, 1972). Both the XYY and the XXY patterns are associated with an increased risk of mental retardation.

People with only a single X chromosome are identified as female, but they lack ovaries and so do not mature sexually unless hormones are given artificially. They are likely to have other birth defects as well, and they tend to be quite short.

HORMONES.   Whether they will ultimately develop into males or females, all human embryos are at first the same. Each possesses a pair of primitive sex glands that can become either ovaries or testes. At 7 or 8 weeks after conception, these glands begin to develop into ovaries if the sex-chromosome pattern is XX, into testes if it is XY. These sex glands or **gonads** each produce a characteristic type of hormone. The ovaries produce the set of related female hormones called **estrogens,** and the testes produce the male hormones called **androgens,** of which the most important is **testosterone.** The hormones secreted by the embryo's gonads determine the kind of internal and external reproductive organs (**primary sex characteristics**) that will develop. If the gonads secrete testosterone, the fetus will develop the characteristics of a male. Otherwise it will develop the characteristics of a female, whether or not its gonads secrete estrogen. In mammals, both male and female embryos are subjected to the influence of the mother's female hormones, so a female is produced unless there is opposition from testosterone. It is interesting that the situation is just the opposite in bird embryos, which are encased in a shell and not exposed to the mother's hormones. A bird embryo will develp into a male unless estrogen is present at the critical stage of development (Wilson & Glick, 1970).

The hormones also control the development of the **secondary sex characteristics,** which appear at puberty. In humans these include breast and hip enlargement in females, beard growth and voice change in males. Puberty is marked by a great increase in the output of sex hormones. The pituitary gland, located in the brain, produces hormones called *gonadotropins,* which stimulate the gonads to produce androgen and estrogen. Oddly enough, both kinds of hormones (which are closely related in biochemical structure) are produced by both sexes, but the testes tend to produce more androgen, the ovaries more estrogen. In males, estrogen produced by the testes is normally destroyed by the liver. Breast enlargement in teen-aged boys sometimes results when the liver fails to destroy all the estrogen.

Hormonal sex can override genetic sex more or less completely, depending on how early in development the hormonal influence occurs. There is a condition that occurs in humans called the **androgen-insensitivity syndrome.** In this condition, the testes of a genetic male fetus secrete testosterone, but for some reason—probably an enzyme deficiency—the testosterone is not used by the body cells and the fetus develops into what appears to be a normal female. The individual is raised as a girl and at puberty the secretion of estrogen is sufficient to cause the development of female secondary sex characteristics. However, menstruation does not occur, be-

Rough and tumble play is more common among boys than among girls; it is also more accepted by parents. As more young girls are encouraged to compete with boys in various sports, the differences in skill between the two seem to be diminishing.

cause there are no ovaries and the uterus is incompletely formed. Although these people cannot become pregnant, they are in most respects unquestionably female. Some have had successful careers as fashion models; many have married and have adopted and parented children (Money, 1970; Money & Ehrhardt, 1972).

Genetic females may also develop malelike characteristics if subjected to male hormones early in fetal life. When injections of testosterone were given to pregnant female monkeys, their female offspring were born with sex organs that were partly male and partly female, a condition known as **hermaphroditism.** These baby monkeys had a small but otherwise well-developed penis. On the other hand, they also had the internal organs (ovaries, uterus) of a normal female (Goy, 1968).

A synthetic hormone called **progestin,** formerly used to prevent miscarriage in pregnant women, was later discovered to have masculinizing effects on unborn female children. Some of these girls were born with an enlarged clitoris and partially fused labia. The condition was corrected surgically, and they were reared as females (Money & Ehrhardt, 1972). (We will look in Chapter 14 at the childhood behavior and development of some of these girls.)

MALENESS AND FEMALENESS.   The differences in behavior between "normal" boys and "normal" girls are relative rather than absolute: A particular kind of behavior will occur more often, *on the average,* in boys than in girls, or in girls than in boys. That such statistical differences *do* exist in many species is unquestionable. For example, young male rhesus monkeys engage in more "rough and tumble" play than do young females (Rosenblum, 1961). What is not clear is how much these differences depend on genetic and hormonal influences, and how much they depend on the way the individual is treated by parents and others. Even in subhuman species, different parental treatment for male and female offspring has been observed. Rhesus monkey mothers with female offspring restrain their infants almost 3 times as often as mothers of male offspring (Mitchell, 1968). *Restraining* was defined as "active interference with the infant's attempts to leave the mother." The importance of social and parental influences on the development of "maleness" and "femaleness" is clearly greatest in the human species, as we will discuss further in Chapter 12.

Even when genetic, hormonal, and environmental factors are all (as far as we know) in agreement, there are people who feel that they have been "assigned" to the wrong sex—men who feel that they "should have been" women, and women who feel that they "should have been" men. These people are called transsexuals. A number of such individuals have requested and received surgical and hormonal treatments that produce a change in apparent sexual identity. However, a recent study (Meyer, 1980) has found that these operations do not produce any long-term beneficial effects on the lives of the people who undergo them. On the basis of this study, some hospitals have stopped performing this type of surgery.

Mating Behavior

Mating behavior begins, in all species, with some preliminaries called *courtship behavior*. The male sniffs, nuzzles, or otherwise expresses interest in the female; the female either rejects or accepts these advances. If she is receptive to them, she will eventually allow the male to mount. In virtually all mammals except humans, the female always has all four feet firmly on the ground. The male gets on top and *intromission* (entry of the penis into the female's vagina) is from behind and above. The female must cooperate by standing still, by arching her back somewhat, and by holding her tail (if she has one) to the side; this response is called *lordosis*.

What follows next differs in its details from species to species, although the outcome is the same. The rat, for instance, will mount the female a number of times and achieve 8 to 15 intromissions, each lasting less than a second. During the final intromission the male will *ejaculate* semen (the fluid containing the sperm) into the female's vagina.

The behavior just described evidently has drive-reducing (or incentive) value not only for the male, but for the female as well. It has been shown that receptive female rats will press a lever to gain access to a male rat (Bermant, 1961).

THE INFLUENCE OF HORMONES ON THE FEMALE.   All mammalian females show cyclical variations in hormonal state, called the **menstrual cycle** in primates, the **estrus cycle** in lower mammals. In most species, ovulation occurs automatically at some specific point in the cycle, and at that time the female becomes both sexually attractive and sexually receptive to the male. One exception to this rule is the rabbit, which is virtually always receptive and which ovulates only upon mating. The other chief exception occurs in those primate species, including humans, in which females ovulate on a cyclical basis but show little or no (there is still some debate on this question) cyclical change in receptivity or sexual attractiveness.

If the ovaries of a nonhuman female mammal are removed (which is done when female dogs and cats are "spayed"), the animal's hormonal cycle ceases, and so do the periods of sexual receptivity and sexual attractiveness. These functions can be restored by the administration of the ovarian hormones estrogen and progesterone. Removal of the ovaries in human females sometimes lowers sexual drive, but sometimes it increases it (perhaps because fear of pregnancy is removed), and often it has no effect at all.

Mating and Parental Behavior in the Ring Dove

The ring dove is a small relative of the domestic pigeon. It gets its name from the semicircle of black feathers that "rings" the back of its neck. These birds breed freely under laboratory conditions and have been used extensively for detailed studies of parental behavior (Lehrman, 1964).

When a male and a female ring dove are placed together in a cage, courtship begins almost at once: The male begins to strut about, bowing and cooing. After several hours the birds choose a nesting site; in the laboratory this consists of a shallow glass bowl put in the cage for that purpose. Nest building takes about a week and is shared by both sexes. During this week the birds also

mate. The female lays the first egg about 9 days after the beginning of the courtship period, and a second egg 2 days later. The parent birds take turns incubating the eggs, with the female doing most of the sitting and the male relieving her for about 6 hours of each day.

The eggs hatch in 2 weeks, and the newly hatched squabs are fed with a substance called "crop milk," a liquid secreted in the crops of both male and female birds. (The crop is a pouchlike enlargement of a bird's esophagus.) The squabs leave the nest when they are about 11 days old, but the parents continue to feed them—with increasing reluctance—for another 10 days. Then courtship begins again, and the cycle repeats itself.

What determines the performance of the actions described above and the physiological changes that accompany them? Experiments have

shown that hormonal factors play an important role, and so do visual and auditory stimuli. (The sense of smell does not seem to be involved; birds are not very sensitive to odors.)

When adult ring doves are caged separately they never make a nest, no matter how much nesting material is available. If these single birds are offered nests with eggs in them they ignore them. If a male and a female bird are put together and immediately presented with a nest and eggs, they will not incubate them. They will do so, however, if the eggs are presented 6 or 7 days later, even though the female has not yet laid her own eggs. Similarly, if the eggs are removed from a nesting pair and baby birds are substituted, the parents will feed the squabs at once, even if their own eggs were not due to hatch for another week. They will have to feed the squabs on regurgitated seeds at first, but very soon

THE INFLUENCE OF HORMONES ON THE MALE. In the male, cyclical variations in hormonal level occur in such animals as the deer, which confine their sexual activities to a certain season of the year. In most species hormonal production is constant, and the male is able and willing to engage in sexual activity at any time.

The effects of castration (surgical removal of the testes) depend on the age at which the operation is performed. A male that is castrated before puberty will never reach sexual maturity and will never show normal sexual behavior unless the hormones normally secreted by the tests are supplied artificially, by injection. Castration after puberty has a variable effect, depending on the species and the amount of previous sexual experience. A male rat will usually cease to attempt to mount a receptive female within 2 or 3 months of castration. An experienced male dog might attempt to mount for a year or more after castration. In humans, castration has an unpredictable effect, sometimes resulting in an immediate loss of potency (probably due to psychological factors) and sometimes in a slow decline over a period of years. In both humans and animals, sexual desire and ability are restored by the administration of testosterone. By the way, *additional* testosterone administered to a male who already has an adequate supply has little effect on sexual activity (Bermant & Davidson, 1974).

THE ROLE OF EXPERIENCE. In many animals the ability to engage in normal sexual activity depends on their having been reared with others of their kind. Guinea pigs raised in isolation do not show sexual behavior (Valenstein, Riss, & Young, 1955). Isolated male rats do mount receptive females, but it takes

(sooner than usual) their crops will start to produce crop milk.

Lehrman and his collaborators showed that a female ring dove that is prevented from mating will lay (infertile) eggs if she can see and hear a male ring dove bowing and cooing in an adjacent cage, behind a glass partition. If the male has been castrated, he will not bow and coo, and the female will not lay eggs. The growth of the oviduct and the laying of eggs is dependent on 2 hormones: estrogen first, then progesterone. Evidently, visual and auditory stimuli from the normal male are enough to stimulate the female's ovaries to produce these hormones. The same hormones determine incubation behavior: If a male and a female that have each been injected with progesterone are put together in a cage and offered a nest with eggs, they will incubate them almost immediately, instead of

after 6 or 7 days. Estrogen injections cause them to incubate the eggs after a delay of 2 or 3 days.

Growth of the crop and production of crop milk has been shown to depend on the hormone *prolactin*, secreted by the pituitary gland. (Prolactin is also responsible for milk production in female mammals.) Injections of prolactin will cause either

single male or single female ring doves to feed baby birds that are put into their cages. Secretion of this hormone (like that of estrogen and progesterone) is affected by external stimuli: Male birds separated from their mates early in the nesting period will fail to produce prolactin and their crops will not grow. But if they are placed in an adjacent cage and can still see the female sitting on the eggs, their crops will grow just as if they were sharing in the incubation. The presence of squabs also stimulates prolactin production and crop growth.

The conclusion is that the visual and auditory stimuli that appear at different stages of the breeding cycle produce changes in hormonal activity. These hormonal changes produce changes in behavior. The changes in behavior may, in turn, be a source of new visual and auditory stimuli.

them much longer (Zimbardo, 1958). Male beagles raised alone attempt to mount as frequently as normally reared dogs, but they often fail because their attempts are directed toward the female's head or side (Beach, 1968).

In monkeys reared in isolation, neither males nor females show normal sexual responses. A group of monkeys was reared in separate cages where they could see and hear—but not touch—other monkeys. In adulthood these animals failed to mate even when a male and a female were caged together for as long as 7 years. When paired with normally reared monkeys, none of the isolated males ever achieved a normal mount, and only one female became pregnant. These effects seem to be due not to the infant monkey's lack of a mother, but to its lack of social interactions with other young monkeys. Infant monkeys raised without mothers but allowed to play with one another for only 20 minutes a day later showed perfectly normal sexual behavior (Harlow, 1962).

HOMOSEXUALITY. **Homosexuality** shows up in all human societies and in most animal species. In animals, mounting is frequently seen in females as well as males, and males will attempt to mount other males. Often this behavior is associated with dominance rather than with sexuality. However, mounting by female rats and by female monkeys is increased if they are exposed to testosterone early in development. Male rats that are castrated at birth will exhibit the female sexual response as adults if they are given estrogen and progesterone.

In humans, male or female homosexual behavior often shows up as isolated episodes in the lives of otherwise heterosexual individuals. In some societies homosexual behavior is considered normal during adolescence. Later most people in these societies marry and show normal **hetero-sexuality** (Money & Ehrhardt, 1972). Another type of homosexuality involves people (male or female) who *never* engage in heterosexual behavior.

Many attempts have been made to link homosexuality to physical factors such as chromosomal errors or hormonal abnormalities. It is true that the incidence of homosexual experience is somewhat higher in men with an XXY or XYY chromosomal pattern. However, the number of such cases is so small that these genetic errors account for a negligible proportion of homosexuals. It is the same with hormonal disorders: They are found in some small proportion of homosexuals, but not in most (Money, 1970).

THE HUMAN SEXUAL RESPONSE. In 1966 Masters and Johnson published the results of their pioneering study of human sexuality. In this study, volunteer subjects engaged in sexual activity to the point of orgasm, while sophisticated devices monitored a number of their physiological responses. Four different stages of the human sexual pattern were defined:

1. **Excitement.** This stage is characterized by vaginal lubrication, thickening of the vaginal walls, and elevation of the clitoris in females. In the male it involves erection of the penis and elevation of the testes. Nipple erection may also occur in both males and females.
2. **Plateau.** In both sexes heart rate, respiration, and muscle tension increase. The male testes increase in size and are pulled up very high in the scrotum. In the female the outer vaginal wall swells and the clitoris retracts.
3. **Orgasm.** In the male the penis throbs in rhythmic contractions and semen is expelled. The female experiences rhythmic contractions of the muscles of the vagina and uterus. In both sexes, muscles throughout the body contract. Physiologically, the female's orgasm is quite similar to the male's. No differences were found between orgasms produced through clitoral stimulation and those produced through vaginal stimulation.
4. **Resolution.** A rapid decrease in physiological arousal follows orgasm in males. In females one or several orgasms may occur before resolution.

Since this description is, of course, rather cold and clinical, perhaps we should add that the whole sequence is usually considered highly pleasurable by both of the parties involved.

PARENTING

In virtually all species, the period immediately following birth is a dangerous time, associated with a high rate of mortality that declines as the organism matures. If the offspring are nurtured and protected by the adult members of a species, more of them are likely to survive. Thus parental care is clearly important to the success of the species as a whole. For this reason, care of the young has evolved in a great variety of species, including those as primitive as insects, spiders, and fish.

As an example, consider the threespine stickleback, a small fish that has successfully colonized almost all the coastal waters of the northern hemisphere (Hartmann, 1979). In this species the male provides the parental care.

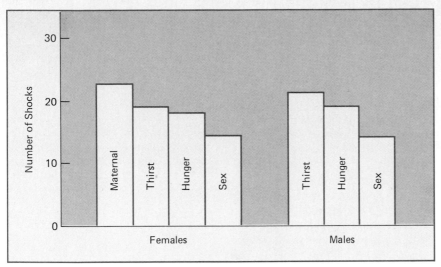

He carefully builds a nest out of bits of plants and covers it with a mixture of sand and a sticky substance secreted by his kidneys. A receptive female is then enticed into the nest, where she lays her eggs. The male fertilizes the eggs by emitting sperm over them and then guards them until they hatch, meanwhile ventilating the nest by fanning water through it. When the young fish hatch, the father continues to guard them and will even retrieve those that stray from the nest. None of the other things this animal can do—obtaining food, fleeing from enemies—is as complex and demanding as the behavior just described.

In most nonhuman mammals the father plays a relatively minor role; nearly all parental care is given by the mother. In the rat and the dog, maternal behavior begins before the birth of the young, in the form of nest building. When the young are born, the mother bites off the umbilical cords and cleans off the pups. Almost immediately after the last pup is born, the mother begins to nurse, by lying or crouching in such a way that the pups can reach her nipples. She will keep the pups warm, guard them against predators, and retrieve any that wander away or are removed from the nest. During the first day or so a mother dog will leave her litter for only a minute or two at a time, and only for the purpose of relieving bowel and bladder. A female rat that has been separated from her pups is so motivated to return to them that, in order to reach them, she will cross an electrfied grid more readily than a hungry or thirsty rat seeking food or water (see Figure 10–4).

These innate patterns of behavior are elicited by a complex combination of hormonal states and external stimuli. For example, in many species nesting can be induced by progesterone injections, or by presenting a female with a ready-made litter of pups. Most animals—mammalian and nonmammalian—do not appear to recognize their own young but will respond appropriately to any infant member of their species. (Or even a different species—cowbirds and cuckoos lay their eggs in the nest of other species, where their offspring are fed and cared for by the foster mother and father, often to the detriment of their own less-demanding young!)

MOTHERLESSNESS IN MONKEYS.   What exact function does parenting serve? What aspect of parenting is most important to the offspring? In an attempt to answer

Sociobiology and Altruistic Behavior

Care of the young is a notable characteristic of the social insects—ants, bees, and wasps. Strictly speaking, this behavior cannot be called "parenting," because the workers that care for the eggs and larva are the sisters of the immature insects. Consideration of the activities of these social insects and of other animals has given rise to a school of thought called **sociobiology** (Wilson, 1971). The sociobiologists believe that group selection, rather than survival of the fittest individual, is responsible for the evolution of altruistic behavior. (**Altruistic behavior** is defined in this context as any act in which an individual organism endangers its own chances of survival in order to increase the survival chances of other individuals. Parental care and protection of the nest by "soldier" ants or bees are two examples of altruistic behavior in nonhuman species.)

According to this theory,

Individuals can afford to sacrifice their own personal genetic fitness if they make up for the loss by increasing the fitness of their relatives. Since many of their own genes are shared with the relatives by common descent, helping the relatives actually multiplies part of their own genetic structure. (Wilson, 1974, p. 9)

In other words, sociobiologists believe that survival value benefits not the individual or even the species, but the genetic material within the chromosomes. In this view the rest of the organism is just an elaborate device for assuring the survival of its genes!

Wilson argues that human altruism has the same genetic basis as the social organization of insects. In fact, he defines sociobiology as the "systematic study of the biological basis of all (animal and human) social behavior" (1975b). Human religion, ethics, tribalism, warfare, conformity, and competition can all be explained as genetically determined "human nature" (Wilson, 1978). There are now at least 3 scientific journals devoted to sociobiology, as well as many collections of edited

papers (e.g., De Vore, 1979). It has also been widely discussed in the popular press, where it has been used to explain everything from the free-market system (*Business Week,* 1978) to the Kent State massacre (Beck, 1979).

Sociobiology is an essentially "instinctual" or hereditarian view of human behavior and, as such, appeals to those who would justify the status quo. For example, Wilson himself argues that because of our genes,

even in the most free and egalitarian of future societies . . . even with identical education and equal access to all professions, men are likely to continue to play a disproportionate role in political life, business, and science. (1975a, p. 47)

Critics of sociobiology see such arguments as the product of underlying social biases masquerading as science (Geertz, 1980; Sahlins, 1976; Washburn, 1978). A general criticism of the hereditarian view of behavior, including sociobiology, is presented in a recent book entitled *Not in Our Genes* (Lewontin, Rose, & Kamin, 1983).

these questions, newborn monkeys were taken from their mothers and raised with "surrogate mothers" of various kinds (Harlow, 1959). It was found that the most important thing for the monkeys was to have something soft to cling to. Given a choice of a surrogate mother made out of wire or one covered with several layers of terrycloth, infant monkeys invariably chose the terrycloth mother. They spent much of their time climbing on or clinging to the cloth-covered object, and when frightened, would run to it for reassurance. Monkeys raised without any mother at all, or with only a wire-covered surrogate mother, withdrew in terror from a strange object, but a monkey with a cloth "mother" would soon gain enough courage to release the soft cloth and investigate the object.

The results were the same for baby monkeys that were fed from a bottle attached to the wire mother. Even though they got their milk from the wire mother, they spent most of their time clinging to the cloth one. Thus nourishment alone does not seem to form the basis for the emotional attachment between a primate infant and its mother.

Warmth appears to play some role, but not a major one. An infant monkey would readily abandon a warm heating pad in favor of its unheated cloth mother. In a later experiment, though, newborn infant monkeys given a

In an experiment by Harlow (1959), if a monkey was separated from its mother at birth and raised with "surrogate" mothers of different kinds, the monkey would invariably choose the terrycloth mother over the wire mother.

choice between warm wire mothers and cool cloth ones favored the warm mother (Harlow, 1971). However, after the age of 20 days they began to prefer the cloth mother.

In the subprimate mammals, warmth may be of greater importance than contact comfort. Puppies given the choice of a fur surrogate mother and a wire one chose the fur mother. But when the fur mother was cooled and the metal one heated, the puppies spent almost all of their time with the metal mother (Jeddi, 1970).

It should be noted, finally, that the infant monkeys "reared" by cloth mothers did not fare so well in the long run. Although they behaved normally as long as their cloth mother was available, they grew up to be very maladjusted monkeys unable to have normal relationships—either social or sexual. If a female monkey raised on a cloth surrogate became pregnant, she never treated her infant with the tender care shown by a normally reared monkey mother. She refused to nurse the infant and either neglected or abused it.

We conclude that successful parenting of a young monkey or a young human (by mother, father, and/or other adults) must necessarily include cuddling. But cuddling is not enough. Infancy is a time of rapid learning as well as of rapid physical growth. One of the most important things an infant must learn is how to get along with other members of its species. That cannot be taught by wire or terrycloth "mothers."

AGGRESSION

The term **aggression** refers to the kinds of behavior that lead to the damage or destruction of something—either another organism or an inanimate object. (In humans, as we shall see in Chapter 18, aggression also may refer to pain-inflicting behaviors.) A coyote killing a lamb, a stallion attacking another stallion, a cat slashing out at a dog, a human destroying an automobile with a sledgehammer—all these actions fall under the definition of aggression.

Clearly, we are not referring to a single type of behavior: There are many different kinds of aggressive responses, and they are elicited by a wide variety of internal and external stimuli (Moyer, 1976). Seven categories of aggressive behavior are described below. It should be noted, however, that it is not always possible to distinguish these types of behavior in practice, because they overlap. A given aggressive act may be the result of two or three factors acting together.

Kinds of Aggressive Behavior

1. **Angry aggression.** This is the classical variety, the type most people think of when they hear the word "aggression." It is generally accompanied by the signs of emotional arousal (see the section on emotion in the next chapter) and is often produced by pain or frustration. For example, two rats put together in a cage and given brief, intermittent electric shocks will attack each other when the shock comes on. Under these circumstances a rat will even attack a doll or a stuffed animal if another rat is not available. A monkey or a mouse whose tail is pinched will bite its tormenter or (if that is impossible) any other nearby object.

Frustration of goal-directed behavior—for example, preventing a hungry animal from reaching a food reward that it has worked for—generally produces an aggressive response. A pigeon that has been taught to peck a key to obtain grain will attack another pigeon if the grain is withheld (Azrin, Hutchinson, & Hake, 1966). However, frustration does not *invariably* have this kind of effect. A theory relating frustration to aggression, as well as other theories of the origins of human aggressive behavior, will be discussed in Chapter 18.

2. **Predatory aggression.** Quite different from the aroused state associated with angry aggression is the dispassionate stalking of its prey by a carnivorous animal such as a fox, a wolf, or any member of the cat family. One would hesitate to call this behavior "aggressive" and would label it "food-seeking" instead, were it not for the fact that the hunger drive need not be present—the response seems to be elicited simply by the presence of the prey and may occur even when the predator is totally satiated.

An interesting finding about predatory behavior is that in some animal species it is partly learned through imitation. A kitten learns to kill rats by the age of 4 months if it is normally reared and allowed to see its mother killing rats. If a kitten is raised in isolation, however, the chances are that it will *not* kill a rat if it is presented with one when it is 4 months old. It can soon learn to do so if it is given the opportunity to watch other cats kill (Kuo, 1930).

3. **Fear-induced aggression.** This is exemplified by the usually meek animal that, when cornerd by a predator, turns on it and attacks it. More generally, any fearful animal is likely to bite when approached too closely by the object of its fear.

4. **Operant aggression.** An organism may perform an aggressive act simply because it is rewarded for doing so, or punished for not doing so. For example, the tendency of a rat to attack another animal or an object when it is given an electric shock can be strengthened if the shock is turned off whenever the rat attacks. Human adults (Loew, 1967) and children (Lovaas, 1961) who are praised for making hostile remarks tend to become more aggressive. The hired killer, who kills because he is paid to do so, is a good example of this class of aggression.

As in other forms of operant conditioning (discussed in Chapter 6), the reinforcement for aggressive behavior need not follow every response. Once the behavior is learned, an occasional reward (or punishment) is enough to maintain it. This is particularly clear in what is known as **obedient aggression.** A guard dog that attacks on command, or a person who harms someone because he or she is "ordered" to do so, is committing obedient aggression.

5. **Territorial aggression.** This category of behavior has been studied more thoroughly by ethologists (such as Konrad Lorenz, 1966) than by psychologists. Animals of many different species will stake out a territory, frequently mark it in some way (by spraying the boundaries with urine, for instance), and then threaten to attack any unfamiliar member of its species that intrudes within its borders. Note that this behavior is confined to the territory itself: If the animal is taken out of its own territory, its territorial aggressiveness vanishes. Some people see parallels in human territorial conflict.

6. **Altruistic aggression.** The aggressiveness of a bird or mammal guarding its young, or of a "soldier" bee or ant defending its hive or nest, are examples of altruistic aggression. Moyer (1976) has used the term **maternal aggression** to describe the fierce behavior of a female mammal whose nestful of pups is threatened. In some species, however—notably humans—the same kind of behavior may be shown by the father, or even by unrelated individuals.

7. **Intermale aggression.** In many species the normal reaction of a full-grown male to another, unfamiliar adult male is a hostile one. Frequently, the animal will attack without provocation. This behavior is distinguished from territorial aggression because it can occur in any location. Studies of intermale aggression in mice and rats have shown that the stimulus that elicits the attack is the scent of the other male. If the animals' odors are masked by an artificial scent, or if their sense of smell is surgically destroyed, they are unlikely to fight (Ropartz, 1968). Furthermore, in many species such as dogs and wolves (Lorenz, 1966), and even bison (Barash, 1977), the fight will not occur if one animal assumes a stereotyped position of submissiveness.

The male hormone testosterone is of critical importance in intermale aggression. Immature or castrated animals do not show this behavior, but if they are injected with testosterone the aggressiveness appears (Levy & King, 1953). It is also clear that intermale aggression is closely connected with the competition for females. In species that breed only in certain seasons, notably the hoofed mammals, almost all aggressive behavior takes place during the mating season.

Physiological Factors in Aggression

The parts of the brain that seem to play the major role in aggressive behavior are the limbic system and the associated areas of the hypothalamus (see Chapter 2). Damage to one of these brain areas, or stimulation of them through implanted electrodes, is likely to affect one or more of the types of aggressive behavior—especially predatory, angry, and fear-induced aggression. Particularly interesting to psychologists and physiologists are those cases in which only a single kind of aggressive behavior is affected. For example, mild electrical stimulation of one part of a cat's hypothalamus will cause it to attack a rat. Stimulation of another area within the hypothalamus, on the other hand, causes it to ignore the rat and instead launch an enraged attack on the experimenter (Wasman & Flynn, 1962; Egger & Flynn, 1963).

Motorcycle clubs have a reputation for aggressive behavior. Which of the types of aggression described in the text would they illustrate?

The amygdala, which is part of the limbic system, appears to be of particular importance in aggressiveness. Surgical destruction of all or part of this brain structure generally results in an animal that is docile, unaggressive, and unfearful. In humans there have been reports of abnormal aggressiveness resulting from tumors in the region of the amygdala. In 1966, a young man named Charles Whitman shot and killed 14 people from the observation tower at the University of Texas, before he himself was cut down by police bullets. In autopsy, a walnut-sized tumor was found in his amygdala (Beck, 1983).

Another factor that has been linked to aggressiveness is the level of glucose in the blood. Ralph Bolton, an American anthropologist, lived for two years among the Qolla, a tribe of Indians in the Andes Mountains of Peru (Bolton, 1976). These people have been described as among the most aggressive on earth—their homicide rate is extremely high, and they are constantly embroiled in arguments and brawls. Bolton found, first of all, that the individuals within this group that were rated most aggressive were likely to be suffering from a moderate degree of hypoglycemia (low blood glucose). The people with normal blood glucose levels were less aggressive, and so were those with *severe* hypoglycemia, doubtless because of the weakening effects of this condition.

Secondly, Bolton found that the overall proportion of hypoglycemics in the Qolla population was far greater than in other populations studied: 55 percent had mild or severe hypoglycemia. (In the United States the proportion has been estimated at between 2 percent and 30 percent, but most researchers believe the 30 percent figure to be very exaggerated.) Bolton attributed the remarkable hypoglycemia rate found among the Qolla to 3 factors: (1) the effects of living at a high altitude; (2) poor nutrition; and (3) the effects of chewing coca leaves, which contain cocaine. Coca (not to be confused with cocoa, which comes from the bean of the cacao tree) deadens hunger pangs and makes its users feel better temporarily, but its long-term effects on the body's metabolism are harmful. Bolton hypothesized that fighting, too, may have temporary beneficial effects: By increasing the secretion of epinephrine by the adrenal glands, it may produce a rise in blood glucose that, though short-lived, results in an increased feeling of well-being while it lasts. Indeed, Qolla individuals sometimes mentioned to Bolton that fighting "makes one feel better."

From as early as 2 or 3 years of age, human males behave in more aggressive fashion than human females (Pederson & Bell, 1970). The same sex difference has been noted in rhesus monkeys (Harlow, 1971) and in a wide variety of mammalian species. This aggressiveness includes not only intermale aggression, but also angry aggression, territorial aggression, and perhaps even operant aggression (male dogs are used as guard dogs more often than females).

In adult male animals, castration greatly reduces all kinds of aggressive behavior. A gelded horse or steer is considerably more tractable and slower to anger than a stallion or bull. The same effect is produced by the administration of estrogens and progesterone to a male animal (Moyer, 1971). Injections of testosterone restore the aggressiveness of castrated animals.

Human motivation is, of course, influenced by many factors other than physiological ones. As we will see in Chapter 11, cognitive, social, and emotional factors are often more important in human behavior than the biological events we have discussed in this chapter.

SUMMARY

1. In motivation theory, James emphasized concepts of impulses and instincts; Cannon put forth the idea of *homeostasis,* or the way the body maintains an equilibrium in its internal environment.

2. The concept of *drives* and *drive reduction* was introduced by Hull. The concept of drives is most useful when we are talking about relatively clearcut states of physiological deprivation such as hunger and thirst.

3. Hunger is one of the most universal sources of *motivation*. Regulation of food intake seems to depend on gastric secretions, a sensation of bulk in the small intestine, blood sugar level, and signals from the hypothalamus.

4. Some experiments support the *set-point theory* and suggest that obese people have a higher set point than nonobese people. When obese people are below their set point, they are in a state of deprivation or homeostatic imbalance, even if their weight is above normal levels.

5. *Osmoreceptors* in the brain seem to respond to dehydration in the cells by causing the organism to be thirsty and by triggering the release of a hormone, causing the kidneys to excrete less water. *Volumetric receptors* respond to a change in the total volume of extracellular fluid by stimulating the thirst receptors in the brain.

6. Sexual behavior apparently has *drive-reducing* (or positive *incentive*) value for both males and females of the species; hormones also play a role in both sexual behavior and the development of secondary sex characteristics.

7. Psychologists have identified at least 10 classes of aggressive behavior; the motivations for *aggression* are diverse, including pain, fear, predatory behavior, and maternal behavior.

8. The innate patterns of behavior that are part of mothering or parenting in many organisms are elicited by a complex combination of hormonal states and external stimuli.

Suggested Readings

BECK, R. C. *Motivation: Theories and principles* (2nd cd.). Englewood Cliffs, N.J.: Prentice-Hall, 1983. Thorough coverage of historical and present-day motivation theories. Also deals with specific motivations such as aggression.

HARLOW, H. *Learning to love*. San Francisco: Albion, 1971. The effects of parental care and peer-group interactions on young monkeys. Describes the development of social, sexual, and aggressive behavior in these animals.

KIMBLE, D. P. *Psychology as a biological science,* 2nd ed. Santa Monica, Calif.: Goodyear, 1977. A general approach to the biological bases of behavior.

LORENZ, K. [*On aggression*] (M. K. Wilson, trans.). New York: Harcourt Brace Jovanovich, 1966. Here Lorenz argues that humans as well as animals have an innate drive to be aggressive.

MAHONEY, B. K., ROGERS, T., STRAW, M. K., et al. *Human obesity: Assessment and treatment*. Englewood Cliffs, N.J.: Prentice-Hall, 1983. A comprehensive review of modern research on obesity and methods of weight reduction.

MONEY, J., & EHRHARDT, A. A. *Man and woman, boy and girl.* Baltimore: Johns Hopkins Press, 1972. Chromosomal and hormonal factors in human sexual identity and behavior.

STUNKARD, A. J. (Ed.). *Obesity*. Philadelphia: Saunders, 1983. A collection of papers by leading experts on obesity.

WONG, R. *Motivation: A biobehavioral analysis of consummatory activities*. New York: Macmillan, 1976. Very detailed discussions of various sorts of motivated behavior, including feeding, drinking, mating, parenting, and stimulus seeking.

11. Human Motivation and Emotion

he previous chapter was concerned with the biological bases of **motivation.** We discussed motives and drives that are common to a wide variety of species: human beings, monkeys, dogs, rats, and even honeybees. In this chapter the focus will be on the human species.

Why do people do what they do? What motivates us to behave at all? And why, of all the things we are capable of doing, do we do a certain thing in a certain situation? Answers to these questions concern the very core of human nature. The answers are, as you might expect, quite complex.

Human motivation ranges from basic physiological drives (such as hunger) through drives for stimulation that are part of our ability to know and understand our environment (such as curiosity) to socially based drives that we acquire from our culture (such as the desire to achieve).

In this chapter we will also consider the topic of emotion. Motivation and emotion are closely linked—indeed, as we shall see, it is often hard to distinguish between them. Emotions can act as motivators, and motivations can produce emotion. We will begin by distinguishing between primary and secondary motivation.

SOURCES OF NEEDS AND MOTIVES

Primary Motivation: Physiological Needs

In the previous chapter we reviewed some of our biological needs: We need food and water to survive. We also require air and an appropriate temperature range. When we encounter deficiencies in any of our basic needs, we typically take action to correct them.

If you think about your typical daily activities, however, you will see that much of your behavior seems to have little or nothing to do with these basic biological needs. At first glance it is hard to see that reading this book, riding a bicycle, talking with friends, or watching television has anything to do with hunger or thirst. But some of these behaviors may have originally been motivated by basic physiological needs, through complex conditioning and learning processes.

Secondary Motivation and Conditioning

In Chapter 6 we saw how Pavlov was able to give previously neutral stimuli the ability to elicit behaviors through the process of classical conditioning. A dog will normally salivate when it sees food, but it will not normally salivate when it hears a tone. After repeated pairings of the tone with the sight of food, Pavlov found that the tone alone could elicit salivation. Furthermore, through higher-order conditioning, the tone could be used to create a link between another stimulus, such as a light, and salivation. Seeing a dog salivate when a light flashes would seem very strange unless you knew the dog's conditioning history.

Skinner, too, has shown that previously neutral stimuli can become secondary reinforcers and can then cause learning of new behaviors, through operant conditioning. When a rat learns that pressing a bar leads to food, the bar acquires the properties of a secondary reinforcer and can be used to reinforce other behaviors. A rat will learn to run a maze to get at the bar, will then learn to open a door to get into the maze, and so on until a complex chain of behavior is formed. An uninformed observer looking at several rats who had received such training might mistakenly conclude that rats have a built-in fondness for mazes.

Human beings, of course, are able to learn even more complex sequences of behaviors. Some of our behaviors that seem to have little relationship with basic physiological needs may in fact be the result of such complex chainings of behaviors. One very common secondary motivator in our society is money. Money serves the same function for us as the bar or lever does for the rat—it gets us the food, drink, clothing, and shelter that we need. We are all familiar with the numerous things people will do to acquire money.

Functional Autonomy of Motivation

With both classical and operant conditioning, previously neutral stimuli eventually lose their acquired reinforcing power if they are not, at least some of the time, paired with the original reinforcer (such as food, in the case of hunger). Humans, however, appear to have many "secondary" reinforcers that do not seem to be paired with primary reinforcers. Color preferences or desires for certain kinds of friends, music, and clothing do not seem to need association with primary reinforcers. This observation has led some motivation theorists to believe that acquired motives can have a "life of their own," independent of any association with the satisfaction of basic biological needs.

Perhaps the clearest example of such a learned or acquired motive comes from the work of Neal Miller and others on fear and anxiety. Miller (1948) demonstrated the motivating power of learned fear in rats. The animals were placed in a box that contained a white compartment and a black compartment with a door between them. First, the rats were given several shocks on the white side of the box through an electrified floor. The animals soon learned

The behavior of the hoarder who collects money for the sheer pleasure of having more and more of it is an example of functional autonomy.

to run from the white compartment through the open door into the black compartment. Following this training period, the animals were placed in the white compartment with the door between the compartments closed. Even though the shock was never turned on again, the rats learned to turn a wheel so that they could get out of the white compartment. Later, when the wheel was disconnected so that it no longer opened the door, the rats learned to press a bar instead to open the door. The bar pressing persisted for hundreds of trials, even though the rats were never shocked again.

Behavior motivated by learned fear, then, can continue indefinitely without the organism ever reexperiencing the pain that originally created the fear. Several theorists have taken this kind of analysis one step further and have argued that many acquired motives can become functionally autonomous (Woodworth, 1918; Allport, 1937). This means that motives that were originally conditioned to basic biological needs can, through repeated use, become motives in their own right. The behavior of the hoarder who collects money for the sheer pleasure of having larger and larger piles of it, and who does not want to spend it even to provide adequate food and clothing, is an example of functional autonomy.

Acquired Motivation or Innate Need?

Many of the complex motives that we see displayed by the people around us are the result of complex learning involving secondary reinforcement. Some of these acquired motives may eventually become functionally autonomous. All of these motives have their origins in basic physiological needs. Some psychologists, indeed, believe that all human motivation can be explained in this way. Others, however, think that there are some innate or built-in motives that do not stem from tissue deficits or physiological imbalances. Such motives are assumed to be part of "human nature." Curiosity is one example of a motive that may reflect built-in characteristics of human nature, rather than being acquired through learning. In the next section we will examine several examples of motives that have been studied extensively by psychologists and that appear to involve fundamental aspects of human nature. These include curiosity, affiliative, and competence needs. Our discussion will also suggest that the expression of all human motives is strongly influenced by learning experiences. This will be particularly clear when we discuss 2 other human needs: the expression of sexual motivation, and the development of achievement motivation. Finally, we will consider motivation in the workplace, a setting in which the variety and complexity of human motivation is expressed.

SOME PROMINENT HUMAN NEEDS

Curiosity and the Need for Stimulation

All animals are equipped with means of gathering and processing information, and human beings are particularly well equipped for these tasks. We routinely gather a wide variety of information through our senses. Through sight, hearing, touch, smell, and taste sensors we take in, organize, interpret, and use information about ourselves and our environment. This enables us to understand our world and to take effective action. We not only have the ability to process information, we also have a need to use that ability.

Humans have a built-in need for stimulation that, in conjunction with a tendency to focus attention on incongruent stimuli, may cause exploration of novel elements in the environment—thus curiosity.

Human information-processing capabilities can be likened to a fine piece of machinery. An automobile engine, for example, can be efficient, powerful, and smooth, but if it is left unused for 6 months, it will probably be balky, dirty, and unreliable. Similarly, if our information-processing abilities are to work well, they need exercise. Unlike an automobile engine, however, we do not need an outside force to "turn us on." Humans and animals have a built-in need for stimulation that motivates them to seek out sensory stimulation from the environment.

A THEORETICAL ACCOUNT OF CURIOSITY.   The fact that we seek stimulation, and exhibit preferences for and interest in certain degrees of complexity in that stimulation, is explained by the concept of an optimal level of stimulation (Hunt, 1965). According to this theory, we tend to pay attention to stimuli that deviate from our standards of comparison (Miller, Galanter, & Pribram, 1960). We develop standards of comparison through experience. The first time you see an object, it interests you and holds your attention. However, as you continue to be exposed to that object, you become used to it or adapt to it, and it is less likely to command your attention. For example, if you are used to seeing birds with two legs, another two-legged bird will not be as likely to arouse your interest as a four-legged bird would be. Standards of comparison are also called adaptation levels (Helson, 1964). For any given stimulus, the adaptation level is the level of stimulation perceived as average or normal. Stimuli that fall within the average or expectable range are not likely to capture our attention; stimuli that fall outside the average range or are exceptional (such as four-legged birds) certainly will.

Using the concepts of adaptation level and focus of attention on incongruous stimuli, Hunt (1965) theorized that there are optimal levels of stimulation. If all incoming stimuli are average, or within our adaptation levels, we become bored. On the other hand, excessive stimulation can be very unpleasant. But stimuli that are somewhat unusual are of interest to us. Optimal levels of stimulation, then, contain enough surprises to keep our interest alive and allow us to exercise our information-processing abilities but are not so different from our experience and expectations that they frighten or overwhelm us. For example, a crowded shopping mall or a museum exhibit with large jostling crowds can be unpleasant because it provides too much stimulation. In contrast, jobs, lectures, or other daily routines that contain no surprises can become unpleasantly boring.

EXPERIMENTS ON SENSORY DEPRIVATION.   If people need stimulation and prefer stimulation to be mildly different from their adaptation levels, then we would expect that a complete absence of stimulation would be very unpleasant and have negative effects on people's efficiency at processing information. In an early experiment on sensory deprivation reported by Bexton, Heron, and Scott (1954), college student volunteers were paid for each day they participated in a study of the effects of reduced sensory input. The subjects spent their time lying on a cot in a sound-deadened room with a constant background noise. They wore translucent goggles, cardboard tubes around their arms, and gloves. This experience was very unpleasant, and most of the subjects refused to continue after a few days. In this experiment and others like it, subjects have experienced visual hallucinations, rapid changes in mood, and an inordinate interest in normally boring material, such as old stock-market reports. After a period of sensory deprivation, subjects also showed reduced competence on a variety of visual, manual-dexterity, and

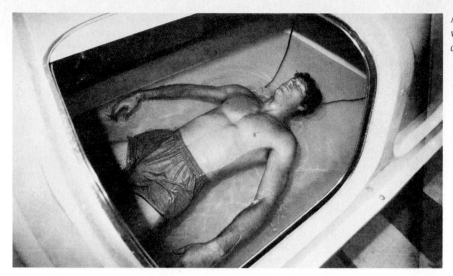

A complete absence of stimulation can be very unpleasant and can have negative effects on information processing abilities.

abstract-reasoning tasks (Held & White, 1959; Bexton, Heron, & White, 1954; Vernon, McGill, Gulick, & Candland, 1959). Taken together, these studies of sensory deprivation underscore the importance of our need for stimulation.

Affiliation

Wherever people are found, whether in a high-rise office building, along the banks of a tropical river, around a desert oasis, or in a crowded discotheque, one clear fact of human existence is that we spend a great deal of our time with other people. We work together, eat together, and play together. We have developed extremely complex languages for the purpose of communicating with one another. At birth we are completely dependent on other people to satisfy our biological needs, and this dependence lasts longer in humans than in any other species. Stories of hermits who live in isolated caves and shun all human contact capture our interest because such behavior is so unusual. For these and other reasons, the human being is often called a social animal.

In the previous chapter we saw that a monkey that is reared alone (or with a terrycloth "mother" instead of a real one) is likely to be permanently impaired in its ability to form normal relationships with other monkeys. Not surprisingly, the deficits caused by lack of proper parental care and attention are even more serious in humans.

EFFECTS OF LACK OF PARENTING. Human babies need more than milk and a warm blanket. They need what is usually called "mothering," but which we will call "parenting," since it can equally well be provided by a father—or, for that matter, any caring adult. Case studies of children who have been subjected to early social deprivation show that it can have very serious ill effects on human development. When infants are reared in institutions in which they receive food and medical care but little social stimulation, they show striking deficits in emotional, intellectual, and even physical development (Goldfarb, 1944, 1945; Spitz, 1946). Provence and Lipton (1962) observed institutionalized infants, aged 4 days to 8 months, whose main contact with other humans was limited to the changing of bottles (which were propped in their cribs) and diapers. Even by 4 months of age, these infants acted differently

Severe Early Isolation— Feral Children

From time to time cases have been reported of children who have been living in the wild from a very early age with little or no human contact. Often these *feral children* are living with, and appear to have been reared by, wild animals.

Sargent and Stafford (1965) reviewed a number of these cases. One of the earliest feral children described in some detail was the Wild Boy of Aveyron, discovered by hunters in southern France in 1799. Apparently he had been foraging for himself for some time (he was about 11 years old). Dr Jean Itard attempted to socialize and teach the boy. Although he did develop some affection for his caretakers and learn a few simple things, he never approached normalcy.

A pair of girls about 2 and 9 years of age were found living with wolves in India in 1920. The younger girl died soon after she was discovered. The older girl, Kamala, had developed wolflike mannerisms: She howled, lapped up liquids, and bared her teeth at anyone who came too close (Gesell, 1941). An even more recent case of a child being thoroughly socialized by an animal community is that of the Gazelle-boy of the Sahara Desert (Armen, 1974) who was found living with a herd of gazelle. He ran with the herd, had gazelle-like mannerisms, and generally seemed to be an accepted part of the gazelle community.

Attempts to resocialize these feral children have met with varied degrees of success. Itard had very limited success with the Wild Boy of Aveyron. Kamala, the wolf girl, was originally completely hostile toward other humans, but eventually she came to like her playmates and learned to use about 100 words. She did not, however, become a normal person. In contrast, Tamasha, the "Wild Boy of Salvador," who was found in the jungle, progressed quite rapidly. He acquired language fairly easily, as well as other habits of human culture, and was able to talk about his experiences in the wild.

It is difficult to compare these children because their experiences and situations varied considerably, but it seems that the longer the period of time away from human contact and society, and the earlier such separation begins, the more difficult it is for the person ever to become integrated into human society.

It is tempting to think that these difficulties of adjustment result from social isolation—that is, to assume that human contact is necessary for normal development and that the absence of such contact is the major source of the feral children's difficulties. There are, however, other possible explanations. For example, how did these feral children get into the wilderness in the first place? One plausible guess is that they were retarded or defective in some other way at birth, and that their parents abandoned them for that reason (Sargent & Stafford, 1965). Another possibility is that the severe malnutrition that most of these children must have experienced caused some central nervous system damage, and that this, rather than their social isolation, was the major problem.

It is because of these ambiguities in the interpretation of isolated cases that the laboratory work on animals by Harlow and others cited in the text is so valuable in trying to understand the effects of extreme social isolation.

from children raised in normal family settings. They vocalized less, were less interested in manipulating objects, and were very passive. H. Gardner (1982) described a group of infants who required hospitalization and had to be removed temporarily from their parents. These infants became listless, showed signs of depression, and failed to gain weight. When they returned to their homes they quickly began to thrive.

It is difficult to pinpoint the specific aspects of social deprivation that led to impaired development in these human infants. It is quite clear, though, that some close human contact is necessary for normal development; humans need far more than merely food and shelter. However, while some instances of extreme early social deprivation seem to cause irreversible damage, several investigators have discovered a remarkable resilience even to severe deprivation. Koluchova (1972) studied the effects of early deprivation on a pair of identical twin boys who were subjected to severe deprivation for the first six years of their lives. When they were discovered they had almost no language and appeared to be severely retarded. By age 14, however, their IQs were average, their speech was normal, and they were doing well in school. This and other examples of rehabilitation give some hope that the negative effects of early social deprivation may be at least partially reversible.

NEED FOR AFFILIATION IN ADULTS.   Fortunately, most of us do not encounter severe social deprivation. Anyone reading this book is already deeply involved in human society and experiences contact with others as a common, daily fact of life. We all spend time with others and time by ourselves, and we all have some control over our social lives. Sometimes we want to be with others: When Saturday evening approaches, dates, parties, and other social activities are often uppermost in our minds. At other times, we want to be alone: A quiet evening with a book or a solitary stroll is sometimes quite appealing. Because we seem to need both socializing and solitude, questions about *when* we seek out social contact and *why* we do so become important.

In one of the first systematic investigations of people's changing desires for **affiliation,** Schachter (1959) did a series of studies of the relationship between anxiety and the desire to affiliate. On the basis of several case studies of college students' reactions to social isolation, he theorized that an increase in anxiety would lead to an increased desire to be with others. In his initial experiment, female college students who volunteered for a psychology experiment were divided into 2 groups. The subjects were met by a person who introduced himself as "Dr. Gregor Zilstein in the Medical School's Departments of Neurology and Psychiatry," who told them that the experiment involved the use of electric shock. Subjects in the high-anxiety condition were told that the shocks would be quite intense and painful, though they were "reassured" that there would be no "permanent damage" and were shown the alleged shock-delivering equipment. This description was, of course, designed to be frightening: No one was ever actually shocked. Subjects in the low-anxiety condition were met by a less ominous "Dr. Zilstein" who, adhering to a reassuring script, told them that the shocks would be extremely mild and that at most they would feel a tickle. Next, all subjects were informed that a number of people were waiting to take part in the experiment and that they too would have to wait. Each subject was asked to indicate whether she would prefer to wait in a room with other people or by herself. Only 33 percent of the low-anxiety subjects asked to wait with other people; almost twice as many

Humans are motivated to seek social contact.

(63 percent) of the high-anxiety subjects asked to wait with others. In subsequent experiments Schachter found that anxiety increased the desire to affiliate, even when the subjects knew that they would not be allowed to talk with the people with whom they would be waiting.

Schachter's studies showed that when people experience anxiety, their desire to be with others increases. Schachter believed he was studying the effects of anxiety on affiliative behavior, but later researchers pointed out that fear might have caused the affiliation pattern he observed. Explanations for the results of these and other experiments point to 2 factors: First, simply being with others often causes a reduction in fear (Wrightsman, 1960). Second, when people are frightened, they want to find out how others in the same situation are reacting, so they can compare their own reactions with those of similar others (Schachter, 1959; Gerard & Rabbie, 1961). The experiments on fear and affiliation thus uncovered 2 of the most important aspects of social contact: emotional support from others, and the provision of standards of correctness through social comparison (Festinger, 1954). (See Chapter 18 for a discussion of social-comparison theory.)

AFFILIATION AVOIDANCE.   There are, of course, times when we do *not* wish to be around others. While people may be motivated to confide their feelings in others when they are under stress, they may avoid affiliation if the stressful situation is an embarrassing one (Fish, Karabenick, & Heath, 1978). When we are embarrassed, the last thing we want is to be around our peers. Our most fervent desire when we have just tripped over a small crack in an otherwise smooth sidewalk, or have just dropped a melting ice-cream cone in our lap, is to be unnoticed by others. When Sarnoff and Zimbardo (1961) told subjects that they would be participating in a study of oral needs and would be sucking on pacifiers, baby bottles, and breast shields, a clear preference to wait alone was expressed. And just as some people typically desire to be around others, chronically shy individuals often take great pains to avoid social contact (Zimbardo, 1977).

Human Sexual Expression

One of the major reasons for affiliating with others is sexual attraction. We will discuss the general question of why we like or dislike others in Chapter 18; the physiology of sexual motivation was described in Chapter 10. In this section we will examine some of the tremendous variability in the expression of our basic sexual needs. Although human sexual behavior has a common physiological basis, its expression varies widely. This variability can be seen in comparisons among different cultures, in historical changes within particular societies, and among subgroups of societies at any given time. Such variability attests to the powerful influence of socialization on the expression of our basic sexual needs.

DIFFERERENCES AND CHANGES IN SEXUAL BEHAVIORS.   The overwhelming influence of socially transmitted standards can be seen clearly in variations in sexual behavior among cultures. In some cultures, for example, homosexuality is approved, but in others it is not (Davenport, 1965); some cultures expose children to their parents' sexual activities and encourage adolescent sexual experimentation, while others make these kinds of behaviors taboo (Marshall, 1971). Cultural standards produce rates of adult sexual intercourse that vary widely (Marshall, 1971). In Mangaia, a South Pacific culture, adoles-

Age	1969		1972	
	Men	Women	Men	Women
Under 30	48%	27%	65%	42%
30 to 44	26	13	45	29
45 and over	12	10	21	12
Total	23	14	37	23
From Udry (1974), p. 108.				

Table 11–1: Percentage of White Men and Women in the United States Who Believe that Premarital Sexual Relations Are Not Wrong, 1969 and 1972.

cents have sex every night and average three orgasms per night (Hyde, 1979). On the island of Ines Beag, off the Irish coast, married couples wear undergarments during intercourse, and the women report that they never have orgasms (Messinger, 1971).

Within our own society, sexual behavior appears to have changed dramatically in this century. The evidence for these changes comes from surveys in which people are asked to report on their attitudes toward various sexual practices and on their own sexual behaviors. The results of such surveys need to be interpreted with some caution. Differences in the reported frequency of particular sexual behaviors from surveys taken in the 1950s and the 1970s, for example, might be due to real changes in behavior, or instead to changes in the willingness to admit to such behaviors. It is also possible that the people who are willing to participate in such surveys are not representative of the population as a whole, and that generalizations from these surveys to the nation are therefore questionable. This problem is particularly acute with surveys conducted by popular magazines, in which the respondents are (1) only people who read such magazines, and (2) only those readers who are motivated to volunteer to respond.

Keeping these cautions in mind, it is fairly clear from the more carefully conducted surveys that substantial changes in sexual attitudes and practices have taken place in the last few decades. Comparisons between the Kinsey studies, which were the first systematic surveys (Kinsey, Pomeroy, & Martin, 1948; Kinsey, Pomeroy, Martin, & Gebhard, 1953), and the study by Hunt (1974) 2 decades later reveal considerable liberalization of both sexual attitudes and behaviors. Attitudes toward premarital sex, masturbation, oral sex, and homosexuality have all become more tolerant. In Table 11–1 and Figure 11–1 you can also see that younger adults have more tolerant attitudes toward various sexual behaviors than older adults. Changes in sexual behavior parallel these changes in attitudes. Both males and females are now more likely to engage in premarital sex, and differences between males and females on this behavior dimension are much smaller than they once were.

THE EFFECTS OF EROTICA ON SEXUAL BEHAVIOR. A topic of current interest and concern is the increasing availability of sexually explicit materials, or *erotica,* in North American society. Psychologists have recently examined similarities and differences in individuals' responses to erotica and have been exploring the possible links between exposure to erotica and the likelihood of subsequent aggression.

In general, erotic material (stories, photographs, and movies) causes physiological arousal in both males and females (Schmidt, Sigush, & Meyberg, 1969; Schmidt & Sigush, 1970) and increases the likelihood of sexual activity for short periods following exposure (Mosher, 1973). There are, however, a number of differences in individuals' responses to erotica, just as there are individual differences in other aspects of sexual behavior. Even though erotica

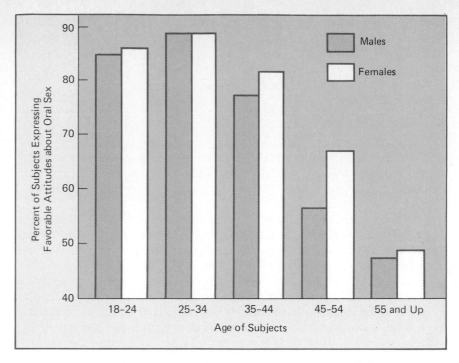

FIGURE 11–1 CHANGES IN ATTITUDES: ORAL SEX?

Survey research indicates that the attitudes of Americans about most sexual topics have been steadily changing in the direction of greater tolerance and permissiveness. In the example shown here, younger individuals consistently express more positive attitudes about oral sex than do older ones. (Adapted from Baron & Byrne, 1981, p. 557, based on data from Hunt, 1974)

can be arousing for everyone, this experience can be either positive or negative in emotional tone. Females, for example, tend to find explicit or "hard-core" sexual materials to be more disturbing than males do (Sapolsky & Zillman, 1981). Individuals classified as sexual liberals or conservatives (based on questionnaire responses to a liberalism–conservatism scale) are equally aroused by sexual material, but while liberals find the most arousing material to be the most entertaining, conservatives find the most arousing material to be the most offensive and least entertaining (Wallace & Wehmer, 1972). And individuals classified as high in sex guilt are less likely to view erotic materials than those low in sex guilt. Schill and Chapin (1972), for example, found that males low in sex guilt tended to look at issues of *Playboy* and *Penthouse* while seated in a waiting room, but males high in sex guilt looked at *Outdoor Life* and *Newsweek*.

EROTICA, VIOLENCE, AND AGGRESSION.   The increased availability of erotic material in North America has produced heated and continuing debates about censorship and personal freedoms, morality, and debasement of women. One issue that has been the subject of recent psychological research is the potential link between erotica and crimes of violence such as rape. Rape cannot be studied in the laboratory, of course, but some experiments have produced evidence that bears on this issue. Aggression in the form of verbal abuse or the willingness to deliver shocks to another subject has been studied in the laboratory (see Chapter 18). In the typical study, subjects view erotica, and their subsequent behavior is measured for aggressiveness and compared to the behavior of subjects who have not viewed erotic stimuli. One general finding is that erotic material by itself does not increase aggression (Sapolsky & Zillman, 1981). But when subjects have been angered before viewing erotic materials (usually by being insulted and/or aggressed against by an experimenter or a confederate posing as another subject), subsequent aggressive behavior increases.

The results of some of these studies seem to be contradictory: Some find that erotica increases the aggressiveness of provoked subjects (e.g., Cantor, Zillman, & Einsiedel, 1978), while others find that erotica reduces aggression (e.g., Baron & Bell, 1977). More recent studies have clarified this contradiction by defining more carefully the nature of erotic content. Erotica can vary in its explicitness and in the extent to which it contains themes of violence. The portrayal of sexually violent erotic scenes has been increasing in both the print and electronic media (Malamuth & Spinner, 1980), and this kind of material does appear to increase subsequent aggression of males against females. Donnerstein and Berkowitz (1981), for example, exposed provoked males to either a neutral movie, an erotic movie with no violent themes, or to a movie portraying a sexual attack. The ending of the violent movie was also varied. In the "positive-ending" film, the woman became a willing participant; in the "negative-ending" film, she was shown to be suffering. As you can see in Figure 11–2, none of these movies affected aggression toward a male target. The female target, however, was given shocks of higher intensity when subjects had viewed either of the violent films.

In a related study, Malamuth and Check (1981) found that males previously exposed to an erotic depiction of a rape showed little sympathy toward the victim of a description of a more realistic rape, and an increase in self-reported willingness to commit rape themselves. The most recent evidence, then, suggests that materials portraying sexual violence do tend to increase subsequent aggression toward women. These effects appear to result because some depictions imply that rape is "acceptable" to potential victims (as in the "positive ending" film in Donnerstein and Berkowitz's study), and because women are presented to angry persons as potential targets for their wrath (Berkowitz, 1974).

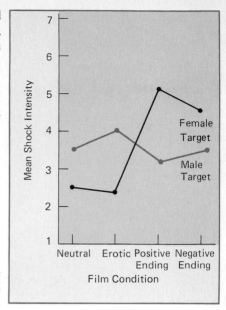

FIGURE 11–2
Mean shock intensity as a function of sex of target and film condition. (From Donnerstein & Berkowitz, 1981, p. 716)

Competence

Imagine trying the following observational exercise: For one day you pretend to be a visitor from another world. You know nothing at all about humans, so you watch them to find out what they are like. One of the most obvious things that you notice, the most accurate description of the humans you saw, would be that they are almost always *doing* something. Except for periods of sleep, and excluding a few abnormal cases of coma or catatonia, people spend nearly all their time *behaving*. They handle machinery, jog around tracks. fly airplanes, ski, scratch their noses, doodle, and tap their feet. What inspires all this activity? Some behaviors clearly serve basic biological needs; hunger, for example, provides the motivation for moving the forkful of spaghetti from the plate to the mouth. But even when all of the basic needs are satisfied, people still talk, drive autos, work crossword puzzles, and do many other things.

This incessant activity has led a number of psychologists to argue that humans *need* to behave. We saw earlier that people need to exercise their information-processing abilities; we now turn to the related notion that they need to exercise their ability to behave. Woodworth (1958), for example, believed that the great variety of behavior that seems to be completely incidental to any primary needs (such as doodling in a notebook) cannot be adequately explained by the theories of secondary motivation reviewed at the beginning of this chapter. He hypothesized that the need to deal with the environment is itself a primary drive. Similarly, Goldstein (1939) gave self-actualization the status of a **primary drive.** His hypothesis, not unlike Woodworth's, was that humans have a basic tendency to actualize or bring into

Efficacy is the feeling that you have when you do something perfectly, whether it be mastering a new skill, conducting an orchestra, or playing a game well. The urge to manipulate the environment and make effective use of your abilities is called effectance motivation.

being their inherent abilities, to do things merely because they are capable of doing them.

After reviewing these and other ideas, White (1959) suggested that people are motivated to develop and exercise **competence** in interacting with their environment. According to this hypothesis, interacting effectively with the environment produces feelings of competence or efficacy. The feeling that you have when you do something perfectly, whether it be making a basketball swish through the net, completing a difficult crossword puzzle, or knitting a row of even stitches in a sweater, are examples of feelings of efficacy. This urge to manipulate the environment, to make effective use of capabilities, was termed **effectance motivation.** Some of White's most interesting examples concerned the play of children. Although dropping a cookie from a highchair might teach a toddler about gravity, and this knowledge might prove useful later in life, White believed that the child is motivated by the desire to create an effect on the environment. He argued that because we need to interact effectively with the environment, effective interaction can be its own reward.

Harter (1978) has proposed a revision of White's model that includes a three-stage analysis of the development of effectance motivation (see Figure 11–3). In infancy, the effectance motive is thought to be an inherent, biologically based striving to affect the environment. Striking at a rattle, pulling on a string, or biting on a squeaky toy are some examples of this kind of behavior. These sorts of things will happen naturally; they do not require any urging from parents. As children grow older, however, they begin to imitate the behavior of other people and to choose behaviors that are shaped by the reinforcements that others give for particular kinds of mastery attempts. As children are given chemistry sets or books and are reinforced for using them, or as they see friends and family members engaged in sports, the arenas in which they express effectance motivation are shaped. The third stage emerges as people internalize values and begin to reward themselves or set goals for themselves based on their own acquired values. As you can see, this theory emphasizes the influences of learning on effectance motivation and the ways in which it is expressed.

Bandura (1977) has proposed a theory of **self-efficacy** that focuses on expectations of efficacy rather than feelings of efficacy. According to this theory, the decision about whether or not to try a particular behavior depends on the person's belief that he or she will be successful. For example, your decision about trying the crossword puzzle in the Sunday newspaper depends on your belief about your ability to complete the puzzle. Expectations of efficacy will also affect how long a person persists at an activity. For instance, once you begin a crossword puzzle, how long you continue to work on it will depend on your beliefs about your ability to finish it. If you decide that it is too hard for you, you will probably quit after a short time. But if you think that you have a good chance of completing it, you might work on it all morning.

FIGURE 11–3 HARTER'S THREE STAGES OF EFFECTANCE MOTIVATION

1. Infancy	Innate desire to affect the environment
2. Early childhood	Imitation of the effective behaviors of others
3. Adolescence and adulthood	Internalized social values channel innate effectance desires through socially approved outlets

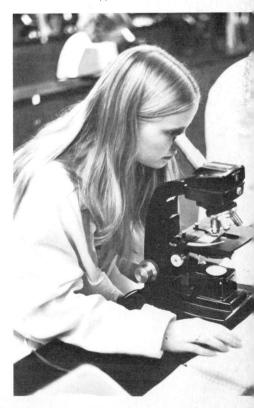

There are four sources of efficacy expectations. One is *past performance accomplishments*. If you have solved a number of crossword puzzles in the past, your expectations will be high. If you have not had much success in the past, your expectations will be low. Expectations are also affected by *vicarious experience*. Seeing other people succeed or fail will influence your own expectations of success. If your roommate solves a lot of crossword puzzles, and you think your verbal skills are equally good, you will be tempted to try one. Another source of expectations comes from *verbal persuasion*. Pep talks from friends or teachers can encourage you to try tasks that you might otherwise avoid. Finally, *emotional arousal* influences efficacy expectations. If thinking about an activity causes nervousness or fear, you will be less likely to think that you can succeed at it.

NEGATIVE EFFECTS OF LOSS OF COMPETENCE. As you can see, competence is a fundamental aspect of human nature. This becomes dramatically apparent when people are deprived of their feelings of competence. Seligman (1975) has shown in a number of studies what happens when people are put through experiences in which they are unable to control their environment. Such experiences lead them to become depressed at the time and to become passive and unresponsive in later settings in which they do have control (Miller & Seligman, 1975; Roth & Kubal, 1975; see Chapters 15 and 16 for a further discussion of loss of control). The more that people expect to have control, the more adversely they are affected by experiences in which they have no control (Pittman & Pittman, 1979). This kind of evidence underscores the vital importance of feelings of competence and efficacy.

TWO SOURCES OF COMPETENCE MOTIVATION—INTRINSIC AND EXTRINSIC. As we have seen, much of an infant's behavior appears to be directed toward producing an effect on the environment. This behavior might seem to be a fairly pure example of effectance motivation. But as a person grows older and becomes socialized, the reasons for a given behavior become more complicated. We might do some things for the pure satisfaction of doing them; many games and other forms of entertainment probably serve this function. But other activities are done with an eye toward gaining something else. We may wash the family car on a Saturday morning motivated more by the thought of next week's allowance than by the sheer joy of seeing a clean automobile. These two kinds of reasons for behaving are called **intrinsic** and **extrinsic motivation** (Pittman, Boggiano, & Ruble, 1982). When we act from intrinsic motivation, we do things because they are fun, or are ends in themselves. When we act from extrinsic motivation, we do things in order to get something else, as a means to an end (Kruglanski, 1975). For many people, these two kinds of motives represent the basic difference between their approaches to play and work.

These definitions of intrinsic and extrinsic motivation imply that activities that lead to other rewards (such as money or candy or other valued possessions) are extrinsically motivated. A clear demonstration of the truth of this idea was provided by Lepper, Greene, and Nisbett (1973). In their study, nursery-school children who liked to draw for the sheer fun of it were asked to draw some pictures under one of three sets of circumstances. Some of the children were told that they would win an attractive Good Player Award if they drew some pictures. This should have encouraged them to think of drawing as an extrinsically motivated activity ("I did it for the reward"). Other children did not find out about the reward until after they had finished drawing. Those

Efficacy expectations are affected by vicarious experience. For example, if your friends are good players of PacMan, you will probably be influenced to try your skills at the game too.

children would not have been thinking of the reward as they drew pictures, so they should have continued to think of drawing as intrinsically motivated ("I did it because I like to draw"). The third group of children simply drew the pictures and were never told about any reward. When all the children were observed during free play periods 2 weeks later, the children who had drawn in order to get the reward were much less interested in drawing as a leisure activity than were the children from the other two groups.

This study shows that the addition of reward to an initially interesting activity causes a shift from an intrinsic to an extrinsic motivational orientation. Once this shift in orientation occurs, we tend to think of the activity (in this case, drawing) as being more like work than play, and therefore we are less likely to choose the activity as something to do in our free time. Shifting to an extrinsic orientation can mean that competence motivation becomes a less important influence, and this in turn leads to decreased creativity (Amabile, 1979) and a preference for the least challenging versions of an activity (Pittman, Emery, & Boggiano, 1982).

Achievement

The need for **achievement** involves competence needs that include the desire to excel, to complete difficult tasks, to meet high standards, and to outperform others. People differ, of course, in the extent to which they express competence motivation in these ways. Those who have a great need for achievement, called high-need achievers, differ from low-need achievers in a number of ways. For example, they tend to do better on problem-solving tasks (French & Thomas, 1958) and show better performance and more rapid improvement on verbal problems (Lowell, 1952). They also tend to set realistic but challenging goals for themselves. (See Chapter 15 for a discussion of a related personality distinction, the Type-A and Type-B behavior pattern.) McClelland (1958) showed this with 5-year-old children who played a game in which they tried to toss rings onto a peg standing on the floor. They were allowed to stand as far away from the peg as they liked. McClelland found that the children who had a high need for achievement typically chose to stand at an intermediate distance from the peg, neither so close that the game was very simple, nor so far away that it was almost impossible. Children who had a low need for achievement did just the opposite. Either they stood so close that they were assured of some success, or they stood unrealistically far away. The same findings have been obtained with college students who played the ring-toss game (Atkinson & Litwin, 1960).

How do children come to have high or low achievement needs? Parental attitudes and child-rearing practices appear to play an important role in the development of achievement motivation. Winterbottom (1953) interviewed the mothers of 8- to 10-year-old boys and found that boys who scored high in achievement motivation had mothers who were more likely to encourage early independence and to reward successful performance with physical affection (such as hugging) than were mothers of boys whose achievement motivation was low. Rosen and D'Andrade (1959) gave young boys a difficult and frustrating task to perform while their parents watched. The watching mothers of boys who scored high in achievement need were more encouraging and supportive than the mothers of low-achievement boys. Fathers of low-achievement boys were most likely to interfere and become irritated when their sons were having difficulty with the task. In general, parents who reward and encourage independent achievement are more likely to have sons who are high in achievement motivation.

ATKINSON'S THEORY OF ACHIEVEMENT MOTIVATION. What determines a person's achievement orientation toward a specific task? Atkinson and Feather (1966) theorized that orientation results from 2 separate motives: to achieve success, and to avoid failure. The motive to achieve success is determined by 3 things: (1) the need to succeed, or need achievement (nAch); (2) the person's estimate of the likelihood of success in performing the particular task; and (3) the incentive for success—that is, how much the person wants to succeed in that particular task. The motive to avoid failure is determined by three similar considerations: (1) the need to avoid failure, which, like the need to achieve success, varies among individuals; (2) the person's estimate of the likelihood of failure at the particular task; and (3) the incentive value of failure at that task, that is, how unpleasant it would be to fail. The relative strengths of the motives to succeed and to avoid failure determine the level of task difficulty people will prefer. When the motive to succeed is stronger, as it is for people who have a high need to achieve, the preferred tasks are those intermediate in difficulty, in which the likelihood of success is reasonable and the pride in accomplishment fairly high. When the motive to avoid failure is dominant, however, people either prefer very simple tasks in which the probability of failure is low, or very difficult tasks where the shame in failing is low. As we have already seen, high and low achievers have shown this pattern of preferences in risk-taking studies. Atkinson has recently expanded this theory to take account of changes in achievement behavior over time (Atkinson & Birch, 1970; Atkinson, 1979). One such change is that people progressively choose more and more difficult tasks (Kuhl & Blankenship, 1979). (See Chapter 18 for an account of another approach to achievement motivation, Weiner's [1971] attribution analysis.)

With such a wide range of needs, can we predict what people will do in a specific setting at a specific time? Unless we have some way of knowing when particular needs are actively influencing current behavior and when they are not, we will have a difficult time figuring out which of the many possible needs are the important or dominant ones at any moment. These kinds of problems have been addressed by psychologists who study motivation in the workplace.

Motivation in the Workplace

What motivates people in their jobs? What need or needs are fulfilled or frustrated in the workplace? As we have seen in this selective review of some prominent needs, human motivation is complex and varied. Organizational psychologists interested in work motivation and job satisfaction have developed a number of theories of work motivation. Each has implications for establishing working conditions to enhance both productivity and human satisfaction.

Schein (1980) has identified three major theoretical approaches to work motivation. The *rational-economic* approach assumes that workers are primarily motivated by economic incentives and that the principles of learning through reinforcement discussed in Chapter 6 are the main determinants of workers' behavior. If workers are primarily motivated by the need to satisfy basic needs, such as the need for food, clothing, and shelter, then specific worker behaviors can be controlled through the application of appropriate rewards. One technique this approach suggests is the use of pay incentives for desired quantity or quality of productivity.

The *social* approach, while recognizing that incentives do have some importance, focuses mainly on the social needs that may be fulfilled in the work environment. People need to affiliate, as we have seen, for self-evaluation, social interaction, and acceptance. To fulfill these needs, people must be able to form social groups and have opportunity for social interaction. Changes in the work environment that ignore or disrupt the fulfillment of social needs can reduce productivity and job satisfaction (Roethlisberger & Dickson, 1939; Schrank, 1978). This approach emphasizes that work motivation can be enhanced in an environment that fosters the formation of work groups so that affiliative needs can be met. Ouchi and Jaeger (1978) report that attention to the social needs of workers is characteristic of Japanese organizations, which have high productivity and quality products.

The **self-actualization** approach focuses on fulfilling curiosity, competence, and achievement needs. We have seen that people need to be stimulated, to feel effective, and to have opportunities to improve and to advance. Whether or not these needs will be fulfilled for a given individual depends on the nature of the work that person does. Boring, repetitive tasks clearly will not satisfy self-actualization needs. This approach asserts that job enrichment can increase worker motivation and satisfaction (Ford, 1973; Robey, 1974) and, therefore, improve productivity. Job enrichment can be accomplished by making work tasks varied instead of repetitive, by allowing workers to participate in setting goals, and by making opportunities for advancement available. In this way, feelings of personal growth can be encouraged.

Each of these three approaches has been used with some success to improve job performance and satisfaction, but no single approach by itself will increase motivation for all workers in all work environments. *All* human needs are important, and programs focused at one need may fail if the workers are unfulfilled in other areas. This points to a general problem with using our knowledge about human motivation. At a particular time, in a particular situation, for a particular person, how can we predict which of the rather sizeable set of human needs will be most important? One potential answer to this question that has been influential in psychology in general and in organizational psychology in particular is Maslow's (1954, 1970) concept of a need hierarchy, the idea that some needs come first and must be satisfied before other needs gain attention.

MASLOW'S HIERARCHY OF NEEDS. Imagine that you are swimming underwater and you accidentally come up under a large raft where there is no air. As you struggle to reach open water before your lungs burst, do you wonder about what you will have for dinner that evening? Or suppose you are on a summer camping trip in a national forest, become separated from your companions, and it is now 5 days since you last ate. You are tired, cold, and you keep hearing noises at night that sound like bears and wolves. Do you think you would be most concerned about food, about safety, or about a need for achievement? Finally, try this more pleasant scene: You have just finished an excellent meal of all your favorite foods and you feel very satisfied, but not stuffed. You are rested, feel somewhat energetic but relaxed, and have no commitments. You can do whatever you like. What would you do? Your answer may reveal something about yourself; it will also reveal something about the nature of needs. In the first two examples, needs for air, food, and safety become paramount when a deficit exists. The third example illustrates

FIGURE 11–4
Maslow's hierarchy of needs.

that once a need is satisfied, it is a much less demanding motive. Whether a particular need will motivate behavior seems to depend on two things: (1) whether that need has been satisfied recently, and (2) how strong other, more fundamental needs may be. For example, no matter how hungry we are, the need to breathe will take precedence over the need to eat. This idea—that some needs come first and must be satisfied before other needs gain attention—is basic to Maslow's theory.

Maslow (1970) believed that there are five categories of needs and that these categories form a sequence or **hierarchy of needs** (see Figure 11–4). For a particular need to guide the person, all the more basic needs must be satisfied first. The most basic needs are *physiological;* these must be met if we are to survive, and they include oxygen, food, water, shelter, and sex (although not necessary to the survival of the individual, sex is essential to the survival of the species). When basic physiological needs are satisfied, then and only then do needs higher in the hierarchy become dominant. *Safety* needs form the next category. Again, these needs are often routinely satisfied, but they can become preoccupations if we live in a high-crime neighborhood or near a defective nuclear power plant, or have a hazardous job. Next come needs for *love and belongingness,* the affiliative needs. Maslow believed that people need to give and receive affection; they also need to feel that they belong to a group or a society. The need to belong has become increasingly difficult to satisfy as society becomes more mobile. Changing homes, jobs, and schools may frustrate an individual's need to belong. Maslow thought that the growth of encounter groups in the 1960s could be attributed to widespread frustration of this need. Once the needs for love and belongingness are satisfied, then needs for *esteem* can arise. These include the desire to think highly of yourself (**self-esteem**) and to have others think highly of you. We need to respect ourselves and to have others respect us. Esteem is what makes us feel confident and worthy; without it we feel inferior and worthless.

You might think that someone who has no worries about food, clothing, or safety, who feels loved and accepted by others, and who commands respect from others and has high self-esteem would be very content. Maslow, however, found such people to be tense and restless, because when all the other needs are satisfied, the need for *self-actualization* becomes dominant. Self-actualization is the realization of our potential, the exercise of our talents to the fullest. A person with musical talents needs to make music; someone with a logical, inquisitive mind devoted to science needs to be a scientist. Most of us do not reach the self-actualization level because most of us never fully satisfy our needs for love and esteem. Those who do become self-actualizers seem to have certain characteristics and talents that set them apart, as we will see in Chapter 14.

Maslow's ideas have been particularly influential for organizational psychologists who have a self-actualization perspective (e.g., McGregor, 1960; Argyris, 1964). However, the research support for the need hierarchy concept is weak at best (Wahba & Bridewell, 1976). There are two problems with the specific assumptions of Maslow's theory: (1) an individual's needs do not always follow the hierarchical order (for example, a person might be guided by esteem needs even though belongingness needs were met); and (2) different needs come to the fore as time on a job increases (see Figure 11–5). Although some of the specifics of Maslow's theory have had to be modified in practice, the general strategy of distinguishing need categories, determining which are most paramount, and making appropriate changes in the work environment has proven to be useful in increasing work motivation.

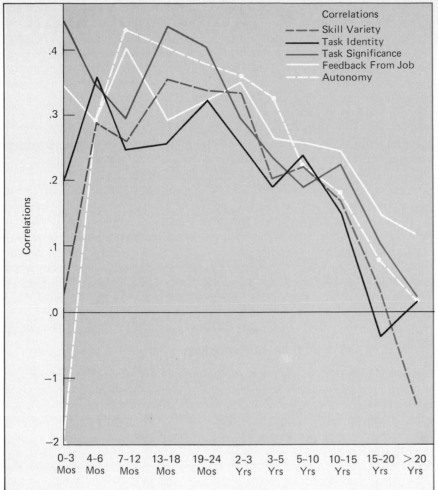

FIGURE 11–5
Correlations between job satisfaction and the five task dimensions for different job-longevity periods. (Katz, 1978)

EMOTION

As we mentioned at the beginning of the chapter, motivation and emotion are very closely intertwined. We usually consider hunger, thirst, and sex to be needs or drives; typical emotions are anger, grief, joy, surprise, and embarrassment. But what about pain? A painful stimulus produces both an emotional response and a drive to escape the pain. In the same way, fear is an emotion but also a motivator—for example, the rats that received electric shocks in the white cage (see page 324) presumably became afraid when they were put into that cage again and were motivated to escape. So an unpleasant emotion can serve as a motivator—the organism is motivated to terminate that feeling.

Drives and needs can produce emotions, too. Consider the example of the person swimming underwater who comes up under a raft. The need for air will produce not only a struggle to reach the edge of the raft, but also intense fear. Extreme hunger or thirst is also likely to result in emotional responses such as grief, anger, or fear. Another source of strong emotional responses is the frustration of the sexual or parental drive.

As these examples indicate, there is sometimes no clear-cut separation between motivation and emotion. Generally, though, we can think of motivation as arising from some internal source such as deprivation of a biological requirement (food, for instance), and of producing some sort of goal-directed behavior (such as searching for food). On the other hand, we can think of **emotion** as being an internal state usually produced by an external stimulus (or stimuli) and not necessarily leading to any particular behavior. In fact, a given emotion can result in many different sorts of behavior, even within the same individual. When a specific emotion is accompanied by specific behaviors, either as a result of predisposition or of learning, then motivation and emotion form a coherent unit. In other cases, though, they act as independent action tendencies and states of being.

Emotion is an extremely difficult subject to study. It is especially hard to study under controlled laboratory conditions, because it is not always possible to produce a genuine emotion in the laboratory or even to know for sure when we have succeeded in producing it. Some behavioral and physiological indications can tell us when a person is fearful or angry, but it is often difficult to tell—except by the person's verbal reports—whether he or she is happy, sad, amused, embarrassed, disgusted, envious, puzzled, worried, relieved, or in love. Thus, these more subtle emotions have been the subject of relatively little research.

Indications of Emotional Responses

You probably know at any given moment whether you are experiencing an emotion, and what the emotion is. It is a lot harder to determine the emotions of *other* people. Some people hide their emotions so well that others never know what they are feeling. And some convincingly feign emotions, or pretend to feel them more strongly than they really do.

How do we judge the emotional state of another individual? There are several kinds of cues on which we usually rely: situational factors, facial expression, verbal report, motor responses, and physiological responses.

SITUATIONAL FACTORS.   You can imagine how someone who has just been told that she won the state lottery feels. Similarly, you can guess the emotions of a person after he has been informed of his mother's death, or after he has slipped on the ice and fallen heavily on his knees. We know how *we* would feel in these situations, and we assume that the other person feels the same way. In addition, we often assume—with less justification—that we know the emotional state of *animals* on the same basis. For example, we might guess that a horse being whipped feels anger or fear, even if there are no outward signs of these emotions.

FACIAL EXPRESSION.   In 1872 Charles Darwin published a book entitled *The Expression of the Emotions in Man and Animals*. In it he described in minute detail the facial expressions of emotion in humans and animals—even naming the particular muscles that come into play in each instance. The principles that Darwin wished to establish were that facial expressions of emotions in humans are innate, not learned; that they are universal in all races of humanity; and that they have their origins in the facial expressions of animals. He pointed out that a human snarl of anger closely resembles the teeth-baring grimace of angry dogs and cats. Young chimpanzees, when tickled under the arms, make a response that looks and sounds very much like human laughter.

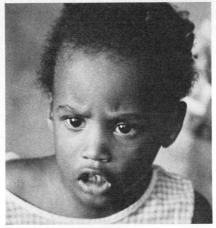
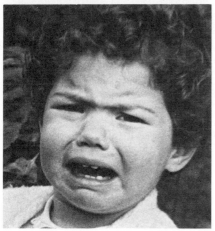

Darwin was the first to observe that facial expression of emotion is innate, is universal, and has its origins in the facial expressions of animals.

Darwin's observations were so thorough and so careful that even today we have little to add to them. We still believe that facial expressions of emotions are not learned. Children blind from birth, who have never even seen a smile or a frown on another person's face, are nonetheless able to smile or frown as well as children with normal vision. The universality of facial expressions has also been confirmed. Ekman and Friesen (1968) photographed people portraying various emotions such as grief, happiness, fear, surprise, and disgust. They showed these photographs to subjects in the United States, Brazil, Chile, Japan, and Borneo. All the subjects tended to identify the same faces with the same emotions.

In another experiment Ekman and Friesen (1971) showed their pictures to the Fore of New Guinea, a people who had had little or no contact with Western or Eastern literate cultures. With the aid of a translator the experimenters read a simple story to the subjects—for example, "She is just now looking at something which smells bad"—and asked the subject to pick which of three faces best agreed with the story. The Fore subjects picked the "correct" picture almost all the time; the main exception was that fear and surprise proved hard to tell apart. Ekman and Friesen also had some Fore subjects feign various emotions. Photos of these portrayed emotions were correctly identified by college students in the United States.

It is important to distinguish between *facial* expressions of emotions—

which are unlearned and universal—and *gestures*—which are culturally determined. Morris, Collett, Marsh, and O'Shaughnessy (1979) made an extensive survey of hand and head gestures in many parts of the world. They reported that a given gesture might mean one thing in one place and something quite different somewhere else. For instance, the "thumb up" sign means either "everything's okay" or "hitching a ride" in most countries studied. But in parts of Greece and Sardinia it is unwise to try to hitch a lift with an upraised thumb. There it is an insult, equivalent to the raised third finger in the United States!

VERBAL REPORT.   The easiest way to find out what a person is feeling is by asking. When someone says "I'm delighted" or "Ugh, that's disgusting," that person is presumably giving us a description of some internal state that otherwise we might have no way of determining.

People learn to make these statements about private aspects of their consciousness in two ways. From childhood, we use given words or labels that help us identify the emotions we feel. For example, parents judge a child's emotion by the situation (did she just fall down? did someone take her toy away?) and by the child's facial expression. The parent then says to the child, "You're sad, aren't you," or "Don't be angry." The child learns to associate the words "sad" and "angry" with a particular internal state. Of course, there is no way of knowing whether that child is *really* sad or angry, or whether her anger or grief feels the same as yours!

The other way we learn to talk about our emotions is by *metaphor*. We often hear and use terms that liken inner feelings to some objective event in the outside world: "I was crushed," "He suffered a stab of regret," "I'm walking on air."

MOTOR RESPONSES.   There are three kinds of motor behavior that result from emotion. The first are postural—a happy person stands and walks erect, a sad person slumps, and an angry or fearful one assumes a tense position.

The startle pattern: The head moves forward, the mouth is open, the muscles of the neck stand out, and the arms and legs jerk.

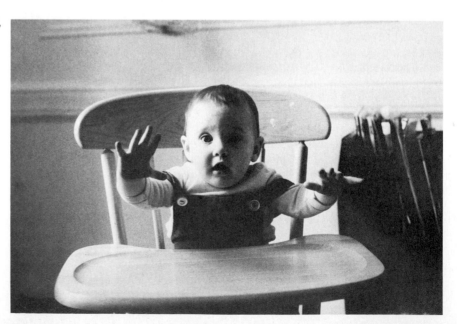

The second is a rapid, automatic motor response. A sudden loud noise or any intense and unexpected stimulus produces a predictable pattern of involuntary actions called the *startle pattern:* The head moves forward, the eyes blink and the mouth may open, the muscles of the neck stand out, and the arms and legs may jerk.

Third are voluntary behavioral actions. People express their feelings by clapping or "jumping for joy," or by running away from something they are afraid of. The most interesting and complex of these behavioral indications are those that result from anger, which were discussed in the section on aggression in Chapter 10.

INTERNAL PHYSIOLOGICAL RESPONSES.   Perhaps the most important characteristic of an emotional response is its physiological component. Many—perhaps all—emotions are associated with some change in the body's condition. The most clear-cut and well-known changes are those that accompany the feeling of fear. Everyone has experienced fear. When you've narrowly escaped an automobile accident, when you think you hear someone breaking into your home, even when you are called upon to answer a difficult question in front of a large audience, you've probably noticed your heart pounding, your knees shaking, your palms sweating, or your mouth feeling dry.

The bodily reactions to a fearful stimulus result from the action of the sympathetic nervous system and from the effects of the hormone *epinephrine* (popularly known as *adrenaline*) secreted by the adrenal glands. These reactions occur:

1. The rate and depth of breathing increase.
2. There is an increase in heart rate and in the amount of blood pumped out with each beat.
3. Blood pressure goes up.
4. Less blood goes to the internal organs, more to the muscles.
5. The liver releases extra blood sugar to supply energy.
6. Production of saliva in the mouth, and of mucus in the respiratory passages, decreases.
7. The pupils of the eyes dilate, letting in more light.
8. The galvanic skin response or GSR (changes in the electrical resistance of the skin) goes up. The GSR is related in a complex way to the functioning of the sweat glands in the skin.

The fact that many of these changes are quite easy to measure provides the basis for the ordinary lie detector, or **polygraph.** This device generally measures heart rate, breathing rate, blood pressure, and GSR. The idea behind the polygraph, as with the voice-stress analyzer, is that most people cannot tell a lie without feeling at least a little uncomfortable—consciously or unconsciously—and this discomfort is often reflected by a change in one or more of the measured functions. These changes must be compared with the baseline measurements obtained when neutral questions (such as "what's your name?") are asked.

One trouble with the polygraph—and this is a problem with the voice-stress analyzer, too—is that some people *don't* get anxious when they tell a lie, and others get anxious under questioning even when they're not telling one. In addition, it may be somewhat easier to produce a false outcome on the polygraph, simply because it is possible to voluntarily increase some or all of the measurements—by breathing faster, tensing one's body, or thinking

Human beings have both innate and learned emotional responses.

about something emotionally arousing. If a person understands the principles underlying polygraph testing and uses these methods when neutral questions are asked, the baseline is raised, and it is often impossible to tell when a lie has actually been told.

Many of the bodily changes that occur with fear also accompany anger, but there are some physiological differences between the two emotions (Ax, 1953). Epinephrine is secreted with anger as well as with fear, but anger involves an additional adrenal hormone, *norepinephrine* (see Chapter 2). Norepinephrine also increases blood pressure, but it does so not by increasing heart rate but by constricting the blood vessels that supply the muscles. In fact, injections of norepinephrine *slow* the heart.

Attempts to differentiate other emotions on the basis of different physiological responses have been less successful. Averill (1969) had one group of subjects watch a sad movie, while another group watched a funny movie. The resulting differences in bodily responses were not statistically significant. In fact, it is likely that a given individual produces a characteristic pattern of physiological responses to almost *any* form of emotional arousal. The physiological reactions of a given subject to different sources of stress are quite similar; the reactions of different subjects to the *same* stimulus are quite different (Lacey & Lacey, 1958). For these reasons, various physiological changes are considered to be associated with emotional change in general, but they cannot be used as reliable indicators of particular kinds of emotion (Grings & Dawson, 1978).

What Produces an Emotional Response?

INNATE VS. LEARNED EMOTIONS.   Human beings, as well as animals, have a number of built-in emotional responses. For example, any sudden intense stimulus is likely to evoke the startle pattern and the emotion of fear. Restraint of motion or the sudden withdrawal of a proffered reward generally leads to anger. An infant's smile elicits feelings of love and delight from its parents. The death of a close relative usually results in grief. Human babies just beginning to crawl are afraid to cross from a table onto a pane of glass 3 or 4 feet above the floor—a device called the **visual cliff,** which will be discussed in Chapter 12.

Other stimuli produce emotional reactions that are clearly acquired through experience. If we administer an electric shock to a rat each time we sound a buzzer, the rat begins to act afraid whenever the buzzer goes on. Rats that became ill after eating a certain food reacted with apparent disgust when offered that food at a later time—they scooped it out of the food dish with their paws and scattered it on the floor of the cage. The delight that some people feel when they listen to a Mozart concerto or when they hear the bell of the ice-cream wagon are other examples of acquired, or secondary, emotional responses.

In one of the most famous—or infamous!—psychological experiments ever conducted, the behaviorist J. B. Watson taught an 11-month-old baby named Albert to be afraid of white rats (Watson & Rayner, 1920). When Albert was first shown a white rat he was not at all afraid of it. Then the experimenters made a loud noise behind the child each time the rat was presented to him. The noise startled Albert and made him cry. After this happened a few times Albert started to cry whenever he saw the rat. In addition, he became afraid of other furry things: a white toy rabbit, a Santa Claus beard.

A great deal of time and effort has gone into attempts to determine whether the human emotional response to a certain stimulus is a primary (innate) or a secondary (learned or acquired) response. For example, is the fear of snakes innate or learned? Some psychologists have said "innate" and pointed to the fact that chimpanzees raised in the laboratory are innately afraid of snakes (Hebb, 1946). Others have shown that children under 2 years of age often seem to have no fear of snakes. Neither of these arguments is very persuasive, however: That chimpanzees are innately afraid of snakes doesn't mean that humans are; and that a fear develops after infancy does not mean that it is learned. Indeed, only two stimuli seem to elicit fear in a newborn: a loud noise and a sudden loss of support. Or, rather, these 2 stimuli elicit a generalized excitement response, which is all that the newborn seems to be capable of (Bridges, 1932). During the first 4 or 5 months of life, this generalized excitement becomes differentiated into separate emotions such as anger, fear, and delight. Moreover, certain stimuli—such as an unfamiliar human face—that at first elicit neutral or favorable emotional responses produce fearful reactions in older babies.

PREPAREDNESS.   Martin Seligman (1972) has proposed a new approach to the old problem of innate versus learned emotional responses. He asks why it was so easy to make little Albert become afraid of furry animals. Other experimenters (English, 1929; Bregman, 1934) tried to repeat Watson's experiment using wooden blocks, wooden ducks, or curtains. They were not able to condition fear at all, even after pairing these objects many times with loud noises. Seligman describes an occasion in his own life when he came down with a violent stomach flu a few hours after eating filet mignon with sauce Béarnaise. After that he couldn't stand sauce Béarnaise, although previously it was a favorite of his. But, as he says, "neither the filet mignon, nor the white plates off which I ate the sauce, nor *Tristan und Isolde,* the opera that I listened to [in the time between the meal and the onset of the illness], nor my wife, Kerry, became aversive. Only the sauce Béarnaise did" (Seligman & Hager, 1972, p. 8). Even though Seligman *knew* the sauce was not responsible (because others had eaten it and had not gotten sick, or had gotten sick without eating it), this knowledge did not affect his feelings—what we might call his "gut reaction."

Seligman accounted for his acquired disgust by a concept he called **preparedness:** Organisms are more prepared to associate a given emotional response with one kind of stimulus, and less prepared to associate it with another kind. An experiment by Garcia and Koelling (1966) illustrates this principle. Rats were given water sweetened with saccharin and then made sick by exposure to radiation. Afterward they didn't want to drink saccharin-flavored water. When the sweetened water was paired with a light and a clicking sound, the rats showed no tendency later to avoid either the light or the sound. But when rats were given electric shocks after drinking water, they avoided water associated with the light and sound but didn't object to the saccharin-flavored water. The conclusion is that rats are *prepared* to associate illness with a taste, or electric shock with a visual or auditory stimulus. They are not prepared—or, rather, are *less* prepared—to associate illness with light or sound, or shock with a taste.

Preparedness is not a yes-or-no, all-or-none situation: It is a continuum. Each possible association of a stimulus and an emotional response can be given a position on this continuum by asking: How many pairings of this stimulus with this response are necessary in order to condition the association? On the extreme, "prepared," end of the continuum, the answer may be *none*—some stimuli elicit the emotional response the very first time they are presented. On the "unprepared" end of the continuum, the answer is an infinite number—some emotional responses may *never* become linked to any specific stimulus. In between are all the associations that are more or less easy to condition. Clearly, little Albert's fear of furry animals was an easy association to make, and fear of a wooden block is a relatively hard one.

Theories of Emotion

We have reviewed some of the ways that emotions are expressed and how they can be measured, and we have discussed whether they are learned or innate. But what are emotions and just how do they arise? What is the relationship between physiological changes and emotion? What role does cognitive interpretation play? Are different kinds of emotion connected or related in any way? Theories of emotion have been developed to answer these kinds of questions.

THE JAMES-LANGE THEORY.   If you are walking home in the dark and someone jumps out at you from behind a tree, two things happen. One is that you feel afraid. The other is that your adrenal glands stimulate the sympathetic nervous system (see Chapter 2), your heart starts to pound, and so on. The question is: Which comes first? It may seem obvious to you that first you become afraid and then your body responds to your fear, but this did not seem so obvious to the Harvard psychologist William James or the Danish physiologist Carl Lange. A century ago, these two scientists both came to the same conclusion: that the bodily changes come *first,* and then—as a result of these changes— you become afraid. In James's words:

> Common-sense says, we lose our fortune, are sorry and weep; we meet a bear, are frightened and run; we are angry and strike. . . . [T]he more rational statement is that we feel sorry because we cry, angry because we strike, afraid because we tremble. . . . Without the bodily states following on the perception, the latter would be purely cognitive in form, pale, colorless, destitute of emotional warmth. We might then see the bear and judge it best to run, receive the insult and deem it right to strike, but we should not actually *feel* afraid or angry. (1890, pp. 449–450)

In 1927 the influential physiologist Walter Cannon published an attack on changes that are associated with emotion. He pointed out, first of all, that the bodily changes that are associated with emotional states occur too slowly. When the bear appears, fear is felt immediately, too quickly to be a byproduct of the physiological reactions.

Second, the physiological changes that occur with emotions take place in other situations too, *without* producing the emotions. Many of the same bodily responses that accompany fear—the increases in heart rate, breathing rate, blood pressure, GSR, and so on—can be produced simply by exercising violently. Yet exercise does not have any noteworthy effect on the state of the emotions. These same physiological changes can also be induced artificially, by injections of stimulants, without resulting in a feeling of fear.

Some recent evidence seems to provide some support for the **James-Lange theory.** A psychologist (Hohmann, 1966) interviewed a group of patients who had suffered serious spinal cord injuries and were unable to feel any sensations in the parts of their bodies below the level of the injury. Some of these people had spinal cord injuries at the neck (cervical) level and therefore could not feel anything from the neck down; in others the injury was at the lower part of the spine (sacral); the rest were somewhere in between. These patients were asked how the emotions they felt since their accidents

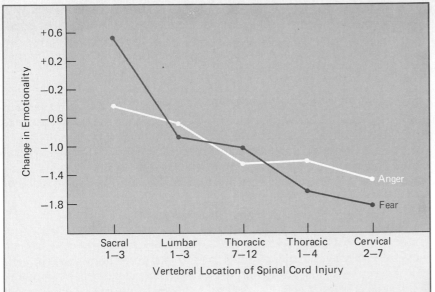

FIGURE 11–6
According to Hohmann's research, the greater the degree of incapacity resulting from spinal injury, the greater the decrease in feelings of fear and anger. Those with sacral injuries (who felt no sensation in their legs) reported only minor changes in emotional feelings, but those with cervical injuries (affecting the entire body) reported a significant decrease in feelings of such emotions as fear and anger. (After Hohmann, 1966)

differed from the emotions they remembered feeling before they were injured. Were they the same as before, or more intense, or less intense? The people with sacral injuries (who felt no sensations in their legs) reported only minor changes in emotional feelings, but the people with cervical injuries (affecting the entire body) reported a decrease in feelings of fear, anger, grief, and sexual drive (see Figure 11–6). Only the emotion that the experimenter labeled "sentiment" was unaffected. The people with intermediate injuries gave mixed reports—some reported decreases in certain emotions, others did not. From these results, Hohmann concluded that in order to experience strong emotions, it is necessary to have some feedback from the body—some indication of the physiological reactions going on. When the sensations produced by these reactions are absent, the emotions may be felt less intensely. If you hear some very sad news and do not cry, you might wonder whether you are really sad, or perhaps whether you really care. Similarly, if you are about to give a speech and you do not feel your heart pounding or "butterflies" in your stomach, you might marvel at how calm you are.

THE CANNON-BARD THEORY.   The theory of emotion that Cannon proposed (1927) and that Bard elaborated (1934) was based on what was known about the brain at that time. Cannon placed the source of emotions in the thalamus, which is located in the center of the brain. According to the **Cannon-Bard theory,** when an emotionally arousing stimulus is perceived, the thalamus sends out impulses to the sympathetic nervous system, which produce the physiological reactions. *At the same time,* the thalamus also sends out impulses to the cerebral cortex, producing the conscious feeling of emotion. This hypothesis implies that the bodily changes and the emotional feelings occur simultaneously.

Modern neurophysiology does not support the association of the thalamus to emotion. It is now believed that the *hypothalamus* and the *limbic system* are the brain parts involved in emotional response. It has, for example, been found that lesions in certain parts of these areas produce permanent changes in emotional behavior in animals: They become passive and unreactive, or they become overactive and fly into a rage with little or no provocation, depending on the location of the brain injury. Neurophysiologists have also investigated the limbic system by implanting electrodes in the brains of animals and giving tiny electric shocks to various areas. Depending on the location of the electrode, the shock may produce fear, rage, passivity, or even pleasure (as we saw in Chapter 2).

ACTIVATION THEORY.   Moruzzi and Magoun (1949) studied the **reticular activating system (RAS),** which consists of pathways in the brain extending from the brain stem upward to the thalamus and the cerebral cortex. Inputs to the RAS come from all the senses except smell. This system controls **arousal:** When an animal's RAS is damaged, it goes into a coma and is unresponsive to stimulation. Drugs such as amphetamines increase RAS activity, while barbiturates depress it.

In a normal individual, the reticular system works "something like a fire alarm that gets people into action but does not really say where the fire is" (Beck, 1983, p. 104). At moderate levels of activity it makes a person alert and attentive; but when incoming stimuli are too intense or numerous, the reticular system produces too much arousal or excitement, and behavior becomes disorganized. This is presumably what happens to people who "lose their heads" in an emergency, or to soldiers who panic under enemy fire. The **activation theory** states that there is some optimal level of emotional arousal—too little produces sleepiness or apathy, too much produces aimless activity and emotional disturbance.

COGNITIVE FACTORS AND THE JUKEBOX THEORY.   This theory is based on an experiment performed by Schachter and Singer (1962); the term **jukebox theory** was coined by Mandler (1962). In Schachter and Singer's experiment, subjects were injected with epinephrine (which, as we know, produces the symptoms of fear: increased blood pressure, heart rate, GSR, and so on). They were told that these injections were a new vitamin compound and that the purpose of the experiment was to study the effects of this compound on visual perception. After the injection each subject was sent into another room to wait, with a second subject, until the compound "took effect." In fact, epinephrine works very quickly, and the 20-minute "waiting period" was really the experiment itself and the "second subject" was really a confederate of the experimenters.

Some subjects had been told the truth about the effects of the injection—that it would produce a slight hand tremor, increased heart rate, and a flushed feeling in the face. Subjects in a second group were misinformed—they were told that the drug would cause numbness in the feet, itching sensations, and a slight headache. A third group of subjects were told nothing at all.

Soon after the real subject entered the waiting room, the confederate began to behave in a bizarre manner. He made paper airplanes and flew them around the room, made a ball of paper and played basketball with a wastepaper basket. He even hula-hooped with a piece of equipment left in the room! During this display of feigned euphoria the confederate invited the real subject to participate in his games.

The experimenters found that the subjects who were *correctly* informed about the effects of the injection behaved normally and did not accept the confederate's invitation to play. But the subjects who were given the wrong information or no information at all often participated in the games, sometimes behaving as foolishly as the confederate. In a variation of the experiment, the confederate feigned anger and aggression instead of euphoria, and again the subjects who were correctly informed about the effects of the epinephrine behaved normally, whereas those who were not informed were affected by the put-on emotion. Thus, the same drug given to different groups of subjects made them happy, made them angry, or had no effect at all on their emotions—depending on their understanding of the situation.

The conclusion drawn from these experiments is that the physiological arousal produced by a drug can set the basis for an emotion, but it is not enough. When subjects *know* what reactions to expect, they correctly interpret their physiological changes as resulting from the injection; when they have no explanation for the effects they are feeling, they interpret these effects in terms of the situation (see Figure 11–7). This is where the name "jukebox" comes in. The injection of the drug—like the coin you drop in a jukebox—starts things going, provides the energy. But the tune played—or the emotion experienced—depends on which button is pushed.

In the years since Schachter and Singer's experiment, a number of similar experiments have been performed. Although some have failed to substantiate the jukebox theory (Maslach, 1979), many have provided support. Some results that are consistent with Schachter and Singer's hypothesis were provided by an experiment in which physiological arousal was induced in some subjects by having them view a sex movie (Zillman, 1971). When the subjects later had a chance to express anger toward a person who had insulted them, the ones who had seen the sex movie were more aggressive than those who hadn't. Even physiological arousal produced by fast pedaling on an exercise bicycle has, under some conditions, produced an enhanced emotional response (Cantor, Zillman, & Bryant, 1975).

Note the contrast between this situation, in which physiological arousal appears to produce emotional arousal, and the situation we examined earlier, that people with severed spinal cords are likely to feel emotions less strongly than before they were injured (Hohmann, 1966). It seems, then, that emotion-producing stimuli affect us in two ways: First, we have a cognitive awareness of the meaning of the stimuli, and second, we make a variety of physiological responses. In order for emotion to be deeply felt, the physiological responses must occur and must be perceived. But the nature of these responses is rather vague and generalized, and signs of physiological arousal can be attributed to several different emotions. The emotion to which they *are* attributed is the emotion that is appropriate to the person's cognitive awareness of the situation.

THE OPPONENT-PROCESS THEORY.   The last theory of emotion we will discuss is compatible with any of the previous theories, because it does not attempt to specify where emotion comes from or what it consists of. This theory, instead, is designed to explain the motivation behind such potentially self-destructive human behaviors as thrill-seeking, masochism, and addiction.

The **opponent-process theory** (Solomon, 1980; Solomon & Corbit, 1973, 1974) begins with several assumptions about emotional states:

1. Whenever a stimulus causes an emotional response, it also causes another emotional response that is opposite to, or the opponent of, the initial response. Thus if the sight of a bear causes the emotion of fear (state A), it will also activate the opponent emotion, which in this case might be relief (state B).
2. The opponent process (state B) is aroused more slowly, and decays more

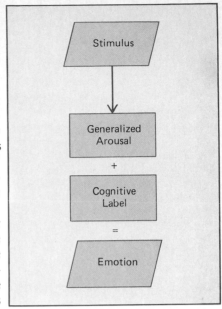

FIGURE 11–7
Schachter's jukebox theory of emotion.

APPLICATION□

Opponent-Process Theory and Addiction

One interesting, important, and sometimes puzzling aspect of human motivation is our ability to become addicted to things that we know are not good for us. Such addictions can be extremely debilitating; heroin addiction and alcoholism are all too common examples. Other addictions are not so clearly dangerous, but are definitely bad for our health; cigarette smoking is one of these dangerous but widespread addictions. One interesting approach to understanding why people become addicted, and why "kicking the habit" is so difficult, is provided by Solomon and Corbit's (1973) application of opponent-process theory to addiction.

Opponent-process theory (see text) assumes that every emotional state (state A) has an opponent emotional state (state B). For positive A states, the associated B states are negative or unpleasant. When an addictive substance is taken, a positive A state is created; examples include the "highs" obtained with alcohol or heroin, and the pleasure associated with inhaling cigarette smoke. Once the pleasant A state is aroused, the opponent process also begins to be aroused, taking the edge off the pleasant experience. Initially, the A state is strong and very pleasant, while the B state is weak and slow to occur. With repeated usage, however, the B state

is strengthened. Experienced users have mild highs but very intense lows following drug use. Originally, addictive substances are taken because of the pleasant effects they produce. After repeated use, however, they are taken to get rid of or avoid the very unpleasant opponent process.

You can probably see that this is a trap. The more a drug is used, the stronger and more intense the unpleasant B state becomes. How can a person get rid of the B state? The most effective way is to take the drug again, to fight the B state with its associated pleasant A state. But taking the drug again will strengthen the B process in the long run, causing an even more unpleasant aftereffect and thereby increasing motivation to take the drug again. This is the vicious cycle of addiction. The firmly addicted heroin user or cigarette smoker is primarily motivated to avoid the unpleasant state that occurs after the last dose rather than to enjoy the positive highs originally associated with the substance.

The various opponent processes, or B states, can be positive or negative depending upon the nature of the associated A state, but they also differ in other ways. Some opponent processes are relatively weak, others are relatively intense; some are long-lasting and some are short-lived. Addictive substances lead to B states that are intense and long-lasting. Very long-lasting B states, which are sometimes experienced as a "craving" for the addictive substance, make it extremely difficult to give up the addiction. Cigarette

smokers, alcoholics, and heroin addicts can experience such cravings for years after their last dose of the substance. These long-lasting B states put great demands on self-control and explain why relapses, even after long periods of abstinence, are common.

One way to break an addiction is to quit all at once, or cold turkey. For a firmly addicted person, this method can be extremely unpleasant. Another way to break an addiction is to reduce gradually the amount of the addictive substance taken. For example, a cigarette smokers who uses two packs a day might gradually reduce the amount of one pack, then switch to a low tar and nicotine brand, then continue to cut down to 15, 10, and then 5 cigarettes a day, finally quitting altogether. Presumably, it is easier to abstain from the one cigarette a day, to which one eventually becomes accustomed, than it is to go immediately from two packs a day to total abstinence. From the opponent-process theory point of view, this makes some sense. As the use of the addictive substance decreases, the B state gradually weakens. There is, however, an insidious catch to this procedure. As the B state weakens, the pleasure of the A state increases—each one of those 5 cigarettes that you allow yourself is wonderful! As the positive side of the addiction becomes stronger during gradual reduction of consumption, the *positive* motivation to smoke reasserts itself. In other words, as anyone who has been addicted to anything knows, it is very hard to quit.

slowly, than the initial response (state A). In the example, the emotion of relief will lag behind the emotion of fear when the bear is sighted. Similarly, when the bear goes away the feeling of relief will linger after the feeling of fear has left us.

3. With repeated experience, states A and B slowly change character. For example, with repeated sightings of the bear, fear may change to alert tension, while relief may change to joy. To indicate such changes we could relabel the two states A′ and B′.

4. This implies that with repeated experience the B (or B′) state gets stronger,

but the A (or A′) state does not. In the example, moderate relief (B) turns into strong joy (B′).

These 4 assumptions explain a very common sequence of emotional reactions: When the eliciting stimulus is presented (the bear appears from behind a tree), a very strong emotional response occurs (stark, petrifying fear). As the exposure to the stimulus continues (the bear continues to stand there), the emotion is reduced a bit and remains steady (plain old fear). Solomon and Corbit explain that this reduction occurs because the opponent process (relief), as it is slowly activated, subtracts from and thus reduces state A. When the stimulus is withdrawn (the bear leaves), a very different emotion is experienced. This happens because state A (fear) disappears rapidly when the stimulus is withdrawn, but state B goes away much more slowly. Therefore, when the stimulus is removed, the person experiences state B (relief). This pattern of emotions has repeatedly been found in experiments; it also agrees with many experiences that people report and that we all have had.

The operation of opponent-process theory is clearly illustrated in a recent study of the emotions associated with blood donation. Piliavin, Callero, and Evans (1982) measured the emotions of a large number of blood donors both before and after donation. First-time donors reported feeling uptight, fearful, and jittery (the A state). After donation, they felt carefree, playful, and warmhearted (the B state). The researchers found that the stronger the A state was, the more intensely the B state was experienced after donation, just as the theory would predict. Furthermore, for veteran donors the A state became less intense as the number of prior donations increased (because an increasingly strong B state was subtracted from it). Over time, then, blood donors' emotional reactions appear to be dominated by the pleasant post-donation B state, while the negative predonation A state becomes progressively weaker.

Solomon and Corbit (1974) have made a similar analysis of the thrill-seeking sport of parachute jumping based on Epstein's (1967) reports of the changes in emotions of veteran jumpers. With repeated experience, prejump anxieties (the A state) weaken, and postjump exhilaration (the B state) increases. This pattern of reactions can explain much thrill-seeking behavior. The increasingly pleasant aftereffects, together with the decreasing aversiveness of the initial anxiety reaction, motivate people to keep taking risks.

Masochistic (self-punishing) behavior can be explained in the same way: The person submits to painful or unpleasant abuse in order to experience the positive opponent process afterward. In sexual masochism, for example, the positive B state associated with the cessation of pain apparently enhances the pleasure of orgasm for some people.

Of course, just as unpleasant initial reactions are followed by a positive opponent process, so will pleasant initial reactions be followed by an unpleasant opponent process. This sequence of reactions appears to be involved in various kinds of addictions (see the Application on opponent-process theory and addiction).

The opponent-process theory seems to explain a number of emotional phenomena very well. But why are emotional reactions arranged this way? What is the reason for the existence of opponent processes? According to Solomon and Corbit, opponent processes allow the organism to damp down emotional reactions, to keep them from becoming too strong or too removed from neutral. Since severe emotional reactions can be debilitating and can interfere with new learning (Spence & Spence, 1966), such an emotional cooling-off system appears to have adaptive survival value.

Mood and Memory

Schachter's cognitive theory of emotion explains that what we think can determine how we feel. Recent research by Gordon Bower (1981) shows the converse: that what we *feel* affects what we *think*. When we are in a positive mood, we tend to remember positive things. When we are in a negative mood, we tend to remember negative things. To show how mood affects memory, Bower had his subjects hypnotized and, in one study, put them successively into sad and happy moods by having them imagine appropriate scenes. The subjects then learned lists of words in each mood. Later they were returned to their original mood and asked to recall the words they had learned. As the figure indicates, words that were learned by subjects in a sad mood were best recalled when the subjects were again in a sad mood, while fewer than half of the words learned by subjects in a sad mood could be recalled when those subjects were in a happy mood. Similarly, nearly all words learned by subjects in a happy mood were recalled when those subjects were again in a happy mood, while about half as many words learned in a happy mood were recalled when subjects

were in a sad mood. This phenomenon is called *state-dependent memory*: Memory is best when the mood that is in effect during recall matches the mood that was in effect during learning.

To show how state-dependent memory might affect everyday thought, Bower again used hypnotic induction to produce happy or sad moods and then asked his subjects to describe as many incidents as they could think of from their pre–high-school years. When the incidents recalled were classified into happy and sad categories, a clear state-dependent memory effect emerged: Subjects in a happy mood remembered more happy incidents, but subjects in a sad mood remembered more sad incidents.

The state-dependent-memory effect has been shown with a number of other moods, such as fear, anger, and joy. Emotions appear to serve as organizing points or *nodes* in memory, and pieces of information are associated and stored with related moods. When a mood is activated or experienced, the information associated and stored with that mood becomes more accessible and is therefore readily remembered. You can see how the association of information with moods can intensify an emotion: You become depressed, you then find it easy to recall things that happened when you were de-

pressed in the past, and since those things are likely to be unpleasant, you become even more depressed. The concept of state-dependent memory can also provide the key to remembering information that is difficult to recall: Such material will be more likely to come to mind if we can reconstruct the mood we were in at the time we learned it in the first place.

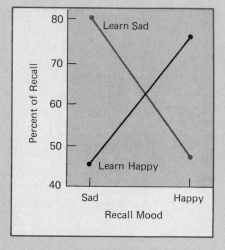

The percentage of learned material that is recalled depends on the match between learning mood and recall mood. The sloping lines represent the recall scores of subjects who learned 2 word lists under different moods. (Adapted from Bower, 1981)

SUMMARY

1. Human *motivation* ranges from basic physiological needs, through needs for stimulation (such as curiosity), to socially based needs.

2. Secondary motivations associated with physiological needs may be acquired through conditioning; these acquired motivations, according to some theorists, can become functionally autonomous.

3. Some prominent human needs are *affiliation, curiosity, competence,* and *achievement.*

4. The optimal level of stimulation theory attempts to explain curiosity motives; stimuli outside the adaptation level allow people to exercise their information-processing abilities and fulfill curiosity needs. Sensory-deprivation studies underscore humans' needs for stimulation.

5. Infants reared in institutions in which they receive food and medical care but little social stimulation show striking deficits in emotional, intellectual, and even physical development.

6. Sexual expression varies among cultures and across time, owing to different learning experiences. Reactions to erotica, for example, may vary according to gender, degree of liberalism or conservatism, and sex guilt.

7. Among the theories of *competence motives* are White's theory of *effectance motivation* and Bandura's theory of *self-efficacy*. Many psychologists believe that loss of competence leads to depression or passivity.

8. *Achievement motives* are related to the desire to excel, to complete difficult tasks, to meet high standards, and to outperform others.

9. Theories based on rational-economic, social, or self-actualization assumptions emphasize different sets of workers' needs. Maslow's hierarchy of needs (physiological, safety, love and belongingness, esteem, and self-actualization) is one of several approaches that attempt to guide the design of the workplace to enhance worker productivity and motivation.

10. The cues we use to judge the emotional state of others include situational factors, facial expression, verbal report, motor responses, and physiological responses.

11. The question of whether emotions are innate or learned is still not absolutely resolved. Seligman's concept of *preparedness* theorizes that organisms may be more prepared to associate a given emotional response with a particular stimulus.

12. The *James-Lange theory* of emotion asserts that bodily changes are experienced first, then emotion; the *Cannon-Bard theory* maintains that bodily changes and emotions occur simultaneously.

13. Modern neurological research focuses on the *limbic system* and the *hypothalamus* as the parts of the brain that play the major role in emotion.

14. The *activation theory* emphasizes the *reticular activation system* (*RAS*) and its effects on arousal, including the idea that there is some optimal level of emotional arousal.

15. According to the *jukebox theory,* physiological arousal provides the basis or energy for emotion, but the emotion experienced depends on cognitive factors.

16. *Opponent-process theory* states that for every emotion, there is a paired opponent or opposite emotion.

Suggested Readings

ATKINSON, J. W., & RAYNOR, J. O. *Personality, motivation, and achievement.* Washington, D.C.: Hemisphere, 1978. This book contains an interesting, updated series of papers representing the "classic" approach to achievement motivation.

IZARD, C. *Emotions in personality and psychopathology.* New York: Plenum Press, 1979. Contains a wide selection of current research on emotions.

LEPPER, M. R., & GREENE, D. (Eds.). *The hidden costs of reward.* Hillsdale, N.J.: Erlbaum, 1978. Much of the research on rewards and intrinsic motivation is covered in this edited volume.

PLINER, P., BLANKSTEIN, K. R., & SPIGEL, I. M. *Perception of emotions in self and others.* New York: Plenum Press, 1979. A variety of perspectives on the cognitive aspects of motivation, reflecting progress made since Schachter's 2-component theory of emotion was introduced.

SCHACHTER, S. *The psychology of affiliation.* Stanford, Calif.: Stanford University Press, 1959. This is a research monograph in which the original studies on affiliation are reported. It is a good example of how a set of studies build upon one another.

SELIGMAN, M. E. P. *Helplessness: On depression, development, and death.* San Francisco: Freeman, 1975. A readable and provocative presentation of the relationship between lack of control and depression.

SOLOMON, R. L. The opponent-process theory of acquired motivation: The costs of pleasure and the benefit of pain. *American Psychologist,* 1980, *35,* 691–712. This is the latest comprehensive statement of the opponent-process theory of acquired motivation.

12. Childhood

The mystery of development—how a fertilized egg becomes a person—has intrigued people from the earliest times. Throughout recorded history there have been two contrasting views of the sources of developmental change: one emphasizing our biological-physical structure, and the other, our experiences.

The extreme form of the biological and structural view emphasizes innate characteristics of people and appeals to **rationalism** as the mechanism for gaining knowledge. René Descartes, the seventeenth-century French philosopher, argued that although the mind arises through interaction with events in the world, it can think and reason innately and without any prior experience or learning. *Reason* was the primary source of all knowledge. In contrast, the **empiricism** of John Locke, the seventeenth-century English philosopher, held that *experience* was the source of all knowledge:

> Let us then suppose the mind to be, as we say, white paper void of all characters, without any ideas—How come it to be furnished: . . . Whence has it all the *materials* of reason and knowledge? To this I answer, in one word, from EXPERIENCE. In that all our knowledge is founded; and from that it ultimately derives itself. Our observation, employed either about external sensible objects, or about the operations of our minds . . . supplies our understanding with all the *materials* of thinking. These two [external perception and internal introspection] are the fountains of knowledge whence all the ideas we have, or can naturally have, do spring. (1690/1973, p. 23)

The controversy continues to this day. One contemporary example is the difference of opinion between the followers of B. F. Skinner on the one hand, and of Noam Chomsky on the other. Skinner (1957) argues that all learning, including language learning, is based on experience. Chomsky (1968) argues that we don't actually learn language—instead we are born with a "language acquisition device" (an innate knowledge of grammar). We use our experience to learn only the superficial aspects of speech, such as the words and sounds of our particular language. The basic structure of language itself, the universal grammar, is wired into the brain (Chomsky, 1975).

Skinner's empiricism and Chomsky's rationalism are extreme and one-sided versions of what must, in fact, be true of all developmental change. Our physical structures and our experiences interact continually to make us what we are. How and when do they do this?

SOURCES OF DEVELOPMENTAL CHANGE

People develop as a result of the joint workings of their genetic and biological endowments and their experiences. Developmental theorists sometimes ignore this critical fact and lean heavily toward one or the other philosophical position, each of which has its counterparts in other aspects of psychology, and in theories of education and social policy as well. Rationalists will weigh the role of instinct more heavily than the role of learning in describing animal behavior. Empiricists will have the opposite bias. In discussions of heredity and nature versus environment and nurture, rationalists lean to the nature side, empiricists to the nurture side. Rationalists thus tend to weigh genetic determinants of behavior quite heavily, while empiricists see the causes of behavior in the past and present environments of organisms.

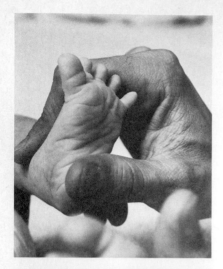

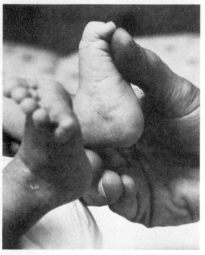

The Babinski reflex is shown here—the immature form in the top photo, the mature form in the bottom photo.

The philosophical orientation of rationalists is generally quite conservative and traditional. If the main source of behavior is innate, then why try to change things by manipulating the environment? For the opposite reason, empiricists tend to believe in social change and social activism. If we are the product of our environments, then we should engineer our environments to improve human nature. We should remember that there are no *necessary* links here. A commited geneticist might quite comfortably believe in socialism and social engineering; a committed learning theorist may well be politically and socially conservative.

In general, though, when political arguments arise over the issue of changing or modifying human conditions—as, for example, over the potential efficacy of Head Start or other early enrichment programs—the debate often hinges on basic beliefs about human nature. Is it pliable and susceptible to change (the basic tenet of empiricism), or is it fixed and determined at birth (as an extreme rationalist would argue)? Neither position is useful to a scientist, however much either position may enhance a political argument. We are interested in how nature and nurture interact to jointly guide development. Change as a function of nature is called maturation; change due to nurture is called experiential change.

Maturation

One way for behavior to change is through the growth and maturation of the nervous and sensorimotor systems. Physical growth and development allow an organism to do something it couldn't do before—for example, when a baby is able to lift its head for the first time. **Maturation** refers to the development of an ability or skill that was made possible by a structural change in the nervous system and in the associated motor and sensory organs. A classic experimental demonstration of maturation was Leonard Carmichael's (1927) study of the development of swimming in the salamander tadpole. When first hatched, salamander tadpoles do not swim; they just float quietly in pond water for about 5 days as they feed on their yolk sac. During this time they have ample opportunity to profit from experience and practice. Is that opportunity necessary? Carmichael took one group of freshly hatched tadpoles and left them in ordinary pond water. He took another group, hatched the same day, and put them in water that contained chloretone—an anesthetic that effectively prevented movement. When the normally treated tadpoles began to swim, he took the anesthetized tads out of their drugged tank and put them into fresh water. Carmichael reasoned that if practice were necessary for swimming to develop, it would take these practice-deprived tads some time to be able to swim. If practice were unnecessary, then they would swim as soon as the drug wore off. In this particular case, it turned out that practice was unnecessary. The drugged tads began to swim normally as soon as the drug effects wore off.

Clear-cut examples of maturation in humans are not so easy to find. One such is the Babinski reflex. When first born, infants flex their toes outward when the sole of the foot is scratched. This reflex changes with the growth of the nervous system so that in babies of 4 to 6 months the toes flex inward, as do the toes of normal adults. If this reflex change fails to develop, or if an adult regresses to the newborn pattern, it is usually a sign of neurological damage. A change in a reflex is not, of course, totally independent of "experience" in its most general sense. After all, the baby must have proper nourishment, oxygen, and other environmental supports in order to develop neurologically. What maturation means, even in this simple case, is that a specific behavior develops with no specific experiential or environmental events, and that this was made possible by physical development. This development did not happen in the total absence of experience or an environment, but rather within a normal range of both.

Human motor development is, in this sense, primarily maturational. Most normal babies will progress through the same sequence of motor skills and abilities—from crawling to walking—whether they are given special practice or not, and whether they are allowed to move freely, as in our culture, or are swaddled and bound softly in cloth (Lipton, Steinschneider, & Richmond, 1965). An experiment by Gesell and Thompson (1929) makes this point rather dramatically. One of a pair of twin boys was given extensive practice climbing stairs. The other was not. When the trained twin acquired skill in this activity, the untrained one was allowed to try it on his own. The advantage of the trained twin over the untrained one lasted only a week or two. Of course, once maturation has taken place, further practice and training can improve skills enormously. There is a world of difference between an ordinary person who can run easily and swiftly and an Olympic-class runner. Part of the trained athlete's superiority is his or her physical structure and condition, and part is technique and style. Physical structure and condition are the maturational components of motor development; the technique and style are the learned components. Even when they walk, children seem to have acquired the style and gait of their mothers and fathers. This component of walking is not maturational; it is learned. Similarly, the ability to handle a knife and fork depends on maturation, but the style (and the particular table manners involved) are learned. The ability to play a piano must mature; whether one can actually play the piano depends on experience.

Experience

Maturational changes occur normally if the experience of the developing organism is within normal ranges. Other developmental changes reflect more directly the particular life experiences of the growing person. Children growing up in Finland learn Finnish, while children growing up in the United States of America learn American English. Just as maturational changes take place against a backdrop of normal environments and experiences, so must learning take place against a backdrop of normal physical growth and development.

This was not always obvious. One of the first recorded experiments in history was reported by the Greek scholar Herodotus. King Psammetchus of Egypt in the 7th century B.C. wanted to demonstrate that Egyptian was the most ancient language in the world. He believed that if children were reared without ever hearing human speech, their first word would be Egyptian! According to Herodotus, he therefore

> contrived the following method of discovery: he took two children of the common sort, and gave them over to a herdsman to bring up at his folds, strictly charging him to let no one utter a word in their presence, but to keep them in a sequestered cottage, and from time to time introduce goats to their apartment, see that they got their fill of milk, and in all other respects look after them. His object herein was to know, after the indistinct babblings of infancy were over, what word they would first articulate. (Herodotus, in Watson, 1968)

Konrad Lorenz as mother surrogate to young geese.

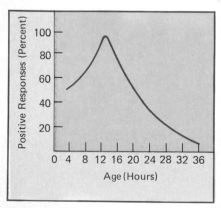

FIGURE 12–1
As shown here, although the critical period for imprinting for ducks lasts from hatching to 36 hours, it is most effective within 13 hours of hatching. (Hess, 1958)

We now know that such an experiment is, in fact, impossible. If children do not hear human speech, they will not utter any words at all, and, as we discussed in Chapter 11, if they are deprived of human interaction and stimulation, they show striking deficits in emotional, intellectual, and physical development (Goldfarb, 1944, 1945; Spitz, 1946). Given normal physical growth, specific kinds of experiences and learning are necessary for most normal human activities, from the development of social attachments to the acquisition of language and reasoning skills.

Critical Periods

There are some types of learning that must take place during a specific time in a developing organism's life. Otherwise, they will not occur at all. The clearest cases can be found in animals other than humans, where experimentation and careful observation are possible. When learning is confined to a specific developmental time, we say that it depends on a **critical period.** Konrad Lorenz, the Austrian ethologist, first discovered such a period in young goslings. Baby geese, as they grow up in their normal world, follow their mother around everywhere, as do baby ducks and other *precocial* birds (birds that can function immediately after hatching). This behavior was considered natural and innate. The birds were born with an **attachment** to their mother, and with the tendency to follow her around. Of course, each baby followed its own mother, whom it had learned to recognize, so that even here some experience was necessary. Lorenz (1937) discovered that during the first 24 hours of its life a young gosling would acquire an attachment to the first moving object it saw. Thereafter even so ungooselike an object as Dr. Lorenz could become a mother surrogate to young geese if he was the first moving object in their view. They would then show no interest whatever in their true mothers. This process, by which very young animals develop an attachment to a particular stimulus, is known as **imprinting.**

Since Lorenz's first demonstrations of imprinting, experiments have shown that young ducks or geese will acquire an attachment to the first moving object they see during the critical period, which is from hatching to about 36 hours of age (Jaynes, 1958). This attachment is revealed in heartfelt and pitiful distress cries when the imprinted mother surrogate is absent, by contentment upon its return, and by diligent following when it moves about (Hoffman, Eisever, Ratner, & Pickering, 1974). The rapid learning grows steadily and reaches its greatest effect within 13 hours for ducks (Hess, 1959; Hoffman, 1978), as shown in Figure 12–1.

In people, such strictly delimited time periods with such specific effects are not readily apparent. For most human skills, long time periods with extended learning and practice are usually required. Even language, which at one time did seem to require a critical period (Lenneberg, 1967), can be learned at any time in the life span, from early childhood to old age (McLaughlin, 1978). For many years, people believed that language was best acquired before the onset of puberty. This seemed reasonable because of the striking contrast between how easily children learned to talk and how difficult it seemed for older students to learn foreign languages in school. This attitude, however, may well be peculiar to North Americans, where few people other than bilingual Canadians and Hispanic Americans learn any language other than English. In countries where bilingualism or second-language learning is expected, people of all ages learn languages without any apparent difficulties. Indeed, the observable age differences seem to favor adult rather than childhood language learning. Among a group of English speakers learning Dutch in the Netherlands, adults and teenagers progressed more quickly and achieved greater mastery than did prepubescent or younger children (Snow & Hoefnagel-Höhle, 1978). The advantages of the older learners included vocabulary, grammar, and even pronunciation. The important factors seem to be motivation and the opportunity to learn and practice the language in natural as opposed to strictly classroom settings.

DEVELOPMENTAL TASKS OF INFANCY

Newborn infants don't do very much. Eating, sleeping, and making various noises occupy much of the day and night (Gesell, 1934). Nevertheless, despite the apparent absence of perceptual or cognitive skills, infants are not totally disorganized and helpless creatures. Newborn babies can discriminate colors, tastes, and smells, and quite early in life can discriminate among certain speech sounds (Eimas, Siqueland, Jusczyk, & Vigorito, 1971). Their eyes can follow moving objects within a day or two of birth and can focus within a month. With this rudimentary but important set of early capabilities, infants must acquire the ability to perceive the world accurately, to move about purposefully, and to develop social relationships with other people. These three areas of competence are the most important tasks of early infancy.

Perceptual Development

The basic machinery for perceiving the world is pretty much ready at birth. Babies' eyes, ears, nose, tongue, and skin act very much like those of adults (Cohen, DeLoache, & Strauss, 1979). What infants must learn is how to use these sensory and perceptual organs, how to control them and interpret the flood of sensations from the world. This integration of the senses does not advance very quickly until 6 to 8 months of age, and it is not complete before 1 year (Gottfried et al., 1977). A case in point is how infants gradually learn to avoid falls from such hazards as chairs, tables, and stair landings. Rudimentary depth discrimination is present by about $1\frac{1}{2}$ months of age. When such a young infant is placed on the deep side of a visual-cliff apparatus (see the Highlight on how perception is studied in infants), its heart rate *decelerates* (slows down) compared to when it is placed on the shallow side. This deceleration indicates that the infant notices a difference between the two sides; it does *not* indicate fear of the deep side. The heart rate *accelerates* (speeds up) in fear situations, and this is just what happens when older children who have already had crawling experience are placed on the deep side of the visual cliff (Campos, Hiatt, Ramsay, Henderson, & Svejda, 1978). Children 7 months or older show heart rate acceleration when placed on the deep side, suggesting that they fear the apparent drop. They also avoid crawling out over the deep side, even when encouraged to do so by their mothers. But 7-month-olds who have not yet begun to crawl do not show a fear response—accelerated heart rate—to the deep side. This suggests that human infants with **depth perception** have to learn to fear and to avoid sharp drops. They can learn either from their own experience of falling, or from the fright reactions shown by their parents when they are in danger of falling (Campos et al., 1978; Walk, 1966). Not surprisingly, many young animals show the same developmental progression. Very young kittens and rabbits do not avoid the

The development of visual perception typifies perceptual development in general. At first the infant has only partial control over eye movements (Ruff & Birch, 1974). Indeed, it is not clear that babies have full voluntary control over what they look at; infants' choices of what to look at are very limited. The main questions about the infant's visual system are about how detailed a newborn's analysis of the visual world is, and about what properties of objects and people infants notice.

It is difficult to answer these questions because infants are limited in the ways that they can respond. One fruitful approach is to compare the amount of time infants spend looking at various things. This visual-preference technique has provided striking evidence that even the youngest infants prefer one pattern to another and thus can discriminate between patterns. For example, Fantz (1963) found that within 48 hours of birth, infants preferred faces to uniformly colored disks.

This method, however, cannot be used when two stimuli are equally appealing, so a **habituation** technique is often used instead. One stimulus is displayed repeatedly, and this suppresses attention to it. Then, the habituated response to this familiar sight is compared with a response to something new. If babies favor this new object, then we can infer that they are able to discriminate between the two stimuli. For example, Friedman (1972) found that newborns who were habituated to one checkerboard pattern preferred to gaze at one with a different number and size of squares.

Although even the youngest infants can tell one form from another, a newborn's perception of a pattern is undoubtedly less detailed than that of an older baby. This may be because the newborn's vision is somewhat limited by incomplete development of the eye. For example, the lens can focus precisely on an object about 19 cm away (the approximate distance of the face of the

deep cliff; older ones do (Walk, 1966). Yet other animals, such as goats, avoid the deep cliff from the very beginning (Walk & Gibson, 1961). Apparently, what may require learning and experience in one species may, in other species, be present at birth. In humans, learning and experience almost invariably play important roles.

Infants also must gradually learn perceptual and object constancies. When an object is moved toward or away from you, its visual size changes, but you perceive it as having the same size. Similarly, when objects rotate in space, their visual shape changes, but you still see the shape as constant. By 2 or 3 months of age babies behave as if they have size and shape constancy (Fagan, 1976; Bower, 1966; Caron, Caron, & Carlson, 1979). However, it is several months before infants display more mature object constancy, looking for the reappearance of an object after it has been hidden from view. For very young infants, disappearance of an object seems total—out of sight, out of mind.

By 6 months babies seem to experience the physical world pretty much as adults do. The world is no longer, as William James once put it, a "blooming buzzing confusion." Things do not change size or shape as they move; babies look accurately toward sources of sound and aim fairly accurately for things within their reach.

Motor Development

While babies are learning to make sense of their perceptual apparatus, they are also becoming more able to do things and act upon the world. The schedule and sequence of development of gross motor abilities is fairly uniform for normal babies. On average, babies are able to roll over between 2 and 3 months of age, sit without support at about 6 months, and walk alone at about 12 months (Shirley, 1931). While there is some variability in these ages (see Figure 12–2), the regularity of the sequence suggests that maturation of muscle, nervous system, and bones is the major pacesetter here.

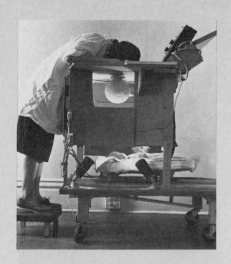

fants scan visual stimuli, Salapatek (1975) discovered that a shift in infants' scanning behaviors occurs at about 2 months of age. At this time the infant progresses to more thorough scanning of a pattern and concentrates more on the internal areas of a figure than on the edges. This developmental shift applies to faces as well as to geometric shapes: Younger infants concentrate on the edges of faces; older infants attend more to eyes (Haith, Bergman, & Moore, 1977).

Infants' heart rates have proved to be useful in the study of depth perception. When placed on a *visual cliff*, a platform of clear glass over what looks like a sharp drop, infants' heart rates are slower on the deep side (Campos, Langer, & Krowitz,

parent when holding the baby), but objects farther away appear blurred (Haynes, White, & Held, 1965). Using infrared cameras to record how in-

1970), suggesting that infants as young as $1\frac{1}{2}$ months have depth perception in this situation.

This conclusion is strengthened by the rather small effects of either early deprivation or early experience. In cultures that swaddle infants and provide them with relatively little chance for early exercise and practice, motor development does not seem to be retarded. Studies of the effects of practice on the acquisition of these motor abilities show little if any permanent effects. A practiced baby might be able to do something slightly earlier than usual, but such early practice seems to confer no permanent advantage (Stone, Smith, & Murphy, 1973). The role of special experience in motor development is thus small. This is not true for other important developmental processes, including early social attachments.

Social Attachments

The first year of life is a critical time for the formation of a person's basic sense of trust in others and faith in the future (Erikson, 1963). A person's feelings in the area of social attachment are rooted largely in the social experiences of this first year of life; among the most important of these experiences are those of the infant with the mother or other primary caregiver.

The infant's social attachment usually begins with an intense bond to the mother. Infants can tell their mothers apart from other people as early as their first few weeks (Carpenter, 1975). Between 6 and 9 months a deep social attachment becomes obvious. At that age, and for the next year or more, infants may protest loudly when their mothers disappear from view (Schaffer & Emerson, 1964a). At first infants are disturbed when anyone leaves them, but gradually they become disturbed primarily when their mother leaves. This developmental pattern is quite similar to the growth of the distress reaction in young ducklings as they become attached to their mothers (Hoffman, 1978).

The quality of infants' attachments to their mothers may vary from "securely attached" to "anxiously attached." In studies using the "strange-situation"

FIGURE 12–2

These photos represent some of the stages in the sequence of motor development. Every baby goes through the same sequence, but some go faster than others. Lags of a few weeks in early infancy and a few months in later infancy are normal.

The stages shown here are: lift head up (1 month), roll over (2½–4 months), creep (7–10 months), pull to stand (7–8 months), climb stair steps (10 months), and, below, getting ready to stand alone (11 months).

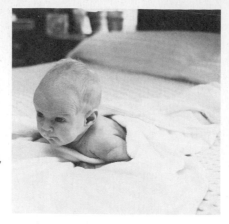

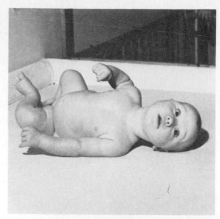

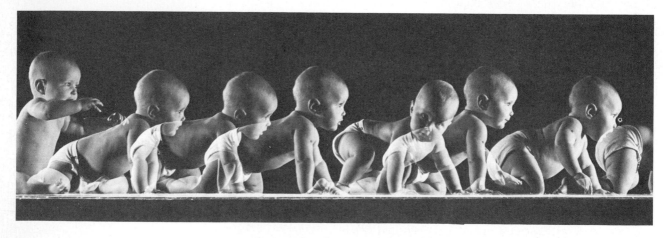

procedure, infants' interactions with their mothers were observed both before and after mothers left the laboratory playroom briefly (Ainsworth & Wittig, 1969). Infants were labeled "securely attached" if they had intermittent pleasant contacts with their mother before the separation, were secure enough to explore the unfamiliar room in her presence, and responded positively when she reappeared. In contrast, "anxiously attached" infants did not explore the room in the preseparation period, acted very distressed during the separation, and sometimes acted ambivalently toward their mother when she returned. Finally, "weakly attached" infants showed little separation distress and little desire to be near the mother when she returned.

Mothers may contribute to the development of "secure attachment" by prompt and sensitive responses to a child's needs. Mothers classified as sensitive in their interactions with their infants seem to have "secure" infants as measured by the strange-situation tests (Ainsworth & Bell, 1969; Ainsworth, Bell, & Slayton, 1971). The more social stimulation mothers provide for their babies, the more securely attached those babies will be to their mothers (Clarke-Stewart, 1973).

How is attachment affected when very young children spend their days away from the mother, as in day-care centers? Fortunately, children in high-quality day-care settings do not seem to differ from children who spend most of their time at home. Day-care infants, aged 3.5 to 29 months, respond no differently than home-reared children in the strange-situation test (Kagan, Kearsley, & Zelazo, 1977). Day-care children also interact normally with their mothers—that is, just as home-reared children do (Ragozin, 1980). These findings are most encouraging, because increasing numbers of mothers of young children are working outside of the home. The overwhelming weight of evidence is that high-quality day care seems to have no short- or long-term adverse effects (Belsky & Steinberg, 1978).

Mother-infant attachments have traditionally received more attention from researchers than father-infant attachments, and therefore more information is available about mother-infant bonds than about father-infant bonds. However, the attachment of infant to father may be just as strong (Lamb, 1977). Of course, infants may have different kinds of relationships with their mothers than with their fathers. Infants may prefer playing with their fathers, as Clarke-Stewart (1978) found for 18-month-olds, but they may tend to look to their mothers rather than their fathers for protection in frightening situations (Lamb, 1976). As family situations change and as fathers participate more in child rearing, it will be interesting to see if patterns of parent-infant attachment change.

EARLY CHILDHOOD

In the first year of life infants gain perceptual and motor control of themselves and of some aspects of their world, and they establish strong social attachments to their mother and other constant companions. From then until they start school (in Western culture, usually at 5 to 6 years of age), children acquire fundamental skills and concepts and learn to cope with their physical and social world. According to the most influential theories of personality development, this time period is also crucial to social and sexual growth and to health in adulthood.

Personal and Social Development

The most influential theories of personality and social development have come from two major sources: Sigmund Freud, whose theory of psycho-analysis revolutionized our thinking about childhood and the development of adult personality, and the more recent social-learning theory, which adapted the principles of learning and conditioning to the phenomena of social development.

PSYCHODYNAMIC GROWTH. According to psychoanalytic (or psychodynamic) theorists such as Sigmund Freud and Erik Erikson, people pass through specific psychosexual and psychosocial stages as they develop from infancy through adulthood and old age. **Psychosexual development** involves the gradual acquisition of identity as a woman or man, as well as basic ways of relating to people and to the world. For Freud (1920/1966), the determinants of adult personality are rooted in early childhood, and the ways that children deal with sexual energy—called **libido**—determine how they will cope with life as adults.

For example, infants' experiences during the first psychosexual stage—the oral stage—will affect both their adjustment to later stages and their needs and attitudes toward events, persons, and things in later life that are associated with orality. If oral needs such as suckling either are not met or are over-indulged, then the adult may develop an "oral" personality. Oral satisfactions such as food or tobacco will be inordinately craved; other people will not be trusted because of the original betrayal by a mother who perhaps weaned a child from the breast too abruptly.

This oversimplified version of oral-stage development does not do full justice to Freud's insights about the importance of early experience in the development of identity and adult personality. We will give here only a bare outline of the theory of psychosexual development, which will be discussed in detail in Chapter 14. The central idea is that a person's energies are focused on various parts of the body during different stages of development. Starting with the mouth at infancy (the **oral stage**), this focus of libidinal energy shifts to the areas of elimination during the years 2 and 3 (the **anal stage**). The focus then shifts to the sexual organs when girls and boys deal with their relationships with and sexual feelings for their parents during the **phallic stage.** Next comes the **latency period,** which lasts from about age 5 to **puberty.** The focus here is more on social and intellectual development. The final goal of psychosexual development is the achievement of **genitality**—firm identification with the person's own gender and the ability to love someone of the opposite sex so the person can marry and have children.

The transition from one psychosexual stage to another is partly matura-tional. As our bodies mature and grow, we acquire new drives, needs, and satisfactions. This kind of change is more dramatic at puberty. For the young child, the changes from the oral to the anal to the phallic stages are partly maturational. They are also very heavily influenced by the social demands of growing up. Erik Erikson (1963) has enriched Freud's stage theory by adding **psychosocial stages** to the bare-boned psychosexual stages proposed by Freud (see Table 12–1). Erikson views each stage as a time in a person's life when certain basic crises must be resolved. The preschool years provide the child with three such crises. During the first year infants must resolve their feelings of trust versus mistrust in the world and in other people. If during this year they learn to place basic trust in others, then an optimistic and trusting adult life is in store for them. During the second year, when infants continue to learn to cope with and control the world around them, the basic conflict is between a sense of autonomy and a doubting, worrisome personality. If they resolve their conflict successfully, infants develop a sense of personal competence and confidence in their ability to control their own fate. The years 3 through 5 are considered critical for acquiring initiative and for

Table 12–1: The Stages of Psychosocial Development Proposed by Erikson.

1. First Year (Trust vs. Mistrust)	Through basic attachment to mother or other caregiver, children develop basic sense of trust or mistrust, come to respond in that way to the world and other people.
2. Second Year (Autonomy vs. Shame and Doubt)	Conflict between child's need to explore, be independent, and basic dependency on parents. Ideal outcome is sense of competence, self-control; poor outcome is shame and doubt through not feeling in control of oneself.
3. Third through Fifth Years **(Initiative vs. Guilt)**	Children develop ability to initiate activities, see them through. Parental encouragement or discouragement of such attempts affect children's sense of ability and purpose or direction.
4. Sixth Year through Puberty **(Industry vs. Inferiority)**	Development of basic competencies in neighborhood and school. Constant testing of child against peers and in school is the basis for feelings of competency (industry) or lack of it (inferiority).
5. Adolescence **(Identity vs. Role Confusion)**	Need to integrate various roles (as son or daughter, sibling, friend, peer, etc.) into one identity. Inability to do this may lead to role confusion—trying out one role after another, trying to be all things to all people.
6. Early Adulthood (Intimacy vs. Isolation)	Important to develop close relationships with others, to commit self to others and to a career. Avoiding this may lead to a general lack of purpose and isolation from other people.
7. Middle Age (Generativity vs. Stagnation, Self-Absorption)	At this stage people need to feel that they are somehow perpetuating themselves—family and work are basic ways to do this, and they are the focus at this time. Resolution of this crisis can mean the difference between a sense of fulfillment, of life being worthwhile, or a sense of boredom or of having somehow missed the boat.
8. Old Age (Integrity vs. Despair)	Need to develop a sense of what one's life has meant, what life itself is all about, and what death means in this context.

Adapted from Erikson (1963).

minimizing feelings of guilt and dismay. During each stage the parents' behavior—whether they encourage or discourage the placing of trust, attempts to control things, and efforts to initiate activities—is crucial in helping children to resolve these basic conflicts. What children learn about themselves during their early years influences how they will cope with later developmental crises.

Learning about oneself involves the central process of **identification.** Children imitate their parents, doing things that their mothers and fathers do, and adopting their mannerisms. But they do more than that. They also adopt parental values and attitudes, and in many ways become symbolic reincarnations of their mother and father. They empathize with them, take joy and pride in their parents' accomplishments, and feel guilt and shame in their parents' failures and shortcomings. Boys' identification with their fathers irreversibly stamps them as males in their society, and girls' identification with their mothers stamps them as females.

Even during the early years of life, sex-role identifications and expectations are apparent. Children as young as 2 or 3 have already absorbed many of society's stereotypes about the behaviors expected from each sex (Kuhn, Nash, & Brucken, 1978). In one study children were introduced to male and female paper dolls, "Michael" and "Lisa," and then asked which doll had made each of various statements. Both boys and girls believed that Lisa liked to help her mother, talked a lot, said "I need some help," and that she would be a nurse and clean the house when she was grown up. And both believed that

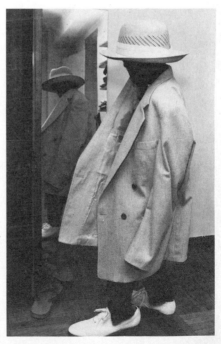

Michael liked to help his father, said "I can hit you," and would be a boss when he grew up.

In the tradition of Freudian psychoanalytic thinking, identification theories have described how people acquire sex roles through their relationships with their mothers in childhood and through the mother's fulfillment of their physical needs. Although various versions of identification theories have ascribed different motivations for identification, they agree with Freud that the same-sex parent is the primary source of information about sex-role behaviors, and that a sex role is acquired as a unit, once and for all, early in life. However, the characteristics of that role can change as society's definitions of sex roles change.

SOCIAL-LEARNING THEORY. In contrast to identification theorists, social-learning theorists (such as Bandura, 1969) propose that sex roles are not adopted as units. Instead, a child learns, one by one, each of the many behaviors and attitudes that eventually will constitute a sex role. The learning is accomplished through imitation and reinforcement. If a child is positively reinforced (that is, rewarded) for a behavior, then the probability of repeating that behavior will increase. For example, suppose that parents give a girl several dolls and pay a lot of attention to her when she mothers the dolls, while giving a boy no opportunities to play with dolls or ignoring his doll play. The girl, but not the boy, will increasingly adopt nurturant behaviors, because they have been reinforced. A girl may learn that, in general, imitation of her mother leads to behaviors that are reinforced, while boys learn to imitate their fathers for the same reason.

Learning theorists differ with identification theorists on other points as well. Because they believe that any learned behavior can be modified, learning theorists do not view sex-role behaviors as fixed. Finally, they view the same-sex parent as only one of many shapers of sex-role behaviors. Reinforcement by nursery-school teachers, for example, may help to shape such behavior. Serbin and O'Leary (1975) found that nursery-school teachers unintentionally rewarded different behaviors from boys than from girls, encouraging boys to be aggressive and to tackle difficult tasks, while encouraging girls to be dependent.

According to social-learning theorists, children imitate both parents, as well as other adults, other children, TV characters, and other models. Environmental influences, not internal motivational states, are the key shapers of sex roles. Thus the traditional ways of portraying men and women in our society shape the way children view themselves. These stereotypes can be further reinforced by most children's books and television programs. Fortunately, this is slowly changing.

Conceptual Growth

Just as children must develop an adult personality and an adult understanding of social relationships, so must they acquire adult ways of thinking, reasoning, and understanding the world. One of the major theorists of cognitive and conceptual development was the Swiss psychologist Jean Piaget. According to Piaget, children go through a series of cognitive stages, beginning with the **sensorimotor stage** of cognitive development (Piaget & Inhelder, 1968). Children of this age—from birth to about 2 years—know the world predominantly through their physical and perceptual interactions with it (see Table 12–2). There are several ways of "knowing." We know how to ride a bicycle

Table 12–2: Piagetian Stages of Cognitive Growth.

1. Sensorimotor Stage (Birth to 2 Years)	Children begin to distinguish between themselves and the rest of the world. Begin to organize their experiences, a first step toward intentional behavior. Learn object permanence, and that actions have consequences (cause and effect).
2. Preoperational Stage (2–7 Years)	Children have a growing ability both to remember and to anticipate. Begin to use symbols to represent external world internally. Egocentric—tend not to put themselves in someone else's place. Tend to focus on one aspect or dimension of an object and ignore all others. Cannot mentally retrace steps to reach a conclusion (irreversibility).
3. Concrete Operational (7–11 Years)	Children learn to retrace thoughts, correct themselves; can consider more than one aspect or dimension at a time. Able to look at a problem in different ways and see other people's points of view. Develop concepts of conservation—number, mass, etc.
4. Formal Operation Stage (12 years and up)	Individuals can think in abstract terms; formulate and test hypotheses through logic. Can think through various solutions to a problem or possible consequences of an action. No longer tied to concrete testing of ideas in external world—can test them internally through logic.

Adapted from Piaget & Inhelder (1968).

through the largely unconscious motor acts and skills that we use—balance, pedal, brake, and steer. This kind of knowledge is "enactive"—knowing by doing.

A baby's knowledge of the world—mental image of things, events, and people—is inextricably bound up with the baby's own interactions with that world. At first, knowledge is acquired primarily through touch, and mostly by the mouth. Young infants get to know what objects are like by mouthing them in addition to looking at them and holding them in their hands. Gradually, the actions performed on objects become more complex, and eye-hand coordination becomes good enough for children to reach accurately for things. Soon the sensorimotor image of objects becomes quite rich and complex. Not only the sight, but the feel, weight, texture, taste, and sounds of an object become an integrated whole.

During this period, as children are learning to differentiate themselves from the larger environment, they also come to appreciate that objects exist even when they are not physically present. They acquire the concept of **object permanence.** Before they have this concept, they believe that anything removed from their sight ceases to exist. For example, if a toy the infant is playing with is removed from view, the infant will not look for it or lift a blanket or cloth to see if the toy is hidden underneath, even if the infant saw the toy being covered with the blanket. To the infant, once the toy is removed from sight, it no longer exists. One of the first signs that a child has attained object permanence is looking-for or searching behavior. At this point, the child knows the toy is somewhere but does not know where.

The next stage, beginning at age 2, is the **preoperational** (or **symbolic**) **stage.** Now children are learning to represent aspects of the world symbolically, in words or in visual images. Children of this age begin to appreciate that some transformations of objects do not matter—the object remains the same. This is the concept of the **conservation of mass.** For example, very young children will often judge that a piece of clay is "more" if it is rolled from a spherical shape to a long cylindrical shape. Older children know that the mass or amount of clay does not change when its shape is changed. This is one of the many mental operations needed for object constancy—the ability to perceive that objects remain stable despite changes in surface appearance (H. Gardner, 1982).

How does the child move from one level of cognitive ability to another? Partly through relatively simple learning—learning eye-hand coordination, for example—and partly through the mechanisms of classical or operant conditioning (see Chapter 6). For example, children can learn to associate one event with another so that the sound of someone's voice becomes associated with that person's face. Children learn that doing one thing will result in praise, whereas doing another will bring punishment.

Cognitive growth, however, requires two other kinds of mechanisms, according to Piaget, and these are the fundamental factors in a child's progression from one stage or level of cognitive functioning to the next. These fundamental instruments of cognitive change are **assimilation** and **accommodation.** When a person encounters something new that doesn't quite fit with his or her experience and knowledge, it is *assimilated* to what the person already knows. In other words, the new thing or event is interpreted in terms of what is already known. The "learning" in this case involves interpreting the new to fit preexisting knowledge. Whenever we interpret new things in terms of their similarity to and differences from the familiar, we are using processes of assimilation.

Sometimes we encounter situations or concepts that are so different from the familiar that they cannot be assimilated. Such events in ordinary adult life are rare. When they do occur, they are either totally ignored or they force us to change our way of thinking—to *accommodate* what we already know to something new and important. In adolescence the facts of sexuality and our new reactions to people of the opposite sex force accommodation—changes in our ways of conceptualizing ourselves and others. In the larger society, great and pervasive new ideas, such as Darwin's theory of evolution, Freud's theory of the unconscious, or Einstein's theory of relativity and the emergence of nuclear power forced people to change their basic conceptions of their biological, social, and physical worlds.

For young children, events and situations that require accommodation are commonplace. Those that cannot be coped with at any given age are ignored. Those that are just beyond the level of the child at any given age, and that cannot be assimilated, force accommodation; they force changes in the way the child views reality as well as changes in the way the child thinks. Learning about language is one example of accommodation. Every child must, at some point in normal development, get the idea that words can represent things—that words "mean" something. This is an important accommodation, usually lost to our memory. But in at least one instance a person could remember that flash of insight, that moment of accommodation. Helen Keller lost her sight and hearing early in childhood, before she learned to speak. When she was about 6 years old, during a session with her tutor, she suddenly understood that a gesture made on one of her hands and the water she felt with her other hand were symbolically related. At that moment she understood the concept of naming, and from then on, Helen Keller thought about the world differently. It was now a place with things that could be named and that, when named, were under control—at least to the imagination (Keller, 1903).

The Roots of Language

Realizations of the nature of words and of language as a medium for communication are major accommodations that can have enormous consequences for children's learning (Sinclair-de Zwart, 1973). The social ties between child and parents, and between child and other children, are equally important for the growth of language abilities. From early infancy children display perceptual behaviors that aid communication between mother and child. By the age of 3 months children will, when playing with their mother, look at the same things their mother looks at (Bruner, 1974/1975). Mother and child usually pay attention to the same things simultaneously. This virtually guarantees that the child will gradually get to know what the mother is talking about—that if the mother names an object, chances are that the child will be looking at and paying attention to that object. The social attachment and shared attention patterns between mother and child set the stage for language learning.

The continual social interaction and communication patterns between mother and child also contribute in important ways. If children are to learn what words mean, they must first know what mother or father intends to say. As Macnamara (1972) put it:

> Infants learn their language by first determining, independent of language, the meaning which a speaker intends to convey to them, and by then working out the relationship between the meaning and the language. To put it another way, the infant uses meaning as a clue to language, rather than language as a clue to meaning. (p. 1)

In other words, the infant plays a guessing game. The infant first tries to figure out what the other person is saying. Then the infant gradually maps out the sounds that are heard onto what he or she understands. Mothers help by using "motherese," a form of talking to young children that uses simplified grammar and is carefully tailored to the linguistic and cognitive level of the child. For example, a typical mother might say to her 2-year-old: "That's a lion. And the lion's name is Leo. Leo lives in a *big* house. Leo goes for a walk every morning. And he always takes his cane along" (Snow, 1972). These ideas rarely, if ever, would be expressed to a 2-year-old by saying: "That is a lion named Leo who lives in a large house and goes for a walk every morning invariably taking his cane along." Parents carefully make sure that children attend to them and to what they are talking about, use questions both to test the child and to continue the conversation, and rarely make the mistake of talking about things the child doesn't understand (Gleason & Weintraub, 1978). Children, for their part, give clear signals when they do not understand—they simply turn off. Babies either fuss or go to sleep, young children fidget and look away. The sensitivity of most people to these conversational signals greatly facilitates early language development (Shatz, 1978). When children are deprived of such important and sensitive social interactions, as in some institutional settings, language development can be delayed and even permanently impaired.

Just as young children's social environment supports their acquisition of language, so does their growing ability to think. During the late sensorimotor and early preoperational stages of growth, children become able to deal with increasingly complex aspects of things, and with relationships between things. Early in this period, between 1 and 2 years, they classify simple sets of objects by dealing with one kind of thing at a time. For example, if a child is given four plates and four blocks to play with, he or she might pick up one plate after another, grouping them together in one pile. The child at this age uses language in a similar way, talking about one thing at a time by saying "plate, plate, plate, plate" (Sugarman, 1982, 1983). Toward the end of this period, between $2\frac{1}{2}$ and 3 years, children become able to consider two classes of objects simultaneously and to talk about the relations between object classes.

A child might pick up a plate and put it in one pile, then pick up a block, say "not plate," and put it in a different pile. These conceptual advances are reflected both in the child's increasingly complex use of language and in such other cognitive abilities as counting (Gelman & Gallistel, 1978).

Moral Development

As children learn to talk and to think about their world, they inevitably encounter problems of interpretation. One area of great importance to people and to society is the attribution of responsibility and concepts of morality. The most direct and simplest way to attribute responsibility for both good and bad actions is to judge them completely by their most obvious characteristics—what people do and the consequences of those actions. This simplistic way of thinking relies entirely on observables and completely ignores *intentions*. Children in the preoperational stage of cognitive development often judge people this way (Piaget, 1932). A child who breaks a plate while trying to be helpful (a bad consequence but a good intention) is blamed as much as someone else who broke a plate deliberately (a bad consequence with a bad intention). Several experiments with young children (e.g., Piaget, 1932) suggest that they tend to weigh consequences more heavily than intentions in judging whether someone should be rewarded or punished. However, it is not clear whether this tendency is peculiar to young children or whether it is a reflection of common, everyday adult patterns. Consider what adults usually do when a child happens to break a treasured vase or spill ice cream on the damask table linen: They usually get angry, despite the child's plea, "I didn't mean it!" Are young children usually imitating their elders, then, even though they may already be capable of taking intentions into account?

When psychologists test children for their ability to use information about someone's intentions, they usually read the children a story in which someone's intentions are described first and then the actions and consequences of those actions are told. If children remember only the *last* part of the story, we may infer that they have not taken intention into account. When the order of information is reversed—action/consequence first, intention last—children do use intentional information, either because they remember it better or because putting it at the end makes it more salient. Children then say that people should not be punished for doing something bad if their intentions were good and honorable (Austin, Ruble, & Trabasso, 1977).

Moral judgment of others is but one aspect of moral development, and perhaps not the most important one at that. Of far greater importance is the development of our own morality and the ways in which we judge ourselves and control our own behavior. Lawrence Kohlberg (1963, 1971, 1981) proposed a theory of moral development modeled after Piaget's theory of cognitive development. Children in the sensorimotor and preoperational stages of cognitive development are thought to be in a premoral stage (see Table 12–3 for a summary of the stages). Their behavior is governed by rewards and punishments rather than by higher principles. It is bad, for example, to hurt puppy dogs because you will be punished if you do it. This theory seems far too simple. Young children are often guided by compassion and empathy in such matters, and it is a rare child indeed whose actions are as completely governed by rewards and punishments as Kohlberg's theory would have us believe. Nonetheless, Kohlberg's stage theory is interesting and does capture what children often *say* about morality, if not what they do. As with many

Table 12–3: Kohlberg's Stage Theory of the Development of Moral Reasoning.

I. Preconventional Level

Rules are set down by others.

Stage 1. Punishment and Obedience Orientation

Physical consequences of action determine its goodness or badness.

Stage 2. Instrumental Relativist Orientation

What's right is whatever satisfies one's own needs and occasionally the needs of others. Elements of fairness, reciprocity are present, but they are mostly interpreted in a "you scratch my back, I'll scratch yours" fashion.

II. Conventional Level

Individual adopts rules, and will sometimes subordinate own needs to those of the group. Expectations of family, group, or nation seen as valuable in own right, regardless of immediate and obvious consequences.

Stage 3. "Good Boy-Good Girl" Orientation

Good behavior is whatever pleases or helps others and is approved of by them. One earns approval by being "nice."

Stage 4. "Law and Order" Orientation

Right is doing one's duty, showing respect for authority, and maintaining the given social order for its own sake.

III. Postconventional Level

Individual defines own values in terms of ethical principles he or she has chosen to follow.

Stage 5. Social Contract Orientation

What's right is defined in terms of general individual rights and in terms of standards that have been agreed upon by the whole society. In contrast to Stage 4, laws are not "frozen"—they can be changed for the good of society.

Stage 6. Universal Ethical Principle Orientation

What's right is defined by decision of conscience according to self-chosen ethical principles. These principles are abstract and ethical (such as the Golden Rule), not specific moral prescriptions (such as the Ten Commandments).

Stage 7. Cosmic Ethical Principle Orientation

What's right is defined in terms of a sense of cosmic unity.

Adapted from Kohlberg (1969, 1981). Stage 7 was added later to provide for a morality that conforms to religious beliefs beyond those of one's personal conscience.

Piagetian tests with children, what children say and what they can do often lead to very different assessments of their capabilities (Gelman, 1978). Preschool children have not yet learned to describe their thoughts and ideas very well. One of the aims of schooling is to produce articulate children who can talk about their own mental life and social beliefs (Flavell, 1978).

Self-Control

Preschool children must also learn to control their own actions. In early childhood, parents can gradually gain control over their children's behavior by talking to them. Children gradually acquire the ability to follow instructions. For example, at about 1 year of age, a child's attention can be directed toward an object. Asked to pick up a toy truck from a nearby table, 1-year-olds will do it easily. They will also be able to follow the request if the truck is across the room. However, if there is another toy between them and the truck, they will often be distracted and bring the other toy back instead.

One-year olds are not yet able to sustain an action in the face of external distraction, but older children can maintain a sequence of actions in spite of distractions.

More importantly, children soon begin to talk to themselves as if they were their own parents, often saying things like "mustn't touch, Daddy spank" when tempted by forbidden objects. Luria, a Russian psychologist who studied the development of self-control in children, expressed this development as a shift from control by others to control by oneself: Speech as a form of communication . . . [between the child and] . . . adults later becomes a means of organizing the child's own behavior. . . . The function which was previously divided between two people later becomes an internal function of human behavior" (Luria, 1959, p. 341). Children first learn to act on the basis of verbal instructions given by other people, then learn to talk to themselves, and finally can think silently to themselves about what and what not to do when.

Preschool children can also be shown how to resist temptation now in order to gain a larger reward later. Young children often seem to choose small rewards early rather than postpone them for a better reward later. For example, children between the ages of 3 and 5 years were told that if they finished a simple task, such as copying letters of the alphabet, they would be allowed to play with some really terrific toys. If they didn't finish, then they would have to play with some broken and rather dull toys. While they worked, a toy clown would pop up from a jack-in-the-box and say things like "Ho ho ho, I love to play with children. Come push my nose and see what happens." Without instructions as to how to resist this temptation, most children stopped working to play with the distracting clown. However, children could easily be taught to use simple plans to resist the temptation. They were told to (1) tell the clown "No, I can't; I'm working"; (2) say to themselves, "I'm going to keep working so I can play with the fun toys and Mr. Clown later"; or (3) pretend that there was a wall between themselves and the distractor. Giving children such simple plans, especially plans that helped to inhibit temptation, proved to be an effective way to teach them self-control (Mischel & Patterson, 1978). Such learning is an essential part of socialization in cultures such as ours, where the postponement of gratification is expected of us, especially during the school years.

THE SCHOOL AGES

In our discussion of the psychosexual, psychosocial, cognitive, and social development of the preschooler, we have forecast the growth of the child during the school year. Children are now faced with a wider social and intellectual world than they knew at home, and they are more open to influences from peers and from adults other than their parents. Indeed, the **peer group** soon becomes a major factor in shaping attitudes, beliefs, and personality (Hartup, 1978).

On the Way to Becoming a Unique Person

The years 6 through 12 are the latency period in Freud's scheme of psychosexual development. On the surface there seems to be no interest in the opposite sex, and little or no interest in sexual matters in general. Boys play with boys and shun little girls; girls play with girls and despise little boys.

Friendships are almost exclusively with children of the same sex (Whiting & Whiting, 1975). For Erikson, psychosocial growth centers on the development of basic competencies, and the neighborhood and the school are the central areas of activity. This is a time for steady, unspectacular, but important growth. Children learn to understand death and such political concepts as nations, states, cities, and government, and they begin to appreciate individual points of view (H. Gardner, 1982).

Children begin to turn more and more to their age mates for information, approval, and models as to what to do when. The school-age child is a conformist through and through. Taste in music, books, games, movies, television programs, and even clothing seem to be mysteriously arrived at by consensus, with little or no deviance tolerated. There are inexorable rules of the seasons—one day in spring, baseball is played. Just as suddenly, in fall it's hockey time, and woe be to those children who mistakenly carry their baseball mitts during hockey season!

Interest in assessing one's own skills and abilities increases during this period, especially in comparison to other children in the same classroom. Younger children show little interest in comparing themselves with others and tend not to use social comparison information in evaluating their own performances. For example, children of 3 or 4 years who observe that others scored 10 in the same game in which they had scored 5 would still rate their own performance as quite good. Older children use such social-comparison information to lower their estimates of their own performance (Ruble, Parsons, & Ross, 1976). (We discuss social comparison further in Chapter 18.)

This time of surface conformity is also the time when individual differences in important personal characteristics emerge. One such characteristic is the motive to achieve. Achievement motivation varies considerably from person to person, as measured by tests devised by David McClelland (McClelland, Atkinson, Clark, & Lowell, 1953; see also Chapter 11). At the beginning of the school years, children do not differ very much from one another on measures of achievement motivation. By age 12 or 13, however, there are clear differences, at least in boys (unfortunately, girls were not tested in this study). Not surprisingly, parental styles can influence children's achievement motivations. Children who are high achievers tend to have parents who set high standards and who give them warm and generous encouragement. Low achievers' parents tend to be authoritarian and directive and tend to punish failure rather than reward success (Rosen & D'Andrade, 1959). Other factors, including

One test of conservation is to pour water from a short wide glass into a tall narrow one and ask if the amount of water is the same. Preoperational children will say that there is more water in the taller glass; concrete operational children will say that the amount of water has not changed.

social and school environments, also have a major effect on achievement motivation.

Cognitive Skills

CONSERVATION.   Some of the most obvious changes in children 5 to 13 take place in the intellectual domain. Reading and writing skills improve enormously, and children's language becomes more complex, subtle, and rich. In Piaget's theory, children pass from the preoperational to the **concrete operations stage** at about the time they move into the second grade. The acid test of whether children have reached the concrete operational stage is whether they can perform the mental operations that are necessary for **conservation** (Elkind, 1961; Flavell, 1963), the knowledge that quantities and other permanent characteristics of objects remain the same despite such superficial transformations as apparent shape, brightness, or size. When, for example, water is poured from a short wide glass into a tall narrow one, preoperational children will say that there is now more water in the taller glass. Concrete operational children will be able to judge that the amount of water has not changed. They can do this by using three basic mental operations. The first of these is **compensation.** For example, the child says that the water is the same because even though it is higher, it is also narrower—one perceptual quality is *compensated for* by another. A second important operation is *identity*—the material itself, the water, is the same in the two conditions, so that identity must extend to amount. The third operation is *reversibility*—what would happen if the water were to be poured back into the short wide container? Children who can carry out this operation mentally are more likely to judge that the amount of water has not changed.

Is the child in the concrete operational stage qualitatively different from the preoperational child? That is, do children in these two stages think in fundamentally different ways? According to Piagetian theory, yes. The older child is capable of certain mental operations that the younger child simply cannot do. If Piaget's theory is absolutely correct, it should be impossible to teach a preoperational child to conserve. Rochel Gelman (1969) tested this notion by taking a group of children who had failed the standard tests of conservation and training them to pay attention to the relevant dimensions of situations. For example, for the water problem, children would be taught to look at and compare *both* the *height* and the *width* of containers. This training produced dramatic results: The children performed just like older children on tests of conservation, whereas their matched age mates without training performed like preoperational children. Of course, it could very well be that these children were on the verge of learning to conserve on their own and that the training simply accelerated their normal growth patterns. To some extent, this must be true—we would hardly expect this kind of training to be effective for 1- or even 2-year-old children. On the other hand, in many situations adults would be revealed as nonconservers as well. Consider how successful creative packagers have been in making us believe that the things we buy are more than they actually are.

Perhaps the most reasonable conclusion is that the emergence of operational cognitive skills depends on the availability of certain mental operations, such as compensation, *and* on the child's knowledge about which aspects of a situation are important and relevant and which are not. Such knowledge comes primarily from experience with similar situations; but ability to perform the necessary mental operations comes from a distillation of a variety of experiences and is more general (Weisberg, 1980). Piaget recognizes this distinction between the potential availability of a mental operation —or a problem-solving strategy—and its actual use in a problem situation. Children will often display conservation, for example, in one test and not display it in another. Fully operational children are consistent across all situations; developing children have yet to learn the specific situations that call for the mental and cognitive skills they may have (Flavell, 1978).

MEMORY.   The same interplay between possessing a skill and knowing when to use it can be seen in the development of another important cognitive skill, *remembering*. The difference between having a skill and applying it helps to explain an apparent paradox. Although young children apparently have poor memories, they learn an enormous amount of complex material in a very short time—for example, they learn a language in about 3 or 4 years! How could a person with a poor memory learn so much vocabulary, to say nothing of the complex grammatical rules that are necessary to produce and understand sentences? How poor can the young child's memory be?

Children in the preschool years perform quite poorly on *tests* of memory compared to school-age children. One such test assesses the ability to remember material immediately after it has been presented, like a telephone number. The number of digits or items that someone can repeat back immediately after hearing them is an estimate of the **memory span.** Most adults have a span of about 7 digits, the usual length of a telephone number (Miller, 1956). At age 6, children have a span of about 5 digits. This difference between young children and adults is real, but not all that dramatic. Where the real differences appear are in tests that require specific strategies to perform well. For example, most of us know that if we hear a telephone number, we will not remember it beyond a few seconds if we don't repeat it to ourselves several times. This knowledge about memory, or meta-memory (Flavell & Wellman, 1977), is something young children do not yet have, though schoolchildren learn it to a great extent by age 7 or 8. Their memory in itself has not improved, but their ability to remember has improved because they have learned how to sustain the fleeting immediate-memory trace (A. Brown, 1975).

The same thing can be seen in children's abilities to remember lists of words. When adults are given a list of words that belong to discrete categories —four names of countries, four tools, four vegetables, and four names of furniture—they memorize the list in terms of these categories. Even if the list is presented in random order, recall is grouped by categories, so that the four country names will be recalled together, then the vegetables, and so on. This strategy greatly aids recall. Young children do not organize their recall by

The Kpelle of Liberia provided an opportunity to study memory skills of people with the same sociocultural background, some of whom had formal schooling and others of whom had not. Here an aide of researcher Michael Cole interviews a subject. Cole found that schooling was a significant advantage for developing memory strategies and ability to recall.

categories spontaneously, although they can if they are instructed to (Bjorkland, Ornstein, & Haig, 1977). Older children, like adults, have learned to organize their recall by categories whenever possible. Their memory performance, as a result, is better than that of younger children. Is this improvement in memory strategies simply a function of increased age—possibly of maturation—or is it a by-product of formal schooling?

This kind of question is almost impossible to answer in a society where everyone goes to school. However, we can investigate the problem in parts of the world where formal schooling is not universal. The Kpelle tribe in Africa provided the American psychologist Michael Cole and his colleagues with a rare natural experiment (Cole, Gay, Glick, & Sharp, 1971). Some Kpelle villages had formal European-type schools for their children, and others did not. Here was a perfect opportunity to compare the memory skills of children who went to school with those of children who did not go to school, since all other factors were equal—age, culture, race, language, and virtually all other relevant factors. Somewhat to Cole's surprise, the Kpelle's strategies for remembering lists of words did not change with age alone. High-school-aged Kpelle children who did not have formal schooling did not cluster words in recall, and their recall of word lists did not improve very much with repeated trials. Comparable Kpelle who went to school remembered pretty much the way Americans do: They had apparently learned how to rehearse and organize word lists and so could recall them fairly well.

Does this mean that people without schooling have terrible memories? Not necessarily. What it does mean is that people have to learn different ways to remember different kinds of material. Schooling seems to teach children how to memorize essentially meaningless material by rote. This may be because so much educational material demands this kind of skill—for example, multiplication tables, spelling rules, and geographical place names. Not surprisingly, this kind of training helps people in similar kinds of situations, including standard tests of memory (Scribner & Cole, 1981).

By the end of the preadolescent years most children have acquired a reasonable working knowledge of their physical, cultural, and social worlds. They are now ready for the transition from childhood to the world of adults— work, career, and perhaps marriage and parenthood.

SUMMARY

1. The changes that a person undergoes throughout the life cycle are of central importance in the study of psychological development.

2. An important source of developmental change is *maturation,* the ability to do something one couldn't do before, through physical growth and development.

3. Experience is important for development to occur; experience also plays an influential role in the maturation process.

4. Some learning must take place at a specific time during development; this specific development time is called a *critical period.* In human development, it is more accurate to say that there are *sensitive periods* for learning, when various traits and abilities are most readily acquired.

5. Perceptual development during infancy involves perceptual and object constancies and a shift in the perception of patterns. At the same time, certain motor abilities, such as sitting without support and walking, are acquired. Finally, the first year of life

is very important in the social experience of the infant with parents, which affects later attitudes toward social attachments in general.

6. Freud theorized that people pass through various *psychosexual stages*—(oral, anal, phallic, latency, and genital)—as they develop from infancy through adulthood.

7. Erikson modified this to *psychosocial stages,* or periods during which basic crises arise and must be resolved.

8. Learning about oneself involves *identification,* including sex-role identification, which is greatly affected by society's expectations. *Social-learning theory* is an explanation of sex-role development based on concepts of reinforcement and imitation.

9. Jean Piaget identified various stages in a child's awareness of the world, or cognitive development. In childhood one passes through the *sensorimotor, preoperational,* and *concrete operational stages.* Development from one cognitive level or stage to another involves the processes of *assimilation* and *accommodation.*

10. Language development is dependent to a certain extent on the child's early social interactions with parents.

11. Moral development progresses from simple ideas of morality, based almost entirely on consequences of an action, to more complicated ideas that take into account such things as principles and *intentions.*

12. Preschool children must learn to control their own actions. First children learn to follow their parents' instructions. Next they tell themselves what to do as if they were their parents. Finally children learn to think silently about what to do when. Preschool children can also be shown how to delay gratification in order to gain a larger reward later.

13. During the school years, children are faced with a wider social and intellectual world, and the peer group becomes a major factor in shaping attitudes, beliefs, and personality. The cognitive abilities of *compensation* and longer *memory span* develop, and basic skills of reading, writing, numbers, and a fair knowledge of the physical, cultural, and social world are acquired.

Suggested Readings

American Psychologist, October 1979, S. Scarr, Guest Editor. This issue, prepared to celebrate the International Year of the Child, contains invited essays on important topics, including children's thinking, their socioemotional development, and issues of social policy affecting children and their families.

BORNSTEIN, M. H., & KESSEN, W. *Psychological development from infancy.* Hillsdale, N.J.: Erlbaum, 1977. Provides a good survey of the major advances in our understanding of infancy.

CHUKOVSKY, K. *From two to five.* Los Angeles: University of California Press, 1968. A poet's observations and reflections on preschool children's language, thought, and imagination.

FLAVELL, J. H. *Cognitive development.* Englewood Cliffs, N.J.: Prentice-Hall, 1977. Piaget's work is somewhat difficult for people just entering the field. This is a clear and concise introduction to his work.

GARDNER, H. *Developmental psychology: An introduction* (2nd ed.). Boston: Little, Brown, 1982. A readable introduction to the major concepts of developmental psychology, providing lucid introductions to the major views in the field, such as those of Piaget, Freud, and Darwin.

GARDNER, J. K. *Readings in developmental psychology* (2nd ed.). Boston: Little, Brown, 1982. A diverse and tasteful selection of articles and essays on the many phases and aspects of child development. The pieces from literary sources are particularly well chosen.

PIAGET, J. *The child's conception of the world.* Totowa, N.J.: Littlefield, Adams, 1960. A very readable account of children's spontaneous explanations of natural phenomena, with detailed observations by Piaget. This is a good introduction to Piaget's ways of looking into the child's mind first-hand.

STONE, L. J., SMITH, H. T., & MURPHY, L. B. (Eds.). *The competent infant: Research and commentary.* New York: Basic Books, 1973. Presents a variety of articles on the capabilities and characteristics of infants. This anthology provides excellent source and background material on this topic.

13. Adolescence, Adulthood, and Aging

The term **puberty** derives from the Latin word "pubescere," meaning "to grow hairy." Puberty is defined as the period during which a child attains sexual maturity. In our culture puberty signals the beginning of adolescence; in some other cultures it marks the transition to adulthood. In cultures where the change from the status of child to adult is abrupt, this transition may be highlighted with an initiation ceremony that specifically signals the attainment of adult status. In some cultures, boys' initiation rites involve a display of courage and skill—qualities required by adult men (Benedict, 1934; Brown, 1969; Munroe & Munroe, 1975). Thus boys may be beaten, thrown into icy waters, circumcised, or scarified. In other societies, the initiation rites for boys involve the teaching of ideas considered important for their culture (Whiting, Klucholm, & Anthony, 1958). Among the Zuni Indians of New Mexico, during initiation rites boys learn that the sacred Kachina who appear at seasonal festivals are really masked adult members of the community, and that "they as mortals, must exercise all the functions which the uninitiated ascribed to the supernaturals themselves" (Benedict, 1934, p. 70).

For girls, initiation rites frequently involve a period of isolation or seclusion from other people. For example, the girl may go to a hut outside the village, and women may teach her the skills needed to be a lover, wife, and mother, including information on lovemaking, contraception, and childbirth. The isolated girl may also undergo certain hardships: She may be subjected to genital mutilation; her skin may be tattooed or scarred; and her teeth may be filed and blackened (Ford & Beach, 1951). When the girl emerges from seclusion, she is usually honored with great ceremony. She often signals her change of status by a change of hair style and by putting on the clothing of an adult woman. All of this announces that she is eligible for marriage.

In Western cultures, the initiation into adulthood is not marked by dramatic initiation rites. Instead, the change from childhood to adulthood takes place during an extended period of adjustment known as adolescence.

ADOLESCENCE

The term **adolescence** derives from the Latin word "adolescere," which means "to grow into maturity." In our culture, adolescence is the period between childhood and adulthood during which the individual learns the skills needed to flourish as an adult. Unlike puberty, adolescence is a socially rather than biologically determined phase of development. The passage to adulthood is marked by a number of small changes in status during or near the end of adolescence. Graduation from high school and the right to vote, drink liquor, and drive a vehicle are all events that, to some degree, signify adult status. These events frequently occur at different times and may or may not coincide with the independence and self-sufficiency usually associated with adulthood. This lack of consistency in the laws and customs signaling the attainment of adult status may be a source of conflict and anxiety for many adolescents in our society (Conger, 1977).

Physical Development

Puberty is marked by dramatic physical changes in both growth rate and sexual characteristics. The initial adolescent growth spurt and the first signs

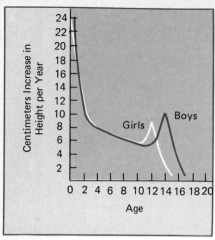

FIGURE 13–1
Typical growth curves for males and females during the first 18 years. Notice that the growth spurt during adolescence occurs 1 or 2 years earlier for females. (Adapted from Tanner, Whitehouse, & Takaish, 1966)

of the developing secondary sex characteristics signal the onset of a period of rapid physical growth that is second only to growth during infancy and early childhood (see Figure 13–1). In boys, active acceleration in growth and the development of coarse pubic hair and facial hair precede such other signs of puberty as voice change. For girls, rapid growth in height begins about $2\frac{1}{2}$ years before **menarche** (the start of menstruation). The growth spurt generally begins at age 12 or 13 for boys and at 10 or 11 for girls; it is, however, normal also for puberty to occur several years later in both boys and girls (see Figure 13–2). In both sexes, it takes about $4\frac{1}{2}$ years from the first appearance of secondary sex characteristics to the development of the adult configuration of sexual characteristics (Conger, 1977; Marshall & Tanner, 1969, 1970; Tanner, 1970).

The age at which puberty occurs varies across individuals and groups. For example, it is clear that better-nourished children reach sexual maturity before those who are undernourished (Tanner, 1970). Genetic factors are also influential (Tanner, 1962, 1970). And the beginning of puberty sometimes varies across time in the same culture. In the United States, for example, menarche has been occurring at younger ages than in the past. The average girl reached menarche at age 14 in 1910, at 13.4 in 1930, at 13.3 in 1940, and at 12.8 in 1955 (Cagas & Riley, 1970; Malina, 1979). The mean age of menarche decreased by 6 months between 1940 and 1955. However, since the mid 1950s

FIGURE 13–2 GROWTH RATES AND SEXUAL DEVELOPMENT DURING PUBERTY. *The bars represent the average age at onset and completion of the events of puberty. (Tanner, 1973)*

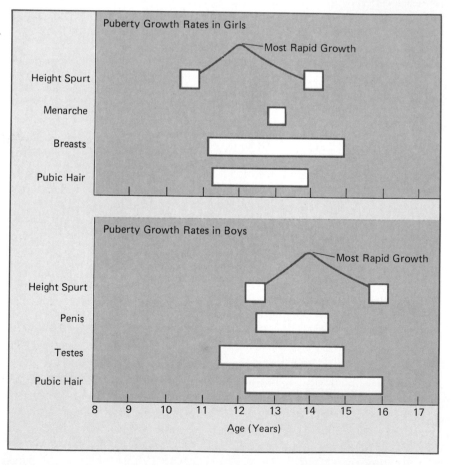

Many psychologists believe that a
person's behavior and personality
are formed in the early years and resist change in adulthood. This point
of view was an outcome, in part, of
Sigmund Freud's emphasis on
trauma and psychosexual crises during early childhood. However, according to data from a well-known
longitudinal study at the University
of California in Berkeley, it is incorrect to assume that there is great
consistency between childhood behavior and personality in later functioning.

The Berkeley researchers have
been following the development of
persons born approximately 50 years
ago. Thus they have data on development throughout childhood and
well into adulthood. One of the
more important findings coming out
of the study is that there is little
continuity in development from
childhood to adulthood (MacFarlane,
1963, 1964). Indeed, 50 percent of
the children turned out to be more
stable and effective adults than any
of the researchers would have predicted; 20 percent were less substantial than would have been
predicted; and the researchers were
correct in their predictions only
about 30 percent of the time.

In other words, many dull, unhappy, and unstable children
matured into wise, satisfied, and
creative adults, and some popular
and seemingly stable children had
significant problems in adulthood. It
appears that many traumatic childhood events can be learning experiences and that behaviors often
change with new experiences and
learning. Furthermore, some people
seem to be "late bloomers" or "slow
jellers" and require time, and perhaps a change of situation, to work
through earlier confusions or inhibitions and achieve their potential.

the mean age of menarche has been stable; in a national sample of American
girls in the 1960s, the median age of menarche was 12.8 (12.5 for black girls,
12.8 for white girls) (MacMahon, 1973). Perhaps nutrition and general health
have risen to such a high level among American girls that the average age for
menarche will not decrease in the future.

THE EFFECTS OF BEING AN EARLY OR A LATE BLOOMER.   The age at which children
go through the dramatic physical changes associated with puberty and later
adolescence varies greatly, and these variations appear to have an effect on the
adolescent's personality. According to an intensive study of boys aged 14 to 17,
early-maturing boys were at an advantage over late-maturing boys. Both their
peers and adults tend to see them as superior (Conger, 1977). Early maturers
were more reserved, self-assured, displayed more socially appropriate behavior, were better able to laugh at themselves, and were more likely to be
needed. Boys who were late bloomers were seen as less attractive physically,
less poised, more prone to attention-getting behavior, more tense, more
eager and expressive, and less popular with their peers (Jones, 1958; Jones &
Bayley, 1950). The late bloomers also reported more feelings of inadequacy
and rejection and held more negative self-concepts (Mussen & Jones, 1957).
Furthermore, the effects of being an early or late maturer were long-term.
When the boys were studied again at age 33, those who had matured later
were relatively less responsible, dominant, and self-controlled, and more
dependent on others than the early maturers. However, early and late maturers did not differ in marital status, family size, or educational level (Jones,
1957).

The picture for girls is more complicated. According to a 1960 study by
Faust, girls who matured early tended to be at a social disadvantage in late
elementary school, but in junior high school and high school they had more
prestige than the late maturers. According to another study, early bloomers
tended to be more adjusted, self-assured, relaxed, secure, and displayed more
adequate thought processes in adolescence (Jones & Mussen, 1958). Thus,
while early-maturing females frequently feel different and vulnerable before

the age at which most girls reach menarche, they seem to be at a social advantage in later adolescence.

Cognitive Development

At about age 11 or 12, children enter into Piaget's final stage of cognitive development—the stage of formal operations. During this stage they acquire several important cognitive capacities they did not have in childhood (Inhelder & Piaget, 1958; Piaget, 1972).

During the stage of concrete operations, which we discussed in Chapter 12, children can do mental operations in their head, but only if they concern concrete material objects or actions already performed. The most basic change in the **formal-operational period** is adolescents' new-found ability to think about the possible and the abstract. In contrast to children at the concrete-operational stage, adolescents can consider that which has not yet occurred, and they can imagine all the diverse possible relationships and outcomes in a given situation. For instance, they can reason about contrary-to-fact situations (e.g., if coal were white) and consider all the ramifications of such a situation. Further, adolescents at the formal-operational stage often display what is called **hypothetico-deductive reasoning.** This is the ability to test systematically a set of possibilities for correctness by using logic and experimental methods. Scientists who test a hypothesis by systematically examining each alternative explanation are using hypothetico-deductive thinking (Flavell, 1963; Inhelder & Piaget, 1958).

Adolescents can also manipulate thoughts and systems of thought mentally. This ability to reason about verbal statements and abstractions is called **propositional thinking.** It enables adolescents to think systematically about the future and about abstract ideology and philosophy.

The development of formal operational thinking makes the adolescent's thought richer and far more flexible than the child's. Adolescents can consider and explore realms of the impossible and improbable, as well as the realm of reality. And they can systematically evaluate the many possibilities in their own lives, as well as the validity of others' assertions and hypotheses (such as political candidates' platforms and ideological claims). This acquisition of the ability to think more abstractly is reflected in the educational system's curriculum. In junior high school and high school, students are generally required to apply propositional and hypothetico-deductive thinking in their classwork.

Not everyone reaches the formal-operations stage. Indeed, according to some studies, only 30 to 40 percent of adolescents and adults in our society display formal-operational thinking (Neimark, 1975). Further, this mode of thinking is apparently absent in some nonliterate cultures (Berry & Dasen, 1974; Neimark, 1975).

To account for these qualifications, Piaget (1972) modified his original proposal, explaining that formal, abstract thought does not necessarily develop without specific schooling and training, particularly in mathematics and science. Piaget suggested that the content, or subject matter, *is* important—people can apply their knowledge of logic in fields they are familiar with, but may not be able to do so in fields they know little about. Thus, a carpenter may successfully use abstract logical thinking in problems of construction and design, but perhaps not in problems of philosophy and the law. The reverse might well be true for a lawyer.

The ability to test a formula for correctness by using experimental methods (as in this high-school chemistry lab) is called hypothetico-deductive reasoning and is an ability that adolescents gain as part of formal operational thinking.

Social Development

Stanley Hall (1904) was the first social scientist to discuss and study the development of adolescence. In his writings about the period, he labeled adolescence as the period of "storm and stress." According to Hall, adolescents typically waver between contradictory and extreme states—for example, between exuberance and lethargy, cruelty and sensitivity, diligence and laziness. He suggested that this storm and stress was a reenactment of an earlier stage of human development during which humans were becoming more civilized.

Hall's theme of storm and stress has been repeated and expanded upon by later theorists (Freud, 1953; Muss, 1975). In Freud's view, the sexual energy of libido repressed during latency reemerges during adolescence, and the adult stage of development begins. Thus the young adolescent not only must adapt to dramatic physical changes but also must deal with the rise in level of sexual energy.

According to Freud, the evolution of independence from parents is an important developmental task during adolescence. Adolescents must break childhood ties of emotional dependency and become capable of functioning autonomously from their parents. Freud pointed out that in the course of freeing themselves from emotional dependency, adolescents will necessarily go through a period in which they reject their parents, and a certain amount of parent–child conflict is a result of this.

Another famous theorist, Erik Erikson, also emphasized the importance of developing an autonomous, integrated identity during adolescence. In fact, Erikson's fifth stage of psychosocial development, called **identity versus role confusion,** occurs during adolescence.

What does one's sense of identity consist of? Intuitively defined, it is the feeling of being a unified, consistent person, with noncontradictory beliefs, consistent values and ideas about important aspects of the world, coupled with a secure sense of one's own worthiness as a human being. Within one's identity are included one's self-concept and level of self-esteem. The self-concept should be realistic about strengths and weaknesses. For optimal mental health, one's self-esteem should be reasonably high—a person should like himself or herself. One's sense of identity also includes a system of values, including attitudes toward the importance of education, athletic skills, manual dexterity, artistic sensitivity, and loyalty to friends or family, as well as more general political orientations such as conservative versus liberal. Morality and religious beliefs are central to one's sense of personal identity as well as to one's identification with a larger group.

The quest for an identity is often uneasy and conflict-laden. Indeed, Erikson coined the term **identity conflict** to represent this struggle. According to Erikson, a number of negative outcomes may result from the quest for an identity. The first is *identity foreclosure,* in which the adolescent consolidates an identity early, before having ample opportunity to experiment with the range of possible identities. Erikson believes that a period of trying out or testing of possible alternatives is healthy. He calls this period *moratorium* and sees it as a time of experimenting with different identities—for example, seeing what it would be like to be an actress or a writer. If adolescents foreclose or decide on an identity without testing a number of alternatives, they may not become all they were capable of becoming. On the other hand, if adolescents do not consolidate an identity, they may exhibit *identity con-*

fusion. These individuals shift from identity to identity without a sense of purpose and may even exhibit delinquent, psychotic, or other negative behaviors (Erikson, 1959, 1963).

Hall, Freud, Erikson, Anna Freud, and other theorists have all viewed adolescence as an especially conflicted period of development. Is this necessarily true? According to research, no.

Anthropological field work in other cultures, notably by Margaret Mead (1928, 1939) in the South Sea community of Samoa, shows us that our stereotypic picture of teenagers as troubled, emotionally beset, and sexually confused is culturally caused. Confusions about sex roles and identities do not exist in the pastoral and relatively uncomplicated life of the Samoans. Who one is, both sexually and in the world of work, is unambiguous and set down clearly and explicitly in the culture.

Mead's picture of the Samoan society as an unconflicted and violence-free paradise has recently (Freeman, 1983) been challenged by other anthropologists. However, other researchers have found that even in our own culture, adolescence need not be an especially stressful period (Douvan & Adelson, 1966; King, 1971). Indeed, from a historical perspective, the "storm and stress" of modern adolescence was unknown before the Industrial Revolution. In ages and places where young people assume adult responsibilities in their teens or even earlier, adolescence as we know it today cannot exist. The prolonged period of testing alternative identities is a luxury allowed by a culture that does not need its young people to be economically productive. Even today, not all teenagers in the United States experience this period as a time of stress and anxiety. For example, in one longitudinal study of midwestern adolescent boys, most of the boys showed little evidence of inner turmoil (Offer, 1969; Offer, Marcus, & Offer, 1970). According to the follow-up study, only a relatively small percentage of the boys (approximately 20 percent) experienced "tumultuous" growth—that is, showed much turmoil during adolescence (Offer & Offer, 1974).

It appears that for most adolescents, the transition from childhood to adulthood is not as rocky as theorists such as Erikson, Hall, and Freud thought. While the changes in adolescence do produce stress for many individuals, the great majority of adolescents appear to be capable of coping with the stresses without a high degree of emotional turmoil (Conger, 1977; King, 1971).

Peer Conformity and the Generation Gap

During early childhood, children are more attached to their parents than to their age mates, though they do find age mates quite interesting (Eckerman, Whatley, & Kutz, 1975). However, orientation to peers and conformity with peers increase from the elementary school years until early adolescence, at least in ambiguous situations (Berndt, 1979; Costanzo & Shaw, 1966; Hoving, Hamm, & Galvin, 1969; Shaffer, 1979). For example, when adolescents are asked to make a judgment and the correct response is ambiguous, they rely on their peers' opinions more than younger children do.

This conformity to the peer group frequently results in conflict between parental and peer influences (Berndt, 1979; Bixenstine, DeCorte, & Bixenstine, 1976). In one study, children aged 8, 10, 12, 14, and 16 were asked what they would do when their parents and peers had different opinions and gave conflicting advice about something. The older children were more likely to say they would follow their peers' advice rather than their parents' (Utech & Hoving, 1969).

Both parents' and peers' opinions, however, seem to influence adolescents' behavior. For example, Kandel (1973) found that adolescents were more likely to use drugs if their friends did—and if their parents did (although their friends' behavior seemed to have a larger influence).

The complexity of peer-group influence is illustrated by the work of Michael Simon (1977). He found that he could predict adolescent behavior by considering (1) the standards endorsed by the adolescent's parents; (2) the extent to which the adolescent's parents conformed to this standard; (3) the standards endorsed by the adolescent's peer group; and (4) the extent to which the individual's values conformed or deviated from the peer group's. Both parental and peer norms affected adolescents' behaviors, according to Simon, and the peer group's acceptance of parental norms affected how the adolescent reacted to parental standards. In other words, the peer group acted as a "filter" for parental norms—an adolescent's values were accepted as valid if they conformed to the peer group's perceptions of the average parental norm.

Adolescents' strong orientation to peers has led many people to talk about a "generation gap," meaning that adolescents disagree with their parents about many issues, including basic values. However, this gap may be illusory (McClelland, 1982). While it is true that adolescents differ greatly from their parents on many relatively unimportant matters such as dress and choice of entertainment, their values concerning important issues are frequently quite similar to those of their parents (Conger, 1977). Even during the height of the counterculture movement in the 1960s, most adolescents and their parents agreed that their differences on ideals and values were not marked (Conger, 1977). According to **self-reports,** white civil rights workers (the Freedom Riders) and college radicals and liberals in the 1960s frequently modeled their values and behaviors on those of their parents (Flacks, 1970; Horn & Knott, 1971; Rosenhan, 1970). More recent studies done in the 1970s found surprising agreement among parents and adolescents on the validity of such traditional values as self-reliance, hard work, and the importance of duty before pleasure (Conger, 1977; Thurnher, Spence, & Fiske, 1974). Thus, although the average parent and the average adolescent may differ somewhat on certain issues such as sex, religion, drugs, and social justice, the generation gap is not as wide as it has been portrayed by the media and social critics.

Adolescence and Sexuality

A widespread opinion in American society is that today's adolescents are more sexually active and more oriented toward sexual concerns than were adolescents in the past. The media, including films, music, and television, reinforce this idea by presenting images of highly sexual adolescents. But how much does this image reflect reality?

Adolescents today are more sexually involved than in the past: Incidence of both petting and sexual intercourse is higher and occurs at earlier ages (Conger, 1977; Hopkins, 1977; Sorenson, 1973). However, this is not a new phenomenon, for the parents of today's adolescents were in their turn more sexually active than their parents. According to the famous research done by Kinsey and his colleagues, only 8 percent of females born before 1900 had premarital intercourse before the age of 20; in contrast, 21 percent of the mothers of today's adolescents had premarital intercourse by the same age (Kinsey, Pomeroy, & Martin, 1953). The figures for intercourse among adolescents in a study published in 1973 were 72 percent for boys and 57 percent for girls by the age 19 (Sorenson, 1973). While this study may overstate the percentages—in another study only 33 percent of males and 55 percent of females in their senior year had had sexual intercourse (Jessor & Jessor, 1975)—there has indeed been a dramatic change in sexual behavior during adolescence during the past century. Although sexual activity has increased, it should be noted that the overall number of births by women under the age of 19 has fallen steadily since 1958. What has increased for adolescent women is the rate of childbearing outside marriage. By 1980, more than one-fourth of the babies born to white teenagers, and 80 percent of those born to black teenagers, were born to unmarried women (National Center for Health Statistics, 1980).

In contrast to behavior, adolescents' attitudes regarding sex have not changed as much as many people believe. Most adolescents strongly oppose sex solely for physical enjoyment, exploitation in sexual relationships, and sex among people too young to know what they are getting into (Conger, 1977; Sorenson, 1973). In a recent survey, for example, over 80 percent of all adolescents disagreed with the statement that the most important thing in a relationship is sex. And when adolescents rated the relative importance of different goals such as learning about themselves, having fun, and being independent, having sex with different people and "making out" were ranked as among the *least* important goals (Sorenson, 1973). So while contemporary adolescents are relatively sexually active, they have not renounced all traditional values relating to sex.

Moral Development

Moral development continues from childhood into adolescence. As discussed in the last chapter (see Table 12–3), most children reason in what Kohlberg calls a preconventional manner. Young children are concerned with obedience to authority, avoidance of punishment, and hedonistic gains for themselves and the people important to them. Around adolescence most people enter Kohlberg's (1969, 1971) conventional level of moral judgment, which contains 2 stages—Stages 3 and 4. In contrast to the preconventional moral reasoning of children, which is essentially nonmoral, individuals reasoning at the conventional level have accepted the moral values and standards of their culture. At the conventional level of moral reasoning, an act is seen as right if it is in accordance with the established rules of society.

Stage 3 is frequently called the "interpersonal concordance" or "good boy–nice girl" orientation. The individual conforms to stereotype conceptions of a "good boy" or a "nice girl." Good behavior is that which fulfills the demands of the roles that society provides. Acts that help others or lead to their approval are moral (Colby, 1979; Kohlberg, 1976, 1978).

During Stage 4, the "law and order" orientation, norms and values of the society become more internalized. Stage 4 individuals are oriented toward duties, defined responsibility, fixed rules, and maintenance of the social order. Right behavior consists of showing respect to authorities, doing one's duty, and maintaining the social order for its own sake.

While Kohlberg's viewpoint has been criticized (Moshman & Neimark, 1982), his description of conventional reasoning captures the flavor of American adolescents' moral judgment.

EARLY ADULTHOOD

As we have seen, in some societies puberty heralds the beginning of adulthood; in others the child does not become an adult until much later. In the United States it is not clear when an adolescent becomes an adult. Is it at graduation from high school, or when the person becomes self-supporting or moves out of the parental home?

In recent years, the question of when an adolescent attains adult status has become even less clear. For example, many college students live away from their parents, and many marry while still financially dependent on their

Keniston has proposed a new stage of life, "youth," for those people in their late teens and early 20s caught between adolescence and adult status. It is an ambiguous stage, with many college and graduate students being married and living away from home and yet still being financially dependent on their parents.

parents. Many people today spend long periods training for a career or trying to determine what their occupation should be.

Because so many people in their late teens and early 20s are caught in limbo between adolescence and adult status, Keniston (1970) proposed that a new stage of life, called "youth," has appeared in our culture. According to Keniston, people in this stage are deeply involved in working out the conflict between maintaining personal integrity and achieving effectiveness in society. Since they realize the potency of societal forces that conflict with their self-identity, youths may refuse to be socialized into the predominant adult society. They may become estranged from the dominant culture and identify with a distinctive "youth culture" instead.

Keniston developed his theory of a "youth" stage to explain the unrest among young people in the 1960s. Regardless of its original use, the theory makes a worthwhile point about the ambiguous status of young people in our society. An adult is generally seen as responsible, mature, self-supporting, and well integrated into adult society, but people may not develop all these attributes and characteristics simultaneously. Thus there is disagreement among both social scientists and people in general as to when an individual becomes an adult.

Social Development

THEORY.   According to a number of theorists, the major task in early adulthood is to establish intimate relationships. Freud believed that successful development during the genital stage meant the ability to "lieben und arbeiten" (to love and to work) (Erikson, 1963). Therefore, he thought that a heterosexual loving relationship was a major component of adult development. Similarly, Erikson's (1963) sixth stage of development, which occurs during early adulthood, is called *intimacy versus isolation*. During this stage,

The major task in early adulthood seems to be to establish intimate relationships. As Erikson noted, young adults emerge from the adolescent stage of searching for identity eager to join their identity with that of others. If young adults do not form some sort of intimate relationship, it can lead to isolation and a kind of self-absorption.

the young adult, emerging from the search for and the insistence on identity, is eager and willing to fuse his identity with that of others. He is ready for intimacy, that is, the capacity to commit himself to concrete affiliations and partnerships and to develop the ethical strength to abide by such commitments, even though they may call for significant sacrifices and compromises. (Erikson, 1963, p. 58.)

Empirical research has supported Freud's and Erikson's claims that the establishment of intimate relationships is a major development task during early adulthood (Gould, 1974; Levinson, Darrow, Klein, Levinson, & McKee, 1978).

According to Erikson (1963), intimacy is not synonymous with sexuality: The mutual respect and caring that create an intimate situation may be expressed in close friendships as well as in sexual relationships. If the young adult does not form some sort of intimate relationship, however, he or she will develop a deep sense of isolation and consequent self-absorption.

THE STATUS OF MARRIAGE.   For many people, the quest for intimate relationships results in marriage. However, the statistics and dynamics relating to marriage have changed greatly over the years.

Consider, first, the age of the individual at the time of his or her first marriage. From about 1900 to the late 1950s, the age at which Americans married for the first time went down. The average bride in 1890 was 22.0 years old; in 1956 she was 20.1. Analogous figures for males were 26.1 and 22.5 years. Since the 1950s the trend has reversed, and the average age at marriage has increased gradually. In 1978 the average ages of females and males at marriage were 21.8 and 24.2, respectively. Further, in the 1970s the percentage of people in early adulthood who had never been married increased. In 1960, 53.1 percent of males and 28.4 percent of females aged 20 to 24 had never been married; by 1975 the figures were 59.9 percent and 40.3 percent. In 1978, 47.6 percent of women aged 20 to 24 had never been married. Obviously, people are marrying later in life than they did in the recent past (Current Population Reports, 1975, 1979a).

Another major demographic trend is the increasing number of marriages that end in divorce. In the 1920s and 1930s, each year only about 1 percent of married women aged 14 to 44 were divorced. In the mid 1940s the rate was 2.4 percent; and in the mid 1950s, 1.5 percent (Glick & Norton, 1973). In 1978, 11 percent of women in the United States who had been married were divorced (Current Population Reports, 1978). The rate of divorce is increasingly rapidly, and it is estimated that 29 percent of women born between 1940 and 1944 will end their first marriage in divorce (Glick & Norton, 1973). Indeed, for persons under 30 years of age, the rate of divorce rose 296 percent between 1960 and 1978 (Current Population Reports, 1978). While approximately 4 out of 5 divorced people remarry, particularly men (Glick & Norton, 1973), the high rate of divorce indicates that many young (as well as older) adults experience the stress of ending a marriage.

The late 1970s, however, saw the beginning of a new trend in both marriage and divorce. The rate and number of marriages have been increasing since 1976, reaching a record in 1982. Meanwhile, the number of divorces decreased in 1982 for the first time in 20 years. The divorce rate declined almost 4 percent, from 5.3 per 1,000 population in 1981 to 5.1 in 1982 (Monthly Vital Statistics Report, 1983).

BIRTHRATES AND PARENTHOOD.   Not only are the rates of marriage and divorce changing, but so are the roles within marriage. One of the most important

Career Choice and Psychology

One of the tasks of early adulthood is the choice of career. Many young people have access to vocational or career counselors in high school and college. Some of the methods used by these counselors to gather information about individuals have been developed by psychologists.

Vocational-interest inventories are frequently used to provide a basis for advising young adults about careers. Two of the most popular are the Kuder Personal Preference Inventory and the Strong-Campbell Interest Inventory. Persons taking the inventory are typically presented with pairs of activities to do or events to watch, and they then report which of the pair they would prefer. The inventory also asks people to report which they prefer from a large number of pairs of school subjects, activities, amusements, and types of people. Sample items include: geometry or physiology; writing reports or pursuing a bandit in a sheriff's posse; skiing or organizing a play; and ballet dancers or business people. An individual's pattern of preferences is then analyzed. One person may generally prefer active outdoor activities that are done alone, a second may prefer sedentary, problem-solving activities, and a third person might enjoy working with groups of people.

Seeing their hundreds of specific choices analyzed in this fashion is often useful for people, but it is the next step that links the outcome of an interest inventory to specific possible careers. To correlate preference patterns with career options, the inventory developers administered the inventory to groups of people already engaged in a wide range of occupations. These criterion groups were used to create a composite profile of the interest patterns of, for instance, doctors, accountants, or forest rangers. Research has shown that many (although not all) occupations do have characteristic interest patterns. The profile derived from the inventory responses of an individual who is seeking a career is compared to these composite profiles. Thus, counselors are able to suggest those careers associated with an interest profile most matched to that of the person being counseled.

Certain problems with vocational interest batteries are worth pointing out. First, no test can magically produce career interests where none exist. Those who are most likely to be confused about careers may not have many interests or like many activities, and so vocational preference batteries are not likely to find many careers to suggest for them. Second, we are today concerned about avoiding sex bias in career choices. But the criterion groups used to create the occupational keys on these tests consisted of people who chose their careers years ago, before the fairly recent changes in occupational patterns of women. As

factors affecting the women's role is the declining birthrate. The average number of births for married women decreased steadily in the United States from 7 in 1880 to 2.3 in 1940, but rose during the baby boom from the 1940s until 1957, when the average number of births per married woman was 3.8. Since 1957, however, the average has dropped to about 2.11 (Current Population Reports, 1979b). Although the rate of births appears to be rising slightly (Sklar & Berkov, 1975), the rate is lower today than in the past. This change in birthrate has accompanied the entrance of married women into the labor force.

Parenthood influences the quality of life in early adulthood. Young fathers report fewer positive feelings about their lives, perhaps because of the economic burdens and other stresses associated with having to support a family (Campbell, 1975). Indeed, parenthood creates a life crisis for most couples (LeMasters, 1957); married couples with children under age 17 report higher levels of stress than couples with no children or those with adult children.

While parenthood may be very stressful, it provides an opportunity for growth and satisfaction. Erik Erikson concluded that being a caring, directive parent is one way to develop successfully during his sixth stage of development, *generativity versus stagnation*. Another way to become a generative adult is to guide young people of the next generation who are not one's own children, for example, by teaching children. According to Erikson, the adult who does not attend to the welfare of the next generation often develops a pervasive sense of stagnation and personal impoverishment (Erikson, 1963).

a result, the standardized career profiles may tend to steer women and men away from careers that have recently been open to them. The psychologists who create and administer the inventories are aware of these problems but have not yet completely overcome them.

A third difficulty with career inventories results from the way in which the occupational keys are constructed. If a large number of surgeons are interested in building small-scale models, that interest may well be linked to a particular component of surgeons' professional tasks. Some interests that may be shared by many members of an occupational group may have no connection to their career tasks. Suppose, for instance that bankers were at one time largely recruited from wealthy families and that "polo" showed up as an interest of many members of that group. While it is true that people who didn't play polo might have received a cold reception in banking at that time, it is quite clear that the sport has no relationship to banking tasks. We should be concerned that the various social class and ethnic biases historically associated with certain occupations might be perpetuated as a result of such accidental associations during construction of career inventories.

Aptitude tests also are used in career counseling. Obviously, people will do best at jobs for which they possess the requisite skills, and employers certainly seek as potential employees those who have the needed skills. Aptitude testing, therefore, is useful if 2 sets of conditions are met: The first condition is that the aptitude test must reliably measure an actual aptitude, and the second is that the aptitude must be central and indispensable to the job. These are not always easy conditions to meet in practice. Probably a plumber should have a reasonable degree of mechanical aptitude, an electronics technician good spatial-relations skills, and an airline pilot good eye–hand coordination.

However, what are the aptitudes required for success as a social worker or college teacher? They are remarkably hard to define. A social worker ought to "be able to get along with people," but is that a specific aptitude or a combination of hard-to-define skills and experiences? Is there such a thing as a single aptitude called "teaching ability"? Probably not. Some teachers are effective in large lectures and less effective in seminars, while others are at their best working intensively with students on individual projects. All these careers seem to require somewhat different bundles of competencies, not necessarily connected, and they should not necessarily be thought of as utilizing single aptitudes.

For these reasons, as well as for others, there is some question whether aptitude-test batteries can precisely determine people's fitness for various careers. Reflecting this, industries that use tests to choose workers must demonstrate that the skills and aptitudes for which they test are directly relevant to the jobs in question.

Moral Development

Moral development may continue into adulthood. While many people attain the highest level of moral judgment during adolescence, others continue to develop their moral reasoning into their 20s and perhaps even later (Kohlberg, 1976; Kohlberg & Kramer, 1969).

During early adulthood, a relatively small percentage of adults achieve Kohlberg's third level of moral development, the *postconventional level* (Kohlberg, 1969, 1971). Previously in Kohlberg's theory, this level consisted of 2 stages—Stages 5 and 6. At Stage 5, the *social-contract orientation,* right behavior is defined in terms of general individual rights and standards that have been critically examined and agreed upon by members of a society. The Stage 5 individual has a clear awareness of the relativism of personal values and opinions, emphasizes procedural rules for reaching consensus in a group, and believes that laws should be changed in accordance with rational considerations. Aside from what is democratically agreed upon by the group, right is considered a matter of personal value.

In Stage 6, the *universal ethical principle orientation,* right is defined by a decision of conscience in accordance with self-chosen ethical principles that are logically comprehensive, universal to all people, and consistent. These principles are abstract, such as ideas of justice, equality of human rights, and respect for the dignity of individual human beings (Kohlberg, 1971). In a recent modification of his theory, Kohlberg (1981) added Stage 7, in which

FIGURE 13–3

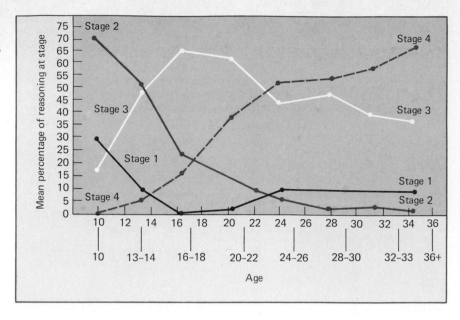

moral choices are suffused with a sense of the oneness of the universe, a cosmic rather than a people- or world-oriented perspective.

Kohlberg's postconventional level is the most criticized of his 3 levels. Many researchers and theorists feel that it is culturally biased—that is, it applies only to Western industrialized societies (Kurtines & Grief, 1974; Simpson, 1974). Furthermore, it is not clear that Stage 6 is developmentally more mature than Stage 5. Indeed, Kohlberg (1978) conceded that Stage 6 may not be separable from Stage 5: At both Stage 5 and Stage 6, the moral person is aware of human rights that exist independent of the social contracts and arrangements of the individual. The person considers a multiplicity of moral and legal options and, in sharp contrast to previous stages, recognizes that there can be real moral disagreements among people.

However, even though many of Kohlberg's original claims regarding the postconventional level of moral judgment have not been substantiated, it is clear that postconventional reasoning is an adult achievement, and that adults who do attain it differ significantly in their moral perspective from adolescents and other adults.

Turiel's (1969) research suggests that most Americans are at Stage 4 of their moral reasoning. Longitudinal studies (Colby, 1979) show that there is an age-linked shift toward Stage 4 reasoning; and despite the predominance of a given kind of moral judgment at a particular time, moral reasoning that is characterstic of other stages can be important, too (see Figure 13–3). Being at a particular stage of development, therefore, does not preclude making occasional moral judgments by other principles. Adults sometimes make rather childish moral judgments and children rather grown-up ones.

THE MATURE YEARS

In the last decade or so, the attitude of both psychologists and people in general toward middle age has undergone a radical transformation. Previously, middle age was regarded as a period in which nothing much happened. Life "ended at forty and there was nothing to do but wait around for retirement and death" (Brim, 1976). Currently, however, it is fashionable to regard middle age as a time of considerable conflict and growth. The term "midlife crisis" has come into vogue. Songs such as "Middle-aged Crazy," movies such as *10,* and numerous popular books and magazine articles popularize the idea that turmoil is natural at this stage of life. In a humorous essay Gerald Nachman (1979) satirizes the current interest in the topic. Focusing on the plight of those who are afraid they will be "left behind again," he suggests the establishment of a Midlife Crisis Camp for men incapable of devising their own traumas.

> You sign up for a week of intensive anguish, located on 227 acres of choice desolation, reminiscent of the usual barren atmosphere of Middle Crises—drab hotel rooms, murky bars, obscure cafés, empty parks. The camp guarantees to produce a maximum sense of worthlessness and tortured self-doubt in a minimum amount of time. (p. 308)

Researchers interested in midlife development disagree on whether a significant number of individuals experience emotional turmoil disruptive enough to constitute a "crisis." Many believe that the transitions that take place during this time may be accomplished smoothly (Brim, 1976). Nonetheless, there is general agreement that between the ages of 40 and 60 changes do take place in several areas of a person's life and that each of these changes presents a challenge to the individual, which may or may not be met successfully.

Physical Changes

Although individuals vary in the rate at which these changes occur, virtually all middle-aged people notice signs of deterioration in some aspects of their physical functioning.

In the 40s, for example, there is usually a decline in near vision, a condition known as presbyopia. The lens of the eye becomes less elastic and loses its ability to accommodate to objects at close range. Reading glasses or bifocals may be required for the first time. The individual may also notice increased sensitivity to glare—on the windshield of the car, for example, or in brightly lit stores. In their 50s people often find that it takes their eyes longer to adapt to the change in illumination when they enter a darkened theater or when they go outside on a bright, sunny day. Some degree of hearing loss is also found in many people over 50.

Changes in outward appearance also occur. Hair thins or grays noticeably, facial wrinkles become more pronounced, the physique alters (as one individual noted ruefully, "The sand shifts"). Weight gains are common, and the ratio of muscle to fat in the body declines. People may also notice a decline in their ability to engage in strenuous activities.

These and other physical changes clearly signal to the individual that he or she is growing older. Both sexes are affected by this realization, but there is some evidence that men are more concerned with health and physical prowess, women with physical appearance. A study by Carol Nowak (1977) found that middle-aged women were less able than women of other ages to separate their assessment of their appearance from their assessment of their other qualities. Developing wrinkles was often equated with being less interesting or less active. In judging the attractiveness of other women, middle-aged women were more likely than those of other ages and all men to equate a youthful appearance with looking attractive and to minimize the attractiveness of other middle-aged women. On the other hand, Neugarten (1968) found in her study of 100 people between the ages of 40 and 60 that men were more likely than women to make such spontaneous comments as, "Mentally, I still feel young, but suddenly one day my son beat me at tennis," or "It was the sudden heart attack in a friend that made the difference. I realized that I could no longer count on my body as I used to" (p. 96).

People adapt to these physical changes on at least 2 levels: At the physical level, they may pay more attention to diet and exercise and stop smoking in order to slow down the rate of deterioration. At the psychological level, theorists such as Robert Peck (1968) suggest that middle-aged people shift from valuing physical power to valuing wisdom, a term Peck uses for the mental skills that are derived from life experience.

Menopause

Women typically experience **menopause,** the cessation of the menstrual cycle, sometime in their late 40s or early 50s. This change generally marks the end of the reproductive period, although there are reports of women becoming pregnant as much as 18 months after menopause has presumably taken place (Talbert, 1977).

Some women experience physical symptoms during this time, including "hot flashes," headaches, nausea, dizziness, and heart palpitations. In a sizable minority of women, such symptoms may cause real physical incapacity. The vast majority of women, however, experience only minor discomfort. There may also be negative psychological effects. A woman may become depressed over the loss of ability to bear children or worry about the effect of menopause on her sexuality. She may become moody and feel less in control of herself. However, in a study of premenopausal and postmenopausal women, Neugarten, Wood, Kraines, and Loomis (1968) found that for many, anticipation may be worse than the event itself. Although about 50 percent of each group agreed that menopause is an unpleasant experience, postmenopausal women were more likely to say that a woman has some degree of control over the symptoms she experiences. They were also more likely to emphasize positive changes, such as an increased sense of freedom and self-confidence.

In men there is no obvious counterpart to menopause. Most men undergo a gradual decline in fertility during middle and old age, although there are reports of men as old as 94 successfully fathering children (Talbert, 1977).

Middle age and the loss of reproductive capacity need not mean the end of sexual functioning for either sex. Although, for example, a middle-aged man may take longer to attain an erection, and a postmenopausal woman may experience some irritation of the vaginal wall during intercourse, the primary barriers to full sexual enjoyment are not physical but psychological. They include tension at home and at work, boredom, and acceptance of the myth that sexual waning is an inevitable part of the aging process (Masters & Johnson, 1966, 1970). In fact, the majority of individuals 40 to 60 continue to engage in regular, satisfying sexual activity (Christenson & Gagnon, 1965; Pfeiffer, Verwoerdt, & Davis, 1974).

The Empty Nest

A major event of the middle years is the departure of children from the home. This period is often called that of the "empty nest" and was once viewed as

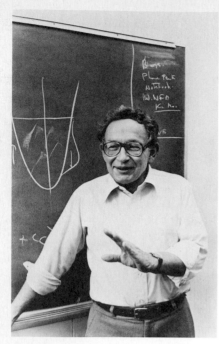

A common physical change in middle age is a decline in near vision, when reading glasses or bifocals may be worn for the first time.

very trying. In fact, some home-centered mothers do feel a great void when their children leave (Bart, 1971). However, according to recent research, many mothers (and fathers) do not. Women whose children have left home tend to be less suppressed, more satisfied, and less self-pitying (Campbell, 1975; Lowenthal, Thurnher, & Chiriboga, 1975; Radloff, 1975). Indeed, feelings of stress are lower for both the husband and wife when the children are over age 17 (Campbell, 1975). Thus, rather than creating a crisis, the "empty nest" may actually relieve parents of drains on their finances and time.

Vocational Changes

The woman whose children have left home sometimes decides to return to work. This decision may carry with it several difficulties. She may find that she no longer has the skills necessary for successful competition in the work world. The jobs that are available to her may be low-paying and monotonous and provide little of the satisfaction for which she is looking. A return to work may also mean a shift in the woman's relationship with her husband, both because she has less time available for household chores and because she is making a greater economic contribution to the family.

Many middle-aged men and women who have been employed throughout their adult life experience increased dissatisfaction with their work. In her book on midlife career changes, Paula Robbins (1978) identifies several sources of this dissatisfaction. Although her research focused primarily on middle- and upper-middle-class men, several of the issues she raises seem equally pertinent to working women and to men in blue-collar occupations. Among the most important complaints were

1. *"Being put on the shelf" or "topping out."* At some point in their careers, most men must face the fact that they have advanced as far as they are likely to. The top jobs within their organization or the positions of greatest recognition within their profession will be held in the future not by them,

Recently, unemployed managerial personnel have begun banding together in clubs and organizations to give each other emotional support and aid in seeking out new positions.

but by others. Although they may view their current position, in and of itself, as satisfying, they may find the loss of potential mobility hard to accept. The blue-collar equivalent of this dilemma was described by Chinoy (1955, as quoted by Brim, 1976) in his study of automobile workers. He found that many workers dealt with the discrepancy between what they wanted when they were young and what they had accomplished by clinging to dreams of becoming a farmer or small businessman.

2. *Lack of challenge.* Once the demands of a particular job are thoroughly mastered, boredom may set in and the individual may seek new challenges.

3. *Change in values.* Middle-aged people may find that they no longer want to pursue the goals that were important to them earlier. The reasons for this shift are varied. It may be the result of exposure to new ideas. For example, many of the men in Robbins's study cited experiences with the antiwar and civil rights movements of the late 1960s and early 1970s as contributing to their changed outlook. It may reflect a shift in orientation. Several authors (Gutmann, 1977; Jung, 1933) have suggested that in middle age, men and women reclaim underutilized parts of themselves. Men become more oriented toward nurturance, women toward competitive interaction. Both sexes may seek occupations that allow freer expression of these new interests. Or it may grow out of a resurgence of interest in early dreams that were pushed aside (Levinson et al., 1978).

4. *Lack of autonomy.* People's desire to have more control over their work life is an important motivator during the middle years.

Another factor, not mentioned by the men in Robbins's study—although she suggests it may be an important source of dissatisfaction for many workers—is income level. Many middle-aged people realize that they will never have certain possessions or worry that they will be unable to prepare adequately for their retirement.

Despite all these possible difficulties, the middle years can be a time of considerable satisfaction vocationally. People are likely to be at their peak in terms of income, status, and responsibility. In a survey of 100 middle-class and upper-middle-class men and women, Neugarten (1968) found that the majority felt that they had the maximum capacity to handle the demands of their job in middle age. To quote a participant:

> I know now exactly what I can do best, and how to make best use of my time. . . . I know how to delegate authority, but also what decisions to make myself. . . . I know how to buffer myself from troublesome people. . . . (p. 98)

Marriage

Several studies (Burr, 1970; Campbell, 1975; Rollins & Feldman, 1970; Thurnher, 1976) show that marital satisfaction, particularly for women, is relatively low at the beginning of this period, until just before the children leave home. Couples report that they are less likely than in the early days of their marriage to confide in each other (Pineo, 1961), to laugh together, or to have a stimulating exchange of ideas (Rollins & Feldman, 1970). A study of midlife marriages by Majda Thurnher (1976) found that couples put greater stress on whether or not the spouse lives up to role expectations (e.g., is a "good mother" or "good provider") and much less stress on personality attributes than do younger or older couples. She suggested that couples may be particularly "out of sync" during this period of life, because each partner is preoccupied with the changes in his or her own life. She quotes a male participant in her study:

> Now I go my way and she goes hers and they don't seem to coincide that much. I think one of these days we'll come to a closer understanding. When I stop being so tense about things at work, we should be able to get back on the beam. (p. 132)

This man's optimism about the future is justified, at least for marriages in general. With the departure of the children from the family center, and perhaps also as the couple comes to terms with the issues of the midlife period, marital satisfaction begins to rise (Campbell, 1970; Rollins & Feldman, 1970; Thurnher, 1976). Many, if not most, couples share more activities and strengthen the emotional bond between them in the later years of this period.

OLD AGE

Just when "old age" begins is not easily determined. Traditionally, researchers in the field of aging have used age 65 or older as the point at which an individual may be considered "old." However, being old is seen as undesirable in American society, so many people continue to think of themselves as middle-aged until they are well into their 70s. Several studies suggest that it is not until people have experienced many of the changes that we associate with aging (retirement, loss of spouse and friends, poor health) that they are willing to apply the label "old" to themselves.

The relative status of the old in our society, as well as people's willingness to think of themselves as old, may be changing. Ronald Reagan's election to the presidency of the United States at age 69 must have altered many people's conception of "old." Organizations such as the Gray Panthers have worked hard to increase the visibility and political power of the elderly. The media also have focused more attention on this age group. In part, these changes reflect changing demographic patterns. Increased life expectancy and a de-

FIGURE 13–4

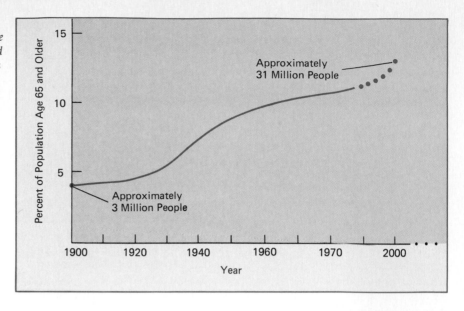

clining birthrate have resulted not only in greater numbers of people over 65 in the United States but also in a greater proportion of people in that age range. Figure 13–4 shows how this trend should lead to almost 15 percent of the population being over 65 by the year 2000—a substantial gain and one likely to lead to increased power and status for the elderly in our society.

Whether or not they label themselves as "old," individuals in their 60s and 70s encounter new changes in their functioning and in their environment. As in earlier periods of life, these changes require adjustment, which may sometimes be easy and sometimes difficult.

Physical Changes

Many of the physical changes of middle age become more marked in the later years of life. Visual and auditory capacities generally show further decline. Decreases in muscle strength, reaction time, and stamina continue to occur. Outward appearance continues to alter.

Health becomes an increasingly important issue during this period. Acute (temporary) problems such as injuries and influenza actually tend to decline with age. However, chronic (long-term) problems increase significantly. It has been estimated that approximately 80 percent of all older people have one or more chronic conditions, including arthritis, rheumatism, hypertension, heart disease, and cancer (Ward, 1979). In 1974, according to the U.S. Public Health Service (1974), 39 percent of people over 65 experienced limitations on major activities (defined as the ability to work, keep house, or engage in school activities) and another 7 percent experienced less serious limitations.

Research suggests that older people learn to live with and accept many of these conditions as an inevitable part of aging. Consequently, self-ratings of health decline less than objective ratings (Riley & Foner, 1968). Nevertheless, perceived and actual health are clearly related to each other—actual health cannot decline too far before perceived health is affected. The importance of this is illustrated in a study by Palmore and Luikart (1972), which found that self-rating of health was the variable most related to life satisfaction among middle-aged and older men and women.

Health is important also because it can affect the individual's ability to function sexually. It is difficult to obtain reliable data on sexual activity in old age, in part because different studies focus on different aspects of sexuality. Sexual functioning has been variously defined as coitus once a week or more, successful coitus at least once a year, or regular orgasmic release through any means including coitus, masturbation, or nocturnal emission. Further, most research has focused on males. Given the limitations, the evidence suggests that even in their 70s the majority of men continue to function sexually (Botwinick, 1973; Kahn & Fisher, 1967). The evidence further suggests that loss of responsiveness is not an inevitable part of aging but is due instead to factors such as chronic physical problems, lack of an available partner, and the belief that sex after 60 is somehow unusual or immoral (Botwinick, 1973).

Cognitive Changes

One of the most controversial issues in the field of gerontology is the extent to which cognitive capacities decline with advancing age. In part, this conflict reflects the fact that researchers have focused on different aspects of intellectual functioning, including memory, problem-solving abilities, and performance on intelligence tests. In addition, methodological issues make it difficult to interpret the results of many of the studies that have been done. Looking first at methodological problems, three seem to be of particular importance:

1. The research design used. Some studies have used cross-sectional designs; others have used longitudinal designs. Each method has its own biases. Cross-sectional approaches tend to overestimate negative age changes, since people in older age groups have had less education than younger people. Longitudinal approaches tend to underestimate negative age changes because subjects may become "test-wise" and also because less able subjects tend to drop out more often than more competent subjects (Botwinick, 1977).
2. The appropriateness of the tests. Some researchers have suggested that the old perform more poorly than the young on many tests not because they have less ability, but because they are not used to being in a testing situation and see the tasks as irrelevant. They, therefore, are not motivated to do well.
3. The effect of extraneous factors. Overarousal in a laboratory situation and a tendency to tire during extended testing also have been suggested as important factors affecting the performance of older people (Arenberg & Robertson-Tchabo, 1977; Botwinick, 1977).

With these methodological limitations in mind, we will review some of the research findings in the area that have probably received the most attention— performance on IQ tests. Studies using tests such as the Wechsler Adult Intelligence Scale have typically found a "classic pattern of aging." Subtests emphasizing verbal skills (vocabulary, information, comprehension) tend to show little or no decline until well into old age. But subtests that measure memory and perceptual-integrative skills (digit span, digit symbol, picture arrangement) show declining scores from middle age on (Botwinick, 1977). One way of conceptualizing these different types of skills is in terms of "crystallized" versus "fluid" intelligence. **Crystallized intelligence** refers to those abilities that can be "expected to improve by the increased learning, the

Digit Presented	Sum to Calculate	Appropriate Response
9	—	—
3	3 + 9	12
1	1 + 3	4
7	7 + 1	8
.	.	.
.	.	.
.	.	.

FIGURE 13–5

An illustration of the continuous-addition task used by Rabbit (1982) to compare young and aged subjects. As each digit was presented, the subject had to report the sum of it and the preceding digit. Aged subjects made more errors in which they seemed to recall the wrong term from short-term memory. For example, when the 1 was presented in the sequence shown above, they might erroneously respond "10," as if they had added the 1 to the first digit (9) instead of to the immediately preceding digit (3). Or when 7 was presented, they might errone- ously respond "11," as if they had added the 7 to the preceding sum (4) instead of to the immediately preceding digit (1). (Rabbit, 1982)

consolidation of knowledge . . . which accompany aging." Crystallized intelligence is best observed in the verbal subtests, which show relatively little age-related decline. **Fluid intelligence,** on the other hand, refers to those abilities that are most sensitive to "any loss or degeneration of the physiological (principally neurological) substratum supporting intellectual behavior," and it is best observed in scores on the more performance-oriented subtests, which do show an earlier decline with age. Theorists who support this conceptualization suggest that whether or not the older individual is at a relative disadvantage in performing a particular task depends in large part on which type of ability the task demands (Horn & Donaldson, 1976).

A psychologist at Oxford University in England (Rabbit, 1982) compared young subjects (18 to 32 years old) and aged subjects (65 to 81 years old) on a simple calculational task that placed a special burden on short-term memory. Subjects listened to a random series of 50 digits. As soon as they heard each digit, they were to add it to the preceding digit and report the sum (the sum of the last two digits). When the digits were presented rapidly (one digit every 2 or 3 seconds) and the subjects had to perform a distracting secondary task, both young and aged subjects made errors. However, the aged subjects were more likely to make a particular type of error, and this type seemed to involve the recall of the wrong item from short-term memory. For example, they would add an earlier digit rather than the preceding digit, or add a preceding sum (see Figure 13–5).

The specific cognitive problem of the aged was not so much a failure to retain information in short-term memory, but a failure to retrieve the appropriate information. Rabbit (1981) found a similar difference between young and old subjects in recalling a series of four sentences spoken by different speakers. Both young and aged recalled the sentences equally well, but the older people were less likely to remember who spoke each sentence. This may be why some older people have difficulty participating in conversations involving several people; they remember what is said, but can't remember who said it.

It must be emphasized that these tests measure changes in intellectual functioning in *groups.* Decrement is not inevitable in every person. Indeed, numerous individuals continue to function at a high level until they are quite old. Factors such as health, education, and earlier level of performance appear to be far more important than age per se in affecting performance during the later years (Botwinick, 1977).

In a vast number of studies, there seems to be a discernible pattern of decline in cognitive performance on the part of the aged. The more the cognitive task in question is unfamiliar, novel, and removed from the day-to-day activities of the individual, and the more its execution requires speed or short-term memory capacities, the more the performance of the aged shows a decline. On the other hand, the more familiar the task, and the more similar to the day-to-day activities of the person, the less the decline seems to be (Birren, Cunningham, & Yamamoto, 1983).

Retirement

Retirement is one of the most important, and most studied, changes associated with old age. Some people see it as a quite negative change, a separation from an important source of satisfaction and self-esteem. Those who take this point of view have been active in the movement to raise and even abolish mandatory retirement ages. But others view retirement as a positive shift to

a life with more free time and more opportunity to pursue non–work-related interests. Some labor unions have demanded "30 and out" plans, allowing workers to retire on full pension after 30 years of service. At present, only about 20 percent of males and 8.5 percent of females continue to work after age 65 (Kalish, 1982).

How retirement is perceived by the individual worker is crucial because attitude toward retirement is among the most important predictors of later adjustment and satisfaction (Kimmel, Price, & Walker, 1978; Streib & Schneider, 1971). Other factors that affect adjustment are

1. *Health.* Several studies have suggested that continued good health is one of the most important predictors of postretirement satisfaction (Kimmel, Price, & Walker, 1978; Streib & Schneider, 1971).
2. *Voluntary versus involuntary retirement.* It is not easy to define "voluntary"—for example, is retiring before a mandatory time because one is in poor health voluntary? But the more voluntary the retirement, the better the adjustment (Kimmel et al., 1978).
3. *Sex.* Some evidence indicates that, contrary to stereotypes, women take longer than men to adjust to retirement (Atchley, 1976).
4. *Adequate income.* Many people face a sharp drop in income upon retirement. Several studies indicate that "the money it brings in" is the most missed aspect of work (Harris poll, 1975) and that the expectation of a reasonable standard of living is a major factor in making a positive adjustment to retirement (Eisdorfer, 1972; Glamzer, 1976).
5. *Social class.* The relationship between social class and adjustment is not clear. On the one hand, upper-status workers generally find more satisfaction in their work roles than blue-collar workers do, and so they might be expected to miss working more. On the other hand, they are more likely to have adequate retirement incomes and to be involved in non–work-related activities that may carry over into retirement (Eisdorfer, 1972).

Overall, most people seem to adjust well to retirement and find it a relatively satisfying experience (Ward, 1979).

Marriage and Widowhood

The upswing in marital happiness that begins in middle age continues into this period of life. Although an increase in tension may occur just before the husband's retirement, the necessary adjustments in the marriage are usually made smoothly, and the majority of older couples report high levels of satisfaction (Dressler, 1973; Rollins & Feldman, 1970; Thurnher, 1976; Kalish, 1982).

The death of a spouse, however, is common during this period. While only 15 percent of the males over 65 years old in the United States are widowers, more than 50 percent of the women over 65 are widows.

In an important study of the process of adjustment, Helen Lopata (1973) focused on 301 widows over the age of 50 living in the Chicago area. She found three general patterns of adaptation. The "self-initiating woman" is both aware that she has to make behavioral and relational adjustments and flexible enough to do so. She selects those aspects of her previous life that can be continued and discards those it would be impossible to maintain. She modifies her relationships with friends and children, builds a life style suited to her individual needs, and attempts to match available resources and personal goals. The second pattern, generally found in widows in lower-class ethnic communities, involves relatively little change after a husband dies. "Being immersed in kin relations, a very close peer group, or a network of neighbors, such a woman may continue many of her involvements with little modification after becoming a widow." Lopata suggests that a similar pattern may be found in some suburbanites. The third pattern is that of the "social isolate," the woman who was never highly engaged in the broader society, whose life was centered on her husband, and who lacks the resources to develop new roles as her old ones fall away.

Other studies have focused on specific factors that affect the adjustment to widowhood. Among the variables found to affect morale are income level, mobility, health, age (older widows tend to adjust more easily), and availability of alternative roles such as employment or family involvement (Atchley, 1975; Morgan, 1976). In general, the data suggest that most people cope adequately, although widows and widowers are somewhat less satisfied with their lives than those who are still married (Campbell, 1975; Riley & Foner, 1968).

Establishment of Ego Integrity

We have focused so far on specific areas requiring adjustment in old age. In his classic description of the stages of life, Erik Erikson (1963) identified what he felt was the crucial broad task confronting individuals who are approaching death—the establishment of a sense of *ego integrity*. They must evaluate their lives and affirm to themselves that they were meaningful and "something that had to be." The alternative is despair, a sense that one's life has been wasted and that it is now too late to find fulfillment.

In a similar vein, Robert Butler (1968) suggests that the older individual engages in a "life review" and that an inability to handle this process may lead to depression. Like Erikson, Butler argues that a possible and ideal outcome is the further evolution of such characteristics as candor, serenity, and wisdom.

DEATH AND DYING

Although death has traditionally been a taboo subject in American culture, interest in this "final stage of development" is currently on the rise. Partly this reflects a recognition that death is "the most mysterious, most threatening, and most tantalizing of all human phenomena" (Shneidman, 1973, p. 23) and that understanding life and development requires coming to terms with death. It also reflects concern that avoidance of the topic leads to dehumanization of the dying (Kübler-Ross, 1969).

Elisabeth Kübler-Ross has been a pioneer in the study of the dying. On the basis of intensive interviews with over 200 terminally ill patients in a Chicago hospital, she outlined five stages that people go through as they approach death (Kübler-Ross, 1969).

The first stage is *denial and isolation*. The initial response by most patients is "No, not me, it cannot be true." They may become convinced that there has been a mixup in laboratory reports, they may turn to faith healers, or they may simply talk cheerfully about their future plans. Kübler-Ross regards this as a healthy reaction, a means of buying time until other, less radical, defenses can be mobilized. The vast majority of patients give up denial and move on to the other stages, although they may temporarily return to this stage later in their illness.

Anger is the next stage and occurs when denial can no longer be maintained. The question becomes "Why me? Why not someone else, who is older or meaner or of less use to society?" These feelings of resentment and envy, as well as concern about being overlooked or treated as of no importance, may result in outbursts of temper. This can be a particularly difficult time for the dying person's family and the hospital staff.

If treated with respect and understanding, the anger usually subsides and people may move on to the third stage, *bargaining*. Now they attempt to reach some sort of agreement, usually with God. "I will be good"—e.g., I will live a life in the service of the church or eventually give my body to science—"if only I am allowed to live." Not all dying patients go through this stage.

The fourth stage is *depression*. Kübler-Ross distinguishes two different types of grief that may be experienced during this time. The first is what she calls *reactive* depression, in which patients respond to current and past losses—the disfigurement caused by the disease, the inability to care for their family because they are ill, the wrongs they committed that cannot be righted. The

The Hospice Movement

In recent years, people have begun to pay more attention to the care of those suffering from terminal illness. Some people believe that the modern hospital, with its emphasis on aggressive therapy and the prolongation of life by any means, does not and cannot provide sufficient support either for the dying person or for the family (Holden, 1976).

One alternative is the hospice movement, which originated in its modern form in England. The term **hospice** is generally used to describe centers established for the care of patients dying of diseases such as cancer. It can also refer to a community of volunteers and professionals who provide support for patients and their families, both at the centers and in the patients' homes. Although hospices differ, most share certain aims (DuBois, 1980; Holden, 1976):

1. Adequate pain control. The first goal is to make the patient free from pain, and from any fear that pain will return. Movement leaders point out that many hospitals fail to control pain adequately, in part because of the pharmacological ignorance of many doctors, and in part because of concern about addiction and side effects,

second is a *preparatory* depression, a reaction to impending losses, the separation from life and loved ones.

At last, given sufficient time and support, people may reach the final stage, *acceptance,* in which they are able to contemplate death with some degree of quiet expectation, without fear or despair. Kübler-Ross emphasizes that this is neither a happy time nor a time of hopelessness and resignation. It is a period of peace.

Several criticisms of this description have been advanced. One of the most frequent is the argument that these reactions do not constitute "stages" in the sense that dying people necessarily advance through them in a predictable sequence. Kübler-Ross herself now acknowledges that the stages do not always occur in the same order and that, indeed, a patient may experience several simultaneously (Kübler-Ross, 1974). Another criticism is that there is no consistent evidence that the "typical" dying patient is characterized by any emotion other than depression (DuBois, 1980). A third criticism is that Kübler-Ross's stages will be taken as a prescription for an "ideal death." To quote Kalish (1977), "Some health caretakers have been observed trying to encourage, or even manipulate, their dying patients through [the] stages; patients occasionally become concerned if they are not progressing adequately, with adequacy also defined in terms of the stages" (p. 494). Finally, it is questionable whether acceptance is the only reasonable way to face death. Weisman (1972) points out that "not going gently into that good night but raging" may be an equally appropriate reaction. Despite these criticisms, Kübler-Ross's work has served the useful purpose of drawing attention to an important area of study.

SUMMARY

1. *Puberty* is marked by dramatic changes in growth rate and the development of primary and secondary sex characteristics.

2. *Adolescence* is the period between childhood and adulthood during which the individual learns the skills needed to survive as an adult; it is a socially rather than biologically determined phase of development.

3. At about age 12, the child enters Piaget's final stage of cognitive development—*formal operations.* The most basic change in this stage is the ability to deal with abstract concepts and use both

concerns that are irrelevant to the dying.

2. Psychological support for the patient. "Support" in this sense means doing whatever will give this particular individual the greatest comfort and peace. This may mean getting the house in order and making plans for the children. It may mean providing opportunities for the patient to be with family and friends as much as possible. Or it may mean giving the person an opportunity to see and talk with other dying patients.

3. Support for the bereaved, both before and after the death. Although some family members will need little follow-up, others will need considerable help. The latter may return to the hospice at any time for further care.

It remains to be seen what impact the hospice concept will have in the United States. There may be resistance from traditional health-care providers. There is also some concern that hospices will become simply another type of nursing home (Holden, 1976). So far, few studies have been done to show how well the hospice meets the needs of the dying and their families. However, the hospice concept appears to be a potentially valuable tool in the effort to make the process of dying less frightening and less dehumanizing.

hypothetico-deductive reasoning and *propositional thinking.*

4. According to Freud, during adolescence the sexual energy of libido, repressed during latency, reemerges, and the adult stage of development begins. Erikson called the search for *self-identity* the key crisis in need of resolution during adolescent years.

5. Keniston suggested the term "youth" for the stage between adolescence and adulthood, when people spend long periods of training for a career while still dependent on their parents financially.

6. According to a number of theorists, the major task in early adulthood is the establishing of intimate relationships.

7. A major event of the middle years is the departure of children from the home. While some parents do suffer from the "empty-nest" syndrome, many welcome their new-found freedom. This is also the time when many women are able to reenter the job market.

8. Physical changes during the midlife years may cause some persons to experience self-doubts or stress; in women, the *menopause* is characterized by physical changes that may be accompanied by psychological effects as well.

9. Among the major changes occurring in old age are physical change, cognitive change, retirement, and widowhood.

10. Erikson has described the crucial task confronting the person entering old age as the establishment of a sense of *ego integrity;* Butler suggests that old age is a time in which "life review" is essential.

11. Kübler-Ross has outlined five stages of dealing with death: denial, anger, bargaining, depression, and acceptance.

Suggested Readings

BIRREN, J. E., & SCHAIE, K. W. *Handbook of the psychology of aging.* New York: Van Nostrand Reinhold, 1977. Physiological and cognitive effects of the aging process.

DAVITZ, J., & DAVITZ, L. *Making it from forty to fifty.* New York: Random House, 1976. Interviews with 200 middle-aged adults reveal thoughts, feelings, and actions characteristic of midlife adjustments.

GOETHALS, G. W., & KLOS, D. S. *Experiencing youth: First person accounts,* 2nd ed. Boston: Little, Brown, 1976. Autobiographical studies of adolescents with focus on interpersonal problems and personality development.

SARASON, S. B. *Work, aging, and social change.* New York: Free Press, 1977. An examination of our current expectations about professional careers, with suggestions for social policy to facilitate career change.

WOODRUFF, D. S., & BIRREN, J. E. *Aging: Scientific perspectives and social issues,* 2nd ed. Belmont, Calif.: Wadsworth, 1983.

14. Personality

There is no single accepted definition of personality; there are many, each resting on different assumptions and stressing different aspects of being. A key theme uniting many definitions, however, is that **personality** is the organized and distinctive pattern of behavior that characterizes an individual's adaptation to a situation and endures over time. Were it not for this distinctiveness, we would not be able to distinguish one person from another; were it not for the relative permanence of personality, we would not recognize the same individual from one moment to the next.

The study of personality is rich with theories about our inherent nature, about what makes us think, feel, behave, and experience life as we do. Each theory involves a different view of the essence, structure, and functioning of humans and their relationship to the environment. The range of concerns in the study of personality thus includes ideas, motives, attitudes, emotions, life crises, beliefs, values, and the processes by which people try to understand their own behavior, that of others, and the world.

Formal personality theories must specify and answer 4 major questions:

1. What is the structure of personality? Are there differing levels of structure and are some elements of personality subordinate to others? If there is no overall structure, what is the alternative concept?
2. What motivates us? Why do we act as we do?
3. How does personality grow and change over time? Does it change fundamentally? If so, in what ways?
4. How do we account for human individuality or uniqueness?

The first 3 questions are concerned with qualities shared by all people, or how we are alike; the last tries to account for uniqueness, or why we are different. Today the focus is on understanding the common qualities, on the characteristics, motives, drives, and behaviors that all people share. Traditionally, however, those studying personality were concerned with what made the individual unique. Our examination of personality theories begins with one of these traditional approaches, the trait theories, which categorize people on the basis of their distinctive attributes and traits.

TRAIT THEORIES

The earliest approaches to personality accounted for human behavior in terms of people's innate traits or dispositions. Traits were said to be stable, enduring, and consistent; continuous rather than discrete. They intertwined with and affected one another—they could be talked about in terms of amount or degree rather than as absolutes. Because of this, however, it was difficult to find a completely satisfactory method for categorizing traits.

Nomothetic Personality Theories: Cattell

Trait theories in personality psychology have traditionally been **nomothetic** in character—that is, based on the belief that all traits are equally applicable to all individuals. In this view, every person occupies some position with regard to every trait. An individual's personality, then, is the sum total of his or her rankings on each of the traits. For example, John may be *very* independent, Jane *moderately* independent, and Ralph *not at all* independent, but the relative independence of each individual is measurable on the same scale. Within this framework there has been some disagreement over the number or kinds of traits that exist (Eysenck, 1977), but the idea that traits are global and universal characteristics is common to most traditional views of personality.

Some theorists who used the nomothetic approach tried to reduce the potentially vast number of traits to a more manageable and efficient list. Raymond Cattell, a leading trait theorist, set out to identify a reasonable number of traits that could be used to describe all individuals and predict their behavior. To accomplish this empirical "mapping of the personality," he used a sophisticated statistical technique known as factor analysis. This procedure makes it possible to analyze data for a large number of variables simultaneously and to group together those variables that are associated with one another. Two or more factors that correlate highly are assumed to reflect the existence of one underlying trait; for example, think of "warm" and "sociable" as against "aloof" and "cool." Using this procedure, Cattell drew up a 16-factor inventory that he believed gave an adequate representation of personality.

For Cattell, personality "permits a prediction of what a person will do in a given situation" (1952, p. 2). So, once he could position a person according to the 16 factors, he would attempt to predict many of that person's behaviors. The method involves several steps. Cattell called the 16 first-order factors the **source traits,** the structural influences underlying personality (see Table 14–1). Source traits interact with one another to produce second-order factors and overt behaviors called **surface traits.**

Idiographic Personality Theories: Allport

Attempts like Cattell's to predict behavior from underlying traits have met with mixed success. Moreover, the assumption that traits are universal characteristics or dispositions has not gone unchallenged. **Idiographic** models of personality are based on the assumption that traits are concrete (i.e., based on specific situations) and unique to particular individuals. Personality is seen as the sum of an individual's experiences. In this view, the same trait may mean different things to different individuals. For example, for John independence may mean being aggressive with peers and unwilling to take advice; Jane's idea of independence may include unorthodox political views and socially outgoing behavior at parties; Ralph, on the other hand, may not think of himself in terms of independence at all. The unique experiences of these 3 individuals have given them ideas of independence that may overlap but are by no means universal.

One of the first personality psychologists to attempt to approach personality in this idiographic way was Gordon Allport. According to Allport, no 2 people are alike, no 2 individuals respond in the same way even to identical stimuli. To study personality, then, one must study the combination of traits as they appear in single individuals. Traits direct action and motivate us to behave the way we do. However, some traits are more impelling than others. Allport distinguished 3 levels of traits according to the degree to which they govern personality:

1. *Cardinal traits.* These are the most powerful and pervasive traits; they dominate a person's life. Few people possess cardinal traits. When they do,

SOURCE TRAIT INDEX	LOW-SCORE DESCRIPTION			SOURCE TRAIT INDEX	HIGH-SCORE DESCRIPTION
A	SIZIA *Reserved, detached, critical, aloof, stiff*	M	PRAXERNIA *Practical, "down-to-earth," concerned*	A	AFFECTIA *Outgoing, warmhearted, easygoing, participating*
B	LOW INTELLIGENCE *Dull*	N	ARTLESSNESS *Forthright, unpretentious, genuine, but socially clumsy*	B	HIGH INTELLIGENCE *Bright*
C	LOW EGO STRENGTH *At mercy of feelings, emotionally less stable, easily upset, changeable*			C	HIGHER EGO STRENGTH *Emotionally stable, mature, faces reality, calm*
		O	UNTROUBLED ADEQUACY *Self-assured, placid, secure, complacent, serene*		
E	SUBMISSIVENESS *Humble, mild, easily led, docile, accommodating*	Q1	CONSERVATISM OF TEMPERAMENT *Conservative, respecting traditional ideas*	E	DOMINANCE *Assertive, aggressive, competitive, stubborn*
F	DESURGENCY *Sober, taciturn, serious*			F	SURGENCY *happy-go-lucky, gay, enthusiastic*
G	WEAKER, SUPEREGO STRENGTH *Expedient, disregards rules*	Q2	GROUP ADHERENCE *Group-dependent, a "joiner" and sound follower*	G	STRONGER SUPEREGO STRENGTH *Conscientious, persistent, moralistic, staid*
H	THRECTIA *Shy, timid, threat-sensitive*	Q3	LOW SELF-SENTIMENT INTEGRATION *Undisciplined, self conflict, follows own urges, careless of social rules*	H	PARMIA *Venturesome, uninhibited, socially bold*
I	HARRIA *Tough-minded, self-reliant*			I	PREMSIA *Tender-minded, sensitive, clinging, overprotected*
		Q4	LOW ERGIC TENSION *Relaxed, tranquil, torpid, unfrustrated, composed*	L	PROTENSION *Suspicious, hard to fool*
L	ALAXIA *Trusting, accepting conditions*			M	AUTIA *Imaginative, bohemian, absent-minded*
				N	SHREWDNESS *Astute, polished, socially aware*
				O	GUILT PRONENESS *Apprehensive, self-reproaching, insecure, worrying, troubled*
				Q1	RADICALISM *Experimenting, liberal, free-thinking*
				Q2	SELF-SUFFICIENCY *Self-sufficient, resourceful, prefers own decisions*
				Q3	HIGHER STRENGTH OF SELF-SENTIMENT *Controlled, exacting will power, socially precise, compulsive, following self-image*
				Q4	HIGH ERGIC TENSION *Tense, frustrated, driven, overwrought*

Table 14–1: Cattell's 16 Source Traits. Note the low-score description for each trait above and the corresponding high-score description for the same trait to the right.

Cattell & Kline, 1977, p. 44.

we often think of them primarily in terms of those traits. If we say someone is Machiavellian, we are referring to the kind of unscrupulous behavior that marks everything this person says, does, and thinks.

2. *Central traits.* These are the few traits that characterize an individual. A study by Allport (1961) showed that people perceive an average of 7.2 central dispositions in those they know well. Central traits are the kind that might be included in a letter of recommendation or a counselor's report (e.g., punctuality, industriousness, honesty).

3. *Secondary traits.* These are the most limited in frequency and least crucial to an understanding of the dynamics of an individual's personality. They include, for example, the kind of music or food one likes.

Although traits must be apparent in an individual's behavior patterns in order to be known, Allport's theory allows room for situational differences in an individual's behavior. These differences occur because there are many traits, many are active at the same time, they overlap, and they are organized in a different way for each individual. This point about differential organization is particularly important. For instance, 2 people may both be accurately described as possessing the trait of "honesty," but for the first, honesty may extend to a prohibition even of "white lies" (telling people that you like their expensive new clothes even though you actually think they are tasteless), while for the second, an apparently harmless deception is acceptable.

Allport's theory has some clear strengths. First, it calls attention to the conscious motives for behavior. Second, it is concerned mainly with current behavior—the way someone reacts now, at this moment. Third, it attempts to specify the ways in which people are different, one of the key questions that a theory of personality must address.

There are also weaknesses in this approach. For instance, people do behave in apparently contradictory ways. How is this to be explained within a trait system that emphasizes consistency? Allport attempted to deal with this problem in 2 ways. First, he pointed out that traits could intertwine with and affect one another, and thus they should be talked about in terms of amount or degree rather than as absolutes. Second, he showed that people have used a vast number of traits—in one analysis, over 5,000—to describe behavior. Thus, trait theories are concerned primarily with identifying the structure of personality and using that structure to predict behavior. But trait theorists still do not agree on the *number* of traits that are applicable to individuals, the *universality* of the traits, and the *stability* of traits across people and situations. The trait models also do not tell us how that personality structure develops. The question of how we develop into the stable, recognizable individuals we are can be answered in a variety of different ways. In the following sections, we will examine 5 different approaches, each providing a unique perspective on the development of personality: on the roles played by heredity and the environment, and on the relative stability of personality traits over time, across people, and across situations.

FIVE MODELS OF PERSONALITY

Although personality is clearly an important area of inquiry for psychologists, they do not agree on any one theoretical approach to this subject. Consequently, there are 5 models of personality: the psychoanalytic, humanistic-existential, biological, learning, and cognitive models. Each of these models incorporates a very different notion about people and how they come to be the way they are. Each holds different views on how active or passive people are in the formulation of their personal behaviors, and on the motivating forces, the role of environment, and the role of internal factors, among other concepts and issues. Each model rests on different assumptions about the best way to understand and explain human behavior. It is important to keep in mind that these are *models*, not reality. Ultimately, a particular model's usefulness depends on how well it helps us to organize and predict human behavior.

THE PSYCHOANALYTIC MODEL

According to Freud's psychoanalytic theory, the most comprehensive and influential of all theories of personality, we are at the mercy of a strict psychic determinism, primarily motivated by "drives" or "instincts" over which we have little control and of which we are only dimly aware. In this view, human personality is like an iceberg: The tip above the water, a small fraction of the total iceberg, represents our conscious awareness, while the vast mass below represents our unconscious life. Thus the primary motivation for our actions is not always directly accessible to us.

One of the most fundamental conceptual discoveries of **psychoanalytic theory** is that of the unconscious mind. To Freud, several different things point toward the existence of unconscious thought processes. Slips of the tongue, memory errors, and other apparently trivial phenomena, which are produced without conscious awareness, often can be shown to be connected by some very systematic and very revealing links. Dreams show the same connectedness; though they contain apparently disconnected leaps and illogical gaps, on analysis the psychological connections between elements are clear. From this, Freud was led to postulate the existence of the unconscious mind, in which the continuity of the thought process unfolds, blocked from the awareness of the thinker. The unconscious, unknown to consciousness, fundamentally affects the thought, feeling, and behavior of the individual; in it are the primary representation and the effects of many of the forces that govern people's behavior.

The Structure of Personality

We can get a clearer picture of Freud's concept of the unconscious and how it exerts its influence by looking more closely at his 3-part structure of personality: the id, ego, and superego. Remember, these concepts refer to processes, not actual physical locations in the brain. Also, although they are interrelated, each of the 3 processes has its own operating principles and functions. Personality and behavior are the products of the interaction of these 3 systems.

ID.   The **id** is the most basic of the 3 personality systems. The ego and the superego develop out of the id and, throughout life, rely on the id as the source of psychic energy for their activities. In a sense, then, their dependence on the id, the power source that runs the human personality, never ceases. The id is formed of the instincts, or drives, that an infant possesses at birth. Freud divided the instincts into two broad categories: life instincts (**Eros**) and death instincts (**Thanatos**). In terms of drives, these are frequently expressed as sex and aggression. The human organism, Freud believed, simultaneously wants to live and die, create and destroy.

Many psychologists have wished that Freud had not attached the label "sexual" to the first class of instincts, for many of the needs he discussed as belonging to this category—affection, warmth, nourishment—are not what most people would term "sexual." But, as we will see shortly, Freud was attempting to make clear the underlying unity of these needs and their connection with the sexual drive. This general class of sexual or life instincts enables the individual organisms of a species to survive and the species as a whole to perpetuate itself. Freud called the energy that fuels the life instincts **libido.**

The death or destructive instincts are less apparent in their operation. Indeed, Freud did not originally include them in his system. Only after the apparently senseless slaughter of World War I did he come to realize that his theory required some such concept. After that, Freud, often a pessimist, expressed the relationship between life and death in a famous dictum: "The goal of all life is death" (1920/1950, p. 38).

According to Freud, the human system is continually experiencing tension caused by both internal and external pressures. The goal of the id is immediate tension reduction. For instance, when a person experiences a need, such as hunger, this is felt as an uncomfortable state of tension. The id automatically strives to reduce this increase in tension and return to a low energy level. Freud called this the **pleasure principle.**

The id seeks immediate gratification without resort to objective reality. For example, if the organism is hungry, the id will create a mental image of "food" or a mother's breast. Creating an image of the desired object is called **wish fulfillment.** This obviously does not enable an organism to survive—an image of food cannot satisfy hunger—so the organism has to evolve a mode of thinking that can relate its needs to the external or objective world, where real, material food exists. This mode of thinking, which is based on logic and reason, Freud called **secondary-process thinking,** as opposed to the id's **primary-process thinking.** This secondary process, which developed out of the id and became differentiated from it, is the ego.

EGO. The **ego,** in contrast to the id, is concerned with, and aware of, objective reality. The ego seeks actual food, not an image of it. In general, the ego attempts to "match" objects in the external world as closely as possible to the images created by the id. The ego is devoted primarily to protecting the organism and to coping with the real world.

The ego will not allow the organism to release tension until it has located the object in the external world that will satisfy the instinctual need. Because the ego resorts to external reality to satisfy needs, it is said to obey the **reality principle** (as against the id's pleasure principle). If necessary, the ego will delay the organism's attempts at immediate gratification and pleasure, either because these attempts are unlikely to be successful or because greater gratification can be gained by waiting. The ego, therefore, is concerned with what is good and bad for the organism on the basis of objective criteria.

The ego is not the "enemy" of the id. In the most fundamental sense, it exists to serve the id's needs, to work in its behalf. The ego and id only come into conflict over the best way to do this. The ego seeks to postpone gratification until a real object in the external world has been found to satisfy an instinctual need. The id, on the other hand, demands immediate gratification and has no awareness of or concern about external reality—it is unsocialized and unconscious.

SUPEREGO. The last personality system to be differentiated from the id is the **superego.** Often referred to as the "conscience" or "moral arm" of the personality, the superego is concerned with moral ideals. These ideals are originally conveyed to the child by the parents; later, other authority figures and the rewards and punishments imposed by society also play a part in shaping the growing child's superego. It is the development of the superego that makes possible the child's development of self-control.

The superego deals in absolute rules. Unlike the ego, which seeks compromise, the superego strives for perfection. It does not function merely to postpone id impulses, as the ego does; it seeks to block them permanently. In this effort, it is as persistent and unyielding as the id. Many of the people Freud saw as patients could be described as being in unbearable conflict between the strong demands laid down by their ids and the absolute prohibitions on fulfilling those demands laid down by their superegos. Their egos were so weakened in the attempt to cope with this psychic conflict that they were no longer able to meet the day-to-day demands of ordinary life.

Jean Cocteau's drawing of Sigmund Freud. The set of eyes peering out from the body is Cocteau's way of symbolizing Freud's emphasis on the effects of the id on human behavior.

Psychic Interplay and Conflict

Freud conceived of the psychic system as having a limited amount of energy. The 3 personality systems compete for this energy and thus are often in competition. When one system—the id, for example—dominates the energy supply, the other systems must grow weaker.

The id, which originally had a monopoly on the psychic energy of the organism, uses it in the service of the pleasure principle. The ego and super-ego, however, postpone and block gratification as well as strive for it. The earlier example of matching real food with an image of food provides a good illustration of this; in this way, the ego diverts the psychic energy of the id and directs it out into the real world. The ego often causes object displacements that form a complex web of preferences, values, interests, and attitudes, which, although they don't directly satisfy the individual's instinctual needs, were originally connected in the history of the individual to objects that did.

Such displacement accounts for the great diversity of human nature and behavior. All our socialized attitudes, interests, and activities, according to Freud, are the result of the displacement of energy from original instinctual desires. It is this process that makes civilization possible, by causing individuals to invest their energies in the activities that make society go, rather than in the immediate gratification of their own needs.

Freud was pessimistic about the relationship between the individual and society—he saw it as one of essential conflict. Society requires repression of the most direct expressions of the person's impulses. The price we all pay for this postponement or blocking of direct instinctual gratification is unhappiness. Many pay a higher price in the form of psychosis or neurosis. This issue is explored by Freud in *Civilization and Its Discontents* (1930/1961), a book whose title reveals its general conclusion.

The Development of Personality

Freud's model of personality assumes that individuals develop in discrete, observable stages. Successful progression from one stage to the next is a critical determinant of adult mental health. As a physician, Freud investigated these developmental stages by observing the behavior of his patients. He believed that the regularity of the stages of personality development could be best understood by examining those individuals in whom the normal progression had been interrupted or subverted. One of Freud's greatest discoveries was that the roots of his adult patients' difficulties could be traced to their early childhood experiences. According to Freud, the basic patterns of behavior are established at an early age, and later development and growth are consistent with or constrained by these patterns.

One major source of these basic behavior patterns is the person's adaptation to each of the 4 psychosexual stages of development through which we all pass (see Chapter 12 for a summary of these stages). According to Freud, people who do not resolve the developmental challenges and problems of any one of these stages become **fixated** at that stage. They then fail to solve properly the problems posed by later stages, and as adults they have neurotic problems reflecting the stage at which the fixation occurred.

A person can also return to an earlier stage of development when experiencing conflict later in life. These individuals **regress,** or proceed backwards, to a stage at which fixation had occured. For example, a child experiencing unresolved conflict may return to an oral stage, with infantile behaviors such

Culture and Personality

Both because of his training in the biological sciences and the intellectual climate of the time, Freud believed that psychological processes are tied to the biological inheritance of the human being. He considered such concepts as the libido, the stages of development, and the **Oedipus complex** as essentially biological in nature.

There were two important intellectual consequences of this emphasis on biology. First, it means that an individual's development has a fixed, immutable character: The sequence of developmental stages is fixed by the biologically produced shifts in the individual's zones of gratification; and the conflicted nature of the Oedipal situation and its resolution is inevitable because of the developing sexual impulses of the child.

Second, since humans are biologically the same in all cultures, Freud felt that his theory was universal and did not require serious modification for people of another culture. Putting this another way, Freud did not think that the specifics of the culture in which one was reared had an important effect on the psychodynamic unfolding of personality development in the early childhood years.

But other intellectual developments of the early twentieth century

as thumb sucking; later, that child, now an adult with other problems, may seek refuge in drink, another type of oral activity.

A person rarely fixates or regresses totally. These are relative conditions. Under a similar set of stresses, one individual may regress to an oral stage, a second to a later stage, and a third may not regress at all.

Freud believed that particular personality problems or behaviors were due to problems in progressing through specific psychosexual stages. For example, a problem in the oral stage, in which the mouth is the primary source of pleasure, can lead to problems with dependency or aggression in the adult. Clinging to authority figures and attempting to draw strength from them can be an oral-stage attempt to solve a problem. Similarly, a "biting," aggressive style of wit can represent a return to the biting, aggressive aspects of the later oral stage. It is important to recognize here that for Freud, these stages represent a very general and even metaphorical way of coping with the world. The oral stage, for instance, involves some very general impulses of dependency.

Regression to the anal stage would be signaled by a person's being obstinate, overly concerned with orderliness, or parsimonious. Misers and, more generally, people who are unable to "let go" of control may be fixated at the anal stage. Attitudes toward authority and sexual activity are determined by the manner in which the conflicts of the phallic stage (in which the genitals become the center of pleasure) are resolved. Little personality development takes place during the latency period, but it is critical to pass through latency to reach the genital stage, in which more altruistic, less self-centered motives become possible. The final resolution of the genital stage allows the individual to function as a mature, well-adjusted member of society.

This has been a short summary of Freud's theory of personality and how it develops. In the chapters to come, we will discuss other aspects of his theory, such as defense mechanisms (Chapter 15), the basis for abnormal behavior (Chapter 16), and psychoanalysis as therapy for abnormal behavior (Chapter 17).

Now we will look at some of the variations of Freudian theory that have developed since the time of Freud.

Neo- and Post-Freudian Theorists

A number of theorists generally agreed with Freud on the importance of unconscious processes but disagreed with him on the origins of the impulses

challenged this biologically based conceptualization of human nature. About the same time that Freud was formulating and developing psychoanalytic theory, sociology and anthropology were changing people's conception of themselves and the factors that influence behavior.

The vivid descriptions of cultural anthropologists, particularly, were making Westerners aware that other cultures existed with elaborate and stable social systems and cultural arrangements that were dramatically different from those of Europe and the United States. And in at least some of these cultures, such Freudian "universals" as the latency period simply did not occur.

From this cross-cultural perspective, people could be seen as a product of social as well as biological forces. Their needs, impulses, and personality patterns were obviously conditioned by institutions such as the family, the educational system, and the social organizations of religion, power, and governance—institutions that differed greatly from culture to culture. Individuals and their personalities did not grow in splendid isolation in which biological patterns dictated a single sequence of development, but in a cultural context that contained its own sequences of growth and development, and its own standards of "normal" behavior and desirable personality.

that motivated those unconscious processes. For instance, Carl Jung shared the emphasis on personality as a "battlefield" of unconscious urges in conflict with the other systems of the personality. However, Jung replaced Freud's sexually motivated unconscious with the idea of a **collective unconscious** composed of **archetypes.** The collective unconscious is the "memory trace" of our ancestral history, including our animal origins, which exists in each individual and is essentially the same for everyone. It is independent of anything personal in the life of the individual, and at times it can overwhelm both the ego and "the personal unconscious" (our repressed thoughts, forgotten experiences, etc.).

Other **neo-Freudians,** such as Alfred Adler, Karen Horney, and Erich Fromm, took issue with Freud and Jung's emphasis on the role of instinct in determining behavior. They emphasized social rather than biological determinants of personality motivation and believed that anxiety and conflict come from the social conditions in which people find themselves as well as from their inherent personality structure.

The neo-Freudians in general shared with Freud and Jung a belief in the importance of the unconscious, but they gave a more independent role to the ego. Because of this emphasis, they have been called "ego psychologists." In suggesting that the ego had its own powers independent of the id, the ego psychologists were in effect saying that people are capable of a wider sphere of rational activities than orthodox psychoanalytic theory would grant. They saw people as freer, at least potentially, to choose their own fates, as compared to Freud's deterministic approach.

To critics, neo-Freudians and ego psychologists seem largely to complicate Freud's theory without moving away from it. We turn now to theories that differ from Freud's in more basic ways.

THE HUMANISTIC-EXISTENTIAL MODEL

The common emphasis of humanistic and existential theories is on the total personality as opposed to the separate behaviors that make up that personality. This is a radically antideterministic view that minimizes not only the effects of environment but also those of biology. The emphasis is on choice and the personal responsibility that being able to make choices implies.

The **humanistic-existential model** stresses personal experience and what that experience means to the individual as the basis of human personality and behavior. In order to understand the behavior of another person, we must first understand the way that person constructs his or her world.

As we have mentioned before, the psychoanalytic model of personality is basically one of *conflict* between the pleasure-seeking id and a restrictive society. Existential psychologists de-emphasize conflict and favor instead a model that emphasizes *striving:* awareness of one's own actions, understanding and acceptance of their consequences, and eagerness to embrace future choices. This condition of striving is known as being *authentic.* Being authentic includes being aware of the fear that one's choices may be wrong. This fear, or *ontological anxiety,* must be accepted as a part of being if an individual is to be authentic. A person who ignores or hides from this fear, or refuses to accept responsibility for his or her actions, becomes inauthentic and riddled with guilt.

We make choices about the actions we perform, and therefore our actions and personalities are explained by a different system from that used in natural sciences. The ax splits the log because of principles of mass and force; you split the log into firewood because you are planning to build a fire. Humans genuinely do engage in conscious, motivated, goal-directed behavior. But since each choice that we make involves giving up all the other choices available to us at that moment, all choices involve some pain because they mean foregoing other possibilities.

Nonetheless, particularly among the American practitioners of humanistic-existential psychology such as Maslow and Rogers, a more optimistic theme emerges. The basic force motivating human behavior is the need for growth and self-direction. People are seen as continually striving for increased awareness, self-actualization, and the fulfillment of their human potential.

Motives for Growth: Goldstein and Maslow

Abraham Maslow developed his approach to personality from the study of healthy, creative people. In general, he objected to the usual emphasis of personality theories on neurosis and maladaptive behavior, which he argued derived from the fact that most personality theorists were therapists who worked with disturbed individuals. Maslow believed that in every person "there is an active will toward health, an impulse toward growth, or toward the actualization of human potentialities" (1967, p. 153). This view stands in sharp contrast to Freudian and other theories that claim we have impulses, instincts, urges, or traits that stand in opposition to society and that need to be repressively socialized through training and education.

Maslow drew on the work of Kurt Goldstein, a neuropsychiatrist who had developed a theory about positive motives for behavior. In Goldstein's theory any need motivates us to satisfy it. But underlying all our needs is one real drive, one true motive: to self-actualize, to continuously realize our own potential by whatever means we can. The drive for **self-actualization** gives unity and organization to the personality. The tasks we perform to satisfy a need are the way we work toward self-actualization.

We may all have the same drive for self-actualization, but the means and ends we seek vary. This is because, according to Goldstein, we have different inherent preferences and potentialities. These not only help define our means and ends, but they also influence our individual development.

According to Goldstein, our drive for self-actualization comes from within, and the healthy individual can overcome "the disturbance arising from the clash with the world, not out of anxiety but out of the joy of conquest" (1939, p. 305). The individual has the possibility of *mastery* or *control* of the environment. However, if the realities of the environment are too inconsistent with the goals of the individual, the individual will break down or redefine his or her goals.

An environment, then, must allow an individual to be in a state that is normal or adequate to his or her nature. If the environment is too unstable, the constancy and identity of the individual are threatened. If, during childhood development, the environment is too stressful or inconsistent with the needs of the individual, Goldstein says, the child will develop behavior patterns that deter the process of self-actualization.

Maslow's need hierarchy, which we discussed in Chapter 11, can be used to clarify the conditions under which this occurs. Maslow divides his need hierarchy into 2 groups, one based on deficiency, the other on growth. The former (for example, the need for food) Maslow calls **basic needs;** the latter (for example, the desire for beauty, justice, and goodness) are called **meta-needs.** Basic needs, according to Maslow, are basic in the sense that if they are unfulfilled, people give them priority over other needs. A starving person seeks food and has no time or energy for appreciating works of art. For Maslow, self-actualization is the final concern of the person: It can only receive attention after the physiological, safety, belonging and love, and esteem needs have been met.

If the physical and social environments do not provide fulfillment of these basic needs, the person will seek to satisfy these needs by whatever means possible. Thus the environment can either temporarily or permanently block or thwart the natural drive for self-actualization. A person who sees the world as threatening or unpredictable may pursue safety or security needs to the exclusion of self-actualization. Maslow believed in the possibilities of personal growth and thought it worthwhile to urge people to self-actualize. He described in detail the characteristics of the self-actualized person (see Table 14–2).

Table 14–2: The Characteristics of Self-Actualized Individuals.

1. Are able to perceive reality accurately.
2. Are able to accept reality readily.
3. Are natural and spontaneous.
4. Can focus on problems rather than on their self.
5. Have a need for privacy.
6. Are self-sufficient and independent.
7. Are capable of fresh, spontaneous, non-stereotyped appreciation of objects, events and people that they encounter.
8. Have peak experiences, and attain transcendence.
9. Identify with mankind, and experience shared social bonds with other people.
10. May have few or many friends, but will have deep relationships with at least some of these friends.
11. Have a democratic, egalitarian attitude.
12. Have strongly held values and do not confuse means with ends.
13. Have a broad, tolerant sense of humor.
14. Are inventive and creative, and able to see things in new ways.
15. Resist the pressures of conformity to society.
16. Are able to transcend dichotomies, bring together opposites.

From Maslow (1967).

Self Theory: Rogers

Like Goldstein and Maslow, Carl Rogers, in his **person-centered personality theory,** viewed the individual as a whole being composed of complex cognitive, emotional, biological, and other processes and capable of self-actualization. Like Jung and Adler, Rogers also emphasized the role of the **self** and conscious awareness in the life of the individual. Like many other personality theorists, he constantly tried to help people with their problems. Perhaps because many of the people he saw were college students, Rogers reached a more optimistic conclusion about personal growth than did other theorists.

In keeping with the humanistic-existential tradition, Rogers placed great emphasis on the individual's total experience at a given moment. This unique personal experience, the **phenomenal field** of the individual, cannot be directly known by another. Rogers believed that knowing how people interpret their experiences is the first step in understanding their personality and behavior. But he also pointed out that elements of people's experience may be incorrectly represented by them, or not represented at all. A healthy, mature condition of adjustment exists, he said, when people accurately symbolize to themselves their phenomenal field. Maladjustment arises when there is a gap between people's actual experience and their awareness of it—in other words, when they deny or distort parts of their experience.

The self-image is particularly important in the development of personality. Each of us has an image of our real self (the self as it is) and of an ideal self (the self we'd like to be). The self-image develops from interaction with others. Our parents reward "worthy" actions and feelings and punish "unworthy" actions and feelings. If children are forced to give up or deny the "unworthy" actions or feelings (rather than learn to express them in more acceptable ways), they are compelled to deny a part of their existence. Their self-image then becomes inconsistent with their actual experience. Because their behavior is regulated not just by their own perceptions and feelings, but also by values they have incorporated from their parents and others, their personality is in effect divided.

The condition for self-actualization, therefore, is trusting one's own experience in the evaluation of oneself rather than evaluating oneself on the basis of the needs and interests of others. According to Rogers, a period of positive regard from parents and others in our lives helps us to do this.

It is difficult in this preliminary discussion to explain fully all the differences between the humanistic-existential theories and all other theories of personality. In Chapters 16 and 17, where we discuss the humanistic perspective on abnormal psychology and the existential modes of therapy, other distinctions will become clear. In brief, the humanistic-existential approaches assert that people have the freedom to choose the actions they take; because they do so, they have the capacity to grow and develop. But the other side of the coin is that they may use that same freedom to choose actions that limit or diminish their lives.

THE BIOLOGICAL MODEL

The biological approach to the study of personality holds that physical constitution, genetic endowment, and other physiological characteristics determine at least some basic features of personality. Older theories claimed that almost all the important elements of personality are biological in origin, while more modern versions state that only some personality characteristics originate in biological factors and that biological and other factors interact in complex ways that affect personality.

The Constitutional Approach: Sheldon

The **constitutional approach** holds that the structure of the body, or body type, determines personality and behavior. Some everyday stereotypes that we all have heard express this view. For instance, all fat people are jolly; thin, frail people are scholarly and ascetic. William Sheldon thought that there was a great deal of truth to these everyday generalizations although they were given short shrift by psychologists. He commented, "It is the old notion that structure must somehow determine function. In the face of this expectation it is rather astonishing that in the past so little relation has been discovered between the shape of man and the way he behaves" (1942, p. 4). After analyzing more than 4,000 photographs, Sheldon concluded that there are 3 basic body structures or **somatotypes** (see Figure 14–1): **Endomorphs** are usually fat and have underdeveloped musculature. **Mesomorphs** are generally muscular and of medium build. **Ectomorphs** tend to be slender and fragile and to have a light muscle structure.

Sheldon also did an extensive analysis of over 500 trait words, using intuitive procedures and correlational methods. He found 3 major groups of traits that make up the primary components of "temperament." He also found that each somatotype was strongly associated with one of the 3 primary temperaments. The chubby endomorph was likely to have an easygoing, sociable temperament; the athletic-looking mesomorph would probably be a risk-taking, assertive type; and the physically fragile ectomorph often was withdrawn and restrained.

Modern researchers tend to discount such facile correlations. They have been particularly critical of the fact that ratings of temperament were made by people (Sheldon and his associates) who had set out to find a body type–temperament correlation. In other words, the high degree of cor-

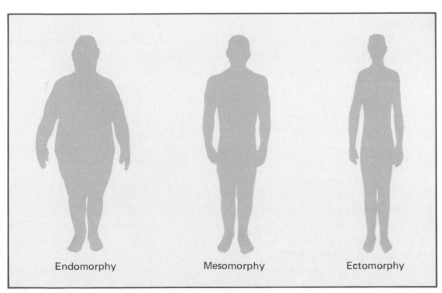

Endomorphy   Mesomorphy   Ectomorphy

FIGURE 14–1
This diagram shows examples of the three body types described by Sheldon: endomorphy, mesomorphy, and ectomorphy.

relation found may reflect a bias in the eye of the beholder. When such studies are done in a methodologically more sophisticated way, the connections between body type and temperament are much less strong.

Still, there *is* a correlation, and Sheldon must be given credit for calling attention to the connection between physique and temperament. Nor did he argue that all of a person's temperamental characteristics mysteriously flowed from that person's physique at birth. He discussed the ways in which a person's physique might cause interactions with other people that could shape temperamental development. For instance, he pointed out that mesomorphs were likely to be recruited for sports because of their physiques and could further develop their competitive temperaments in this setting.

Genetic Theories of Personality Characteristics

Many investigators have been struck by the continuities in behavior from infancy to later life. For instance, in their study of temperament, Thomas, Chess, and Birch (1970) followed the development of 150 children for almost a decade, gathering information from interviews with parents and home observation. They concluded that there are evident temperamental patterns in children at birth and that these patterns endure. For example, "moody" babies are likely to become "moody" children and to have more behavior problems later in life than even-tempered babies.

Introversion/extroversion is a temperamental pattern that has also been suggested to have a genetic component. Whether as adults people are shy and anxious or friendly and outgoing in their relationships with others and the environment correlates with expressions of these orientations at birth: Friendly infants tend to become friendly teenagers, while cold infants are also somewhat unfriendly as adolescents (Schaeffer & Bayley, 1963). Babies also appear to differ at birth in the way they prefer to be calmed when they are upset: Some like to be held, others want to be left alone. The names "cuddlers" and "noncuddlers" have been applied to these two types (Schaffer & Emerson, 1964). Cuddlers are described by their mothers as snuggling, loving to be held, and cuddling back; mothers of noncuddlers say their children don't like to be held, resist all attempts to do so, and fret and wriggle until they are put down.

Of course, it is also important to assess environmental influences. A child who at first doesn't seek attachment with the parent may be perceived and treated by the parent as more independent; continued noncuddling behavior could be the product of interaction with a parent who expects the baby to avoid warm behavior. Similarly, friendly, extroverted babies may draw reinforcing responses from their parents that encourage further development of that pattern. Thomas, Chess, and Birch (1970) observed parental reactions to children's temperamental displays, such as moodiness, and saw how these reactions could support the temperamental patterns that were first used by the child.

Genetic theories of personality, then, may actually be genetic-environmental theories of development. These theories suggest that the influence of genetics will be greatest when the first signs of a predisposition draw from the environment some reaction that supports the continuation of that predisposition. It should also be pointed out that even behaviors that appear extremely early in life are not necessarily genetic in origin. They can be very quickly learned reactions, and there is evidence that some learning can take place soon after birth.

THE LEARNING MODEL

The learning and conditioned-response theories of personality are based on studies of lower-order organisms such as rats and pigeons described in Chapter 6. Learning theorists believe that human beings, like rats and pigeons, respond to stimuli presented by other people or by the external world. Thus the environment controls our behavior through the reinforcement contingencies it delivers. Learning theorists hold that the human personality is a set of patterns of learned behaviors. A set of stimulus conditions is presented, the person responds to it, and reinforcement may follow. If it does, the response will be repeated if the stimulus conditions recur.

A problem that all personality theories must address is the development of uniqueness. Learning theorists believe that people's personalities differ because of childhood differences in stimulus patterns, reinforcement contingencies, and punishment patterns. If we know someone's reinforcement history, therefore, we should be able to predict that person's present behavior patterns. Even though the human personality is complex, it is based on simple learning principles, such as generalization of previous learning to new situations and the increasing ability to discriminate, through experience, among the stimuli that lead to reinforcement.

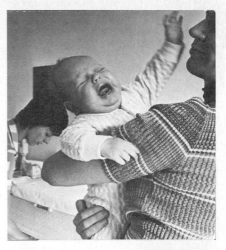

Conditioned Anxiety: Dollard and Miller

One of the important contributions of learning theory to personality dynamics is the theory of conditioned anxiety conceived of by John Dollard and Neil Miller (1950). As we saw in our discussion of conditioning in Chapter 6, a tone originally may be a neutral stimulus, but if it is frequently followed by an electric shock, the tone itself becomes a cue for fear responses originally produced by the shock. Animals tested by Dollard and Miller were able to learn new responses to escape from or terminate an anxiety cue. In the same way, a child who is hurt by a fall from a swing may become anxious when near any swing. By stimulus generalization, the child may become afraid of other play equipment and come to avoid playgrounds in order to avoid the anxiety caused by the sight of the equipment.

Do we encourage an infant's fretfulness by picking up the baby when he or she cries? Traditional learning theory would say yes. Smiling and laughing can also be encouraged by playful parents.

Two properties of conditioned anxiety make it a particularly important concept in learning theories of personality. First, anxiety may be conditioned to a previously neutral stimulus by just a few pairings, and sometimes by a single pairing. Given the normal hurts and harms of an ordinary childhood, we probably all have many conditioned fears. Second, because people learn responses that get them out of an anxiety situation, they may never discover that the original reason for the anxiety—the physical or emotional pain that once followed the cue—is no longer present. The child who avoids the swing from which he or she once fell may not discover that with a little practice the swing is easy to manage. Conditioned anxiety theory gives us an insight into why many people continue to engage in patterns of action that seem to be useless or even self-defeating: They do so because these patterns remove them from anxiety cues and do not allow them to discover that the original source of the fear is gone.

Operant Conditioning: Skinner

Skinner's learning principles (see Chapter 6) proved useful in specifying the ways in which a person's history of reinforcements determines the person's behavior. The simplest kind of learning is based on classical conditioning, in which an initially neutral stimulus is paired with an unconditioned stimulus that causes an unconditioned response. Pavlov's famous demonstration of a dog being conditioned to salivate at the sound of a tone is an example of this, as is the conditioning of fear to a previously neutral stimulus, which Dollard and Miller used as the basis of conditioned anxiety.

Skinner, however, was most concerned with reinforcement in operant conditioning. In this type of conditioning, the likelihood that a response will be emitted is affected by whether that response was followed by reinforcement in the past. Reinforcement to Skinner is the primary way in which people learn responses and control the responses of others.

In the course of personality development, a child learns to respond to certain stimuli with certain responses and to give very different responses to other stimuli. This learning takes place through stimulus generalization and discrimination. A child cuddles a furry toy and is reinforced by its pleasing texture and the parents' smiles. Because of stimulus generalization, the child will at first respond to a real furry cat by cuddling it—it looks like the furry toy and therefore elicits the response given to the toy. The scratches of the squashed cat teach the child stimulus discrimination: The child learns to discriminate between 2 physically similar stimuli because the environment rewards the response to one and not the other.

Is it possible to use this model to account for the acquisition of behavior that is maladaptive, harmful, or abnormal? Skinner and other learning theorists have proposed several mechanisms to explain such behavior. The first we have already mentioned: Conditioned anxiety can cause a person to try to escape from a once-threatening stimulus situation in which no real reasons for fear remain.

Skinner suggests 3 other mechanisms that may produce maladaptive behavior. The first is "random" or chance reinforcement. Occasionally the environment delivers a reward to people that is quite independent of their actions. Nonetheless, the reinforcement increases the probability that a person will repeat whatever action he or she was emitting when the reward was delivered. This type of reinforcement, where there is no cause-and-effect relation between action and reward, can lead to "superstitious" behavior. For example, a person may wear a particular shirt just before winning a big game and wear it again because it "brought luck." While this example is fairly harmless, accidental or random reinforcement can result in self-destructive behavior, as when depressive symptoms are accidentally rewarded by love and attention from a caring friend. Thus the individual is reinforced to use this means to obtain the same love and affection again.

A second reward mechanism for producing unwanted behaviors centers on ambiguities about what exactly is reinforcing, and in what way. Tired or preoccupied parents may not pay attention to their children until the children get out of hand. The attention may then take the form of scolding, but it may also have rewarding elements. Sadly, some people get so little attention that almost any form of it is rewarding. A patient in a mental hospital, for instance, gradually became too uncoordinated to eat and had to be fed by an attendant. The few words the harassed but kindly attendant addressed to her while feeding her were the only pleasant human interactions the patient had all day and led her to behave in ways that demanded more and more of the attendant's time.

The third mechanism accounting for maladaptive behavior is provided by the Skinnerian discovery of schedules of reinforcement. For any of the reasons we just discussed, undesirable behavior may have been at least occasionally reinforced in the past. The problem is why that behavior does not become extinct in the present. (*Extinction* is Skinner's term for the gradual decrease and final elimination of responses that are not reinforced.) Because they are undesirable, responses such as crying or hostility usually receive reinforcement only intermittently. You will recall that responses learned under conditions of intermittent reinforcement are much more resistant to extinction than those that are always reinforced. So the occasional reinforcement of a maladaptive response may be enough to cause it to persist.

Social-Learning Theory: Bandura

Bandura and other **social-learning theorists** agree that personality consists of patterns of human responses that are learned, and they acknowledge the validity of the learning mechanisms as defined by Dollard and Miller and Skinner in conditions of direct reinforcement. Their major contribution has been to point out that there is a second kind of learning that is very important for personality development: They show that people can learn through **imitating,** by observing the responses of others.

In fact, it can be argued that most of our learning is of this indirect, observational kind. Children, for example, learn a new response just by watching others, without having ever before made that response themselves and without being reinforced themselves or even having seen anyone else reinforced for the response. In one study (Bandura, Ross, & Ross, 1961), some nursery school children watched adults behave aggressively toward an oversized doll, while other children watched nonaggressive adults sit quietly, ignoring the doll. The children were later placed in a room with the doll, and their behavior toward it was observed. Those who had watched the more aggressive adult models were more aggressive toward the doll than the children who had observed nonaggressive models.

It has been found that modeling can take place when the model is presented symbolically, as in films or on TV, as well as in real-life situations. Models in films and TV are very influential—children watching a model behave aggressively on TV or in a film were just as likely to imitate that behavior as children who observed a model who was physically present (Bandura, Ross, & Ross, 1963b).

Observing models may help to reduce inhibitions, especially if the model is doing something that is not socially acceptable. In this case the person observing may not so much be learning a new response as gaining the nerve to make a response that before was only imagined (Walters & Llewellyn Thomas, 1963). Again, imitation may depend on the observer's ability to discover the reinforcement structure of the situation. A model who is not punished for an action may be particularly effective in removing inhibition of a similar action in the observer.

Certain aspects of the modeling situation affect the influence of the model:

1. *Whether the model being observed is rewarded or punished.* Although people may imitate a model who is not rewarded, they are much more likely to imitate models who have been rewarded for their behavior than those who have been punished or have not received any reward (Bandura, Ross, & Ross, 1963a). However, even when a model has been punished, people may still imitate the model's behavior if the threat of punishment is subsequently removed (Bandura, 1965).

Role models seen on TV can be as influential as those who are physically present. There has been a great deal of concern over the effect that the violence shown on TV has on the children who watch it.

2. *Characteristics of models.* These characteristics include age, sex, and social status, but the most important is whether or not the model is seen as powerful or weak. Children are much more likely to imitate a model who seems powerful to them than one who seems weak (Jakubczak & Walters, 1959). Thus, for a young child the most commonly imitated model is likely to be the same-sex parent, although the effectiveness of models presented through the mass media, particularly through television, cannot be overlooked (Liebert, Neale, & Davidson, 1973).

According to Bandura, people do not merely learn to imitate specific behaviors; they are also capable of generalizing from one situation to another. However, the degree to which the generalization occurs has not been entirely spelled out by empirical research. In addition, there is still a great deal of disagreement concerning the conditions under which imitation will occur. For example, empirical research into the effects of television violence on aggressive behavior in children has yielded a mixed bag of findings. In some situations, viewing aggressive behavior led to more aggression (Liebert & Baron, 1972; Parke, Berkowitz, Leyens, West, & Sebastian, 1977); in others, viewing an aggressive sequence decreased viewers' levels of aggressive behavior (Feshbach & Singer, 1971); still other studies indicate that the degree of imitation of aggressive behavior may be a function of individual personality characteristics of the viewers involved (Stein & Friedrich, 1972).

Although a large body of research in social learning deals with the imitation of aggression, it is important to note that aggressive behavior is not the only kind of behavior that can be learned. Research has also shown that with the right models, individuals can learn to imitate altruistic behavior such as sharing (Midlarsky, Bryan, & Brickman, 1973) or helping (Bryan & Test, 1967). Thus, whether or not imitation will occur does not seem to depend on the *type* of behavior being observed, but rather on characteristics of the models themselves and the situation in which they are presented.

Bandura and Rosenthal (1976) pointed out another type of learning that is important in social-learning theory, and that is the vicarious learning of classically conditioned emotional responses. For example, if a person observes a model reacting with extreme fear and repugnance to a stimulus, the next time that stimulus is presented, the observer may react the same way, even if the model is no longer present. For example, small children, before they are toilet trained often play with their fecal material with no signs of disgust. But their parents react to the children's activities with expressions of repugnance. Soon, even in the parent's absence, the child responds to his feces with the disgust. Through vicarious conditioning the child has learned the response that is appropriate in our culture.

Fears, particularly, are easily learned this way. Bandura has shown that the conditioned anxiety avoidance sequence described by Dollard and Miller may begin not as the person's *own* anxiety experience, but as a second-hand fear acquired from observing another. This other may even be a character in a drama. It is interesting to speculate about how many of our anxieties are acquired from the overcharged excitements of television and the movies.

Social-learning theorists have made 3 important additions to a learning theory of personality: People can learn indirectly by observing the actions of others and the consequences of those actions; people are often sensitive to the social context in which learning takes place; and people interpret experience in the process of learning.

More recently, Bandura (1977, 1978) has been considering the influence of the goals people set for themselves and their evaluations of their success or failure in meeting their goals. People's self-evaluation standards affect their reactions to their own performances. They gain self-respect by living up to their standards and experience disappointment from not reaching them. These self-standards, Bandura points out, are an important part of all of our experience, and "to ignore the influential role of self-evaluation reactions in the self-regulation of behavior is to disavow a uniquely human capacity" (1978, p. 351).

Bandura has explored self-evaluation in a therapeutic context as well, in developing the concept of **self-efficacy** (Bandura, 1977). A sense of self-efficacy refers to a person's expectation of having the power to control situations and influence events in a positive way. Achieving a sense of self-efficacy is a little like becoming "authentic" in the existential sense. The difference between them lies in the grounding of self-efficacy in actual behavior. According to social-learning theory, one can *learn* to be efficacious through imitation of others. People who lack a sense of self-efficacy may be fearful, depressed, or feel unable to cope with stressful situations. Indeed, Bandura suggests that such mental-health problems as phobias can be alleviated by giving sufferers a sense of self-efficacy. This sense of competence would then generalize to competence, or at least more effective coping, in problem areas.

Therapists can teach people to feel more efficacious by allowing them to interact with efficacious models. In this technique, known as participant modeling, the model is gradually phased out as the individual takes a larger and more positive role in a series of tasks (Bandura, Jeffery, & Wright, 1974). This approach was tried with individuals who feared (had a phobia of) snakes. Snake-phobics became less fearful (as measured by their willingness to approach snakes) after being exposed to an efficacious model and taught to feel efficacious themselves (Bandura, Adams, & Beyer, 1966).

THE COGNITIVE MODEL

Cognitive theories of personality draw on what psychologists have learned about the information-processing strategies of human beings. Like humanistic-existential theories, they begin the study of personality by determining the categories and systems people use for organizing their image of the world. Like social-learning theories, they assume that people learn from past experience and use that learning as a guide to future behavior. Personality, for the cognitive psychologist, is people's particular and unique representations of the interpersonal and physical situations in which they find themselves: Their actions flow from their perspectives.

Kelly (1955), for example, focuses on how people make sense out of, or construe, experience. In his view, people create their own picture, or **personal construct,** of reality by actively perceiving, evaluating, and organizing their own experience. Kelly suggests that it is useful to think of ourselves as scientists, going about making sense out of our own world in the same way that scientists make sense out of their field of study. Not only do we construe events and objects, but we also try to find cause-and-effect relationships. We use our understanding of these to predict future events and to intervene in the world in effective ways, trying to control events and produce outcomes that we desire.

People constantly try to make more accurate predictions about their world,

Like scientists, we go about making sense of our world.

One of the major controversies in personality psychology (usually debated between personality and social psychologists) is the degree to which people's behavior is a function of their fixed personality characteristics or a relatively free response to the situation in which they find themselves. Which is more powerful in the determination of behavior, situational variables or personality variables?

Trait and psychodynamic approaches state that constant, internal, relatively stable forces of personality have a consistent effect on behavior. Lately, personality researchers—most notably Walter Mischel (1968, 1976)—have put forth a different view. Mischel feels that individual responses in any situation are not reflections of constant traits, but rather depend on and vary according to the situation.

The classic study in this area was conducted by Hartshorne and May (1928) on honesty in children. In this study, children were put in a number of situations in which they had a chance to be dishonest and believed they would not be detected. For example, they were given money to play with that they could have kept, they were asked to report about work done at home, or they were observed taking tests to see who would cheat and who would not. The children were neither honest nor dishonest consistently. Rather, their behavior seemed specific to the situation.

Mischel argues that to account for variability in behavior, personality theorists must shift their orientation from a focus on the characteristics of the person to a focus on the characteristics of the situation. Rather than global traits or states, the basis for developing theories of personality should be the manner in which personality reflects contingencies in the environment.

Mischel uses the stimulus-discrimination principle of learning theory as a basis for the argument that people can learn to make very different responses to similar stimulus situations if their past reinforcement contingences have led them to do so. But he does not believe that

and to Kelly, this is the primary motivating force in personality. Our ability to predict may improve with experience, because experience changes our anticipations (predictions), according to whether or not it fulfills them. Like scientists, we change our hypotheses as we acquire new information, and so, learning from experience that one of our anticipations was wrong is a particularly important opportunity for growth.

The Person and the Situation

Cognitive models have redefined the debate between nomothetic and idiographic theories of personality. Research using a cognitive perspective has produced a variety of theories about the ways in which people construct their social worlds. Common to these theories is the idea that the thoughts and feelings that are "in the head" of perceivers interact with the situations in which they find themselves and the needs and purposes they bring to those situations.

The debate concerning the relative strength of the person—in terms of traits and dispositions—and the situation (see the Application on the situation vs. the person) has led to attempts to assess empirically the ways in which certain situations predispose certain kinds of individuals to react in particular ways. In trying to assess the "personality of situations" (Bem & Funder, 1978), researchers have conceived of the person-situation interaction as a *template,* which can be used to match the personality of the perceiver with characteristics of the situation to predict an individual's behavior in any situation. In this view, traits are a function of the situation in which people find themselves; in addition, a given situation can have a range of meanings, depending on the characteristics of the individual perceiver.

This kind of interactionist view has been described by Walter Mischel in the realm of person perception:

current responses can be completely accounted for in terms of past environmental reinforcement contingencies and the currently presented external stimuli. He says that besides conditions in the environment, it is necessary to take into account a person's perceptual and cognitive processes—how someone uniquely perceives, organizes, and interprets the social environment.

First, individuals may differ in their competencies, or ability to generate particular cognitions. These competencies would be related to intelligence or social capacity. Second, individuals may differ in the way they interpret and label events or other people. Third, individuals may also have different expectations about what will happen if they do this or that in any one situation.

Fourth, individuals' subjective values, motives, and incentives are likely to differ. Finally, there may be individual differences in self-regulatory systems—people's unique rules for performance—and their plans.

Mischel argues that it doesn't make sense to ask whether personality or the situation is more important. It is more appropriate to determine when situation variables are more important and when person variables are more important.

According to Mischel, this depends on the strength or weakness of a situation. When a situation leads everyone to make the same interpretation, induce uniform expectancies, and require skills that everyone can perform, situational variables are more important. A red light is an example of such a powerful situation—it will be perceived and processed uniformly by nearly everyone and consequently leads to stable, predictable patterns of behavior. However, if you ask how someone will behave at a cocktail party the answer will be much less certain. When situations are ambiguous, person variables exert a greater influence on behavior.

Adopting this approach to personality may be difficult for most of us. We are accustomed to describing people in terms of what we "know" of their personality characteristics, and we all have a tendency to perceive more consistency in our own and other people's behavior than may actually exist. We will discuss these quirks of attribution at greater length in Chapter 18.

> Structure, I believe, exists neither "all in the head" of the perceiver nor "all in the person" perceived; it is instead a function of an interaction between the beliefs of observers and the characteristics of the observed. . . . Perceivers surely go beyond the information they are "given," but they just as surely do not invent regularly the information itself. Information in the head of the perceiver and in the world of the perceived interacts in the course of person perception. (1981, p. 15)

What kinds of structures exist "in the head" of the perceiver? Recently, these structures have been given several names: prototypes (Cantor & Mischel, 1977), schemas (Markus, 1977), or scripts (Schank & Abelson, 1976). Sometimes these words are used to refer to clusters of traits or behaviors that seem to go together in certain situations; for example, I might consider that intelligence, a graduate degree, and a tweed jacket are all features of my category of "psychology professors." Cognitive structures may also be much more like theories about people. I might have quite clear expectations about what kinds of people behave in particular ways, as well as complex explanations of why that behavior occurs. These *implicit personality theories* (Schneider, 1973; see Chapter 18) help me to interpret the world around me, even though they might not always be accurate. For example, I might believe that all psychology professors are intelligent, sympathetic, and easy graders; these beliefs may guide my behavior toward psychology professors, help me to interpret their comments about my work, and may even evoke sympathetic behavior in them (Snyder & Swann, 1978)!

Identification of individual differences in the way people structure the social world, and the effects these difference have on behavior, has become an important focus for cognitive personality psychology. Traditional measures of memory, like recognition, recall, and reaction time, are being used to investigate the nature of these differences and their implications for personality theories. A great deal of this research has focused on how people view *themselves.* This research is founded on the notion that, while we all share some common categories and labels for our own behavior and that of others, each person sees him or herself as a unique individual, whose personality is the result of his or her own unique experience. In this view, personality is indeed idiographic, and the universal applicability of global traits is called into question as the emphasis has shifted to individual differences.

One area in which individual differences in cognitive functioning have been examined is **self-monitoring.** The concept of self-monitoring refers to the degree to which an individual attends to the social context in planning social behavior. High self-monitors "regard themselves as rather flexible and adaptive creatures who shrewdly and pragmatically tailor their social behavior to fit situational and interpersonal specifications of appropriateness" (Snyder, 1981, p. 322). Low self-monitors, on the other hand, see themselves as stable, enduring, and consistent individuals, whose behavior across situations can be seen as following a similar pattern. These differences in the way people see their own personalities have important consequences for the stability of trait measurements across situations and individuals. Low self-monitors behave consistently even in different situations, while high self-monitors fit their behavior to the situation and may appear quite inconsistent as a result. Whether a person is a high or low self-monitor may be very important in understanding his or her responses to a particular situation.

In a variety of domains, it has been demonstrated that a person's self-image is a powerful component of social perception. Recent research on the relationship of self-image to sex-role–related behavior has attempted to shed some light on this relationship. In these studies (Markus, Crane, & Siladi, 1978; Markus, Crane, Siladi, & Bernstein, 1982), individuals whose self-image contained a masculine or feminine component were asked whether a series of "masculine" and "feminine" words were relevant to themselves personally. Subjects quickly and confidently endorsed those words that were consistent with their self-image; when presented with an inconsistent word, subjects experienced difficulty in admitting its self-relevance, even when the characteristic was desirable. The general conclusion of this and similar studies is that a person's self-image helps to filter stimuli from the environment, so that consistent information gets priority and inconsistent information is ignored or avoided. Subsequent research (Markus & Smith, 1981) has shown that this filtering process occurs even when the stimulus is not directly self-relevant.

THE ASSESSMENT OF PERSONALITY

All the models of personality we have examined—the psychoanalytic, humanistic-existential, learning, biological, and cognitive—require some sort of procedure to identify and locate the various characteristics, traits, and personalities they are studying. This is true for 2 reasons. First, practical decisions may hinge on it. One would not want to put a paranoid schizophrenic in charge of a missile-testing base, nor a psychopathic deviant in a police uniform. More positively, it is desirable to match people with jobs that suit their personalities. Some people enjoy stress and ought to have jobs in which they will be presented with challenging tasks; others would fall apart in a job in which there was constant stress, challenging or not.

A second reason for assessing personality is scientific—it is useful for testing personality theories. For instance, according to Maslow's theory, there should be a distinct group of people who are self-actualized. These people should share certain qualities or characteristics described by Maslow—a broad and tolerant sense of humor, the tendency to stand by their friends, and so on. But we cannot prove that there are such people unless we measure people's sense of humor, tendency to back their values in the face of pressure to conform, and other qualities that Maslow hypothesizes for self-actualized individuals.

Reliability and Validity

Tests for personality assessment, as for any effective test instruments, must possess both reliability and validity. A personality test should give the same result each time it is administered to the same person, assuming there is no reason to believe that his or her personality has changed between tests; this is **reliability.** In general, there are two ways to check a test for reliability. For a test with a relatively straightforward output such as "true/false" or "agree/disagree" answers, reliability is assessed by comparing equivalent parts or versions of the test. Thus we might judge the correlation between 2 halves of the same test (split-half method), 2 versions of the same test (alternate-forms method), or 2 successive versions of the same test (test-retest method). For a test whose outcome consists of ratings made by an observer or judge, then interrater reliability is used: The person being tested is rated by a second, equally qualified observer, and the correlation between the 2 judges' ratings is calculated.

Validity determines whether the test actually measures those factors it is intended to measure. Psychologists distinguish different kinds of validity. **Predictive validity** is of concern when an assessment is being made for a practical purpose—when, for instance, the object is to predict how well a person will do in college, as an airplane pilot, or in another job. The future performance being tested is called the **criterion,** and the purpose of the test is to predict it as accurately as possible. Therefore if the maximum correlation ($+1$ or -1) between the assessment instrument and the criterion could be obtained, the test would be considered wildly successful because it would predict without error whether a person would do well ($+1$) or poorly (-1) at the criterion. The predictive validity of an instrument, then, is the degree of correlation between that instrument and the criterion performance that is to be predicted. Establishing the predictive validity of a performance measure can have important practical consequences. For example, Equal Employment Opportunity legislation now requires that all tests used to screen job applications have a measurable degree of predictive validity. This was done to ensure that individuals are hired on the basis of their ability to perform the actual tasks of a job (the criterion) and not on the basis of extraneous or irrelevant variables such as sex, age, or race.

Construct validity is generally of interest when personality assessment is being done for theoretical rather than practical purposes. It is possible to think of a theory as a set of constructs or ideas and the relationships among them. There is a difference between the construct itself (which is always hypothetical and constructed by the theorizer) and measures or ways to identify or test the construct. Constructs, although they can be defined, described, and discussed, are not directly observable; but measures are. A construct whose presence cannot be inferred by some measure is useless in psychology, which takes an empirical approach to knowledge. Thus, a measure must be relevant to the ideas or constructs it is supposed to identify; this

Sex-Role Behavior
and Personality

The search for stable, enduring traits in personality is nowhere more clearly defined than in the area of sex roles. Many researchers have attempted to catalog masculinity and femininity and to characterize differences in behavior as a function of the fundamental personality differences they see as inherent in men and women (Murdock, 1965). It has been argued that this emphasis on *differentiation* has led to an exaggeration of the number of differences between the sexes that cannot be attributed to situational factors.

Using an entirely different perspective, Maccoby and Jacklin (1974) conducted an extensive review of the sex-role literature in an attempt to discover which of the many alleged behavioral differences between men and women really exist. Their research yielded only 4 basic distinctions: Females have better verbal ability; males have better spatial judgment; males are better at mathematics; females are less aggressive.

This disagreement concerning the nature of sex-role behaviors is also reflected in the ongoing debate concerning how individuals develop their particular sex-role identity. Research has shown that sex-role identity is an early component of the child's self-concept; even children who are younger than 2 years old can reliably identify themselves as male or female (Thompson, 1975). Where does this knowledge come from? The most radical biological view suggests that sex-role identity is largely determined by an individual's genetic identity (Daly & Wilson, 1978). In this view, a "masculine" or "feminine" personality grows out of the individual's response to his or her own sex-linked behavior. In the psychoanalytic tradition, on the other hand, Freud cited case studies of his patients as proof that all individuals are born with the potential for both sex-role identities. His often-quoted assertion that "anatomy is destiny" refers to his notion that normal sex-role development is centered around proper resolution of the conflicts associated with an individual's first awareness of his or her sex organs. The goal of this resolution—identification with the same-sex parent—ensures that the individual will adopt sex-appropriate behavior and personality traits.

Because sex differences are associated with a large number of obvious, directly observable biological differences, some researchers have sought biological explanations for observed behavioral differences between the sexes. The sex hormones are obvious targets for such research. Among lower animals, there is a great deal of evidence that sexual differentiation in behavior is an adaptive function of the gonadal hormones—androgens in males, and estrogen in females (see Daly & Wilson, 1978, for a review). In laboratory experiments, for example, female rhesus monkeys injected with the male hormone testosterone at various stages of prenatal development exhibit alterations not only of sexual behavior but in such things as aggressiveness, play, and interest in babies (Phoenix, 1974). It is extremely tempting to generalize from the behavior of monkeys to that of humans, especially since we obviously cannot perform the same kinds of experiments on humans. But while such experiments are suggestive, they are not sufficient evidence. We have to rely on different kinds of evidence in searching for sex differences in human personality.

Most of the biological evidence that has been examined has been the result of abnormality or medical malpractice. One such study involved genetic females with a clinical condition called *adrenogenital syndrome* (AGS), in which the adrenal glands wrongly produce an androgen. At birth, AGS girls show some genital masculinization; with hormone treatments and minor surgery, however, these girls can have normal lives and even bear children. AGS girls are normally raised as girls; the only obvious difference between AGS girls and normal girls is their exposure to male hormones before birth. Erhardt and

is construct validity. Since constructs themselves are not observable, there is no direct empirical way to assess the relevance of a given measure to a given construct. This must be assessed indirectly, by using other, related constructs.

Suppose that a psychologist has developed the construct of "test anxiety," defined as a tendency to become anxious in test situations and thus to perform more poorly than would otherwise be the case. What kind of measure would the psychologist want to develop to assess this construct? What pattern of correlations with other behaviors should the assessment instrument show? To demonstrate construct validity, the researcher must be able to specify what the relationship *should be* between the construct under scrutiny and other constructs. From this relationship, the researcher can infer what the relationship should be between the *measure* of this construct and the measures of other constructs. If these measures are related in ways expected by the

Baker (1974) conducted extensive interviews with AGS girls and their families, in which they discovered that both the subjects and their families saw the AGS girls as more "tomboyish" than normals.

Similar results were found in an earlier study (described in Chapter 10) of children whose mothers had been injected with androgens to prevent miscarriage (Money & Erhardt, 1972). The daughters of these women, like the AGS girls, preferred "boyish" games to more traditional female occupations and thought of themselves as tomboys. Even though the behavior of these girls was well within the range of "acceptable" feminine behavior, their "masculine" tendencies were taken as evidence for the effect of fetal hormones on the development of sex-typed behavior. A final example, also described by Money and Erhardt, concerns the strange case of a pair of identical male twins. When they were being circumcised, the penis of one of the twins was accidentally mutilated. The child's parents decided to raise the child as a girl, and genital surgery was performed before the child's second birthday. Money and Erhardt report that the twins' mother made every effort to make her daughter "quiet and ladylike" (p. 122) and to differentiate her from her twin brother; even though the child did exhibit some "tomboyish" behavior, she did on the whole accept her girlhood completely, while her brother was seen as a normal male. These results were seen as evidence that socialization could sometimes override genetic tendencies.

Such studies, though, do not really clarify the effects of biological factors on personality development. They are not controlled experiments, and thus their outcomes may be due to interacting multiple factors. For example, in the studies mentioned here, the parents knew of the abnormalities in their children's development. The differences found may have been due to differential treatment by the parents, or to some other aspect of the children's environments. Also, most of these children received hormone therapy after birth, which may have had additional behavioral effects. For instance, Money and Erhardt's "feminized" twin will have received large amounts of estrogen to facilitate development of appropriate secondary sex characteristics at puberty. Biology and the environment clearly could interact in complex ways in such cases.

Both social-learning and cognitive models of personality assert that sex-role development is the result of experience, but each model places a different interpretation on that experience. As one psychologist put it:

The social-learning syllogism is: "I want rewards, I am rewarded for doing boy things, therefore, I want to be a boy." In contrast, a cognitive theory assumes this sequence: "I am a boy, therefore I want to do boy things, therefore the opportunity to do boy things (and to gain approval for doing them) is rewarding." (Kohlberg, 1966, p. 89)

Learning theory, then, argues that sex-role identity is learned in much the same way as other kinds of behavior; if a male child is rewarded for displaying aggressive, masculine behavior, he will continue to act in a way that will allow observers to categorize him as a "masculine" personality. Cognitive theories, however, assume that the child is aware of himself as a boy or herself as a girl and uses this awareness to interpret the social world. The male child in the example sees himself as masculine and uses that category to give meaning to his behavior. Expanding this view, recent research (Bem, 1981) has suggested that sex-role differences in personality may be the result of individual differences in the range of circumstances in which gender is used by individuals to categorize behavior.

Thus the development of sex-role identity—and the search for masculinity, femininity, and androgyny— are rich, relevant topics for the student of personality. Biological, psychoanalytic, learning, and cognitive models of personality each have their own unique perspective on these important questions.

theory, the measure of the experimental construct has construct validity. In the construct of "test anxiety," then, we would look for an assessment instrument that would show moderate correlations with a number of other behaviors. (Contrast this to the predictive-reliability requirement of a high correlation with some single-criterion measure.)

Let us consider the factors that determine performance on a math test. Certainly anxiety about taking the test is one such factor, but so is mathematical ability and how much time the person has spent studying for the test. The actual test scores, of course, provide the measure of performance.

Now imagine 6 individuals who have the test anxiety, math ability, and math test scores shown in Table 14–3. Notice that the people with low test anxiety tend to work at the level of their abilities, whereas people who are highly "test anxious" do a bit worse than their ability alone would lead us to expect. But

Table 14–3: The Construct
Validation of a Test.

Person	Math Ability 1 = low, 10 = high	Test Anxiety 1 = low, 10 = high	Math Test Performance 1 = low, 10 = high
1	8	1	8
2	8	9	6
3	4	2	4
4	4	8	2
5	7	5	6
6	2	7	1

what about the correlation between performance on the math test and the test-anxiety measure? In Table 14–4, the test-anxiety scores are listed in ascending order and the math scores are listed in the right-hand column. The correlation is $-.41$, indicating that there is a negative relationship between test anxiety and test performance (recall that a negative correlation is just as useful as a positive one—it simply indicates that scoring at the high end of one scale correlates with scoring at the low end of the other scale). This is, though, a moderate, and not a perfect correlation. To understand why, consider Person 2, who did fairly well on the math test, even though she was highly test anxious, because she had a high level of mathematical ability. Now you can see why the first requirement for construct validity is a moderate rather than a high correlation between the construct test and some other measure that we expect to be influenced by that test. Notice that demonstrating the construct validity of test anxiety is not terribly different from demonstrating the construct validity of math ability. Notice further that the *theory* is also strengthened by establishing construct validity and vice-versa.

The second requirement for validation is that the construct test show not just a single correlation but a pattern of correlations with a number of other behaviors. This is because a construct that is theoretically useful should have general implications. If our measure of test anxiety correlated only with people's scores on a single test of math performance, then we could not be sure that we had a general measure of test anxiety. A general measure ought to correlate with performances on English and social-studies tests, written and oral tests, and so on. Figure 14–2 diagrams the different correlational patterns that are desirable in predictive versus construct validation.

There are many other kinds of validity. Indeed, a recent article (Brinberg, 1981) actually described as many as 40! To illustrate the variety of special kinds of validity, we will conclude our discussion by describing two variations of construct validity. A measure has **convergent validity** when other measures that purport to measure the same construct correlate well with the target measure. Thus, if I am trying to measure "intelligence" by asking subjects to interpret inkblots, I would expect that individuals who achieved high scores on my measure would have high scores on other measures of

Table 14–4: Performance Scores as
a Function of Test Anxiety.

Person	Test Anxiety 1 = low, 10 = high	Math Test Performance 1 = low, 10 = high
1	1	8
3	2	4
5	5	6
6	7	1
4	8	2
2	9	6
$r = -.41$		

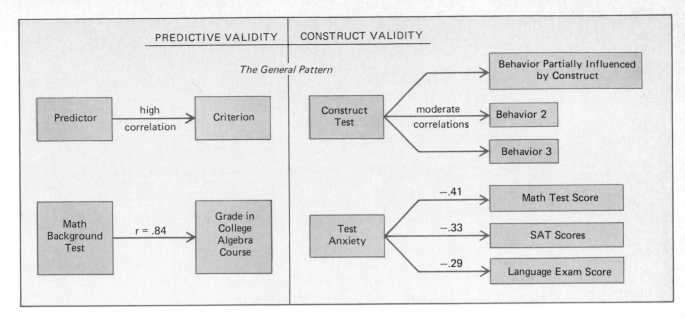

The different correlational patterns desirable in predictive and construct validation. Notice that in our specific example the correlations differ in 2 ways. Only one difference is important. The math background test–algebra grade correlation is a high one, indicating a strong association between the test and the grade, while the set of correlations between the measure of test anxiety and the various behaviors are all much lower. This is exactly what is desired: high correlations when predictive validity is at issue, moderate ones for construct validity. Note the second difference. The predictive validity correlation is positive, while the construct validity correlations are negative. This is less important. It simply reflects the fact that a high score on the test anxiety measure goes along with lower scores on the other tests, which is exactly what one would expect. (See the Appendix for more on the mathematics of correlations.)

intelligence as well. Conversely, I would also expect low scorers on my inkblot measure to have low scores on other measures of intelligence. Thus, several measures would converge in evaluating intelligence.

Is it sufficient for an assessment device to have convergent validity? Can I safely conclude that my inkblot measure is a valid measure of intelligence? Before I apply for the copyright, I must also make sure that my inkblot test measures the construct of "intelligence" *at least as well* as it measures other things. The **discriminant validity** of my inkblot test depends on the specificity with which it measures intelligence. For example, if my inkblot scores correlate highly with IQ but also correlate equally well with socioeconomic status, sex, and shoe size, I cannot be sure whether my test is measuring intelligence or some other construct in which intelligence plays a role. If my measure fails to discriminate between intelligence and other constructs, it lacks discriminant validity.

To introduce our discussion of personality assessment we have presented the measurement (sometimes called psychometric) characteristics of assessment devices. To summarize, a successful assessment device must be *reliable*—it must give approximately the same result when applied repeatedly to the same individual. This is a precondition for *validity*, the second requirement for a successful assessment device. Validity requirements differ according to the purpose of the test. A test designed to predict a person's performance on some practical task should have predictive validity; a test designed to measure an individual's disposition or style should have construct validity. We now turn to 4 different kinds of procedures used to assess personality: observational techniques, scales and self-reports, projective tests, and personality inventories.

Observational Techniques

As we observe other people, we come to certain conclusions about their personalities. If we write these observations in list or paragraph form, a sort of personality assessment emerges. Personal observation is perhaps the oldest assessment technique, and it is still in great use today. But different observers may have seen different samples of the person's behavior and may have different questions in mind when they write their assessments. For these and other reasons, personal assessments have often proved unreliable (and therefore of low validity). Consequently, psychologists have come up with ways to make such judgments more precise and systematic. These include structuring the assessment techniques, either by structuring the rating system itself or by structuring the methods of gathering the information on which the assessment is based.

STRUCTURING THE RATINGS. Instead of making a general summary of someone's characteristics, observers rate the person on certain specific, defined dimensions. This assures that every observer will rate the same qualities by using a common vocabulary to describe them. The scales can be used during or just after an interview and can be based on the person's answers to questions, general behavior during the interview, or both.

Sometimes observers are given a set of adjectives and asked to select those that apply to the person they're evaluating. The adjectives can describe various personality characteristics or can refer to the person's moods, skills, or physical appearance, depending on the purpose of the assessment.

A variation of this is the **q-sort technique.** Here the observer is given a large set of cards with an adjective or phrase printed on each. The observer then sorts the cards from 9 groups, Group 1 being those statements that best describe the person, and Group 9 those that don't apply to the person at all. Sometimes the judge is told to make the distribution of items conform to a normal distribution (see Appendix), with the fewest cards in Groups 1 and 9, and the most in Groups 3–5. The idea behind this direction is that only a few qualities best describe most of us, a few never apply to us at all, and most are intermediate. Conforming with this direction makes observers more careful about qualities at either end of the scale. It also facilitates comparisons among individuals because exactly the same number of adjectives are reported as most or least typical of each individual.

STRUCTURING THE OBSERVATIONS. Another way to make observations more reliable and valid is to structure the information on which they are based. In the interview setting, this would involve structuring the kinds of questions asked of the person.

An interview in which the observer talks to a person and follows the conversation wherever it leads is called an **unstructured** or **open-ended interview.** In a **structured interview,** everyone is asked the same questions in the same order. This makes it easier to sort, rate, and analyze the answers. It is also more reliable in that the same results are likely if the interview is repeated. With the open-ended interview, very different outcomes may result the second time (or with a different interviewer). A compromise format, often called a *semistructured* or *structured/open-ended interview,* sets out a prearranged schedule of questions, but allows the interviewer to explore in depth any of the respondent's answers that seem particularly revealing or important.

STRUCTURING THE SETTINGS OR SITUATIONS. Observers sometimes form impressions of others by watching their behavior rather than by interviewing them. A clinical or developmental psychologist, for instance, may gain impressions of a child by observing that child interact with parents in the home, teachers in the classroom, and children on the playground.

This kind of observation is more reliable if the situations in which the person performs are structured. In addition, research shows that the predictive validity of observations increases as the test situation more closely resembles the situation for which one is attempting to predict behavior.

One of the most extensive attempts at arriving at personality data from structured settings was made by American Army Intelligence during World War II. At several secret locations in the United States, elaborate training centers were built to simulate some of the situations in which undercover agents sent into Nazi-occupied Europe might find themselves. The primary function of these centers was training, but their secondary function was to enable observers to make behavioral assessments of the future agents, focusing on their behavior under stress.

The test situations were structured to be as close as possible to real situations the agents would face. What was supposed to be an after-hours tavern on the base is a good example. Here agents were not on their guard, not expecting any sort of test, so when an acquaintance tried to extract secret information from them, their reactions were revealing of how they would behave in a similar future situation in which their lives might depend on just such an unguarded reaction.

Teams of observers rated the agents at the training centers. Then, overseas, their superior officers and colleagues rated them again in actual situations. Unfortunately, the observers' ratings did not reliably predict success in the field. There were many reasons for this, but the major one was that most of the war situations were different from the test situations in unpredictable ways.

Two kinds of moderately structured setting assessments reflect the theoretical principle involved in the Army Tests. In the first, the test is constructed to be as similar to actual job conditions as possible. Samples of the kinds of work done by people on the job are taken and appear on the test in a simplified version. Second, on the premise that a particularly important component of every job is decision making under stress, stress-producing incidents are included in the test.

Scales and Self-Reports

Often people are asked to report on their own personalities. As Allport pointed out, the easiest way to find out about a person is to ask that person. There are many aspects of our own personalities that we are quite aware of and capable of reporting on. The same rating scales and adjective cards that we described for observational techniques are used when people make observations about themselves. The reliability of the self-rating is assessed by test-retest correlations, and the predictive and construct validity of the self-report is assessed in the same way that it is with observers' judgments.

The problem with this procedure is that people sometimes do not wish to reveal certain things about themselves that they feel are embarrassing or socially undesirable. If asked whether they are "flexible or rigid," or "organized or disorganized," they would probably report that they are flexible and organized because these are seen as the socially desirable answers. So researchers working with **self-reports** have found it wise to try to balance their scales so that neither end of the scale is the "good" or "bad" end. This is surprisingly hard to do, because many words used to describe people carry positive or negative connotations.

One way around this difficulty is to ask people to rate their behavior patterns rather than their personalities. Instead of asking them whether they are "dependable," for instance, the tester would ask questions about missed appointments, forgotten meetings, and tasks left incomplete. Again, though, because it is not socially desirable to respond "frequently" to questions about missed meetings, people may falsely report that they act in socially desirable ways (much as they would, in a personality test, report that they are socially desirable people).

Another problem with this technique is that people have certain personality characteristics and behavior patterns of which they are unaware. These include, in Freud's terms, defense mechanisms such as repression; or, in behaviorist terms, patterns of behavior such as learned helplessness.

In an effort to reveal underlying problems, conflicts, or qualities that people are unaware of themselves or are unwilling to report, psychologists have used indirect ways to gain information. For example, they may ask questions about some seemingly harmless thought or act that they believe correlates with or reveals the underlying conflict or difficulty. These tests are divided into two groups on the basis of how the correlation between test question and characteristic is established. **Projective tests** generally rely on theoretically asserted correlations; **personality inventories** rely on empirical correlations.

Projective Tests

The typical projective test presents an ambiguous visual stimulus, which a subject must describe. The key that allows interpretation is the assumption that respondents reveal something about their underlying dynamics—project their internal psychological processes—by the structure or content their answers impose on the situation.

RORSCHACH TEST.   The **Rorschach inkblot test** is one of the oldest of the projective tests. Each inkblot is a pattern that can look like many things: animals, people, devils, masks, birds.

Rorschach tested thousands of inkblots for years before choosing the 10 that are still in use today. He tested the blots both on patients who had been classified by disorder in a mental hospital and on normal people. The final 10 were those that best discriminated reactions of patients from those of normal people, and also showed some ability to discriminate among patients according to disorder.

The 10 inkblots are on cards. Most are black, others contain one or more colors. The cards are presented one at a time in a certain order. The person being tested can make one interpretation or many. After showing all the inkblots, the tester goes back over the cards, asking why the person saw what he or she did in the card, what part of the blot looked like that, and so on.

As in some other testing procedures, the tester observes the person's behavior and style of answering as well as actual answers. The answers are scored in several ways. Does a subject see the whole blot or just parts? What is the subject matter or content? To what qualities does the subject respond (color, shape, etc.)? In all of this, the tester is looking for consistencies, patterns of reponding.

From the answers, the tester makes inferences about the underlying personality structure of the respondent, in accordance with psychoanalytic prin-

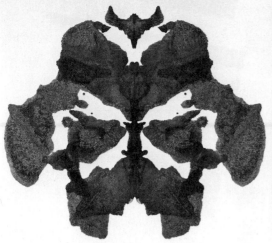

A sample Rorschach inkblot. Some of the inkblots are in one or more colors, but most are black, like this one.

ciples: Recurring themes across pictures are thought to hint at recurring underlying conflicts; sequential responses to the same images reveal material that is causally linked in the unconscious. Stylistic characteristics of the response may also be meaningful: A person who consistently focuses on a part rather than the whole inkblot may be revealing an obsessional concern with detail; someone who persistently sees movement in the figures may be revealing something important about his or her internal functioning.

THE THEMATIC APPERCEPTION TEST.   Henry Murray (1943) developed the **Thematic Apperception Test (TAT)** in an attempt to find out more about an individual's functioning with other people. Murray collected a set of photographs and sketches of people, often shown in some ambiguous relationship with other people, and asked the respondent to make up a story based on the picture.

The person is asked to tell what led up to the scene on the card, what is happening in the scene, and what the outcome will be. Basically the tester is interested in several elements of respondents' stories: which character on the card is seen as central to the story, which character respondents identify with, what needs and drives are expressed in their story, and what seems to be helping or hindering the achievement of them. By interpreting the themes of the stories, the detail the respondent uses to illustrate it, and the pattern of consistent themes and images that recur across stories, a skilled interpreter can arrive at surprisingly rich and detailed interpretations of the respondent's character.

But these are still only interpretations. Both the Rorschach and the Thematic Apperception Test result in a complex and free-form mix of descriptive and evaluative statements by the interpreter about the respondent, and, like any other test result, they require validation. If the clinician interprets the fussy, orderly way an individual organizes the TAT answers as revealing an underlying trait of anal compulsivity, this interpretation requires checking. The respondent may simply have been attempting to live up to what were perceived as the demands of the test situation. Hundreds of studies have attempted to validate elements of projective interpretations, and while they are far too numerous to review in detail here, it is fair to say that many psychologists are not impressed with the validity of the material emerging

The psychologist shown here is administering the Thematic Apperception Test (TAT). In this test the person being interviewed is asked to tell what is happening in the scene shown, what led up to it, and what the outcome will be.

from projective testing. To develop better test instruments, a new system of test construction was adopted.

Personality Inventories

One of the best known personality tests is the *Minnesota Multiphasic Personality Inventory (MMPI)*. The psychologists who constructed the MMPI started with several hundred statements or test items that were thought to be useful in diagnosing and detecting serious behavior disorders such as depression, paranoia, and hysteria. The test consists of statements to which the person answers "true," "false," or "cannot say." They include statements on the person's past experiences, attitudes, physiological and psychological symptoms, and views of the world. For example:

> I daydream a little.
> People are following me.
> My mother often made me obey even when I thought it was unreasonable.

A test for a specific characteristic is contructed in the following way: The items on the inventory are treated as a source pool. First, the test constructor decides what the test will be used for. For instance, it could be used to identify people who perform poorly in highly stressful situations. Then the test constructor identifies a group of people who actually have the characteristic for which the test is being developed. It may, for example, be a group of students who "fall apart" under the pressure of timed tests, or a group of workers who have been identified as poor performers under stress. The test is given to these *criterion groups* and their pattern of answers is compared to the answers given by the normal population. The questions that the criterion and normal groups answer differently (the "discriminating items") are the ones selected to go on the test for poor performance under stress. So research

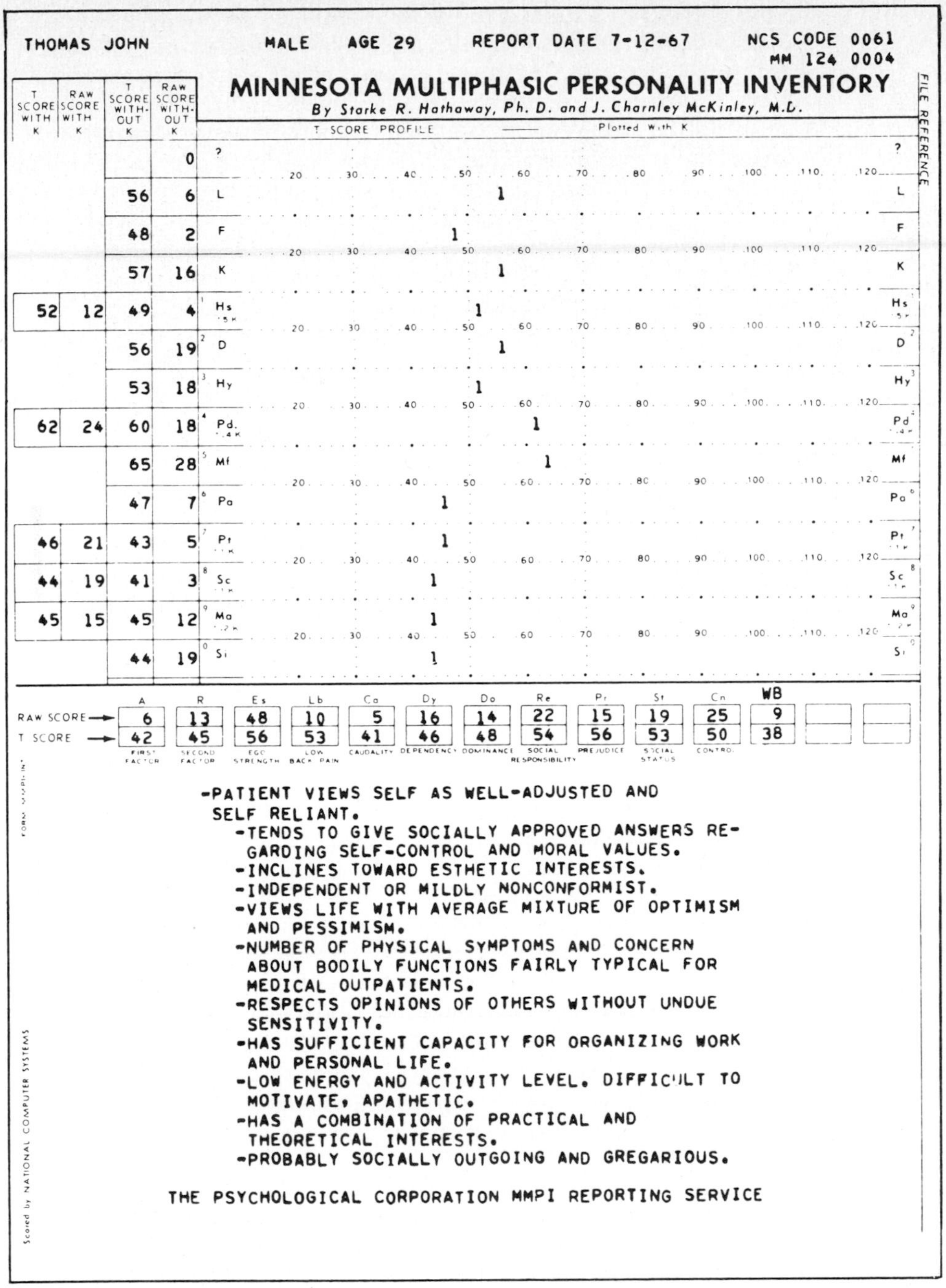

| THOMAS JOHN | | | | MALE   AGE 29 | REPORT DATE 7-12-67 | NCS CODE 0061 |
| | | | | | | MM 124 0004 |

MINNESOTA MULTIPHASIC PERSONALITY INVENTORY
By Starke R. Hathaway, Ph. D. and J. Charnley McKinley, M.D.

T SCORE PROFILE ————— Plotted with K

T SCORE WITH K	RAW SCORE WITH K	T SCORE WITH-OUT K	RAW SCORE WITH-OUT K			
			0	?		?
		56	6	L	1	L
		48	2	F	1	F
		57	16	K	1	K
52	12	49	4	Hs	1	Hs
		56	19	D	1	D
		53	18	Hy	1	Hy
62	24	60	18	Pd	1	Pd
		65	28	Mf	1	Mf
		47	7	Pa	1	Pa
46	21	43	5	Pt	1	Pt
44	19	41	3	Sc	1	Sc
45	15	45	12	Ma	1	Ma
		44	19	Si	1	Si

	A	R	Es	Lb	Ca	Dy	Do	Re	Pr	St	Cn	WB
RAW SCORE →	6	13	48	10	5	16	14	22	15	19	25	9
T SCORE →	42	45	56	53	41	46	48	54	56	53	50	38
	FIRST FACTOR	SECOND FACTOR	EGO STRENGTH	LOW BACK PAIN	CAUDALITY	DEPENDENCY	DOMINANCE	SOCIAL RESPONSIBILITY	PREJUDICE	SOCIAL STATUS	SOCIAL CONTROL	

-PATIENT VIEWS SELF AS WELL-ADJUSTED AND
SELF RELIANT.
   -TENDS TO GIVE SOCIALLY APPROVED ANSWERS RE-
   GARDING SELF-CONTROL AND MORAL VALUES.
   -INCLINES TOWARD ESTHETIC INTERESTS.
   -INDEPENDENT OR MILDLY NONCONFORMIST.
   -VIEWS LIFE WITH AVERAGE MIXTURE OF OPTIMISM
   AND PESSIMISM.
   -NUMBER OF PHYSICAL SYMPTOMS AND CONCERN
   ABOUT BODILY FUNCTIONS FAIRLY TYPICAL FOR
   MEDICAL OUTPATIENTS.
   -RESPECTS OPINIONS OF OTHERS WITHOUT UNDUE
   SENSITIVITY.
   -HAS SUFFICIENT CAPACITY FOR ORGANIZING WORK
   AND PERSONAL LIFE.
   -LOW ENERGY AND ACTIVITY LEVEL. DIFFICULT TO
   MOTIVATE, APATHETIC.
   -HAS A COMBINATION OF PRACTICAL AND
   THEORETICAL INTERESTS.
   -PROBABLY SOCIALLY OUTGOING AND GREGARIOUS.

THE PSYCHOLOGICAL CORPORATION MMPI REPORTING SERVICE

FIGURE 14–3
This is a computer printout of a profile and its interpretation for the Minnesota Multiphasic Personality Inventory (MMPI). (Hathaway & McKinley, 1967)

reports developing this kind of test often contain such lists as "25+" and "37−." This means that a true (+) answer to Question 25 on the MMPI is characteristic of (for example) a poor performer under stress, and a false (−) answer to Question 37 is also characteristic of that pattern. The set of questions that proves to discriminate the criterion from the normal group, not only on the first application, but through successive sets of trials with different specific criterion groups, becomes the scale for the factor or characteristic in question. For instance, the depression scale of the MMPI has between 40 and 50 items that have been shown to discriminate between depressed people and the rest of the population, and also between depressed people and people with other behavior disorders. Answers are not expressed as raw scores; they are plotted as deviations from the general patterns of answers given by thousands of previous respondents.

The initial use of the MMPI was in diagnostic settings, such as mental hospitals, and this is reflected in the scales that appear on the standard MMPI report form. So, for instance, the "Hy" scale is the "hysteria scale" and was developed with a criterion group of patients in mental hospitals whose observing psychiatrists and psychologists reported them to be high on hysterical symptomatology. Suppose that a person has a high "Pa" scale score. Does this mean that person is a raving paranoid who is or ought to be hospitalized? Certainly not. Many normally functioning individuals have MMPI profiles that are elevated on one or more scales. The MMPI is fruitfully used to characterize the personality profiles of normal individuals. Someone who thinks ahead to anticipate dangers in order to avoid them is a useful person to have around. On the MMPI this tendency might be indicated by an elevated psychasthenia (Pt) scale score, since this scale contains items that reflect a tendency to worry. The MMPI has been used to identify many characteristics, including some that we do not ordinarily think of as personality traits. For instance, it has been keyed to identify individuals who will be relatively successful salespersons and college teachers (Welsh & Dahlstrom, 1965).

Since the development of the MMPI, other multiphasic inventories have been contructed on the same principles. (*Multiphasic* means that a test measures many aspects of personality, in contrast to a test that measures only one construct—neurotic anxiety, for instance.) These new tests focus less on behavior disorders and more on normal personality characteristics. For instance, the California Psychological Inventory contains scales measuring such attributes as self-acceptance, sociability, and several kinds of achievement strivings. The content of the items and the labels of the scales of these inventories make them less threatening to respondents, but the developers of the MMPI would point out that research with these new inventories produces dimensions that are quite similar to those included in the MMPI. Apparently, empirical scale construction is a powerful technique for identifying subgroups of individuals whose personality elements differ from those of the population at large.

SUMMARY

1. *Personality* refers to an organized and distinctive pattern of behavior that shows endurance over time and characterizes a person's adaptation to a situation.

2. The earliest ideas about personality attempted to account for a person's behavior in terms of innate *traits*.

3. The *psychoanalytic model* assumes that we are primarily motivated by drives and instincts over which we have little control; these motivations exist, for the most part, in our unconscious. Personality is made up of 3 processes, or systems—the id, the ego, and the superego. A person's behavior is the product of the interaction, and often conflict, of these 3 systems.

4. According to Freud, personality development takes place during 4 psychosexual stages: oral, anal, phallic, and genital.

5. In the *biological model,* genetic endowment and biological features are assumed to be the determinants of personality. Sheldon's constitutional theory classified personality types according to body type: endomorphy, mesomorphy, and ectomorphy.

6. *Humanistic-existential* models focus on the total personality as opposed to separate behaviors that make up personality; biology and the environment are minimized as determinants, and personal choice is emphasized.

7. Maslow emphasized the drive for self-actualization, whereas Rogers emphasized the role of self and conscious awareness in the life of the individual.

8. According to *learning theorists,* personality is a set of patterns of behavior that we learn to make in response to specific stimuli, according to how such responses have been reinforced in the past.

9. *Social-learning theory* points out that a second type of learning—imitation based on observation of others—also affects behavior and thus personality.

10. *Cognitive models* view personality as being the result of a person's unique cognitive organization of the world; in other words, a person's actions flow from his or her perspective. *Personal-construct theory* focuses on how people make sense of their experience.

11. Among the methods used in assessing personality are: *q-sort technique, open-ended interviews, projective tests,* and *personality inventories.*

Suggested Readings

BANDURA, A., & WALTERS, K. *Social learning and personality development.* New York: Holt, Rinehart & Winston, 1963. Presents the principles of the social-learning approach to personality and reviews modeling, imitation, and identification in the development of personality and the learning of social behaviors.

FREUD, S. [*New introductory lectures on psychoanalysis*] (W. J. H. Sproutt, trans.). New York: Norton, 1933. An introduction to the psychodynamic approach to personality. Included is Freud's most concise explanation of id, ego, and superego provinces and functioning; anxiety; and the development of the female psyche. In the final lectures the implications of psychoanalysis for religion and social order are presented.

HALL, C. S., & LINDZEY, G. (Eds.). *Theories of personality* (3rd ed.). New York: John Wiley, 1978. Concise and detailed digest of the major theories of personality. Presents each theorist's conceptualization of the human being, the structure of personality, mechanisms of development and change, assessment, and (when applicable) therapeutic procedure.

MASLOW, A. H. *Toward a psychology of being* (2nd ed.). New York: Van Nostrand, 1968. Describes the humanistic approach to personality, exploring the fundamental motive of growth and the characteristics of the self-actualized personality. Contrasts the humanistic model with the psychodynamic model and makes comparisons with other humanistic, existential, and neo-Freudian theories.

MISCHEL, W. *Personality and assessment.* New York: John Wiley, 1968. A complete exposition of Mischel's unsuccessful search for cross-situational consistency in behavior, explaining his position regarding the inadequacies of nomothetic trait theories of personality.

PERVIN, L. A. *Current controversies and issues in personality.* New York: John Wiley, 1978. Personality theories are presented in light of their conflicting positions on a number of current controversies in personality—role of the environment, aggression, altruism, sex differences, and the role of affect. An evaluation of each theoretical viewpoint in terms of social and political implications is provided.

SKINNER, B. F. *Science and human behavior.* New York: Macmillan, 1953. Details an approach to personality based on a functional analysis of cause-and-effect relationships and the application of the principles of operant conditioning to the study of personality and behavior.

VERNON, P. E. *Personality assessment: A critical survey.* New York: John Wiley, 1964. Presents the merits and drawbacks of the methods suggested by major personality theorists for the assessment of personality. Includes psychoanalytic and Rogerian interview techniques, the objective approaches of psychometric measurement suggested by the trait theorists Eysenck and Cattell, and techniques that assess major trends in personality, such as the MMPI and self-concept scales.

15. Stress and Coping

Stress is a universal human experience. Unpleasant experiences bring on stress—getting fired, having an illness in the family, or failing an important exam are all stressful. But even generally pleasant events and experiences can have stressful components—a promotion, going away to college, or the purchase of a new house will also cause stress. The common element among these experiences, both pleasant and unpleasant, is that they require some kind of **adjustment** or **adaptation.** Sometimes people are able to adapt to stressful situations fairly easily; at other times they have more difficulty coping with them. Certain people react badly to certain kinds of stresses but cope well with other kinds; others have different coping patterns.

Stress can be defined as a state that occurs when people are faced with demands from the environment that require them to change in some way. One question this definition raises is whether stress is the environmental demand itself or rather people's responses to that demand. It is helpful to think of stress as including both environmental demands, or **stressors,** and the person's reaction to them, the **stress responses.** In this chapter we will discuss stress, its causes and consequences, people's reactions to it, and the methods people use to cope with it. All of us at one time or another experience many of the sources of stress and show many, if not all, of the reactions that we will discuss. As we go through the chapter we will refine our definitions of stress and coping, make them clearer, and show how they apply to us.

SOURCES OF STRESS

According to our definition, stress arises from demands placed on the person by the environment. That environmental demand, or *stressor,* can be physical or psychological, intrinsic to a situation or attributed to it by the person involved, universal or unique to one person's experience. Some specific stressors are traumatic events, life events and chronic difficulties, conflict, and frustration.

Traumatic Events

Perhaps the most easily understood sources of stress are traumatic events. These are situations of exceptional danger generally outside the range of usual experience. Examples of traumatic events include natural disasters (floods, earthquakes), disasters caused by other human beings (being held hostage, military combat, air-raid attack), catastrophic accidents (car accidents, airplane crashes), and physical assaults (torture, attempted murder, rape). These extreme situations produce severe symptoms of stress in nearly everybody and require extensive and prolonged adaptive efforts. Adjusting to traumatic events can be very costly in physical and psychological terms. We will talk about the consequences of adapting to such severe stressors later in the chapter.

Life Events and Chronic Difficulties

Although most people do not experience traumatic events, they do go through many eventful changes and encounter persistent difficulties in the course of their lives. Such events and difficulties can pose considerable chal-

Extreme Situational Stress

Situations of exceptional tension—war, catastrophe, physical assault—often produce characteristic stress reactions. One of the most common of these is combat fatigue. First described during World War I by a British pathologist who named it "shell shock," combat fatigue is characterized by psychic numbing or diminished responsiveness to the external world, and also by severe depression, hypersensitivity, sleep disturbance, nightmares, anxiety, and tremors. It can result from prolonged exposure to battle conditions or from some traumatic experience during combat, such as the death of a comrade. Sometimes combat fatigue strikes after the battle is over. A minor stress may suddenly trigger the stress symptoms the soldier managed to suppress in the field.

One study conducted during World War II indicated that wounded soldiers were less likely to experience combat fatigue than the unwounded. In fact, according to this

One of the most common examples of extreme situational stress is combat fatigue. Interestingly, it is not the wounded soldier who is most likely to suffer from combat fatigue, but the nonwounded.

study, the more seriously wounded men tended to have the least anxiety of all. The researchers suggested that wounded soldiers had less anxiety because they were removed from the stress of battle, at least temporarily, and seriously wounded men knew they probably would never have to return to the field. The unwounded could not only anticipate future combat, but also wonder, sometimes guiltily, why they had been spared while their buddies had fallen.

In civilian life, catastrophic events can produce a stress reaction not unlike combat fatigue. The victims may show a wide range of symptoms depending on the nature and severity of the catastrophe, its degree of unexpectedness, and their own unique personalities. The common behavior pattern following a catastrophic event has been called the **disaster syndrome** (Lifton, 1968; Erikson, 1976). It consists of 3 stages: In the shock stage, victims appear to be unaware of their injuries or of danger. They are stunned, dazed, and apathetic. In extreme cases, they may be disoriented or show

lenge or even hazard to an individual. Changes that disrupt or threaten to disrupt people's usual activities are called *life events*. These include normal and even happy life-stage transitions such as graduation, marriage, birth of a first child, and retirement. They also include more unexpected life changes such as divorce, illness or injury, job promotion, and change in career. Life events, both positive and negative, require substantial readjustments in behavior, and these readjustments can be quite stressful (Holmes & Rahe, 1967). Think, for example, of the myriad adjustments new parents must make to take care of their first baby. Career plans and work schedules are disrupted, sleeping patterns are altered, schedules and responsibilities must be rearranged, and social activities are altered. Even more readjustment is required by such negative events as the loss of a job or the death of a spouse.

Major life events can produce chronic difficulties as well, although events and difficulties can exist independently. Chronic difficulties are problems that cause individuals to make ·adjustments more or less continuously in the course of daily life. Poverty, marital troubles, crowded living conditions, urban noise, job and academic pressures, continuous ill health—all of these and many other situations pose problems requiring daily adaptation. The wear and tear on individuals experiencing such demands can be considerable, especially when they have no control over those conditions. We will examine the physical as well as psychological consequences of life events and chronic difficulties at some length later in the chapter.

signs of partial amnesia. In the suggestible stage, victims continue to be passive. They will take orders readily but are often unable to perform even the simplest tasks. The recovery stage, which is the final stage, is a time of great stress. Victims are anxious, tense, apprehensive. They may have difficulty sleeping or concentrating and may repeat the story of the catastrophe over and over.

Like combat fatigue and other extreme stress reactions, the disaster syndrome may not occur immediately after the trauma but, instead, may be brought on by some minor stress several weeks or even months later. The new *Diagnostic and Statistical Manual of Mental Disorders* (DSM-III) (American Psychiatric Association, 1979) terms this syndrome "post-traumatic stress disorder" and distinguishes among acute, chronic, and delayed types. In the acute type, symptoms occur within 6 months of the trauma but are not prolonged beyond 6 months, as they are in the chronic type. Delayed post-traumatic stress disorder is diagnosed if symptoms begin at least 6 months after

the crisis situation.

Post-traumatic stress disorder was introduced into DSM-III in part through the lobbying efforts of veterans and psychiatric professionals following the Vietnam War. Although there is a lack of reliable data as yet, veterans of Vietnam seemed especially likely to have experienced this syndrome because of the unusual aspects of this war: the absence of clear front and back lines, unpredictable attacks in dense jungle conditions, an inability to distinguish easily between Vietnamese allies and enemies, the horrors of napalm bombing, and the lack of unified support at home. Vietnam vets, like other victims of extreme stress, complain of reexperiencing traumatic events in painful, recurrent memories or dreams. In rare instances, they relive the events for a few minutes or hours, behaving as though experiencing the crisis situation at that moment; this may occur in response to circumstances that are similar to or symbolize the original traumatic events.

Associated with post-traumatic stress disorder are feelings of es-

trangement from previously important persons and activities, severe depression often brought on by guilt for having survived when others did not, and occasional unpredictable explosions of rage or aggression with little provocation. Aggressive reactions are particularly characteristic of war veterans; death-camp survivors more often experience failing memory and an impaired ability to concentrate.

Methods of treatment for post-traumatic stress disorder are still being devised. It appears that among soldiers in battle, removal to back lines or a return home can be counterproductive, stabilizing the disorder rather than relieving it (Glass, 1953). Rest and care behind front lines, coupled with the expectations of a quick return to combat, appear to prevent chronic disorder from developing. Among civilian survivors of disaster, participation in volunteer community clean-up and rebuilding efforts can speed recovery (Barton, 1969). Much still has to be learned, however, regarding effective treatment for the effects of extreme situational stress.

Conflict

Another kind of demand that results in stress is **conflict,** which occurs when a person must choose between incompatible, contradictory, or mutually exclusive goals or courses of action. Two goals are mutually exclusive when the action needed to achieve one automatically prevents the person from reaching the other. Conflict can occur when 2 inner needs are in opposition, when 2 external demands pull the person in different directions, or when an inner need is incompatible with an external demand. Psychologists who have described and studied conflict (Lewin, 1931; Miller, 1944) have categorized some basic categories of conflict according to the person's tendency to approach or to avoid a goal.

APPROACH-APPROACH CONFLICT.   In **approach-approach conflict,** people are faced with 2 equally attractive but mutually exclusive goals, a situation in which choosing one automatically means giving up the other. This is bound to make people more discontented than if they faced only one attractive goal. Someone who receives 2 good job offers, for example, may agonize over the decision and feel doubts after making the choice; this stress probably would not have occurred with only one job offer.

APPROACH-AVOIDANCE CONFLICT.   Here the person is confronted with a single goal that has both positive and negative consequences. If you have ever tried to feed a wild animal, you have seen **approach-avoidance conflict**—the animal wants the food yet is naturally afraid to come close to a human to get it. People generally experience this sort of stress when they want to do something but know that some of the consequences will be unpleasant. Many people approach marriage with these feelings—love for the other person leads them to approach marriage, but uneasiness about new responsibilities and loss of freedom makes them want to avoid it.

AVOIDANCE-AVOIDANCE CONFLICT. This type of stressful situation involves an inescapable choice between 2 equally unattractive goals or outcomes. A baseball player caught between 2 bases is faced with **avoidance-avoidance conflict:** Going forward or going back will result in being tagged out. A middle-aged man may hate the thought of spending the rest of his working years in a field that he finds boring. At the same time he knows the problems of changing careers at his age, and he probably has family responsibilities that make it hard for him to start over. The response to this type of conflict is often to try not to make any decision at all.

DOUBLE APPROACH-AVOIDANCE CONFLICT. In this complex situation, 2 possible courses of action each present an approach-avoidance conflict. Think of a college senior attempting to choose between 2 job offers, each of which has both desirable and undesirable components. One job, for example, promises challenging work (approach) but low pay (avoidance). The other promises a good deal of tedium (avoidance) but a lucrative salary (approach). The student in this situation is in a **double approach-avoidance conflict** and, quite understandably, may respond with some stress.

Frustration

Frustration is both a result of conflict and a source of stress in itself. We experience frustration when the attainment of some desired goal has been blocked or thwarted.

Researchers (Coleman & Hammen, 1974) have identified 5 sources of frustration, most of which are a natural outgrowth of our society:

1. *Delays.* In a society in which the value of time (and thus of being on time) is emphasized, any kind of delay is frustrating.
2. *Lack of resources.* We are constantly bombarded by advertising that makes goods seem attractive and necessary to our status and self-worth. When we cannot afford these goods, we feel frustrated.
3. *Loss.* This can be the death of a loved one, or simply the loss of friendships when we move to another part of the country. Loss causes grief, of course, but also frustration, because it makes us feel helpless and reminds us that we have no control over many things that affect our lives.
4. *Failure.* Since our society is a very competitive one, we are bound to experience failure almost all the time. One of the most frustrating aspects of failure is the feeling that we are in some way responsible for it—if only we had done this instead of that, it might never have happened. Whether this feeling is realistic or not, it is frustrating.
5. *Meaninglessness.* It is not easy to live a meaningful life, although this is an ideal in our society and may even be a basic human need, as suggested by existential psychologists. Many people do not have meaningful or fulfilling jobs, for instance, and many are unable to find any work at all. This kind

Frustration is both a result of conflict and a source of stress. In our society the automobile is certainly a common source of (or at least the scene of) many frustrating and stressful occurrences.

of frustration is made worse by the feeling that society is to blame and there is nothing to be done about it.

CONSEQUENCES OF STRESS

It is now widely believed that exposure to severe or prolonged environmental stress can produce physical and even mental illness. Stress has been linked to a variety of disorders—high blood pressure, heart disease, ulcers, even cancer and schizophrenia. But exactly how these illnesses are produced by stress is not yet well understood. Studies of physiological reactions to stress suggest important answers, especially with respect to physical illness.

The Biological Model

Psychologists who assert a physiological basis for behavior consider stress a biological event. In this view, stress is a set of physiological responses to demands placed upon the individual. (Indeed, physiological change is one of the most widely used indicators of stress reactions because it is concrete and measurable.) Most psychologists who take a biological approach to stress believe that physiological reactions to external demands overwhelm the body's resistance to disease or impair the ability of body organs to function.

Much of our understanding of the physiology of stress comes from the pioneering work of Hans Selye (1956). As a young medical student in the mid-1920s, Selye observed physical reactions that were common to most patients, no matter what their illness. This gave him the idea that there might be a general pattern of reaction to stress that did not differ according to the source of the stress. He called this pattern the **General Adaptation Syndrome.**

THE GENERAL ADAPTATION SYNDROME.   This syndrome is described by Selye (1956) as a 3-stage response. It begins with an *alarm reaction* characterized by a number of physical changes: increases in heart rate, respiratory activity, endocrine secretions, sweat-gland activity, temperature, and blood pressure, as well as muscle tension. You may have observed many of these reactions in yourself when you are under stress.

In the *stage of resistance,* people recover from the initial alarm and try to cope with the stressful situation. The external physical symptoms of stress disappear and the internal responses to stress—hormone activity, heart rate, and blood pressure—become normalized. In this stage everything appears to be under control, but the appearance is deceptive. In fact, the person's emotional and physical resources are being consumed by his or her efforts to control the stress. If the stressful condition continues, the person will enter the third stage—*exhaustion.* If a new stress arises during the stage of resistance, a person will often break down and enter the exhaustion phase immediately.

Selye's (1956) biochemical studies showed that the adrenal glands play a major role in the General Adaptation Syndrome. The adrenal medulla is controlled by the sympathetic nervous system (see Chapter 2). When it is stimulated in response to some form of excitement, it secretes quantities of epinephrine and norepinephrine into the blood. These hormones increase metabolism and help the body to release energy stores, which causes the physical reactions described as part of the alarm reaction.

The stage of resistance is characterized by increased activity of the adrenal cortex. In order to function, the adrenal cortex must be stimulated by the hormone ACTH, which is produced by the pituitary gland. When an organism is subjected to stress, the pituitary secretions increase. This, in turn, causes the adrenal cortex to produce more hormones. Some of the effects of these hormones on other parts of the body are maintenance of blood pressure, manufacture of red blood cells, blocking of the inflammatory response, and increased blood sugar level.

It is not surprising that with all these physiological responses to stress, people who are exposed to stress over a long period of time often become ill. In the next section we will look at some of these stress-linked disorders.

PSYCHOSOMATIC ILLNESSES.   Stress-linked disorders, such as ulcers, migraine, asthma, eczema, and high blood pressure, are called **psychosomatic illnesses.** It is important to note that the term psychosomatic illness is often misused. Quite often, because such disorders appear to be due to psychological stress, they are confused with types of neurotic physical symptoms (to be discussed in Chapter 16) that exist primarily in the patient's mind. Psychosomatic disorders are real physical illnesses that should be treated by a medical doctor.

Scientists who have studied these disorders have been confronted with a number of questions. Why, for example, do some people become ill from stress while others do not? Why does stress cause a physical illness instead of an emotional one? Why does one person get ulcers from stress while another has a heart attack?

Many theories have been developed to answer these questions. One, the *general-reaction, somatic weakness theory,* holds that any stressor can generate a reaction similar to the General Adaptation Syndrome (Selye, 1956; Levi, 1965; Lazarus, 1977). The type of psychosomatic illness that develops from prolonged stress depends upon the person's weakest or most vulnerable body system, and not upon the specific nature of the stressful stimulus. For example, people whose lungs have been weakened by smoking are predisposed to asthma when they come under stress. In people whose lungs are healthy, some other area of the body may be affected. Genetic factors, diet, and life style all interact to produce a somatic weakness.

The *specific-reaction theory,* on the other hand, says that psychosomatic illnesses depend upon the type of stressor experienced by a person (Alexander, 1950; Mason, 1971; Lazarus, 1966) or upon the idiosyncratic physical reactions of a stressed person (Engel, 1960). For example, Alexander argued that particular unconscious emotional conflicts (types of stress) produce particular psychosomatic disorders. Others have pointed to possible variations in illness outcomes that depend on acute versus chronic stress (Mahl, 1952), type of emotional reaction (Mason, 1971), or perceptions of the stressful situation (Lazarus & Launier, 1978). Engel, another specific-reaction theorist, suggested that people develop disorders in the system in which they show the greatest response to stress. These unique reactions, which vary from person to person, may be genetically determined. One individual, for example, experiences rapid acceleration of heartbeat under stress. Another produces excessive stomach acid. These unique reactions may determine which specific system of the body will be prone to a stress-linked disorder.

Finally, the *diasthesis-stress theory* (Schwartz, 1977; Gannon, 1981; Sternbach, 1966) holds that specific disorders are produced by some combination of environment, stress, and biological predisposition. According to this model, both a diasthesis, or predisposing organic condition, and precipitating stressful events are necessary to produce psychosomatic symptoms. This view explains, in part, why different people exposed to the same stressor develop different symptoms. A person with a predisposition to secrete high levels of pepsinogen is likely to develop an ulcer when exposed to prolonged environmental stress, while one who has a weak respiratory system may develop breathing difficulties instead.

We do not know the exact mechanisms through which short-term physiological changes in response to stress can result in chronic disease. Specific environmental, psychological, and physiological factors undoubtedly interact to produce particular psychosomatic illnesses, but how these factors work together has yet to be determined (Weiner, 1977; Lazarus, 1977). We turn now from theories of physiological stress processes to describe specific psychosomatic disorders.

Hypertension, or high blood pressure, is one disorder that has been linked to stress. Essential hypertension is chronic high blood pressure that cannot be traced to an organic cause. Acceleration of the heartbeat, often experienced under stress, has something to do with high blood pressure. More important, experts feel, is the constriction of the walls of the arteries, a phenomenon that also occurs under stress, which forces the heart to work harder to drive the blood through the narrowed arteries.

Much research has been done on the link between stress and hypertension. Numerous studies show an association between stress and a short-term rise in blood pressure (Hokanson, DeGood, Forrest, & Britton, 1971; Dembroski, MacDougall, Heid, & Shields, 1979). These studies consistently demonstrate that people respond to the threat of shock or to challenge with increased blood pressure. However, the blood pressure returns to normal after a short time. Long-term or chronic hypertension has been found in people who have lost their jobs (Kasl & Cobb, 1970), people who experience daily traffic congestion while commuting (Stokols, Novaco, Stokols, & Campbell, 1978), and even people who are undergoing the stressful experience of hospitalization (Volicer & Volicer, 1977). How these episodic environmental stressors translate into chronic hypertension has not yet been established.

Another set of physiological responses to stress occurs in the *gastrointestinal* system. The body reacts to a stressor by secreting certain hormones that increase the flow of the stomach's acidic digestive juices as well as

Table 15–1: Social Readjustment Rating Scale.

Life Event	Mean LCU Value
Death of spouse	100
Divorce	73
Marital separation	65
Jail term	63
Death of close family member	63
Personal injury or illness	53
Marriage	50
Fired at work	47
Marital reconciliation	45
Retirement	45
Change in health of family member	44
Pregnancy	40
Sex difficulties	39
Gain of new family member	39
Business readjustment	39
Change in financial state	38
Death of close friend	37
Change to different line of work	36
Change in number of arguments with spouse	35
Mortgage over $10,000	31
Foreclosure of mortgage or loan	30
Change in responsibilities at work	29
Son or daughter leaving home	29
Trouble with in-laws	29
Outstanding personal achievement	28
Wife begin or stop work	26
Begin or end school	26
Change in living conditions	25
Revision of personal habits	24
Trouble with boss	23
Change in work hours or conditions	20
Change in residence	20
Change in schools	20
Change in recreation	19
Change in church activities	19
Change in social activities	18
Mortgage or loan less than $10,000	17
Change in sleeping habits	16
Change in number of family get-togethers	15
Change in eating habits	15
Vacation	13
Christmas	12
Minor violations of the law	11

From Holmes & Rahe (1967), p. 216

engorge the stomach with blood. As a result, the mucus lining of the stomach is stretched out and the entire gastrointestinal system is subjected to excessive amounts of gastric acid. After prolonged exposure to such acids, the mucus layer is eaten through, resulting in ulceration of the stomach or small intestine (producing *gastric ulcers* or *duodenal ulcers,* respectively). The most common ulcers are duodenal (Walker & Sandman, 1981), which have been clearly related to excess hydrochloric acid secretion. Gastric ulcers, on the other hand, may be due less to excess acid than to inadequate secretions of protective mucus in the stomach lining. Certain individuals seem predisposed to produce high levels of gastric acid (Weiner, 1977). If these people are exposed to prolonged stress, they have an increased likelihood of developing an ulcer.

STRESS AND GENERAL HEALTH. Recently the focus of research has shifted from how stress leads to a particular psychosomatic illness to how stress affects our health in general. One approach follows from Selye's General Adaptation Syndrome stress-response model. One of the physical consequences of the stage of exhaustion is lowered resistance to infection. Lowered resistance should increase the likelihood of the occurrence of disease. This phenomenon has been studied especially in connection with the kind of stress that accompanies life events. The Social Readjustment Rating Scale has proved to be an invaluable tool in studying this kind of stress.

Holmes and Rahe (1967) asked people to judge each of 43 life events according to the degree of social readjustment called for in response to them. All comparisons were made against marriage, which was assigned an arbitrary value; judges were supposed to decide whether each event listed called for more or less readjustment than marriage. Ratings did not depend on the desirability of the event—it could be positively or negatively viewed—but only on the amount of readjustment required. Consensus was high among participants in the first rating study, and it has continued to be high in subsequent studies, even among adolescents who presumably have not themselves experienced a number of these life changes (Holmes, 1979).

These readjustment ratings were averaged to yield a value for each life event. These were called Life Change Units (LCUs). The more stressful an event, the higher its LCU value. But again, the emphasis is on change rather than on the psychological meaning, emotion, or social desirability of the event. The events ranged in stressfulness from death of a spouse down to a vacation or a minor law violation.

The resulting Social Readjustment Rating Scale has proved to be a useful tool in measuring the relationship between life change and health change (see Table 15–1). In the typical study using the Social Readjustment Rating Scale, people are asked to indicate which of the events listed on the questionnaire happened to them over a fixed time period, either 6 months to 1 year ago or 1 year to 2 years ago. The stress value for each event is multiplied by the number of times the event occurred and the values for all events are totaled to produce a score in Life Change Units for the specific time period. Researchers then look at the relationship between Life Change Units, a quantified amount of adaptation, and illness in the individuals.

In one study, for example, the magnitude of Life Change Units was recorded for victims of coronary heart disease as reported by their kin (Rahe, Romo, Bennett, & Siltanen, 1974). Compared to a 6-month interval 1 year before the coronary, victims had experienced a 50 to 100 percent increase in LCUs in the 6 months *immediately* before the heart attack. An even more dramatic finding was that victims who died from the coronary had experienced an average

A Cautionary Note on Life-Events Research

For several reasons, we should be cautious in interpreting the findings of studies based on the Holmes and Rahe (1967) Social Readjustment Rating Scale (SRRS) and other life-events scales like it. First, the SRRS may not adequately measure the extent of life change for most people. Many common stressful life events are not listed on the scale, for example, being the victim of a crime, going on strike, receiving a promotion or demotion, having a traffic accident, obtaining an abortion. You can probably think of many others as you examine the scale (see Table 15–1). The SRRS tends to underrepresent events that occur to the poor, to students, to women, and to various ethnic and specific occupational groups.

Second, ratings of the amount of readjustment required by each event, averaged into Life Change Unit (LCU) scores, can vary depending upon the sex, age, race, ethnicity, and nationality of the raters (Miller et al., 1974; Hough et al., 1978; Rosenberg & Dohrenwend, 1975). Notice, too, that the most socially undesir-able, or negative events (death of spouse, divorce, etc.) have the highest LCU values. This suggests that rather than measuring the amount of life *change*, the SRRS may be measuring the amount of *negative* change in a person's life. In fact, numerous studies do suggest that negative changes are more predictive of ill health than either total change or positive change (Glass, 1977; Sarason et al., 1978; Vinokur & Selzer, 1975; Mueller et al., 1977).

Third, studies using the SRRS often rely on retrospective reports that may not be highly accurate. The longer the time period for which people are asked to report, the less accurate may be their recall. (What has happened to *you* in the last 5 years?) On the other hand, people who are trying to explain their illness may recall more events, especially undesirable ones, in an "effort after meaning" (Brown, 1974). Such biased recall may inflate the associations between LCU scores and illness. For this reason, many life-events researchers have designed prospective studies (Holmes & Masuda, 1974). That is, they collect data on the SRRS at one point in time, and several months to a year later they assess their subjects' health status. In this way, bias from retrospective reporting can be avoided.

But finally, even prospective studies must be viewed cautiously: The SRRS contains many items that are changes in health (personal illness and injury) or may be symptoms of health change (change in eating habits, change in sleeping habits, sex difficulties). A researcher who thinks he or she is examining the relationship between *life* changes and future illness may simply be finding a relationship between *health* changes and future illness (Thoits, 1981)! The SRRS contains items that are contaminated by the outcomes that they are intended to explain. This problem affects both prospective and retrospective life-events studies.

In short, it pays to be a critical consumer of life-events research. Many flaws may undermine the significance of many of the findings thus far. However, those researchers who have carefully controlled for these problems (cf. Tausig, 1982) still report that there are indeed associations between life changes, especially negative ones, and physical and psychological disorders. The SRRS has served as a useful springboard for research in this area; however, a more sensitive scale that reflects the impact upon people's well-being of the full range and complexity of life events remains to be devised.

increase in LCUs of 100 to 200 percent over the 6-month period immediately before the illness.

Since its publication in 1967, literally hundreds of studies have utilized the Social Readjustment Rating Scale. Scores on the scale have been positively associated with sudden cardiac death, onset of heart disease, fractures, diabetes, leukemia, and influenza as well as minor illnesses (Holmes & Masuda, 1974). Scores on the Social Readjustment Rating Scale (and other life-event scales developed subsequently) have also been associated with neurosis, depression, schizophrenia, and symptoms of serious psychological distress (Dohrenwend & Dohrenwend, 1974; Barrett, 1979). Although there have been numerous criticisms of life-event studies in general and the Social Readjustment Rating Scale in particular, the bulk of the evidence does suggest that the cumulative effects of adapting to environmental demands lowers the body's resistance to disease.

So far we have been concerned with the consequences of stress for the physical and psychological health of individuals. Although illness or disturbance often follows from severe or prolonged stress exposure, such consequences are far from inevitable. This is because people often successfully cope with the stressors in their lives, thus eliminating or reducing their harmful physiological effects. We turn now to consider the different ways that people cope with environmental demands. Many coping patterns that we will discuss are used to eliminate a general psychological response elicited by most stressors—anxiety. We will examine various models of anxiety and the adjustments that people make to control it.

STRESS, ANXIETY, AND COPING

Anxiety is a term with many connotations. It is used to refer to symptoms of psychopathology, to realistic fears, to irrational emotional states, and to normal reactions experienced by everyone. Although anxiety is usually considered negative, it can sometimes serve a positive function. It will become clear from our discussion that under different circumstances anxiety can take all of these forms. The fact that "anxiety" has so many meanings in everyday usage may stem, in part, from the different views of anxiety held by different schools or models of psychology. As we look at how each model explains anxiety, we will see that while anxiety is a fearful psychological *reaction* to stressful events, it often becomes itself a *source* of stress to which the individual must adjust. That is, anxiety may be so intense that the person must cope with it first before turning attention to its causes. Some coping patterns, then, may be used to adapt to stressors while others are used to reduce (or avoid) anxiety itself.

The Psychoanalytic Model

Sigmund Freud saw anxiety as a consequence of **intrapsychic conflict.** You will recall that Freud divided the mind into three parts. The id is the source of our primal impulses and drives. The superego is analogous to the conscience or moral sense; it is the product of socialization, the collective voice of parents, church, state, and custom. The superego's demands are often contrary to those of the id. The ego is the mediator between these two opposing forces. Conflict often arises when the ego attempts to reconcile the demands of the id and the superego, and this conflict produces anxiety.

Freudian theorists identify three different types of anxiety: **Reality anxiety** occurs when we are threatened by something in the environment. The threat may be either physical or psychological, but it signifies real danger in the external world. **Moral anxiety** is fear of conscience—we feel guilty when we do, or even think of, something contrary to our moral code. **Neurotic anxiety** is the fear that our instincts will get out of control and make us do something for which we will be punished. It is not so much a fear of the instincts themselves as of punishment for following them.

In Freudian terms, reality anxiety and moral anxiety are appropriate responses to some situations that inevitably occur in life. However, neurotic anxiety can be counterproductive. It occurs when the unconscious forces of the id are in conflict with the superego. The anxiety is a warning signal to the ego that some unacceptable id impulse is about to surface. When this warning is sounded, the ego develops a strategy to reduce the anxiety by reducing the conflict. Thus we may either inhibit or ignore the impulse or obey our

Job-related difficulties can be a great source of anxiety.

conscience; in either case, the conflict is resolved (for the moment). When the ego cannot cope by these direct methods, we turn to defense mechanisms.

Defense Mechanisms

Defense mechanisms are automatic and unconscious reactions in response to intrapsychic conflict. A defense mechanism works in 1 of 2 ways: (1) It blocks a sexual or aggressive impulse and thus relieves the anxiety and guilt caused by such impulses; or (2) it changes the nature of the impulse itself and both relieves the guilt and anxiety and allows some gratification of the now-transformed impulse.

Freud and his followers identified several strategies that people use to cope with stress or anxiety stemming from intrapsychic conflict.

REPRESSION.   People who use this coping method exclude their unacceptable-drive thoughts and feelings from consciousness. Evidence of **repression** is underreaction to a relevant situation and indirect indications that the repressed tendencies are actually present. For example, a woman may feel angry at having to pay taxes but blocks that feeling from her awareness. That her anger is actually present is shown indirectly—she forgets to sign or enclose the check with the tax return.

DISPLACEMENT.   Repression can lead directly to **displacement** because the most common type of repressive barricade is to focus attention on a substitute—to displace attention. If you have ever been angry at a boss or a professor and were unable to express that anger to that person, you may have found yourself lashing out at your roommate or a stranger in the street. Because you could not show anger at the person who provoked it, you displaced that anger onto a more acceptable target.

PROJECTION.   One way to block unacceptable thoughts and feelings is to attribute them to another person. This is called **projection.** A person who feels guilty about aggressive business practices may attribute to competitors the same practices and claim that their actions made it necessary to retaliate. Projection locates the responsibility for one's behavior outside oneself and removes the guilt and conflict that behavior would otherwise cause.

REACTION FORMATION.   In **reaction formation** we reverse our unacceptable feelings. For example, a man may hate his mother because she nags him and makes extraordinary demands on him. The conflict between his angry impulses and his superego's command to honor and love his parents causes him anxiety and guilt. To relieve those feelings, he unconsciously converts his hatred into exaggerated love and devotion and acts like a model son. We sometimes hold a number of deeply felt attitudes that are the direct opposites of our repressed attitudes.

NEGATION.   This is another way of refusing to acknowledge unacceptable feelings. In **negation,** the feeling is expressed, but with a "negative sign" next to it. Take the example of the man who hates his mother. If his method of coping is reaction formation, he will say, "I love my mother." If he uses negation to cope, he will state, emphatically, "I don't hate my mother." And often he will make this statement out of the blue, when no one has been questioning or challenging his feelings about his mother. If he states his love angrily, he will be able to get rid of the anger he is feeling without acknowledging its unacceptable source.

INTELLECTUALIZATION. This is simply an exaggerated preference for thought over feeling. A person who uses **intellectualization** will talk about sexual or aggressive matters in a very cool, detached way. This prevents experiencing any of the feelings most of us would have discussing these subjects. Teenagers often use this defense mechanism in "bull sessions" in which sexual matters are discussed in the abstract. Intellectualization helps teenagers to get through many of the conflicts that are inevitable in growing up.

UNDOING. **Undoing** means following an unacceptable act with one that negates it, thus relieving the guilt and anxiety that resulted from the first act. It is the only defense mechanism that is an "after-the-fact" response. The other defense mechanisms operate to prevent unacceptable thoughts or feelings from occurring. A husband who habitually argues with his wife in the morning and then brings her flowers when he comes home from work is using the undoing defense. He would be quite surprised if you confronted him with this pattern, though, and would deny that was what he was doing.

REGRESSION. In **regression,** a person flees anxiety by retreating into behavior appropriate to an earlier, seemingly safer stage in life. A little girl going through the stress of entering school for the first time may begin to act in a very babyish way: She may suck her thumb, wet her bed, or insist on being carried by her mother or father instead of walking.

SUBLIMATION. **Sublimation** is the channeling of unacceptable urges and feelings into acceptable activities. Freud interpreted the madonnas painted by the great Leonardo da Vinci as an example of sublimation of Oedipal feelings—in other words, he believed Leonardo dealt with an unresolved Oedipal conflict by transforming his feelings about his mother into art. Sublimation allows an individual to express repressed, sadistic urges in constructive activities such as surgery. Freud believed that the intellectual curiosity of adults was a sublimation of childhood sexual curiosity. The inhibitions of creativity that he saw in adults seemed to him to derive from the strong repression of childhood sexual curiosity.

Defense mechanisms are very much a part of normal behavior. But, according to Freud, their overuse is a symptom of neurosis. Overuse means either carrying a defense to an extreme (such as marked regression to a childish state) or habitually resorting to the same defense (such as a lifelong repression of sexual feelings).

The Freudian theory of defense mechanisms is but one interpretation of the way people cope with psychological stress. We will now look at coping habits from a number of other approaches.

The Learning Model

When experimental psychologists began to study anxiety, they translated Freud's theories into stimulus-response terms and concluded that anxiety is a learned autonomic or internal response. The experimental data produced by Mourer (1939) and Miller (1948) are the basis of this learning model of anxiety.

You will recall from our discussion of classical conditioning in Chapter 6 that an organism can be conditioned to fear a neutral stimulus through *classical conditioning* techniques. In one experiment (Miller, 1948), for example, rats were shocked repeatedly while a tone was sounded; after many trials, the rats showed fear at the sound of the tone alone. The tone had become a conditioned stimulus for the fear response.

The rats also learned new responses to avoid the sound of the tone (the conditioned stimulus), and thus they learned new responses to avoid fear (the conditioned response). This part of the learning model uses the principles of *operant conditioning*. The new response was rewarded by a reduction of the fear caused by a previously conditioned stimulus, the tone. The interesting point here is that the rats learned new behavior to avoid a stimulus that in itself was harmless—the tone didn't hurt them, and yet to escape the tone was reinforcing.

Learning theory suggests, then, that the various methods people use to cope with stress are the result of specific response–reinforcement relationships. An interesting extension of this idea can be found in the work of Martin Seligman (1975) and his colleagues. They discovered that dogs exposed to uncontrollable and inescapable shock later failed to try to escape, even in situations where escape was possible. What is most interesting about these studies is that the animals appear to give up—they stop responding entirely and endure the shocks passively. Seligman has labeled this state "learned helplessness," because what the animals are learning is that no response that they make will affect the outcome or change what happens to them.

Learned helplessness has also been demonstrated in humans (Hiroto & Seligman, 1975). It has been shown that repeated inability to affect or control a situation can lead to deficits in learning. People learn that their responses do not affect the outcome of events, and their learned expectation prevents them from acquiring other knowledge or behavior patterns that would help them to gain control over their environment. In particular, reduced responding leads to later learning deficits. However, learned helplessness is not necessarily an inappropriate or negative response in some situations. It is at times a beneficial strategy, since giving up can be accompanied by reduced stress responses (Gatchel & Proctor, 1976).

While learning theorists see learned helplessness as an entirely learned mode of responding, recent research disputes this. The inability to control a situation is a key factor in the experience of helplessness, and the expectation of control depends in part on a person's perceptions and attributions. It is the individual's *interpretation* of the situational demand that determines the stress reaction. Recently, learned-helplessness theory has been reformulated to take these interpretational or attributional factors into account. We will discuss this approach when we examine cognitive models of coping with stress and anxiety.

The Humanistic-Existential Model

Humanistic and existential psychologists believe that anxiety is due to people's failure to achieve their fullest potential and take full responsibility for their lives. Humanists assume that people are motivated to "self-actualize," that is, to realize personal fulfillment. Through faulty learning or the diversion of energies to more basic needs, they may fail to achieve self-actualization. This failure to live up to one's potential leads to anxiety-producing self-devaluation that, as in the psychoanalytic model, must be defended against.

What the existentialists add to this theory is the idea that people are re-

"Type-A" Behavior and Coronary Heart Disease

Most discussions of **coping** imply that making an active effort to solve problems is a good way to combat or reduce stress in our lives. However, one particular kind of coping response calls this idea into question. This response is called Type-A or coronary-prone behavior pattern (Friedman, 1969).

You have probably observed many Type-A people in your own life. They tend to be impatient, aggressive, competitive individuals who are filled with a sense of urgency. A traffic jam can send a Type-A person into a fit of anger; Type-A people cannot stand to be kept waiting even for a few minutes. Type-B people, in contrast, tend to be more relaxed and accepting of events and occurrences.

Does the Type-A behavior pattern fit you? If so, then watch out. There is a considerable amount of evidence that Type-A behavior is related to heart disease. One study followed more than 3,000 employed, college-educated, middle-aged California men over an 8½-year period (Rosenman et al., 1975; Brand et al., 1976). These men were interviewed in 1960 and classified as Type A or Type B. At regular intervals over the next 8 years, Rosenman and his colleagues assessed blood pressure, serum cholesterol, weight, cigarette smoking, and other measures of risk for heart disease. They found that the rate of coronary heart disease among Type A men was *twice* that of Type Bs, even when standard risk factors were controlled.

Although Type-A behavior is strongly associated with coronary heart disease, the mechanisms by which this behavior brings about illness has yet to be established. One hypothesis suggested by Glass (1977) is that Type-A individuals overrespond to stress, and in particular, to loss of control.

In a series of studies, Glass showed that when confronted by a stressful situation in which they feel they do not have control, Type-A individuals struggle to assert their control. They work faster, strive harder, and become more aggressive. After extended exposure to situations that they feel unable to control, however, Type-A people show a dramatic decline in their attempts to manage the situation. In contrast, when Type-B people encounter uncontrollable situations, their reactions are calmer and more even. They show neither frantic attempts to gain control in the beginning nor a lack of assertive energy when stress is prolonged.

Attributional processes have also been linked to Type-A behavior. Studies have shown that the need of Type-A individuals to be in control results from their general tendency to see themselves as the cause of all events in their lives (Rhodewalt, 1979).

Physiological comparisons of Type-A and Type-B people indicate that extreme blood pressure elevations characterize Type A individuals under stress but not Type Bs (Goldband et al., 1979). Blood pressure, then, may represent the physiological link between the Type-A behavior pattern, uncontrollable stress, and coronary heart disease. These self-destructive coping responses may be amenable to change. Learning theory suggests that Type-A people might be taught to replace these behaviors with more constructive responses to stress.

sponsible for their own self-actualization. According to the existentialists, the individual is constantly aware of the possibility of death or ultimate "nonbeing." This awareness forces one to question the meaning of one's life. Concern with nonbeing leads to *existential anxiety,* the fear that one is not leading a meaningful life. Existentialists point to the breakdown of tradition, the increasing number of unfulfilling, repetitive jobs, and the dehumanization of relationships in complex technological societies as conditions fostering meaninglessness (Frankl, 1963). Although it is painful, existential anxiety is viewed positively by humanistic and existential psychologists. This anxiety can lead to new growth if the person can be encouraged to cease defending against it and instead actively seek a purpose for being.

The Cognitive Model

So far, we have been concerned with how individuals respond to anxiety that results from environmental demands or to intrapsychic conflict. But individuals also differ widely in their perception of what is or is not stressful, and this perception determines the degree of anxiety they experience. For this view, we will turn to the cognitive model.

From a cognitive perspective, the stress experience is more than the sum total of the stressors to which one is exposed. A cognitive psychologist acknowledges the role that the individual plays in the experience of stress. Lazarus (1966) has described stress as a transaction between people and their environments in which the critical mediating variable is people's *perception* of demand and of their own ability to cope with it. Stress, then, in this view is composed of 3 elements: First, there is a set of environmental events that may or may not be potentially stressful. Second, there is the individual's cognitive appraisal of the degree to which those environmental events represent serious harm, threat, or challenge to well-being (*primary appraisal*). And finally, there is the individual's appraisal of the adequacy of his or her resources and abilities to cope with that threat or challenge (*secondary appraisal*). Secondary appraisal helps determine the type of coping response the person will use in the face of stress.

The crucial importance of appraisal was demonstrated in an early set of studies by Lazarus and his colleagues (Speisman et al., 1964; Lazarus & Alfert, 1964). They showed subjects a silent film of Australian aboriginal puberty rites. The film focused on the crude surgical operations performed on the genitals of male adolescents (subincision). The film's graphic depiction of pain and genital mutilation elicited strong physiological stress reactions and self-reports of stress among a group of control subjects (Lazarus et al., 1962), so the film was clearly highly threatening. Three different sound tracks were then superimposed upon the film. In one sound track, the "trauma" track, the commentary emphasized the pain, mutilation, and health hazard to the boys. The "denial" track emphasized the happiness of the boys at becoming fully accepted members of the tribe and denied the harm of the operation. The "intellectualization" track took a detached, unemotional, anthropological view of these strange rites.

Some cognitive researchers have suggested that coping responses are either emotion-focused or problem-focused. The threat to one's home and family by raging storms would certainly elicit both.

As measured by skin conductance and heart rate, the trauma track significantly increased the stress reactions of experimental subjects compared to controls. The denial and intellectualization tracks both significantly reduced subjects' distress. Moreover, the effectiveness of the denial and intellectualization tracks in decreasing stress was enhanced for subjects with denying and intellectualizing personality dispositions, respectively (see Figure 15–1).

These findings, which have been replicated in subsequent studies (Lazarus et al., 1965; Alfert, 1964), are important for two reasons. First, they show that people's *interpretations* of an event alter the amount of anxiety they will feel in response to it. The same threatening event evoked different amounts of stress in subjects who differed only in their appraisals of its meaning. Second, these findings suggest that the use of defense mechanisms can be beneficial for individuals, a theme usually underemphasized by psychoanalytical theorists. Note that in Lazarus's cognitive approach, intrapsychic defense mechanisms are viewed as ways of interpreting environmental stressors, rather than as potentially neurotic responses to internal conflict.

One factor that also seems to make a difference in stress-reduction is the degree to which people believe they have some control over a stressor. When they think they can escape it, avoid it, or even just predict it, they will have a milder stress reaction to it. This reduction of stress is based entirely on people's *perception* of their control, not on how much control they actually have.

Several studies have demonstrated that perceptions of control over avoidance responses can actually reduce stress responses (Glass & Singer, 1972). Hokanson and his colleagues (1971) tested the stress-avoidance hypothesis

FIGURE 15–1

Effects of the subincision film on skin conductance for subjects high and low in denial disposition. (Lazarus & Alfert, 1964, p. 201)

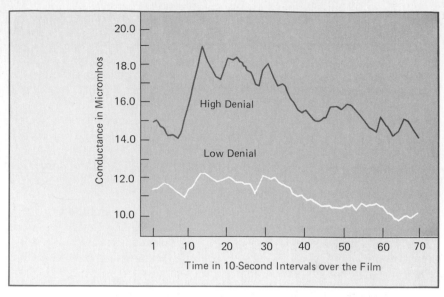

with 2 groups of college students. Both groups were assigned a learning task. Students who failed to achieve it received an electrical shock. One group was given the option of asking for "time out" from the stress of learning. The other group received the same number and length of rest periods as the first group, but these students had no control over when the "time outs" occurred.

The students' blood pressure was measured to indicate their stress level. When the researchers analyzed and compared the blood pressure levels of the 2 groups, they found that the students who believed they could control their escape from the shock showed less stress (had lower blood pressure) than those who did not (see Figure 15–2).

Not only do perceptions of control make a difference in stress reduction, but attributions regarding the cause of stress experiences do, too. When we attribute stress to our own failings, we have a much more unpleasant reaction than when we are able to attribute it to some external uncontrollable factor (Abramson et al., 1978). (See Chapter 18 for more on attribution theory.)

Cognitive factors appear to affect the amount of stress one feels, as well as the types of coping one will attempt. This may explain why some people develop physical or psychological disorders in the face of stress while others do not. Recently, a new field, health psychology, has developed within psychology and focuses on the relationship between psychological and physical variables.

HEALTH PSYCHOLOGY.   Researchers and medical practitioners alike have become increasingly aware of the importance of psychological factors in the development, course, treatment, and prevention of disease. The contribution of psychological factors to health and illness is the focus of *health psychology,* or *behavioral medicine* (Taylor, 1978; Stone, Cohen, & Adler, 1979; Matarazzo, 1980).

We have already discussed a number of studies that implicate psychosocial forces in the development of disease. Life events (particularly negative and loss events) and ongoing difficulties (especially occupational strains and urban stress) have been linked to a variety of physical and psychological disorders (Dohrenwend & Dohrenwend, 1974; Glass & Singer, 1972; Glass,

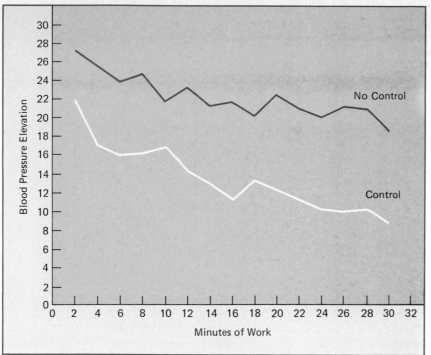

FIGURE 15–2
The graph shows the results of a study by Hokanson et al. (1971). Students who perceived that they had control over when they escaped the shock showed less stress (had lower blood pressure) than students who perceived that they had no control.

1977). Personality dispositions, such as the aggressive, striving Type-A behavior pattern (see the Highlight on Type-A behavior), have been associated with coronary heart disease (Friedman, 1969; Jenkins et al., 1974; Glass, 1977). The possibility of an association between feelings of helplessness and hopelessness and the development of cancer has even been raised (Schmale & Iker, 1971).

Psychological studies of coping processes are also contributing to our understanding of disease prevention and control. Perceptions of situational control have been shown to reduce physiological stress reactions, which in turn are related to psychosomatic illnesses (Geer, Davison, & Gatchel, 1970; Langer, Janis, & Wolfer, 1975; Pennebaker & Skelton, 1978). Defense mechanisms such as denial and intellectualization can reduce stress (Lazarus, 1966), although the long-term consequences of these coping mechanisms on health or recovery from illness are much less clear (Cohen & Lazarus, 1979; Silver & Wortman, 1980). Through the use of cognitive reattributions, people can even be taught ways to cope with pain, fear, and unpleasant medical procedures (Ross et al., 1969; Johnson & Leventhal, 1974; Corah & Boffa, 1970; Langer et al., 1975).

Psychological studies also suggest ways to improve relationships between patients and medical personnel. Studies of communications between patients and physicians have identified factors that may lead patients to disobey doctors' orders (Korsch & Negrete, 1972; Davis, 1966). Studies have also indicated that nurses and physicians can be taught techniques to alleviate the stresses and fears of their patients (Janis, 1958; Skipper & Leonard, 1965).

Finally, psychological studies may suggest more effective ways of promoting public health. To prevent disease, millions of people must be persuaded to change their diet, smoking and drinking habits, and sedentary lifestyles. Knowledge of effective persuasion and behavior-change techniques may facilitate a mass preventive effort (Taylor, 1978).

Thus the new field of health psychology may contribute substantially in the future to our ability to alleviate stress, change destructive coping or health habits, prevent disease, and improve treatment experiences and outcomes for patients.

Stress, Coping, and Disease: Toward an Integrated Model

The terms *health psychology* and *behavioral medicine* suggest an integration of psychology with the disciplines of medicine, physiology, and biology. This is indeed occurring, not only in research but also in medical practice, where psychologists are increasingly being hired by medical schools and general hospitals to work in collaboration with medical practitioners (Matarazzo, 1980). Nowhere in the field of health psychology is the integration of disciplines more clear than in research on stress, coping, and disease.

As we reviewed the biological, psychoanalytic, learning, and cognitive models of stress and coping, it may have struck you that no one of these approaches seemed adequate to explain why some people become ill under stress while others do not, or why a person develops one psychosomatic disease rather than another. To explain these phenomena, a combination of models appears necessary.

For example, biological theory alone seems unable to identify the conditions under which reactions to prolonged or severe stress will overwhelm the body's defenses and lead to particular physical or psychological disorders. Rather, some knowledge of people's past learning histories, their perceptions of stress, their coping behaviors, and their psychological defense mechanisms seems necessary. Cognitions and coping responses (both active and intra-psychic) seem to mediate the stress–disease relationship.

These considerations suggest that a more elaborate model of stress, coping, and illness is required, incorporating learning, cognitions, physiological processes, and even aspects of psychoanalytic theory. For example, people's past reinforcement history may determine the kinds of skills and defensive attitudes they have available to meet environmental demands. More importantly, past learning may determine people's expectations for successful coping with those demands. These learned behavioral and cognitive responses in turn should influence the degree to which new environmental demands are perceived as threatening. The intensity of physiological stress reactions should vary directly with the degree of perceived threat. Physiological reactions may be dampened or eliminated as the person utilizes learned skills to actively master the situation or successfully defends against its threat intrapsychically. To the degree that these learned coping mechanisms fail, prolonged or recurrent physiological stress reactions may weaken genetically vulnerable body systems and produce illness. In short, disease is quite likely the end product of a multiplicity of factors, both psychological and physiological.

To understand the extremely complex interrelationships between the mind and the body, we clearly require a combination of theoretical models and interdisciplinary efforts. But many difficult questions remain to be answered. Why do some people become psychologically disturbed while others become physically ill in response to stress? What is the mechanism by which stress reactions weaken the body? How can we change people's environments, particularly work settings, to reduce their stressfulness? What types of coping mechanisms are most effective in reducing what types of stress?

Much still has to be done to increase our knowledge of the relationships among stress, coping, and disease, but these questions are exciting ones, rich in potential payoffs for significantly improving the lives and the health of many.

COPING AND ADAPTATION.   Because we are confronted with psychological stress in some form every day of our lives, we become adept at coping with it. If we are continually confronted with a certain stressor, our coping results in adaptation. The pressure of a new job, for example, is stressful to a person who has just taken on added responsibility, but he or she will rise to the challenge and gradually adapt to the pressure.

The ability to adapt to the environment has been one key to the success and survival of the human species. Adaptation has made it possible for people to thrive in a wide range of climates. It has enabled people to endure and emerge from the horrors of war, concentration camps, and natural disasters. On a personal level, it helps us to overcome the pains of surgery, the trauma of a loved one's death, the noise and overcrowding of cities. But we pay a price for our adaptability.

When people adapt to demands, their stress responses seem to be minimized. Noise, for example, that might once have disturbed them is hardly noticed. Crowds that might have once made them feel panicky no longer arouse their fears. This adaptation, however, may only be superficial. Continued exposure to a stressor may cause a buildup of stress effects that explode when the stressor is removed. When the period of coping is over, a double dose of reaction may set in, both to the stressor *and* to the strain of coping (Glass & Singer, 1972).

When people adapt to the noise and crowds of city living, their stress responses seem to be considerably minimized. The hidden risk is that it may only be superficial, and the stress effects may appear later.

One study of men who had just completed a stressful and demanding army training course bears this out. Although the men adapted successfully to the training, they experienced severe anxiety right after graduation. In accord with Selye's General Adaptation Syndrome, Glass and Singer conclude that "adaptive effort may leave the individual less able to cope with subsequent environmental demands and frustrations, and this reduction in coping ability can be described as the psychic cost of adaptation to stressful events" (p. 11). Sooner or later, then, the effects of stress are felt. Coping may help for the moment, but then an aftershock may come along.

The constant use of a coping response may in itself produce stress, as in the Type-A coronary-prone behavior pattern. Glass and Singer note that the aftereffects of adaptation may take the form of physical and mental disease, psychosomatic disorders, performance and learning deficits, and general social-emotional maladjustments. These aftereffects may not be apparent for a long time. Milgram (1970), studying the effects of urban living, observed that cognitive overload typified city dwellers. Because they have to evaluate and adapt to so many stimuli, they devote less and less attention to each one. This eventually may result in the cold attitude often said to be associated with city people: lack of interest in others, unwillingness to aid strangers, rudeness, and lack of social responsibility.

But the phenomenon of stress has a positive side. As some research has shown, laboratory animals and children who experience stress early in life function better as adults than do their nonstressed peers. They outperform them and are more adaptable to novel or stressful situations. One way to appreciate the beneficial aspects of stress is to observe the effects of a lack of stress. Sensory-deprivation studies, in which both animal and human subjects have been deprived of all stimulation, suggest that the total absence of stress is in itself stressful (Suedfeld, 1980). Perhaps stress and adaptation are curvilinearly related: Both too much and too little stress may overwhelm our coping abilities and leave us poorly adapted.

HARDINESS. It is encouraging to note that some personality traits actually make it *easier* for a person to handle stress. A recent study by Kobasa (1979) suggests that our personalities differ in terms of *hardiness*. When "hardy" people are confronted by stress, they are less likely to feel overwhelmed or to become ill. What characteristics make up this trait?

Kobasa studied executives who had experienced stressful life events within the past 3 years. Those in one group had become physically ill following the events, while those in another group had not. The hardy executives possessed 3 characteristics that the others did not: They had a great feeling of control; they had a strong sense of commitment to specific goals in their lives; and they viewed change as a challenge rather than as a threat.

Once again, we see the importance of people's perceptions of demands placed upon them. Those who experience themselves as victims of unwanted or threatening change are less able to adapt. Those who have somehow learned to view themselves as active determinants of the outcomes of change more easily overcome the objective difficulties and stressful reactions that change produces.

Further work in the area of stress and coping may enable social scientists to do more than merely warn people to avoid stressful lives. New studies may show us how to develop the characteristics and coping skills that can aid in a productive and healthy life.

SPECIAL ISSUES IN STRESS AND ADJUSTMENT

Aging: Stress and Control

Aging is a normal life change that brings a good deal of stress. Retirement from work, decline in health, the deaths of friends and family members—all inevitable events of old age—cause feelings of loss and anxiety. Another source of stress during this period is loss of control. Illness, decline in income and mobility, and compulsory retirement are a few of the conditions that make old people feel dependent.

We have seen repeatedly throughout this chapter how loss of control heightens stress. In old age, this stress accelerates the natural decline in mental and physical abilities. Old people who are institutionalized lose more control over their lives than do those who live in their own homes or with their families.

To demonstrate the effects of institutionalized loss of control, psychologists Ellen Langer and Judith Rodin (1976) studied the residents of a nursing home. They divided their subjects into 2 groups. Members of one group were encouraged by the staff to take more control over their daily lives. They were given choices about where to see their visitors, how their rooms would be arranged, what night they would go to a movie. In addition, they were each offered a plant to care for. Those who decided to take a plant had to choose the one they wanted. Members of the second group were encouraged to let the staff help them and look after them. They were told where they would be allowed to see visitors and what night they were scheduled to attend the movies. They were given plants and told that the nurses would water and care for them.

The attitudes and behaviors of the 2 groups were studied as these treatments continued over a 3-week period. The staff and the residents were interviewed, and the activity level of the residents was monitored. The group that was encouraged to be independent showed an improvement in several areas of behavior. They were more active, happier, and more alert than before. The dependent group, in only 3 weeks' time, became generally more debilitated, less active, and more withdrawn.

Eighteen months later, Rodin and Langer (1977) returned to the nursing home to do a follow-up study of their subjects. Using the same methods of interviewing and observation, they discovered that the level of health, happiness, activity, and involvement continued to be higher for the subjects in the responsibility-induced group. Also, only 15 percent of the responsibility-induced group had died during that time, while 30 percent of the dependency-induced group had died. This study seemed to have great implications for improving the lives of the institutionalized aged.

In another study, however, Richard Schulz and Barbara Hanusa (1978) obtained results that suggest the Rodin-Langer findings should be viewed with caution. Like Rodin and Langer, these researchers studied the changes that occurred in the behavior of nursing home residents who were given more control over their daily lives, but they found that the effects of increased control were short-lived. Forty-two months after the study, they found no difference between the dependent and responsible groups.

Schulz and Hanusa suggest that attribution played a powerful role in this situation. The aged subjects attributed their increased autonomy not to themselves but to the home's administration. Knowing that their increased freedom was something granted by the administration, which could withdraw it if it wished, they continued to feel dependent. Thus any positive reactions were doomed to be temporary.

Social Support as a Buffer against Stress

Recently, a good deal of interest among behavioral scientists has been stimulated by the apparent stress-reducing properties of social support. Social support can be viewed as a coping resource. If a person can obtain emotional concern, material aid, information, and/or helpful feedback from others, that person has social support (House, 1981).

A set of experiments by Schachter (1959) demonstrated that people anticipating a stressful experience actually seek out social support, if given the opportunity. Subjects who thought they were going to receive a series of painful electric shocks and subjects who anticipated only very mild shocks were given a choice of waiting alone or waiting with another subject before the experiment would begin. The greater the expected pain, the more subjects chose to wait with others. An experiment by Sarnoff and Zimbardo (1961) added a qualifier to Schachter's findings: Subjects who feel their anxi-

The beneficial effects of social support have led to the development of a variety of formal and informal support groups. For example, people reentering the job market or going through divorce will find groups organized to help them with these stressful transitions.

eties are inappropriate or socially unacceptable will seek to avoid others.

People tend to seek out social support when facing stress, but does this support actually protect them physically and psychologically? The answer appears to be yes. Berkman and Syme (1979) showed that among roughly 5,000 adults randomly sampled from Alameda County, California, the presence or absence of four types of social ties in 1965—marriage, friends, church participation, and formal and informal group membership—strongly affected the probability of the person dying over the next 9 years, even when factors such as age, sex, and income were controlled. People lacking social ties were from 30 to 300 percent more likely to die than those with each kind of relationship. Nuckolls and her colleagues (1972) studied 170 pregnant army wives. Wives who experienced stressful events *and* who lacked social support during pregnancy were three times more likely to develop medical complications at birth than wives who experienced little stress or had high amounts of support.

It is important to emphasize that *how* social support operates to buffer stress is still poorly understood. Does support increase people's self-confidence or self-esteem under stress? Does it reduce uncertainty? Does it give people a sense of control? Does it help them use more effective coping methods? And what sources and types of support buffer what kinds of stress most effectively? There is still a good deal that we must discover about this important coping resource.

SUMMARY

1. *Stress* occurs when a person is faced with environmental demands, whether pleasant or unpleasant, that require some kind of *adjustment* or *adaptation*. Traumatic events are extremely stressful situations involving grave physical risk.

2. *Approach-approach conflict* occurs when a person is faced with two equally attractive but mutually exclusive goals. In *approach-avoidance conflict,* the person faces a single goal that has both positive and negative consequences. *Avoidance-avoidance conflict* is the situation in which a person faces an unavoidable choice between 2 equally unattractive goals. The final category, *double approach-avoidance conflict,* occurs when a person is faced with 2 goals that each present an approach-avoidance conflict of its own.

3. *Frustration* is both a result of conflict and a source of stress on its own. Five sources of frustration identified by Coleman and Hammen are delays, lack of resources, loss, failure, and meaninglessness.

4. In the biological model, anxiety is viewed as a set of physiological responses (such as increased heart rate or sweat-gland activity) that occur because of demands placed on the individual. Selye observed a general pattern of physiological reactions to stress that occurs no matter what stressor is involved; this is called the *General Adaptation Syndrome.*

5. Physical disorders linked to stress (such as ulcers or asthma) are known as *psychosomatic illnesses.* Among the theories devised to explain these illnesses are the *general-reaction, somatic weakness theory,* the *specific-reaction theory,* and the *diasthesis-stress theory.*

6. In the psychoanalytic model, anxiety is seen as a consequence of *intrapsychic conflict,* or conflict between the id and the superego. Freudians identify three types of anxiety: reality anxiety, moral anxiety, and neurotic anxiety. In the psychoanalytic model, common ways of coping with stress are *defense mechanisms.* They include repression, displacement, projection, reaction formation, negation, intellectualization, undoing, regression, and sublimation.

7. In the learning model, anxiety is seen as a learned autonomic or internal response. *Learned helplessness,* according to the learning model, occurs when animals and humans learn that there is no connection between their responses and what happens to them, which leads to a reduced rate of active coping.

8. The humanistic-existential psychologists view anxiety as a result of an individual's failure to live up to his or her fullest potential.

9. In the cognitive model, the definition of stress includes three elements: the set of environmental events that are potentially stressful; the person's cognitive appraisal of the events; and the person's appraisal of abilities to cope with those events. Lazarus has classified coping responses into two types. Studies by cognitive researchers indicate that stress is based on people's *perception* of their control, not on how much control they actually have.

10. Continually being confronted with and having to cope with a certain stressor results in *adjustment,* or *adaptation,* the process of becoming less sensitive to a particular stressor. However, researchers note aftereffects of adaptation, including illness, performance and learning deficits, social-emotional maladjustments, and a possible inability to cope with later environmental demands.

11. Social support consists of emotional concern, material aid, information, and/or helpful feedback from others. Studies have shown that support is a coping resource that buffers or reduces the harmful effects of stress situations.

Suggested Readings

COELHO, G. V., HAMBURG, D. A., & ADAMS, J. E. (Eds.). *Coping and adaptation.* New York: Basic Books, 1974. A collection of theoretical articles on coping, including discussions of the development of coping competence in children and coping with real-life crises.

DOHRENWEND, B. S., & DOHRENWEND, B. P. (Eds.). *Stressful life events: Their nature and effects.* New York: John Wiley, 1974. Papers by leading researchers in the field discuss the ways in which stress can be measured in terms of life events, and the connection between stress and physical illness.

FRANKL, V. E. *Man's search for meaning: An introduction to logotherapy.* Boston: Beacon Press, 1968. Basic principles of existential psychology as they emerged from the author's concentration-camp experiences.

FRASER, M. *Children in conflict.* Garden City, N.Y.: Doubleday, 1973. Deals with the way children in Northern Ireland have learned to cope with an immensely stressful situation in the conflict between Catholics and Protestants.

GARGER, J., & SELIGMAN, M. E. P. (Eds.). *Human helplessness: Theory and applications.* New York: Academic Press, 1980. Presents the reformulation of learned helplessness theory and its applications to depression, anxiety, intellectual achievement, Type-A behavior, and aging.

GLASS, D. C., & SINGER, J. E. *Urban stress: Experiments on noise and social stressors.* New York: Academic Press, 1972. This book presents an interesting series of experiments on human responses to noise as a function of predictability and control.

LAZARUS, R. S. *Psychological stress and the coping process.* New York: McGraw-Hill, 1966. Lazarus's cognitive coping theory, with dozens of interesting experiments that help substantiate it. A classic.

MAHL, G. F. *Psychological conflict and defense.* New York: Harcourt Brace Jovanovich, 1971. An outline of the psychoanalytical mechanisms involved in coping with stress. Presents an excellent review of psychoanalytic theory.

MONAT, A., & LAZARUS, R. S. (Eds.). *Stress and coping: An anthology.* New York: Columbia University Press, 1977. A collection of classic articles on stress and coping, including Cannon's study of sudden death.

SELYE, H. *The stress of life.* New York: McGraw-Hill, 1956. Selye's autobiographical account of his discovery of the General Adaptation Syndrome and a very readable explanation of the physiological processes involved.

SELYE, H. (Ed.). *Selye's guide to stress research,* Vol. 1. New York: Van Nostrand Reinhold, 1980. First in an annual series on current topics in stress research, this volume covers such topics as stressful life events research, the effects of learning on physical symptoms, and hormones and stress.

STONE, G. C., COHEN, F., & ADLER, N. E. (Eds.). *Health psychology.* San Francisco: Jossey-Bass, 1979. This collection of articles examines psychology's contributions to the development, course, and treatment of disease and to the maintenance of health. There is special focus both on the health-care delivery system and on trends and new directions in health psychology as a field.

16. Abnormal Psychology

W ho is an "abnormal" person? Is he or she a person who exhibits abnormal behavior? Then what are the differences between "abnormal" and "normal" behavior?

Is normal behavior simply behavior that is predictable and socially acceptable? Or might it be behavior that is considered acceptable by the individual, however bizarre other people think it is? In this chapter, we will look at some of the answers that have been proposed to these basic questions; we will also discuss models of abnormality and examine some patterns of abnormal behavior.

ABNORMAL VS. NORMAL BEHAVIOR

At first glance it seems easy enough to define abnormal behavior. Since abnormal means "not normal," all we have to do is define normal behavior and conclude that anything other than that is abnormal. But most people, if asked, would probably define normal behavior as the absence of abnormal behavior. This doesn't help us.

Theorists have tried to establish criteria to distinguish between the normal and the abnormal. Some have used a statistical approach: Normal behavior is simply behavior that is typical of most people. Therefore, all people who stray from the statistical average are behaving abnormally. Others argue that such a definition is too broad and too vague: The abnormal category would include very intelligent people and nearsighted people.

Others have tried to define normal and abnormal behavior in terms of cultural boundaries and expectations. In this view, behavior can only be judged in the context of the culture in which it takes place—there are no absolutes. Behavior that is abnormal in some cultures may be acceptable, and thus normal, in others. Heavy drug use or constant aggression are accepted as normal in some cultures. In ours, they are not.

Normal behavior can also be thought of in absolute or ideal terms. For example, you could define a normal person as one who is happy, effective with other people, sincere, and free of anxiety. However, this describes an ideal rather than a real person. If normal behavior is an ideal, we cannot define abnormality as the absence of the ideal; if we did, just about everyone would be abnormal.

Because it has proved surprisingly difficult to define abnormal behavior in statistical, cultural, or ideal terms, another approach to the problem of definition can be taken. Let us think about the kinds of behavior we ourselves tend to label "abnormal":

1. *Bizarreness and extremeness.* Typical examples would be hallucinations, **delusions,** and uncontrolled violence. Some normal and even ordinary behaviors, such as hand-washing, could fall into this category as well if done dozens of times a day.
2. *Disturbance of others.* Unusual behavior that interferes with the well-being of others is generally regarded as abnormal. Drunken driving, molesting a child, or talking incoherently to strangers on a bus are examples of such disturbances. (Some of these acts, it is important to notice, we regard as "abnormal" in the sense of mentally disturbed. Other, more calculating acts we regard as criminal.)

3. *Inappropriate or excessive emotional display.* People with obvious outward manifestations of distress, panic, overwhelming happiness, or uncontrollable depression, when circumstances don't seem to warrant it, are often regarded by others as abnormal.
4. *Interference with daily functioning.* If people are unable to meet society's standards of daily functioning and personal relationships, they often are considered abnormal. Disheveled dress or chronic self-destructive tardiness are some examples.

Descriptively, these seem to be some behaviors that ordinary people regard as abnormal. This gives us enough understanding of what is meant by "abnormality" to continue our discussion of it. By now, though, you can appreciate the problems of trying to diagnose abnormal behavior. To help us further appreciate this difficulty, a brief history of the diagnosis of mental disorders is in order.

Clinical Classification and Diagnosis

For antiquity, observers have noticed that much abnormal behavior seems to reflect underlying confusions of thought and behavior. Since Hippocrates, many attempts have been made to classify abnormal behavior patterns. Recently, many of these classification schemes have been based on the *medical* model, in that they assumed that these abnormalities were produced by the same kinds of problems that cause physical illnesses. This was not always the case. In medieval times, certain kinds of abnormal behavior patterns were regarded as evidence of possession by evil spirits or devils, and the cure was to drive the devil out, perhaps with exorcism, perhaps with beatings.

In more recent times, we have generally regarded many kinds of abnormal behaviors as being caused by some underlying "mental illness." In 1883, Emil Kraepelin, a German psychiatrist, developed a classification system that is influential to this day. His effort was a most comprehensive one in that he attempted to include all mental disorders, and to distinguish the various mental disorders from one another on the basis of each disorder's *symptoms, origin, course,* and *outcome.*

Since his time, many other individuals and groups have attempted to establish comprehensive diagnostic schemes. Beginning in 1952, the American Psychiatric Association issued a classification system called the *Diagnostic and Statistical Manual of Mental Disorders,* known as the *DSM,* the current revision (1980) being referred to as *DSM-III* (see Table 16–1), and the 1968 revision being called *DSM-II.*

The authors of DSM-III wanted the diagnostic system to be reliable; they wanted to enable two different clinicians, faced with patients presenting the same or similar symptoms, to make similar diagnoses. The reason for this is obvious: A diagnostic system that doesn't foster consistent diagnoses does not serve clinicians or patients well. No previous systems had achieved an acceptable consistency. Researchers have even found that the same observer presented with virtually identical descriptions of a patient on two different occasions would often give different diagnoses (Beck, 1962; Wilson & Meyer, 1962). In a review of studies of the reliability of psychiatric diagnosis, Spitzer and Fleiss (1974) concluded that only a few broad categories (such as mental retardation or alcoholism) were reliable.

Those constructing DSM-III attempted to achieve better diagnostic re-

Table 16–1: Psychological Disorders as Classified in DSM-III.

DISORDERS USUALLY FIRST EVIDENT IN INFANCY, CHILDHOOD, OR ADOLESCENCE

Mental retardation

Mild mental retardation
Moderate mental retardation
Severe mental retardation
Profound mental retardation
Unspecified mental retardation

Attention deficit disorder,
  with hyperactivity
  without hyperactivity
  residual type

Conduct disorder,
  undersocialized, aggressive
  undersocialized, nonaggressive
  socialized, aggressive
  socialized nonaggressive
  atypical

Anxiety disorders of childhood or adolescence

Separation anxiety disorder
Avoidant disorder of childhood or adolescence
Overanxious disorder

Other disorders of infancy, childhood or adolescence

Reactive attachment disorder of infancy
Schizoid disorder of childhood or adolescence
Elective mutism
Identity disorder

Eating disorders

Anorexia nervosa
Bulimia
Pica
Atypical eating disorder

Stereotyped movement disorders

Transient tic disorder
Chronic motor tic disorder
Tourette's disorder
Atypical tic disorder
Atypical stereotyped movement disorder

Other disorders with physical manifestations

Stuttering
Functional enuresis
Functional encopresis
Sleepwalking disorder
Sleep terror disorder

Pervasive developmental disorders

Infantile autism
Childhood onset pervasive developmental disorder
Atypical

Specific developmental disorders

Developmental reading disorder
Developmental arithmetical disorder
Developmental language disorder
Developmental articulation disorder
Mixed specific developmental disorder
Atypical specific developmental disorder

ORGANIC MENTAL DISORDERS

Section 1. Organic mental disorders whose etiology or pathophysiological process is listed below

Dementias arising in the senium and presenium

Primary degenerative dementia, senile onset
  with delirium
  with delusions
  with depression
  uncomplicated
Primary degenerative dementia, presenile onset
Multi-infarct dementia

Substance-induced

Alcohol
  intoxication
  idiosyncratic intoxication
  withdrawal
  withdrawal delirium
  hallucinosis
  amnestic disorder
  dementia associated with alcoholism

Barbiturate or similarly acting sedative or hypnotic
  intoxication
  withdrawal
  withdrawal delirium
  amnestic disorder
Opioid
  intoxication
  withdrawal
Cocaine
  intoxication
Amphetamine or similarly acting sympathomimetic
  intoxication
  delirium
  delusional syndrome
  withdrawal
Phencyclidine (PCP) or similarly acting arylcyclohexylamine
  intoxication
  delirium
  mixed organic mental disorder
Hallucinogen
  hallucinosis
  delusional disorder
  affective disorder
Cannabis
  intoxication
  delusional disorder
Tobacco
  withdrawal
Caffeine
  intoxication
Other or unspecified substance

Section 2. Organic brain syndromes whose etiology and pathophysiological process are either noted as an additional diagnosis or is unknown

Delirium
Dementia
Amnestic syndrome
Organic delusional syndrome
Organic hallucinosis
Organic affective syndrome
Organic personality syndrome
Atypical or mixed organic brain syndrome

SUBSTANCE USE DISORDER

Alcohol abuse
Alcohol dependence (Alcoholism)

Table 16–1 (continued)

Barbiturate or similarly acting sedative or hypnotic abuse
Barbiturate or similarly acting sedative or hypnotic dependency
Opioid abuse
Opioid dependence
Cocaine abuse
Amphetamine or similarly acting sympathomimetic abuse
Amphetamine or similarly acting sympathomimetic dependence
Phencyclidine (PCP) or similarly acting arylcyclohexylamine abuse
Hallucinogen abuse
Cannabis abuse
Cannabis dependence
Tobacco dependence

SCHIZOPHRENIC DISORDERS

Schizophrenia
  disorganized
  catatonic
  paranoid
  undifferentiated
  residual

PARANOID DISORDERS

Paranoia
Shared paranoid disorder

Acute paranoid disorder
Atypical paranoid disorder

PSYCHOTIC DISORDERS NOT ELSEWHERE CLASSIFIED

Schizophreniform disorder
Brief reactive psychosis
Schizoaffective disorder
Atypical psychosis

AFFECTIVE DISORDERS

Major affective disorders

Bipolar disorder
  mixed
  manic
  depressed
Major depression
  single episode
  recurrent

Other specific affective disorders

Atypical affective disorders

Atypical bipolar disorder
Atypical depression

ANXIETY DISORDERS

Phobic disorders
  Agoraphobia with panic attacks

Agoraphobia without panic attacks
Social phobia
Simple phobia
Anxiety states
  Panic disorder
  Generalized anxiety disorder
  Obsessive compulsive disorder
Post-traumatic stress disorder
  acute
  chronic or delayed
Atypical anxiety disorder

SOMATOFORM DISORDERS

Somatization disorder
Conversion disorder
Psychogenic pain disorder
Hypochondriasis
Atypical somatoform disorder

DISSOCIATIVE DISORDERS

Psychogenic amnesia
Psychogenic fugue
Multiple personality
Depersonalization disorder
Atypical dissociative disorder

PSYCHOSEXUAL DISORDERS

Gender identity disorders

Transsexualism

liability in several ways. First, they eliminated or redefined diagnostic terms that had been used inconsistently. Second, they used the results of reliability studies to suggest which categories should be retained. Third, much more than previous diagnostic systems, they specified in much more detail the *behavioral elements* that were to be taken as signs of each diagnostic category. Fourth, vague or broad categories were broken down into more precise categories. Finally, one of the most important changes concerned the attempt to eliminate hidden theoretical biases in the system. It did this by deciding not to identify the origins, or *etiology* of each mental condition. Those working on DSM-III essentially concluded that for most disorders they defined, the etiology is unknown (p. 6). This omission was a radical departure for a diagnostic system. Since Kraepelin, virtually all systems had tried to establish an etiology for each disorder.

If this omission surprises you, it might help you to understand their decision if you recall the five classes of personality theories reviewed in the personality chapter. As you recall, each theory makes different claims about the origins of many disorders. For instance, Freudian theorists hold that phobic disorders are generated by "a displacement of anxiety resulting from the breakdown of defensive operations for keeping internal conflict out of consciousness" (p. 7). Learning theorists, on the other hand, regard phobias

Gender identity disorder of childhood
Atypical gender identity disorder

Paraphilias

Fetishism
Transvestism
Zoophilia
Pedophilia
Exhibitionism
Voyeurism
Sexual masochism
Sexual sadism
Atypical paraphilia

Psychosexual dysfunctions

Inhibited sexual desire
Inhibited sexual excitement
Inhibited female orgasm
Inhibited male orgasm
Premature ejaculation
Functional dyspareunia
Functional vaginismus
Atypical psychosexual dysfunction

Other psychosexual disorders

Ego-dystonic homosexuality
Psychosexual disorder not elsewhere
  classified

DISORDERS OF IMPULSE CONTROL
NOT ELSEWHERE CLASSIFIED

Pathological gambling
Kleptomania
Pyromania
Intermittent explosive disorder
Isolated explosive disorder
Atypical impulse control disorder

ADJUSTMENT DISORDER,

  with depressed mood
  with anxious mood
  with mixed emotional features
  with disturbance of conduct
  with mixed disturbance of
    emotions and conduct
  with work (or academic) inhibition
  with withdrawal
  with atypical features

PSYCHOLOGICAL FACTORS
AFFECTING PHYSICAL CONDITION

Psychological factors affecting
  physical condition

PERSONALITY DISORDERS

Paranoid
Schizoid
Schizotypal
Histrionic

Narcissistic
Antisocial
Borderline
Avoidant
Dependent
Compulsive
Passive-Aggressive
Atypical, mixed or other personality
  disorder

CONDITIONS NOT ATTRIBUTABLE
TO A MENTAL DISORDER

Malingering
Borderline intellectual functioning
Adult antisocial behavior
Childhood or adolescent antisocial
  behavior
Academic problem
Occupational problem
Uncomplicated bereavement
Noncompliance with medical
  treatment
Phase-of-life problem or other life-
  circumstance problem
Marital problem
Parent–child problem
Other specified family circumstances
Other interpersonal problem

Adapted from American Psychiatric Association (1980), pp. 15–19.

as being learned avoidance responses to conditioned anxiety. In order to generate diagnostic categories on which clinicians could agree, it was necessary to eliminate most etiological claims from the diagnostic process.

To achieve more reliable diagnoses, DSM-III therefore attempts to be more descriptive than previous diagnostic systems. This reliability would be useful for a more accurate prediction of the course of the diagnosed disorder and for a better prescription for treatments of the disorder. These were the major goals in revising the DSM system. The diagnostic manual lists both essential features of the diseases and features frequently associated with it; it indicates which features must be present for the diagnostic category to be used and describes how to distinguish a particular disorder from other disorders with which it is often confused.

The DSM-III *Category System*

One of the most central changes in DSM-III is the use of five axes in assessing an individual's problem. Previous systems generally required clinicians to come up with one simple label; the present system provides the diagnostician with five different dimensions on which to evaluate a patient's functioning. Axis I is called the *clinical psychiatric syndrome*. This is a statement of the

Table 16–2: Axis IV: Scale for Rating Severity of Psycho-social Stressors.*

Table 16–2: Axis IV: Scale for Rating Severity of Psycho-social Stressors.*

1 None—No apparent psychosocial stressor

2 Minimal—Minor violation of the law; small bank loan

3 Mild—Argument with neighbor; change in work hours

4 Moderate— New career; death of close friend; pregnancy

5 Severe—Serious illness in self or family; major financial loss; marital separation; birth of child

6 Extreme—Death of close relative; divorce

7 Catastrophic—Concentration camp experience; devastating natural disaster

0 Unspecified—No information, or not applicable

*Compare this scale with the Life-Change Units Scale presented in Chapter 15.

Adapted from American Psychiatric Association (1980), p. 27

person's most central problem, usually the problem that has caused the patient to seek or be referred for help. More specifically, the first axis is a statement of the specific psychiatric syndrome that the individual displays, such as depression or phobic disorder. The second axis involves *personality or developmental disorders* in adults or children. It focuses on any long-term personality disorder that the person has shown, such as a compulsive personality disorder. Axes I and II include all of the mental disorders and therefore give what most people would consider a full diagnosis of the mental condition of the patient being diagnosed. Axis III concerns *physical disorders.* Here the diagnostician's attention is called to the possibility of the person having some physical syndrome that may be a factor in the presenting condition. Axis IV (see Table 16–2) asks the diagnostician to rate the *severity of psychosocial stress* being experienced by the person. This implies a recognition of the main point of our chapter on stress, which is that the stresses a person is experiencing in life can play a considerable role in exacerbating internal conflicts and providing abnormal behaviors. Axis V (see Table 16–3) concerns the person's *highest level of adaptive functioning in the past year.* Both Axis IV and Axis V are useful in planning treatments for the diagnosed individual and predicting the success such treatments might achieve. For example, a person having psychological problems after several deaths in the family but who had functioned very well in the preceding year would have a better prognosis than someone who usually functioned poorly and was experiencing minor life stresses.

UNRESOLVED PROBLEMS WITH DSM-III.   In many ways the multiaxial diagnostic system of DSM-III represents a considerable gain over previous systems. As we have already discussed, it is important that a diagnostic system be reliable. Field trials (Spitzer, Forman, & Nee, 1979) on the first two axes of DSM-III show that agreement is quite high on diagnosis of many categories. Although more research is needed, the reliability results on DSM-III are promising. Second, making DSM-III more acceptable to theoreticians of various persuasions is also likely to enhance its utility. However, many criticisms of it remain. Describing these criticisms here will also highlight some of the differences in the ways in which the concept of abnormality is dealt with by the five theoretical approaches we have focused on.

To begin with, a diagnosis, and particularly one for a "mental disorder," attaches a label to an individual in a way that can have negative effects. For example, a clinician, once committed to a diagnosis, may be less likely to recognize signs that suggest the label does not fit the individual. Then, too, the label often becomes part of an individual's records, something that may be carried throughout life. It may frighten off potential friends or employers. It may also cause the person to look differently at himself or herself. If a diagnostic label leads to positive consequences, such as genuinely helpful treatment, then these negative consequences may be outweighed, but it is important to be aware of the possibility of negative consequences.

The diagnosis of a condition often contains some implicit assumptions about its cause. Clinicians of various schools have different assumptions about the origins of various syndromes. Therefore, even though DSM-III is more descriptive and less theoretical than its predecessors, clinicians using it may still be influenced by their causal theories. In fact, since the factors causing a condition can be important in determining its treatment, a completely non-theoretical diagnostic system might not be desirable.

Some critics argue that the diagnostic system still has a pervasive medical

Levels	Adult examples
1 SUPERIOR—Unusually effective functioning in social relations, occupational functioning, and use of leisure time.	Single parent living in deteriorating neighborhood takes excellent care of children and home, has warm relations with friends, and finds time for pursuit of hobby.
2 VERY GOOD—Better than average functioning in social relations, occupational functioning, and use of leisure time.	A 65-year-old retired widower does some volunteer work, often sees old friends, and pursues hobbies.
3 GOOD—No more than slight impairment in either social or occupational functioning.	A woman with many friends functions extremely well at a difficult job, but says "the strain is too much."
4 FAIR—Moderate impairment in either social relations or occupational functioning, or some impairment in both.	A lawyer has trouble carrying through assignments; has several acquaintances, but hardly any close friends.
5 POOR— Marked impairment in either social relations or occupational functioning, or moderate impairment in both.	A man with one or two friends has trouble keeping a job for more than a few weeks.
6 VERY POOR—Marked impairment in both social relations and occupational functioning.	A woman is unable to do any of her housework and has violent outbursts toward family and neighbors.
7 GROSSLY IMPAIRED—Gross impairment in virtually all areas of functioning.	An elderly man needs supervision to maintain minimal personal hygiene and is usually incoherent.
0 UNSPECIFIED	No information.

Table 16–3: Axis V: Scale for Rating Level of Functioning.

Adapted from American Psychiatric Association (1980), pp. 29–30.

and psychiatric bias. Some kinds of mental retardation fit well with a medical approach, but what about "developmental arithmetical disorder"? Or fear of crowds or open spaces? Or frequent shoplifting? Or setting fires? Many clinicians do not think that these are medical conditions like fevers or flues, best "treated" by individuals with medical degrees, according to standard medical practices. Humanists and existentialists, as well as cognitive and learning personality theorists, all worry about the overinclusiveness of the medical aspects of the system.

MODELS OF ABNORMAL BEHAVIOR

In Chapter 14 we discussed models of the normal personality; here we will examine the views that these same models have of abnormal behavior and the abnormal personality. Since each model focuses on different aspects of human behavior, particular behaviors may be interpreted quite differently by each model. It is not uncommon to find the same behavior pattern viewed as normal by one model and abnormal by another.

The *psychoanalytic model* generally views abnormal behavior as evidence of unresolved conflicts among the id, ego, and superego. This model suggests that life is a constant struggle among these three parts of our personality. Somehow we have to harmonize the instinctual and unreasoning desires of the id, the rational and realistic requirements of the ego, and the moral and restrictive demands of the superego. Because conflicts among them can lead to unpleasant and anxious feelings, we develop defense mechanisms to help us avoid such conflicts. Defense mechanisms may reduce our anxiety by keeping from us the conscious awareness of those conflicts which would be too painful for us to acknowledge. Our defense mechanisms, then, do not actually reduce conflicts, but rather hide them from us. Abnormal behavior can result from faulty defense mechanisms that allow conflict and anxiety to break through, or from overuse of defense mechanisms.

According to the *learning model,* abnormal behaviors are learned in the same way that all behaviors are learned. People acquire them through either classical conditioning, operant conditioning, or modeling. Abnormal behaviors can be understood through such concepts as stimulus, response, and reinforcement.

The *biological model* argues that abnormal behaviors can be traced in part to physical disorders. The link between the mind and the body can work in two directions: (1) Biological abnormalities can affect mind and behavior; or (2) emotional stress can have a physical effect on us, thus setting the stage for yet a further impact on our behavior. According to the biological model, it makes no sense to separate the mind from the body in explaining abnormal behavior, because to do so obscures the ciritical role played by physical factors.

In the *humanistic-existential model,* abnormal behaviors are caused by people's failure to fulfill their personal potential. These failures may occur when people lose sight of or distort their real emotions and thoughts, cut themselves off from those around them, or come to view their lives as totally meaningless.

The *cognitive model* finds the roots of abnormal behavior in the way we think about and perceive the world. People who distort or misinterpret their experiences, the intentions of those around them, and the kind of world they live in are bound to act abnormally.

Neurosis: An Earlier Construct

In considering abnormal patterns of life, we run right into a problem we noted earlier—the problem of theoretical orientations dictating classification systems. The term **neurosis** was traditionally used within the medical, psychodynamic system to describe a set of problems (namely, an individual with generally intact skills at reality testing who was nonetheless possessed of one or more symptoms that caused him or her "psychic" pain). The concept of neurosis was also used as a theory about the etiology of these symptoms.

Psychodynamic theory holds that neuroses are caused by unconscious conflicts that arouse anxiety; the anxiety is then coped with by the maladaptive use of defense mechanisms. It is this maladaptive use of defense mechanisms that produces the symptoms causing the victim pain. Thus the traditional Freudian view is that neurotic behavior patterns share some common elements. One is the central role of anxiety in the problem. Another is the self-defeating aspect of neurotic behaviors. While they may ease or prevent anxiety in the short run, they create greater problems for the person in the long run. A third feature is the exaggerated nature of neurotic behaviors. Usually a neurotic person's anxiety, defenses, or other reactions are reasonable to a point; it is their persistence beyond that point that becomes abnormal.

As we will see, the other models of personality do not share the view that all behavior or thought patterns labeled by psychodynamic theorists as "neurotic" are caused by anxiety and unconscious conflict. Indeed, the growing sense that "neurosis" was not a useful construct led to the new classification system of DSM-III. The cognitive and humanistic approaches have been in the forefront of attempts to redefine abnormal behavior patterns and to treat them in new ways.

ANXIETY DISORDERS

Under this head DSM-III includes conditions in which anxiety is either the major symptom in itself, or in which a person feels anxiety when attempting to overcome another symptom. We will look at phobic, anxiety, and panic disorders, and at obsessive-compulsive disorders. In each of these categories, anxiety is manifested in different, but very dysfunctional, ways.

Phobic, Anxiety, and Panic Disorders

Phobic disorders involve a persistent and irrational fear of a particular object or situation, a fear far out of proportion to the actual threat present. For example, it is quite natural to be afraid of a snarling dog that lunges at you; it is not so natural to feel the same fear when faced with any dog in any situation. Examples of phobic disorders would include such simple phobias as **claustrophobia** (fear of closed spaces) or **acrophobia** (fear of heights), and more complex phobias such as **agoraphobia** (a fear of being alone, particularly in public places from which escape might be difficult). The usual defense against this type of fear is to avoid the source of it. Most of us have some irrational fears; we may feel uncomfortable in the presence of snakes or at the top of a ladder. But we still function normally most of the time—unless we suddenly become the local dog catcher or take up snake dancing, we are fine. Agoraphobia, on the other hand, is often more serious, because it is not easily compartmentalized; ordinary activities are increasingly restricted. Often, agoraphobic individuals will not venture out of the house without a friend or relative at their side.

Generalized anxiety disorder involves the same kind of discomfort as phobic disorders, but the person's anxiety is not clearly linked to a specific object or situation. Since the feeling of anxiety is present in so many situations, it has sometimes been called "free-floating anxiety." Symptoms include tenseness, autonomic system hyperactivity, apprehensive expectations, and increased scanning of the external environment for dangers. Sufferers feel that their lives are out of control and that disaster is imminent. They are unable to make decisions or form relationships with other people. Physical effects include excessive sweating, nausea, fatigue, and muscular tension.

The essential features of a **panic disorder** are recurrent panic attacks that

A study is being made in Houston (Mathew, 1980) of what may be a new phobia—now tentatively referred to as "traffic phobia." This disabling fear is most often associated with freeway driving and has become a problem in big cities where freeway, thruway, or expressway driving is a major part of everyday life.

occur unpredictably, although they may more frequently occur in certain situations such as riding an elevator or flying in an airplane. The essential feelings are ones of overwhelming terror or impending doom, with sensations of pain, choking, dizziness, and vertigo. Normally these attacks last for minutes, occasionally for hours.

The *psychoanalytic model* says that phobic, anxiety, and panic disorders can be traced to an unresolved clash between the id and the ego and supergo. If the id's drive for sexual or aggressive expression was harshly punished in childhood, these early punishments have left a mark on the individual. As a result, the individual has come to fear either the person who meted out the punishment or his or her own id impulses.

People who fear their punisher are likely to develop phobic or panic disorders. Typically, the fear of the punisher is displaced to a more neutral object or situation, perhaps something that only symbolizes the punisher. In this way people manage to avoid fearing the punisher, who is often very important to them—for instance, their mother or father.

People who fear their own id impulses live in constant fear, since such impulses are always fighting for expression. These people will have generalized anxiety disorders: free-floating anxiety in all kinds of situations. Their ego constantly struggles to contain their impulses—which is a losing battle. Thus these people experience danger in every kind of situation.

The *learning model* does not make a clear distinction among phobic, anxiety, and panic disorders. A phobia is seen as a conditioned fear reaction followed by a learned avoidance response. For example, as a child you were frightened one night by the loud noises of a thunderstorm. Afterward, you developed an intense fear of the color blue—the color of the bedroom in which you spent that frightening night. The color blue (conditioned stimulus), which just happened to be present at the same time as the loud noises of thunder (unconditioned stimulus), now brings about the same intense fear reaction. According to Mowrer (1947), this classically conditioned fear is negatively reinforced by a reduction in anxiety as you avoid the color blue over and over again. Constant avoidance prevents you from realizing that the color blue is really quite harmless. As the fear gets further locked in, so does

Richard Benson, age 38, applied to a psychiatrist for therapy because he was suffering from severe and overwhelming anxiety which sometimes escalated to a panic attack. During the times when he was experiencing intense anxiety, it often seemed as if he were having a heart seizure. He experienced chest pains and heart palpitations, numbness, shortness of breath, and he felt a strong need to breathe in air. He reported that in the midst of the anxiety attack, he developed a feeling of tightness over his eyes and he could only see objects directly in front of him (tunnel vision). He further stated that he feared that he would not be able to swallow.

As the anxiety symptoms became more severe and persistent, the client began to worry about when another acute attack would occur and this apprehension made him more anxious still. He expressed a general concern about his physical well-being, and he became extremely sensitive to any fluctuations in his breathing or difficulties in swallowing. He began to note the location of doctors' offices and hospitals in whatever vicinity he happened to be, and he became extremely anxious if medical help was not close by.

Mr. Benson stated that he could not fight off his constant feelings of anxiety, and he was unable to control his behavior when the anxiety symptoms occasionally spiralled to a panic attack. He could not sit still when he felt acutely and painfully anxious, and the only way he could find relief from his symptoms was to go home and pace back and forth in his yard. Gradually, he stopped perspiring and the rapid heart rate and other somatic symptoms subsided as well. He went back into the house as soon as he felt calmer, but after a half hour the symptoms often reappeared and the anxiety episode started all over again. At that point, the only way he could bring the anxiety attack under control was to contact his physician for a tranquilizer injection.

From Leon (1977), pp. 113–118.

the pattern of avoidance behavior. In this case you would be displaying a phobic reaction.

The learning model goes on to say that a pattern of anxiety can be explained in essentially the same way. The only difference is in the number of conditioned stimuli that come to cause the fear reaction. Going back to the thunderstorm example, in addition to fearing the color blue, you may also fear many other stimuli present on the night of the storm (that is, the fear generalizes to other stimuli). The point is that with a thorough enough search, anxiety that appears to be general can be identified as a set of specific fears triggered by specific stimuli. These many fears may come from one situation that yields many conditioned stimuli, or from a series of situations, each yielding a variety of conditioned stimuli.

The *humanistic-existential model* views phobic and anxiety disorders as produced by a failure to fulfill one's potential. You may recall from Chapter 14 that Carl Rogers believed that all people have a need for positive regard right from the beginning. However, we do not always receive unconditional regard from others—some people are criticized a great deal as children and in turn become intensely self-critical. These people later find it very hard to accept themselves and their actions because everything they do falls far short of their strict standards of self-evaluation. They come to perceive their experiences in a selective fashion, denying or distorting any experiences that are contrary to or threaten their self-concept. So much denial and distortion requires a lot of energy. They experience anxiety and have no energy left for self-actualization. According to this model, anxiety, panic, and phobic disorders are the results of comparing one's actual behaviors to an unrealistically high standard of performance which causes individuals to fear and avoid situations in which they might otherwise grow. *Existentialists* would change this explanation somewhat. They stress the person's need to act in an authentic fashion in a world that often requires inauthentic behavior. Panic and anxiety are produced in people who remain too aware of the degree to which their actions do not correspond to their desired authentic selves.

The *cognitive model* explains phobic, anxiety, and panic disorders as problems that can be traced to troublesome thought processes. Albert Ellis (1958, 1973, 1975) argues that such disorders develop because of people's irrational assumptions. For example, some people believe that if they receive any disapproval at all, they must be totally worthless. Thus they try to avoid disapproval in all their interactions, and they die a thousand deaths whenever they are criticized. Other people assume they must do everything perfectly, thus setting impossible standards for themselves. Since these assumptions lead to expectations that are impossible to fulfill, they assure the very high level of anxiety and dysfunction that characterize phobic and anxiety disorders. Research has indeed suggested that such irrational assumptions are related to anxiety disorders. For example, Newmark, Frerking, Cook, and Newmark (1973) found that people classified as having anxiety disorders endorse such extreme beliefs or assumptions significantly more often than other people.

The *biological* perspective, naturally, examines the possibility of inheritance of these patterns, but there is no clear evidence for such heritability. However, researchers have found physiological contingencies for some of these problems. For instance, a person may possess either an autonomic nervous system or a reticular activation system that is particularly easily aroused by stressful or other negative events. This sensitivity may come from inherited tendencies (Lacey, 1967) or chronic stress (Seligman, 1971). Any of these patterns would produce an individual who "overreacts" to negative events, and whose overreactions, according to learning principles, might become attached to different real-world stimuli.

Obsessive-Compulsive Disorders

Obsessive-compulsive disorders are shown by people who feel forced to repeat unwanted thoughts or ideas over and over, or to repeat certain actions or rituals again and again. Examples are the need to count every step when you walk or to wash your hands every time you touch a doorknob. A minor example that most of us have experienced is having a tune or part of an advertising jingle repeat itself in our heads in spite of our attempts to get rid of it. Such an experience is usually no more than mildly annoying; for people with an obsessive-compulsive disorder, the intrusion may be so severe and constant that they find it almost impossible to function normally.

Obsessions and compulsions represent different aspects of a disorder. **Obsessions** are thoughts that repeatedly intrude against one's will and defy one's efforts to ignore them. They may occur in various forms. For example, there are obsessive doubts, such as "Did I turn off the stove before I left the house?" There are also obsessive impulses, which may range from whimsical ideas like winking at passers-by to the thought of violent acts such as stabbing one's child. Other people are plagued by obsessive fears, such as "I am going to shout something in church" (Akhter, Wig, Varma, Pershad, & Verma, 1975).

In the vast majority of cases, such obsessive thoughts never translate into action. However, they often are so dramatic and unpleasant that they cause very high levels of anxiety. Many people who obsess worry most about the possibility that they will someday act out their terrible obsessive thoughts.

Compulsions are acts or rituals that are repeated against a person's will. There are minor compulsions that most people have and that fall well within the realm of normal behavior—for example, stepping over cracks in the sidewalk. Also, it is common to have daily rituals—for example, many people

Repetitive compulsive actions are characteristic of the obsessive personality disorder.

go through their morning routines without variation day after day and are quite upset if something forces them to change the routine.

When compulsive actions become extremely frequent, intense, unyielding, and disruptive to a person's life, they are no longer within the realm of normal behavior. For example, people who feel compelled to take 10 showers a day or to wash their hands 50 times a day are displaying significant compulsive patterns (see Table 16–4).

People may have obsessive thoughts without many compulsive acts, or may act compulsively without experiencing much in the way of obsessive thinking. However, often the two occur together in the same person—in fact, one is frequently a response to the other. A person who compulsively checks the locks on doors and windows is often yielding to an obsessive fear of burglars. And sometimes compulsive acts are used to control obsessive thoughts: People may recite certain words or phrases over and over again to keep an obsessive and frightening image from occupying their minds.

The *psychoanalytic model* regards obsessive-compulsive disorders as inappropriate defenses against the anxiety produced by unconscious aggressive conflicts. Freudians suggest that the difficulty begins with id impulses that were dealt with too harshly in childhood. Take, for example, the id impulses that were severely punished during the toilet-training period of the anal stage. Because these impulses could not be expressed during that stage, they demand expression later in life. Frequently, they come to the surface in the form of obsessive thoughts; at other times they are prevented or overcome by counterthoughts or actions. In short, the id and the ego's defense mechanisms are in a seesaw battle. For example, the id impulse to partake in a forbidden sexual encounter (obsessive thought) may be countered by repeatedly thinking other thoughts or by engaging in purifying rituals (compulsive acts) that help deny such obsessive ideas.

The *learning model* views obsessions and compulsions as learned reactions reinforced by their ability to reduce anxiety. For example, compulsively washing one's hands many times a day might be regarded as an escape mechanism from obsessive fears of disease. It is not even necessary that the

Is there resistance to carrying out the rituals?	Definitely Yes 32%	Somewhat 22%	Definitely No 46%
How sensible do you consider the rituals?	Sensible 22%	Rather Silly 13%	Absurd 65%
Does reassurance from others reduce the occurrence of the rituals?	Definitely Yes 27%	Some 15%	Definitely No 68%
Does the presence of others affect the rituals?	Occurs When Alone 20%	Company Irrelevant 76%	Occurs in Company 4%
Amount of family distress caused by the rituals.	Little or None 29%	Moderate 22%	A Great Deal 49%

Adapted from Stern & Cobb (1978).

Table 16–4: Obsessive-Compulsives Rate Aspects of Their Rituals.

fear be so specific. As long as a person's general anxiety has regularly been reduced or avoided by such activity, the person will tend to repeat it in the face of danger, real or imagined.

The learning model has not always been clear about the causal factors in obsessions or compulsions. The compulsive hand-washer may have at first imitated such behavior on the part of a parent, a peer, or a friend. Washing one's hands as a child may have been followed by rewards such as parental approval.

It is possible that some obsessional actions originally are learned by a process Skinner (1948) described for the acquisition of what he called *superstitious behaviors*. He observed that if a reinforcer is delivered at a random time to a pigeon, the bird will frequently continue to emit whatever response it was making just before the reinforcer was delivered. Suppose a man feels anxious and these feelings come and go. One day, just before the anxiety feelings naturally dissipated, he was washing his hands. Because of this fortuitous reinforcement, he increases the frequency of hand washing when he becomes anxious, without becoming particularly aware of it. This in turn increases the probability that hand washing may be followed by a decrease in anxiety. Hand washing is now on a schedule of reinforcement, and possibly a variable interval schedule, which is known to produce a high rate of responding.

The *cognitive model* views at least some forms of obsessive-compulsive disorders as an attempt to assure order and predictability. People who perceive the world as highly threatening may become obsessed with a ritual of meticulous orderliness, arranging their personal environment in exacting ways to maintain their sense of order and control. When the smallest detail becomes disarranged—say, the handle of a cup points the wrong way—their entire sense of order is threatened, and they have to repeat the ritual in order to relieve the anxiety once again.

DISSOCIATIVE DISORDERS

The behaviors to be described here are quite dramatic: Rarely does a year go by in which a multiple personality, an amnesiac protagonist, or a mysterious sleepwalker does not appear in books, movies, and television. (These are among the disorders that psychoanalytic theorists considered to be hysterical neuroses.) Given this, it is artistically disappointing, although scientifically correct, to report that such disorders are rare and represent only a very small proportion of the abnormal behaviors seen by clinicians.

Dissociative disorders are characterized by sudden, temporary changes in consciousness, activity, or identity. They include amnesia, fugue, somnambulism, and multiple personality. We will discuss each of these in turn, presenting where possible both the modern clinical perspective and the more classical theories.

Amnesia is a partial or total loss of memory for a period lasting from several hours to several years. Although people with amnesia usually retain the ability to communicate and reason, they may forget who they are or where they live; they generally fail to recognize relatives and friends. The forgotten material is sometimes but not always irretrievable; it may reappear spontaneously or under hypnosis.

Modern research on amnesia (Hirst, 1982) does not draw heavily on psychodynamic reasoning. Instead, the complex relationship between neurological damage and memory deficit has become the focus of attention. Since Scoville and Milner (1957), researchers have tended to study **anterograde amnesia,** which is loss of memory for events that occur after the neurologically damaging event; these are the easiest kind to study experimentally. One recent researcher (Hirst, 1981) suggests that amnesiacs must expend effort to encode material that is automatically encoded in normal people; the evidence is not conclusive, however. This interpretation uses the depth-of-coding theory of memory (see Chapter 7) and suggests that people with neurological deficits either must expend more effort to encode material or must encode it with less richness than do normal people.

Fugue (from the Latin word meaning "to flee") is amnesia accompanied by actual physical flight—a person in a state of amnesia may simply wander away for several hours, or even move to another area and set up a new life. Years later, the amnesia may suddenly reverse—the person then "awakens" in a strange place with a full memory of his or her original identity but with amnesia now about the fugue period.

Somnambulism, or sleepwalking, has been traditionally viewed within *psychoanalytic theory* as a dissociative disorder because the individual's body movements are apparently being controlled without the knowledge or participation of the conscious mind. As researchers have learned more about sleep and its difficulties, a different picture of what is now called "sleepwalking disorder" has emerged. It usually occurs during stage 3 or stage 4 sleep and involves the carrying out of what looks like purposive sequences of behavior—walking, dressing, or going to the bathroom. Its major danger is that sleepwalkers may accidentally injure themselves during their excursions. Up to 15 percent of children may show isolated instances of sleepwalking; clinicians estimate that between 1 and 6 percent of children do it often enough to be labeled as having this condition. For the great majority of children, the condition disappears in a few years (American Psychiatric Association, 1980, p. 82). The conservative course of treatment is no treatment at all.

Multiple personality means the presence of two or more separate personalities in the same person. These personalities compete for access to consciousness. Often they alternate, with one personality being in control for a few hours or days and then the other. The most famous accounts of multiple personalities are the books *Three Faces of Eve* (Thigpen & Cleckley, 1954) and *Sybil* (Schreiber, 1974).

Because dissociative disorders are relatively rare, well-documented literature on the subject is scarce. It therefore remains one of the least clearly understood patterns. Nevertheless, the psychoanalytic and learning models have offered some explanations.

The *psychoanalytic model* considers these as a massive repression that actually splits off part of consciousness. In this view, a person becomes so upset and threatened by his or her own thoughts or acts that the only way to resolve the resulting conflict is to separate that part of consciousness completely and become totally unaware that it ever existed.

The *learning model* regards these denials as avoidance responses. This model does not use such concepts as unconsciousness or split consciousness. Rather, people are seen as ignoring or not thinking about significant dimensions of themselves because in this way they are able to escape or avoid anxiety. While the avoidance pattern in dissociative disorders is quite extreme, it is nevertheless due to basic learning principles. In the person's past, such behaviors were reinforced by the immediate reduction of anxiety they brought about. It may be true that other less extreme behaviors would also reduce anxiety, but the individual has not learned such alternative behaviors. The dissociative responses have become the ones used by the individual to cope with certain anxiety-arousing situations.

SOMATOFORM DISORDERS

DSM-III distinguishes several **somatoform disorders,** or physical symptoms that have no apparent organic cause. In **converson disorders,** the person develops symptoms in response to some stressful event. The symptom serves a twofold purpose: It gains sympathy for the individual from others, and it makes it possible for the person to avoid the stress-producing situation. The physical disabilities that appear in conversion disorders may take many forms:

1. *Sensory symptoms:* partial or complete loss of sight or hearing, insensitivity to pain, and unusual tactile sensations, such as itchiness or tingling.
2. *Motor symptoms:* paralysis, tremors, rigid joints, and inability to talk above a whisper.
3. *Visceral symptoms:* chronic coughing, headaches, nausea, and shortness of breath.

Freud believed that people transformed or converted their unacceptable desires or psychological conflicts into a bodily symptom that was tangible and socially acceptable. The *psychoanalytic model* begins its explanation of conversion disorders by focusing on id impulses (for example, sexual desires) that were dealt with too harshly during childhood. For example, during the Oedipal stage, children come to desire the parent of the opposite sex. If this desire is not resolved adequately in the form of identification with the same-sex parent, children may feel threatened and anxious about such sexual impulses. Later in life, when these or similar id impulses emerge in a particularly strong manner, the individual may convert them into a physical channel. Of course, a conversion disorder need not always involve sexual impulses. Abse (1959) described a case in which a man's desire to kill his wife and her lover was so threatening to him that he repressed this desire and instead developed paralysis of the legs. In this case of a conversion disorder, as in others, the conversion to the physical channel helps protect people from their disturbing impulses.

The *learning model,* on the other hand, does not see a conversion process in such physical disabilities. Rather, this model sees them as learned behaviors that are reinforced by their role in helping the individual avoid stressful situations. This does not mean that such individuals are pretending. Rather, such physical difficulties have in the past been reinforced by serving to reduce or avoid the anxiety of key stressful events. Their illness may serve to protect them from social, occupational, or family pressures and may be further reinforced by the attention and comfort elicited from others. The similarities between such disorders and organic-based disorders indicate that the person may have had some experience with a relative or acquaintance who had a real physical disease that served as a model.

As in the case of dissociative disorders, the empirical evidence for these explanations of conversion disorders is rather sparse. Indeed, DSM-III states that a case of true conversion disorder is rare and that numerous other explanations must be tested before this diagnosis can be made.

AFFECTIVE DISORDERS

Affect is the term used by psychologists to refer to the expression of emotion. (Affect does not refer to the emotion itself, but to the signs of feelings that people show to others.) **Affective disorders** are patterns of behavior in which an individual expresses emotional states excessively, inappropriately, or inadequately.

Depression

In contrast to other disorders such as multiple personalities, which we are more likely to encounter in movies or television than real life, we are all likely to know a person, a friend, or family member who experiences **depression** at some time. Approximately 5 to 10 percent of men and 10 to 20 percent of women in our society will suffer at least one bout of serious depression during their lives (Weissman & Myers, 1978; Woodruff, Goodwin, & Guze, 1974). In addition to feelings of sadness, depression often involves a change in appetite, sleeping difficulties, and a decrease in activities, interests, and energy (see Table 16–5). Severely depressed persons think of themselves negatively and self-reproachingly. Their sex drive is low, and they experience either insomnia or an increased need for sleep. They avoid social contact and may consider suicide. Not all depressed persons have all these symptoms, nor are these symptoms unique to depression. (Because the same symptoms are found in many other categories, diagnostic reliability is far from high.)

There seem to be different kinds of depression. For example, there is a range of severity from relatively mild symptoms of depression to patterns so severe as to make daily functioning all but impossible. DSM III differentiates between *major depression* that seems to arise from within the individual, and that caused by adjustment to a stressful life situation. *Adjustment disorder with depression* is precipitated by some external event, usually a loss such as death, illness, or departure of a family member, but it may also be caused by stresses such as divorce, job loss, or change in work conditions (Paykel, 1973). The-

Table 16–5: Changes from Normal to Depressed States.

ITEMS	NORMAL STATE	DEPRESSED STATE
Stimulus	Response	
Loved object	Affection	Loss of feeling, revulsion
Favorite activities	Pleasure	Boredom
New Opportunities	Enthusiasm	Indifference
Humor	Amusement	Mirthlessness
Novel stimuli	Curiosity	Lack of interest
Abuse	Anger	Self-criticism, sadness
Goal or Drive	Direction	
Gratification	Pleasure	Avoidance
Welfare	Self-care	Self-neglect
Self-preservation	Survival	Suicide
Achievement	Success	Withdrawal
Thinking	Appraisal	
About self	Realistic	Self-devaluating
About future	Hopeful	Hopeless
About environment	Realistic	Overwhelming
Biological and Physiological Activities	Symptom	
Appetite	Spontaneous hunger	Loss of appetite
Sexuality	Spontaneous desire	Loss of desire
Sleep	Restful	Disturbed
Energy	Spontaneous	Fatigued

From Beck (1974).

orists (Bowlby, 1973) have suggested that the present loss or stress connects with earlier loss of a parent, to cause the current feelings of depression. Evidence shows that people who suffered the death of a parent during childhood are more likely to have depressions as adults (Heinicke, 1973).

Major depression is not a response to an external situation. It is characterized by long-lasting and overwhelming sadness of mood, with many of the behaviors described above. Those who are psychotically depressed have delusions, or hallucinations, or may be mute and unresponsive. Classically, such pervasive depressions were thought to be biological in origin, but many modern depression researchers do not agree. They also suggest that major depression may be rarer than previously thought, because situationally depressed individuals may repress, forget, or minimize the external circumstances that triggered their depression.

The *psychoanalytic model* generally regards major depression as anger turned inward. Freud believed that the tendency toward depression starts in early childhood, specifically during the first phase of development, the oral period. If our infantile needs during this time are over- or undergratified, a fixation occurs which results in overdependence on others. Later in life, after the loss of a loved one through separation or death, our overdependent ego identifies with this lost person. We "introject" or incorporate the person and essentially make the person part of ourselves. According to Freud, we all have unconscious feelings of hate toward those we love, and we now turn those feelings against ourselves, and depression results.

The psychoanalytic formulation has several problems, some of which are theoretical. If we incorporate the loved one within us, why do feelings of hate rather than love dominate? Second, people who have not experienced the death of a loved one during childhood also become depressed. Why? The psychoanalytic answer is that it is possible to become depressed without actually losing a loved one. A person may experience a "symbolic loss" in which some action or event creates a trauma equivalent to the loss of a loved one. For instance a father is drafted into the military and called away; the mother enters the work force; or the father does something the child interprets as rejection. If these sorts of events are considered losses, then it seems that they must occur in everybody's life; and the Freudians must tell us why only some people become depressed.

Some evidence goes against the Freudian view of depression. Researchers (Beck & Ward, 1961) find images of loss and failure in the dreams of depressed people, not the anger and hostility Freudians would expect to be present, given their view that unconscious material is represented in dreams. Despite the psychoanalytic view that depression is anger turned inward, researchers have found that depressed people are quite capable of expressing rage and hostility at other people (Weissman, Klerman, & Paykel, 1971).

Learning and *cognitive models* combine to form an account of depression that more clearly fits the empirical results. Learning theorists (Eastman, 1976; Lewinsohn, 1974) suggest that depressed feelings are produced when the reinforcers a person is receiving from the outside world drop to a low rate. Because of this decrease in reinforcement (which may be caused by some external event such as loss of job or death of spouse), activities that would have called forth positive responses in the past decrease, leading to an even further loss of reinforcers and dejection, so a vicious circle begins.

For example, a woman's husband may die, leading to a major reduction in the pleasures and reinforcers she receives. Without her husband, she is less rewarded for being active, initiating conversations, dressing attractively, or acting cheerfully. Her range of behaviors becomes more limited and depressive in nature. Such behaviors make it difficult for others to be around her, converse with her, have fun with her, and reward her. This isolation makes her feel more depressed.

A related viewpoint is that of Seligman's helplessness model. Seligman proposes that depressed people have developed a **learned helplessness** from earlier experiences and now believe themselves unable to influence and control events. Thus they develop negative symptoms, including helplessness, passivity, and depressed and negative expectations when faced with stressful situations. An experiment by Miller and Seligman (1975) demonstrated that depressed subjects, unlike nondepressed subjects, did not expect success in performing a skilled task even after they had done it successfully several times. In other words, even success did not give them faith in their ability; helplessness, once learned, apparently does not dissipate easily.

Notice that the research on reinforcement and learned helplessness was done to clarify the *learning perspective* on depression, but that the results recognize a very important *cognitive component*. Both are concerned with the reinforcement patterns the individual experiences and the mental representations of the world the individual constructs from these patterns of reinforcement.

In an influential modification of the theory of learned helplessness (Abramson, Seligman, & Teasdale, 1978), the cognitive components were made even more explicit. They found that the interpretations people make about the causes of their failure will determine both whether or not they become depressed by that failure and what effects that failure will have in the future. Thus attribution is part of this cognitive process. (See Chapter 18 for a further discussion of theories of attribution.) If I believe that the reasons for my failure are global, stable, and internal to me, then depression and loss of self-esteem are likely to result, and I will feel helpless as well. I may then decide that I will not try similar tasks in the future, since I will only fail at them. For instance, if I fail a math test and decide that I failed because I lack intelligence, I will be very depressed indeed.

A more specific attribution, although still internal and stable, would be that I lacked math ability. An even more specific attribution, and a correspondingly less depressing one, would be that I perform poorly on high pressure, multiple-choice tests. Note the difference in the consequences that I expect to follow from each attribution. If I really believe that I'm unintelligent, then I am likely not to aspire to college and a whole set of "intellectual" careers. If I believe that I'm poor at math, the effects, while still general, are less so. I may well go to college, and simply stay away from mathematics courses. Finally, if my interpretation of my failure was simply that I was bad at a certain kind of test-taking skill, then I might even take math courses, if I were sure the tests would be of the take-home variety.

Researchers postulate that some people have a *depressive attributional style;* such a person attributes frequently poor outcomes to global, stable, internal causes. Research (Seligman, Abramson, Semmel, & von Baeyer, 1979) supports the notion that depressed students are more likely to attribute failure in this way. Other research (Metalinsky, Abramson, Seligman, Semmel, Peterson, & von Baeyer, 1982) showed that students who indicated a depressive attributional style on a beginning-of-term questionnaire became more depressed if they received a lower-than-expected midterm grade.

Aaron Beck has developed an exceedingly influential *cognitive* model of depression. According to Beck (1967), depression is one point on a continuum that includes ordinary forms of everyday "blues" and sadness, rather than some special state. Beck sees depression as the result of a series of logical errors made by depressed people in interpreting the causes of events that happen to them. These "negative schemas" converge to produce negative self-evaluation in the depressed person.

A depressed person shows consistent tendencies of self-deprecation and self-blame, and these tendencies are evidenced in several ways. Negative self-evaluations are reached based on insufficient evidence, by wildly over-generalized conclusions from few and possibly unimportant events. One poorly received lecture causes a lecturer to be depressed about his teaching abilities and self-worth. The negativity of small events, such as an ill-considered remark, is maximized, while positive outcomes are minimized. We all know that many events in life are multiply caused, but the depression-prone individual abstracts from this multiplicity of causes the ones that support feelings of low self-worth. Depressed people regularly draw conclusions without evidence, attend to only certain aspects of a situation (usually the wrong ones), and overgeneralize from specific occurrences to their whole lives. These kinds of repeated cognitive distortions seem quite reasonable and natural to depressed people and add strength to their negative self-view and world view. This negative view flavors decisions, behaviors, emotions, and interactions, thus locking in a pattern of depression.

There is evidence that depressed individuals do show the thought patterns Beck describes (Beck, 1967; Beck, Weissman, Lester, & Trexler, 1974; Nelson, 1977). However, Beck's theory postulates more than this correlational finding; it postulates that the negative reasoning processes should be the cause of depression. Studies need to be done that first assess individuals' negative thought patterns and see whether these individuals become depressed when negative events occur in their lives.

Bipolar Disorders

Bipolar disorders add manic behavior to the symptoms of depression. A person with this type of disorder will at times go through periods of intense depression and at other times be energetic and excessively lively.

Manic behavior may at first appear to be simply a very positive and enthusiastic approach to life. But it soon becomes clear that the behavior and reactions of people in a manic period are extreme and inappropriate. Often they have feelings of great joy or elation, show great agitation, become involved in many different undertakings, and show a heightened pace in activity and thinking, extreme impatience, poor concentration, and poor judgment. In some cases, they will make expensive and extravagant plans that are totally unrealistic. Most people think of manic behavior as happy behavior, but this is not always so. Sometimes people in a manic pattern are quite irritated and unpleasant. They may be quite aggressive or may become confused, incoherent, disoriented, or even violent.

The periods of depression and mania are of varying duration—sometimes they go on for months at a time—and seem unrelated to particular situational factors or changes. For this reason, bipolar disorders have often been analyzed in biological terms. Since Pavlov, researchers have characterized the nervous system as having an excitatory, action-producing component, and an inhibitory, action-suppressing component. It has been suggested that depressive disorders are caused by a neurophysiologically produced activation of the inhibitory system, and that bipolar disorders are produced by some cyclical neurophysiological process that involves first the relative dominance of the excitatory system, then the inhibitory system.

Most neuroscientists now regard this as an oversimplification, but several more sophisticated versions of neurophysiological explanations for bipolar disorders are being investigated. As we discussed in Chapter 2, neurotransmitters regulate the transmission of impulses across synapses between neurons in the brain. This suggests that excesses or deficiencies of *norepinephrine* (a neuro-transmitter) are the cause of **manic or depressive** behavior (Schildkraut, 1965). That many of the drugs that affect bipolar disorders also affect norepinephrine levels is taken as evidence for this.

Again, further research (Barchas, Akil, Elliott, Holman, & Watson, 1978; Berger, 1978) tells a more complicated story. A second neurotransmitter, *serotonin,* has been linked to depression (Prange, Wilson, Lynn, Lacoe, & Stikeleather, 1974). The current tentative formulation is that lowered levels of serotonin predispose an individual to bipolar disorders. Given a serotonin deficiency, a high or low level of norepinephrine leads to manic or depressive behavior, respectively.

SCHIZOPHRENIA

When we turn to a discussion of **schizophrenia,** we are confronted with the most controversial and puzzling of mental disorders. Schizophrenia always involves a deterioration from a previous level of functioning. To family, friends, or work colleagues, schizophrenics seem not be to be doing (or thinking) as well as they once did.

The diagnosis of schizophrenia has been applied to such a wide variety of behaviors that many professionals argue that it is a wastebasket category. Still, there are some characteristics that most persons diagnosed as schizophrenic do seem to share: a distortion of reality in some significant way, social with-

"Life story" as depicted by a schizophrenic patient. Many of the typical concerns of schizophrenia can be seen in the various scenes.

drawal, and prominent disturbances in thought, perception, motor activity, or emotionality.

Disturbances of Thought, Perception, Emotion, and Motor Abilities

The thought disturbances of schizophrenia are centered on the individual's inability to organize ideas coherently. Often such individuals have trouble sticking to one topic at a time (loose associations). The ends of their statements are only distantly related to the beginnings. For some, the only rule is that key words in their statements rhyme (clang associations). And yet others are so unaffected by the usual rules of communication that they use their own private words (neologisms) that have meaning to no one else.

Sometimes it is not the organization of thought but its content that is disturbed. This is best illustrated by the delusions that often form part of schizophrenic thinking, beliefs that seem totally unfounded and are frequently bizarre. People with delusions of grandeur view themselves as magnificent or powerful persons such as Christ, Einstein, or Joan of Arc. Those who have delusions of influence or control may believe that others are trying to contact them by radar, television, or other means. And those with delusions of persecution imagine that others are trying to hurt them.

The perceptual disturbances of schizophrenia center on individuals' inability to selectively filter out the millions of stimuli surrounding them at any given moment and to give order and meaning to their world. The result is that schizophrenics often pay great attention to seemingly irrelevant stimuli and ignore important stimuli. Distraction is a way of life.

Often the perceptual difficulties extend to **hallucinations,** the perception of things that are not actually there. People with visual hallucinations may see imaginary persons or objects. Those with auditory hallucinations may hear imaginary voices that command, advise, criticize, or praise them. Other senses may also be involved in hallucinations, as in the case of people who feel millions of insects crawling on their skin or taste poison in their food.

There can be other sorts of emotional disturbances. Some individuals show extremely inappropriate emotional reactions—for example, laughing at the death of someone dear to them. Others show ambivalent reactions, repeatedly expressing both intensely positive and negative emotions toward the same person or object. And yet others show virtually no reaction at all, no matter what the situation.

The motor activities of a schizophrenic are often quite disturbed. Some people spend hour upon hour gesturing in systematic ways. For example, an individual may bend each finger of each hand in succession, or may raise and lower an arm over and over again. Some schizophrenics move about with much excitement, waving, and activity. Others show virtually no movement at all. They stay in the same position for long periods of time, whether sitting, squatting, or lying. Such people often show a "waxy flexibility"—their hands, arms, and legs can be molded into any position by another person and the position will be maintained.

Different Types of Schizophrenia

Because schizophrenia is characterized by such a wide range of behavioral and perceptual disturbances, it can be considered as a number of subtypes based on the predominant symptoms. For example, if the person has delusions of grandiosity or of persecution, has unfocused anxieties, or tends to be argumentative or aggressive, the diagnosis is likely to be **paranoid schizophrenia. Catatonic schizophrenics** are generally immobile and resistant to instructions or attempts to move them; they occasionally have bursts of purposeless excited motor activity. The number of subtypes of schizophrenia has both grown and decreased over the years in line with contemporary thinking. Some clinicians have questioned the usefulness of distinguishing so many subtypes.

Research has indicated, however, that it is useful to distinguish schizophrenics according to at least a few dimensions. Paranoid schizophrenics, for example, have been found to be distinctly more alert than nonparanoid schizophrenics, and more coherent in their thoughts and statements. One may not agree with their view of things, but they are capable of stating them quite coherently. Another useful distinction is between chronic schizophrenics, whose symptoms emerge gradually and last a long time, and acute schizophrenics, whose symptoms emerge rapidly and improve rapidly. The prior social adjustment (the premorbid adjustment) of schizophrenic persons has also proved to be an important distinction. A schizophrenic person with a "good premorbid adjustment" tends to improve significantly faster.

Models of Schizophrenia

The explanations of schizophrenia vary greatly. Psychoanalytic theorists are themselves divided in their interpretations. One *psychoanalytic* perspective, that proposed by Freud, views schizophrenia as regression to a pre-ego stage, that very early period in childhood when self-absorption ruled the day. To function without an ego is to function without reality testing (understanding that something exists outside of you), which is certainly consistent with the separation from reality that is so typical of schizophrenia.

An alternative psychoanalytic perspective sees schizophrenia as a total ego-defense strategy. According to this interpretation, schizophrenic persons are coping with their early and ongoing traumatic experiences by overrelying on a wide range of ego-defense mechanisms. For example, delusions and hallucinations are said to be exaggerated uses of such defenses as projection, fantasy, and wish fulfillment. Delusions of influence are simply the projections of blame onto others for one's own unacceptable thoughts, behaviors, and failures. Delusions of grandeur represent extreme fantasy and wish fulfillment. And hallucinations enable one to tolerate one's own negative thoughts and ideas by externalizing them as "voices" outside oneself.

Learning theorists also offer more than one explanation for schizophrenia, although all involve reinforcement principles. One account (Ullman & Krasner, 1975) suggests that schizophrenics are people who were not reinforced for responding to the social stimuli to which most of us learned to respond. This is because of disturbed contact with their families while growing up. In social situations, there is a sense in which schizophrenics are not "paying attention" to the cues. They are then ostracized or punished for their inappropriate behavior, which can contribute to their "paranoid" beliefs that people are talking about them. Their peers probably do talk about their weird behavior, and they may even be cruel to them.

Deprived of normal reinforcement, these people are particularly "in search of" whatever few reinforcements that the environment does provide, and these may come from the attention or sympathy they receive when they make schizophrenic responses. In other words, in the reward-deprived worlds of these people, crazy behavior may produce most of the reinforcements that they receive. Support for this view comes from research that shows that schizophrenic talk can be reduced by systematic efforts to ignore such talk and to reward "normal" talk.

Yet a third learning perspective suggests that schizophrenic individuals learn their behaviors by imitating other schizophrenic people in their environment. Some studies suggest that sometimes the parents of schizophrenics are schizophrenic themselves, thus providing an influential model. This perspective does not account for that vast number of schizophrenics who did not have schizophrenic parents or other such models; nor does it explain why so many children of schizophrenic parents are apparently uninfluenced by having such models and remain normal.

Humanistic and *existential* perspectives are more easily applied to less psychotic and flamboyant difficulties of life than schizophrenia. In terms of this disorder, the leading spokesperson for this point of view is British psychiatrist R. D. Laing (1964), who has approached schizophrenia from a humanistic and thought-provoking perspective. Laing suggests that schizophrenia is a sane response to a social world gone mad. To be successful and "normal" in our society, Laing continues, requires us to accept false, depersonalizing, trivial, or destructive goals and modes of behavior. Because schizophrenic individuals have suffered intolerable pressures and contradictory demands from their environment, they react appropriately negatively to all of society. People who become schizophrenic may have had "worse" family situations, which simply made them more sensitive to societal contradictions than the rest of us. Their schizophrenia is a withdrawal from others to make an inward search. This search, if allowed to continue, will result in a strong, well-adjusted person who has come appropriately to terms with living authentically in a world that frequently demands less-than-authentic behavior. Laing believes that the standard, well-meaning efforts of family members, therapists, and others to alleviate schizophrenic symptoms actually interfere with this constructive process. Such interventions suspend the person in an endless journey and prevent the natural positive outcome of the search.

Not surprisingly, Laing's theory has raised a great deal of controversy. The main difficulty is his notion that schizophrenic symptoms are constructive. Critics point to the apparent suffering and limited lives of schizophrenic persons and ask how these can be viewed as positive. Laing responds that the suffering and limitations result from the environment's inappropriate interference with the natural growth process.

The *biological approach* to schizophrenia has generated high excitement for various physiological or biochemical explanations. Unfortunately, many of these did not hold up when subject to more tightly controlled scientific scrutiny. For example, Heath and Krupp (1967) believed that the problem was an antibody named *taraxein* found in the blood of schizophrenics. There was a great deal of excitement when Heath and his colleagues first found that normal individuals would sometimes show schizophrenic symptoms when they were injected with taraxein or when they were given rapid blood transfusions from schizophrenic persons. However, later research produced ambiguous findings.

For a while there was much interest in the *transmethylation process* researched by Hoffer and Osmond (1966, 1968). They argued that in schizophrenics the production of neurotransmitters (see Chapter 2) such as norepinephrine is somehow sidetracked so that hallucinogens are produced instead. These self-made hallucinogens, produced by transmethylation, were thought to produce ongoing schizophrenic behavior, just as synthetic hallucinogens such as mescaline and LSD produce temporary psychotic-like behaviors.

This theory has acquired some support over the years. For example, it was found that the body's neurotransmitters and such synthetic hallucinogens as mescaline and LSD-25 have similar biochemical structures. Also, Friedhoff and Van Winkle (1962) found a hallucinogenic compound called DMPEA in the urine of 15 out of 19 schizophrenics. However, urinary measures can be affected by a number of factors. Moreover, subsequent findings on the trans-methylation process were mixed, and the enthusiasm for this explanation of schizophrenia declined.

Recall that in discussing the possible physiological causes of bipolar disorders, we raised the possibility that manic and depressive disorders were caused by certain complex patterns of neurotransmitter imbalances. Similarly, it has been suggested that schizophrenics have too much of the neurotransmitter *dopamine* at certain brain centers. Dopamine, among other functions, plays a key role in our ability to attend to, perceive, and integrate information. It may help us to link sensations such as a smell or a color with our memories or internal feelings. If a person had too much dopamine, almost every smell, color, or other perception would trigger a distinct memory or feeling until the person was overloaded with sensations demanding attention. How upsetting and confusing this would be—and how similar this experience is to schizophrenic symptoms.

The support for this theory is indirect but intriguing. For example, *phenothiazines* (antipsychotic medications such as thorazine) not only remove schizophrenic symptoms, but also bring on the Parkinsonian symptoms of extreme muscle tremors. We know that Parkinsonian symptoms are caused by too little dopamine in the brain. Antipsychotic medications apparently reduce schizophrenic symptoms by severely reducing dopamine, perhaps from a level that was much too high in the first place.

It has also been observed that chronic amphetamine abuse often leads to the appearance of schizophrenic symptoms, and amphetamines are now known to stimulate dopamine production. In fact, schizophrenic persons who take even small dosages of an amphetamine show more intense symptoms. At this point, high dopamine levels do seem to be involved in schizophrenia. But as with much other physiological research, the complete explanation is probably more complex. In general, it is unlikely that any complex psychological syndrome will have any simple correlation to simple patterns of neuro-transmitter surpluses or deficiencies. Second, even when the links between neurotransmitter patterns of activity and personality disorders are known, we will still need to understand the events that produce these neurotransmitter dysfunctions. Those events may well be psychological in nature, including those events specified in the psychodynamic, learning, cognitive, and humanistic models.

The possibility may be illustrated by considering one interesting *cognitive model* of schizophrenia. In a sense, it begins its explanation where the biological model leaves off. Maher (1970) argues that there is nothing wrong with the thinking processes of schizophrenics. Rather, such people have a very real biochemical problem that leads them to experience sensory distortions such as odd sensations, visions, or sounds. Their apparent delusions result from their efforts to make sense of these unusual experiences. Since everyone around them denies that they could be experiencing such sensations, they learn to ignore or discount the opinions of others. Thus schizophrenic individuals apply their logical processes to their unique but real experiences, and they apply them in relative isolation.

In trying to explain these experiences, the person may well decide that such odd sounds are coming from a source that other people apparently cannot hear. The individual may further believe that he or she is a special person to be receiving such communications. Or the person may feel that others are lying about not hearing these sounds or are even secretly sending the sounds and voices. Either way, a delusional system emerges, all from trying to log-

Schizophrenia—Nature or Nurture?

Schizophrenia is one area in which both genetic and environmental factors have been thought to operate. Early studies seemed to indicate that schizophrenia was particularly likely to develop in a person who has one or more schizophrenic genetic relatives, particularly an identical twin. (Be cautioned that these studies are subject to many of the same methodological criticisms as the studies on the inheritance of intelligence discussed in Chapter 9.) Although controversy remains, many research studies (Gottesman & Shields, 1972) are generally interpreted as affirming an inherited component to the syndrome of schizophrenia; whether or not this component is the result of the direct action of the genes or of some complex biochemical process in the brain is open to question. Moreover, this heritability is viewed as much less determining than earlier researchers claimed.

Even those who assert a genetic role, however, assign a considerable and possibly determining role to the environment. People with a presumed strong hereditary disposition to become schizophrenic may not do so if their physical and interpersonal environment remains benign at critical points in their lives. At the same time, people with no apparent hereditary disposition to schizophrenia can become schizophrenic as the result of consistently destructive experiences.

Still remaining, however, is the question of the extent to which the presence of a schizophrenic in the family itself creates an environmental proclivitiy to developing this condition in other family members. Does having a schizophrenic father in some way "teach" a child to become schizophrenic as well? Since we all know that children learn how to behave from their parents, can one learn schizophrenic behavior and thought processes? Obviously the issues involving this serious disorder are compelling, and researchers struggle to sort out the nature–nurture issues involved.

ically understand events that cannot be logically explained within the person's framework of knowledge.

PERSONALITY DISORDERS

All people show characteristic patterns of behavior and ways of thinking about and perceiving the environment and other people. When these characteristic patterns become maladaptive, causing individuals distress or impairing their normal functioning in occupational or social situations, these individuals are characterized as having a **personality disorder** (American Psychiatric Association, 1980, p. 305). We will discuss the antisocial personality disorder as an example of this group of disorders.

Antisocial Personality Disorder

In a society in which criminal behavior is increasing, many people take advantage of others, and many behave unethically and immorally; people often look to psychology for reasons why this is so. Is antisocial behavior (including behavior by seemingly respectable persons) a form of abnormality? What accounts for some people's indifference to the moral standards of their society? One answer provided by psychology is the **antisocial personality disorder,** previously called the **psychopathic** or **sociopathic personality.**

Many psychologists have felt uncomfortable about even considering such behaviors as a form of abnormal functioning. Clearly, such patterns are deviant, but "deviant" does not necessarily equal abnormal. Perhaps because the kinds of behavior involved have so harmful an impact on society, clinicians struggle to understand the antisocial personality disorder. Researchers are

"I can't understand the girl, no matter how hard I try," said the father, shaking his head in genuine perplexity. "It's not that she seems bad or that she means to do wrong. She can lie with the straightest face, and after she's found in the most outlandish lies she still seems perfectly easy in her own mind."

He had related . . . how Roberta at the age of 10 stole her aunt's silver hairbrush, how she repeatedly made off with small articles from the dime store, the drug store, and from her own home. . . .

Neither the father nor the mother seemed a severe parent. . . . [However], there was nothing to suggest that this girl had been spoiled. The parents had, so far as could be determined, consistently let her find that lying and stealing and truancy brought censure and punishment.

As she grew into her teens [she] began to buy dresses, cosmetics, candy, perfume, and other articles, charging them to her father. He had no warning that these bills would come. . . . For many of these things she had little or no use; some of them she distributed among her acquaintances. . . . As a matter of fact, the father, previously in comfortable circumstances, had at one time been forced to the verge of bankruptcy.

In school Roberta's work was mediocre. She studied little and her truancy was spectacular and persistent. No one regarded her as dull, and she seemed to learn easily

very aware that this investigation involves some complex legal, moral, and societal problems.

Certainly, not everyone who is a criminal should be categorized as having an antisocial personality disorder. The label has been applied to those individuals whose personality characteristics pervasively include unsocialized behavior in conflict with society: inability to display loyalty to others; gross selfishness, callousness, irresponsibilty, and impulsiveness; inability to feel guilt or learn from experience; and low tolerance of frustration. At the same time, such individuals can be quite intelligent. Obviously, these characteristics fit many different actions and people. It is important to know that the label of antisocial personality disorder has been used for those whose whole life style is typified by such characteristics. The essential feature of the disorder is that there has been a history of continuous, chronic antisocial behavior. This antisocial behavior characteristically emerges during the person's teenage years, and it affects on-the-job performance. Generally, these people are unable to sustain genuinely close friendships or loving relationships with other people.

A brief look at the history of psychological perspectives on antisocial behavior will help us to understand the current theories about this disorder. Throughout most of history, people who committed crimes generally were treated as criminals with the standard punishments that this implied. During the nineteenth century, people became aware that some criminals seemed different from the others, and observers began to describe what we now call the antisocial personality disorder. Because the scientific thinking of the time was dominated by a hereditarian perspective, the disorder was originally thought to be genetic in its origins. Later observers suggested that the origins of the syndrome lay in an early breakdown in the individual's relations to society, particularly to his family. (The "his" in the previous sentence is not inappropriate. DSM-III estimates that the disorder is about three times as likely to appear in males as in females: less than 1 percent in females and 3 percent in males.)

In the 1950s and 1960s, the tendency was for many clinicians to view all antisocial acts as the product of an antisocial personality disorder. Broadly stated, the view was that all people who committed crimes were "sick" or "mentally ill" and probably had been made so "through no fault of their own"—by a failure of their family or of society in general. Current diagnostic

when she made any effort at all. (Her IQ was found to be 135.)...

"I wouldn't exactly say she's like a hypocrite," her father said. "When she's caught and confronted with her lies and other misbehavior she doesn't seem to appreciate the inconsistency of her position. Her conscience seems still untouched...."

Having failed in many classes and her truancy becoming intolerable to the school, Roberta was expelled from the local high school....

Roberta was sent to 2 other boarding schools from which she had to be expelled.... Employed in her father's business as a book-keeper, she used her skill at figures and a good deal of ingenuity to make off with considerable sums.

[Eventually she was hospitalized for psychiatric observation.] During her hospitalization she ... discussed her mistakes with every appearance of insight. She spoke like a person who had been lost and bewildered but now had found her way.... (Roberta returned home but her old behavior patterns continued.)

Despite her failures she would, in her letters ... write as if she had been miraculously cured: "This time we have got to the very root of my trouble and I see the whole story in a different light.... If, in your whole life you had never succeeded with one other patient, what you have done for me should make your practice worthwhile.... I wish I could tell you how different I feel. How different I am! ..."

Abridged from Cleckley, Hervey: *The mask of sanity*, ed. 5, St. Louis, 1976, The C. V. Mosby Co.

practice requires the clinician to be more discriminating. We now distinguish between crimes committed by antisocial personalities and those committed by normal individuals for motives such as gain or revenge.

Theories and research into antisocial personality patterns have centered on two areas: (1) socialization and family background, and (2) biological factors. The *biological* factor first suggested, as in almost every other case, was genetic inheritance. It was, for example, suggested that a tendency to commit crimes was inherited. More recently, it was suggested that a rare chromosomal abnormality is a cause of criminality (Jacobs, Branton, & Melville, 1965). Some individuals, called "XYY types" carry an extra male chromosome (the second Y chromosome). Researchers questioned whether this extra male chromosome transmitted some extra tendency toward the commission of active, physical, "male" activities that sometimes manifested as violent crime.

After much empirical research, the conclusion is that the extra Y chromosome is not a predictor of criminal behavior. Researchers still argue about whether the chromosomal abnormality is found more often in criminals than in the general population, but there is general agreement that the abnormality is rare and not found in many violent criminals. In addition, most identified XYY types are not violent criminals but ordinary, peaceable individuals. There is considerably less enthusiasm for the "chromosomal hypothesis" than there once was.

Other theories of the causes of antisocial personality disorder have cut across the psychoanalytic, learning, and cognitive models. They have focused on such variables as identification, modeling, poor value acquisition, and attitude development. *Psychoanalytic theory* suggests that the disorder is shown by people who have not developed superego control of their behavior. Without these superego controls, the person is much more likely to succumb to some of the id's demands for immediate gratification, regardless of the moral dictates of the situation. Developing an adequate superego, you will recall, involves absorbing parental standards at an early stage. As researchers (Greer, 1964; Robins, 1966) have in fact found, the absence of a parent, because of death, separation, or desertion, is a rather common factor in the background of antisocial individuals.

Learning theorists suggest that antisocial responses are learned by imitation from parents, peers, and even from the violence seen on the entertainment media. Second, parents of well-socialized children have been found (Snyder,

1977) to reinforce cooperative behavior and to punish or not reinforce anti-social behavior. Parents of antisocial children frequently punish their children and rarely reinforce them; and their punishments, at least from the child's point of view, are arbitrary, rather than following antisocial actions. *Cognitive theorists* might suggest that such children are likely to realize that the moral rules of conduct they hear preached do not really govern who gets punished and who gets rewarded and that they might as well act as their impulses direct them.

As will be apparent from this discussion, psychologists have many questions about the exact nature of this disorder, and much work is still in progress.

OTHER DIMENSIONS OF ABNORMALITY

During the past few decades, we have seen an enormous increase in the discovery and manufacture of mind-affecting drugs. We increasingly recognize that many of these substances—new and old—can have rather complex negative effects. For example, many of these substances can cause brain damage. Chronic consumption of alcohol can lead to an amnesia syndrome called Korsakoff's disease; other substances can lead to strong states of dependency, the maintenance of which may dominate an addict's life. DSM-III reflects this awareness of drug problems by the inclusion of many more drug-related disorders than did the previous diagnostic systems.

In general, a diagnosis of **organic mental disorder** is made when the substance use has acute or chronic effects on the central nervous system. **Substance-use disorders** are diagnosed from the maladaptive behavior patterns that users show. These behaviors generally include impairment in social and occupational functioning, inability to control or limit use of the substance, and withdrawal symptoms. In some cases these two diagnoses are interrelated; frequently, a person who has an alcohol-produced organic mental disorder of intoxication and withdrawal will have an alcohol-abuse and -dependence disorder.

The list of abuse and dependence characteristics of substance-use disorders has proven depressingly long. In other words, there are a variety of addictions. Alcoholism is certainly an addiction. Surprisingly, many people do not think of alcohol as a drug, mainly because it is legal and accessible. Narcotic addiction (addiction to opium, heroin, and morphine) is a major problem and is linked to crime because narcotics are relatively inaccessible and illegal in our society. Yet another very serious one is barbiturate addiction (certain kinds of sedatives and sleeping pills). Amphetamine and cannabis (marijuana) have more recently been added to the list. Cocaine, PCP, and various hallucinogens clearly provoke abusive behavior, but physiological dependence has not yet been shown for these substances. Tobacco, oddly, is not thought of as producing abusive behaviors (apparently death by cancer is not an abuse), but it does produce acute physiological dependency.

Substance-Use Disorders

We will focus, in the next few pages, on those disorders that are classified as addictions. **Addiction** or **substance dependence** typically involves increasing physical tolerance, psychological dependence, and severe with-

HIGHLIGHT □

Diet and Abnormal Behavior

Many people believe that diet affects mental health. For instance, many parents have been led to believe that sugar and some food additives cause hyperactivity in children or criminality in adults. There are several problems with these contentions: So far, the evidence for them has been more anecdotal than experimental. In addition, the mechanisms by which the food additives are postulated to affect activity patterns have generally not been specified. Finally, those proposing such relationships between food additives and human actions were highly committed to their claims and therefore not in the best position to be objective about them. An example of this last point is useful: A group of boys whose parents believed that refined sugar immediately caused them to behave hyperactively were chosen as subjects. The boys were given drinks of sugar or saccharin water and then were fitted with activity monitoring devices and watched by trained observers. Neither the observers nor the activity monitors detected any increased hyperactivity in the boys who ingested the sugar. If anything,

a slight decrease in activity was observed.

Very recently, scientists studying the behavioral effects of diet have met in order to assess the state of the art. Their conclusions are tentative but potentially intriguing. Many researchers in this area have done studies with animals because the high precision of measurement and control obtainable in these circumstances has been most valuable. Their results (Kolata, 1982) demonstrate that the presence or absence of various nutrients in the diet alters the rate of synthesis of various neurotransmitters, including serotonin, dopamine, norepinephrine, and acetylcholine. (Look to Chapter 2 for a description of the role of these neurotransmitters in brain functioning.) For instance, high-carbohydrate meals cause an increased release of insulin, which in turn triggers a differentially high concentration of tryptophan in the bloodstream, which in turn facilitates the production of serotonin. Serotonin, as the reader will recall, has its effects on sleep.

In human beings, effects of diet are much more subtle than popular accounts would have us believe, at least as they can be measured in research. Even though the body's only source of tryptophan is dietary pro-

tein, it is high-carbohydrate diets, rather than high-protein diets, that differentially increase the amount of tryptophan in the blood, and therefore the amount of serotonin produced. Hartmann (reported in Kolata, 1982) concludes that a high-carbohydrate meal makes mildly insomniac patients fall asleep more quickly, but not normal sleepers or serious insomniacs.

There are a number of possible reasons for this complex pattern, and further research is needed to clarify the entire area, but several cautionary points can be extracted: The effects of diet on behavior are likely to be complex and subtle. There is no reason to believe that neurochemically produced changes will lead to an increase in *abnormal* behaviors, as opposed to complex shifts in many behaviors. As we recognized at the beginning of the chapter, abnormality is a category with societally imposed elements in its definition, and the connections between shifting patterns of neurotransmitters in the brain and increasing patterns of deviant or socially condemned behavior are generally going to be remote and complex. It certainly looks as though researchers are on to a generally exciting area of inquiry, but much of the story remains to be discovered.

drawal symptoms, both physical and psychological, when use of the substance is discontinued.

It is difficult in a textbook to capture the dynamics of drug or alcohol addiction. While some people are able to carry on a fairly normal life despite substance dependency, others show disturbing effects fairly soon. At first people get pleasurable effects from the drug, but often they come to need greater and greater amounts to achieve the same pleasurable effects. In fact, they come to need greater and greater amounts to reach even the basic level of comfort they originally had without any drugs. If they try to stop taking the drug, they experience painful physical symptoms (**withdrawal** symptoms), including hypertension, severe cramps, and restlessness. (See also Chapter 5 and the Application on the opponent-process theory and addiction in Chapter 11.) People who are dependent on drugs are on an escalating cycle— they must take more and more of the drug just to break even. If they stay off the drug long enough, they can break this cycle; but withdrawal is a most painful and feared experience.

In an attempt to understand substance dependence, it is useful to describe three related aspects of the problem: the *host* (mental or physical makeup of the individual); the *environment;* and the *agent* or nature of the substance involved.

Host. Although psychologists have been unable to come up with a personality profile that leads inevitably to dependency, studies suggest that certain characteristics are fairly consistent. Among these are emotional immaturity, a low tolerance for frustration or tension, and a strong tendency to avoid reality. Because addicts or problem drinkers often seem to run in families, a genetic influence has long been suspected. One study by Goodwin, Shulsinger, Hermansen, Guze, and Winokur (1973) showed a higher than normal rate of drinking problems among adopted children whose biological parents were alcoholics, even though the children were unaware of their background. However, there are also circumstances under which drug use leading to dependence does not seem related to any particular "addiction personality pattern." A wounded soldier might be treated for real pain with morphine and later develop a dependence. During the 1950s and 1960s, a number of people who experienced occasional anxieties or depressions were rather casually prescribed tranquilizers that were later found to have addictive properties.

Environment. Social acceptability plays a major role in substance dependence. As might be expected, both drug and alcohol abuse are more prevalent in sociocultural environments where these substances are readily available. It is easier for a susceptible individual to become dependent on drugs that are considered "normal," as alcohol is in our culture. Economic factors may also be influential. In times of prosperity, money is available to spend on drugs and alcohol. Conversely, during a financial depression these substances provide an eagerly sought escape mechanism.

Agent. Obviously, people become dependent on some drugs more easily than other drugs. Users of the opiates (heroin in particular) or barbiturates may become dependent in a relatively short time, no matter how psychologically stable they are. Other drugs, including amphetamines, may become addictive through conditioned response to their tension-releasing properties.

ALCOHOLISM. **Alcoholism** is an easy dependence to drift into because alcohol is both readily available and socially acceptable in our society. Alcoholism affects a wide range of age groups and cuts across all levels of occupation, wealth, and religion. Male alcoholics have traditionally outnumbered female alcoholics, but the gap seems to be narrowing.

The destructiveness of alcoholism is pervasive and dramatic. Alcoholics can cause themselves grave bodily damage (including liver damage, malnutrition, hypertension, endocrine gland and heart problems), psychological damage (for example, overdependence, poor social judgment, and loss of self-respect), and damage to the quality and purposefulness of their lives (loss of job, friends, others' trust, and sense of accomplishment).

The family and friends of alcoholic people suffer greatly as they observe loved ones destroying their lives. Family and friends are themselves often subjected to abuse, embarrassment, frustration, and financial instability in the course of their relationships with individuals dependent on alcohol.

Alcoholics also inflict suffering on members of society whom they have never met. The number of crimes and accidents related to alcohol is staggering:

Alcohol has been associated with over half the deaths and major injuries suffered in automobile accidents each year, and with about 50 percent of all murders, 40 percent of all assaults, 35 percent or more of all rapes, and 30 percent of all suicides. About one out of every three arrests in the United States results from the abuse of alcohol. (Coleman, Butcher, & Carson, 1980, p. 314)

Because alcoholism is so prevalent, there have been numerous efforts to understand the causes and cures. The *psychoanalytic model* provides several viewpoints. One of the more common is that alcoholics are fixated at the oral stage of development—their needs as infants during the oral stage were either not met or were met excessively. In either case, the frustrated needs, especially dependence and oral needs, may later take the form of alcoholism under a particular set of life events and circumstances.

The *learning model* sees the use of alcohol as a learned method of reducing stress. At first glance, this theory seems at odds with the obvious punishment and increased stress that ultimately result from long-term usage. One explanation for this seeming contradiction is provided by the concept of a *delay-of-reward gradient* (Dollard & Miller, 1950). Rewards and punishments decrease in value the further off they seem, and the alcoholic individual chooses the immediate gratification of temporary tension relief.

The *biological model* points to the withdrawal symptoms that occur when a chronic alcohol drinker suddenly stops as evidence that some physiological changes are involved in alcoholism. A group of withdrawal symptoms that occur in many chronic drinkers is called *delerium tremens* (*DTs*). A sudden drop in the blood's alcohol level can cause profuse sweating, eye pupil irregularity, delirious experiences, and hallucinations of the most disturbing sort. Of course, such withdrawal reactions do not prove that alcoholism is primarily a physical event that causes psychological dependency, but there is a lot of interest in this possibility. Many people have proposed that alcoholism is indeed a problem "caused" by biological predispositions, metabolic or organic weaknesses, genetic factors, and the like (Williams, 1959; Segovia-Riguelme, Varela, & Mardones, 1971; Goodwin et al., 1973). Others have argued against this perspective, saying that the evidence has yet to clearly establish this point.

Alcohol dependence, although more socially acceptable, can be as damaging as other drug dependencies—and as depressing.

DRUG DEPENDENCE.   Other forms of addiction are unique in certain ways but basically involve the same dimensions as alcoholism. For example, in narcotic addiction and barbiturate addiction there are significant physiological addiction, bodily and psychological damage, personal damage, family and social impact, and societal implications. And the explanations offered by the various models parallel those offered for alcoholism.

Narcotic dependence has stirred a great deal of attention in recent years because of some critical research findings that may ultimately point to a clear understanding of what dependence is all about, at least in biological terms. A few years ago researchers (Pert & Snyder, 1973) discovered that the body had certain receptor sites for opiates, including certain sites in the brain, intestines, and other locations. Apparently, opiates operate on a person through their impact on these receptor locations. For example, there are a high number of opiate receptors in the area of the brain that regulate pupil dilation. One effect of opiates is constriction of the pupils. Obviously, they do this by their impact on these particular receptor sites in the brain.

Researchers were able to map the opiate receptor sites throughout the body. They then asked why we have receptor sites in our bodies for foreign substances like opium, morphine, and heroin. A possible answer was that perhaps our bodies have naturally occurring opiates that regularly operate on these receptor sites in all people. The search was on for the body's natural opiates, and indeed, natural opiatelike substances were found in the bodies of human beings and other animals—*enkephalins* and *endorphins*. Enkephalins and endorphins are apparently naturally produced substances that help us cope with pain and stress. Our bodies automatically produce them, use them, and need them at certain times.

Putting this startling discovery together with what is known about narcotic dependence, researchers think that dependence may operate in the following way. When first taken, opiates relieve pain or give an extra push to the emotions by filling those receptor sites that have not yet been filled by the body's natural opiates—enkephalins and endorphins. But if a person takes opiates too often, these receptor sites get overloaded and the body's own production of enkephalins and endorphins is decreased or cut off because these substances simply aren't needed as much. At this point, the opiates are needed not just for an extra push but to *make up for* the decreases in normal bodily production of enkephalins and endorphins. Thus the dependent person needs to take more and more opiates to fill this increasing number of empty receptor sites.

This explanation is certainly consistent with the increasing tolerance we noted earlier. If opiates are withheld from the dependent person, the receptor sites will remain empty for a period of time because enkephalin production has been cut off. With no opiates—foreign or natural—at these sites, the body has no tools to fight pain or stress or to perform certain regulatory functions. The person will feel and react in a most uncomfortable and debilitated manner. This explanation is consistent with the experience of withdrawal. Withdrawal symptoms will continue until the body renews its production of enkephalins and endorphins.

Research in this area is now moving at a rapid pace. As our insights into the biological mechanisms involved in narcotic dependence grow, so should the implications for treating dependence. Possible connections with other forms of dependence may also emerge in the near future.

Abnormal Categories: A Perspective

What can we say about the reasons for abnormal behavior? In the past, researchers, clinicians, and theoreticians assumed that most disorders could be explained with one theoretical structure; we no longer believe that is possible. For some disorders, biological explanations are relevant; for other problems, the psychoanalytic, learning, cognitive, and humanist-existential explanations clearly provide more insight into their causation. Research has sometimes provided clarification of a particular type of abnormal functioning, but more often it has simply given us further clues. Few disorders are completely understood. It is clear, though, that the psychoanalytic explanations are not the whole story.

Society is presenting us with an urgent set of questions here. Clearly, abnormal functioning in its various forms represents a major problem in our society. People are increasingly seeking the services of mental health personnel and facilities. This rise in numbers may be due in part to the lessening of the stigma associated with emotional and behavioral problems, but it probably also reflects an increase in the actual prevalence of such problems. The

Table 16-6: *Estimated* Incidence of Abnormal Behavior Patterns in the United States.

500,000	reported cases of child abuse per year (1.5 million cases are estimated to go unreported).[1]
27,300	deaths from suicide per year.[2]*
1,200,000	individuals are actively schizophrenic.[3]
16,000,000	individuals suffer from anxiety, phobia or other related disorder.[3]
18,000,000	individuals suffer from major depression and other affective disorders.[3] (300,000 persons are hospitalized each year for disabling depressive disorders.[4])
2,200,000	individuals suffer from drug dependence.[3]
13,000,000	individuals suffer from alcohol abuse, including 10,000,000 adults and 3,000,000 teenagers. (Alcohol abuse includes both alcoholism and problem drinking.)[3]
10,200,000	individuals are arrested per year in connection with serious crimes.[5] (315,000 individuals are in state and federal prisons.[6]*)
29,000	children in the United States are estimated to be afflicted by some form of psychosis. (From 2 to 5 college students out of every 1,000 will develop psychosis while they are in college.[7])
3,500,000	elementary school children in the U.S. have moderate to severe emotional problems requiring some kind of mental health care.[7]
34,000,000	persons are affected by a mental disorder each year.[8]

*The incidence of suicide attempts and serious crimes may be much higher due to the large number that are not reported.

[1] Michael de Courcy, "Child-Abuse Parley Deplores Fund Cuts," *The New York Times*, April 8, 1981, III, 1:3.

[2] U.S. Bureau of the Census, *Statistical Abstract of the United States* (Washington, D.C.: U.S. Government Printing Office, 1981), table 113, p. 74.

[3] U.S. Public Health Service, *The Alcohol, Drug Abuse, and Mental Health National Data Book* (Alcohol, Drug Abuse and Mental Health Administration, DHEW Publication No. (ADM) 80-938) (Washington, D.C.: U.S. Government Printing Office, 1980), p. 19.

[4] Judith Norback, *The Mental Health Yearbook/Directory 79-80.* (New York: Van Nostrand Reinhold, 1979), p. 745.

[5] *Sourcebook of Criminal Justice Statistics 1981*, table 4.1, p. 338.

[6] *Statistical Abstract of the U.S.*, table 336, p. 191.

[7] *The Mental Health Yearbook/Directory 79-80*, p. 745: *Statistical Abstract of the U.S.*, table 31, pp. 28-29.

[8] *The Mental Health Yearbook/Directory 79-80*, p. 746.

estimated incidence of major maladaptive behavior patterns in the United States is summarized in Table 16-6.

Many perspectives are relevant in the diagnosis of abnormal functioning, and at the moment, psychology is in some conflict about the definitions of abnormal behavior. This is not an unreasonable state of affairs in this complex area. Progress will require (1) further research on the causation of abnormal behavior, and (2) careful, logical, psychological delineation of the questions being asked, given the multiple meanings of "abnormal behavior" and "abnormal personal functioning."

SUMMARY

1. Defining normal and abnormal behavior in statistical, cultural, or ideal terms has proved difficult. Instead, it has been found useful to establish criteria that, taken together, give a picture of abnormal behavior. These criteria are bizarreness and extremeness; disturbance of others; inappropriate or excessive emotional display; and interference with daily functioning.

2. The *Diagnostic and Statistical Manual of Mental Disorders* (*DSM-III*) is the official classification system of the American Psychiatric Association. In contrast to previous systems, it is multiaxial: It requires a person to be evaluated on five different dimensions. This procedure is designed to give a more complete picture of the individual. DSM-III also uses highly explicit and detailed descriptions in order to achieve high diagnostic reliability.

3. *Phobic disorders* involve a persistent, disproportionate fear of a particular object or situation, such as a fear of heights (acrophobia). *Generalized anxiety disorders* involve the same fear and discomfort as in phobic disorder, but are not linked to a specific object. A *panic disorder* consists of recurrent panic attacks that occur unpredictably.

4. *Obsessive-compulsive disorders* are those that compel a person to repeat unwanted thoughts over and over or to repeat certain actions or rituals.

5. *Dissociative disorders* involve problems of memory and consciousness, such as amnesia, fugue, somnambulism, and multiple personality. *Conversion disorders* are a subdivision of *somatoform disorders,* in which people develop physical symptoms, such as blindness, body aches, or paralysis, with no apparent physical cause.

6. *Depression* describes a wide range of complaints from mild sadness to a highly disabling state. The various schools of thought differ as to the cause of depression. For example, the cognitive theorists suggest that depression results from a person making uniquely personal and broad-reaching interpretations of the negative events that happen to all of us.

7. *Bipolar disorders* occur when the "lows" of depression alternate with the "highs" of a manic phase, which is characterized by euphoria and energetic activity.

8. *Schizophrenia* is another term that is applied to a wide range of disorders; schizophrenia includes disturbances of thought, perception, emotion, and motor abilities. Thoughts may be disorganized or the content of thoughts may be delusional. Disturbances of perception may range from distraction to *hallucinations*. Emotional disturbances may include inappropriate reactions or ambivalent reactions; motor disturbances may include systematic gesturing or catatonic states.

9. A biological explanation of schizophrenia is that schizophrenics have an abnormally high amount of the neurotransmitter dopamine in certain brain centers. Dopamine affects attention, perception, and integration of information. This research is not conclusive. It seems likely that environmental factors interact with a biologically-based predisposition to produce schizophrenia in some individuals.

10. The *antisocial personality disorder* has been a difficult one for psychologists and psychiatrists to come to terms with, and theories about its causes have changed as society's thinking about criminality has changed.

11. *Substance-use disorders* involve both impaired functioning (such as poor social or occupational functioning), and withdrawal symptoms when the drug is withheld. Neuroscientists are making promising discoveries about the workings of drugs on the chemicals in the brain. The three interconnected areas of influence in drug dependence have been described as the host, the environment, and the agent.

Suggested Readings

AGRAS, W. S., CHAPIN, H. N., & OLIVEAU, D. C. The natural history of phobia: Course and prognosis. *Archives of General Psychiatry,* 1972, *26,* 315–317. Presents a study following the natural course of phobias over a 5-year period in people whose phobias were not treated by psychotherapy.

BECK, A. T. *Cognitive therapy and emotional disorders.* New York: International Universities Press, 1976. A thoughtful statement of the cognitive theory of depression and other disorders by one of its leading proponents.

BECKER, J. *Affective disorders.* Morristown, N.J.: General Learning Press, 1977. Provides an overview of the problem of depression, citing theories and research from the various models.

FADIMAN, J., & KEWMAN, D. (Eds.). *Exploring madness: Experience, theory, and research.* Monterey, Calif.: Brooks/Cole, 1973. Looks at abnormal functioning through an interesting mixture of personal and literary accounts, research, and theoretical perspectives, including both traditional and radical perspectives.

LEON, G. R. *Case histories of deviant behavior* (2nd ed.). Boston: Holbrook, 1977. Interesting case histories are presented along with interpretations and discussions reflecting the behavioral and cognitive models.

McNEIL, E. G. *The quiet furies.* Englewood Cliffs, N.J.: Prentice-Hall, 1967. Presents interesting case histories in detail from a psychodynamic perspective.

SELIGMAN, M. E. P. *Helplessness.* San Francisco: W. H. Freeman & Company, Publishers, 1975. Offers the learned-helplessness interpretation of depression, a cognitive-behavioral view that has stirred a great deal of research in recent years.

SZASZ, R. The myth of mental illness. *American Psychologist,* 1960, *15,* 113–118. Presents a controversial position on the nature and definition of mental illness by one of the field's most interesting figures.

17. Therapy

Therapy can be defined as a set of procedures that attempts to improve the well-being of individuals. Guided by one or more theories of **personality** (discussed in Chapter 14), a therapist attempts to help a person to change his or her life, usually because the individual is experiencing one of the problems or disorders that we examined in Chapter 16.

Change is a key element in therapy. The change may be cognitive, behavioral, or emotional—that is, therapy may change the way a person thinks, behaves, or feels—or it may change all three.

As we have seen, there is little agreement on the probable causes of various kinds of abnormal behavior. As you might expect, there is a correspondingly vast array of therapeutic procedures, dependent on the presumed cause of the disorder being treated. One broad distinction often made is between **psychotherapies** (talk therapies) and **drug therapies.** The talk therapies characteristically involve a client "talking through" problems with a therapist, seeking to gain some insight into their causes. Generally, these therapies are guided by *psychoanalytic, cognitive,* or *humanistic* and *existential* thinking. Drug therapy involves prescribing medications that alter mood or behavior by alteration of the underlying physiological causes.

More recently, other techniques have emerged. A therapist using principles of learning theory may set up mechanisms to selectively reinforce or punish certain behaviors of the client. A therapist may have clients reenact old scenes of conflict in their lives, or realistically role-play new social skills modeled by other people. Recently, too, many therapists have become more eclectic, drawing on several kinds of theories about the origins of a patient's problems, and using a correspondingly eclectic mix of therapeutic techniques to deal with these problems. In this chapter we will look at various theories and approaches to therapy, their intended purposes, and their demonstrated effectiveness.

THE HISTORY OF THERAPY

The first attempt at treatment we know of took place roughly half a million years ago, during the Stone Age (Coleman, 1980). There is evidence from the period of a practice known as *trephining,* in which people were treated by chipping a round hole in their skulls with a stone tool, presumably to allow an evil spirit or demon to escape. Some of the unearthed skulls show evidence of healing around the hole, so at least some patients survived this drastic remedy and lived for several years afterward.

From early recorded history there seems to have been agreement among the Chinese, Hebrews, Egyptians, and Greeks that mental abnormalities were the result of possession by demons. The accepted method of treatment was *exorcism,* which involved rites of prayer and a variety of techniques designed to make the possessed person's body a most undesirable place for evil spirits. These techniques included drinking vile liquids, which were then regurgitated, presumably along with the offending demon. Other approaches, perhaps designed for more stubborn cases, involved flogging and starvation.

In every age, the dominant influence in the choice of therapy has been the particular model of human behavior used by the therapist.

Hippocrates rejected the prevailing idea of demons and formulated an early medical model. He divided mental illness into three categories: mania, mel-

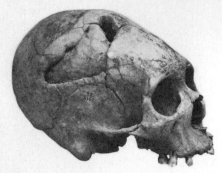

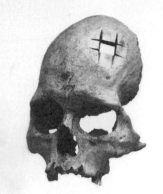

Trephining, or making a hole in the skull, presumably to allow an evil demon or spirit to escape, was one of the first attempts at treatment. Notice how in the lower skull the hole has actually begun to grow over—this means that the patient actually survived this drastic treatment and lived for several years afterward.

ancholia, and phrenitis, or brain fever. All three were thought to be caused by a disturbance of the body. Treatment, therefore, was aimed at the body and, depending on the category, included vegetarianism, exercise, sexual abstinence, and bleeding.

By the late Middle Ages, however, the demons had returned. Priests took over the treatment of abnormal behavior, first with prayers and sprinkling of holy water, and later with more violent forms of exorcism (driving out the devil). By the fifteenth century, abnormal behavior was thought to be due to witchcraft. Treatment consisted of torturing the victims until they confessed, and then burning them to death.

The demon approach was still accepted by both church and state in the early sixteenth century. It was not, however, without opposition. One of the leading attackers was Johann Weyer, who published a book based on a humanitarian model, arguing that witches were mentally ill rather than "possessed." He advocated treatment centered on understanding and help instead of torture and burning at the stake. Although Weyer is regarded as the founder of modern psychopathology, his theories were met at the time with scathing criticism.

Mentally disturbed people who escaped the treatment for witchcraft were usually confined to monasteries or prisons. From the sixteenth century onward, special asylums, or mental hospitals, gradually took over this responsibility. Patients in institutions were usually treated more like animals or prisoners than human beings in need of help. Then, in 1792, a Frenchman, Philippe Pinel, was put in charge of a hospital for the insane near Paris. Pinel made some radical changes. He removed the patients' chains; he moved them from dark dungeons to sunny rooms; and he allowed them to work and exercise outdoors. The results were almost miraculously beneficial.

About the same time, reforms were taking place in American mental institutions. One notable advocate of the humanitarian approach was Benjamin Rush, who became known as the father of American psychiatry. Another energetic reformer was a retired schoolteacher from New England, Dorothea Dix. Dix took her humanitarian crusade throughout the country (and several other countries as well) and is credited with the establishment or reform of more than 30 mental hospitals.

Throughout the nineteenth century, many state hospitals for mental patients were founded on the optimistic belief that proper treatment in proper surroundings would lead to recovery. The result was an increase in admissions, which by the mid-nineteenth century had reached such proportions that the institutions were forced to shift their priority from curing mental illness to simply providing custodial care. Bars reappeared on windows, doors were locked, and the atmosphere once more became more like that of a prison than a hospital.

Private mental hospitals were usually superior to public ones. Since they had better financing and a lower staff-to-patient ratio, they were often able to provide the quiet therapeutic atmosphere and patient attention that could lead to improvement. However, private hospitals were usually available only to the wealthy. Most people requiring hospitalization went to the inadequate public facilities.

As our knowledge of abnormal functioning improved, it became clear that many people who needed treatment did not have to be in a hospital. Outpatient treatment proved helpful to many people. Again, the therapy was available only to those who could afford it. Others in need tended to receive no outpatient treatment or were hospitalized even though they might have

improved even more with outpatient psychotherapy treatment.

Thus effective outpatient and inpatient care was available only to a small number of people with emotional and behavioral problems. The less wealthy received inadequate custodial care or no care at all. This situation continued until after World War II, when two major developments brought about changes. First, psychoactive drugs were discovered in the 1950s. These drugs provided an easier way to control violent patients and reduce anxiety and depression in others. Such drugs helped to lower the population of public mental hospitals, and this in turn improved the treatment prognosis.

The second major postwar development in psychotherapy came about in the 1960s, partly in response to dissatisfaction with mental institutions. The community mental-health movement was formed to deal with mental-health problems on a local level, if possible before hospitalization was needed. Community mental-health centers were established to provide help for the many people who could not afford private and sometimes distant treatment. Another objective was to overcome some people's resistance to the idea of psychotherapy.

Services at community mental-health centers were tailored to the needs of the local population and might include: ongoing psychotherapy; hotline phones so that anyone with a problem could find someone who would listen; public education on problems such as drug abuse; and active participation in controlling factors that may have an effect on the emotional stability of the community, such as poor housing. This tradition of local agencies providing ongoing therapy and other innovative interventions continues today (see Figure 17–1).

In short, inpatient and outpatient treatment has improved considerably in recent years. Yet there is still room for more improvement. For example, treatment in some public mental hospitals consists of little more than regular doses of tranquilizing drugs and group therapy with other patients. Regular sessions alone with a hospital psychiatrist or clinical psychologist are often the exception rather than the rule. Many observers believe that treatment in such mental institutions is of little value, especially when the negative effects of being labeled an "ex–mental patient" are considered. Our mental institutions need further reform, and we still have to find a way to make quality, effective mental-health care available at a cost most people can afford.

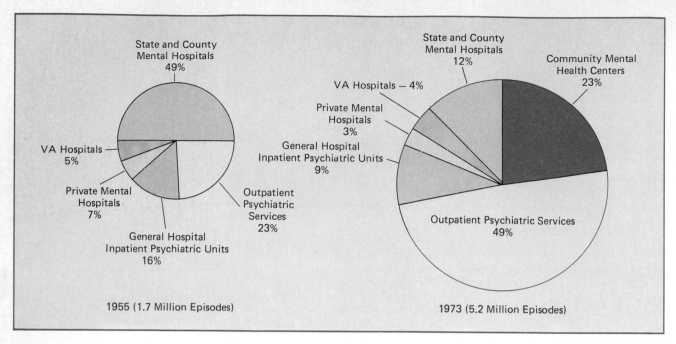

State and County Mental Hospitals 49%

VA Hospitals — 5%

Private Mental Hospitals 7%

General Hospital Inpatient Psychiatric Units 16%

Outpatient Psychiatric Services 23%

1955 (1.7 Million Episodes)

State and County Mental Hospitals 12%

VA Hospitals — 4%

Private Mental Hospitals 3%

General Hospital Inpatient Psychiatric Units 9%

Community Mental Health Centers 23%

Outpatient Psychiatric Services 49%

1973 (5.2 Million Episodes)

FIGURE 17–1
This chart shows the percentage of patients treated in a number of different facilities and by different agencies in 1955 and 1973. Note the increase in patients treated by community mental-health agencies and the increase in outpatient treatment in general in 1973. (National Institute of Mental Health, 1975)

WHO PRACTICES THERAPY?

Practitioners of psychotherapy are divided into four groups, largely on the basis of the type of training they have undergone: clinical psychologists, psychiatrists, psychiatric social workers, and counselors. The type of training is also likely to have a strong influence on the model used by a particular therapist.

Clinical psychologists do 4 to 5 years of graduate work after graduating from college and obtain a Ph.D. Their training includes laboratory work, research design, and specialized training in abnormal behavior and therapy techniques, usually followed by an internship in which candidates work with clients under professional supervision.

Psychiatrists are the only one of the four groups that have an M.D. degree. After earning their medical degree, they undertake a residency program in psychiatry for several years. Psychiatrists are the only psychotherapists who are permitted to prescribe psychoactive drugs and electroshock treatment. Because psychiatrists are doctors, they are often thought of as being more extensively trained in psychotherapy than other kinds of therapists. This is not necessarily true, because the 4-year period of medical training involves little **psychiatry.**

Psychiatric social workers study for 2 years to earn a master's degree, including a year's internship in social work. The number of social workers involved in psychotherapy is growing rapidly in this country. This growth reflects our society's increasing use of psychotherapy services, as well as the heightened degree of training and professionalism now available in the field of social work.

Counseling psychologists and *counselors* earn graduate degrees in psychology or counseling and then do internships in a counseling setting. Often their training and attention are concentrated in specific areas such as student, marriage, or family counseling. Often their practice focuses on problems in adjustment rather than abnormal functioning.

It is not uncommon for these different mental-health practitioners to practice similar kinds of therapy or focus on similar problems. For example, marriage and couple counseling is a field of specialization practiced not only by counselors but also by psychiatrists, psychologists, social workers, and other professionals in the field. Another example is family counseling, which focuses on faulty relationships among members of the family rather than merely on the personality problems of the individual. Practitioners work with all family members rather than focusing on one person.

Many people practice psychotherapy in the course of performing other functions. For example, psychiatric nurses not only carry out the medication orders of staff psychiatrists but also interact with patients in psychotherapeutic ways. While the main function of school psychologists and social workers is the assessment of emotional and behavioral difficulties, they often engage in therapeutic interactions with pupils. Therefore, there is an increasing trend to include therapeutic techniques in the training of these professionals.

Thus there are many different types of therapists operating in many different settings. There are also different approaches to therapy, which we shall look at next. The five basic approaches are the same ones that we discussed in relation to abnormal behavior in Chapter 16: the *psychoanalytic, learning, biological, humanistic-existential,* and *cognitive models.*

There are many different types of therapies which take place in many different settings. Here, a student participates in a psychotherapy session with a counseling psychologist.

THE PSYCHOANALYTIC MODEL OF THERAPY

The **psychoanalytic model,** formulated by Freud, locates the origin of abnormal functioning in emotionally painful childhood situations or events that have resulted in arrested personality development. The adult patient is unable to resolve unconscious conflicts and impulses except by maladaptive defense mechanisms such as excessive repression.

Psychoanalytic therapy—or **psychoanalysis,** as it is called—is based on verbal techniques. Its basic purpose is to solve psychological problems by bringing the unconscious conflicts into the conscious mind, where they may be confronted and resolved by the person. The focus is on feelings rather than on behavior. Psychoanalysis aims to change the patient's entire life style and personality rather than just certain behaviors. In Freudian terms, psychoanalysis is designed to strengthen the ego, increase the awareness of the id, and bring the superego under control.

Psychoanalysis is usually an involved process that takes years to complete. The role of the psychoanalyst is largely passive; it is that of a guide and interpreter rather than a teacher. One of the major problems the analyst must deal with is the emotional resistance of the patient to the painful awareness that an emotional problem exists. Therefore, analysis must do more than uncover the emotional origins of problems; if effective therapy is to take place, it must enable the person to acknowledge and confront these problems.

Techniques of Psychoanalysis

Psychoanalysis uses several techniques—most of them originated by Freud—as part of the therapeutic process. One of the best known is **free association,** in which the patient is encouraged to say whatever thoughts come to mind, regardless of how illogical, irrelevant, or embarrassing they seem. Freud said that free association should be like someone viewing scenes from a train window, smoothly flowing by. The theory is that by disregarding intellectual judgment and interpretation, the person will bypass the ego's defenses and produce clues to the unconscious source of the problems. Of course, it rarely happens this easily. What gets in the way is the person's own **resistance,** which occurs in the form of blanks, obviously contrived associations, or disputes with the therapist. The form or source of this resistance is regarded as significant by the psychoanalyst and a possible opportunity for insight and interpretation, because it is a clue that the person is getting close to the source of a problem.

Interpretation is another key technique used by the psychoanalyst to make the unconscious conscious, to bring hidden emotions to the surface. When the person seems ready to face underlying problems, the analyst suggests possible hidden meanings or defense mechanisms revealed by the person's actions or statements. The analyst points out connections and associations the person may not have seen—connections between belief and actions, or between current attitudes and something that happened in the past. The person may deny these connections (this is one form of resistance, and it is usually taken by the analyst as a sign that the interpretation is correct) or use them to gain insight into the unconscious source of the problem.

In addition to interpreting a person's resistance, psychoanalysts also interpret the person's dreams. Freud (1933) called dreams the "royal road to the unconscious." By interpreting dreams, the psychoanalyst tries to help people recognize unconscious impulses that are threatening to them. By looking at such impulses in the light of day, people can see that they are no longer as scary or as unacceptable as they seemed when they were children. Once people see this, they are able to relax their defenses and bring out more unconscious material.

When we are asleep, the ego and superego are not as much in control as when we are awake, and unconscious impulses surface—but usually in disguise. According to Freud, dreams have two levels of content. One is the **manifest content,** which involves the overt and concrete happenings of the dream. This is the dream as dreamers experience and remember it. The other level is the **latent content,** the hidden and symbolic meaning of the dream, the disguise that the impulse appears in. It is the latent content that the psychoanalyst helps people to understand and use to gain insight into their hidden motivations.

As psychoanalysis progresses, a special relationship, called **transference,** begins to develop between patient and analyst. Patients begin to form irrational emotional expectations of the analyst. They may feel that the analyst is angry with them, bored by them, disappointed in them, trying to seduce them, or expecting too much of them. Their own reaction may be anger, fear, love, or an effort to dominate the analyst. According to Freud, these unrealistic interpretations are a result of transferring past relationships with important adults (usually parents) onto the analyst, relating to the analyst as if he or she were the parent figure. Although this transference is unconscious, patients expect the analyst to react the way their parents would, so they reenact repressed wishes and experiences. A patient with a stern, demanding father, for example, may express the fear that the analyst is displeased with the progress of the therapy. A patient who was emotionally abandoned by an unresponsive mother might feel that the analyst is not really interested in helping with the problem (that is, abandoning the patient again).

Psychoanalysis since Freud

Psychoanalysis as a therapeutic approach has been modified by many people over the years. Just as different psychoanalytic theorists have attached greater importance to social drives (as opposed to sexual drives) or to the ego (as opposed to the id), different psychoanalytic therapists have emphasized interpersonal relationships or insights into the role of the ego. Thus there may be significant differences among psychoanalytic therapies, though all share the belief that intrapsychic conflict is at the core of the problem and that insight is essential to improvement. However, the precise elements of the intrapsychic conflict and the precise kind of insight that is achieved in therapy may vary significantly depending on the particular psychoanalytic school of thought.

Psychoanalysis has also undergone some significant changes in technique. Sessions 5 days a week in which the patient lies on a couch, once the hallmark of this approach, still take place, but much less often. More common are sessions once a week in which the patient and the therapist sit face to face. In some psychoanalytic circles, there are even efforts to shorten the duration of psychotherapy or to have the therapist play a much more active role. The goals also differ somewhat from Freud's. Today there is more emphasis on present problems and ways to solve them and less on building a psychodynamic history of the person. Techniques are also more flexible—transference may or may not be used, and the therapist may vary techniques to deal with different individuals' problems, or even to deal with one individual's different needs at various points in the therapy.

Criticism of Psychoanalysis

Psychoanalytic approaches have received a great deal of criticism—this after an extended period during which psychoanalysis was almost the only approach to therapy available. Some critics argue that analysis simply takes too long and costs too much money for most people. Others point out that the techniques and complexities of psychoanalysis make it helpful only to people who are in touch with reality and coherent, and to those who possess verbal abilities and verbal interaction skills.

The requirement of coherence is particularly troubling when it comes to treating people whose major symptom is a lack of coherence. It is not surprising, therefore, that psychoanalytic approaches have been regularly applied to problems of anxiety and depression, where the person's intellectual ability is intact, and less often to cases of psychosis, such as schizophrenia. Many psychoanalysts, including Freud, have admitted that psychoanalysis is not an effective therapy for schizophrenia. Beyond the issue of coherence and reality testing, one of the major problems with the psychoanalytic approach is the necessity for establishing a bond of trust between therapist and patient. This can be discouragingly difficult to achieve with schizophrenics, since they often are extremely withdrawn and have strong defenses against the intimacy and transference essential to psychoanalysis.

Finally, there is the criticism that psychoanalysis may be a good way to get at the source of the patient's problem, but not necessarily to change it. It may be that the quickest and most effective way to solve present problems is to focus on the problems themselves rather than on what caused them. That, at least, is the viewpoint of the learning model.

LEARNING MODELS OF THERAPY

Learning models see abnormal functioning as patterns of behavior that are learned by the individual—"bad habits," if you will. Thus the learning approach to psychotherapy involves extinguishing the maladaptive patterns and learning more appropriate ones. The extinction and learning follow the principles of classical conditioning, operant conditioning, and modeling that were discussed in Chapters 6 and 14.

Therapy is centered on the problem behaviors themselves; there is no attempt to work back to their origin in the person's childhood. Thus most learning therapy approaches come under the heading of **behavioral therapy.** The first step in a behavioral approach is to define the problem in terms of measurable behavior. Behavioral therapists are not content with descriptions of feeling or undefined fears. If, for example, a person wants to overcome feelings of helplessness, the therapist will begin by working with the person to better describe these feelings and to pinpoint what behaviors are affected by these feelings. Helpless to do what? To get to work on time? To complete assignments? To relate to other people? Once the specific behaviors in need of change are defined, treatment programs using conditioning techniques are worked out. In this way the therapist adapts the method used to the particular problem, rather than using the same method with all problems.

Systematic Desensitization

Behavioral approaches have been applied quite often to problems of anxiety and neurosis. One of the best-known approaches is **systematic desensitization.** It is based on the principle of reciprocal inhibition, in which the person substitutes for the undesired response a response that is incompatible or competitive with it. For example, anxiety responses may be extinguished by gradually associating the anxiety-producing situation or stimulus with a relaxation response.

First the person is trained in relaxation techniques over a period of several sessions and homework assignments. The next step is to make up a hierarchy in which various aspects of the anxiety-producing situation are ranked from

to speak, by this accident.

PATIENT: But I gained attention and love from mother for the first time. I felt so good. I'm ashamed to tell you this. Before I healed I opened the cast and tried to walk to make myself sick again so I could stay in bed longer.

THERAPIST: How does that connect up with your impulse to be sick now and stay in bed so much? (*The patient has these tendencies, of which she is ashamed.*)

PATIENT: Oh . . . (*pause*)

THERAPIST: What do you think?

PATIENT: Oh, my God, how infantile, how ungrown-up (*pause*). It must be so. I want people to love me and be sorry for me. Oh, my God. How completely childish. It is, *is* that. My mother must have ignored me when I was little, and I wanted so to be loved. (*This sounds like insight.*)

THERAPIST: So that it may have been threatening to go back to being self-willed and unloved after you got out of the cast (*interpretation*).

PATIENT: It did. My life changed. I became meek and controlled. I couldn't get angry or stubborn afterward.

THERAPIST: Perhaps if you go back to being stubborn with *me*, you would be returning to how you were before, that is, active, stubborn but unloved.

PATIENT: (*excitedly*) And, therefore, losing your love. I need you, but after all you aren't going to reject me. But the pattern is so established now that the threat of the loss of love is too overwhelming with everybody, and I've got to keep myself from acting selfish or angry.

(Wolberg, 1977, pp. 560–561)

extremely mild to extremely tense and anxiety filled. The client is asked to relax and then to experience or imagine each step in the hierarchy, starting at the lower or mild end. (It is best if the person actually undergoes the experience, but that is not always possible. The alternative to experiencing the anxiety-provoking situation directly is to imagine or visualize it.)

Through repeated short exposures while using the relaxation technique, the person learns to imagine each step without feelings of anxiety. As each step in the hierarchy is "conquered," the person moves on until he or she can experience or imagine the most disturbing level without anxiety. The final step is for the person to carry the learned relaxed responses into the actual environment.

In order for systematic desensitization to work, it is obviously necessary that people be able to identify what they are afraid of. For this reason the approach has been most successfully applied to **phobias** (such as specific fears of animals or heights) and **anxieties** that can be broken down into basic elements (such as the fear of performing in public).

Systematic desensitization includes two central ingredients: a gradual hierarchy of fears, and relaxation training (Wolpe, 1958). Therapists who use this approach argue that the experience of fearful stimuli by themselves—without the relaxation training—will only intensify anxiety. In the next behavioral therapy that we will look at, implosive therapy, therapists argue just the opposite.

Implosive Therapy

In this type of behavioral therapy, people are instructed to tackle an undesirable behavior head on by imagining themselves in the worst anxiety-producing situations for long periods of time. A person with a fear of heights, for example, might be told to imagine standing on a narrow ledge on top of a skyscraper or crossing Niagara Falls on a tightrope in a high wind. Rather than ease the anxiety, the therapist attempts to increase it by adding frightening details to the imagined scene. The theory is that prolonged exposure to the anxiety-producing stimulus in the absence of reinforcement (without the expected or feared consequences) defuses its power.

Proponents of **implosive therapy** argue that the technique of desensi-

Implosive Therapy

The following is an example of a scene used in implosive therapy with snake phobics.

[Imagine that the snakes are] touching you, biting you, try to get that helpless feeling like you can't win, and just give up and let them crawl all over you. Don't even fight them anymore. Let them crawl as much as they want. And now there is a big giant snake, it is as big as a man and it is staring at you and it is looking at you; it's ugly and it's black and it has got horrible eyes and long fangs, and it is coming towards you. It is standing on its tail and it is looking down at you, looking down on you. I want you to get that feeling, like you are a helpless little rabbit, and it's coming toward you closer and closer; feel it coming towards you. Horrible, evil, ugly, slimy, and it's looking down on you, ready to strike at you. Feel it in your stomach, feel it coming, oooh, it is getting closer and closer and it snaps out at you. Feel it biting at your head now, it is biting at your head; it opens its giant mouth and it has your whole head inside of its mouth. And it is biting your head right off. Feel it; feel it biting, the fangs going right through your neck. Feel it, and now it is starting to swallow you whole. It is pulling you right inside its body, feel yourself being pulled and dragged into its body. Feel yourself inside, helpless, lost, and now you are starting to turn into a snake. Feel yourself turning into a slimy snake. And you are crawling out if its mouth. All the other snakes see you. And they start to attack you. Feel them; they are coming to rip you apart. Do you know how animals attack each other? Look at the snakes attacking you, feel them biting you, ripping you to shreds.

(Hogan, 1968, p. 429)

tization successfully reduces anxiety only because it fosters exposure to the feared objects or situations without negative consequences, not because of its gradualism or relaxation training. Thus, they say, why bother with these components? There is evidence, especially in the animal research, that merely preventing escape from a feared stimulus can indeed sometimes extinguish anxiety reactions (Stampfl & Levis, 1967; Baum, 1970). On the other hand, it is not yet clear how to best interpret the research into human desensitization and implosion therapy. At this point, desensitization techniques are more often used, probably because many therapists are concerned that implosive techniques may be too fast and harsh for their clients.

Aversive Counterconditioning

With some problems, it is thought to be helpful to develop a negative response, rather than to attempt to eliminate one. Undesirable habits such as smoking, overeating, or excessive drinking are hard for many persons to break. The behavioral approach of **aversive counterconditioning** seeks to help people to extinguish their excessive attraction to smoking, food, or alcohol by associating a negative reaction, such as nausea or anxiety, with the same stimulus.

The undesirable attraction to the object is extinguished by repeatedly pairing it with an unpleasant consequence such as verbal ridicule, nausea-producing drugs, or electric shock. For example, a chronic overeater is repeatedly offered a large serving of a favorite food, and then given a mild electric shock with each bite. Thus, in conditioning terms, the attractive stimulus, the food, is the conditioned stimulus; it is paired with the unattractive stimulus, the shock, which is the unconditioned stimulus. This pairing produces a fear or revulsion response. When the food comes to elicit fear (or nausea or whatever), its attraction no longer exists—the food is no longer tempting. It is important, however, to replace the overeating with a more desirable response that is somehow fulfilling or tension-releasing. Otherwise, relapse rates in this kind of treatment are high.

Aversive counterconditioning is more exciting in theory than in actuality.

Research has shown that its effects are short-lived in many cases. There is also the problem that the learned negative reaction will generalize too much. For example, in addition to feeling nauseated in the presence of chocolate cake, a person may become nauseated at the sight of a wide range of healthful foods. As a result, aversion therapies are usually recommended only after other approaches have failed.

Operant Conditioning

Operant approaches to therapy borrow from Skinner's (1953) notion that you can shape desired behaviors by rewarding them and by not rewarding undesirable alternative behaviors. One of the best-known operant conditioning therapies is the use of a **token economy.** This approach has been used with such problems as schizophrenic disorders, retardation, and school misbehavior and has had some success in problems typically resistant to change.

Token-economy programs are often practiced in controlled environments such as mental hospitals or psychiatric wards. Positive behavior is reinforced by the reward of tokens that can be exchanged later for special privileges. Thus behavior is reinforced right away by the token, but what it's traded in for and when it's traded in are controlled by the therapist. It is a simple system, which is a big advantage—even severely retarded children quickly catch on to the use of tokens.

The therapist (and sometimes the patient as well) controls the choice of specific behaviors that are to be reinforced and the items or privileges for which the tokens may be exchanged. They may, for example, be good for admission to movies, special meals, or other favors that are available only through the program. An advantage of using tokens is that with one item you can reinforce many different people having many different needs or desires.

The target behaviors that are reinforced may range from increased socialization to the completion of assigned chores, depending on each person's problem areas. With the token-economy program, the therapist can also shape behavior. This has the advantage that the therapist can start with the behavior

Behavioral therapies are quite effective in helping people overcome specific anxieties and phobias—for example, a fear of snakes.

Table 17–1: Token Economy:
A Sample Treatment Program.

Behavior	Reinforcer	Schedule	Control Stimuli
Smiling	Tokens	Each time detected	As part of greeting
Talking to other patients	Tokens	Each time detected	
Sitting	Tokens	Each time detected	Patients must be with others; not alone
Reading (patient looking at printed material)	Tokens	Each time detected	Appropriate time and place: especially not in group meetings or at medications
Grooming—hair	Tokens or praise	Each time detected	Only when hair is not pulled tightly against head; prefer "feminine" style
Completion of specific assignment	Tokens or free trip out-of-doors	Each time detected	Prior to reinforcement patient must say something positive about the job she completed

Schaefer & Martin (1969).

the person is already demonstrating. The token-economy approach therefore is good with very apathetic or withdrawn patients, who are not likely to spontaneously show the final, desired behavior (see Table 17–1).

Remarkable results have been claimed for token-economy programs in improving behavior within institutions (Goldfried & Davison, 1976; Hersen, 1976). Since in many institutions no behavior—positive *or* negative—has any effect on subsequent rewards, rewarding positive behavior is bound to increase it to a certain point. There are problems, however. First, a token-economy program requires a lot of staff training, time, and cooperation, and this is a major drawback for many institutions. A second problem is producing behavioral changes that will transfer to the outside world, when patients are discharged and their behavior is no longer affected by the direct token-reward relationship. Therapists have begun to work on this problem by trying to shift gradually from tokens to social approval (which *can* be obtained outside the institution).

Of course, an operant approach need not actually use tokens. It may use more direct means of reinforcement, as Lovaas (1977) has in treating autistic children. Lovaas developed an intensive behavior-modification program to condition appropriate behaviors in psychotic children. His approach focused on speech training, which was carried out 6 days a week for as long as 7 hours a day. The children were rewarded with food for imitating the sounds produced by the trainer. Lovaas also used punishment in the form of shouting and spanking to suppress undesirable behaviors such as self-destructive acts. Some children took as many as 7,000 trials to learn their first words. As the program progressed, they learned at a faster rate. Treatment lasted 12–14 months, after which the children were transferred to a state hospital. A follow-up study showed that their behavior deteriorated discouragingly over the next 4 years. Better results were achieved with the next group by training the parents to continue the program at home after the child's initial training was finished.

Modeling

Another behavioral approach is **modeling.** In this relatively new technique, a person who fears a certain object repeatedly observes another person—the model—interacting with the object. For example, a person who fears snakes watches a model handling a snake. After the observer sees that the model survives the experience with no bad consequences, he or she comes to believe that there is no basis for an anxiety response (Bandura, 1968). This is a kind of social learning: The person learns something by observing rather than by experiencing it directly.

Modeling is very effective in overcoming fears and anxieties because it gives the person a chance to see someone else go through the anxiety-producing situation without getting hurt. Usually people avoid these situations and therefore never learn that they won't hurt them.

Social-Skills Training

Recently therapists have developed a set of techniques that are designed to help clients perform more skillfully in social situations. They reason, for instance, that a child may become socially isolated because he or she does not have the action or interaction skills necessary to draw forth reinforcing actions from other children or teachers. This may lead not only to increased social isolation, but to depression, to a failure to learn more advanced social skills, and to a tendency to seek attention by destructive or disruptive actions. Therapists are increasingly willing to teach social skills. They begin with behavioral-rehearsal procedures (Lazarus, 1971) in which the therapist coaches the client in appropriate ways to behave in a specific, concrete social setting; they then move on to role-playing techniques in which the therapist takes the part of a teacher, or peer, or potential date and coaches the client through a set of responses that will be socially effective.

THE BIOLOGICAL MODEL OF THERAPY

According to the biological model, abnormal behavior is caused by a malfunction of the body. Treatment is therefore designed to make a particular change in the person's biological functioning. This may be done through such means as drugs, electroshock therapy, or psychosurgery.

Chemotherapy

Chemotherapy, the treatment of abnormal behavior with drugs, is the most widespread biological technique. The drugs used in chemotherapy can be classified as antianxiety, antidepressant, or antipsychotic. As the names imply, each type of drug is aimed at treating a specific type of abnormal functioning. Antianxiety drugs are essentially tranquilizers that calm people who are tense or anxious. Antidepressant drugs are designed to lift the mood of a depressed person, and antipsychotic drugs modify the severe manifestations of psychosis.

The treatment of anxiety with antianxiety drugs is widely practiced not only by therapists, but also by medical doctors who give their patients something to "calm their nerves" and by individuals who swallow a tranquilizer whenever they feel emotionally upset. The popularity of these drugs is due, in large part, to the speed with which they work. (They are also less expensive than psychotherapy.) When they do work, they seem almost to be an instant cure. The "instant cure," however, may be little more than a temporary alleviation of symptoms. There is growing evidence that the so-called minor tranquilizers, such as Librium, Miltown, and Valium, are physically and psychologically addictive when used consistently in high dosages over a long period of time. They are also dangerous (sometimes fatal) and even more addictive when used with alcohol.

Antidepressant drugs are the most common biological treatment for depression. The two main types of antidepressants are *tricyclics* and *monoamine oxidase (MAO) inhibitors,* both of which were discovered by accident. The tricyclics were being tested as a treatment of schizophrenia, and, although they proved to be ineffective, researchers noted that subjects showed an unexpected increase in positive mood. The same result was found when MAO inhibitors were administered as a treatment for tuberculosis.

Tricyclic drugs are usually preferred over MAO inhibitors for depressed persons, first because they have been proven more effective, and second because the MAO inhibitors sometimes have very dangerous side effects, including brain and liver damage, when mixed with certain foods.

The tricyclics, in those cases where they do help, start lifting a person's spirits after a period of approximately 10 days. Further adjustments in dosage are then made until maintenance level is reached.

There are a growing number of antidepressant medications. A given person may be helped significantly by one kind yet be virtually untouched by another. One form of depressed functioning that is relatively unresponsive to these antidepressant medications is the manic-depressive pattern. As you will recall from the chapter on abnormal psychology, this form of depression, with its dramatic manic phase, is distinctly different from other forms. In recent years a different type of drug, not an antidepressant, has been found to significantly reduce the manic-depressive symptoms of people who have experienced them for many years without relief. The drug, *lithium,* must be taken at just the right level to be effective. Below the necessary level, it offers little therapeutic value; above that level, it can be quite toxic and dangerous. For this reason, careful monitoring of people on lithium is critical.

It is not yet clear why lithium works with manic-depressives. One notion is that the problem itself reflects an imbalance of intracellular sodium and potassium and that lithium, which has properties similar to those of sodium, corrects this imbalance (Coppen, 1967). Since the net effect of lithium is to produce a marked reduction in intracellular sodium, it is not surprising that taking too much lithium can be so dangerous.

Chemotherapy has become the most dramatically effective form of treatment for schizophrenia, largely because of the *phenothiazines,* a group of drugs introduced in the 1950s. Because of their success in relieving schizophrenic symptoms, the phenothiazines and related drugs became known as antipsychotic drugs. Before these drugs were discovered, the populations of schizophrenic persons in mental hospitals had been increasing, with no end in sight. With these drugs, however, there has been a reversal in this trend, and in the past few decades the number of schizophrenics in mental hospitals has been reduced dramatically. Indeed, many state hospitals have closed altogether. New philosophies of treatment (for instance, community mental health) and new approaches (for example, token economy) have helped to bring about this trend, but the antipsychotic medications have been the single most important factor (see Figure 17–2).

Research has repeatedly demonstrated the effectiveness of these medications (Casey, Bennett, & Lindley, 1960; Cole, 1964; Freedman, 1977). However, research also points to other issues surrounding the use of these drugs. For example, some people experience uncomfortable and sometimes serious side effects that must be dealt with, such as tremors and problems in motor control. Moreover, those people who have improved on these drugs and have been released from hospitals often show high readmission rates. This has led to what is often called the "revolving-door syndrome"—patients improve enough to be released, but they are not really capable of coping with the outside world. Some stop taking their medication and the symptoms recur; others simply do not have the social or vocational skills to cope outside the institution.

Thus these drugs cannot be said to be a "cure." Some research suggests that the best treatment for schizophrenic functioning is a mixture of psychotherapy and antipsychotic medications. This is where a real value of the drug lies—it brings patients to the point where more traditional forms of psychotherapy are *possible*. Thus, while a more complete understanding of how they operate is needed, these medications have already made possible significant progress in the treatment of schizophrenia, where before the prognosis was very poor.

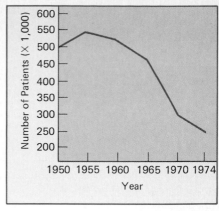

FIGURE 17–2
The use of antipsychotic drugs (phenothiazines and related drugs) since the 1950s has led to a dramatic reduction in the number of schizophrenics in mental hospitals in this country. (National Institute of Mental Health, 1975)

Genetic Counseling and Genetic Engineering

The biological approach suggests certain kinds of interventions that are not "therapeutic" in any normal sense of the word, yet are indirectly aimed at dealing with abnormal behavior. Genetic counseling is one such intervention. This kind of counseling begins by identifying certain diseases that are inherited. Next potential parents are interviewed about the existence of that disease in their families. Sometimes this information is supplemented by information from physical examination of the individuals. As electromicroscopic techniques become more sophisticated, direct examination of chromosomes may also be used to provide information. Fitting this information into the models of genetic inheritance available, the genetic counselor attempts to give the prospective parents some estimate of the odds that their offspring will have certain physical conditions. They then make their parenting decision in the light of that information.

Many of the disorders so identified are physical ones such as Tay-Sachs disease. However, at least some of the disorders, although physical in nature, will have among their symptoms various kinds of mental disorganization which may motivate potential parents to avoid conceiving a child that would have one of these conditions. Amnioscentesis testing of the fluid in the womb after the fetus is conceived is also possible and may lead to a decision to abort the fetus if massive abnormalities are detected.

All of these are grim possibilities, involving wrenching decisions for the people involved. And there is some possibility that the genetic damage situation is growing bleaker. In the first half of this century there has been an incredible proliferation in the manufacture and use of complex chemicals. Many scientists now suspect that overexposure to some of these chemicals or certain manufacturing processes may cause chromosomal damage in an individual and that damage may be genetically passed on to the descendants of that individual. There is good evidence that this occurs in nonhuman mammals (National Academy of Science, 1983). Although the evidence is indirect, since the transmission mechanisms are similar it is likely that it occurs in humans as well. In the future, genetic counselors are likely to add questions about chemical hazards at the workplace to their lists of questions.

Some other forms of biologically based interventions are less bleak. One day, "genetic repair" interventions may be possible, perhaps by early manipulation of the genetic material itself. Today it is sometimes possible to compensate for a genetic deficiency with drugs or control of diet. PKU is a genetically transmitted disease that was often fatal; the underlying cause involves an abnormal build-up of amino acids when elimination mechanisms malfunction. This build-up can be avoided by control of diet.

Electroshock Treatment

One of the more controversial biological treatments is **electroshock.** It is usually used only with people for whom other forms of therapy have not been effective. Therapists have resorted to it less frequently since the antidepressant drugs became available. In electroshock, which was first introduced in the 1930s, a brief electric current is sent through the brain by means of electrodes placed on either side of the forehead.

Before receiving electroshock, people generally are given a sedative and a muscle relaxant, which reduce the risk of injury and seem to minimize the discomfort. A standard course of treatment would consist of 2 or 3 weeks of treatments of 3 electroshocks a week. The result of the shock is a convulsive seizure that lasts for about a minute, following which the person loses consciousness for several minutes. The treatment is often accompanied by a memory loss of unpredictable length, ranging from a few minutes to several hours.

In many cases of depression, electroshock reduces symptoms, and it works quickly (Greenblatt, 1977). No one knows for sure how or why it works. Some experimenters think that it temporarily stimulates the syntheses of norepinephrine in the brain (Kety, 1974). However it works, it is not an absolute cure––the depression often recurs later in the person's life. Also, in some cases it has produced long-term, severe memory loss that seriously hampers a person's life. Finally, it is a treatment that is feared by a great many patients, not surprisingly. For all of these reasons, it is a controversial treatment, which is now used sparingly and with great caution.

Psychosurgery

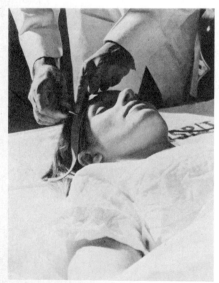

One of the more controversial biological treatments is electroshock. Once used to reduce symptoms of depression, electroshock is currently used sparingly and with great caution.

The last biological method, **psychosurgery,** is even more controversial. The **prefrontal lobotomy** has been particularly controversial. This brain surgery was based on the notion that the frontal lobes of the brain strengthen or increase emotional responses, which arise in the limbic system and hypothalamus. Thus it was thought that cutting the connections between the frontal lobes and these other brain regions would help in such problems as schizophrenia and depression. In the 1940s and 1950s an enormous number of lobotomies were performed with claims of great success. Subsequent research, however, found that people who had had lobotomies showed very bad side effects, such as seizures, stupor, and extreme listlessness, to say nothing of impaired mental functioning. This Nobel Prize–winning procedure fell into disfavor as it became evident that its side effects represented a very significant and serious problem. As a result, all forms of psychosurgery are now treated with great caution by both the professional community and the public at large. Ironically, many psychosurgical techniques are now more precise and better controlled than they were in the 1940s and 1950s; however, because of the lobotomy lesson, as well as the success of the relatively less severe medication approaches, psychosurgery today is infrequently used.

Electroshock and lobotomy share a similar history (Davison & Neale, 1982). Both were discovered "by accident" because they were originally used for other purposes, and their "psychological effects" were noticed later. Both had a period of initial and faddish acceptance, followed by a decline in use once it became clear that the benefits were not as great as originally claimed and that undesirable side effects occurred. More disturbingly, both were used on patients for whom their use was not indicated, and both were used on patients who did not give their consent and often did all they could to resist the procedures. (Many of you will have seen the movie *Frances,* in which Jessica Lange reenacts a dramatized version of the life of the film actress Frances Farmer. In an absolutely terrifying set of scenes, she is lobotomized in a mental hospital. As bizarre and frightening as these scenes are, the portrayal is historically accurate.) Modern researchers and practitioners are appalled by the way these treatments were put into practice.

THE HUMANISTIC-EXISTENTIAL MODEL OF THERAPY

For humanistic and existential psychologists, abnormal functioning results from a failure to reach or strive toward one's full potential. In humanistic theories, this is often called a failure to self-actualize; that is, a failure to move toward the fulfillment of one's natural potential as a human being and to be in close touch with who one is, how one feels, and what one actually thinks. In existential theories, too, abnormality represents a failure to reach one's full potential, but this failure is rooted in one's inability to overcome the sources of anxiety built into the existential situation of life; this is an inability to meet life assertively, give it meaning, and take responsibility for one's life. Both theories define abnormal functioning as a failure to be and fulfill oneself, and the humanistic-existential approach to therapy seeks to help people get in touch with their real selves, and then to make deliberate choices regarding their lives and behaviors, rather than letting outside events determine their behavior.

Years ago, humanistic forms of therapy mainly involved some form of careful and intense self-examination (for instance, Carl Rogers's approach to therapy). In more recent years, the search for fulfilling one's potential has also used altered states of consciousness such as meditation or yoga.

Many therapy approaches fall under the humanistic or existential heading. We will examine two that are quite different in everything but their overall humanistic orientation and goals—Carl Rogers's client-centered therapy and Fritz Perls's Gestalt therapy. Each works toward enhanced self-awareness in a different way.

Client-Centered Therapy

You will recall from Chapter 16 on abnormal psychology that client-centered therapists believe that because of the threatening and evaluative environ-

CLIENT: Well, it happened again yesterday. I got back that exam in American Lit.

THERAPIST: I see.

CLIENT: Just like before. I got an A all right—me and 8 others. But on the third question the instructor wrote a comment that I could have been a little clearer or else could have given more detail. The same old crap. I got an A all right, but it's pretty damn clear that I'm like a machine that can generate correct answers without ever understanding. That's it. I memorize, but there's no spark, no creativity. Boy!

THERAPIST: What else can you tell me about the exam?

CLIENT: Well, it was like we talked about before. I'm doing OK, but I just don't feel like I really measure up. I remember my brother bringing home a paper in high school. It was a C, but the instructor said John had real potential. I just don't think I've got it.

THERAPIST: Even though you got an A you are not satisfied.

CLIENT: I know I should be satisfied with an A. Other guys would be. They'd be glad to get an A.

THERAPIST: Mm-hmm.

CLIENT: But I can't. No wonder the folks are so proud of John. He got decent grades, and he was satisfied—not like me. It's a wonder they don't get fed up with my moping around.

THERAPIST: So even with good grades your unhappiness is enough to turn people off.

CLIENT: Sure. But somehow I've got to get rid of this defeatist attitude.

I've got to think about the good side.

THERAPIST: Mm-hmm.

CLIENT: A lot of times I've tried to forget my lack of potential. Just go on and plug along.

THERAPIST: Yeah, I guess you really felt people put you down because of this lack of potential?

CLIENT: Boy, did they! Especially my folks. They never really said so, but I could tell from the way they acted.

THERAPIST: Mm-hmm.

CLIENT: They'd say that John really has a head on his shoulders, or (*pause*) . . . he can think his way out of anything.

THERAPIST: And this made you feel sort of worthless—not hearing things like that about yourself.

CLIENT: That's right!

(Phares, 1979, pp. 360–361)

ments of their childhood, people find it hard to look at themselves accurately and feel the positive self-regard that everyone needs. Thus they have developed a style of self-distortion, selectively perceiving events and behaviors in a way that is consistent with their self-view. Their inaccurate self-view and the energy invested in this constant self-deception make it impossible for them to fulfill their potential.

The idea underlying **client-centered therapy** is that therapy must create a totally nonthreatening atmosphere in which people can honestly look at and accept themselves and make relevant decisions. More accurate self-awareness and acceptance will in turn lead to the more functional and productive life style of self-actualization.

Thus the humanistic technique created by Rogers (1950, 1961, 1967) allows the client a large role in directing the course of the therapy. For therapy to be effective, the client must perceive the therapist as showing unconditional positive regard, empathy, and genuineness.

Unconditional positive regard is essential to the concept of client-centered therapy. The therapist must consider the client a worthy human being, without qualification. No judgment should be passed, either against or in support of the client's viewpoint or actions. (Rogers referred to this as AT&T, or Attitude of Tentativeness and Tolerance.) The therapist must, however, show a deep faith in the ability of the client to discover the right path to follow. As a result of this unconditional positive regard, clients begin to accept themselves, partly because even when they reveal bizarre or seemingly terrible thoughts, they are still accepted by their therapist.

Unlike psychoanalysis, in which the therapist attempts to observe and analyze the patient's conception of reality, the client-centered therapist *empathizes* with the client's world by trying to enter it and experience it from the same viewpoint as the client. When listening to their clients, therapists make remarks reflecting the emotional content of what is being said. They do this to make sure they are in touch with it, but also to make sure that clients recognize all that they are saying, or the implications of what they're saying. This has been described as mirroring clients' feelings so that they will see all that is there.

Genuineness means that the therapist must establish a human-to-human relationship with the client, not one that could be interpreted by the client as doctor-patient, expert-amateur, or savior-sinner. For Rogers, the therapist must *feel* a genuine concern and empathy for the client in order for therapy to be effective.

Gestalt Therapy

Another humanist approach, **Gestalt therapy,** is largely the work of Frederick (Fritz) Perls (1965, 1969). Like Rogers, Perls believed all people are innately good. Abnormal functioning originates in the denial of this goodness and the blocking of its expression. Ordinarily, in whatever we perceive, whether it be ideas, events, or emotions, we concentrate on only part of our whole experience. We focus on the *figure,* or foreground, and largely ignore the *background* against which the figure appears. If we are holding a conversation with a professor who has rejected a term paper, for example, we concentrate our attention on the conversation and our efforts to defend our work (the foreground) and are only partly aware of our anger and frustration against which this conversation takes place (the background). Perls wanted people to perceive the wholeness, or **Gestalt,** of their experiences. (The concept of Gestalt, or whole perception, was discussed in Chapter 4.)

The purpose of Gestalt therapy is to help people become aware of this wholeness by bringing more of the background into the foreground experience. Great importance is placed on the *here and now.* For Perls, nothing else existed. Therapy encourages people to recognize the immediate experience in its entirety, which means knowing what they are feeling as well as thinking, so that their behavior is in harmony with their whole being. To achieve this goal, they must free themselves from trying to live up to the expectations of others. They must be responsible for their own behavior and recognize their capabilities for self-improvement.

Among the techniques practiced by Gestalt therapists, role playing and projection are used to bring out problems caused by expectations or rules of behavior that were originally applied by parents and other authority figures and that people have internalized. The purpose is to show that these problems are really self-imposed, that they do not result from universal rules that everyone must follow.

In the empty-chair technique, for example, clients are asked to imagine that some person with whom they have an emotionally charged relationship (father, mother, spouse) is sitting in the empty chair opposite them. They then talk to this person about the problems in their relationship and their specific feelings toward that person. Then the client switches chairs and talks as if he or she were the other person speaking—this brings out how clients think other persons see them. The empty-chair technique may also be used to encourage clients to talk to different parts of themselves—to their fears, desires, dreams—and to try to confront their feelings and accept them as part of their total makeup.

Another Gestalt technique is to ask clients to act out the opposite of what they feel. People who feel emotionally unresponsive, for example, would be instructed to react as if they were extremely sensitive and emotionally uninhibited. Through this exercise, Perls felt that clients could discover a very real part of their being that had never been allowed open expression.

Throughout Gestalt therapy, an effort is made to experience feelings, to acknowledge them, and then work toward changing them if necessary. Gestalt concentrates on the present and how people are now, encouraging them to accept themselves as they are and not as they think they should be.

THE COGNITIVE MODEL OF THERAPY

Cognitive therapies start with the assumption that emotional upsets or abnormal patterns of behavior result from what we think (content) or how we think (process), not from what we feel. Even if the problem appears to be one of emotion, behavior, or circumstance, it is our cognitive mediation—our thoughts—that plays the most critical role. Thus cognitive theorists are less concerned with the symptoms than with the thinking process that led to them, and they try to change these thoughts or thinking processes in therapy. The cognitive therapies that are best known are the rational-emotive therapy of Albert Ellis and the cognitive therapy of Aaron Beck. The newest cognitive therapy is called cognitive-behavioral therapy.

Ellis: Rational-Emotive Therapy

Ellis's **rational-emotive therapy (RET)** focuses primarily on thought content: that is, on specific irrational thoughts or assumptions that Ellis says lie at the core of abnormal functioning. This approach, which has been most often applied to problems in anxiety and neurotic functioning, argues that therapy should be directed at pointing out the false beliefs that neurotic persons hold and that lead to their feelings of anxiety. Some of the more common false beliefs at the root of abnormal functioning are the following (Ellis, 1962):

1. I must be loved or approved of by virtually every significant other person around me.
2. I must be thoroughly competent, adequate, and achieving in all possible respects or I can't consider myself worthwhile.
3. Certain people are bad, wicked, or villainous . . . they should be severely punished for it.
4. It is awful and catastrophic when things are not the way I want them to be.

Rational-emotive therapy tries to show the client how to separate rational from irrational thoughts and accept reality. Ellis emphasizes tolerance of oneself, of others, and of inevitable frustration in the real world. Instead of irrationally thinking "I ought to succeed" or "I must succeed," the client learns to accept the rational thought, "It would be better to succeed," or "I may fail in this one thing, but that doesn't mean I'm a total failure."

This requires, in many cases, big changes in one's basic values and beliefs. In leading clients to this change, RET therapists tend to be more active than therapists of some other approaches. Unlike Rogers's client-centered therapy, for example, in RET therapists openly challenge statements that they consider irrational: They don't wait for clients to discover irrationality on their own.

APPLICATION □
Rational-Emotive Therapy

CLIENT: I had another anxiety attack yesterday. I was having lunch with some friends in this really nice restaurant in North Dallas. I felt like I couldn't finish my meal. It was just terrible.

THERAPIST: Okay. Now think back to when you were in the restaurant yesterday, and tell me what you experienced. You know, how you felt and what you were thinking.

CLIENT: Okay. . . . Well, the waiter had just served the main course. I noticed I was really tense. I remember thinking . . . What if I have another panic attack, right here? I might not be able to continue eating. I might even faint. That would be terrible.

THERAPIST: Well, you said that you've never actually fainted in situations like this before. And so my guess is you won't . . . but what if you did? How would it be terrible? Do you mean that you would injure yourself physically or something like that?

CLIENT: No . . . not really. I think I imagine myself, you know, slumped over in my chair. And my friends and everybody else are looking at me, just staring.

THERAPIST: And what are those people thinking?

CLIENT: (*Her eyes begin to tear*) That . . . I can't even have lunch without making an ass of myself . . . that I'm incompetent . . . worthless.

THERAPIST: Okay. Now it looks to me like you think the worst thing that could happen would be that you'd faint. First, that's pretty unlikely, right?

CLIENT: Sure, but what if I *did*?

THERAPIST: Suppose you were in a restaurant and you saw somebody else faint. What would you think about them? Would you judge them to be incompetent and worthless?

CLIENT: I guess I'd think they were, you know, sick. . . . I'd probably try to help them. No . . . I wouldn't think they were . . . bad . . . or worthless. I see what you mean. Maybe they wouldn't ridicule me.

THERAPIST: I think they wouldn't. But *suppose* they did. There you are, slumped in your chair, and you are just regaining consciousness. And everyone in the restaurant . . . your friends . . . everyone . . . they are jeering at you . . . making fun of you. We just agreed that isn't likely to happen, but suppose everybody in the restaurant just happened to behave like purple meanies?

CLIENT: That would be awful . . . I couldn't stand it. I'd just wither up and die.

THERAPIST: You'd literally, physically wither up and die?

CLIENT: Well, when you put it that way . . . I guess not.

(Rimm & Masters, 1979, pp. 383–384)

They give their own personal opinion when asked by clients and, often, when not asked. Instead of occasionally interpreting something, like psychoanalysts, or restating, like Rogerians, they spend a good deal of time telling their clients the way things are and what is wrong with their thinking.

Among the techniques used by RET therapists are role playing and modeling. Both of these techniques may be used in individual sessions or in groups to show clients in what ways their thinking is unrealistic and what the consequences of this irrationality are for their relationships with others and their own self-perceptions.

RET therapists also try to show unconditional acceptance of their clients. Unlike Rogerian therapists, who strive to give unconditional acceptance in a nonjudgmental way, RET therapists will criticize their clients for faulty thinking but still demonstrate that they accept them unconditionally even with their flaws. The hope is that clients can learn to accept themselves in the same unconditional way.

Beck: Cognitive Therapy

Aaron Beck's **cognitive therapy** (1972, 1973, 1975) has been most often applied to the problems of depression. Beck traces depressed patterns to both problematic thoughts and distorted thinking processes. He argues that depressed persons have basic "rules," not unlike Ellis's irrational thoughts or assumptions, that underlie their depression. For example, "It would be terrible if someone else had a low opinion of me," or "Anything less than total success would be a disaster." While Beck does not describe these rules as irrational, he does see them as very limiting because of their arbitrary, extreme, and unyielding nature. These rules give rise to "automatic thoughts"—negative self-verbalizations that pop into a person's head continually throughout the day.

In addition to problematic thoughts (such as the rules and automatic thoughts just described), Beck is concerned with distorted thinking processes, which he says characterize depressed functioning. These distortions in thinking include jumping to conclusions without having enough evidence and overgeneralizing from a single event. Usually these distorted thinking processes help to lock in a negative self-view and view of the future.

Beck's cognitive therapy seeks to reveal and change these rules, automatic thoughts, and distorted thinking processes (without trying to find out how or why they arose). Therapy begins with some tasks that lead the person to experience the joy of success—a pleasure that typically escapes very depressed people. People are assigned a series of tasks within their range of ability. This may start with a very simple task, such as buying some items at a nearby supermarket, and move upward to harder ones. As the person's mood becomes somewhat more elevated in the face of undeniable successes, the therapy becomes more cognitive. Clients are helped to recognize and even record their automatic thoughts. They are taught to evaluate and challenge these thoughts rather than accept them automatically. Through a series of cognitive maneuvers, the person comes to further identify and challenge the rules and style of thinking attached to these automatic thoughts.

The treatment program is expected to significantly improve depressed clients in 20 1-hour sessions. Research suggests that Beck's cognitive viewpoint of depression has its merits (for instance, Beck, Weissman, Lester, & Trexler, 1974), and that this cognitive form of psychotherapy significantly reduces depression and even compares well to the treatment effectiveness of antidepressive medications (Rush, Beck, Kovacs, & Hollon, 1977).

Cognitive-Behavioral Therapy

Cognitive-behavioral therapy represents a fusion of several approaches. Like the humanistic perspective, it emphasizes the important role that people's present contructions of the world play in determining their behavior. Cognitive therapists are also aware of recent theories of the workings of human memory and seek to use these theories to describe how people remember the childhood events that are so important in psychoanalytic theory.

Most importantly, and as its name implies, this approach represents the convergence of behavioral and cognitive models. Many behavioral therapists have moved away from complete reliance on the manipulation of reinforcement contingencies. More and more, these therapists have recognized that a person's learning can be enhanced by explicit focus on the generalizations they draw from their experiences or by observing the behavior of others. In short, a good many behaviorists have become more cognitive in their therapeutic perspective. In recent years, there has been a growing appreciation of the unique and subtle role of cognition and mediation in determining human functioning, including abnormal functioning. The cognitive-behavioral therapists are developing a variety of approaches and techniques for intervening in a wide range of abnormal difficulties. Most of these therapists are research-minded, and their influence in the field is growing rapidly.

OTHER KINDS OF THERAPY:
MIXING THE MODELS

As our discussion of the models of psychotherapy indicates, the field of psychotherapy is indeed varied. The various models of psychotherapy approach abnormal patterns in very different ways. Indeed, even within a given model there is often a diversity of viewpoints and specific approaches. In addition, there are several therapies that do not readily fit into any one model. A case in point is biofeedback.

Biofeedback

Biofeedback training is an approach that has gained notice in recent years. The basic notion of this approach is that anxiety and other discomforts will be lessened if a person can learn to control the bodily responses involved. Experiments have shown that when subjects are given feedback of their present bodily states in the form of audible tones, moving graphs, or dials, they can in turn learn to control such bodily reactions as brain wave pattern, blood pressure, and muscle tension. Since heart rate normally increases as a reaction to fear, for example, people who can be taught to control their heart rate can control their fear.

Biofeedback procedures have been used effectively to deal with hypertension, heartrate arrhythmia, epilepsy, and tension migraine headaches (Runck, 1980). However, it has not always been easy to transfer biofeedback techniques to the world outside the laboratory, where people are subject to the normal tensions of life and cannot be hooked up to the biofeedback device. Amid the activity and stress of a normal work day, for instance, a person may find it hard to remember and to practice the exact techniques used in the laboratory to reduce heartrate. Also, a person who is not hooked up to the feedback device may be unable to tell whether attempts to reduce heartrate and muscle tension have been effective. Perhaps for these reasons, general relaxation training has often proved to be about as effective as more elaborate biofeedback procedures.

One of the most promising future applications of biofeedback is to compensate for accident- or disease-induced neuromotor disability. In such cases there has been deterioration of muscle and motor functioning. It has been suggested that the deterioration occurs because the central nervous system cannot sense the signals that flow back to it from the muscles. The use of biofeedback to amplify the faint signals and to bypass damaged signal pathways may enable the victim to bring muscle movements under voluntary control once again. It is possible to leave miniature feedback devices permanently in place to provide a constant source of feedback information.

Clearly, the biofeedback approach cuts across the biological, learning, and humanistic models. The biological perspective is represented by the focus on the bodily functions as the center of the problem. The learning approach is at the heart of the training program in which direct control over involuntary processes is learned by observation and feedback. The function of biofeedback training as a technique that enables people to get in touch with hidden dimensions of their bodily responses has sometimes led to its classification as a humanistic approach.

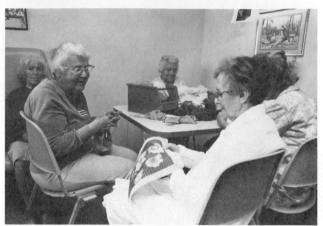

Group therapy takes on many configurations and purposes and also draws on various theories of personality. Although most forms of treatment involve a one-to-one relationship between a client and therapist, group settings often have therapeutic advantages over individual therapy.

Group Therapy

Most of the forms of treatment that we have described involve a one-to-one relationship between client and therapist; that is, a client meets privately with his or her therapist. An alternative format whose popularity has grown in the past few decades is **group therapy,** in which several clients simultaneously meet with a therapist. Obviously, such a format is an efficient use of the therapist's time and is usually cheaper for clients. Moreover, group therapy formats seem to have certain therapeutic advantages over individual therapy. For one thing, members of a group may learn from one another's difficulties. It is sometimes easier to observe oneself by looking at and listening to others. For another, people whose problems have a distinct interpersonal dimension often find the group setting the ideal place to develop the interpersonal skills, perspective, and feelings of relaxation they sorely need.

Groups vary in several ways. First, they differ in membership and makeup. For example, many groups consist of strangers whose problems have something in common. In other group formats, such as the increasingly popular *family therapy* and *couple (marital) therapy groups,* the members are hardly strangers.

Family therapy brings the family members together to work on such issues as communication and interaction. As members become better able to relate to one another, the problems of the family and of individual members should improve significantly. This approach has been particularly helpful in dealing with the problems of children. Working with children alone has often led to only limited success. However, working with them along with their parents and siblings often enables a therapist to deal with children's problems in a more comprehensive and successful way.

This is so, family therapists would assert, because the problems at issue (e.g., anorexia nervosa) are being *shown* by the child but are a *product* of the tensions within the family system. This becomes particularly true in families that do not acknowledge conflicts; the anorexia of a daughter or delinquent behavior of a son deflects attention from more basic conflicts. The therapy, to be successful, must turn attention back to those conflicts and must show how the disorder of the "identified patient" is due to these conflicts rather than to the individual pathology of the patient. Obviously, working with families, with their many problems and channels of interaction, can be a complex task, and family therapists receive special training in family psychotherapy.

Problem-Oriented Approaches

Certain problems are particularly resistant to the application of traditional models or forms of therapy. Sometimes a new form of treatment has emerged just for such a resistant problem. Some examples are (1) self-help approaches for alcoholism and addiction, (2) treatment for problems in sexual dysfunctioning, and (3) suicide prevention.

SELF-HELP APPROACHES: ALCOHOLISM AND ADDICTION.   Traditional therapeutic approaches to alcoholism have had very little success over the years. In 1935 two alcoholic men helped each other recover and began a group known as Alcoholics Anonymous. Today AA is a worldwide organization with thousands of groups and more than a million members. It is primarily a nonprofessional program in which alcoholics, past and present, help one another in one-to-one and group formats. The emphasis is on support, insight, self-acceptance, and spiritual development.

At regular meetings, problem drinkers and alcoholics are encouraged to give up their drinking habit and to gain insight into their problems and how to deal with them. Alcoholism is regarded by AA as a physiological disease in which the person's body cannot tolerate alcohol, rather than as a sign of psychological weakness or self-indulgence. AA sees alcoholism, therefore, as a lifelong problem, with the only cure being total abstinence. The effectiveness of the AA approach has not been objectively tested. Obviously, it does not work for all alcoholics. The number it does reach and help, however, is considerable.

SEXUAL DYSFUNCTION.   In recent years, exciting gains have been made in the field of **sexual-dysfunction therapy.** Masters and Johnson, in their influential book *Human Sexual Inadequacy* (1970), suggest that for sexual dysfunctions, 2 causes are predominant: a person's tendency to adopt a spectator role during the act of sexual intercourse, and a person's fear of performing inadequately. By focusing undue attention on *performance* during intercourse, either of these problems can inhibit the normal un–self-conscious enjoyment of sensations that leads to sexual satisfaction.

Even a transitory cause of sexual dysfunction can lead to long-term sexual dysfunction in couples. Suppose an executive is going through a particularly anxious period of his life and uses tranquilizers to get through this time. Certain tranquilizers dull sexual arousal. The effect of the medication, coupled with whatever effect the job anxieties are having on him, may make it difficult for him to maintain an erection. After a few failures, his performance anxieties build up. Unfortunately, almost any way the wife responds may contribute to the problem. If she continues to be physically affectionate, her husband may interpret her manner as a demand for sexual intercourse, a demand he fears he cannot satisfy. His anxieties cause him to give his wife cues to keep her distance. He may develop avoidance patterns—for instance, working so late that his wife is asleep before he comes to bed. Or, if his wife is less affectionate physically in order not to make demands on him, this decrease may be defensively interpreted by the anxious husband as a rejection of his sexually inadequate self.

One can see how these problems might persist long after the specific events that began them have disappeared. Depending on a therapist's perceptions of the background causes of sexual dysfunction, the therapeutic techniques used will vary. The difficulties that many couples experience when talking directly about sex may exacerbate the situation; in such a situation, sex therapists often seek to improve the couple's communication skills about sexual matters. Because of a psychosexual trauma or a set of religious, ethnic, or cultural beliefs, a person may fear sexual intercourse or believe that it is wrong, evil, or not pleasurable. Because of inadequate instruction, a man or a woman may not know how the rather complicated human reproductive system works. Excessive intake of alcohol or physiological problems may hamper sexual performance. Once the therapist identifies what conditions are contributing to the couple's problems, an eclectic set of therapeutic techniques is available.

One element in almost all treatments of sexual dysfunction is anxiety reduction. The visualization techniques of desensitization hierarchies developed by Wolpe (1958) are used, but the therapist also usually arranges desensitization experiences in real sexual encounters between the couple. These real-life anxiety-reduction techniques are often effective in reducing sexual dysfunction, as one might anticipate from the central role of performance anxiety in causing sexual dysfunction. Information about the human reproductive system and the physical aspects of sexual intercourse is also frequently given by sex therapists. Many people know surprisingly little about their sexuality, and education can be very helpful, particularly if it teaches the range of experiences and feelings that are normal aspects of the process. Many other standard therapeutic techniques, often of a cognitive-behavioral sort, are used to explore whatever negative feelings or attitudes might be contributing to the sexual dysfunction. Finally, a medical consultation might be suggested to explore any physiological conditions contributing to the problem.

Fortunately, sexual-dysfunction therapy seems to work. Although evidence from tightly controlled outcome studies is scarce, a great deal of clinical evidence supports this conclusion (Lo Piccolo & Lo Piccolo, 1978). It is interesting to note, too, that sex therapists draw on all the perspectives we have discussed, although the behavioral and cognitive approaches are most central to this type of therapy.

SUICIDE PREVENTION.   Suicide is one of our most serious yet least understood problems. One of the greatest difficulties is that there are a great many myths about suicide that tend to lull relatives, friends, and even professionals into a false sense of security about the likelihood of a particular person committing suicide. The recent increase in suicide attempts and actual suicides has led to the establishment of the suicide-prevention centers around the country. They

Crisis-intervention programs have emerged to help people deal with many types of personal crises. These programs take a variety of forms, but all serve to make a trained person available, either over the phone or in person, to people in distress. The program shown is a suicide prevention one. The person standing is the center director, who has the responsibility for training those who respond to the potential suicide's call.

provide around-the-clock hotline telephone services for people in distress.

A telephone worker at such a center will seek to (1) establish a relationship with the caller and obtain information, (2) clairfy the central problem, (3) assess the potential for suicide, (4) assess the person's strengths and resources, and (5) develop with the person a constructive plan of action, including involvement in an appropriate treatment program.

Suicide-prevention centers typically provide in-person treatment services and personnel for longer-term intervention in addition to the hotline, assessment, and referral service. These centers are staffed by psychiatrists, psychologists, social workers, other professionals, and trained nonprofessionals (paraprofessionals).

These programs have in turn led to the development of **crisis-intervention** programs for a wide range of difficulties. These take different forms, but all serve to make a trained person available, either over the phone or in personal interviews, to help people faced with a crisis. All sorts of problems may be encountered—from floods, accidents, or illness to crises such as desertion by a spouse, sexual anxieties, or abuse of some sort.

THE EFFECTIVENESS OF THERAPY

Over the past few decades, with the emergence of many new approaches to therapy, there has also emerged a debate in which the effectiveness of therapy itself has been questioned. This debate includes questions not only about the effectiveness of therapy in general, but also about how the different forms of therapy compare in terms of effectiveness.

The issue of general therapy effectiveness is a very difficult one for several reasons. First of all, how are we to define success? Is our criterion to be partial change or total change? change in the behavioral, emotional, or cognitive spheres? change seen by the person, the therapist, a friend, or a relative? Second, there are so many forms of therapy that we cannot speak of "therapy" as if it represents a general process. Moreover, there are many different kinds of problems in abnormal functioning, so it is impossible to talk about the general effectiveness of psychotherapy. Furthermore, many other life events have an impact on people while they are involved in therapy. How can we sort out these factors in evaluating the role of therapy?

When we seek to compare the effectiveness of particular therapies, we run into these same questions, plus additional difficulties. A major problem is that the various forms of psychotherapy differ in their definitions of psychotherapy success and goals. Then we are faced with the fact that every therapist practices his or her orientation in at least a slightly different manner. For example, there are many differences in technique and interpretation among psychoanalytic psychotherapists. Similarly, there are many variations among behavioral therapists. How, then, can we confidently compare the effectiveness of psychoanalysis to that of behavioral therapy? Are we comparing processes or therapists? Furthermore, there are many different variables and factors that bear on therapy outcome: different settings, formats, personality factors, and so on. Certainly these will complicate our comparison of the effectiveness of various therapies.

It is not surprising, therefore, that despite a great deal of research over the past few decades, our conclusions about the effectiveness of psychotherapy are still tentative. Here are some of the things we do seem to know:

1. Psychotherapy can be a helpful and effective process for certain problems and individuals (Bergin, 1971; Smith & Glass, 1977).
2. Sometimes psychotherapy will provide no help or even have a negative effect (Eysenck, 1952).
3. Often a spontaneous remission will occur after a period of time whether or not the person has been in therapy. Such improvements may be due to factors in the individual's personal life or to some internal factors.
4. In direct comparisons, the major psychotherapy approaches (psychoanalytic, behavioral, humanistic) often demonstrate similar overall rates of effectiveness (Smith & Glass, 1977; Luborsky, Singer, & Luborsky, 1975).
5. At the same time, some therapy approaches seem superior with specific difficulties (Luborsky & Spence, 1971). For example, the behavioral approach seems most effective with phobias, and the biological approach of antipsychotic medications seems most effective with schizophrenic disorders (May, 1968).

Research efforts in psychotherapy are accelerating, and their results should lead to more effective therapy. We are becoming increasingly aware of the strengths and weaknesses, the similarities and differences, of the various forms of therapy, as well as the key variables of each. One very promising result of this awareness has been a movement to match specific problems and people to specific kinds of therapy and therapists. Of course, if this kind of matching is to become more productive and accurate, we will need much more research.

SUMMARY

1. *Therapy* can be defined as a set of procedures designed to produce positive change in an individual's cognitions, emotions, and behaviors. It involves applying various theories of personality in an effort to reduce or eliminate abnormal behavior.

2. Psychoactive drugs, discovered in the 1950s, had a major effect on the quality of care in public hospitals by making possible outpatient care, reduced inpatient population, and improved treatment prognoses.

3. In the 1960s, the community health movement introduced practices such as: public education about mental health; crisis hotlines; ongoing psychotherapy services; and community treatment centers offering free or inexpensive care.

4. *Psychoanalysis* uses verbal techniques and attempts to solve problems by bringing unconscious conflicts into consciousness where they may be confronted and resolved by the person. Techniques include *free association, interpretation,* and *transference.*

5. The learning model of therapy involves extinguishing maladaptive patterns and learning more appropriate ones. Techniques include *systematic desensitization, implosive therapy, aversive counterconditioning, token economies,* and *modeling.*

6. In the biological model of therapy, the role of treatment is to change the person's biological functioning. This may be done through *chemotherapy* (drugs), *electroshock treatment,* or *psychosurgery.*

7. The humanistic-existential approach to therapy involves an attempt to help people become in touch with their selves and subsequently take charge of their lives and behaviors. Among the various kinds of humanistic-existential therapies are Carl Rogers's *client-centered therapy* and Fritz Perls's *Gestalt therapy.*

8. In cognitive therapies, the focus is on thoughts and thinking processes and how they must be changed. Ellis's *rational-emotive therapy (RET)* attempts to show the client how to separate rational from irrational thoughts and to accept reality through role-playing and modeling techniques. Beck's cognitive therapy attempts to reveal a person's basic "rules" and distorted thinking processes and subsequently change the "rules."

9. Cognitive-behavioral therapy emphasizes the multiple influences on human thinking and behaviors. This approach combines several perspectives and uses a variety of techniques.

10. Problem-oriented approaches to therapy include self-help groups, such as Alcoholics Anonymous; therapist-controlled procedures such as sexual-dysfunction therapy; and suicide-prevention services that mix self-help, peer help, and therapist intervention.

Suggested Readings

BELKIN, G. S. *Contemporary psychotherapies.* Chicago: Rand McNally, 1980. Offers an overview of the many forms of psychotherapy practiced in the United States today and includes a wide range of clinical case studies.

BRODSKY, A., & HARE-MUSTIN, R. (Eds.). *Women and psychotherapy.* New York: Guilford Press, 1980. A book with the general purpose of drawing together the research literature on women and psychotherapy. Topics include gender differences in rates of experiencing various disorders, gender differences in therapeutic process and outcome, and some alternatives to traditional therapeutic approaches to "the problems of women."

ELLIS, A., & GREIGER, R. (Eds.). *Handbook of rational-emotive therapy.* New York: Springer, 1977. A compendium of chapters on rational-emotive therapy, its uses, and its successes. This book includes a chapter by Ellis on the clinical theory underlying the therapy.

GARFIELD, S. L., & BERGIN, A. E. (Eds.). *Handbook of psychotherapy and behavior change* (2nd ed.) New York: John Wiley, 1978. Good appraisal of the research in the field of psychotherapy, with leading theorists focusing on such issues as methodology, psychotherapeutic processes, outcomes, various approaches, and new developments in the field.

HOFFMAN, L. *Foundations of family therapy.* New York: Basic Books, 1981. This book gives a thoughtful presentation of the systems approach to family therapy, often from a historical perspective.

LICHTENSTEIN, E. *Psychotherapy: Approaches and applications.* Monterey, Calif.: Brooks/Cole, 1980. A broad look at psychotherapy, including economic, social, and political influences, with an evaluative framework.

PERLS, F. T. *Gestalt therapy verbatim.* Monterey, Calif.: Real People Press, 1969. Provides a good introduction to Gestalt therapy by the intriguing theorist and therapist who developed this approach.

ROGERS, C. R. *Client-centered therapy.* Boston: Houghton Mifflin, 1951. A comprehensive introduction to the client-centered approach by the originator of this form of therapy.

18. Social Behavior

In this chapter and the next we will be discussing the behavior of individuals interacting with each other and with groups, the content of **social psychology.** As we have seen, psychoanalytic thinking stresses that human actions are often driven by unconscious motives that are inaccessible to the individual and formed by past experience. Social psychologists, like cognitive personality theorists, stress instead the present causes of a person's actions and look for many of those causes in the interpersonal situations in which people find themselves. The constant theme of social psychology concerns the ways in which people perceive the social situations around them, and how they base their actions on these perceptions.

In this chapter we will study how people's attitudes are determined, and how people analyze the motives and intentions of others, and thus become attracted to or aggressive against those other people. In Chapter 19 we will see how individuals join, act in, and are acted upon by the groups in which they find themselves.

ATTRIBUTION

The processes of interpersonal perception have similarities to the general processes of perception discussed in Chapter 4. Like object perception, person perception is a categorical process. That is, the details we perceive about other people—their clothes, their body postures, and so on—lead us to make inferences about the categories to which people belong. The middle-aged person in the coat and tie standing in front of the classroom is the teacher, the young person in blue jeans talking to the teacher is obviously a student, and so on.

Person perception, like object perception, is done by making rapid inferences from fragments of information received by the senses. As with all guessing processes, the perceptual inferencing process can "go wrong" and lead the perceiver to make incorrect categorical decisions. The middle-aged person in the coat and tie may suddenly sit down with the other students, and the person in blue jeans may start lecturing.

In one way, person perception is obviously different from object perception. Unlike rocks, trees, and other physical objects, people have intentions, plans, and personalities. This means that part of the task of perceiving other people is "looking behind" their actions to discover what they are "really like." **Attribution theories** describe the ways in which we go about developing explanations for and interpretations of the actions of others.

The process of attributing characteristics and motives to another person is a complex one, involving interpretation and judgment. Consequently, different perceivers will see a certain person in different and even contradictory ways, because different observers have (1) different experiences with the person, (2) different impressions of the person, (3) different beliefs about the nature of personality, (4) different rules for making attributions, (5) different opportunities to observe the person, or (6) different perspectives on the situation in which they encounter the person. In the following sections we will consider each of these factors in turn.

Experience and Attribution

People may have different experiences with another person because they meet that person in different roles or settings. Students who see a professor only in a large lecture class may attribute some of the inevitably formal nature of that situation to the character of the professor and perceive her as distant, ironic, witty, and pedantic. But the professor's children may see her as close, warm, and relaxed. Her colleagues may have yet a third view of her. The point is that these different perspectives are held by people who have had systematically different experiences with a person and have thereby been led to systematically differing attributions of her personality.

First Impressions and Attribution

It can be expected that the first impressions we form of others will be highly influential in our final impressions of their personalities. An experiment by Luchins (1942) vividly illustrates this. Read the following description and see what impressions you draw about Jim:

> Jim left the house to get some stationery. He walked out into the sun-filled street with two of his friends, basking in the sun as he walked. Jim entered the stationery store, which was full of people. Jim talked with an acquaintance while he waited for the clerk to catch his eye. On his way out, he stopped to chat with a school friend who was just coming into the store. Leaving the store, he walked toward school. On his way out he met the girl to whom he had been introduced the night before. They talked for a short while, and then Jim left for school.
>
> After school Jim left the classroom alone. Leaving the school, he started on his long walk home. The street was filled with brilliant sunshine. Jim walked down the street on the shady side. Coming down the street toward him, he saw the pretty girl whom he had met on the previous evening. Jim crossed the street and entered a candy store. The store was crowded with students, and he noticed a few familiar faces. Jim waited quietly until the counterman caught his eye and then gave his order. Taking his drink, he sat down at a side table. When he had finished his drink he went home.

Why do you think Jim crossed the street? Why did he sit by himself? When Luchins showed subjects these paragraphs, they usually said that Jim crossed the street not to avoid the girl, but to buy something at the store, and that he then sat by himself not because he wanted to be alone, but because he had some work to do. But these interpretations of Jim's actions are caused by people's first impression of Jim as a gregarious person. The first paragraph does indeed describe actions that seem characteristic of an outgoing, extroverted individual. But the actions described in the second paragraph are those of a withdrawn, introverted person. Indeed, when Luchins reversed the order of these two paragraphs, subjects thought Jim was a shy person who avoided contact with other people.

Often, as in this example, the first information received has more influence than that received later, a phenomenon known as the **primacy effect.** Under other circumstances, the last information carries more weight, a phenomenon known as the **recency effect** (see Chapter 7). First impressions of people do tend to stay with us.

Implicit Personality Theories

Social psychologists have recognized that we all have our own implicit personality theories that we apply to people we meet. An implicit personality theory consists of our beliefs about which traits are likely to occur together in people; for example, some people believe that musical ability and a sense of humor go hand in hand, or that someone who does not look you straight in the eyes is bound to be generally untrustworthy.

Because of this, different people can make very different judgments about the same individual, for two reasons: Either their first impressions differ, or their different implicit personality theories cause them to come to different conclusions based on the same first impression.

Attribution Rules

Sometimes our implicit personality theories don't help us—for instance, in a case in which we are able to observe only one action of another person and yet need to make a judgment about what the person is like from this scanty information. When, for example, do we conclude that a kind action means that the person who commits that action is kind? Jones and Davis (1965) pointed out that we learn relatively little from the socially desirable actions of a person. We cannot tell if someone who makes cheerful conversation when we meet him or her for the first time really likes us or is just fulfilling social norms of politeness. However, an unusual, unexpected, or inappropriate behavior is assumed to reflect an intention by an individual to act in that way. We infer that the person had an intention that corresponded to the choice of behavior.

Attributions from Multiple Observations

The attribution rules we have just discussed are those we use to infer a person's momentary intentions and enduring personality characteristics from a single action. But we are able to learn a lot more about other people by observing not one but many of their actions. Kelley (1967) has proposed a set of rules that people use in determining the meaning of a set of observations of another person's actions. When, for example, we observe changes in a person's behavior, we ask ourselves what changes in circumstances might be the cause.

Suppose that you see John laughing at a certain comedian. What sorts of information will help you understand *why* John laughed? Kelley (1967) suggests three dimensions around which we organize new information—the actor, the entity or stimulus, and time—and illustrates them with the following example:

Observations of John's behavior over a long period of time give us information about the *consistency* of his response. If John laughs at this comedian every time he sees him, this highly consistent information helps us judge that John really likes the comedian. If John laughs one time but not the next, this inconsistency may lead us to different conclusions.

Distinctiveness information refers to a person's reaction to similar entities or stimuli. Does John laugh at all comedians? If he does, then his behavior shows low distinctiveness, because it does not vary from one comedian to the next. His reaction, then, would not be distinctive to just this comedian.

Consensus information refers to a similar reaction by many actors to one entity. If John laughs at the comedian and everyone else does too (high consensus information), then we conclude that John's reaction is not unique; the comedian is genuinely funny.

Kelley next suggested that certain patterns of these three kinds of information lead naturally to certain kinds of conclusions. For instance the combination of high consistency, low distinctiveness, and low consensus information

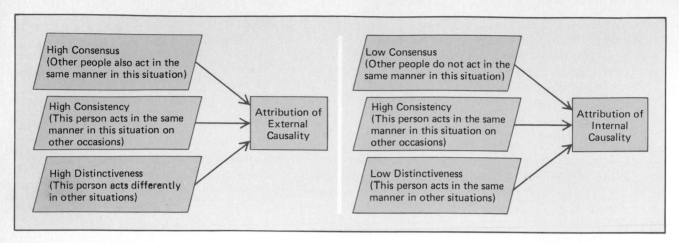

FIGURE 18–1 KELLEY'S THEORY OF
ATTRIBUTION FROM MULTIPLE
OBSERVATIONS
*The combination of high consistency, low
distinctiveness, and low consensus information
usually leads to an attribution of internal
causality—an attribution about the actor.
High consistency, high consensus, and high
distinctiveness lead to an attribution of
external causality—an attribution about the
entity or stimulus.*

leads to an attribution about the actor (see Figure 18–1). If John always (high consistency) laughs at any and all comedians (low distinctiveness), even when other people don't (low consensus), then we know something about John, namely that he is a fool for comedians. On the other hand, high consistency and high consensus information lead to another type of attribution. That is, if everybody (high consensus) always (high consistency) laughs at a particular comedian, particularly if there are some other comedians at whom they don't laugh (high distinctiveness), then we know that the comedian (the entity) is indeed very funny—but this tells us nothing in particular about John. The results of several studies (McArthur, 1972; Karaz & Perlman, 1975; Ruble & Feldman, 1976) generally confirm Kelley's suggestions about the attribution rules used by most of us, with some interesting extensions we will discuss below.

Individual Perspectives and Attribution

Sometimes a difference in the perspective from which people view an exchange between others leads them to make systematically different attributions about the role of the participants in the exchange. For instance, Taylor and Fiske (1975) showed that the physical perspective from which an observer witnessed a discussion led to different attributions of the contributions to the discussion of the different participants (see Figure 18–2). Apparently, the focus of our attention in a situation determines to some extent the attributions we make about the participants.

The Consequences of Attributions: Social Interactions

Attributional theories describe the ways in which people perceive the behavior of other people and interpret the meanings of events and interactions. This is a sufficiently fascinating problem to warrant paying attention to attribution research, but there is another reason as well, and that reason may be even more important: Our interpretation of the personalities of others, and the meanings we assign to the acts of others, determine our behavior toward them. In other words, our attributions guide our social interactions. We act toward people on the basis of our interpretation of their actions, and some important social consequences flow from this fact (Darley & Fazio, 1980).

PERCEPTUAL CONFIRMATION EFFECTS.   First, when we make judgments about a person over whom we have power, we assign that person to the treatments that our judgments imply are correct. We punish a child, hire or fire a worker, or make a friend miserable on the basis of our attributions of their behaviors. To the extent that our judgments are inaccurate because they are based in biases in the attribution process, then our treatments of those individuals will be flawed.

One researcher (Rist, 1970), who observed the treatment of children when they entered school for the first time, has provided poignant documentation of this. In the first few days the kindergarten teacher assigned each child to one of three tables. The table groupings were apparently based on such things as the children's grooming and the cleanliness of their clothes, whether they were from "intact" or "broken" homes, and whether their families were on welfare. With no test results in the children's files, the teacher used their appearances and caseworker reports to make attributions about their maturity and ability to learn.

As you might surmise, Table 1 got more of the teacher's attention and more intensive training in reading and mathematics than Tables 2 or 3. For example, when the teacher was working at Table 1, children from Table 3 worked in workbooks or on assignments. If they had a question, the teacher kept them waiting until she finished with Table 1, but when she was working with the Table 3 children she was more likely to accept interruptions by Table 1 students.

Follow-up observations showed that, as those students moved through the school sytem, they continued to be grouped and treated on the basis of their initial table assignments: Most of the Table 1 children were at Table A in the first grade and the "tiger's table" in the second grade, whereas the children from Table 3 went to Table C and then to the "clown's table."

In our society, judgments about people that can have lifelong effects on them are made every day. A judge decides which delinquent is a prospect for rehabilitation and which one is "incorrigible" and then sentences them accordingly. A psychiatrist decides which mentally ill patients will benefit from

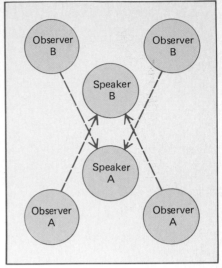

FIGURE 18–2

Observers watched Speaker A and Speaker B in conversation. "A" observers, who paid more attention to Speaker A because of the location of their seats, believed that Speaker A set the tone of the conversation and chose the conversational topics. "B" observers, whose field of vision was focused on Speaker B, thought B had more to do than A with choosing the topics and setting the tone. In actuality, both speakers were following a script that gave each equal conversational control. The results of this experiment suggest that one's physical point of view determines one's causal attributions. (Adapted from Taylor & Fiske, 1975)

Rist (1972) has demonstrated that a teacher's erroneous attributions about young children's maturity and ability to learn can have serious long-term effects.

Distorted and Biased Attributions

As might be expected, people are not perfectly accurate "attributors." Indeed, the attribution process has been found to be skewed by several different kinds of misperceptions. These systematic biases are of practical significance as well as being theoretically intriguing.

THE FUNDAMENTAL ATTRIBUTION ERROR

Reviewing many studies, Jones (1979) concluded that when people judge the behavior of others, they generally attribute the causes of behavior to those who take action, rather than to the situations in which they are involved. Since this error occurred in experiments in which there was an independent definition of the accurate attribution, this person-attribution bias is clearly an attribution *error*. Because of its central theoretical character, it is called the **fundamental attribution error** (Ross, 1977).

Consider the following circumstances: A college student is asked to write a speech that happens to be contrary to his true beliefs. He might be personally in favor of establishing coeducation at a men's college, but a coin toss has determined that he is to write a speech in favor of staying in an all-men's college. But (and this is the important part) he is given plenty of good reasons for taking this position: For instance, it is necessary to have speeches on both sides of the issue, the topic assignment was fairly made by a coin toss, and so on. In these circumstances, people usually are willing to write a speech even if it goes against their own beliefs. Since we know the student was under pressure, we would not expect the speech he wrote to tell us about his true beliefs. But even when observers are told that the position advocated in the speech was assigned by a coin flip, and told all of the reasons that compelled the student to go along with his assignment, the observers still falsely believe that the true underlying opinion is somehow reflected in the speech, and they rate the writer as having beliefs that are consistent with the speech.

The social implications of the fundamental attribution error are interesting to contemplate. It is as if we attempt to control our complex world by overestimating people's ability to determine their own behavior and the outcomes of their acts. A primary school teacher, for instance, may decide that a child's poor performance on an arithmetic quiz indicates poor arithmetic ability rather than considering the possibility that the child is temporarily distracted by some event taking place at home, such as the birth of a new sibling. Or a person observing the angry response of a worker may, not knowing the cause of her anger, conclude that the worker is a hostile and cantankerous person.

THE "JUST WORLD" BELIEF

Another general tendency that leads to attributional bias involves our desire to believe in a just world: We want, for instance, to believe that victims of horrible events must have done something to deserve their fate, because such explanations preserve our ability to believe that people generally receive fair and equitable treatment (Lerner, Miller, & Holmes, 1975). This tendency to see the world as we would like it to be may explain the "blame the victim" phenomenon. Thus, poor people are often categorized as "shiftless," and women who have been raped are

psychotherapy as outpatients and which are to be confined to a state hospital. The attributor has the power to assign the perceived individual to a treatment that may make the first impressions come to be true. These are the processes that sociologists discuss under the heading of "labeling effects" (Gove, 1975) and are akin to the self-fulfilling prophecy, which we will discuss in the following section.

Self-Fulfilling Prophecies

Our initial attributions about other people can cause us to have certain expectations about them. For instance, many people expect mental patients to behave in weird and hostile ways. Suppose such a person then discovers that a co-worker was briefly hospitalized for mental illness. Last week he acted in a friendly way toward her, and even invited her to lunch. This week, because of this expectation, he acts toward her in a cautious and guarded distant way, although he may even be aware that he is doing so. When his co-worker reciprocates his lunch invitation, he panics and makes up excuses not to go. The co-worker becomes aware that this person has begun to act differently

frequently said to have acted enticingly. In some cases this is a form of the general attribution error; the causality for the event is attributed to the person rather than to the surrounding situation. For other cases though, it is more. Both the victim and the attacker are persons, and therefore the fundamental attribution error does not suggest to whom causality will be assigned; while the just world rule does: Causality is assigned to some past bad action or enduring negative characteristic of the victim, so that the rest of us can continue our belief that such things will not happen to us.

THE PERSPECTIVE BIAS

As we have noted in the text, a person's perspective can and often will influence that individual's attributional interpretations of a situation. "Perspective" can mean the physical position from which an observer witnesses an interaction, but it can also have the more general meaning of "point of view." In one experiment, subjects were told they would perform a task as workers or as supervisors. While waiting for the task to be assigned, they witnessed an incident in which a "supervisor" bumped into a table, which tipped over an elaborate construction built by a "worker." As a consequence, the worker would not get paid for his efforts. Subjects who anticipated taking the job of worker blamed the supervisor for the accident. But subjects who believed they would be supervisors blamed the experimenter for having a set-up so flimsy that it led to accidents (Chaikin & Darley, 1973).

We have seen that a person's perception of others is guided by implicit theories of personality and subjected to several biases. If the perceiver is completely rational, as objective as a scientist, taking all the time necessary to come to a perfectly accurate picture of others, then these discoveries imply that perceptions are bound to be inaccurate. However, the perfect perceivers who wait for all the information to be in before making a decision are likely to find life's events passing them by and the time for making the decision long past. Increasingly, social psychologists are realizing that people do not need to be *perfect* decision makers but *efficient* ones. Viewed from this perspective, the existence of widespread and systematic biases does not necessarily mean that people are poor judges of the world around them. Indeed, quite the opposite is generally true.

First, a point-of-view bias is not necessarily irrational; it may in fact be based on accurate information. As a parent I am of course *motivated* to see my child as having high ability, but I also have a great deal of information about what sort of math problems she can do, what French lessons she has completed, and so on. So when she does poorly on a test I will use all of the other information I have to discount this test result to maintain my perceptions of her high ability. A stranger, seeing only the test result, can decide the child has low ability. The difference in our attributions may not simply be due to the fact that our motivations lead us to opposing perceptions. Rather, we have access to different sources of information that lead to different conclusions.

Second, to say that "biases determine perceptions" is true—but only up to a point. It does not mean that people interpret situations in ways that have no relation to reality. Numerous studies make clear that people are quite accurate perceivers of the social world around them, even when they might prefer to see things otherwise.

and distantly toward her and becomes quite angry, for as far as she can see, she has done nothing to deserve this sudden cold treatment. She may respond in kind, and the situation may escalate until, perhaps, harsh words are exchanged.

So the interaction ends. But notice how it ends from the perspective of the first individual. He is convinced that he is right about former mental patients, and he now has one more case to prove it. But in fact it was his own expectations, translated into actions, that caused his "prophecy" to be "fulfilled."

In the course of our own interactions, it seems to us that we are simply responding to the actions of others, and it is hard to see that our expectations about them can channel the interaction. A careful and important experiment demonstrated this effect (Snyder, Tanke, & Berscheid, 1977). Men students who were to have a get-acquainted telephone conversation with a woman student were first shown a photograph of her. The researchers had arranged that some of the men would see a picture of an attractive woman, while others would see a plain-looking woman. Questioning revealed that the men who expected to talk to the attractive woman thought she would be poised, humor-

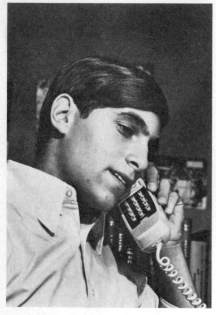

Although we generally believe that we respond to the actions of others in the course of our interactions with them, Snyder, Tanke, and Berscheid (1974) vividly demonstrated how our initial expectations of others can determine our interactions with them.

ous, and socially adept, while those who expected to talk to the unattractive woman thought she would be awkward, serious, and socially inept.

The women whom the men actually spoke to were not those whose photos they had seen and were in fact of equal attractiveness. But those men who believed the woman to be attractive carried on animated, warm, friendly, and humorous conversations with her. Not surprisingly, she responded in a similar way. But those men who conversed with a woman they believed to be plain had colder, less interesting, and more reserved conversations, and the women to whom they spoke gave cool, aloof, and distant responses. Thus the men's stereotypes were confirmed: Those women thought to be attractive were indeed more socially adept, but not because they were so by nature. They seemed more poised and sociable because the men's conversations created the opportunities for them to be so. But the men emerged from the conversations convinced that the women were as they seemed to be. Interestingly, observers agreed with them. People who listened to taped recordings of the women's side of the conversations judged that those women who had been randomly labeled as attractive were more socially adept than those who were originally identified by a less attractive photograph.

Other researchers have shown that women's stereotypes of men can also shape the interaction (Anderson & Bem, 1981). Studies in the work place have shown that instructors who are told that workers labeled at random as having high aptitude learn faster and perform better on objective tests after being trained by instructors with these originally false expectations. These and other studies confirm the wide influence of self-fulfilling prophecies on our daily lives.

Stereotypes and Prejudice

Stereotypes are assumptions we make about people on the basis of their membership in a group. For example, a stereotyped view of women is that they are emotional, talkative, prone to hysteria, and bad drivers. Negative stereotypes can obviously be quite damaging. First, they usually are excessively negative. Second, they often are erroneously attributed to individuals who are members of the stereotyped group, without regard for their individuality.

One source of stereotypes is our tendency to pay more attention to the similarities between ourselves and members of groups to which we belong and more attention to the differences between ourselves and members of groups to which we do not belong (Wilder & Allen, 1978). This tendency to focus on the dissimilarity of outgroup members probably encourages the formation of negative stereotypes.

A second source of stereotypes comes from our tendency to form illusory correlations (Chapman, 1967). Two things are correlated when they appear or occur together, and most stereotypes are actually assumed correlations. For example, the stereotyped belief that the Welsh are good singers implies that if a man is of Welsh descent, he is probably a good singer. In forming such correlations we are disproportionately influenced by distinctive or unusual events. Unusual personal characteristics such as skin color or physical deformity draw our attention (Langer, Taylor, Fiske, & Chanowitz, 1976). Unusual behaviors, particularly negative ones, also draw our attention. Hamilton and Gifford (1976) found that people overestimate the extent to which unusual group membership and unusual behavior go together. Even when such pairings are actually quite infrequent, the combination of unusual personal characteristics and unusual behavior is so memorable that it is difficult to avoid overestimating the extent to which they go together and thus to avoid forming a negative stereotype. In a sense, then, stereotypes are implicit personality theories "run wild," formed on the basis of limited evidence and too frequently applied to broad groups of individuals.

Just like any attributions, stereotypes can become the basis for self-fulfilling prophecies that can further damage the stereotyped individual. If a school system tester believes that Mexican-Americans are not intelligent, she may assign a Mexican-American child to a lower grade level than the child's age would suggest. Pushed only as fast as the rest of the children in that grade, the child may not ever catch up with his age group. Moreover, if the teacher shares the stereotype, the Mexican-American child may get relatively little of the teacher's teaching energies. Bored and frustrated, the child may become a behavior problem and his or her education may further suffer. To others, the child will certainly end up looking like a person of low abilities and intelligence. As we will see later, such a child may even come to believe that about himself or herself.

Ward, Zanna, and Cooper (1977) demonstrated experimentally the ways in which racial stereotypes can lead to destructive self-fulfilling prophecies in a job interview.

ATTITUDE FORMATION AND CHANGE

As we have seen, attributional theories are concerned with the ways in which we make inferences about other people's behavior. Social psychologists have also been concerned with another, similar, problem: how people form attitudes about objects, groups (such as political parties), issues (such as capital punishment), and events. An **attitude** is a broad general disposition to react a certain way to categories of events, objects, or persons.

Classically, attitudes have been thought to have several components: The first is **evaluation.** We are all generally able to say how favorably or unfavorably disposed we are toward things, how good or bad we think certain politicians are, and so on. A second component involves our cognitions or beliefs about the facts pertaining to the person, event, or object—for instance, what do we think are the planks of the 1984 Democratic Party platform, or what was the sequence of events that led up to a favored team losing the big game? The third component is the set of actions that we believe are appropriate toward the attitudinal object. Two people may have the same evaluation of, for instance, a political candidate, but have very different guidelines for acting in regard to that candidate. One person may feel obliged, if the weather isn't too bad, to go to the polls to vote for the candidate. But another may feel obliged to help campaign for the candidate.

The Formation of Attitudes

Some of our attitudes are formed by direct contact and experience with the attitudinal object. A person reads a party platform or spends time with a person, or a child has a chance to play with a new toy at a friend's house. Other attitudes are formed more indirectly. A person reads about a party platform in a news magazine or hears a friend's opinion of another person, or a child sees a television advertisement for a toy. As researchers (Fazio & Zanna, 1981, p. 185) have shown, directly and indirectly formed attitudes may be held with apparently equal intensity. Attitudes formed through direct experience, however, are more clearly defined, held with greater certainty, more stable over time, and more resistant to counterinfluence than attitudes that are formed indirectly.

Attitude Change

Attempts to change people's attitudes are widespread in modern life. Millions of dollars are spent on attempting to convince us that Brand X is better, less expensive, and more effective than Brand Y or Brand Z. In a depressingly similar fashion, millions more are spent to convince us that Candidate X is better, less expensive, and more effective than Candidate Y or Candidate Z. What factors about a communication cause changes in attitudes? The first investigators to systematically study attitude change (Hovland et al., 1949; Hovland, Janis, & Kelley, 1953) formulated a remarkably succinct categorization of these factors: "*Who* says *what,* to *whom,* and with what effect?" In other words, the factors that cause attitude change fall into three categories: aspects of the person doing the communicating, aspects of the communication message itself, and aspects of the audience receiving the communication.

Aspects of the Communicator

In different experiments, many aspects of the communicator have been found to affect the changes in attitudes brought about by a communication. There is evidence that the attractiveness, prestige, power, trustworthiness, and expertise of a communicator increase the persuasiveness of a communication. Among the first variables psychologists examined were the expertise and prestige—the credibility—of the communicator. Hovland and Weiss (1951) gave subjects four communications, each of which was attributed to a source that was either very credible or not very credible. For example, a message about the feasibility of building atomic submarines was attributed either to Robert Oppenheimer, an eminent American physicist (high credibility), or to *Pravda,* a Soviet newspaper (low credibility). After receiving the message, subjects reported their attitudes toward the issues that had been presented. The messages attributed to the highly credible sources proved significantly more effective in changing subjects' attitudes than those attributed to the low-credibility sources. These results are compatible with the intuitive belief that a source perceived as prestigious, knowledgeable, and expert in a given field will have more influence than a negatively perceived source.

While some communicators may be perceived as trustworthy in general, all are seen as more trustworthy when they argue for a position that is against their own self-interest. The listener seems to reason that "if even *this* person sees X as true, then it really must be true." This perhaps explains why, at election time, advertisements appear signed by "Democrats for Reagan" or "Republicans for Kennedy," or why advertisements show a "former user of Brand Y detergent" throwing it away to use new improved Brand X. For slightly different reasons, expertise may have certain limits; a physicist may have expertise about nuclear weapons, and therefore be persuasive on issues related to that, but would not be more persuasive about such an unrelated topic as the relative merits of pro football quarterbacks.

Aspects of the Communication

What factors in a communication or message make it persuasive? Among the characteristics that psychologists have found effective are the logical content of the communication (Wyer & Goldberg, 1970), its comprehensibility (Eagly, 1974), its presentation of only one side of an issue or inclusion of arguments for both sides, and the degree of fear that it arouses.

ONE-SIDED VERSUS TWO-SIDED COMMUNICATIONS.   One issue that confronts a speaker trying to influence an audience is whether to present only *one* side of the issue or whether to include points from the opposite side and then refute them. The classic study examining the effectiveness of one-sided versus two-sided communications was conducted in response to a serious problem. In early 1945, Germany had lost the Battle of the Bulge, and the European war was nearing an end. The Allied command, therefore, began to concentrate more heavily on the war in the Pacific. There was, however, a morale problem among the soldiers. The troops stationed in Europe were tired of war and wanted to go home, and yet months of war with Japan lay ahead of them. In order to solve this problem, Army psychologists prepared radio broadcasts designed to persuade soldiers that the war in the Pacific theater would not be over soon, as the soldiers wished to believe, but that victory was attainable within 2 years.

In studying the Army's problem, psychologists (Hovland et al., 1949) saw the opportunity to examine the one-sided versus two-sided communication question. Two radio programs were prepared. One script presented only reasons for expecting another 2 years of war with Japan (one-sided); the other script presented the same reasons plus contradictory reasons for why the United States might win the war more quickly (two-sided). The experimental question was whether there would be a persuasion advantage in trying to give an impression of fairness through the two-sided communication, or whether it would be a disadvantage to publicize contradictory ideas.

Several hundred soldiers were divided into 2 experimental groups and 1 control group. Their initial opinions about the probable duration of the war with Japan were determined in a survey. The soldiers then heard 1 of the 2 radio broadcasts, after which their attitudes were measured again. The control group, which did not hear either broadcast, also responded to both attitude surveys. In this way, the researchers could determine whether any observed changes in attitudes were due to the radio broadcasts or to other events that might occur at that time.

Before listening to the broadcast, about 37 percent of the subjects in all 3 groups estimated that it would take 18 months or longer to win the war. On the second questionnaire, about the same amount (34 percent) of the control group made the same estimate. The experimental groups, however, showed significantly more attitude change than the control group. Fifty-nine percent of the soldiers in *both* the one-sided and two-sided communication conditions made the 18-month-or-longer estimate. Thus, the persuasive communications significantly altered the soldiers' attitudes about the duration of the war, but whether the broadcasts presented one or two sides of the issue did not appear to make a difference in the amount of attitude change.

Intrigued by this finding, Hovland examined the data in terms of the soldiers' initial opinions on the probable duration of war with Japan. They found that soldiers whose initial attitudes were in *opposition* to the point of view

FIGURE 18–3

Effects of one-sided versus two-sided communications on those who initially agreed with the point of view of the communicator and those who initially disagreed. (Adapted from Hovland et al., 1949)

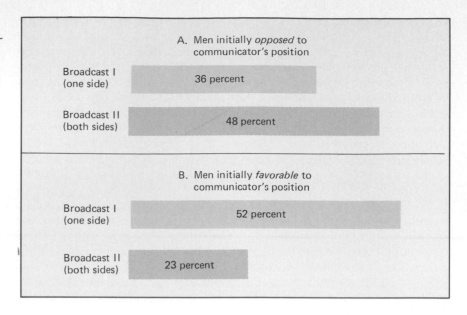

A. Men initially *opposed* to communicator's position

Broadcast I (one side): 36 percent

Broadcast II (both sides): 48 percent

B. Men initially *favorable* to communicator's position

Broadcast I (one side): 52 percent

Broadcast II (both sides): 23 percent

expressed in the broadcast showed more attitude change when they heard the *two-sided* instead of the one-sided communication. These soldiers were obviously very much aware that there were two sides to the issue, and the one-sided communication probably struck them as too blatant an attempt at persuasion. On the other hand, the two-sided communication mentioned those points that the soldiers supported, but stressed the evidence for the other side. For those soldiers who initially *agreed* with the viewpoint of the broadcast, the *one-sided* communication was more effective in further strengthening their attitudes. These soldiers, already in agreement with the Army's position, probably began to doubt the correctness of their opinions when they heard the other side of the issue discussed in the two-sided communication. The one-sided communication, on the other hand, provided them with more reasons to support their already formed attitudes, and presented no discordant ideas (see Figure 18–3).

Aspects of the Listener

Our discussion of the communication or message itself has suggested that even the most carefully constructed message may not have its intended effect because of particular characteristics of the listener. For example, we have seen in the study by Hovland et al. (1949) that the prior opinions of the audience interact very strongly with the one-sided or two-sided manipulation of the communication. What other aspects of the listener affect attitude formation and change?

INTELLIGENCE, EDUCATION, AND SELF-ESTEEM.   Probably many people believe that a highly intelligent person would be more difficult to persuade than a person of low intelligence. However, several studies conducted by Hovland and his colleagues (Hovland & Janis, 1959; Hovland & Mandell, 1952) failed to find any reliable relationship between intelligence and a resistance to persuasion. Hovland et al. (1949) did find evidence for an interesting relationship between amount of education and attitude change. They examined their data from the one-sided versus two-sided communication study in terms of the soldiers' educational background and found that the two-sided communication was more effective with better educated soldiers, while the one-sided communication was more effective with less educated soldiers. Miller and Buckhout (1973) hypothesize that the educated soldiers acquired habits of thought during their schooling that made them more resistant to the one-sided presentation. The less educated soldiers, on the other hand, were not as critical in their reception of the message and thus were more impressed by the supporting evidence of the one-sided presentation.

Communication outside the Laboratory

The communication variables we have been discussing have been effective in influencing attitude change in an experimental setting. What variables affect attitude change in the real world beyond the laboratory? There seem to be at least two—the audience selection effect and the diffusion of communication through a two-step process.

AUDIENCE SELECTION EFFECT.   In a controlled experimental setting, researchers can ensure that the people serving as subjects attend completely to the communication without any distraction. Outside the laboratory, on the other hand, distractions are always present, and speakers can rarely expect that their message will receive the total attention of their audience. More importantly, in the experimental setting each and every subject is fully exposed to the message. In the real world, however, people tend to listen to messages they agree with and to shun persuasive communications that argue for the other side of the issue. This is called the **audience selection effect.** For example, a person who believes that capital punishment is an effective deterrent to crime will pass over a newspaper editorial or change the television channel when someone is writing or speaking against capital punishment. Thus, the people who choose not to expose themselves to a communication can be highly biased; unfortunately, this is often the very audience that persuasive speakers try to reach.

MEN VERSUS WOMEN.   An enduring question is whether women are more easily persuaded than men. An early study by Janis and Field (1959) found that women were indeed more easily persuaded, which the researchers attributed to stereotyped sex differences in female and male roles—men are raised to

The audience selection effect *describes the tendency of listeners to attend to messages they agree with and shun persuasive communications that argue for the other side of an issue.*

be relatively independent thinkers, they reasoned, while women are raised to be submissive and to yield to social influence. These early studies helped establish a belief in the greater persuasibility of women.

One explanation of this finding was that the subjects of the speech, such as the technical feasibility of nuclear submarines, were generally issues about which men were better informed than women. It is known that people are less persuasible on issues about which they are informed, so the observed difference in persuasibility between men and women might be a consequence of this underlying difference.

Plausible though this idea seems, Eagly and Carli (1981) could find no evidence of it. Instead, they found that experiments run by male researchers tended to show that women were more readily persuaded, whereas experiments run by female researchers found no differences in persuasibility between men and women! A number of explanations for this occur to the reader: For instance, the male experimenters, who did many of the earlier studies, may have expected women to be more persuasible, which may somehow have been conveyed to the subjects and affected the experimental results. Whatever the reason, further research is needed to clarify this finding. Meanwhile, the result reminds us that experiments are, among other things, social interactions between subject and experimenter and therefore influenced by all of the complex factors present in any social interaction.

DIFFUSION OF COMMUNICATION.   In an experimental setting, subjects sit alone, respond to an attitude questionnaire, are given a persuasive communication, and then respond to another questionnaire. Comparison of the "before" and "after" questionnaires indicates the shift in attitudes. In the real world, attitude change takes place in less artificial, and much more social, settings. People discuss and exchange information, and by so doing, influence and are influenced by those around them. Katz and Lazarsfeld (1955) have studied attitude formation and change in many real-world issues such as voting in an election. They have found that people tend to vote the same way their family, friends, or fellow employees vote. They found also that certain individuals in these formal or informal groups of people exert a particularly great influence on the attitudes of others. These "opinion leaders" were found at all occupational and socioeconomic levels of society and did not necessarily have the characteristics we usually think of as belonging to a leader. Furthermore, opinion leadership does not seem to be a personality trait that some people have and others do not; different people are opinion leaders in regard to different topics or issues. Thus, there is a two-step process by which information gets spread in a population: Ideas flow from the media and other sources to opinion leaders, and from opinion leaders to the less active sections of the population (Katz & Lazarsfeld, 1955).

Do Attitudes Cause Behavior?

It seems logical to assume that attitudes do guide behavior, and that if we know a person's attitudes, we can predict how that person will behave. But this logical assumption was called into question by one of the earliest attitude-behavior studies. In fact, a number of experiments over the years have shown that in some instances, attitudes and behaviors have little or nothing to do with each other. In the first of these failures to find a consistent relationship between attitudes and behaviors, LaPiere (1934) reported on his experiences in traveling in the United States with a young Oriental couple. In the course of their travels, LaPiere and his companions stopped at a large number of restaurants and hotels. In only one case was the couple not treated hospitably because of their ethnic origin. However, when LaPiere later measured the attitudes of the owners of the establishments that they had visited, over 90 percent of those who responded were negative—they said that as a matter of policy Orientals would not be served in their establishment. The reported attitudes and the actual behavior seemed to be completely unconnected. The LaPiere study contains many procedural flaws—for example, it is quite likely that the people who answered the attitude questionnaire (i.e., owners) were not the same people who had actually provided service (i.e., waiters, hostesses, and desk clerks). But a number of subsequent investigators have found similar discrepancies between attitudes and behavior. Most recently, Nisbett and Wilson (1977) reported a series of experiments that seem to show that even when people think they have acted on their attitudes, they may really have acted in response to outside influences of which they are completely unaware.

Somewhat surprised by these and other findings of a lack of consistency between attitudes and behavior, psychologists have recently reexamined their thinking and carried out more research on the problem (Ajzen & Fishbein, 1980; Fazio & Zanna, 1981). As a result, the following generalizations can be made:

First, in some circumstances it is inappropriate or undesirable to express certain attitudes. For instance, I may intensely dislike Shakespeare's *Henry IV,* but when my son excitedly tells me that he has been selected to play the lead role in it I will not announce my feelings about the play. Researchers have generally found that constraints imposed by social norms inhibit the expression of inappropriate attitudes (Warner & DeFleur, 1969).

Second, individuals who value being consistent also show a greater tendency to guide their behaviors by their attitudes (Snyder & Tanke, 1976; Zanna, Olson, & Fazio, 1980). Third, attitudes that are based on direct experience relate more closely to behavior than attitudes based on indirect experience; so do more confidently held, well-defined attitudes.

Finally, if the action one wants to predict is very specific, it is better to predict it for attitudes specifically related to that action (Ajzen & Fishbein, 1977). If you want to know whether a person will vote for a particular Democratic candidate, for example, it will help to ask about the voter's attitudes toward Democrats in general, but it will help even more to ask about his attitudes toward that candidate. On the other hand, if you want to predict general behavior patterns, then measure general attitudes: To determine a person's voting pattern in regard to all Democratic candidates, ask about attitudes toward the Democratic Party.

Using the more precise guidelines indicated by these examples instead of the overgeneralized approach tried earlier, recent research has identified consistent relationships between attitudes and behaviors. The consistencies are by no means one-to-one or simple, but they are there. The study of the effects of people's attitudes on their behavior is interesting in its own right, because of the insights it gives us into people's behaviors, and because the findings have practical applications in many areas of modern life.

Behavior Affects Attitudes: Cognitive Dissonance Theory

We have just examined some situations in which attitudes do, or do not, influence a person's behavior. The time has come to put the question in reverse: What effect does behavior have on attitudes?

Much of the research on this question has been stimulated by Leon

Festinger's (1957) theory of **cognitive dissonance,** which attempts to explain what happens when people behave in ways that are contrary to their beliefs or attitudes. The basic elements in Festinger's theory are **cognitions,** or bits of knowledge that we have about the world. When two cognitions are inconsistent—that is, when one thought or cognition contradicts another—a dissonant relationship is said to exist between the two. For example, knowledge that one is a Democrat is dissonant with knowledge that one has just voted for a Republican. According to Festinger, this state of cognitive dissonance produces a psychological tension that a person is motivated to reduce: In other words, having two inconsistent cognitions is unpleasant, and people will find a way to get rid of that unpleasant, dissonant feeling.

How can dissonance be reduced? One way would be to change one or both cognitions to make them less dissonant. Voters, for instance, might convince themselves that they are not rigidly loyal to the Democrats, after all. This strategy had been proposed by others before Festinger (Heider, 1946; Newcomb, 1953). Festinger's contribution, and the real hallmark of cognitive dissonance theory, was to state more explicitly the process by which cognitions are made to become less dissonant, and to express it in terms that could be experimentally tested.

Festinger proposed that certain of our cognitions are more resistant to change than others. For instance, cognitions based on physical reality, such as the knowledge that ice is cold or that you have just eaten spinach, will be particularly difficult to alter. In contrast, cognitions based on opinions and attitudes ("I dislike spinach") are more open to change. Festinger believed that dissonance can be reduced by altering those cognitions that are *least* resistant to change. It is through this process that your behaviors may come to influence your attitudes. Suppose that your behavior (eating spinach) is dissonant with your attitude ("I dislike spinach"). It is difficult to deny that the behavior has occurred; the easier course of action is to bring the attitude into line with the behavior ("Spinach isn't so bad, after all" "I really do like spinach").

Support for these notions came from a now-classic experiment conducted by Festinger and Carlsmith (1959). They recruited subjects for what was supposedly an experiment on task performance. When individual subjects arrived, they were given a series of exceedingly dull, boring tasks to occupy their time. For example, they were required to turn each peg along a number of rows on a pegboard, first a quarter turn to the left, then back a quarter turn to the right. After the tasks were finished the experimenter explained that the actual experiment had to do with mental sets or expectations, which were to be created by a confederate of the experimenter who met subjects before they performed the tasks and convinced them that the tasks were going to be interesting and fun.

Subjects were then told that they were in the *control* condition of the experiment—that is, the condition that assessed task performance without the confederate raising any expectations. At this point the subjects assumed that they had completed the experiment, but in fact the crucial part was yet to come. Acting somewhat perplexed, the experimenter stated that the confederate had yet to arrive for the next subject, who was to be in the "positive expectation" condition. The experimenter then had what appeared to be a flash of insight: Perhaps the present subject could help by filling in as the confederate. All that was required was to convince the next "subject" (actually a confederate of the experimenter) that the tasks were in fact interesting and fun. For this, subjects were offered $1. After complying with the experimenter's request, subjects then indicated their own "true" attitudes toward the tasks on a questionnaire.

Festinger and Carlsmith had created a situation ripe for dissonance arousal. Subjects' behavior in attempting to influence the confederate was clearly dissonant with their original attitudes about the tasks. Moreover, the $1 inducement does not seem enough to justify the behavior (that is, to serve as a supportive cognition). It is unlikely that subjects would change their cognitions about the behavior (they could hardly be persuaded that they hadn't performed the tasks). Dissonance theory would predict a change in the least resistant cognitions (the attitudes toward the tasks), so that they would no longer be inconsistent with the behavior. In other words, subjects should rate the tasks as having actually been interesting. Compared to a second group of subjects, who were paid $20 for attempting to influence the confederate, and a control group, who simply rated the tasks after completing them, subjects in the $1 condition in fact brought their attitudes into line with their behavior and rated the tasks as more interesting (see Table 18–1). Subjects in the $20 condition should have experienced little dissonance in the first place, since the $20, especially in 1959, provided a ready explanation for their behavior.

This finding of greater attitude change with lower incentive has come to be known as the **induced compliance effect,** and has been repeated in numerous other experiments (Cohen, 1962; Zimbardo, Weisenberg, Firestone, & Levy, 1965).

A second line of research has also provided support for cognitive dissonance theory. This is in the area of **effort justification,** which is perhaps best captured by the idea that we learn to like what we have suffered to achieve. The basic notion is that when we expend a great deal of effort for little or no reason, we will experience dissonance. The cognition that we are working hard is dissonant with the knowledge that we are not gaining anything worthwhile by doing it. As with induced compliance, we can reduce the dissonance by bringing our attitude into line with our behavior. In this case, the positive benefits of the activity being undertaken can be elevated to justify the expenditure of effort. Anyone who has encountered (or been) a zealous jogger will probably have a good intuitive understanding of these notions.

Self-Perception and Attitude Change

PERCEIVING OUR OWN BEHAVIOR.   Cognitive-dissonance theory helps us to understand what happens when we act in ways that are inconsistent with our attitudes. But what about those occasions when our actions are consistent with our attitudes? Or when we don't have a particular attitude in the first place? Darryl Bem (1965, 1972) has suggested that we frequently form our beliefs about ourselves, about what we prefer and what our attitudes are, by observing our own behavior in the same way that other people observe us. If, for example, you find yourself doing things that don't require the company of others, you might conclude that you are a "loner."

Of course, others' attributions about our behavior can influence our perceptions of ourselves as well. A comment such as, "You must be a history buff—you keep taking history courses" may make us conclude that what we previously thought of as a pastime is instead a major concern in our life. This is, in fact, the way we learn about ourselves during our growing-up years. If as children we didn't hesitate to greet strangers, our parents might say "What a friendly child you are!" and we would then say to ourselves "I must be a friendly person—Mother said so."

Table 18–1: Attitude Toward the Task.*

Inducement	Attitude
$1	+ 1.35
$20	− 0.5
Control	− .45

*Based on a −5 to +5 scale, where −5 means "extremely boring" and +5 means "extremely interesting."
Festinger and Carlsmith (1959).

But tomorrow this person will choose to run again! Anyone who has ever encountered (or been) a zealous jogger will probably have a good intuitive understanding of effort justification.

PERCEIVING OUR ABILITIES AND COMPETENCIES. Most of us are quite concerned with discovering our abilities. How intelligent are we? how good looking? how socially adept? Much of the information we have about ourselves is acquired through making comparisons with others. Festinger's **social-comparison theory** (1954) addresses this important source of self-knowledge. Two of the central points of this theory have to do with social reality and appropriate sources of comparison. In many ways, we depend on others to help us determine what is right and wrong, correct and incorrect, or good and bad. Particularly in new or ambiguous circumstances, the actions of others help us to define what is real. A student transferring to a new high school learns, by the reaction of other students to his clothes, what are the "right" or "wrong" things to wear to signal the appropriate "cool" personality. But even in school or employment settings, where our performance is evaluated explicitly and such evaluations are communicated in the unmistakable form of grades and salaries, the meaning of such evaluations is not clear until we have compared ourselves with others. For example, a salary increase of 10 percent can be taken as a reward or a punishment, depending on whether your co-workers' raises were generally larger or smaller. We are, then, most interested in comparing ourselves with others who are similar to us in relevant ways. The meaning of your B grade in a college course in English will not be clarified by finding out how your little brother's friend fared in his 7th-grade English quiz. Even within your own class, you will probably be more interested in comparing yourself with other freshmen (if you are a freshman) than with seniors.

Recently social psychologists have turned their attention to the other side of the coin: When do we *not* wish to compare ourselves with others and find out exactly how we measure up?

Jones and Berglas (1978) have coined the term **self-handicapping** to describe some of the ways that individuals strive to protect their self-concepts from negative information. Do you really want to know *for certain* that 40 percent of the people around you are smarter than you are? Would you like to know *exactly* how much other people like you? Jones and Berglas have argued that most of us don't really care to receive unequivocal feedback that might destroy some of our favorite illusions about ourselves. One good way to avoid such unpleasant information is to give ourselves handicaps that can be used as excuses. For example, if you don't study for an examination, then a poor grade does not necessarily imply that you are stupid. Or if you have a hangover or a sore leg when you play tennis, your losses don't have to be taken as an indication of physical inferiority. And if, with such handicaps, you should happen to do well, so much the better; you can take even more pride in your triumph in the face of adversity.

Weiner (1971, 1974) has offered a useful system for classifying the kinds of explanations that people give for their own performances and the performances of others. To illustrate this system, imagine that you have just learned that you received a grade of C on your midterm psychology examination. How might you explain your performance? According to Weiner, you would probably use one or more of the following types of explanations:

1. *Ability:* "I am not too good at this psychology stuff."
2. *Effort:* "I knew I should have studied last night instead of partying."
3. *Task Difficulty:* "That exam was ridiculous—I'll bet most of those psych professors couldn't have done better than a C."

4. *Luck:* "What rotten luck—that professor emphasized all the things I didn't know and didn't ask anything about the stuff I studied."

The first of these attributions is avoided by most of us in the face of failure: ability. The self-handicapping strategies described here are designed to allow us to attribute our bad performances to causes that are not damaging to our self-esteem, such as task difficulty, or luck. Task difficulty or bad luck may be plausible excuses for a poor performance, but they become implausible as explanations for a whole set of poor performances.

CONSTRUCTIVE RELATIONSHIPS—ATTRACTION

What causes people to like each other? Why do we like some people very much and dislike others? Whenever two or more people interact, they form attitudes and opinions about each other. These evaluations combine to determine how much attraction people feel for each other. In between the extremes of passionate love and hatred lies a range of positive and negative evaluations that have pervasive consequences for us all. Where do these evaluations come from?

Liking and Propinquity

There are thousands—perhaps millions—of people in the world whom we could like. Which ones we *do* come to like depends on which ones we meet. Thus, our physical proximity or *propinquity*—nearness—to other people is an important precondition for future liking, because it makes possible the encounter which may begin the liking process. People can come to like one another after encounters due to accidents as various as being assigned to the same section of a course or being placed next to one another in a state police training program in which seating was by alphabetical order (Segal, 1974). Even racial barriers to friendship have crumbled as the propinquity effect takes over (Deutsch & Collins, 1951).

Studies have shown that all of the essentially accidental reasons that bring people together can lead to liking relationships. Why is this so? Propinquity doesn't always work. When it does, it is often because it gives people a chance to discover that they have shared interests, matching opinions, and similar values. As you will read immediately below, these are important determinants of liking. A second reason for the effects of propinquity is more subtle. When people are presented with new situations or conditions they at first react negatively and with feelings of strangeness, but gradually become more familiar with the material and more positively disposed toward it. Think, for example, of what happens when you hear a new song. At first it seems strange and perhaps you don't care for it; but after you have heard it a few times you begin to like it.

It is part of conventional wisdom that birds of a feather flock together. While there is a general tendency to like people who are like us, there are also a number of exceptions to this rule. One obvious one is implied by another piece of conventional wisdom: Opposites attract. Although we like people who are like us, we also may get along better with people who have complementary characteristics.

Liking and Similarity

It is part of conventional wisdom that birds of a feather flock together. In this case, conventional wisdom has been proven correct by a number of experimental studies. As the degree of similarity of attitudes and values held by two

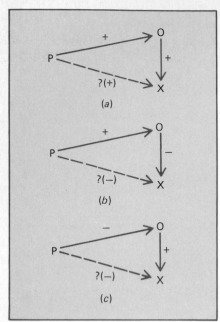

FIGURE 18–4: Balanced
and Unbalanced Triads

So strong is the effect of the balance principle that people often use it as a predictive guide. If I (P) like one person (O), and that person likes another (X), I guess that probably I will like X also (see a). If I like O, and O dislikes X, what am I likely to guess about whether I will like or dislike X? Balance theory suggests, and research shows, that I will expect to dislike X (see b). Extensions of balance theory are also possible: If I disagree violently with the political opinions of person O, and if all I know about candidate X is that he is endorsed by person O, what am I likely to suspect about candidate X's political views? And, therefore, am I likely to vote for candidate X (see c)?

Table 18–2: Means for Liking
the Confederate.

Experimental Condition	Mean
Gain (Negative-positive)	+ 7.67
(Positive-positive)	+ 6.42
(Negative-negative)	+ 2.52
Loss (Positive-negative)	+ 0.87

Aronson and Linder (1965).

people increases, so does the attraction between them (Byrne & Rhamey, 1965). Most of these investigations have been conducted in laboratory settings, in which the degree of apparent similarity can be controlled and manipulated, but there is also evidence of a relationship between similarity and attraction in such varied settings as marriage (Kerckhoff & Davis, 1962) and bomb shelters (Griffitt & Veitch, 1974).

Why do we tend to like similar others? One major explanation employs the principle of cognitive consistency. As we have seen, Festinger's (1957) theory of cognitive dissonance makes it clear that people try to reduce or eliminate inconsistency, and a number of other theorists have observed that people prefer consistency (e.g., Heider, 1958). Newcomb (1956, 1971) has applied the principle of cognitive consistency to interpersonal relationships. According to this **balance theory,** we tend to like relationships that are consistent or balanced. If we are very similar to another person, it "makes sense" (is consistent or balanced) to like that person (see Figure 18–4).

Still another reason why we tend to like similar others is because they reinforce and validate our opinions and values. It is always reassuring and rewarding to discover that another person agrees with you or has similar values (Byrne & Clore, 1970; Lott & Lott, 1968, 1974).

While we have a general tendency to like people who are like us, there are also a number of exceptions to this rule. One obvious one is implied by another piece of conventional wisdom: "Opposites attract." Although we may like people who are like us, we may get along better with people who have complementary characteristics. For example, a person who talks a lot is likely to have some friends who are listeners; a dominant person needs someone to dominate and therefore might be disposed to like submissive acquaintances; a sadist is a natural partner for a masochist. Need complementarity is primarily important in long-term relationships. Kerckhoff and Davis (1962), for example, found that couples in the early stages of a relationship were more likely to move toward forming a permanent relationship when they had similar needs; later in the relationship, however, complementary needs became more important.

The Reciprocation of Liking

A second major determinant of our attraction for another comes from our belief about whether or not that person likes us. Liking tends to be reciprocated. If people obviously like you, then you will probably like them. If people clearly dislike you, you will probably dislike them (Byrne & Rhamey, 1965; Sigall & Aronson, 1969; Tagiuri, Blake, & Bruner, 1953). Being liked by others makes you feel good, but being disliked makes you feel bad. It is not surprising that both liking and disliking are reciprocated (Byrne & Clore, 1970).

You might expect, then, that the more good things Tom says about Bill, the more Bill will like Tom. Similarly, the more critical or disparaging remarks Ann makes about Sue, the less Sue should like Ann. However, a study by Aronson and Lindner (1965) makes it clear that such predictions must be qualified. They found that the *sequence* of liking information can be as important as its positive or negative quality. To become liked by someone who formerly disliked you, or to lose the approval of someone who formerly liked you, has a greater impact than sustained liking or disliking from another person (see Table 18–2).

Liking and Loving

Is romantic love simply a deeper, more extreme form of liking, or does it have different characteristics altogether? Probably, most of us feel that the two emotions are importantly different in kind, and a set of research studies by Rubin (1973) tends to bear this out. First, Rubin invented a large number of statements that could describe one person's feelings toward another person. He then had subjects sort these into two categories: those that were characteristic of loving relationships and those characteristic of liking relationships. There was general agreement on which statements belong in each category: relatively few items were judged by subjects to be descriptive both of loving and of liking relationships. This suggests, first, that people generally agree on descriptions of loving and liking; and second, that these two feelings are described—and experienced—quite differently. Loving seems to involve

feelings of attachment and intimacy, while liking implies a favorable evaluation of the other on such positive characteristics as good judgment and maturity and on what Rubin refers to as the "associated tendency to view the other person as similar to oneself" (1973, p. 217). (Recall our earlier discussion about opinion similarity and liking.)

Rubin brought together couples who reported being deeply in love with each other (as measured by the Rubin scale; see table). They made more eye contact with each other than did members of pairs who were not as much in love, and the more deeply in love they reported being, the more likely they were six months later to report that their relationship had progressed. Interestingly, this last finding was true only for those respondents who believed that love should "conquer all." For those who held a less romantic ideology and who felt that there were considerations of economic gain and social status to be considered in choosing a marriage partner, there was no as-

sociation between depth of love and progress of the relationship toward marriage. Apparently, the effects of love on one's relationship are tempered by one's ideology about the meaning of love for marriage.

Selected Love-Scale and Liking-Scale Items

Love Scale

1. I would do almost anything for _____.
2. I would forgive _____ for practically anything.
3. I feel responsible for _____'s well-being.
4. It would be hard for me to get along without _____.

Liking Scale

1. I think that _____ is unusually well adjusted.
2. I have great confidence in _____'s good judgment.
3. I think that _____ is one of those people who quickly wins respect.
4. _____ is one of the most likable people I know.

Adapted from Rubin, 1973, p. 219.

Physical Attractiveness and Liking

Anyone who has watched television, leafed through a popular magazine, or looked at billboard advertisements knows that our culture values physical attractiveness very highly. Manufacturers spend millions of dollars on advertising for products that are designed to make us look good, and we spend even more millions buying those products. The popularity of diets, exercise clubs, and the latest fashions all attest to our interest in improving our appearance. There is good reason for this great interest in our appearance: A large number of investigations all point to the conclusion that the more physically attractive a person is, the more he or she is liked by others.

Walster, Aronson, Abrahams, and Rottman (1966), for example, measured liking for various partners at a "computer dance" at which each participant was matched with a series of partners of the opposite sex by a computer. A number of personal characteristics of the dance participants were measured in an attempt to discover which would influence liking. The researchers found, however, that the only one that mattered was physical attractiveness. The more physically attractive the partner was, the more he or she was liked.

In addition to being liked, physically attractive people are generally assumed to have a number of more positive qualities than their more average-looking counterparts. For example, Dion, Berscheid, and Walster (1972) showed photographs of attractive and ordinary-looking people to their subjects. The subjects attributed more positive personality traits, greater occupational success, and higher marital competence to the physically attractive people.

The Development of Long-Term Relationships

As you have probably noticed, most of the causes of liking that we have been discussing are those most likely to determine only our initial reactions to other people. Once we have gained a favorable first impression and decided that we like someone, how do we move into short-term early relationships, and then how do such acquaintances develop into long-term, close relationships? A number of psychologists (Levinger, 1974; Levinger & Snoek, 1972; Murstein, 1976) have watched the actual course of long-term relationships as they develop and have reported on the processes that they observed. Levinger (1974) identified three levels of relationships, each level being distinguished from an earlier stage by an increasing degree of interdependence between the participants.

The first level is one of *unilateral awareness* of each other. At this level, the other variables we have discussed have their effects. Proximity creates the possibility of contact. Brief contact, perhaps not even involving the exchange of words, creates the possibility of an assessment of the other's behavior, manners, and looks. Other cues, such as the absence of an engagement ring, signal availability. Manner of dress—trendy or conventional—can tell much about attitudes. At this level of awareness, the attraction one person feels toward another depends largely on the image projected by the other person. Our perceptions of another's image, in turn, depends on the visible characteristics of the other's appearance, filtered through our own conceptualizations of the desirability or attractiveness of those characteristics.

The second level of a relationship is that of *surface contact*. Many of the initial contacts between two people are likely to take place in the settings in which they first encountered each other, and so, quite naturally, their conversation will be formed by these settings and the social role played by each within it. Two people who meet at a political club will begin talking to each other about their candidates and issues. Even when these early conversations are relatively superficial, they create chances for the discovery of similarities—both may, for instance, agree on which issues are more relevant at the time.

It is at this second level that *self-disclosure* begins. Psychologists (Jourard, 1968), have noted that a key component of the process that leads to intimacy involves the mutual sharing of increasingly important and intimate personal information. Generally (Jourard, 1968), one individual tells the other some fact that he considers important about himself, and the other responds by telling a similar confidence about herself that is equally or a little more revealing. In this way, the two people may discover that they have important similar experiences, likes, and dislikes that could not be discovered from the superficial impressions of the first stage. (Or, of course, they may discover that, although their superficial similarities drew them together, the more important things they learn about each other through self-disclosure suggest they are mismatched. In this case the relationship may go no further.)

Self-disclosure between two people marks the beginnings of a relationship that sets them apart from others. All of us have had this experience—and it is quite a wonderful one—of discovering that there is another person who thinks, feels, and experiences the world "just like I do." So, people in this stage generally are motivated to continue their relationship. Each will seek to discover if the other's time and other commitments permit a deepening of the relationship.

Mutuality characterizes the third stage of close relationships. Deeper self-disclosures create greater feelings of intimacy. The two partners, who previously discovered shared attitudes, now come to work out a joint position on new topics. Empathy develops between them; they each become highly aware of how the other feels. Each adapts his or her behavior to decrease actions that might hurt or dissatisfy the other person. In this state, people experience a "we" rather than "I" identification.

The major theme that runs through the three stages in the development of a relationship is *interdependence*. As relationships grow and deepen, the participants come to depend on each other more, and in a greater number of ways: for need gratification, for confirmations of the ways each sees the world, for reward, and for the experiences of being secure and unthreatened within a relationship and of providing that security for another. This sequence describes the development of romantic relationships, but it is true of the ways people develop intimate friendships as well.

Social Exchange in Long-Term Relationships

One theory of long-term relationships suggests that people with attitudinal similarity are able to supply something—in this case confirmation of ideas and attitudes—that is of value to one another. Obviously one reason for liking another is that the other provides one with rewards. One reason people stay together is that they continue to provide rewards for each other. These social-exchange principles, which will be discussd further in Chapter 19, are at work in most interpersonal relationships. In the traditional marriage, for example, the husband was thought to give economic and emotional security to the wife, who because of her dependency valued these commodities. Meanwhile she gave domestic services, children, and sexual favors to the male. This is a nice example of an exchange in which the participants have complementary resources that allow for a satisfactory exchange of rewards. In other words, different people need different things and exchange relationships can become successful and endure because one person can relatively easily give what another person needs. The example also makes it clear that the traditional image of marriage relies on social diagnoses of the needs of men and women which are not valid for many people today and which, indeed, are currently much argued about.

Changes in a person's view of marriage can lead to dissatisfaction. For example, if a traditional woman begins to be more concerned about intellectual and professional goals than about homemaking, she may also become less satisfied. In such cases, the previous situation is viewed less favorably because the person's set of expectations or *comparison level* has changed (Thibaut & Kelley, 1959; Kelley & Thibaut, 1978). If both partners can change together, then a new satisfactory relationship may be established on a new basis. However, if one party cannot or will not change, or if the resources available to either person prevent the kind of change desired by the partner, then the relationship may dissolve.

Dissolution of marital relationships is much more common now than in the past. One reason may be that changes in traditional male and female roles and expectations have created new stresses in marriages that are difficult to resolve. But there is another important consideration. If the outcomes in a relationship fall below a person's minimum requirements, or comparison level, the person will not be satisfied. This by itself does not necessarily mean that the relationship will end. The alternatives must be considered. If the satisfactions obtainable from other relationships seem even lower than the few satisfactions gained from the existing relationship, then the person will seek to preserve the present relationship even though it is unsatisfactory in an absolute sense. The phrase "the lesser of two evils" contains this idea; if the relationship you are in is better than any of your alternatives, then you will stay in it even though you are dissatisfied.

Kelley and Thibaut (1978) point out that leaving a relationship also has *exit costs.* Exit costs are those costs incurred when one terminates a relationship. They include whatever negative events the former partner inflicts, such as tears and recriminations. They can also include any guilt the person ending the relationship feels. Finally, they can include whatever costs society inflicts on the terminator. In the past, divorce had all of these costs. A man divorcing a woman who had been a good wife, for instance, could expect bitter recriminations from his wife, guilt, and severe condemnation from society. These exit costs, although still substantial, appear to have been reduced recently. The increased frequency of divorce has coincided with a more lenient public attitude toward such behavior. In addition, many states have liberalized divorce laws, again reducing exit costs so that unsatisfactory relationships are less likely to persist.

It is clear that viewing marriage as an exchange relationship is a useful analytic approach. It is also clear, however, that participants in such long-term relationships as marriage, or even close friendship do not like to view their behavior in such an analytical way. Indeed, a person would probably feel rejected if a friend or spouse kept a balance sheet of favors rendered and received, and immediately returned every kindness with a similar favor of equal value. Clark and Mills (1979) argue that relationships are thought of in two different categories. In *exchange* relationships, such as business transactions, it is appropriate and fair to keep close track of the benefits that accrue to each participant, and to be concerned with the equity of reward distribution. In *communal* relationships, such as marriage, these concerns are not so appropriate. In these relationships favors are given as affirmations of attraction or to satisfy the needs of the other; they need not and should not be returned "tit-for-tat." In a series of studies, Clark and Mills demonstrated that in exchange relationships, requests for favors and unreturned favors are viewed negatively. In communal relationships, however, requests for favors are viewed favorably, but promptly returning the favor of the other will be taken as a rebuff. One implication we can draw from these ideas is that the renegotiation of a traditional marriage into some new form, in addition to other difficulties, runs the risk of changing the fundamental character of the interaction from a communal focus to an exchange focus, a change that could have negative connotations for the participants.

DESTRUCTIVE RELATIONSHIPS—AGGRESSION

Unfortunately, one all-too-frequent form of human interpersonal interaction involves the injury (physical and/or psychological) of one person by another. The term **aggression** (when applied to humans) refers to attempts by one individual to inflict pain or injury on another. Almost any daily newspaper or television newscast is sufficient to remind us that many relationships are destructive. Human aggression takes many forms, ranging from verbal insults and individual mayhem and murder to the numerous wars throughout human history.

Instinct Theories of Aggression

Why is aggression so common? What makes one person want to harm another? The frequency and persistence of violence in human history has led some to believe that we possess an aggressive instinct. Freud, for example, assumed that aggression resulted from displacement of a universal urge to return to an inert state. Because our death instinct is usually kept in check by instincts for self-preservation, it finds expression in hostile actions toward others rather than toward ourselves.

Naturalistic observations of a number of animal species led Lorenz (1966) to argue that an aggressive instinct is the natural product of evolution, in which the strong and ruthless tend to weed out the weak and passive. This is so, Lorenz suggested, for several reasons. First, a male animal who uses aggressive acts to dominate other males of the same species will have the opportunity to impregnate more females. This increases the number of animals in subsequent generations who possess the genes of aggressive forebearers. Second, among carnivorous animals who prey on animals of other species for their food, successful aggressiveness has obvious survival value, and thus provides an evolutionary advantage.

Most psychologists who study human aggressive behavior would assign relatively little causal role to instinctive or innate processes. From a human perspective, there are a discouragingly large number of ways in which aggression is learned and rewarded; and it is usually not necessary to refer to instinct in explaining acts of human aggression.

The Frustration-Aggression Theory

We all seem to have an occasional urge to harm another person. One attempt to explain this, first formulated by Dollard, Doob, Miller, Mower, and Sears (1939), was the **frustration-aggression hypothesis.** These researchers believed that **frustration** (the blocking of the path to a goal) always leads to aggression, and that aggression is always the result of frustration.

It has become clear that the initial form of this hypothesis is wrong. Frustration does not *always* led to aggression; it can, for example, cause depression and lethargy instead (Seligman, 1975). Likewise, aggression is not *always* the result of frustration; soldiers and executioners, for example, engage in aggression when they are ordered to do so. There is, however, considerable support for a more modest form of the hypothesis. Frustration does, under certain circumstances, tend to increase the likelihood of aggression.

One determinant of the frustration-aggression link is the nature of the frustration. *Arbitrary* frustrations do lead to aggression, but nonarbitrary frustrations (those that seem to have an acceptable reason for occurring) do not (Zillman & Cantor, 1976). Capricious or inexplicable sources of frustration thus appear to be most likely to provoke aggressive reactions.

One implication of the frustration-aggression analysis is that each new frustration will increase the instigation to aggress, until the person finally "blows up." After this, the person's arousal level is presumably lowered, until new frustrations begin to build it up again. This view implies that if aggressive impulses could be drained off in some harmless, socially acceptable way, then the negative effects of uncontrolled aggression could be eliminated. The process of draining off aggressive impulses is called **catharsis.** The most obvious form of catharsis would be aggression directed toward the source of frustration. Aggression against a person not related to the original source of frustration may also reduce aggressive arousal. A more controversial notion is that *vicarious catharsis,* such as the observation of someone else aggressing, serves to reduce the tendency to aggress. A large number of studies testing the validity of the catharsis hypothesis lead to the conclusion that catharsis only occurs when the person actually aggresses against the source of frustration (Doob & Wood, 1972; Konecni & Doob, 1972). Aggressing against some other person, or watching someone else aggress, does not produce a cathartic effect. In fact, as we shall see in the next section, watching someone else aggress *increases* the likelihood of subsequent aggression from the observer.

The Aggression-Cues Theory

Berkowitz (1973, 1974) has suggested a reformulation of the frustration-aggression hypothesis that better fits the research results. Frustration, in his theory, leads to the emotional response of anger. That anger creates a readiness for aggressive acts, but those acts do not actually take place unless cues to aggressive actions are present. For example, Berkowitz and LePage (1967) first had a confederate make subjects angry. The subjects were then given the opportunity to aggress against the confederate by giving him electric shocks. When no aggressive cues were present, subjects engaged in little aggression against the confederate. When aggressive cues were present, in the form of a shotgun and a revolver lying on a table next to the subject, the confederate was much more likely to be given powerful electric shocks. (The confederate was not actually shocked in this and similar experiments. For a description of the device used in such studies, see Chapter 19.)

The classic frustration-aggression hypothesis holds that frustration can be reduced by committing against any person aggression that was similar but not identical to the act that instigated the aggression. Berkowitz rejects this and instead suggests that the frustrated individual's anger will not be reduced unless harm is inflicted directly on the instigator.

Berkowitz and his students have generated an impressive body of research supporting his theory (Berkowitz, 1974), but controversy remains (see, for instance, Feshback & Fraczek, 1979). One area of disagreement involves the sources of aggression. According to social-learning theory (which we will examine below), the sources of aggression are multiple. But according to Berkowitz, frustration first instigates anger, but cues associated in the past with aggression must be present for aggressive acts to occur in the present. Here the controversy may be more apparent than real. Sources of frustration are frequent in our culture, and cues associated with aggression are also plentiful. So there is a sense, in Berkowitz's theory, that the "sources" of aggression may be multiple. Moreover, the original frustration-aggression theory suggests that the aggressive tension produced by frustration can be reduced when it is directed against something or someone other than the source of the frustration. In contrast, the aggression-cues theory suggests that the cause of the frustration must be the target of the aggression. The evidence reviewed earlier suggesting that catharsis does not necessarily reduce aggression supports the aggression-cues theory. On the other hand, there is evidence that activities other than aggression can reduce the arousal produced by frustration. Further research is needed to clarify this issue.

The Instrumental Theory of Aggression

While the frustration-aggression hypothesis, in its recently modified form, has some validity, there is a second explanation for aggressive behavior that is also clearly valid in our society. Aggression is learned and practiced because it leads to rewards for the aggressing person (**instrumental aggression**). According to the leading proponents of this **social-learning theory** (Bandura & Walters, 1963; Bass, 1971), the laws of operant learning that we discussed in Chapter 6 provide good explanations for much of the aggression that we see around us.

One "good" reason for attacking another person is that such aggression will lead to a reward. In the case of mugging or armed robbery, the potential reward is obvious. The rewards can, of course, be more subtle, involving feelings of power and control or social approval. In street gangs or military organizations, aggressive behavior may be explicitly or implicitly approved by group members. Geen and Stonner (1971), for example, found that verbal approval is very effective in increasing aggression.

The other major way in which we learn aggressive behavior is through imitating others. An excellent demonstration that aggression can be learned by imitating the behavior of others was provided by Bandura, Ross, and Ross (1963) in their "Bobo doll" experiment. Young children were shown either a live or filmed adult model or a cartoon figure hitting an inflatable punching-bag doll. Children who saw any of the three kinds of models displayed more aggression toward the Bobo doll than did children who had not been exposed to an aggressive model.

Aggression, then, can be learned either directly or by observation. But, as you will remember, learning theory suggests that aggressive action will continue to be emitted only if there are reinforcing contingencies that maintain

Perhaps the most common instigator of aggression is aggression itself. If someone gives you a shove, the likelihood that you will shove back is high.

it. This does unfortunately often seem to be the case (Baron, 1977). Bullies sometimes get their way, or the best position on the team, or the best toys in the preschool, and their adult equivalents sometimes get the adult equivalents of such rewards. First, aggression is sometimes rewarded. Second, recall (from Chapter 6) that intermittently delivered reinforcements have strong sustaining effects on responses. Reward does not need to occur after *every* aggressive act for aggressive behavior to be maintained. It has, rather, been shown that intermittent reinforcement can maintain a high rate of responding (see the discussion of partial reinforcement and reinforcement schedules in Chapter 6). There seem to be three kinds of rewards that the real world may offer aggressors. First, as in the above examples, there are tangible rewards in the form of commodities such as toys or scarce supplies of food. Second, approval and other social rewards are often available to aggressors. The calls of "kill the quarterback" from the crowds, even at children's football games, are a convincing example of this. And in neighborhood gangs the "toughest kid" often gets status and power. Third, self-reward mechanisms that maintain aggressive action may develop. When "toughness" becomes a part of one's self-image, living up to it through aggressive acts may bring self-satisfaction.

Situational Determinants of Aggression

We have seen that such environmental conditions as the presence of weapons and the viewing of violence can increase the likelihood of aggression. A number of other precipitating factors have also been studied. Perhaps the most obvious instigator of aggression is aggression itself. For example, if someone gives you a shove, it is quite likely that you will shove back (Taylor & Pisano, 1971). Laboratory studies have often made use of aggression as an instigator of aggression.

High levels of arousal, even arousal from a source that has nothing to do with frustration or aggression, also facilitate aggression. Geen and O'Neal (1969), for example, found that subjects aroused by loud noise were more affected by an aggression-laden film than subjects who were not exposed to noise. Zillman (1971) found that increased sexual arousal also made subsequent aggression more likely when subjects were irritated by a confederate. Zillman (1971) believes that heightened, generalized arousal can be attached to aggressive behavior when an inducement to aggress is present. (Note the similarities between this theory of aggression and Schachter's general theory of emotion presented in Chapter 11.)

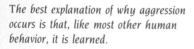

The best explanation of why aggression occurs is that, like most other human behavior, it is learned.

Does Violence on Television Cause Violent Behavior?

Like many of us, George Gerbner and his colleagues at the Annenberg School of Communication watch a great deal of television. Unlike the rest of us, they keep careful records of what they watch. They find that they watch a great deal of physical violence. Seventy percent of prime time shows contain one or more episodes of physical violence, and children's programs contain even more (Gerbner & Gross, 1976). Based on estimates of the numbers of hours children spend watching television, Walters and Malamud (1975) figured that the average 16-year-old has "witnessed" 13,000 television murders, while heavy television watchers have viewed many more.

Parents and other citizens, observing the barrage of television violence, have become concerned about its effects on children's development. Does viewing violent acts on television lead to violent behavior? For ethical and practical reasons, this is a very difficult question on which to gather proof. We cannot perform true long-term controlled experiments, sentencing some children, chosen at random, to watch only violent shows for months or years and others to watch only nonviolent shows. Only field studies are possible. (We can, of course, set up a short-term experiment in which we control what children watch for the duration of the experiment and test immediately for its effects. However, it is usually the long-term effects of television viewing that we are concerned with, and we cannot have 24-hour-a-day control over children's viewing habits.)

Some researchers have watched the development of children's viewing patterns over time (e.g., Huesmann, 1982). Often, but not always, these studies have found that children who watch a great deal of television or who prefer to watch violent television shows, do display higher levels of violent behavior later in childhood. Obviously this is consistent with the interpretation that watching violence provokes violence, but does not prove it. It could be that some children are predisposed toward violence and that they, therefore, tend to watch more violent television shows at an early age and to behave violently as they get older. The watching of violent television, then, may be a symptom of a violence-disposed personality rather than a cause of violence.

Another research approach is to look at the world views of people—including children—who are heavy television viewers. By extensive analyses of random samples of shows, researchers can determine the rates at which fictional crimes happen to television people. Government statistics, of course, document real-life incidences of various crimes. As you might expect, the crime rate is higher on television than in real life. (It is higher still on children's cartoon shows: Just watch some weekend morning and observe the crashing, bashing, and crushing typical of the "kiddy ghetto" programs!) When asked about the rates at which various events happen in the real world, heavy television viewers tend to overestimate the likelihood that they will be crime victims, whereas light viewers have a more accurate perspective (Gerbner et al., 1979). How do you think this affects the relationships of heavy television viewers with their neighbors, acquaintances, and strangers, or their votes for public officials?

States of Awareness and Aggression

The likelihood that people will act aggressively appears to be closely related to their *state of awareness*. Evidence for this assertion comes from research inspired by Duval and Wicklund's (1972) theory of **objective self-awareness.** The central idea of this theory is that we can be either *objectively* or *subjectively* self-aware. In a state of subjective self-awareness, attention is focused outward. For example, if we are driving down a twisting road at high speed, most of our attention will be concerned with staying on the road. Subjective awareness is probably the most typical state of consciousness.

When we are objectively self-aware, however, we turn our full attention onto ourselves. Seeing yourself in a mirror or on closed circuit television would make you consider yourself as an object of attention. When we focus on ourselves, we tend to evaluate ourselves compared to the standards and values which we hold and which are salient or relevant at the time.

There is a third state of awareness, one in which the self is completely submerged as the person is totally caught up in concerns of the moment, with no thought of what others or oneself might think of the behavior being emitted. In the state of *deindividuation* (Zimbardo, 1969), the person loses all concern for himself or herself as an individual, and instead focuses on the present environment with little thought of the past or future. In this state, the normal self-controls (such as values, concerns about the reactions of others, and feelings such as shame and guilt) are disconnected. In a sense, deindividuation is the opposite of objective self-awareness and is more like an extreme form of subjective self-awareness.

Deindividuation often occurs in crowds. One thinks of the mobs of people who occasionally gather under building ledges on which would-be suicides are perched, agonizing about whether to jump. One person in the crowd calls out "jump," and suddenly others pick up the chant as well. When people are in a deindividualized state, their behavior tends to be vigorous, repetitive, and difficult to stop. Behaviors that are normally inhibited may occur, and the person may not respond to cues that normally would trigger self-control mechanisms. This means that the behavior of a person who begins to aggress while deindividuated may be of high intensity, difficult to stop, and indiscriminate in its choice of targets. This description fits that of someone who has "gone berserk." It may explain the violent crimes one hears of in which victims are stabbed scores or even hundreds of times.

The social-learning model of aggression and its offshoots have been substantially supported by empirical evidence in recent years (Baron, 1977). What, then, are its implications? First, unlike instinctive or drive theories, learning theory suggests that aggressive behavior has multiple causes. Second, there seem to be a large number of ways in which aggressive actions are directly learned or indirectly modeled. For this reason, learning theorists see aggression as deeply rooted in our society. But, unlike drive and instinct theorists, they do not view aggression as an inevitable and inescapable human behavior. They do not see human aggression as the product of an ever-filling internal reservoir of aggressive energy, or as an automatic response to frustration or some other innate releasing mechanism. In fact, from a social-learning perspective, human aggression can be reduced by eliminating the conditions under which it is learned and reducing the reinforcements by which it is maintained. The message of social-learning theory contains elements of both pessimism and optimism: pessimism at the number of elements in our social system supporting violence, and optimism that these can be changed and violence decreased.

SUMMARY

1. *Attribution* is the process by which we perceive people and make judgments about what they are like. It can be influenced by a number of factors, including experience with the person, first impressions, implicit personality theories, attribution rules, and different opportunities to observe the person.

2. There are three dimensions around which we can organize information about a person's behavior: the actor, the entity, and time. The *fundamental-*

attribution error is a tendency to attribute behavior to actors rather than to the situations they are in.

3. Two personal perspectives that also may sway people's attributions are the *liking bias* and the *attractiveness bias*. Mitigating factors, however, usually prevent systematic biases from causing us to err frequently in our attributions.

4. Our attributions produce our conceptualizations

of others, and we then act toward others on the basis of these conceptualizations. If our attributions are initially incorrect, then interactions with others may serve to correct them. But our interactions may also reflect a *self-fulfilling prophecy*.

5. *Stereotypes,* or assumptions we make about people based on their membership in a group, are an extreme example of *implicit personality theories,* the common sense notions we have about how personality traits "go together." Stereotyping tends to give disproportionate weight to personal characteristics, such as skin color or sex, and to ignore attributes more pertinent to the situation.

6. Psychologists have long attempted to determine how, if at all, attitudes influence behavior. Present thinking holds that the relationship is complex. Attitudes that closely relate to the behaviors in question are the best predictors of future behavior, and this is particularly true for attitudes based on previous experience with the attitude object.

7. We experience *cognitive dissonance* when two or more of our beliefs or attitudes (cognitions) are contradictory or inconsistent (dissonant). According to Festinger's theory, we are so uncomfortable in a state of cognitive dissonance that we alter one or more of our cognitions to make them more compatible with one another.

8. Some characteristics of a communicator that make a communication more effective are expertise or credibility, trustworthiness, and similarity to the receiver. Aspects of a communication that make it more persuasive include clarity and, oftentimes, presentation of both sides of an issue.

9. When we make attributions about our own behavior, we often use the same principles that we use when we observe others. However, because we have privileged information and beliefs about ourselves, the same attributional rules may cause us to attribute very differently when we look at ourselves and when we look at others. For instance, we are more likely to see our own behavior as caused by a situation, but other people's behavior as due to their personalities.

10. Proximity generally encourages the development of liking relationships. In the early stages of a relationship, relatively superficial characteristics, such as physical attractiveness and similarity, determine whether we like another person.

11. Explanations of the causes of aggression include instinct theories, the *frustration-aggression hypothesis,* and *social-learning theory.* The situational determinants of aggression are also important in understanding its occurrence. Social-learning theory suggests that just as aggression is learned, nonaggressive behaviors can also be learned.

Suggested Readings

BARON, R. A. *Human aggression.* New York: Plenum Press, 1977. An excellent introduction to theories of human aggression and the empirical evidence for these theories.

BERSCHEID, E., & WALSTER, E. H. *Interpersonal attraction* (2nd ed.). Reading, Mass.: Addison-Wesley, 1978. This is a good overall summary of recent research on attraction.

NISBETT, R. E., & ROSS, L. *Human inference: Strategies and shortcomings of social judgment.* Englewood Cliffs, N.J.: Prentice-Hall, 1980. The authors present a recent, readable summary of findings on our strengths and weaknesses as intuitive psychologists.

PETTY, R. E., & CACIOPPO, J. T. *Attitudes and persuasion: Classic and contemporary approaches.* Dubuque, Iowa: Brown, 1981. An up-to-date, thoughtful summary of classic and recent perspectives on attitudes and attitude change.

SCHNEIDER, D. J., HASDORF, A. H., & ELLSWORTH, P. C. *Person perception* (2nd ed.). Reading, Mass.: Addison-Wesley, 1979. An integrative review of modern research and thinking on the core topics of person perception and stereotyping.

SHAVER, K. G. *An introduction to attribution processes.* Cambridge, Mass.: Winthrop, 1975. A thoughtful orientation to attribution theories.

WICKLUND, R. A., & BREHM, J. W. *Perspectives on cognitive dissonance.* Hillsdale, N.J.: Erlbaum, 1976. The huge amount of dissonance research is summarized in this comprehensive review.

19. Social Influence and Group Processes

The extent to which human beings lead their lives in groups is striking. As children we are dependent on the family group for our care and our survival. Primary school brings with it the peer groups of classmates. By high school, we develop sets of friends with whom we spend hours of our time. In college, classes, discussion groups, and extracurricular activities are all done in groups. Next we choose a career, and most careers are located in hierarchical organizations such as business, government, or health delivery services—groups in another guise. Our hobbies and special interests are often pursued in groups, clubs, associations, or volunteer societies. And if we marry and have children we rejoin our earliest group of all, the family, and recreate the cycle for another generation.

These groups shape our perceptions, guide our actions, limit and structure our choices, and affect our lives. Because this is so, it is important that we understand the processes by which groups change our lives. Fortunately, social and organizational psychologists have discovered some common tendencies and processes that function in all groups. An understanding of these general processes can give insight into the particular—and often peculiar and puzzling—happenings that occur in specific groups.

THE INDIVIDUAL IN THE GROUP

For reasons that will become apparent, groups develop both habitual ways of looking at the world and accepted methods of procedure. In other words, groups have rules that apply to its members. Group members, therefore, are sometimes confronted with the choice of conforming to the group's rules or deviating from them. If they deviate, then they may find themselves under pressure to get back into line or leave the group. However, their choices are not always this bleak—their deviant actions may come to be accepted by the group and regarded as an innovation. They may even become group leaders.

Conformity

Social psychology often deals with value-laden issues. **Conformity** is one of these, and it is important to recognize this early in the discussion. "Conformity" is a negative word that calls up images of submissive actions by weak-willed people. But consider the following definition of a conforming response: one that agrees with the response of a group, when respondents have insufficient evidence themselves to know that their response is correct. Next consider the following example: You are guiding your sailboat into a harbor in which you have never anchored before. Your charts and the harbor markers show two possible entrances, and you are on course for the nearest one. Then you notice that several other boats near you are choosing the other entrance. From the home port markings on those boats, you realize that this harbor is the home harbor for all of them. What's going on? One obvious explanation is that there is some hidden obstruction in the near channel—a recent wreck, perhaps, or a shift in the channel depth—that occurred too recently to get on the charts. You don't know, but to be safe you alter course and follow the other boats to the more distant entrance.

This fits the definition of conformity: You have gone along with the response of the group without having sufficient evidence yourself to judge whether that is the correct response. Yet, because it is so obviously the sensible action to take, it seems wrong to label it "conformity." That is the point: It seems wrong because conformity has negative connotations, but conformity, like other actions, can be good or bad, rational or irrational, depending on the context in which it occurs.

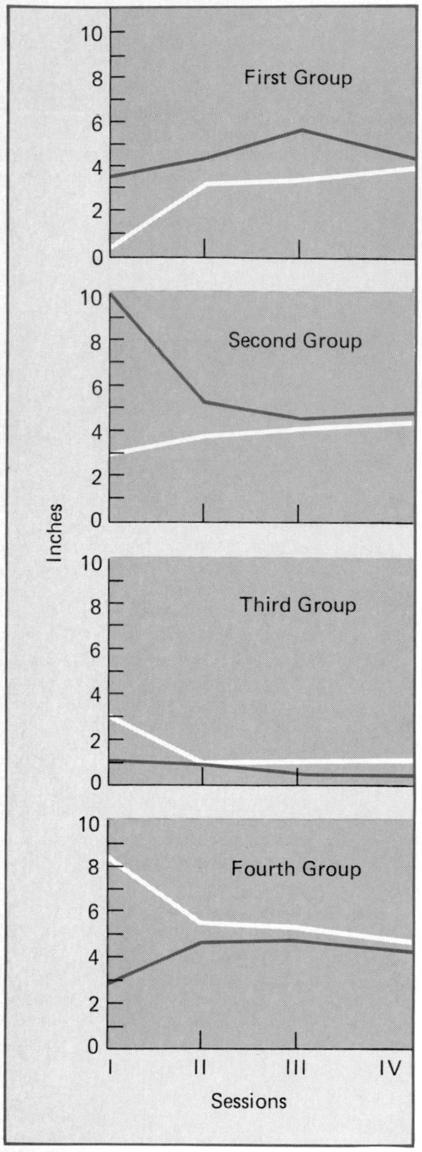

INFORMATIONAL SOCIAL INFLUENCE.   The kind of conformity found in our example, a rational kind of conformity that can be thought of as learning about the world from the actions of others, is called **informational social influence** (Kelley, 1952). It is likely to arise in two cases: when the realities to be learned about are essentially social in nature, and when they have physical components.

In the United States we drive our automobiles on the right-hand side of the road, and in the English language we use the word *chair* to describe a piece of furniture on which a person sits. That these are socially agreed on ways of doing or labeling things rather than physically necessary ways of doing or labeling things is demonstrated by the fact that in England vehicles are driven on the left and the German word for "chair" is *Stuhl*. People are the best source of information about these social customs. Indeed, they are the only source. Therefore, the only sensible way for a person who is new to a group to learn about its customs is by observing the actions of the group members. This is the normal learning process of socialization, without which no child could become a functioning member of a culture. It continues into adult life, producing what often could be called conformity.

Another word for social realities is *conventions,* those social rules about the "right" clothes to wear, the "right" way to address a faculty member, and so on. We learn about social conventions from others. But when what we need to know are not social but *physical* realities—things that can be measured and monitored—we still may look to the opinions of others. In some circumstances direct learning about events or objects might be too time-consuming or costly. Think back, for instance, to the example at the beginning of the chapter, in which, as the boat owner, you tried to determine if the channel were clear of obstructions. You could have sailed in and investigated. But you knew that to do this was likely to be hazardous and that you were better off simply going along with the decision of the other sailors.

In one of the earliest studies of conformity, Musafer Sherif made elegant use of an ambiguous event to demonstrate the ways in which individuals, when making judgments about physical events, are influenced by the judgments of others (Sherif, 1936). To appreciate what he did, you need to know the following: When you look at a stationary, pinpoint source of light in a totally darkened room, the light appears to move, even though it actually doesn't (the **autokinetic effect** discussed in Chapter 4). Furthermore, to each person the "movement" is somewhat different. Sherif realized that this was an excellent experimental context in which to demonstrate how people can be made to conform to a belief about a physical reality.

Next Sherif had pairs of subjects watch the light, each making an estimation of movement. At first, each member of the pair quite naturally gave a judgment that was different from the other's. One subject might report movement of 12 inches, for instance, while the other might report movement of only 3 inches. As the experiment progressed, however, the estimates of movement came closer and closer together. Each subject was influenced by the judg-

FIGURE 19–1

In each of the graphs above, you can see that when the two subjects guessed how far a light had "moved," their guesses varied widely. However, as soon as the pairs of subjects began making judgments in each other's presence, their guesses conformed with each other. (Sherif & Sherif, 1948/1956).

ments of the other, and a joint standard emerged (see Figure 19–1). New people, introduced into the group after the other members had developed a standard, then converged in their judgments toward that standard (Jacobs & Campbell, 1961), thus demonstrating the power of a group in influencing our interpretations and descriptions of physical realities.

Clearly, other people provide information that we use in making judgments about what is going on in the real world. The Sherif experiment proves that, but it does so in a rather artificial context.

Many examples of studies, however, show conformity effects on judgments of other physical stimuli, thus demonstrating that the informational conformity effect generally occurs. These studies follow a format designed by Solomon Asch (1951, 1955). Imagine yourself in the following position: You volunteer to be in a psychology study, and you and seven other students are waiting for the session to begin. The experimenter has everyone take a seat and then explains that the task is to guess which of three lines is the same length as a comparison or standard line. When you look at the first set of lines, the correct answer is very obvious. The first subject is asked and gives the correct answer; and so does everyone else in the group. The next few sets of lines are just as easy; everyone is correct, and you settle back anticipating a boring experience.

On the next trial, the answer is again obvious, but this time the first subject picks a line that is clearly not the same length as the standard. The second person, in a casual tone of voice, makes the same mistake! The third subject agrees with the first two! You look at the lines again, squinting your eyes and moving your head to get a different angle. Everyone else has agreed, and now it is your turn to speak up. What would you do?

Asch placed a number of students in just such a predicament (see Figure 19–2). In his line-judging groups, all participants but one were confederates of the experimenter who gave unanimous but incorrect answers on some trials, thereby placing conformity pressure on the one "real" subject. Overall, Asch found that his subjects conformed on about one-third of the trials when there was a unanimous majority.

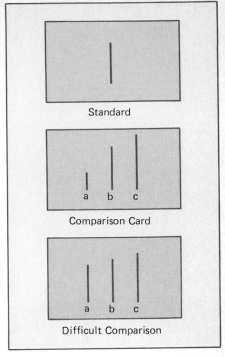

FIGURE 19–2

Asch (1951) presented subjects with a series of cards like the top one ("standard"). Their task was to select the line from the comparison card that was matched in length to the standard line. Other researchers made the task more difficult by giving the subjects a comparison set in which lines were of similar lengths.

NORMATIVE SOCIAL INFLUENCE. Up to this point, we have been discussing the kind of conformity that results from using information provided by other people about social conventions or physical realities. We called this kind of conformity informational social influence. But there is another kind of social influence that occurs when people suppress or downplay their own opinions and "go along with" the group because they want to gain the rewards or avoid the punishments that the group has to give. This kind of conformity can be called compliance to the **normative social influence** of the group. Although it may be rational to give in to social influence for this reason, it is not always admirable, hence the "bad name" conformity has come to have. But certainly this kind of conformity does occur, as was demonstrated in a landmark study by Deutsch and Gerard (1955).

Deutsch and Gerard wanted to demonstrate the existence of both normative and informational social influence. They reasoned that if people were conforming because they were using the judgments of other people to help them form their impressions (informational social influence), it should make no difference whether they gave their judgments publicly or privately. All that should matter is that they hear the judgments of the others. On the other hand, if people felt pressure to conform because they wanted to avoid looking foolish to the others, or did not want to be criticized or rejected by them

HIGHLIGHT□

Bystander Responses to Emergencies

Some years ago, in a case that attracted national attention, a woman returning home late at night was attacked and repeatedly stabbed until she was dead, while other people watched from their apartment windows. The onlookers neither directly intervened to help nor called the police. This was a shocking but not an isolated case. In numerous situations witnesses have failed to help people in trouble, even when there was relatively little danger to themselves in offering help. Research on bystander responses to emergencies illustrates some of the social psychological principles we have discussed.

First, this research illustrates the differences between the theoretical approaches of personality and of social psychologists. Personality theoreticians sought to identify personality traits that might distinguish nonresponders from responders. They suggested that nonresponders would be characterized by apathy and anomie, and perhaps also by hostility that caused them to get secret satisfaction from the suffering of people in distress.

Analyzing such situations from a social psychological perspective, Latané and Darley (1970) suggested a different set of reasons for failure to help, and discoverd that these affect all who witness a potential emergency. Among these reasons for failure to help is the information transmission process discussed in the text.

An event that becomes an emergency may not seem so at the beginning. The observable details may be ambiguous. For instance, suppose that in a big city you see a poorly dressed, unshaven man reeling along the street. He then sits on a park bench, holding his head in his hands. What is going on? The man could be having a heart attack and need immediate medical attention. Or he could be dazed and drunk. Or he could simply be tired. What, if anything, should you do? What you decide to do will depend on which of the possible interpretations of the situation you adopt. Suppose other people also witness the incident. You will look to their reactions to determine their interpretations of the event, and their interpretations may influence your own.

To see the effect of information-produced conformity on decisions about emergencies, Latané and Darley (1968) set up an experiment in which an ambiguous but potentially dangerous event was staged. Subjects' reactions would be determined by their interpretation of the event. Students came one at a time to a waiting room to fill out a preliminary information form before taking part in an interview on "urban settings." While each subject filled out the questionnaire, white smoke began to jet through a vent in the wall. The cause of the smoke was not immediately apparent, but one possibility was that it signalled a fire somewhere in the building. Those waiting for the interview generally reacted in terms of this possibility. They didn't panic, but they did walk out and find a person to whom they could report. To that person they said something like, "I don't know if there is anything wrong, but smoke is coming into the waiting room; could you please check?"

Other subjects were presented with the same event but in a different social context: Two strangers were also in the waiting room filling out questionnaires and apparently also waiting for interviews. Actually, the two other people were confederates of the experimenters who had been instructed to continue filling out their questionnaires even after the smoke appeared.

What did their behavior convey to the subjects? Apparently it indicated that they knew the smoke did not signal a dangerous fire. Perhaps they had had previous experiences with smoke in the building, or perhaps they had figured out something the subjects did not figure out. But they seemed to have concluded that it was safe to stay.

The results of this experiment are shown in Figure A: Most subjects remained in the waiting room, continuing to fill out their questionnaires even as the smoke poured into the room.

It would be easy to condemn them as "conformers," but it is probably more accurate to think that they followed a generally rational process that in this instance led to a less than rational conclusion. The lack of action on the part of the other people in the room conveyed

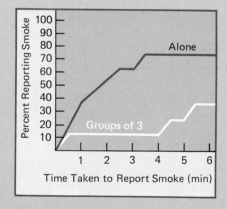

Figure A

the information that no danger was present. The subjects integrated this information with the other information available to them, and came to their conclusions. Some reported afterward that they thought that the smoke signalled the presence of a chemistry lab nearby, or was somehow connected with the heating system, or with the changeover from the heating to the cooling system. The inaction of the confederates had given them some cues about the meaning of the smoke, and had caused them to conclude that it was not a sign of danger.

Another study (Darley & Latané, 1968) in this series illuminates a different situational determinant of nonresponding. (This situation was described in the first chapter of this text, so only a reminder of it is necessary here.) It concerned the different perceptions of responsibility in an emergency when many people are present. In this situation, it seems that each potential responder feels a decrease in his or her responsibility to help.

To test this notion of diffusion of responsibility, an experiment was arranged in which people talked to each other over communications systems. One participant (whose presence was actually simulated by a tape recording) apparently had an epileptic seizure and called for help. Because his call for help preempted the single communication channel there was no way the other participants could discuss the incident with each other or even know whether others were responding. (The situation was designed in this way to remove the influence of visible behavioral responses, as in the previously described experiment.) Some participants believed that they were in a two-person discussion group, and therefore

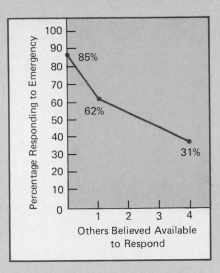

Figure B

reasoned that they alone heard the victim's call for help. Others believed that they were in three-person groups; still others that they were in six-person groups. Therefore there was one other person, or four others, who could help.

As Figure B shows, the more people a subject thought were available, the less likely he or she (both men and women showed the same effect) was to offer help. Apparently the diffusion of responsibility notion is an accurate portrayal of how people think during emergencies.

Figure C diagrams the researchers' suggestions about the ways in which the definition and diffusion processes interact. Notice that only if the situation is defined as an emergency does the question of personal responsibility even become relevant. Only one path through the set of decisions leads to a helping response; several paths lead to the response of not helping.

Thus, it seems that the influence processes set up by the presence of other observers actually accounts for nonresponding. Why, then, are we so shocked and upset when we read

about incidents of nonhelping in the real world, in which not one but many people fail to help? In this and other experiments (i.e., Gergen & Morse, 1971), it has been found that personality characteristics of participants do not predict their likelihood of responding. Yet many of us, reading reports of emergencies in which spectators do not respond, cannot help but feel that the nonresponders are somehow different from the rest of us normal, helpful people. Does this sound familiar? It should: We have again made the fundamental attribution error, attributing to personality behavior that is actually caused by the situation.

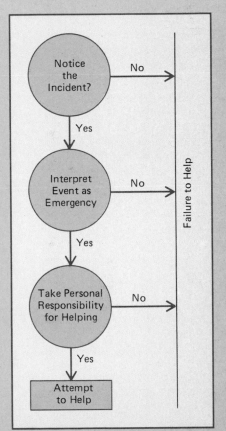

Figure C

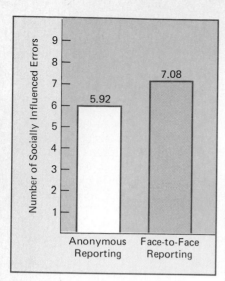

FIGURE 19–3

As shown here, the number of socially influenced errors in the experiment was a function of whether subjects reported anonymously or in the presence of others.

(normative social influence), then it should make a significant difference. Their deviance would become apparent and punishable only if the others knew their pattern of answers.

The experimenters arranged a social-influence test. In a control group, individuals judged the lengths of a series of lines. The right answers were very obvious, and these subjects made virtually no mistakes. Two experimental groups of subjects were asked to make the same judgments, but only after hearing the responses of another group of people to the same task. Although the subjects were unaware of it, the answers of the others were prearranged, and they all gave an identical wrong answer. All experimental subjects faced the same dilemma: Should they trust their own opinion (which was actually correct), or should they conform to the response of the group? One group of subjects knew that their answers would be heard by the other group members. The other group of subjects believed that the people in the other group could not hear their answers. If subjects were influenced only by the informational content of the others' answers (if they believed that the others were actually correct), then the conformity rate of the two groups would be alike. However, if subjects were also concerned about violating group norms and the possible sanctions the group might inflict on them for doing so, then the group that gave their answers publicly should have a higher conformity rate than the group that gave their answers privately. As Figure 19–3 shows, the data support this hypothesis. Clearly, there is a difference between informational and normative social influence. More precisely, a good deal of the conformity is of an informational variety (the approximately six errors made by the average subject in the anonymous condition). In the face-to-face reporting condition, however, the increase in conformity was caused by the desire of subjects not to violate group norms.

Deviation

What if people continue to deviate even in the face of group pressure to conform because they hold a strong opinion or have a prior public commitment to a particular viewpoint? Research by Schachter (1951) and Newcomb (1953) shows us what happens in this kind of **deviation.** In both experiments, an actor was planted in a small group of people who were supposed to reach an agreement about the solution to a problem. The experimenter instructed the actor to oppose the solution of the other group members, and to speak out for a different one. For instance, the group was asked to make a decision regarding the future of a juvenile delinquent. They were told that the boy had a terrible and rejecting home environment, but was committing increasingly harmful crimes. Should the boy be given another chance in a foster home, or should he be sent to a relatively severe house of detention? As instructed, the "plant" deviated from the group opinion. If the group favored the foster home, the deviant argued for the house of detention.

An interesting pattern emerged in some of the experimental groups. Once the group's position became clear, some group members directed more attention to those who disagreed, trying to get them to change their position. The experimenters had instructed the deviant in some of the groups to "become convinced" at this point and conform to the group's opinion. Once this person became convinced, the group turned more attention to the remaining deviant. This conformity made them acceptable as group members. Other deviants were instructed to stand firm and not conform to the group's opinion. Communication directed toward them dropped off: Previously they had received more attention than the average group member, but now they received less. It seemed as if the other group members were giving up on the deviants, and further evidence indicates that this was so.

The experimenters wondered whether the group members wished to punish the deviants or even exclude them from the group. Group members were asked to assign several jobs. As the experimenters predicted, deviants were frequently nominated for the relatively boring and menial tasks. The experimenters then explained that it might be necessary to have future meetings with a smaller group. Deviants were frequently "nominated" to be the ones left out—the processes of exclusion were under way.

Consider what this means in real-life situations for those who deviate from the group. Frequently, they find themselves excluded when their opinions are discovered. Because the opinions of deviants have been contradicted, their values have been threatened and are in need of bolstering. An excellent way of doing this is by finding a group of people who think as they do, thereby receiving social support from them. Thus deviants' future associations are likely to include a disproportionate number of people who agree with them on this one opinion. Naturally, they come to spend more time with these other people and less time with the rejecting majority. They become members of an *outgroup*.

Innovation

At this point, the fate of deviants may seem rather bleak. If people don't conform to the opinions of the groups in which they find themselves, they are rejected; if rejected, they seek out a supporting group, only to find themselves subjected to conformity pressures from this new source. But there is another side to this picture: Sometimes a majority will tolerate views that differ. Sometimes it may come to adopt the very views that it once resisted. Under what conditions will the majority either tolerate or even adopt deviant opinions?

Hollander (1958, 1960) demonstrated that high-status individuals can hold deviant opinions and still stay in favor with the group. He told subjects that a hypothetical person had "been in a group for some while," and had been "an extremely capable performer in the group's activity," or, alternatively, that the person was a new member of the group and had performed in an average or even below-average way on the group's tasks. The subjects were then asked to rate the person about whom they read. As expected, the capable performer who had been in the group for some time was accorded a higher status than the new member. Next, the subjects were asked to rate their degree of approval of certain actions initiated by these people. Seventy-two percent of the subjects reported that they would disapprove of a suggestion for a change in group plans if a low-status individual initiated it. Only 18 percent disapproved of the same suggestion when it was initiated by a high-status individual.

It is clear, then, that people's status in a group will affect their ability to have their deviant opinions accepted. High-status individuals whose opinions have been valid in the past are likely to have their innovative suggestions accepted by the group.

Leadership

Over half a century's research has been devoted to the study of **leadership.** Originally, these studies took a *trait-centered approach*—that is, they searched for people who possessed the **trait** of "leadership" or who pos-

Obedience to Authority

One of the most disturbing forms of human interaction occurs when a person harms or kills another. Often this happens in response to orders from a third person.

Are people so cowed by a person "in authority" that they will inflict harm on another human being because they are "under orders?" Stanley Milgram (1963, 1965) was determined to find out.

In his experiment, an individual who was apparently receiving power-ful electric shocks called out from an adjoining room begging the subject to stop giving him the shocks. Yet because the experimenter said something as minor as "please continue" or "the experiment requires that you continue," the subject did continue to administer (as he thought) electric shocks. Many who read Milgram's results concluded that, if concentration camps were to be established in North America, we would not have to look far for people to staff them. (It should be noted that actual shocks were never delivered, and "victims" were experimental confederates.)

In some variations of the experiment, Milgram brought the "victim" physically closer to the shock-giving subject. This reduced the likelihood that the subject would deliver the full series of shocks. (But even when the subject was seated right next to the "victim" and told to forceably push the "victim's" hand down on the shock device, 35 percent of the subjects did so, giving the maximum shocks.) The fact that being physically distant from the pain being inflicted makes it easier to continue does remind one of the experience of bomber crews during the Vietnam war. They flew so high above the countryside that the damage done by their bombs was so distant and remote they had trouble conceiving of it at all.

possessed other traits such as "dominance" or "extroversion." It was assumed that these traits would guarantee their selection as leaders, regardless of the groups in which they found themselves or the tasks faced by these groups. This approach had very limited success, however (Mann, 1959; Stogdill, 1948). Very few traits that were predictive of leadership were found in more than one study. Worse, a trait that was positively related to leader effectiveness (for example, sensitivity) in one study was found to be negatively related in another.

COMPONENTS OF LEADERSHIP.   Pressed by this evidence to rethink their models of leadership, many organizational psychologists turned to the study of leadership behavior to see if they couldn't come to a better understanding of the

Leadership styles can vary with the purposes for which the group comes together. Very different styles are called for in conducting an orchestra, supervising factory workers, and heading a government. Yoshimi Takeda conducts the New Mexico Symphony; a Johns-Manville supervisor consults with a line worker; and Indian Prime Minister Indira Gandhi addresses voters.

But before we make the generalization that all of Milgram's subjects were revealing latent capacities for evil, we should examine a few more aspects of their behavior. First, when subjects were paired with two peers who defied the experimenter and refused to continue delivering shocks, 90 percent of the subjects refused to obey the experimenter. Second, when the experimenter was "unexpectedly called away" and a prearranged "replacement" ordered subjects to continue, they generally refused. Indeed, when this person then stepped forward to administer further shocks himself, subjects frequently foreceably restrained him.

This gives us a clue to what is going on in the subject's mind: It is not so much the presence of the *authority* that is critical as it is the presence of the *expert* authority. When the expert says "please continue," more is implied. The phrase means something like, "I'm the expert here. Even though that other person says he doesn't want to continue, I know he's not really being harmed, so it's O.K. Please continue." Apparently, such an implied assurance was an important determinent of the subjects' continued participation.

Thus it seems that, in the context of a scientific experiment, when there is a convincing rationale for inflicting electric shocks on another person, subjects continue to participate even though the person seems to be in considerable pain. This differs in some ways from prison camp guards and other real-world settings, but it is in many ways similar also. There are striking similarities between a person causing pain for "the good of science" and a person harming another for "the good of the state." The obedience phenomena uncovered by Milgram remain disturbing from a societal perspective. They also illustrate a number of the principles discussed in these chapters on social psychology, and demonstrated how group processes can lead to acts of violence.

phenomenon itself, before attempting to predict success at it. A useful distinction that has stood up well over the years is that much of leadership behavior has two components: consideration and initiation (Fleishman, 1957; Halpin & Winer, 1975). Acts of *consideration* generally are supportive acts that show concern for other group members. Examples include praising the work other group members do or listening attentively to their opinions. Leaders show consideration by being friendly or helpful to subordinates, listening to their suggestions, being concerned for their welfare, going to bat for them with the company, and so on.

Acts of *initiation* involve undertaking the tasks of the group and structuring the group to achieve its goals most effectively. A group member who volunteers to do one part of the group's task is demonstrating initiating behavior. In a business setting, a superior who sets deadlines, assigns tasks, sets quotas, coordinates the production of subordinates, and criticizes poor performance is fulfilling an initiating role (Wexley & Yukl, 1977).

CONTINGENCY MODEL OF EFFECTIVE LEADERSHIP. Theories of leadership have grown much more complicated since their beginnings with the simple trait approach. It has become increasingly clear that a leader's success depends not only on his or her personal qualities, but also on numerous situational factors such as the skills necessary to accomplish the task, the existing rules by which the group operates, the resources and skills available in the group, the competition, and often sheer luck.

Fiedler (1967, 1972) has demonstrated that the effectiveness of a given leadership style depends on the acceptance of the leader by the group and on the kinds of problems the group must deal with. Fiedler used an ingenious method to identify two different types of leadership styles. Subjects were asked to think of the person they would most like to work with and the person they would least like to work with in the future. They then rate these two workers negatively or positively on a number of dimensions (for example, intelligence or determination). Typically, there is little difference among people's ratings of their most preferred co-worker, who is generally highly pos-

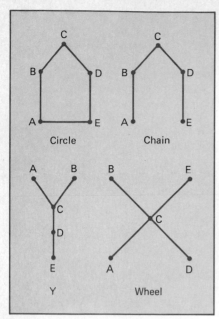

FIGURE 19–4

These are the communication networks studied by Leavitt. The circle configuration is the most decentralized: Everyone can talk directly to the person on either side. The wheel is the most centralized: All communications must go through the person in the center or hub position. (Leavitt, 1951)

itively rated. On the other hand, there is some divergence in the way people rate their *least preferred co-worker* (*LPC*). Some people give this person relatively positive ratings, while others give him or her sharply negative ratings. Those who give high ratings turn out to be people who are concerned with having good interpersonal relations and with being well regarded by people with whom they work (**relation-oriented leaders**). Those who give negative ratings to their least preferred co-worker tend to be people who are concerned with successfully completing tasks, even if they must risk poor interpersonal relations with their co-workers (**task-oriented leaders**).

As might be expected, these two different kinds of orientations lead to two different styles of leadership, each of which can be effective, depending on the setting. For instance, when the group's human relationships are of primary importance, the successful leader is one who is oriented toward developing good interpersonal relations; a task-oriented leader would be ineffective and resented. If, however, the group's relationships are going well and pressure to complete the task successfully is high, then the task-oriented leader would be more successful. Successful leadership depends on complex relationships between leaders and group members and is strongly affected by the nature of the task the group faces (Fiedler, 1972).

COMMUNICATION NETWORKS.   Sometimes people may become leaders simply by virtue of their position in an organization's communication network. Leavitt (1951), for example, studied the four kinds of communication networks shown in Figure 19–4. The figure indicates in what directions communication can flow (that is, who can talk to whom). In the *circle,* no position conveys an advantage. In the *chain,* those at each end are at a disadvantage since they can talk to only one other person. In both the *Y* and *wheel* arrangements, however, there is one position on which communications tend to concentrate. Leavitt found that the person occupying such a central position was most likely to become the group leader. This study illustrates how particular roles, no matter who occupies them, tend to produce leaders.

Understanding conformity pressures and leadership qualities and styles is clearly important when assigning groups to perform various tasks. For example, relation-oriented leaders are generally better for groups that are either very poorly or very well organized and integrated; task-oriented leaders do better with groups that are intermediate on these dimensions. It has also been found that when a group faces a complex task, a decentralized communication network is more effective in transmitting essential information, whereas centralized networks function well for simple group tasks (Leavitt, 1951; Shaw, 1954).

GROUP DECISIONS AND ACTIONS

One kind of group performance of special significance is the process of group decision making. Many of the most important decisions that affect our lives—such as the size and nature of the federal budget, admissions to college and graduate school, and the marketing and production actions of business organizations—are made by groups. Stoner (1961) made a discovery about group decision making that triggered a great deal of interest. Stoner had his subjects read a series of problems and make choices among several recommendations that varied in the risk of failure they carried. Subjects made

HIGHLIGHT☐
Groupthink and Group Decision Making

Irving Janis (1982) has documented a number of cases in which groups have made disastrous decisions. He reminds us of John Kennedy's decision to invade Cuba (the Bay of Pigs fiasco) and Richard Nixon's decision to suppress evidence of White House complicity in illegal activities (the Watergate coverup). By studying such events as these, Janis discovered a process that he calls **groupthink**, in which a cohesive group lets concerns for unanimity "override their motivation to realistically appraise alternative courses of action" (p. 9).

Through analyses of such materials as the tape-recorded transcripts of meetings of Nixon's close advisors, and the recollections of Kennedy's advisors, Janis has identified a number of symptoms characteristic of group processes on the way to a disastrous decision. A prime symptom, he reports, is the group's sense of its own invulnerability. The group has an exaggerated sense of its own power to control events, and tends to ignore or minimize cues from the real world that suggest dangers to the group's plan. One of Nixon's key staff members, for example, reported that he was confident that Nixon, whom he regarded as the most astute politician in the country, would avoid any negative political fallout from revelations of White House personnel being linked to the burglary attempt at the Democratic campaign headquarters in the Watergate building complex. He was equally certain that Nixon's power would be sufficient to force staff members to commit perjury. He was, of course, wrong on both counts. But even as more and more negative reactions from the nation became evident, the conspirators, instead of changing their course of action, reassured one another by belittling their detractors and seized on any external support as evidence that the "tide of popular sentiment" was about to swing in their favor. The group seemed to engage in some of the defense mechanisms that Freud had identified in individuals. To preserve its internal harmony and collective well-being, it became more and more out of touch with reality.

Janis' analysis of groupthink symptoms is shown in the figure. Groupthink is likely to occur in socially homogeneous, cohesive groups that are isolated from outsiders, that have no tradition of careful consideration of alternatives, and that face a decision with high costs for failure.

Lest we conclude that group decision making is inevitably disastrous, Janis suggests a number of ways in which groups can be structured and led to avoid poor decision making. These include encouraging dissent, assigning some members to the task of being "devil's advocates" to advance unpopular alternatives, and holding "second chance" meetings to reexamine the wisdom of the previously accepted decision.

Organizational psychologists have naturally looked into the problem of group decision making, since it is frequently practiced in businesses and other organizations. They point out that, if the group can avoid the dangers of groupthink, there are several advantages of making decisions in groups: Because of differing sources of information, a group will generally have more knowledge than will a single individual; this should help both in defining the problem and generating and assessing alternative solutions. Second, in the course of a group discussion the nature of the problem being solved and the nature of the solution to the problem can become clearer to all participants. Each, therefore, is more knowledgeable about the actions

Concurrence-Seeking (Groupthink) Tendency

Symptoms of Groupthink
Type I. Overestimation of the Group
1. Illusion of Invulnerability
2. Belief in Inherent Morality of the Group
Type II. Closed-Mindedness
3. Collective Rationalizations
4. Stereotypes of Out-Groups
Type III. Pressures Toward Uniformity
5. Self-Censorship
6. Illusion of Unanimity
7. Direct Pressure on Dissenters
8. Self-Appointed Mindguards

Symptoms of Defective Decision-Making
1. Incomplete Survey of Alternatives
2. Incomplete Survey of Objectives
3. Failure to Examine Risks of Preferred Choice
4. Failure to Reappraise Initially Rejected Alternatives
5. Poor Information Search
6. Selective Bias in Processing Information at Hand
7. Failure to Work Out Contingency Plans

Low Probability of Successful Outcome

needed to implement the decision. Third, each person is likely to feel that he or she participated in making the decision and therefore to be more committed to making it work well.

Continued on page 580

It has been amply demonstrated that groups can come to decisions that are both better and more likely to be successfully implemented. Yet the phenomenon of groupthink to which Janis directs our attention cannot be ignored. How can we integrate these apparently contradictory insights? Janis suggests that a group that is vulnerable to groupthink, with the resulting likelihood of making poor decisions, is under high stress from its environment. In such a situation members are excessively dependent on one another for support. Unless they have internal traditions and decision-making safeguards, they can be led to suppress dissent and strive for consensus—even when that means a consensus on a disastrous decision.

- A low ranked participant in a national chess tournament, playing an early match with the top-favored man, has the choice of attempting or not trying a deceptive but risky maneuver which might lead to quick victory if successful or almost certain defeat if it fails.
- A college senior with considerable musical talent must choose between the secure course of going on to medical school and becoming a physician, or the risky course of embarking on the career of a concert pianist.
- A research physicist, just beginning a 5-year appointment at a university, may spend the time working on a series of short-term problems which he would be sure to solve but which would be a lesser importance, or on a very important but very difficult problem with the risk of nothing to show for his 5 years of effort.

FIGURE 19–5
Researchers (Wallach, Kogan, & Bem, 1962) developed a choice-dilemma questionnaire consisting of problems such as these. Individuals, having read a problem, then reported the probability of success (1 chance in 10 of success, 7 chances in 10) that must hold before they would recommend the action. The researchers found that many (but not all) individuals made a more risky recommendation following a group discussion of the dilemmas than they made alone. For instance, an individual deciding alone might recommend an action only if it had 9 chances in 10 of succeeding. Following group discussion, the same individual might recommend the operation even if there were only 5 or 7 chances in 10 of success. The reasons for this risky shift are discussed in the text.

private decisions, had a group discussion, and then made the decision again. After the group discussions, the recommendations tended to become riskier; this phenomenon was termed the *risky shift* (see Figure 19–5). A number of other investigators also found risky shifts following group discussions (Wallach, Kogan, & Bem, 1962). The existence of risky shifts seemed to have obvious importance, since it implied that groups might need to be aware of (and wary of) a tendency to take too many risks. However, it soon became clear that groups often show conservative rather than risky shifts (Zajonc, Wolosin, Wolosin, & Sherman, 1968; Pruitt, 1971). It is now clear that both of these effects can be thought of as specific instances of a more general **group polarization effect.** Group discussion tends to make the average decision of the group members more extreme in one direction or the other than it is when there is no discussion. This occurs in areas as widely diverse as attitudes, ethical decisions, judgments about other people, and decisions about bargaining and negotiating postures.

Making Decisions in Groups

Several explanations offer insight into this phenomenon. **Value theory** emphasizes the kinds of social comparisons that tend to occur in groups (Brown, 1965). When alone, individuals try to avoid being either too cautious or too risky; thus they avoid making extreme recommendations. When they find out that others have a more extreme inclination, however, each member may be willing to go with a more extreme decision because of the emerging group support. Our cultural norms do generally favor risk taking, and thus an individual may feel that his or her position is more moderate than the social norm.

Whether a particular decision leads to a risky or conservative shift will be determined by the average group tendency, which presumably will reflect the dominant cultural value for that kind of problem. **Information exchange theories** point out that during group discussion, persuasive arguments that some members would not have thought of on their own will be raised, and these arguments tend to convince people to be more extreme than they would have been (Vinokur, 1971; Burnstein, Vinokur, & Trope, 1973). In other words, it is not just the awareness of more extreme positions that causes people to change their minds; it is the presentation of new information or arguments that makes them alter their decision.

Finally, **diffusion of responsibility theory** points out that the responsibility for a potentially bad decision is diffused when decisions are made in a group. This frees some individuals to be more extreme than if they made their decision alone (Wallach, Kogan, & Bem, 1962). Examples of extremity shifts have been found in numerous contexts, including bargaining (Lamm & Sauer, 1974), and court decisions (Walker & Main, 1973).

Group discussion tends to make the average decision of the group members more extreme in one direction or the other (either risky or conservative).

Various of the explanations cited above have been found to account for the shifts in different contexts, and this in general makes sense. When an individual is likely to be blamed if a decision goes badly, it helps if others came to the same decision so that any blame can be shared. Those people in a group decision-making context need not moderate their true opinions in the interest of avoiding blame for the final decision, if they sense that others will be equally extreme and thus share responsibility for the decision.

Facilitation of Individual Performances

What about individual performance in groups? How are performances affected by the presence of audiences or of co-workers? Performance in groups has a long history of study, beginning with Triplett's (1897) investigation of the effects of co-workers on performance. As additional studies accumulated, the findings seemed to be quite contradictory, with some studies showing that individuals performed better alone, and others finding better performance in groups. Robert Zajonc (1965) made sense out of this confusion by proposing a **social facilitation theory.** The central assumption of the theory is very simple: The mere presence of others is a source of arousal. Increases in arousal have been found to enhance performance on easy tasks and to interfere with performance on complex tasks (Spence & Spence, 1966; Spence, Farber, & McFann, 1956). Therefore, if the task is easy, performance should be better in a group; if the task is difficult, performance should be worse in a group. In addition to making sense out of the previous work, Zajonc and his colleagues were able to demonstrate the correctness of their analysis in a number of subsequent studies (Zajonc & Sales, 1966; Matlin & Zajonc, 1968).

Some social facilitation research has indicated that the "mere presence" of others is sufficient to cause arousal. It has also, however, been shown that concern about being evaluated plays a large part in producing these arousal effects (Cottrell, 1972; Good, 1973).

Cooperation and Social Exchanges

We all seek resources, whether they be as simple and tangible as food and money or as complex and intangible as status or power. To gain these resources, we must make transactions with other people who have resources to exchange but who also have their own motives. They may complement or conflict with our motives. When people depend on one another for the fulfillment of their needs, they are in a relationship of interdependence. Psychologists have developed their analysis of interdependence in the context of bargaining games (in which subjects compete for shares of limited resources such as points, money, or prizes) but have then applied it very generally to a wide variety of human interactions.

MATRIX ANALYSIS. Social scientists use a **matrix** format to show interdependencies between people (Thibaut & Kelley, 1959). This type of analysis can be applied to real and complex social situations, such as the following: Two men have been arrested. There is clear evidence that they have committed a minor crime for which they could receive a year in jail, and there is circumstantial evidence that they may have committed a major crime, for which they could receive a 12-year sentence. The police separate the men and offer each a deal: If one immediately confesses to the major crime and provides evidence incriminating the other, then the prosecutor will recommend only a 1-year sentence for that person. Of course, once a confession is obtained from one of the suspects, a second confession adds little to the prosecution's case, so only the first person to confess will get a light sentence. The other person would receive the major sentence.

If you were one of the prisoners, what would you choose? This exercise, called the **prisoner's dilemma,** is represented in matrix format in Figure 19–6. Think about it—it's not an easy decision. If neither confesses, then both may get off with minor sentences because there is not enough evidence to sustain a heavier sentence for either. If A confesses first, he is certain to get the lighter sentence, while B is equally certain to get a 12-year jail term. Meanwhile B, not knowing whether A will incriminate him, must decide whether *he* should turn state's evidence against A.

Some of the most general properties of interdependent interaction are shown by this example. One of the key properties is the way in which one's fate—*outcome* in the matrix format—depends not on one's own choice or action, but on one's choice *in conjunction* with the choice of another. For the prisoner, the choice not to confess may get him off with the light sentence of one year—*if* the other doesn't confess. But if the other does confess, then the later-confessing prisoner will get a 12-year sentence. The fate of each rests in the hands of the other.

A second point made by this example is the wide range of human situations that can be represented in the matrix format. Consider a boy who has gone out with a girl for several months and who now feels he is in love with her. Should he tell her? If he does and she responds that she is beginning to love him too, then we can imagine the increase in his happiness that this will

FIGURE 19–6
This is a matrix format representing the various choices and outcomes open to the 2 prisoners in our example in the text. Note that people's outcomes in the matrix format depend not on their own choice, but on their choice in conjunction with the choice of another. (Thibaut & Kelley, 1959)

		Prisoner A	
		Confess	Not Confess
Prisoner B	Confess	Whoever is first gets 1 year; the other gets 12 years	A = 12 years B = 1 year
	Not Confess	A = 1 year B = 12 years	A = 1 year B = 1 year

produce. On the other hand, she might say that although she likes going out with him, she doesn't feel that she loves him. And no matter how gently and tactfully this is conveyed, it still would hurt. Again, this is a situation in which the consequences of the boy's choice, to speak or not to speak, depend heavily on the other person's response to his actions.

SOCIAL EXCHANGE THEORY.   Psychologists, economists, mathematicians, and sociologists have taken seriously the proposition that much of life can be thought of as a series of **social exchanges** in which people provide each other with mutually satisfying rewards. These rewards (Foa & Foa, 1976) can be money or services or goods, but they also can be less tangible commodities such as information, status, or love. All of these diverse entities are desired by or needed by a person at one time or another and, therefore, can become the "currencies" people use in social exchanges with one another. Using the matrix-analysis format, scientists have explored the ramifications of this idea in many areas of life. Many social interactions can be thought of as exchanges between individuals. When a boy helps his younger brother, he "earns" the brother's gratitude and his father's praise and approval. A worker's successful completion of a task "earns" her the praise of her boss, possible raises, and so on.

Several useful insights arise from this view of social interaction. First, people are unlikely to continue a relationship voluntarily unless both are receiving reasonable "payoffs" from it. This is a useful thing to remember when you are studying human relationships— if you observe a relationship in which one person seems to be receiving no benefits and much grief, dig deeper. Perhaps that person has hidden needs and is receiving some benefits, after all.

Social exchange theory gives us another insight into the way people interact. Our decision as to whether or not we should continue a relationship is based not on the absolute value of the profits we are getting from it, but on the relative magnitude in comparison to what we could get elsewhere (Thibaut & Kelley, 1959). This can be seen, for example, in the way workers will cling to even menial and degrading jobs during a depression because they perceive that no other jobs are available. It also helps us to understand cases in which someone ends a long-term relationship that continues to produce the same level of satisfactions that it always did. The possibility of a new relationship has opened up, holding out the promise of an even higher level of satisfaction.

COOPERATION VS. COMPETITION.   Much of the research on social exchange has focused on whether individuals will choose to cooperate or to compete with each other in certain situations. Researchers in this area have found that people govern their behavior according to the contingencies offered by the environment. That is, the pattern of "payoffs"—which can be represented in a matrix as gains or losses—does strongly control people's choices. Consider the three matrices in Figure 19–7.

Assume a pair of individuals will give a set of 10 joint responses. If both choose choice 1 all 10 times, each will make 30 points (10 × 3). However, if person A can select choice 2 even once, person A will make 32 points (9 × 3 + 1 × 5). This will work *unless* person B selects choice 2 at the same time. (What happens to the total payoffs then?) As you might expect, this matrix provokes some complex moves by each player, and they both frequently end up making fewer than the 30 points they could have achieved.

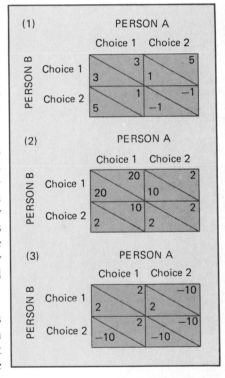

FIGURE 19–7
Outcomes in three different sets of payoff contingencies shown as gains (positive numbers) or losses (negative numbers). In each case, the number above the diagonal is Person A's outcome, and the number below the diagonal is Person B's outcome. For example, in Matrix 1, if A selects choice 1 and B selects choice 2, then A's outcome is 1 and B's outcome is 5.

Matrices 2 and 3 differ from matrix 1 in that they both, in different ways, almost compel the cooperative response of choice 1 out of both participants. Matrix 2 does this by making choice 1, and only choice 1, highly profitable for any player who makes it. Matrix 3 accomplishes the same result by making choice 2 highly punishing for any participant who chooses it. Research has shown that people are responsive to such changes in payoff contingencies.

Researchers have also come up with another, more subtle finding. In many bargaining situations, an optimal strategy, which means the greatest gains for both players, can be mapped out. But many times people played the games in such a way that their actual payoffs were far below the maximum levels possible. This was most likely to occur when the possibilities of negative outcomes existed. In many real-life situations, participants can cause negative outcomes for each other. Lovers can quarrel, labor can strike and management can lock workers out, faculty can give failing grades and students can give low course evaluations. In such situations the behavior of the participants often seems to take on tones of mistrust and suspicion.

A landmark study of the role of threat in bargaining settings was made in 1960 by Deutsch and Krauss. They developed a realistic situation that contained the possibilities of threat and conflict. Participants found the *trucking game* highly involving. In this game, one player is in charge of the Acme Trucking Company and the other is in charge of Bolt. Both are to deliver goods from their own start to their own destination; the more quickly they do so, the more profit they make. Each player could take the slow, winding, alternate route, shown in Figure 19–8, but at a small loss of time. The center route is more direct, so it presented the possibility of profit. However, it also contained a one-lane stretch that could accommodate only one truck at a time.

Confronted with this choice, subjects generally arrived at an alternating strategy, taking turns with the long and short routes. Over the 20 trials played, this earned a reasonable payoff for each player. For some subjects, the game was complicated by the addition of weapons, in the form of gates at the points marked in Figure 19–8. One gate was controlled by Acme and therefore could be used to block the progress of Bolt; the other gate was controlled by Bolt and could block the progress of Acme. When both players had the use of gates, the situation became a payoff disaster: Often both trucks would sit at each other's gates while seconds ticked away. The addition of the bilateral threat was actually a hindrance to the players' resolving their potential conflicts and coming to terms with each other.

FIGURE 19–8
This sketch shows the basic layout of the Deutsch and Krauss Trucking Game. Note that both Acme and Bolt controlled gates that could be used to block the progress of the other.

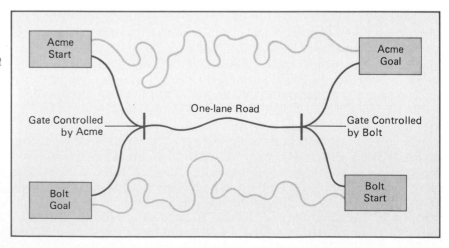

For a third set of players the trucking game was altered so that Acme was given a gate and Bolt was not. This meant that Acme had the unilateral capability to block Bolt's path. Not surprisingly, Acme sometimes used this capacity, and at the end of the game Bolt's payoffs were well below zero, indicating losses rather than profits (although not as bad as those incurred in the bilateral threat condition). Interestingly, Acme, the high-power participant in the interaction, also had a negative payoff over the 20-trial series, because the one-lane section of the center highway gave Bolt the capacity to block Acme's truck if they met head-on in that lane. This blocked Acme's chances of a quick and profitable run. This version of the trucking game demonstrated that the person who has relatively more power suffers from its availability, because it causes others to use whatever negative sanctions are at their disposal. The results of the trucking games are shown in Table 19–1.

Some psychologists, although impressed with the Deutsch and Krauss studies, suggest that the presence of threats or negative sanctions may not always hinder the resolution of conflict. For instance, Kelley (1965) pointed out that the gate in the trucking game was first an actual block, and only secondarily a threat. That is, the intention to use it in the future (the threat component) had to be communicated by actually using it as a block. Other researchers (Shomer, Davis, & Kelley, 1966) devised a version of the trucking game that gave subjects both a way of signaling a threat and a way of actually blocking the other player. Use of the threat-signaling capability caused participants to increase their gains. This suggests that the ability to communicate a threat is an effective conflict-resolution tool.

Other investigators have found that communication promotes cooperative behavior (Wichman, 1970; Caldwell, 1976), and Nemeth (1972) pointed out that communication between participants was not possible in the original Deutsch and Krauss games. Communication is usually possible in most of the real-world situations to which psychologists wish to apply their findings. However, in later studies that allowed participants to communicate, the course of the bargaining or the payoff outcomes were not necessarily affected (Deutsch & Krauss, 1962). We are not yet sure of the precise conditions under which communication enhances cooperation.

A picture begins to emerge of the complexity of bargaining research and the difficulties of making such general conclusions as "the presence of threat always increases conflict." Each bargaining situation has its own complex characteristics, so that the interrelationship of possibilities of communication, threats, and the balance of alternative causes of action and relative payoffs determines the role of each factor in the bargaining outcome. In addition, there are the bargaining participants, each trying to "decode" the situation in terms of the underlying motives and dispositions of the other player.

Table 19–1: Payoffs in the Deutsch and Krauss Trucking Game.

Variable	No Threat	Means Bilateral Threat (Acme and Bolt both control gates)	Unilateral Threat (Acme controls gate)
Summed Payoffs (Acme and Bolt)	203.32	−875.12	−405.87
Acme's payoff	122.44	−406.56	−118.56
Bolt's payoff	80.88	−468.56	−287.31

Deutsch & Krauss, 1960

APPLICATION□

A Matrix Analysis of the Armaments Race

Consider yourself the leader of superpower A with a decision to make. You have enough missiles to wipe out 50 percent of the major population centers of potentially hostile superpower B, and it has enough missiles to do the same to you. You know you will never launch a first strike, but you suspect the other side might. You also know that if your opponent attacks first, your retaliatory strike will be able to destroy only 20 percent of its population centers, and vice-versa. Assume, too, for purposes of this exercise, that each nation has 100 missiles and 100 major population centers.

All of this can be represented in a matrix as follows:

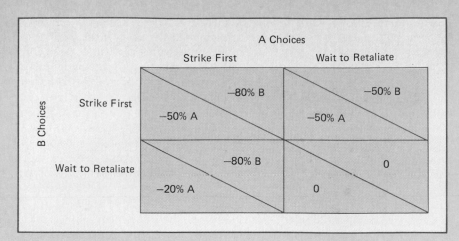

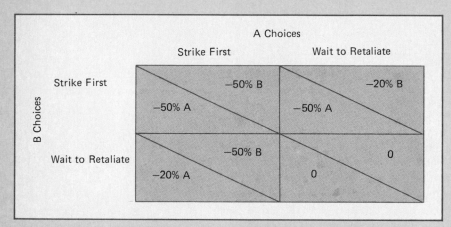

This, then, is your problem: If the other side strikes first, it will thereafter be sufficiently stronger than you to win the subsequent conflict. (It will have 80 percent of its population left after you retaliate, while you are left with 50 percent of yours.) So you decide to increase your missiles until you will be able to destroy 50 percent of your opponent's population even after it strikes first. Naturally, your increase in armaments gives you additional first strike capability as well.

This changes the matrix as follows:

Notice first that your addition of missiles has done what you want; it has changed the matrix terms so that power B will now lose 50 percent of its population if it strikes first and you retaliate. As the leader of superpower A, you feel that you have increased the protection of your country, and you are ready to stop adding missiles.

As the leader of superpower A, you know that your country will never strike first, but the leader of superpower B does not know this. Notice the second change in the matrix: If superpower A strikes first, B loses 80 percent of its population centers, putting it in a hopeless position to fight a subsequent war against A. (This occurs because, by increasing its retaliatory capacity to destroy B's population from 20 percent to 50 percent, A added 30 percent to its first strike capability as

well.) Now what are B's options? Obviously, one is to increase the number of its missiles. The other is to strike first and gamble on winning the war that follows.

The action A took to increase its stock of missiles to protect the country is perceived by B as sufficiently threatening to require a response. In the real world, defense planners are aware of this and attempt to avoid it—for instance, by storing missiles in hidden locations not recognized by potential enemies as first-strike weapons. Still, they could function as first-strike weapons, so they are actually a threat to the other side.

In working through this exercise, you are carrying out in very much oversimplified terms the kind of calculations that any group in charge of national security must consider. As you have done so, you have been thinking rationally about a nearly unthinkable possibility, nuclear holocaust resulting in the death of half of the men, women, and children in this and other countries. There is research evidence that merely thinking about a particular outcome increases people's estimate of the likelihood that it will actually occur. How might this "thinking the unthinkable" affect real world national defense planners who must consider various scenarios for nuclear war? Would they be likely to overestimate the probability that such a war may actually occur? If so, what changes might they make in their analyses?

Bargaining takes place in many areas of life—shown here are talks between the National Football League and the Players Association. Seated in the foreground are a player representative and a union leader. At the table in the light suit is the representative of the owners and his aides. The players went on strike for several weeks in the fall of 1982.

One of the conclusions that arises from the social exchange perspective and matrix analysis is that the *kinds* of situational interdependency can strongly influence the behavior of the individuals involved. Many individuals in interactive situations (such as the prisoner's dilemma) are afraid of unfavorable outcomes if they make the cooperative choice and the other person does not. Thus they may choose not to cooperate, beginning a series of destructive exchanges that each side would prefer to avoid. There are also bargaining exchanges in which an individual chooses a cooperative strategy that is contingent upon the opponent cooperating rather than competing. Otherwise, one person would react competitively to competitive moves by the opponent. This contingent cooperative strategy does induce cooperative responses in the other person (Kuhlman & Marshello, 1975; Rapaport, 1973).

When we said above that certain situations of interdependency may be destructive by driving participants into "destructive exchanges that each would prefer to avoid," were you reminded of any real-world situations? You should have been, for this type of conflict is reported daily on the front pages of our newspapers in stories about local strikes or international arms limitation negotiations. The fact that the social exchange model, and particularly its typical analytic method, matrix analysis, can be fitted to conflicts between groups, and between nations, as well as between individuals, is not coincidental. Much of the original impetus for developing these techniques came from the need to analyze conflicts between nations.

THE CONTEXTS OF GROUP ACTIVITIES

Social exchange research has shown that the actions of individuals, whether alone or in groups, are strongly affected by the contexts in which these activities take place. Special exchanges take place in contexts that are both *interpersonal* and *structural*. The interpersonal component reflects the interactional goals of the participants, while the structural component reflects the situational balance of power.

Other contexts of group actions affect participants' behavior as well. Groups conduct their activities in physical settings that influence the nature of those activities. Every college student knows this—think of a lecture hall, with rows and rows of chairs, all facing ahead, all bolted to the floor, and imagine trying to have a group discussion in that room. Nobody could face the person with whom he or she was talking. Students in the first rows would be talking to empty air, those in the back row to the backs of heads. At best, the discussion would be awkward to carry out; more likely, it would simply not take place. Clearly, the physical and spatial context within which group interactions take place can foster or inhibit those interactions.

Behavior Settings and Environmental Psychology

Environmental psychology is a branch of social psychology that is concerned with the relationships of behavior to the setting in which it occurs. On a baseball field, pitchers, catchers, batters, and fielders carry out their activities. In a bank, tellers, officers, and customers carry out their transactions, watched over by guards. Sometimes the behavior setting is a neighborhood, for example, or a city. Other settings studied by environmental psychologists include college dormitories, inner-city housing projects, and a variety of business organizations. Environmental psychologists have also been concerned with the ways in which people view themselves within their settings (see the Highlight on cognitive maps).

Institutions can differ in the number and range of the behavior settings they provide, and this makes a great deal of difference to the lives of people in those settings. Roger Barker (1960) and his colleagues painstakingly catalogued all of the behavior settings available to adolescents in a small Kansas town called "Midwest" and in a town about the same size in England called "Yoredale." They found that the 2 towns differed markedly: Midwest had a larger number of behavior settings than did Yoredale, and it also had a larger number of people acting in each setting. So, for instance, the American adolescents took positions of responsibility in 3.5 times as many behavior settings as their English counterparts.

This is important, first of all, in what it says about the social learning experiences of the two sets of adolescents. Compared to their English counterparts, the American teenagers have many more possibilities for learning how to play various roles and for practicing the various skills associated with those roles. The high-school newspaper editor, for instance, learns a whole set of skills concerning clear writing and how to prepare copy for the press. But this person also has the chance to learn skills in working with people, in coordinating their activities, and in being in a position of authority. Such skills originally learned in an adolescent behavior setting may create career possibilities later in life.

Second, behavior settings can generate forces that cause people to want to maintain the settings. A high school wouldn't seem complete without a newspaper, and since a newspaper traditionally requires an editor, a person is needed to serve that function. So arms are twisted and an editor appears in that behavior setting. Generalizing from this, environmental psychologists realized that the ratio of people needed to people available to fill behavior settings can have very general effects on the social climate of an institution.

Destructive Environments

Some physical surroundings are destructive because they inhibit the development of certain group processes. The rigidly row-organized lecture hall that inhibits group discussion is an example of this. Robert Sommer (1974) has studied interactions in a number of environments and has called attention to some specific settings that have negative consequences for human interactions. Given some of the earlier discussions in this text, you will not be surprised to discover that the mental hospital was the source of many of his examples. The common room of a geriatric ward was remodeled, painted a more cheerful color, carpeted, and decorated with new furniture, in the hope that this would combat some of the apathy and isolation observed among the patients. Long lines of chairs were neatly placed against the walls and in the center of the room, an arrangement that the staff felt was sensible and that the custodial staff found easy to keep clean. Despite the redecoration, patients seldom used the common room. Even when they did, there was little interaction among them. What are the possibilities for human interaction in such an environment? Picture yourself trying to converse with a person sitting shoulder to shoulder with you. It's awkward, isn't it? Usually people face one another when they talk, so that they can give the nonverbal signals that enhance conversation. That is not possible when chairs are placed side by side.

Or imagine trying to converse with someone sitting across the room. You can look at each other when you talk, and that helps, but the distance between you is too great. Normal conversations take place at distances between 2 and 4 feet, and intimacy is lost at greater distances (Hall, 1966). Also, other people walking through the room will pass between the two who are conversing, further disrupting their interaction. Such seating layouts are not structured to promote social interaction. In fact, they are structured to inhibit it.

How would you arrange the furniture to encourage social interactions? The researchers convinced the hospital management to add some square tables to the room and to group the chairs in sets of four around these tables (this is the pattern normally seen in dining rooms, office meeting rooms, and other spaces designed to aid communication; see Figure 19–9). The new arrangement worked: The interactions among the patients increased, nearly doubling within a few weeks. The change in the furniture arrangement produced a behavioral setting that encouraged social contact.

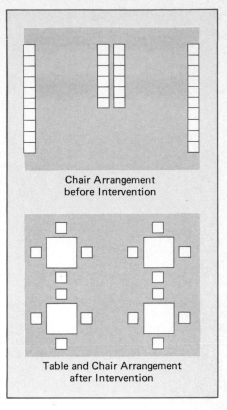

Chair Arrangement before Intervention

Table and Chair Arrangement after Intervention

FIGURE 19–9
Here are the 2 seating arrangements in the geriatric ward. Which do you guess would promote social interaction?

Density, Crowding, and Privacy

The **density** of a group of individuals refers to the number of people present in a particular environment, expressed in terms of persons per square foot. For instance, if 10 people are in a room that is 8 feet wide and 12 feet long (96 square feet), the density is 1 person per 9.6 square feet.

Intuitively, high-density situations feel unpleasant to us, and a great deal of research has attempted to demonstrate this in large-scale urban environments. A number of demographic studies examined the relationship between density indices, such as the number of people who lived in a city block, and the rates of disease, crime, and mental pathology for that area. The results of these studies were confusing, sometimes supporting the idea of the existence of a relationship between density and pathology, but sometimes contradicting it. Hong Kong, for instance, has population densities 4 times as great as even the most crowded American cities, but it has lower rates of hospitalization for mental illness and criminal violence than American cities.

These contradictions led researchers to think more carefully about population density and how it relates to other elements of human experience. They found that high density was not always experienced as negative, and that its effects could be altered by the physical arrangements within which it existed.

Physical settings can create behavioral settings that encourage or discourage social interaction, as can be seen in the informal arrangement in a student cooperative and the formal arrangement of pews in a church.

The concept of **crowding** was developed to describe the psychological state of feeling crowded, surrounded, and intruded on by other people (Altman, 1975; Stokols, 1972). Crowding occurs when there are too many people present or too many activities going on. This excessive stimulation can lead to a feeling of stimulus overload (Milgram, 1970). The feeling of being crowded also occurs when one is subjected to a higher degree of social contact than is desired, and so one feels one's privacy or personal space is being violated. High density does not always lead to these conditions and therefore will not always be stressful. And sometimes the potential negative effects of high density can be avoided by changing the interaction space to limit overload and create the possibilities of privacy.

Researchers have applied these concepts in studies of social interactions in college dormitories. In Figure 19–10 you will certainly recognize the upper

Crowding is the term used by environmental psychologists to describe the psychological state of feeling crowded, surrounded, and intruded on by other people. Crowding occurs in high-density environments, but it is not endemic to them.

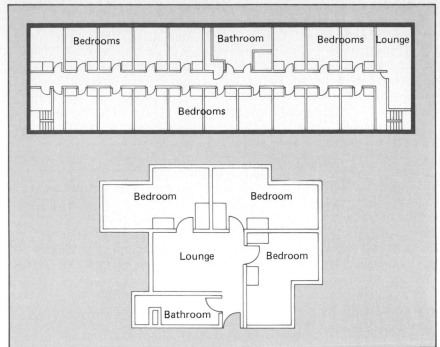

FIGURE 19–10
The sketch on top is the familiar "long-corridor" dormitory plan that is found in most campuses. The sketch underneath it is a newer plan organized by suites, in which the lounge space is shared only by those who have rooms in that suite, not with all the residents on the corridor, as in the older plan. This difference in arrangement in turn leads to different kinds of social interactions. (Baum & Valins, 1977)

floor plan as the familiar "long-corridor dormitory" that exists on nearly every residential campus in the country. The bottom plan is a newer suite floor plan. It can accommodate as many residents as the equivalent amount of space in the corridor arrangement. Its important feature is that the lounge space is shared only by the people who have rooms in the suite. In the long-corridor plan, the lounge at the end of the hall is used by all the residents in the hall. Baum and Valins (1977) found that even though both kinds of dorms had the same population density, the long-corridor dorm residents felt more crowded. And they, more than the residents of suite-organized dorms, reported that they felt it was useless to try to change things in their dormitory. To see how far the effects of the dormitories generalized, Baum and Valins set up in a psychology laboratory a task in which rather little information was given to the participants. Participants who lived in long-corridor dorms were relatively unlikely to seek out additional information. (Compare this result with the discussion of learned helplessness in Chapters 11 and 15.)

Organizational Settings

So far we have considered the ways people are influenced by and influence the small groups in which they are involved, the ways small groups influence one another, and the ways in which individuals and small groups are influenced by the physical contexts of their activities. We will now look at the ways in which people's activities are influenced by the *organizational* contexts in which their activities take place—the effects of social organizations on human behavior. Actually, we have already examined some effects of motivation and job design on people's behavior in organizations (Chapter 11) and on industrial testing (Chapter 14). Here we will reconsider some of these themes and bring up new ones in the context of work organizations.

STRUCTURING THE ORGANIZATION. How should work organizations be structured? Initial answers to this question were provided by classical theorists, who saw an organization as essentially a hierarchical authority structure in which superiors controlled the performance of subordinates. Subordinates were to be given a clear, definite, and preferably limited and repetitive set of duties and responsibilities. Each person should have one and only one boss, who would reward or punish the worker based on productivity. Any problems were to be referred upward, and information was to be passed upward as well. Decisions and orders were passed downward. Rules were to be carefully followed.

As critics have pointed out, this classical theory of organizational design has a number of problems. First, it rests on a rather dehumanizing set of assumptions about the worker. The worker is seen as requiring external motivation and as possessing none of his or her own. For modern workers, however, being given a constant stream of orders while doing repetitive work often leads to hostility or withdrawal. Second, today's organizations function in a changing and demanding environment. (An organization's environment includes outside forces, such as competitors and union rules, and internal conditions, such as employee morale and working conditions.) Standard rules cannot be set up to cover every situation, because unpredictable events occur frequently. By the time each decision is referred up the hierarchy to a point at which the authority exists to make the decision, it may be too late for an optimal response. Finally, workers who resent rigid organization rules can develop an overprecise way of following them, which actually subverts the goals of the organization.

In response to these kinds of problems, *humanistic theories of organization* were developed in the 1950s and 1960s (Argyris, 1957; Likert, 1967; McGregor, 1960). This new approach saw the organization as a network of supportive relationships, operating through group decision-making processes, with interactions furthered by a free flow of communication. Critics of these organizational theorists (Wexley & Yukl, 1977) have commented that in reacting to the classical structure, they have gone too far in the other direction. Their assumptions about worker motivations are too idealistic, and their

Organizational structures have changed considerably in this century. Recent research has shown that the key factor in designing an optimal organizational structure is a careful consideration of the organization's external environment and its internal needs.

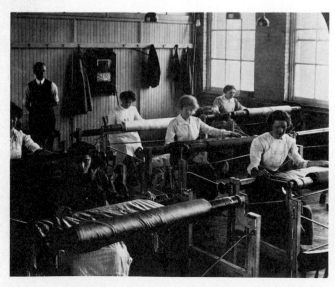

assumption that workers' motivations are always compatible with organizational goals may also be naïve. Nor is quick adaptation to a shifting outside environment guaranteed by the sometimes complex and time-consuming process of group decision making.

More recent research (Burns & Stalker, 1961; Morse & Lorsch, 1970) suggests that an organization's external environment and its internal needs are the key factors in designing an optimal structure. The contingencies a company must deal with—competitive market, technological innovations, employee characteristics, for example—must be taken into account in establishing its structure. Many organizational structures today include some elements of both the classical and humanistic prescriptions. An organization with stable markets, relatively unchanging production technologies, and low demands for new product development might well use something close to the classical organizational structure. Companies that need to respond to rapidly changing markets and that are affected by new technologies tend to do better with a more group-centered organization. Of course, they must have a group that is capable of making decisions rapidly. These newer theories of organization, which postulate that an organization's structure must be determined by each company's unique set of external and internal factors, are called *contingency theories of organizational design*. This approach recognizes that no one perfect structure will work for all organizations.

CONFLICT IN ORGANIZATIONS AND ITS RESOLUTION.   **Conflict** is said to occur when two parties in a dispute begin to interfere intentionally with each other's goal attainment (Wexley & Yukl, 1977). Conflicts occur in all organizations and, therefore, have been studied intensively by organizational psychologists. As we well know, conflicts also occur between nations, between student organizations, and between individuals; and it is hoped that the analyses of conflict and conflict resolution in organizational settings might have implications for the analysis and resolution of these other conflicts as well.

A number of causes of conflicts in business organizations have been identified (Robbins, 1974; Walton & Dutton, 1969; Wexley & Yukl, 1977). These include competition for scarce resources, dependence on others for completion of one's own tasks, ambiguous responsibilities, status and power problems, and concerns about promotion or compensation. Generally conflict arises when an individual or a group in an organization is frustrated in pursuit of important goals. When these situations arise, we can expect reactions similar to those we discussed in the section of Chapter 18 on frustration and aggression.

A common source of conflict is poor communication, which often leads to the perception that some frustrating circumstances exist even when they really don't. One of the most frequent research findings is that there is insufficient upward communication in organizations, and managers are often misinformed about workers' motivations as a result. For example, Kahn (1958) discovered that supervisors overestimate the importance of fulfillment of such workers' needs as pay and security, and underestimate the importance of the intrinsic satisfactions of doing the job well. Communication problems are frequently exacerbated because workers neither understand nor trust management's goals (Athanassiades, 1973). Meanwhile, people in management are sure that they are aware of the real concerns of workers, even though evidence suggests that they are not (Hamann, 1956).

Conflict in an organization can disrupt communication and production and can cause feelings of hostility among participants. Conflict can also have positive consequences because its resolution can lead to needed changes. For example, college students frequently experience conflict with parents over issues of independence— choice of friends, life patterns, late hours, and so on. These conflicts are necessary for the parent to understand that the student is no longer a child, and for the student to realize that he or she is responsible for conducting his or her own life. The resolution of these conflicts can lead to real growth for parent and student. It is important to remember that conflict can have positive outcomes.

Often the intervention of third parties is useful in resolving conflict, and standard roles for third parties have been developed. For instance, labor and management can agree to submit a dispute to a respected *arbitrator,* who customarily is given the power to reach a decision that is binding on the disputants. A *mediator* fulfills a similar role but does not have the power to make binding decisions, and so must use persuasion, insight, and conflict-managment techniques to achieve a solution. These techniques range from separating the two bargaining parties in order to eliminate hostilities expressed in face-to-face disputes, to accurately understanding each party's real solution preferences (which they may not have thought through for themselves), from which compromise solutions may be proposed (Pruitt,

Table 19–2: Five Modes of Conflict Resolution.

Conflict-handling Modes	Appropriate Situations
Competing	1. When quick, decisive action is vital—e.g., emergencies.
	2. On important issues where unpopular actions need implementing—e.g., cost cutting, enforcing unpopular rules, discipline.
	3. On issues vital to company welfare when you know you're right.
	4. Against people who take advantage of non-competitive behavior.
Collaborating	1. To find an integrative solution when both sets of concerns are too important to be compromised.
	2. When your objective is to learn.
	3. To merge insights from people with different perspectives.
	4. To gain commitment by incorporating concerns into a consensus.
	5. To work through feelings that have interfered with a relationship.
Compromising	1. When goals are important, but not worth the effort or potential disruption of more assertive modes.
	2. When opponents with equal power are committed to mutually exclusive goals.
	3. To achieve temporary settlements to complex issues.
	4. To arrive at expedient solutions under time pressure.
	5. As a backup when collaboration or competition is unsuccessful.

1975). Finally, a third party intervener may focus less on the immediate dispute and more on the *process* by which the parties resolve their disputes.

Thomas (1977) has classified various modes of handling conflicts within organizations (see Table 19–2). His taxonomy is useful for those concerned with resolving disputes between any parties in a conflict, family members, roommates, students and teachers, as well as organizations. The taxonomy contains one important insight, which is that all modes of resolving conflict, including avoiding it, may be appropriate depending on the circumstances.

Conflict resolution relies first on the social exchange analysis and second on attribution theory. It is vital to recognize that participants in a dispute are making attributions about the attitudes, personalities, goals, purposes, and motives of other disputants, and that flawed communications can cause false attributions about these factors. As you can see, conflict resolution specifically, and organizational psychology generally, rely heavily on the analytic perspectives that they share with social psychology, so it is worth emphasizing these once again. How is the surrounding situation perceived by the actor? What are the motives, goals, and needs of a sibling, a new acquaintance, a possible dating partner, or a boss? What are their personalities? What meanings should be placed on the actions of others? Then through a system of social exchanges and interactions, the perceiver can act in order to reach desired goals.

Conflict-handling Modes	Appropriate Situations
Avoiding	1. When an issue is trivial, or more important issues are pressing.
	2. When you perceive no chance of satisfying your concerns.
	3. When potential disruption outweighs the benefits of resolution.
	4. To let people cool down and regain perspecitve.
	5. When gathering information supersedes immediate decision.
	6. When others can resolve the conflict more effectively.
	7. When issues seem tangential or symptomatic of other issues.
Accommodating	1. When you find you are wrong—to allow a better position to be heard, to learn, and to show your reasonableness.
	2. When issues are more important to others than yourself—to satisfy others and maintain cooperation.
	3. To build social credits for later issues.
	4. To minimize loss when you are outmatched and losing.
	5. When harmony and stability are especially important.
	6. To allow subordinates to develop by learning from mistakes.

Thomas (1977), p. 487.

SUMMARY

1. Four dimensions of the interaction between individuals and groups are conformity, deviation, innovation, and leadership.

2. *Conformity* often has a negative connotation, but in some situations it is a sign of rational behavior, not weakness. Examples of rational conformity are conforming actions arising from *informational social influence.* Another type of conformity, *normative social influence,* often involves the suppression of one's own opinions.

3. People who deviate from the group opinion are often ostracized and punished by the group; they then may become members of *outgroups.*

4. Status in a group determines how much influence a person will have in getting his or her opinions adopted by the group; this adoption of an opinion not originally held by the majority is called *innovation.*

5. Theories of *leadership* include the trait-centered approach, relational theory, and the contingency model of leadership effectiveness.

6. Several theories have been proposed to explain the *group polarization effect:* value theory, information exchange theories, diffusion of responsibility theory.

7. *Social facilitation theory* is based on the assumption that the presence of others is a source of arousal; depending on the difficulty of the task involved, this can lead to poor or good performance.

8. *Social exchange theory* analyzes human interaction as a series of exchanges of desired commodities such as money, goods, information, or more intangible commodities such as respect. The *matrix* format is frequently used to analyze the particular nature of the possible exchanges between people and to predict the particular cooperative or competitive relationships that will emerge.

9. *Environmental psychologists* study setting–interaction relationships; the basic unit of their studies is the *behavior setting.*

10. *Density* refers to the number of people present in a particular environment. High-density situations seem to be negative only when these situations create crowding—the psychological state of feeling crowded, surrounded, and intruded on by other people.

11. Environmental psychologists have shown how space can be manipulated to create the possibilities of privacy and to reduce the potential negative effects of density.

12. Psychologists have tried to understand people's behavior in organizational settings. There is no single organizational structure that seems to work for all organizations.

13. Research on *conflict* and conflict resolution deals with social exchange analysis and attribution processes.

Suggested Readings

BAUM, A., & VALINS, S. *Architecture and social behavior: Psychological studies in social density.* Hillsdale, N.J.: Erlbaum, 1977. Contains some good examples of recent developments in ecological research.

DAVIS, J. H. *Group performance.* Reading, Mass.: Addison-Wesley, 1969. Interesting but complex findings on group performance variables are reviewed here.

FIEDLER, F. E., & CHEMERS, M. H. *Leadership and effective management.* Chicago: Scott, Foresman, 1974. An excellent review of leadership research, necessary reading for those who wish to pursue the subject further.

FREEDMAN, J. L. *Crowding and behavior.* San Francisco: W. H. Freeman & Company, Publishers, 1975. This is an award-winning analysis of crowding research that is both readable and entertaining.

KELLEY, H. H. *Personal relationships: Their structures and processes.* Hillsdale, N.J.: Erlbaum, 1979. Using attributional and social exchange principles, Kelley illuminates many of the events that take place in intimate relationships.

KIESLER, C. A., & KIESLER, S. B. *Conformity.* Reading, Mass.: Addison-Wesley, 1969. Well organized and clear, this text reviews the conformity literature in comprehensive but succinct fashion.

LATANÉ, B., & DARLEY, J. M. *The unresponsive bystander: Why doesn't he help?* Englewood Cliffs, N.J.: Prentice-Hall, 1970. This research monograph shows how informational and normative pressures interact when one is faced with the decision to help or not to help in an emergency.

MILGRAM, S. *Obedience to authority.* New York: Harper & Row, 1974. The controversial research on obedience to authority is reported by its author.

STOKALS, D. *Perspectives on environment and behavior.* New York: Plenum, 1977. A thoughtful presentation of many of the issues in environmental psychology, by one of the major figures in the field.

SULS, J., & MILLER, R. J. (Eds.). *Social comparison processes: Theoretical and empirical perspectives.* Washington, D.C.: Hemisphere/Halsted, 1977. This edited volume contains a number of recent papers on social comparison.

WHEELER, L., DECI, E., HEIS, H., & ZUCKERMAN, M. *Interpersonal influence,* 2nd ed. Boston: Allyn & Bacon, 1978. This well-written book explores many of the issues discussed in this chapter, e.g., conformity and social facilitation.

Appendix: Statistics

"You haven't told me yet," said Lady Nuttal, "what it is your fiancé does for a living."

"He's a statistician," replied Lamia, with an annoying sense of being on the defensive.

Lady Nuttal was obviously taken aback. It had not occurred to her that statisticians entered into normal relationships. The species, she would have surmised, was perpetuated in some collateral manner, like mules.

"But Aunt Sara, it's a very interesting profession," said Lamia warmly.

"I don't doubt it," said her aunt, who obviously doubted it very much. "To express anything important in mere figures is so plainly impossible that there must be endless scope for well-paid advice on how to do it. But don't you think that life with a statistician would be rather, shall we say, humdrum?"

Lamia was silent. She felt reluctant to discuss the surprising depth of emotional possibility which she had discovered below Edward's numerical veneer.

"It's not the figures themselves," she said finally, "it's what you do with them that matters." (K. A. C. Manderville, *The Undoing of Lamia Gurdleneck*)

Psychologists often use numbers to describe behavior—for example, how long it takes for a stimulus to evoke a response, the number of correct answers on a test, a subject's rating of preference on a scale from 1 to 9, and so on. These are all measurement procedures, as are the more familiar procedures for measuring length and weight. In this appendix we will discuss how some aspects of a group of numbers (for example, test scores) can be characterized by other numbers called **statistics** (for example, the average test score), and how inferences can be drawn from such statistics, a process called *statistical inference*.

DESCRIPTIVE STATISTICS

Frequency Distributions

Descriptive statistics is a set of methods for organizing and summarizing numerical data. The data may be any set of measurements of a group of objects, people, or events. For example, if we are interested in the annual incomes of domestic workers, we might conduct a survey by asking some domestic workers what their annual income is. Here the **population** is incomes of all domestic workers, and the **sample** we take is the actual records of incomes we have at the conclusion of the survey. Table 1A gives the incomes reported by each of 17 hypothetical domestic workers. These data could be described as mostly in the $4,000 range, with some much higher and a few lower. A more precise way of characterizing the incomes in the sample is to specify

Table 1A: Annual Incomes Sampled from 17 Domestic Workers.

3,000	4,000	6,000
5,000	5,000	4,000
10,000	7,000	10,000
20,000	10,000	4,000
8,000	9,000	4,000
4,000	4,000	

Table 1B: Frequency Distribution of Annual Incomes Grouped in Intervals of $1,000.

Income Interval	Frequency
3,000–3,999	1
4,000–4,999	6
5,000–5,999	2
6,000–6,999	1
7,000–7,999	1
8,000–8,999	1
9,000–9,999	1
10,000–10,999	3
11,000–11,999	0
12,000–12,999	0
13,000–13,999	0
14,000–14,999	0
15,000–15,999	0
16,000–16,999	0
17,000–17,999	0
18,000–18,999	0
19,000–19,999	0
20,000–20,999	1
	17

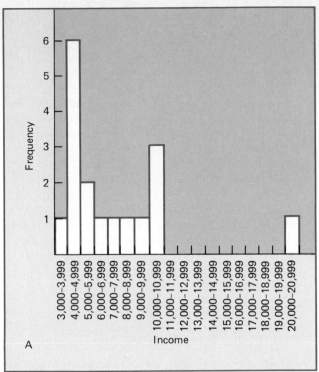

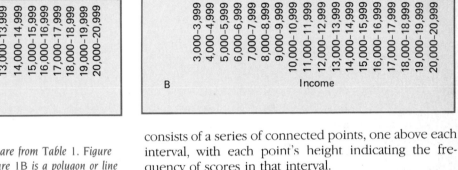

A Income

B Income

FIGURE 1

The data in these frequency distributions are from Table 1. Figure 1A is a histogram or bar graph, and Figure 1B is a polygon or line graph.

exactly how many there are in the $3,000 range, $4,000 range, $5,000 range, and so on. This is a **frequency distribution.** It can be presented as a table (Table 1B) or as a graph (Figure 1). Notice that in Table 1 and Figure 1 we have classified incomes into *class intervals* of $1,000.

Two types of graphs are shown in Figure 1: A **histogram,** or bar graph (Figure 1A), indicates the frequency of scores in a class interval by the height of a bar above that interval. A **polygon,** or line graph (Figure 1B),

consists of a series of connected points, one above each interval, with each point's height indicating the frequency of scores in that interval.

Tables and graphs are helpful for showing how numbers are distributed. It is also useful to summarize certain characteristics of distributions in terms of a single number. Figure 2 presents three frequency distributions. The centers of distributions A and B are similar, in that each lies above the class interval 50–59. In contrast,

FIGURE 2

Three frequency distributions. Distribution A has less variability than B but a similar central tendency. Distribution C has a higher central tendency than B, but a similar variability.

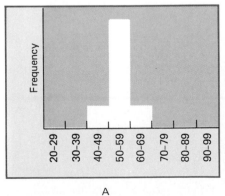

A

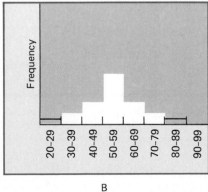

B

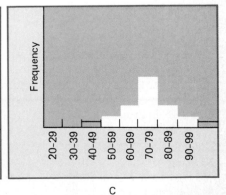

C

the center of distribution C lies above the class interval 70–79. In other words, a "typical" score in both distribution A and B is around 55, whereas it is around 75 in distribution C. This typical value of a distribution is called its **central tendency.**

A second major feature of a distribution is its spread or **variability.** For example, the scores in distribution A are all closely grouped around the center of the distribution, while they are much more spread out or variable in distributions B and C. Thus distribution B is similar to distribution A in central tendency, but similar to distribution C in variability.

Central tendency and variability can be more precisely characterized with specific measures or numbers. Such numbers, or statistics, characterize particular aspects of a group of numbers.

Measures of Central Tendency

Three different statistics are commonly used to characterize the central tendency of a distribution. These are the mode, the median, and the mean. The **mode** is the number that occurs most frequently in a distribution. For example, suppose your data consist of these numbers: 11, 7, 7, 10, 11, 8, 11. The mode would be 11, because it occurs more often than any other number. In a frequency distribution graph, the mode would be the interval having the highest bar above it in a histogram, or the highest point in a polygon (for example, the interval from 4,000 to 4,999 in Figure 1). (Exactly which number within that interval you use to denote the mode involves issues we need not consider here.)

The **median** is the middle number in an ascending or descending sequence of numbers. If you order or *rank* the numbers in a distribution, beginning with the largest and ending with the smallest, the median is in the very middle. For example, suppose your data consist of these numbers: 9, 2, 5, 4, 6, 10, 12. If you rank them (12, 10, 9, 6, 5, 4, 2), the number 6 would be the median, because there are as many numbers ranked above it (12, 10, 9) as below it (5, 4, 2). Again, there are some complexities when you use grouped data or when 2 numbers have the same rank.

The third and perhaps most frequently used way of characterizing central tendency is called the arithmetic **mean** or **average.** To calculate the mean, you add all the entries in the distribution and divide by the number of entries. For example, suppose your data consist of 7 numbers: 8, 6, 1, 9, 5, 10, 3. To calculate the mean, first add all of the entries ($8 + 6 + 1 + 9 + 5 + 10 + 3 = 42$). Then divide by the number of entries ($42 \div 7$

$= 6$). Thus the mean or average of 8, 6, 1, 9, 5, 10, and 3 is 6.

Usually we use different symbols to refer to the mean of a sample and the mean of a total population: $\overline{X}$ stands for the mean of a sample, and the Greek letter μ (mu) stands for the mean of a total population. For example, the mean of the sample of incomes in Table 1 is \$6,882; therefore, $\overline{X} = \$6,882$. We would not, however, know the value of μ, the mean of all incomes, unless we were able to determine the income of every domestic worker in the country.

Often the popular press reports an "average" of a frequency distribution without specifying whether it is the mode, the median, or the arithmetic mean. Which of these it is can make a difference. Consider the hypothetical income data we have been discussing: The mode is about \$4500; the median is \$5500; and the arithmetic mean is \$6,882. How well you think domestic workers are paid will certainly depend on which of these "averages" is reported!

Measures of Variability

Three statistics commonly used to characterize the variability of a distribution are the range, the variance, and the standard deviation. The **range** is simply the difference between the largest and smallest number in the distribution. For example, suppose your data consist of the following numbers: 20, 15, 5, 30, 10. The range equals the largest number (30) minus the smallest number (5), or 25. Thus the range is based on the largest and smallest numbers in a distribution.

A more commonly used measure of variability is the **variance,** the average squared *deviation* or difference of each number from the mean of all the numbers. The variance of a sample is called s^2, and the variance of a population is called σ^2, the Greek letter sigma, squared. As an example of how to compute a variance, say that the data consist of these numbers: 1, 4, 2, 1. First the mean, $\overline{X}$, would be calculated:

$$\overline{X} = \frac{1 + 4 + 2 + 1}{4} = \frac{8}{4} = 2$$

Next, the deviation of each of these numbers from the mean (2) would be squared, as follows:

$$(1 - 2)^2 = 1$$
$$(4 - 2)^2 = 4$$
$$(2 - 2)^2 = 0$$
$$(1 - 2)^2 = 1$$

To compute the variance, you then find the average or

Table 2: The Results of Five Different Measurements on Truway and Accuway Scales.

	Truway	Accuway
1st weighing	1.5 grams	1.7 grams
2nd weighing	1.0 grams	1.4 grams
3rd weighing	2.0 grams	1.5 grams
4th weighing	2.5 grams	1.3 grams
5th weighing	.5 grams	1.6 grams
	$\overline{X} = 1.5$ grams	$\overline{X} = 1.5$ grams
	$s^2 = .5$ grams^2	$s^2 = 0.2$ grams^2
	$s = .71$ grams	$s = .14$ grams

mean of these squared deviations, which is their sum divided by 4:

$$s^2 = \frac{1 + 4 + 0 + 1}{4} = \frac{6}{4} = 1.5$$

The variance is just as important as the mean in interpreting data. For example, look at the hypothetical data in Table 2. An object known to weigh 1.5 grams was weighed on a Truway scale and on an Accuway scale on five different occasions. Though the average weight for the two scales is the same, the *Truway scale is more variable* ($s^2 = .5$ grams^2 versus .02 grams^2), and so it is less reliable. Thus, Accuway is clearly the preferred scale, but knowing only the average value of the measurements would not tell you this and, thus, would not help you make the best choice.

The variance of the measurements in Table 2 is shown in grams squared, an awkward kind of quantity to think about. If we take the square root of the variance ($s = \sqrt{s^2}$ and $\sigma = \sqrt{\sigma^2}$), we have another measure of variability, the **standard deviation.** For example, the variance of .5 grams^2 corresponds to a standard deviation of .71 grams. The standard deviation is easier to use because the units are the same as in the original measurements (grams instead of grams squared).

Position in a Distribution

Two commonly used indices of a number's relative position in a distribution are standard deviation and percentiles. The standard deviation of a distribution of numbers provides a convenient way of expressing how far away any given measurement is from the average of a set of measurements. Look again at the measurements for the Accuway Scale: 1.3, 1.4, 1.5, 1.6, 1.7. The average, $\overline{X}$, is 1.5 grams; the standard deviation is .14 grams. The measurement of 1.7 grams, then, for instance, is 1.4 standard deviation units above the mean ($1.7 = \overline{X} +$

1.4s or $1.7 = 1.5 + (1.4)(.14) = 1.5 + .20$). Similarly, the measurement of 1.4 grams is .71 standard deviation unit below the mean ($1.4 = \overline{X} - .71s = 1.5 - .1$). Thus we can express any measurement in terms of how many standard deviations it is above or below the mean of the set of measurements. Thus, if we let X be any measurement, we may express X as the mean ($\overline{X}$) plus some multiple (z) of the standard deviation (s): $X = \overline{X} + z(s)$.

As an example, look again at the Truway measurements in Table 2. How many standard deviation units above the mean is the measurement of 2.5? In other words, what is z equal to in $2.5 = 1.5 + z(.71)$? To find out the value of z we first subtract the mean, 1.5, from the measurement, 2.5:

$$2.5 - 1.5 = z(.71)$$

The last step in finding z is to divide both sides of the equation by the standard deviation, or .71:

$$\frac{1}{.71} = \frac{z(.71)}{.71} \qquad 1.41 = z$$

The score of 2.5 is 1.41 standard deviation units above the mean, 1.5. We can do the same thing for measurements below the mean. In Table 2 the Truway Score of .5 is -1.41 standard deviation units *below* the mean, since

$$.5 = 1.5 - (1.41)(.71) \quad \text{or} \quad Z = \frac{.5 - 1.5}{.71} = -1.41.$$

Table 3 gives each Truway and Accuway measurement and its standard score (how many standard deviations above or below the mean it is). When we reexpress a number in terms of how many standard deviation units it is from the mean, we call that its **standard score,** or **z-score.**

A second way of expressing a number's relative position in a distribution is in terms of the percentage of numbers that are at the same level or below it—that is, give the number's **percentile rank.** For example, by

Table 3: Truway and Accuway Measurements and Their Standard Scores.

TRUWAY		ACCUWAY	
Raw Score	Standard Score	Raw Score	Standard Score
1.5	0	1.7	$+1.43$
1.0	$- .70$	1.4	$- .71$
2.0	$+ .70$	1.5	0
2.5	$+1.41$	1.3	-1.43
.5	-1.41	1.6	$+ .71$

definition of the median, the percentile rank of the median is the 50th percentile. As another example, a score of 80 on a given test is in the 40th percentile if 40 percent of the scores are below it. On another test, however, a score of 80 might be in the 90th percentile, because 90 percent of the scores were at or below 80.

RELATIVE FREQUENCY AND PROBABILITY

Frequencies can be deceiving! University A reports admitting 20 women to graduate school; University B reports admitting 40. Does this indicate a pattern of discrimination on the part of University A as compared to B? Before reaching any conclusions, it would be important at least to determine for each university what proportion or **relative frequency** of admittances were women. Suppose A's total number of admittances is 40 and B's is 80. The picture is now different; it is clear that each university is admitting about 50 percent men and women. Figure 3 shows a relative frequency distribution for the data given in Table 1 and Figure 1.

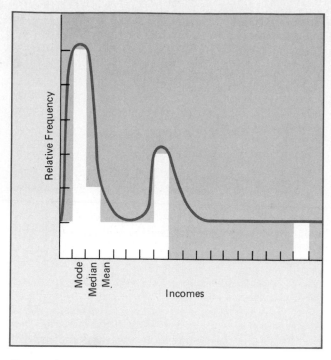

FIGURE 4
Comparison of a theoretical probability distribution of incomes (smooth curve) and the relative frequency distribution of the sampled incomes.

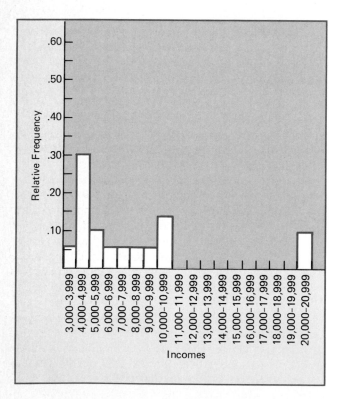

FIGURE 3
Relative frequency distribution for the scores in Table 1.

Suppose we took the incomes in Table 1A, painted each of the numbers on a marble, and then put them all in an urn, which we then shook up. What are the chances that we would draw a marble with a number between 7,000 and 7,999 on it? Since there are 17 marbles and only one is in the interval 7,000 to 7,999, we can readily see that the chances are 1 in 17. But what about our original sample of incomes—what were our chances of drawing one income between $7,000 and $7,999? Without knowing the true proportion or *probability* of incomes in this interval in the population, we cannot answer this question. We can, however, say that the true proportion of incomes in the interval $7,000 to $7,999 is the probability that if we randomly sample one income from the population, then that income will be between $7,000 and $7,999. In a *random sample,* every income in the population has an equal chance of being selected. In a random sample, then, there are no biases that would favor some incomes over others. Such a bias might occur if, for example, we surveyed domestic workers in only one part of the country.

Figure 4 compares a theoretical probability distribution of incomes to the relative frequency distribution of incomes in our sample of 17 incomes. Though we can see that the distribution of incomes in the sample is not exactly the same as the theoretical probability distribution of incomes, it is very similar. When we don't know the true probability distribution for the population, we can use the distribution of a random sample as our best guess as to the true proportion in the population. Thus, for example, our best guess as to the true proportion of incomes between $7,000 and $7,999 is .059, the proportion or relative frequency in our sample. When statisticians use quantities or statistics such as relative frequency to guess the true quantity, we say that the sample statistic is used to estimate the population value or *parameter*.

Just as we can use the sample proportion to estimate the true proportion or probability, we can use the mean of the sample, $\overline{X}$, as an estimate of the population mean, μ. In the income example, we would estimate the average income as the sample average: $6,882. Similarly, we can use the variance of the sample to estimate the variance of the population.

NORMAL DISTRIBUTION

Many kinds of empirical data are distributed in a pattern that is approximately symmetrical, or bell-shaped—as in the sample of IQ data shown in Figure 5. When this occurs, it is often assumed that the true probability dis-

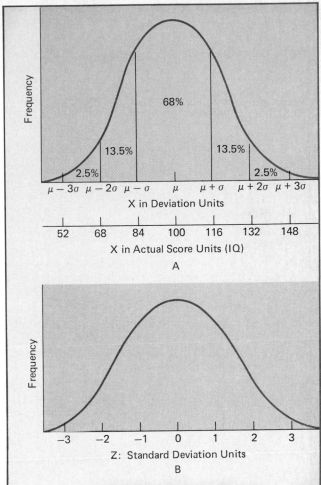

FIGURE 6
Normal curve: (A) Percent areas from mean to specified distance in deviation units. (B) Standard normal curve.

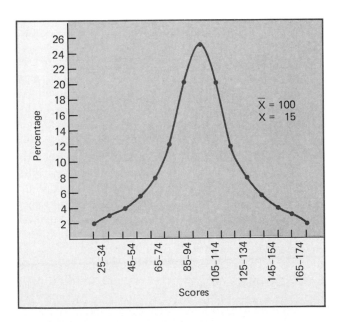

FIGURE 5
IQ data from a hypothetical sample of 500 tests.

tribution is the **normal distribution curve** shown in Figure 6A. In a normal distribution, 68 percent of the numbers are between 1 standard deviation below the mean and 1 standard deviation above the mean ($\mu \pm 1\sigma$). Looking at the IQ data in Figure 5, we see that the sample mean is 100 and the sample standard deviation is 15 points. The graph shows us that in this sample of IQ scores, 65 percent of the measurements are in the interval from 85 to 114. So for this interval, the proportion of numbers in the sample is similar to a normal distribution. When the sample proportions are so close to the theoretical probabilities of the normal distribution, we say the normal curve gives a good approximation of the empirical, sample distribution. The theoretical proportion .68 is arrived at by computing the area under the curve and over the interval 1 standard

Table 4: Area under Normal Curve as Proportion of Total Area.

Standard Deviation	(1) Area to the Left of This Value	(2) Area to the Right of This Value	(3) Area Between This Value and the Mean
−3.00	.001	.999	.499
−2.50	.006	.994	.494
−2.00	.025	.975	.475
−1.50	.067	.933	.433
−1.00	.159	.841	.341
− .50	.309	.691	.191
.00	.500	.500	.000
+ .50	.691	.309	.191
+1.00	.841	.159	.341
+1.50	.933	.067	.433
+2.00	.975	.025	.475
+2.50	.994	.006	.494
+3.00	.999	.001	.499

Table 5: Graduate Record Examination Scores and Their Respective Standard Scores.

GRE Scores	Standard Score
200	−3.0
300	−2.0
400	−1.0
500	0.0
600	+1.0
700	+2.0
800	+3.0

Mean = 500
Standard Deviation = 100

deviation below and above the mean, as shown in Figure 6A. Similarly, the area under the curve and above the interval from $\mu + 1\sigma$ to $\mu + 2\sigma$ is equal to the proportion .135. This is very near the sample proportion in the data of Figure 5A. It is very difficult to compute areas under the normal curve, so statisticians have provided tables of different fractions of areas under this curve. Table 4 gives area under the normal curve as a proportion of the total area.

There are many uses for the proportions given in Table 4. One of them is the interpretation of standard scores and the other is in tests of significance.

Standard Scores and the Normal Distribution

It is often useful to express a measurement in relation to the rest of the measurements—either as a percentile rank or as a standard score. If the population sampled has a normal probability distribution, then the set of standard scores of that population also has a normal distribution. Figure 6B is the normal distribution of standard scores: The mean of the standard scores is 0 (that is, $\mu = 0$), and its standard deviation is equal to 1 (that is, $\sigma = 1$). Standard scores of a distribution are useful for finding the probability that an observation from a normal population will fall in a given interval. For example, the Graduate Record Exam has a mean of 500 and a standard deviation of 100, as shown in Table 5. The probability that a score picked at random will be

below −.5 standard deviations (−.5σ below the mean) is given in Table 4 in the row containing −.5; it is .309. The GRE score corresponding to a standard score of −.5 can be computed as follows: We let X denote the unknown GRE score. We know X can be written as

$$X = \overline{X} - (.5)(\sigma)$$

So for the GRE we have

$$X = 500 - (.5)(100) = 450$$

So the chance of sampling a GRE score *below* 450 is .309.

STATISTICAL INFERENCE AND DECISION MAKING

Statistical inference is the process of interpreting sample data. Here we will discuss how to interpret differences among sample means from several groups. First, though, we need to consider just how typical the sample mean really is.

Does the sample mean accurately predict the true population mean? Table 6 gives the results of two different experiments on how long it takes rats to complete a maze. The two experiments were conducted under the same procedure, but with different rats. As might be expected, the mean times for the two groups of rats are different. Even if the two groups of rats are from the same population, we would still expect the sample means to be different, because random samples drawn from a population do vary. Thus there is a *distribution of sample means,* whose mean, μ, is the same as the mean of the population from which the samples are drawn. The distribution of sample means can be ap-

Table 6: Raw Scores and Statistics from Two Experiments.

The experiments measured the time it takes a rat to traverse a maze.

TIME (MIN)			
Experiment 1		Experiment 2	
Rat 1	2.1	Rat 1	2.3
Rat 2	2.4	Rat 2	2.2
Rat 3	1.8	Rat 3	1.9
Rat 4	2.3	Rat 4	1.5
Rat 5	1.9	Rat 5	1.2
$\overline{X} = 2.1$		$\overline{X} = 1.82$	
$s^2 = .052$		$s^2 = .1736$	
$s = .228$		$s = .417$	

proximated with the normal curve as shown in Figure 7.

The standard deviation of the distribution of sample means is called the **standard error of the mean,** $\sigma_{\overline{X}}$, since it reflects the accuracy with which the sample mean estimates the population mean. The formula for the standard error of the mean is

$$\sigma_{\overline{X}} = \frac{\sigma}{\sqrt{N}}$$

where σ is the population standard deviation and N is the number of measurements added together in computing the sample mean.

The more samples there are, the smaller the size of the standard error. This is just what we would expect; a more reliable (i.e., less variable) estimate of the mean *should* be obtained by taking larger samples. A few sample computations will make this observation clear. First, let's consider the theoretical distribution of IQ scores in Figure 5. Let the standard deviation of the population, σ, be assumed to be 16. Now, suppose we administer an IQ

test to a group suspected to differ from the norm in their average IQ. Thus, we wish to estimate their average IQ. Suppose we give the IQ test to a sample of 64 people in this group. How much variability will there be in our estimate of the group's average IQ? To answer this, we compute the standard error of the mean:

$$\sigma_{\overline{X}} = \frac{\sigma}{\sqrt{N}}$$

For our example,

$$\frac{\sigma}{\sqrt{N}} = \frac{16}{\sqrt{64}} = 2.0$$

Thus, one standard deviation in the distribution of sample means is 2.0 To interpret this, we recall that for the normal probability curve, the chances of being between 1 standard deviation above and below the mean is about 68 percent—in other words, the probability that a sample mean based on 64 test scores is between 98 and 102 is .68. Consider, however, taking a sample mean based on only 16 scores. The standard error of the mean in this case is

$$\frac{\sigma}{\sqrt{N}} = \frac{16}{\sqrt{16}} = 4$$

Thus, the standard error in the mean is twice as great as when N = 64. Now there is a 68 percent chance that the observed sample mean lies between 96 and 104—a much wider interval than when the sample size is 64. Thus, *the smaller the sample size, the less reliable or accurate is the sample mean as an estimator of the population mean.* Furthermore, given the sample size and standard deviation of the population, it is possible to specify the probability that the sample mean will be in a given interval.

Statistical Significance

The interpretation of many experiments in psychology depends on comparisons of measurements made on 2 different populations. Each population is sampled, and the sample mean for each group is computed. Deciding whether the population means differ involves assessing the variability of the sample means to determine if an observed difference between the sample means is reliable, or **statistically significant.** The basic question, then, is whether a difference between two sample means reflects a true difference between population means or is simply the result of the variability inherent in sample means—that is, sampling error.

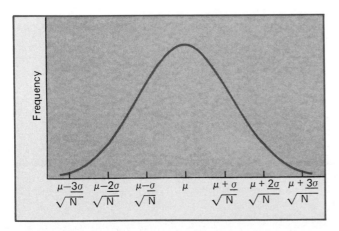

FIGURE 7
The normal curve distribution of sample means.

Table 7: Hypothetical Comprehension Scores for Two Methods for Teaching Reading.

Teaching Method I	Teaching Method II
80	80
85	85
60	60
75	75
90	30
Mean = 78	Mean = 66

Table 8: A Second Set of Hypothetical Comprehension Scores.

Reading Method I	Reading Method II
70	60
72	58
78	66
84	74
86	72
Mean = 78	Mean = 66

As an example, let's look at the data from an experiment to test reading comprehension. There are two groups in this experiment. Each group consists of 5 children who were randomly selected from elementary schools in the area. Each group is exposed to a different reading method. At the end of the learning period, a comprehension test is given; the test scores are shown in Table 7. What can be inferred from the data? Is Method I significantly better than Method II? Note that the difference between the means is 12, but the two groups only differ on one score. Thus we would not want to conclude that the groups differ significantly, even though their means differ.

Table 8 shows another set of hypothetical data. Again, the mean difference is the same, but now most of the scores for Method I are higher than most of the scores for Method II. This gives us greater confidence that Method I is better than Method II, but this is just an intuitive judgment—what a test of statistical significance gives us is a precise way to evaluate the reliability of an observed difference between sample means.

The examples comparing reading methods suggest that the reliability of a difference between means depends both on the *size* of the difference in means and on the *variability* of the means. By comparing the magnitude of the difference between the means to the standard error of the difference between the means, we can evaluate precisely the reliability of the difference be-

tween the means. This comparison is done by computing a *test statistic,* which is the ratio of the difference between the means, D, and the standard error of the difference between means, σ_D:

$$\text{test statistic} = \frac{D}{\sigma_D}$$

If the difference in the means is sufficiently larger than σ_D, then the difference, D, is classified as statistically significant or reliable. As a rule of thumb, a ratio of 2.0 or more is considered statistically significant. The formula for the standard error of the difference between means is

$$\sigma_D = \sqrt{\frac{\sigma_1^2}{N_1} + \frac{\sigma_2^2}{N_2}}$$

where $\frac{\sigma_1^2}{N_1}$ is the variance of the first group mean and $\frac{\sigma_2^2}{N_2}$ is the variance of the second group mean.

We will use the data from the reading methods example to illustrate the computation of a test statistic. For the data in Table 7, the difference between the sample means is

$$D = 78 - 66 = 12$$

The estimated standard error of the difference between means, $\hat{\sigma}_D$, is

$$\hat{\sigma}_D = \sqrt{\frac{106}{5} + \frac{394}{5}} = 10$$

Dividing D by $\hat{\sigma}_D$, we find that

$$\text{test statistic} = \frac{12}{10} = 1.2$$

Since this value is smaller than 2.0, we conclude that the difference between the means is not statistically significant. Using the same procedure, we can compute the test statistic for the data in Table 8. The difference between the sample means is

$$D = 78 - 66 = 12$$

The standard error of the difference between means is

$$\hat{\sigma}_D = \sqrt{\frac{40}{5} + \frac{40}{5}} = 4$$

Thus, we compute

$$\text{test statistic} = \frac{12}{4} = 3$$

Because the test statistic is well above 2.0, we may conclude that the difference between the sample means is statistically significant. This confirms our intuition about the data in Table 8.

Notice that the sign of the test statistic could be positive or negative, depending on which mean is subtracted from the other ($78 - 66$ or $66 - 78$). In interpreting the test statistic only the number, not the sign, is relevant.

Why is a test statistic of 2.0 the critical value? Just as the normal curve is the distribution of sample means, it is also the distribution of the *differences* between sample means. Since we can treat the test statistic as a standard score when there is no difference between the population means, the chances of a standard score bigger than 2.0 is .025, and the chances of a standard score smaller than -2.0 is .025. Thus, the total probability of a standard score being more than 2 standard deviations away from the mean is .05, the sum of the 2 probabilities. This means that, on the average, 5 out of 100 times the test statistic will be more than 2 standard deviations from the mean by chance, even though there is no difference between the population means. A test statistic greater than 2.0 is often said to be *significant at the .05 level.*

Correlation

When two measures vary together so that it is possible to predict one measure from the other, the two measures are said to be *correlated.* Height and weight, for example, are correlated, since taller people also tend to be heavier, and vice versa. Similarly, good grades in the freshman year of college tend to go with good grades in the senior year of college. (Of course, there are excep-

tions. We all know short, heavy people; tall, lightweight people; people who have poor grades as freshmen and good grades as seniors.)

The **correlation coefficient** is a measure of the degree to which two measures are related, or the degree to which one is predictable from the other. For example, weight is a pretty good predictor of height, while parents' IQ is not quite as good a predictor of child's IQ. In other words, weight is more predictable from height than child's IQ is from parents' IQ. When two measures are completely *un*related, they are said to be independent or uncorrelated. For example, hair color and IQ are not correlated, and so the correlation coefficient is 0.

Two measures are *positively correlated* when high values of one go with high values of the other (e.g., height and weight). Two measures are *negatively correlated* when high values of one go with low values of the other. For example, there is a negative correlation between the number of cigarettes smoked per day and length of life. A perfect positive correlation is assigned the number $+1$, while a perfect negative correlation is given the number -1. Less than perfect correlations range between -1 and $+1$, with 0 (no correlation) being in the middle.

A rough estimate of the relationship between two measures can be shown in a **scatter diagram.** Figure 8 shows three such diagrams. The points in Figure 8A were obtained by testing the IQ of a number of parents and their children, as shown in Table 9. Thus, each point represents a *pair* of measurements. To plot a point in

FIGURE 8

Scatter diagrams for hypothetical data. Each point represents the IQ scores for a given parent-child pair (left); the book length-rated quality for a given book (middle); and the reading ability-reading time scores for a given student (right).

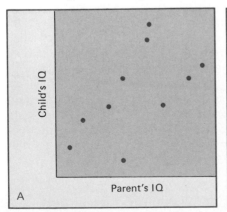

A — Child's IQ vs Parent's IQ

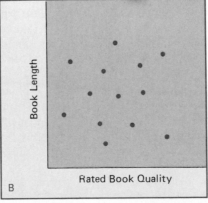

B — Book Length vs Rated Book Quality

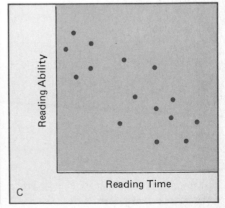

C — Reading Ability vs Reading Time

Table 9: IQ Scores from Pairs of Parents and Children.

Observation Number	Parents' IQ	Child's IQ	Product of Deviations from Mean
1	125	110	$(125 - 100.3)(110 - 100) = 247.0$
2	120	105	$(120 - 100.3)(105 - 100) = 98.5$
3	110	95	$(110 - 100.3)(95 - 100) = -48.5$
4	105	125	$(105 - 100.3)(125 - 100) = 117.5$
5	105	120	$(105 - 100.3)(120 - 100) = 94.0$
6	95	105	$(95 - 100.3)(105 - 100) = -26.5$
7	98	75	$(98 - 100.3)(75 - 100) = 57.5$
8	90	95	$(90 - 100.3)(95 - 100) = 51.5$
9	80	90	$(80 - 100.3)(90 - 100) = 203.0$
10	75	80	$(75 - 100.3)(80 - 100) = 506.0$
Mean	100.3	100	SUM DEV = 1300
Variance	232.81	235	
Standard Deviation	15.26	15.33	

Figure 8A, we first find the parent IQ on the horizontal axis and the child IQ on the vertical axis and then put a point where the lines intersect. Notice that in Figure 8A there is a tendency for high parent IQ to go with high child IQ, so the graph indicates a *positive correlation*. Figure 8B illustrates *no correlation* whatsoever between the rated quality of a book and its length. Here the points seem randomly scattered about the graph. Figure 8C illustrates a *negative correlation* between

reading time and reading ability—greater reading ability goes with shorter reading time. Figure 9 gives a number of idealized scatter diagram shapes together with an appropriate numerical value of the correlation coefficient.

Product-Moment Correlation

The product-moment method is the most frequently used method for determining the correlation coefficient (r) of a sample of pairs of measurements. This method provides a way to estimate the true population correlation, which is denoted by the Greek letter ρ (rho).

The formula for computing the sample correlation coefficient is

$$r = \frac{\text{SUM DEV}}{N s_1 s_2}$$

where SUM DEV is the sum of the product of deviation scores, N is the number of pairs of measures, s_1 is the standard deviation of one set of measures, and s_2 is the standard deviation of the other set of measures. To illustrate the computation of r, we will use the data in Table 9. The far right column of this table gives the product of deviation scores for each pair of measurements. The product is obtained by taking the deviation of the parent IQ from the mean parent IQ times the deviation of the child IQ from the mean child IQ. After all these products are computed, we add them up to get *SUM DEV*. In Table 9, *SUM DEV* = 1300. Thus

$$r = \frac{\text{SUM DEV}}{N(s_1 s_2)} = \frac{1300}{10(15.26 \times 15.33)}$$

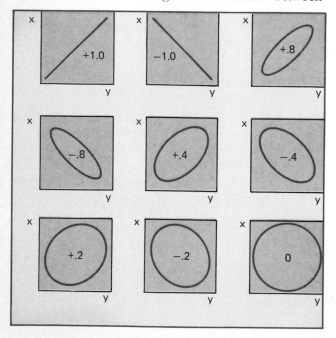

FIGURE 9
Idealized scatter diagrams and an appropriate correlation coefficient.

$$r = \frac{1300}{2339.36}$$

$$r = .56$$

INTERPRETATION OF THE CORRELATION COEFFICIENT. Since the correlation coefficient tells us how predictable the value of one measure is, given a value of a second measure, it is often tempting to think that a correlation indicates a cause-and-effect relationship. In the case of height and weight there is not much temptation, since it seems silly to say height "causes" weight. We know that both height and weight are the result of a complex of factors—thus they share common causes. In the case of the relation between parent and child IQ it seems more reasonable to infer a cause for the relationship—the child inherits his or her IQ from the parent. However, it is just as reasonable to interpret this correlation the same way we did in the height-weight example: Scores on IQ tests are the result of a complex of factors. Parents and children share a number of environmental as well as heritable factors. As another example, there is a positive correlation between years of education and later income, but this does not mean more education *causes* higher income. Other factors may cause both: People with money are more likely to send their children to college, more intelligent people attend college, and social pressures that select for college attendance versus nonattendance covary with the job opportunities available.

Suggested Readings

HUFF, D. *How to lie with statistics.* New York: Norton, 1954. An excellent introductory book on the use and misuses of statistics.

KIMBLE, G. A. *How to use (and misuse) statistics.* Englewood Cliffs, N.J.: Prentice-Hall, 1978. A more advanced book on this subject.

MOSTELLER, F., ROURKE, R. E. K., & THOMAS, G. B., JR. *Probability with statistical applications.* Reading, Mass.: Addison-Wesley, 1973. A more advanced introduction to probability and statistics.

MYERS, J. L. *Fundamentals of experimental design,* 3rd ed. Boston: Allyn & Bacon, 1979. An advanced book on experimental design for students who have had some elementary statistics.

WELKOWITZ, J., EWEN, R. B., & COHEN, J. *Introductory statistics for the behavioral sciences,* 3rd ed. New York: Academic Press, 1982. A very elementary introduction to statistics.

Glossary

Absolute refractory period The period just after the firing of a neuron when the neuron cannot be excited, no matter how great the stimulus.

Absolute threshold The minimum amount of stimulus required to produce sensation at least 50 percent of the time.

Accommodation (1) the reshaping of the lens that allows the eye to focus on both near and distant objects; (2) according to Piaget, the child's adjustment to new objects or new stimuli by acquiring new responses.

Acetylcholine A chemical believed to be the major neurotransmitter.

Achievement Expression of competence motivation through the desire to excel, to complete difficult tasks, to meet high standards, and to perform better than others.

Achievement tests Test designed to measure how much material has been previously learned by the testee.

Acquisition The first part of a learning experiment, during which, as a result of reinforcement, a new response is gradually learned.

Acronym A word made up of parts of a more complex phrase (e.g., the word NASA to denote National Aeronautics and Space Administration).

Acrophobia Fear of heights.

Action potential The rapid change in electrical charge that flows along a neuron and is associated with nerve and muscle activity; this potential is caused by a change in the permeability of the cell membrane.

Activation theory A theory based on the idea that emotional expressions are not unique or independent but exist on a continuum ranging from inactivity (sleep) to maximum activity (violent emotion).

Adaptation Decreased reactivity to environmental stressors. Stress responses are often reduced with coping techniques.

Addiction See **substance dependence**.

Additive mixture A color mixture that is produced by focusing light of different wavelengths on the same spot.

Adjustment Changes in behavior, skills, or personal traits that enable environmental demands upon the individual to be met.

Adolescence In our culture, the period between childhood and adulthood during which a person learns the skills needed to function as an adult.

Adoption studies Studies that examine the behavior of adopted children, especially twins reared apart, to separate the effects of genes (biological parents) and environment (adoptive parents).

Adrenal glands. The two endocrine glands situated above the kidneys; the hormones they secrete affect the body's reaction to stress (epinephrine and norepinephrine) and regulate the functions of metabolism and sexual activity (steroids).

Adrenaline A commonly used term for **epinephrine**.

Adrenocorticotropic hormone (ACTH) A hormone that is released by the pituitary gland and causes the adrenal cortex to release **adrenalin (epinephrine)**.

Affect The expression of emotion; the signs and feelings of emotion shown to others.

Affective disorders Patterns of behavior in which an individual expresses emotional states to excess, inappropriately, or inadequately.

Affective meaning The emotional connotation of a word. For example, the affective meaning of "sunshine" is generally positive for most people. See **semantic differential**.

Afferent Neuronal impulses that are directed toward the brain or spinal cord.

Affiliation. The need or desire to be connected to or to associate with others.

Aggression The kinds of behavior that lead to the damage or destruction of something—either another organism or an inanimate object.

Agoraphobia Fear of open places.

Alcohol A drug that acts as a depressant of the central nervous system and is found in beer, wine, and distilled spirits.

Alcoholism A condition in which dependence on alcohol results in impairment of some significant part of the drinker's life and progressively leads to physical damage.

Alleles Pairs of related genes (such as those determining eye color); one allele is usually dominant and the other recessive.

Allophones The different versions of a phoneme (speech sound) that sound different but are equivalent (e.g., the sound of the letter "r" in "bird" can vary depending on the speaker's accent, but these variations are all allophones of the basic phoneme /r/).

All-or-none property The rule that a neuron will always respond with its complete strength (action potential) to a stimulus or will not respond at all, regardless of the stimulus magnitude.

Alpha waves Brain waves produced when the body is in a state of relaxation.

Altruistic behavior Behavior that helps others and does not result in any personal gain.

Alzheimer's disease A disease that causes rapid aging and loss of cognitive ability.

Amnesia Memory loss caused by head injury or psychological trauma; can be partial or total. See also **anterograde amnesia, retrograde amnesia, organic amnesia,** and **repression**.

Amphetamines Stimulants that affect the central nervous system and can cause edginess, anxiety, and increased heart rate; sometimes prescribed for mood or weight control.

Amplitude The magnitude of a sound or light wave; the main determinants of loudness and brilliance.

Anal stage According to Freud, the second stage of personality development, when retention and elimination of feces become the focus of a child's erotic feelings.

Analysis-by-synthesis A mechanism for perception of complex patterns whereby the person generates a best guess of what the pattern is (i.e., synthesizes the pattern) and then evaluates that guess against the original input.

Androgens Hormones that regulate the growth of secondary sex characteristics, principally in males but also in females.

Androgen-insensitivity syndrome Occurs in genetic males whose embryonic testes secrete testosterone, but this testosterone is not used by the body cells, and the fetus develops into what appears to be a normal female.

Anesthetic An agent that blocks the transmittal of nerve impulses so that anesthesia, a loss of sensation and often consciousness, is produced.

Anterograde amnesia Following the onset of amnesia, the inability to learn or retain new information.

Antisocial personality disorder Refers to a wide range of chronic problem behavior patterns which commonly include unsocialized behavior and conflict with society; examples include inability to display loyalty to others, gross selfishness, callousness, irresponsibility, impulsiveness, inability to feel guilt or learn from experience, and low tolerance of frustration. Previously called **psychopathic or sociopathic personality.**

Anxiety Emotional arousal similar to fear or apprehension, but lacking a specific object of threat.

Aphasia Impairment or loss of speech production or comprehension, usually because of damage to language areas of the brain.

Approach-approach conflict Occurs when a person confronts simultaneously two attractive but incompatible goals.

Approach-avoidance conflict Occurs when a person is simultaneously attracted to and repelled by the same goal.

Aptitude The capability of learning; aptitude tests are designed to measure a person's ability for future learning.

Aptitude tests Tests designed to predict the future performance, often academic performance, of the testee.

Archetypes According to Jung, primary ideas shared by all humans; contents of the collective unconscious.

Arousal A general state of alertness and increased physiological activity following sensory stimulation.

Assertiveness-training Behavioral techniques that help individuals to more effectively and appropriately assert themselves, their needs, and their interests in interactions with others.

Assimilation Interpreting new information in terms of what is already known; fitting new ideas into existing cognitive schema or frameworks.

Association Linking or a response to a stimulus through learning; also, the connection between words, ideas, or concepts in semantic memory.

Association areas. Areas of the cerebral cortex believed to serve in integrating the complex flow of information and responses related to learning, memory, speech, and thinking.

Attachment Development of emotional bonds and dependencies between individuals, especially between an infant and its parents.

Attention The process of focusing awareness on a limited set of stimuli.

Attitude A specific and consistent way of reacting to certain people, things, or concepts. Attitudes are learned and have both behavioral and cognitive components.

Attribution theory A theory concerned with the rules people use in attempting to infer the causes of behavior they observe in others.

Audience-selection effect The tendency to listen selectively to messages and information agreed with and to shun persuasive communications that argue for the other side.

Audiometric function The function relating absolute threshold to the frequency of a pure tone.

Autokinetic effect The illusion that a stationary spot of light is moving when viewed in a darkened room.

Autonomic nervous system That portion of the peripheral nervous system that regulates the mostly involuntary functions of internal muscles and glands.

Autonomy A sense of independence and control over one's own life.

Aversive counterconditioning By associating an unwanted behavior with negative sensations (pain, discomfort), this kind of therapy attempts to eradicate maladaptive behaviors such as alcoholism and drug abuse.

Avoidance-avoidance conflict Occurs when a person is faced with opposing, equally undesirable choices from which there is no escape—a choice must be made.

Avoidance learning A form of operant conditioning in which timely performance of a specified response prevents the occurrence of an otherwise inevitable aversive stimulus.

Axon The extended portion of nerve fiber that carries impulses away from the nerve cell body to other cells and to muscles and glands.

Axonal transport In a neuron, all replacement parts are manufactured in the cell body and carried down the axon to their destination in a slow-moving system called axonal transport.

Bait shyness In animal studies, the tendency of the animal to avoid food it once favored if it has been made sick by it. This avoidance often occurs even if the animal does not get sick until hours after eating the food.

Balance theory A cognitive theory that states that people prefer consistency in the relationship between their evaluation of another person and that person.

Barbiturates An hypnotic form of depressant often used to induce sleep.

Basic needs According to Maslow, the part of the need hierarchy having to do with *deficiency:* for example, the need for food or the need for shelter.

Basilar membrane A membrane within the cochlea containing sense receptors that, when vibrated, produce the neuronal effects of auditory stimulation.

Behavior All responses or activity of an organism, including thinking, dreaming, and physiological functions; in psychology the emphasis is on behaviors that are observable by others, including cognitive processes related verbally.

Behavioral therapy A type of therapy based on learning theory and focused on problem behaviors themselves. Abnormal functioning is viewed as maladaptive patterns of behavior that are learned; the goal of therapy is to extinguish these patterns and help the client learn new, adaptive ones.

Behavior modification Attempts to alter an individual's behavior through operant conditioning techniques.

Bel Unit of measurement for the intensity of sound. One bel represents a tenfold (10^1) increase in energy, two bels a hundred-fold (10^2), etc. See also **decibel.**

Bel scale Zero on the bel scale corresponds to the normal threshold energy for a 1,000 Hz tone. Named in honor of Alexander Graham Bell.

Binocular cues Visual cues from both eyes, combined through **binocular fusion.**

Binocular disparity The way the same object is seen from two slightly different angles due to the separation of the right and left eyes.

Binocular fusion. The combination of both left and right eye perspectives so that they are experienced as one.

Binocular rivalry The competition between disparate monocular views for inclusion in the cyclopian view (e.g., if one eye sees vertical stripes and the other horizontal, then vertical and horizontal views alternate every few seconds in the combined (cyclopian) view.

Biofeedback A technique usually employing physiological sensing devices for providing feedback to an individual, in the form of tones, moving graphs, or dials, on his or her present bodily states. Through these feedback procedures, the individual may learn to monitor and control such functions as brain wave patterns, blood pressure, muscle tension, and heart rate.

Bipolar disorders Previously known as manic-depressive psychosis, bipolar disorders are defined by extreme swings in mood: The individual goes through periods of severe depression and periods of energetic mania of varying durations—from days to months.

Blind spot The region of the retina insensitive to light because the blood vessels and nerves exit there.

Blocking A psychological barrier to acknowledging or remembering an element of reality one fears.

Blood-brain barrier A system for protecting the brain from toxic substances: Blood vessels are less permeable in the brain than in other parts of the body. It has prevented the effective use of some new drugs, which will not pass this barrier (e.g., use of GABA in the treatment of Huntington's chorea).

Brain stem Lower part of the brain; consists of the hindbrain (medulla, pons, and cerebellum) and midbrain.

Brain transplant Since the normal rejection mechanisms do not operate through the blood-brain barrier, it is possibe to transplant tissue into the brain without rejection.

Broca's area A zone in the left cerebral hemisphere that is believed to control speech.

Cannon-Bard theory of emotion States that when an emotionally arousing stimulus is perceived, the thalamus sends out impulses both to the sympathetic nervous system and to the cerebral cortex—thus bodily changes and emotional feelings occur at the same time. See **James-Lange theory of emotion; jukebox theory of emotion.**

Case study A psychological method in which an exhaustive study is made of an individual's history in an attempt to determine past causes of present behavior.

Cataplexy Immobility following an experience of intense fright or shock; occurs sometimes as a sleep disorder.

Catatonic schizophrenia A severe mental disorder characterized by immobility; resistance to comprehending communication; low levels of coherent verbalization; and occasional outbursts of purposeless, excited motor activity.

Catharsis (1) the process of draining off aggressive impulses; (2) relief from tension associated with repression; obtained by remembering or expressing the experiences that were originally repressed.

Cell body The part of a cell containing its nucleus (which contains **chromosomes**).

Central nervous system The brain and the spinal cord.

Central tendency The "typical" or central value in a distribution characterized by measures such as the mean, median, or mode.

Cerebellum The portion of the hindbrain that governs body movement and balance.

Cerebral cortex The deeply folded gray matter that composes the surrounding layer of the cerebrum.

Cerebral hemispheres The two large half-sections of the mammalian brain.

Cerebrum The brain's largest division, consisting of the two cerebral hemispheres and their enveloping layer of cerebral cortex.

Chemotherapy The treatment of abnormal behavior with drugs.

Chimeric stimuli Images made up of incompatible left and right halves (e.g., halves of 2 different faces) used in research on split-brain patients.

Chromosome Threadlike particle in the cell nucleus that contains genes.

Chronological age A person's age in years.

Classical conditioning In this type of learning, a neutral stimulus (CS) is repeatedly paired with an unconditioned stimulus (US), and the subject comes to respond to the neutral stimulus even when it is presented alone.

Claustrophobia Fear of enclosed spaces.

Client-centered therapy An approach that assumes the client is the most qualified person to identify and solve his or her own problems; the therapist's role is to create a supportive environment and to facilitate the client's self-discovery.

Clinical psychologist A psychologist with a Ph.D. who is trained in the diagnosis and treatment of emotional and behavioral problems.

Cocaine A local anesthetic; produces a state of euphoria, talkativeness, and sometimes muscle tremors.

Cochlea The inner ear structure shaped like a snail's shell in which sound energy is converted into nerve impulses.

Code Any way of representing information.

Cognition A term that encompasses all the kinds of knowing an individual may have, including thoughts, knowledge, interpretations, and ideas.

Cognitive-behavioral therapy A form of **behavioral therapy** in which **cognition**—a person's unique ways of seeing and thinking about the world—is considered to be an important determinant of abnormal behavior.

Cognitive dissonance A situation in which a person perceives fundamental discrepancies between two or more beliefs he or she holds or between beliefs and behaviors; when such cognitive dissonance occurs, it often stimulates action to bring opposing beliefs or beliefs and behaviors back into agreement.

Cognitive psychology A branch of psychology that focuses on mental processes such as thinking, reasoning, and language.

Cognitive therapy A therapy developed by Aaron Beck and most often applied to problems of depression. It seeks to reveal and change the problematic thoughts and distorted thinking processes that underlie depression.

Collective unconscious According to Jung's theory of personality, the part of an individual's unconscious that is inherited and shared by all people; contains the archetypes.

Color blindness Having some degree of inability to perceive color. See **dichromats** and **monochromats.**

Color constancy The tendency to perceive a well-known object as being a single color, even if its actual color is modified by changes in illumination.

Compensation The mechanism of covering up aspects of oneself and substituting more desired traits or behaviors in an exaggerated form.

Competence A person's desire or ability to interact effectively with his or her environment.

Compulsions Acts or rituals that are repeated against a person's will.

Computerized axial tomography (CAT) A method of computing images (e.g., brain "slices") based on a series of X-rays generated as the X-ray source is rotated about the head.

Concrete operational stage The third major stage of Piaget's theory of cognitive development (from 7–11 years), during which children develop logical reasoning abilities and concepts of conservation.

Conditioned response The learned response to a conditioned stimulus (CS).

Conditioned stimulus (CS). A neutral stimulus that is repeatedly paired with an unconditioned stimulus (US) in classical conditioning.

Conditioning An elementary form of learning involving the formation of associations among stimuli, responses, and reinforcers.

Cones Sensory receptors on the retina, primarily responsible for the ability to see fine detail and color; function best in daylight or bright light.

Conflict A state of disturbance or tension resulting from opposing motives, drives, needs, or goals.

Conformity Behavior that goes along with group standards or opinions.

Conjunctive concept A concept that is defined in terms of 2 or more criteria or rules. For example, the concept of eligible voter defines a person who is both a citizen and at least 18 years of age.

Connotative meaning The emotional or attitudinal component of word meaning. See **denotative meaning.**

Conservation Understanding that changes

in the appearance of objects do not change such intrinsic properties as numerosity, total volume, or mass.

Consolidation theory Theory suggesting that for a particular memory to be retained permanently, it must have the benefit of an undisturbed period of consolidation (continued neural activity).

Constitutional approach The biological models of personality that hold that body structure or body type determine personality and behavior.

Construct validity A determination of whether or not a test actually measures what it proposes to measure.

Contrast A difference in brightness. For example, the difference between the lightest and darkest parts of a sinusoidal grating (akin to the amplitude of a pure tone).

Control group The group of subjects in an experiment who are treated exactly the same as the experimental group(s) except that they are not given the "treatment" under study and thus serve as the basis for comparison.

Convergence (1) In the nervous system, the process in which nerve impulses from many receptor cells are directed toward the same neuron effector cell. (2) Inward rotation of the eyes to produce fusion of the differing views from each eye.

Convergent thinking A term employed by Guilford to describe problem-solving thought processes which involve narrowing down to a single correct solution.

Convergent validity The degree to which a test or measure of a target concept correlates with other measures of that concept.

Conversion disorders The types of **somatoform disorders** in which an individual develops physical symptoms that have no organic basis in response to some traumatic event.

Coping a person's learned behavior for dealing with conflict or stress.

Cornea The slightly protruding clear outer cap over the iris of the eye.

Corpus callosum The thick band of fibrous white matter that connects the cerebral hemispheres to each other and to other parts of the nervous system.

Corpus striatum An area of the cerebrum that receives dopamine-containing fibers from the midbrain. A deficiency of dopamine affects the cells of the corpus striatum, producing Parkinson's disease.

Correlation A relationship or association between two variables.

Correlation coefficient A measure indicating the strength of association (lack of independence) between two variables.

Cortex The grayish, thin, unmyelinated

covering of the cerebrum; also called **gray matter.**

Covariance A situation in which a change in one variable is associated with a change in another variable.

Creativity Designing, building, or thinking of something that is novel and useful; solving a problem in a unique and clever way.

Crisis intervention Programs that provide a trained person to help people faced with a personal crisis—either over the phone or in person.

Criterion In personality assessment, the *performance* an assessment instrument is trying to predict.

Criterion groups Groups of individuals thought to exhibit a trait or behavior that is being tested. The answers of criterion groups to test items are compared to "normal" subjects in constructing valid test items.

Critical period A limited time period during development when specific learning must occur if it is to occur at all (e.g., imprinting of ducks or geese).

Cross-sectional studies Studies and surveys that involve comparisons of people from a variety of age groups, backgrounds, etc.

Cross-tolerance If repeated use of substance A produces tolerance for substances A and B, then A and B show cross-tolerance.

Crowding The psychological state of feeling crowded, surrounded, and intruded on by the people around you; occurs in situations in which there are too many people or too many activities for the individual to attend to comfortably.

Crystallized intelligence The kind of intellectual functioning that shows little age-related decline, such as that measured by the verbal subtest of the **Weschler Adult Intelligence Scale.**

Culture-fair test An IQ test designed to be fair to persons of all backgrounds.

Dark adaptation. The process in which visual sensitivity increases after one enters a dark room as pigment in the rods reaches its highest concentration.

Decibel A unit of measurement for the intensity of sound; 10 decibels equal 1 bel.

Declarative knowledge Another name for **propositional knowledge.**

Deductive reasoning Reaching a conclusion by accepting the premises of an argument and then following formal logical rules. See **inductive reasoning.**

Deep structure In linguistic theory, the underlying organization of a sentence. See **surface structure.**

Defense mechanisms Strategies used by the ego to fight off instinctual outbursts of

the id and attacks of the superego; examples include repression, reaction formation, rationalization, projection, etc.

Delusion A false belief that cannot be shaken by presentation of facts or reasoning; examples include delusion of grandeur, delusion of persecution, etc.

Dendrites Fibers with many branches extending from the receptor end of a neuron.

Denotative meaning The conceptual aspect of word meaning—the concept that the word refers to. See **connotative meaning.**

Density The number of people present in a specific environment.

Dependent variable In an experiment, the variable that changes or is expected to change when the experimenter manipulates the independent variable.

Depressant A drug that depresses or lowers the activity of the nervous system.

Depression An **affective disorder** of varying degrees of severity, but including common difficulties such as feelings of sadness; a change in appetite; sleeping difficulties; and a decrease in activities, interests, and energy.

Depth of processing The idea that information can be processed (associated, elaborated, recoded, reorganized) to varying degrees (depth); and the more processing, the better recall.

Depth perception The ability to perceive three-dimensional space and objects.

Descriptive statistics Methods of summarizing and describing large amounts of data; for example, the average or mean.

Determinism The theory that all events in nature (including behaviors) are preceded by specific causes; if the relevant causes are known, an event can be predicted.

Developmental psychologist The branch of psychology concerned with physiological and behavioral changes throughout the life span.

Deviation IQ A person's IQ score calculated by comparing his or her test performance to the performance of age-mates on the same test.

Dichromats People who are color blind to either yellow-blue or red-green.

Difference threshold The level of stimulus change necessary in order for a person to perceive a difference; also known as **just noticeable difference (JND).**

Diffusion of responsibility theory Emphasizes that in groups people are more likely to make extreme choices because the responsibility for the choice will be shared by many people.

Digit span The number of digits a person can recall immediately after hearing them spoken.

Disaster syndrome A stress reaction to a

catastrophic event characterized by 3 stages: shock, suggestibility, and recovery.

Discriminant validity (also called **divergent validity**) The degree to which a test or measure measures a target concept better than it measures any other concept.

Discrimination In conditioning, the process of being able to distinguish among stimuli, ignore irrelevant stimuli, and respond to a specific stimulus.

Disjunctive concept A category that is defined in terms of an either-or criterion, for example, the category of *citizen* may be defined as someone who is either born in a country, OR marries a citizen of that country.

Displacement In psychoanalysis, a defense mechanism in which a person directs an emotional response from its actual object to a safer one.

Dissociative disorders A set of disorders characterized by sudden, temporary changes in consciousness, activity, or identity.

Distance cues Cues that assist a person in perceiving distance, such as relative size of similar objects.

Divergent thinking A term employed by Guilford to describe problem-solving thought processes that involve a set of innovative, original, and alternative possible solutions, rather than a single correct answer.

Dizygotic twins Twins resulting from the fertilization of two separate eggs at the same time; also called fraternal twins. See **monozygotic twins**.

Dominant gene The member of the gene pair (allele) that takes precedence and determines the particular bodily characteristic.

Dorsal Referring to the back.

Double approach-avoidance conflict A complex situation in which two possible courses of action each present an approach-avoidance conflict. A person is faced with both approaching and avoiding two goals simultaneously.

Double blind Studies or experiments in which *neither* the experimenter *nor* the subject knows which condition or group is the control and which condition or group is the experimental.

Down's syndrome (mongolism) A congenital defect characterized by mental deficiency (usually moderate retardation) and some physical abnormalities. Down's Syndrome children have an extra, 47th, chromosome.

Dream Vivid imagery occuring during sleep.

Drive The state of arousal or unlearned motivation that occurs when a need is not met.

Drive reduction The theory that motivated behavior is the response to a drive and that responses that satisfy drives are reinforced by the subsequent drive reduction.

Drug Any substance other than food that alters our bodily or mental functioning.

Drug abuse See **substance dependence**.

Drug dependence A physiological and/or psychological need for a drug accompanied by increased tolerance of the drug and withdrawal symptoms if the drug is removed.

Drug therapy See **chemotherapy**.

Eardrum The thin, flexible membrane separating the middle ear from the outer ear.

Echoic memory system A theoretical human memory system that briefly retains auditory information in a form similar to its initial acoustic code.

Ectomorph In Sheldon's constitutional theory, a person with a thin, fragile build who probably has a corresponding introverted, highly sensitive personality.

Effectance motivation The desire to develop and exercise competence in interacting with the environment.

Efferent Refers to neurons leaving the central nervous system; motor neurons.

Effort justification. An area of research supporting cognitive dissonance theory that suggests that people learn to like what they have suffered to achieve.

Ego In Freudian terms, the part of the personality that distinguishes between self and the environment and that mediates the demands of the id and the superego.

Eidetic imagery The ability to retain a mental image of something one has seen for a long period of time; often referred to as **photographic memory.**

Elaboration A recoding of information in an elaborated form (such as adding your own illustration of a point made by a lecturer).

Electroencephalogram (EEG) The record of the electrical activity of the brain.

Electroshock therapy A controversial therapy in which an electric shock is transmitted to the brain to induce convulsions and unconsciousness. Used in cases of severe and prolonged depression.

Elevation A depth perception cue operating on the principle that the higher an object appears in the visual plane, the farther away it appears.

Emotion A complex reaction consisting of both physiological change and a subjective experience of feeling.

Empiricism In theories of development, the idea that all knowledge is based on experience. In philosophy of science, the reliance on observation and experiment—the empirical method.

Encoding The way information is first stored or represented in a memory system.

Encoding specificity Tulving's view that stimuli present during **encoding** are usually good **recall cues**.

Endocrine gland A ductless gland that secretes hormones directly into the bloodstream.

Endogenous Naturally produced within the body.

Endomorph In Sheldon's constitutional theory, a person with a round, heavy build who is likely to have a lethargic, comfort-seeking personality.

Endorphin and enkephalin Naturally produced, opiate-like substances in the body that help people cope with pain and stress.

Energy spectrum The amount of energy from each part of the visible spectrum in a particular source of light.

Enkephalin See **endorphin and enkephalin.**

Environmental psychology A field of scientific inquiry concerned with the interrelationships between the physical environment—the natural or human-made environment—and human behavior.

Epinephrine A hormone secreted by the adrenal glands; increases blood pressure and heart rate as a response to an emergency.

Episodic knowledge Knowledge of events that occurred at specific times earlier in one's experience. A type of **propositional knowledge.**

Equilibratory sense The sense of balance. **Semicircular canals** and **vestibular sacs** are the sensory organs responsible for this sense.

Erogenous zones Areas of the body associated with sexual pleasure.

Eros According to Freud, the life instincts; love directed toward oneself and others.

Estrogens The female hormones that stimulate the development of secondary sex characteristics.

Estrus cycle Cyclical variations in hormonal state in females of the lower mammal species. Ovulation occurs automatically at some specific point in the cycle, and at that time the female becomes both sexually attractive and sexually receptive to the male.

Ethology The study of animal behavior, generally in the animal's own environment.

Evaluation A comparison of a score, object, behavior, or situation with another, and subsequent determination of its relative value.

Excitement The first of Masters and Johnson's 4 stages of human sexual response.

Existential model A personality theory focusing on individual freedom and responsibility for one's own actions. (See also **humanistic model**.)

Exogenous   Something introduced into the body from outside; not occurring naturally within the body.

Expectancy   A person's estimate or belief that a specific behavior will lead to a specific reinforcement or outcome.

Experiential change   Behavioral development that is primarily caused by experience, practice, or training. Contrasted with **maturation**.

Experimental group   The group in a scientific observation (experiment) upon whom the effect of some particular treatment is observed.

Experimental method   A system of testing an idea or theory in a carefully controlled situation involving independent variables and a dependent variable.

Expressive jargon   Speech produced by young children that uses adult speech sounds and intonations but is unintelligible. Precedes stage of single-word utterances and disappears when child begins to produce real words.

Extinction   The gradual reduction of a conditioned response that occurs because of lack of reinforcement.

Extrinsic motivation   Engaging in activities or behaviors because they lead to other rewards; for example, learning course material well in order to win the praise of the professor; a means to an end.

Extrovert   A person who is more concerned with the outside world than with self; an outgoing person.

Factor analysis   A statistical procedure for estimating the correlations of several variables with a common factor; a process by which variables can be grouped in categories.

Family studies   Studies that examine the occurrence of certain traits within families. Taken alone, they do not clearly separate the effects of a common genetic pool and a common environment.

Family therapy   Psychotherapy in which the interactive processes of the family as a group as well as the individual family members are treated.

Fear-induced aggression   Aggressive acts taken by an organism to protect itself when threatened.

Feature detectors   Systems (neural or electronic) that respond to the presence of a specific stimulus component (e.g., an edge, intersection, or particular speech format).

Fechner's law   A law concerning the relationship between a stimulus and a sensation. States that the relation between physical stimulus intensity and the strength of

sensation is a logarithmic one, in which a constant ratio of stimulus intensity produces a constant difference in sensation.

Figure-ground organization   A basic tendency (which Gestalt psychologists argued is innate) to perceive things (figures) standing out against a background (ground).

Filtering   The process whereby certain wavelengths of light are selectively blocked out as the light passes through a substance (filter).

Fixation   In Freudian terms, arrested development characterized by the failure to successfully pass through an earlier psychosexual stage; a persistent behavior which has outlived its usefulness.

Fixed-interval schedule   A schedule of reinforcement in which the animal or person is reinforced for a response only after the passage of a specific interval of time—every 3 minutes, for example.

Fixed-ratio schedule   A schedule of reinforcement in which the animal or person is reinforced after a specific number of correct responses.

Fluid intelligence   The sort of intellectual functioning that shows a decline with age, such as that measured by the performance-oriented subtests of the **Weschler Adult Intelligence Scale**.

Formal operational stage   The fourth and final major stage of cognitive development (Piaget), during which children and adults become able to think and reason in abstract terms (age 12 and up).

Fovea   A small area on the retina on which the cones are concentrated; thus, the area of greatest visual acuity.

Framing effects   The consequences of the particular way in which a problem is worded, or framed. People can be easily biased by the words used to describe a situation or problem.

Fraternal twins   Twins resulting from the fertilization of two separate eggs at the same time; also called dizygotic twins. See **identical** or **monozygotic twins**.

Free association   (1) A process in psychoanalysis in which the patient reports whatever thoughts come to mind in a freefloating, nonstructured way; (2) a type of word-association test.

Free recall   A type of memory test in which the subject recalls items in a list in any order, rather than in the specific order in which they were presented.

Free will   The doctrine that humans are influenced by outside stimulation and bodily states but free to choose their actions on rational grounds.

Frequency   The number of cycles per second of a sound wave; a primary factor in pitch.

Frequency distribution   The frequencies of various values (or ranges of values) occurring in a set of values.

Frequency theory   In hearing, the theory that pitch is determined by the rate of firing of sound receptors. The rate of pulses traveling up the auditory nerve to the brain matches that of a tone over a wide range of frequencies.

Frustration   The psychological state a person experiences when something prevents him or her from reaching a desired goal. Coleman and Hammen (1974) have identified five sources of frustration: delays, lack of resources, loss, failure, and meaninglessness.

Frustration-aggression hypothesis   An explanation of aggression that states that frustration always leads to aggression and that aggression is always a result of frustration.

Fugue   Amnesia accompanied by actual physical flight—the person may wander away for several hours or move to another area and establish a new life.

Functional fixedness   An inability to solve a problem because of a perception of only one function (use) of a particular object.

Fundamental attribution error   The tendency in people to attribute behavior to internal, dispositional states rather than external, situational causes.

Fundamental tone   The dominant frequency of a note sounded on a musical instrument.

Galvanic skin response (GSR)   A response indicated by electrical changes on the skin; common physiological response to fear is a rise in GSR.

Ganglia   Clusters of nerve cell bodies found outside the spinal cord and brain.

Gene   The basic unit of heredity, located on the chromosomes.

General Adaptation Syndrome   Selye's theory of the way people tend to react to stress, beginning with the alarm reaction and progressing through resistance and exhaustion.

Generalization   Responding in a similar way to a broad category of stimuli.

Generalized anxiety disorders   Involves the same kind of discomfort as **phobic disorders,** but the person's anxiety is not clearly linked to a specific object or situation.

Genetics   The study of heredity, or how biological traits are passed on from parents to offspring.

Genital stage   In Freud's theory of psychosexual development, the attainment of firm identification with one's own gender and the capacity for heterosexual love and commitment.

Genotype The specific genetic makeup of an organism.

Gestalt (1) A whole form or figure; (2) a branch of psychology in which behavior is viewed as an integrated whole, greater than the sum of its parts.

Gestalt therapy A humanistic approach, based on the work of Fritz Perls, in which abnormal functioning is viewed as an imbalance in figure-ground perceptions and the denial of one's innate goodness. The goal of Gestalt therapy is to help people become aware of the wholeness of their experiences.

Glial cells Cells of the nervous system that: (1) are responsible for myelination of axons in the brain; (2) direct the growth of neural pathways or interconnections; and (3) play a general role in nervous system metabolism.

Gonads Sex glands: ovaries in females produce estrogen, testes in males produce androgens.

Gray matter See **cortex.**

Group polarization effect The finding that members of a group, after discussion of an issue, are likely to take a more extreme position collectively than they would as individuals. A number of explanations exist for this finding, including information exchange theory and value theory.

Group therapy Psychotherapy involving a number of people working with one another and with a therapist, rather than each person seeing a therapist alone in private or individual sessions.

Groupthink A group decision-making process in which a cohesive group of decision makers lets its concern for group unanimity override making good decisions by carefully appraising alternative courses of action. Obviously, this can, and frequently does, lead to bad decisions being made.

Habituation In behavior studies, a decrease in the strength of a response as the eliciting stimulus is repeated.

Hallucination A perception that is not based on reality; a false mental image.

Hallucinogen A drug, such as LSD, that causes a person to experience hallucinations.

Harmonic Some multiple of the **fundamental tone.**

Hashish A concentrated form of cannabis or marijuana.

Heredity The passing on of traits from parents to offspring.

Hering's opponent-process theory See **Opponent-process theory of color vision.**

Heritability ratio The ratio depicting the proportion of variability in a trait associated with genetic, as opposed to environment, factors.

Hermaphrodite A person with both male and female sexual organs.

Heroin An opiod often used by addicts.

Hertz (Hz) A unit of sound wave frequency equal to one cycle per second.

Heterosexuality Attraction for persons of the opposite sex.

Heuristics General strategies for solving problems or making decisions.

Hierarchy of needs (Maslow) Maslow's system for categorizing human motivation; ascending from basic, physiological needs which must be satisfied before the higher-level needs such as love, esteem, and finally, self-actualization can be satisfied.

Histogram A bar graph indicating a **frequency distribution.**

Holophrastic speech A type of speech used by infants in which one word or phrase stands for a whole idea. "Milk" in this sort of usage can stand for "I want more milk," "Mommy is pouring the milk," or "I spilled the milk."

Homeostatic mechanisms The bodily functions that help maintain homeostasis.

Homeostasis The physiological tendency to maintain an internal, bodily state of balance in terms of food, water, air, sleep, and temperature.

Homosexuality Preference for sexual relations with members of the same sex.

Hormones Substances secreted by endocrine glands that activate and/or regulate many bodily processes.

Hospice A center designed for the care of dying patients.

Hue Color.

Humanistic model A theory of personality focusing on the worth of the individual and the particular and unique experiences of the individual. (See also **existential model.**)

Hypertension A chronic condition of high blood pressure. Early stages of hypertension can be caused by stress.

Hyperthyroidism An overactive thyroid causes irritability, restlessness, and weight loss in adults.

Hypnosis An artificially induced, sleeplike state in which the subject is extremely open to the hypnotist's suggestions.

Hypnotics Depressant substances such as **barbiturates** that are used to induce sleep.

Hypothalamus The lower part of the thalamus in the brain; appears to have a regulatory function in motivation and emotion.

Hypothesis An assumption that serves as a possible explanation for some response or phenomenon.

Hypothyroidism An underactive thyroid causes reduced growth and mental retardation in the young and depression and fatigue in the adult.

Iconic memory A kind of short-term memory involving visual images.

Id The most primary of Freud's three-part personality system; the instinctual impulses which supply psychic energy to the system and seek immediate gratification.

Identical twins Twins that develop from the splitting of a single fertilized egg; also called **monozygotic twins.**

Identification The process during psychosexual development by which a child comes to adopt the behaviors, values, and attitudes of significant adults through imitation.

Identity conflict The conflicts that arise during an adolescent's quest for an adult identity.

Identity versus role confusion According to Erikson, the crisis occurring in adolescence in which the individual must develop a self-concept, adult role, and adult sexuality.

Idiographic Pertaining to the concrete, the individual, the unique. For example, idiographic approaches to personality are based on the assumption that traits are based on specific situations and are unique to individuals.

Illumination (1) The stage in problem solving or creativity when an idea suddenly comes to mind as when the light bulb flashes above the head of a cartoon character; (2) the amount of light falling on a surface.

Illusion A mistaken perception or a distortion of perception.

Imitation Mimicking the behavior of another—plays an important role in child development.

Implosive therapy A type of behavioral therapy based on the theory that prolonged exposure to an anxiety-producing stimulus (by imagining it) in the absence of reinforcement (the feared consequences) extinguishes the fear-provoking power of the stimulus.

Imprinting The behavioral responses, such as following, which are learned rapidly and very early in life, and which are not reversible. In ducks and geese the **critical period** for imprinting is from birth to about 36 hours of age.

Incentive An external stimulus that has the capacity to motivate behavior.

Incubation Unconscious problem solving—when not deliberately thinking about a problem, a solution suddenly appears in consciousness.

Independent variable The factor in an experiment that is deliberately varied by the experimenter in order to test its effects on some other factor.

Induced compliance effect The finding in cognitive dissonance research that greater amounts of attitude change can be achieved with lower incentives for change.

Induced motion The apparent motion of one object in the visual field produced by motion of some other object.

Inductive reasoning Drawing a general conclusion from a set of particular instances. See **deductive reasoning.**

Industry vs. inferiority According to Erikson, the developmental crisis that occurs and should be resolved during the elementary school years, when children develop basic academic and social competence.

Informational social influence A positive form of conformity in which one learns about social realities or conventions from the actions of others.

Information exchange theory A partial explanation for the group polarization effect that points out how, in the course of group decision making, many persuasive arguments will be raised and will tend to convince group members to be more extreme in their decisions.

Information reduction A loss of information such as that which often occurs in **recoding** information from one form to another (e.g., lecture notes to a summary).

Initiative vs. guilt According to Erikson, the developmental crisis from ages 3–5, when children should acquire the ability to initiate activities and develop a sense of purpose.

Innate Unlearned; present at birth.

Insight (1) Understanding of self and awareness of one's motivations, goals, needs; (2) in thinking or problem solving, the sudden solution to a problem or a sudden flash of understanding.

Insight learning Learning based on a sudden grasp of a problem; frequently involves a novel approach to a situation or problem.

Insomnia A common sleep disorder in which a person has trouble going to sleep initially or wakes up during the night and has trouble going back to sleep.

Instinct An innate, unlearned behavior characteristic of a particular species.

Instrumental aggression Aggression that occurs for the gain of the aggressor rather than to just inflict harm; for example, a mercenary soldier's aggression occurs for money.

Intellectualization A defense mechanism in which one avoids the emotional content of a situation by using abstract, intellectual understandings to explain the situation.

Intelligence quotient (IQ) The ratio of a person's mental age to his or her chronological age. (See **deviation IQ.**)

Interneurons Neurons that connect sensory and motor neurons.

Intrapsychic conflict Expressions of the existence of two opposing motivations or impulses within a person.

Intrinsic motivation Engaging in activities or behaviors for the pure satisfaction and pleasure of doing them; for example, learning course material well because it's interesting, challenging, and enjoyable; an end in itself.

Introspection The process of looking inward to one's feelings and attempting to report on what one observes and experiences. Wilhelm Wundt was a pioneering figure in this approach in Germany in the mid-nineteenth century.

Introvert A person more involved with self than with the outer world.

IQ See **Intelligence quotient.**

Iris The colored portion of the eye; the pigments in the iris determine whether the eye is blue, brown, green, etc.

James-Lange theory A theory of emotion which states that physiological arousal, followed by awareness and labeling of that arousal, is what we experience as emotion.

Jukebox theory A theory of emotion based on the experimental finding that physiological arousal (produced by a drug) can set the basis for an emotion. It is, however, an individual's interpretation or understanding of the arousal that determines the emotional response.

Just noticeable difference (JND) A difference in a stimulus that is noticed 50 percent of the time. Also called **difference threshold.**

Key word method A mnemonic technique in which the meaning of a foreign word is recalled by using an English word (the key word) that rhymes with the foreign word as a **recall cue** for the meaning of the foreign word.

Kinesthetic sense The sense of movement of the body (and its parts—muscles, tendons, and joints) and body position.

Korsakoff's syndrome A disorder of memory and orientation resulting from alcoholism.

Language acquisition device (LAD) The innate mechanism (posited by Noam Chomsky) that enables children to learn language and language rules as part of their development.

Latency stage According to Freud, the period between the phallic stage and the onset of puberty, in which the Oedipal and aggressive wishes have been repressed.

Latent content (psychoanalysis) The hidden, symbolic meaning of a dream as caused by unconscious wishes and impulses.

Latent learning Learning that occurs but is not necessarily manifested in behavior or performance.

Lateral hypothalamus The portion of the hypothalamus that appears to stimulate eating.

Lateral inhibition A reduction of sensitivity in one neuron produced by stimulation of an adjacent neuron.

Law of effect A term originally used by Thorndike to describe his observation that responses followed by reward (by a "good effect") tended to be repeated.

Leadership Qualities such as intelligence, ambition, skill, and optimism that enable a person to guide, motivate, and control relevant aspects of the behavior of others.

Learned helplessness The idea that an organism may learn to be helpless as a result of the repeated demonstration that its responses have no effect on its surroundings.

Learning A relatively permanent change in behavior as a result of experience or practice.

Learning set The learning of a particular method or approach that can be applied to the solving of a number of similar problems.

Left hemisphere In most persons, the dominant hemisphere of the cerebrum, which controls motor activity and speech.

Lens The transparent part of the eye that focuses light onto the retina.

Libido Freud's term for instinctive sexual energy that drives the personality system; the combination of the life instincts and the death instincts.

Light adaptation The adjustment of the rods and cones in the eye to changes in illumination.

Limbic system Interrelated structures in the brain that appear to play a role in emotions.

Linear perspective A depth perception cue based on the apparent converging of two parallel lines at the horizon.

Linguistic relativity A theory that language determines how people think and conceptualize the world, such that people who speak different languages think differently.

Literacy The ability to read and write.

Location constancy A perception of stability in position even though the retinal image is moved about.

Longitudinal studies Studies involving a single group of persons over time (e.g., Terman's study of high-IQ children, which has followed them through life for over 50 years). See **cross-sectional studies.**

Long-term memory The relatively permanent storage of information—storage that continues even when the information is not being used.

Long-term memory system Any memory system capable of retaining information over long periods of time.

LSD (lysergic acid diethylamide) A powerful **hallucinogen** that radically alters sensation and perception with minute doses (e.g., 1 milligram).

Magnitude estimation A psychophysical procedure in which the subject indicates the intensity of a sensation by assigning it a number.

Manic-depression A behavioral disorder characterized by feelings of sadness and lethargy alternating with feelings of ecstasy and excitement.

Manifest content (psychoanalysis) The covert, concrete happenings in a dream.

Marijuana A mild hallucinogen with varying effects on its many users, ranging from mood exaggeration to distorted time sense.

Masochism A pathological desire to inflict pain on oneself, or deriving pleasure from being mistreated or suffering.

Maternal aggression Aggressive acts by the mother to protect her young.

Matrix A table of outcomes arranged in rows and columns to graphically demonstrate interdependencies between and among the participants to the interaction.

Maturation The development of a behavior or an ability solely as a result of physical growth; also, the process of physical development itself.

Mean The average value in a distribution (Σ X/N).

Mean length of utterance (MLU) A measurement of sentence length used in language studies of children.

Mechanism A belief that all events in nature (including behaviors) are determined by mechanical causes and that by understanding chemical and physical causes, we can understand the resulting events.

Median The "middle" value in a distribution (as many values exceed it as fall below it).

Meditation A method of relaxation in which one concentrates his or her attention on a single unchanging or repetitive stimulus.

Medulla Swelling of the brain stem just above the spinal cord; controls important involuntary functions such as breathing, heart beat, and digestion.

Memory The ability to retain learned information.

Memory span The number of items that can be recalled after a single presentation.

Memory system Any system capable of retaining information over time (e.g., a photograph, book, electronic computer, or human memory).

Menarche The start of menstruation in young girls.

Menopause In adult women, the stopping of menstruation and the loss of the ability to reproduce, occuring in the 40s–50s.

Menstrual cycle The regular cycle of discharge of blood and uterine materials in human females.

Mental age A measure of a person's intelligence based on the abilities a person is expected to have at that particular age.

Mental retardation Below-normal intelligence; usually an IQ below 70, coupled with social inadequacy.

Mesomorph According to Sheldon's constitutional theory, a person with a muscular, well-developed build who is likely to have an outgoing, risk-taking, athletic personality.

Meta-needs According to Maslow, the "higher" needs, such as beauty, truth and justice.

Method of adjustment A psychophysical method in which the subject simply adjusts a stimulus until it evokes a certain sensation (e.g., until it is as "loud" as some comparison sound or is "just visible," etc.).

Method of constant stimuli A psychophysical method in which a fixed set of stimuli is presented in random order to determine the subject's typical response to each one (e.g., the subject "heard it" 20 percent of the times it was presented).

Method of loci A memory-improving technique in which one associates items to be recalled with specific places or locations, such as the various rooms of one's house.

Midbrain The region of the brain containing the reticular activating system.

Middle ear The portion of the ear lying between the eardrum and the cochlea.

Mnemonics or mnemonic technique Method used to improve one's memory and to aid in remembering something (such as the **method of loci**).

Mode The most frequently occurring value in a distribution.

Modeling A form of behavior training in which a subject learns to make a response by watching others make a response to a particular stimulus.

Mongolism See **Down's syndrome**.

Monochromats People who are missing both color systems and see the world only in shades of gray.

Monocular cues Visual cues from one eye only.

Monozygotic twins Twins that develop from the splitting of a single fertilized egg; also called identical twins.

Moral anxiety In psychoanalytic theory, fear of conscience. We feel guilty when we contemplate or do something contrary to our moral code (superego).

Morpheme The smallest linguistic unit that has meaning.

Morphine An **opioid** often used to control pain.

Motion parallax The relative motion of objects at different distances from a moving observer.

Motivation A general term used to describe an internal state which arouses, maintains, and directs an individual's or animal's behavior toward a goal.

Motor area The area of the brain responsible for integrating the responses of the motor neurons, thereby affecting muscular activity.

Motor homunculus A graphic depiction of a map of the motor cortex, in which each part of the body is shown larger or smaller according to how much motor cortex is devoted to it (see Figure 2–20).

Motor neurons Neurons that carry nerve impulses to the muscles.

Multiple personality A relatively rare **dissociative disorder** in which 2 or more distinct personalities are present in one individual. These personalities alternate over a period of hours or days and compete for access to consciousness.

Mutation An alteration in the genetic code (often caused by chemicals or radiation) that results in an alteration of cell growth.

Myelin The fatty white covering on some axons.

Narcotics Opium and its derivatives, such as heroin and morphine; drugs with pain-killing powers that produce high drug dependence.

Need A biological or psychological requirement; a state of deprivation that motivates a person to take action toward a goal.

Negation A defense mechanism, like **reaction formation**, for refusing to acknowledge unacceptable feelings. The denial of a feeling; for example, I *don't* hate my mother.

Negative afterimage An afterimage that occurs when a person who has been looking at a stimulus looks away; the negative afterimage is perceived in complementary colors to the original stimulus.

Negative reinforcer An event (such as electric shock) that, if stopped when a response is made, increases the likelihood that the response will be repeated.

Negative set A habitual way of approaching a problem that interferes with solving it; a tendency to do things the same old way even when a change of strategy is required.

Neo-cortex The outer layers of the cerebrum.

Neo-Freudian A school of psychological thought based on a modification of Freud's theories: includes such theorists as Horney and Fromm.

Nerve impulse The traveling wave of depolarization that carries information along a neuron.

Neuromodulators Chemicals that control the action of **neurotransmitters** at synaptic junctions.

Neuron The basic unit of the nervous system: consists of a cell body, nucleus, axon, and dendrites.

Neurosis A term traditionally used within the Freudian and Neo-Freudian psychodynamic framework to describe an extremely broad pattern of disorders characterized by anxiety, fear, and self-defeating behaviors.

Neurotic anxiety In psychoanalytic theory, fear that an unacceptable id impulse will surface, causing behavior that will be punished.

Neurotransmitter One of several chemical substances that play a role at the synapse in transmitting messages from neuron to neuron.

Nodes Transfer of ions in neurons can only take place at breaks in the myelin sheath, called nodes, that occur every 1 or 2 millimeters along the axon.

Nomothetic Dealing with general statements or laws. For example, nomothetic approaches to personality are based on the belief that all traits are equally applicable to all individuals.

Norepinephrine A hormone secreted by the adrenal glands; promotes the release of sugar into the blood and also acts as a neurotransmitter; also called noradrenaline.

Normal distribution curve A diagram of scores in which 68 percent of the scores occur between one standard deviation below the mean and one standard deviation above the mean.

Normative social influence Conformity through social influence; occurs when a person suppresses his or her own opinions and complies with group standards in order to avoid punishment or gain reward from the group.

NREM sleep Sleep during which the physiological processes slow down: consists of four stages of sleep through which the person moves in a regular cycle during the night. For the most part, dreaming does not occur in NREM sleep. See **REM sleep.**

Obedient aggression Aggression that occurs as a response to a command from an authority figure.

Obesity In humans, defined as being more than 15 percent over the "ideal" weight, given the person's height and overall body build.

Objective self-awareness A state in which full attention is focused inward, on oneself, in an evaluative way; contrasted with subjective self-awareness in which one's attention is directed outward to activities and others.

Object permanence The knowledge that an object that is hidden from view does not cease to exist.

Obsessions Thoughts that repeatedly intrude against one's will and defy one's efforts to ignore them. Sometimes used more generally to describe the behaviors that are done repetitively to temporarily terminate these thoughts, for example, excessive hand washing.

Obssessive-compulsive disorders Behavior patterns characterized by a compelling drive to repeat unwanted thought or actions over and over agin.

Oedipus complex In Freudian terms, a boy's erotic involvement with his mother and jealousy of his father.

Olfaction The sense of smell.

Open-ended interview An assessment interview in which a judge talks to a person and follows the conversation wherever it leads.

Operant conditioning A type of learning in which specific voluntary behaviors are reinforced.

Opioids Psychoactive derivatives of the opium poppy, or similar but synthetic substances such as methadone.

Opponent-process theory of color vision One of the two leading theories of color vision. States that there are three separate color systems: red-green, blue-yellow, and black-white. The effect of the two components in each system is opposite, so that each system's signal to the brain indicates how much is in the stimulus.

Opponent-process theory of emotion Formulated to explain the motivation behind some self-destructive behaviors, this theory does not address where emotion comes from or what it consists of. Instead, it hypothesizes that the stimulus that causes an emotion also causes another, opposite, emotional reaction (e.g., fear and relief).

Optic chiasm The point at which the optic nerves cross to go to opposite sides of the brain.

Oral stage In Freudian terms, the first psychosexual stage during which the infant's sexual pleasure is derived from stimulation of the mouth.

Organic amnesia Amnesia caused by physiological problems such as stroke or disease or by injury.

Organic mental disorders A diagnostic category from DSM-III for the acute or chronic effects of drug use on the central nervous system.

Orgasm The third of Masters and Johnson's 4 phases of human sexual response characterized by ejaculation in the man and vaginal contractions in the woman.

Osmoreceptors Receptors, sensitive to the amount of fluid inside the body's cells, that play a role in drinking regulation.

Osmosis The movement of fluids through a semipermeable membrane (e.g., water through the walls of a cell).

Otoliths Small calcium deposits in the inner ear which appear to have a function in maintaining equilibrium.

Oval window The membrane across the opening between the inner ear and the middle ear.

Overextension Stretching the meaning of a word beyond its correct usage, as when young children use the word "dog" to refer to all small, furry four-legged animals.

Overtones Harmonics of the fundamental tone which impart a special quality or timbre to notes played on different instruments.

Panic disorders A type of anxiety disorder in which the essential feature is the unpredictable recurrence of panic attacks. These attacks may occur more frequently in situations such as riding an elevator or flying in an airplane.

Paranoid schizophrenia A severe psychological disorder in which delusions of persecution play a major role.

Parasympathetic system The branch of the autonomic nervous system that maintains the routine "vegetative" functions such as digestion; tends to conserve energy.

PCP (Phencyclidine or "angel dust") Originally developed as a powerful pain killer, it has become a highly dangerous "street drug" which often produces unpredictable outbursts of violence.

Peer group A group of social and chronological equals.

Peg words A mnemonic technique in which the information to be remembered is associated with specific words (peg words) that are more easily recalled. These peg words then serve as **recall cues** for the associated information (such as "bun" in "one is a bun, two a shoe, etc.").

Percentile rank If a value has a percentile rank of X, it exceeds X percent of the other values in a distribution; e.g., the median is defined as having a percentile rank of 50.

Perception Interpretation of the information provided by one's sensory receptors.

Perceptual constancy The ability, in perception, to draw similar inferences about the world from different patterns of sensory activity (e.g., a person seen from many different angles is still perceived as the same person).

Performance   The act of displaying what has been learned or using learned skills.

Peripheral nervous system   The entire nervous system outside the brain and spinal cord.

Peripheral streaming   The linear "streaming" or movement of stimulus contours toward the periphery of the retina as one moves through space. A strong cue for motion.

Personal construct   A view of reality created by actively perceiving, evaluating, and organizing one's own experience.

Personality   An individual's complex and unique patterns of behavior, motives, emotions.

Personality disorders   Patterns of behavior, thinking, and perceiving that have become maladaptive, causing distress or impairing normal functioning in the work place or in social situations.

Personality inventories   Scales or measures that ask people to report on some thought or behavior that has been empirically shown to correlate with some underlying conflict or difficulty.

Person-centered personality theory   Carl Rogers's humanistic personality theory which emphasizes viewing the individual as a whole being capable of self-actualization and the importance of the self and conscious awareness in the life of the individual.

Phallic stage   According to Freud, the developmental stage in which sex urges are directed toward a parent and in which one establishes a sexual identity (usually between ages 3–5).

Phenomenal field   The boundaries of an individual's awareness and influence.

Phenotype   The manner in which an organism's genetic makeup (**genotype**) is expressed as it develops in a particular environment.

Phenylketonuria (PKU)   An inherited form of mental retardation caused by a disorder of amino acid metabolism.

Phi illusion   An illusion of movement caused by flashing lights off and on one after another, which makes them appear to move.

Phobia   A persistent and irrational fear of some class of stimulus objects and events.

Phobic disorders   A persistent and irrational fear of a particular object or situation, usually far out of proportion to the actual threat.

Phoneme   The smallest functional unit of speech sound in a language.

Photographic memory   An ability to remember things as if you were seeing them in full detail. (Also called **eidetic imagery**.)

Phrase-structure rules   Rules that govern the organization of the various parts of a sentence (such as nouns, verbs, adjectives, etc.)

Pitch   The sensory experience of highness or lowness of a tone corresponding to the frequency of sound waves.

Pituitary gland   An endocrine gland located at the base of the brain and attached to the hypothalamus. Secretes tropic hormones, which affect other endocrine glands, causing them to secrete other hormones. Often called the "master gland" for this reason.

Placebo   An inert substance (e.g., an empty pill) that is used as a control in drug experiments.

Place theory   The idea that different tone frequencies affect **neurons** located at different places along the **basilar membrane** in the **cochlea**.

Plateau   According to Masters and Johnson, the second of 4 phases of sexual excitation.

Pleasure principle   According to Freud, the dominant force in id activity which calls for immediate reduction of tension through gratification of instinctual impulses.

Polygenic trait   A trait determined by more than one gene pair.

Polygon   A series of points connected by straight lines indicating a frequency distribution.

Polygraph   An apparatus used for measuring and recording various physiological reactions such as GSR. Often referred to as a lie detector.

Pons   Part of the hindbrain, just above the spinal cord; acts mainly as a way station for neural pathways going to other brain areas.

Population   A clearly defined set of potential measurements from which samples may be drawn.

Positive reinforcer   An event (such as food) that, if presented just after a response, increases the likelihood that the response will be repeated.

Positron emission tomography (PET)   A computer generated image of the brain based on the emission of positrons when radioactively tagged chemicals enter into neural activity.

Posthypnotic suggestion   A suggestion to take some action, change a way of thinking, or alter behavior. Given to a subject under hypnosis, it takes effect after the subject has come out of hypnosis.

Predatory aggression.   Aggression that occurs for hunting purposes—the action of a predator against its prey.

Predictive validity   The determination that a test can accurately predict future results.

Prefrontal lobotomy   The surgical removal of the prefrontal part of the frontal lobes in the brain; a controversial form of psychosurgery rarely used today.

Preoperational stage   The second major stage of cognitive development (Piaget), during which children begin to use symbols, including linguistic symbols (words); ages 2–7 years.

Preparation stage   The first stage of creative thinking, in which an individual absorbs the data and ideas needed to solve a problem creatively.

Preparedness   Seligman's theory that organisms are more prepared to associate a given emotional response with one stimulus than another. Has been used to explain why it is more common to develop phobias about some stimuli than others.

Primacy effect   Under certain conditions the first item(s) in a series will be remembered better than those that follow.

Primary drive   A universal drive based on biological needs.

Primary process   According to Freud, the process in the id by which it gains immediate satisfaction of instinctual wishes. Primary processes are unconscious and often irrational.

Primary sex characteristics   Internal and external reproductive organs.

Priming   The increased accessibility or retrievability of information in memory produced by the prior presentation of related cues.

Prisoner's dilemma   A bargaining game used to illustrate properties of interdependent social interactions; participants can cooperate or compete. The outcome for each individual is dependent on what the other person chooses to do.

Proactive interference   Forgetting or memory difficulties caused by interference of information learned earlier.

Procedural knowledge   "How to" knowledge, such as how to ride a bicycle or tie a shoe. It is usually evidenced by how well you do something (rather than by being right or wrong as in **propositional** or **declarative knowledge**).

Progestin   A female sex hormone that has a role in pregnancy and nursing.

Projection   The attribution of one's own faults to others.

Projective tests   Personality tests in which a person's responses to ambiguous stimuli are analyzed.

Propositional knowledge   Knowledge in the form of relations between two or more concepts (propositions), also called **declarative knowledge**. It is a statement of fact that can be true or false.

Propositional thinking The ability to reason about verbal statements and abstractions.

Psychiatry The branch of medicine that deals with mental illness.

Psychoactive drugs Drugs that affect mental processes.

Psychoanalysis (psychoanalytic therapy) A variety of psychotherapies that share the foundational belief that intrapsychic conflict is the cause of abnormality and that insight is essential to improvement.

Psychoanalytic model Model of personality, abnormal functioning, and therapy based on Freud's dynamic system of psychology which seeks the understanding of behavior in unconscious motivation and conflict.

Psychoanalytic theory Sigmund Freud's theory of human personality, stressing unconscious motives, largely sexual and aggressive in nature.

Psychogenic Something that can be attributed to psychological causes rather than organic.

Psychopathic disorders See **antisocial personality disorders.**

Psychophysical relations Relations between physical stimulus variables and the sensations they evoke (as indicated by a subject's responses).

Psychosensory Pertaining to sensations not originating in the sense organs.

Psychosexual development Freud's theory of development, in which gratification of sexual energies is focused on various parts of the body during different stages of development.

Psychosis The main difference between neurosis and psychosis is a more extreme or bizarre manifestation of behavior, thought, and emotion with psychosis. In psychosis the individual loses contact with reality in some central way, and from this loss a variety of severe problems emerges.

Psychosocial stages Erikson's stages of development in which a person passes through particular social crises at particular ages.

Psychosomatic illness A physical disorder or illness that is psychologically determined and often stress-related.

Psychosurgery Cuts, lesions, and removal of brain sections; based on the biological theory that abnormal behavior is determined by a malfunction in the brain.

Psychotherapy A set of procedures by which one person attempts to change the life of another by using talk-oriented change procedures based on psychoanalytics or other theories.

Puberty The developmental time when people reach physical sexual maturity.

Punishment An aversive (negative) stimulus that follows a response for the purpose of eliminating that response.

Pupil The dark circular opening within the iris of the eye through which light passes into the eye.

Q-sort technique A personality measure in which individuals are given a set of cards containing adjectives or phrases to sort into groups based on the degree to which they describe themselves or a target person.

Range The difference between the largest and smallest value in a numerical distribution.

Rational-emotive therapy (RET) A form of **cognitive therapy** developed by Albert Ellis. RET focuses primarily on thought content; identifying and changing irrational thoughts which lead to anxiety and neurotic functioning are the goals of RET.

Rationalism The philosophical position that assumes that people are born with innate knowledge of the world. Contrasted to **empiricism,** the position that knowledge is acquired through experience.

Rationalization A defense mechanism·in which one deceives oneself by giving an acceptable reason to explain an unacceptable outcome or motive.

Reaction formation A defense mechanism in which the way one feels about something is the opposite of the way one behaves toward it.

Reality anxiety In psychoanalytic theory, a reaction of fear to a real danger, physical or psychological, in the external world.

Reality principle According to Freud, the process of the ego mediating the demands of the id and the environment.

Reasoning Drawing conclusions from known or assumed premises, as in deductive reasoning, or making inferences from known or assumed facts, as in inductive reasoning; step-by-step thought processes.

Recall A measure of retention of memory in which a person reproduces or reconstructs the information learned earlier with a minimum of cues.

Recall cues Cues that assist in retaining and retrieving items of memory.

Recency effect Under certain conditions, the last item(s) in a series will be remembered better than the ones preceding them.

Receptive fields If the electrical activity of a neuron in the visual system is affected by a particular type of visual stimulus on a particular part of the retina, the type of stimulus and location on the retina define that neuron's receptive field (e.g., a vertical white bar in the center of the retina).

Receptor organ A body part that receives sensory information; eyes, for example, are the receptor organs of vision.

Recessive gene The member of the gene pair (allele) that carries a weaker characteristic and can determine a trait only when paired with another recessive gene.

Recoding Coding information that was encoded previously in either the same form or a related form.

Recognition A measurement of memory retention in which a person is asked to pick out from a list items that were learned previously.

Reconstruction or redintegration In memory, the process of reconstructing or filling in missing information through educated guessing based on information still available and stimulus redundancy.

Redundancy The idea that activity in one's various sensory receptors is highly correlated, or redundant. For example, when people speak to you, the movement of their lips is highly correlated with the sound of their voice.

Reduplicated babbling Type of vocalization produced by 6–9 month old infants, usually consisting of repeated consonant-vowel syllables such as "da da da da."

Reflection The process whereby light bounces off a surface into a new path.

Reflexes Automatic sequences of stimulus and response, which in some cases may involve only a single synapse between sensory and motor neurons (monosynaptic reflex).

Regression A defense mechanism in which a person returns to less mature levels of behavior when faced with anxiety.

Rehearsal Repeating learned information in one's mind to enhance memory.

Reinforcement In classical conditioning, following the conditioned stimulus with presentation of the unconditioned stimulus. In operant conditioning, following a response by presentation of a reward or by removal of an aversive stimulus. Reinforcement promotes the learning of responses.

Relation-oriented leader A leadership style that emphasizes the leader's relationships to the group and relationships within the group; most effective for groups that are either very well or very poorly organized and integrated.

Relative frequency The frequency of a value in a distribution divided by the total number of values (the proportion of such values in the distribution).

Relative refractory period The period following the absolute refractory period when it is more difficult, but not impossible, to trigger a nerve impulse.

Relearning Even when people seem to have forgotten something they learned earlier, relearning will take place faster than the original learning did. This reduction in time to learn, or **savings,** means they actually did retain some of the information from the first time.

Reliability The determination of whether a test will produce consistent results on repeated measurements under the same circumstances.

REM (rapid eye movement) Rapid movements of the eyes during sleep which seem related to dreaming.

REM Sleep One of the two types of sleep, characterized by rapid movements of the eyes; is the period during which dreaming is most likely to occur.

Reorganization A process in which a person orders items of memory and classifies the items into categories to assist in memory.

Repression A defense mechanism in which a person avoids unpleasant thoughts by blocking these thoughts out of consciousness.

Resistance In psychoanalysis, the unwillingness or the inability to discuss certain painful areas of experience, by preventing these experiences and ideas from becoming part of consciousness.

Resistance to extinction A measure of the ability of a conditioned response to resist being eliminated by later trials with no reinforcement.

Resolution According to Masters and Johnson, the final phase of sexual intercourse; resolution follows orgasm and is the phase in which physiological activity returns to normal.

Response The measurable behavior of an organism, particularly as a reaction to a stimulus.

Resting potential The normal polarity of a neuron in which its interior is about −70 mV negative in respect to its exterior.

Retention The storage of memory; the maintaining of information.

Reticular activating system (RAS) A network of fibers beginning in the spinal cord and extending up through the midbrain into the higher centers; has a role in attention and arousal.

Reticular formation See **reticular activating system (RAS).**

Retina The inside layer of the eye containing the light-sensitive **rods** and **cones.**

Retrieval The process of obtaining memory from storage in the brain.

Retroactive interference The interference of new information with the memory of something learned earlier.

Retrograde amnesia The inability to remember events and information that were immediately followed by a brain injury or shock.

Right hemisphere The nondominant cerebral hemisphere believed to have a role in spatial perception and artistic interpretation.

Rods Light-sensitive receptor cells found on the retina; sensitive to black and white stimuli but not color.

Rorschach test A projective personality test in which a person is asked to describe what images come to mind upon viewing ten ordered inkblots.

Round window The membrane-covered opening on the far end of the **cochlea** which absorbs the waves of energy entering earlier through the **oval window.**

Saccade The rapid rotation of the eye that occurs between successive fixations

Saltatory conduction The more rapid transmission of a nerve impulse along myelinated neurons where the action potential "leaps" (saltates) from node to node of myelin.

Sample A subset of measurements from some population.

Saturation The purity of a color; as a color becomes less saturated, it becomes progressively whiter.

Savings In relearning, the amount of time saved when seemingly forgotten information or responses are learned again.

Scatter diagram A graph showing pairs of values for 2 variables as points in a Cartesian coordinate system.

Schedule of reinforcement The schedule determining whether a correct response will be reinforced according to a time interval or after a number of correct responses; the schedule can be fixed or variable.

Schema The conceptual framework that people use to organize their knowledge of the world.

Schizophrenia A term applied to a wide variety of severe abnormal behaviors including distortions of reality, social withdrawal, and prominent disturbances in thought, perception, motor activity, or emotionality. Many professionals argue that the term is no longer a useful diagnostic category.

Secondary process In Freudian terms, the activity of the conscious part of the psyche which governs the ego's attempts to meet the id's demands through rational thought and conscious activity directed toward satisfying specific drives.

Secondary reinforcement Reinforcement that does not directly satisfy a need but that in the past has been associated with a primary reinforcing stimulus and thus comes to take on reward value.

Secondary sex characteristics Sexually differentiating features which normally emerge at puberty, such as breast and hip enlargement in females and beard growth and voice change in males.

Sedatives Drugs that help people sleep and are highly addictive; **barbiturates** are a class of sedatives.

Selective breeding The breeding of laboratory animals for heredity studies; the animals are selected for specific characteristics and are bred with animals with similar characteristics in an attempt to get as pure a genetic strain as possible.

Self The individual as a unique and conscious being.

Self-actualization According to Maslow, the ultimate goal of human beings and the pinnacle of the hierarchy of needs; self-actualized persons have fulfilled their innate, positive potentials.

Self-efficacy The expectation that one has the power to take control of situations and influence events in a positive way.

Self-esteem A person's own judgment of his or her worth and abilities.

Self-handicapping The strategies that allow one to attribute poor performance to causes that do not damage self-esteem; for example, partying late the night before a final exam provides a "safe" explanation for failing the exam.

Self-monitoring The degree to which an individual attends to the social context in planning his/her behavior.

Self-perception theory A theory proposing that people make judgments about themselves based on qualities they view in other people.

Self-report An observation and rating of an individual made by that individual.

Self theories Humanistic theories of personality that suggest that people are basically good and have an inborn desire to change for the better and reach self-fulfillment.

Semantic differential Osgood's technique for rating the connotative meanings of words.

Semantic knowledge Factual knowledge that is independent of the individual or when it is learned; another type of **propositional knowledge.**

Semantic memory Our conceptual knowledge, which includes our knowledge of language, the concepts that we have, and general world knowledge. Compare with **episodic memory**—memory for discrete events in our past.

Semicircular canals Three canals in the inner ear that function in the perception of body movement.

Sensation Psychological experience of a stimulus.

Sensorimotor stage The first major stage of cognitive development (Piaget) during which children know the world primarily through their perceptual-motor interactions with the immediate environment and during which they acquire the concept of **object permanence** (also known as object constancy).

Sensory areas   Areas of the cerebral cortex that function in the integration of sensory information from each of the various receptor organs.

Sensory codes   The specific patterns of neural activity that carry information from the various senses to the brain.

Sensory memory   A type of short-term memory in which information lasts for only a few seconds.

Sensory memory system   A theoretical human **memory system** which briefly retains information in a form similar to its initial sensory code (e.g., **echoic, iconic**).

Sensory neurons   Neurons that carry information from receptors to the central nervous system.

Separation anxiety   An infant's fear of losing the mother whenever she disappears for even a few moments.

Serial position effect   In memory, the tendency for the position of items in a list to affect one's ability to recall them—the first and last items are more easily remembered than the rest of the list.

Set-point theory   Nisbett's theory that feeding behavior tends to hold weight at a specific value (set point); that is, some rats or humans simply have a higher set point.

Sex-linked trait   An inherited trait linked specifically to a sex chromosome.

Sex-related aggression   Aggression directly related to sexual potency or sexual rivalry.

Sexual-dysfunction therapy   An eclectic set of therapeutic techniques—although primarily cognitive and behavioral—to specifically address and overcome problems of sexual dysfunction.

Shape constancy   The knowledge that even when an object is viewed from a different angle its shape remains the same.

Shaping   An operant conditioning technique in which behavior is gradually molded into a desired form through reinforcement of successive approximations of the target behavior.

Short-term memory   A type of memory with a somewhat limited capacity; items must be consciously rehearsed to be retained in short-term memory.

Signal detection theory   A theory that attempts to explain perceptual judgments through analysis of a person's sensitivity to sensory stimuli in addition to the criteria a person uses in decision making.

Sine wave   A simple pressure wave representing one frequency of sound at one amplitude.

Sinusoidal grating   A cyclical (sinusoidal) variation in brightness across the visual field.

Size constancy   A tendency to perceive familiar objects as being the same size even when they cast a different-sized image on the retina because of one's distance from them.

Skinner box   A chamber containing a lever or some other device that an animal can manipulate to obtain reinforcers (e.g., food or water) during an operant conditioning experiment.

Skin senses   The senses of pressure, pain, hot, and cold.

Social-comparison theory   Festinger's theory of how people come to know and understand their own relative abilities, strengths, and weaknesses by comparing themselves with others.

Social exchanges   The social and emotional "rewards" exchanged within social interactions; typically participants have complimentary resources to exchange so that one person can fairly easily give what the other needs, and vice versa. The traditional marriage is a good example of the social exchange process.

Social facilitation theory   A theory suggesting that a person's behavior becomes stronger or more extreme when others are

Social-learning theory   The theory that people can learn important things about themselves and about others through observation of other people's behaviors, without having to go through trial and error on their own.

Socialization   The process in which a person acquires attitudes and values of his or her culture.

Social psychology   A branch of psychology that studies individual's interactions

Sociobiology   The study of the biological basis of social behavior in man and animals.

Sociopathic disorders   See **antisocial personality disorders**.

Somatic nervous system.   The part of the peripheral nervous system that controls voluntary muscles.

Somatoform disorders   Physical symptoms that have no apparent organic cause.

Somatosensory areas   Areas of the cerebral cortex that function in the integration of stimuli from the kinesthetic sense and the skin senses.

Somatosensory homunculus   Graphic depiction of a map of the somatosensory cortex, in which each part of the body is shown larger or smaller, according to how much somatosensory cortex is devoted to it (see Figure 2–20).

Somatotype   Body type.

Somnambulism   Sleep walking.

Source trait   According to Cattell, one of the basic traits that accounts for a person's behavior and personality.

Spatial frequency   The frequency of a sinusoidal variation in brightness across the visual field expressed in cycles per degree visual angle.

Split-brain subjects   Subjects who, for medical or for experimental reasons, have had their cerebral hemispheres surgically separated at the corpus callosum and who subsequently have unconnected cerebral hemispheres which appear to function somewhat separately and differently.

Spontaneous recovery   The return of a conditioned response after extinction and without further training trials.

Spread of activation   The process by which a cue progressively activates (primes, makes accessible) related information in memory.

Standard deviation   The square root of the average squared deviation from the mean (a measure of variability).

Standard error of the mean   The standard deviation of sample means about the population mean.

Standard score or z-score   The number of standard deviations (σ) between a score (X) and the mean ($\bar{X}$) of the distribution of scores; i.e., $z = (X - \bar{X})/\sigma$.

Stanford-Binet test   A modified version of Binet's original IQ test used to assess intelligence in children.

State-dependent learning   The idea that learning a response in a particular environment or emotional or physical state will enable the person to remember the response much better in a similar environment or state.

Statistically significant   A pattern of data that is so unlikely to have occurred by chance (probability less than .01 or .05) that it can be interpreted as a real rather than a random occurrence.

Statistics   Mathematical relationships and representations that describe events and other data.

Stereopsis   Visual perception of three dimensional objects.

Stereotype   A preconceived notion of how a group or individual will behave.

Steven's power law   Assertion that sensation (S) is proportional to stimulus intensity (I) raised to some power (b): $S = kI^b$ where k is a constant that depends on the unit of measurement.

Stimulants   Drugs, such as **amphetamines,** which accelerate brain and nervous system functioning.

Stimulus-response psychology   The branch of psychology concerned with behavior as seen through stimulus-response relationships and principles of conditioning and simple learning.

Stress A term that includes demands from the environment requiring the individual to change (stressors) and the state of physiological and psychological tension resulting from those demands (the stress response).

Stressors The environmental demands that lead to a stress response. Stressors can be physical or psychological, universal or unique, intrinsic to a situation or attributed to it.

Stress response A person's reaction to a threatening demand from the environment, including changes in the autonomic nervous system, requiring some kind of adjustment or adaptation.

Stroboscopic motion See phi illusion.

Structured interview A personality assessment technique in which an interviewer asks a subject specific questions designed to provide information about particular areas of personality.

Sublimation A defense mechanism in which unacceptable urges and feelings are channeled into acceptable activities.

Substance dependence Addiction typically involving increasing physical tolerance to the substance, psychological dependence, and severe withdrawal symptoms when use is discontinued.

Substance-use disorders Maladaptive behavior patterns shown by chronic drug users; including impaired social and occupational functioning, an inability to control or limit use of the substance, and withdrawal symptoms.

Subtractive mixture A form of color mixing in which pigments absorb part of the spectrum and the result is color produced by a subtraction of a particular color wavelength.

Successive approximations In shaping, the process of gradually coming closer and closer to the desired behavior.

Superego In Freudian terms, the part of the personality that is the conscience and reflects parental and societal codes of morality.

Suppression A defense mechanism in which incompatible ideas are unconsciously inhibited or eliminated.

Surface structure The characteristics and organization of the verbatim form of a sentence. See **deep structure.**

Surface trait According to Cattell, one of the behavioral patterns through which source traits are expressed.

Survey method A method of research involving the collection of data from a large number of individuals.

Sympathetic nervous system The branch of the autonomic nervous system that functions as the arousal center during emergencies or stress situations.

Synapse The point between neurons where nerve impulses are transmitted from neuron to neuron.

Synaptic cleft The tiny gap between an axon terminal and another neuron into which the axon releases neurotransmitters.

Syntactic scene analysis A hierarchical structural analysis of the components of a scene, much like the parsing of a sentence into its constituent syntactic parts.

Syntax Grammar; rules for organizing and combining words into phrases and sentences.

Systematic desensitization A type of behavior therapy in which the person substitutes for an undesired response a response that is incompatible or competitive with it.

Tachistoscope An instrument used in learning and memory studies; exposes cards or slides for very brief periods of time.

Task-oriented leader A leadership style that emphasizes successful completion of tasks, even at the risk of poor interpersonal relations with group members; most effective for groups that are neither well or poorly organized and integrated.

Taste buds The receptors on the tongue that respond to substances in your mouth and contribute to your experience of taste.

Telegraphic speech Utterances with the unimportant and the function words left out. Characteristic of an early stage of language and called "telegraphic" because of its resemblance to the way that telegrams are written.

Temporal contiguity Occurring close together in time; a primary cause of association in many theories of learning and memory.

Territorial aggression Aggression that occurs to protect a territory or to let an enemy know which boundaries cannot be crossed.

Testosterone One of the androgens (male hormones) that promotes secondary sex characteristics.

Texture gradient. Distance cues based on the fact that objects lose definition and detail the farther away they are.

Thalamus A fairly large, bilobed area at the midline of the brain; an important way station for receiving information from the various sense organs and relaying it to the cortex.

Thanatos According to Freud, the death instinct.

Thematic Apperception Test (TAT). A projective personality test in which a person is shown pictures and must make up stories about what he or she feels is going on in the various pictures, what has led up to this situation, and what will come of it afterwards.

Theory A formalized statement of particular principles and concepts designed to explain a particular phenomenon or behavior.

Therapy A set of procedures by which one person uses language to change the life of another (Davidson & Neale, 1978).

Threshold The minimum stimulus necessary to elicit a response.

Timbre The characteristic quality of a tone produced by the combination of overtones heard along with the pure tone.

Tip-of-the-tongue (TOT) phenomenon When trying to remember something, the feeling that one is just about to recall it, that it is on the "tip of the tongue."

Token economy A behavior therapy technique in which tokens are given to reward desired behavior; the tokens can later be exchanged for a specific reward that the patient desires, such as specific privileges, candy, etc.

Tolerance The phenomenon in which increasing amounts of a drug are required to produce the same physiological effects.

Traces A hypothetical impression of memory in the nervous system.

Trait A characteristic of a person's behavior/personality that can be measured.

Tranquilizer Drugs that depress nervous system activity and reduce anxiety and tension.

Transference In psychoanalysis, the process in which a patient transfers love or other emotional attachment from another person in his or her past to the therapist.

Transformational rules Rules that specify how one sentence can be "transformed" into another; grammatical rules that spell out the relationships between sentences.

Twin studies Studies that compare the common traits of monozygotic (genetically identical) and dyzygotic (fraternal) twins.

Unconditioned reflex or response A response that is elicited by a stimulus without learning (e.g., a dog's salivation when presented with meat powder is an unconditioned response).

Unconditioned stimulus A stimulus that provokes a response in the absence of learning or conditioning.

Unconscious That part of one's mental life of which one is unaware and over which one has little or no control.

Undoing A defense mechanism characterized by engaging in a positive act in order to negate a previous, unacceptable act, thus relieving guilt and anxiety associated with the first act.

Unstructured interview A personality assessment technique in which the interviewer and the subject engage in free-flowing conversation.

Validity The extent to which a test measures what it purports to measure.

Value theory A theory that explains how, in the course of group decision making, social comparison leads members to shift their own position to one that is consistent but more extreme; whether the shift is risky or cautious is determined by the average group tendency, reflecting the dominant cultural value for that type of problem.

Variability The amount of variation among scores in a distribution. Characterized by such measures as the range, variance (σ^2), or standard deviation (σ).

Variable-interval schedule A reinforcement schedule in which the first correct response after unpredictably varying periods of time is reinforced.

Variable-ratio schedule A schedule of reinforcement in which an unpredictably varying number of correct responses must occur before reinforcement occurs.

Variance The mean-square deviation; in other words, the square of the standard deviation. A useful measure of the amount of scatter around the mean or average of a set of numerical observations.

Ventral Pertaining to the abdominal side of the body.

Ventromedial hypothalamus A portion of the hypothalamus believed to have a role in satiation or inhibition of eating.

Verification The part of the creative process in which the person evaluates the results of the illumination (sudden solution to the problem).

Vestibular sacs Bony stuctures of the head that send sensory stimuli about head movement to the brain.

Visual acuity Ability to discern fine details in spatial patterns of light.

Visual angle Used to describe the size of an object in terms of how much of your visual field it occupies—that is, how many degrees of the imaginary surrounding circle's circumference it would cover. This is referred to as an object's size in degrees of visual angle.

Visual cliff The depth illusion device developed to determine whether human infants and other species have depth perception.

Visual field The three-dimensional space in which all objects are perceived by the eyes at a given time.

Visual spectrum. ("Light"). The range of electromagnetic energy to which our eye is sensitive (normally about 400 to 700 nm).

Volley principle The hearing theory based on the idea that hearing receptors respond one after another in rapid succession, signaling pitch of higher frequencies in this way.

WAIS The Wechsler Adult Intelligence Scale, a battery of tests devised to assess intelligence and cognitive abilities in adults.

Weber's constant The constant of proportionality (k) in Weber's law (JND = kI).

Weber's law The principle that the just noticeable difference (JND) of a stimulus is a constant fraction of the intensity of the original stimulus.

Wernicke's area An association area located on the lower side of the lateral fissure, near the auditory cortex. Damage to this area produces Wernicke's aphasia, in which people speak fluently, but with bizarre and nonsensical content.

White matter The fibrous portion of the nervous system; the white appearance is due to the myelin sheath covering the axons.

WISC-R The revised version of Wechsler's intelligence scale for children; an individual IQ test used with children aged 6 to 16.

Wish fulfillment According to Freud, the id's need for immediate gratification causes it to create an image of the desired object. It is up to the ego to actually acquire the object.

Withdrawal A pattern of severe physiological symptoms, such as nausea, intense sweating, muscular cramps, possible coma, as well as psychological effects that occur when one stops taking a drug one has become dependent on (addicted to).

X Chromosome The female sex chromosome.

Y Chromosome The male sex chromosome.

Young-Helmholtz theory of color vision States that there are three types of cones, each sensitive to a different part of the visual spectrum.

References

Abramsom, L. Y., Seligman, M. E. P., & Teasdale, J. D. (1978). Learned helplessness in humans: Critique and reformulation. *Journal of Abnormal Psychology, 87,* 49–74.

Abse, D. W. (1959). Hysteria. In S. Arieti (Ed.), *American handbook of psychiatry* (Vol. 1). New York: Basic Books. Pp. 272–292.

Adolph, E. F. (1939). Measurements of water drinking in dogs. *American Journal of Physiology, 125,* 75–86.

Agras, W. S., Chapin, H. N., & Oliveau, D. C. (1972). The natural history of phobia: Course and prognosis. *Archives of General Psychiatry, 26,* 315–317.

Aiken, L. R. (1979). *Psychological testing and assessment* (3rd ed.). Boston: Allyn & Bacon.

Ainsworth, M. D. S. (1967). *Infancy in Uganda: Infant care and the growth of love.* Baltimore, Md.: John Hopkins Press.

Ainsworth, M. D. S., & Bell, S. M. (1969). Some contemporary patterns of mother-infant interaction in the feeding situation. In A. Ambrose (Ed.), *Stimulation in early infancy.* New York: Academic Press.

Ainsworth, M. D. S., Bell, S. M., & Stayton, D. J. (1971). Individual differences in strange situation behavior of one-year-olds. In H. R. Schaffer (Ed.), *The origins of human social relations.* New York: Academic Press.

Ainsworth, M. D. S., Blehar, M. C., Waters, E., & Wall, S. (1978). *Patterns of attachment: A psychological study of the strange situation.* Hillsdale, N.J.: Erlbaum.

Ainsworth, M. D. S., & Wittig, B. A. (1969). Attachment and exploratory behavior of one-year-olds in a strange situation. In B. M. Foss (Ed.), *Determinants of infant behavior* (Vol. 4). London: Methuen.

Ajzen, I., & Fishbein, M. (1979). Attitude-behavior relations: A theoretical analysis and review of empirical research. *Psychological Bulletin, 84,* 888–918.

Ajzen, I., & Fishbein, M. (1980). *Understanding attitudes and predicting behavior.* Englewood Cliffs, N.J.: Prentice-Hall.

Akhter, S., Wig, N. N., Varma, V. K., Pershad, D., & Verma, S. K. (1975). A phenomenological analysis of symptoms in obsessive-compulsive neurosis. *British Journal of Psychiatry, 127,* 342–348.

Alexander, F. (1950). *Psychosomatic medicine: Its principles and applications.* New York: W. W. Norton.

Alfert, E. (1964). Reactions to a vicariously experienced and a direct threat. Unpublished doctoral dissertation, University of California, Berkeley.

Allen, V. L. (1975). Social support for nonconformity. In L. Berkowitz (Ed.), *Advances in experimental-social psychology* (Vol. 8). New York: Academic Press. Pp. 7–43.

Allport, G. W. (1937). *Personality: A psychological interpretation.* New York: Holt, Rinehart and Winston.

Allport, G. W. (1954). *The nature of prejudice.* Reading, Mass: Addison-Wesley.

Allport, G. W. (1961). *Pattern and growth in personality.* New York: Holt, Rinehart and Winston.

Altman, I. (1975). *The environment and social behavior.* Monterey, Calif.: Brooks-Cole.

Amabile, T. M. (1979). Effects of external evaluation on artistic creativity. *Journal of Personality and Social Psychology, 37,* 221–233.

American Psychiatric Association. (1979). *Diagnostic and statistical manual of mental disorders* (3rd ed.). Washington, D.C.: American Psychiatric Association.

Amoore, J. E. (1964). Current status of stereochemical theories of odor. *Annals of the New York Academy of Sciences, 116,* 457–476.

Amsel, A. (1967). Partial reinforcement effects on vigor and persistence: Advances in frustration theory derived from a variety of within-subjects experiments. In K. W. Spence & J. T. Spence (Eds.), *The psychology of learning and motivation* (Vol. 1). New York: Academic Press.

Anderson, J. R. (1976). *Language, memory, and thought.* Hillsdale, N.J.: Erlbaum.

Anderson, J. R. (1978). Arguments concerning representation for mental imagery. *Psychological Review, 85,* 249–277.

Anderson, J. R. (1980). *Cognitive psychology and its implications.* San Francisco: Freeman.

Anderson, J. R., & Bower, G. H. (1973). *Human associative memory.* Washington, D.C.: Winston.

Anderson, J. R., & Kintsch, W. (1974). *Human associative memory.* Washington, D.C.: Winston.

Anderson, J. R., & Paulson, R. (1977). Representation and retention of verbatim information. *Journal of Verbal Learning and Verbal Behavior, 16,* 439–451.

Anderson, S. M., & Bem, S. L. (1981). Sex typing and androgyny in dyadic interaction: Individual differences in responsiveness to physical attractiveness. *Journal of Personality and Social Psychology, 41,* 74–86.

Andersson, B. (1952). Polydipsia caused by intrahypothalamic injections of hypertonic NaCl solutions. *Experientia, 8,* 157.

Andersson, B., & McCann, S. M. (1955). A further study of polydipsia evoked by hypothalamic stimulation in the goat. *Acta Physiologica Scandinavica, 33,* 333–346.

Annett, M. (1972). The distribution of manual asymmetry. *British Journal of Psychology, 63,* 343–358.

Appelle, S., & Oswald, L. E. (1974). Simple reaction time as a function of alertness and prior mental activity. *Perceptual and Motor Skills, 38,* 1263–1268.

Appleyard, D. (1976). *Planning a pluralistic city.* Cambridge, Mass.: M.I.T. Press.

Arenberg, D., & Robertson-Tchabo, E. A. (1977). Learning and aging. In J. E. Birren & K. W. Schaie (Eds.), *Handbook of the psychology of aging.* New York: Van Nostrand Reinhold.

Argyris, C. (1964). *Integrating the individual and the organization.* New York: Wiley.

Arkin, A. M., Antrobus, J. S., & Ellman, S. J. (Eds.). (1978). *The mind in sleep: Psychology and psychophysiology.* New York: Halsted.

Arkin, A. M., Hastey, J. M., & Reiser, M. F. (1966). Post-hypnotically simulated sleep talking. *Journal of Nervous and Mental Disease, 142,* 293–309.

Armen, J. C. (1974). *Gazelle-boy: A child brought up by gazelles in the Sahara Desert.* London: Bodley Head.

Aronson, E., & Linder, D. (1965). Gain and loss of esteem as determinants of interpersonal attractiveness. *Journal of Experimental Social Psychology, 1,* 156–171.

Aronson, E., & Mills, J. (1959). The effect of severity of initiation on liking for a group. *Journal of Abnormal and Social Psychology, 59,* 177–181.

Asch, S. E. (1946). Forming impressions of personality. *Journal of Abnormal and Social Psychology, 41,* 258–290.

Asch, S. E. (1951). Effects of group pressure upon the modification and distortion of judgment. In H. Guetzkow (Ed.), *Groups, leadership and men.* Pittsburgh: Carnegie.

Asch, S. E. (1955). Opinions and social pressure. *Scientific American, 11,* 32.

Asch, S. E. (1956). Studies of independence and conformity: I. A minority of one against a unanimous majority. *Psychological Monographs, 70,* 9 (Whole No. 416).

Asher, S. R. (1979). Referential communication. In G. J. Whitehurst & B. J. Zimmerman (Eds.), *The functions of language and cognition.* New York: Academic Press.

Atchley, R. C. (1975). Dimensions of widowhood in later life. *The Gerontologist, 15,* 176–178.

Atchley, R. C. (1976). Selected social and psychological differences between men and women in later life. *Journal of Gerontology, 31*(2), 204–211.

Athanassiades, J. (1973). The distortion of upward communication in hierarchical organization. *Academy of Management Journal, 16,* 207–226.

Atkinson, J. W. (Ed.). (1958). *Motives in fantasy, action and society.* Princeton, N.J.: Van Nostrand.

Atkinson, J. W. (1977). Motivation for achievement. In T. Blass (Ed.), *Personality variables in social behavior*. Hillsdale, N.J.: Erlbaum.

Atkinson, J. W., & Birch, D. (1970). *The dynamics of action*. New York: Wiley.

Atkinson, J. W., & Feather, N. T. (Eds.).(1966). *A theory of achievement motivation*. New York: Wiley.

Atkinson, J. W., & Litwin, G. H. (1960). Achievement motive and test anxiety conceived as motive to approach success and motive to avoid failure. *Journal of Abnormal and Social Psychology, 60,* 27–36.

Atkinson, R. C., & Raugh, M. R. (1975). An application of the mnemonic keyword method to the acquisition of a Russian vocabulary. *Journal of Experimental Psychology: Human Learning and Memory, 104,* 126–133.

Atkinson, R. C., & Shiffrin, R. M. (1971). The control of short-term memory. *Scientific American, 225,* 82–90.

Atkinson, R. C., & Shiffrin, R. M. (1977). Human memory: A proposed system and its control processes. In G. H. Bower (Ed.), *Human memory: Basic processes*. New York: Academic Press.

Austin, V. C., Ruble, D. N., & Trabasso, T. (1977). Recall and order effects as factors in children's moral judgements. *Child Development, 48,* 470–474.

Averill, J. R. (1969). Autonomic response patterns during sadness and mirth. *Psychophysiology, 5,* 399–414.

Ax, A. F. (1953). The physiological differentiation between fear and anger in humans. *Psychosomatic Medicine, 14,* 433–442.

Ayllon, T. (1963). Intensive treatment of psychotic behavior by stimulus satiation and food reinforcement. *Behavior Research and Therapy, 1,* 53–61.

Ayllon, T., & Azrin, N. H. (1968). *The token economy: A motivational system for therapy and rehabilitation*. Englewood Cliffs, N.J.: Prentice-Hall.

Ayres, C. E. (1921). Instinct and capacity: I. The instinct of belief-in-instincts. *Journal of Philosophy, 18,* 561–566.

Azrin, N. H., Hutchinson, R. R., & Hake, D. F. (1965). Extinction induced aggression. *American Psychologist, 20,* 583.

Bales, R. F. (1951). Channels of communication in small groups. *American Sociological Review, 16,* 461–468.

Bandura, A. (1965). Behavior modification through modeling procedures. In L. Krooner & L. P. Ullman (Eds.), *Research in behavior modification*. New York: Holt, Rinehart & Winston.

Bandura, A. (1968). Social learning interpretation of psychological dysfunctions. In P. London & D. Rosenhan (Eds.), *Foundations of abnormal psychology*. New York: Holt, Rinehart and Winston.

Bandura, A. (1969). Social-learning theory of identificatory processes. In D. A. Goslin (Ed.), *Handbook of socialization theory and research*. Chicago: Rand McNally.

Bandura, A. (1973). *Aggression: A social learning analysis*. Englewood Cliffs, N.J.: Prentice-Hall.

Bandura, A. (1978). The self system in recipro-

cal determinism. *American Psychologist, 33,* 344–358.

Bandura, A. (1979). Self-efficacy: Toward a unifying theory of behavior change. *Psychological Review, 84,* 191–215.

Bandura, A., Adams, N. E., & Beyer, J. (1966). Cognitive processes mediating behavioral classical conditioning as a function of arousal level. *Journal of Personality and Social Psychology, 3,* 54–62.

Bandura, A., Adams, N. E., & Beyer, J. (1977). Cognitive processes mediating behavioral change. *Journal of Personality and Social Psychology, 35,* 125–139.

Bandura, A., Jeffery, R., & Wright, C. (1974). Efficacy of participant modeling as a function of response induction aids. *Journal of Abnormal Psychology, 83* (1), 56–64.

Bandura, A., & Rosenthal, T. L. (1976). Vicarious change. *Journal of Personality and Social Psychology, 35,* 125–139.

Bandura, A., Ross, D., & Ross, S. (1961). Transmission of aggression through imitation of aggressive models. *Journal of Abnormal and Social Psychology, 63,* 575–582.

Bandura, A., Ross, D., & Ross, S. (1963). Imitation of film-mediated aggressive models. *Journal of Abnormal and Social Psychology, 66,* 3–11. (a)

Bandura, A., Ross, D., & Ross, S. (1963). Vicarious reinforcement and imitative learning. *Journal of Abnormal and Social Psychology, 67,* 601–607. (b)

Bandura, A., & Walters, R. H. (1963). *Social learning and personality development*. New York: Holt, Rinehart and Winston.

Barash, D. P. (1977). *Sociobiology and behavior*. New York: Elsevier.

Barber, T. X., Spanos, H. P., & Chaves, J. F. (1974). *Hypnosis, imagination, and human potentialities*. New York: Pergamon.

Barber, T. X., & Wilson, S. C. (1977). Hypnosis, suggestions, and altered states of consciousness: Experimental evaluation of the new cognitive behavioral theory and the traditional trance-state theory of hypnosis. In W. D. Edmonston, Jr. (Ed.), *Conceptual and investigative approaches to hypnosis and hypnotic phenomena. Annals of The New York Academy of Sciences* (Vol. 296), 34–47.

Barchas, J., Akil, H., Elliott, G., Holman, R., & Watson, S. (1978). Behavioral neurochemistry: Neuroregulators and behavioral states. *Science, 200,* 964–973.

Bard, P. (1934). On emotional expression after decortication with some remarks on certain theoretical views. Parts I and II. *Psychological Review, 41,* 309–329 and 424–449.

Barker, R. G. (1960). Ecology and motivation. In M. R. Jones (Ed.), *Nebraska Symposium on Motivation* (Vol. 8). Lincoln: University of Nebraska Press.

Barker, R. G. (1968). *Ecological psychology: Concepts and methods for studying the environment of human behavior*. Stanford, Calif.: Stanford University Press.

Barker, R. G., & Associates. (1978). *Habitats, environments, and human behavior*. San Francisco: Jossey-Bass.

Barmark, S. M., & Caunitz, S. C. B. (1979).

Transcendental meditation and heterohypnosis as altered states of consciousness. *International Journal of Clinical and Experimental Hypnosis, 27,* 227–239.

Baron, R. A. (1977). *Human aggression*. New York: Plenum Press.

Baron, R. A., & Bell, P. A. (1975). Aggression and heat: Mediating effects of prior provocation and exposure to an aggressive model. *Journal of Personality and Social Psychology, 31,* 825–832.

Baron, R. A., & Bell, P. A. (1977). Sexual arousal and aggression by males: Effects of type of erotic stimuli and prior provocation. *Journal of Personality and Social Psychology, 35,* 79–87.

Baron, R. A., & Byrne, D. (1981). *Social psychology: Understanding human interaction* (3rd ed.). Boston: Allyn & Bacon.

Barrett, J. E. (Ed.). (1979). *Stress and mental disorder*. New York: Raven.

Barron, F., Jarvik, M., & Bunnell, S., Jr. (1964, April). The hallucinogenic drugs. *Scientific American*.

Bart, P. (1971). Depression in middle-aged women. In V. Gormick & B. K. Moran (Eds.), *Woman in sexist society: Studies in power and powerlessness*. New York: Basic Books.

Bartlett, F. C. (1932). *Remembering: A study in experimental and social psychology*. Cambridge: Cambridge University Press.

Barton, A. H. (1969). *Communities in disaster*. Garden City, N.Y.: Doubleday.

Baum, A., & Valins, S. (1977). *Architecture and social behavior: Psychological studies in social density*. Hillsdale, N.J.: Erlbaum.

Baum, M. (1970). Extinction of avoidance responding through response prevention (flooding). *Psychological Bulletin, 74,* 276–284.

Bavelas, A., Hastorf, A. H., Gross, A. E., & Kite, W. R. (1965). Experiments on the alteration of group structure. *Journal of Experimental Social Psychology, 1,* 55–71.

Baley, N., & Oden, M. H. (1955). The maintenance of intellectual ability in gifted adults. *Journal of Gerontology, 10,* 91–107.

Beach, F. A. (1968). Coital behavior in dogs: III. Effects of early isolation on mating in males. *Behavior, 30,* 218–238.

Beck, A. T. (1962). Reliability of psychiatric diagnosis: A critique of systematic studies. *American Journal of Psychiatry, 119,* 210–216.

Beck, A. T. (1967). *Depression: Clinical, experimental and theoretical aspects*. New York: Harper & Row.

Beck, A. T. (1972). *Depression: Causes and treatment*. Philadelphia: University of Pennsylvania Press.

Beck, A. T. (1973). *Diagnosis and management of depression*. Philadelphia: University of Pennsylvania Press.

Beck, A. T. (1974). The development of depression: A cognitive model. In R. Friedman & M. Katz (Eds.), *Psychology of depression: Contemporary theory and research*. Washington D.C.: Winston.

Beck, A. T. (1975). *Cognitive therapy and emotional disorders*. New York: International Universities Press.

Beck, A. T., & Ward, C. H. (1961). Dreams of

depressed patients: Characteristic themes in manifest context. *Archives of Social Psychology.* 5, 462–467.

Beck, A. T., Weissman, A., Lester, D., & Trexler, L. (1974). The measurement of pessimism. *Journal of Consulting and Clinical Psychology.* 42, 861–865.

Beck, H. (1979). The Ocean-Hill Brownsville and Cambodian-Kent State crises: A biobehavioral approach to human sociobiology. *Behavioral Science.* 24 (1), 25–36.

Beck, R. C. (1983). *Motivation: Theories and principles* (2nd ed.). Englewood Cliffs, N.J.: Prentice-Hall.

Becker, J. (1977). *Affective disorders.* Morristown, N.J.: General Learning Press.

Békésy, G. von. (1955). Human skin perception of traveling waves similar to those on the cochlea. *Journal of the Acoustical Society of America.* 27, 830–841.

Békésy, G. von. (1966). Taste theories and the chemical stimulation of single papillae. *Journal of Applied Physiology.* 21, 1–9.

Belkin, G. S. (1980). *Contemporary psychotherapies.* Chicago: Rand McNally.

Bellack, A. S., & Hersen, M. (1980). *Introduction to clinical psychology.* New York: Oxford University Press.

Belsky, J., & Steinberg, L. D. (1978). The effects of day care: A critical review. *Child Development.* 49, 929–949.

Bem, D. J. (1965). An experimental analysis of self-persuasion. *Journal of Experimental Social Psychology.* 1, 199–218

Bem, D. J. (1977). Self-perception theory. In L. Berkowitz (Ed.), *Advances in experimental social psychology* (Vol. 6). New York: Academic Press.

Bem, D. J., & Funder, D. C. (1978). Predicting more of the people more of the time: Assessing the personality of situations. *Psychological Review.* 85, 485–501.

Bem, S. L. (1974). The measurement of psychological androgyny. *Journal of Consulting and Clinical Psychology.* 42, 155–162.

Bem, S. L. (1981). Gender schema theory: A cognitive account of sex typing. *Psychological Review.* 88, 354–364.

Benedict, R. (1934). *Patterns of culture.* Boston: Houghton Mifflin.

Benson, H. (1975). *The relaxation response.* New York: Morrow.

Benson, H. (1977). Systemic hypertension and the relaxation response. *New England Journal of Medicine.* 296, 1152–1156.

Benson, H., Alexander, S., & Feldman, C. L. (1975). Decreased premature ventricular contractions through use of the relaxation response in patients with stable ischaemic heart disease. *Lancet, 2,* 380.

Berger, P. (1978). Medical treatment of mental illness. *Science, 200,* 974–981.

Berger, R. J. (1963). Experimental modification of dream content by meaningful verbal stimuli. *British Journal of Psychiatry, 109,* 722–740.

Berger, R. J., & Oswald, I. (1962). Eye movements during active and passive dreams. *Science, 137,* 601.

Bergin, A. E. (1971). The evaluation of thera-peutic outcomes. In A. E. Bergin & S. L. Garfield (Eds.), *Handbook of psychotherapy and behavior change: An empirical analysis.* New York: Wiley.

Berglas, S., & Jones, E. E. (1978). Drug choice as a self-handicapping strategy in response to noncontingent success. *Journal of Personality and Social Psychology, 36,* 405–417.

Berkman, L. F., & Syme, S. L. (1979). Social networks, host resistance, and mortality: A nine-year follow-up study of Alameda County residents. *American Journal of Epidemiology, 102* (2), 186–204.

Berko, J. (1958). The child's learning of English morphology. *Word, 14,* 150–177.

Berkowitz, L. (1962). *Aggression.* New York: McGraw-Hill.

Berkowitz, L. (1969). The frustration-aggression hypothesis revisited. In L. Berkowitz (Ed.), *Roots of aggression.* New York: Atherton.

Berkowitz, L. (1973). Control of aggression. In B. M. Caldwell & H. M. Ricciutti (Eds.), *Review of child development research* (Vol. 3). Chicago: Chicago University Press.

Berkowitz, L. (1974). Some determinants of impulsive aggression: Role of mediated associations with reinforcements for aggression. *Psychological Review.* 81, 165–176.

Berkowitz, L., & Le Page, A. (1967). Weapons as aggression-eliciting stimuli. *Journal of Personality and Social Psychology, 1,* 202–207.

Berkun, M. M., Kessen, M. L., & Miller, N. E. (1952). Hunger-reducing effects of food by stomach fistula versus food by mouth measured by a consummatory response. *Journal of Comparative and Physiological Psychology, 45,* 550–554.

Berlyne, D. E. (1957). Conflict and information-theory variables as determinants of human perceptual curiosity. *Journal of Experimental Psychology, 53,* 399–404.

Bermant, G. (1961). Response latencies of female rats during sexual intercourse. *Science, 133,* 1771–1773.

Bermant, G., & Davidson, J. M. (1974). *Biological bases of sexual behavior.* New York: Harper & Row.

Berndt, T. J. (1979). Developmental changes in conformity to peers and parents. *Developmental Psychology, 15,* 608–616.

Bernheim, H. A., Vaughn, L. K., & Kluger, M. J. (1974). Induction of fever in lizards in response to gram-negative bacteria. *Federation Proceedings, 33,* 457.

Berry, J. W., & Dason, P. (Eds.). (1974). *Culture and cognition: Readings in cross-cultural psychology.* London: Methuen.

Bettelheim, B. (1967). *The empty fortress.* New York: Free Press.

Bexton, W. H., Herm, W., & Scott, T. H. (1954). Effects of decreased variation in the sensory environment. *Canadian Journal of Psychology, 8,* 70–76.

Birren, J., Cunningham, W., & Yamamoto, K. (1983). Psychology of adult development and aging. *Annual Review of Psychology, 34,* 543–575.

Bixenstine, V. E., Decorte, M. S., & Bixenstine, B. A. (1976). Conformity to peer-sponsored misconduct at four grade levels. *Developmental Psychology, 12,* 226–236.

Bjorklund, D. F., Ornstein, P. A., & Haig, J. R. (1977). Developmental differences in organization and recall: Training in the use of organizational techniques. *Developmental Psychology, 13* (3), 175–183.

Blakemore, C. (1977). *Mechanics of the mind.* Cambridge: Cambridge University Press.

Block, N. J., & Dworkin, G. (1976). *The IQ controversy.* New York: Pantheon.

Bloom L. (1970). *Language development: Form and function in emerging grammars.* Cambridge, Mass.: MIT Press.

Bloom, L. (1973). *One word at a time.* The Hague: Mouton.

Bolton, R. (1976). Aggression and hypoglycemia among the Qolla: A study in psychobiological anthropology. In K. E. Moyer (Ed.), *Physiology of aggression and implications for control.* New York: Raven Press.

Bootzin, R. R. (1975). *Behavior modification and therapy.* Boston: Winthrop.

Boring, E. G. (1950). *A history of experimental psychology* (2nd ed.). Englewood Cliffs, N.J.: Prentice-Hall.

Bornstein, M. H., & Kessen, W. (1979). *Psychological development from infancy.* Hillsdale, N.J.: Erlbaum.

Botwinick, J. (1973). *Aging and behavior.* New York: Springer.

Botwinick, J. (1977). Intellectual abilities. In J. E. Birren & K. W. Schaie (Eds.), *Handbook of the psychology of aging.* New York: Van Nostrand Reinhold.

Bouchard, T. J., & McGue, M. (1981). Familial studies of intelligence: A review. *Science, 212,* 1055–1059.

Bower, G. H. (1981). Mood and memory. *American Psychologist, 36,* 129–148.

Bower, T. G. R. (1966). Slant perception and shape constancy in infants. *Science, 151,* 832–834.

Bowers, D. G., & Seashore, S. E. (1966). Predicting organizational effectiveness with a four-factor theory of leadership. *Administrative Science Quarterly, 11,* 238–263.

Bowers, K. S. (1967). The effects of demands for honesty on reports of visual and auditory hallucinations. *International Journal of Clinical and Experimental Hypnosis, 15,* 31–36.

Bowers, K. S. (1977). Hypnosis: An informational approach. In W. E. Edmonston, Jr. (Ed.), *Conceptual and investigative approaches to hypnosis and hypnotic phenomena.* Annals of the New York Academy of Sciences (Vol. 296), 222–237.

Bowlby, J. (1973). *Attachment and loss* (Vol. 1): *Attachment.* New York: Basic Books.

Bowlby, J. (1973). *Attachment and loss* (Vol. 2): *Separation.* New York: Basic Books.

Bowman, C. H., & Fishbein, M. (1978). Understanding public reaction to energy proposals: An application of the Fishbein model. *Journal of Applied Social Psychology, 8,* 319–340.

Brady, J. V. (1958, October). Ulcers in "executive monkeys." *Scientific American.* Pp. 95–100.

Bramwell, S. T., Masuda, M., Wagner, N.

N., & Holmes, T. H. (1975). Psychosocial factors in athletic injuries: Development and application of the Social and Athletic Readjustment-Rating Scale (SARRS). *Journal of Human Stress, 1* (2), 6–20.

Brand, R. J., Rosenman, R. H., Sholtz, R. I., & Friedman, M. (1976). Multivariate prediction of coronary heart disease in the Western Collaborative Group Study compared to the findings of Framingham Study. *Circulation, 53,* 348–355.

Bransford, J. D., & Franks, J. J. (1971). The abstraction of linguistic ideas. *Cognitive Psychology, 2,* 331–350.

Bregman, E. (1934). An attempt to modify the emotional attitude of infants by the conditioned response technique. *Journal of Genetic Psychology, 45,* 169–198.

Brennan, W. M., Ames, E. W., & Moore, R. W. (1966). Age differences in infants' attention to patterns of different complexities. *Science, 151,* 354–356.

Bridges, K. M. B. (1932). Emotional development in early infancy. *Child Development, 3,* 324–354.

Brigham, C. C. (1923). *A study of American intelligence.* Princeton, N.J.: Princeton University Press.

Brigham, C. C. (1930). Intelligence tests of immigrant groups. *Psychological Review, 37,* 158–165.

Brim, O. J. (1976). Theories of the male midlife crisis. *The Counseling Psychologist, 6* (1), 2–9.

Broadbent, D. E. (1958). *Perception and communication.* London: Pergamon.

Broadbent, D. E. (1977). The hidden preattentive processes. *American Psychologist, 32,* 109–118.

Brock, T. C. (1965). Communicator-recipient similarity and decision change. *Journal of Personality and Social Psychology, 1,* 650–654.

Brody, E. B., & Brody, N. (1976). *Intelligence: Nature, determinants, and consequences.* New York: Academic Press.

Bronzaft, A. L., Dobrow, S. B., & O'Hanlon, T. J. (1976). Spatial orientation in a subway system. *Environment and Behavior, 8,* 575–594.

Brooks, L. R. (1968). Spatial and verbal components of the act of recall. *Canadian Journal of Psychology, 22,* 349–368.

Brown, A. L. (1975). The development of memory: Knowing, knowing about knowing, and knowing how to know. In H. W. Reese (Ed.), *Advances in child development and behavior* (Vol. 10). New York: Academic Press.

Brown, G. W. (1974). Meaning, measurement, and stress of life events. In B. S. Dohrenwend & B. P. Dohrenwend (Eds.), *Stressful life events: Their nature and effects.* New York: Wiley.

Brown, J. K. (1969). Adolescent initiation rites among preliterate people. In R. E. Grinder (Ed.), *Studies in adolescence* (2nd ed.). New York: Macmillan.

Brown, J. S. (1948). Gradients of approach and avoidance responses and their relation to the level of motivation. *Journal of Comparative and Physiological Psychology, 41,* 450–465.

Brown, R. (1965). *Social psychology.* New York: Free Press.

Brown, R. (1973). *A first language: The early

stages.* Cambridge, Mass: Harvard University Press.

Brown, R. (1976). In memorial tribute to Eric Lenneberg. *Cognition, 4,* 125–153.

Brownwell, K., & Venditti, B. (1983). The etiology and treatment of obesity. In W. E. Fann, I. Karacan, A. D. Pokorney, & R. L. Williams (Eds.), *Phenomenology and the treatment of psychophysiologic disorders.* New York: Spectrum.

Bruner, J. S. (1974/75). From communication to language. *Cognition, 3,* 255–287.

Bruner, J. S., & Goodnow, J. J. (1956). *A study of thinking.* New York: Wiley.

Bryan, J. H., & Test, M. A. (1967). Models and helping: Naturalistic studies in aiding behavior. *Journal of Personality and Social Psychology, 6,* 400–407.

Burks, B. S. (1928). The relative influence of nature and nurture upon mental development: A comparative study of foster parent–foster child resemblance and true parent–true child resemblance. *Yearbook of the National Society for the Study of Education, 27* (Part 1), 219–316.

Burns, T., & Stalker, G. M. (1961). *The management of innovation.* London: Tavistock.

Burnstein, E., Vinokur, A., & Trope, Y. (1973). Interpersonal comparison versus persuasive argumentation: A more direct test of alternative explanations for group-induced shifts in individual choice. *Journal of Experimental Social Psychology, 9,* 236–245.

Burr, W. (1970). Satisfaction with various aspects of marriage over the life cycle: A random middle class sample. *Journal of Marriage and the Family, 32* (1), 29–37.

Burt, C. L. (1943). Ability and income. *British Journal of Educational Psychology, 13,* 83–98.

Burt, C. (1966). The genetic determination of differences in intelligence: A study of monozygotic twins reared together and apart. *British Journal of Psychology, 57,* 137–153.

Buswell, G. T. (1922). Fundamental reading habits: A study of their development. *Supplementary Educational Monographs, No. 21.*

Butler, R. A. (1957). Discrimination learning by rhesus monkeys to visual-exploration motivation. *Journal of Comparative and Physiological Psychology, 50,* 239–241.

Butler, R. N. (1968). The life review: An interpretation of reminiscence in old age. In B. L. Neugarten (Ed.), *Middle age and aging.* Chicago: University of Chicago Press.

Byrne, B. (1974). Item concreteness vs. spatial organization as predictors of visual imagery. *Memory and Cognition, 2,* 53–59.

Byrne, D. (1971). *The attraction paradigm.* New York: Academic Press.

Byrne, D., & Clore, G. L. (1970). A reinforcement model of evaluative responses. *Personality: An International Journal, 1,* 103–128.

Byrne, D., & Rhamey, R. (1965). Magnitude of positive and negative reinforcements as a determinant of attraction. *Journal of Personality and Social Psychology, 2,* 884–889.

Cagas, C. R., & Riley, H. D., Jr. (1970). Age of menarche in girls in a west-south-central community. *American Journal of Diseases of Children, 120,* 303–308.

Caldwell, M. D. (1976). Communication and sex effects in a five-person Prisoner's Dilemma

game. *Journal of Personality and Social Psychology, 33,* 273–280.

Campbell, A. (1975). The American way of mating. Marriage si, children only maybe. *Psychology Today, 8,* 37–41.

Campbell, A., Converse, P. E., Miller, B., & Stokes, D. E. (1964). *The American Voter.* New York: Wiley.

Campbell, D. T. (1963). Social attitudes and other acquired behavioral dispositions. In S. Koch (Ed.), *Psychology: A study of a science* (Vol. 6). New York: McGraw-Hill.

Campbell, E. Q. (1969). Adolescent socialization. In D. A. Goslin (Ed.), *Handbook of socialization theory and research.* New York: Russell Sage Foundation. Pp. 821–859.

Campos, J. J., Hiatt, S., Ramsay, D., Henderson, C., & Svejda, M. (1978). The emergence of fear on the visual cliff. In M. Lewis & L. A. Rosenblum (Eds.), *The development of affect.* New York: Plenum. Pp. 149–182.

Campos, J. J., Langer, A., & Krowitz, A. (1970). Cardiac responses on the visual cliff in prelocomotor human infants. *Science, 170,* 196–197.

Cannon, W. B. (1927). The James-Lange theory of emotion: A critical examination and an alternative theory. *American Journal of Psychology, 39,* 106–124.

Cannon, W. B. (1939). *The wisdom of the body.* New York: Norton.

Cannon, W. B. (1942). Voodoo death. *American Anthropologist, 44,* 169–181.

Cantor, J. R., Zillman, D., & Bryant, J. (1975). Enhancement of experienced sexual arousal in response to erotic stimuli through misattribution of unrelated residual excitation. *Journal of Personality and Social Psychology, 32,* 69–75.

Cantor, J. R., Zillman, D., & Einsiedel, E. F. (1978). Female responses to provocation after exposure to aggresive and erotic films. *Communication Research, 5,* 395–411.

Cantor, N., & Mischel, W. (1977). Traits as prototypes: Effects on recognition and memory. *Journal of Personality and Social Psychology, 35,* 38–48.

Carey, S., & Bartlett, E. (1983). Acquiring a single new word. *Papers and reports on child language development.* Palo Alto: Stanford University Committee on Linguistics.

Carlisle, H. J. (1969). The effects of preoptic and anterior hypothalamic lesions on behavioral thermoregulation in the cold. *Journal of Comparative and Physiological Psychology, 69,* 391–402.

Carlson, N. R. (1980). *Physiology of behavior* (2nd ed.). Boston: Allyn & Bacon.

Carmichael, L. (1926). The development of behavior in vertebrates experimentally removed from the influence of external stimulation. *Psychological Review, 33,* 51–58.

Carmichael, L. (1927). A further study of the development of vertebrates experimentally removed from the influence of external stimulation. *Psychological Review, 34,* 34–47.

Carmichael, L., Hogan, H. P., & Walter, A. A. (1932). An experimental study of the effect of language on the representation of visually perceived form. *Journal of Experimental Psychology, 15,* 73–86.

Caron, A. H., Caron, R. F., & Carlson, V. R. (1979). Infant perception of the invariant shape of objects varying in slant. *Child Development, 50,* 716–721.

Carpenter, G. (1975). Mother's face and the newborn. In R. Lewin (Ed.), *Child alive.* London: Temple Smith.

Carpenter, P. A., & Just, M. A. (1977). Reading comprehension as the eyes see it. In M. A. Just & P. A. Carpenter (Eds.), *Cognitive processes in comprehension.* Hillsdale, N.J.: Erlbaum.

Carrington, P. (1977). *Freedom in meditation.* New York: Anchor Press/Doubleday; Doubleday Paperback, 1978.

Carrington, P. (1978). *Clinically standardized meditation (CSM) instructor's kit.* Kendall Park, N.J.: Pace Educational Systems.

Carrington, P., Collings, G. H., Benson, H., Robinson, H., Wood, L. W., Lehrer, P. M., Woolfolk, R. L., & Cole, J. W. (1980). The use of meditation-relaxation techniques for the management of stress in a working population. *Journal of Occupational Medicine, 22,* 221–231.

Carter, H., & Glick, P. C. (1976). *Marriage and divorce.* Cambridge, Mass.: Harvard University Press.

Cartwright, D. (1971). Risk taking by individuals and groups: An assessment of research involving choice dilemmas. *Journal of Personality and Social Psychology, 20,* 361–378.

Cartwright, D. S. (1979). *Theories and models of personality.* Dubuque, Iowa: William C. Brown.

Cartwright, R. D. (1978, December). Happy ending for our dreams. *Psychology Today.*

Carver, C. S. (1974). Facilitation of physical aggression through objective self-awareness. *Journal of Experimental Social Psychology, 10,* 365–370.

Carver, R. P. (1972). Speed readers don't read: They skim. *Psychology Today.*

Casey, J. F., Bennett, I. F., & Lindley, C. J. (1960). Drug therapy in schizophrenia: A controlled study of the relative effectiveness of chlorpromazine, promazine, phenobarbital and placebo. *Archives of General Psychiatry, 2,* 210–220.

Cattell, R. B. (1949). *The culture free intelligence test.* Champaign, Ill.: Institute for Personality and Ability Testing.

Cattell, R. B. (1950). *Personality: A systematic, theoretical, and factual study.* New York: McGraw-Hill.

Cattell, R. B., & Kline, P. (1937). *The scientific analysis of personality and motivation.* New York: Academic Press.

Chaikin, A. L., & Darley, J. M. (1973). Victim or perpetrator?: Defensive attribution of responsibility and the need for order and justice. *Journal of Personality and Social Psychology, 25,* 268–275.

Chaikin, S., & Eagly, A. (1976). Communication modality as a determinant of message persuasiveness and message comprehensibility. *Journal of Personality and Social Psychology, 34,* 605–614.

Chapman, L. J. (1967). Illusory correlation in observational report. *Journal of Verbal Learning and Verbal Behavior, 6,* 151–155.

Chomsky, N. (1957). *Synactic structures.* The Hague: Mouton.

Chomsky, N. (1968). *Language and mind.* New York: Harcourt Brace Jovanovich.

Chomsky, N. (1975). *Reflections on language.* New York: Pantheon.

Christensen, C. V., & Gagnon, J. H. (1965). Sexual behavior in a group of older women. *Journal of Gerontology, 20,* 351–356.

Chukovsky, K. (1968). *From two to five.* Los Angeles: University of California Press.

Clark, H. H., & Clark, E. V. (1977). *Psychology and language: An introduction to psycholinguistics.* New York: Harcourt Brace Jovanovich.

Clark, M. S., & Mills, J. (1979). Interpersonal attraction in exchange and communal relationships. *Journal of Personality and Social Psychology, 37,* 12–24.

Clarke-Stewart, K. A. (1973). Interactions between mothers and their young children: Characteristics and consequences. *Monographs of the Society for Research in Child Development, 38* (6-7, Serial No. 153).

Clarke-Stewart, K. A. (1978). And daddy makes three. *Child Development, 49,* 466–478.

Clarke-Stewart, K. A., & Apfel, N. (1979). Evaluating parental effects on child development. In L. S. Shulman (Ed.), *Review of research in education* (Vol. 6). Itasca, Ill.: Peacock.

Clarparede, E. (1911). La genèse de l'hypothese. *Arch. de Ps., 24,* 1–154.

Cleary, T. A., Humphreys, L. G., Kendrick, S. A., & Wesman, A. (1975). Educational uses of tests with disadvantaged students. *American Psychologist, 30,* 15–41.

Cleckley, H. (1976). *The mask of sanity* (5th ed.). St. Louis, Mo.: Mosby.

Cohen, A. R. (1962). An experiment on small rewards for discrepant compliance and attitude change. In J. W. Brehm & A. R. Cohen, *Explorations in cognitive dissonance.* New York: Wiley.

Cohen, D. B. (1979). *Sleep and dreaming: Origins, nature and functions.* Oxford: Pergamon Press.

Cohen, F., & Lazarus, R. S. (1979). Coping with the stresses of illness. In G. C. Stone, F. Cohen, & N. E. Adler (Eds.), *Health psychology.* San Francisco: Jossey-Bass.

Cohen, L. B., DeLoache, J. S., & Strauss, M. S. (1979). Infant perceptual development. In J. D. Osofsky (Ed.), *Handbook of infant development.* New York: Wiley.

Cohen, L. B., & Gelber, E. R. (1975). Infant visual memory. In L. B. Cohen & P. Salapatek (Eds.), *Infant perception: From sensation to cognition* (Vol. 1): *Basic visual processes.* New York: Academic Press.

Colby, A. (1978). Evolution of a moral-development theory. In W. Damon (Ed.), *Moral development.* San Francisco: Jossey-Bass.

Cole, J. O. (1964). Phenothiazine treatment in acute schizophrenia: Effectiveness. *Archives of General Psychiatry, 10,* 246–261.

Cole, M., Gay, J., Glick, J. A., & Sharp, D. W. (1971). *The cultural context of learning and thinking.* New York: Basic Books.

Coleman, J. C., Butcher, J. N., & Carson, R. C. (1980). *Abnormal psychology and modern life.* (6th ed.). Glenview, Ill.: Scott, Foresman.

Collier, G., & Hirsch, E. (1971). Reinforcing properties of spontaneous activity in the rat. *Journal of Comparative and Physiological Psychology, 7,* 155–160.

Collier, G., Hirsch, E., & Hamlin, P. (1972). The ecological determinants of reinforcement. *Journal of Physiology and Behavior, 9,* 705–716.

Collier, G., Hirsch, E., & Kanarek, R. (1977). The operant revisited. In W. K. Honig & J. E. R. Staddor (Eds.), *Handbook of operant behavior.* Englewood Cliffs, N.J.: Prentice-Hall.

Colt, E. W., Wardlaw, S. L., & Frantz, A. G. (1981). The effect of running on plasma β-endorphin. *Life Sciences, 28,* 1637–1640.

Coltheart, M., & Glick, M. J. (1974). Visual imagery: A case study. *Quarterly Journal of Experimental Psychology, 26,* 438–453.

Conger, J. J. (1977). *Adolescence and youth: Psychological development in a changing world* (2nd ed.). New York: Harper & Row.

Converse, P. E. (1964). The nature of belief systems in mass publics. In D. E. Apter (Ed.), *Ideology and discontent.* New York: Free Press.

Cooper, J. (1971). Personal responsibility and dissonance; the role of foreseen consequences. *Journal of Personality and Social Psychology, 18,* 354–363.

Cooper, J. (1979). Dissonance and psychotherapy: The use of effort justification in the reduction of snake phobia. Unpublished manuscript. Princeton University.

Cooper, J., & Axsom, D. (1982). Cognitive dissonance and psychotherapy. In G. W. Weary & H. Mirels (Eds.), *Emerging integration of clinical social psychology.* New York: Oxford University Press.

Cooper, L. A., & Shepard, R. N. (1973). Chronometric studies of the notation of mental images. In W. G. Chase (Ed.), *Visual information processing.* New York: Academic Press.

Cooper, M. J., & Aygen, M. M. (1979). A relaxation technique in the management of hypercholesterolemia. *Journal of Human Stress, 5,* 24–27.

Cooper, R., & Zubek, J. (1958). Effects of enriched and restricted early environments on the learning ability of bright and dull rats. *Canadian Journal of Psychology, 12,* 159–164.

Coppen, A. (1967). The biochemistry of affective disorders. *British Journal of Psychiatry, 113,* 1237–1264.

Corah, N. L., & Boffa, J. (1970). Perceived control, self-observation, and response to aversive stimulation. *Journal of Personality and Social Psychology, 16,* 1–4.

Corballis, M. C. (1980). Laterality and myth. *American Psychologist, 35,* 284–295.

Corballis, M. C., & Beale, I. L. (1976). *The psychology of left and right.* Hillsdale, N.J.: Erlbaum.

Coren, S., & Porac, C. (1977). Fifty centuries of righthandedness: The historical record. *Science, 298,* 631–632.

Corsini, R. J. (1977). A medley of current personality theories. In R. J. Corsini (Ed.), *Current personality theories.* Itasca, Ill.: Peacock.

Costanzo, P. R., & Shaw, M. E. (1966). Conformity as a function of age level. *Child Development, 37,* 967–975.

Cottrell, N. B. (1972). Social facilitation. In C. G. McClintock (Ed.), *Experimental social psy-*

chology. New York: Holt, Rinehart and Winston.

Cowan, W. M. (1979). The development of the brain. *Scientific American, 241* (3), 112–133.

Cox, T. (1978). *Stress*. Baltimore, Md.: University Park Press.

Craik, F. I. M., & Lockhart, R. S. (1972). Levels of processing: A framework for memory research. *Journal of Verbal Learning and Verbal Behavior, 11,* 671–684.

Craik, F. I. M., & Tulving, E. (1975). Depth of processing and the retention of words in episodic memory. *Journal of Experimental Psychology, 104,* 268–294.

Cumming, E. (1963). Further thoughts on the theory of disengagement. *International Social Science Journal, 15,* 377–393.

Cumming, E., & Henry, W. E. (1961). *Growing old*. New York: Basic Books.

Current Population Reports. (1975). Population Characteristics Series p-20, No. 287: Marital status and living arrangements: March 1975. Washington, D.C.: U.S. Government Printing Office.

Current Population Reports. (1979). Population Characteristics Series p-20, No. 338: Marital status and living arrangements: March 1978. Washington, D.C.: U.S. Government Printing Office.

Current Population Reports. (1979). Population Characteristics Series p-20, No. 341: Fertility of American women: June 1978. Washington, D.C.: U.S. Government Printing Office.

Daly, M., & Wilson, M. (1978). *Sex, evolution and behavior*. Boston, Mass.: Duxbury Press.

Daniels, D. (1977). Cited in Carrington, P. *Freedom in meditation*. New York: Anchor Press/Doubleday. P. 60.

Darley, J. M., & Fazio, R. H. (1980). Expectancy confirmation processes arising in the social interaction sequence. *American Psychologist, 35,* 867–881.

Darley, J. M., & Latané, B. (1968). Bystander intervention in emergencies: Diffusion of responsibility. *Journal of Personality and Social Psychology, 8,* 377–383.

Darley, J. M., Moriarty, T., Darley, S., & Berscheid, E. (1974). Increased conformity to a fellow deviant as a function of prior deviation. *Journal of Experimental Social Psychology, 10,* 211–223.

Dart, R. A. (1949). The predatory implemental technique of *Australopithecus. American Journal of Physical Anthropology, 7,* 1–38.

Darwin, C. (1872). *The expression of the emotions in men and animals*. London: Murray.

Darwin, C. (1859). *On the origin of species by means of natural selection, or the preservation of favoured races in the struggle for life*. London: Murray.

Davenport, W. (1965). Sexual patterns and their regulation in a society of the Southwest Pacific. In F. A. Beach (Ed.), *Sex and behavior*. New York: Wiley.

Davis, C. M. (1928). Self-selection of diet by newly weaned infants. *American Journal of Diseases of Children, 36,* 651–679.

Davis, J. D., Gallagher, R. J., & Ladlove, R. F. (1967). Food intake controlled by a blood factor. *Science, 156,* 1247–1248.

Davis, M. S. (1966). Variations in patients' compliance with doctors' orders: Analysis of

congruence between survey responses and results of empirical investigations. *Journal of Medical Education, 41,* 1037–1048.

Davison, G. C., & Neale, J. M. (1978). *Abnormal psychology: An experimental clinical approach* (2nd ed.). New York: Wiley.

Dekker, E., & Groen, J. (1956). Reproducible psychogenic attacks of asthma. *Journal of Psychosomatic Research, 1,* 58–67.

Dember, W. N. (1964). Birth order and need affiliation. *Journal of Abnormal and Social Psychology, 68,* 555–557.

Dembroski, T. M., MacDougall, J. M., Herd, J. A., & Shields, J. L. (1979). Effects of level of challenge on pressor and heart rate responses in Type A and B subjects. *Journal of Applied Social Psychology, 9,* 209–228.

Dement, W. C. (1974). *Some must watch while some must sleep*. San Francisco: Freeman.

Dement, W. C., & Kleitman, M. (1957). The relation of eye movements during sleep to dream activity: An objective method for the study of dreaming. *Journal of Experimental Psychology, 53,* 339–346.

Denes, P. D., & Pinson, E. N. (1963). *The speech chain*. New York: Doubleday.

Derlega, V. J., & Chaikin, A. (1975). *Sharing intimacy*. Englewood Cliffs, N.J.: Prentice-Hall.

Deutsch, J. A. (1960). *The structural basis of behavior*. Chicago: University of Chicago Press.

Deutsch, M., & Collins, M. E. (1951). *Interracial housing: A psychological evaluation of a social experiment*. Minneapolis: University of Minnesota Press.

Deutsch, M., & Gerard, H. B. (1955). A study of normative and informational social influences upon individual judgment. *Journal of Abnormal and Social Psychology, 51,* 629–636.

Deutsch, M., & Krauss, R. M. (1960). The effect of threat upon interpersonal bargaining. *Journal of Abnormal and Social Psychology, 61,* 181–189.

Deutsch, M., & Krauss, R. M. (1962). Studies of interpersonal bargaining. *Journal of Conflict Resolution, 6,* 52–76.

De Vore, I. (1979). *Sociobiology and the social sciences*. Chicago: Aldine Atherton.

Dion, K. (1972). Physical attractiveness and evaluation of children's transgressions. *Journal of Personality and Social Psychology, 24,* 207–213.

Dion, K. K., Berscheid, E., & Walster, E. (1972). What is beautiful is good. *Journal of Personality and Social Psychology, 24,* 285–290.

Ditter, J., & Kelley, H. H. (1956). Effects of different conditions of acceptance upon conformity to group norms. *Journal of Abnormal and Social Psychology, 53,* 100–107.

Diven, K. (1936). Certain determinants in the conditioning of anxiety reactions. *Journal of Psychology, 3,* 291–308.

Dohrenwend, B. S., & Dohrenwend, B. P. (Eds.). (1974). *Stressful life events: Their nature and effects*. New York: Wiley.

Dollard, J., Doob, L., Miller, N. E., Mower, O., & Sears, R. (1939). *Frustration and aggression*. New Haven, Conn.: Yale University Press.

Dollard, J., & Miller, N. E. (1950). *Personality and psychotherapy*. New York: McGraw-Hill.

Donnerstein, E., & Berkowitz, L. (1981). Victim reactions in aggressive erotic films as a factor in violence against women. *Journal of Personality and Social Psychology, 41,* 710–724.

Doob, A. N., & Wood, L. (1972). Catharsis and aggression: The effects of annoyance and retaliation on aggressive behavior. *Journal of Personality and Social Psychology, 22,* 156–162.

Douvan, E. A., & Adelson, J. (1966). *The adolescent experience*. New York: Wiley.

Dressler, D. M. (1973). Life adjustment of retired couples. *International Journal of Aging and Human Development, 4*(4), 335–349.

DuBois, P. M. (1980). *The hospice way of death*. New York: Human Sciences Press.

Duncker, K. (1945). On problem-solving. *Psychological Monographs, 58,* 5(Whole No. 270).

Duval, S., & Wicklund, R. A. (1972). *A theory of objective self-awareness*. New York: Academic Press.

Dweck, C. S., & Goetz, T. E. (1978). Attributions and learned helplessness. In J. H. Harvey, W. Ickes, & R. F. Kidd (Eds.), *New directions in attribution research* (Vol. 2). New York: Wiley.

Eagly, A. (1978). Sex differences in influenceability. *Psychological Bulletin, 85,* 86–116.

Eagly, A. H., & Carli, L. L. (1981). Sex of researcher and sex-typed communications as determinants of sex differences in influenceability: A meta-analysis of social influence studies. *Psychological Bulletin, 90,* 1–20.

Eagly, A. H., Wood, W., & Chaiken, S. (1978). Causal inferences about communicators and their effect on opinion change. *Journal of Personality and Social Psychology, 36,* 424–435.

Eastman, C. (1976). Behavioral formulations of depression. *Psychological Review, 83,* 277–291.

Ebbinghaus, H. (1885). *Memory: A contribution to experimental psychology* (H. A. Ruger & C. E. Bussenius, trans.). New York: Teachers College.

Eckerman, C. O., Whatley, J. L., & Kutz, S. L. (1975). Growth of social play during the second year of life. *Developmental Psychology, 11,* 42–49.

Edmonston, W. E., Jr. (Ed.). (1977). Conceptual and investigative approaches to hypnosis and hypnotic phenomena. *Annals of The New York Academy of Sciences* (Vol. 296).

Efran, M. G. (1974). The effect of physical appearance on the judgment of guilt, interpersonal attraction, and severity of recommended punishment in a simulated jury task. *Journal of Research in Personality, 8,* 45–54.

Egger, M. D., & Flynn, J. P. (1963). Effect of electrical stimulation of the amygdala on hypothalamically elicited attack behavior in cats. *Journal of Neurophysiology, 26,* 705–720.

Eimas, P., Siqueland, E. R., Jusczyk, P., & Vigorito, J. (1971). Speech perception in infants. *Science, 171,* 303–306.

Eisdorfer, C. (1972). Adaptation to loss of work. In Frances M. Carp (Ed.), *Retirement*. New York: Behavioral Publications.

Ekman, P., & Friesen, W. V. (1968). The repertoire of nonverbal behavior—categories, origins, usage and coding. *Semiotica, 1,* 49–98.

Ekman, P., & Friesen, W. V. (1971). Constants across cultures in the face and emotion. *Journal of Personality and Social Psychology, 17*, 124–129.

Elkind, D. (1961). Children's discovery of the conversation of mass, weight, and volume: Piaget's replication study II. *Journal of Genetic Psychology, 98*, 219–227.

Ellis, A. (1958). Rational psychotherapy. *Journal of Social Psychology, 59*, 35–49.

Ellis, A. (1962). *Reason and emotion in psychotherapy.* New York: Lyle Stuart.

Ellis, A. (1973). *Humanistic psychotherapy: the rational-emotive approach.* New York: Julian.

Ellis, A. (1975). *A new guide to rational living.* Englewood Cliffs, N.J.: Prentice-Hall.

Engel, B. T. (1960). Stimulus-response and individual-response specificity. *Archives of General Psychiatry, 2*, 305–313.

English, H. B. (1929). Three cases of the "conditioned fear response." *Journal of Abnormal and Social Psychology, 34*, 221–225.

Epstein, A. N., Fitzsimons, J. T., & Rolls, B. J. (1970). Drinking induced by injections of angiotensin into the brain of the rat. *Journal of Physiology* (London), *210*, 457–474.

Epstein, S. M. (1967). Toward a unified theory of anxiety. In B. A. Maher (Ed.), *Progress in experimental personality research* (Vol. 4). New York: Academic Press.

Erhardt, A. A., & Baker, S. (1974). Fetal androgens, human CNS differentiation, and behavioral sex differences. In R. C. Friedman, R. M. Richart, & K. L. VandeWiele (Eds.), *Sex differences in behavior.* New York: Wiley.

Erikson, E. H. (1959). Identity and the life cycle. *Psychological Issues, 1.*

Erikson, E. H. (1963). *Childhood and society.* New York: Norton.

Erikson, K. T. (1976). *Everything in its path: Destruction of community in the Buffalo Creek Flood.* New York: Simon & Schuster.

Estes, W. K. (1949). A study of motivating conditions necessary for secondary reinforcement. *Journal of Experimental Psychology, 39*, 306–310.

Evans, F. J. (1977). Hypnosis and sleep: The control of altered states of awareness. In W. E. Edmonston, Jr. (Ed.), Conceptual and investigative approaches to hypnosis and hypnotic phenomena. *Annals of The New York Academy of Sciences* (Vol. 296), 162–174.

Eyferth, K. (1961). Leistungen verschiedner Gruppen von Besatzungskindern in Hamburg—Wechsler Intelligenztest für Kinder (HAWIK). *Archiv für die gesamte Psychologie, 113,* 222–241.

Eysenk, H. J. (1952). The effects of psychotherapy: An evaluation. *Journal of Consulting Psychology, 16,* 319–324.

Eysenck, H. J. (1977). The case of Sir Cyril Burt. *Encounter, 48,* 19–24.

Fadiman, J., & Kewman, D. (Eds.). (1973). *Exploring madness: Experience, theory, and research.* Monterey, Calif.: Brooks/Cole.

Fagan, J. F. (1976). Infants' recognition of invariant features of faces. *Child Development, 47,* 627–638.

Fantz, R. L. (1963). Pattern vision in newborn infants. *Science, 140,* 296–297.

Faust, M. S. (1960). Developmental maturity as a determinant in prestige of adolescent girls. *Child Development, 31,* 173–184.

Fazio, R. H., & Zanna, M. P. (1981). Direct experience and attitude-behavior consistency. In L. Berkowitz (Ed.), *Advances in experimental social psychology* (Vol. 14). New York: Academic Press.

Fazio, R. H., Zanna, M. P., & Cooper, J. (1979). On the relationship of data to theory: A reply to Ronis and Greenwald. *Journal of Experimental Social Psychology, 15,* 70–76.

Feather, N. T., & Simon, J. G. (1975). Reactions to male and female success and failure in sex-linked occupations: Impressions of personality, causal attributions, and perceived likelihood of different consequences. *Journal of Personality and Social Psychology, 31,* 20–31.

Fechner, G. (1966). *Elements of psychophysics* (H. E. Adler, trans.). New York: Holt, Rinehart and Winston. (Originally published in 1860.)

Feldman, M. W., & Lewontin, R. C. (1975). The heritability hand-up. *Science, 190,* 1163–1168.

Ferster, C. B. (1961). Positive reinforcement and behavioral deficits of autistic children. *Child Development, 32,* 437–456.

Ferster, C. B., & Skinner, B. F. (1957). *Schedules of reinforcement.* Englewood Cliffs, N.J.: Prentice-Hall.

Feshback, S., & Fraczek, A. (1979). *Aggression and behavior change: Biological and social processes.* New York: Praeger.

Feshback, S., & Singer, R. D. (1971). *Television and aggression.* San Francisco: Jossey-Bass.

Festinger, L. A. (1954). A theory of social comparison processes. *Human Relations, 7,* 117–140.

Festinger, L. (1957). *A theory of cognitive dissonance.* Evanston, Ill.: Row, Peterson.

Festinger, L., & Carlsmith, J. M. (1959). Cognitive consequences of forced compliance. *Journal of Abnormal and Social Psychology, 58,* 203–210.

Fiedler, F. E. (1967). *A theory of leadership effectiveness.* New York: McGraw-Hill.

Fiedler, F. E. (1972). Personality, motivational systems, and behavior of high and low LPC persons. *Human Relations, 25,* 391–412.

Fish, B., Karabenick, S., & Heath, M. (1978). The effects of observation on emotional arousal and affiliation. *Journal of Experimental Social Psychology, 14,* 251–265.

Fishbein, M. (1967). Attitude and the prediction of behavior. In M. Fishbein (Ed.), *Readings in attitude theory and measurement.* New York: Wiley.

Fisher, S., & Greenberg, R. P. (1977). *The scientific credibility of Freud's theories and therapy.* New York: Basic Books.

Fitzgerald, J., & Brackbill, Y. (1976). Classical conditioning in infancy. *Psychological Bulletin, 83,* 353–376.

Fitzsimmons, J. T. (1972). Thirst. *Psychological Review, 52,* 468–561.

Flacks, R. (1970). The revolt of the advantaged. In R. Sigel (Ed.), *Learning about politics.* New York: Random House.

Flaherty, C. F., Hamilton, L. W., Gandleman, R. J., & Spear, N. E. (1977). *Learning and memory.* Chicago: Rand McNally.

Flavell, J. H. (1963). *The developmental psychology of Jean Piaget.* Princeton, N.J.: Van Nostrand.

Flavell, J. H. (1977). *Cognitive development.* Englewood Cliffs, N.J.: Prentice-Hall.

Flavell, J. H. (1978). Metacognitive development. In J. M. Scandura & C. J. Brainerd (Eds.), *Structural/process theories of complex human behavior.* Alphen a.d. Rijn, The Netherlands: Sijthoff & Noordhoff.

Flavell, J. H., & Wellman, H. M. (1977). Metamemory. In R. V. Kail, Jr. & J. W. Hagen (Eds.), *Perspectives on the development of memory and cognition.* Hillsdale, N.J.: Erlbaum.

Fleishman, E. A. (1957). A leader behavior description for industry. In R. M. Stogdill & A. E. Coons (Eds.), *Leader behavior: Its description and measurement.* Columbus: Ohio State University, Bureau of Business Research.

Foa, E., & Foa, V. (1976). Resource theory of social exchange. In J. Thibaut, J. Spence, & R. Carson (Eds.), *Contemporary trends in social psychology.* Morristown, N.J.: Social Learning Press.

Foldman, S., & Lazarus, R. S. (1978). An analyis of coping in a middle-aged community sample. *Journal of Health and Social Behavior, 21,* 219–239.

Foltz, E. L., & Millett, F. E. (1964). Experimental psychosomatic disease states in monkeys. I. Peptic ulcer—"Executive monkeys." *Journal of Surgical Research, 4,* 445–453.

Ford, C. W., & Beach, F. A. (1951). *Patterns of sexual behavior.* New York: Harper & Row.

Ford, R. N. (1973). Job enrichment lessons from AT&T. *Harvard Business Review,* pp. 96–106.

Foree, D. D., & LoLordo, V. M. (1973). Attention in the pigeon: The differential effect of food-getting vs. shock avoidance procedures. *Journal of Comparative and Psychological Psychology, 85,* 551–558.

Foulkes, D., Larson, J. D., Swanson, E. M., & Rardin, M. (1969). Two studies of childhood dreaming. *American Journal of Orthopsychiatry, 39,* 627–643.

Frankl, V. E. (1963). *Man's search for meaning.* New York: Washington Square Press.

Fraser, M. (1973). *Children in conflict.* Garden City, N.Y.: Doubleday.

Freedman, D. X. (1977). Pharmacotherapy. In F. J. Braceland et al. (Eds.), *Year book of psychiatry and applied mental health.* Chicago: Year Book Medical Publishers.

French, E. G., & Thomas, F. H. (1958). The relation of achievement to problem-solving effectiveness. *Journal of Abnormal and Social Psychology, 56,* 45–48.

Freud, S. (1933). *New introductory lectures on psychoanalysis* (W. J. H. Sproutt, trans.). New York: Norton.

Freud, S. (1953). The interpretation of dreams. In J. Strachey (Ed. and trans.), *The standard edition of the complete psychological works.* London: Hogarth. (Originally published in 1900.)

Freud, S. (1955). Beyond the pleasure principle. In J. Strachey (Ed. and trans.), *The standard edition of the complete psychological works.* London: Hogarth. (Originally published in 1920.)

Freud, S. (1961). Civilization and its discontents. In J. Strachey (Ed. and trans.), *The standard edition of the complete psychological works*

(Vol. 21). London: Hogarth. (Originally published in 1930.)

Freud, S. (1960). [*Introductory lectures on psychoanalysis*] (J. Strachey, Ed. and trans.). New York: Norton. (First English edition New York: Boni & Liveright, 1920, titled *A general introduction to psychoanalysis*.)

Frew, D. (1977). *Management of stress.* Chicago: Nelson-Hall.

Friedhoff, A. J., & Van Winkle, E. (1962). Isolation and characterization of a compound from the urine of schizophrenics. *Nature, 194,* 897–898.

Friedman, M. (1969). *Pathogenesis of coronary artery disease.* New York: McGraw-Hill.

Friedman, S. (1972). Habituation and recovery of visual response in the alert human newborn. *Journal of Experimental Child Psychology, 13,* 339–349.

Fromkin, V. A. (1976). Personal communication.

Gannon, L. (1981). The psychophysiology of psychosomatic disorders. In S. N. Haynes & L. Gannon (Eds.), *Psychosomatic disorders.* New York: Praeger.

Garcia, J., & Koelling, R. A. (1966). Relation of cues to consequence in avoidance learning. *Psychonomic Science, 4,* 123–124.

Garcia, J., McGowan, B. K., & Green, K. F. (1972). Biological constraints on conditioning. In A. H. Black & W. F. Prokasy (Eds.), *Classical conditioning II: Current theory and research.* New York: Appleton-Century-Crofts.

Gardner, H. (1982). *Developmental psychology* (2nd ed.). Boston: Little, Brown.

Gardner, J. K. (1982). *Readings in developmental psychology* (2nd ed.). Boston: Little, Brown.

Gardner, L. (1972). Deprivation dwarfism. *Scientific American, 227,* 76–82.

Gardner, R. A., & Gardner, B. T. (1969). Teaching sign language to a chimpanzee. *Science, 165,* 664–672.

Gardner, R. A., & Gardner B. T. (1980). Reply to Terrace. Personal communication.

Garfield, S. L., & Bergin, A. E. (Eds.). (1978). *Handbook of psychotherapy and behavior change* (2nd ed.). New York: Wiley.

Gatchel, R., & Proctor, J. D. (1976). Physiological correlates of learned helplessness in man. *Journal of Abnormal Psychology, 85,* 27–34.

Gauron, E., & Dickinson, J. K. (1966). Diagnostic decision making in psychiatry. *Archives of General Psychiatry, 14,* 233–237.

Gazzaniga, M. S. (1967). The split brain in man. *Scientific American, 217* (2), 24–29.

Geen, R. G., & O'Neal, E. C. (1969). Activation of cue-elicited aggression by general arousal. *Journal of Personality and Social Psychology, 11,* 287–292.

Geen, R. G., & Stonner, D. (1971). Effects of aggressiveness habit strength on behavior in the presence of aggression-related stimuli. *Journal of Personality and Social Psychology, 17,* 149–153.

Geer, J. H., Davison, G. C., & Gatchel, R. I. (1970). Reduction of stress in humans through nonveridical perceived control of aversive stimulation. *Journal of Personality and Social Psychology, 16,* 731–738.

Geertz, C. (1980, July 24). Sociosexology. *New York Review of Books,* pp. 3–4.

Gelman, R. (1969). Conservation acquisition: A problem of learning to attend to relevant attributes. *Journal of Experimental Child Psychology, 7,* 176–187.

Gelman, R. (1978). Cognitive development. In L. W. Porter & M. R. Rosenzweig (Eds.), *Annual Review of Psychology* (Vol. 29). Palo Alto, Calif.: Annual Reviews.

Gelman, R., & Gallistel, C. R. (1978). *The child's understanding of number.* Cambridge, Mass.: Harvard University Press.

Gerard, H. B., & Mathewson, G. C. (1966). The effects of severity of initiation on liking for a group: A replication. *Journal of Experimental Social Psychology, 2,* 278–287.

Gerard, H. B., & Rabbie, J. M. (1961). Fear and social comparison. *Journal of Abnormal and Social Psychology, 62,* 586–592.

Gerard, H. B., Wilhelmy, R. A., & Conolley, E. S. (1968). Conformity and group size. *Journal of Personality and Social Psychology, 8,* 82.

Gerbner, G., & Gross, L. (1976). Living with television: The violence profile. *Journal of Communications, 26,* 173–199.

Gerbner, G., Gross, L., Signorielli, N., Morgan, M., & Jackson-Beeck, M. (1979). The demonstration of power: Violence profile No. 10. *Journal of Communication, 29,* 177–196.

Gergen, K., Gergen, M., & Meter, K. (1972). Individuals' orientations to prosocial behavior. *Journal of Social Issues, 28,* 105–130.

Gesell, A. L. (1934). *Infant behavior.* New Haven, Conn.: Yale University Press.

Gesell, A. L. (1941). *Wolf child and human child, being a narrative interpretation of the life history of Kamala, the wolf girl; based on the diary account of a child who was reared by a wolf and who then lived for nine years in the orphanage of Midnapore, in the province of Bengal, India.* New York: Harper & Brothers.

Gesell, A. L., & Thompson, H. (1929). Learning and growth in identical twins: An experimental study by the method of co-twin control. *Genetic Psychology Monographs, Vol. 6* (1).

Geshwind, N. (1979). Specializations of the human brain. *Scientific American, 241* (3), 180–199.

Gewirtz, J. L. (1969). Mechanisms of social learning: Some roles of stimulation and behavior in early human development. In D. A. Goslin (Ed.), *Handbook of socialization theory and research.* Chicago: Rand-McNally.

Gibb, C. A. (1969). Leadership. In G. Lindzey & E. Aronson (Eds.), *Handbook of social psychology* (2nd ed.) (Vol. 4). Reading, Mass.: Addison-Wesley.

Gibbs, J., Young, R. C., & Smith, G. P. (1973). Cholecystokinin decreases food intake in rats. *Journal of Comparative and Physiological Psychology, 84,* 488–495.

Gibson, J. J. (1966). *The senses considered as perceptual systems.* Boston: Houghton Mifflin.

Gick, M. L., & Holyoak, K. J. (1980). Analogical problem solving. *Cognitive Psychology, 12,* 306–355.

Gilligan, C. (1982). *In a different voice: Psychological theory and women's development.* Cambridge, Mass.: Harvard University Press.

Glamzer, F. D. (1976). Determinants of a positive attitude toward retirement. *Journal of Gerontology, 31*(1), 104–107.

Glass, A. J. (1953). Psychotherapy in the combat zone. In *Symposium on stress.* Washington, D.C.: Army Medical Service Graduate School.

Glass, D. (1977). *Behavior patterns, stress and coronary disease.* Hillsdale, N.J.: Erlbaum.

Glass, D., & Singer, J. (1972). *Urban stress.* New York: Academic Press.

Gleason, J. B., & Weintraub, S. (1978). Input language and the acquisition of communicative competence. In K. Nelson (Ed.), *Children's language* (Vol. 1). New York: Gardner Press.

Glick, P. C., & Norton, A. J. (1973). Perspectives on the recent upturn in divorce and remarriage. *Demography, 10,* 301–314.

Glucksberg, S., & Danks, J. H. (1975). *Experimental psycholinguistics.* Hillsdale, N.J.: Erlbaum.

Glucksberg, S., & King, L. J. (1967). Motivated forgetting mediated by implicit verbal chaining. *Science, 158,* 517–519.

Glucksberg, S., Krauss, R. M., & Weisberg, R. (1966). Referential communication in nursery school children. Method and some preliminary findings. *Journal of Experimental Child Psychology, 3,* 333–342.

Glucksberg, S., & Weisberg, R. W. (1966). Verbal behavior and problem solving: Some effects of labelling in a functional fixedness problem. *Journal of Experimental Psychology, 71,* 659–64.

Glueck, B. C., & Stroebel, C. F. (1975). Biofeedback and meditation in the treatment of psychiatric illness. *Comprehensive Psychiatry, 16,* 302–321.

Goddard, H. H. (1917). Mental tests and the immigrant. *Journal of Delinquency, 2,* 243–277.

Goddard, H. H. (1920). *Human efficiency and levels of intelligence.* Princeton, N.J.: Princeton University Press.

Goldband, S., Katkin, E. S., & Morrell, M. A. (1979). Personality and cardiovascular disorder: Steps toward demystification. In I. G. Sarason & C. D. Spielberger (Eds.), *Stress and anxiety* (Vol. 6). New York: Wiley.

Goldfarb, W. (1944). Infant-rearing as a factor in foster home placement. *American Journal of Orthopsychiatry, 14,* 162–167.

Goldfarb, W. (1945). Effects of psychological deprivation in infancy and subsequent stimulation. *American Journal of Psychiatry, 102,* 18–33.

Goldfried, M. R., & Davison, G. C. (1976). *Clinical behavior therapy.* New York: Holt, Rinehart and Winston.

Goldstein, K. (1939). *The organism, a holistic approach to biology derived from pathological data in man.* New York: American Book.

Goleman, D. J., & Schwartz, G. E. (1976). Meditation as an intervention in stress reactivity. *Journal of Consulting and Clinical Psychology, 44,* 456–466.

Gollob, H., & Dittes, J. (1965). Different effects of manipulated self-esteem on persuasibility depending on the threat and complexity of the communication. *Journal of Personality and Social Psychology, 2,* 195–201.

Good, K. J. (1973). Social facilitation: Effects of performance anticipation, evaluation, and response competition on free associations. *Journal of Personality and Social Psychology, 28,* 270–275.

Goodenough, D. R. (1978). Dream recall: History and current status of the field. In A. M. Arkin, J. S. Antrobus, & S. J. Ellman, *The mind in sleep: Psychology and psychophysiology.* New York: Halsted.

Goodwin, D. W. (1979). Alcoholism and heredity: A review and hypothesis. *Archives of Social Psychiatry, 36,* 57–61.

Goodwin, D. W., Powell, B., Bremer, D., Hoine, H., & Stern, J. (1969). Alcohol and recall: State-dependent effects in man. *Science, 163,* 1358–1360.

Goodwin, D. W., Schulsinger, F., Hermansen, L., Guze, S. B., & Winokur, G. (1973). Alcohol problems in adoptees raised apart from alcoholic biological parents. *Archives of General Psychiatry, 28,* 238–243.

Goranson, R. E., & King, D. (1970). Rioting and daily temperature: Analysis of the U.S. riots in 1967. Unpublished manuscript, York University, Toronto.

Gordon, E. S. (1960). Nonesterified fatty acids in the blood of obese and lean subjects. *American Journal of Clinical Nutrition, 8,* 704–747.

Gottesman, I., & Shields, J. (1972). *Schizophrenia and genetics.* New York: Academic Press.

Gottfried, A. W., Rose, S. A., & Bridger, W. H. (1977). Cross-modal transfer in human infants. *Child Development, 48* (91), 118–123.

Gould, R. (1974, March). Adult life stages: Growth toward self-tolerance. *Psychology Today,* pp. 74–78.

Gove, W. R. (Ed.). (1975). *The labeling of deviance.* New York: Wiley.

Goy, R. W. (1968). Organizing effects of androgen on the behavior of rhesus monkeys. In R. P. Michael (Ed.), *Endocrinology and human behavior.* London: Oxford University Press.

Green, D. M., & Swets, J. A. (1966). *Signal detection theory and psychophysics.* New York: Wiley.

Greenblatt, M. H. (1977). Efficacy of ECT in affective and schizophrenic illness. *American Journal of Psychiatry, 134.* 1001–1005.

Greenman, G. W. (1963). Visual behavior of newborn infants. In A. J. Solnit & S. A. Provence (Eds.), *Modern perspectives in child development.* New York: Hallmark.

Greer, S. (1964). Study of parental loss in neurotics and sociopaths. *Archives of Social Psychiatry. 11.* 177–180.

Gregory, R. L. (1970). *The intelligent eye.* New York: McGraw-Hill.

Gregory, R. L. (1973). *Eye and brain* (2nd ed.). New York: World University Library.

Grice, G. R. (1948). The relation of secondary reinforcement to delayed reward in visual discrimination learning. *Journal of Experimental Psychology. 38.* 1–16.

Grice, H. P. (1975). Logic and conservation. In D. Davidson & G. Harman (Eds.), *The logic of grammar.* Encino, Calif.: Dickenson.

Griffitt, W., & Veitch, R. (1971). Influences of population density on interpersonal affective behavior. *Journal of Personality and Social Psychology, 17,* 92–98.

Griffitt, W., & Veitch, R. (1974). Preacquaintance attitude similarity and attraction revisited: Ten days in a fall-out shelter. *Sociometry, 37,* 163–173.

Grings, W. W., & Dawson, M. E. (1978). *Emotions and bodily responses.* New York: Academic Press.

Grinspoon, L. (1969, December). Marijuana. *Scientific American.*

Guilford, J. P. (1967). *The nature of human intelligence.* New York: McGraw-Hill.

Guildford, J. P., & Hoepfner, R. (1971). *The analysis of intelligence.* New York: McGraw-Hill.

Gutmann, D. (1977). The cross-cultural perspective: Notes toward a comparative psychology of aging. In J. E. Birren & K. W. Schaie (Eds.), *Handbook of the psychology of aging.* New York: Van Nostrand Reinhold.

Guttman, N., & Kalish, H. I. (1956). Discriminability and stimulus generalization. *Journal of Experimental Psychology, 51,* 79–88.

Haefner, D. (1956, August 15). Some effects of guilt arousing and fear arousing persuasive communications on opinion change. Technical Report, Office of Naval Research, Contract No. N 6 ONR 241. (Abridgement of unpublished doctoral dissertation, University of Rochester.)

Haith, M. M. (1966). The response of the human newborn to visual movement. *Journal of Experimental Child Psychology, 3,* 235–243.

Haith, M. M., Bergman, T., & Moore, M. J. (1977). Eye contact and face scanning in early infancy. Unpublished manuscript, University of Denver.

Hall, E. T. (1966). *The hidden dimension.* New York: Doubleday.

Hall, G. S. (1904). *Adolescence.* New York. Appleton.

Halpin, A. W., & Winer, B. J. (1957). A factorial study of the leader behavior descriptions. In R. R. Stodgill & A. E. Coons (Eds.), *Leader behavior: Its description and measurement.* Columbus: Ohio State University, Bureau of Business Research.

Halverson, H. M. (1931). An experimental study of prehension in infants by means of systematic cinema records. *Genetic Psychology Monographs, 10,* 107–286.

Hamann, J. R. (1956). Panel discussion. American Management Association. *General Management Service.* No. 182, pp. 21–23.

Hamilton, D. L., & Gifford, R. K. (1976). Illusory correlation in interpersonal perception: A cognitive basis of stereotypic judgments. *Journal of Experimental Social Psychology, 12,* 392–407.

Hanson, H. M. (1961). Stimulus generalization following three-stimulus discrimination training. *Journal of Comparative and Physiological Psychology. 54.* 181–185.

Hardyk, C., & Petrinovich, L. F. (1977). Left-handedness. *Psychological Bulletin. 84.* 385–404.

Hare, R. D. (1970). *Psychopathy: Theory and research.* New York: Wiley.

Harlow, H. F. (1949). The formation of learning sets. *Psychological Review, 56,* 51–65.

Harlow, H. F. (1958). The nature of love. *American Psychologist, 13,* 673–685.

Harlow, H. F. (1959, July). Love in infant monkeys. *Scientific American, 201* (1).

Harlow, H. F. (1962). The heterosexual affectional system in monkeys. *American Psychologist, 17,* 1–9.

Harlow, H. F. (1971). *Learning to love.* San Francisco: Albion.

Harlow, H. F., & Harlow, M. K. (1966). The affectional system. In A. M. Schrier, H. F. Harlow, & F. Stollnitz (Eds.), *Behavior of nonhuman primates* (Vol. 2). New York: Academic Press.

Harlow, H. F., & Harlow, M. K. (1969). Effects of various mother—infant relationships on rhesus monkey behaviors. In B. M. Foss (Ed.), *Determinants of infant behavior* (Vol. 4). New York: Barnes & Noble.

Harlow, H. F., Harlow, M. K., & Meyer, D. R. (1950). Learning motivated by a manipulation drive. *Journal of Experimental Psychology, 49,* 228–234.

Harlow, H. F., & Suomi, S. J. (1970). Nature of love—simplified. *American Psychologist, 25,* 161–168.

Harlow, H. F., & Zimmermann, R. R. (1959). Affectional responses in the infant monkey. *Science, 130,* 421–432.

Harrell, T. W., & Harrell, M. S. (1945). Army General Classification Test scores for civilian occupations. *Educational and Psychological Measurement, 5,* 229–239.

Harter, S. (1975). Developmental differences in the manifestation of mastery motivation on problem-solving tasks. *Child Development, 46,* 370–378.

Harter, S. (1978). Effectance motivation reconsidered. *Human Development, 21,* 34–64.

Hartmann, F. (1979). Three spines on a stickleback. *Natural History. 88*(10), 32–35.

Hartshorne, H., & May, M. A. (1928). *Studies in the nature of character: Studies in deceit.* New York: Macmillan.

Hartup, W. W. (1978). Children and their friends. In H. McGurk (Ed.), *Issues in childhood social development.* London: Methuen.

Hathaway, S. R., & McKinley, J. C. (1951). *The MMPI Manual.* New York: The Psychological Corporation; revised 1967.

Hayes, C. (1951). *The ape in our house.* New York: Harper & Row.

Haynes, H., White, B. L., & Held, R. (1965). Visual accommodation in human infants. *Science, 148.* 528–530.

Hearnshaw, L. S. (1979). *Cyril Burt: Psychologist.* Ithaca, N.Y.: Cornell University Press.

Heath, J. E. (1970). Behavioral regulation of body temperature in poikilotherms. *Physiologist, 13,* 399–410.

Heath, R. G., & Krupp, I. M. (1967). Schizophrenia as an immunologic disorder. *Archives of General Psychiatry, 16,* 1–33.

Hebb, D. O. (1946). On the nature of fear. *Psychological Review, 53,* 259–276.

Heidbreder, E. (1947). The attainment of concepts: III. The problem. *Journal of Psychology, 24,* 93–138.

Heider, E. R., & Olivier, D. C. (1972). The structure of the color space in naming and memory for two languages. *Cognitive Psychology, 3,* 337–354.

Heider, F. (1946). Attitudes and cognitive organization. *Journal of Psychology, 21,* 107–112.

Heinicke, C. M. (1973). Parental deprivation in early childhood: A predisposition to later depression? In J. P. Scott & E. C. Senay (Eds.), *Separation and depression: Clinical and research aspects.* Washington, D.C.: American Association for the Advancement of Sciences.

Held, R. (1965, November). Plasticity in sensory-motor systems. *Scientific American,* pp. 84–94.

Held, R., & White, B. (1959). Sensory deprivation and visual speed: An analysis. *Science, 130,* 860–861.

Helmholtz, H. von. (1962). *Treatise on physiological optics* (J. P. C. Southall, trans.). New York: Dover. (This translation originally published in 1925.)

Helson, H. (1964). *Adaptation-level theory.* New York: Harper & Row.

Henry, J. P., & Cassel, J. C. (1969). Psychosocial factors in essential hypertension. *Journal of Epidemiology, 90* (3), 171–200.

Herman, C. P., & Mack, D. (1975). Restrained and unrestrained eating. *Journal of Personality, 43,* 647–660.

Herman, C. P., & Polivy, J. (1975). Anxiety, restraint, and eating behavior. *Journal of Abnormal Psychology, 84,* 666–672.

Heron, W., Doane, B. D., & Scott, T. H. (1956). Visual disturbances after prolonged perceptual isolation. *Canadian Journal of Psychology, 10,* 13–16.

Herrnstein, R. J. (1973). *IQ in the meritocracy.* Boston: Atlantic Monthly Press.

Herrnstein, R. J., & Hineline, P. N. (1966). Negative reinforcement as shock frequency reduction. *Journal of Experimental Analysis of Behavior, 9,* 421–430.

Hersen, M. (1976). Token economies in institutional settings: Historical, political, deprivation, ethical and generalization issues. *Journal of Nervous and Mental Disease, 162,* 206–214.

Hess, E. W. (1959). Two conditions limiting critical age for imprinting. *Journal of Comparative and Physiological Psychology, 52,* 515–518.

Hibscher, J. A., & Herman, C. P. (1977). Obesity, dieting, and the expression of "obese" characteristics. *Journal of Comparative and Physiological Psychology, 91,* 374–380.

Hilgard, E. R. (1975). Hypnosis. *Annual Review of Psychology, 26,* 19–44.

Hilgard, E. R. (1977). The problem of divided consciousness: A neodissociation interpretation. In W. E. Edmonston, Jr. (Ed.), *Conceptual and investigative approaches to hypnosis and hypnotic phenomena. Annals of the New York Academy of Sciences* (Vol. 296), 48–59.

Hilgard, E. R., & Bower, G. H. (1975). *Theories of learning* (4th ed.). Englewood Cliffs, N.J.: Prentice-Hall.

Hilton, I. (1967). Differences in the behavior of mothers toward first- and later-born children. *Journal of Personality and Social Psychology, 7,* 282–290.

Hindley, C. B., & Owen, C. F. (1978). The extent of individual changes in I.Q. for ages between 6 months and 17 years, in a British longitudinal sample. *Journal of Child Psychology and Psychiatry, 19,* 329–350.

Hiroto, D. S., & Seligman, M. E. P. (1975). Generality of learned helplessness in man. *Journal of Personality and Social Psychology, 31,* 311–327.

Hirst, W. (1982). The amnesiac syndrome: Descriptions and explanations. *Psychological Bulletin, 91,* 435–460.

Hochberg, J. (1978). *Perception* (2nd ed.). Englewood Cliffs, N.J.: Prentice-Hall.

Hochchild, A. R. (1976). Disengagement theory: A logical, empirical, and phenomenological critique. In J. F. Gurbrium (Ed.), *Time, roles, and self in old age.* New York: Behavioral Publications.

Hoebel, B. G. (1971). Feeding: Neural control of intake. In V. E. Hall, A. C. Giese, & R. Sonnenschein (Eds.), *Annual Review of Physiology, 33.*

Hoffer, A., & Osmond, H. (1966). Nicotinamide adenine dinucleotide (NAD) as a treatment for schizophrenia. *Journal of Psychopharmacology, 1,* 79–95.

Hoffer, A., & Osmond, H. (1968). Nicotinamide adenine dinucleotide in the treatment of chronic schizophrenic ptients. *British Journal of Psychiatry, 114,* 915–917.

Hoffman, H. S. (1978). Experimental analysis of imprinting and its behavioral effects. In G. Bower (Ed.), *The psychology of learning and motivation* (Vol. 12). New York: Academic Press.

Hoffman, H. S., Eisever, L. A., Ratner, A. M., & Pickering V. (1974). Development of distress vocalization during withdrawal of an imprinting stimulus. *Journal of Comparative and Physiological Psychology, 86,* 563–568.

Hoffman, M. I. (1970). Moral development. In P. H. Mussen (Ed.), *Carmichael's manual of child psychology* (Vol. 2). New York: Wiley.

Hogan, R. A. (1968). The implosive technique. *Behavior Research and Therapy, 6,* 423–431.

Hogarty, G. E., & Goldberg, S. C. (1973). Drug and sociotherapy in the aftercare of schizophrenic patients. *Archives of General Psychiatry, 28,* 54–64.

Hohmann, G. W. (1966). Some effects of spinal cord lesions on experienced emotional feelings. *Psychophysiology, 3,* 143–156.

Hokanson, J., DeGood, D. E., Forrest, M., & Britton, T. (1971). Availability of avoidance behaviors in modulating vascular stress responses. *Journal of Personality and Social Psychology, 19,* 60–68.

Holden, C. (1976). Hospices: For the dying, relief from pain and fear. *Science, 193,* 389–391.

Hollander, E. P. (1958). Conformity, status and idiosyncrasy credit. *Psychological Review, 65,* 117–127.

Hollander, E. P. (1960). Competence and conformity in the acceptance of influence. *Journal of Abnormal and Social Psychology, 61,* 361–365.

Holmes, T. H. (1979). Development and application of a quantitative measure of life change magnitude. In J. E. Barrett (Ed.), *Stress and mental disorder.* New York: Raven.

Holmes, T. H., & Masuda, M. (1974). Life change and illness susceptibility. In B. S. Dohrenwend & B. P. Dohrenwend (Eds.), *Stressful life events: Their nature and effects.* New York: Wiley.

Holmes, T. H., & Rahe, R. H. (1967). The social readjustment rating scale. *Journal of Psychosomatic Research, 11,* 213–218.

Honig, W. K., & Staddon, J. E. R. (Eds.). (1977). *The handbook of operant behavior.* Englewood Cliffs, N.J.: Prentice-Hall.

Honsberger, R. W., & Wilson, A. F. (1973). Transcendental meditation in treating asthma. *Respiratory Therapy: The Journal of Inhalation Technology, 3,* 79–80.

Honzik, M. P., Macfarlane, J. W., & Allen, L. (1948). The stability of mental test performance between two and eighteen years. *Journal of Experimental Education, 17,* 309–334.

Hopkins, J. R. (1977). Sexual behavior in adolescence. *Journal of Social Issues, 33,* 67–85.

Horn, J. L., & Donaldson, G. (1976). On the myth of intellectual decline in adulthood. *American Psychologist, 31,* 701–719.

Horn, J. L., & Knott, P. D. (1971). Activist youth of the 1960's: Summary and prognosis. *Science, 3975,* 977–985.

Horn, J. M., Loehlin, J. C., & Willerman, L. (1979). Intellectual resemblance among adoptive and biological relatives: The Texas Adoption Project. *Behavior Genetics, 9,* 177–208.

Horner, M. (1974). Toward an understanding of achievement-related conflicts in women. In J. Stacey, S. Béreaud, & J. Daniels (Eds.), *And Jill came tumbling after: Sexism in American education.* New York: Dell.

Horner, M. S. (1978). The measurement and behavioral implications of fear of success in women. In J. W. Atkinson & J. O. Raynor (Eds.), *Personality, motivation, and achievement.* New York: Halsted Press.

Hough, R. L., Fairbank, D. T., & Garcia, A. M. (1976). Problems in the ratio measurement of life stress. *Journal of Health and Social Behavior, 17,* 70–82.

House, J. S. (1981). *Work stress and social support.* Reading, Mass.: Addison-Wesley.

Hoving, K. L., Hamm, N., & Galvin, P. (1969). Social influences as a function of a stimulus ambiguity at three age levels. *Developmental Psychology, 6,* 631–636.

Hovland, C. I. (1937). The generalization of conditioned responses: I. The sensory generalization of conditioned responses with varying frequencies of tone. *Journal of General Psychology, 17,* 125–148.

Hovland, C. I., Janis, I. L., & Kelley, H. H. (1953). *Communication and persuasion.* New Haven: Yale University Press.

Hovland, C. I., & Janis, I. L. (1959). *Personality and persuasibility.* New Haven, Conn.: Yale University Press.

Hovland, C. I., Lumsdaine, A. A., & Sheffield, F. D. (1949). *Experiments on mass communication.* Princeton, N.J.: Princeton University Press.

Hovland, C. I., & Mandell, W. (1952). An experimental comparison of conclusion drawing by the communicator and by the audience. *Journal of Abnormal and Social Psychology, 47,* 581–588.

Hovland, C. I., & Weiss, W. (1951). The influence of source credibility on communication effectiveness. *Public Opinion Quarterly, 15,* 635–650.

Howe, K. G., & Zanna, M. P. (1975). Sex-appropriateness of the task and achievement behavior. *Eastern Psychological Association*, New York.

Hubel, D. (1979). The brain. *Scientific American, 241*(3), 44–53

Hubel, D. H., & Wiesel, T. N. (1959). Receptive fields of single neurons in the cat's striate cortex. *Journal of Physiology, 148*, 574–591.

Hubel, D. H., & Wiesel, T. N. (1979). Brain mechanisms of vision. *Scientific American, 241*(3), 150–162.

Huesmann, L. R. (1982). Television violence and aggressive behavior. In D. Pearl & L. Bouthilet (Eds.), *Television and behavior: Ten years of scientific progress and implications for the 80's*. Washington, D.C.: Superintendent of Documents, U.S. Government Printing Office.

Huff, D. (1954). *How to lie with statistics*. New York: Norton.

Hughes, J., Smith, T. W., Kosterlitz, H. W., Fothergill, L. A., Morgan, B. A., & Morris, H. R. (1975). Identification of two related pentapeptides from the brain with the potent opiate agonist activity. *Nature, 258*, 577–579.

Hull, C. L. (1943). *Principles of behavior*. New York: Appleton-Century-Crofts.

Hunt, E., & Love, T. (1972). How good can memory be? In A. N. Melton & E. Martin (Eds.), *Coding processes in human memory*. Washington, D. C.: Winston Wiley.

Hunt, J. McV. (1965). Intrinsic motivation and its role in psychological development. In D. Levine (Ed.), *Nebraska Symposium on Motivation, 1965*. Lincoln, Neb.: University of Nebraska Press.

Hunt, M. (1974). *Sexual behavior in the 70s*. Chicago: Playboy.

Hurvich, L. M. (1978). Two decades of opponent processes. In F. W. Billmeyer, Jr. & G. Wyszecki (Eds.), *Color 77*. Bristol, Eng.: Adam Hilger.

Hurvich, L. M., & Jameson, D. (1957). An opponent-process theory of color vision. *Psychological Review, 64*, 384–404.

Hutchings, B., & Mednick, S. A. (1974). Registerd criminality in the adoptive and biological parents of registered male adoptees. In S. A. Mednick, F. Schulsinger, J. Higgins, & B. Bell (Eds.), *Genetics, environment and psychopathology*. New York: Elsevier.

Hutt, C. (1966). Exploration and play in children. In P. A. Jewell & C. Lorzos (Eds.), *Play, exploration and territory in mammals. Symposium of the Zoological Society of London* (No. 18). New York: Academic Press.

Hyde, J. S. (1979). *Understanding human sexuality*. New York: McGraw-Hill.

Inhelder, B., & Piaget, J. (1958). *The growth of logical thinking from childhood to adolescence*. New York: Basic Books.

Insko, C. A. (1967). *Theories of attitude change*. New York: Appleton-Century-Crofts.

Iverson, L. I. (1979). The chemistry of the brain. *Scientific American. 241*(3), 134–149.

Izard, C. E. (1979). *Emotions in personality and psychopathology*. New York: Plenum.

Jacobs, P. A., Branton, M., & Melville, M. M. (1965). Agressive behavior, mental abnormality, and the XYY male. *Nature, 208*, 1351–1352.

Jacobs, R. C., & Campbell, D. T. (1961). The perpetuation of an arbitrary tradition through several generations of a laboratory microculture. *Journal of Abnormal and Social Psychology, 62*, 649–658.

Jacquet, Y. F. (1980). Stereospecific, dose-dependent antagonism by noloxone of non-opiate behavior in mice. *Pharmacology, Biochemistry, and Behavior, 13*, 585–587.

Jacquet, Y. F., & Marks, N. (1976). The C-Fragments of β-lipotropin: An indogenous neuroleptic or antiphychotogen. *Science, 194*, 632–635.

Jakubczak, L. F., & Walters, R. H. (1959). Suggestibility as dependency behavior. *Journal of Abnormal and Social Psychology, 59*, 102–107.

James, W. (1890). *Principles of psychology*. New York: Holt.

Janda, L., O'Grady, K., & Capps, C. (1978). Fear of success in males and females in sex-linked occupations. *Sex Roles, 4*, 43–50.

Janis, I. L. (1958). *Psychological stress*. New York: Wiley.

Janis, I. L. (1982). *Groupthink* (2nd ed.). Boston: Houghton Mifflin.

Janis, I. L., & Feshbach, S. (1953). Effects of fear-arousing communications. *Journal of Abnormal and Social Psychology, 48*, 78–92.

Janis, I. L., & Field, P. B. (1959). Sex differences and personality factors related to persuasibility. In I. L. Janis et al. (Eds.), *Personality and persuasibility*. New Haven, Conn.: Yale University Press.

Jarvik, L. F., Klodin, V., & Matsuyama, S. S. (1973). Human aggression and the extra Y chromosome: Fact or fantasy? *American Psychologist, 28*, 674–682.

Jaynes, J. (1958). Imprinting: The interaction of learned and innate behavior: III. Generalization and emergent discrimination. *Journal of Comparative and Physiological Psychology, 51*, 234–237.

Jeddi, E. (1970). Confort du contact et thermo-regulation comportementale. *Phsiology and Behavior, 5*. 1487–1493.

Jencks, C. (1972). *Inequality*. New York: Basic Books.

Jenkins, C. D., Rosenman, R. H., & Zyzanski, S. J. (1974). Prediction of clinical coronary heart disease by a test for the coronary-prone behavior pattern. *New England Journal of Medicine, 290*, 1271–1275.

Jensen, A. R. (1969). How much can we boost IQ and scholastic achievement? *Harvard Educational Review, 39*, 1–123.

Jensen, A. R. (1972a). *Genetics and education*. New York: Harper & Row.

Jensen, A. R. (1972b). Sir Cyril Burt (obituary). *Psychometrika, 37*, 115–117.

Jensen, A. R. (1974). Kinship correlations reported by Sir Cyril Burt. *Behavior Genetics, 4*, 1–28.

Jensen, A. R. (1976, December 9). Heredity and intelligence: Sir Cyril Burt's findings. Letter to the *London Times*, p. 11.

Jensen, A. R. (1980). *Bias in mental testing*. New York: Free Press.

Jessor, R., & Jessor, S. L. (1975). The transition from virginity to non-virginity among youth: A social -psychological study over time. *Developmental Psychology, 11*, 473–484.

Johnson, J. E., & Leventhal, H. (1974). Effects of accurate expectations and behavioral instructions on reactions during a noxious medical examination. *Journal of Personality and Social Psychology, 29*, 710–718.

Johnson, W. G. (1971). The effect of prior-taste and food visibility on the food-directed instrumental performance of obese individuals. Unpublished doctoral dissertation, Catholic University of America, 1970. Cited in S. Schachter, Some extraordinary facts about obese humans and rats. *American Psychologist, 26*, 129–144.

Johnson-Laird, P. N., Legrenzi, P., & Legrenzi, M. (1972). Reasoning and a sense of reality. *British Journal of Psychology, 63*, 395–400.

Johnson-Laird, P. N., & Wason, P. C. (1977). A theoretical analysis of insight in a reasoning task. In P. N. Johnson-Laird & P. C. Wason (Eds.), *Thinking: Readings in cognitive science*. Cambridge: Cambridge University Press.

Johnson-Laird, P. N., & Wason, P. C. (1977). *Thinking: Readings in cognitive science*. Cambridge: The University Press.

Jones, E. E. (1979). The rocky road from act to dispositions. *American Psychologist, 34*, 107–117.

Jones, E. E., & Berglas, S. (1978). Control of attributions about the self through self-handicapping strategies: The appeal of alcohol and the role of underachievement. *Personality and Social Psychology Bulletin, 4*(2), 200–206.

Jones, E. E., & Davis, K. E. (1965). From acts to dispositions: The attribution process in person perception. In L. Berkowitz (Ed.), *Advances in experimental social psychology* (Vol. 2). New York: Academic Press.

Jones, E. E., & Nisbett, R. E. (1972). The actor and the observer: Divergent perceptions of the causes of behavior. In E. E. Jones, D. Kanouse, H. H. Kelley, R. E Nisbett, S. Valins, & B. Weiner (Eds.), *Attribution: Perceiving the causes of behavior*. Morristown, N.J.: General Learning Press. Pp.79–94.

Jones, H. E., & Conrad H. S. (1933). The growth and decline of intelligence: A study of a homogeneous group between the ages of ten and sixty. *Genetic Psychology Monographs, 13*, 223–298.

Jones, H. E., & Jones, M. C. (1928). A study of fear. *Childhood Education, 5*, 136–143.

Jones, M. C. (1957). The later careers of boys who were early or late maturing. *Child Development, 28*, 113–128.

Jones, M. C. (1958). A study of socialization patterns at the high school level. *Journal of Genetic Psychology, 92*, 87–111.

Jones, M. C., & Bayley, N. (1950). Physical maturing among boys as related to behavior. *Journal of Educational Psychology, 41*, 129–148.

Jones, M. C., & Mussen, P. H. (1958). Self-conceptions, motivations and interpersonal attitudes of early and late maturing girls. *Child Development, 29*, 491–501.

Jourard, S. M. (1968). *Disclosing man to himself*. New York: Van Nostrand.

Jouvet, M. (1967, February). The states of sleep. *Scientific American.*

Juel-Nielsen, N. (1965). Individual and environment: A psychiatric-psychological investigation of monozygous twins reared apart. *Acta psychiatrica et neurologica Scandinavica* (Monograph Supplement, 183).

Julesz, B. (1971). *Foundations of cyclopian vision.* Chicago: University of Chicago Press.

Jung, C. G. (1954). *The development of personality.* New York: Pantheon Books.

Jung, C. G. (1971). The stages of life. In J. Campbell (Ed.), *The portable Jung.* New York: Viking.

Just, M. A., & Carpenter, P. A. (1980). A theory of reading: From eye fixations to comprehension. *Psychological Review,* 87(4), 329–354.

Kagan, J. (1976). New views on cognitive development. *Journal of Youth and Adolescence, 5,* 113–129.

Kagan, J., Kearsley, R. B., & Zelazo, P. R. (1977). The effects of infant day care on psychological development. *Educational Quarterly, 1,* 109–142.

Kahn, E., & Fisher, C. (1967). REM sleep and sexuality in the aged. Presented at the Seventh Annual Scientific Meeting of the Boston Society for Gerontologic Psychiatry.

Kahn, R. L. (1958). Human relations on the shop floor. In E. M. Hugh-Jones (Ed.), *Human relations in modern management.* Amsterdam: North Holland Publishing Co.

Kahneman, D., & Tversky, A. (1982). The psychology of preferences. *Scientific American, 246,* 160–173.

Kalish, R. R. (1976). Death and dying in a social context. In R. H. Binstock & E. Shanas (Eds.), *Handbook of aging and the social sciences.* New York: Van Nostrand Reinhold.

Kalish, R. A. (1982). *Late adulthood: Perspectives on human development.* Monterey, Calif.: Brooks/Cole.

Kamin, L. J. (1956). The effects of termination of the CS and avoidance of the US on avoidance learning. *Journal of Comparative and Physiological Psychology, 49,* 420–424.

Kamin, L. J. (1957). The gradient of delay of secondary reward in avoidance learning. *Journal of Comparative and Physiological Psychology, 50,* 445–449.

Kamin, L. J. (1965). Temporal and intensity characteristics of the conditioned stimulus. *Classical conditioning: A symposium.* New York: Appleton-Century-Crofts.

Kamin, L. J. (1968). Predictability, surprise, attention, and conditioning. In B. A. Campbell & R. M. Church (Eds.), *Punishment: A symposium.* New York: Appleton-Century-Crofts.

Kamin, L. J. (1973). Heredity, intelligence, politics and society. Invited address, Eastern Psychological Association, Washington.

Kamin, L. J. (1974). *The science and politics of IQ.* Hillsdale, N.J.: Erlbaum.

Kandel, D. (1973). Adolescent marijuana use: Role of parents and peers. *Science, 181,* 1067–1070.

Kangas, J., & Bradway, K. (1971). Intelligence at middle age: A thirty-eight year follow-up. *Developmental Psychology, 5(2),* 333–337.

Karaz, V., & Perlman, D. (1975). Attribution at the wire: Consistency and outcome finish strong. *Journal of Experimental and Social Psychology, 11,* 470–477.

Kase, S. V., & Cobb, S. (1970). Blood pressure changes in men undergoing job loss: A preliminary report. *Psychosomatic Medicine, 6,* 95–106.

Kassin, S. M., & Wrightsman, L. S. (1980). Prior confessions and mock juror verdicts. *Journal of Applied Social Psychology, 10,* 133–146.

Katz, E., & Lazarsfeld, P. F. (1955). *Personal influence.* Glencoe, Ill.: Free Press.

Katz, R. (1978). Job longevity as a situational factor in job satisfaction. *Administrative Science Quarterly, 23,* 204–233.

Kaufman, A. S., & Doppelt, J. E. (1976). Analysis of WISC-R standardization data in terms of the stratification variables. *Child Development, 47,* 165–171.

Keele, S. W., & Summers, J. J. (1976). The structure of motor programs. In G. E. Stelmach (Ed.), *Motor control: Issues and trends.* New York: Academic Press.

Keenan, J. M., MacWhinney, B., & Mayhew, D. (1977). Pragmatics in memory: A study of natural conversation. *Journal of Verbal Learning and Verbal Behavior, 16,* 549–560.

Keesey, R. E., & Porvley, T. L. (1975). Hypothalamic regulation of body weight. *American Scientist, 63,* 558–565.

Keller, H. (1903). *The story of my life.* New York: Doubleday, Page.

Kelley, H. H. (1952). Two functions of reference groups. In G. E. Sovanson, T. M. Newcomb, & E. L. Hartley (Eds.), *Readings in social psychology* (2nd ed.). New York: Holt, Rinehart and Winston.

Kelley, H. H. (1965). Experimental studies of threats in interpersonal negotiations. *Journal of Conflict Resolution, 9,* 79–105.

Kelley, H. H. (1967). Attribution theory in social psychology. In D. Levine (Ed.), *Nebraska Symposium on Motivation, 15,* 192–238.

Kelley, H. H., & Stahelski, A. J. (1970). Errors in perceptual intentions in a mixed-motive game. *Journal of Experimental Social Psychology, 6,* 379–400.

Kellogg, W. N., & Kellogg, L. A. (1933). *The ape and the child.* New York: McGraw-Hill.

Kelly, G. A. (1955). *The psychology of personal constructs.* New York: Norton.

Kelly, H. H., & Thibaut, J. (1978). *Interpersonal relations: A theory of interdependence.* New York: Wiley.

Kelman, H. C., & Hovland, C. I. (1953). "Reinstatement" of the communicator in delayed measurement of opinion change. *Journal of Abnormal and Social Psychology, 48,* 326–335.

Keniston, K. (1969). Moral development, youthful activism and modern society. *Youth and Society, 1,* 110–127.

Kerckhoff, A., & Davis, K. E. (1962). Value consensus and need complementarity in mate selection. *American Sociological Review, 27,* 295–303.

Kety, S. (1974). Biochemical and neurochemical effects of electroconvulsive shock. In M. Fink, S. Kety, & J. McGraugh (Eds.), *Psychobiology of convulsive therapy.* Washington, D.C.: Winston, 285–294.

Kiesler, C. A., & Kiesler, S. B. (1969). *Conformity.* Reading, Mass.: Addison-Wesley.

Kiesler, C. A., & Pallak, M. S. (1976). Arousal properties of dissonance manipulation. *Psychological Bulletin, 83,* 1014–1025.

Kihlstrom, J. (1981). On personality and memory. In N. Cantor & J. Kihlstrom (Eds.), *Personality, cognition and social interaction.* Hillsdale, N.J.: Erlbaum.

Kimble, G. A. (1978). *How to use (and misuse) statistics.* Englewood Cliffs, N.J.: Prentice-Hall.

Kimmel, D. C., Price, K. F., & Walker, J. W. (1978). Retirement choice and retirement satisfaction. *Journal of Gerontology, 33(4),* 575–585.

Kinchla, R. A. (1980). The measurement of attention. In R. Nickerson (Ed.), *Attention and performance: VIII.* Hillsdale, N.J.: Erlbaum.

Kinchla, R. A., & Allan, L. G. (1969). A theory of visual movement perception. *Psychological Review, 76,* 537–558.

Kinchla, R. A., & Wolfe, J. M. (1979). The order of visual processing: "Top-down," "bottom-up," or "middle-out." *Perception and Psychophysics, 25(3),* 225–231.

King, S. H. (1971). Coping mechanisms in adolescents. *Psychiatric Annuals, 1,* 10–46.

Kinsey, A. C., Pomeroy, W. B., & Martin, C. E. (1948). *Sexual behavior in the human male.* Philadelphia: Saunders.

Kinsey, A. C., Pomeroy, W. B., Martin, C. E., & Gebhard, P. H. (1953). *Sexual behavior in the human female.* Philadelphia: Saunders.

Kintsch, W. (1974). *The representation of meaning in memory.* Hillsdale, N.J.: Erlbaum.

Kintsch, W., & Bates, E. (1977). Recognition memory for statements from a classroom lecture. *Journal of Experimental Psychology: Human Learning and Memory, 3,* 150–159.

Kleinhauz, M., Dreyfuss, D. A., Beran, B., Goldberg, T., & Azikri, D. (1979). Some after-effects of stage hypnosis: A case study of psychopathological manifestations. *International Journal of Clinical and Experimental Hypnosis, 27,* 219–226.

Kluger, M. J. (1976). The importance of being feverish. *Natural History, 85(1),* 70–75.

Knittle, J. L. (1975). Early influences on development of adipose tissue. In G. A. Bray (Ed.), *Obesity in perspective.* Washington, D.C.: U.S. Government Printing Office.

Knittle, J. L., & Hirsch, J. (1968). Effect of early nutrition on the development of rat epididymal fat pads: Cellularity and metabolism. *Journal of Clinical Investigation, 47,* 2091.

Kobasa, S. C. (1979). Stressful life events, personality, and health: An inquiry into hardiness. *Journal of Personality and Social Psychology, 37,* 1–11.

Koestler, A. (1964). *The act of creation.* New York: Macmillan.

Koffka, A. (1935). *The principles of Gestalt psychology.* New York: Harcourt, Brace.

Kohlberg, L. (1961). Stage and sequence: The

cognitive-developmental approach to socialization. In D. A. Goslin (Ed.), *Handbook of socialization theory and research.* New York: Rand-McNally.

Kohlberg, L. (1963). Development of children's orientation toward a moral order. 1. Sequence in the development of moral thoughts. *Vita Humana, 6,* 11–36.

Kohlberg, L. (1966). A cognitive-developmental analysis of children's sex-role concepts and attitudes. In E. E. Maccoby (Ed.), *The development of sex differences.* Palo Alto, Calif.: Stanford University Press.

Kohlberg, L. (1969). Stage and sequence: The cognitive developmental approach to socialization. In D. A. Goslin (Eds.), *Handbook of socialization theory of research.* Chicago: Rand McNally. Pp. 347–480.

Kohlberg, L. (1971). From is to ought: How to commit the naturalistic fallacy and get away with it in the study of moral development. In T. Mischel (Ed.), *Cognitive development and genetic epistemology.* New York: Academic Press.

Kohlberg, L. (1976). Moral stage and moralization: The cognitive-developmental approach. In T. Lickona (Ed.), *Moral development and behavior: Theory, research, and social issues.* New York: Holt, Rinehart and Winston.

Kohlberg, L. (1978). Revisions in the theory and practice of moral development. *New Directions for Child Development, 2,* 83–88.

Kohlberg, L. (1981). *The philosophy of moral development.* New York: Harper & Row.

Kohlberg, L., & Kramer, R. B. (1969). Continuities and discontinuities in childhood and adult moral development. *Human Development, 12,* 93–120.

Kohler, I. (1962, May). Experimental with goggles. *Scientific American,* p. 62.

Kohler, W. (1940). *Dynamics in psychology.* New York: Liveright.

Kohler, W. (1947). *Gestalt psychology.* New York: Liveright.

Kohler, W. (1973). *The mentality of apes* (rev. 2nd ed.) (E. Winter, trans.). London: Routledge and Kegan. (Originally published in 1925.)

Kolata, C. (1982). Food affects human behavior. *Science, 218,* 1209–1210.

Kolb, L. C. (1977). *Modern clinical psychiatry* (9th ed.). Philadelphia: W. B. Saunders.

Koluchova, J. (1972). Severe deprivation in twins: A case study. *Journal of Child Psychology and Psychiatry, 13,* 107–114.

Komaki, J., Barwick, K., & Scott, L. R. (1978). A behavioral approach to occupational safety: Pinpointing and reinforcing safe performance in a good manufacturing plant. *Journal of Applied Psychology, 63,* 434–445.

Komorita, S. S., Sheplosh, J. P., & Braver, S. L. (1969). Power, the use of power, and cooperative choice in a two-person game. *Journal of Personality and Social Psychology, 8,* 134–142.

Konečni, V. J., & Doob, A. N. (1972). Catharsis through displacement of aggression. *Journal of Personality and Social Psychology, 23,* 379–387.

Korsch, B., & Negrete, V. (1972). Doctor-patient communication. *Scientific American,* pp. 227.

Kosslyn, S. M., Ball, T. M., & Reiser, B. J. (1978). Visual images preserve metric spatial information: Evidence from studies of image scanning. *Journal of Experimental Psychology: Human Perception and Performance, 4,* 47–60.

Kraeplin, E. (1902). *Clinical psychiatry: A textbook for physicians* (A. Diffendorf, trans.). New York: Macmillan.

Kraus, S., El-Assal, E., & DeFleur, M. L. (1964). Fear threat appeals in mass communications: An apparent contradiction. Mimeo.

Krauss, R. M., & Glucksberg, S. (1977). Social and nonsocial speech. *Scientific American, 236,* 100–105.

Kruglanski A. W. (1975). The endogenous—exogenous partition in attribution theory. *Psychological Review, 82,* 387–406.

Kruuk, H. (1972). *The spotted hyena: A study of predation and social behavior.* Chicago: University of Chicago Press.

Kübler-Ross, E. (1969). *On death and dying.* New York: Macmillan.

Kübler-Ross, E. (1974). *Questions and answers on death and dying.* New York: Macmillan.

Kuenne, M. R. (1946). Experimental investigation of the relation of language to transposition behavior in young children. *Journal of Experimental Psychology, 36,* 471–490.

Kuhl, J., & Blankenship, V. (1979). Behavioral change in a constant environment: Shift to more difficult tasks with constant probability of success. *Journal of Personality and Social Psychology, 37,* 551–563.

Kuhlman, D. M., & Marshello, A. F. (1975). Individual differences in game motivation as moderators of preprogrammed strategy effects in prisoner's dilemma. *Journal of Personality and Social Psychology, 32,* 992–931.

Kuhn, D., Nash, S. C., & Brucken, L. (1978). Sex role concepts of two- and three-year-olds. *Child Development, 49,* 445–451.

Kuiper, N. A., & Derry, P. A. (1981). The self in person perception and depression. In N. Cantor & J. Kihlstrom (Eds.), *Personality, cognition and social interaction.* Hillsdale, N.J.: Erlbaum.

Kuo, Z. Y. (1930). The genesis of the cat's response to the rat. *Journal of Comparative Psychology, 11,* 1–30.

Kurtines, W., & Grief, E. B. (1974). The development of moral thought: Review and evaluation of Kohlberg's approach. *Psychological Bulletin.* pp. 453–470.

Lacey, J. I. (1967). Somatic response patterning and stress: Some revisions of activation theory. In M. Appley & R. Trumbell (Eds.), *Psychological stress.* New York: McGraw-Hill.

Lacey, J. I., & Lacey, B. C. (1958). Verification and extension of the principle of autonomic response-stereotypy. *American Journal of Psychology, 71,* 50–73.

Laing, R. D. (1964). Is schizophrenia a disease? *International Journal of Social Psychiatry, 10,* 184–193.

Laing, R. D. (1965). *The divided self.* Middlesex, England: Penguin.

Lamb, M. E. (1973). The effects of maternal deprivation on the development of the concepts of object and person. *Journal of Behavioral Science, 1,* 355–364.

Lamb, M. E. (1976). Twelve-month-olds and their parents: Interaction in a laboratory playroom. *Developmental Psychology, 12,* 237–244.

Lamb, M. E. (1977). Father-infant and mother-infant interaction in the first year of life. *Child Development, 48,* 167–181.

Lamm, H., & Sauer, C. (1974). Discussion-induced shift toward higher demands in negotiation. *European Journal of Social Psychology, 4,* 85–88.

Landauer, T. K., & Whiting, J. W. M. (1964). Infantile stimulation and adult stature of human males. *American Anthropologist, 66,* 1007–1028.

Lang, P. J., Rice, D. G., & Sternbach, R. A. (1972). The psychophysiology of emotion. In N. S. Greenfield & R. A. Sternbach (Eds.), *Handbook of psychophysiology.* New York: Holt, Rinehart and Winston. Pp. 623–643.

Langer, E., Janis, I. L., & Wolfer, J. A. (1975). Reduction of psychological stress in surgical patients. *Journal of Experimental Social Psychology, 11,* 155–165.

Langer, E., & Rodin, J. (1976). The effects of choice and enhanced personal responsibility for the aged: A field experiment in an institutional setting. *Journal of Personality and Social Psychology, 34,* 191–198.

Langer, E. J., Taylor, S. E., Fiske, S., & Chanowitz, B. (1976). Stigma, staring, and discomfort: A novel stimulus hypothesis. *Journal of Experimental Social Psychology, 12,* 451–463.

LaPiere, R.T. (1934). Attitudes and actions. *Social Forces, 13,* 230–237.

Latané, B., & Darley, J. M. (1968). Group inhibition of bystander intervention in emergencies. *Journal of Personality and Social Psychology, 10,* 215–221.

Latané, B., & Darley, J. M. (1970). *The unresponsive bystander: Why doesn't he help?* Englewood Cliffs, N.J.: Prentice-Hall.

Layzer, D. (1974). Heritability analyses of IQ: Science or numerology? *Science, 183,* 1259–1266.

Lazarus, A. (1971). *Behavior therapy and beyond.* New York: McGraw-Hill.

Lazarus, R. S. (1966). *Psychological stress and the coping process.* New York: McGraw-Hill.

Lazarus, R. S. (1977). Psychological stress and coping in adaptation and illness. In Z. J. Lipowski, D. R. Lippsitt, & P. C. Whybrow (Eds.), *Psychosomatic medicine: Current trends and clinical applications.* New York: Oxford University Press.

Lazarus, R. S., & Alfert, E. (1964). The short-circuiting of threat. *Journal of Abnormal and Social Psychology, 69,* 195–205.

Lazarus, R. S., & Launier, R. (1978). Stress-related transactions between person and environment. In L. A. Pervin & M. Lewis (Eds.), *Perspectives in interactional psychology.* New York: Plenum.

Lazarus, R. S., Opton, E. M., Nomikos, M. S., & Rankin, N. O. (1965). The principle of short-circuiting threat: Further evidence. *Journal of Personality, 33,* 622–635.

Lazarus, R. S., Speisman, J. C., Mordkoff, A. M., & Davison, L. A. (1962). A laboratory study of psychological stress produced by a motion picture film. *Psychological Monographs*, 76(34, Whole No. 553).

Leahy, A. (1935). Nature-nurture and intelligence. *Genetic Psychology Monographs*, 17, 241–306.

Leask, J., Haber, R. N., & Haber, R. B. (1969). *Eidetic imagery in children, II: Longitudinal and experimental results. Psychonomic Monograph Supplements*, 3, 25–48.

Leavitt, H. J. (1951). Some effects of certain communication patterns on group performance. *Journal of Abnormal and Social Psychology*, 46, 38–50.

Lee, E. S. (1951). Negro intelligence and selective migration: A Philadelphia test of the Klineberg hypothesis. *American Sociological Review*, 16, 227–233.

Lehrer, P. M., Schoicket, S., Carrington, P., & Woolfolk, R. (1980). Psychophysiological and cognitive responses to stressful stimuli in subjects practicing progressive relaxation and clinically standardized meditation. *Behavior Research and Therapy*, 18(4), 293–303.

Lehrman, D. S. (1962). Interaction of hormonal and experiential influences on development of behavior. In E. L. Bliss (Ed.), *Roots of behavior*. New York: Harper & Row.

Lehrman, D. S. (1964, November). The reproductive behavior of ring doves. *Scientific American*, 211(5), 48–54.

LeMasters, E. E. (1957). Parenthood as crisis. *Marriage and Family Living*, 19, 352–355.

Lemon, B. W., Bengston, V. L., & Peterson, J. A. (1972). An exploration of the activity theory of aging: Activity types and life satisfaction among in-movers to a retirement community. *Journal of Gerontology*, 27(4), 511–523.

Lenneberg, E. (1967). *Biological foundations of language*. New York: Wiley.

Leon, G. R. (1977). *Case histories of deviant behavior, an interactional perspective* (2nd ed). Boston: Allyn & Bacon.

Lepper, M. R., Greene, D., & Nisbett, R. E. (1973). Undermining children's intrinsic interest with extrinsic rewards: A test of the "overjustification hypothesis." *Journal of Personality and Social Psychology*, 28, 129–137.

Lerner, M. J., Miller, D. T., & Holmes, J. G. (1975). Deserving versus justice: A contemporary dilemma. In L. Berkowitz & E. Walster (Eds.), *Advances of experimental social psychology* (Vol. 12). New York: Academic Press.

Lerner, M. J., Miller, D. T., & Holmes, J. G. (1976). Deserving and the emergence of forms of justice. In L. Berkowitz & E. Walster (Eds.), *Advances in experimental social psychology* (Vol. 9). New York: Academic Press. Pp. 133–162.

Leventhal, H. (1970). Findings and theory in the study of fear communications. In L. Berkowitz (Ed.), *Advances in experimental social psychology* (Vol. 5). New York: Academic Press.

Leventhal, H., & Niles, P. (1965). Persistence of influence for varying duration of exposure to threat stimuli. *Psychological Reports*, 16, 223–233.

Leventhal, H., & Singer, R. (1966). Affect arousal and positioning of recommendation in persuasive communications. *Journal of Personality and Social Psychology*, 4, 137–146.

Levi, L. (1965). The urinary output of adrenalin and nonadrenalin during pleasant and unpleasant emotional states: A preliminary report. *Psychosomatic Medicine*, 27, 80–85.

Levinger, G. (1974). A three-level approach to attraction: Toward an understanding of pair relatedness. In T. L. Huston (Ed.), *Foundations of interpersonal attraction*. New York: Academic Press. Pp. 100–120.

Levinger, G. (1977). Re-viewing the close relationship. In G. Levinger & H. Raush (Eds.), *Close relationships: Perspectives on the meaning of intimacy*. Amherst, Mass.: University of Massachusetts Press. Pp. 137–162.

Levinger, G., & Snoek, J. D. (1972). *Attraction in relationships: A new look at interpersonal attraction*. Morristown, N.J.: General Learning Press.

Levinson, D. J., Darrow, C. N., Klein, E. B., Levinson, M. H., & McKee, B. (1978). *The seasons of a man's life*. New York: Knopf.

Levinthal, C. F. (1979). *The physiological approach in psychology*. Englewood Cliffs, N.J.: Prentice-Hall.

Levy, J., Trevarthian, C., & Sperry, R. W. (1972). Perception of bilateral chimeric figures following hemispheric deconnexion. *Brain*, 95, 61–78.

Levy, J. V., & King, J. A. (1953). The effects of testosterone proprionate on fighting behavior in young male C57 BL/10 mice. *Anat. Record*, 117, 562–563.

Lewin, K. (1931). Environmental forces in child behavior and development. In C. Murchison (Ed.), *A handbook of child psychology*. Worcester, Mass.: Clark University Press.

Lewin, K. (1951). *Field theory in the social sciences*. New York: Harper & Brothers.

Lewinsohn, P. H. (1974). A behavioral approach to depression. In R. J. Friedman & M. M. Katz (Eds.), *The psychology of depression: Contemporary theory and research*. Washington, D.C.: Winston-Wiley.

Liberman, A. M., & Studdert-Kennedy, M. (1978). Phonetic perception. In R. Held, H. W. Leibowitz, & H. L. Tueber (Eds.), *Handbook of sensory physiology* (Vol. 8). Berlin: Springer-Verlag.

Lichtenstein, E. (1980). *Psychotherapy: Approaches and applications*. Monterey, Calif.: Brooks/Cole.

Liddell, H. (1950). Some specific factors that modify tolerance for environmental stress. In H. G. Wolff, S. G. Wolff, & C. C. Hare (Eds.), *Life stress and bodily disease*. Baltimore: Williams and Wilkins.

Liebert, R. M., & Baron, R. A. (1972). Some immediate effects of televised violence on children's behavior. *Developmental Psychology*, 6, 469–475.

Liebert, R. M., Neale, J. M., & Davidson, E. S. (1973). *The early window: Effects of television on children and youth*. New York: Pergamon Press.

Lifton, R. J. (1968). *Death in life: Survivors of Hiroshima*. New York: Random House.

Likert, R. (1967). *The human organization: Its management and value*. New York: McGraw-Hill.

Linder, D. E., Cooper, J., & Jones, E. E. (1967). Decision freedom as a determinant of the role of incentive magnitude in attitude change. *Journal of Personality and Social Psychology*, 6, 245–254.

Lindsay, P. H., & Norman, D. A. (1977). *Human information processing* (2nd ed.). New York: Academic Press.

Linn, R. (1979). *You can drink and stay healthy*. New York: Watts.

Lipton, E. L., Steinschneider, A., & Richmond, J. B. (1965). Swaddling, a child care practice: Historical, cultural, and experimental observations. *Pediatrics*, 35, 521–567.

Lipton, J. M. (1968). Effects of preoptic lesions on heat-escape responding and colonic temperature in the rat. *Physiology and Behavior*, 3, 165–169.

Locke, J. (1690). An essay concerning human understanding. London: Basset.

Loehlin, J. C., Lindzey, G., & Spuhler, J. N. (1975). *Race differences in intelligence*. San Francisco: Freeman.

Loehlin, J. C., & Nichols, R. C. (1976). *Heredity, environment and personality*. Austin, Tex.: University of Texas Press.

Loew, C. A. (1967). Acquisition of hostile attitude and its relationship to aggressive behavior. *Journal of Personality and Social Psychology*, 5, 335–341.

Loftus, E. F. (1979). *Eyewitness testimony*. Cambridge, Mass.: Harvard University Press.

Lopata, H. Z. (1973). *Widowhood in an American city*. Cambridge, Mass.: Schenkman.

Lo Piccolo, J., & Lo Piccolo, L. (1978). *Handbook of sex therapy*. New York: Plenum.

Lorenz, K. Z. (1937). The companion in the bird's world. *Auk*, 54, 245–273.

Lorenz, K. Z. (1966). *On aggression*. New York: Harcourt, Brace and World.

Lott, A. J., & Lott, B. E. (1968). A learning theory approach to interpersonal attitudes. In A. G. Greenwald, T. C. Brock, & T. Ostrom (Eds.), *Psychological foundations of attitudes*. New York: Academic Press.

Lott, A. J., & Lott, B. E. (1974). The role of reward in the formation of positive interpersonal attitudes. In T. L. Huston (Ed.), *Foundations of interpersonal attraction*. New York: Academic Press.

Lovaas, O. I. (1961). Effect of exposure to symbolic aggression on aggressive behavior. *Child Development*, 32, 37–44.

Lovaas, O. I. (1977). *The autistic child*. New York: Halsted.

Lovaas, O. I., Schreibman, L., Koegel, R., & Rehm, R. (1971). Selective responding by austistic children to multiple sensory input. *Journal of Abnormal Psychology*, 77, 211–222.

Lowell, E. L. (1952). The effect of need for achievement on learning and speed of performance. *Journal of Psychology*, 33, 31–40.

Lowenthal, M. F., Thurnher, M., & Chiriboga, D. (1975). *Four states of life; A comparative study of women and men facing transitions*. San Francisco: Jossey-Bass.

Luborsky, L., Singer, B., & Luborsky, L.

(1975). Comparative studies of psychotherapies: Is it true that "Everyone has won and all must have prizes"? *Archives of General Psychiatry, 32,* 995–1008.

Luborsky, L., & Spence, D. P. (1971). Quantitative research on psychoanalytic therapy. In A. E. Bergin & S. L. Garfield (Eds.), *Handbook of psychotherapy and behavior changes: An empirical analysis.* New York: Wiley.

Luce, G. G., & Segal, J. (1966). *Sleep.* New York: Coward, McCann & Geoghegan.

Luchins, A. J. (1942). Mechanization in problem solving: The effect of *Einstellung. Psychological Monographs, 54,* 6 (Whole No. 248).

Ludel, J. (1978). *Introduction to sensory processes.* San Francisco: Freeman.

Ludwig, A. M., Brandsman, J. M., & Culbert, C. B. (1972). The objective study of multiple personality. *Archives of Social Psychiatry, 26,* 298–310.

Luria, A. R. (1959). Development of the directive function of speech in early childhood. *Word, 15,* 341–352.

Luria, A. R. (1968). *The mind of a mnemonist.* New York: Basic Books. (Originally published in 1920.)

Lynch, K. (1960). *The image of the city.* Cambridge, Mass.: MIT Press.

Lynd, H. (1971). *On shame and the search for identity.* New York: Harcourt Brace Jovanovich.

Maccoby, E. E., & Jacklin, C. N. (1974). *The psychology of sex differences.* Palo Alto, Calif.: Stanford University Press.

MacFarlane, J. W. (1963). From infancy to adulthood. *Childhood Education, 39,* 336–342.

MacFarlane, J. W. (1964). Perspectives on personality consistency and change from the guidance study. *Vita Humana, 7,* 115–126.

Mackintosh, N. J. (1974). *The psychology of animal learning.* New York: Academic Press.

Mackintosh, N. J. (1975). A theory of attention. *Psychological Review, 82,* 276–298.

MacLean, P. D. (1958). Contrasting functions of limbic and neocortical systems of the brain and their relevance to psychophysiological aspects of medicine. *American Journal of Medicine, 25,* 611–626.

MacMahon, B. (1973). *Age at menarche, United States* (Vital and Health Statistics, Series 11, No. 133, DHEW Publication No. [HRA] 74-1615). Washington, D.C.: U.S. Government Printing Office.

Macnamara, J. (1972). Cognitive basis of language learning in infants. *Psychological Review, 79,* 1–13.

Madden, J., Akil, H., Patrick, R. L., & Barchas, J. D. (1977). Stress induced parallel changes in central opioid levels and pain responsiveness in the rat. *Nature, 265,* 358–360.

Madigan, S. A. (1969). Intraserial repetition and coding processes in free recall. *Journal of Verbal Learning and Verbal Behavior, 8,* 828–835.

Maher, B. A. (1970). Delusional thinking and cognitive disorder. Paper presented at annual meeting of the American Psychological Association.

Mahl, G. F. (1952). Relationship between acute and chronic fear and the gastric acidity and blood sugar levels in *macaca mulatta* monkeys. *Psychosomatic Medicine, 14,* 182–210.

Mahl, G. F. (1971). *Psychological conflict and defense.* New York: Harcourt Brace Jovanovich.

Main, M. (1973). Exploration, play and level of cognitive functioning as related to child—mother attachment. Unpublished dissertation, Johns Hopkins University.

Malamuth, N. M., & Check, J. V. P. (1981). The effects of mass media exposure on acceptance of violence against women: A field experiment. *Journal of Research in Personality, 15,* 436–446.

Malamuth, N. M., & Spinner, B. (1980). A longitudinal content analysis of sexual violence in the best-selling erotic magazines. *The Journal of Sex Research, 16,* 226–237.

Malina, R. M. (1979). Secular changes in size and maturity: Causes and effects. *Monographs of the Society of Research in Child Development, 44*(3-4, Serial No. 179), 59–120.

Mandler, G. (1962). Emotions. In T. M. Newcomb (Ed.), *New directions in psychology.* New York: Holt, Rinehart and Winston.

Maniscalco, C. I., Doherty, N. E., & Ullman, D. G. (1980). Assessing discrimination: An application of social judgment technology. *Journal of Applied Psychology, 65,* 284–288.

Mann, R. D. (1959). A review of the relationships between personality and performance in small groups. *Psychological Bulletin, 56,* 241–270.

Markus, H. (1977). Self-schemata and processing information about the self. *Journal of Personality and Social Psychology, 35,* 63–78.

Markus, H., Crane, M., Bernstein, S., & Siladi, M. (1982). Self-schemas and gender. *Journal of Personality and Social Psychology, 42,* 38–50.

Markus, H., Crane, M., & Siladi, M. (1978). Cognitive consequences of androgyny. Paper presented at the annual meeting of the American Psychological Association, Chicago, Ill.

Markus, H., & Smith, J. (1981). The influence of self-schemas on the perception of others. In N. Cantor & J. Kihlstrom (Eds.), *Personality, cognition and social interaction.* Hillsdale, N.J.: Erlbaum.

Marshall, D. S. (1971). Sexual behavior in Mangaia. In D. S. Marshall & R. G. Suggs (Eds.), *Human sexual behavior.* Englewood Cliffs, N.J.: Prentice-Hall.

Marshall, W. A., & Tanner, J. M. (1969). Variations in pattern of pubertal changes in girls. *Archives of Disease in Childhood, 44,* 291–303.

Marshall, W. A., & Tanner, J. M. (1970). Variations in the pattern of pubertal changes in boys. *Archives of Diseases in Childhood, 45,* 13–23.

Maslach, C. (1979). The emotional consequences of arousal without reason. In C. Izard, *Emotions in personality and psychopathology.* New York: Plenum.

Maslow, A. H. (1954). *Motivation and personality.* New York: Harper.

Maslow, A. H. (1962). *Toward a psychology of being.* Princeton, N.J.: Van Nostrand. Pp. 23–24.

Maslow, A. H. (1967). Neurosis as a failure of personal growth. *Humanitas, 3,* 153–170.

Maslow, A. H. (1970). *Motivation and personality* (2nd ed.). New York: Harper & Row.

Mason, J. W. (1971). A re-evaluation of the concept of "non-specificity" in stress theory. *Journal of Psychiatric Research, 8,* 323–333.

Mason, W. A. (1968). Early social deprivation in the nonhuman primates. Implications for human behavior. In D. C. Glass (Ed.), *Environmental influences.* New York: Rockefeller University Press and Russell Sage Foundation.

Massaro, A. J. (1970). Retroactive interference in short-term recognition memory for pitch. *Journal of Experimental Psychology, 83,* 32–39.

Masters, W. H., & Johnson, V. E. (1966). *Human sexual response.* Boston: Little, Brown.

Masters, W. H., & Johnson, V. E. (1970). *Human sexual inadequacy.* Boston: Little, Brown.

Matarazzo, J. D. (1980). Behavioral health and behavioral medicine: Frontiers for a new health psychology. *Psychologist,* 807–817.

Matas, L., Arend, R. A., & Sroufe, L. A. (1978). Continuity of adaptation in the second year: The relationship between quality of attachment and later competence. *Child Development, 49,* 547–556.

Matlin, M. W., & Zajonc, R. B. (1968). Social facilitation of word associations. *Journal of Personality and Social Psychology, 10,* 455–460.

May, P. R. A. (1968). *Treatments of schizophrenia: A comparative study of five treatment methods.* New York: Science House.

Mayer, D. J. (1980). The centrofugal control of pain. In L. Ng & J. J. Bonica (Eds.), *Pain, discomfort, and humitarian care.* Amsterdam: Elsevier. Pp. 83–105.

Mayer, D. J., & Hayes, R. L. (1975). Tolerance to repeated electrical stimulation of the brain. *Science, 188,* 941.

Mayer, J. (1953). Genetic, traumatic and environmental factors in the etiology of obesity. *Physiological Reviews, 33,* 472–508.

Mayer, J. (1955). Regulation of energy intake and the body weight: The glucostatic theory and the lipostatic hypothesis. *Annals of the New York Academy of Science, 63,* 15–43.

McArthur, L. A. (1972). The how and what of why: Some determinants and consequences of causal attribution. *Journal of Personality and Social Psychology, 22,* 171–193.

McCarley, R. W. (1978, December). Where dreams come from: A new theory. *Psychology Today.*

McClelland, D. C. (1958). Risk-taking in children with high and low need for achievement. In J. W. Atkinson (Ed.), *Motives in fantasy, action, and society.* Princeton, N.J.: Van Nostrand.

McClelland, D. C. (1975). *Power: The inner experience.* New York: Irvington.

McClelland, D. C., Atkinson, J. W., Clark, R. A., & Lowell, E. L. (1953). *The achievement motive.* New York: Appleton-Century-Crofts.

McClelland, D. C., & Watson, R. I. (1973). Power motivation and risk-taking behavior. *Journal of Personality, 41,* 121–139.

McClelland, K. (1982). Adolescent subculture in the schools. In F. Field, A. Huston, H.

Quay, L. Troll, & G. Finley (Eds.), *Review of human development*. New York: Wiley.

McClelland, L., & Cook, S. W. (1980). Promoting energy conservation in master-metered apartments through group financial incentives. *Journal of Applied Social Psychology, 10,* 20–31.

McCullough, D. (1981). *Mornings on horseback.* New York: Simon & Schuster.

McGinniss, J. (1969). *The selling of the presidency.* New York: Simon & Schuster.

McGlothlin, W. H. (1975). Drug use and abuse. *Annual Review of Psychology, 26.*

McGregor, D. M. (1960). *The human side of enterprise.* New York: McGraw-Hill.

McGuire, W. J., & Papageorgis, D. (1961). The relative efficacy of various types of prior belief-defense and producing immunity against persuasion. *Journal of Abnormal and Social Psychology, 62,* 327–337.

McIntyre, M. E., Silverman, F. H., & Trotler, W. D. (1974). Transcendental meditation and stuttering: A preliminary report. *Perceptual and Motor Skills, 39,* 294.

McLaughlin, B. (1978). *Second-language acquisition in childhood.* Hillsdale, N.J.: Erlbaum.

McNemar, Q. (1942). *The revision of the Stanford-Binet scale: An analysis of the standardizatin data.* Boston: Houghton Mifflin.

Mead, M. (1928). *Coming of age in Samoa.* Chicago: University of Chicago Press.

Mead, M. (1939). *From the South Seas: Studies of adolescence and sex in primitive societies.* New York: Morrow.

Mechanic, D. (1962). *Students under stress.* New York: Free Press.

Mednick, S. A. (1962). The associative basis of the creative process. *Psychological Review, 69,* 220–232.

Mendels, J., Fieve, A., Fitzgerand, R. G., Ramsey, T. A., & Stokes, J. W. (1972). Biogenic amine metabolites in cerebrospinal fluid of depressed and manic patients. *Science, 175,* 1380–1382.

Merriam-Webster. (1973). *Webster's New Collegiate Dictionary.* Springfield, Mass.: Merriam.

Messe, L. A., Arnoff, J., & Wilson, J. P. (1972). Motivation as a mediator of the mechanisms underlying role assignments in small groups. *Journal of Personality and Social Psychology, 24,* 84–90.

Messinger, J. C. (1971). Sex and repression in an Irish folk community. In D. S. Marshall & R. G. Suggs (Eds.), *Human sexual behavior.* Englewood Cliffs, N.J.: Prentice-Hall.

Metalsky, G. I., Abramson, L. Y., Seligman, M. E. P., Semmel, A., & Peterson, C. (1982). Attributional styles and life events in the classroom: Vulnerability and invulnerability to depressive mood reactions. *Journal of Personality and Social Psychology, 43,* 612–617.

Meyer, D. E., & Schvaneveldt, R. W. (1971). Facilitation in recognizing pairs of words: Evidence of a dependence between retrieval operations. *Journal of Experimental Psychology, 90,* 227–234.

Midlarsky, E., Bryan, J. H., & Brickman, P. (1973). Aversive approval: Interactive effects of modeling and reinforcement on altruistic behavior. *Child Development, 44,* 321–328.

Milgram, S. (1963). Behavioral study of obedi-ence. *Journal of Abnormal and Social Psychology, 67,* 371–378.

Milgram, S. (1964). Group pressure and action against a person. *Journal of Abnormal and Social Psychology, 69,* 137–143.

Milgram, S. (1965). Some conditions of obedience and disobedience to authority. *Human Relations, 18,* 57–76.

Milgram, S. (1970). The experience of living in cities: Adaptations to urban overload create characteristic qualities of city life that can be measured. *Science, 167,* 1461–1468.

Milgram, S. (1974). *Obedience to authority.* New York: Harper & Row.

Milgram, S. (1976). Psychological maps of Paris. In H. Proshansky, W. Ittelson, & L. Rivlin (Eds.), *Environmental psychology* (2nd ed.). New York: Holt, Rinehart and Winston.

Milgram, S. (1977). *The individual in a social world.* Reading, Mass.: Addison-Wesley.

Miller, A. G., Jones, E. E., & Hinkle, S. (1980). A robust attribution error in the personality domain. *Journal of Experimental Social Psychology, 17,* 587–600.

Miller, D. T., & Ross, M. (1975). Self-serving biases in the attribution of causality: Fact or fiction? *Psychological Bulletin, 82,* 213–225.

Miller, F. T., Bentz, W. K., Aponte, J. F., & Brogan, D. R. (1974). Perception of life crisis events: A comparative study of rural and urban samples. In B. S. Dohrenwend & B. P. Dohrenwend (Eds.), *Stressful life events: Their nature and effects.* New York: Wiley.

Miller, G. A. (1956). The magical number seven plus or minus two: Some limits on our capacity for processing information. *Psychological Review, 63,* 81–97.

Miller, G. A. (1981). *Language and speech.* San Francisco: Freeman.

Miller, G. A., & Buckhout, R. (1973). *Psychology: The science of mental life.* New York: Harper & Row.

Miller, G. A., Galanter, E., & Pribram, K. H. (1960). *Plans and the structure of behavior.* New York: Holt, Rinehart and Winston.

Miller, G. A., & Isard, S. (1963). Some perceptual consequences of linguistic rules. *Journal of Verbal Learning and Verbal Behavior, 2,* 217–228.

Miller, N., Maruyama, G., Beaber, R. J., & Valone, K. (1976). Speed of speech and persuasion. *Journal of Personality and Social Psychology, 34,* 615–624.

Miller, N. E. (1935). The influence of past experience upon the transfer of subsequent training. Unpublished doctoral dissertation, Yale University.

Miller, N. E. (1944). Experimental studies of conflict. In J. McV. Hunt (Ed.), *Personality and the behavior disorders.* New York: Ronald Press.

Miller, N. E. (1948). Studies of fear as an acquirable drive: I. Fear as motivation and fear-reduction as reinforcement in the learning of new responses. *Journal of Experimental Psychology, 38,* 89–101.

Miller, N. E. (1951). Learnable drives and rewards. In S. S. Stevens (Ed.), *Handbook of experimental psychology.* New York: Wiley.

Miller, N. E. (1969). Learning of visceral and glandular responses. *Science, 163,* 434–445.

Miller, N. E. (1978). Biofeedback and visceral learning. *Annual Review of Psychology, 29,* 373–404.

Miller, N. E., Bailey, C. J., & Stevenson, J. A. F. (1950). Decreased "hunger" but increased food intake resulting from hypothalamic lesions. *Science, 112,* 256–259.

Miller, N. E., & Brucker, B. S. (1979). A learned visceral response apparently independent of skeletal ones in patients paralyzed by spinal lesions. In N. Birbaumer & H. D. Kimmel (Eds.), *Biofeedback and self-regulation.* Hillsdale, N.J.: Erlbaum.

Miller, N. E., & DiCara, L. (1967). Instrumental learning of heart-rate changes in curarized rats: Shaping, and specificity to discriminative stimulus. *Journal of Comparative and Physiological Psychology, 63,* 12–19.

Miller, N. E., & Dworkin, B. R. (1974). Visceral learning: Recent difficulties with curarized rats and significant problems for human research. In P. A. Obrist, A. H. Black, J. Brener, & L. V. DiCara (Eds.), *Cardiovascular psychophysiology: Current issues in response mechanisms, biofeedback, and methodology.* Chicago: Aldine.

Miller, N. E., & Kessen, M. L. (1952). Reward effects of food via stomach fistula compared with those of food via mouth. *Journal of Comparative and Physiological Psychology, 45,* 555–564.

Miller, W. R., & Seligman, M. E. P. (1975). Depression and learned helplessness in man. *Journal of Abnormal Psychology, 84,* 228–238.

Milner, B. (1970). Memory and the medial temporal regions of the brain. In K. H. Pribram & D. E. Broadbent (Eds.), *Biology of memory.* New York: Academic Press. Pp. 29–50.

Milner, B., Branch, C., & Rasmussen, T. (1966). Evidence for bilateral representation in non–right-handers. *Transactions of the American Neurological Association, 91,* 306–308.

Milton, G. A., & Lipetz, M. E. (1968). The factor structure of needs as measured by the EPPS. *Multivariate Behavioral Research, 3,* 37–46.

Mischel, W. (1968). *Personality and assessment.* New York: Wiley.

Mischel, W. (1976). *Introduction to personality* (2nd ed.). New York: Holt, Rinehart & Winston.

Mischel, W. (1981). Personality and cognition: Something borrowed, something new? In N. Cantor & J. Kihlstrom (Eds.), *Personality, cognition and social interaction.* Hillsdale, N.J.: Erlbaum.

Mischel, W., & Patterson, C. J. (1978). Effective plans for self-control in children. In W. A. Collins (Ed.), *Minnesota symposia on child psychology* (Vol. 11). Hillsdale, N.J.: Erlbaum.

Mitchell, G. D. (1968). Attachment differences in male and female infant monkeys. *Child Development, 39,* 611–620.

Mohler, H., & Okada, T. (1977). Bezodiazepine receptor: Demonstration in the central nervous system. *Science, 198,* 849–851.

Molfese, D. L., & Molfese, V. J. (1980). Cortical responses of preterm infants to phonetic and nonphonetic speech stimuli. *Developmental Psychology, 6,* 574–581.

Money, J. (1970). Sexual dimorphism and homosexual gender identity. *Psychological Bulletin, 74,* 425–440.

Money, J., & Ehrhardt, A. A. (1972). *Man and woman, boy and girl.* Baltimore: Johns Hopkins University Press.

Montgomery, M. F. (1931). The role of the salivary glands in the thirst mechanism. *American Journal of Physiology, 96,* 221–227.

Moore, C., & Shiek, D. (1971). Toward a theory of early infantile autism. *Psychological Review, 78,* 451–456.

Morgan, A. H., & Hilgard, E. R. (1971). Age differences in susceptibility to hypnosis. *International Journal of Clinical Experimental Hypnosis.*

Morgan, C. D., & Murray, H. A. (1935). Method for investigating fantasies—the Thematic Apperception Test. *Archives of Neurology and Psychiatry, 34,* 289–306.

Morgan, C. T., & Morgan, J. D. (1940). Studies in hunger: II. The relation of gastric denervation and dietary sugar to the effect of insulin upon food-intake in the rat. *Journal of Genetic Psychology, 57,* 153–163.

Morgan, L. A. (1976). A re-examination of widowhood and morale. *Journal of Gerontology, 31(6),* 687–695.

Morris, D., Collett, P., Marsh, P., & O'Shaughnessy, M. (1979). *Gestures.* New York: Stein & Day.

Morse, D. R. (1977). An exploratory study of the use of meditation alone and in combination with hypnosis in clinical dentistry. *Journal of the American Society of Psychosomatic Dental Medicine, 24(4),* 113.

Morse, J. J., & Lorsch, J. W. (1970, May-June). Beyond theory Y. *Harvard Business Review.* pp. 61–68.

Moruzzi, G., & Magoun, H. W. (1949). Brain stem and reticular formation and activation of the EEG. *Electroencephalography and Clinical Neurophysiology, 1,* 455–473.

Moscivici, S., & Nemeth, C. (1974). Social influence II: Minority influence. In C. Nemeth (Ed.), *Social psychology: Classic and contemporary integrations.* Chicago: Rand McNally.

Mosher, D. L. (1973). Sex differences, sex experience, sex guilt, and explicitly sexual films. *Journal of Social Issues, 29,* 95–112.

Moshman, D., & Neimark, E. (1982). Four aspects of adolescent cognitive development. In T. Field, A. Huston, H. Quay, L. Troll, & G. Finley (Eds.), *Review of human development.* New York: Wiley.

Mosteller, F., Rourke, R. E. K., & Thomas, G. B., Jr. (1973). *Probability with statistical applications.* Reading, Mass.: Addison-Wesley.

Mowrer, O. H. (1939). A stimulus-response analysis of anxiety and its role as a reinforcing agent. *Psychological Review, 46,* 553–565.

Mowrer, O. H. (1947). On the dual nature of learning—a reinterpretation of "conditioning" and "problem solving." *Harvard Educational Review, 17,* 102–148.

Mowrer, O. H., & Mowrer, W. M. (1938). Enuresis—a method for its study and treatment. *American Journal Of Orthopsychiatry, 8,* 436–459.

Moyer, K. E. (1971). The physiology of aggression and the implications for aggression control. In J. L. Singer (Ed.), *The control of aggression and violence: Cognitive and physiological factors.* New York: Academic Press.

Moyer, K. E. (1976). Kinds of aggression and their physiological basis. In K. E. Moyer (Ed.), *Physiology of aggression and implications for control.* New York: Raven Press.

Mueller, D., Edwards, D. W., & Yarvis, R. M. (1977). Stressful life events and psychiatric symptomatology: Change or undesirability? *Journal of Health and Social Behavior, 18,* 307–316.

Müller, G. E., & Pilzecker, A. (1900). Experimentelle Beiträge zur Lehre von Gedächtnis. *Zeitschrift für Psychologie* (Supplement no. 1).

Munroe, R. L., & Munroe, R. H. (1975). *Cross-cultural human development.* Monterey, Calif.: Brooks/Cole.

Munsinger, H., & Kessen, W. (1964). Uncertainty, structure, and preference. *Psychological Monographs, 78* (Whole No. 586), 1–24.

Munsinger, H., Kessen, W., & Kessen, M. L. (1964). Age and uncertainty: Developmental variation in preference for variability. *Journal of Experimental Child Psychology, 1,* 1–15.

Murdock, G. P. (1965). *Culture and society.* Pittsburgh, Penn.: University of Pittsburgh Press.

Murray, H. A. (1938). *Exploration in personality.* New York: Oxford University Press.

Murray, H. A. (1943). *Thematic Apperception Test manual.* Cambridge, Mass.: Harvard University Press.

Murstein, B. I. (1976). *Who will marry whom.* New York: Springer.

Muss, R. (1975). *Theories of adolescence* (3rd ed.). New York: Random House.

Mussen, P. H., & Jones, M. C. (1957). Self-conceptions, motivations and interpersonal attitudes of late and early maturing boys. *Child Development, 28,* 243–256.

Myers, J. L. (1979). *Fundamentals of experimental design* (3rd ed.). Boston: Allyn & Bacon.

Nachman, G. (1979). The menopause that refreshes. In P. I. Rose (Ed.), *Socialization and the life cycle.* New York: St. Martin's Press.

Natelson, B. (1977). The "executive" monkey revisited. In F. P. Brooks & P. W. Evens (Eds.), *Nerves and the gut.* Philadelphia: C. B. Slack.

National Academy of Sciences. (1983). *Identifying and estimating the genetic impact of chemical mutagens.* Washington, D.C.: National Academy Press.

National Center for Health Statistics (1983, March), Births, marriages, divorces, and deaths, United States. *Monthly Vital Statistics Report.* Vol. 31, No. 12. DHHS Pub. No. (PHS) 83-1120. Public Health Service, Hyattsville, Md.

Nauta, W. J. H., & Feirtag, M. (1979). The organization of the brain. *Scientific American, 241(3),* 88–111.

Navon, D. (1977). Forest before trees: The precedence of global features in visual perception. *Cognitive Psychology, 9,* 353–383.

Neimark, E. D. (1975). Intellectual development during adolescence. In F. D. Horowitz (Ed.), *Review of child development research* (Vol. 1). Chicago: University of Chicago Press.

Neisser, U. (1967). *Cognitive psychology.* Englewood Cliffs, N.J.: Prentice-Hall.

Neisser, U. (1976). *Cognition and reality: Principles and implications of cognitive psychology.* San Francisco: Freeman.

Nelson, K. (1973). Structure and strategy in learning to talk. *Monographs of the Society for Research in Child Development, 38* (1–2, Serial No. 149).

Nelson, R. E. (1977). Irrational beliefs in depression. *Journal of Consulting and Clinical Psychology, 45,* 1190–1191.

Nemeth, C. (1972). A critical analysis of research utilizing the prisoner's dilemma paradigm for the study of bargaining. In L. Berkowitz (Ed.), *Advances in experimental social psychology* (Vol. 6). New York: Academic Press.

Nemiah, J. (1975). Hysterical neurosis, dissociative type. In A. Freedman, H. Kaplan, & B. Sadlock (Eds.), *Comprehensive textbook of psychiatry* (2nd ed.) (Vol 1). Baltimore: Williams & Wilkins.

Nerem, R., Levesque, M. J., & Cornhill, J. F. (1980). Social environment as a factor in diet-induced arteriosclerosis. *Science, 208,* 1475–1476.

Neugarten, B. L. (1968). The awareness of middle age. In B. L. Neugarten (Ed.), *Middle age and aging.* Chicago: The University of Chicago Press.

Neugarten, B. L., & Gutman, D. L. (1968). Age-sex roles and personality in middle age: A thematic apperception study. In B. L. Neugarten (Ed.), *Middle age and aging.* Chicago: University of Chicago Press.

Neugarten, B. L., Wood, V., Kraines, R. J., & Loomis, B. (1963). Women's attitudes toward the menopause. *Vita Humana, 6,* 140–151.

Newcomb, T. (1953). An approach to the study of communicative acts. *Psychological Review, 60,* 393–404.

Newcomb, T. (1956). The prediction of interpersonal attraction. *American Psychologist, 11,* 575–586.

Newcomb, T. M. (1971). Dyadic balance as a source of clues about interpersonal attraction. In B. I. Murstein (Ed.), *Theories of attraction and love.* New York: Springer.

Newell, A. (1973). You can't play 20 questions with nature and win. In W. G. Chase (Ed.), *Visual information processing.* New York: Academic Press.

Newman, H. H., Freeman, F. N., & Holzinger, K. J. (1937). *Twins: A study of heredity and environment.* Chicago: University of Chicago Press.

Newmark, C. S., Frerking, R. A., Cook, L., & Newmark, L. (1973). Endorsement of Ellis' irrational beliefs as a function of psychopathology. *Journal of Clinical Psychology, 29,* 300–302.

NIMH. (1969). *The mental health of urban America.* Washington, D.C.: U.S. Government Printing Office.

NIMH. (1976). *Emergency services in psychiatric fa-*

cilities. Washington, D.C.: U.S. Government Printing Office.

NIMH. (1978, March). Changes in the age, sex, and diagnostic composition of the resident population of state and county mental hospitals (statistical note #146). Washington, D.C.: U.S. Government Printing Office.

Nisbett, R. E. (1972). Hunger, obesity, and the ventromedial hypothalamus. *Psychological Review, 79,* 433–453.

Nisbett, R. E., & Ross, L. (1980). *Human inference: Strategies and shortcomings.* Englewood Cliffs, N.J.: Prentice-Hall.

Nisbett, R. E., & Wilson, T. D. (1977). Telling more than we can know: Verbal reports on mental processes. *Psychological Review, 84,* 231–259.

Norman, D. A. (1979). *Memory and attention,* (3rd ed.). New York: Wiley.

Norman, D. A., & Rumelhart, D. E. (1975). *Explorations in cognition.* San Francisco: Freeman.

Novak, D., & Lerner, M. (1968). Rejection as a consequence of perceived similarity. *Journal of Personality and Social Psychology, 9,* 147–152.

Novak, M. A., & Harlow, H. F. (1975). Social recovery of monkeys isolated for the first year of life: I. Rehabilitation and therapy. *Developmental Psychology, 11,* 564–565.

Nowak, C. A. (1977). Does youthfulness equal attractiveness? In L. E. Troll, J. Israel, & K. Israel (Eds.), *Looking ahead: A woman's guide to the problems and joys of growing older.* Englewood Cliffs, N.J.: Prentice-Hall.

Nuckolls, K. B., Cassel, J., & Kaplan, B. H. (1972). Psychosocial assets, life crisis, and the prognosis of pregnancy. *American Journal of Epidemiology, 95,* 431–441.

Offer, D. (1969). *The psychological world of the teenager: A study of normal adolescent boys.* New York: Basic Books.

Offer, D., Marcus, D., & Offer, J. L. (1970). A longitudinal study of normal adolescent boys. *American Journal of Psychiatry, 126,* 917–924.

Offer, D., & Offer, J. (1974). Normal adolescent males; The high school and college years. *Journal of the American College Health Association, 22,* 209–215.

Ojemann, G., & Mateer, C. (1979). Human language cortex: Localization of memory, syntax, and sequential motor-phoneme identification systems. *Science, 205,* 1401–1403.

Olds, J. (1956). Pleasure centers in the brain. *Scientific American, 195,* 105–116.

Olds, J., & Milner, P. (1954). Positive reinforcement produced by electrical stimulation of septal area and other regions of rat brain. *Journal of Comparative and Physiological Psychology, 47,* 419–427.

O'Leary, V., & Hammock, B. (1975). Sex-role orientation and achievement context as determinants of the motive to avoid success. *Sex Roles, 1,* 225–234.

Oller, D. K., & Warren, I. (1976). On the nature of phonological capacity. *Lingua, 39,* 183–199.

Orne, M. T. (1977). The construct of hypnosis: Implications of definition for research and practice. In W. E. Edmonston, Jr. (Ed.), *Con-ceptual and investigative approaches to hypnosis and hypnotic phenomena.* Annals of the New York Academy of Sciences (Vol. 296), 14–33.

Orne, M. T., Sheehan, P. W., & Evans, F. J. (1968). Occurrence of posthypnotic behavior outside the experimental setting. *Journal of Personality and Social Psychology, 9,* 189–196.

Osgood, C. E., Suci, G. J., & Tannenbaum, P. H. (1957). *The measurement of meaning.* Urbana, Ill.: University of Illinois Press.

Ouchi, W. G., & Jaeger, A. M. (1978). Social structure and organizational type. In W. W. Meyer et al. (Eds.), *Environments and organizations.* San Francisco: Jossey-Bass.

Owen, D. R. (1972). The 47, XYY male: A review. *Psychological Bulletin, 78,* 209–233.

Paivio, A. (1971). *Imagery and verbal processes.* New York: Holt, Rinehart and Winston.

Paivio, A. (1978). Comparisons of mental clocks. *Journal of Experimental Psychology: Human Perception and Performance, 4,* 61–71.

Pallak, M. S., & Pittman, T. S. (1972). General motivational effects of dissonance arousal. *Journal of Personality and Social Psychology, 21,* 349–358.

Palmore, E., & Luikart, C. (1972). Health and social factors related to life satisfaction. *Journal of Health and Social Behavior, 13,* 68–80.

Palumbo, S. R. (1978). *Dreaming and memory: A new information-processing model.* New York: Basic Books.

Panksepp, J. (1973). Reanalysis of feeding patterns in the rat. *Journal of Comparative and Physiological Psychology, 82,* 78–94.

Parke, R. D., Berkowitz, L., Leyens, J. R., & Sebastian, R. (1975). The effects of repeated exposure to movie violence on aggressive behavior in juvenile delinquent boys: Field experimental studies. In L. Berkowitz (Ed.), *Advances in experimental social psychology* (Vol. 8). New York: Academic Press.

Parke, R. D., Berkowitz, L., Leyens, J. R., West, S. G., & Sebastian, R. J. (1977). Some effects of violent and nonviolent movies on the behavior of juvenile delinquents. In L. Berkowitz (Ed.), *Advances in experimental social psychology.* New York: Academic Press.

Parker, G., & Lipscombe, P. (1979). Parental overprotection and asthma. *Journal of Psychosomatic Research, 23,* 295–300.

Partridge, G. (1930). Current conceptions of the psychosomatic personality. *American Journal of Psychiatry, 87,* 53–99.

Patel, C. H. (1973). Yoga and biofeedback in the management of hypertension. *Lancet, 2,* 1053–1055.

Patel, C. H. (1975). Twelvemonth follow-up of yoga and biofeedback in the management of hypertension. *Lancet, 1,* 62–64.

Pavlov, I. P. (1927). *Conditioned reflexes* (G. V. Anrep, trans.) London: Oxford University Press.

Pearlin, L. I., & Schooler, C. (1978). The structure of coping. *Journal of Health and Social Behavior, 19,* 2–21.

Peck, R. C. (1968). Psychological developments in the second half of life. In B. L. Neugarten (Ed.), *Middle age and aging.* Chicago: The University of Chicago Press.

Pedersen, F. A., & Bell, R. Q. (1970). Sex dif-ferences in preschool children without histories of complications of pregnancy and delivery. *Developmental Psychology, 3,* 10–15.

Pederson, L. L., Scrimgeour, W. G., & Lefcoe, N. M. (1979). Variables of hypnosis which are related to success in a smoking withdrawal program. *International Journal of Clinical and Experimental Hypnosis, 27,* 14–20.

Pennebaker, J. W., & Skelton, J. A. (1978). Psychological parameters of physical symptoms. *Personality and Social Psychology Bulletin, 4,* 524–540.

Perls, F. S. (1969). *Gestalt therapy verbatim.* Lafayette, Calif.: Real People Press.

Perls, F. S. (1970). Four lectures. In J. Fagan & I. L. Shepherd (Eds.), *Gestalt therapy now: Therapy, techniques, applications.* Palo Alto, Calif.: Science Behavior Books.

Perry, C. (1977). Variables influencing the posthypnotic persistence of an uncancelled hypnotic suggestion. In W. E. Edmonston, Jr. (Ed.), *Conceptual and investigative approaches to hypnosis and hypnotic phenomena.* Annals of The New York Academy of Science (Vol. 296), 264–273.

Pert, C. B., Kuhar, M. J., & Snyder, S. H. (1976). Autoradiographic localization of opiate receptor in rat brain. *National Academy of Science (USA): Proceedings, 73,* 3729–3733.

Pert, C. B., & Snyder, S. H. (1970). Opiate receptors: Demonstration in nervous tissue. *Science, 179,* 1011–1014.

Peterson, L. R., & Peterson, M. J. (1959). Short-term retention of individual items. *Journal of Experimental Psychology, 58,* 193–198.

Pfeiffer, E., Verwoordt, A., & Davis, G. C. (1974). Sexual behavior in middle life. In E. Palmore (Ed.), *Normal aging II: Reports from the Duke longitudinal studies, 1970–1973.* Durham, N.C.: Duke University Press.

Phares, E. J. (1979). *Clinical psychology: Concepts, methods, and profession.* Chicago: Dorsey.

Phoenix, C. H. (1974). Prenatal testosterone in the nonhuman primate and its consequences for behavior. In R. C. Friedman, R. M. Richart, & K. L. VandeWiele (Eds.), *Sex differences in behavior.* New York: Wiley.

Piaget, J. (1932). *The moral judgment of the child.* New York: Harcourt, Brace.

Piaget, J. (1960). *The child's conception of the world.* Totowa, N.J.: Littlefield, Adams.

Piaget, J. (1972) Intellectual evolution from adolescence to adulthood. *Human Development, 15,* 1–12.

Piaget, J., & Inhelder, B. (1968). *The psychology of the child.* New York: Basic Books.

Piliavin, J. A., Callero, P. L., & Evans, D. E. (1982). Addiction to altruism?: Opponent-process theory and habitual blood donation. *Journal of Personality and Social Psychology, 43,* 1200–1213.

Pineo, P. C. (1961). Disenchantment in the later years of marriage. *Marriage and Family Living, 23,* 3–11.

Pittman, N. L., & Pittman, T. S. (1979). Effects of amount of helplessness training and internal–external locus of control on mood and performance. *Journal of Personality and Social Psychology, 37,* 39–47.

Pittman, T. S. (1975). Attribution of arousal as a mediator in dissonance reduction. *Journal of Experimental Social Psychology, 11,* 53–63.

Pittman, T. S., Boggiano, A. K., & Ruble, D. N. (1982). Intrinsic and extrinsic motivational orientations; Interactive effects of reward, competence feedback, and task complexity. In J. Levine & M. Wang (Eds.), *Teacher and student perceptions: Implications for learning.* Hillsdale, N.J.: Erlbaum.

Pittman, T. S., Emery, J., & Boggiano, A. K. (1982). Intrinsic and extrinsic motivational orientation: Reward-induced changes in preference for complexity. *Journal of Personality and Social Psychology, 42,* 789–797.

Pliner, P., Blankstein, K. R., & Spigel, I. M. (1979). *Perception of emotion in self and others.* New York: Plenum.

Plomin, R., & DeFries, J. C. (1980). Genetics and intelligence: Recent data. *Intelligence, 4,* 15–24.

Poincare, H. (1929). *The foundations of science* (G. R. Halstead, trans.). New York: The Science Press.

Pollack, I., Rubenstein, H., & Decker, L. (1959). Intelligibility of known and unknown message sets. *Journal of the Acoustical Society of America, 31,* 273–279.

Pollard-Gott, L., McCluskey, M., & Todres, A. (1979). Subjective story structure. *Discourse Processes, 2,* 251–281.

Porteous, J. D. (1977). *Environment and behavior.* Reading, Mass.: Addison-Wesley.

Porter, R. W., Brady, J. V., Conrad, D., Mason, J. W., Galambos, R., & Rioch, D. (1958). Some experimental observations on gastrointestinal lesions in behaviorally conditioned monkeys. *Psychosomatic Medicine, 20,* 379–394.

Posner, M. I. (1969). Abstraction and the process of recognition. In G. H. Bower & J. T. Spence (Eds.), *The psychology of learning and motivation: Advances in research and theory* (Vol. 3). New York: McGraw-Hill.

Prange, A., Jr., Wilson, I., Lynn, W., Lacoe, B., & Strikeleather, R. (1974). L-tryptophan in mania—contribution to a permissive hypothesis of affective disorders. *Archives of General Psychiatry, 30,* 56–62.

Premack, D. (1976). *Intelligence in ape and man.* Hillsdale, N.J.: Erlbaum.

Provence, S., & Lipton, R. C. (1962). *Infants in institutions.* New York: International Universities Press.

Pruitt, D. G. (1975). Power and bargaining. In B. Seidenberg & A. Swadowsky (Eds.), *Social psychology: An introduction.* New York: Free Press.

Pruitt, D. G. (1976). Conclusions: Toward an understanding of choice shifts in group discussion. *Journal of Personality and Social Psychology, 20,* 495–510.

Rabbitt, P. M. (1982). Breakdown of control processes in old age. In T. Field, A. Huston, H. Quay, L. Troll, & G. Finnley (Eds.), *Review of human development.* New York: Wiley.

Rachlin, H. (1976). *Introduction to modern behaviorism* (2nd ed.). San Francisco: Freeman.

Rachman, S. (1966). Sexual fetishism: An ex-perimental analogue. *Psychological Record, 16,* 293–296.

Radloff, L. (1975). Sex differences in depression: The effects of occupation and marital status. *Sex Roles, 1,* 249–281.

Ragozin, A. S. (1980). Attachment behavior of day-care children: Naturalistic and laboratory observation. *Child Development, 51,* 409–415.

Rahe, R., Romo, M., Bennett, L., & Siltanen, P. (1974). Recent life changes, myocardial infarction, and abrupt coronary death: Studies in Helsinki. *Archives of Internal Medicine, 133,* 221–228.

Raines, H. (1979, December 23). Marijuana from many sources softening cancer chemotherapy. *New York Times.*

Rao, D. C., Morton, N. E., Lalouel, J. M., & Lew R. (1982). Path analysis under generalized assortative mating. II. American I.Q. *Genetical Research, 39,* 187–198.

Raphael, B. (1976). *The thinking computer: Mind inside matter.* San Francisco: Freeman.

Rappaport, A. (1973). *Experimental games and their uses in psychology.* Morristown, N.J.: Social Learning Press.

Raven, J. C. (1947). *Progressive matrices.* London: Lewis.

Rees, L. (1963). The significance of parental attitudes in childhood asthma. *Journal of Psychosomatic Research, 7,* 181–190.

Regan, D. T., Strauss, E., & Fazio, R. H. (1974). Liking and the attribution process. *Journal of Experimental Social Psychology, 10,* 385–397

Rescorla, R. A. (1967a). Inhibition of delay in Pavlovian fear conditioning. *Journal of Comparative and Physiological Psychology, 64,* 114–120.

Rescorla, R. A. (1967b). Pavlovian conditioning and its proper control procedures. *Psychological Review, 74,* 71–80.

Rescorla, R. A. (1969). Conditioned inhibition of fear resulting from negative CS-US contingencies. *Journal of Comparative and Physiological Psychology, 67,* 504–509.

Rescorla, R. A., & Wagner, A. R. (1972). A theory of Pavlovian conditioning: Variations in the effectiveness of reinforcement and nonreinforcement. In A. H. Black & W. F. Prokasy (Eds.), *Classical conditioning II: Current research and theory.* New York: Appleton-Century-Crofts.

Reynolds, G. S. (1975). *A primer of operant conditioning* (rev. ed.). Glenview, Ill.: Scott Foresman.

Rheingold, H. L., & Adams, J. L. (1980). The significance of speech to newborns. *Developmental Psychology, 6,* 397–403.

Rhodewalt, F. (1979). The coronary-prone behavior pattern, psychological reactance, and the self-attributor. Unpublished doctoral dissertation, Princeton University.

Rice, J., Cloninger, C. R., & Reich, T. (1980). Analysis of behavioral traits in the presence of cultural transmission and assortative mating: Applications to I.Q. and SES. *Behavior Genetics, 10,* 73–92.

Rife, D. C. (1940). Handedness, with special reference to twins. *Genetics, 25,* 178–186.

Riley, M., & Foner, A. (1968). *Aging and society. Vol. 1: An inventory of research findings.* New York: Russell Sage.

Rimland, B. (1964). *Infantile autism.* New York: Appleton-Century-Crofts.

Rimm, D. C., & Masters, J. C. (1979). *Behavior therapy: Techniques and empirical findings* (2nd ed.). New York: Academic Press.

Rist, R. (1970). Student social class and teacher expectations: The self-fulfilling prophecy in ghetto education. *Harvard Educational Review, 40,* 411–451.

Robbins, P. (1978). *Successful midlife career change.* New York: AMACON.

Robbins, S. P. (1974). *Managing organizational conflict: A nontraditional approach.* Englewood Cliffs, N.J.: Prentice-Hall.

Roberts, C. L., Marx, M. H., & Collier, G. (1958). Light onset and light offset as reinforcers for the albino rat. *Journal of Comparative and Physiological Psychology, 51,* 575–579.

Roberts, L. E. (1979). Operant conditioning of autonomic responses: One perspective on the curare experiments. In G. E. Schwartz & D. Shapiro (Eds.), *Consciousness and self-regulation: Advances in research* (Vol. 2). New York: Plenum.

Robey, D. (1974). Task design, work values, and work response: An experimental test. *Organizational Behavior and Human Performance, 12,* 264–273.

Robin, J., & Langer, E. (1977). Long-term effects of control-relevant intervention with the institutionalized aged. *Journal of Personality and Social Psychology, 35,* 897–902.

Robins, N. L. (1966). *Deviant children grow up.* Baltimore: Williams & Wilkins.

Rock, I. (1975). *An introduction to perception.* New York: Macmillan.

Rodin, J. (1981). Current status of the internal-external hypothesis of obesity: What went wrong? *American Psychologist, 36,* 361–372.

Rodin, J., & Langer, E. (1977). Long-term effects of a control-relevant intervention with the institutionalized aged. *Journal of Personality and Social Psychology, 35,* 897–902.

Roethlisberger, F. J., & Dickson, W. J. (1939). *Management and the worker.* Cambridge, Mass.: Harvard University Press.

Roffwarg, H. P., Muzio, J. N., & Dement, W. C. (1966). Ontogenetic development of the human sleep-dream cycle. *Science, 152,* 604–619.

Roffwarg, H. P., Herman, J. H., Bowe-Anders, C., & Tauber, E. S. (1978). The effects of sustained alterations of waking visual input on dream content. In A. M. Arkin, J. S. Antrobus, and S. J. Ellman (Eds.), *The mind in sleep: Psychology and psychobiology.* Hillsdale, N.J.: Erlbaum.

Rogers, C. R. (1951). *Client-centered therapy.* Boston: Houghton Mifflin.

Rogers, C. R. (1960). *On becoming a person: A therapist's view of psychotherapy.* Boston: Houghton Mifflin.

Rokeach, M. (1968). *Beliefs, attitudes, and values.* San Francisco: Jossey-Bass.

Rokeach, M., & Kliejunas, P. (1972). Behavior as a function of attitude-toward-object and attitude-toward situation. *Journal of Personality and Social Psychology, 22,* 194–201.

Rollins, B. C., & Feldman, H. (1970). Marital satisfaction over the family life cycle. *Journal of Marriage and the Family, 32*(1), 20–28.

Ropartz, P. (1968). The relation between olfactory stimulation and aggressive behavior in mice. *Animal Behavior, 16,* 97–100.

Rosch, E. (1977). Human categorization. In N. Warren (Ed.), *Advances in cross-cultural psychology* (Vol. 1). London: Academic Press.

Rosch, E., & Lloyd B. B. (Eds.). (1978). *Cognition and categorization.* Hillsdale, N.J.: Erlbaum.

Rose, A. M. (1968). A current theoretical issue in social gerontology. In B. L. Neugarten (Ed.), *Middle age and aging.* Chicago: The University of Chicago Press.

Rose, S. (1975). *The conscious brain.* New York: Knopf.

Rosen, B. C., & D'Andrade, R. (1959). The psychosocial origins of achievement motivation. *Sociometry, 22,* 188–218.

Rosenberg, E. J., & Dohrenwend, B. S. (1975). Effects of experience and ethnicity on ratings of life events as stressors. *Journal of Health and Social Behavior, 16,* 127–129.

Rosenberg, M. J. (1960). Cognitive reorganization in response to hypnotic reversals of attitudinal affect. *Journal of Personality, 28,* 39–63.

Rosenblum, L. A. (1977). The development of social behavior in the rhesus monkey. Unpublished Ph.D. dissertation, U. of Wisconsin, 1961. Cited in D. P. Kimble, *Psychology as a biological science.* Santa Monica, Calif.: Goodyear.

Rosenhan, D. L. (1970). The natural socialization of altruistic autonomy. In J. Macaulay & L. Berkowitz (Eds.), *Altruism and helping behavior.* New York: Academic Press.

Rosenman, R. H., Brand, R. J., Jenkins, C. D., Friedman, M., Straus, R., & Wurm, M. (1975). Coronary heart disease in the Western Collaborative Group Study: Final follow-up experience of 8½ years. *Journal of the American Medical Association, 233,* 872–877.

Rosenthal, R. (1967). Covert communication in the psychological experiment. *Psychological Bulletin, 67,* 356–367.

Rosenzweig, M. R. (1966). Environmental complexity, cerebral change and behavior. *American Psychologist, 21,* 321–332.

Ross, L. (1977). The intuitive psychologist and his short-comings: Distortions in the attribution process. In L. Berkowitz (Ed.), *Advances in experimental social psychology* (Vol. 10). New York: Academic Press.

Ross, L., Rodin, J., & Zimbardo, P. (1969). Toward an attribution therapy: The reduction of fear through induced cognitive-emotional misattribution. *Journal of Personality and Social Psychology, 12,* 279–288.

Roth, S., & Kubal, L. (1975). The effects of noncontingent reinforcement on tasks of differing importance: Facilitation and learned helplessness. *Journal of Personality and Social Psychology, 32,* 680–691.

Rozin, P., & Kalat, J. (1971). Specific hungers and poison avoidance as adoptive specializations of learning. *Psychological Review, 78,* 459–486.

Rozin, P., & Mayer, J. (1961). Thermal reinforcement and thermoregulatory behavior in the goldfish, *Carassius auratus. Science, 134,* 942–943.

Rubin, D. (1977). Very long term memory for prose and verse. *Journal of Verbal Learning and Verbal Behavior, 16,* 611–621.

Rubin, Z. (1973). *Liking and loving: An invitation to social psychology.* New York: Holt, Rinehart & Winston.

Rubin, Z. (1974). From liking to loving: Patterns of attractions in dating relationships. In T. L. Huston (Ed.), *Foundations of interpersonal attraction.* New York: Academic Press.

Ruble, D. N., & Feldman, N. S. (1976). Order of consensus, distinctiveness, and consistency information and causal attributions. *Journal of Personality and Social Psychology, 34,* 930–937.

Ruble, D. N., Parsons, J. E., & Ross, J. (1976). Self-evaluative responses of children in an achievement setting. *Child Development, 47,* 990–997.

Ruff, H. A., & Birch, H. G. (1974). Infant visual fixation: The effects of concentricity, curvilinearity, and number of directions. *Journal of Experimental Child Psychology, 17,* 460–473.

Rumbaugh, D. M. (1977). *Language learning by a chimpanzee: The LANA project.* New York: Academic Press.

Rumbaugh, D. M., Savage-Rumbaugh, E. S., & Gill, T. V. (1979). The chimpanzee as an animal model in language research. In R. L. Schiefelbusch & J. H. Hollis (Eds.), *Language intervention from ape to child.* Baltimore, Md.: University Park Press.

Rumelhart, D. E. (1977). Understanding and summarizing brief stories. In D. Lolberge & J. Samuels (Eds.), *Basic processes in reading: Perception and comprehension.* Hillsdale, N.J.: Erlbaum.

Runck, B. (1980). *Biofeedback—Issues in treatment assessment.* Rockville, Md.: National Institute of Mental Health.

Rundus, D. (1971). Analysis of rehearsal processes in free recall. *Journal of Experimental Psychology, 89,* 63–77.

Rush, A. J., Beck, A. T., Kovacs, M., & Hollon, S. (1977). Comparative efficacy of cognitive therapy and pharmacotherapy in the treatment of depressed outpatients. *Cognitive Therapy and Research, 1,* 17–37.

Ryle, G. (1949). *The concept of mind.* London: Hutchinson.

Saarinen, T. F. (1969). *Perception of the environment.* Resource Paper no. 5. Association of American Geographers.

Sachs, J. S. (1967). Recognition memory for syntactic and semantic aspects of connected discourse. *Perception and Psychophysics, 2,* 437–442.

Saegert, S., Swap, W., & Zajonc, R. B. (1973). Exposure, context, and interpersonal attraction. *Journal of Personality and Social Psychology, 25,* 234–242.

Sakurai, M. M. (1975). Small group cohesiveness and detrimental conformity. *Sociometry, 38,* 340–357.

Salapatek, P. (1975). Pattern perception in early infancy. In L. B. Cohen & P. Salapetek (Eds.), *Infant perception: From sensation to cognition* (Vol. 1): *Basic visual processes.* New York: Academic Press.

Salapatek, P., Bechtold, A. G., & Bushnell, E. W. (1976). Infant visual acuity as a function of viewing distance. *Child Development, 47,* 860–863.

Salapatek, P., & Kessen, W. (1966). Visual scanning of triangles by the human newborn. *Journal of Experimental Child Psychology, 3,* 155–167.

Samuda, R. J. (1975). *Psychological testing of American minorities: Issues and consequences.* New York: Dodd, Mead.

Sapir, E. (1958). Language and environment. In D. G. Mandelbaum (Ed.), *Selected writings of Edward Sapir in language, culture and personality.* Berkeley: University of California Press. (Originally published, 1912.)

Sapolsky, B. S., & Zillman, D. (1981). The effect of soft-core and hard-core erotica on provoked and unprovoked hostile behavior. *Journal of Sex Research, 17,* 319–343.

Sarason, I. G., Johnson, J. H., & Siegel, J. M. (1978). Assessing the impact of life changes: Development of the life experiences survey. *Journal of Consulting and Clinical Psychology, 46,* 932–946.

Sarbin, T. R. (1962). Attempts to understand hypnotic phenomena. In L. Postman, *Psychology in the making.* New York: Knopf. Pp. 745–784.

Sarbin, T. R., & Coe, W. C. (1972). *Hypnosis: A social psychological analysis of influence communication.* New York: Holt, Rinehart and Winston.

Sargent, S. S., & Stafford, K. R. (1965). *Basic teachings of the great psychologists.* Garden City, N.Y.: Doubleday.

Sarnoff, I., & Zimbardo, P. G. (1961). Anxiety, fear, and social affiliation. *Journal of Abnormal and Social Psychology, 62,* 356–363.

Satinoff, E. (1974). Neural integration of thermoregulatory responses. In L. V. DiCara (Ed.), *Limbic and autonomic nervous system: Advances in research.* New York: Plenum.

Satinoff, E., & Henderson, R. (1977). Thermoregulatory behavior. In W. K. Honig & J. E. R. Staddon (Eds.), *Handbook of operant behavior.* Englewood Cliffs, N.J.: Prentice-Hall.

Savage-Rumbaugh, E. S., Rumbaugh, D. M., Smith, S. T., & Lawson, J. (1980). Reference: The linguistic essential. *Science, 210,* 922–925.

Scarr, S., & Weinberg, R. A. (1976). IQ test performance of black children adopted by white females. *American Psychologist, 31,* 726–739.

Scarr, S., & Weinberg, R. A. (1977). Intellectual similarities within families of both adopted and biological children. *Intelligence, 1,* 170–191.

Schachter, S. (1951). Deviation, rejection, and communication. *Journal of Abnormal and Social Psychology, 46,* 190–207.

Schachter, S. (1959). *The psychology of affiliation: Experimental studies of the sources of gregariousness.* Stanford, Calif.: Stanford University Press.

Schachter, S. (1971). Some extraordinary facts about obese humans and rats. *American Psychologist, 26,* 129–144.

Schachter, S., & Singer, J. E. (1962). Cognitive, social, and physiological determinants of emotional state. *Psychological Review, 69,* 379–399.

Schaefer, E. S., & Bayley, N. (1963). Maternal behavior, child behavior, and their intercorrelations from infancy through adolescence. *Monographs of the Society for Research in Child Development, 28* (3, Serial No. 87).

Schaefer, H. H., & Martin, P. L. (1969). *Behavior therapy.* New York: McGraw-Hill.

Schaffer, H. R., & Emerson, P. E. (1964a). The development of social attachments in infancy. *Monographs of the Society for Research in Child Development, 29* (3, Serial No. 94).

Schaffer, H. R., & Emerson, P. E. (1964b). Patterns of response to physical contact in early human development. *Journal of Child Psychology and Psychiatry, 5,* 1–13.

Schaie, K. W., Labouvie, G., & Buech, B. V. (1973). Generational and cohort-specific differences in adult cognitive functioning: A fourteen-year study of independent samples. *Developmental Psychology, 9,* 151–166.

Schank, R., & Abelson, R. (1976). *Scripts, plans, goals, and understanding.* Hillsdale, N.J.: Erlbaum.

Scheier, M. F., Fenigstein, A., & Buss, A. (1974). Self-awareness and physical aggression. *Journal of Experimental Social Psychology, 10,* 264–273.

Schein, E. H. (1980). *Organizational psychology.* Englewood Cliffs, N.J.: Prentice-Hall.

Schelling, T. C. (1960). *The strategy of conflict.* Cambridge, Mass.: Harvard University Press.

Schiff, M., Duyme, M., Dumaret, A., & Tomkiewicz, S. (1982). How much *could* we boost scholastic achievement and I.Q. scores? A direct answer from a French adoption study. *Cognition, 12,* 165–196.

Schiff, W. (1980). *Perception: An applied approach.* Boston: Houghton Mifflin.

Schildkraut, J. (1965). The catecholamine hypothesis of affective disorders: A review of supporting evidence. *American Journal of Psychiatry, 122,* 509–522.

Schill, T., & Chapin, J. (1972). Sex guilt and males' preference for reading erotic literature. *Journal of Consulting and Clinical Psychology, 39,* 516.

Schmale, A. H., & Iker, H. (1971). Hopelessness as a predictor of cervical cancer. *Social Science and Medicine, 5,* 95–100.

Schmidt, G., & Sigush, V. (1970). Sex differences in responses to psychosexual stimulation by film and slides. *Journal of Sex Research, 6,* 268–283.

Schmidt, G., Sigush, V., & Meyberg, V. (1969). Psychosexual stimulation in men: Emotional reactions, changes of sex behavior, and measures of conservative attitudes. *Journal of Sex Research, 5,* 199–217.

Schmidt, H. O., & Fonda, C. (1956). The reliability of psychiatric diagnosis. *Journal of Abnormal and Social Psychology, 52,* 262–267.

Schneider, D. J. (1973). Implicit personality theory: A review. *Psychological Bulletin, 79,* 294–309.

Schneider, W., & Shiffrin, R. M. (1977). Controlled and automatic human information processing. I. Detection, search, and attention. *Psychological Review, 84,* 1–66.

Schrank, R. (1978). *Ten thousand working days.* Cambridge, Mass.: MIT Press.

Schreiber, F. R. (1974). *Sybil.* New York: Warner.

Schulsinger, F. (1972). Psychopathology: Heredity and environment. *International Journal of Mental Health, 1,* 190–206.

Schutz, R., & Hanusa, B. (1978). Long-term effects of control and predictability-enhancing interventions: Findings and ethical issues. *Journal of Personality and Social Psychology, 36,* 1194–1201.

Schwartz, B. (1978). *Psychology of learning and behavior.* New York: Norton.

Schwartz, G. E. (1977). Psychosomatic disorders and biofeedback: A psychobiological model of disregulation. In J. D. Maser & M. E. P. Seligman (Eds.), *Psychopathology: Experimental models.* San Francisco: Freeman.

Schwartz, M. (1978). *Physiological psychology.* Englewood Cliffs, N.J.: Prentice-Hall.

Schwartz, M. D., & Errera, P. (1963). Psychiatric care in a general hospital emergency room. *Archives of General Psychiatry, 9,* 113–121.

Scoville, W. B., & Milner, B. (1957). Loss of recent memory after bilateral hippocampal lesions. *Journal of Neurology, Neurosurgery, and Psychiatry, 20,* 11–21.

Scribner, S., & Cole, M. (1981). *The psychology of literacy.* Cambridge, Mass.: Harvard University Press.

Seagert, S. C., Swap, W., & Zajonc, R. B. (1973). Exposure, context, and intepersonal attraction. *Journal of Personality and Social Psychology, 25,* 234–242.

Searle, J. (1979). *Expression and meaning: Studies in the theory of speech acts.* Cambridge: Cambridge University Press.

Sears, R. R., Maccoby, E. E., & Levin, H. (1957). *Patterns of child rearing.* New York: Harper & Row.

Segal, M. W. (1974). Alphabet and attraction: An unobtrusive measure of the effect of propinquity in a field setting. *Journal of Personality and Social Psychology, 30,* 654–657.

Segal, S. J., & Fusella, V. (1970). Influence of imaged pictures and sounds in detection of visual and auditory signals. *Journal of Experimental Psychology, 83,* 458–474.

Segovia-Riguelma, N., Varela, A., & Mardones, J. (1971). Appetite for alcohol. In Y. Israel & J. Mardones (Eds.), *Biological basis of alcoholism.* New York: Wiley.

Selfridge, O. G. (1959). Pandemonium: A paradigm for learning. In D. V. Blake & A. M. Uttley (Eds.), *Proceedings of the symposium on the mechanisation of thought processes.* London: Her Majesty's Stationery Office.

Seligman, M. E. P. (1971). Phobias and preparedness. *Behavior Therapy, 2,* 307–320.

Seligman, M. E. P. (1972). Phobias and preparedness. In M. E. P. Seligman & J. L. Hager (Eds.), *Biological boundaries of learning.* New York: Appleton-Century-Crofts.

Seligman, M. E. P. (1974). Depression and learned helplessness. In R. J. Friedman & M. M. Katz (Eds.), *The psychology of depression: Contemporary theory and research.* Washington, D.C.: Winston-Wiley.

Seligman, M. E. P. (1975). *Helplessness: On de-* pression, development, and death. San Francisco: Freeman.

Seligman, M. E. P., Abramson, L. Y., Semmel, A., & von Baeyer, C. (1979). Depressive attributional style. *Journal of Abnormal Psychology, 88,* 242–247.

Seligman, M. E. P., & Hager, J. L. (1972). *Biological boundaries of learning.* New York: Appleton-Century-Crofts.

Selye, H. (1956). *The stress of life.* New York: McGraw-Hill.

Selye, H. (1976). *The stress of life* (2nd ed.). New York: McGraw-Hill.

Selye, H. (Ed.). (1980). *Selye's guide to stress research* (Vol. 1). New York: Van Nostrand Reinhold.

Sem-Jacobsen, C. W., & Torkildsen, A. (1960). Depth recording and electrical stimulation in the human brain. In E. R. Ramey & D. S. O'Doherty (Eds.), *Electrical studies on the anesthetized brain.* New York: Hoeber. Pp.275–290.

Serbin, L. A., & O'Leary, K. E. (1975). How nursery schools teach girls to shut up. *Psychology Today, 9,* 57–58, 102–103.

Shaffer, D. R. (1979). *Social and personality development.* Monterey, Calif.: Brooks/Cole.

Shafii, M., Lavely, R. A., & Jaffe, R. D. (1974). Meditation and marijuana. *American Journal of Psychiatry, 131,* 60–63.

Shafii, M., Lavely, R. A., & Jaffe, R. D. (1975). Meditation and the prevention of alcohol abuse. *American Journal of Psychiatry, 132,* 942–945.

Shatz, M. (1978). The relationship between cognitive processes and the development of communication skill. In C. B. Keasey (Ed.), *Nebraska Symposium on Motivation* (Vol. 26). Lincoln, Neb.: University of Nebraska Press.

Shatz, M., & Gelman, R. (1973). The development of communication skills: Modification in the speech of young children as a function of listener. *Monographs of the Society for Research in Child Development, 38*(5, Whole No. 152).

Shaw, D. M. (1966). Mineral metabolism, mania, and melancholia. *British Medical Journal, 2,* 262–267.

Shaw, M. E. (1954). Some effects of unequal distribution of information upon group performance in various communication nets. *Journal of Abnormal and Social Psychology, 49,* 547–553.

Shaw, R., & Bransford, J. (1977). Approaches to the problem of knowledge. In R. Shaw & J. Bransford (Eds.), *Perceiving, acting, and knowing.* Hillsdale, N.J.: Erlbaum.

Sheldon, W. H. (1942). *The varieties of temperament: A psychology of constitutional differences.* New York: Harper.

Shepard, R. N., & Metzler, J. (1971). Mental rotation of three-dimensional objects. *Science, 171,* 701–703.

Sheppard, H. L. (1976). Work and retirement. In R. H. Binstock & E. Shanas (Eds.), *Handbook of aging and the social sciences.* New York: Van Nostrand Reinhold.

Sherif, M. (1936). *The psychology of group norms.* New York: Harper & Row.

Sherif, M., & Sherif, C. W. (1948/1956). *An outline of social psychology* (rev. ed.). New York: Harper & Row.

Shields, J. (1962). *Monozygotic twins brought up*

apart and brought up together. London: Oxford University Press.

Shirley, M. M. (1931). *The first two years: A study of twenty-five babies: Postural and locomotor development.* Minneapolis, Minn.: University of Minnesota Press.

Shneidman, E. S. (1973). *Deaths of man.* New York: New York Times Book Co.

Shomer, R. W., Davis, A., & Kelley, H. H. (1966). Threats and the development of coordination: Further studies of the Deutsch and Krauss trucking game. *Journal of Personality and Social Psychology, 4,* 119–126.

Sidman, M. (1953). Two temporal parameters of the maintenance of avoidance behavior by the white rat. *Journal of Comparative and Physiological Psychology, 46,* 253–261.

Siegel, S. (1976). Morphine analgesic tolerance: Its situation specificity supports a Pavlovian conditioning model. *Science, 193,* 323–325.

Sigall, H., & Aronson, F. (1969). Liking for an evaluator as a function of her physical attractiveness and nature of the evaluations. *Journal of Experimental Social Psychology, 5,* 93–100.

Sigall, H., & Ostrove, N. (1975). Beautiful but dangerous: Effects of offender attractiveness and nature of the crime on juridic judgment. *Journal of Personality and Social Psychology, 31,* 410–414.

Silver R. L., & Wortman, C. B. (1980). Coping with undesirable life events. In J. Garber & M. E. P. Seligman (Eds.), *Human helplessness: Theory and applications.* New York: Academic Press.

Simon, H. A. (1978). Information-processing theory of human problem solving. In W. K. Estes (Ed.), *Handbook of learning and cognitive processing.* Hillsdale, N.J.: Erlbaum.

Simon, M. L. (1977). Application of a new model of peer group influence to naturally existing adolescent friendship groups. *Child Development, 48,* 270–274.

Simpson, E. L. (1974). Moral development research: A case of scientific bias. *Human Development, 17,* 81–106.

Sinclair-de Zwart, H. (1973). Language acquisition and cognitive development. In T. E. Moore (Ed.), *Cognitive development and the acquisition of language.* New York: Academic Press.

Skinner, B. F. (1948). "Superstitition" in the pigeon. *Journal of Experimental Psychology, 38* 168–172.

Skinner, B. F. (1953). *Science and human behavior.* New York: Macmillan.

Skinner, B. F. (1957). *Verbal behavior.* Englewood Cliffs, N.J.: Prentice-Hall.

Skinner, B. F. (1971). *Beyond freedom and dignity.* New York: Knopf.

Skipper, J. K., & Leonard, R. (Eds.). (1965). *Social interactions and patient care.* Philadelphia: J. B. Lippincott.

Sklar, J., & Berkov, B. (1975). The American birth rate: Evidences of coming rise. *Science, 189,* 693–700.

Skodak, M., & Skeels, H. (1949). A final follow-up study of one hundred adopted children. *Journal of Genetic Psychology, 75,* 85–125.

Slobin, D. I. (1971). *Psycholinguistics.* Glenview, Ill.: Scott, Foresman.

Smith, E. E., & Medin, D. L. (1981). *Categories*

and concepts. Cambridge, Mass.: Harvard University Press.

Smith, F. (1970). *Understanding reading.* New York: Holt, Rinehart and Winston.

Smith, M. E. (1926). An investigation of the development of the sentence and the extent of vocabulary in young children. *University of Iowa Studies in Child Welfare, 3,* No. 5.

Smith, M. L., & Glass, B. V. (1977). Meta-analysis of psychotherapy outcome studies. *American Psychologist, 32,* 752–760.

Snow, C. E. (1972). Mother's speech to children learning language. *Child Development, 43,* 549–565.

Snow, C. E., & Hoefnagel-Höhle, M. (1978). The critical period for learning acquisition: Evidence from second-language learning. *Child Development,* pp. 1114–1128.

Snyder, J. (1977). Reinforcement and analyses of interaction in problem and nonproblem families. *Journal of Abnormal Psychology, 86,* 528–535.

Snyder, M. (1981). On the influence of individuals on situations. In N. Cantor & J. Kihlstrom (Eds.), *Personality, cognition and social interaction.* Hillsdale, N.J.: Erlbaum.

Snyder, M., & Swann, W. B., Jr. (1978). Behavioral confirmation in social interaction: From social perception to social reality. *Journal of Experimental Social Psychology, 14,* 148–162.

Snyder, M., Tanke, E. D. (1976). Behavior and attitude: Some people are more consistent than others. *Journal of Personality, 44,* 501–517.

Snyder, M., Tanke, E. D., & Berscheid, E. (1977). Social perception and interpersonal behavior: On the self-fulfilling nature of social stereotypes. *Journal of Personality and Social Psychology, 35,* 656–666.

Snyder, S. H. (1981). Opiate and benzodiazepine receptors. *Psychosomatics, 22* (11), 986–989.

Sohlins, M. (1976). *The use and abuse of biology: An anthropological critique of sociobiology.* Ann Arbor, Mich.: University of Michigan Press.

Solomon, R. L. (1980). The opponent-process theory of acquired motivation: the costs of pleasure and the benefits of pain. *American Psychologist, 35,* 691–712.

Solomon, R. L., & Corbit, J. D. (1973). An opponent-process theory of motivation: II. Cigarette addiction. *Journal of Abnormal Psychology, 81,* 158–171.

Solomon, R. L., & Corbit, J. D. (1974). An opponent-process theory of motivation. I. Temporal dynamics of affect. *Psychological Review,* 119–145.

Solomon R. L., Kamin, L. J., & Wynne, L. C. (1953). Traumatic avoidance learning: The outcomes of several extinction procedures with dogs. *Journal of Abnormal and Social Psychology, 48,* 291–302.

Sommer, R. (1974). *Tight spaces.* Englewood Cliffs, N.J.: Prentice-Hall.

Sorenson, R. C. (1973). *Adolescent sexuality in contemporary America: Personal values and sexual behavior ages 13–14.* New York: Abrams.

Sorrentino, R. M., & Boutillier, R. G. (1975). The effect of quantity and quality of verbal interaction on ratings of leadership ability. *Jour-*

nal of Experimental Social Psychology, 11, 403–411.

Speisman, J. C., Lazarus, R. S., Mordkoff, A. M., & Davison, L. A. (1964). The experimental reduction of stress based on ego-defense theory. *Journal of Abnormal and Social Psychology, 68,* 367–380.

Spence, J. T., & Spence, K. W. (1966). The motivational components of manifest anxiety: Drive and drive stimuli. In C. D. Spielberger (Ed.), *Anxiety and behavior.* New York: Academic Press.

Spence, K. W., Farber, I. E., & McFann, H. H. (1956). The relation of anxiety (drive) level to performance in competitional paired-associates learning. *Journal of Experimental Social Psychology, 52,* 296–305.

Sperling, G. (1960). The information available in brief visual presentations.. *Psychological Monographs, 74* (11, Whole No. 498).

Sperry, R. W. (1964). The great cerebral commissure. *Scientific American, 210* (1), 42–52.

Sperry, R. W., & Hibberd, E. (1968). In G. E. W. Wolstenholme & M. O'Connor (Eds.), *Growth of the nervous system.* London: Churchill.

Spiegel, H. (1970). A single-treatment method to stop smoking using ancillary self-hypnosis. *International Journal of Clinical Hypnosis, 18,* 235–250.

Spitz, R. A. (1945). Hospitalism: An inquiry into the genesis of psychiatric conditions in early childhood. In R. S. Eissler et al. (Eds.), *The psychoanalytic study of the child* (Vol. 1). New York: International Universities Press.

Spitz, R. A. (1946). Hospitalism: A follow-up report. In R. S. Eissler et al. (Eds.), *Pyschoanalytic study of the child* (Vol. 2). New York: International Universities Press.

Spitzer, R. L., & Fleiss, J. L. (1974). An analysis of the reliability of psychiatric diagnosis. *British Journal of Psychiatry, 125,* 341–347.

Spitzer, R. L., Forman, J. B. W., & Nee, J. (1979). DSM-III field trials: 1. Initial interrater diagnostic reliability. *American Journal of Psychiatry, 136,* 815–817.

Spooner, A., & Kellogg, W. N. (1947). The backward conditioning curve. *American Journal of Psychology, 60,* 321–334.

Squires, R. R., & Braestrup, C. (1977). Bezodiazepine receptors in rat brain. *Nature, 266,* 732–734.

Staats, C. K., & Staats, W. W. (1957). Meaning established by classical conditioning. *Journal of Experimental Psychology, 54,* 74–80.

Stafford-Clark, D., & Smith, A. C. (1978). *Psychiatry for students* (5th ed.). London: Allen & Unwin.

Stampfl, T. G., & Levis, D. J. (1967). Phobic patients: Treatment with the learning theory approach of implosive therapy. *Voices: The Art and Science of Psychotherapy, 3,* 23–27.

Standing, L., Conezio, J., & Haber, R. N. (1970). Perception and memory for pictures: Single-trial learning of 2560 visual stimuli. *Psychonomic Science, 19,* 73–74.

Stein, A. H., & Friedrich, L. K. (1972). Television content and young children's behavior. In J. P. Murray, E. A. Rubenstein, & G. S. Comstock (Eds.), *Television and social behavior. Vol. 2: Television and social learning.*

Washington, D.C.: U.S. Government Printing Office.

Stern, G. G. (1970). *People in context*. New York: Wiley.

Stern, J. A., Brown, M., Ulett, G. A., & Sletten, I. (1977). A comparison of hypnosis, acupuncture, morphine, valium, aspirin, and placebo in the management of experimentally induced pain. In W. E. Edmonston, Jr. (Ed.), *Conceptual and investigative approaches to hypnosis and hypnotic phenomena. Annals of The New York Academy of Sciences* (Vol. 296), 175–193.

Stern, R. S., & Cobb, J. P. (1978). Phenomenology of obsessive-compulsive neurosis. *British Journal of Psychiatry, 132*, 233–234.

Sternbach, R. A. (1966). *Principles of psychophysiology*. New York: Academic Press.

Sternberg, S. (1966). High-speed scanning in human memory. *Science, 53*, 421–457.

Stevens, K. N., & House, A. S. (1972). Speech perception. In J. V. Tobias (Ed.), *Foundations of modern auditory theory* (Vol. 2). New York: Academic Press.

Stevens, S. S. (1956). The direct estimate of sensory magnitudes—loudness. *American Journal of Psychology, 69*, 1–25.

Stevens, S. S. (1957). On the psychophysical law. *Psychological Review, 64*, 153–181.

Stinett, N., Carter, L. M., & Montgomery, J. E. (1972). Older persons' perceptions of their marriages. *Journal of Marriage and the Family, 34*, 665–670.

Stodgill, R. M. (1948). Personal factors associated with leadership. *Journal of Psychology, 25*, 35–71.

Stodgill, R. M. (1974). *Handbook of leadership*. New York: Free Press.

Stokols, D. (1972). On the distinction between density and crowding: Some implications for future research. *Psychological Review, 79*, 275–278.

Stokols, D., Novaco, R. W., Stokols, J., & Campbell, J. (1978). Traffic congestion, type A behavior and stress. *Journal of Applied Psychology, 63*, 467–480.

Stone, G. C., Cohen, F., & Adler, N. E. (1979). *Health psychology*. San Francisco: Jossey-Bass.

Stone, L. J., Smith, H. T., & Murphy, L. B. (Eds.). (1973). *The competent infant: Research and commentary*. New York: Basic Books.

Stoner, J. (1961). A comparison of individual and group decisions, including risk. Unpublished master's thesis, MIT.

Stratton, G. M. (1896) Some preliminary experiments on vision without inversion of the retinal image. *Psychological Review, 3*, 611–617.

Streib, G. F., & Schneider, C. J. (1971). *Retirement in American society*. Ithaca, N.Y.: Cornell University Press.

Stromeyer, C. F., & Psotka, J. (1973). The detailed texture of eidetic images. *Nature, 225*, 346–349.

Stroop, J. R. (1935). Studies of interference in serial verbal reactions. *Journal of Experimental Psychology, 18*, 643–662.

Stunkard, A. J. (1983). *Obesity*. Philadelphia: Saunders.

Suedfeld, P. (1980). *Restricted environmental stimulation: Research and clinical applications*. New York: Wiley.

Sugarman, S. (1982). Developmental change in early representational intelligence: Evidence from spatial classification strategies and related verbal expressions. *Cognitive Psychology, 14*, 410–449.

Sugarman, S. (1983). *Children's early thought: Development in classification*. Cambridge: Cambridge University Press.

Suls, J., & Miller, R. J. (Eds.). (1977). *Social comparison processes: Theoretical and empirical perspectives*. Washington, D.C.: Hempishere/Halsted.

Suomi, S. J. (1977). Development of attachment and other behaviors in rhesus monkeys. In T. Alloway, P. Pliner, & L. Krames (Eds.), *Advances in the study of communication and affect* (Vol. 3): *Attachment behavior*. New York: Plenum.

Suomi, S. J., & Harlow, H. F. (1972). Social rehabilitation of isolate-reared monkeys. *Developmental Psychology, 6*, 487–496.

Szasz, T. (1960). The myth of mental illness. *American Psychologist, 15*, 113–118.

Tagiuri, R., Blake, R., & Bruner, J. (1953). Some determinants of the perception of positive and negative feelings in others. *Journal of Abnormal and Social Psychology, 48*, 585–592.

Talbert, G. B. (1977). Aging of the reproductive system. In C. E. Finch & L. Hayflick (Eds.), *Handbook of the biology of aging*. New York: Van Nostrand Reinhold.

Tanner, J. M. (1962). *Growth at adolescence*. Philadelphia: Davis.

Tanner, J. M. (1970). Physical growth. In P. H. Mussen (Ed.), *Carmichael's manual of child psychology* (Vol. 2) (3rd ed.). New York: Wiley.

Tanner, J. M., Whitehouse, R. H., & Takaishi, M. (1966). Standards from birth to maturity for height, weight, height velocity, and weight velocity; British children 1965. *Archives of Diseases in Childhood, 41*, 454–471.

Tarshis, B. (1979). *The "average American" book*. New York: Atheneum/SMI.

Tausig, M. (1982). Measuring life events. *Journal of Health and Social Behavior, 23*, 52–64.

Tavris, C. (1982, May 2). Women and men and morality. (Review of *In a different voice: Psychological theory and women's development* by C. Gilligan). *New York Times Book Review*.

Taylor, S., & Metlee, D. (1971). When similarity breeds contempt. *Journal of Personality and Social Psychology, 20*, 75–81.

Taylor, S. E. (1978). A developing role for social psychology in medicine and medical practice. *Personality and Social Psychology Bulletin, 4*, 515–523.

Taylor, S. E., & Fiske, S. T. (1975). Point of view and perceptions of causality. *Journal of Personality and Social Psychology, 32*, 439–445.

Taylor, S. P., & Pisano, R. (1971). Physical aggression as a function of frustration and physical attack. *Journal of Social Psychology, 84*, 261–267.

Teghtsoonian, R. (1971). On the exponent in Stevens' Law and the constant in Ekman's Law. *Psychological Review, 78*, 71–80.

Teitelbaum, P. (1957). Random and food-directed activity in hyperphagic and normal rats. *Journal of Comparative and Physiological Psychology, 50*, 486–490.

Teitelbaum, P. (1961). Disturbances in feeding and drinking behavior after hypothalamic lesions. In M. R. Jones (Ed.), *Nebraska Symposium on Motivation*. Lincoln, Neb.: University of Nebraska Press.

Teitelbaum, P., & Epstein, A. N. (1962). The lateral hypothalamic syndrome: Recovery of feeding and drinking after lateral hypothalamic lesions. *Psychological Review, 69*, 74–90.

Tennen, H., & Ellir, S. (1977). Attributional components of learned helplessness and facilitation. *Journal of Personality and Social Psychology, 35*, 265–271.

Terman, L. M. (1916). *The measurement of intelligence*. Boston: Houghton Mifflin.

Terman, L. M. (1917). Feeble-minded children in the public schools of California. *School and Society, 5*, 161–165.

Terman, L. M. (1925). *Mental and physical traits of a thousand gifted children. Genetic studies of genius*. (Vol. 1). Stanford, Calif.: Stanford University Press.

Terrace, H. S. (1979). *Nim*. New York: Knopf.

Terrace, H. S., Petitto, L. A., Sanders, R. J., & Bever, T. G. (1979). Can an ape create a sentence? *Science, 206*, 891–901.

Thibaut, J. W., & Kelley, H. H. (1959). *The social psychology of groups*. New York: Wiley.

Thigpen, C. H., & Cleckley, H. (1954). *The three faces of Eve*. Kingsport, Tenn.: Kingsport Press.

Thoits, P. (1981). Undesirable life events and psychophysiological distress: A problem of operational confounding. *American Sociological Review, 46*, 97–109.

Thomas, A., Chess, S., & Birch, H. G. (1970). The origin of personality. *Scientific American, 223*, 102–109.

Thomas, K. W. (1977). Toward multidimensional values in teaching: The example of conflict behaviors. *Academy of Management Review, 2*.

Thomas, M. Horton, R., Lippincott, E., & Drabman, R. (1977). Desensitization to portrayals of real-life aggression as a function of exposure to television violence. *Journal of Personality and Social Psychology, 35*, 450–458.

Thompson, W. R., & Heron, W. (1954). The effects of restricting early experience on the problem-solving capacity of dogs. *Canadian Journal of Psychology, 8*, 17–31.

Thorndike, E. L. (1911). *Animal intelligence*. New York: Macmillan.

Thorson, G., Hochhaus, L., & Stanners, R. F. (1976). Temporal changes in visual and acoustic codes in a letter-watching task. *Perception and Psychophysics, 19*(4), 346–348.

Thurnher, M. (1976). Midlife marriage: Sex differences in evaluation and perspectives. *International Journal of Aging and Human Development, 7*(2), 129–135.

Thurnher, M., Spence, D., & Fiske, M. (1974). Value confluence and behavioral conflict in intergenerational relations. *Journal of Marriage and the Family, 36*, 308–319.

Thurstone, L. L. (1938). Primary mental abilities. *Psychometrika Monographs*, No. 1.

Tinbergen, N. (1951). *The study of instinct*. Oxford: Clarendon Press.

Tizard, B., & Hodges, J. (1978). The effect of early institutional rearing on the development of eight-year-old children. *Journal of Child Psychology and Psychiatry*, 19, 99–118.

Tolman, E. C., & Honzik, C. H. (1930). Introduction and removal of reward, and maze performance in rats. *University of California Publications in Psychology*, 4, 257–275.

Tolman, J., & King, J. A. (1956). The effects of testosterone propionate on aggression in male and female C57 BL/10 mice. *British Journal of Animal Behavior*, 4, 147–149.

Treisman, A. M. (1964). Selective attention in man. *British Medical Bulletin*, 20, 12–16.

Triplett, N. (1897). The dynamogenic factors in pacemaking and competition. *American Journal of Psychology*, 9, 507–533.

Tyron, R. C. (1942). Individual differences. In F. A. Moss (Ed.), *Comparative psychology*. Englewood Cliffs, N. J.: Prentice-Hall. Pp. 330–365.

Tseng, L. F., Loh, H. H., & Li, C. H. (1976). β-endorphin as a potent analgesic by intravenous injection. *Nature*, 263, 239–240.

Tuddenham, R. D. Blumenkrantz, J., & Wiklin, W. R. (1968). Age changes on AGCT: A longitudinal study of average adults. *Journal of Consulting and Clinical Psychology*, 32, 659–663.

Tulving, E. (1972). Episodic and semantic memory. In E. Tulving & W. Donaldson (Eds.), *Organization of memory*. New York: Academic Press.

Tulving, E. (1978). Relation between encoding specificity and levels of processing. In L. S. Cermak & F. I. M. Craik (Eds.), *Levels of processing and human memory*. Hillsdale, N.J.: Erlbaum.

Tulving, E., & Watkins M. J. (1973). Continuity between recall and recognition. *American Journal of Psychology*, 86, 739–748.

Turiel, E. (1974). Conflict and transition in adolescent moral development. *Child Development*, 45, 14–29.

Turnbull, C. (1962). *The forest people*. New York: Simon & Shuster.

Turvey, M. T., & Shaw, R. E. (1978). Memory (or, knowing) as a matter of specification not representation: Notes towards a different class of machines. In L. S. Cermak & F. I. M. Craik (Eds.), *Levels of processing and human memory*. Hillsdale, N.J.: Erlbaum.

Tversky, A., & Kahneman, D. (1974). Judgment under uncertainty: Heuristics and biases. *Science*, 185, 1124–1131.

Udry, J. R. (1974). *The social context of marriage*. Philadelphia: Lippincott.

Ullman, J., & Krasner, L. (1975). *A psychological approach to abnormal behavior* (2nd ed.). Englewood Cliffs, N.J.: Prentice-Hall.

U.S. Census Bureau. Demographic aspects of aging and the older population in the United States. Current Population Reports, Series P-23, No. 59. Washington, D.C.: U.S. Government Printing Office.

U.S. Public Health Service (1974). Current estimates from the health interview survey: United States. Vital and Health Statistics, Series 10, No. 100, National Center for Health Statistics. Washington, D.C.: U.S. Government Printing Office.

Utech, D. A., & Horing, K. L. (1969). Parents and peers as competing influences in the decisions of children of differing ages. *Journal of Social Psychology*, 78, 267–274.

Valenstein, E., Riss, W., & Young, W. C. (1955). Experiential and genetic factors in the organization of sexual behavior in male guinea pigs. *Journal of Comparative and Physiological Psychology*, 48, 397–403.

Valenstein, E. S. (1973). *Brain control: A critical examination of brain stimulation and psychosurgery*. New York: Wiley.

Van Praag, H., Korf, J., & Schut, D. (1973). Cerebral monoamines and depression: An investigation with the probenecid technique. *Archives of General Psychiatry*, 28, 827–831.

Vernon, J. A., McGill, T. E., Gulick, W. L., & Candland, D. R. (1959). Effect of sensory deprivation on some perceptual and motor skills. *Perceptual and Motor Skills*, 9, 91–97.

Veroff, J., Wilcox, S., & Atkinson, J. W. (1953). The achievement motive in high school and college-age women. *Journal of Abnormal and Social Psychology*, 48, 102–119.

Verplanck, W. S. (1955). The control of the content of conversation: Reinforcement of statements of opinion. *Journal of Abnormal and Social Psychology*, 51, 668–676.

Vinokur, A. (1971). Effects of group processes upon individual and group decisions involving risk. *Dissertation Abstracts International* (Vol. 31) (12-A), 6721–6722.

Vinokur, A., & Selzer, M. L. (1975). Desirable versus undesirable life events: Their relationship to stress and mental distress. *Journal of Personality and Social Psychology*, 32, 329–337.

Vogel, G. W. (1978). Sleep-onset mentation. In A. M. Arkin, J. S. Antrobus, & S. J. Ellman (Eds.), *The mind in sleep psychology and psychobiology*. Hillsdale, N.J.: Erlbaum. Pp. 97–112.

Volicer, B. J., & Volicer, L. (1978). Cardiovascular changes associated with stress during hospitalization. *Journal of Psychosomatic Research*, 22, 159–168.

von Frisch, K. (1967). Honeybees: Do they use direction and distance information provided by their dances? *Science*, 158, 1072–1076.

Wagner, A. R., & Rescorla, R. A. (1972). Inhibition in Pavlovian conditioning. Application of a theory. In R. A. Boakes & M. S. Halliday (Eds.), *Inhibition and learning*. London: Academic Press.

Wahba, M. A., & Bridwell, L. G. (1976). Maslow reconsidered: A review of research on the need hierarchy theory. *Organizational Behavior and Human Performance*, 15, 212–240.

Walk, R. (1966). The development of depth perception in animals and human infants. *Monographs of the Society for Research in Child Development*, 31 (Whole No. 5).

Walk, R., & Gibson, E. (1961). A comparative and analytic study of visual depth perception. *Psychological Monographs*, 75 (15, Whole No. 519).

Walker, B. B., & Sandman, C. A. (1981). Disregulation of the gastrointestinal system. In S. N. Haynes & L. Gannon (Eds.), *Psychosomatic disorders*. New York: Praeger.

Walker, T. G., & Main, E. C. (1973). Choice-shifts in political decision making: Federal judges and civil liberties cases. *Journal of Applied Social Psychology*, 2, 39–38.

Wallace, D. H., & Wehmer, G. (1972). Evaluation of visual erotica by sexual liberals and conservatives. *Journal of Sex Research*, 8, 147–153.

Wallace, M., Kogan, N., & Bern, D. (1962). Group influence on individual risk taking. *Journal of Abnormal and Social Psychology*, 65, 75–86.

Walster, E., Aronson, V., Abrahams, D., & Rottman, L. (1966). Importance of physical attractiveness in dating behavior. *Journal of Personality and Social Psychology*, 4, 508–516.

Walters, H. F., & Malmud, P. (1975, March 10). "Drop that gun, Captain Video." *Newsweek*, 85(10), 81–92.

Walters, R. H., & Llewellyn Thomas, E. (1963). Enhancement of punitiveness by visual and audiovisual displays. *Canadian Journal of Psychology*, 16, 244–255.

Ward, C. H., Beck, A. T., Mendelson, M., Mock, J. E., & Erbaugh, T. K. (1962). The psychiatric nomenclature: Reasons for diagnostic disagreement. *Archives of General Psychiatry*, 7, 198–205.

Ward, C. O., Zanna, M. P., & Cooper, J. (1974). The nonverbal mediation of self-fulfilling prophecies in interracial interaction. *Journal of Experimental Social Psychology*, 10, 109–120.

Ward, R. A. (1979). *The aging experience*. New York: Lippincott.

Warner, L. G., & DeFleur, M. L. (1969). Attitude as an interactional concept: Social constraint and social distance as intervening variables between attitudes and action. *American Sociological Review*, 34, 153–169.

Washburn, S. (1978). Animal behavior and social anthropology. *Society*, 15–6, 35–41.

Wasman, M., & Flynn, J. P. (1962). Directed attack elicited from hypothalamus. *Archives of Neurology*, 6, 220–227.

Wason, P. C., & Johnson-Laird, P. N. (1972). *Psychology of reasoning: Structure and content*. London: Batsford.

Waters, E., Wippman, J., & Sroufe, L. A. (1979). Attachment, positive affect, and competence in the peer group: Two studies in construct validation. *Child Development*, 50, 821–829.

Watkins, L. R., & Mayer, D. J. (1982). Organization of opiate and non-opiate pain control systems. *Science*, 216, 1185–1192.

Watson, J. B., & Rayner, R. (1920). Conditioned emotional reactions. *Journal of Experimental Psychology*, 3, 1–14.

Watson, R. I. (1968). *The great psychologists: Aristotle to Freud*. Philadelphia: Lippincott.

Webb, W. B. (1975). *Sleep: The gentle tyrant*. Englewood Cliffs, N.J.: Prentice Hall.

Webb, W. B., & Cartwright, R. D. (1978). Sleep and dreams. *Annual Review of Psychology*, 29.

Weigman, A. D. (1972). *On dying and denying*. New York: Behavioral Publications.

Weiner, B. (1974). *Achievement motivation and at-*

tribution theory. Morristown, N.J.: General Learning Press.

Weiner, B., Frieze, I., Kukla, A., Reed, L., Rest, S., & Rosenbaum, R. M. (1971). Perceiving the causes of success and failure. In E. E. Jones et al. (Eds.), *Attribution: Perceiving the causes of behavior*. Morristown, N.J.: General Learning Press.

Weiner, H. (1977). *Psychobiology and human disease*. New York: Elsevier.

Weisberg, R. (1980). *Memory, thought and behavior*. New York: Oxford University Press.

Weisberg, R., DiCamillo, M., & Phillips, D. (1978). Transferring old associations to new situations: A nonautomatic process. *Journal of Verbal Learning and Verbal Behavior, 17*, 219–228.

Weiss, J. M. (1977). Ulcers. In J. Maser & M. E. P. Seligman (Eds.), *Psychopathology: Experimental models*. San Francisco: Freeman.

Weissman, M. M., Klerman, G. L., & Paykel, E. S. (1971). Clinical evaluation of hostility in depression. *American Journal of Psychiatry, 128*, 261–266.

Weissman, M. M., & Meyers, J. K. (1978). Affective disorders in a U.S. urban community. *Archives of General Psychiatry, 35*, 1304–1310.

Welkowitz, J., Ewen, R. B., & Cohen, J. (1977). *Introductory statistics for the behavioral sciences*. New York: Academic Press.

Welsh, G. S., & Dahlstrom, W. G. (Eds.). (1965). *Basic readings on the MMPI in psychology and medicine*. Minneapolis: University of Minnesota Press.

Wertheimer, M. (1945/1959). *Productive thinking*. New York: Harper.

Wever, E. G., & Bray, C. W. (1937). The perception of low tones and the resonance-volley theory. *Journal of Psychology, 3*, 101–114.

Wexley, K. N., & Yukl, G. A. (1977). *Organizational behavior and personnel psychology*. Homewood, Ill.: Irwin.

White, R. W. (1959). Motivation reconsidered: The concept of competence. *Psychological Review, 66*, 297–333.

Whiting, B. B., & Whiting, J. W. M. (1975). *Children of six cultures*. Cambridge, Mass.: Harvard University Press.

Whiting, J. W. M., Kluckolm, R. C., & Anthony, A. (1958). The function of male initiation ceremonies at puberty. In E. Maccoby, T. M. Newcomb, & E. L. Hartley (Eds.), *Readings in social psychology*. New York: Holt, Rinehart and Winston.

Whiting, J. W., Landauer, T. K., & Jones, T. M. (1968). Infantile immunization and adult stature. *Child Development, 39*, 58–67.

Whorf, B. L. (1940). Science and linguistics. *Technology Review* (MIT), pp. 229–231, 242–248.

Whorf, B. L. (1956a). Languages and logic. In J. B. Carroll (Ed.), *Language, thought and reality: Selected writings of Benjamin Lee Whorf*. Cambridge, Mass.: MIT Press.

Whorf, B. L. (1956b). Science and linguistics. In J. B. Carroll (Ed.), *Language, thought and reality: Selected writings of Benjamin Lee Whorf*. Cambridge, Mass.: MIT Press.

Wichman, H. (1970). Effects of isolation and communication on cooperation in a two-

person game. *Journal of Personality and Social Psychology, 16*, 114–120.

Wickens, D. D. (1972). Characteristics of word encoding. In A. W. Melton & E. Martin (Eds.), *Coding processes in human memory*. Washington, D.C.: Winston.

Wicker, A. (1969). Attitudes versus actions: The relationship of verbal and overt behavioral responses to attitude objects. *The Journal of Social Issues, 25*, 1–78.

Wicklund, R. A., & Brehm, J. W. (1976). *Perspectives on cognitive dissonance*. Hillsdale, N.J.: Erlbaum.

Wicklund, R. A., Cooper J., & Linden, D. E. (1967). Effects of expected effort on attitude change prior to exposure. *Journal of Experimental Social Psychology, 3*, 416–428.

Wiesel, T. N., & Hubel, D. H. (1963). Single-cell responses in striate cortex of kittens deprived of vision in one eye. *Journal of Neurophysiology, 26*, 1003–1017.

Wilder, D. A., & Allen, V. L. (1978). Group membership and preference for information about others. *Personality and Social Psychology Bulletin, 4*, 106–110.

Willerman, L. (1979). *The psychology of individual and group differences*. San Francisco: Freeman.

Willerman, L., Naylor, A. F., & Myrianthopoulos, N. C. (1974). Intellectual development of children from interracial matings: Performance in infancy and at four years. *Behavior Genetics, 4*, 83–90.

Williams R. J. (1959). Biochemical individuality and cellular nutrition: Prime factors in alcoholism. *Quarterly Journal of Studies on Alcohol, 20*, 452–463.

Wilson, E. O. (1971). *The insect societies*. Cambridge, Mass.: The Belknap Press of Harvard University Press.

Wilson, E. O. (1974). *Introduction to ecology, evolution and population biology* (Readings from Scientific American). San Francisco: Freeman.

Wilson, E. O. (1975a, October 12). Human decency in animals. The New York Times Magazine.

Wilson, E. O. (1975b). *Sociobiology: The new synthesis*. Cambridge, Mass.: Harvard University Press.

Wilson, G. T. (1978). Methodological considerations in treatment outcome research on obesity. *Journal of Consulting and Clinical Psychology, 46*, 687–702.

Wilson, J. A., & Glick, B. (1970). Ontogeny of mating behavior in the chicken. *American Journal of Physiology, 218*, 951–955.

Wilson, M. S., & Meyer, E. (1962). Diagnostic consistency in a psychiatric liaison service. *American Journal of Psychiatry, 119*, 207–209.

Winston, P. H. (1975). *The psychology of computer vision*. New York: McGraw-Hill.

Winterbottom, M. R. (1953). The relation of childhood training in independence to achievement motivation. Unpublished doctoral dissertation, University of Michigan.

Wolberg, L. R. (1977). *The technique of psychotherapy* (3rd ed.). New York: Grune & Stratton.

Wolff, E. (no date). *Practical hypnotism*. New York: Louis Tannen.

Wolpe, J. (1958). *Psychotherapy by reciprocal inhi-*

bition. Stanford, Calif.: Stanford University Press.

Woodruff, R. A., Goodwin, D. W., & Guze, S. B. (1974). *Psychiatric diagnosis*. New York: Oxford University Press.

Woods, P. J. (Ed.). (1976). *Career opportunities for psychologists*. Washington, D.C.: American Psychological Association.

Woodworth, R. S. (1918). *Dynamic psychology*. New York: Columbia University Press.

Woodworth, R. S. (1958). *Dynamics of behavior*. New York: Holt, Rinehart and Winston.

Woolfolk, R. L., Carr-Kaffashan, K., Lehrer, P. M., et al. (1976). Meditation training as a treatment for insomnia. *Behavior Therapy, 7*, 359–365.

Word, C. H., Zanna, M. P., & Cooper, J. (1974). The nonverbal mediation of self-fulfilling prophecies in intersocial interaction. *Journal of Experimental Social Psychology, 10*, 109–120.

Wortman, C., Panciera, L., Shusterman, L., & Hibscher, J. (1976). Attributions of causality and reactions to uncontrollable outcomes. *Journal of Experimental Social Psychology, 12*, 301–306.

Wrightsman, L. S. (1960). Effects of waiting with others on changes in level of felt anxiety. *Journal of Abnormal and Social Psychology, 61*, 216–222.

Wuerthele, S. M., Freed, W. J., Olson, L., Morihisa, J., Spoor, L., Wyatt, R. J., & Hoffer, B. J. (1981). Effect of dopamine agonists and antagonists on the electrical activity of substantia nigra neurons transplanted into the lateral ventrical of the rat. *Experimental Brain Research, 44*, 1–10.

Wyer, R., & Goldberg, L. (1970). A probabilistic analysis of the relationships among beliefs and attitudes. *Psychological Review, 77*, 100–120.

Wyld, H. C. (1931). The superiority of received standard English. *Society for Pure English, Tract XXXVII*, 603–617.

Yarbus, A. L. (1967). *Eye movements and vision*. New York: Plenum.

Yarrow, L. J., Rubenstein, J. L., & Pedersen, F. A. (1975). *Infant and environment: Early cognitive and motivational development*. New York: Wiley.

Yerkes, R. M. (Ed.). (1921). Psychological examining in the United States Army. Washington, D.C.: *Memoirs of the National Academy of Sciences* (No. 15).

Yerkes, R. M., & Foster, J. C. (1923). *A point scale for measuring mental ability*. Baltimore, Md.: Warwick and York.

Young, W. C., Goy, R. W., & Phoenix, C. H. (1964). Hormones and sexual behavior. *Science, 143*, 212–218.

Young, W. S., III, & Kuhar, M. J. (1980). Radiohistochemical localization of benzodiazepine receptors in rat brain. *Journal of Pharmacological Experimental Therapy, 212*, 337–346.

Zajonc, R. B. (1965). Social facilitation. *Science, 149*, 269–274.

Zajonc, R. B. (1968). Attitudinal effects of mere exposure. *Journal of Personality and Social Psychology, Monograph Supplement, 9*, 1–27.

Zajonc, R. B., & Sales, S. M. (1966). Social facilitation of dominant and subordinate responses. *Journal of Experimental Social Psychology, 2,* 160–168.

Zajonc, R. B., Wolosin, R. J., Wolosin, M., & Sherman, S. J. (1968). Individual and group risk taking in a two-choice situation. *Journal of Experimental Social Psychology, 4,* 89–106.

Zanna, M. P., & Cooper, J. (1974). Dissonance and the pill: An attribution approach to studying the arousal properties of dissonance. *Journal of Personality and Social Psychology, 29,* 703–709.

Zanna, M. P., Olson, J. M., & Fazio, R. H. (1980). Attitude-behavior consistency: An individual difference perspective. *Journal of Personality and Social Psychology, 38,* 432–440.

Zellner, M. (1970). Self-esteem, reception and influenceability. *Journal of Personality and Social Psychology, 15,* 87–93.

Zelnik, M., & Kanter, J. F. (1972). The probability of premarital intercourse. *Social Science Research, 1,* 335–341.

Zillman, D. (1978). *Hostility and aggression.* Hillsdale, N.J.: Erlbaum.

Zillman, D. (1971). Excitation transfer in communication-mediated aggressive behavior. *Journal of Experimental Social Psychology, 7,* 419–434.

Zillman, D., & Cantor, J. R. (1976). Effects of timing of information about mitigating circumstances on emotional responses to provocation and retaliatory behavior. *Journal of Experimental Social Psychology, 12,* 38–55.

Zimbardo, P. G. (1958). The efforts of early avoidance training and rearing conditions upon the sexual behavior of the male rat. *Journal of Comparative and Physiological Psychology, 51,* 764–769.

Zimbardo, P. G. (1965). The effect of effort and improvisation on self-persuasion produced by role playing. *Journal of Experimental Social Psychology, 1,* 103–120.

Zimbardo, P. G. (1970). The human choice: Individuation, reason, and order versus deindividuation, impulse, and chaos. In W. Arnold & D. Levine (Eds.), *Nebraska Symposium on Motivation.* Lincoln, Neb.: University of Nebraska Press.

Zimbardo, P. G. (1977). *Shyness: What it is, what to do about it.* Reading, Mass.: Addison-Wesley.

Zimbardo, P. G., Weisenberg, M., Firestone, I., & Levy, B. (1965). Communicator effectiveness in producing public conformity and private attitude change. *Journal of Personality, 33,* 233–255.

Zimmerman, D. W. (1957). Durable secondary reinforcement: Method and theory. *Psychological Review, 64,* 373–383.

Zuckerman, M. (1979). Sensation seeking and risk taking. In C. Izard, *Emotions in personality and psychopathology.* New York: Plenum.

Zuckerman, M., & Wheeler, L. (1975). To dispel fantasies about the fantasy-based measure of fear of success. *Psychological Bulletin, 82,* 932–946.

Acknowledgments

Figures, Tables, Text

Fig. 1-1 Tinbergen, N. *The study of instinct.* © 1951 by Oxford University Press. Reprinted by permission. **Table 1-1** Latané, B., & Darley, J. Group inhibition of bystander intervention in emergencies. *Journal of Personality and Social Psychology,* 1968, *10,* 215-221. Copyright 1968 by the American Psychological Association. Reprinted by permission of the author.

Fig. 2-1 Dr. James L. German, III. **Fig. 2-4** Fritz Goro **Fig. 2-6** *Scientific American,* September 1979. **Fig. 2-7** Carl Olsen and Henry Hall, Princeton University. **Fig. 2-8** Courtesy Dr. David H. Hubel, Harvard Medical School. **Fig. 2-9** Photos from Blakemore, C. *Mechanics of the mind.* Cambridge, Eng.: Cambridge University Press, 1977. **Fig. 2-11** Adapted from McFarland, R. A. *Physiological psychology.* Palo Alto, Calif.: Mayfield, 1981. **Fig. in box on pp. 40-41** From "The Chemistry of the Brain" by Leslie L. Iversen. Copyright © by Scientific American, Inc. All rights reserved. **Fig. 2-17** From Nauta, W. J. H., & Feirtag, M. The organization of the brain. Copyright © 1979 by Scientific American, Inc. All rights reserved. **Table 2-1** Milner, B., Branch, C., & Rasmussen, T. Evidence for bilateral representation in non-righthanders. *Transactions of the American Neurological Association,* 1966, *91,* 306-308. Reprinted by permission. **Fig. B in box on pp. 56-57** Adapted from Levy, J., Trevarthen, C., & Sperry, R. W. Perception of bilateral chimeric figures following hemispheric disconnection. *Brain,* 1972, *95,* fig. 4, p. 68.

Table 3-1 Teghtsoonian, R. On the exponent in Stevens' Law and the constant in Ekman's Law. *Psychological Review,* 1971, *78,* 71-90. Copyright 1971 by the American Psychological Association. Reprinted by permission of the author. **Fig. 3-3** Stevens, S. S. On the psychophysical law. *Psychological Review,* 1957, *64,* 153-181. Copyright 1957 by the American Psychological Association. Reprinted by permission of the author. **Fig. 3-5** From *The Speech Chain* by Peter B. Denes and Elliot N. Pinson. Copyright © 1963 by Bell Telephone Laboratories, Inc. Reprinted by permission of Doubleday & Company Inc. **Photo in Fig. B of box on pp. 78-79** From Cornsweet, T. N. *Visual perception.* New York: Academic Press, 1970. **Fig. 3-13** Courtesy Dr. Francis A. L'Esperance, Jr. **Fig. A in box on pp. 80–81** Blakemore, C. *Mechanics of the Mind.* Cambridge: Cambridge University Press, 1977, page 78. **Fig. 3-14** From *The Psychology of Being Human,* Second Edition by Zick Rubin and Majorie McNeil. Copyright © 1977 by Majorie McNeil and Zick Rubin. Reprinted by permission of Harper & Row, Pub., Inc. **Fig. 3-21** Photo courtesy of Inmont Corporation **Fig. 3-23** Fritz Goro, Life Magazine, © Time Inc. **Fig. 3-26** Photo © Douglas Faulkner/Photo Researchers, Inc. Color chips courtesy of Scientific Publishing Co. **Fig. 3-28** Photo Sybil Shackman/Monkmeyer Press Photo Service.

Fig. 4-3 Broadbent, D. E. The role of auditory localization in attention and memory span. *Journal of Experimental Psychology,* 1958, *47,* 191-196. Copyright 1958 by the American Psychological Association. Reprinted by permission. **Fig. 4-5** (top) Public Information Office/Jet Propulsion Laboratory (bottom left) Gregory, R. L. *The intelligent eye.* New York: McGraw-Hill, 1970. Reproduced with permission. **Fig. 4-7** Murich, G. *Visual and Auditory Perception.* New York: Bobbs-Merrill, 1973. Figure 4-27, p. 146. **Fig. 4-11** (photo) Willian Vandivert. **Extract in box on pp. 112–113** From *The Forest People* by Colin M. Turnbull. Copyright © 1961 by Colin M. Turnbull. Reprinted by permission of Simon & Schuster, Inc. **Fig. in box on pp. 112-113** Adapted from McBurney, D. H., & Collins, V. B. *Introduction to sensation and perception.* Englewood Cliffs, N.J.: Prentice-Hall, 1977. Figure 13-3, p. 257. Reprinted by permission. **Fig. 4-14** Yarbus, A. L. *Eye movements and vision.* Fig. 116. Copyright 1967 by Plenum Publishing Corporation. Reprinted by permission. **Fig. 4-15** Lindsay, P. H., & Norman, D. A. *Human information processing* (2nd ed.). New York: Academic Press, 1977. Reprinted with permission. **Fig. 4-16** M. C. Escher, *Reptiles.* Collection Haags Gemeentemuseum—The Hague. **Fig. 4-18** (photo) © 1977 Bernard Pierre Wolff/Photo Researchers, Inc.

Fig. 4-20 Adapted from William Schiff: *Perception: An Applied Approach,* p. 245. Copyright © 1980 by Houghton Mifflin Company. **Figs. 4-22, 4-23** Buswell, G. T. Fundamental reading habits: A study of their development. *Supplementary Educational Monographs,* No. 21, 1922.

Fig. 5-1 Photo courtesy Teri Leigh Stratford, Sleep-Wake Disorders Center, Montifiore Medical Center; brain wave patterns reprinted by permission of Bill Berger Associates, from *Sleep* by Gay Gaer Luce and Julius Segal. Copyright © 1966 by Gay Gaer Luce and Julius Segal. **Fig. 5-2** Dement, W. C. *Some must watch while some must sleep.* P. 114. New York: Norton, 1974. **Fig. 5-3** Roffward, H. P., Muzio, J. N., & Dement, W. C. Ontogenetic development of the human sleep-dream cycle. *Science,* 1966, *152,* 604-619. Copyright 1966 by the American Association for the Advancement of Science. **Fig. 5-4** Morgan, A. H., & Hilgard, E. R. Age differences in susceptibility to hypnosis. Reprinted from the April 1973 *International Journal of Clinical and Experimental Hypnosis.* Copyrighted by the Society for Clinical and Experimental Hypnosis, April 1973. **Box fig. p. 151** Young, W. S., & Kuhar, M. J. Radiohistochemical localization of benzodiazepine receptors in rat brain. *Journal of Pharmacology and Experimental Therapeutics,* 1980, *212,* 337–346. © 1980.

Fig. 6-4 Hovland, C. I. The generalization of conditioned responses. I. The sensory generalization of conditioned responses with varying frequencies of tone. *Journal of General Psychology,* 1937, *17,* Fig. 2, p. 136. **Fig. 6-5** Spooner, A., & Kellogg, W. N. The backward conditioning curve. *American Journal of Psychology,* 1947, *60,* 321–334. **Fig. 6-7** Photo courtesy of Irene Springer. **Fig. 6-11** Grice, G. R. The relation of secondary reinforcement to delayed reward in visual discrimination learning. *Journal of Experimental Psychology,* 1948, *38,* 1-16. **Figure in box on p. 179** Miller, N. E., & Brucker, B. S. A learned visceral response, apparently independent of skeletal ones, in patients paralyzed by spinal lesions. In N. Birbaumer & H. D. Kimmel (Eds.), *Biofeedback and self-regulation.*

Hillsdale, N.J.: Erlbaum, 1979. **Fig. 6-12** (left) Harlow, H. F. The formation of learning sets. *Psychological Review*, 1949, *56*, Fig. 2. (right) Photo courtesy of University of Wisconsin Primate Laboratory. **Fig. 6-13** (left) Tolman, E. C., & Honzik, C. H. Introduction and removal of reward, and maze performance in rats. *University of California Publications in Psychology*, 1930, *4*, 257–275. (right) Photo courtesy of Forsyth/Monkmeyer. **Fig. 6-14** Tolman, E. C., & Honzik, C. H. Introduction and removal of reward, and maze performance in rats. *University of California Publications in Psychology*, 1930, *4*, 257–275.

Fig. 7-2 Photo by Paolo Koch, Photo Researchers, Inc. **Fig. 7-4** Madigan, S. A. Intraserial repetition and coding processed in free recall. *Journal of Verbal Learning and Verbal Behavior*, 1969, *8*, 828–835; reprinted by permission of Academic Press, Inc. **Fig. 7-5** Frederick C. Barlett, *Remembering: A Study in Experimental and Social Psychology* (New York: Cambridge University Press, 1967), p. 65. (Originally published in 1932.) **Fig. 7-6** Tulving, E., & Watkins, M. J. Continuity between recall and recognition. *American Journal of Psychology*, 1973, *86*, 739–748. Reprinted by permission of the University of Illinois Press. **Fig. 7-7** Ebbinghaus, H. *Memory: A contribution to experimental psychology*. Leipzig: Altenberg, 1885. **Fig. 7-8** Peterson, L. R., & Peterson, M. J. Short-term retention of individual items. *Journal of Experimental Psychology*, 1959, *58*, 193–198. Copyright 1959 by the American Psychological Association. Reprinted by permission of the author. **Fig. 7-10** Wickens, D. D. Characteristics of work encoding. In A. W. Melton & E. Martin (Eds.), *Coding processes in human memory*. Washington, D.C.: Winston, 1972. **Fig. 7-12** Sperling G. The information available in brief mental presentations. *Psychological Monographs*, 1960, 74 (11, Whole No. 498). **Fig. A in box on p. 206** Sternberg, S. High-speed scanning in human memory. *Science*, 1966, *153*, 652–654. **Table 7-2** Adapted from *Cognitive Psychology and Its Implications* by J. R. Anderson. Copyright © 1980 by W. H. Freeman and Company. All rights reserved. **Fig. A in box on p. 206** "High-Speed Scanning in Human Memory," Sternberg, S., *Science*, Vol. 153, pp. 652–654. Copyright 1966 by the American Association for the Advancement of Science. **Table 7-3** Photo by Laimute Druskis. **Fig. 7-16** Pollard-Gott, L., McCluskey, M., & Todres, A. Subjective story structure. *Discourse Processes*, 1979, *2*, 251–281. **Fig. A in box on pp. 214–215** Paivio, A. Comparisons of mental clocks. *Journal of Experimental Psychology: Human Perception and Performance*, 1978, *4*, 61–71. Copyright 1978 by the

American Psychological Association. Reprinted by permission of the author. **Fig. B in box on pp. 214–215** Kosslyn, S. M., Ball, T. M., & Reiser, B. J. Visual images preserve metric spatial information: Evidence from studies of image scanning. *Journal of Experimental Psychology: Human Perception and Performance*, 1978, *4*, 47–60. Copyright 1978 by the American Psychological Association. Reprinted by permission of the author.

Fig. 8-1 Glucksberg, S., & Danks, K. H. *Experimental psycholinguistics*. Copyright 1975 by Lawrence J. Erlbaum Associates. Reprinted by permission. **Fig 8-4** Lenneberg, E. *Biological foundations of language*. New York: Wiley, 1967. Reprinted with permission. **Table 8-1** From *Psycholinguistics* by Dan I. Slobin. Copyright © 1971 Scott, Foresman and Company. Reprinted by permission. **Fig. 8-5** Brown, R. A. First language: The early stages. Cambridge, Mass.: Harvard University Press, 1973. **Fig. 8-6** Berko, J. The child's learning of English morphology. *Word*, 1958, *14*, 150–177. Copyright International Linguistic Association. Reprinted by permission. **Figs. 8-7 and 8-8** From Social and nonsocial speech by R. M. Krauss & S. Glucksberg. Copyright © 1977 by Scientific American, Inc. All rights reserved. **Figure in box on p. 241** Premack, D. The education of S*A*R*A*H. *Psychology Today*, September 1970, pp. 54–58. Copyright 1970 by Psychology Today. Reprinted by permission. **Fig. 8-9** Heidbreder, E. The attainment of concepts: III. The problem. *Journal of Psychology*, 1947, *24*, 93–138. Reprinted by permission. **Fig. 8-11** Carmichael, L., Hogan, H. P., & Walter, A. A. An experimental study of the effect of language on the presentation of visually perceived form. *Journal of Experimental Psychology*, 1932, *15*, 73–86. **Table 8-2** Luchins, A. J. Mechanization in problem solving: The effect of *Einstellung*. *Psychological Monographs*, 1942, 54, 6 (Whole No. 248). **Fig. 8-15** Figures 4, 5A, 5B, and 6 from *Productive Thinking*, enlarged edition by Max Wertheimer, edited by Michael Wertheimer. Copyright 1945, © 1959 by Valentin Wertheimer. Reprinted by permission of Harper & Row, Publishers, Inc. **Fig. 8-16** Glucksberg, S., & Weisberg, R. W. Verbal behavior and problem solving: Some effects of labeling in a functional fixedness problem. *Journal of Experimental Psychology*, 1966, *71*, 659–664. Copyright 1966 by the American Psychological Association. Reprinted by permission of the author **Table 8-3** Mednick, S. A. The associative basis of the creative process. *Psychological Review*, 1962, *69*, 220–232. Copyright 1962 by the American Psychological Association. Reprinted by permission of the author.

Table 9-2, Fig. 9-2 Honzik, M. P., Macfarlance, J. W., & Allen, L. The stability of mental test performance between two and eighteen years. *Journal of Experimental Education*, 1948, *17*, 309–334. **Fig. 9-3** Adapted from Schaie, K. W., Labouvie, G., & Buech, B. V. Generational and cohort specific differences in adult cognitive functioning: A fourteen-year study of independent samples. *Development Psychology*, 1973, *9*, 151–160. Copyright 1973 by the American Psychological Association. Adapted by permission of the author. **Tables 9-4, 9-5** Horn, J. M., Loehlin, J. O., & Willerman, L. Intellectual resemblance among adoptive and biological relatives: The Texas Adoption Project. *Behavior Genetics*, 1979, *9*, 177–208. Scarr, S., & Weinberg, R. A. Intellectual similarities within families of both adopted and biological children. *Intelligence*, 1977, *1*, 170–191. Courtesy Mensa, 1791 West 3rd St., Brooklyn, NY 11223. **Fig. 9-5** Harrell, T. W., & Harrell, M. S. Army General Classification Test scores for civilian occupations. *Educational and Psychological Measurement*, 1945, *5*, 229–239.

Table 10-2 Schachter, S. Some extraordinary facts about obese humans and rats. *American Psychologist*, 1971, *26*, 129–144. Copyright 1971 by the American Psychological Association. Reprinted by permission of the author. **Fig. 10-2** From Johnson, W. G., unpublished doctoral dissertation, Catholic University of America, 1970; cited in Schacter, S. Some extraordinary facts about obese humans and rats. *American Psychologist*, 1971, *26*, 129–144. **Fig. 10-3** Hibscher, J. A., & Herman, C. P. Obesity, dieting, and the expression of "obese" characteristics. *Journal of Comparative and Physiological Psychology*, 1977, *91*, 374–380. Copyright 1977 by the American Psychological Association. Reprinted by permission of the author. **Fig. 10-4** Warden, C. J. Animal motivation: Experimental studies on the albino rat. New York: Columbia University Press, 1931.

Table 11-1 Udry, J. R. *The social context of marriage*. Philadelphia: Lippincott, 1974. **Fig. 11-1** Baron, R. A., & Byrne D. *Social psychology: Understanding human interaction* (3rd ed.). Boston: Allyn & Bacon, 1981, p. 557. **Fig. 11-2** Donnerstein, E., & Berkowitz, L. Victim reaction in aggressive erotic film as a factor in violence against women. *Journal of Personality and Social Psychology*, 1981, *41*, 710–724. Copyright 1981 by the American Psychological Association. Reprinted by permission of the author. **Fig. 11-5** Reprinted from Job longevity as a situational factor in job satisfaction by R. Katz published in *Administrative Science Quarterly, 23*, by permission of *The Administrative*

Science Quarterly. © 1978 by The Administrative Science Quarterly. **Fig.** 11-6 Hohmann, G. W. Some effects of spinal cord lesions on experienced emotional feelings. *Psychophysiology,* 1966, *3,* 143–156. Copyright © 1966, The Society for Psychophysiological Research. Reprinted by permission of the publisher. **Figure in box on p.** 354 Bower, G. H. Mood and memory. *American Psychologist,* 1981, *36,* 129–148. Copyright 1981 by the American Psychological Association. Reprinted by permission of the author.

Fig. 12-1 From "Imprinting in Animals" by Edkhard H. Hess. Copyright © 1958 by Scientific American, Inc. All rights reserved. **Fig.** 12-2 (upper left) © 1981 Suzanne Szasz/ Photo Researchers, Inc. (upper right) © Martine Franck/Magnum (center left) W. W. Wilson/Monkmeyer Press Photo Service (center middle) Raimondo Borea/Editorial Prohocolor Archives (center right) Teri Leigh Stratford (bottom) Richard Checani/Kay Reese & Associates. **Table** 12-1 Adapted from, *Childhood and society* by Erik H. Erikson, by permission of W. W. Norton & Company, Inc. and The Hogarth Press, Ltd. Copyright © 1950, 1963 by W. W. Norton & Company, Inc. and The Hogarth Press, Ltd. **Table** 12-2 From *The Psychology of the Child* by Jean Piaget and Barbel Inhelder. © 1969 by Basic Books Inc. and Routledge, Kegan, Paul Ltd. By permission of the publishers.

Fig. 13-2 From "Growing Up" by J. M. Tanner. Copyright © 1973 by Scientific American, Inc. All rights reserved. **Fig.** 13-5 Rabbitt, P. M. Breakdown of control processes in old age. In T. Field, A. Huston, H. Quay, L. Trol, and G. Finnley (Eds.), *Review of human development.* New York: Wiley, 1982.

Table 14-1 Cattell, R. B., & Kline, P. *The scientific analysis of personality and motivation.* Copyright 1977 by Academic Press Inc. (London) Ltd. **Table** 14-2 Maslow, A. H. Self-actualization and beyond. In J. F. T. Bugental (Ed.), *Challenges of humanistic psychology.* Copyright 1967 by McGraw-Hill Book Company. Used with permission. **Fig.** 14-3 Hathaway, S. R., & McKinley, J. C. *Minnesota Multiphasic Personality Inventory Revised 1967.* New York: The Psychological Corporation, 1970. Copyright 1970 by the Psychological Corporation and reproduced with permission.

List on pp. 448-449 From *Contemporary psychology and effective behavior* by James C. Coleman and Constance L. Hammen. Copyright © 1974 Scott, Foresman and Company. Reprinted by permission. **Table** 15-1 Reprinted with permission from *Journal of Psy-*

chosomatic Research, 11. T. H. Holmes & R. H. Rahe, The social readjustment rating scale. Copyright 1967 by Pergamon Press, Ltd. **Fig.** 15-1 Lazarus, R. S., & Alfert, E. The short-circuiting of threat. *Journal of Abnormal and Social Psychology,* 1964, *69,* 195–205. Reprinted by permission. **Fig.** 15-2 Hokanson, J., DeGood, D. E., Forrest, M., & Britton, T. Availability of avoidance behaviors in modulating vascular stress responses. *Journal of Personality and Social Psychology,* 1971, *19,* 60–68. Copyright 1971 by the American Psychological Association. Reprinted by permission of the author.

Tables 16-1, 16-2, 16-3 American Psychiatric Association, Diagnostic and Statistical Manual of Mental Disorders, Third Edition, Washington, D. C., APA, 1980. **Case History on p.** 479 Abridged from Leon, G. R., *Case histories of deviant behavior* (2nd ed.). Boston: Allyn and Bacon, 1977, pp. 113–118. **Table** 16-4 Adapted from Stern, R. S., & Cobb, J. P. (1978) Phenomenology of obsessive compulsive neurosis. *The British Journal of Psychiatry, 182,* 233–239. **Case History on p.** 485 Stafford-Clark, D., & Smith, A. C. *Psychiatry for students* (6th ed.). Winchester, Mass.: Allen & Unwin, 1978. **Table** 16-5 Beck, A. T. The development of depression: A cognitive model. In R. J. Friedman & M. M. Katz (Eds.), *The psychology of depression: Contemporary theory and research.* Copyright © 1974 by Hemisphere Publishing Corporation, Washington, D. C. Reprinted by permission. **Case History on p.** 491 Abridged from Kolb, D. *Modern clinical psychiatry* (8th ed.). Philadelphia: W. B. Saunders Co., 1973, pp. 334–335. **Case History on pp.** 496–497 Abridged from Cleckley, Hervey: *The mask of sanity,* ed. 5. St. Louis, 1976. The C. V. Mosby Co.

Application on pp. 514-515 Wolberg, L. *The technique of psychotherapy* (3rd ed.). New York: Grune & Stratton, 1977, pp. 560–561. Copyright © 1977 by Lewis R. Wolberg, M.D. **Application on p.** 516 Reprinted with permission from *Behavior Research and Therapy,* 1968, *6,* R. A. Hogan, The implosive technique. Copyright 1968, Pergamon Press, Ltd. **Table** 17-1 From *Behavior therapy* by H. H. Schaefer & P. L. Martin. Copyright 1969. Used by permission of McGraw-Hill Book Company. **Application on p.** 524 Abridged from Phares, E. J. *Clinical psychology: Concepts, methods, and profession.* Copyright 1979 by The Dorsey Press. Reprinted by permission. **Application on p.** 527 Abridged from Rimm, D. C., & Masters, J. C. *Behavior therapy: Techniques and empirical findings* (2nd ed.). New York: Academic Press, 1979, pp. 383–394. Copyright © 1979 by Academic Press. Reprinted by permission.

Fig. 18-1 Kelley, H. H. The processes of casual attribution. *American Psychologist,* February 1973, 107–128. Copyright 1974 by the American Psychological Association. Reprinted by permission of the author. **Fig.** 18-3 Carl I. Hovland, Arthur A. Lumsdane, and Fred D. Sheffield, *Experiments on Mass Communication,* Vol. III, Studies in Social Psychology in World War II. Copyright 1949, © renewed 1977 by Princeton University Press. Adapted from 2 figs., p. 213, by permission of Princeton University Press. **Table** 18-1 Festinger, L., & Carlsmith, J. M. Cognitive consequences of forced compliance. *Journal of Abnormal and Social Psychology,* 1959, *58,* 203–210. Copyright 1959 by the American Psychological Association. Reprinted by permission of the author. **Table** 18-2 Aronson, E., & Linder, D. Gain and loss of esteem as determinants of interpersonal attractiveness. *Journal of Experimental Social Psychology,* 1965, *1,* 156–171. Copyright © 1965 by Academic Press.

Fig. 19-1 From *An outline of social psychology,* revised edition, by Muzafer Sherif and Carolyn W. Sherif. Copyright 1948, 1956 by Harper & Row, Publishers, Inc. Reprinted by permission of the publisher. **Fig.** 19-4 Leavitt, H. J. Some effects of certain communication patterns on group performance. *Journal of Abnormal and Social Psychology,* 1951, *46,* Fig. 4, p. 42. Copyright 1951 by the American Psychological Association. Reprinted by permission. **Figure in box on p.** 579 Janis I. L. *Groupthink* (2nd. ed.). Boston: Houghton Mifflin, 1982. **Fig.** 19-5 M. Wallach, N. Kogan, & D. Bem. Group influence on individual risk taking. *Journal of Abnormal and Social Psychology,* 1962, *65,* 75–86. Copyright 1962 by the American Psychological Association. Reprinted by permission of the author. **Fig.** 19-6 Thibaut, J. W., & Kelley, H. H. *The social psychology of groups.* New York: Wiley, 1959. **Fig.** 19-8, **Table** 19-1 Deutsch, M., & Krauss, R. M. The effect of threat upon interpersonal bargaining. *Journal of Abnormal and Social Psychology,* 1960, *61,* 181–189. Copyright 1960 by the American Psychological Association. Reprinted by permission of the publisher and author. **Fig.** 19-10 Baum, S., & Valins, S. *Architecture and social behavior: Psychological studies in social density.* Hillsdale, N.J.: Erlbaum, 1977. **Table** 19-2 K. W. Thomas, Toward multidimensional values in teaching: The example of conflict behaviors. *Academy of Management Review* (1977), Vol. 2, p. 487. Reprinted by permission.

Photographs

4 Edmund Engelman 6 Laimute E. Druskis 7 Owen Franken/Stock, Boston 9 Sybil

Shackman/Monkmeyer 13 Jan Lukas/Photo Researchers, Inc. 14 (top) Ken Karp (bottom) Ken Karp 15 (top) Ken Karp (bottom) Ken Karp 24 Abbot Laboratories 34 United Press International Inc. **Fig. A in box on pp. 48–49** Courtesy Cabrini Medical Center **Fig. B in box on pp. 48–49** Courtesy Dr. Fred J. Hodges, III, Washington University School of Medicine, St. Louis. **Fig. C in box on pp. 48–49** Courtesy Dr. Fred J. Hodges, III, Washington University School of Medicine. **Fig. D in box on pp. 48–49** Courtesy Dr. Michel M. Ter-Pogossian 76 Courtesy Steven Goodman, SUNY College of Optometry, Center for BioCommunication. 89 Teri Leigh Stratford 90 Art Resources 95 Courtesy Fragrance Foundation 97 © M. A. Geissinger/ Photo Researchers, Inc. **Fig. A in box on p. 104** (left) USDA Photo (right) U. S. Forest Service **Fig. B in box on p. 104** © Gerry Cranham/Photo Researchers, Inc. **Box on p. 112** (lower left) cover photo *The Forest People* by Colin M. Turnbull (upper right) © Richard Frieman/Photo Researchers, Inc. 115 (upper left) M. C. Escher, *Rippled Surface.* Collection Haags Gemeentemuseum—The Hague (lower right) M. C. Escher, *Three Worlds.* Collection Haags Gemeentemuseum—The Hague 121 Courtesy Museum of Modern Art/Film Stills Archive 133 The Bettmann Archive, Inc. 136 (left) New York Public Library (right) The Bettmann Archive, Inc. 141 Laimute Druskis 144 Charles Gatewood 167 Ken Karp 168 Ken Karp 169 Irene Springer 171 George Eastman House 173 United Press International 175 Dr. Judy Komaki, Purdue University 179 Sybil Shelton/Monkmeyer 190 Roy Ellis, Photo Researchers, Inc. 191 (left) Mark Mangold, U.S. Census Bureau (right) AT&T Photo, Superior Fototech, Inc. 198 Ann Zane Shanks, Photo Researchers, Inc. 199 Elisabeth Weiland, Photo Researchers, Inc. 210 Myron Wood, Photo Researchers, Inc. 214 Van Bucher, Photo Researchers, Inc. 234 (left) Ken Karp (right) Teri Leigh Stratford 240 The New York Public Library Picture Collection 241 United Press International 255 The New York Public Library Picture Collection 267 Bruce Roberts/Photo Researchers, Inc. 269 Photos courtesy The Psy-

chological Corporation 283 Alice Kandell/ Photo Researchers, Inc. 291 The New York Public Library 298 © Teri Leigh Stratford/ Photo Researchers, Inc. 299 Teri Leigh Stratford 300 Dr. Neal E. Miller 303 © 1977 Robert Houser/Photo Researchers, Inc. 306 © 1983 Bernard Pierre Wolff/Photo Researchers, Inc. 310 (left) Paul S. Conklin/ Monkmeyer Press Photo Service (right) Mimi Forsyth/Monkmeyer Press Photo Service 311 United Press International 313 © Ylla/Photo Researchers, Inc. 315 © 1972 Barbara Young/Photo Researchers, Inc. 317 Photo courtesy Harry F. Harlow, University of Wisconsin Primate Laboratory 320 © Esias Baitel/Rapho-Photo Researchers, Inc. 324 © 1976 Guy Gillette/Photo Researchers, Inc. 326 (top) © 1977 Lynn McLaren/Photo Researchers, Inc. (bottom) © Michael Hayman/ Photo Researchers, Inc. 327 Mark Perlstein/ The New York Times 329 Ken Karp 334 (left) Keith Gunnar/National Audubon Society/Photo Researchers, Inc. (upper right) United Press International (bottom right) Marc Anderson 335 (left) © 1982 Erika Stone/Photo Researchers, Inc. (center) © Alice Kandell/Photo Researchers, Inc. (right) © Teri Leigh Stratford 336 © Barbara Rios/ Photo Researchers, Inc. 343 (top left) Ken Karp (bottom left) © 1979 Hella Hammid/ Photo Researchers, Inc. (top right) © 1976 Bob Combs/Rapho-Photo Researchers, Inc. (bottom right) © 1981 Suzanne Szasz/Photo Researchers, Inc. 344 Teri Leigh Stratford 346 David A. Krathwohl/Stock, Boston 358 (top and bottom) Ken Karp 360 Thomas McAvoy, Time-Life Picture Agency © Time Inc. **Box on p. 363** (left) David Linton, Scientific American (right) © William Vandivert 367 Ken Karp 375 Ken Karp 376 Mimi Forsyth/Monkmeyer Press Photo Service 377 Courtesy Dr. Michael Cole, University of California, San Diego 381 Ken Karp 384 Mimi Forsyth/Monkmeyer Press Photo Service 387 Ken Karp 389 © Melissa Hayes English/Photo Researchers, Inc. 390 (left) Teri Leigh Stratford (right) Nancy Harp/ Monkmeyer Press Photo Service 396 A.T.&T. Co. Photo Center 398 Fred R. Conrad/The New York Times 403 Courtesy Action 404 Ken Karp, Sirovich Senior Center

414 The Bettmann Archive 423 (top) Yan Lukas/Photo Researchers, Inc. (bottom) Bob Combs/Photo Researchers, Inc. 425 Alice Kandell/Photo Researchers, Inc. 427 © 1981 Suzanne Szasz/Photo Researchers, Inc. 439 (left) Courtesy University of Florida Clinical Psychology Department (right) Van Bucher/ Photo Researchers, Inc. 440 (left) Van Bucher/Photo Researchers, Inc. (right) Harvard University Press 446 United Press International 449 © 1982 De Sazo/Rapho Photo Researchers, Inc. 454 Arthur Tress/ Photo Researchers, Inc. 459 United Press International 463 Peter de-Krassel/Photo Researchers, Inc. 465 Sybil Shelton/Monkmeyer Press Photo Service 478 © Georg Gerster/ Photo Researchers, Inc. 480 Lew Merrim/ Monkmeyer Press Photo Service 485 © 1979 Ed Lettau/Photo Researchers, Inc. 490 United Press International 501 © 1982 Amy Stromsten/Photo Researchers, Inc. 508 The American Museum of Natural History 509 (left and right) The Bettmann Archive, Inc. 511 Ken Karp 517 © 1982 Susan Rosenberg/ Photo Researchers, Inc.; snake courtesy of Academy of Natural Sciences of Philadelphia 522 Courtesy National Institute of Mental Health 530 (left) © 1980 Linda Ferrer/ Woodfin Camp & Associates (top right) Van Bucher, Courtesy Wagner College Psychology Department/Photo Researchers, Inc. (bottom right) Conklin/SCP 533 United Press International 541 Ken Karp 544 (top and bottom) Courtesy A.T.&T. 545 1973 Robert Houser/Photo Researchers, Inc. 549 AFL-CIO News 553 © 1979 Maureen Fennelli/Photo Researchers, Inc. 555 Ken Karp 563 © Michael Hayman/Photo Researchers, Inc. 564 Bonnie Freer/Photo Researchers, Inc. 576 (left) Mimi Forsyth/ Monkmeyer Press Photo Service (center) © 1980 Will McIntyre/Photo Researchers, Inc. (right) United Press International Photo 581 © 1982 Bill Bachman/Photo Researchers, Inc. 587 United Press International Photo 590 (top left) Catholics for a Free Choice (top right) © Frank Siteman MCMLXXX/Stock, Boston (bottom) © Yan Lukas/Photo Researchers, Inc. 592 (left) Library of Congress (right) © 1981 Guy Gilette/Photo Researchers, Inc.

Name Index

Jameson, D., 93
Janis, I. L., 461, 546, 548, 549, 579–580
Jaynes, J., 360
Jeddi, E., 317
Jeffery, R., 427
Jencks, C., 286
Jenkins, C. D., 461
Jensen, A. R., 273, 276, 279, 284, 287, 288
Jessor, R., 388
Jessor, S. L., 388
Johnson, J. E., 461
Johnson, V. E., 314, 396
Johnson, W. G., 304
Johnson-Laird, P. N., 248, 249
Jones, E. E., 539, 542, 554
Jones, H. E., 266
Jones, M. C., 383
Jones, T. M., 152
Jourard, S. M., 558
Juel-Nielsen, N., 278
Jung, C. G., 398, 417
Jusczyk, P., 361
Just, M. A., 122

Kagan, J., 365
Kahn, E., 401
Kahn, R. L., 584, 593
Kahneman, D., 252–254
Kalat, J., 302
Kalish, R. A., 403, 404, 406
Kallman, L., 495
Kamin, L. J., 161, 174–175, 182, 278, 279,
   316
Kanarek, R., 301, 302
Kandel, D., 387
Karabenick, S., 330
Karaz, V., 540
Kase, S. V., 451
Kassin, S. M., 16–17
Katz, E., 485, 550
Kaufman, A. S., 285, 287
Kearsley, R. B., 365
Keele, S. W., 209
Keenan, J. M., 228
Keesey, R. E., 301
Keller, Helen, 370
Kelley, H. H., 539–540, 546, 559, 560, 570,
   582, 585
Kellogg, L. A., 240
Kellogg, W. N., 161, 240
Kelly, G. A., 427
Kendrick, S. A., 265
Keinston, K., 389
Kennedy, John F., 579
Kerckhoff, A., 556
Kessen, M. L., 299, 300
Kety, S., 522
Kiang, J. A., 75
Kimmel, D. C , 403
Kinchla, R. A., 103, 118
King, J. A., 319
King, S. H., 386
Kinsey, A. C., 331, 338
Kintsch, W., 207
Klein, E. B., 391
Kleitman, N., 129, 130
Klerman, G. L., 487
Klucholm, R. C., 381
Knittle, J. L., 305

Knott, P. D., 387
Kobasa, S. C., 464
Koelling, R. A., 180, 302, 347
Koestler, A., 255–256
Koffka, K., 103
Kogan, N., 580
Kohlberg, Lawrence, 372, 388–389, 393–394,
   433
Köhler, W., 80, 81, 103
Kolata, M., 499
Kolb, L. C., 491
Koluchova, J., 328
Konečni, V. J., 562
Korsch, B., 461
Kosslyn, S. M., 215
Kosterlitz, H. W., 40
Kovacs, M., 528
Kraepelin, Emil, 470
Kraines, R. J., 396
Kramer, R. B., 393
Krasner, L., 492
Krauss, R. M., 239, 584–585
Krowitz, A., 363
Kruglanski, A. W., 336
Krupp, I. M., 493
Kruuk, H., 302
Kubal, L., 336
Kübler-Ross, Elisabeth, 405, 406
Kuenne, M. R., 245
Kuhar, M. J., 40, 150
Kuhl, J., 338
Kühler, Wolfgang, 181
Kuhlman, D. M., 587
Kuhn, D., 367
Kuo, Z. Y., 318
Kurtines, W., 394
Kutz, S. L., 386

Labouvie, G., 266
Lacey, B. C., 346
Lacey, J. I., 346, 480
Lacoe, B., 489
Ladlove, R. F., 300
Laing, R. D., 493
Lalouel, J. M., 284
Lamb, M. E., 365
Lamm, H., 580
Lange, Carl, 348
Langer, A., 363
Langer, Ellen, J., 461, 464, 465, 544
LaPiere, R. T., 550–551
Latané, B., 12, 572
Launier, R., 451
Layzer, D., 276
Lazarsfeld, P. F., 550
Lazarus, A., 519
Lazarus, R. S., 450, 451, 459–461
Leahy, A., 281
Leary, Timothy, 149
Leask, J., 216
Leavitt, H. J., 578
Lee, E. S., 289
Lehrer, P. M., 142
Lehrman, D. S., 312, 313
LeMasters, E. E., 392
Lenneberg, E., 234, 360
Lepper, M. R., 336
Leon, G. R., 479
Leonard, R., 461

LePage, A., 562
Lerner, M. J., 152, 542
Lester, D., 488, 528
Levens, J. P., 426
Leventhal, H., 461
Levi, L., 450
Levinger, G., 558
Levinson, D. J., 391, 398
Levinson, M. H., 391
Levis, D. J., 516
Levy, B., 553
Levy, J. V., 56, 319
Lew, R., 284
Lewin, Kurt, 16, 17
Lewin, K., 447
Lewinsohn, P. H., 487
Lewontin, R. C., 276, 316
Li, C. H., 40
Lieberman, A. M., 76
Liebert, R. M., 426
Lifton, R. J., 446
Likert, R , 592
Lind, James, 302
Lindley, C. J., 521
Lindner, D., 556
Lipton, E. L., 359
Lipton, R. C., 327
Litwin, G. H., 337
Llewellyn Thomas, E., 425
Locke, John, 357
Lockhart, R. S., 210
Loehlin, J. C., 282, 283
Loew, C. A., 318
Loftus, Elizabeth, 213
Loh, H. H., 40
LoLordo, V. M., 180
Loomis, B., 396
Lopata, Helen, 404
Lo Piccolo, L., 532
Lorenz, Konrad, 319, 360, 561
Lorsch, J. W., 593
Lott, A. J., 556
Lott, B. E., 556
Lovaas, O. I., 318, 518
Love, T., 216
Lowell, E. L., 375
Lowenthal, M. F., 397
Luborsky, L., 534
Luce, G. G., 128
Luchins, A. J., 538
Ludwig, A. M., 482
Luikart, C., 400
Luria, A. R., 216, 374
Lynn, W., 489

McArthur, L. A., 540
McCann, S. M., 306
McCarley, R. W., 131
McClelland, David C., 375, 387
McClelland, L., 16, 337
McCluskey, M., 212
Maccoby, E. E., 432
MacDougall, J. M., 451
McFann, H. H., 581
Macfarlane, J. W., 263, 383
McGill, T. E., 327
McGowan, B. K., 180
McGregor, D. M., 340, 592
McGue, M., 283, 284

Rabbie, J. M., 330
Rabbitt, P. M., 402
Radloff, L., 397
Ragozin, A. S., 365
Rahe, R. H., 446, 452, 453
Ramsay, D., 361
Rao, D. C., 284
Raphael, B., 119
Rappaport, A., 587
Ratner, A. M., 360
Raugh, M. R., 217
Ray, S., 146
Rayner, R., 346
Reich, F., 284
Reiser, B. J., 215
Rescorla, R. A., 165
Rhamey, R., 556
Rheingold, H. L., 232
Rhodewalt, F., 458
Rice, J., 284
Richmond, J. B., 359
Rife, D. C., 55
Riley, H. D., Jr., 382
Riley, M., 400, 404
Rimm, D. C., 527
Rimol, A. G. P., 140
Riss, W., 312
Rist, R., 541
Robbins, Paula, 397
Robbins, S. P., 593
Roberts, C. L., 179, 298
Robertson-Tchabo, E. A., 401
Robey, D., 339
Robins, N. L., 497
Rodin, Judith, 304, 464, 465
Roethlisberger, F. J., 339
Rogers, Carl, 420, 479, 523–525
Rollins, B. C., 399, 404
Rolls, B. J., 307
Romo, M., 452
Ropartz, P., 319
Rosch, E., 243, 244
Rose, Steven, 53, 316
Rosen, B. C., 337, 375
Rosenberg, E. J., 453
Rosenblum, L. A., 310
Rosenhan, D. L., 387
Rosenman, R. H., 458
Rosenthal, T. L., 16, 426
Ross, D., 425, 563
Ross, J., 375
Ross, L., 254, 542
Ross, S., 425, 563
Roth, S., 336
Rottman, L., 557
Rozin, P., 302
Rubenstein, H., 222
Rubin, Z., 228, 557
Ruble, D. N., 336, 372, 375, 540
Ruff, H. A., 362
Rumbaugh, D. M., 241, 245
Rumelhart, D. E., 207
Runck, B., 529
Rundus, D., 204
Rush, A. J., 528
Rush, Benjamin, 508
Ryle, G., 205

Sachs, Jacqueline, 228
Salapatek, P., 363
Sales, S. M., 581
Sanders, R. J., 241
Sandman, C. A., 452
Sapir, Edward, 245
Saplosky, B. S., 332
Sarason, I. G., 453
Sarbin, T. R., 135, 137
Sargent, S. S., 328
Sarnoff, I., 330, 465
Sauer, C., 580
Savage-Rumbaugh, Sue, 241
Scarr, S., 281, 282, 289
Schachter, S., 303, 304, 329, 330, 350, 465, 574
Schaefer, E. S., 422
Schaefer, H. H., 518
Schaffer, H. R., 363, 422
Schaie, K. W., 266
Schank, R., 209, 429
Schayler, S., 485
Schein, F. H., 338
Schildkraut, J., 489
Schill, T., 280
Schmale, A. H., 461
Schmidt, G., 331
Schneider, C. J., 403
Schneider, D. J., 429
Schneider, W., 103
Schrank, R., 339
Schreiber, F. R., 483
Schulz, Richard, 465
Schvaneveldt, R. W., 208
Schwartz, G. E., 140, 451
Scott, L. R., 175
Scott, T. H., 326
Scoville, W. B., 483
Scribner, S., 378
Searle, John, 231
Sears, R., 561
Sebastian, R. J., 426
Segal, M. W., 555
Segal, S. J., 128, 215
Segovia-Riguelme, N., 501
Selfridge, O. G., 118
Seligman, Martin E. P., 336, 347, 457, 480, 487, 488, 561
Selye, Hans, 449, 450
Selzer, M. L., 453
Semmel, A., 488
Serbin, L. A., 368
Seymour, J., 148
Shaffer, D. R., 386
Shafii, M., 140
Sharp, D., 378
Shatz, M., 239, 371
Shaw, M. E., 386, 578
Shaw, R., 102
Sheenan, P. W., 135
Sheldon, William, 421–422
Sherif, M., 570–571
Sherman, S. J., 580
Shields, J., 277–278, 451, 495
Shiffrin, R. M., 103, 201, 203, 204, 210
Shirley, M. M., 362
Shneidman, E. S., 405
Shomer, R. W., 585

Shulsinger, F., 500
Sidman, M., 175
Siegal, S., 152, 162
Sigall, H., 556
Sigush, V., 331
Siladi, M., 430
Siltanen, P., 452
Silver, R. L., 461
Siman, Michael, 387
Simmons, H., 152
Simon, T., 209, 259
Simpson, E. L., 394
Sinclair-de Zwart, H., 370
Singer, B., 534
Singer, J., 459, 460, 463
Singer, J. E., 350
Singer, R. D., 426
Siqueland, E. R., 361
Skeels, H., 280
Skelton, J. A., 461
Skinner, B. F., 23, 166–167, 172–173, 176–177, 296, 323, 357, 482, 517
Skipper, J. K., 461
Sklar, J., 392
Skodak, M., 280
Slayton, D. J., 365
Sletten, I., 136
Slobin, D. I., 237
Smith, A. C., 485
Smith, F., 122
Smith, G. P., 300
Smith, H. T., 363
Smith, J., 430
Smith, M. E., 234
Smith, M. L., 534
Snoek, J. D., 558
Snow, C. E., 361, 371
Snyder, J., 497
Snyder, M., 429–430, 543, 551
Snyder, S. H., 40, 150, 501
Sohlins, M., 316
Solomon, R. L., 174, 351–353
Sommer, Robert, 589
Sorenson, R. C., 389
Spanos, H. P., 137
Spearman, Charles, 273–274
Speisman, J. C., 459
Spence, D., 387
Spence, D. P., 534
Spence, J. T., 353, 581
Spence, K. W., 353, 581
Sperling, George, 122, 202, 203
Sperry, R. W., 56, 57
Spinner, B., 333
Spitz, R. A., 327, 360
Spitzer, R. L., 470, 474
Spooner, A., 161
Spoor, L., 45
Squires, R. R., 150
Staats, C. K., 230
Staats, W. W., 230
Stafford, K. R., 328
Stafford-Clark, D., 485
Stalker, G. M., 593
Stampfl, T. G., 516
Stanners, R. F., 204
Stein, A. H., 426
Steinberg, L. D., 365

Subject Index

Feral children, 328
Festinger's theory: of cognitive dissonance, 552–553, 556; of social comparisons, 554
Figure-ground organization, 105–106
Filter theory, 103
First impressions, attribution and, 538
Fixation, 111, 415
Fixed-interval schedule, 170–171
Fixed-ratio schedule, 171
Flicker fusion, 77
Fluid intelligence, 402
Food intake regulation, 299–302; set-point theory of, 301, 304–305
Forebrain, 47
Forgetting. *See* Amnesia; Information loss
Formal operations, stage of, 384
Fovea, 78
Framing effects, 252
Free association, 511–512
Free will, doctrine of, 295
Frequency: of a pure tone, 71; relative, 602–603; spatial, 78
Frequency distributions, 598–602
Frequency theory of pitch perception, 75
Freudian theory: of aggression, 561; of anxiety, 454–456; of defense mechanisms, 455–456; of dreams, 130–131; of forgetting, 198–199; of neurosis, 476–477; of personality, 366, 383, 412–417; of psychoanalysis, 4–5 (*See also* Psychoanalytic theory); of psychosexual development, 366, 374–375, 385, 390, 391, 415–416; of schizophrenia, 492
Frustration: aggression and, 561–562; stress and, 448–449
Fugue, 199, 483
Functional fixedness, 251
Fundamental attribution error, 542
Fundamental tone, 72

GABA (gamma-aminobutyric acid), 45, 150–151
Galvanic skin response (GSR), 345; conditioned, 158–159
Ganglia, 32
Gastrointestinal system, stress and, 451–452
Gazelle-boy, 328
General Adaptation Syndrome, 449–450, 463
Generalization, 158–159; in operant conditioning, 171–172
Generalized anxiety disorder, 477
General-reaction, somatic weakness theory, 450
Generation gap, 387–388
Genes, 23–26
Genetic counseling, 521
Genetics. *See* Heredity
Genetic sex, 308–309
Genetic theories of personality, 422
Genitality, 366
Genotype, 27
Gestalt principles of organization, 103–106
Gestalt psychology, 3
Gestalt therapy, 525–526
Gestures, 344
Gibsonian invariants, 104
Glaucoma, 88–89
Glial cells, 34
Glucose: aggression and, 320; food intake regulation and, 300
Gonadotropins, 309

Gonads, 309
Grammar, 223; children's acquisition of, 237–238; phrase structure rules and transformational rules of, 226–227. *See also* Syntax
Graphs, 599–600
Group polarization effect, 580
Groups, 569–595; conformity in, 569–574; contexts of activities of, 587–595; cooperation and social exchanges in, 581–587; decision making in, 578–581; deviation in, 574–575; innovation in, 575; leadership in, 575–578
Group therapy, 530–531
Groupthink, 579–580

Hallucinations, 490
Hallucinogens, 149–150
Hallucinogenic drugs, 46
Handedness, 54–55
Hardiness, 464
Harmonics, 72
Hashish, 150
Health: in old age, 400–401, 403; stress and, 452. *See also* Illnesses
Health psychology, 460–462
Hearing, 70–76; auditory stimuli and, 70–73; theories of, 74–76
Hearing aids, 72, 73
Hearing loss, 72–73
Heredity, 23–28; genes and chromosomes and, 23–26; intelligence tests and, 275–289; study of, 26–28
Hermaphroditism, 310
Heroin, 147
Hertz (Hz), 71
Heterozygosis, 25–26
Heuristics, 253–254
Hierarchy of needs, Maslow's, 339–340
Hindbrain, 46
Histogram, 599
Holophrastic utterances, 234
Homeostasis, 297; food intake regulation and, 301–302
Homeostatic mechanisms, 297
Homosexuality, 313–314
Homozygosis, 25–26
Hormones, 60–62; adrenocorticotropic, 61; mating behavior and, 311–312; sexual differentiation and, 309–310
Hospice movement, 406–407
Hubel-Wiesel Experiment, 84
Hue, 86
Humanistic-existential model: of abnormal behavior, 476; of anxiety, 457–458; of organizations, 592–593; of personality, 417–420; of phobic and anxiety disorders, 479–480; of schizophrenia, 493
Hunger, 297, 299–305
Huntington's chorea, 45
Hyperopia (farsightedness), 88
Hypertension, 451
Hyperthyroidism, 60
Hypnosis, 132–138; definition and nature of, 132–133; history of, 136–137; pain reduction through, 135–138; posthypnotic suggestion and, 138; responsiveness to, 134–135
Hypnotics, 148
Hypoglycemia, aggression and, 320

Hypothalamus, 47; aggression and, 319; emotions and, 349–350; food intake regulation and, 300, 303; thirst and, 306–307
Hypothetico-deductive reasoning, 384
Hypothyroidism, 60

Iconic memory system, 202–203
Id, 413–417, 454
Identification, 367–368
Identity, sex role, 433
Identity conflict, 385–386
Idiographic personality theories, 410–412
Illnesses (disease): coronory heart disease, 458; health psychology and, 460–462; psychosomatic, 450–451; stress and, 460–462. *See also* Health
Imitation, in social-learning theory of personality, 425, 426
Immigration policy, intelligence tests and, 290–291
Implicit personality theories, 429, 538–539
Impolsive therapy, 515–516
Imprinting, 360
Incentive, 298
Independent variables, 14
Induced compliance effect, 553
Inductive reasoning, 247
Industrial psychology, 10
Infancy, developmental tasks of, 361–365
Infants, perceptions of, 232
Informational social influence, 570–571
Information exchange theories, 580
Information loss, 189–190, 196–200; distraction and attentional problems and, 197; emotional factors and, 198–199; interference from other memories and, 197–199; organic causes of, 199–200, 204–205; retention time and, 196–197
Information reduction, 190
Inhibition, conditioned, 160, 165
Innovation, 575
Insight learning, 181
Insomnia, 127
Instict(s), 296; aggression as, 561
Instrumental theory of aggression, 563–564
Intellectualization, 456
Intelligence: age and, 265–267; crystallized, 401–402; fluid, 402; intelligence tests as defining, 263–264
Intelligence quotient (IQ): adoption studies of, 280–282; black-white differences in, 287–289; concept of, 261–262; deviation, 269–270; family studies of, 284; genetic relatedness, 277–284; group differences in, 284–298; heritability of, 275–289; high, 268; low, 267–268; sex differences in, 284–285; social-class differences in, 285; stability of, 263–264; twin studies of, 263–264; twin studies of, 277–280, 282–284
Intelligence tests (IQ tests), 259–292; abuse of, 272; Binet's, 259–262; culture-fair, 273; as diagnostic instruments, 264; of divergent thinking, 274–275; factorially designed, 273–274; group, 270–271; hereditary factors and, 275–289; intelligence as defined by, 263–264; performance, 271–273; reliability of, 263; social issues and, 289–292; Standford-Binet, 268–270, 272, 285, 287;

Sleepwalking, 483
Smell, sense of (olfaction), 93–94
Snellen test, 76
Social attachments, development of, 363–365
Social classes: IQ and, 285; retirement and, 403
Social comparison theory, 554
Social deprivation, 327–329
Social development: during adolescence, 385–386; during childhood, 365–368; during early adulthood, 390–392
Social exchanges: in groups, 583–587; in long-term relationships, 559–560
Social faciliation theory, 581
Social influence: informational, 570–571; normative, 571, 574
Social-learning theory: of aggression, 563–566; of personality, 425–427, 433; of sex-role development, 368
Social psychology, 11, 16–17, 537. *See also* Groups
Social Readjustment Rating Scale, 452–453
Social-skills training, 519
Social support, as a buffer against stress, 465–466
Sociobiology, 316
Somatic motor system, 39
Somatoform disorders, 484
Somatosensory cortex, 52–53
Somatosensory homunculus, 52
Somatotypes, 421–422
Somnambulism, 483
Sounds, infants' perception and production of, 232–233
Spatial frequency, 78
Specific-reaction theory, 450–451
Speech, 222; development of, 232–233; handedness and, 54, 55; infants' perception of, 232; sounds and perception of, 222. *See also* Language
Speech-act theory, 231
Speech areas of the neocortex, 53–54
Speed-reading courses, 122–124
Spikes, 129
Spinal cord, 42–43
Spinal nerves, 39
Split-brain operation, 56
Split-brain subjects, 56–57
Spontaneous recovery, 158
Spread of activation, 208–209
Standard deviation, 601
Standard error of the mean, 605
Standard scores, 604
Stanford-Binet test, 262–264, 268–270, 272, 285, 287
Startle pattern, 345
State-dependent learning, 193
State-dependent memory, 354
Statistical inference, 604–609
Statistical significance, 605–607
Statistics, 598–609; descriptive, 598–602
Stereopis, 111
Stereotypes, 544–545
Steroids, 61
Stevens's power law, 69
Stimulants, 143–144
Stimulation: need for, 325–326; optimal levels of, 326
Stomach, food-intake regulation and, 299–300

STP, 150
Stress, 445–466; aging and, 464–465; biological model of, 449–454; cognitive model of, 458–462; coping responses to, 462–463; defined, 445; extreme, 446–447; meditation for reduction of, 139–142; social support as a buffer against, 465–466; sources of, 445–448
Stress hormones, 61
Stroboscopic motion, 120
Stroop effect, 103
Structural code, 204
Sublimation, 456
Substance abuse, 141–152
Substance P, 41
Substance-use disorders, 498–502
Successive approximations, reinforcement of, 168
Suicide, prevention of, 532–533
Superego, 414–415
Superstitious behaviors, 482
Surface structure, 228
Surprise, conditioning and, 182
Survey method, 5–7
Symmetry, 104, 106
Sympathetic system, 58–60
Synapses, 37–38
Synaptic cleft, 38
Synaptic knobs, 37
Synesthesia, 216
Syntactic scene analysis, 118
Syntax, 225–229, 230–231; children's acquisition of, 237–238
Systematic desensitization, 514–515

Tabes dorsalis, 96
Tables, 599–600
Tachistoscope, 121–122
Tag questions, 238
Taraxein, 493
Taste, sense of, 93
Taste buds, 93
TAT (Thematic Apperception Test), 439–440
Tay-Sachs disease, 521
Television, violent behavior and violence on, 565
Temporal contiguity, learning and, 200
Territorial aggression, 319
Testosterone, 309
Tests: achievement, 264–265; aptitude, 265; intelligence, *see* Intelligence tests; for personality assessment, 431–435, 438–440; projective, for personality assessment, 438–440
Texas Adoption Project, 282
Texture gradient, 104, 110
Thalamus, 47; emotions and, 349
Thanatos (death instincts), 413
THC (tetrahydrocannabinal), 150, 151
Thematic Apperception Test (TAT), 439–440
Theories, 9
Therapy, 507–534; biofeedback, 529; biological model of, 519–523; cognitive model of, 526–530; effectiveness of, 533–534; family, 530–531; group, 530–531; history of, 507–509; humanistic-existential model of, 523–526; learning models of, 514–519; problem-oriented approaches to, 531–533; psychoanalytic model of, 511–515
Thinking, 247–256; creative, 254–256; decision making, 252–254; divergent, tests of,

274–275; hypothetico-deductive, 384; primary-process and secondary-process, 414; problem solving, 250–252; propositional, 384; reasoning, 247–250; schizophrenic, 490. *See also* Cognitive development
Thirst, 305–308
Three-dimensional world, two-dimensional images as evoking, 113–115
Three-receptor theory, 90–91
Thyrotropin, 60
Thyroxin, 60
Timbre, 72
Tip-of-the-tongue (TOT) phenomenon, 193, 208
Token-economy programs, 517–518
Tonal gap, 72
Tones, pure, 71–72
Touch, sense of, 94–96
Trait theories, of personality, 409–412
Tranquilizers, 148, 150–151, 519–520
Transcendental Meditation (TM), 139
Transference, 512, 513
Transformational rules, 227
Transmethylation proccss, 493
Traumatic events, as sources of stress, 445–447
Trephining, 507
Trial-and-error learning, 165
Tricyclic drugs, 520
Trucking game, 584–585
Twin studies, 27–28; of IQ, 227–280, 282–284
Two-dimensional images, three-dimensional world evoked by, 113–115
Type-A behavior, 458, 461

Unconditional positive regard, 524
Unconditioned response (UR), 157
Unconditioned stimulus (US), 157
Unconscious, the, 4–5, 413; dreams and, 130–131
Unconscious inferences, 102
Undoing, 456

Validity, of tests for personality assessment, 431–435
Value theory, 580
Variability, measures of, 600–601
Variable-interval schedule, 171
Variable-ratio schedule, 171
Variables, experimental methods and, 14
Variance, 600–601
Vestibular sacs, 96
Violent behavior: erotic materials and, 332–333; violence on television and, 565. *See also* Aggression
Vision (visual perception), 76–92; adaptation to a righted or displaced retinal image, 80–81; color, 86–92; development of, 362; Gibsonian invariants and, 104; sinusoidal gratings and, 78–79; visual stimuli and, 76–77. *See also* Eye, the
Visual acuity, 76
Visual adaptation, 82–83
Visual angle, 77
Visual cliff, 346
Visual cortex, 53, 86
Visual field, 77
Visual illusion: Ames room, 108; moon, 113; phi, 120; two-dimensional depth cues and, 114–115

About the Authors

John Darley is a professor of psychology at Princeton University. He received his B.A. from Swarthmore College and his M.A. and Ph.D. degrees from the Department of Social Relations at Harvard University where he worked with Elliot Aronson. Before coming to Princeton University he taught for four years in the graduate program of the Washington Square unit of New York University. His own research is in social psychology, and over the years has included work on bystander responses to emergencies, the dynamics of self-fulfilling prophecies, and stereotyping and prejudice. John Darley recently co-authored the chapter on environmental psychology in the forthcoming *Handbook of social psychology*.

Sam Glucksberg was born in Montreal, Canada, and moved to New York City, where he attended The Bronx High School of Science, City College of New York, and, finally, New York University, where he received his Ph.D. in experimental psychology in 1960. He then spent three years in the army with the Human Engineering Laboratories at Aberdeen Proving Ground Maryland, where he worked on basic human engineering research problems. He joined the faculty of Princeton University in 1963, where he has been ever since. He has served as chairman of the psychology department, as chair of an NIMH research review committee, and as consulting editor on numerous journals, including *American Scientist, Cognitive Psychology,* and *Developmental Psychology Journal of Experimental Psychology: Learning, Memory and Cognition.* He is now editor of the *Journal of Experimental Psychology: General.* His research focuses on cognitive processes, with emphasis on language and thought processes.

Leon Kamin is the Dorman T. Warren Professor of Psychology at Princeton University. He received his A.B., A.M., and Ph.D. degrees at Harvard University. Before coming to Princeton, he had taught at McGill, Queen's and McMaster Universities in Canada. He served as chairman of the department of psychology at McMaster and at Princeton. He is a past president of the Eastern Psychological Association. He received the Martin Luther King Junior Award of the New York Society of Clinical Psychologists and a special award from the National Education Association Committee on Human Relations. He is the author of many experimental papers, mostly concerned with animal learning and conditioning. He is also the author of *The Science and Politics of I.Q.,* and co-author of *The Intelligence Controversy* and of *Not in Our Genes.* His current research is in the area of psychopathology.

Ron Kinchla has been a professor of psychology at Princeton since 1969. He received his B.A. and Ph.D. degrees from the University of California, Los Angeles, followed by postdoctoral research on human perception at Stanford University and the NASA Ames Research Center. Before coming to Princeton he taught at New York University in Greenwich Village and McMaster University in Ontario, Canada. He has published numerous research articles and book chapters on visual and auditory perception, attention, and mathematical psychology. He has been a reviewer or consulting editor on a number of journals including *Perception and Psychophysics*, *The Journal of Mathematical Psychology*, *The Journal of Experimental Psychology*, and *Psychological Review*. He has also been a member of The Advisory Committee of the International Society for Studies of Attention and Performance. He is presently Director of Graduate Studies in the Psychology Department at Princeton and is working on a book relating the study of perception and memory.